TABLES OF WEIGHTS AND MEA

METRIC UNITS	ENGLISH UNITS

LENGTH

10 millimeters (mm) = 1 centimeter (cm)	12 inches (in) = 1 foot (ft)
100 centimeters (cm) = 1 meter (m)	3 feet (ft) = 1 yard (yd)
1,000 millimeters (mm) = 1 meter (m)	1,760 yards (yd) = 1 mile (mi)
1,000 meters (m) = 1 kilometer (km)	5,280 feet (ft) = 1 mile (mi)

LIQUID VOLUME

1,000 milliliters (ml) = 1 liter (l)	16 ounces (oz) = 1 pint (pt)
1,000 liters (l) = 1 kiloliter (kl)	2 pints (pt) = 1 quart (qt)
	4 quarts (qt) = 1 gallon (gal)
	128 ounces (oz) = 1 gallon (gal)
	8 pints (pt) = 1 gallon (gal)

DRY VOLUME

1,000 cubic millimeters (mm^3) = 1 cubic centimeter (cm^3)	1,728 cubic inches (cu in) = 1 cubic foot (cu ft)
1,000,000 cubic centimeters (cm^3) = 1 cubic meter (m^3)	27 cubic feet (cu ft) = 1 cubic yard (cu yd)
	46,656 cubic inches (cu in) = 1 cubic yard (cu yd)

WEIGHT

1,000 milligrams (mg) = 1 gram (g)	16 ounces (oz) = 1 pound (lb)
1,000 grams (g) = 1 kilogram (kg)	2,000 pounds (lb) = 1 ton
1,000 kilograms (kg) = 1 metric ton	

METRIC PREFIX MEANINGS

kilo- = one thousand

deci- = one tenth

centi- = one hundredth

milli- = one thousandth

micro- = one millionth

EIGHTH EDITION

SCIENCE FOR THE ELEMENTARY AND MIDDLE SCHOOL

Edward Victor

Richard D. Kellough

Merrill, an imprint of Prentice Hall

Upper Saddle River, New Jersey   Columbus, Ohio

Library of Congress Cataloging-in-Publication Data
Victor, Edward, 1914–
 Science for the elementary and middle school / Edward Victor,
Richard D. Kellough.—8th ed.
  p. cm.
  Rev. ed. of: Science for the elementary school. c1993.
  Includes bibliographical references and index.
  ISBN 0-13-457037-5
 1. Science—Study and teaching (Elementary) 2. Middle schools.
I. Kellough, Richard D. (Richard Dean) II. Victor, Edward. 1914–
Science for the elementary school. III. Title.
LB1585.V46 1997
372.3'5—dc20   96-22861
                                                        CIP

Cover photo: © Joel Dexter/Unicorn Stock Photos
Editor: Bradley J. Potthoff
Production Coordination: Betsy Keefer
Photo Researchers: Anthony Magnacca and Angela Jenkins
Design Coordinator: Jill E. Bonar
Text Designer: Betsy Keefer
Cover Designer: Brian Deep
Production Manager: Deidra M. Schwartz
Electronic Text Management: Marilyn Wilson Phelps, Matthew Williams, Karen L. Bretz, Tracey Ward

This book was set in Goudy by Carlisle Communications, Ltd. and was printed and bound by Courier/Kendallville, Inc. The cover was printed by Phoenix Color Corp.

 © 1997 by Prentice-Hall, Inc.
Simon & Schuster/A Viacom Company
Upper Saddle River, New Jersey 07458

Earlier editions, entitled *Science for the Elementary School,* © 1989, 1993 by Macmillan Publishing Company and © 1965, 1970, 1975, 1980, and 1985 by Edward Victor.

Photo credits: pages 2, 28, 41, 71, 99, 132, 150, 152, 171, 210 by Scott Cunningham/ Merrill/Prentice Hall; pages 6, 51, 81, 109, 122, 158, 169, and 183 by Impressions; pages 83, 97, 113, 120, 121, 134, 190, 173, 217, 226, 253, and 257 by Anthony Magnacca/ Merrill/Prentice Hall; page 404, Courtesy of NASA; page 116 by Linda Peterson/Merrill/Prentice Hall; pages 50, 66 by Barbara Schwartz/Merrill/Prentice Hall; pages 29, 36, 63, 95, 108, 111, 140, 146, 161, and 208 by Anne Vega/Merrill/Prentice Hall.

Excerpts on pages 265, 423, and 578 are courtesy of the National Academy Press, Washington, DC. Taken from the National Research Council, *National Science Education Standards,* © 1996 National Academy of Sciences, pp. 127, 130, 138, 149, 155, 158, and 166.

Printed in the United States of America

10 9 8 7 6 5 4 3 2

ISBN: 0-13-457037-5

Prentice-Hall International (UK) Limited, *London*
Prentice-Hall of Australia Pty. Limited, *Sydney*
Prentice-Hall of Canada, Inc., *Toronto*
Prentice-Hall of Hispanoamericana, S.A., *Mexico*
Prentice-Hall of India Private Limited, *New Delhi*
Prentice-Hall of Japan, Inc., *Tokyo*
Simon & Schuster Asia Pte., Ltd., *Singapore*
Editora Prentice-Hall do Brasil, Ltda., *Rio de Janeiro*

Preface

INTRODUCTION

Current trends in science education include the ascendancy of cognitive learning theory and its view of intelligence, the rise of the constructivist approach to learning, the use of social-interactive learning as an important instructional practice, and the revival of interest in inquiry teaching—all of which involve students in metacognition and real-life problem-solving. Additional trends include developments in the reorganization and restructuring of schools and an emphasis on activities that celebrate student differences and diversity. These trends prompted major changes for the eighth edition of this textbook. From a sound research base, the valuable and appreciated input of the users of the previous edition and reviewers of the manuscript for this edition, major revisions have been made throughout the book—in essence, for this edition the book has been partially reorganized and completely rewritten—from cover to cover.

PURPOSE OF THIS BOOK

The purpose of this book is to provide a current source of pedagogy, subject-matter content, and exploratory activities in science teaching for

- college and university students preparing to teach science in elementary or middle schools,
- experienced science teachers who desire to continue developing their knowledge and skills for elementary or middle school science teaching, and
- administrators and curriculum specialists who desire to have available for reference purposes a current, practical, and concise book of methods, content, and resources about elementary and middle school science teaching.

OUR BELIEFS: HOW AND WHERE THEY ARE REFLECTED IN THIS BOOK

As a teacher, your greatest resources are the young people you teach and the adults with whom you work. We cannot tell you what will always succeed best with your students; you will know them better than we. In this book we share the best of practice, the most useful of research findings, and the richest of experiences. The numbered statements that follow are statements of our beliefs about elementary and middle school science teaching and how those beliefs are incorporated in this book.

1. *Integrated learning by inquiry is the cornerstone of effective science instruction.* In preparing this new edition we present strategies that integrate learning and provide illustrations of how they may be used. In Chapter 5, "Planning for Science Instruction," for example, we present a theory of the "Spectrum of Integrated Curriculum," and in various chapters of Part II we provide sample methods for integrating student learning of science with other disciplines. Active learning by student inquiry and teaching for thinking are emphasized throughout the book.

2. *Because science teaching at the elementary and middle school level is such an exciting, complex, and ever-changing profession, we believe that to be most effective you should use an eclectic teaching style.* Rather than focusing your attention on particular "models of teaching," this text emphasizes the importance of an eclectic model, whereby you select the best from various instructional approaches. For example, there are times when you will want to use a direct, expository approach, perhaps by lecturing to the students; however, there are other times when you will want to use an indirect, social-interactive, student-centered approach that features cooperative learning or project-based learning. Our desire is to present understanding and guidelines that will both (a) help you decide which approach to use at a particular time and (b) provide the knowledge that will assist you in developing the skills necessary for using a specific approach. These approaches are the essence of the presentation in Chapter 3, "Methods of Teaching Science."

3. *Skill in classroom management is critical to effective teaching, in general, and especially for the science teacher using a project-centered, inquiry-based approach.* Procedures for establishing and maintaining an accepting and safe environment are important to the effective learning of science, and this is also addressed in Chapter 3. General and specific guidelines for safety in the science classroom are presented throughout, especially in Chapters 3, 13, 18, and 21.

4. *Regardless of gender, social class, physical abilities, and ethnic or cultural characteristics, all students must have equal opportunity to participate and learn in the science classroom.* That belief is reflected throughout this book, especially in Chapters 1 and 3.

HOW THIS EDITION DIFFERS FROM THE PRECEDING EDITION

In preparing this edition, besides doing the usual things that authors do when preparing a new edition of an existing book—such as updating the research base and readings—we went much further. As a matter of fact, preparation of this eighth edition began even before the seventh edition was on the bookstore shelves. Our goals were to have this edition released in time to coincide with the publication and for it to be consistent with the content of the *National Science Education Standards*,[1] which, itself, is consistent with the earlier publications, *Science for All Americans*[2] and *Benchmarks for Science Literacy*.[3]

Other specific and major changes in this edition include:

- *The book is rewritten and renamed* Science for the Elementary and Middle School. This was done to reflect the reorganization of many schools—middle schools, for example, now often include grades 6–8, and sometimes even grade 5—and because the National Science Education Standards are organized and presented for grades K–4, 5–8, and 9–12.

- *Every effort was made to reduce the size and, therefore, the cost of the book.* The reason was to make the book more affordable to its student-users.

- *Part II was reorganized with the addition of exploratory activities for sciencing.* Major reorganizational changes made to Part II include (a) the deletion of activities in the prior edition that are dated or no longer relevant; (b) the inclusion of appropriate and useful demonstrations and activities within the science content sections; and (c) the addition of student-centered exploratory activities to complement the content section of each chapter.

- *The science content of Part II was completely rewritten.* The purposes for this rewrite were to (a) correct and update content; (b) delete content that was no longer relevant; (c) connect the science content to modern technology; and (d) assure the inclusion of content most appropriate for grade levels K–8.

ADDITIONAL FEATURES OF THIS BOOK

Other pedagogical features of this edition include:

- Questions for Class Discussion at the end of each chapter in Part I, developed to ensure relevancy, currency, and appropriate levels of thinking and action;

- Resources and Guidelines throughout the book that are current, useful, practical, and tested, as exemplified by the sample interdisciplinary thematic units in Chapters 4 and 10, the guidelines for using copyrighted materials and media and for selecting media in Chapter 4, and the guidelines for using assessment strategies in Chapter 6; and

- Suggested Readings section at the end of each chapter of Part I and a Student Books and Other Resources section at the end of each chapter of Part II to provide current and useful resources.

PEOPLE WE WANT TO THANK

The preparation of this eighth edition has resulted in a major revision; we hope you find the book useful now and throughout your professional career. We appreciate the help we have received from our former students, from teachers and colleagues who have shared their ideas and success and have permitted us to include their names in the book, from authors and publishers who have graciously permitted us to reprint their materials, and from chapter and manuscript reviewers who have helped us immensely to avoid errors and to improve the book's content. As always, though, we assume full responsibility for any errors or shortcomings that slipped through the screening processes.

Persons who have provided important contributions, for which we are deeply grateful, but who are not mentioned elsewhere in this book, include:

Richard L. Bennit, Wayne State University
Evan Bloom, Kaiser Hospital, Sacramento
Michael E. Browne, University of Idaho
Marilyn Cundiff-Gee, Wetlands Program Manager, State of California
Betty Crockar, University of North Texas
Warren Hyde, Valley High School Physics Teacher, Elk Grove, California

Adrian Jund, retired, University of California, Davis
G. Robert Moore, University of Nevada, Las Vegas
Linda Scott-Halverson, St. Cloud State University
Roger B. Wilson, Millersville University of Pennsylvania

We express our special admiration and continued appreciation to the efficacious professionals at Merrill Education at Prentice-Hall.

R. D. K.
E. V.

NOTES

1. National Research Council, *National Science Education Standards*, (Washington, DC: National Academy Press, 1996).
2. American Association for the Advancement of Science, *Science for All Americans* (New York: Oxford University Press, 1989).
3. American Association for the Advancement of Science, *Benchmarks for Science Literacy* (New York: Oxford University Press, 1993).

Brief Contents

Contents

PART II   BASIC SCIENCE INFORMATION, DEMONSTRATIONS, EXPLORATORY ACTIVITIES, AND OTHER RESOURCES   263

EARTH AND THE UNIVERSE   265

Chapter 8   The Universe   266

Chapter 9   The Earth   296

Chapter 10   Water, Weather, and Climate   333

Chapter 11   Air, Aircraft, and Space Travel   395

PART I

TEACHING SCIENCE IN THE ELEMENTARY AND MIDDLE SCHOOL

All teachers of science need to
- *Understand the nature of scientific inquiry, its central role in science, and how to use the skills and processes of scientific inquiry,*
- *Understand the fundamental facts and concepts in the major science disciplines,*
- *Be able to make conceptual connections within and across science disciplines, as well as to mathematics and technology, and*
- *Use scientific understanding and ability when dealing with personal and societal issues.*[1]

CHAPTER 1

Science Teaching in the Elementary and Middle School: An Overview

*Teachers of **grades K–4** usually are generalists who teach most, if not all, school sub-jects. A primary task for these teachers is to lay the experiential, conceptual, and atti-tudinal foundation for future learning in science by guiding students through a range of inquiry activities. To achieve this, elementary teachers of science need to have the op-portunity to develop a broad knowledge of science content in addition to some in-depth experiences in at least one science subject. Such in-depth experiences will allow teach-ers to develop an understanding of inquiry and the structure and production of science knowledge.*

*Science curricula are organized in many different ways in the **middle grades.** Science experiences go into greater depth, are more quantitative, require more sophisti-cated reasoning skills, and use more sophisticated apparatus and technology. These re-quirements of the science courses change the character of the conceptual background re-quired of middle-level teachers of science. While maintaining a breadth of science knowledge, they need to develop greater depth of understanding than their colleagues teaching grades K–4. An intensive, thorough study of at least one scientific discipline will help them meet the demands of their teaching and gain appreciation for how scientific knowledge is produced and how disciplines are structured.[2]*

Welcome to the exciting, ever-changing world of elementary and middle school science teaching. Whether, as a teacher, you will ever be responsible for teaching science, you need to know why learning science in elementary and middle grades is so important for children. If you are now or will be teaching science in any grade, preschool through eight, then you need to know what to teach and how to teach it well. This book is designed to help you make the necessary decisions, to gain appropriate understandings and skills, and to implement them effectively.

The quest begins in this chapter as you learn about (1) the reasons science is taught in the elementary and middle schools, (2) the goals and objectives for elementary and middle school science, and (3) the knowledge and skills you need to teach science effectively.

To understand why science is taught today in elementary and middle grades, it is helpful to review the history of twentieth-century elementary and middle school science. As an es-teemed subject of the school curriculum in the twentieth century, science has had a roller coaster ride. During the final years of this century, however, there is renewed emphasis, both nationally and locally, on the importance of children having early and continued experiences in science. Science is at last recognized as a basic discipline. As stated in *Educating Americans for the 21st Century,* "The basics of the twenty-first century are not only reading, writing and arithmetic . . . [but also] include communication and higher problem-solving skills, and sci-entific and technological literacy."[3] Furthermore, 1990 publication of the American Association for the Advancement of Science adds, "Human survival and the quality of life depend on liberally educated citizens who are able to make informed assessments of the op-portunities and risks inherent in the scientific enterprise. . . . Science must be taught as one of the liberal arts, which it unquestionably is."[4]

There are a steadily increasing variety of effective techniques for teaching science. These advances result from (1) a recognition of the importance of science as a basic discipline in the school curriculum, (2) the continuing rapid development of new technologies, and (3) recent research findings on thinking and about how children learn. Each of these areas is presented and discussed in this book, complemented by the presentation of a broad array of exciting teaching ideas.

To be effective as a science teacher you need to know "what" science is taught and "how" to teach it, and you need to have a firm understanding of "why" you are teaching it. First, let's discuss the "why."

REASONS FOR SCIENCE IN THE ELEMENTARY AND MIDDLE SCHOOL CURRICULUM

Historically, in the United States, science was the last of the major disciplines to be included in the curriculum of elementary and middle school grades. Today it is taught in those grades because (1) learning science can build attitudes that are important, (2) science learning attends to and nourishes the child's natural curiosity about the environment, (3) science learning builds a base for important understanding, and (4) learning science develops skills necessary for survival in the real world. As stated by *Project 2061: Science Literacy for a Changing Future,* "K–12 education . . . should be reformed so that all American high school graduates are science literate—that is, equipped with the knowledge and skills they need to make sense of how the world works, to think critically and independently, and to lead interesting, responsible, and productive lives in a culture increasingly shaped by science and technology. . . . The common core of learning in science, mathematics, and technology should center on science literacy . . . [and] should emphasize connections among the natural and social sciences, mathematics, and technology and between those areas and the arts, humanities, and vocational subjects."[5]

To help your understanding of the role of science in the elementary and middle school curriculum today, let's review how the science curriculum has evolved.

In the Beginning

The history of science in the school curriculum is a reflection of economic and political events in our society. Until the economic depression of the 1870s practically no science was taught in the elementary schools; the emphasis was on reading, writing, spelling, and arithmetic. Science learning was the privilege only of children of well-to-do parents who could afford private tutoring. Their tutoring was accomplished with the use of didactic reading materials about natural phenomena, reading materials that were brought from abroad, primarily from England. The organization of the National Education Association in 1857 helped to make some of that literature available for use in school classrooms in the United States.

PESTALOZZI AND OBJECT TEACHING
In the 1870s, science taught in schools was based on the writings of the Swiss educator Johann Pestalozzi (1746–1827). Pestalozzi believed that emphasis in teaching should be on training of the mind and that students should learn by observing and experimenting, using all their senses, rather than by merely memorizing facts from books. However, at the time of America's Industrial Revolution in the late nineteenth century, Pestalozzi's "object-centered" approach lost its appeal because of its lack of emphasis on content and sequential organization. As a direct result of the Industrial Revolution, with its exodus of people from rural areas into cities and a mass migration of people to the United States, elementary science programs were developed that emphasized content and vocational technology—utilitarian science.

THE NATURE STUDY MOVEMENT
In the final decade of the nineteenth century, to balance the content of a vocational-oriented science curriculum, nature study was introduced in a few schools, mostly in the state of New

York. Its purpose was to help children develop a balanced life by getting to know the natural environment through firsthand observation, classification, and measurement of objects and organisms—e.g., birds, flowers, and rocks—in natural habitats.

Almost from its beginning, however, the nature study movement met obstacles and criticism, and resistance only increased with time. This movement was introduced by people who were both specialists in science and master teachers. They were able to make the study of nature a dynamic and unforgettable learning experience for the children. However, once entrusted to other teachers, with little or no background in science and with varying degrees of teaching effectiveness, the study of nature in the elementary schools deteriorated. Undue emphasis was placed on incidental items. Identification and classification assumed increasing importance and eventually became the end, rather than the means. Learning activities involving firsthand observations gave way to reading about nature in books, where much of the science content was only partially correct and fable and fancy were often interspersed with the science. By 1920 it was clear that nature study, as being taught in the schools, was not successful. Nature study was dead; utilitarian science was alive.

Landmarks in the Development of the Elementary and Middle School Science Curriculum

As we approach the end of this millenium and reset our compass for the start of a voyage into the next century of science education, it seems most appropriate to reflect and to learn from the history of the past 100 years of elementary and middle level science education in this country. There have been significant and important landmarks indeed.

JOHN DEWEY
A century ago, John Dewey demonstrated in his laboratory school in Chicago the importance of children being given responsibility for their own learning, of their being allowed to pursue their natural curiosity. He further posited that children learn best through direct experience. Shortly thereafter, in his 1910 publication, Dewey spoke of the importance of *science as inquiry,* and argued for *curriculum integration*.[6]

SCHOOL RESTRUCTURING
During those early years of the twentieth century, the nation's population markedly increased. Schools were undergoing reorganization. One of the changes was the organization and development of the junior high school, with an initiation of courses in general science. Influenced by colleges and universities, and because of the change from an 8–4 pattern of organization (eight years of elementary school and four years of high school) to a 6–3–3 pattern (six years of elementary school, three years of junior high school, and three years of high school), the science curriculum at each level changed. The development of the junior high school with courses in general science was a landmark that caused changes in the elementary school science curriculum.

GERALD CRAIG
In 1927, while a student at Columbia University, Gerald S. Craig wrote his doctoral dissertation, which became another landmark in the historical development of science curriculum. Responding to economic and political situations, his thesis, titled *Certain Techniques Used in Developing a Course of Study in Science for the Horace Mann Elementary School,* led to the development of a science curriculum that dominated elementary school science for more than three decades. In essence, Craig organized the existing chaos of science instruction into a sequence of what and how. Craig strongly favored teaching science through *investigations by the children*.

The goals of elementary and middle school science require programs that emphasize experiences designed to further the intellectual, emotional, physical, and social development of children. Firsthand observation and learning by doing have nearly always been recognized as important in achieving those goals.

YEARBOOKS OF THE NATIONAL SOCIETY FOR THE STUDY OF EDUCATION

In 1932, shortly after the publication of Craig's thesis and while the nation started to recover from economic depression, yet another landmark appeared—the publication of the National Society for the Study of Education's (NSSE) *Thirty-first Yearbook*,[7] which dealt exclusively with science in public schools. The yearbook recommended a continuous science program from kindergarten through the twelfth grade. Further, it proposed that the objectives of science teaching were to develop an understanding of (1) the major generalizations of science and (2) associated scientific attitudes. Emphasizing scientific understandings, science as a body of factual information, and the applications of science and technology, the *Thirty-first Yearbook* had profound influence on the direction of textbooks, course syllabi, and curriculum development. The importance of problem-solving strategies and the development of certain attitudes and appreciations, however, were neglected.

Another landmark for elementary school science was reached in 1947, following the end of World War II—publication of the second yearbook of NSSE to be devoted to science education. Recognizing the impact of science on society, the *Forty-sixth Yearbook*[8] reaffirmed NSSE's earlier recommendation for a continuous K–12 science program. Further, it stressed that the learning outcomes should be functional and proposed the following general goals: (1) the functional understanding of facts, principles, and concepts, and (2) the development of functional scientific skills, attitudes, appreciations, and interests. Although facts and understandings of science still dominated as the major focus of science instruction, problem-solving skills and development of attitudes and appreciations were also addressed.

In 1960, in its *Fifty-ninth Yearbook,*[9] the third to be devoted to science education, the NSSE expressed awareness of the increasing dependence of society on science. It now took for granted that schools had a continuous and articulated K–12 science program. It repeated the basic goals stated in the *Forty-sixth Yearbook*, deleting the word "functional" and adding critical thinking, emphasis on problem solving, and a stress on the importance of teaching science as a process of inquiry. By the early 1960s it had become clear to science educators that what scientists do is to invent and use conceptual schemes, which are then modified over time and occasionally even discarded.[10] Conceptual schemes, then, became the framework for an articulated kindergarten through twelfth-grade science program.

In the early 1960s children's learning of science became a national concern, triggered by several factors. First, in 1957 the Soviet Union had sent up the world's first orbiting space satellite, Sputnik. Second, in the world race for technological superiority, the United States was not winning, but was experiencing a critical shortage of scientists and technicians. Third, scientists and science educators were deploring that insufficient attention in schools was being given to teaching science as a process of inquiry.

THE NATIONAL CURRICULUM DEVELOPMENT PROJECTS OF THE 1960s

Out of this national concern, many programs, sponsored mostly by the National Science Foundation (NSF), were initiated for improving the teaching and learning of science in public schools. At first, the NSF-sponsored projects were developed to upgrade science teaching at the high school level. Projects were then created for improving middle level science programs. Attention eventually focused on elementary school science, and several projects were developed at that level.

The national curriculum projects were the most exciting events to have happened in science education. They were extensively publicized because their heavy financial support made possible the large-scale involvement of scientists, science educators, teachers, psychologists, and children. For guidance and direction in developing their programs, the projects turned to the theories and research of child development psychologists on how children develop intellectually and learn. The projects were actively concerned with teaching science as a process of inquiry—*teaching science as it is practiced*. After several years of testing, scientific supply houses packaged, advertised, and sold the materials needed for the learning activities that were an integral part of the projects.

Although the NSF-sponsored projects did not agree on the role, quantity, and emphasis of content or on the degree of freedom for student exploration, they did agree that science should be taught as a process of inquiry. A major contribution of the projects was to ensure that an inquiry approach to teaching science assumed its rightful place in the school science program. This inquiry-based approach is an emphasis that continues today. For example, "Teaching Standard A" of the *National Science Education Standards,* published in 1996, states that "teachers of science plan an inquiry-based science program for their students."[11]

A second major contribution of the NSF-sponsored science curriculum projects, concomitant with teaching science as a process of inquiry, was the change from the teacher as a teller about science, to the teacher as a guide who facilitates students doing *hands-on science*—another emphasis that continues today.

A third contribution was the movement from a textbook-centered curriculum to a materials-centered one, with the presentation of fewer areas of content, to be studied in greater detail. Knowing less but understanding it better is also a recommended emphasis today. For example, a fundamental premise of *Project 2061* (discussed later in this chapter) is that schools do not need to teach more but should teach less so that what is taught is learned better.[12]

Of the elementary science curriculum projects developed in the 1960s, three emerged as most popular: the *Elementary Science Study* (ESS), the *Science Curriculum Improvement Study* (SCIS), and *Science—A Process Approach* (SAPA). Although all have undergone revision, they continue in use in some schools. Figure 3.11 (p. 119) illustrates specifics about these programs and others.

Although the NSF-sponsored inquiry-based, activities-oriented programs were more effective in raising student performance and attitudes about science than were traditional reading-based programs,[13] in the 1970s their popularity began to wane, for several reasons. School systems found it difficult to adapt the prepackaged materials to local curricula. Schools' finances diminished as a long inflationary period steadily eroded their budgets. For many teachers, the activities were too complex and required too much preparation time in an already busy school day. So the trend again was for schools to develop their own science programs, adapted to their individual needs and conditions. The NSF-funded curriculum projects, and similar ones that followed, disappeared from many schools, leaving perhaps a few of their activities and teaching ideas incorporated into existing local science programs.

Also in the 1970s there was concern about the decreasing verbal and mathematical scores of children on national examinations. A growing "back to the basics" movement undoubtedly distracted schools from the interest in science generated during the previous decade.

BACK TO THE "BASICS"

In the 1970s and throughout much of the 1980s, schools were accused of relaxing their demands for children to learn thoroughly the basics of reading, spelling, grammar, composition, and mathematics. Consequently, a strong back-to-basics movement arose (and may be on the rise again as this twentieth century comes to a close). Simultaneously, there was a steadily increasing shortage of well-trained science and mathematics teachers, making it difficult to find teachers capable of teaching science as inquiry. Although, in the 1970s and 1980s, the original NSF-sponsored projects underwent revision and new projects emerged, by 1990 a preoccupation with learning scientific facts was accompanied by an increased emphasis on textbook learning of the "fundamentals."

As stated in 1990 by Bruce Watson and Richard Konicek,

> Today's texts, which have the greatest influence on how science is taught in American schools, have come almost full circle, and teachers who rely primarily on them are little closer to teaching science as inquiry than were their counterparts in the 1920s. In too many classrooms across the U.S., science is still taught as a cohesive set of facts to be absorbed, and children are viewed as blank slates on which teachers are to write.[14]

In the late 1970s and throughout the 1980s, science teaching stressed acquisition of science knowledge, with little or no attention given to application or to the reforms offered by the science curriculum projects of the 1960s. In 1982, the National Science Teachers Association published a position statement that urged new goals for science teaching, emphasizing the education of students for scientific literacy.[15]

A Nation at Risk. National Commission on Excellence in Education. Washington, DC: United States Office of Education, 1983.

A Nation Prepared: Teachers for the 21st Century. Washington, DC: Carnegie Forum on Education and the Economy, 1986.

Anderson, R. C.; Heibert, E. H.; Scott, J. A.; and Wilkinson, I. A. G. *Becoming a Nation of Readers: The Report of the Commission on Reading.* Washington, DC: National Institute of Education, 1985.

Applebee, A. N., et al. *The Writing Report Card: Writing Achievement in American Schools.* Princeton, NJ: National Assessment of Educational Progress at Educational Testing Service, 1986.

————. *Who Reads Best?* Princeton, NJ: National Assessment of Educational Progress at Educational Testing Service, 1988.

Berliner, D. C., and Biddle, B. J. *The Manufactured Crisis: Myth, Fraud, and the Attack on America's Public Schools.* New York: Addison-Wesley, 1995.

Criteria for Excellence. Washington, DC: National Science Teachers Association, 1987.

Educating Americans for the 21st Century. Washington, DC: National Science Board, 1983.

Goodlad, J. I. *A Place Called School.* New York: McGraw-Hill, 1984.

————. *Teachers for Our Nation's Schools.* San Francisco: Jossey-Bass, 1990.

Glasser, W. *The Quality School.* New York: Harper & Row, 1990.

Project Synthesis. Washington, DC: National Science Foundation, 1981.

Jacobson, W., and Doran, R. *Science Achievement in Western Countries.* Elmsford, NY: Pergamon Press, 1989.

The Continuing Crisis in Science Education: The AAAS Responds. A Report to the Board of Directors. Washington, DC: The American Association for the Advancement of Science, 1986.

The Liberal Art of Science: Agenda for Action. Washington, DC: The American Association for the Advancement of Science, 1990.

FIGURE 1.1   Sample of the influential publications that began in the 1980s.

DECADE OF THE REPORTS

Certainly, no facet of education receives more attention from the media, causes more concern among parents and teachers, or gets larger headlines than a reported decline in students' achievement in the public schools. Reports are issued, polls taken, debates organized, and blue-ribbon panels formed. Community members write letters to local editors about this trend, news editors devote editorial space to it, television anchors comment about it, and documentaries and specials focus on it. Headlines proclaim, for example, "America's Children Study and Know Less Science Than Do Children of Most Other Countries."

Never were so many reports about education published in such a short time as there were in 1983 and 1984. More than 120 national studies were published during just those two years. The interest continues today. Consider the brief sample list of influential publications shown in Figure 1.1.

THE 1990s

In response to the reports, educators and politicians acted. Around the country, their actions resulted in:

- Changes in standards for teacher certification.[16]
- Commitments to upgrade the teaching force.
- Emphasis on helping students make connections between what is being learned and real life, as well as connections between subjects in the curriculum.
- Emphasis on rising test scores, reduced dropout rates, increasing class time, and changing curricula.
- Emphasis on education for cultural diversity.
- Financial recognition and new roles for teachers as mentors.
- Formation of school-home-community partnership to enhance the education of children.
- Federally enacted "Goals 2000: Educate America Act," and the development of national education standards for all major subject areas.[17]

- Increased involvement of parents and guardians in their children's education.
- New "basics" requirements for a high school diploma.
- Ways of teaching children who have limited proficiency in English.[18]
- Teacher-competency testing.

KEY PRACTICES TODAY

Key practices today include

- Dividing the student body and faculty into smaller groups, i.e., "houses" (school-within-a-school concept), and using nontraditional scheduling and teaching teams.
- Facilitating children's social skills as they interact, relate to one another, and develop relationships and friendships.
- Facilitating the developing of children's values as related to their families, the community, and schools.
- Holding high expectations for all children.
- Integrating the curriculum, especially the language arts, and introducing reading and writing across the curriculum.
- Introducing the Internet and using it with children in the classroom.
- Involving communities in the schools; developing community learning centers.
- Involving parents and guardians in school decision-making.
- Involving students in self-assessment and student-directed parent conferences.
- Making multicultural education work for all children.
- Providing students with the opportunity to learn to think and be creative, rather than simply to memorize and repeat information.
- Using heterogeneous grouping and cooperative learning, peer and cross-age tutoring as instructional strategies.

Today: Focus on Science and Technology Literacy

In 1990, in a publication titled *The Liberal Art of Science: Agenda for Action*, the American Association for the Advancement of Science (AAAS), a leading federation of scientific societies with more than 141,000 individual members and nearly 300 affiliated scientific and engineering societies and academics of science, emphasized that science is fundamental to a liberal education and that people need to understand:

- The nature of the scientific endeavor, concepts, principles, and theories that describe the natural world;
- Unifying concepts that integrate the sciences with other disciplines; and
- How scientific knowledge influences and is influenced by the intellectual tradition of the culture in which that knowledge is embedded.[19]

However, nearly a decade before that publication, the AAAS began its *Project 2061*, a long-term multiphase project to work in collaboration with school-district teams to "radically improve science, mathematics, and technology education for the 21st century." The approach to Earth of Halley's Comet in 1985 prompted the project's originators to imagine all the scientific and technological changes that a child entering school in 1985 would likely live to witness before the return of the comet in 2061—hence the name *Project 2061*.[20]

Initially, *Project 2061* focused on the substance of science literacy. Publication of *Science for All Americans (SFAA)*[21] was the major product of that effort. SFAA proposes the dimensions of scientific literacy—the knowledge, skills, and attitudes—that students should have as a result of their K–12 science experiences. As defined by that publication, the dimensions of scientific literacy are:

- Being familiar with the natural world and recognizing both its diversity and its unity
- Understanding key concepts and principles of science
- Being aware of some of the important ways in which science, mathematics, and technology depend on one another
- Knowing that science, mathematics, and technology are human enterprises and knowing what that implies about their strengths and limitations
- Having a capacity for scientific ways of thinking
- Using scientific knowledge and ways of thinking for individual and social purposes[22]

Emphasizing the connectedness of knowledge from various disciplines, SFAA recommends softening the boundaries so as to make better connections between and among traditional subject disciplines. It also recommends reducing the amount of detail that students are required to remember.

Project 2061 involves teams of educators and scientists transforming SFAA into a number of alternative curriculum models. A product of that effort, and the second major tool developed by *Project 2061*, is the publication *Benchmarks for Science Literacy*.[23] *Benchmarks* elaborates on the SFAA recommendations in terms of students' progress toward each of the learning goals in SFAA—specifically, what students should be able to do by the end of grades 2, 5, 8, and 12.

Project 2061 teams are now working on the identification of useful current materials, units of instruction and curriculum models, a resource database for curriculum and instruction, and blueprints for reforming other aspects of the educational system to accommodate new curriculum models.

Until 1989 national curriculum standards did not exist in the United States. The National Council on Education Standards and Testing recommended that national standards for subject content in education be developed for all core subjects—the arts, civics/social studies, English/language arts/reading, geography, history, mathematics, and science. In 1989, the National Council of Teachers of Mathematics (NCTM) issued standards for mathematics for grades K through 12. Within just three years, more than 40 states, usually through state curriculum frameworks, were following those standards to guide what and how mathematics is taught and how student progress is assessed.

In 1991, coordinated by the National Research Council (NRC), the operating arm of the National Academy of Science, began work on national standards for science curriculum, teaching, and assessment, which were published in their final form in 1996. In preparing these standards, the *National Science Education Standards* drew extensively from, and made independent use and interpretation of, the statements concerning what students should know and be able to do that were published earlier in the AAAS publications *Science for All Americans* and *Benchmarks for Science Literacy*.

Today science teaching may not yet be all it can be, but science itself has undoubtedly become a basic subject at the elementary and middle school levels. As a new teacher, you may understand this well. However, some experienced teachers and school administrators may not. Part of your task as a teacher may be to convince your colleagues of the importance and value of science in the school curriculum.

EDUCATIONAL REFORM IS A SLOW PROCESS: PROBLEMS AND ISSUES THAT AFFECT THE SCHOOL SCIENCE PROGRAM

Improvement in the teaching and learning of science in the elementary and middle schools does not occur just because influential individuals and organizations say it should. As someone once remarked, reorganizing and restructuring schools is like trying to rebuild a 747 jetliner while it is in flight; changing tradition and people's minds is analogous to trying to stop an onrushing tank with only your hands. Changing what people do and think is often a long process, which may be one reason that *Project 2061* is designed as a long-term project. As a new teacher for the twenty-first century you will become an integral and important agent in this change process.

The improvement of science teaching and learning does not occur in a vacuum. As indicated in the preceding summary of landmarks in science education, the importance of science teaching coexists with many other significant problems and important issues shared by public schools and society, such as the following examples:

- A national pressure to end traditional ability grouping or tracking of children in school.[24]
- A national system of uniform educational standards and assessment practices.[25]
- Controversy over the content of textbooks.
- Inconsistent concensus among politicians on education issues from one year to the next.
- Inner-city school dropout rates.
- Overcrowded classrooms.
- Staff development related to the scarcity of minority teachers to serve as role models for minority students and the need to assist teachers to work effectively with students who are culturally different from the teacher.
- School security and the problem of weapons, crime, violence, and drugs on school campuses and in school neighborhoods.[26]
- Sexual harassment (i.e., unwanted and unwelcomed sexual behavior that interferes with a child's life) of children while they are at school, mostly from other students but sometimes from school employees.
- Teaching and assessing for higher-order thinking skills and the development of national performance-based assessment strategies.
- The education of teachers to work effectively with students who may be too overwhelmed by family and other problems to focus on learning and succeed in school.
- The continuing, long-running controversy over the teaching of values and sex education.[27]

Consideration of these complex issues, along with a strong back-to-basics movement and recent research on how children learn concepts in science, have helped correct some of the imbalances produced by the earlier science curriculum projects. For example, the preoccupation of earlier projects with the key processes of science often led schools and teachers to discourage reading in science and, in many cases, to eliminate reading completely from the science program. Today, new knowledge about learning and a renewed emphasis on human issues and fundamentals needed to live useful and meaningful lives have served to integrate subjects in the curriculum. Today's science teacher is no longer isolated from the rest of the school curriculum. Although Dewey professed synthesis of the curriculum with children's life experiences, it was with *Project 2061: Science for All Americans*, more than 70 years after Dewey, that in science education there began a concerted national effort to develop a curriculum that focuses on helping children make connections between disciplines and real-life experiences, and that emphasizes ideas and thinking, rather than the traditional preservation of boundaries between academic disciplines, with importance given to specialized vocabulary and memorization. Furthermore, in the earlier curriculum projects, emphasis on the key operations of science resulted in a tendency to assign the learning of concepts to a position of secondary importance in the program. Now, however, concepts, processes, the internalization of values, and the human aspects of the scientific enterprise are recognized as equal in importance, as interdependent and interrelated not only among themselves, but also to the entire curriculum. Today, science has become a vital, balanced, integrated school activity. Exemplary science teaching today is concerned with teaching science and integrating it into the curriculum in a way that is meaningful to the everyday lives of all students, and in a way that is helpful to each child's developing self-esteem.

Perhaps the words of Herbert Smith, written in 1963, are equally appropriate today:

One may summarize the historical overview [of elementary and middle school science] by pointing out that the past century has been a century of unprecedented social, economic, scientific, and technological change. The schools are to a very large degree a mirror of the ambient culture, and they are probably more sensitive to social change than any other educational level. They are always, to a degree, consonant with the prevailing philosophies and state of knowledge in existence at any particular time. Fundamental changes in philosophy, in theories of child rearing and educability, in the need for universal and extended educational training for all children and adolescents of our society with capacity to learn, have been accepted within this century. Science, itself, has progressed from the dilettantism of the leisured intellectual to a basic and fundamental activity of a substantial percentage of [all humankind].[28]

From the preceding survey of the historical landmarks that have led to today's emphases in science education, the key reasons science is taught in elementary and middle schools today are summarized in the paragraphs that follow.

Building Attitudes That Are Important

Dogmatic teaching is lethal to effective learning in science, whereas unrestrained thought enhances a child's natural curiosity. You should teach your class as if it were a think tank, encouraging skepticism, suspension of judgment, guessing, and intuitive thought. As teacher, you must model these behaviors yourself.

Values and attitudes begin forming at an early age. Thus there are attitudinal objectives for science learning for the earliest grades—objectives that should be incorporated into the science curriculum starting in kindergarten. Examples of sound learning objectives for all grades, which begin in kindergarten, are:

- The child demonstrates curiosity about the natural world.
- The child demonstrates respect for humans and other living things.
- The child demonstrates conservation practices.

Children must learn that science and scientific ways of thinking are important to their daily living and that careers in science and technology are open to all, not only to Caucasian males. The teacher can and should help dispel myths, superstitions, and stereotypes about science, sciencing,[29] and scientists.

Through science, children can develop intellectual and communication skills—skills that improve their ability to get along with each other and to understand the natural world. Our environment is a rich "classroom" in which to teach science to children. We should strive always to leave it a better place. This includes avoiding unnecessary collecting and general "ripping off" of the outdoors. It means encouraging practices of preservation and enhancement of the environment. Such practice should begin with the child's *inner environment* (the child's own self), then proceed to the child's *immediate environment* (the child's own "turf"), which includes the classroom and other places where the child lives. When these environmental aspects of the child's world have been nourished and cared for, the *global environment* can be considered. A child cannot be expected to show concern for the future of an endangered species in a faraway place if the world of the child's own inner self is being inadequately tended. For example, a child from an urban environment on the East Coast who comes to school hungry can't be expected to show much concern for the future of the spotted owl in the timberlands of the Northwest.

A skillful teacher strives for a balance between objective behaviors and intuitive thinking and creates a classroom climate where all children are welcomed and feel free to learn within a rich environment of shared responsibilities and decision making.

Building Foundations for Understandings

In science, children should practice inquiry skills that lead to higher-order thinking. For example, kindergarten children can be taught the importance of listening fully to the ideas of others—a step toward the development of a critical, questioning attitude. They can be taught skills needed to generate data, such as observing, recalling, identifying, and measuring. Children should also be taught how to handle and care for plants, for animals, and for each other.

Children should learn cognitions in science that build as they progress from one level of schooling to the next. Kindergarten children learn to *identify* objects with similar characteristics, to *compare* and match pictures of animals and their offspring, to *predict* what will happen in some particular case, and to *experiment* to discover whether their predictions were correct. These are but a few of the intellectual skills that lead to a child's developing understanding of the larger conceptual organizations around which the K–12 science curriculum is built.

Science is taught in the kindergarten and primary grades not only because that is where we must begin laying the foundation for conceptual understandings and positive attitudes and feelings about science and technology, but because it is at this time we must stimulate and develop the child's innate curiosity about the natural environment. By doing science and learning science, children can:

- Develop and apply values that contribute to their affective development
- Develop positive attitudes about science and technology
- Develop an awareness of the relationship and interdependence of science, technology, and society
- Develop an awareness of careers in science and technology
- Develop higher-order thinking skills
- Develop knowledge, understandings, and skills that contribute to their intellectual growth
- Develop their psychomotor skills

GOALS AND OBJECTIVES FOR ELEMENTARY AND MIDDLE SCHOOL SCIENCE

As a teacher, you will often encounter the compound structure "goals and objectives." There is a distinction however, and the easiest way to understand the difference between the two words, "goals" and "objectives," is to look at your intent.

Goals are ideas that you intend to reach, i. e., ideals that you would like to have accomplished. Goals may be stated as teacher goals, as student goals, as course goals, or even more broadly, as goals of elementary or middle school science (the broadest goals are sometimes referred to as "aims"). Ideally, in all, the goal is the same. If, for example, the broad goal (aim) is to improve students' scientific literacy, it can be stated as follows:

Teacher or course goal
   "To help students become scientifically literate"
or
Student goal
   "To improve my literacy in science"

Goals are general statements of intent[30] and are prepared by others or by teachers early in curriculum planning. From goals, objectives are prepared and written, preferably, in behavioral terms so that assessment strategies can be prepared that best align with the objectives. Objectives are *not* intentions; they are the actual behaviors teachers intend to cause students to display. In short, objectives are what students *do*.

As implied in the preceding paragraphs, goals guide the science curriculum and the instructional methods; objectives drive student performance. Instructional goals are general statements, usually not even complete sentences, often beginning with the infinitive "to." They identify what the teacher intends for the students to learn. Objectives, stated in performance (behavioral) terms,[31] are specific anticipated student actions. Objectives are complete sentences that include the verb "will" to indicate what each student is expected to be able to do as a result of the instructional experience. Objectives that are written in behavioral terms are more clearly measurable. Although goals may not always be quantifiable, that is, readily measurable, objectives when correctly written are always measurable. This subject is discussed further in Chapter 5.

Goals for Elementary and Middle School Science

An articulated K–12 science curriculum is held together by at least six broad goals that have evolved during the past century or more of science education in this country. The broad goals are to help students:

1. To become scientifically literate
2. To learn to solve real problems by thinking critically and creatively
3. To understand our environment and the problems of preserving it and making it better
4. To understand how science, technology, and society are interrelated
5. To live successfully and productively in a constantly changing world
6. To grow intellectually, emotionally, and socially according to their individual abilities, interests, and needs

TO BECOME SCIENTIFICALLY LITERATE

One goal of science education is to develop scientifically literate and personally concerned citizens who will think and act rationally and productively. The elementary and middle school science programs play an important role in getting children off to a good start toward achieving this goal.

The scientifically literate person (SLP) is one who has an understanding of the products and processes of science and will use them daily in making decisions while interacting with other people and the environment. The products of science include facts, concepts, principles, and theories. The processes include specific skills, attitudes, and values.

Let us define some terms that seem particularly relevant to the goal of scientific literacy. "One of the greatest barriers to scientific literacy is the specialized vocabulary of science and its relationship to concepts. Students must recognize the importance of this language and learn the basic terminology for accurate communication and shared understanding."[32] As a teacher of science, you must model correct usage, and to do that you must understand terms.

Definitions Relevant to Understanding Science and the Goal of Scientific Literacy

1. **Fact.** A fact can be defined as something known by observation or experience to be true or to have happened. Generally, two criteria are used to identify a scientific fact: (a) it is directly observable, and (b) it can be readily demonstrated. Although facts, such as the

fact that you are reading these lines now, have little meaning by themselves, they serve as the foundation for the development and understanding of concepts, principles, and theories. Thoughtful reasoning is necessary to make meaningful sense from a fact.

2. **Concept.** One acceptable definition is that a concept is an abstraction that organizes the world of objects and events into a smaller number of categories.[33] Examples of concepts are "combine," "human," "plant," "star," "acid," "water," and "electron flow." A concept results from the accumulation of facts with a common attribute. To comprehend the full meaning of a concept we must understand its definition, its attributes, and its value.

3. **Principle** (or generalization or law). Principles can be concepts or rules, but are those that involve some sort of relationship between two or more concepts. An example of a principle is "An acid and a base will combine to form water." Within this principle are four separate concepts—acid, base, combine, and water.

4. **Theory** and **hypothesis.** To understand the term "theory," as used in science, requires that you understand the term "hypothesis." In ordinary usage, outside science, the terms are used interchangeably. In science, they are not; they mean different things. A hypothesis is a speculation—a guess that remains untested. In everyday usage, when someone says "I have a theory about . . . ," that person actually has a hypothesis. Theories have more empirical support than do hypotheses, even more than so-called "educated guesses." A theory is a speculation about a rather large idea that has been empirically supported. Examples of scientific theories include "molecular structure," "biological evolution," and "cell structure."

The scientifically literate person knows the difference between facts and theories. Whereas facts are accepted truths, that is, realities that are directly observable and consistently demonstrated, theories, on the other hand, are in a constant state of revision. The scientific name of humans is *Homo sapiens,* and that is a fact. That the sun consists of helium, however, is a conclusion.

5. **Conclusion.** A conclusion is not a fact, but an inference based on fact. As opposed to a fact, a conclusion has not been directly observed.

6. **Model.** Sometimes, in science, we use the term "model." A scientific model is a visual or mental image of something we cannot see. It is a representation of either a phenomenon or an abstract idea.

Of course, terms and their definitions are words invented by people for ease and efficiency in communication. As we emphasize again in Part II of this book, natural phenomena do not always fit textbook definitions. Sometimes the distinctions between hypotheses, theories, and models are obscure. On the other hand, to be scientifically literate requires that we understand the language so that we can communicate effectively. To help students increase their literacy in science, the teacher must model scientific literacy.

As well as being able to communicate articulately, being scientifically literate also includes being able to self-reflect.

7. **Self-reflection** means being conscious of one's own opinions and judgments and the role of humans in the natural world. Self-reflection derives from an ability to analyze one's own arguments, to determine the factual basis for information, to evaluate the quality of evidence, and to identify and assess one's premises and values. Self-reflection frees an individual from egocentrism, intellectual provincialism, and an anthropocentric worldview.[34]

8. The **scientifically literate person** knows the social implications of science and recognizes the role of rational thinking in arriving at value judgments and solving social problems. The SLP knows how to learn, to inquire, to gain knowledge, and to solve new problems. Throughout life the SLP continues to inquire, to increase his or her knowledge base, and uses that knowledge to self-reflect and to promote the development of people as rational human beings.

TO SOLVE PROBLEMS BY THINKING CRITICALLY AND CREATIVELY

Children are natural problem identifiers and solvers. The school science program should help them develop their skills in identifying and solving problems. The methods of problem solving should not be presented to students so rigidly that they are discouraged from trying to do things their own way. Creative problem solving must allow for serendipity and intuitive thought. Like scientists, children can and do learn from their own mistakes. When given latitude, children sometimes devise surprisingly interesting, creative, and satisfactory solutions.

A good science program takes advantage of the fact that children have inquiring minds and encourages students to inquire into the cause and effect of things that are happening to them. It raises problems that will allow meaningful learning, not just rote memorization. A good science program also whets the students' natural curiosity and enthusiasm. It is designed to help students develop their thinking skills and to think about their own thinking (metacognition). Each time a student uses a rational and reflective thinking approach in trying to solve a problem, that student is one step closer to being a scientifically literate person.

TO UNDERSTAND OUR ENVIRONMENT AND THE PROBLEMS OF PRESERVING IT AND MAKING IT BETTER

Children are interested and curious about almost everything. They are interested in themselves, the sky, the earth, the air, matter and energy, and living things. Because of their interests, the science program should be designed to help students learn concepts that enable them to understand and interpret their environment. Facts should be used primarily for building students' understandings of concepts, not as ends to their learning.

The program should be organized so there is opportunity to reinforce the students' understanding of concepts and their relationships. It must help students realize that scientific knowledge is cumulative and that often it is necessary to use prior knowledge to gain new knowledge. In the process, students become familiar with historical incidents in science and thus assimilate the historical flavor of science. Finally, in learning science, children develop a vocabulary that they will find useful for years to come.

Today our environment is faced with many complex problems, such as air and water pollution, global warming and ozone depletion, solid and nuclear waste disposal, depletion of natural resources, and ecological imbalances. It is obvious that science, society, and technology must play collaborative roles to solve these problems. The science program, then, must be vitally concerned with helping students learn how to work collaboratively and to learn about the delicate balance of nature and ways of preserving and enhancing what is left of it.

TO UNDERSTAND HOW SCIENCE, TECHNOLOGY, AND SOCIETY ARE INTERRELATED

The science program must consider the relationship and interdependency of science, technology, and society. Although they are interrelated and interdependent, science and technology are not the same, and their goals are sometimes quite different. **Science** is the knowledge gathered through systematic inquiry about the natural world. **Technology** is the translation of scientific knowledge into the development of products and processes. To put it another and perhaps more meaningful way, "Technology is the process and product of human skill and ingenuity in designing and making things out of available resources to satisfy personal and societal needs and wants."[35] The following list is useful in differentiating technology and science:

Technology	Science
Concerned with "how to."	Concerned with "what is."
Knowledge is created.	Knowledge is discovered.
Guided by trial and error.	Guided by theory.
Oriented toward action.	Oriented toward research.[36]

Science usually has a long-range effect on humans and on the course of civilization, whereas technology has an immediate effect on the physical, economic, social, and cultural aspects of our existence. The achievements of science and technology often call for social and economic innovations if such achievements are to be used advantageously for the benefit of humans and without detrimental effects to the environment. Consequently, a science program must be designed to help students develop an awareness and understanding of the social and economic aspects of science and technology, and the values derived from them. We want our children to become informed citizens who understand these relationships and can make intelligent decisions when called upon.

TO LIVE SUCCESSFULLY AND PRODUCTIVELY IN A CONSTANTLY CHANGING WORLD

It is human nature to be comfortable and secure with the known and familiar, but it is also true that we live in a world of ongoing change. Scientific knowledge is rapidly changing, and societies of people are forever changing. The science program must help students understand that scientific knowledge is tentative and continues to change as evidence accumulates. Understanding the tentative and cumulative nature of scientific knowledge, and of the thinking skills used in sciencing, can help students better deal with ambiguity, with the tentative nature of knowledge, and with the problems that result from the continued changes in society and in their own lives.

TO GROW INTELLECTUALLY, EMOTIONALLY, AND SOCIALLY ACCORDING TO INDIVIDUAL ABILITIES, INTERESTS, AND NEEDS

The science program must provide for the individual and emotional growth of all children. You must be prepared not only to teach science but to do so effectively with students of various cultural backgrounds, diverse linguistic abilities, and different learning styles, as well as with students who have been identified as having special needs. The science program should offer a wide range of learning activities for students, making it possible to provide for their varied abilities, interests, and needs. An exemplary educational program helps each child grow to the utmost of that child's ability.

These are six broad goals that should guide the elementary and middle school science program. They are compatible with the four goals for school science that underlie the *National Science Education Standards* (see Figure 1.2). The principles that underlie those standards are shown in Figure 1.3. From such goals, teachers derive specific objectives.

The goals for school science that underlie the *National Science Education Standards* are to educate students who are able to

- Experience the richness and excitement of knowing about and understanding the natural world.
- Use appropriate scientific processes and principles in making personal decisions.
- Engage intelligently in public discourse and debate about matters of scientific and technological concern.
- Increase their economic productivity through the use of the knowledge, understanding, and skills of the scientifically literate person in their careers.

FIGURE 1.2 NSES goals for school science. (*Source:* From *National Science Education Standards* © 1996, National Academy of Science. Courtesy of National Academy Press, Washington, DC: 1996, p. 13.)

> The development of the *National Science Education Standards* was guided by these principles.
>
> - Science is for all students.
> - Learning science is an active process.
> - School science reflects the intellectual and cultural traditions that characterize the practice of contemporary science.
> - Improving science education is part of systemic education reform.

FIGURE 1.3   Principles underlying the NSSE Standards. (*Source:* From *National Science Education Standards* © 1996, National Academy of Science. Courtesy of National Academy Press, Washington, DC: 1996, p. 19.)

Objectives for Elementary and Middle School Science

Whereas goals and their underlying principles guide the science curriculum, objectives drive student performance. Objectives provide the basis for the selection of specific content and activities, and they are the criteria by which student achievement is assessed.

Objectives for teaching science are found in various textbooks and in the teacher's manual for specific programs. At first glance, objectives from various sources may seem to differ, and some may appear to be more complete than others. However, on closer scrutiny, objectives from various lists will be found to be in close agreement, differing only in how they are written. (Understanding, preparing, and writing objectives are topics discussed in Chapter 5.) The consensus is that the objectives of elementary and middle school science programs fall into three broad areas: (1) developing an understanding of science concepts, (2) developing process skills, and (3) developing attitudes, appreciations, and values. Learning in these three areas helps students grow in scientific literacy and to become proficient problem solvers and critical thinkers. It helps them to understand the differences and relationships between science and technology, and the interrelationship of both those enterprises with society. Finally, the feeling of accomplishment in these areas leads to improvement in a student's self-esteem, which in turn leads to further achievement.

We assume that one reason you have chosen to be an elementary or middle school teacher is because you enjoy children. To be an effective teacher, that is a good start. To be an effective teacher of science, you also need certain understandings and skills.

KNOWLEDGE AND SKILLS NEEDED TO TEACH SCIENCE IN THE ELEMENTARY AND MIDDLE SCHOOL

It is impossible for you to have comprehensive knowledge of all the areas of science that you are likely to teach—e. g., animals, astronomy, earth science, human biology, physical science, plants, and weather. However, you should have a strong, broad base of scientific understanding in each of the content standards (see Figures 1.4 and 1.5). Part II of this book provides useful content references and instructional ideas for those and other areas.

Effective science teaching is more than knowing science content and some teaching strategies. Skilled teachers of science have special understandings and abilities that integrate their knowledge of science content, curriculum, learning, teaching, and students. Such knowledge allows teachers to tailor learning situations to the needs of individuals and groups. This special knowledge, called "pedagogical content knowledge," distinguishes the science knowledge of teachers from that of scientists. It is one element that defines a professional teacher of science.[37]

Science as Inquiry	Physical Science	Life Science	Earth and Space Science	Science and Technology	Science in Personal and Social Perspectives	History and Nature of Science	Unifying Concepts and Processes
Abilities necessary to do scientific inquiry Understandings about scientific inquiry	Properties of objects and materials Position and motion of objects Light, heat, electricity, and magnetism	Characteristics of organisms Life cycles of organisms Organisms and environments	Properties of earth materials Objects in the sky Changes in earth and sky	Abilities to distinguish between natural objects and objects made by humans Abilities of technological design Understandings about science and technology	Personal health Characteristics and changes in populations Types of resources Changes in environments Science and technology in local challenges	Science as a human endeavor	Systems, order, and organization Evidence, models, and explanation Change, constancy, and measurement Evolution and equilibrium Form and function

FIGURE 1.4   Content standards, grades K–4.

Science as Inquiry	Physical Science	Life Science	Earth and Space Science	Science and Technology	Science in Personal and Social Perspectives	History and Nature of Science	Unifying Concepts and Processes
Abilities necessary to do scientific inquiry Understandings about scientific inquiry	Properties and changes of properties in matter Motions and forces Transfer of energy	Structure and function in living systems Reproduction and heredity Regulation and behavior Populations and ecosystems Diversity and adaptations of organisms	Structure of the earth system Earth's history Earth in the solar system	Abilities of technological design Understanding about science and technology	Personal health Populations, resources, and environments Natural hazards Risks and benefits Science and technology in society	Science as a human endeavor Nature of science History of science	Systems, order, and organization Evidence, models, and explanation Change, constancy, and measurement Evolution and equilibrium Form and function

FIGURE 1.5   Content standards, grades 5–8.

Teachers of grades K–4 usually are generalists who teach most, if not all, areas of the school curriculum. A primary task for these teachers is to lay the experiential, conceptual, and attitudinal foundation for future learning and exploration in science by guiding students through a range of inquiry activities. To achieve this, elementary teachers of science possess broad knowledge of science content, supplemented by in-depth experiences in at least one subject area that includes an understanding of inquiry and the structure and production of science knowledge. Such knowledge prepares teachers to guide student inquiries and appraise student understanding, and then to use that information in furthering students' intellectual development. Clearly, deep science knowledge benefits the work of an elementary teacher, but realistically, the elementary teacher knows a wide range of subjects and cannot possibly engage in-depth with all.[38]

Because grades 5–8 take different configurations in different school districts, science curricula are organized in many different ways in the middle grades. However, science for students at this level goes into greater depth, is more quantitative, requires more sophisticated reasoning skills, and uses more sophisticated apparatus and technologies than it does at elementary levels. Thus, middle-level teachers of science maintain breadth and develop greater depth of understanding of science than those at the K–4 level. That understanding can be gained by deep study of at least one scientific discipline so that teachers gain appreciation for how scientific knowledge is produced and how disciplines are structured. An important test of the appropriate level of understanding for middle-level teachers is their ability to elicit student understandings and beliefs about scientific ideas and to use these data to formulate activities that will aid the development of sound scientific ideas.[39]

All teachers of science need a working understanding of the nature of science and of sciencing. Furthermore, because science is a useful vehicle for interdisciplinary teaching, which makes students' learning more meaningful and longer lasting, you need to know how to use science in an integrated thematic approach. Chapter 5 and some of the "exploratory activities" in Part II of this text illustrate how that can be done.

Teachers have found theme teaching to be a valuable curriculum approach. For example, a second-grade teacher may select a theme in science, perhaps "plants," and then, around that theme, build a teaching unit during which the children learn not only science, but language arts, mathematics, social studies, and all the other subject areas expected to be learned at that grade level. Thematic teaching units are important components of many state science frameworks. (For sample thematic units, see activities 10.2 and 14.2 of Chapters 10 and 14, respectively.)

Many at-risk youngsters disengage from school during the upper-elementary and middle-grade years, before physically dropping out later. One study found that as many as 50 percent of one large city's school dropouts left immediately after grade eight.[40] The number becomes staggering when students who drop out during high school are added.

Many states have advised their schools to increase their emphasis on dropout prevention at early grade levels. Making learning meaningful for students at school, at home, and in life is an imperative responsibility of middle-grade teachers, who, for many students, are the last hope for formal schooling and for their becoming scientifically literate.

One way to make learning meaningful for students is by using interdisciplinary thematic units (ITU). *Science for All Americans* identifies common abstract themes that cut across many scientific disciplines, some of which are systems, models, scale, constancy, and patterns of change. Although these themes have been used as the basis for current development of science curriculum frameworks, they were not intended for designing units of study for elementary or middle school students, who do not yet have the experiences and intellectual maturity necessary to understand such abstract conceptual schemes.[41] Like the "oceans" unit of Chapter 10, the interdisciplinary thematic units of most use in teaching science are much less abstract. Moreover, rather than integrating science disciplines, they are designed to integrate subject disciplines, such as the core subjects of language arts/English/reading, mathematics, social studies/history, and science.

Although the specifics of the use of ITUs are presented later, in Chapter 5, for now please understand that the purpose of the approach is to integrate content from various subject areas to show the interconnectedness of life and learning. Students need to know that the information they are learning will be practical not only in school, but in the workplace and throughout life. Sometimes an interdisciplinary thematic unit is taught to a group of children by an interdisciplinary team of teachers.

In many exemplary schools the teachers are part of a professional team. Usually, four or five teachers with different subject area strengths work together to plan the curriculum for a common group of students. In middle schools, the teaching team is usually composed of one teacher each from language arts/English/reading, mathematics, science, and history/social studies. In addition to teachers of these core subjects, specialty area teachers may be part of the teaching team. These may include teachers with expertise in physical education, art, and music, even specialists for children with learning disabilities and children who may be at risk. Some teams may ask a school counselor or a community resource person to be a member. Because the teachers come from a variety of disciplines, the teams are commonly called interdisciplinary teaching teams or simply interdisciplinary teams.

An interdisciplinary teaching team and the cluster of students with whom it works can be thought of as a "house," "village," or "school within a school," where each team of teachers is assigned each day to the same group of about 125 students for a common block of time. Within this block of time, teachers on the team are responsible for making the professional decisions, such as how to make school meaningful to students' lives, what specific responsibilities each teacher has each day, which guidance activities are to be implemented, what special attention is needed by individual students, and how students will be grouped for instruction.

The "school within a school" concept helps students to make important and meaningful connections among disciplines, and it provides them with peer and adult group identification, with an important and concomitant sense of belonging.

Understanding the Nature of Science

If you are apprehensive about teaching science because you feel that you do not have sufficient knowledge of content, you will be delighted when you read the words in this section. In fact, the teacher who has stored many scientific facts in long-term memory but does not comprehend or agree with the concept that follows, may be dangerous indeed, as that teacher believes and behaves as if teaching science is nothing more than telling students what the teacher knows, having them memorize it by rote, and then tell it back to the teacher. That is *not* science teaching, but merely the presentation of a series of exercises in short-term recall.

There is perhaps no quicker way to discourage student interest in science than to teach science as though it were "an organized body of knowledge to be learned." A teacher who teaches as if everything scientific is already known, and what students must do is memorize a certain number of facts, has learned nothing from the more than 100 years of science education in this country. Although in teaching science it is unavoidable to have students learn some of the information that has been developed through science, rote memorization is not science! A teacher who does nothing more than to transmit information is merely an orchestrator of factual-recall memory tests.

A DEFINITION OF SCIENCE

Science is a continuing process and human endeavor to discover order in nature. The products of that endeavor are human knowledge—facts, which are building blocks, reference points for the understandings of the bigger ideas, the principles, generalizations, and concepts. These products of science are *tentative* and *cumulative*. The tentative and cumulative nature of science is exceedingly important for teachers and their students to understand.

In science teaching, attention must be given to the processes of science, as well as the products, and intuitive thought and guessing must be valued. Guesses are hypotheses, the possible explanations to recognized problems and discrepancies. Hypotheses are then tested, data are collected and analyzed, and tentative conclusions reached. These conclusions may lead to further understanding of concepts, which in turn provide further comprehension toward the major themes that make up the structural framework for the K–12 science curriculum.

THEME STRUCTURE

A theme structure unites the facts and activities of the daily content of lessons. Examples of major themes, sometimes called conceptual schemes, are order and organization, form and function, evolution and equilibrium, matter-energy relationships, systems and interaction. Students build their understandings of concepts and develop their skills in science as they engage in and practice the processes, learning that they can science, and that science is a human activity.

Understanding the Interrelatedness of Science, Technology, and Society

You need an understanding of the important role of elementary and middle school science in building a society of scientifically literate citizens. Discussed earlier were the meaning and importance of a citizenry that understands the interrelatedness and interdependence of science, technology, and society (STS) and can use this knowledge, not only in science-related careers, but also in daily decision making.

In addition, you must understand that despite the national tendency toward improved mean performance of students on standardized tests, and a national commitment to keeping children in schools, the student dropout rate in schools in urban areas is still close to 50 percent. As mentioned earlier, many of those students drop out during late elementary and middle school years. This means that for many youngsters, the elementary school years may be the last chance for receiving formal education leading to their becoming scientifically literate persons.

Understanding the Nature of the Learner, Learning, and Teaching

In your preparation as a teacher, you have probably learned much about children, perhaps through direct observation and experience, through theory classes in child development, and in learning psychology. You have learned that among themselves, elementary and middle school students differ in many ways, for instance, in their abilities to learn, readiness to learn, learning skills, and how they learn. In recent years, there has been a wealth of information developed about children and their intellectual development, about how they learn, and about how they are taught. It may sometimes seem to you that you are expected to know it all!

You probably know something about how children develop intellectually and emotionally, and you have learned, or will learn, about the contributions of Ausubel (cognitive theory of meaningful learning; advance organizers), Bloom (cognitive taxonomy; mastery learning), Bruner (concept learning; guided discovery), Maslow (hierarchy of needs), Novak

---

Teachers of science must have a firm grounding in learning theory—understanding how learning occurs and is facilitated. Learning is an active process by which students individually and collaboratively achieve understanding. Effective teaching requires that teachers know what students of certain ages are likely to know, understand, and be able to do; what they will learn quickly; and what will be a struggle. Teachers of science need to anticipate typical misunderstandings and to judge the appropriateness of concepts for the developmental level of their students. In addition, teachers of science must develop understanding of how students with different backgrounds, experiences, motivations, learning styles, abilities, and interests learn science. Teachers use all of that knowledge to make effective decisions about learning objectives, teaching strategies, assessment tasks, and curriculum materials.[42]

(concept mapping), Piaget (stages of intellectual development; cognitive disequilibrium), Vygotsky (cooperative learning in a supportive environment), and other cognitive psychologists and researchers. You need to understand the importance of their contributions. That is our next focus in Chapter 2.

Understanding Sciencing

Sciencing is what the scientist does; it is what students should do when they study science. We do not believe that you should teach children that there are "steps" to the scientific method. To ask children to learn and memorize steps in the scientific method implies that the process of sciencing is linear—it is not. It implies that there is a beginning and an end that is final—that is misleading. It further implies to students that, for them, science is a repetition of experiments or the memorization of facts, of learning what is already "known"—that is dull.

By the time children reach the upper elementary grades, those taught in such a dogmatic way are bored to death. This kind of teaching is lethal to a child's natural interest in science. We can all recall teachers who taught us in such a dreary fashion. They taught us to memorize such "facts" as: "Pluto is the outer planet of our solar system" (not always). "Saturn has nine rings." (It has hundreds.) "Human cells have 48 chromosomes." (They don't.) "Roots of trees grow down, and stems grow up." (Some do.) "Green plants produce food." (So do red plants and brown plants.) "Plants produce oxygen for animals." (Plants need oxygen too.)

As professed by Dewey 100 years ago and observed by Pestalozzi even before that, children should learn science by observing and investigating, using all their senses, rather than by merely memorizing facts from books and as presented by a teacher. We repeat the point made earlier (p. 22): A teacher who does nothing more than have students memorize and repeat "facts" is not teaching science; that teacher is simply orchestrating repetitive tests in memorizing.

Understanding That the Process of Sciencing Is Cyclic

Rather than linear, with an orderly sequence of steps, the process of sciencing is cyclic. See Figure 1.6. One enters the cycle whenever a discrepancy or problem is observed. Furthermore, discrepancy or problem recognition can occur at any point in the cycle.

When a person is sciencing, the cycle proceeds as follows. The person

- recognizes a problem or discrepancy;
- makes a guess as to its explanation;
- designs an experiment to test the guess;
- collects data from the experiment;
- analyzes the data; and
- arrives at a tentative conclusion.

Consider the following illustration. When a biochemist believes she has discovered a new enzyme, there is no textbook or teacher "expert" to whom she can go to find out whether she is right. She arrives at her tentative conclusion resulting from her self-confidence in collection, processing, and analysis of available data. Later, new data may cause her to revise that conclusion.

In the same way that scientists develop their knowledge and understanding as they seek answers to questions about the natural world, students develop an understanding of the natural world when they are actively engaged in scientific inquiry—alone and with others.[43]

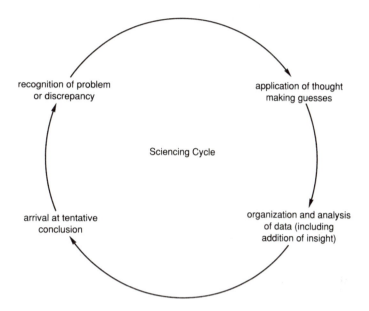

FIGURE 1.6   The Sciencing Cycle.

In everyday living, real-life problems are resolved in the same fashion by any scientifically literate person (SLP). For example, a problem may arise: "Should I marry this person or not?" After this recognition, a guess is made, "Yes, I should" or "No, I should not." Whichever the case, data are collected (e.g., from friends, parents, and intuitive thought about one's own future) and analyzed. Finally, a decision (conclusion) is made. "Yes, I will marry this person." Remember, however, the conclusion is tentative. The process does not end with the conclusion. The process is cyclic. At some later time, perhaps after the marriage has taken place, further data may show a need for revision of the earlier conclusion.

In sciencing, as in real-world problem solving, we do not think in terms of "absolute" truths. Data support ideas; data never prove conclusively.[44] What your students will do while learning science, then, is *generate their own ideas and test them.* That is sciencing. The processes involved are varied: some are concerned with generating and organizing data, others are concerned with building and using ideas. Figure 1.7 illustrates processes in each of these operations.

PEDAGOGY FOR SCIENCING: THE LEARNING CYCLE
For an understanding of conceptual development and change, J. Piaget developed a theory of learning that involves children in what later became described as a three-phase learning cycle. Although there have been many other descriptions and variations of the learning cycle, perhaps that with the most lasting impact on science education was described in 1962 by Atkin and Karplus.[45] Their three phases are (1) an *exploratory hands-on phase,* wherein students explore materials that lead to their own questions and tentative answers, (2) a *concept development phase,* in which under the guidance of a teacher, children invent concepts and principles that help them answer their questions and reorganize their ideas, and (3) a *concept application phase,* in which the children try out their new ideas by applying them to situations

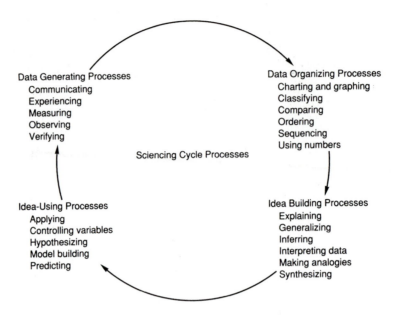

Figure 1.7   Sciencing cycle processes.

that are relevant and meaningful to them. When a learner is applying a concept (third phase), the learner is again involved in a hands-on activity. During application of a concept the learner may discover new information that causes a change in his or her understanding of the concept being applied. Thus, the process of learning is cyclic.

This learning cycle represents a pedagogy recommended and often used by teachers in planning their lessons and in involving students in actively learning science, that is, in sciencing. Omitting any of the three phases or presenting the phases out of sequence greatly reduces the effectiveness of the learning cycle.

At the exploration phase students' notions about a certain phenomenon are challenged through a hands-on and minds-on (see beginning of Chapter 2) activity, in which they are instructed in how to make observations and to collect data but are not given any new vocabulary or explanation about what to expect. Students' prior knowledge is the basis for the organization of ideas during this phase. During the exploration phase the teacher assumes the role of facilitator, posing questions and assisting students as they work in small groups. Hands-on and minds-on learning are the primary activities during the exploration phase.

At the concept introduction phase, under the guidance of the teacher, students are encouraged to form new ideas, based on the observations they made and on the data that were collected during the exploration phase, and to link their new ideas with their former notions. The teacher helps students see how patterns in data reveal the concepts being defined in the lesson. Reading is an important part of the concept introduction phase. It is during this phase that the teacher may further develop conceptual understanding through the use of textbooks, media, and other resource materials.

In the concept application phase, students extend their understanding of the topic by using what they have learned to solve a new problem or conduct an experiment. It is during this phase that the students' previously held misconceptions are dealt with.

The three phases of this learning cycle are comparable to the three levels of questioning and thinking, described variously by others. For example, in Elliot Eisner's *The Educational Imagination* (Macmillan, 1979), the levels are referred to as "descriptive," "interpretive," and "evaluative." In Chapter 3, in the discussion of the use of questioning strategies, we use "input," "processing," and "application."[46]

The three-phase learning cycle was the basis for the NSF-sponsored SCIS elementary science program. Today, there are variations and modifications of the learning cycle, most of which have added an "assessment phase" to reflect constructivist learning theory and to emphasize the importance of student self-assessment.[47] However, because we believe that assessment of what students know or think they know should be a continuous process, permeating all three phases of the learning cycle, we reject the notion of "assessment" as a self-standing phase.

Understanding the Sciencing Cycle Processes

In this chapter we have spoken of the three aspects of the science learning enterprise: the learning of content; the developing of process skills; and learning that sciencing is a human activity that is important to all people and that all people can do.

As a science teacher you need to understand the processes of sciencing and to be skilled in using these processes and in aiding your students in their development of their own skills. These skills are also important for teaching and learning in language arts, mathematics, and social science.

SCIENCING CYCLE AND THE LEARNING CYCLE

In the sciencing cycle processes (Figure 1.7) we illustrate the processes by clustering them into four groups: data generating, data organizing, idea building, and idea using.

Generally, the data-generating processes are those students perform during the exploration phase of the learning cycle; data-organizing and idea-building processes take place during the concept introduction phase; idea-using processes occur during concept application phase. As emphasized earlier, discrepancy recognition can occur at any time and at any place within the cycle.

Some processes in the sciencing cycle are "discovery" processes; others are "inquiry." (Additional explanations about discovery and inquiry follow in Chapter 3.) Inquiry processes are more complex intellectual operations (all the idea-using processes); they are sometimes referred to as integrated processes. Early grades should concentrate on discovery skills. By the time children are adolescents, many are in the process of developing formal operational thought (discussed in Chapter 2) and should be provided experiences requiring the integrated skills of inquiry. However, most students of middle school age (ages 10–14) are not ready to perform mental operations required by true inquiry. Nevertheless, teachers of upper elementary grades should introduce integrated skills and begin the process of aiding students in developing those skills, thus facilitating their readiness for formal-operation thinking.

The Processes: Thinking Skills

The processes of sciencing are thinking skills. As students develop maturity in the use of these skills, they will be able to do more sophisticated work in science, in other subjects, and in real-life problem solving. In the descriptions that follow, you will see how the processes of

Through science learning, children develop their language skills, communicate with others, and learn by direct observation through listening, investigating, and sharing their experiences.

the sciencing cycle relate to the learning cycle. Assessment, including student self-assessment, should be a component built into *each* of the four phases of the sciencing cycle, not just at the completion of a study.

Data-generating processes (the exploratory phase of the learning cycle). These are the processes needed to produce data, a major product of student investigation during the exploratory phase of the learning cycle. Teachers help children develop their skills in these processes beginning in kindergarten. Children produce data by developing their language skills, by communicating with others, by listening and sharing their experiences. The test of a child's developing skill in communication is whether the child's written and spoken communication is understood by others. Communication skill development is enhanced as children are provided a variety of exciting, carefully planned opportunities to experience their environment. As they experience their natural environment, they are taught skills in measuring, in observing with all their senses, and in verifying by looking, touching, perhaps tasting, listening, or smelling again. The planned development of skills in these data-generating processes begins in kindergarten and continues throughout schooling.

Beginning in the primary grades, children are taught how to order, sequence, and classify—important data-organizing processes.

Data-organizing processes (the beginning of the concept introduction phase of the learning cycle). For data to make sense, they must be organized. The planned development of skills in organizing data also starts in kindergarten. Beginning in the primary grades, children are taught how to order ("Arrange these objects from smallest to largest"), to sequence ("Which duck do you suppose came first, and which came last—the mother, the young duckling, or the baby?"), to classify ("If each of us places a shoe into the center of the room, how do you suppose we could arrange the shoes?"). They are taught how to chart and graph data and to use numbers so that comparisons can be made. From the things they do and make, children may recognize discrepancies and, if so, they may begin the cycle all over again. While doing these things, the children are also integrating their learning of mathematics and science and perhaps other disciplines as well.

Idea-building processes (a continuation of concept introduction, and the concept building phase of the learning cycle). As data are collected and organized, students can begin to make sense out of the data, to build ideas, to develop concepts, and to arrive at tentative decisions about the information. As they bring together ideas generated by the data (synthesizing), and try to interpret or make sense of their data, they arrive at tentative conclusions about the data (generalizing) and test their conclusions by explaining to others. As they are reasoning or thinking through their explanations, they are developing the skill of inferring (a more sophisticated form of drawing a conclusion). During the explaining and inferring processes children may think of analogies, and they may recognize discrepancies that may cause them to start the learning cycle all over again.

Interpreting data, making analogies, and synthesizing, which are higher thinking skills than explaining, inferring, and generalizing, are not usually stressed until the late primary or early intermediate grades.

Idea-using processes (the concept application phase of the learning cycle). When a person gets an idea, he or she usually wants to try it out, to test it, to put it to work, to apply it. After getting an idea, *wanting to test it is a nearly unavoidable impulse*. Various skills are involved in using ideas. Predicting "what will happen if" is a skill that should be encouraged and practiced from the earliest grades. From ideas generated, children can predict "what will happen if" and then test their hypotheses by designing experiments in which all variables but one are controlled. Sometimes the experiment is one of designing, building, and testing a model. Skill in concept application can be demonstrated by testing one's ideas through experimenting or by applying a fully tested idea, such as Jonas Salk did once his polio vaccine had been fully tested in a controlled environment. Although most of the skills in the idea-using category are complex mental operations, at some degree of sophistication all children can be helped in their development of these skills.

These are the skills with which intelligent people behave. They are skills that are used not just in science, but in all disciplines, and that help one to live productively and intelligently throughout life.

Understanding the Origin and Nature of Misconceptions

While teaching science you will discover that your children often have false understandings, or misconceptions, about certain science concepts. It is difficult enough to teach science concepts to children; it is even more difficult to reverse their understandings. Chapter 2 discusses the reteaching of concepts; here we provide guidelines on how to *avoid* teaching misconceptions.

Avoid prejudices about the natural world. *Artificialism* is the term used by Piaget to represent the natural tendency for young children to believe that everything in the world is for the benefit of humans, more specifically, for the individual. Although natural for children in early grades, artificialism does represent a selfish, prejudiced, nonobjective attitude, which a science teacher has an obligation, and an opportunity, to correct. Unfortunately, as evidenced along highways and city streets, many adults have yet to learn that the world is not their own private trash can.

Avoid prejudices about human beings. Good science teaching can help dispel attitudes and superstitions that are detrimental to world peace. For example, we have observed teachers requiring students to "learn the differences between racial groups." If there are differences between racial groups, they are so insignificant that they are of no consequence. Requiring students to learn differences is to overemphasize those differences (which is to place a lesser importance on similarities or likenesses) and to perpetuate attitudes that cause social stratification and the oppression of groups of people.

Use caution when simplifying science concepts. While trying to simplify concepts for students, teachers sometimes unintentionally teach misconceptions. For example, in the middle and upper grades, the science program considers the concept of photosynthesis. With the intention of simplifying what occurs in photosynthesis, teachers and textbooks may use the following equation: $CO_2 + H_2O + chlorophyll \rightarrow sugar + energy$. If this equation were accurate, any student should be able to perform photosynthesis simply by shaking carbon dioxide with water and chlorophyll in a jar. Of course, it will not happen, because in photosynthesis water and carbon dioxide do not combine to form sugar, or anything else. This example of a misconception continues to be taught, perhaps because of a combination of tradition and lack of knowledge. Traditionally, that equation has been illustrated in science books, and many teachers and textbook writers continue to perpetuate the misconception. Perhaps, in this instance, the damage is only minor. In another example, to follow, the danger is greater. The point is this: *To avoid teaching misconceptions, and, most certainly, to correct children's misconceptions about science, teachers themselves must understand the concepts they are trying to teach* *and must be aware that, in their effort to simplify a concept for student understanding, they may, in fact, teach a misconception.*

The exact explanation of photosynthesis is very complex; however, it is possible to offer a simplified explanation that does not foster misconceptions. In the presence of chlorophyll, the water molecule is split into hydrogen and oxygen. This is the light reaction; it can be shown as $H_2O \rightarrow [H] + O_2$. While the oxygen is released into the environment, the hydrogen is combined with carbon dioxide to form a carbohydrate. Sometimes that carbohydrate is a sugar; at other times it is a more complex carbohydrate. This reaction is the carbon-fixing reaction, or dark reaction, which continues in the absence of light and can be illustrated as $[H] + CO_2 \rightarrow (CH_2O)_x$. The brackets around hydrogen indicate that it is never freed. Instead, it is attached to other molecules in transport to carbon dioxide. For elementary or middle school science, words can be substituted for the chemical symbols. Light (such as sunlight) is necessary to start photosynthesis, but the process continues in the absence of light. Water and carbon dioxide do not combine. So, when teaching about photosynthesis, rather than perpetuating a misconcept it is just as easy to summarize the concept correctly as involving two processes—the light reaction, whereby hydrogen is released from water; and the dark reaction, in which the hydrogen is combined with carbon dioxide to form a carbohydrate. The oxygen released from the water is released into the air unless the plant uses it for its own cellular respiration.

This brings us to our second example, perhaps more important for understanding by elementary and middle school students. When we surveyed science teachers and their students and asked where the oxygen comes from that is in water, that fish need in order to breathe, we found a significant number of children *and their teachers* held a misconception. They thought the oxygen that fish needed to breathe came from the oxygen in the water molecule, rather than from oxygen dissolved in the water. Holding that misconception, students (and their teachers) will never comprehend the nature of water pollution; that is, resulting from bacteria and other organisms consuming the dissolved oxygen, or from oil or detergents on the surface of a polluted stream keeping oxygen in the air from dissolving in the water. In both cases, fish and other organisms in the stream will die from lack of oxygen.

Finally, as a result of their misconception about photosynthesis, as discussed earlier, we have observed many teachers and books emphasizing or implying that cellular respiration (the breakdown of sugar into water and carbon dioxide and the release of energy) is the opposite of photosynthesis. As you can understand now, that is not quite the case. Although both reactions somehow involve water and carbon dioxide, cellular respiration and photosynthesis are not opposites.

As we teach toward an understanding of science concepts, let's not teach misconceptions. To avoid teaching misconceptions about science, it is important for the teacher to shun dogmatic teaching and to be aware of his or her own lack of understanding of certain concepts.

Summary

In this chapter we have surveyed the history of science education in this country, specifically, how it has developed for elementary and middle school science teaching. You gained knowledge of why science learning is so important for children today. In essence, you acquired an overview of (1) why science is taught in the elementary and middle schools, (2) the goals and objectives for elementary and middle school science, and (3) the understandings and skills that you need to teach science effectively.

In Chapter 2, to guide you in your continuing quest to become an exemplary science teacher, you will learn more about children and their learning.

QUESTIONS FOR CLASS DISCUSSION

1. Provide a rationale as to why science should or should not be taught in grades K–2, 3–5, and 6–8. Support your rationale.
2. Describe the contributions of at least five major landmarks in the history of science teaching in this country.
3. Explain why some people consider science to be a basic subject. Do you agree or disagree that science is a basic? Explain your answer.
4. In a sentence, describe what it means to say a person is scientifically literate. Do you feel that you are scientifically literate? Explain your answer.
5. Explain the differences and similarities between science and technology. Is it important for children to understand the difference? Explain your answer, and, if so, describe some ways you could help their understanding.
6. What achievements in science and technology can you think of that have affected the social, economic, or cultural aspects of people's existence? Explain the effects.
7. What is the best way to assess whether children understand the meaning of the term "science?" Explain how you would do it.
8. Do you think students should be encouraged to make guesses about explanations of scientific phenomena? Explain your answer.
9. From your recent observations and field work as related to this teacher preparation program, identify one specific example of educational practice that seems contradictory to exemplary practice or theory as presented in this chapter. Present your explanation for the discrepancy.
10. What questions do you have about the content of this chapter? How might answers be found?

NOTES

1. National Research Council, reprinted from *National Science Education Standards*, © 1996 National Academy of Sciences, p. 59. Courtesy of National Academy Press, Washington, DC.
2. National Research Council, reprinted from *National Science Education Standards*, © 1996 National Academy of Sciences, p. 60. Courtesy of National Academy Press, Washington, DC.
3. The National Science Board Commission on Precollege Education in Mathematics, Science and Technology, *Educating Americans for the 21st Century* (Washington, DC: NSB, September 12, 1983), v.
4. *The Liberal Art of Science: An Agenda for Action* (Washington, DC: American Association for the Advancement of Science, 1990), xi.
5. American Association for the Advancement of Science, *Project 2061: Science Literacy for a Changing Future: Update 1994* (Washington, DC: Author, 1994), 6.
6. J. Dewey, *How We Think* (Boston: Heath, 1910).
7. *Thirty-first Yearbook*. Part I. (Bloomington, IL: National Society for the Study of Education, Public School Publishing, 1932).
8. *Forty-sixth Yearbook*. Part I. (Chicago: National Society for the Study of Education, University of Chicago Press, 1947).
9. *Fifth-ninth Yearbook* (Chicago: National Society for the Study of Education, University of Chicago Press, 1960).
10. J. D. Novak, "Application of Advances in Learning Theory and Philosophy of Science to the Improvement of Chemistry Teaching," *Journal of Chemistry Education* 61(7) (July 1984), pp. 607–612.
11. Reprinted from *National Science Education Standards*, © 1996 National Academy of Sciences, p. 30. Courtesy of National Academy Press, Washington, DC.
12. American Association for the Advancement of Science, *Science for All Americans: Project 2061 Summary* (Washington, DC: Arthur, 1995), 3.

13. J. A. Shymansky, "A Reassessment of the Inquiry-Based Science Curricula of the 60s on Student Performance," *Journal of Research in Science Teaching* 27(2):127–144 (February 1990).
14. B. Watson and R. Konicek, "Teaching for Conceptual Change: Confronting Children's Experience," *Phi Delta Kappan* 71(9):680–685 (May 1990), 681. For a historical perspective, see also N. C. Harms, Project *Synthesis* (Boulder: School of Education, University of Colorado, 1979), and N. C. Harms and R. E. Yager, eds. *What Research Says to the Science Teacher, vol. 3* (Washington, DC: National Science Teachers Association, 1982).
15. *Science-Technology-Society: Science Education for the 1980s* (Washington, DC: National Science Teachers Association, 1982).
16. Model standards describing what prospective teachers should know and be able to do in order to receive a teaching license have been drafted by the Interstate New Teacher Assessment and Support Consortium, a project of the Council of Chief State School Officers. Representatives of seventeen states and professional associations—including the National Education Association (NEA), the American Federation of Teachers (AFT), the American Association of Colleges for Teacher Education (AACTE), and the National Council for the Accreditation of Teacher Education (NCATE) comprise the group. Instead of identifying the courses teachers should take to become licensed, the standards are performance-based and revolve around a common core of principles of knowledge and skills that cut across disciplines.
17. See, for example, Anne C. Lewis, "An Overview of the Standards Movement," *Phi Delta Kappan* 76(10):744–750 (June 1995) and the several other articles on standards in that same issue of *Phi Delta Kappan*.
18. See, for example, Scott Willis, "Teaching Language-Minority Students," *ASCD Update* 36(5): 1, 4–5 (June 1994).
19. *The Liberal Art of Science: Agenda for Action* (Washington, DC: American Association for the Advancement of Science, 1990), 16.
20. American Association for the Advancement of Science, *Project 2061: Science Literacy for a Changing Future: Update 1994* (Washington, DC: Author, 1994), 6.
21. F. J. Rutherford and A. Ahlgren, *Science for All Americans* (New York: Oxford University Press, 1989).
22. American Association for the Advancement of Science, *Science for All Americans: Project 2061 Summary* (Washington, DC: Author, 1995), 4.
23. American Association for the Advancement of Science, *Benchmarks for Science Literacy* (New York: Oxford University Press, 1993).
24. See, for example, the several articles on "detracking" and "untracking" in *Phi Delta Kappan* 77(3), November 1995.
25. See, for example, the entire theme issue of *Phi Delta Kappan* 76(10) June 1995.
26. A useful publication for educators is David W. Johnson and Roger T. Johnson, *Reducing School Violence Through Conflict Resolution* (Alexandria, VA: Association for Supervision and Curriculum Development, 1995).
27. See, for example, Linda A. Berne and Barbara K. Huberman, "Sexuality Education: Sorting Fact from Fiction," *Phi Delta Kappan* 77(3):229–232 (November 1995).
28. H. A. Smith, "Historical Background of Elementary Science," *Journal of Research in Science Teaching* 1(3) (1963), p. 203.
29. The word *sciencing* is an acceptable word and is very useful in stressing the importance of process in talking about what it is a scientist does.
30. Some writers use the phrase "general goals and objectives," but that is redundant and incorrect. Goals *are* general; objectives are specific.
31. For this text, the terms *performance objective* and *behavioral objective* are considered to be synonymous.
32. *The Liberal Art of Science: Agenda for Action* (Washington, DC: American Association for the Advancement of Science, 1990), xiii.
33. P. L. Dressel, "How the Individual Learns Science: Rethinking Science Education," in N. B. Henry, ed., *Fifty-ninth Yearbook of the National Society for the Study of Education* (Chicago: University of Chicago Press, 1960), 60.
34. *The Liberal Art of Science: Agenda for Action* (Washington, DC: American Association for the Advancement of Science, 1990), 11.
35. Cecily C. Selby, "Technology: From Myths to Realities," *Phi Delta Kappan* 74(9):684–689 (May 1993).
36. William Dugger, Jr., and J. Eldon Yung, *Technology Education Today* (Bloomington, IN: Fastback 380, Phi Delta Kappa Educational Foundation, 1995), 9.
37. Reprinted from *National Science Education Standards,* © 1996 National Academy of Sciences, p. 62. Courtesy of National Academy Press, Washington, DC.

38. Reprinted from *National Science Education Standards,* © 1996 National Academy of Sciences, pp. 60, 109. Courtesy of National Academy Press, Washington, DC.
39. Reprinted from *National Science Education Standards,* © 1996 National Academy of Sciences, pp. 60, 110. Courtesy of National Academy Press, Washington, DC.
40. Massachusetts Advocacy Center, *The Way Out: Student Exclusion Practices in Boston Middle Schools* (Boston, MA, 1986).
41. *National Science Resource Center Newsletter* 4(2) Washington, DC: Smithsonian Institution, National Academy of Sciences (Fall 1991), 3, 6.
42. Reprinted from *National Science Education Standards,* © 1996 National Academy of Sciences, p. 62. Courtesy of National Academy Press, Washington DC.
43. Reprinted from *National Science Education Standards,* © 1996 National Academy of Sciences, p. 29. Courtesy of National Academy Press, Washington, DC.
44. Scientific research relies on the statistical analysis of data that are obtained. Because of that statistical treatment, there is always a possibility of variation. Thus, the researcher can only be fairly certain about the conclusion, not absolutely certain. In addition, data are usually collected by means that are indirect and dependent on reliability of instruments.
45. J. M. Atkin and R. Karplus, "Discovery or Invention?" *The Science Teacher* 29(5):45, 1962.
46. For a comparison of thinking models, see Arthur L. Costa, *The School as a Home for the Mind* (Palatine, IL: Skylight Publishing, 1991), 44.
47. For further discussion of use of the learning cycle model in a constructivist classroom, see Jacqueline G. Brooks and Martin G. Brooks, *In Search of Understanding: The Case for Constructivist Classrooms* (Alexandria, VA: Association for Supervision and Curriculum Development, 1993), 116–118.

SUGGESTED READINGS

American Association for the Advancement of Science. *Benchmarks for Science Literacy* (New York: Oxford University Press, 1993).
———. *Sourcebook for Science, Mathematics, and Technology Education.* Washington, DC: American Association for the Advancement of Science, 1993.
———. *Project 2061: Science for All Americans.* Washington, DC: American Association for the Advancement of Science, 1989.
Barman, C. R., et al. "The Learning Cycle: A Basic Tool for Teachers, Too." *Perspectives in Education and Deafness* 11(4):7–11 (March/April 1993).
Beyer, B. K. *Critical Thinking.* Fastback 385. Bloomington, IN: Phi Delta Kappa Educational Foundation, 1995.
Brooks, J. G., and M. G. Brooks. *In Search of Understanding: The Case for Constructivist Classrooms.* Alexandria, VA: Association for Supervision and Curriculum Development, 1993.
Chiappetta, E. L., G. H. Sethna, and D. A. Fillman. "Do Middle School Life Science Textbooks Provide a Balance of Scientific Literacy Themes?" *Journal of Research in Science Teaching* 30(7):787–797 (1993).
Craig, G. S. "Elementary School Science in the Past Century." *Science Education* 24(4):11–14 (February 1957).
Duber, Jr., W., and J. E. Yung. *Technology Education Today.* Fastback 380. Bloomington, IN: Phi Delta Kappa Educational Foundation, 1995.
Fort, D. C. "Science Shy, Science Savvy, Science Smart." *Phi Delta Kappan* 74(9):674–683 (May 1993).
Kibby, M. W. *Student Literacy: Myths and Realities.* Fastback 381. Bloomington, IN: Phi Delta Kappa Educational Foundation, 1995.
Linn, M. C., et al. "Can Research on Learning and Instruction Inform Standards for Science Education?" *Journal of Science Education and Technology* 3(1):7–15 (March 1994).
Lopez, R. E., and J. Tuomi. "Student-Centered Inquiry." *Educational Leadership* 52(8):78–79 (May 1995).
MacDonald, D. "Predictions and Pedagogy." *Science and Children* 30(7):16–19 (April 1993).
Pollak, V. L. "Science Education II: Scientific Literacy and the Karplus Taxonomy." *Journal of Science Education and Technology* 3(2):89–97 (June 1994).
Ramsey, J. "Developing Conceptual Storylines with the Learning Cycle." *Journal of Elementary Science Education* 5(2):1–20 (Spring 1993).

Rutherford, F. J., and A. Ahlgren. *Science for All Americans*. New York: Oxford University Press, 1990.

Selby, C. C. "Technology: From Myths to Realities." *Phi Delta Kappan* 74(9):684–689 (May 1993).

Sennett, M. L. "Everyday Chemical Experiences." *Science and Children* 31(5):17–19 (February 1994).

Shamos, M. H. *The Myth of Scientific Literacy*. New York: Macmillan, 1995.

Underhill, O. E. *The Origin and Development of Elementary School Science*. Chicago: Scott, Foresman and Company, 1941.

Yager, R., ed. *The Science, Technology, Society Movement: What Research Says to the Science Teacher*. Vol. 7. Washington, DC: National Science Teachers Association, 1993.

CHAPTER 2

Learning, Thinking, and Intellectual Development

In addition to a solid understanding of science and sciencing, teachers of science have a firm grounding in learning theory—understanding how learning occurs and how it is facilitated.

- *Student understanding is actively constructed through individual and social processes.*
- *Actions of teachers are deeply influenced by their understanding of and relationships with students.*[1]

To be the most effective teacher, that is, among other things, one who is competent in the use of varied and developmentally appropriate methods of instruction, it is essential that you understand children and young adolescents—how they develop intellectually, how they think, what they think about, and how they learn and process information. Much of what is known about how children learn and process information has been gained from cognitive research in recent years. During the next few years, we may expect many more advances in our knowledge of neurological processing. Meanwhile, it is important to understand the complexity and ramifications of the quest.

It has become quite clear that for the diversity of children in today's schools, learning in each discipline is most effective and longer lasting when it is integrated with the whole curriculum and made meaningful to their lives, rather than simply taught as an unrelated and separate subject at the same time each day. (Such integration of science with other disciplines of the curriculum is discussed in Chapter 5.) This chapter focuses on how children learn and process information.

MEANINGFUL LEARNING: THE CONSTRUCTION OF UNDERSTANDING

If learning is defined as only the accumulation of bits and pieces of information, then we already know how that is learned and how to teach it. However, the accumulation of pieces of information is at the lowest end of a spectrum of types of learning, and it may even be dysfunctional to meaningful learning.

We are still learning about learning and teaching for higher forms of learning, that is, for meaningful understanding and the reflective use of that understanding. Meanwhile, for higher levels of thinking and for learning that is most meaningful, the results of recent research support the use of instructional strategies that help students to make connections to what is being learned, strategies such as the whole-language approach to reading, discovery and inquiry learning, and interdisciplinary thematic teaching, with a curriculum that is integrated and connected to children's life experiences.

We begin this chapter with a review of important work, both historical and recent, of cognitive psychologists, which has led to a modern view of teaching for meaningful understanding. In opposition to the traditional view that sees teaching as covering the prescribed material, this modern view stresses the importance of learning as being a personal process, by which each learner builds on his or her own personal knowledge and experiences.

Meaningful learning is learning that results when the learner makes connections between a new experience and prior knowledge and experiences that were stored in long-term memory. For meaningful learning to occur, correct instruction, then, is to begin where the students are, with what they have experienced and know, or think they know, and to correct any misconceptions they might have while building upon and connecting their understandings and experiences. In assessment for meaningful learning "we look not for what students can repeat, but for what they can generate, demonstrate, and exhibit."[2]

Curriculum Evolves

Like the construction of a skyscraper, meaningful learning is a gradual and sometimes painstakingly slow process. As emphasized by Watson and Konicek, as compared with traditional instruction, teaching in a constructivist mode is slower, involving more discussion, debate, and the re-creation of ideas. Rather than following clearly defined and previously established steps, the curriculum evolves, depends heavily on materials, and, to a great extent, is determined by the students' interests and questions. Less content is covered, fewer facts are memorized and tested for, and progress is sometimes very slow.[3] Consider Figure 2.1, which shows how two teachers go about teaching seventh graders about photosynthesis, the first using the traditional approach, the second using a constructivist approach.

Hands-On/Minds-On Learning Is the Methodology

Modern methodology uses what is referred to as a *hands-on doing* (i.e., the learner is learning by doing) and *minds-on learning* (i.e., the learner is thinking about what she or he is learning and doing) approach to constructing, and often reconstructing, the student's perceptions. Hands-on learning engages young learners' minds, encouraging them to question and then to devise ways of investigating tentative but temporarily satisfactory answers to their own questions. As a classroom teacher, your instructional task is essentially twofold: (1) to plan for and provide the hands-on experiences, supplying the materials and the supportive environment necessary for students' meaningful exploration and discovery; (2) to facilitate the most meaningful and longest lasting learning possible once the students' minds have been activated by the hands-on experience. To accomplish this, then, requires knowledge about and competence in the use of varied and developmentally appropriate methods of instruction. To assist you in beginning the acquisition of that knowledge and competence is the primary purpose of this book.

SIGNIFICANT LEARNING CHARACTERISTICS OF ELEMENTARY AND MIDDLE SCHOOL STUDENTS

If you are to be effective as an elementary or middle school science teacher, you must be aware of and use what is known about children and young adolescents. Knowing and understanding these characteristics will do much to make the teaching and learning of science an enjoyable and rewarding experience for you and your students. The following characteristics apply to elementary and middle school students, regardless of their individual genetic or cultural differences.

EGOCENTRIC

To some degree or another, most young people are egocentric. To egocentric youth, everything is important to them insofar as it relates to themselves. In young children, such egocentricity is quite natural, because they find themselves in a strange yet wonderful world, filled with phenomena that are constantly affecting them. They tend to interpret phenomena according to how the phenomena effect them and to use everything they learn for the express purpose of adjusting to the world in which they live, whether for better or for worse. As a teacher you can help students to understand this world and to adjust to it in positive ways. Usually, as children develop psychologically, emotionally, and intellectually, they will overcome their egocentricity.

In Mr. A's seventh grade, science students are taught through a combination of textbook work and teacher demonstration. Students perform experiments from time to time, depending on the availability of materials and space. Students read a seventh-grade science text that explains that photosynthesis is the chemical change that produces food in plants that have chlorophyll. It explains that carbon dioxide gas and water are combined to produce sugar and oxygen, that the sugar may be changed to starch, and that sunlight supplies the energy for photosynthesis to occur. The energy from sunlight becomes locked in the sugar and starch molecules that are produced. The teacher talks about the role of chlorophyll and presents the chemical equation for photosynthesis: $6CO_2 + 6H_2O \rightarrow C_6H_{12}O_6 + 6O_2$. After a careful explanation of the equation, and how the sugar is used by the plant to make cellulose, which forms its cell walls, and so on, Mr. A also describes the process of respiration. Then he reviews with the students in preparation for a test on the material. Test questions include several item types, such as:

- True or False: "Food is produced in leaves."
- Circle one: "Carbon dioxide, Sugar, Water is produced in photosynthesis."
- Fill in the blank: "Photosynthesis occurs inside plant cells that contain _____."
- Give a short answer: "Explain how respiration is different from photosyntheis."

This is the mimetic approach to learning, whereby students commit new information to short-term memory for the purpose of mimicking an understanding of photosynthesis on an end-of-chapter test. There is little in the presentation of the information or in the assessment strategies that challenges students' current beliefs about the way plants grow and the relationships between plants and other life forms. In fact, both the way in which the content is presented and the manner in which learning is assessed militate against the development of such understandings and, instead, encourage rote memorization of a symbolic, chemical equation.

In Ms. B's seventh-grade science class, during the same study (photosynthesis), the teacher not only deleted the molecular equation and references to cell walls in her introductory lesson plan, but actually deleted all references to photosynthesis. Ms. B asked her students to think of systems with which they might have some experience and familiarity and to indicate the product created, the energy source needed, and the raw materials used. She asked her students to consider, for example, their art classes and what they create there. Several students taking a home technologies class at the time were making malted milk shakes. They combined ingredients (malt, milk, and cocoa) in the presence of an external energy source (an electric blender) to produce a product (the milk shake). They did not readily come up with a by-product, but when they lit on an "appetite-whetting aroma" as a possibility, they became quite animated. Another student, thinking of his health education class, described exercise as a system consisting of ingredients (a human body, weights, and exercise machines) acted on by an energy source (one's muscles) to generate a product (increased strength and muscle tone) and a by-product (a sense of well-being). Because these analogies generated enthusiasm about their home technologies and health class activities, the students engaged in interdisciplinary discussions with each other and Ms. B.

Ms. B structured her initial lessons on photosynthesis so that her students might consider and consolidate the aspects of a system. The term *photosynthesis* was not mentioned during the initial lesson.

Ms. B. asked her students to think of photosynthesis as a system in which certain ingredients (carbon dioxide and water) are changed by an outside energy source (sunlight) to produce a product (sugar) and a by-product (oxygen). The concept of a by-product, in and of itself a new idea for most students, an important precursor to understanding the "system."

It was important to Ms. B that her students consider the relationships between plants and other life forms and the role of photosynthesis in those relationships. The depth to which she might eventually pursue the chemical explanation of the topic depends on the strength of the framework the students construct as a result of the opening lessons.

Although Ms. B's students didn't construct a biochemical understanding of photosynthesis, and their examples were not completely analogous to the system of photosynthesis in terms of reversibility and complexity, they did begin to appreciate that one way of understanding photosynthesis is to see it as a system process yielding both a product and a by-product. This understanding can provide a basis for the construction of a more sophisticated understanding of photosynthesis and the ability to use the unit's vocabulary.

Ms. B's analogic activity served as an invitation for students to look at photosynthesis as a whole system. The students' own creation of analogies helped them to construct a framework. In order to complete the task, students asked questions about photosynthesis, no mean feat for seventh-graders, and struggled to put the "answers" into a meaningful context.

FIGURE 2.1 A comparison of two methods of teaching seventh graders about photosynthesis: a traditional and a constructivist approach. (*Source:* Adapted from Jacqueline Grennon Brooks and Martin G. Brooks, *In Search for Understanding: The Case for Constructivist Classrooms* (Alexandria, VA: Association for Supervision and Curriculum Development, 1993), pp. 16, 18–20. By permission.)

An important skill needed in overcoming egocentricity is the ability to listen to others with understanding and empathy. However, many young adolescents, and even many adults, are not very good at listening. Teachers must help students to develop this skill. One way to facilitate the development of skill in listening is to ask a student to paraphrase what another has said, and then ask the first student if, in fact, that is what he or she said. If it isn't, then have the child repeat what he or she said, and then, again, ask another student to paraphrase that statement. Repeat the process until the original student's statement is correctly understood. Practicing this skill in the classroom helps students not only to develop their listening skill but to learn the subject content being taught, simply because practicing the skill of listening forces the learner to focus her or his attention on the essence of what is being heard.

INTERPRETIVE

Children and young adolescents are constantly interpreting their environment. Interpreting our experiences is an unavoidable mental process. However, these interpretations are often incomplete, or even incorrect, as discussed in the last part of Chapter 1 (and are referred to variously in the literature as naive theories, misconceptions, conceptual misunderstandings, and incongruent schemata, as discussed in the next paragraph). Even when their conceptions are incomplete or in error, students will continue to arrive at interpretations that satisfy them and allow them to function adequately in their own daily lives.

Learners try to construct meaning to their experiences by referring to a body of related information stored in long-term memory from past experiences and knowledge (called networks or schemata).[4] Learning continues by assimilating new information into a schema and modifying it or forming a new schema (a process known as accommodation), thus allowing the learner to function adequately. Children's interpretations of phenomena change with their increasing maturity. Consequently, children are engaged in a constant process of revising interpretations as they mature in ability to understand and to think abstractly. A technique called concept mapping, discussed later in this chapter, is a learning strategy useful in helping students bridge their knowledge and understandings to result in useful schemata.[5]

Students come to your classroom with existing schemata about most everything, which from an adult's point of view may or may not always be sound (that is, may sometimes be incongruent with accepted views) but, nevertheless, are valid. As their teacher, one of your more important tasks is to help students to correct their misconceptions. Not unlike many adults, young adolescents are naturally resistant to changes to their interpretations, so changing their misconceptions and building their understandings is no easy task. Even after they have had corrective instruction, students will often persist in their misconceptions.

Correcting students' misconceptions about the natural world is often a long and arduous task, demanding your understanding, patience, and creative instruction. Students are much more likely to modify data from their experiences to accommodate their schemata than they are to change their beliefs as a result of new experiences.[6] Perhaps this isn't difficult to understand. After all, there are stories of reputable scientists and other professionals who themselves were tempted to modify data to support their beliefs. Stubborn persistence and remaining open to change are virtuous, although conflicting, human attributes. In the words of Brooks and Brooks,

> Students of all ages develop and refine ideas about phenomena and then tenaciously hold onto these ideas as eternal truths. Even in the face of "authoritative" intervention and "hard" data that challenge their views, students typically adhere staunchly to their original notions. Through experiences that might engender contradictions, the frameworks for these notions weaken, causing students to rethink their perspectives and form new understandings.[7]

PERSISTENT

As implied in the preceding discussion, children and young adolescents are tenacious. They like to achieve their objectives and will spend unusual lengths of time and effort at activities that are important and interesting to them. With a student's persistent efforts comes a feeling of personal satisfaction and a sense of accomplishment. It is your challenge to take advantage of this persistence and desire to achieve by helping students to acquire ownership in what is being learned and by providing instruction in the form of interesting and meaningful learning activities.

CURIOUS

Children are naturally curious. While a younger child's world is filled with wonder and excitement, a middle school student's curiosity varies, depending on what catches that student's interest. Generally speaking, young adolescents are more interested in things that move than things that don't. Often they are more interested in objects that make things happen than in those to which things are happening. Their curiosity reaches a peak with things that appear mysterious and magical. To initiate effective learning in the science classroom, good instruction takes advantage of this natural curiosity. That is why, for example, the use of "magic" and discrepant events are so popular and often successful in motivating student learning in science. The greatest challenge to teachers is to sustain this natural curiosity and to keep it alive throughout the school years.

ADVENTUROUS

Children are by nature adventurous and inquisitive—they love to explore. They love to touch and feel objects. They are always wondering "what will happen if . . ." and suggesting ideas for

Children love to participate in hands-on science learning.

finding out. They are natural questioners. The words *what, why,* and *how* are common in their vocabulary. While investigating, young adolescents work and learn best when they experience firsthand. Therefore, you should provide a wide variety of experiences that involve hands-on learning. Hands-on learning engages the learner's mind, causing questioning. When a learner is allowed to question and to explore, her mind is engaged. Consequently, rather than discourage student questions, the competent science teacher encourages and builds the learning around student questions.

ENERGETIC
Children are energetic. They would rather not sit for a long time—for some it is near impossible. They would rather do than to listen, and even while listening, they move their bodies restlessly. This difficulty in sitting quietly has a direct bearing on a student's attention span. As a result, teaching should provide for kinesthetic learning, that is, by offering many activities that give students the opportunity to be physically active.

SOCIAL
Children are social beings. They like to be with and to be accepted by their peers. They like to work together in planning and carrying out their activities. Regardless of any differences within a group of children—socioeconomic, intellectual, ethnic, or physical—children work very well together when given proper encouragement, when they understand the procedures, and when they are given clear direction and worthwhile opportunity. Each student forms a self-concept through these social interactions in school. A student will develop satisfactory self-esteem when given an opportunity to work with others, to offer ideas, and to work out peer relationships. Your teaching can foster not only learning but also the development of each student's self-esteem by incorporating social-interaction teaching strategies, such as co-operative learning, peer tutoring, and cross-age teaching.[8]

VARIETY OF PSYCHOLOGICAL NEEDS
Young people have psychological needs. Abraham Maslow presented a continuum of psychological needs beginning with the most basic—physiological (provision of food, clothing, and shelter), then security (feeling of safety), social (sense of love and belonging), sense of self-esteem, and the highest—self actualization (full use of talents, capacities, abilities, acceptance of self and others).[9]

When children are frustrated because of lack of satisfaction of one or more of these needs, their classroom behavior is affected, and their learning is stifled.[10] Some students become aggressive and disrupt normal classroom procedures, hoping in this way to satisfy a basic need for recognition. Others become antisocial, apathetic, and fail to participate in classroom and school activities. Perhaps this is best explained by D. S. Eitzen:

> Everyone needs a dream. Without a dream, we become apathetic. Without a dream, we become fatalistic. Without a dream and the hope of attaining it, society becomes our enemy. We educators must realize that some young people act in antisocial ways because they have lost their dreams. And we must realize that we as a society are partly responsible for that loss. Teaching is a noble profession whose goal is to increase the success rate for *all* children. We must do everything we can to achieve this goal. If not, we—society, schools, teachers, and students—will all fail.[11]

You must be alert to any student whose basic psychological needs are not being satisfied. Perhaps it is the child who comes to school hungry. Perhaps it is the one who comes to school feeling insecure because of problems at home. Maybe it is the one who comes to school tired from having to spend each night sleeping and living in an automobile, or from being abused by a parent, friend, or relative. Although the classroom teacher cannot solve all the ailments of society, the teacher does have an opportunity and responsibility to make all students feel welcome, respected, and wanted, at least while in that teacher's classroom.

INTELLECTUAL DEVELOPMENT AND HOW STUDENTS LEARN

Jean Piaget, Lev Vygotsky, Robert Gagné, Jerome Bruner, and David Ausubel are learning theorists who have played major roles in the development of today's theory of effective instruction. Of the several psychologists whose theories of learning made an impact during the last half of the twentieth century, perhaps no other had such a wide-ranging influence on education than did Swiss psychologist Jean Piaget (1896–1980). Although Piaget began to publish his insights in the 1920s, his work was not popularized in this country until the 1960s.

Piaget's Theory of Cognitive Development

Piaget was an advocate of constructivism. Maintaining that knowledge is created as children interact with their social and physical environment, he postulated four stages (or periods) of cognitive development, which occur in a continuing progression from birth to post-adolescence. Mental development begins with the first stage and, without skipping a stage, progresses developmentally through each succeeding stage.

AGE RANGES IN PIAGET'S STAGES OF COGNITIVE DEVELOPMENT

Although the ages assigned to Piaget's stages of cognitive development indicate when the majority of children are likely to attain each stage of development, these ages can actually vary widely depending on a number of factors, including the assessment procedures used. Consequently, one must be cautious about placing much reliance on these age ranges. For example, about 5 percent of middle school children, that is, children ages 10–14, operate at the preoperational level. Furthermore, when confronted with perplexing (discrepant) situations (i.e., information or evidence contrary to what they already think they know), evidence indicates that many learners, including adults, tend to revert to an earlier developmental stage. Some researchers refer to this mental phenomenon as **downshifting,** the times that we revert to earlier learned behaviors and programming.

The following sets of conditions, some of which have special significance for teachers of science, can induce situational downshifting, and under these conditions the search for meaningful understanding is sabotaged: (1) prespecified "correct" outcomes have been established for the student; (2) what is learned does not connect well with what students already know; (3) rewards and/or punishments are externally controlled and relatively immediate; (4) time lines are restrictive and inflexible; (5) the work to be done is relatively unfamiliar, with little support available for it.[12]

Sensorimotor Stage (Birth to Age 2)   At this stage, children are bound to the moment and to their immediate environment. Learning and behaviors at this stage result from the direct interaction with stimuli that the child can see or feel. Objects that are not seen are found only by random searching. Through direct interaction the child begins to build mental concepts, associating actions and reactions, and later in the stage begins to label people and objects and to show imagining. For example, seeing a parent preparing the child's food tells the child that he or she will soon be eating. The child, then, is developing a practical base of knowledge that forms the foundation for learning in the next stage.

Preoperational Stage (Ages 2–7)   Children at the preoperational stage can imagine and think before acting, rather than only responding to external stimuli. This stage is called pre-operational because the child does not use logical operations in thinking. In this stage the child is egocentric. The child's worldview is subjective rather than objective. Because of ego-centrism, it is difficult for the child to consider and accept another person's point of view. The child is perceptually oriented, that is, judgments are made according to how things look to the child. The child does not think logically and, therefore, does not reason by implication. Instead, an intuitive approach is used. At this stage, when confronted with new and dis-crepant information about a phenomenon, the child adjusts the new information to accom-modate his or her existing beliefs about it.

At this stage the child can observe and describe variables (properties of an object or as-pects of a phenomenon) but concentrates on just one variable at a time, usually one that stands out visually. The child cannot coordinate variables, so has difficulty in realizing that an object has several properties. Consequently, it is difficult for the child to combine parts into a whole. The child can make simple classifications according to one or two properties, but finds it difficult to realize that multiple classifications are possible. Also, the child can arrange objects in simple series, but has trouble arranging them in a long series or inserting a new object in its proper place within a series. To the child, space is restricted to the his or her own neighborhood, and time is restricted to hours, days, and seasons.

The child in this stage has not yet developed the concept of conservation. This means the child does not understand that several objects can be rearranged and that the size or shape or volume of a solid or liquid can be changed, yet the number of objects and the amount of solid or liquid will be unchanged—or conserved. For example, if two rows of 10 objects are arranged so they take up the same area, the child will state that the two rows are the same and there are the same number of objects in each row. If the objects in one row are spread out so the row is longer, the child is likely to maintain that the longer row now has more objects in it. Similarly, if the child is shown two identical balls of clay, the child will agree that both balls contain the same amount of material. When, in full view of the child, one of the balls is stretched out into the shape of a sausage, the child is likely to say the sausage has more clay because it is larger, or less clay because it is thinner. Either way, the child at this stage is "cen-tering" his or her attention on just one particular property (here, length or thickness) to the neglect of the other properties.

In both of the preceding examples the reason for the child's thinking is that the child does not yet understand reversibility. The child's thinking cannot yet reverse itself back to the point of origin. As a result, the child does not understand that since nothing has been re-moved or added, the extended row of objects can be rearranged to its original length and the clay sausage can be made back into the original ball. The child does not yet comprehend that action and thought processes are reversible.

Not yet able to use abstract reasoning, and only beginning to think conceptually, students at this stage of development learn best by manipulating objects in concrete situations, rather than by abstract, verbal learning alone. For children at this stage of development, conceptual change comes very gradually.

Concrete Operations Stage (Ages 7–11)   In this stage the learner can now perform log-ical operations. The child can observe, judge, and evaluate in less egocentric terms than in the preoperational stage, and can formulate more objective explanations. As a result, the learner knows how to solve physical problems. Because a child's thinking at this stage is still concrete and not yet abstract, the student is limited to problems dealing with actual concrete situations. Early in this stage the learner cannot generalize, deal with hypothetical situations, or weigh possibilities.

The child can make multiple classifications, arrange objects in long series, and place new objects in their proper places in the series. The child can begin to comprehend geographical space and historical time. The child develops the concepts of conservation according to their ease of learning: first, number of objects (ages 6–7), then matter, length, area (age 7), weight (ages 9–12), and volume (age 11 or more). The child also develops the concept of reversibility and can now reverse the physical and mental processes when numbers of objects are rearranged or when the size and shape of matter are changed.

Later in this stage children can hypothesize and do higher-level thinking. Not yet able to use abstract reasoning, and only beginning to be able to think conceptually, students at this stage of development still learn best by manipulating objects in concrete situations, rather than by verbal learning alone. Attempting to change children's understanding of the natural world through direct instruction does not work well at this stage. Indirect instruction through hands-on, active learning is more effective.

Formal Operations Stage (Age 11 and Up)   Piaget initially believed that by age 15 most adolescents reach formal operational thinking, but now it is quite clear that even many high school students and even some adults do not yet function at this level. Essentially, students who are quick to understand abstract ideas are formal thinkers. Most elementary and middle school students, however, are not at this stage. For them, metacognition (planning, monitoring, and evaluating one's own thinking) may be very difficult. (In essence, metacognition is today's term for what Piaget referred to as reflective abstraction, or the reflection upon one's own thinking, without which continued development cannot occur.)[13] Many middle school students are at a stage preparatory to formal operations, a substage in which they may make correct discoveries and handle certain formal operations but do so in an awkward manner and without the skill to provide methodical proof. Furthermore, when confronted with new and perplexing situations, there is a tendency among children and adults alike to downshift, that is, revert to an earlier stage of mental operation.

In the formal operations stage the individual's method of thinking shifts from the concrete to the more formal and abstract. The learner can now relate one abstraction to another and grows in ability to think conceptually. It is in this stage that the learner can develop hypotheses, deduce possible consequences from them, then test these hypotheses with controlled experiments in which all the variables are identical except that being tested. When approaching a new problem, the learner begins by formulating all the possibilities and then, through experimentation and logical analysis, determining which ones are substantiated. After solving the problem, the learner can reflect upon or rethink the thought processes that were used.

Three-Phase Learning Cycle

As discussed in Chapter 1, for an understanding of conceptual development and change, researchers developed a Piaget-based theory of learning whereby students are guided from concrete, hands-on learning experiences to abstract formulations of concepts and their applications. This theory, known as the three-phase learning cycle, was the philosophical basis for the NSF-sponsored *SCIS* program developed in the 1960s by Robert Karplus and his researchers at the University of California at Berkeley. There have been more recent interpretations or modifications of that three-phase cycle, such as 4MAT, discussed later in this chapter. The three phases are (1) an *exploratory hands-on phase,* in which students explore materials that lead to their own questions and tentative answers, (2) a *concept development phase,* in which, under the guidance of the teacher, students invent concepts and principles that help them answer their questions and reorganize their ideas, and (3) a *concept application phase,* another hands-on phase in which the students try out their new ideas by applying them to situations that are relevant and meaningful to them. During application of a concept, the learner may discover new information that causes a change in the learner's understanding of that concept. Thus, as emphasized in Chapter 1, the process of learning is cyclic.

Multilevel Instruction

Students in your classroom will likely be at different stages (and substages) of cognitive development. It is important to attend to where each student is developmentally, that is, to individualize the instruction. To do that, many teachers use multilevel instruction (known also as multitasking). Multilevel instruction is an approach whereby various students or groups of students are working at different tasks to accomplish the same objective, or are working at different tasks to accomplish different objectives. When integrating student learning, multitasking is an important and useful, perhaps even necessary, strategy. Project-centered teaching (discussed in the next chapter) is an instructional method that easily allows for the provision of multilevel instruction.

Factors Affecting the Rate of Cognitive Development

As researched by Piaget, the four stages are general descriptions of the psychological processes in cognitive development, but, as we cautioned earlier, the rate of development varies widely among children. The rate of cognitive development is affected by the individual's (1) maturation, which is controlled by inherited biological factors and by her health, (2) the richness of the student's experiences, (3) social interactions, and (4) the learner's equilibration. Equilibration, discussed later in "Concept Development," is the process of mentally neutralizing the effect of cognitive disequilibrium, that is, moving from disequilibrium to equilibrium, merging new and discrepant information with established knowledge.

Lev Vygotsky: Cooperative Learning in a Supportive Environment

A contemporary of Piaget, the Soviet psychologist Lev Vygotsky (1896–1934) studied and agreed with Piaget on most points, but differed with Piaget on the importance of a child's social interactions. Vygotsky argued that learning is most effective when children cooperate with one another in a supportive learning environment under the careful guidance of a teacher. Cooperative learning, group problem solving, and cross-age tutoring are instructional strategies used today, which have grown in popularity as a result of research evolving from the work of Vygotsky.

Concept Development

Equilibration is the regulator of the relationship between assimilation (input of new information into existing schemata) and accommodation (development of new or modification of old schemata). Equilibrium is a balance between assimilation and accommodation; the brain is always striving internally for this balance. Disequilibrium is the state of imbalance. When disequilibrium occurs, the brain is motivated to assimilate and to accommodate. With or without a teacher's guidance a learner's brain *will* assimilate information. The task of the teacher, then, is to facilitate the learner's continuing accurate construct of old and new schemata. Concept mapping (discussed later in this chapter) has been shown to be an excellent tool for facilitating a learner's assimilation and accommodation.

CONCEPT ATTAINMENT: A CONTINUING CYCLIC PROCESS

As previously emphasized, we can think of the learner's developing understanding of concepts (concept attainment) as being a cyclical (continuing) three-stage process. The first stage is an increasing awareness, which is stimulated by the quality and richness of the learning environment, essentially brought about in science learning by the hands-on/minds-on experiences during the exploratory phase of instruction.

The second stage is disequilibrium, which in science instruction is most likely to occur during the exploratory and concept introduction phases. The third stage is reformulation of the concept, which is accomplished by the learner's process of equilibration. The concept is then set in the learner's mind until new data cause a return of mental disequilibrium.

Maturation Differences

New principles are emerging from neuroscience that may have profound effects on teaching and on how schools are organized. For example, as stated by Caine and Caine, "Because there can be a five-year difference in maturation between any two 'average' children, gauging achievement on the basis of chronological age is inappropriate."[14] Some researchers have argued that brain growth patterns show "plateaus" for most adolescents (although often different between boys and girls), and that these patterns should be considered in organizing schools and programs. For example, Sylwester believes that the range of differences is great enough between boys and girls that boys may be ill-equipped to handle formal operations, but girls may do so more easily, as girls' brains, specifically the rear right hemisphere, *angular gyrus*, and prefrontal cortex, are growing at a rate three times that of boys'.[15] Hensley outlines a need to consider brain growth research before making policies on grade organization.[16] Research indicates brain growth spurts for students in grades 1, 2, 5, 6, 9, and 10. If schools were organized solely on this criterion, they would be configured in grade clusters K, 1–4, 5–8, and 9–12.[17] From 1981 to 1992 the number of middle-level schools using a 5–8 grade span tripled, and as compared with the 1981 figures, only about one third of middle-level schools in 1992 used the 7–9 grade span.[18] With an increasing use of the 5–8 grade span, the middle school may be an indicator of an advance in that direction.

Robert Gagné and the General Learning Hierarchy

Robert Gagné is well known for his hierarchy of learning levels. According to Gagné, learning is the establishing of a capability to do something that the learner was not capable of doing previously. Notice the emphasis on the learner's "doing."

Gagné postulates a hierarchy of learning capabilities. Learning one particular capability usually depends on having previously learned one or more simpler capabilities. For Gagné, observable changes in behavior constitute the *only* criteria for inferring that learning has occurred. It follows, then, that the beginning, or lowest, level of a learning hierarchy includes very simple behaviors. These behaviors form the basis for learning more complex behaviors in the next level of the hierarchy. At each higher level, learning requires that the appropriate simpler, or less complex, behaviors have been acquired in the lower learning levels.

Gagné identifies eight levels of learning in this hierarchy. Beginning with the simplest and progressing to the most complex, these levels are (1) signal learning, whereby the individual learns to make a general conditioned response to a given signal, (2) stimulus-response learning, where the individual acquires a precise physical or vocal response to a discriminated stimulus, (3) chaining, sometimes called skill learning, involving the linking together of two or more units of simple stimulus-response learning, (4) verbal association, a form of chaining, but in which the links are verbal units, (5) multiple discrimination, in which individual learned chains are linked to form multiple discriminations, (6) concept learning, which means learning to respond to stimuli by their abstract characteristics (such as position, shape, color, and number), as opposed to their concrete physical properties, (7) principle learning, whereby the learner must relate two or more concepts, and (8) problem solving. According to Gagné, and as most learning theorists agree, problem solving is the most sophisticated type of learning. In problem solving the individual applies principles learned in order to achieve a goal. While achieving this goal, however, the learner becomes capable of new performances by using the new knowledge. When a problem is solved, new knowledge has been acquired and the individual's capacity moves forward. The individual is now able to handle a wide class of problems similar to the one solved. What has been learned, according to Gagné, is a higher-order principle, which is the combined product of two or more lower-order principles.

Thus, when a child has acquired the capabilities and behaviors of a certain level of learning, we assume that the child has also acquired the capabilities and behaviors of all the learning levels below this level. Furthermore, if the child were having difficulty in demonstrating the capabilities and behaviors for a certain level, the teacher could simply test the child on the capabilities and behaviors of the lower levels to determine which one or ones were causing the difficulty.

Gagné stresses the importance of structure and sequence in science learning. His work provided the theoretical model of a simple-to-complex hierarchy of types of learning. One of the NSF-sponsored elementary science programs of the 1960s, *Science—A Process Approach* (SAPA), was built on this model.

Jerome Bruner and Discovery Learning

A leading interpreter and promoter of Piaget's ideas, Jerome Bruner also made his own significant contributions on how children learn. *Elementary Science Study* (ESS), one of the popular NSF science curriculum projects of the 1960s, was developed around Bruner's model of how children learn.

Like Piaget, Bruner maintains that each child passes through stages that are age-related and biologically determined and that learning depends primarily on the developmental level that the child has attained. Bruner's theory also encompasses three major sequential stages that he refers to as representations. These representations, which can be thought of as ways of knowing, are *enactive representation* (knowing that is related to movement, i.e., through direct experience or concrete activities); *ikonic representation* (knowing that is related to visual and spatial, or graphic, representations, e.g., films and still visuals); and *symbolic representation* (knowing that is related to reason and logic, i.e., that depends on the use of words and abstract symbolization). These correspond to Piaget's sensorimotor, concrete operations, and formal operations stages.

Bruner's thinking was influenced somewhat by the work of Vygotsky.[19] Although Bruner's description of what happens during these three representations corresponds to what happens in Piaget's stages, he differs from Piaget in his interpretation of the role of language in intellectual development, believing that language and prior experiences are more closely associated with the development of new mental constructs than is the quest for cognitive equilibrium.

Piaget believes that although thought and language are related, they are different systems. He posits that the child's thinking is based on a system of inner logic that evolves as the child organizes and adapts to experiences. Bruner, however, maintains that thought is internalized language. The child translates experience into language and then uses language as an instrument of thinking.

Bruner and Piaget differ also in their attitude toward the child's readiness for learning. Piaget concluded that the child's readiness for learning depends on maturation and intellectual development. Bruner, however, as well as other researchers, believe that a child is always ready to learn a concept at some level of sophistication. Bruner states that any subject can be taught effectively in some intellectually honest form to any child at any stage of development. According to Bruner, a child can learn concepts only within the framework of whichever stage of intellectual development the child is in at the time. In teaching children, then, it is essential that each child be helped to pass progressively from one stage of intellectual development to the next. Schools can do this by providing challenging but usable opportunities and problems for children that tempt them to forge ahead into the next stages of development. As a result, the children acquire a higher level of understanding.

BRUNER AND THE ACT OF LEARNING

Bruner describes the act of learning as involving three almost simultaneous processes. The first is the process of acquiring new knowledge. The second is the process of manipulating this knowledge to make it fit new tasks or situations. The third is the process of evaluating the acquisition and manipulation of this knowledge. A major objective of learning is to introduce the child at an early age to the ideas and styles that will help the child become literate. Consequently, the science curriculum should be built around major conceptual schemes, skills, and values that society considers to be important. These should be taught as early as possible in a manner consistent with the child's stages of development and forms of thought, and then revisited many times throughout the school years to increase and deepen the learner's understanding.

Bruner has been an articulate spokesperson for discovery learning. He advocates that, whenever possible, teaching and learning should be conducted in such a matter that children be given the opportunity to discover concepts for themselves.

Benefits of Discovery Learning

Bruner cites four major benefits derived from learning by discovery. First, there is an increase in intellectual potency—this means that discovery learning helps students learn how to learn. It helps the learner to develop skills in problem solving, enabling the learner to arrange and apply what has been learned to new situations and, thus, to learn new concepts.

Second, there is a shift from extrinsic to intrinsic rewards. Discovery learning shifts the motive for learning away from that of satisfying others to that of internal self-rewarding satisfaction, that is, satisfying oneself—the source of motivation is intrinsic rather than extrinsic.

Third, there is an opportunity to learn the working heuristics of discovery. By *heuristics* Bruner means the methods through which a person is educated to find out things independently. Only through the exercise of problem solving and by the effort of discovery can the learner find out things independently. The more adept the learner becomes in the working heuristics of discovery, the more effective the decisions the learner will make in problem solving, the decisions leading to quicker solutions than can be achieved by any trial-and-error approach.

Fourth, there is an aid to memory processing. Knowledge resulting from discovery learning is more easily remembered, and it is more readily recalled when needed. Bruner's work, strongly supported by recent brain research, provides a rationale for using discovery and hands-on learning activities.

Gagné and Bruner differ in emphasis in their approach to learning. Whereas Gagné emphasizes primarily the product of learning (knowledge), Bruner's emphasis is on the process of learning (the skills). For Gagné the key question is, "*What* do you want the child to know?"

Discovery learning helps children learn how to learn.

but for Bruner it is, "*How* do you want the child to know?" For Gagné the emphasis is on learning itself, whether by discovery, review, or practice. For Bruner the emphasis is on learning by discovery; it is the method of learning that is important.

Gagné cites problem solving as the highest level of learning, with the lower learning levels prerequisite to this highest level. The appropriate sequence in learning (and teaching), he says, is from these lower levels toward problem solving. The teacher begins with simple ideas, relates all of them, builds on them, and works toward the more complex levels of learning. On the other hand, Bruner *begins* with problem solving, which in turn leads to the development of necessary skills. The teacher poses a question to be solved and then uses it as a catalyst to motivate children to develop the necessary skills.

Piaget, Bruner, and Gagné also differ in their attitude toward the child's readiness for learning. As stated earlier, Piaget believes that readiness depends on the child's maturation and intellectual development. Bruner believes that the child is always ready to learn a concept at some level of sophistication. Gagné, however, feels that readiness is dependent on the successful development of lower-level skills and prior understandings.

Science Learning: A Process of Discovery

Like Bruner and Piaget, Gagné believes that science should be taught and learned as a process of discovery. Indeed, numerous studies support the notion that children taught science by a

The use of discovery learning helps to shift sources of motivation for learning from extrinsic to intrinsic.

process approach outperform students taught traditional science that emphasizes content knowledge.[20] Giving the student practice in discovery involves giving the learner opportunities to carry out inductive thinking, to hypothesize, and to test hypotheses in a large variety of situations in and outside the classroom. A corresponding value in teaching science by hands-on discovery strategies is that of changing students' misconceptions about science.

Gagné posits that there are two major prerequisites to successful practice of scientific inquiry. First, the child must have a broad science background that can be applied to the solving of new problems. Second, the child must be able to discriminate between a good idea and a bad one, that is, between a probably successful course of action and a probably unsuccessful one.

David Ausubel and Meaningful Verbal Learning

David Ausubel is an advocate of reception learning, the receipt of ideas through transmission.[21] He agrees with other psychologists that the development of problem-solving skills is a primary objective in teaching. However, like Gagné, he feels that effective problem solving and discovery are more likely to take place after children have learned key and supporting concepts, primarily through reception learning, that is, through direct instruction (expository teaching).

Ausubel strongly urges teachers to use learning situations and examples that are familiar to the students. This helps students to assimilate what is being learned with what they already know, making their learning more meaningful. Differing from Bruner, Ausubel believes that discovery learning is too time-consuming to enable students to learn all they should know within the short time allotted to learning. Like Bruner and Gagné, he suggests that children in the primary grades should work on as many "hands-on" learning activities as possible, but for children beyond the primary grades, he recommends the increased use of learning by transmission, using teacher explanations, concept mapping, demonstrations, diagrams, and illustrations. However, although it is not always avoidable, Ausubel cautions against learning by rote memorization.

An example of learning by rote is memorizing your Social Security number. Sometimes, such as in memorizing a Social Security number, one must learn by rote information that is not connected to any prior knowledge. To do that, it is helpful to break the information to be learned into small chunks, such as dividing the eight-digit Social Security number into small groups of digits. Learning by rote is also easier if one can connect that which is to be memorized to some prior knowledge. Strategies such as these, used to bridge the gap between rote learning and meaningful learning, are known as **mnemonics.** Examples of common mnemonics in science include:

1. The periods of the Paleozoic Era are Cavemen Object Strenuously During Most Polite Parties (Cambrian, Ordovician, Silurian, Devonian, Mississippian, Pennsylvanian, and Permian).
2. The hierarchy of the biological classification system is Kindly Professors—or Doctors—Can Only Fail Greedy Students (Kingdom, Phylum—or Division—Class, Order, Family, Genus, and Species).
3. The order of colors in the visible spectrum is ROY G. BIV (red, orange, yellow, green, blue, indigo, and violet). (Today, however, blue and indigo are usually combined and considered only as blue.)

To avoid rote memorization, Ausubel encourages teachers to make learning meaningful and longer lasting by using **advance organizers,** ideas that are presented to the students before the new material and that mentally prepare them to integrate the new material into previously built cognitive structures. Most textbook programs today are designed in this way. When Mrs. B (Figure 2.1) began the unit on photosynthesis by asking her students to think of systems with which they might have some experience and familiarity and to indicate the product created, the energy source needed, and the raw materials used, and promoted student thinking by suggesting to the students that they consider, for example, their art classes and what they create there, she was using an advance organizer.

There is no doubt that the most effective teaching is that which allows students to see meaning in what is being taught. A danger in expository teaching (i. e., in which the student is listening to the teacher, reading, and memorizing), however, is a tendency to rely too heavily on spoken communication, which for many learners may be highly abstract and, thus, unlikely to be very effective. This is especially likely in today's public school classrooms of students who may vary widely in their language proficiency, cultural backgrounds, and skill levels.

Concept Mapping

Based on Ausubel's theory of meaningful learning, a technique that has been found useful for helping students change their science misconceptions is concept mapping. Simply put, concepts can be thought of as classifications that attempt to organize the world of objects and

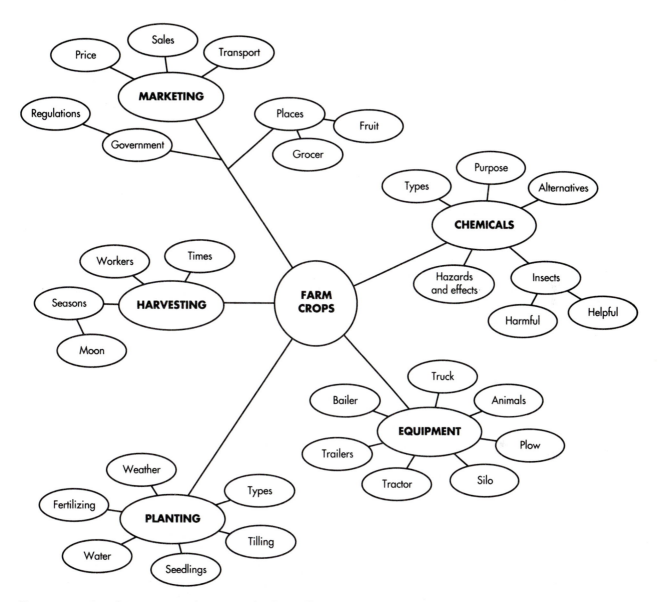

FIGURE 2.2   Sample concept map. (*Source:* Richard D. Kellough, *A Resource Guide for Teaching: K–12* (New York: Macmillan, 1994), p. 332. By permission of Prentice Hall.)

events into a smaller number of categories. In everyday usage, the term *concept* means idea, as when someone says, "My concept of love is not the same as yours." A concept embodies a meaning that develops in complexity with experience and learning over time. For example, the concept of love held by a fifth or sixth grader is unlikely to be as complex as that held by an adult, or even that held by a ninth grader.

A concept map typically refers to a visual or graphic representation of concepts with connections (bridges) to show their relationships. See Figure 2.2, a concept map done in a seventh-grade integrated language arts/social studies/science class showing students' connections of relationships while studying concepts in fruit farming and marketing.

The general procedure for concept mapping is to have students (1) identify important concepts in materials being studied, often by circling those concepts, (2) rank order the concepts from the most general to the most specific, and then (3) arrange the concepts on a sheet of paper, connect related ideas with lines, and define the connections between the related ideas. Concept mapping has been found to help students in their ability to organize, represent their thoughts, and connect new knowledge to their past experiences and schemata.[22]

TEACHING FOR THINKING

Based on what they have learned about learning and brain functioning, teachers are encouraged to integrate explicit thinking instruction into daily lessons. In other words, teachers should help students develop their thinking skills.

> In teaching for thinking, we are interested not only in what students know but also in how students behave when they don't know. . . . Gathering evidence of the performance and growth of intelligent behavior is difficult through standardized testing. It really requires "kid-watching": observing students as they try to solve the day-to-day academic and real-life problems they encounter in school, at home, on the playground, alone, and with friends. By collecting anecdotes and examples of written, oral, and visual expressions, we can see students' increasingly voluntary and spontaneous performance of these intelligent behaviors.[23]

Costa presents 14 characteristics of intelligent behavior that teachers can teach toward and observe developing in students.[24] These characteristics are described here as follows:

Persistence. Sticking to a task until it is completed. Consider these examples of persistence.

> *Clara Barton*, in 1882, nearly single-handedly and against formidable odds, established the American Red Cross.
> *Rachel Carson.* Refusing to be intimidated by mighty leaders from the chemical industry, powerful politicians, and influential persons in the media, Carson was persistent and relentless in her pursuit to educate society about the ill effects of pesticides on humans and the natural world, refusing to accept the premise that damage to nature was the inevitable cost of technological and scientific progress. In 1963, her book *Silent Spring* was the seed that began the development of today's more responsible ecological attitude.
> *Amelia Earhart*, born in 1898, from the time she was a young girl demonstrated creativity, curiosity, and persistence. After learning to fly in 1920, it was only eight years later that she became the first woman to fly the Atlantic Ocean, thereby paving the way for other women to become active in aviation.
> *Thomas Edison.* In designing the light bulb, Thomas Edison tried approximately 3,000 filaments before finding one that worked.

Decreasing impulsivity. When students develop this behavior they think more before acting. Students can be taught to think before shouting out an answer, before beginning a project or task, and before arriving at conclusions with only limited data.

Listening to others with understanding and empathy. Some psychologists believe that the ability to listen to others, to empathize with and to understand their point of view, is one of the highest forms of intelligent behavior. Piaget refers to this behavior as overcoming egocentrism. In research laboratories scientists periodically convene to share their research, to explore their ideas and findings, and to broaden their perspectives by listening to the ideas and reactions of others. While sciencing, children can be taught to listen to, and build upon, the ideas of others.

Cooperative thinking—social intelligence. Humans are social beings. Real-world problem solving has become so complex that seldom can any person go it alone. Not all children come to school knowing how to work effectively in groups. They may exhibit competitiveness, narrow-mindedness, egocentrism, ethnocentrism, or criticism of others' values, emotions, and beliefs. Listening, consensus seeking, giving up an idea to work on someone else's, empathy, compassion, group leadership, cooperative learning, knowing how to support group efforts, altruism—these are behaviors indicative of intelligent human beings, and they can be learned within the science classroom.

Flexibility in thinking. Intelligent people can approach a new problem from a new angle, using a novel approach. De Bono refers to this as *lateral thinking.*[25] Students can learn to consider alternative points of view and to deal with several sources of information simultaneously.

Metacognition. Being able to plan, monitor, and evaluate one's own thinking is another characteristic of intelligent behavior. Students can be helped to develop this intelligent behavior while sciencing.

Striving for accuracy and precision. Science teachers can observe growth in this behavior when students (1) take time to check their experiments, (2) review procedures, (3) repeat the experiment, (4) refuse to draw conclusions until they have obtained sufficient data, and (5) use more concise language.

A sense of humor. The positive effects of humor on the body's physiological functions are well established: a drop in the pulse rate, the secretion of endorphins, an increase of oxygen in the blood. Humor liberates creativity and provides high-level thinking skills, such as anticipation, finding novel relationships, and visual imagery. The acquisition of a sense of humor follows a developmental sequence similar to that described by Piaget[26] and Kohlberg.[27] Initially, children may find humor in all the wrong things—human frailty, ethnic differences, sacrilegious riddles, ribald profanities. Later, creative children thrive on finding incongruity and will demonstrate a whimsical frame of mind during problem solving.

Questioning and problem posing. As mentioned earlier, children are full of questions and do not hesitate to ask them. We want students to be alert to, and to recognize, phenomena and discrepancies in their environment and to freely inquire about their causes. In exemplary science programs students ask questions and then, from those questions, develop a problem-solving strategy to investigate their ideas.

Drawing on past knowledge and applying it to new situations. A major goal of education is that students apply school-learned knowledge to real-life situations. To develop skills in drawing on past knowledge and applying it to new situations, students must be given opportunity to practice doing that very thing.

Risk taking. Students should be encouraged to venture forth and explore their ideas. Science teachers can provide this opportunity with techniques such as brainstorming, exploratory investigation, experimentation, and cooperative learning. Exemplary science teachers model this behavior for their students whenever they show enthusiasm and willingness to venture into the realm of the less known.

Using all the senses. Whenever appropriate, students must be encouraged to use all their senses to learn, and not to depend on only one or two. (See the Learning Experiences Ladder in Chapter 3.)

Ingenuity, originality, and insightfulness: Creativity. In science all students must be encouraged to do, and discouraged from saying "I can't." They must be taught in such a way as to encourage intrinsic motivation, rather than to rely on extrinsic sources. Teachers must be able to offer criticism so the student understands that the criticism is not a criticism of self. In exemplary educational programs, students learn the value of feedback. They learn the value of their own intuition, of guessing.

Wonderment, inquisitiveness, curiosity, and the enjoyment of problem solving: A sense of efficacy as a thinker. Young children typically express wonderment. Through effective science teaching, all students can recapture that sense of wonderment as they are guided by an effective teacher to a feeling of "I can," and express a feeling of "I enjoy." This expression must never be stifled. The science teacher can encourage a cognizant and compassionate behavior toward other life forms as students are able to understand the need for protecting their environment, respecting the roles and values of other human beings, and perceiving the delicate worth, uniqueness, and relationships of everything and everyone they meet.

As science teachers, we should strive to help our own students develop these 14 characteristics of intelligent behavior. In Chapter 3 we present specific teacher behaviors that facilitate this development. We turn now to additional research findings that are important considerations in helping children learn.

STYLES OF LEARNING

Teachers who are most effective are those who adapt their teaching styles and methods to their students, using approaches that interest the students, that are neither too easy nor too difficult, that match the students' learning styles, and that are relevant to the students' lives. This adaptation process is further complicated by the individuality of the students, who can vary widely in interests, abilities, backgrounds, and learning styles. As a matter of fact, not only do students differ from one another, but each student can change to some extent from day to day. What appeals to a student today may not have the same appeal tomorrow. Therefore, you need to consider both the nature of students in general (for example, methods appropriate for a particular second-grade class are unlikely to be the same as those that work best for most eighth graders) and each student in particular. What follows is a synopsis of recent findings about aspects of student learning styles.

Brain Laterality

Research has shown that how a person learns is, in part, related to differences in the left and right hemispheres of the brain. This theory is sometimes referred to as brain laterality or brain hemisphericity. Verbal learning, logical and convergent thinking, and the academic cognitive processes are dominated by the left cerebral hemisphere, whereas affective, intuitive, spatial, emotional, divergent thinking, and visual elements are dominated by the right cerebral hemisphere. Some students are oriented toward right cerebral hemisphere learning, and others toward the left. This means that some students learn better through verbal interactions and others learn through visual, kinesthetic, and tactile involvement. However, "in a healthy person the two hemispheres are inextricably interactive, irrespective of whether a person is dealing with words, mathematics, music, or art."[28]

Brain Laterality and Its Implications for Science Teaching. In integrating the disciplines and helping students to connect what is being learned with real life situations, the teaching is more likely to be addressing both hemispheres.

Learning Modalities

Learning modality refers to *the sensory portal means by which a student prefers to receive sensory reception (modality preference), or the actual way a student learns best (modality adeptness)*. Some students prefer learning by seeing, a visual modality; others prefer learning through instruction from others (through talk), an auditory modality; and still others prefer learning by doing and being physically involved, a kinesthetic modality, and by touching objects, a tactile modality.

Sometimes a student's modality preference is not that student's modality strength. Although primary modality strength can be determined by observing students, it can also be mixed and can change as the result of experience and intellectual maturity. As one might suspect, modality integration (using several modalities at once) has been found to contribute to better achievement in student learning.

Learning Modality and Its Implications for Science Teaching. Because most elementary and middle school students have neither a preference for nor a strength in auditory reception, teachers should limit their use of the lecture method of instruction, that is, avoid too much reliance on teacher talk. Furthermore, instruction that uses a single approach, such as auditory (e.g., lecturing), cheats students who learn better another way. This difference can affect student achievement. Finally, if a teacher's verbal communication conflicts with his or her nonverbal messages, students can become confused, and this too can affect their learning. (When there is a discrepancy between what the teacher says and what that teacher does, the teacher's nonverbal signal will win every time.)

As a general rule, elementary and middle school students prefer to learn by touching objects, by feeling shapes and textures, by interacting with each other, and by moving things around. In contrast, sitting and listening are difficult for many of these students.

You are advised to use strategies that integrate the modalities. Combining reception learning and cognitive mapping is an example of modality integration. When well designed, thematic units incorporate modality integration too. Therefore, in teaching a group of students of mixed learning abilities, mixed modality strengths, mixed language proficiencies, and mixed cultural backgrounds, for the most successful teaching the integration of learning modalities is a must.

Learning Styles

Related to learning modality is learning style, which can be defined as *independent forms of knowing and processing information*. Although some elementary and middle school students may be comfortable with beginning their learning of a new idea in the abstract (e.g., visual or verbal symbolization), most will need to begin with the concrete (e.g., learning by actually doing). Some prosper while working in groups, and others prefer to work alone. Some are quick in their studies, whereas others are slow and methodical, cautious and meticulous. Some can sustain attention to a single topic for a long time, becoming more absorbed in their study as time passes. Others are slower starters and more casual in their pursuits but are capable of shifting with ease from subject to subject. Some can study in the midst of music, noise, or movement, whereas others need quiet, solitude, and a desk or table. The point is this: students vary not only in their skills and preferences as to the way knowledge is received, but also in how they mentally process that information once it has been received. This latter is a person's style of learning, "a gestalt combining internal and external operations derived from the individual's neurobiology, personality, and development and reflected in learner behavior."[29]

CLASSIFICATIONS OF LEARNING STYLES

Although there are probably as many types of learning styles as there are individuals, most learning style classifications center on the recognition of four general types, based on the earlier work of Carl Jung.[30] It is important to note that learning style is not an indicator of intelligence, but rather an indicator of how a person learns.

David Kolb describes two major differences in how people learn: how they perceive situations and how they process information.[31] In the area of perceiving and processing, Bernice McCarthy has described the following four major learning styles:[32]

- The *imaginative learner* perceives information concretely and processes it reflectively. Imaginative learners learn well by listening and sharing with others, integrating the ideas of others with their own experiences. Imaginative learners often have difficulty adjusting to traditional teaching, which depends less on classroom interactions and students' sharing and connecting of their prior experiences. In a traditional classroom, the imaginative learner is likely to be an at-risk student.

- The *analytic learner* perceives information abstractly and processes it reflectively. The analytic learner prefers sequential thinking, needs details, and values what experts have to offer. Analytic learners do well in traditional classrooms.
- The *common sense learner* perceives information abstractly and processes it actively. This type of learner is pragmatic and enjoys hands-on learning. Common sense learners sometimes find school frustrating unless they can see immediate use to what is being learned. In the traditional classroom the common sense learner is likely to be a learner who is at risk of not completing school, of dropping out.
- The *dynamic learner* perceives information concretely and processes it actively. He also prefers hands-on learning and is excited by anything new. Dynamic learners are risk takers and are frustrated by learning if they see it as being tedious and sequential. In a traditional classroom the dynamic learner also is likely to be an at-risk student.

With a system developed by McCarthy (called the 4MAT System), teachers employ a learning cycle of instructional strategies that reach each student's learning style. As stated by McCarthy, in the cycle learners "sense and feel, they experience, then they watch, they reflect, then they think, they develop theories, then they try out theories, they experiment. Finally, they evaluate and synthesize what they have learned in order to apply it to their next similar experience. They get smarter. They apply experience to experiences."[33] Furthermore, in this process they are likely to be using all four learning modalities.[34]

THEORY OF MULTIPLE INTELLIGENCES

In contrast to Jung's four learning styles, Howard Gardner introduces seven learning styles that individuals exhibit in differing ways: *Verbal-Linguistic; Logical-Mathematical; Intrapersonal; Visual-Spatial; Musical-Rhythmic; Body-Kinesthetic;* and *Interpersonal.*[35] As implied earlier in the presentation of McCarthy's four types of learners, many educators believe that students who are at risk of not completing school are those who may be dominant in a cognitive learning style that is not in sync with traditional teaching methods. Traditional methods are largely of McCarthy's analytic style, whereby information is presented in a logical, linear, sequential fashion, and of the first three Gardner types: Verbal-Linguistic, Logical-Mathematical, and Intrapersonal. Consequently, to better synchronize methods of instruction with learning styles, some teachers[36] and schools[37] have restructured the curriculum and instruction around Gardner's seven ways of knowing.

Learning Style and Its Implications for Science Teaching. The importance of the preceding information about learning styles is that it demonstrates two points that you must realize:

1. Intelligence is not a fixed or static reality, but can be learned, taught, and developed.[38] This concept is important for students to understand too. When students understand that intelligence is incremental, something that is developed through use over time, they tend to be more motivated to work at learning than when they believe intelligence is a fixed entity.[39]
2. Not all students learn and respond to learning situations in the same way. A student may learn differently according to the situation or according to his or her ethnicity, cultural background, or socioeconomic status.[40] A teacher who, for all students, uses only one style of teaching or who teaches through only one or a few styles of learning, day-after-day, is short-changing those students who learn better another way. As stated by Rita Dunn, "When children do not learn the way we teach them, then we must teach them the way they learn."[41]

SUMMARY

As a teacher you must acknowledge that your students have different ways of receiving information and different ways of processing that information—different ways of knowing and of constructing their knowledge. These differences are unique and important, and they are what you should address in your teaching. You should try to learn as much as you can about how each student learns and processes information. However, because you can never know everything about each student, the more you vary your teaching strategies and assist students in integrating their learning, the more likely you are to reach more of the students more of the time.

To be an effective teacher of elementary or middle school science, you should: (1) learn as much about your students and their preferred styles of learning as you can; (2) use planning and lessons that are based on the learning cycle, but also develop an eclectic style of teaching, one that is flexible and adaptable; and (3) integrate the various disciplines, thereby assisting students in their conceptual understandings by helping them to make bridges or connections between what is being learned and what is experienced in their lives.

QUESTIONS FOR CLASS DISCUSSION

1. Identify an elementary or middle school science teacher whom you consider to be very competent, and compare what you recall about that teacher's classroom with the variables listed in this chapter.
2. For a specific age or grade level, research and describe the common science misconceptions of students. Share your findings with your colleagues. Describe how you would go about helping students change their misconceptions of specific ideas in science.
3. In small groups, discuss this question; then share a summary of your group's discussion with the entire class. Two teachers were asked the question: "What do you teach?" One teacher responded, "Children." The other teacher responded, "Science." From their responses, what tentative conclusions might we draw about these two teachers?
4. It has been reported that approximately 20 percent of children ages 6 to 11 in this country are living in poverty (*Phi Delta Kappan* 71, no. 10, June 1990). Explain any relevance that this may have for you as a science teacher.
5. Explain why knowledge of teaching styles and student learning styles is important for a science teacher.
6. Ms. Keefer, a science teacher, has a class of 33 seventh graders who, during her lectures, teacher-led discussions, and recitation lessons, are restless and inattentive, creating a major problem for her in classroom management. At Ms. Keefer's invitation the school psychologist tests the children for learning modality and finds that of the 33, 29 children are predominately kinesthetic learners. Of what use is this information to Ms. Keefer? Describe what, if anything, she should try as a result of having this information.
7. What examples of mnemonics can you recall or invent that might be useful in your own teaching? Share them with your classmates.
8. Describe any concepts you held previously that changed as a result of your experiences with this chapter. Describe the changes.
9. From your recent observations and field work as related to this teacher preparation program, clearly identify one specific example of educational practice that seems contradictory to exemplary practice or theory as presented in this chapter. Present your explanation of the discrepancy.
10. What questions do you have about the content of this chapter? Where might answers be found?

NOTES

1. Reprinted from *National Science Education Standards*, © 1996 National Academy of Sciences, pp. 62, 69. Courtesy of National Academy Press, Washington, DC.

2. Jacqueline Grennon Brooks and Martin G. Brooks, *In Search for Understanding: The Case for Constructivist Classrooms* (Alexandria, VA: Association for Supervision and Curriculum Development, 1993), p. 16.

3. Bruce Watson and Richard Konicek, "Teaching for Conceptual Change: Confronting Children's Experience," *Phi Delta Kappan* 71(9) (May 1990), p. 685.

4. A *schema* (plural, *schemata*) is a mental construct by which the learner organizes his or her perceptions of the environment.

5. Joseph D. Novak, "How Do We Learn Our Lesson?" *The Science Teacher* 60(3):50–55 (March 1993).

6. Watson and Konicek, "Teaching for Conceptual Change," 683.

7. Brooks and Brooks, *In Search for Understanding*, 113.

8. See, for example, Laura Robb, "A Cause for Celebration: Reading and Writing with At-Risk Students," *New Advocate* 6(1):25–40 (Winter 1993), which describes a program of remediation for seventh- and eighth-grade students who had failed a state literacy test and were reading below grade level. The successful program included paired-reading and questioning, and reading to kindergarten and first-grade children. See also John W. Fanuzzo et al., "Effects of Reciprocal Peer Tutoring on Mathematics and Social Adjustment: A Component Analysis," *Journal of Educational Psychology* 84(3):331–339 (September 1992). The importance of cooperative learning and cross-age tutoring as developmentally appropriate strategies for middle schools is discussed in Robert L. Gilstrap et al., *Improving Instruction in Middle Schools* (Fastback 331, Bloomington, IN: Phi Delta Educational Foundation, 1992).

9. See Abraham H. Maslow, *Motivation and Personality* (New York: Harper & Row, 1970).

10. See, for example, Sally Reed and R. Craig Sautter, "Children of Poverty: The Status of 12 Million Young Americans," *Phi Delta Kappan* 71(10):K1–K12 (June 1990).

11. D. Stanley Eitzen, "Problem Students: The Sociocultural Roots," *Phi Delta Kappan* 73(8):584–590 (April 1992), 590.

12. Renate Nummela Caine and Geoffrey Caine, "The Critical Need for a Mental Model of Meaningful Learning," *California Catalyst* (Fall 1993): 20.

13. For further clarification of the concept of "metacognition," see I. Braten, "Vygotsky as Precursor to Metacognitive Theory: I. The Concept of Metacognition and Its Roots," *Scandinavian Journal of Educational Research* 35(3):179–192 (1991).

14. Renate Nummela Caine and Geoffrey Caine, "Understanding a Brain-Based Approach to Learning and Teaching," *Educational Leadership* 48(2):66–70 (October 1990), 66.

15. R. Sylwester, "A Child's Brain, Part I," *Instructor* 92(2):90–92, 94, 96 (1982).

16. See R. B. Hensley, "Does Brain-Stage Theory Suggest a Need for a Major Overhaul of Junior High School Curricula?" *Clearing House* 59:39–41 (September 1985).

17. R. Sylwester, J. S. Chall, M. C. Wittrock, and L. A. Hart, "The Educational Implications of Brain Research," *Educational Leadership* 39(1):6–17 (October 1991).

18. Jerry W. Valentine et al., *Leadership in Middle Level Education* (Reston, VA: National Association of Secondary School Principals, 1993), 19.

19. See Jerome Bruner, "Vygotsky: A Historical and Conceptual Perspective." In J. Wertsch (ed.), *Culture, Communication and Cognition: Vygotskian Perspectives*. Cambridge, England: Cambridge University Press, 1985.

20. See J. Shymansky et al., "How Effective Were the Hands-On Science Programs of Yesterday?" *Science and Children* 20(3):14–15 (November/December 1982); and J. Shymansky et al., "Research Synthesis on the Science Curriculum Projects of the Sixties," *Educational Leadership* 40(1):63–66 (October 1982).

21. See David P. Ausubel, *The Psychology of Meaningful Verbal Learning* (New York: Grune & Stratton, 1963).

22. For further information about concept mapping, see Joseph D. Novak, "Concept Maps and Vee Diagrams: Two Metacognitive Tools to Facilitate Meaningful Learning," *Instructional Science* 19(1):29–52 (1990).

23. A. L. Costa, *The School as a Home for the Mind* (Palatine, IL: Skylight Publishing, 1991), 19.

24. Ibid., 20–31.

25. E. de Bono, *Lateral Thinking: Creativity Step by Step* (New York: Harper & Row, 1970).

26. J. Piaget, *The Psychology of Intelligence* (Totowa, NJ: Littlefield Adams, 1972).

27. I. Kohlberg, *The Meaning and Measurement of Moral Development* (Worcester, MA: Clark University Press, 1981).
28. Caine and Caine, "Understanding a Brain-Based Approach to Learning and Teaching," 67.
29. James W. Keefe and Barbara G. Ferrell, "Developing a Defensible Learning Style Paradigm," *Educational Leadership* 48(2):57–61 (October 1990), 59.
30. See Carl G. Jung, *Psychological Types* (New York: Harcourt Brace, 1923). See also Anthony Gregorc, *Gregorc Style Delineator* (Maynard, Ma: Gabriel Systems, 1985); and Rita Dunn and Kenneth Dunn, *Teaching Students Through Their Individual Learning Styles* (Reston, VA: Reston Publications, 1978).
31. Davis Kolb, *The Learning Style Inventory* (Boston: McBer and Co., 1985).
32. Bernice McCarthy, "Using the 4MAT System to Bring Learning Styles to Schools," *Educational Leadership* 48(2):31–37 (October 1990).
33. Ibid., 33.
34. Compare the learning cycle described here with the sciencing cycle and learning cycle concepts discussed earlier in Chapter 1.
35. See Howard Gardner and Thomas Hatch, "Multiple Intelligences Go to School: Educational Implications of the Theory of Multiple Intelligence," *Educational Researcher* 18(8):4–9 (November 1989); or Tina Blythe and Howard Gardner, "A School for All Intelligences," *Educational Leadership* 47(7):33–37 (April 1990); or Howard Gardner, "The Theory of Multiple Intelligences," *Annals of Dyslexia* 37:19–35 (1987).
36. See, for example, Launa Ellison, "Using Multiple Intelligences to Set Goals," *Educational Leadership* 50(2):69–72 (October 1992).
37. See, for example, Thomas R. Hoerr, "How Our School Applied Multiple Intelligences Theory," *Educational Leadership* 50(2):67–68 (October 1992).
38. David G. Lazear, *Teaching for Multiple Intelligences,* Fastback 342 (Bloomington, IN: Phi Delta Kappa, 1992), 8. See also Gerald W. Bracey, "Getting Smart(er) in School," *Phi Delta Kappan* 73(5):414–416 (January 1992).
39. Lauren B. Resnick and Leopold E. Klopfer, *Toward the Thinking Curriculum: Current Cognitive Research,* 1989 ASCD Yearbook (Alexandria, VA: Association for Supervision and Curriculum Development, 1989), 8.
40. For further information about students' cultural differences and learning styles, see Pat Guild, "The Culture/Learning Style Connection," *Educational Leadership* 51(8):16–21 (May 1994).
41. Rita Dunn, *Strategies for Educating Diverse Learners,* Fastback 384 (Bloomington, IN: Phi Delta Kappa Educational Foundation, 1995), 30.

SUGGESTED READINGS

Armstrong, T. *Multiple Intelligences in the Classroom.* Alexandria, VA: Association for Supervision and Curriculum Development, 1994.

Blake, S. "Are You Turning Female and Minority Students Away from Science?" *Science and Children* 30(7):32–35 (April 1993).

Brooks, J. G., and M. G. Brooks. *In Search of Understanding: The Case for Constructivist Classrooms.* Alexandria, VA: Association for Supervision and Curriculum Development, 1993.

Bruner, J. S. *Acts of Meaning.* Cambridge, MA: Harvard University Press, 1990.

———. *The Process of Education.* Cambridge: Harvard University Press, 1960.

———. *Toward a Theory of Instruction.* Cambridge, MA: Harvard University Press, 1966.

Cambell, M., and V. Burton. "Learning in Their Own Style." *Science and Children* 31(7):22–24, 39 (April 1994).

Cooper, J. D. *Literacy: Helping Children Construct Meaning.* 2d ed. Burlington, MA: Houghton Mifflin, 1993.

Cronin, J. F. "Four Misconceptions About Authentic Learning." *Educational Leadership* 50(7):78–80 (April 1993).

Dunn, R. *Strategies for Educating Diverse Learners.* Fastback 384. Bloomington, IN: Phi Delta Kappa Educational Foundation, 1995.

Erb, T. O. "Teaching Diverse Students: Focus on the Learning Cycle." *Schools in the Middle* 4(1):16–20 (September 1994).

Gabel, D., ed. *Handbook of Research on Science Teaching and Learning*. New York: Macmillan 1994.

Gallegos, G. "Learning Styles in Culturally Diverse Classrooms." *California Catalyst* 36–41 (Fall 1993).

Gardner, H. *Creating Minds*. New York: Basic Books, 1993.

Gardner, H., and V. Boix-Mansilla. "Teaching for Understanding Within and Across the Disciplines." *Educational Leadership* 51(5):14–18 (February 1994).

Gil-Perez, D., and J. Carroscosa-Alis. "Bring Pupils' Learning Closer to a Scientific Construction of Knowledge: A Permanent Feature in Innovations in Science Teaching." *Science Education* 78(3):301–305 (June 1994).

Glasson, G. E., and R. V. Lalik. "Reinterpreting the Learning Cycle from a Social Constructivist Perspective: A Qualitative Study of Teacher's Beliefs and Practices." *Journal of Research in Science Teaching* 30(2):187–207 (February 1993).

Guild, P. "The Culture/Learning Style Connection." *Educational Leadership* 51(8):16–21 (May 1994).

Hendry, G. D., and R. C. King. "On Theory of Learning and Knowledge: Educational Implications of Advances in Neuroscience." *Science Education* 78(3):223–253 (June 1994).

Kranz, B. *Identifying Talents Among Multicultural Children*. Fastback 364. Bloomington, IN: Phi Delta Kappa Educational Foundation, 1994.

Novak, J. D. "How Do We Learn Our Lesson?" *The Science Teacher* 60(3): 50–55 (March 1993).

Perkins, D., and T. Blythe. "Putting Understanding Up Front." *Educational Leadership* 51(5):4–7 (February 1994).

Piaget, J. *The Development of Thought: Elaboration of Cognitive Structures*. New York: Viking, 1977.

Rafoth, M. A., et al. *Strategies for Learning and Remembering*. Washington, DC: National Education Association, 1993.

Reyhner, J. *American Indian/Alaska Native Education*. Fastback 367. Bloomington, IN: Phi Delta Kappa Educational Foundation, 1994.

Roth, W., and M. Bowen. "The Unfolding Vee." *Science Scope* 16(5):28–32 (February 1993).

Sylwester, R. "What the Biology of the Brain Tells Us About Learning." *Educational Leadership* 51(4):46–51 (December 1993/January 1994).

Vygotsky, L. *Thought and Language*. Cambridge, MA: MIT Press, 1926.

Wang, M. C. G. D. Haertel, and H. J Walberg. "What Helps Students Learn?" *Educational Leadership* 51(4):74–79 (December 1993/January 1994).

Woods, R. K. "A Close-Up Look at How Children Learn Science." *Educational Leadership* 51(5):33–35 (February 1994).

Zahorik, J. A. *Constructivist Teaching*. Fastback 390. Bloomington, IN: Phi Delta Kappa Educational Foundation, 1995.

CHAPTER 3

Methods of Teaching Science

Teachers of science guide and facilitate learning. In doing this, teachers

- *Focus and support inquiries while interacting with students.*
- *Orchestrate discourse among students about scientific ideas.*
- *Challenge students to take responsibility for their own learning.*
- *Recognize and respond to student diversity and encourage all students to participate fully in science learning.*
- *Encourage and model the skills of scientific inquiry, as well as the curiosity, openness to new ideas and data, and skepticism that characterize science.*[1]

Chapter 1 provides a historical and current overview of elementary and middle school science curriculum and instruction. Chapter 2 provides a historical and current review of how children and young adolescents process information and develop intellectually. Pulling together concepts from these two chapters, this chapter focuses on the practical application of strategies that facilitate student learning in science.

Throughout your career as a teacher, you will continue to develop your repertoire of strategies and skills in using specific strategies. To be most effective you need a large repertoire from which to select a specific strategy for a particular goal with a distinctive group of students. In addition, you need skill in using that strategy. This chapter will help you to build your strategy repertoire for the most effective teaching of elementary and middle school science and to begin developing your skill in the use of specific strategies.

You must know why you have selected a particular strategy. An unknowing teacher is likely to use the strategy most common in teaching college classes—the lecture. Although commonly used in college teaching, for reasons explained in Chapter 2 the lecture is seldom, if ever, an effective way to instruct elementary or middle school students. By preference and by adeptness, students of elementary and middle school age are not strong auditory learners. For most of them, learning by sitting and listening is difficult. By preference and by skill, they learn best when physically and intellectually active—that is, through tactile and kinesthetic experiences, by touching objects, by feeling shapes and textures, by moving objects around, and by talking about and sharing what they are learning. We return to this subject later in this chapter; now we introduce teacher behaviors necessary to facilitate student learning, almost without regard to strategy used or subject being taught.

The basic teacher behaviors that create the conditions needed to enable students to think and to learn are those that produce the following results:

- Students are physically and mentally engaged in the learning activities.
- Instructional time is efficiently used.
- Classroom distractions and interruptions are minimal.
- Students progress in their intellectual development.

The effectiveness with which a teacher carries out these basic behaviors can be measured. The bottom line is that the students learn.

BASIC TEACHER BEHAVIORS THAT FACILITATE EXPLORATORY LEARNING IN SCIENCE

The effective teacher's basic classroom behaviors create the conditions that enable students to learn, whether the learning is a further understanding of science concepts, the internalization of attitudes and values, the development of cognitive processes, or the actuating of the most complex psychomotor behaviors.

Teachers of science design and manage learning environments that provide students with the time, space, and resources needed for learning science. In doing this, teachers

- *Structure the time available so that students are able to engage in extended investigations.*
- *Create a setting for student work that is flexible and supportive of science inquiry.*
- *Ensure a safe working environment.*
- *Make the available science tools, materials, media, and technological resources accessible to students.*
- *Identify and use resources outside the school.*
- *Engage students in designing the learning environment.*[3]

The basic teacher behaviors that facilitate student learning are 1) structuring the learning environment, 2) accepting instructional accountability, 3) demonstrating withitness and overlapping, 4) providing a variety of motivating and challenging lessons, 5) modeling appropriate behaviors, 6) facilitating student acquisition of data, 7) creating a psychologically safe environment, 8) clarifying whenever necessary, 9) using periods of silence, 10) questioning thoughtfully.[2]

Structuring

The teacher establishes an intellectual, psychological, and physical environment that enables all students to act and react productively. Specifically, the teacher:

a. Plans lessons that have clear and concise beginnings and endings, with much of the planning done collaboratively with the students.
b. Learns and uses student names beginning with the first class meeting.
c. Helps students assume tasks and responsibilities, thereby empowering them in their learning.
d. Communicates clearly with an instructive vocabulary.
e. Establishes and maintains clearly understood classroom procedures and expectations.
f. Organizes the students, helping them to organize their learning.
g. Provides clear definitions.
i. Helps students in the identification of time and resource constraints.
j. Helps students to clarify the learning expectations and to establish clearly understood learning objectives.
k. Provides for frequent summary reviews, often through the use of student self-assessment of what is being learned.
l. Attends to the organization of the learning laboratory to establish a positive, safe, and efficient environment for all student learning.
m. Structures and facilitates ongoing formal and informal discussion based on a shared understanding of the rules of scientific discourse.

Accepting Instructional Accountability

While holding students accountable for their learning, the teacher is willing to be held accountable for the effectiveness of the learning outcomes. Specifically, the teacher:

a. Attends to students' questions, discussions, and recitations.
b. Provides opportunities for students to demonstrate their learning, to refine and explore their questions, and to share their thinking and results.

The teacher structures a learning environment that physically and mentally engages the children in the learning process.

c. Signals to students that they may be called upon to demonstrate their learning.
d. Plans exploratory science activities that engage students in learning.
e. Provides continuous cues for desired learning behaviors.
f. Provides incentives contingent upon desired performance, such as grades, points, rewards, and privileges.
g. Communicates to the students that accomplishment of learning objectives is a responsibility they share with the teacher.
h. Makes active and cooperative efforts to improve the effectiveness of the instruction and learning.
i. Communicates clearly to parents, administrators, and colleagues.
j. Establishes a clearly understood and continuous program of assessment.
k. Assumes responsibility for professional decision making and the risks associated with that responsibility.[4]
l. Shares some responsibility for decision making and risk taking with the students.
m. Requires students to provide objective evidence to support their tentative conclusions.

Teachers of science develop communities of science learners that reflect the intellectual rigor of scientific inquiry and the attitudes and social values conducive to science learning. In doing this, teachers

- *Display and demand respect for the ideas, skills, and experiences of all students.*
- *Enable students to have a significant voice in decisions about the content and context of their work and require students to take responsibility for the learning of all members of the community.*
- *Nurture collaboration among students.*
- *Structure and facilitate ongoing formal and informal discussion based on a shared understanding of rules of scientific discourse.*
- *Model and emphasize the skills, attitudes, and values of scientific inquiry.*[5]

Demonstrating Withitness and Overlapping

In 1936, in *School Begins at Two* (New York: New Republic), Harriet Johnson wrote of the early childhood educator's need to be "with it," by which she was referring to the teacher's awareness of each child's emotions and needs as well as those of the whole group.[6] In 1970, Jacob Kounin wrote of another kind of teacher "withitness," an awareness of the whole group.[7] As described by Kounin, withitness and overlapping are two separate but closely related behaviors. A teacher demonstrates withitness by being able to intervene and redirect potential undesirable student behavior, and overlapping by being able to attend to several matters simultaneously. Specifically, the teacher:

a. Attends to the entire class while working with one student or with a small group of students, communicating this awareness with hand gestures, body language, and clear, but rather quiet, verbal cues.
b. Refocuses or shifts activities for a student whose attention begins to fade.
c. Dwells on one topic only as long as necessary for the students' understandings.
d. Continually and simultaneously monitors all classroom activities to keep students at their tasks and provide them assistance and resources.
e. Demonstrates an understanding of when comprehension checks are needed.
f. Continues monitoring the class during any distraction, such as when a visitor enters the classroom.

Providing a Variety of Motivating and Challenging Activities

The teacher uses a variety of activities that motivate and challenge all students to work to the utmost of their abilities, and that engage and challenge the preferred learning styles of more of the students more of the time. Specifically, the teacher:

a. Shows pride, optimism, and enthusiasm in science learning, thinking, and teaching.
b. Demonstrates the expectation that each student will work to the best of his or her ability.
c. Demonstrates optimism toward each student's ability.
d. With the students, plans exciting and interesting sciencing activities.

e. Paces activities so they move along smoothly and briskly.

f. Plans activities that take advantage of the students' natural interest in the mysterious and novel.

Modeling Appropriate Behaviors

Effective science teachers model the behaviors that are expected of the students and that are consistent with the behaviors related to effective sciencing. Specifically, the teacher:

a. Demonstrates rational problem-solving skills and explains to the students the processes being engaged during problem solving.

b. Models and emphasizes the skills, attitudes, and values of scientific inquiry.

c. Thinks aloud while solving a problem.

d. Models higher-order intellectual processes.

e. Shows respect for all students.

f. Uses "I" when "I" is meant, "we" when "we" is meant.

g. Demonstrates that making "errors" is a natural event during problem solving, and readily admits and corrects a mistake made by him- or herself.

h. Spells correctly, uses proper grammar, and writes clearly and legibly.

i. Arrives promptly in the classroom and demonstrates on-task behaviors for the entire class meeting, just as is expected of the students.

j. Practices communication that is clear and to the point.

k. Is prompt in returning student papers and offers comments that provide instructive and encouraging feedback to the students.

l. Does not interrupt when a student is showing rational thinking, even though the teacher may disagree with the direction of the student's thinking.

m. Thinks aloud while reading to the students.

n. Turns out the lights upon leaving the classroom for recess, especially after a lesson on energy conservation.

o. Practices moments of silence (see the later paragraph entitled "Silence"), thus modeling thoughtfulness, reflectiveness, and restraint of impulsiveness.

p. Provides concrete evidence to support his or her tentative conclusions.

Facilitating Student Acquisitions

The teacher insures that data is accessible to students as input they can process. Specifically, the teacher:

a. Provides clear and specific instructions.

b. Emphasizes major ideas.

c. Creates a responsive classroom environment.

d. Provides concrete learning experiences.

e. Serves as a resource person.

f. Uses cooperative learning, thus regarding the students as resources.

g. Uses older students, other teachers, and the community as resources.

h. Assures that sources of information are readily available to students for their use.

i. Selects books, media, and materials that facilitate student learning.

j. Selects instructional strategies that help students make connections between what is being learned and what they already know.

k. Provides feedback about each child's performance and progress.

l. Encourages students to organize and maintain their own devices to monitor their progress in learning and thinking.

m. Assures that equipment and materials are readily available for students to use.
n. Identifies and uses resources beyond the walls of the classroom and the boundaries of the school campus.

Creating a Psychologically Safe Environment

To encourage the positive development of student self-esteem, to provide a psychologically safe learning environment, and to encourage the most creative thought and behavior, the teacher offers appropriate nonevaluative and nonjudgmental responses. Specifically, the teacher:

a. Avoids the use of criticism. Criticism is a negative value judgment, and "when a teacher responds to a student's ideas or actions with such negative words as 'poor,' 'incorrect,' or 'wrong,' the response tends to signal inadequacy or disapproval and ends the student's thinking about the task."[8]
b. For upper grade and middle school students the teacher infrequently uses strong praise.[9] By the time students are in upper grades, teacher praise, a positive value judgment and the opposite of criticism, has little or no value as a form of positive reinforcement. When praise is used with older students, it should be mild, private, and for student accomplishment rather than for effort, and for each student, frequency in the use of praise should be gradually reduced. When praise is reduced, a more diffused sociometric pattern develops; that is, more of the students become directly and productively involved in the learning. As emphasized by Good and Brophy, praise should be simple and direct, delivered in a natural voice without dramatizing. Even very young children see such theatrics as insincere.[10] (See also item 6 on page 77.)
c. Frequently uses minimal reinforcement (i. e., nonjudgmental acceptance behaviors, such as nodding your head, writing a student's response on the board, or saying, "I understand").
d. Uses paraphrasing and reflective listening.
e. Uses empathic acceptance of a student's mood or expression of feelings.
f. Plans within the lessons behaviors that show respect for the experiences and ideas of individual students.
g. Uses nonverbal cues to show awareness and acceptance of individual students.
h. Writes reinforcing, personalized comments on student papers.
i. Provides positive individual student attention as often as possible.
j. Provides incentives and rewards for student accomplishments.

Clarifying Whenever Necessary

The teacher's responding behavior seeks further elaboration from a student about that student's idea or comprehension. Specifically, the teacher:

a. Provides frequent opportunity for summary reviews and self-assessment of the learning.
b. Politely invites a student to be more specific, offers an opportunity for a student to elaborate on or rephrase an idea or to provide a concrete illustration of an idea.[11]
c. Repeats or paraphrases a student's response, allowing the student to correct any teacher misinterpretation.
d. Helps students to connect new content to that previously learned.
e. Helps students to relate the content of a lesson to their other school and nonschool experiences (as exemplified by Mrs. B in Figure 2.1).
f. Selects instructional strategies that help students correct their misconceptions.

Using Periods of Silence

The teacher effectively uses periods of silence in the classroom. Specifically, the teacher:

a. Pauses for thinking and reflection while talking.
b. Waits longer than two seconds after asking a question or posing a problem.
c. Uses teacher silence to stimulate group discussion.
d. Keeps silent when students are working quietly.
e. Actively listens when a student is talking.
f. Uses teacher silence when students are attending to a visual display.
g. Maintains classroom control with nonverbal signals.

Questioning Thoughtfully

The teacher uses thoughtfully worded questions to induce cognitive learning and to stimulate thinking and the development of students' thinking skills. Specifically, the teacher:

a. Uses a variety of questions, including questions that stimulate divergent thinking as well as those that cause convergent thinking.
b. Helps students develop their own questioning skills and provides opportunities for students to design experiments to find temporary answers to their own questions.
c. Plans questioning sequences that elicit a variety of thinking skills and that maneuver students to higher levels of cognition.
d. Uses questions designed to help students to explore their knowledge, to develop new understandings, and to discover ways of applying their new understandings.
e. Encourages student questioning, without judging the quality or relevancy of a student's question.
f. Attends to student questions and responds, often by building on the content of their questions.

QUESTIONING: THE FOUNDATION FOR EFFECTIVE SCIENCING

In the preceding list of basic behaviors needed to facilitate student learning, questioning is last, not because of its lesser importance, but because it is so important and frequently used—and abused. Questioning is the basic foundation for the most effective science teaching and learning. You will use questioning for so many purposes that there is no way you can teach effectively unless you are skilled in its use.

Purposes for Using Questions

Effective teachers adapt the type and form of each question to the purpose for which it is asked. Effective science teachers encourage students to question and then build the curriculum around their students' questions.

The purposes for which you might use questioning can be separated into five types:

1. *To give instructions* (as in a rhetorical question). For example, "Caesar, will you please get the magnets out of the cupboard for us?"
2. *To review and remind students of classroom procedures.* For example, if students continue to talk without first raising their hands and being recognized by you, you can stop the

The teacher seeks further elaboration from a student about the child's idea.

lesson and say, "Class, I think we need to review the procedure for answering my questions. For talking, what is the procedure that we agreed upon?"

3. *To gather information.* For example, "How many of you have been to a tide pool?" or, as a preassessment to find out what students already know. For example, "Gretchen, can you please tell us what is meant by the *greenhouse effect?*"

4. *To discover student interests.* For example, "How many would be interested in going to the marine aquarium?"

5. *To guide student thinking and learning.* It is this category of questioning that is the focus here. In teaching, questions in this category are used to:

   - *Develop appreciation.* For example, "Do you now understand the ecological relationship between that particular root fungus, voles, and the survival of the large conifers of the forests of the Pacific Northwest?"

   - *Develop student thinking.* For example, "What do you suppose the effects to the ecology are when standing water is sprayed with an insecticide that is designed to kill all mosquito larvae?"

- *Diagnose learning difficulty.* For example, "What part of the formula don't you understand, Sally?"
- *Emphasize major points.* For example, "If we have never been to the sun, how do we know what it is made of?"
- *Encourage students.* For example, "OK, so you didn't remember the formula for glucose. What really impressed me in your essay is what you did understand about photosynthesis. Do you know what part impressed me?"
- *Establish rapport.* For example, "We have a problem here, but I think we can solve it if we put our heads together. What do you think ought to be our first step?"
- *Evaluate learning.* For example, "Sean, what is the effect when two rough surfaces are rubbed together?"
- *Give practice in expression.* For example, "Yvonne, would you please share with us the examples of magnetism that you found in your home?"
- *Help students in their own metacognition.* For example, "Yes, something did go wrong in the experiment. Do you still think your original hypothesis is correct? If not, then where was the error in your thinking? Or if you still think your hypothesis is correct, then where might the error have been in the design of your experiment? How might we find out?"
- *Help students interpret materials.* For example, "Something seems to be wrong with this compass. How do you suppose we can find out what is wrong with it? For example, if the needle is marked N and S in reverse, how can we find out if that is the problem?"
- *Help students organize materials.* For example, "If you really want to carry out your proposed experiment, then we are going to need certain materials. We are going to have to deal with some strategic questions here, such as, what do you think we will need, where can we find those things, who will be responsible for getting them, and how will we store and arrange them once we are ready to start the investigation?"
- *Provide drill and practice.* For example, "Team A has prepared some questions that they would like to use as practice questions for our unit exam, and they are suggesting that we use them to play the game of Jeopardy on Friday. Is everyone in agreement with their idea?"
- *Provide review.* For example, "Today, in your groups, you are going to study the unit review questions I have prepared. After each group has studied and prepared its answers to these written questions, your group will pick another group and ask them your set of review questions. Each group has a different set of questions. Members of Team A are going to keep score, and the group that has the highest score from this review session will receive free pizza at tomorrow's lunch. Ready?"
- *Show agreement or disagreement.* For example, "Some scientists fear that the Antarctic ice shelf is breaking up and melting and that there will be worldwide flooding. With evidence that you have collected from recent articles, do you agree with this conclusion? Explain why or why not."
- *Show relationships, such as cause and effect.* For example, "What do you suppose would be the global effect if just one inch of the total Antarctic ice shelf were to rather suddenly melt?"
- *Build the curriculum.* It is the students' questions that provide the basis for the learning that occurs in an effective program of science that is inquiry based and project centered. More on this subject follows later in this chapter.

Types of Cognitive Questioning

Before going further let us define, describe, and provide examples for each of the types of cognitive questions that you will use in teaching. Then, in the section that follows, we focus your attention on the levels of cognitive questions.

CLARIFYING QUESTION

The clarifying question is used to gain more information from a student to help the teacher better understand a student's ideas, feelings, and thought processes. Often, when asked to elaborate on an initial response, a student will think more deeply, restructuring his thinking, and while doing so, will discover a fallacy in the original response. An example of a clarifying question is: "What I hear you saying is that you would rather work alone than in your group. Is that correct?" Research has shown a strong positive correlation between student learning and development of metacognitive skills, and the teacher's use of questions that ask students for clarification.[12] In addition, by seeking clarification, the teacher is likely to be demonstrating an interest in the student and her or his thinking.

CONVERGENT THINKING QUESTION

Convergent-thinking questions (also called "narrow" questions) are low-order-thinking questions that have a single answer (such as the recall question exemplified in the next section). An example of a convergent question is, "What are the products of photosynthesis?"

CUEING QUESTION

If you ask a question to which, after sufficient wait time (longer than 2 seconds and as long as 9 seconds), no students respond or their inadequate responses indicate they need more information, then you can ask a question that cues the answer or response you are seeking. In essence, you are going backward in your questioning sequence in order to cue the students. For example, as an introduction to a lesson on the study of arthropods, a teacher asks her students a recall question such as, "How many legs do crayfish, lobsters, and shrimp have?" If there is no accurate response, she might cue the answer with the following information and question, "The class to which those animals belong is class Decapoda. Does that give you a clue about the number of legs they have?"

DIVERGENT-THINKING QUESTION

Divergent-thinking questions (also known as "broad," "reflective," or "thought" questions) are open-ended (i.e., usually having no single correct answer), high-order-thinking questions (requiring analysis, synthesis, or evaluation), requiring students to think creatively, to leave the comfortable confines of the known and reach out into the unknown. An example of a question that requires divergent thinking is, "What measures could be taken to improve the habitats of the animals at our city zoo?"

EVALUATIVE QUESTION

Some types of questions, whether convergent or divergent, require students to place a value on something, and these are referred to as evaluative questions. If the teacher and the students all agree on certain premises, then the evaluative question would also be a convergent question. If original assumptions differ, then the response to the evaluative question would be more subjective, and therefore that evaluative question would be divergent. An example of an evaluative question is, "Should the United States allow clear-cutting in its national forests?"

FOCUS QUESTION
A focus question is any question that is designed to focus student thinking. For example, the sample question in the preceding paragraph is a focus question when the teacher asking it is attempting to focus student attention on the ecologic issues involved in clear-cutting.

PROBING QUESTION
Like a clarifying question, a probing question requires student thinking to go beyond superficial "first-answer" or single-word responses. An example of a probing question is, "Why, Sean, do you think that each state should have total control over its wetlands?"

Levels of Cognitive Questions and the Relationship to Student Thinking

Questions posed by the teacher are cues to the students as to the level of thinking expected by the teacher, ranging from the lowest level of mental operation, requiring simple recall of knowledge (convergent thinking), to the highest, requiring divergent thought and application of that thought. It is not crucial that a question be absolutely classified. However, you must (1) be aware of the levels of thinking, (2) understand the importance of attending to student thinking, from low to higher levels of operation, and (3) understand that what for one child may be a matter of simple recall of information, for another may require a higher-order mental activity, such as figuring something out by deduction.

You need to structure questions in a way designed to guide students' thinking to higher levels. To help your understanding, three levels of questioning and thinking are described in the following paragraphs.[13] You should recognize a similarity between these three levels of questions, the three phases of Piaget's learning cycle, and the six levels of thinking presented in Bloom's taxonomy of cognitive objectives in Chapter 5. When preparing lesson plans (Chapter 5) and assessment items (Chapter 6), you may want to refer to the key words illustrated in the descriptions of these three levels of questioning:

1. *Lowest level (the data input phase): Gathering and recalling information.* At this level questions are designed to solicit from students concepts, information, feelings, or experiences that were gained in the past and stored in memory. Sample key words and desired behaviors are:

> complete, count, define, describe, identify, list, match, name, observe, recall, recite, select

Thinking involves receiving data through the senses, followed by the processing of those data. Inputting without processing is brain-dysfunctional. Information that has not been processed is stored only in short-term memory.

2. *Intermediate level (the data processing phase): Processing information.* At this level questions are designed to draw relationships of cause and effect, to synthesize, analyze, summarize, compare, contrast, or classify data. Sample key words and desired behaviors are:

> analyze, classify, compare, contrast, distinguish, explain, group, infer, make an analogy, organize, plan, synthesize

Thinking and questioning that involve processing of information can be conscious or unconscious. When students observe the teacher thinking aloud, and when they are urged to think aloud, to think about their thinking, and to analyze it as it occurs, they are in the process of developing their intellectual skills.

At the processing level, this internal analysis of new data may challenge a learner's preconceptions (and misconceptions) about a scientific phenomenon. As emphasized in Chapter 2, the learner's brain will naturally resist this challenge to existing beliefs. The greater the

---

Balloon Will Not Pop

Practice this first. Partially blow up a balloon, tie it off. Take a large but sharp sewing needle and slowly push it into the balloon. Because the needle immediately plugs the hole, the balloon remains filled. Sure, you say, students have seen this done by magicians or birthday party clowns. But wait. Now for the real discrepant event: slowly remove the needle, and Voila! The balloon does not collapse. The balloon material expands to plug the hole. Make several holes. Take a long needle (as used in doll making) and push it through the balloon and out through the other side, keeping the needle in both holes. The balloon stays filled. (*Hint:* push the needle into the thickest portion of the balloon, opposite the opening.) If students believe you are using a fake balloon, take the same needle and quickly puncture the balloon, popping it.

FIGURE 3.1   An example of a discrepant event demonstration.

mental challenge, the greater will be the brain's effort to draw upon data already in storage. With increasing data, the mind will gradually examine existing concepts and ultimately, as necessary, develop new mental concepts.

If there is a match between new input and existing mental concepts, no problem exists. Piaget called this process *assimilation*. If, however, in processing new data there is not a match with existing mental concepts, then the situation is what Piaget called *cognitive disequilibrium*. The brain does not "like" this disequilibrium and will drive the learner to search for an explanation for the discrepancy. Piaget called this process *accommodation*. However, although learning is enhanced by challenge, in situations that are threatening the brain is less flexible in accommodating new ideas. That is why each student must feel welcomed in the classroom and the classroom environment must be perceived by the learner as challenging but nonthreatening—what researchers refer to as an environment of *relaxed alertness*.[14]

Questions and experiences must be designed to elicit more than merely recall memory responses (assimilation). Many science teachers have found it profitable to use *discrepant events* to introduce science concepts.[15] Discrepant events are phenomena that cause cognitive disequilibrium, thus stimulating higher-level mental functioning. However, merely exposing students to a discrepant event will not in itself cause them to develop new conceptual understandings. It simply stirs the mind into processing, without which mental development does not occur. (See Figure 3.1.)

3. *Highest level (the data output phase): Applying and evaluating in new situations.* Questions at the highest level encourage learners to think intuitively, creatively, and hypothetically, to use their imagination, to expose a value system, or to make a judgment. Sample key words and desired behaviors are:

> apply a principle, build a model, evaluate, extrapolate, forecast, generalize, hypothesize, imagine, judge, predict, speculate

You must use questions at the level best suited for the purpose, use questions of a variety of different levels, and structure questions in a way intended to move student thinking to higher levels. When teachers use higher-level questions, their students tend to score higher on tests of critical thinking and on standardized tests of achievement.[16]

With the use of questions as a strategy to move student thinking to higher levels, the teacher is facilitating the students' intellectual development. Developing your skill in the use of questioning requires attention to detail. The guidelines that follow will be useful as you develop your skill in using this important instructional strategy.

GUIDELINES FOR THE USE OF QUESTIONING: THE IMPORTANCE OF STUDENT QUESTIONS

Your goals are to help your students learn how to solve problems, to make decisions, to think creatively and critically, and to feel good about themselves and their learning—rather than just to fill their minds with bits and pieces of science information. How you construct your questions and how you implement your questioning strategy is important to the realization of these goals.

Preparing Questions

Use the following guidelines in preparing questions.

1. *Cognitive questions should be planned, thoughtfully worded, and written into your lesson plan.* Although you will not be able to anticipate all questions that you will use in a lesson, the thoughtful preparation of major questions helps to assure that they are clear and specific, not ambiguous, that the vocabulary is appropriate, and that each question matches its purpose. Incorporate questions into all of your lessons as instructional devices, welcomed pauses, attention grabbers, and checks for student comprehension.

2. *Match questions with their purposes.* Carefully planning the questions you ask allows them to be sequenced and worded to match the levels of cognitive thinking expected of the students. Sequencing is reviewed later, but consider now the wording of questions.

To help students in developing their thinking skills, you need to model for them how to do it. For this, you must use terminology that is specific and that provides students with examples of experiences consonant with the meanings of the cognitive words. You need to do this every day so students learn the cognitive terminology. As stated by Brooks and Brooks, "framing tasks around cognitive activities such as analysis, interpretation, and prediction—and explicitly using those terms with students—fosters the construction of new understandings."[17] Here are three examples:

Instead of saying:	Say:
"Are you going to get quiet?"	"If we are going to hear what Mark has to say, what do you need to do?"
"How do you know that is so?"	"What *evidence* do you have?"
"How else might it be done?"	"How could you *apply* . . . ?"

Implementing Questioning

Careful preparation of questions is a part of the necessary skill. Implementation is the other part. Here are guidelines for effective implementation:

1. *Avoid bombarding students with too much teacher talk.* Sometimes teachers talk too much and listen too little. This is especially true of teachers who are nervous, as is often the case during the first weeks of student teaching. Knowledge of these guidelines will be helpful in avoiding talking too much. Remind yourself to ask a question that you have carefully formulated, then be silent. Sometimes, especially when a question hasn't been carefully planned by the teacher, the teacher asks the question, then, with some change in wording, asks it again, or asks several questions, one after another. Too much teacher talk and that kind of "shotgun" questioning only confuses students and allows too little time for thinking.

2. *After asking a question, provide students with adequate time to think.* Knowing the subject better than their students, and having given prior thought to it, too many teachers, after ask-

ing a question, allow insufficient time for students to think. In addition, by the time they have reached middle school grades, students have learned pretty well how to play the "game"; that is, they have learned that if they remain silent long enough, teachers will answer their own questions. So, after asking a well-worded question you should remain silent for a while, allowing students time to think and time to respond. And, if you wait, they usually will.

After asking a question, how long should you wait before you do something? You should wait at least two seconds, and as long as nine. Stop reading now and look at your watch or a clock to get a feeling for how long two seconds is. Then observe how long nine seconds is. Does it seem to be a long time? Because we are not used to silence in the classroom, nine seconds of silence can seem eternal. If, for some reason, students have not responded after a period of two to nine seconds of wait-time, ask the question again (avoid rewording an already carefully worded question, or else students may think it is a different question) and pause for several seconds. Then, if you still haven't received a response, you can call on a specific student, then another if necessary, after sufficient wait-time. Soon you will get an adequate response, at least one that can be built upon.[18] Avoid answering your own question!

3. *Practice calling on all students, not just the bright or the slow, or those in the front of the room, or what some teachers refer to as the "chosen few," but all of them.* To do this requires your concentration, but it is important.

4. *Give the same amount of wait-time to all students.* This, too, will require effort on your part, but it also is important. A teacher who waits for less time when calling on a slow student or students of one gender more than the other is showing prejudice or lack of confidence in certain students, both of which are detrimental to the efforts of a teacher striving to establish for all students a positive, equal, and safe environment for classroom learning. Show confidence in all students, and never discriminate by expecting less or more from some than from others.

5. *When you ask questions, don't let students randomly shout out their answers, but, instead, require them to raise their hands and to be called on before they respond.* Establish this procedure and stick with it. It will help to assure that you call on all students equally, evenly distributing your interactions with the students, and that you do not interact less with just girls because boys tend to be more obstreperous. Even at the college level, male students tend to be more vociferous than female students, and when allowed by the instructor, tend to outtalk and to interrupt their female peers. Every teacher has a responsibility to guarantee a nonbiased and equal distribution of interaction time in the classroom.

In addition, expecting students to raise their hands before shouting out helps them to control their impulsivity. Controlling impulsivity is one of the 14 characteristics of intelligent behavior presented in Chapter 2.

6. *Use strong praise sparingly.* Use of strong praise is sometimes okay, especially when working with kindergarten and primary-grade children, special education students, and students who are culturally different, and when asking questions of simple low-level recall, such as, "Susan, which color is this?" However, when you want students to think divergently and creatively, be stingy with your use of strong praise to student responses. Strong praise from a teacher tends to terminate divergent and creative thinking.

One of your goals is to help students find intrinsic sources for motivation, that is, an inner drive of intent or desire that causes them to want to learn. The use of strong praise tends to build conformity, causing students to depend on outside forces, that is, the giver of praise for their worth, rather than on themselves. An example of a strong praise response is when a teacher reacts to a student answer with, "That's right! Very good." On the other hand, passive acceptance responses, such as "OK, that seems to be one possibility," keep the door open for further thinking, particularly for higher level, divergent thinking.

Another example of a passive acceptance response is one used in brainstorming sessions, when the teacher says, "After asking the question, and giving you time to think about it, I will hear your ideas and record them on the board." Only after all student responses have been heard and recorded does the class begins its consideration of each. In the classroom that kind of nonjudgmental acceptance of all ideas can generate a great deal of expression of high-level thought.[19]

7. *Avoid bluffing an answer to a question for which you do not have an answer.* Nothing will cause you to lose credibility with students more quickly than your faking an answer. There is nothing wrong with admitting that you do not know something. It helps students realize that you are human. It helps them maintain adequate self-esteem, realizing that they are OK. What *is* important is that you know where and how to find possible answers and that you help students to develop those same skills.

Encourage Student Questioning

Effective science teachers encourage students to ask questions: questioning is the cornerstone of sciencing. To encourage student inquiry, follow these guidelines.

1. *Encourage students to ask questions about content and process.* No question is a dumb question. Sometimes students, like everyone else, ask questions that could just as easily have been looked up. Such questions can consume valuable class time. For a teacher, that can be frustrating, and the teacher may be tempted to brush off a question of that type with sarcasm, assuming that the student is simply trying to avoid looking up an answer. In such instances, our advice is to think before responding and to respond kindly and professionally, even though, in the busy life of a classroom teacher, this may not always be easy. However, be assured that there is a reason for a student's question. Perhaps the student is signaling a need for your recognition.

In school it is sometimes easy for a child to feel alone and insignificant, and we believe that when a child makes an effort to interact with the teacher, that is a positive sign. So gauge carefully your responses to such efforts. If a student's question is really off the track, out of order, or does not relate to the content of the lesson, as a possible response, consider this: "That is an interesting question (or comment), and I would very much like to talk with you more about it. Could we meet at lunchtime, or before or after school?"

2. *Student questions should be used as springboards for further questions, discussion, and investigations.* One teacher, for example, built her entire science program on questions that her elementary schoolchildren wrote in their "I Wonder" journal entries.[20] Students should be encouraged to ask questions that challenge the textbook, the process, or another person's statement and to seek the facts or evidence behind a statement.

3. *Being able to ask questions may be more important than having right answers.* Knowledge is derived from asking questions. Being able to recognize problems and to formulate questions are skills, and these are fundamental to the development of the skills involved in problem solving and critical thinking. As a science teacher, you have a responsibility to encourage students to formulate questions, to help them word their questions in such a way that tentative answers can be sought. This is the process necessary to build a base of knowledge that can be called upon again and again to connect, interpret, and explain new information in new situations.[21]

4. *Questioning is the cornerstone to critical thinking and real-world problem solving.* In real-world problem solving, there are usually no absolute right answers. Rather than being "correct," some answers are better than others. The person with a problem (a) recognizes and identifies the problem, (b) formulates a question about that problem—e.g., Should I buy a house or rent? Should I date this person or not? Should I take this job or not? Which car should I buy? (c) collects data, and (d) arrives at a temporarily acceptable answer to the problem, realizing that at some later time new data may dictate a review of the former conclusion.

For example, if an astronomer believes she has discovered a new galaxy, there is no textbook (or teacher) to which she may refer to find out whether she is right. Rather, on the basis of her self-confidence in problem identification, asking questions, collecting sufficient data, and arriving at a tentative answer based on those data, she assumes that for now her conclusion is safe. (Begun earlier, in Chapter 1, this important concept for science teaching is revisited in the section on "inquiry" teaching.)

SELECTION OF SPECIFIC INSTRUCTIONAL STRATEGIES

Inquiry is emphasized as a tool for learning science. The science curriculum connects to other school subjects.[22]

In selecting an instructional strategy, there are two distinct choices: whether as teacher you should deliver information to the students (teacher-centered teaching), or whether you should provide students with access to information (student-centered teaching). The pros and cons of these two approaches are discussed next.

Delivery and Access Modes of Instruction

The traditional mode of science instruction is to deliver information; that is, knowledge is transmitted from those who know (the teacher and the textbook) to those who do not (the students). Within the delivery mode, traditional and time-honored strategies include textbook reading, formal teacher talk (the lecture and questioning), and informal teacher talk (the discussion and recitation). For the classroom teacher, teacher talk is an important and unavoidable teaching tool, and it can be valuable when used judiciously. However, being told about science without being allowed to *do* science is like learning the alphabet without being encouraged to put letters together to make words.

With the second approach, the access mode, instead of direct delivery of information and direct control of what is learned, the teacher provides access to information by collaboratively designing with the students experiences that facilitate their obtaining new knowledge and skills. Within this mode an important instructional strategy is inquiry, which most certainly will use questioning, although the questions more often should come from the students. Discussions and other strategies, too, may be involved in inquiry.

It is likely that you are more experienced with the delivery mode, and although this chapter provides guidelines for the use of strategies within that mode, to be most effective as a science teacher you must become knowledgeable and skillful with the use of access strategies. Although our intent is not to imply that one mode is unquestionably always better, strategies within the access mode do facilitate the positive learning of students. As mentioned earlier, we believe that to be most effective, elementary and middle school teachers should be eclectic in selecting strategies, that is, they should appropriately select and effectively use strategies from both modes, but with a strong focus on access, or facilitating, strategies. Thus, in this section you become knowledgeable about use of techniques within each mode in order to make intelligent decisions in choosing the best strategy for particular goals and objectives for your unique group of students. Figures 3.2 and 3.3 presents a review of specific strengths and weaknesses of each mode.

As you can see from Figures 3.2 and 3.3, the strengths and weaknesses of one mode are nearly mirror opposites of those of the other. Although competent teachers should be skillful in the use of strategies from both modes, to be most effective science teachers should

The strengths of the delivery (traditional) mode are:

- Much content can be covered within a short span of time, usually by formal teacher talk and guided discussions, which may be followed by an experiential activity.
- The teacher is in control of what content is covered.
- The teacher is in control of time allotted to specific content coverage.
- Strategies within the delivery mode are consistent with performance-based teaching.
- Student achievement of specific content is predictable and manageable.

The potential weaknesses of delivery strategies are:

- The sources of student motivation are mostly extrinsic.
- Students have little control over the pacing of their learning.
- Students make few important decisions about their learning.
- There may be little opportunity for divergent or creative thinking.
- Student self-esteem may be inadequately attended.

FIGURE 3.2   Delivery mode: its strengths and weaknesses.

The strengths of access strategies are:

- Students learn content, and in greater depth.
- The sources of student motivation are more likely intrinsic.
- Students make important decisions about their own learning.
- Students have more control over the pacing of their learning.
- Students develop a sense of personal self-worth.

The potential weaknesses of access strategies are:

- Content coverage may be more limited.
- Access strategies are time-consuming.
- The teacher has less control over content and time.
- The specific results of student learning are less predictable.
- The teacher may have less control over class procedures.

FIGURE 3.3   Access mode: its strengths and weaknesses.

concentrate more on the use of strategies from the access mode. Strategies within that mode are more student centered, hands-on, and direct, with students actually doing what they are learning to do—they are physically and mentally engaged in sciencing.

Multilevel Teaching: A Blend of Modes

Many science teachers arrange their classrooms so that various groups of students can be learning in different ways (and sometimes even different content) at the same time. While some may be receiving direct instruction (delivery mode), others can be learning by discovery activities (access mode). Direct instruction can be given by the teacher or at a self-paced learning activity center. Simultaneously, in other areas of the classroom, other groups of students may be doing laboratory investigations, creating bulletin board displays, or brainstorming how they are going to investigate a problem.

When the class is divided into groups of students doing different things, that is, learning in different ways at the same time, the process is called multilevel (or multitask) teaching. Multilevel teaching demands careful planning to assure that materials are ready and that the needs of individual students are being carefully considered. Multilevel teaching is very appropriate for teaching science in today's classroom of mixed-ability students; it allows the teacher to attend to individual learning styles, language proficiencies, and levels of understanding and doing.

When several groups of students are doing different kinds of tasks, you must plan carefully.

Direct learning is likely to engage more of the senses, thus to better effect learning.

You must also exercise well-developed withitness and overlapping skills; otherwise, classroom management can become a nightmare.

General Rule in Selecting Learning Activities

In planning and selecting science learning activities, an important rule is to select activities that are as concrete as possible. When students are involved in concrete experiences, they are using more of their sensory modalities (e.g., auditory, visual, tactile, kinesthetic), and when all the senses are engaged, learning is most effective and longest lasting. This is "learning by doing" or, as it is commonly called today, "hands-on learning"—one end of the spectrum on the Learning Experiences Ladder.

Conversely, at the other end of the spectrum are abstract experiences, whereby the learner is exposed only to symbolization (i.e., words and numbers), using only one or two senses. Visual and verbal symbolic experiences, although impossible to avoid in teaching, are less effective in assuring that the planned learning occurs. So, as was said earlier, when planning experiences and selecting materials, you are urged to select activities that engage the students in the most direct experiences possible. Hands-on, or firsthand experience, learning is more educationally potent than vicarious activity, provided that the hands-on learning is combined with reflection—that is, that the mind is engaged.[23]

The Learning Experiences Ladder (Figure 3.4) depicts this range of experiences, from direct to abstract. As implied in the example in the ladder, when teaching about tidal pools,

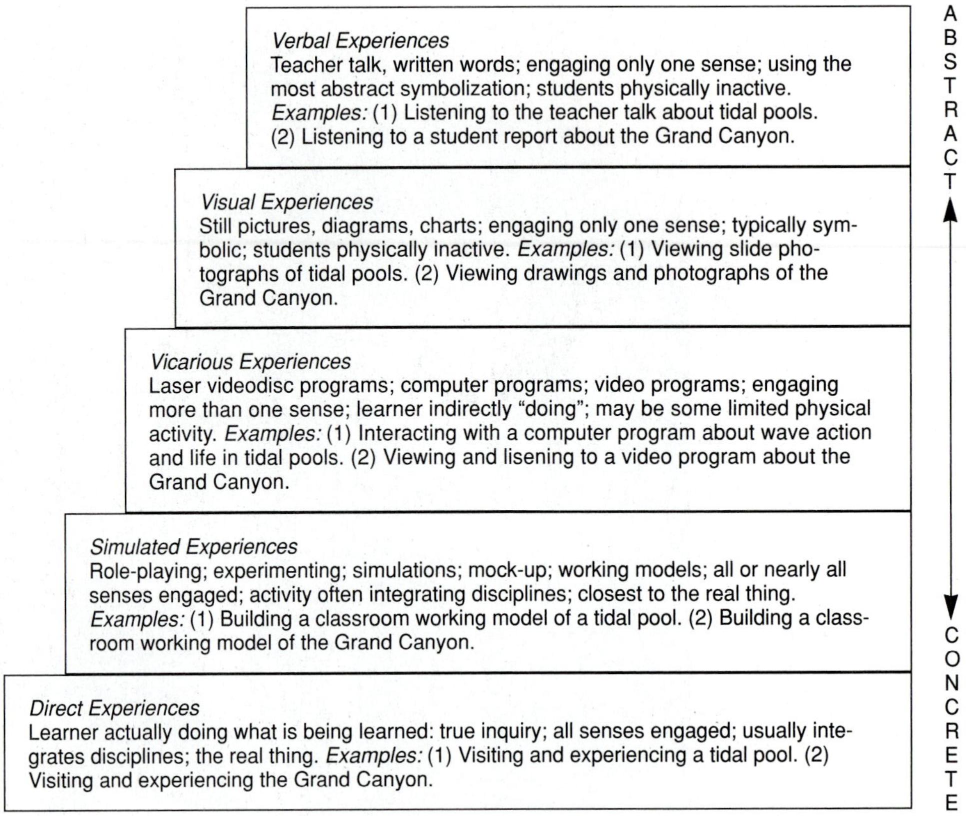

Verbal Experiences
Teacher talk, written words; engaging only one sense; using the most abstract symbolization; students physically inactive. *Examples:* (1) Listening to the teacher talk about tidal pools. (2) Listening to a student report about the Grand Canyon.

Visual Experiences
Still pictures, diagrams, charts; engaging only one sense; typically symbolic; students physically inactive. *Examples:* (1) Viewing slide photographs of tidal pools. (2) Viewing drawings and photographs of the Grand Canyon.

Vicarious Experiences
Laser videodisc programs; computer programs; video programs; engaging more than one sense; learner indirectly "doing"; may be some limited physical activity. *Examples:* (1) Interacting with a computer program about wave action and life in tidal pools. (2) Viewing and lisening to a video program about the Grand Canyon.

Simulated Experiences
Role-playing; experimenting; simulations; mock-up; working models; all or nearly all senses engaged; activity often integrating disciplines; closest to the real thing. *Examples:* (1) Building a classroom working model of a tidal pool. (2) Building a classroom working model of the Grand Canyon.

Direct Experiences
Learner actually doing what is being learned: true inquiry; all senses engaged; usually integrates disciplines; the real thing. *Examples:* (1) Visiting and experiencing a tidal pool. (2) Visiting and experiencing the Grand Canyon.

ABSTRACT ↑

CONCRETE ↓

FIGURE 3.4   The learning experiences ladder. (*Source:* Earlier versions of this concept can be found in: Charles F. Hoban, Sr., et al., *Visualizing the Curriculum* (New York: Dryden, 1937), p. 39; Jerome S. Bruner, *Toward a Theory of Instruction* (Cambridge: Harvard University Press, 1966), p. 49; Edgar Dale, *Audio-Visual Methods in Teaching* (New York: Holt, Rinehart & Winston, 1969), p. 108; and, Eugene E. Kim and Richard D. Kellough, *A Resource Guide for Secondary School Teaching*, 6th ed. (Englewood Cliffs, NJ: Merrill/Prentice Hall, 1995), p. 330.)

the most effective strategy is to take the students to a tidal pool (bottom of ladder; most direct, or concrete, experience) where students can see, hear, touch, smell, and perhaps even taste the tidal pool. The least effective strategy is for the teacher simply to talk about the tidal pool (top of the ladder; most abstract, symbolic experience), engaging only one sense—the auditory.

Of course, for various reasons—such as matters of safety, lack of resources for a field trip, location of your school—you may not be able to take students to a tidal pool. Because it is not always possible to use the most direct experience, sometimes you must select an experience higher on the ladder. In addition, self-discovery teaching is not always appropriate. Sometimes it is more appropriate to build on what others have discovered and learned, rather than to "reinvent the wheel." However, the most effective and longest-lasting learning *is* that which engages most or all of the learner's senses, and in the Learning Experiences Ladder, those are the experiences that fall within the bottom three rungs—the direct, simulated, and vicarious categories.

The science classroom is designed as a learning laboratory where children are motivated to explore phenomena.

Of particular significance is that direct, simulated, and vicarious experiences are usually interdisciplinary; that is, they frequently cross subject content boundaries. That makes these experiences especially useful for integrated learning. Direct, simulated, and vicarious experiences are more like real life, thereby providing an important benefit to students' learning.

THE CLASSROOM AS A LEARNING LABORATORY

The science classroom should be a learning laboratory where students can explore scientific phenomena. Exploring is the heart and soul of science teaching and learning. Of all methods used specifically to teach science, the use of investigations with hands-on/minds-on learning is the one that evokes the greatest curiosity, interest, excitement, and satisfaction among students. It is the means whereby students develop proficiency in many process skills while they are developing their understanding of concepts. Other teaching strategies are valuable for teaching and learning science, but they are usually most effective when used either with or as a result of exploratory investigations.

Exploratory investigations can be used to arouse interest and raise questions or problems, to answer questions or solve problems, to help students develop their thinking skills while applying what they have learned to new, unfamiliar situations, and to encourage and challenge students of various backgrounds and experiences.

Arousing Interest and Raising Questions or Problems to Investigate

Nothing does more to start a unit or lesson successfully than an investigation that arouses the interest of the class and raises questions or problems. On a cold, dry winter day, with a volunteer to assist you, rub an inflated rubber balloon briskly against a wool suit or with a piece of wool cloth, then place the balloon against the wall. This initiating activity may be done by the teacher or, if enough balloons are available, by the students as a class investigation. Students' interest is aroused immediately when they observe the balloon sticking to the wall.

Plan an alternate initiating activity. Sometimes your students may have already experienced the initiating activity that you had planned to do, and to prepare for that situation, it is always good to have an alternative activity ready. For alternative investigations dealing with static electricity, see Figure 3.5. Their interest will naturally provoke comments, questions, and discussion. Student questions can serve as springboards for further investigations. When questions are raised and problems are stated, the class is well on its way to the study of static electricity.

An initiating activity gives students an orientation to the science topic, establishing a "mind set." At the same time, by raising questions or problems, it helps to make the students aware that they must learn much more about the science topic before they can fully understand the event.

Helping to Solve Problems

Exploratory investigation is ideal for problem solving, one of the key objectives for school science. In the process of solving problems, students learn to think critically and creatively and to develop proficiency in the key operations of sciencing. They learn how to define the problem and the terms involved, to make accurate observations and to classify them, to formulate and test hypotheses, to understand the nature of controls and the value of repeated trials to ensure reliability and validity, and to draw tentative conclusions.

Alternate 1. Teachers often demonstrate static electricity by using plastic and glass rods with fur and silk cloths to move balloons and bits of paper. Students in upper-level elementary classrooms may already be familiar with this activity. The following demonstration, however, is one they may not have experienced. Suspend a large piece of lumber (an 8-foot 2 × 4 works well) on a string from the classroom ceiling, or balance the board on a large watch glass using a few drops of oil at the pivot point. Make sure the board is balanced and that it freely rotates. Hold a charged plastic rod (or a comb) near the end of the board. Voila! The board moves toward the rod.

Alternate 2. Rub a rubber comb (or rubber rod), then hold the comb close to water running slowly from a faucet (or poured from a pitcher). The charge on the comb will cause the column of running water to bend toward the comb.

FIGURE 3.5   Alternate static electricity investigations.

Applying What Has Been Learned to New Situations

In a sense, when students apply what they have learned to new situations, to new problems that they have stated, this application serves as an assessment technique. If students have really learned the desired science skills and understandings, they should be able to apply what they have learned to a new situation.

Application to new situations is the third phase of the learning cycle, the one that helps to connect what has been learned to the students's environment and life. Furthermore, the process of applications depends on critical thinking, because the students must now review the various aspects of the investigation, weigh and sift the evidence, call upon their store of scientific knowledge and experiences, make and suspend judgments, hypothesize, and, finally, come to a satisfactory, although perhaps temporary, conclusion.

Encouraging and Challenging Students of Different Learning Styles, Intelligences, Backgrounds, and Experience

Performing exploratory investigations provides an excellent opportunity to enhance the learning of students in your classroom who come from varying backgrounds. Because investigations tend to be concrete, using most or all of the senses, and do not rely heavily on abstract verbal symbolization, they help students to develop the ability to observe and report—to communicate. Experience in exploratory investigations can give students needed confidence in organizing data, in sensing problems, and in solving problems scientifically. For any student, moreover, there is a certain satisfaction in the status involved in explaining to one's peers the reasons or principles underlying the content and procedures of an investigation.

Exploratory investigations can challenge the more intellectually mature learner. While experimenting, students can help and learn from each other in cooperative learning groups or by peer-tutoring. It is axiomatic that a person knows a subject well when he or she can explain or demonstrate it effectively to another person.

In addition, exploratory investigations can afford the opportunity to use multilevel teaching and to incorporate the many intelligences and abilties of students in the classroom. Consider the scenario in Figure 3.6.

Guidelines for Doing Exploratory Investigations

If you adhere to the following guidelines for doing exploratory investigations, your teaching should run smoothly and your students will be motivated and will learn.

For one afternoon during the study of a thematic unit on weather, a fourth-grade teacher and her students are concentrating on learning about the water cycle. She has divided her class into several groups of three or four students each. All are working simultaneously to learn about the water cycle. Several students are conducting and repeating an experiment to discover how many drops of water can be held on one side of a new one-cent coin. Another group is preparing graphs to illustrate the results of those experiments. A third group is creating and composing the words and music of a rap song about the water cycle. A fourth group is creating a colorful bulletin board about it. A fifth group is reading about the water cycle in books they obtained from the school library and from the city water commission. Finally, a sixth group is creating a puppet show about the water cycle. When all groups have finished their projects, they will share them with the whole class.

FIGURE 3.6   A classroom scenario of exploratory investigations and the incorporation of the theory of multiple intelligences.

1. *The investigation should have a purpose*. The purpose should be clearly understood by the students. An investigation can be designed to serve any one or more of the following purposes:

- As a closure to a lesson or unit of study
- As a mind-capturing introduction to a lesson or unit of study
- As a review to a unit of study
- To provide for discrepancy recognition
- To assist in the recognition of a solution to an existing problem
- To establish problem recognition
- To give students an opportunity to participate in active sciencing
- To illustrate a particular concept

2. *Students should understand procedures, expected behavior, and the consequences for not following established procedures*. Two important points must be made. First, the science classroom should be a learning laboratory, where students are actively learning and multitasking, where there are different things happening simultaneously, some of which will cause excitement, curiosity, and purposeful movement about the classroom. Second, the science classroom is a place where, without an enforcement of procedures, serious injuries to students can result. Unfortunately, some science teachers, because of their fear of liability or that the class will get out of control, do not allow students to actively science, or they allow it only in rare instances, perhaps to reward students for their sustained good behavior. To prevent this unfortunate situation, your students must understand classroom procedures and you must consistently enforce those procedures.

From the first day of school, you must establish classroom procedures. In addition, you should assure that students understand basic safety guidelines and the consequences for not following procedures. These consequences should be fair and consistent, and they must be relevant to the grade level you teach.

3. *Planning is important and should involve the students*. The necessary materials must be collected, prepared in advance, and ready for assembling or distribution so there is no delay or "dead time" during class. Try to do the experiments yourself in advance, remembering the adage "If anything can go wrong, it probably will." Students should be involved in various phases of planning their exploratory investigations. Aim for thinking and discussion about the investigation. Talk about it before you begin and again after it is completed. Keep investigations as simple as possible. If an investigation is too complex for the intellectual maturity level of your students, they may never know what it was all about.

4. *Help students connect what is learned to their own world*. To be most meaningful, exploratory investigations should have relevance to the students' real world of everyday living, which is one of the reasons students should be involved in the planning phase of their investigations.

5. *Use controls and repeated trials whenever possible*. The use of controls in investigations is one of the key operations in sciencing. Students are able to understand very early the need for, as well as the nature of, a controlled experiment. In an experiment using a control, all the conditions are duplicated except one, and this single condition (the variable) is the one that is being tested. For example, when studying the effect of heat on the rate of evaporation, a control helps to prove conclusively that heat makes liquids evaporate more quickly. The same measured quantity of water is poured into each of two identical pie pans. One pan is placed on a warm radiator, and the other pan is placed on a table on the other side of the room. The windows and door are kept closed to prevent any effect caused by wind or air circulation. Now all conditions are the same except one, namely, the heat to which the water is exposed. Consequently, as a result of the control, the results of the investigation are clear.

After students have learned the nature and value of control, they should also be exposed to the necessity, sometimes, of having to perform repeated trials to secure results that are both reliable and valid. The consistency with which a technique measures that which it is meant to measure is called its *reliability*. The accuracy with which it makes the measurement is called its *validity*. If, for example, a scale consistently records 10-grams when we place a 10-gram weight on it, we can say the scale has reliability. However, if a scale consistently records 5 grams when we place a 10-gram weight on it, we can still say the scale has reliability. Through this example, it should be clear that an experiment can be reliable without being valid—that is, accurate. In addition, students need to understand the concept of instrument calibration.

Students are quick to understand the need for repeated trials. If a teacher were to suggest that the class should conduct an experiment to see which was the faster runner, a right-handed or a left-handed student, the students would be quick to object to an experiment involving just one right-handed and one left-handed student. The need for testing several students to make the experiment reliable would be obvious to all. (To make an experiment valid, all variables but one, handedness in this instance, would have to be controlled.)

Similarly, when you are finding the dew point (the temperature at which water vapor in the air will condense back into water), it will be so difficult to note the exact temperature when the dew point is reached that the students will recognize the need to repeat the experiment several times and perhaps take an average to obtain satisfactory results. Consequently, experiments requiring several repetitions can help prevent students from making broad generalizations from just one test.

6. *Aim for quantitative as well as qualitative results.* Students are exposed to the "why" and the "what" of science, but should also be exposed to the "how much." Dealing with quantitative aspects gives students an opportunity to practice measurement, a key process of science.

Take, for example, investigations designed to show how the strength of an electromagnet may be increased. It is customary to prove this either by increasing the number of turns of wire around the piece of iron or by using more dry cells. However, consider how much more effective a learning situation this becomes if we make the experiments quantitative as well. When first making the electromagnet, the students wrap 30 turns of wire around the iron nail or bolt. They count the number of tacks the electromagnet will pick up. Then, when the students wrap 60 turns of wire around the iron nail, they find that this second electromagnet will pick up twice as many tacks. There should be little difficulty in realizing that if they double the number of turns of wire, they double the number of tacks that will be picked up. Consequently, the electromagnet has been made twice as strong. If the experiment is repeated, however, this time using the same number of turns of wire in each case and using first one and then two dry cells (connected in series), the results will be the same as when the number of turns of wire was doubled. That is, if the students double the number of dry cells, using the same number of turns, they double the number of tacks that will be picked up, and again they have made the electromagnet twice as strong. The students could then be asked to find out what would happen if they doubled both the number of dry cells and the number of turns.

In this investigation the students not only learn a science concept, but are also given an opportunity to discover mathematical ratios and relationships. There are many opportunities in the teaching of science to include the teaching of measurement, numbers, size, and simple ratios.[25]

7. *When an experiment "fails."* Sometimes experiments fail to work as expected. Recall Thomas Edison and his trial of some 3,000 filaments before finding one that worked satisfactorily. When an experiment is unsuccessful, grab that opportunity to model problem solving

---

The science program should be coordinated with the mathematics program to enhance student use and understanding of mathematics in the study of science and to improve student understanding of mathematics.[24]

---

and creative thinking. Involve the students in proposing and testing hypotheses about why it didn't work. Adhere to the philosophy that "no experiment fails."

One teacher, for example, took advantage of an unsuccessful experiment when the class was studying expansion and contraction. To observe what happens to gases when heated, she selected an experiment involving a rubber balloon and a soda bottle. The balloon was snapped over the neck of the bottle, and the bottle was placed on the radiator in the classroom. The teacher had expected the balloon to expand as the air inside the bottle was heated and expanded into the balloon. The experiment had worked in her other classes, but this time nothing happened. Although initially disconcerted, the teacher immediately seized the opportunity and called upon the class for suggestions. After discussion, the students concluded that either the balloon was punctured, the bottle was cracked, or the radiator was not hot. Each reason was checked, and the cause of the failure—a radiator that had cooled—was quickly found. Instead of being annoyed or frustrated, both the teacher and the students were pleased that they had solved this problem so quickly and scientifically.

Establishing Classroom Procedures

When establishing classroom procedures, remember this: the learning time must run efficiently (i.e., with no "dead spots"), smoothly (i. e., routine procedures are established; transitions between activities are smooth), and with minimum disruption. When stating your expectations for student classroom behavior, try to do so in a positive manner, emphasizing procedures and desired behaviors, stressing what students should *do*, rather than what they should *not* do.

In working with individual learning styles, Dunn suggests posting and enforcing classroom rules such as these:

When we work with learning styles in this class
- If your style interferes with anyone else's style, you lose the privilege of having your style accommodated.
- Every assignment must be completed.
- Your test grades must be better than ever before—or this experiment is not working and there is no reason to continue.
- You must sit like ladies and gentlemen—even when working on the floor—I also have to be able to see you.
- When I ask for your attention, everyone must stop and attend.[26]

As you prepare your procedures for behavior in the classroom, you have to consider what students need to know from the start. Your procedures should be reviewed and rehearsed with the students several times during the first week of school, then followed consistently throughout the school year. Things that students need to know from the start include the following:

- *How to obtain your attention and help.* Most teachers who are effective classroom managers expect their students to raise their hands, and for only as long as necessary, that is, until the teacher acknowledges (usually by a nod) that a student's hand has been seen. With that acknowledgment, the student should lower his or her hand. Try to avoid situations in which a student sits for a long time with his or her hand raised, waiting for you to respond. To prevent a student becoming bored and restless because of waiting, attend to the student as quickly as possible. Expecting students to raise their hands before speaking allows you to control the noise and confusion level and to be proactive in deciding who speaks and encourages students to learn to control their impulsivity (as discussed in Chapter 2).

To avoid dependence on the teacher and having too many students raising their hands for the teacher's attention, and to encourage positive dialogue among the students, many teachers use some form of the "three before me" procedure. That is, when a student has a question, the student must ask three peers for help before asking for the teacher's help.

- *How to maintain, obtain, and use both materials for learning and items of personal use.* Students need to know where, when, and how to store, retrieve, and care for items such as their coats, backpacks, books, pencils, and medicines, how to obtain papers, materials, and laboratory items, and when they may use the pencil sharpener and wastebasket. Classroom control is easiest to maintain when (a) items that students need for class activities and for their personal use are neatly arranged and located in places that require minimum foot traffic, (b) there are established procedures that students clearly understand and that are enforced, (c) there is the least amount of student off-task time, and (d) students do not have to line up for anything. Therefore, you will want to plan the room arrangement, equipment and materials storage, preparation of equipment, materials, and transitions between activities so as to avoid needless delays and confusion. Problems in classroom control will most certainly occur whenever some or all students have nothing to do, even if only for a brief time.

- *When students may go to the drinking fountain and the bathroom.* Normally, students should be able to take care of these matters before or after school and during lunchtime. However, sometimes they do not or, for medical reasons, cannot. Be flexible enough for the occasional student who has an immediate need and follow the established school policy.

- *How to behave during a class interruption.* Unfortunately, class interruptions do occur, and in some schools they occur far too often. For an important (or, unfortunately, sometimes unimportant) reason the principal, a vice-principal, or another person from the school's office may interrupt the class to see the teacher or a student or to make an announcement to the entire class. Students need to know the behavior that is expected of them during these interruptions. When there is a visitor to the class, the expected procedure should be for students to continue working on their learning activity unless directed otherwise by the teacher.

- *What to do when students are late to your class, or when they will be leaving early.* You need to understand and reinforce school policies on early dismissals and tardies. Routinize your own procedures so students clearly understand what they are to do if they must leave your classroom early (e.g., for a medical appointment) or when they arrive late. The procedures should be such that students arriving late or dismissed early do not disturb you or the learning activities in process.

- *The consequences for inappropriate behavior.* Most teachers who are effective classroom managers have routinized their procedures for handling inappropriate behavior and assure that the students understand the consequences for inappropriate behavior. The consequences should be posted in the classroom and, when not counter to school policy, may be similar to the following five-step model.

First offense results in a reminder (warning) to the student.

Second offense results in a 10-minute time out for the student in an isolation area but one that still has adult supervision.

Third offense results in a 15-minute time out.

Fourth offense results in a communication to the student's parents or guardian.

Fifth offense results in the student being sent to the vice-principal or principal's office, sometimes followed by a limited or permanent suspension from school.[27]

■ *Rules for behavior and procedures to follow during emergencies, either real or practice drills.* Students need to know what to do, where to go, and how to behave in emergencies, such as might occur because of a fire, storm, earthquake, or disruptive campus intruder.

Safety Guidelines for the Science Classroom

In addition to the safety guidelines presented here (Figure 3.7), the National Science Teachers Association (NSTA) publishes safety guidelines (see Suggested Readings at the end of this chapter) and your local school district or state department of education may have a publication about safety in the science classroom. For activities involving electricity and magnetism additional safety guidelines are found in Part II of this book.

Teachers ensure a safe working environment. Safety is a fundamental concern in all experimental science. Teachers of science must know and apply the necessary safety regulations in the storage, use, and care of the materials used by students. They adhere to safety rules and guidelines that are established by national organizations and local regulatory agencies.[28]

---

1. Teachers are responsible to prevent accidents and assure that the science classroom is as safe as possible. Whenever an accident happens, notify the school office immediately by phoning or sending a pair of runners to the office.
2. Rules for investigatory work should be taught to the students, posted in a conspicuous place, and reviewed continually. Instruct and rehearse the students in the procedures for classroom behavior and the consequences for misbehavior.
3. When taking students on a field trip, solicit adult help, even when the trip is only a short distance from the school. A recommended guideline is one adult for every ten students.
4. Maintain a neat classroom, with aisles kept clear and books and coats in designated storage areas. Students should not be allowed to wear coats while doing laboratory investigations. Loose-fitting clothing can too easily knock over equipment.
5. Be aware of eye safety precautions and regulations regarding eye protection.
6. Avoid using flammable materials and alcohol burners, and use lighted candles and hot plates with caution.
7. A well-supplied first aid kit should be available in the classroom.
8. Know exactly what to do in case of emergencies, and have emergency procedures posted conspicuously in your classroom.
9. Have an ABC-type fire extinguisher available always, and be sure it is adequately charged.
10. Use proper waste disposal methods. Learn from your school district the regulations for disposing of various kinds of waste materials.
11. Maintain accurate labels on all drawers, cupboards, and containers.
12. Students should not taste unknown substances.
13. Avoid using dangerous plants, animals, chemicals, and apparatus in the classroom.
14. Handle pets with care and caution. For example, birds can carry psittacosis, and turtles and other animals can carry salmonellosis. Dogs, rabbits, and other animals may have parasites. Some children may be allergic to animal dander.
15. Do not allow students to handle or to bring dead animals into the classroom.
16. Do not store heavy items above the heads of the students.
17. Do not allow students to climb or to be in positions where they may fall.
18. Do not leave dangerously sharp objects or those that may shatter where students can obtain them without approval and supervision.
19. Avoid allowing students to overheat or to overexert themselves.
20. Never leave students unattended for any reason.
21. Inspect electrical equipment for frayed cords and, if frayed, do not use.
22. Avoid overloading an electrical circuit.
23. Employ caution in the use of any mechanical equipment with moving parts.
24. Under no circumstances should blood or any other body fluids be extracted from your students.
25. Be alert for students who have allergies or other medical problems, and be aware of what to do if a student is having a medical problem while in your classroom.

FIGURE 3.7   Safety guidelines for the science classroom.

FIRST AID AND MEDICATION

Accidents to students at school do occur. While doing a laboratory experiment, a student may be cut by glass. It is also possible that a student may be burned by a hot item or injured by a falling window pane when the teacher is trying to open a window. A student may fall and be hurt during on a excursion outside the classroom. Do you know what to do if a student in injured while under your supervision?

First, you should give first aid *only* when necessary to save a child's limb or life. When life or limb is not threatened, you should follow school policy in referring the student to *immediate* professional care. When immediate care is not available but you believe it is necessary, you may take prudent action as if you were the child's parent or legal guardian. However, you must be cautious and knowledgeable about what you are doing so that you do not cause further injury.

Unless you are a licensed medical professional, you should *never* give medication to students, whether precription or over-the-counter. Students who need to take medication should bring from home a written parental statement of permission and instructions. Under your supervision or that of the school nurse (if there is one available), they can then take their own medicine.

To test their hypotheses, children understand the importance of repeated trials and careful observations.

TEACHER TALK

Although teacher talk is unavoidable, you need to be aware of several risks associated with using it. First, there is the danger of talking too much. When a teacher talks too much, the significance of the teacher's words is lost while students tune the teacher out. Another danger is talking too fast. Students hear faster than they can understand what is heard. Yet another danger is believing that students have learned something just because you told them about it. Recall, from the Ladder of Learning Experiences, that verbal communication is the least effective form of communication. That is because of its reliance on the use of abstract symbolization, in this case words, and on listening, a skill that many students have not developed very well. Finally, students who have limited proficiency in English can be in double jeopardy. The use of words in a language that is not native to them makes it even more difficult for them to learn science, which in itself can be like a foreign language.

Asking that you keep these risks in mind, we now present general and specific guidelines for the productive and effective use of teacher-talk strategies.

General Principles

Whether your teacher talk is formal (a lecture) or informal (talking, questioning, demonstrating, and discussing), there are certain principles to be followed:

1. Begin the talk with an advance mental organizer. As discussed in Chapter 2, advance mental organizers are introductions that mentally prepare students for new material. They do this by helping students make connections with material already learned—comparative organizing—or by expository organizing, providing them with a conceptual arrangement of what is to be learned. An advance organizer can be a brief introduction or statement about the main idea you intend to get across, an outline of the topic, or the presentation of a discrepant event. Preparing an organizer helps you in planning and organizing the sequence of ideas. Its presentation helps students to organize their own learning and helps make their learning more meaningful. An adage that may be useful here is: Tell them what you are going to tell them; tell them; then tell them what you told them.

2. Your talk should be planned so that it has a beginning and an end, with a logical order between. During your talk, reinforce the various points with visual materials. Visuals may include your explaining and writing unfamiliar terms on the board, presentation of still visuals such as graphs, flannel boards, flip charts, and pictures, or presentation of audiovisuals such as films and videos.

3. The pacing of the talk is important. Your talk should be brisk, but not too fast. Many beginning teachers talk too fast and too much; however, your ability to pace your instruction will improve with experience. Until you have perfected your skill in pacing lessons, constantly remind yourself to slow down and to provide silent pauses. We suggest that your talk should be brisk but with occasional slowdowns to change the pace and to check for student understanding. For older students, a talk should be adequately paced to allow them time to make notes and to ask questions. Finally, have a time plan, but remember that a talk planned for 10 minutes, if it's interesting to the students, will probably take longer.

4. Encourage student participation during your talk. Active participation enhances learning. Encouragement can be planned as questions that you ask the class, or as time allowed for students to comment and ask questions. You can also have students do individual or paired concept mapping during the talk.

Specific Guidelines

Specific guidelines for the use of teacher talks are as follows:

1. *Purposes for teacher talk.* Teacher talk, formal or informal, can serve for any one, or a combination, of the following:

- Discuss the progress of a unit of study.
- Explain an inquiry.
- Introduce a unit of study.
- Present a problem focus.
- Promote student inquiry or critical thinking.
- Provide a transition from one unit of study to the next.
- Provide "cutting edge" information otherwise unavailable to students.
- Share the teacher's experiences.
- Summarize a problem.
- Summarize a unit of study.

2. *Objectives of the talk.* A talk should center on one major concept or idea, and the objectives—not too many for one talk—should be made clear to the students; otherwise, the students may never know what it was about.

3. *Informal vs. formal talk.* Although an occasional brief formal lecture may, for a few upper grade or middle school classes, be appropriate, spontaneous interactive informal talks of about 10 minutes maximum duration are preferable. You should never give long lectures with no teacher-student interaction. And remember, in today's world students are used to "commercial breaks," so, about 10 minutes into most lessons, student attention is likely to begin to drift. That is when you need to have elements planned that will recapture their attention.

Elements planned to recapture student attention can be verbal cues, such as voice inflections, pauses to allow information to sink in, and humor; or visual cues, such as the use of slides, real objects, or body gestures; or proximity cues, such as moving around the room; or tactile cues, such as casually touching the shoulder of a student without interrupting the talk. Perhaps most useful for capturing student attention is to change to an entirely different strategy. This can mean changing from a talk activity to a student-centered activity, such as a hands-on experiment, as opposed to changing from a lecture (mostly teacher talk) to a teacher-led discussion (mostly more teacher talk).

4. *Use notes to guide your teacher talk.* Planning your talk and preparing notes to be used during teacher talk are as important as implementing the talk. There is nothing wrong with using notes during your teaching. We suggest that you do so and that you carry your notes with you on a clipboard (perhaps an attractive neon-colored one) as you move around the room. Your notes should be prepared first in narrative form and then, for class use, reduced to an outline form. Teacher talks should always be given from an outline, never read from prose.

5. *Rehearse the talk.* Rehearse your talk using a camera and a videorecorder, or an audiorecorder, and remember to allow more time for implementation than it takes for rehearsal. Including a time plan for each subtopic allows you to gauge your timing during implementation of the talk.

6. *Don't race through your talk solely to complete it by a predetermined time.* It is more important that students understand some of the planned content than it is for you to cover all the material and the students to understand none of it. If you don't finish, continue later.

7. *Augment teacher talk with multisensory stimulation.* Your presentation should not rely too heavily on the spoken word. When using visuals, such as slides and overhead transparencies, it is not necessary to talk constantly; after clearly explaining the purpose of a visual, give students enough time to look at it, to think about it, and to ask questions about it.

8. *Content of teacher talk*. Rather than simply rehashing material from the textbook, teacher talk should supplement and enhance this information. Students may never read their book if the teacher tells them everything that is in it.

9. *Teacher's voice*. Your voice should be pleasant and interesting to listen to, rather than a steady, boring monotone or a constantly shrieking, irritating, high pitched delivery. On the other hand, it is good to show enthusiasm for what you are talking about. Use dramatic voice inflections to emphasize important points and meaningful body language to give students a visual focus.

10. *Vocabulary of teacher talk*. The words you use should be easily understood by the students, while still modeling professionalism and helping students to increase their vocabulary. When you use a word that you think may be foreign to students, stop to ask a student to help explain its meaning and to demonstrate its derivation. This is a good way to help students remember. Keep in mind that, regardless of their primary teaching subject, all teachers are teachers of language arts.

Good science teachers simultaneously use two vocabularies, the new science vocabulary and the vocabulary necessary to help children learn the new science vocabulary.

11. *Provide older students with a skeletal outline, a study guide, or a concept map of the talk*. An outline, study guide, or concept map (an expository organizer) can facilitate students' understanding and organization of the content of a talk. Students should be coached on how to take notes and shown how to use their notes to build their understanding of concepts.[29]

12. *Use familiar examples*. Incorporate ideas and events with which the students are already familiar. The most effective talk is that which makes frequent connections between what students already know, or think they know, and what they are learning.

13. *Consider students who are different*. While preparing a talk, consider students who are culturally and linguistically different or who may have special needs. Personalize the talk for them through the use of analogies, examples, and audiovisuals.

14. *Establish eye contact with your students frequently*. Whenever you are teaching, your primary eye contact should always be with your students. You should make only momentary eye contact with your notes, visuals, writing board, and other objects in the classroom. With practice, you can learn to visually scan a class of 30 students and establish eye contact with each student about once every minute. To *establish* eye contact means that the student is aware that you are looking at him or her.

Frequent eye contact can have two major benefits. First, as you read your students' body posture and facial gestures, you gain clues about their attentiveness and comprehension. Second, eye contact helps to establish rapport between you and your students. Be alert, however, for students in your classroom who may be from cultures in which eye contact is infrequent or unwanted.

Frequent eye contact is easier when using an overhead projector than when writing on a board. When writing on a board, you have to turn at least partially away from your students, and you may have to move back and forth between writing on the board and maintaining your proximity to the students.

GROUPING FOR INSTRUCTION

An important strategy for effective science instruction is to group students in ways that enhance positive interaction and quality learning. During any given week of school, a student may experience a succession of group settings. In discussing the various ways of grouping students for instruction, we proceed from individualized instruction to working with dyads, small

For children to work cooperatively and productively in groups requires the development of certain social skills, and these skills are not innate, they are learned.

groups, and large groups. We also discuss how to ensure equality in the classroom, how to use assignments and homework, and how to coordinate various forms of independent and small-group study and presentations.

Mastery Learning and Individualizing the Instruction

Learning is an individual experience. Yet a teacher is expected to work effectively with students on other than an individual basis—more likely thirty-five to one. Much has been written of the importance of individualizing instruction. As used here, the concept of *individualizing instruction* refers to "making explicit provisions for adapting the curriculum to students' particular abilities and needs," which is much broader than the narrow view of providing for self-paced instruction.[30]

We know of the individuality of the learning experience. And we know that although some children are primarily verbal learners, many more are primarily visual, tactile, or kinesthetic learners. As teacher, you find yourself in the difficult position of simultaneously "treating" from twenty-five to thirty-five separate and individual learners with individual learning styles and preferences. To individualize instruction in such circumstances seems an impossible expectation—yet, occasionally, teachers do succeed.

Common sense tells us that student achievement in learning is related to both the quality of attention and the length of time given to learning tasks. In 1968, Benjamin Bloom, building on a model developed earlier by John Carroll, developed a concept of individualized instruction called mastery learning, saying that students need sufficient time on task (i. e., engaged time) to master content before moving on to new content.[31] From that concept Fred Keller developed an instructional plan called the Keller Plan, or the Personalized System of Instruction (PSI), which involves the student's learning from printed modules of instruction (which, today, would likely be presented as computer software programs) and which allows the student greater control over the learning pace. This sort of modular instruction is mastery oriented; that is, the student demonstrates mastery of one module before proceeding to the next.

Today's emphasis is on mastery of content, or *quality learning*, rather than coverage of content, or quantity of learning.[32] Because of this emphasis, the importance of the concept of mastery learning has resurfaced, although the strategies for implementing it are different from those of the 1970s. In the current effort to restructure schools, two prevalent approaches— Outcome-Based Education (OBE) and the Coalition of Essential Skills Schools (CESS)—are built on the premise that each student can learn and both focus on the construction of individual knowledge through mastery.[33] Sometimes, unfortunately, attention may be on the mastery of only minimum competencies, and thus students are not encouraged to work and learn to the maximum of their talents and abilities. By mastery of content is meant that *the student demonstrates use of what has been learned.*[34]

ASSUMPTIONS ABOUT MASTERY, OR QUALITY, LEARNING

Mastery, or quality, learning is based on certain assumptions, which are:

1. Mastery (or quality) learning is possible for all students.
2. For quality learning to occur, it is the instruction that must be modified and adapted, not the children. Tracking and ability grouping do not fit with the concept of mastery learning.
3. Although all students can achieve mastery, some may require more time than others to master a particular content. The teacher and the school must provide for this difference in the time needed to complete a task successfully.
4. Most learning outcomes can be specified in terms of observable and measurable performance.
5. Most learning is sequential and logical.
6. Mastery learning can ensure that students experience success at each level of the instructional process. Experiencing success at each level provides incentive and motivation for further learning.[35]

COMPONENTS OF THE MASTERY LEARNING MODEL

Any instructional model designed to teach toward mastery contains the following components:

- Objectives that are stated in specific behavioral terms (i. e., a behavioristic approach to instructional design).
- Preassessment of the learner's present knowledge.
- An instructional component, with practice, reinforcement, frequent comprehension checks (diagnostic or formative assessment), and corrective instruction at each step to keep the learner on track.
- Postassessment to determine the extent of mastery of the objectives.

The theory of cooperative learning is when a small group of children of mixed backgrounds and capabilities increase their liking and respect for each other by working together toward a common goal. The result is an increase in each child's self-esteem and academic achievement.

Dyad Grouping

Sometimes it is advantageous to pair students (dyads) for studying and learning. Examples include:

- *Peer tutoring*, whereby one classmate tutors another. Peer tutoring is useful, for example, when one student helps another who has limited proficiency in English or when a student skilled in math helps another who is less skilled.
- *Cross-age coaching*, whereby one student is coached by another from a higher grade level.[36] Cross-age coaching is similar to peer tutoring, except that the coach is from a higher grade level than the student being coached.
- *Think-pair-share*, whereby two students examine a new concept about to be studied. Perhaps the concept is "digestion." The students of each dyad discuss what they already

know or think they know about digestion, and then each dyad presents its perceptions to the whole group. This is an excellent technique for discovering students' misconceptions. A modification of this is *think-write-pair-share*, whereby the pair of students think and write their ideas before sharing those ideas with the larger group.

The Learning Activity Center (LAC)

Another significantly beneficial way of pairing students for instruction (as well as individualizing instruction) is through the use of learning activity centers, which provide a technique for both integrating and individualizing learning. An LAC is a special station located in the classroom where one student (or two, if student interaction is necessary or preferred at the center) can quietly work and learn at his or her own pace. All materials needed are provided at that station, including clear instructions for operation of the center. A learning activity center might be one that focuses on an experiment dealing with a particular phenomenon or concept in science. A familiar example is the personal computer station. Long popular in elementary schools, the learning activity center can also be an effective and developmentally appropriate instructional device for use in middle school classrooms.[37]

The value of learning centers as instructional devices undoubtedly lies with the facts that (1) the learning center can provide instructional diversity; (2) while working at a center, the student is giving time and quality attention to the learning task (learning toward mastery), and (3) while working at the center, the student is likely to be engaging her or his most effective learning modality, or integrating several or all modalities.

TYPES OF LEARNING ACTIVITY CENTERS

Learning activity centers are of three types:

- *Direct-learning center.* Performance expectations for cognitive learning are quite specific, and the focus is on mastery of content. For example, the LAC may have a setup that involves the student in a designed experiment with magnets.
- *Open-learning center.* The goal is to provide opportunity for exploration, enrichment, motivation, and creative discovery. For example, the LAC may have a variety of magnets and materials designed to allow the student to explore with those materials.
- *Skill center.* As in a direct-learning center, performance expectations are quite specific, but the focus is on the development of a particular skill or process, such as manipulating the mathematics involved in determining the power of an electromagnet according to its wire wrappings and the number of batteries supplying electricity.

PURPOSES OF A LEARNING ACTIVITY CENTER

Although in all instances the primary reason for using a learning center is to individualize the learning, there are additional reasons. These are to provide:

- A mechanism for learning that crosses discipline boundaries
- A special place for a student with special needs
- An opportunity for creative work
- Enrichment experiences
- Multisensory experiences
- Opportunities for students to learn from learning packages that utilize special equipment or media of which only one or a limited supply may be available for use in your classroom (e.g., science materials, a computer, a laser videodisc, a compact disk player, or a combination of these items).

Learning centers are the focal point of many active science classrooms.

GUIDELINES FOR SETTING UP A LEARNING ACTIVITY CENTER

In setting up an LAC, you can be as elaborate and as creative as your time, imagination, and resources allow. Students can even help you plan and set up learning centers, which can relieve the burden imposed on your busy schedule. Here are some guidelines for setting up an LAC.

1. Materials used in the center should be safe for student use.
2. The center should be self-directing; that is, specific instructional objectives and instructions for use of the center should be clearly posted and understandable to the student user. An audio or video cassette is sometimes used for this purpose.
3. The center should be easily supervised by you or an adult aide.
4. The purpose of the center should be understood by the students.
5. Centers should always be used for educational purposes, and *never* for punishment.
6. Topics for the center should be related to the instructional program—for review, remediation, or enrichment.
7. The center should contain a variety of activities geared to the varying abilities and interest levels of the students. Offering a choice of two or more activities at each center is one way to provide for this.

8. Materials used at the center should be readily available, with descriptions for use provided to the student user.
9. The center should be attractive, purposeful, and uncluttered.
10. The design of the center should incorporate a theme, one that integrates the student's learning by featuring activities that cross discipline boundaries.
11. Learning activity centers should be self-correcting; that is, student users should be able to tell by the way they have completed a task whether or not they have done it correctly and have learned.
12. Learning activity centers should be activity-oriented, i.e., dependent on the student's manipulation of materials, not just providing paper-and-pencil tasks.

To adapt their instruction to students' individual needs and preferences, many elementary and middle school teachers design a learning environment that includes several learning centers, each of which uses a different medium and modality or focuses on a special aspect of the curriculum. Students rotate through learning centers according to their needs and preferences.[38]

Cooperative Learning Groups (CLG)

The cooperative learning group is a heterogeneous group (i.e., mixed according to one or more criteria, such as ability or skill level, ethnicity, learning style, gender, and language proficiency) *of three or four students who work together in a teacher- or student-directed setting, emphasizing support for one another, as each student contributes to and learns from the group task.* Most often, a CLG consists of four students of mixed ability, learning styles, gender, and ethnicity, with each member of the group assuming a particular role. Normally, the group is rewarded on the basis of group task achievement, though individual members within the group can later be rewarded for individual contributions. Teachers usually change the membership of each group a few times during the year.

The theory of cooperative learning is that when small groups of students of mixed backgrounds and capabilities work together toward a common goal, members of the group increase their friendship and respect for one another. As a consequence, each individual's self-esteem is enhanced and academic achievement is improved. This theory is well supported by many research studies (see the Suggested Readings at the end of this chapter).

Although there are several techniques for using cooperative learning, the primary purpose of each is for the groups to learn—which means, of course, that individuals within a group must learn. Group achievement in learning, then, is dependent on the learning of individuals within the group. Rather than competing for rewards for achievement, members of the group cooperate with one another by helping one another learn so that the group reward will be a good one.

Because peer support needs to be stronger than peer pressure, you must be cautious about the use of group grading.[39] For grading purposes, bonus points can be given to all members of a group; individuals add to their own scores when everyone in the group has reached preset standards. The preset standards must be appropriate for all members of a group. Lower standards or improvement criteria can be set for students with lower ability, so that everyone feels rewarded and successful. To determine each student's quarter and semester grades, individual student achievement is measured later through individual student results on tests and by other criteria, as well as through each student's performance in the group work (discussed further in Chapter 6).

ROLES WITHIN THE COOPERATIVE LEARNING GROUP

With CLGs it is advisable to assign roles (specific functions) to each member of the group (as exemplified in Figure 5.5, showing a sample unit plan with one daily lesson plan). These roles should be rotated, either during the activity or from one time to the next. Although titles may vary, typical roles are:

> *Group facilitator*—role is to keep the group on task.
> *Materials or equipment manager*—role is to obtain, maintain, and return materials needed for the group to function.
> *Recorder*—role is to record all group activities and processes, and perhaps to periodically assess how the group is doing.
> *Reporter*—role is to report group processes and accomplishments to the teacher and/or to the entire class.
> *Thinking monitor*—role is to identify and record the sequence and processes of the group's thinking and actions. This role encourages metacognition and the development of thinking skills.

WHAT STUDENTS DO IN COOPERATIVE LEARNING GROUPS

Typical cooperative learning strategies involve student teams in which students work on group projects that emphasize the processes in sciencing, especially analysis and evaluation. Sometimes, the students study together what has been previously taught and then are later tested individually. Usually, each member of the group learns about a specific part of a general topic assigned to the group.

OUTCOMES OF USING COOPERATIVE LEARNING GROUPS

When the process is well planned and managed, the outcomes of cooperative learning include: improved communication and relationships between students of different ethnic groups, improved communication and relationships between students with learning disabilities and other students, increased academic achievement, and quality learning with fewer off-task student behaviors.

Small Groups

Small groups include those involving five to eight students, in either a teacher- or student-directed setting. The use of small groups for instruction, including the cooperative learning group, enhances the opportunities for students to assume greater control over their own learning, sometimes referred to as *empowerment*.[40]

PURPOSES FOR SMALL GROUPS

Small groups can be formed to serve a number of purposes. They can be useful for a specific learning activity, such as the completion of a science experiment, or a work project, lasting only as long as the project does. Teachers have various rationales for assigning students to groups. Groups can be formed by combining students according to personality type (e.g., sometimes a teacher may want to team less assertive students in order to give them an opportunity for greater management of their own learning), social pattern (e.g., sometimes it may be necessary to break up a group of rowdy friends, or desirable to broaden the association among students), common interest, or their abilities in a particular skill.

GROUP PRESENTATIONS AND WHOLE-CLASS DISCUSSIONS

Large groups are those that involve more than eight students, usually the entire class. Most often, they are teacher directed. Student presentations and whole-class discussions are two activities that often involve the use of large groups.

Student Presentations

You can encourage students to be presenters for discussion of the ideas, opinions, and knowledge obtained from their own independent and small-group study. Several techniques encourage the development of certain skills in sciencing, such as studying and organizing material, discovery, discussion, rebuttal, listening, analysis, suspending judgment, and critical thinking. Possible forms of discussion involving student presentations include:

- *Debate*. The debate is an arrangement in which formal speeches are made by members of two opposing teams, on topics preassigned and researched. The speeches are followed by rebuttals from each team.
- *Panel*. The panel is a setting in which four to six students, with one designated as chairperson, discuss a topic they have studied, followed by a question-and-answer period involving the entire class. The panel usually begins with each member giving a brief opening statement.
- *Research report*. One student, a dyad, or a small group of students gives a report on a topic that has been investigated; this presentation is followed by questions and discussion by the entire class.
- *Round table*. The round table is a small group of three to five students who sit around a table and discuss among themselves (perhaps with the rest of the class listening and later asking questions) a problem or issue that they have studied.[41]
- *Symposium*. Similar to a round-table discussion but more formal, a symposium is an arrangement in which each student participant presents an explanation of his or her position on a preassigned topic researched by that student. After the presentations, questions are accepted from the rest of the class.

To use these techniques effectively, you will need to coach your students, individually or in whole-class sessions, on procedures: how and where to gather information; how to take notes, to select major points, to organize material, to present a position succinctly and convincingly, and to listen; how to play roles; and how to engage in dialogue and debates with one another. Be patient, the results will be worth it!

Whole-Class Discussion

Whole-class discussion is a technique frequently used in teaching. Having been a student in formal learning for at least 12 years, you are undoubtedly knowledgeable about the advantages and disadvantages of whole-class discussions. In deciding to use this strategy, there are certain questions you will want to ask yourself. Some of these are as follows.

For what reasons would I hold a whole-class discussion? When using a whole-class discussion, as opposed to small-group discussions or cooperative learning groups, a teacher has more precise control over the direction of the discussion, its content and outcome, and the time needed for completion. In addition, the teacher has greater assurance of involvement by certain students.

How can I arrange student seating (in a classroom with moveable seats)? For a discussion that will last long enough to justify moving seats, you will probably want to arrange the students in a circle so each student can see every other student's face.

What ground rules should be established before starting the discussion? The first ground rule is that each student is to be listened to while talking. Talking is expected only when students are recognized by the teacher. An effort will be made to allow every student to speak. This is to assure that the discussion is not dominated by a few students. Adequate think-time and response-time will be allowed, but each speaker has a limited amount of time. When relevant, students are expected to have done their homework on the discussion topic.

Should student participation be forced? To maintain a classroom environment that is non-threatening, student participation should not be forced.

How can I handle digression from the topic? Regardless of how thoroughly you plan your lessons, you can never predict with certainty where the lesson will go, nor should you expect to. A teacher must make many on-the-spot decisions, one of which is whether to allow a digression to continue. Sometimes you will want to allow digression, other times not. That is a professional decision that you are expected to be able to make. And remember, a good science teacher allows for serendipity, but cannot plan for it.

Another consideration is your own role during a class discussion. For example, there may be a time during a whole-class discussion when you will want to turn the discussion leadership over to a student while you step aside to monitor it. Brainstorming can be a form of whole-class discussion, and your role during part of a brainstorming session might simply be that of recorder and monitor.

You will also have to decide on the sorts of activities that should precede a class discussion, and the activities that would be appropriate as follow-up to a whole-class discussion session. For example, an exploratory investigation might precede a discussion; student investigations, motivated by the discussion, might follow. Sometimes discussions follow or precede achievement testing.

Another decision that teachers invariably have to make is whether students should be graded for their participation in class discussion. Why or why not? If so, how? On what basis? By whom? Our answer to this general question may not be entirely satisfactory to you, but here it is. Over the long term, we think, yes, students should be evaluated by the teacher on the basis of their participation in class discussions; but, no, they should not be given grades for every discussion. Knowing that they are being evaluated can create an artificial and less productive atmosphere.

For effective discussions, 10 to 12 feet is the maximum recommended distance between participants. During any discussion, keep this in mind. If you are leading a discussion, you may need to move slowly around the room to stay within the recommended distance.

EQUITY IN THE CLASSROOM

Especially when conducting whole-group discussions, it is easy for a teacher to fall into the trap of interacting with only the brightest, or only those in the front of the room or on one side, or only the most vocal and assertive. You must exercise caution to avoid falling into that trap. To ensure a psychologically safe and effective environment for learning for every person in your class, you must attend to all students and try to involve all students equally in all class activities. You must avoid any biased expectations about certain students, and you must avoid discriminating against students according to their gender or any other personal characteristic. Many classroom studies provide convincing evidence that disadvantaged students in particular—those who come from poor families and from ethnic and linquistic minority backgrounds—receive less instruction in higher-order intellectual skills than do their advantaged peers.[42]

You must avoid the unintentional tendency of teachers of *both* sexes to discriminate on the basis of gender. For example, teachers, along with the rest of society, tend to have lower expectations for girls than for boys in mathematics and science. They tend to call on and encourage boys more than girls. They often let boys interrupt girls, but praise girls for being polite and waiting their turn.[43] To avoid such discrimination may take special effort on your part.

To guarantee equity in interaction with students, many teachers have found it useful to ask someone secretly to tally classroom interactions between the teacher and students during a class discussion. Such an observation should include the percentage of your interactions with children according to gender. After an analysis of the results, you can arrive at a decision about your attending and facilitating behaviors. If, for example, the ratio of boys to girls in your class is one to one, then your interactions according to student gender should closely reflect the same ratio. If your interactions seem to favor one gender or the other, then you need to work at achieving a better balance.

In addition to the analysis according to student gender, observations can include responses and their frequencies according to other teacher-student interactions, such as your calling on students for responses to your questions, or calling on students to assist you with classroom jobs, or chastising students for their inappropriate behavior.

Ensuring Equity   There are several ways of ensuring that students are treated fairly in the classroom:

- Encourage students to demonstrate an appreciation for one another by applauding all individual and group presentations.
- Set and maintain high expectations for all students.
- Insist on appreciation in the classroom. For example, a student can be shown appreciation—such as with a sincere "thank you" or "I appreciate your contribution," or with a whole-class applause, or with a genuine smile—for her or his contribution to the learning process.
- Insist that students be allowed to finish what they are saying without being interrupted by others. Be certain that you model this behavior yourself.
- Insist that students raise their hands and are called on before they are allowed to speak.
- Keep a stopwatch handy to unobtrusively control the wait-time given for each student. Although at first this idea may sound impractical, we assure you it works.
- Use a laminated seating chart (one that can be written on and erased each day) attached to a clipboard, and next to each student's name make a tally for each interaction you have with a student. This also is a good way to maintain records over a period of time in order to eventually reward students for their contributions to class discussions.

PROJECT-CENTERED SCIENCE TEACHING

Independent study, individual writing, group projects, and oral and written group reports should be major features of science instruction. A project is usually a form of small-group (or whole-class) study in which students produce something as a culmination of that study, such as a paper, model, a skit, or a report. Many teachers center their science instruction around themes with student-centered, project-oriented investigations as the primary mode of instruction, hence what is sometimes referred to as project-centered teaching. Exploratory investigations afford the opportunity students need to explore their own interests and to develop their sciencing skills; project work can help satisfy their need to have worthwhile experiences with their peers; the opportunity to share a project with the rest of the class can contribute to their feelings of self-worth and competence.

Values of Using Project-Centered Teaching

The values of using project-centered teaching in science include:

- A student can become especially knowledgeable and experienced in one area of science or in one process skill, thus adding to the student's knowledge and sense of importance and self-worth.
- A student can develop skill in communication through sharing this special knowledge and experience with the teacher and with her or his peers.

- Because a project can accommodate individual interests, learning styles, and life experiences, the learning can have greater personal meaning for the student.
- Students become intrinsically motivated to learn when working on topics that have personal meaning to them, and that have outcomes and time limits that are relatively open ended.
- Students can practice and develop independent learning skills.
- Students learn to work independently, or somewhat independently of the teacher in small groups.
- With proper guidance and coaching by the teacher, students develop skills in writing and in higher-level thinking.

Unless students are given guidance, a project can often be a frustrating experience, for both the teacher and the students. Students should do projects because they want to and because they think the projects are important. Therefore, students should, under guidance of the teacher, decide what project to do and how to go about doing it. The teacher's role is to advise and guide students so they experience success. If a project is laid out in too much detail by the teacher, it becomes a procedure rather than a project. If a project is too broad, students become frustrated and lose interest.

Guidelines for Using Project-Centered Teaching

Students will need some structure, and sometimes considerable guidance, to successfully complete exploratory projects. But with the provision of structure and proper guidance by the teacher, the results can be well worth the effort. For the experience to be educationally beneficial, the teacher should:

1. *Help students generate ideas.* Stimulate ideas by providing lists of things students might study; by mentioning, each time an appropriate idea comes up in class, that this would be a good idea for a group project; by having former students tell about their projects; by showing the results of other students' projects; by suggesting readings that are likely to give students ideas; and by using class discussions to brainstorm ideas.

2. *Provide options, but insist that writing be a part of the students' work.* Research examining the links between writing, thinking, and learning has helped to emphasize the importance of writing. Writing is a complex intellectual behavior and process that helps the learner create and record his or her understanding, that is, to construct meaning.

Allow students to decide whether they will work alone or in small groups. If they choose to work in groups, then help them delineate job descriptions for each member of the group. Groups of four or fewer students seem to work better than groups of more than four.

3. *Provide coaching and guidance.* Work with each student or student team in topic selection, in designing the study, and in the writing and oral reporting. Allow students to develop their own procedures, but guide their preparation of work outlines and preliminary drafts, giving them constructive feedback and encouragement along the way. Help students in identifying potential resources and in the techniques of research.

Frequent drafts and progress reports from the students are a must. At each of these stages, provide students with constructive feedback and encouragement. Provide written guidelines and negotiate time lines for the outlines, drafts, and completed project.

4. *Evaluation.* The final project report should be graded. The method of determining the grade should be clear to students from the beginning, as well as the weight of the project grade toward the term grade. Provide students with clear descriptions of how evaluation and grading will be done. Evaluation should include meeting deadlines for drafts and progress reports. The final grade for the study should be based on four criteria: (a) how well it was organized, including meeting draft deadlines; (b) the quality of the sciencing involved and the quantity of knowledge

Mr. Geral's class was studying a unit on weather and the atmosphere. Mr. Geral asked his students if they would be interested in setting up a weather station on the school grounds as a class project. The students became excited about the idea and agreed that it would be a good learning experience for the whole class. To start the project, one student suggested that they invite a local weather forecaster to help them plan their weather station. Another student said that the weather forecaster seen on local television often announced her willingness to visit schools to instruct classes on weather. The students thought that it would be an excellent idea to invite her to their class to discuss their project idea. Several students volunteered to make an appointment with her at the TV station to explain the project and invite her to visit their class. Ms. Maher, the weather forecaster, accepted the invitation and visited the class. She indicated that she would help them with the project, provided that all students in the class participated in the activities and that they took their assignments seriously.

After giving an introduction to weather observing and forecasting, Ms. Maher told the students that some weather equipment was needed to establish the weather station and that some pieces could be constructed using cheap and simple materials. She recommended that for a class project it would be a good idea for them to make some of the equipment rather than purchase it from a supply house. Ms. Maher said that she would divide the class into small groups and give each group instructions for making one piece of equipment. She provided instructions for making a rain gauge, a hygrometer, a psychometer, and a wind velocity instrument. She said that the other items needed, such as barometers and thermometers, were probably available in the science equipment inventory, but if they were not, she could provide them. She also said that she would provide the class with other specialized equipment needed for the station for an extended period of time. Ms. Maher also gave a group of students the specifications for building a weather shelter in a specified area on the school grounds. With the help of the industrial arts teacher, they built the shelter and placed it in an area designated by Ms. Maher.

After two weeks the weather station was set up and operating. Two students were assigned each day to collect and record data. They recorded the temperature and dew point, relative humidity, barometer readings, type of clouds, height of clouds, rain gauge measurements, wind direction and velocity, and other pertinent data.

The data were given to Ms. Maher during her weekly visits. She showed them how the data were used in producing a weather map for forecasting the weather. She visited the class for four consecutive weeks and exposed the students to some of the principles of weather observing and weather forecasting. The students prepared their own weather maps from data Ms. Maher collected from other weather stations all over the country. With Ms. Maher's help, they attempted to forecast the weather using the weather maps they had plotted. The students collected and recorded weather data on a daily basis for the remainder of the term and found that their data compared well with data collected by professional weather observers.

FIGURE 3.8   One class's semester science project. (*Source:* Alfred T. Collette and Eugene L. Chiappetta, *Science Instruction in the Middle and Secondary Schools*. 3d ed. (Columbus, OH: Merrill, 1994), pp. 264–265. By permission of Merrill/Prentice Hall.)

gained from the experience; (c) the quality of the student's sharing of that learning experience with the rest of the class; and (d) the quality of the student's final written and oral report.

5. *Sharing.* Insist that students share both the progress and the results of their study with the rest of the class. The amount of time allowed for this sharing will, of course, depend on many variables. The value of this type of instructional strategy derives not only from individual contributions but also from the learning that results from the experience and the communication of that experience with others.

See Figure 3.8 for a description of a whole-class semester-long science project.

WRITING ACROSS THE CURRICULUM: GUIDELINES FOR THE SCIENCE TEACHER

Research examining the links between writing, thinking, and learning has emphasized the importance of writing across the curriculum. Writing instruction received attention in *The Writing Report Card: Writing Achievement in American Schools*.[44] That report indicated that students who use techniques known as *process writing* (whereby both students and teacher focus on the process of writing rather than solely on the products of the writing) produce superior results. In process writing, the emphasis is on planning and feedback from other students, and revising and editing. Also helpful in revising the writing of students are word processors and computers and accompanying word processing programs. With these tools, a student can make revisions without copying material by hand. This freedom from hand copying allows a student to focus on revising rather than on the labor of recopying.

Student Journals

Science teachers should have their students maintain journals, another tool that encourages writing, thinking, and reflection. Many teachers require *response journals*, journals in which the students write their thoughts about what they are investigating and studying. Some teachers have their students maintain *dialogue journals*. Dialogue journals are used for students to write anything that is on their minds; teachers, parents or guardians, and other students respond, thereby "talking with" the journal writer.

PURPOSE AND ASSESSMENT OF STUDENT JOURNAL WRITING

The purpose of journal writing is to encourage students to write, to think about their writing, to record observations, and to record their creative thoughts about what they are learning. Students are encouraged to write about experiences, both in school and out, that are related to the subject being studied. They should be encouraged to record their feelings about what and how they are learning.

Journal writing provides a mechanism for record keeping for exploratory activities in science and practice in expression, and should *not* be graded by the teacher. Negative comments and evaluations from the teacher will discourage creative and spontaneous expression by students. Teachers should read the journal writing (except for those things a student might not want the teacher to read, which should be covered or folded over by the student before giving the journal to the teacher) and then offer constructive and positive feedback. However, teachers should avoid giving negative comments and grading the journals. For grading purposes, most teachers simply record whether or not a student does, in fact, maintain the required journal.

THE TEACHING OF THINKING

The curriculum of any school science program should include the development of skills that are used in thinking, which, as discussed shortly, are the skills of inquiry. Because the academic achievement of students increases when they are taught thinking skills directly, many researchers and educators concur that direct instruction should be given to students on how to think.[45] They also agree that learning to think is as valid an educational goal for students who have special needs or who are at risk, disadvantaged, or limited in speaking English as it is for those who are recognized as being gifted and talented.

The direct teaching of thinking has been influenced by four research perspectives (see Chapter 2): (1) the cognitive view of intelligence, which asserts that intellectual ability is not fixed but can be developed; (2) the constructivist approach to learning, which maintains that learners actively and independently construct knowledge by creating and coordinating relationships in their mental repertoire; (3) the social psychology view of classroom experience, which focuses on the learner as an individual who is a member of various peer groups and a society; and (4) the perspective of information processing, which deals with the acquisition, elaboration, and management of information.[46]

Thinking skills are the skills of sciencing, which include classifying, comparing, concluding, generalizing, inferring, and others (see Figure 1.7). Rather than assuming that students

Thinking skills are the skills of sciencing. Rather than assume that students have developed these skills, direct instruction must be given to students on how to think through the analysis of a problem.

have developed these skills, classroom time should be devoted to teaching them directly. As explained by Costa:

> We often find a science textbook which asks students to make a *conclusion* based upon data observed during an experiment. We assume students know how to draw conclusions, yet we seldom teach students that skill. We may hear ourselves or other teachers ask questions that presuppose students' knowing how to perform certain thinking skills: "Who can *summarize* some of the things we've learned about the nomads of the desert?" "Let's *analyze* this problem." . . . While we may assume that students know how to perform the thinking skills implied in the subject matter and the instructional interactions being used in the classroom, we often find they have never learned what it means to perform these basic thinking skills. As a result, students are often dismayed, confused, and handicapped when asked to perform them.[47]

When teaching a thinking skill directly, the subject content becomes the vehicle for thinking. Inquiry teaching and discovery learning are both useful tools for learning and for teaching thinking skills.

INQUIRY TEACHING AND DISCOVERY LEARNING

Intrinsic to the effectiveness of both inquiry and discovery is the assumption that students would rather actively seek knowledge than receive it through expository (i.e., information delivery) methods such as lectures, demonstrations, and textbook reading. Although inquiry and discovery are important teaching tools, there is sometimes confusion about exactly what inquiry teaching is and how it differs from discovery learning. The distinction should become clear as you study the descriptions of these two important tools for teaching and learning science.

The science teacher encourages children to solve problems. Problem solving is not a teaching strategy but a high intellectual behavior that facilitates learning. The development of a child's problem-solving skills is a major goal in school science teaching.

Problem Solving

Perhaps a major reason that inquiry and discovery are sometimes confused is that in both, students are actively engaged in problem solving. Problem solving is *the ability to define or describe a problem, determine the desired outcome, select possible solutions, choose strategies, test trial solutions, evaluate outcomes, and revise these steps where necessary.*[48]

Inquiry Vs. Discovery

Problem solving is not a teaching strategy but a high-order intellectual behavior that facilitates learning. *When teaching science, what a teacher can and should do is to provide opportunities for students to identify and tentatively solve problems.* Experiences in inquiry and discovery can provide those opportunities. With the processes involved in inquiry and discovery, teachers can help students develop the skills necessary for effective problem solving. A major difference between discovery and inquiry is *who* identifies the problem. Another important difference lies in the decisions that are made by the students. Figure 3.9 shows three levels of inquiry, each defined according to what the students does and decides.

From Figure 3.9, it should be evident that what is called Level I inquiry is not true inquiry but actually traditional, didactic, "cookbook" teaching, whereby both the problem and the

Problem identification	Level I (not true inquiry)	Level II	Level III
Process of solving the problem	Identified by teacher of textbook	Identified by teacher or textbook	Identified by student
	Decided by teacher or textbook	Decided by student	Decided by student
Identification of tentative solution to problem	Resolved by student	Resolved by student	Resolved by student

FIGURE 3.9   Levels of inquiry.

process for resolving it are defined for the student. The student then works through the process to its inevitable resolution. If the process is well designed, the result is inevitable, because the student "discovers" what was intended by the writers of the program. This level of learning is also called *guided inquiry* or *discovery*, because the students are carefully guided through the investigation to (the predicable) "discovery."

Level I is in reality a strategy within the delivery mode, as discussed earlier in this chapter, the advantages of which were described then. Because Level I "inquiry" is highly manageable and the learning outcome is predictable, it is probably best for teaching some basic concepts and principles. Students who never experience learning beyond Level I are missing an opportunity to engage their highest mental operations, and they seldom (or never) get to experience more motivating, real-life problem solving. Furthermore, those students may come away with the false notion that problem solving (and sciencing) is a linear process, which it is not. As illustrated in Figure 1.6 (page 25) of Chapter 1, true inquiry is cyclic rather than linear. Therefore, Level I is *not* true inquiry, because it is a linear process. Real-world problem solving is a cyclic rather than linear process. In science (and in social science), addressing a problem is a cyclic rather than a linear process. One enters the cycle whenever a discrepancy or problem is observed and recognized, and that can occur at any point in the cycle.

TRUE INQUIRY

As clearly emphasized by the National Research Council's *National Science Education Standards*, students at all levels of science instruction should be provided experiences for true inquiry, which begins with Level II, whereby students, under the guidance of their teacher, actually decide and design processes for their inquiry. In true inquiry teachers emphasize the tentative nature of conclusions, which makes the activity more like real-life problem solving, in which decisions are always subject to revision if and when new data so prescribe.

At Level III inquiry students recognize and identify the problem, as well as decide the processes and reach a conclusion. Level III inquiry should be a major strategy for science instruction. And, in many exemplary schools that use cross-age teaching and interdisciplinary thematic instruction, that is often the case.

The program of study must emphasize student understanding through inquiry. Inquiry is a set of interrelated processes by which scientists and students pose questions about the natural world and investigate phenomena. . . . Inquiry is a critical component of a science program at all grade levels and in every domain of science, and designers of curricula and programs must be sure that the approach to content, as well as the teaching and assessment strategies, reflect the acquistion of scientific understandings through inquiry.[49]

In guided discovery, children are carefully escorted through an investigatory activity to discovery.

*As a result of activities in **grades K–8,** all students should develop abilities necessary to do scientific inquiry. Abilities that underlie this standard include*

- *Identify questions that can be answered through scientific investigations.*
- *Design and conduct a scientific investigation.*
- *Use appropriate tools and techniques to gather, analyze, and interpret data.*
- *Develop descriptions, explanations, predictions, and models using evidence.*
- *Think critically and logically to make the relationships between evidence and explanations.*
- *Recognize and analyze alternative explanations and predictions.*
- *Communicate scientific procedures and explanations, by communicating experimental methods, following instructions, describing observations, summarizing the results of other groups, and telling other students about investigations and explanations.*[50]

THE PROCESSES OR CRITICAL THINKING SKILLS OF DISCOVERY AND INQUIRY

In true inquiry, students generate ideas and then design ways to test those ideas. The various processes used represent the many critical thinking skills. Some of these skills are concerned with generating and organizing data; others are concerned with building and using ideas. As presented in Chapter 1, Figure 1.7 provides four main categories of these thinking processes and illustrates the place of each within the inquiry cycle. Some processes in the cycle are discovery processes and others are inquiry processes. Inquiry processes include the more complex mental operations (including all of those in the idea-using category). Students of the middle school years, because they are likely to be in the process of developing their higher-level thinking capabilities (see discussion of Piaget in Chapter 2), should be provided experiences that require these more complex, higher-level inquiry skills.

Inquiry learning is a higher-level mental operation that introduces the concept of the discrepant event, something that establishes cognitive disequilibrium (using the element of surprise, as discussed in Chapter 2) to help students develop skills in observing and being alert for discrepancies. Such a strategy provides opportunities for students to investigate their own ideas about explanations. Inquiry, like discovery, depends on skill in problem solving; the difference between the two is in the amount of decision-making responsibility given to students. Experiences in inquiry help students understand the importance of suspending judgment, as well as the tentativeness of answers and solutions. With these understandings, students eventually are better able to deal with life's problems and ambiguities.

INTEGRATING STRATEGIES FOR INTEGRATED LEARNING

Teaching strategies are often combined to establish the most effective teaching-learning experience. For example, in an integrated language arts program, teachers are interested in their students' speaking, reading, listening, thinking, study, and writing skills. These skills (and not textbooks) form a holistic process that is the primary aspect of integrated language arts.

In the area of speaking skills, oral discourse (discussion) in the classroom has a growing research base that promotes methods of teaching and learning through oral language. These methods include cooperative learning,[51] instructional scaffolding (such as with concept mapping),[52] and inquiry teaching.[53] Today's science teacher uses these techniques to help students not only to understand science but to develop holistic learning.

In cooperative learning groups, students discuss and use language for learning that benefits both their content learning and skills in social interaction. Working in heterogeneous groups, students participate in their own learning and can extend their knowledge base and cultural awareness with students of different ethnic backgrounds. When they share information and ideas, they are completing difficult learning tasks, using divergent thinking and decision making, and developing their understanding of science concepts. As issues are presented and responses are challenged, student thinking is clarified. Students assume the responsibility for planning within the group and for carrying out their assignments. When needed, the teacher models an activity with one group in front of the class, and when integrated with student questions, the modeling can become inquiry teaching.

Integrating strategies for integrated learning can include many activities, such as the following:

- *Brainstorming.* Members generate ideas related to a key word and record them. Clustering or chunking, mapping, and the Venn diagram (all discussed below) are variations of brainstorming.
- *Chunking.* Groups of students apply mental organizers by clustering information into chunks for easier manipulation and remembering.
- *Comparing and contrasting.* Similarities and differences between items are discovered and recorded.
- *Concept mapping.* (Discussed in Chapter 2.)
- *Inferring.* For instance, students assume the behaviors of animals (real or fictional) and infer their motives.

Comparing and contrasting are two important science process skills.

- *Making tests*. Each group creates a test and members of another group take it.
- *Memory strategies*. Sometimes information that is not connected to any prior knowledge must be learned by rote, such as memorizing a social security number. It is helpful to break the information to be learned into smaller chunks, such as dividing the eight digit social security number into smaller chunks of information (in this instance, each chunk separated by a hyphen). Learning by rote is also easier if a student can connect the information to be memorized to some prior knowledge. Strategies such as these are used to bridge the gap between rote learning and meaningful learning and are known as mnemonics (examples were presented in Chapter 2).
- *Outlining*. Each group completes an outline that contains some of the main ideas but with subtopics omitted.

- *Paraphrasing.* In a brief summary, each student restates a short selection from an author's text.
- *Reciprocal teaching.* In small group dialogue, students take turns at predicting, questioning, summarizing, and clarifying.
- *Study strategies, such as SQ4R.* Students *survey* the reading, ask *questions* about what was read, *read* to answer the questions, *recite* the answers, *record* important items in their notebooks, then *review* it all.
- *Summarizing.* Each student gives a brief oral summary to the whole group.
- *Think-pair-share.* A concept is presented by the teacher, and students are paired to discuss that concept. They share what they already know or have experienced about the concept, and then share that information with the rest of the class. This strategy is an excellent technique for preassessing and discovering student misconceptions. A modification on the technique is called *think-write-pair-share.* After thinking about and discussing the introduced concept, the pair of students writes their ideas about it before sharing their ideas with the entire group.
- *Vee mapping.* Vee mapping is a kind of road map completed by students, as they learn, showing the route they followed from prior knowledge to new and future knowledge.[54]
- *Venn diagraming.* Venn diagramming is a technique for comparing two concepts or explanations to a phenomenon to show similarities and differences. For example, a student is asked to draw two circles that intersect, mark the circles one and two, and where they intersect, mark that with a three. In circle one, the student lists characteristics of one explanation, and in circle 2, he lists the characteristics of the second. In the area of the intersection, marked 3, the student lists characteristics common to both explanations.

DEMONSTRATIONS

Students like demonstrations, especially when they are performed by the teacher, because the teacher is modeling scientific behavior and is actively engaged in a learning activity, rather than merely verbalizing about it. (Many demonstrations for science teaching are presented in the content section of Part II of this book.)

A demonstration can be designed to serve any of the following purposes:

- As a mind-capturing introduction to a lesson or unit of study
- As a review
- As an unusual closure to a lesson or unit of study
- To assist in the recognition of a solution to an existing problem
- To establish problem recognition
- To give students opportunity for vicarious participation in active learning
- To illustrate a particular point of content
- To reduce potential safety hazards (in which the teacher demonstrates, using materials too dangerous for student use)
- To save time and resources (as opposed to the entire class doing that which is demonstrated)
- To set up a discrepancy recognition

Guidelines for Using a Demonstration

When planning a demonstration, consider the following:

1. Decide which is the most effective way to conduct the demonstration, i.e., as a verbal or a silent demonstration; by a student or by the teacher; by the teacher with a student

helper; to the entire class or to small groups, or by a guest. An inquiry-based demonstration is usually much more effective than a teacher-centered procedure. Involve the students in the demonstration by asking them questions and allowing them to ask questions before, during, and after the demonstration.

2. Be sure that the demonstration is visible to all students.
3. Practice with the materials and procedure before demonstrating to the students; consider what might go wrong, because if anything can, it probably will.
4. Consider your pacing of the demonstration, allowing for enough wait-see and think time.
5. At the start of the demonstration explain its purpose and the learning objectives. Remember the adage: Tell them what you are going to do; show them; then tell them what they saw. As with any lesson, plan your demonstration closure and allow time for questions and discussion.
6. During the demonstration, as in other types of teacher talk, stop frequently to check for student understanding and to allow time for student questions.
7. Consider the use of special lighting to highlight the demonstration. For example, a slide projector can be used as a spotlight.
8. Be sure that the demonstration table and area are free of unnecessary objects that could distract, be in the way, or pose a safety hazard.
9. With potentially hazardous demonstrations, consider wearing safety goggles, having fire safety equipment at hand, or placing a protective shield between the demonstration table and nearby students.

TEXTBOOKS, SCIENCE PROGRAMS, AND OTHER PRINTED MATERIALS

Public schools have periodic textbook adoptions (usually every five years), after which the books are used for several years before the next adoption cycle. For you, the student teacher or first-year teacher, this means that most likely someone will tell you, "Here are the textbooks you will be using." Starting now you should become familiar with textbooks and programs you are likely to be using, and how they can be used.[55]

Because of several factors—the recognition of different individual learning styles of students, the increasing costs of textbooks and the decreasing availability of funds, and the availability of alternative learning materials—science textbook appearance, content, and use has changed considerably in recent years. For example, the State of Texas allows its schools to adopt Optical Data's Windows on Science videodisc-based program. The program comes with a Curriculum Publishing Kit that allows teachers to design their own curriculum from the Windows on Science program, and users periodically receive updated data discs. For specific curriculum areas, Texas, Utah, and West Virginia were the first states to provide schools the option to choose between a textbook-centered program and one that is videodisc centered. By the time you read this, other states have probably done likewise.

How can science textbooks (or media programs) be of help? Textbooks can be of help because they can provide an organization of basic or important content, previously tested activities and suggestions for learning experiences, information about other readings and resources to enhance the learning experiences of students, and a base for building higher-order thinking activities that help develop critical thinking skills.

The student science textbook, however, should not be the "be all and end all" of the instructional experience. The textbook is just one of many teaching tools and should not be cherished as the ultimate word. Of the many methods for using student textbooks in science, the

Science textbooks can provide children with important content organization and resources in learning science.

least acceptable is to give in to a complete dependence on a single book and require students simply to memorize content from it. That is the lowest level of cognitive learning; furthermore, it implies that you are unaware of other significant reading materials and that you have nothing more to contribute to student learning.

Another potential problem caused by reliance on a single textbook is that because textbook publishers prepare books for use in a larger market, that is, for national or statewide use, your state and district-adopted textbook may not, in the minds of your school community, adequately address issues of special interest and importance to your community of students and their parents or guardians.[56]

Still another problem caused by reliance on a single source is that for many students the adopted textbook may just not be one at the appropriate reading level. The reading level in a classroom of students can range by as much as two-thirds of the chronological age of the students in the class. This means that if the chronological age is 9 years (typical for fourth-grade students), then the reading-level range would be 6 years; that is, the class may include students reading at only a first-grade level and others reading at a middle school (seventh-grade) level.

All teachers need to devote time to helping their students develop their reading skills. All teachers need to know about the various kinds of problems readers can experience. All teachers share the responsibility of assuring that students with such difficulties get help in developing their skills in reading.

Guidelines for Using the Science Textbook

There are a number of general guidelines about the use of the textbook in science teaching. We believe that even in programs that are materials-centered, students benefit from having a science textbook, and that textbook should be the current edition. However, because of budget constraints experienced by many school districts today, the textbook may not be the current edition; in some schools students may have to share a book, in which case they may not always be allowed to take the books home. And in yet other classrooms there may be no textbook at all.

Teachers should maintain supplementary reading materials for student use in the classroom. School and community librarians are usually delighted to cooperate in the selection and provision of such materials.

Some students may benefit from the drill, practice, and reinforcement afforded by accompanying science workbooks, but this does not mean that all students benefit from an identical activity. The traditional science workbook, now nearly extinct, is being replaced with materials and units from activity-centered programs (see Figures 3.10 and 3.11) or by programs made possible through modern technology afforded by computer software, CD-ROMs and videodisc programs.

It is important to help students learn how to read and comprehend from their science books. Because science books have their own modes of presentation, styles of language, logic, and density of ideas, it is helpful to students for their teachers to read aloud to them from their science books, and to model thinking skills by thinking aloud about what is being read.[57] Provide vocabulary lists to help students learn meanings of important words and phrases. Teach students how to study from their textbook, perhaps by using the SQ4R method mentioned earlier.

Progressing from one cover of the textbook to the other within the school year is not necessarily indicative of good science teaching. Encourage students to search other sources for content to update the textbook. This is especially important in those areas of science where there is tremendous change and growth in information, and when the student textbook is several years old.

Encourage students to be alert for errors in the textbook, perhaps giving them some sort of credit reward, such as points, when they bring an error to your attention. Such incentives promote critical reading, critical thinking, and healthy skepticism.

When possible, individualize learning for students of varying reading and learning abilities and cultural backgrounds. Consider differentiated reading assignments, in the textbook and in supplementary materials.

Within the span of your professional career you may witness and be a part of a revolution in the design of school textbooks. The prediction has been made that with the revolution in microcomputer chip technology student textbooks will soon take on a whole new appearance. With that will come dramatic changes in the importance and use of student texts, as well as new problems for the teacher, some of which are predictable. Student "texts" may become credit-card size, increasing the chance of students "losing their books." On the positive side, it is probable that the classroom teacher will have available a variety of "textbooks" to better address the reading levels, interests, learning styles, intelligences, and abilities of

Name	Grades	Address	Characteristics
AIMS	K–8	Creative Teaching Associates P.O. Box 8120 Fresno, CA 93747	*Activities for Integrating Math and Science.* Integration of math skills with science processes in a series of investigatory activities; accompanying teacher booklets.
BSCS	K–6	Kendall/Hunt 4050 Westmark Drive Dubuque, IA 52004	*Science for Life and Living: Integrating Science, Technology, and Health.* A complete curriculum with designated scope and sequence organized around themes, using the "5Es" approach: students are engaged in activities, then they explore, explain, elaborate, and evaluate to construct their own understanding of the concept being investigated.
ESS	K–6	Delta Education P.O. Box 916 Hudson, NH 03051-0915	*Elementary Science Study.* A program of 56 nonsequential, open-ended exploratory activities that are not grade-level specific.
FOSS	3–6	Encyclopaedia Britannica Educational Corporation 310 S. Michigan Ave., 6th Floor Chicago, IL 60604-9839	*Full Option Science System.* Designed for both regular and special education students. 16 modules with lab kits, including: measurement; earth materials; physics of sound; structures of life; solar energy.
GEMS	P–10	Lawrence Hall of Science University of California Berkeley, CA 94720	*Great Explorations in Math and Science.* A series of more than 40 teacher's guides for hands-on learning activities using easily obtained materials. Sample titles are: *Animal Defenses; Hide a Butterfly; Investigating Artifacts; Fingerprinting; Oobleck; Vitamin C Testing; Bubble-Ology; Earthworms; and Global Warming.*
HumBio	6–9	Addison-Wesley 2725 Sand Hill Road Menlo Park, CA 94025	*Human Biology Middle Grades Curriculum Project.* Developed at Stanford University and expected to be available for the 1996–97 school year, this project consists of activity-based curriculum units specifically developed for middle school students. The more than 20 unit titles include: *The Changing Body; Reproduction; Sexuality; Becoming an Adult; Your Place in the History of Life.*
IUES	K–6	Educational Development Center 55 Chapel St. Newton, MA 02160	*Improving Urban Elementary Science.* This program contains open-ended, activity-based modules.
NGKN	4–6	Technical Education Resources 1696 Massachusetts Ave., Cambridge, MA 02138	*National Geographic Kids Network.* Extended problem-centered units, computer networked with scientists.
OBIS	(Ages 10–15)	Delta Education P.O. Box 915 Hudson, NH 03051-0915	*Outdoor Biology Instructional Strategies.* Program of outdoor activity packets originally developed at the Lawrence Hall of Science (University of California, Berkeley).
STC	1–6	Carolina Biological Supply 2700 York Road Burlington, NC 27215	*Science and Technology for Children.* Units of hands-on instruction that integrate science and mathematics with other disciplines. A primary focus of program developers is to interest more females and and minority children in science. STC is a science curriculum development project of the National Science Resources Center (NRSC). Many units are completed (e.g., *Organisms; The Life Cycle of Butterflies; Chemical Tests; Electric Circuits; Floating and Sinking*), and others are in various stages of development.
SAPA	K–6	Delta Education P.O. Box 915 Hudson, NH 03051-0915	*Science: A Process Approach.* Highly structured, process-oriented and module-based, developed around sequenced objectives.
SAVI/SELPH	2–10	Center for Multisensory Learning Lawrence Hall of Science University of California Berkeley, CA 94720	*Science Activities for the Visually Impaired/Science Enrichment Learning for the Physically Handicapped.* Nine modules for disabled students in special classes or included in regular classrooms.
SCIS 3	K–6	Delta Education P.O. Box 915 Hudson, NH 03051-0915	*Science Curriculum Improvement Study.* Originally developed by a team at the University of California, Berkeley, there have been several generations of SCIS, with the most recent being SCIS 3. The SCIS programs are built around a hierarchy of science concepts. Process skills are integrated into the activities-centered program, which uses an inductive approach and a three-phase learning cycle: (1) student exploration, (2) concept explanation, and (3) concept application.
TOPS	3–10	TOPS Learning Systems 10970 S. Mulino Rd. Canby, OR 97013	Structured hands-on activity modules that are not sequenced. Sample modules include *Balancing, Electricity, Magnetism, Pendulums, Metric Measure, Animal Survival,* and *Green Thumbs.*

FIGURE 3.10 Elementary and middle school science curriculum projects.

Publishers	Program Name	Grades	Address
Addison-Wesley	Destinations in Science	K-6	2725 Sand Hill Road
	Science Insights	6–9	Menlo Park, CA 94025
Curriculum Research and Development Group	Foundational Approaches in Science Teaching (FAST)	6–9	University of Hawaii 1776 University Avenue Honolulu, HI 96822
Glencoe/McGraw-Hill	Life Science	6–9	P.O. Box 544
	Physical Science	6–9	Blacklick, OH 43004-0544
	Earth Science	6–9	
Harcourt Brace	HBJ Science (Nova)	K–6	Harcourt Brace School Publishers
	Holt Science	K–6	Orlando, FL 32887
	Concepts in Science	K–9	
	Science Anytime	K–6	
Holt, Rinehart and Winston	Holt Science	7–9	1120 South Capital of Texas Hwy. Austin, TX 78746-6487
	HBJ Science	7–9	
	Science Plus	7–9	
Houghton Mifflin	Spaceship Earth	7–8	One Beacon Street Boston, MA 02108
Macmillan/McGraw Hill	Macmillan Life Science	6–9	School Division
	Macmillan Earth Science	6–9	1221 Avenue of the Americas
	Macmillan Physical Science	6–9	New York, NY 10020
	Journeys in Science	K–6	
	Merrill Science	K–6	
	Macmillan/McGraw-Hill Science	K–8	
Prentice Hall	PH Science Integrated Learning System	6–9	School Division
	PH Earth Science	6–9	1 Lake Street
	PH Physical Science	6–9	Upper Saddle River, NJ 07458
	PH Life Science	6–9	
	General Science: A Voyage	6–9	
Scott, Foresman and Co.	Discover the Wonder	K–6	1900 E. Lake Ave.
	Discover Science	K–6	Glenview, IL 60025
	SF Discover Science	K–6	
	SF Life Science	7–9	
	SF Earth Science	7–9	
	SF Physical Science	7–9	
Silver Burdett Ginn	Science Horizons	K–6	299 Jefferson Rd.
	Silver Burdett & Ginn Science	K–6	P.O. Box 480
	Life Science	7–9	Parsippany, NJ 07054
	Earth Science	7–9	
	Physical Science	7–9	
	General Science	7–8	

FIGURE 3.11   Sample listing of elementary and middle school science textbook programs.

individual students. The responsibility for distribution and maintenance of these materials could create an even greater demand on the teacher's time. In any case, dramatic and exciting events have begun to happen to a teaching tool that previously had not changed much throughout the history of education in this country. As an electronic, multimedia tool, the textbook of the twenty-first century will likely be an interactive device that offers text, sound, and video.

ASSIGNMENTS AND HOMEWORK

Whether completed at home or at school, assignments can ease student learning in many ways, such as:

- Constructively extending the time that students are engaged in on-task learning.
- Helping students to develop personal learning.

While learning science, children are encouraged to develop their research skills.

- Helping students to organize their learning.
- Helping students to practice research and study skills.
- Individualizing the learning.
- Involving parents in their students' learning.
- Providing a mechanism whereby students receive constructive feedback from the teacher.
- Providing an opportunity for the teacher to discover student misconceptions.
- Providing students with opportunity to review and practice what has been learned.
- Reinforcing classroom experiences.
- Teaching new content.

Guidelines for Using Assignments and Homework

Plan early the types of assignments you will give (e.g., daily and long-range, minor and major, to be completed in class or at home), and prepare assignment specifications and, in some cases, scoring rubrics (see Chapter 6). Assignments must correlate with specific instructional objectives and should never be given as "busywork" or as punishment.

Written work reinforces the learning process and helps children develop their skills in written expression.

As mentioned earlier, every teacher must give attention to the development of students' reading and writing skills. This attention should be obvious in your assignment specifications and in your assignment grading policy. Homework assignments should "arouse student curiosity, raise questions for further exploration, and foster the self-discipline required for independent study."[58] Furthermore, constructive and corrective feedback from the teacher on the homework, and grading of homework, raises the positive contributions of homework dramatically.[59]

Provide differentiated assignments, that is, assignment variations given to or selected by students on the basis of their interests and abilities. To accomplish the same objective, students can select or be assigned different activities, such as "read and discuss," or they can participate with others in a more direct learning experience. After completion, they share what they have learned.

Determine the resources that students will need to complete assignments, and check the availability of those resources. In this regard, the school librarian is an excellent source of help.

Follow up on assignments. If they are important for students to do, then you must give your full attention to the product of their efforts. Read everything they write. Students are more willing to do an assignment when they believe it is useful, when teachers treat it as an integral part of instruction, when it is evaluated by the teacher, and when it counts as a part of the grade.[60]

Children should be given ample opportunity to present their ideas, opinions, and knowledge gained from their own individual and small-group investigations.

Provide written or oral responses to each student's work, and be positive and constructive in those comments. Always think about the written comments that you make to be relatively certain that they will convey your intended meaning to the students. When writing comments on their papers, you may want to consider using a color other than red. To many people, red has negative connotations—blood, hurt, danger, stop. Use positive reward reinforcers as frequently as possible in order to continue to encourage, rather than discourage, students.

When giving assignments in class, it is best to write them on the board or on an assignment sheet for each student, with extra care to be sure that assignment specifications are clear. Never call out assignments as students are leaving the classroom.

Maintain assignment due dates, allowing, of course, for legitimate and reasonable excuses. Consider permitting students to select their due dates from a list of options.

Allow time in class for students to begin work on homework assignments, so that you can give individual attention to those who need help.

Finally, use caution whenever you plan to give an assignment that could be controversial or that could pose a safety hazard to students. In such cases, especially if you are new to the community, before giving the assignment you may wish to talk it over with other teachers or the principal. You may also want to have students obtain parental permission to do an assignment.

Airports, Apiaries, Aquariums, Archeological digs, Automobile service stations, Backyards, Bird and wildlife sanctuaries, Botanical gardens, Buildings under construction, Chemical plants, Dairies, Farms, Fire departments, Flower shows, Forests and forest preserves, Gardens, Gas companies, Geological sites, Gravel pits, Greenhouses, Health departments, clinics, and hospitals, Heating plants, Highway construction sites, Industrial plants, Lumber companies, Mines, Museums, Nature preserves, Newspaper plants, Observatories, Orchards, Parks, Photography establishments, Planetariums, Power plants, Quarries, Radio stations, Recycling centers, Research laboratories, Sanitation departments, Sawmills, Scientific supply companies, Shorelines (streams, lakes, oceans), Telecommunications centers, Telephone companies, Television stations, Universities and colleges, Water reservoir and treatment plants, Wildlife parks and preserves, Weather bureau and storm centers, Zoos

FIGURE 3.12   Possible field trip locations.

EXTENSIONS OF THE CLASSROOM: THE COMMUNITY AS A LABORATORY AND RESOURCE

Teachers identify and use resources outside the school.[61]

One of the richest resources for learning science is the local community, and the people and places in it. You will want to build your own file of community resources—speakers, sources of free materials, and field trip locations. Your school may already have a community resource file available for your use. However, it may need updating.

A community resource file should contain information about (a) possible field trip locations, (b) community resource people who can serve as guest speakers or mentors, and (c) local agencies that can provide information and instructional materials. Figure 3.12 lists some of the places that can be visited in cities, towns, or rural areas with profitable results for the learning of science.

Field trips to community locations can make the instruction real, exciting, and educationally valuable for the students, but, when not carefully planned and carried out, a field trip can cause you more grief than you could ever imagine.

The Field Trip

For many teachers and schools, the term *field trip* is interpreted as a visit by the teacher and students to a museum, aquarium, planetarium, or industrial plant. Actually, the term has a broader and more inclusive meaning. The field trip is normally thought of as any learning activity that is carried on by the students as a group outside the classroom, such as an excursion to a somewhat distant location, or simply moving from the classroom to a stream on or near the school grounds. But a field trip may also be taken without leaving the classroom. For example, at Romeville Elementary School, in St. James Parish, Louisiana, students use the interactive multimedia program by IBM and Children's Television Workshop (CTW), *Nature of Science Visit Series* (grades 1–6) that allows students to take field trips, such as a trip to the seashore, right in the classroom, to learn about the relationships of animals and their environment. However, in this section we will be dealing with the traditional away-from-the classroom field trip.

Rather than a simple change in location accompanied by an abstract and boring lecture by someone not directly affiliated with the school, the field trip should provide the students firsthand observations and even hands-on (concrete) experiences with materials and phenomena that cannot usually be brought into the classroom. A field trip often enables students to see these things in their natural relationships. It can help them to see more clearly how the science content they have learned applies to their environment.

When visiting industries in their community, museums containing indigenous materials, or geographical points of interest, students can begin to understand and appreciate the contributions of their community to the state, area, or country. The field trip has the added advantage of being an activity that lends itself very easily to integration with other phases of the school's curriculum. There will be reading, oral and written reports to do, and letters to write. There will undoubtedly be implications for social studies, problems in mathematics, and a need for artwork.

WAYS OF USING FIELD TRIPS

A field trip can be used (1) as an introduction to a unit of instruction, (2) to obtain information during the study of a unit, or (3) as a culminating activity at the end of a unit.

To Introduce a Unit   This purpose is particularly effective when the students have had little or no experience with the topic to be studied. The field trip then serves as a motivating factor to create interest in the topic. Thus, the students are able to obtain an overview of the topic and a desire to learn more about it. When using a field trip to introduce a unit, keep in mind that the main purpose is to arouse interest and to raise questions or problems, not especially to find answers. If you use a field trip to introduce a unit, it is often beneficial, later or at the end of the study, to return to the field trip site or to invite a resource person to class so as to bring closure to the unit, particularly if questions have been raised during the study that warrant such a culminating activity.

During the Unit   While studying a unit, students can use a field trip to find answers to their questions and problems, as well as to check on previous experiments, readings, discussions, and conclusions. In addition, a field trip at this time may raise further questions and problems that lead into the next phase of the unit.

As a Culminating Activity   The field trip can also be used to summarize highlights or important understandings of a science topic that students have been studying. It can help fix the learning firmly in the students' minds. As the final activity for a unit of study, it gives students an opportunity to observe those things they have been reading and studying about.

PLANNING A FIELD TRIP

To prepare for and carry out a field trip, there are three important areas of planning to consider. These are (1) details of preparation before the field trip occurs, (2) planning the details of the actual trip, and (3) planning follow-up activities. The following paragraphs consider guidelines for each.

Before the Field Trip   Today's public schools often have only limited funds to support transportation and insurance costs for field trips, and some have no field trip funds at all. Sometimes, when field trip funds are lacking, parent-teacher and civic organizations supply the financial resources necessary to ensure that students get these valuable firsthand experiences. When thinking about and planning a particular field trip for your students, follow these steps:

1. Discuss your idea for a field trip with the principal or your colleagues, especially when transportation will be needed, before introducing it to the students. There is no purpose served in getting students excited about a field trip before you are sure the trip is feasible. Furthermore, if most of your students have made the same trip during a prior school experience, it may not be worth repeating.

2. Once you have obtained initial approval from school officials, take the trip yourself, if possible. A pre-visit allows you to determine how to make the field trip most productive and to discover the arrangements that will be necessary. If you cannot make a pre-visit, you will still need to get information and arrange for (1) enroute travel directions, (2) scheduling of arrival and departure times, (3) parking, (4) briefing by the host, if there is one, (5) storage of students' personal items, such as coats and lunches, (6) provisions for eating and rest rooms, and (7) fees, if any. If there are fees connected with the field trip, you need to talk with your administration about who will pay the fees. If paid by students or their parents and guardians, what about those who may not be able to afford the fee? Is any student going to say, "I can't afford it"? If the trip is worth taking, the school should cover the costs. If that isn't possible, then perhaps financial support can be obtained from the school's parent-teacher organization or another source. If this is not an option, perhaps you should consider an alternative experience that doesn't involve costs to students. No student should ever be left out of a field trip because of lack of money, or because of the student's race, religion, or ethnicity. When planning a field trip, avoid scheduling it on a religious holiday.

3. Arrange for official permission from the school administration. There is probably a school or district form for planning and reporting field trips.

4. You can now discuss the field trip with your students and arrange for permissions from their parents or guardians. You must realize that although parents or guardians sign official permission forms allowing their children to participate in a field trip, these are only forms that show that parents and adult guardians are aware of what is going on. Although the permission form should also include a statement that the parent absolves the teacher and the school from liability should an accident occur, that does not lessen the teacher's and school's responsibilities during the off-campus trip if there is negligence by a teacher, driver, or chaperone.

5. Arrange for students to be excused from their other classes while on the field trip. Using an information form prepared and signed by you, and perhaps by the principal, the students should then assume responsibility for notifying their other teachers of the planned absence from classes, and for making up whatever work is missed because of the field trip. In addition, you will need to see that arrangements are made for your other teaching duties left "uncovered." Teachers in some schools cooperate by covering classes for teachers who will be gone. In other schools, substitute teachers are hired. Teachers in some schools, where budgets are limited, must hire their own substitutes.

6. Arrange for necessary transportation. Your principal, or the principal's designee, will help you with the details. Although sometimes unavoidable, the use of private automobiles is not recommended, because the teacher and the school could be liable for the acts of the drivers.

7. Arrange for collection of any money that is needed for fees. If there are out-of-pocket costs to be paid by the students, this information must be included on the parental permission form.

8. Plan the details for student safety and the monitoring of safety from departure to return. Included should be a first-aid kit and the use of a system of student control, such as a "buddy system," whereby students travel in pairs and must remain paired throughout the trip. The pairs are given numbers that are recorded and kept by the teacher and the chaperones. The pairs should be checked at departure time, periodically during the trip, and upon arrival back at school.

9. Plan for adult chaperones to travel with the class field trip. As a rule of thumb, there should be one adult supervisor for every ten students.

10. Plan the complete route and schedule, including all stops along the way. If transportation is being provided, you may need to discuss the route with whoever is providing the transportation.

11. Establish and discuss rules of behavior with the students. Included in this discussion should be details of the trip, its purpose, directions about where they are going, what they should wear and bring, your academic expectations of them (consider giving each student some sort of study guide) and of the follow-up activities. Include information about what to do if anything should go awry, for example, if a student is late for the departure or return, loses a personal possession, gets lost along the way, is injured, becomes sick, or misbehaves. (In regard to the last circumstance, never send a misbehaving student back to school alone. While on a field trip, all students should be under the direct supervision of an adult always.) Involve the adult chaperones in the pre-visit discussion.

12. If a field trip is supposed to promote some kind of learning, as is probably the case, then to avoid leaving the learning to happen by chance, the learning expectations need to be clearly defined and the students given an explanation of how and where they may encounter the learning experience. Before the field trip, students should be pretested with, "What do we know about _____?" What do we want to find out about _____?" How can we find out?" and then an appropriate guide can be prepared for the students to use during the field trip.

13. Plan follow-up activities. As with any other lesson plan, the field trip lesson is complete when it has, in addition to a proper introduction, a well-planned closure.

During the Field Trip   If your field trip has been carefully planned according to the preceding guidelines, then it should be a valuable and safe experience for all. While at the field trip location, you and your adult chaperones should monitor student behavior and learning just as you do in the classroom.

On the field trip students may take notes and follow a prepared study guide. You may want to take recorders and cameras so records of the experience can be shared in class upon return. All sorts of field trip follow-up activities can be planned as an educational wrap-up to this valuable and exciting firsthand experience. For example, a bulletin board committee can plan and execute an attractive bulletin board display summarizing the experience. Students can write about their experiences in their journals. Small groups can give oral reports to the entire class about what they experienced and learned. These reports can then serve as springboards for further class discussion.

After the Field Trip   Follow-up activities must be planned carefully and should come soon after the field trip. When the students are in class the next day, it would be wise to recall things they saw or did, to review any recordings made, and to review their study guide activities. The intent of follow-up activities is to establish understandings, highlight relationships, and arrive at conclusions.

During follow-up you should be prepared for new questions that may be raised as a result of the field trip. If these questions are related to the unit being studied, they can serve as springboards for further study. If the questions are in areas unrelated to the science content, they may provide excellent leads for future units, for integration with other disciplines, or for discussions with special resource persons, such as a guest speaker. In any case, such new questions will help students develop meaningful learning about the unit.

The follow-up is the time for the teacher and the students to prepare necessary thank-you letters to persons who made the field trip possible. It is not advisable to make the follow-up a test, a procedure that could spoil the field trip for the students and destroy their interest in subsequent trips. Finally, for future planning, all who were involved should contribute to an evaluation of the field trip.

Summary

In this chapter we have discussed and presented guidelines for the use of specific strategies for teaching, some of which are fundamental to good science teaching. However, methods without visual and audio instructional supplements would be empty and boring indeed. For teaching science, there are a large variety of aids and resources from which you can select. Those aids and resources are the topic of the next chapter.

Questions for Class Discussion

1. Explain any reservations you have about teaching by inquiry.
2. Divide into teams, and have each team build a working activity center for teaching science at a particular grade level. Share your centers with the rest of your class.
3. Identify a specific science concept and explain how you would teach toward an understanding of that concept to students in the first, fourth, and sixth grades.
4. Return to the "experiment that failed," the expanding balloon experiment, discussed in this chapter. Discuss how the teacher's experience could have been a Level I inquiry, a Level II inquiry, and a Level III inquiry. At which level of inquiry do you believe the teacher actually handled the experiment that failed? Why?
5. When helping students understand a concept in science, should the teacher first assess what the students already know about it? Explain why or why not. If so, how would you do it?
6. Identify ways that a field trip can be planned to incorporate the three phases of learning: input of data, processing of data, and application of data; or the three stages of Piaget's learning cycle: exploration, invention, and discovery.
7. Explain the concept of multilevel teaching. Describe a situation in which you would use multilevel teaching.
8. Describe any concepts you held that changed as a result of your experiences with this chapter. Describe the changes.
9. From your recent observations and field work as related to this teacher preparation program, clearly identify one specific example of educational practice that seems contradictory to exemplary practice or theory as presented in this chapter. Present your explanation for the discrepancy.
10. Do you have any questions about the content of this chapter? How might answers be found?

Notes

1. Reprinted from *National Science Education Standards* © 1996 National Academy of Sciences, p. 32. Courtesy of National Academy Press, Washington, DC.
2. Clearly at least some of these ten behaviors are also instructional strategies (questioning, for example). While the behaviors must be in place for the most effective teaching to occur, the strategies (as discussed later) are more or less discretionary—that is, they are pedagogical techniques the teacher may select but is not obligated to use. For example, questioning and the use of silence are fundamental teaching behaviors, whereas lecturing and showing slides are not.
3. Reprinted from *National Science Education Standards* © 1996 National Academy of Sciences, p. 43. Courtesy of National Academy Press, Washington, DC.
4. For example, there is a certain amount of risk-taking associated with hands-on inquiry teaching as opposed to the traditional, teacher-centered way of teaching science. See Alan D. Rossman, "Managing Hands-On Inquiry," *Science and Children* 31(1):35–37 (September 1993).

5. Reprinted from *National Science Education Standards* © 1996 National Academy of Sciences, pp. 45–46. Courtesy of National Academy Press, Washington, DC.

6. Carol Seefeldt and Nita Barbour, *Early Childhood Education: An Introduction.* 3d ed. (New York: Macmillan, 1994), p. 284.

7. Jacob S. Kounin, *Discipline and Group Management in Classrooms* (New York: Holt, Rinehart and Winston, 1970).

8. A. L. Costa, *The School as a Home for the Mind* (Palatine, IL: Skylight Publishing, 1991), p. 54.

9. See H. J. Walberg, "Productive Teaching and Instruction: Assessing the Knowledge Base," *Phi Delta Kappan* 71(6):470–478 (February 1990).

10. Thomas L. Good and Jere E. Brophy, *Looking in Classrooms.* 6th ed. (New York: HarperCollins, 1994), pp. 148–149.

11. For a concrete example of asking a student to elaborate in a constructivist sixth-grade science classroom, see Jacqueline G. Brooks and Martin G. Brooks, *In Search of Understanding: The Case for Constructivist Classrooms* (Arlington, VA: Association for Supervision and Curriculum Development, 1993), p. 66.

12. Costa, *The School as a Home for the Mind,* p. 63.

13. Arthur L. Costa, *The Enabling Behaviors* (Orangevale, CA: Search Models Unlimited, 1989). This three-tiered model of thinking has been described variously by others. For example, in Elliot Eisner's *The Educational Imagination* (Macmillan, 1979), the levels are referred to as "descriptive," "interpretive," and "evaluative." For a comparison of thinking models, see Costa, *The School as a Home for the Mind,* p. 44.

14. R. N. Caine and G. Caine, "Understanding a Brain-Based Approach to Learning and Teaching," *Educational Leadership* 48(2) (October 1990), p. 69.

15. See, for example, J. B. Beaver and B. D. Cheney, "What's Wrong with This Picture?" *Science and Children* 26(4):28–29 (January 1989); and C. L. Thompson, "Discrepant Events: What Happens to Those Who Watch?" *School Science and Mathematics* 89(1):26–29 (January 1989).

16. See, for example, B. Newton, "Theoretical Basis for Higher Cognitive Questioning—An Avenue to Critical Thinking," *Education* 98(3):286–290 (March-April 1978); and D. Redfield and E. Rousseau, "A Meta-Analysis of Experimental Research on Teacher Questioning Behavior," *Review of Educational Research* 51(2):237–245 (Summer 1981).

17. Brooks and Brooks, *In Search of Understanding,* p. 105.

18. For wait-time studies, now classics in science education, see M. B. Rowe, "Wait-Time and Rewards as Instructional Variables, Their Influence on Language, Logic and Fate Control: Part One—Wait-Time," *Journal of Research in Science Teaching* 11(2):81–94 (June 1974); and M. B. Rowe, "Wait-Time: Slowing Down May Be a Way of Speeding Up," *American Educator* 11(1):38–47 (Spring 1987). For a further discussion of the importance of wait-time in a constructivist classroom, see Brooks and Brooks, *In Search of Understanding,* pp. 114–115.

19. For further discussion of research findings on the use of praise and rewards in teaching, see B. Joyce and B. Showers, *Student Achievement Through Staff Development* (New York: Longman, 1988); and M. Lepper and D. Green (eds.), *The Hidden Cost of Rewards: New Perspectives on the Psychology of Human Motivation* (New York: Erlbaum, 1978).

20. See Linda Lingenfelter Kulas, "I Wonder . . . Teaching Through Children's Questions Leads to a Rich, Student-Driven Science Curriculum," *Science and Children* 32(4):16–18, 32 (January 1995).

21. L. B. Resnick and L. E. Klopfer (eds.), *Toward the Thinking Curriculum: Current Cognitive Research,* 1989 ASCD Yearbook (Alexandria, VA: Association for Supervision and Curriculum Development, 1989), p. 5.

22. Reprinted from *National Science Education Standards* © 1996 National Academy of Sciences, p. 32. Courtesy of National Academy Press, Washington, DC.

23. M. Haberman, "The Pedagogy of Poverty Versus Good Teaching," *Phi Delta Kappan* 73(4) (December 1991), p. 293.

24. Reprinted from *National Science Education Standards* © 1996 National Academy of Sciences, p. 32. Courtesy of National Academy Press, Washington, DC.

25. See, for example, Richard D. Kellough, *Integrating Mathematics and Science for Kindergarten and Primary Children* and *Integrating Mathematics and Science for Intermediate and Middle School Students* (Columbus, OH: Prentice Hall, 1996).

26. Rita Dunn, *Strategies for Educating Diverse Learners,* Fastback 384 (Bloomington, IN: Phi Delta Kappa Educational Foundation, 1995), p. 13.

27. For various strategies regarding consequences for misbehavior, see Eleanor B. Baron, *Discipline Strategies for Teachers,* Fastback 344 (Bloomington, IN: Phi Delta Kappa Educational Foundation, 1992); and Jack Blendinger et al., *Win-Win Discipline,* Fastback 353 (Bloomington, IN: Phi Delta Kappa Educational Foundation, 1993).

28. Reprinted from *National Science Education Standards* © 1996 National Academy of Sciences, p. 44. Courtesy of National Academy Press, Washington, DC.
29. See H. Stein, "On That Note . . .," *Science and Children* 26(3):16–18 (November-December 1988).
30. As used in Allan G. Glatthorn, *Developing a Quality Curriculum* (Alexandria, VA: Association for Supervision and Curriculum Development, 1994), pp. 104–105.
31. See Benjamin Bloom, *Human Characteristics and School Learning* (New York: McGraw-Hill, 1987); and John Carroll, "A Model of School Learning," *Teachers College Record* 64(8):723–733 (May 1963).
32. See, for example, Frank N. Dempster, "Exposing Our Students to Less Should Help Them Learn More," *Phi Delta Kappan* 74(6):433–437 (February 1993).
33. Cheryl T. Desmond, "A Comparison of the Assessment of Mastery in an Outcome-Based School and a Coalition of Essential Skills School." Paper presented at the annual meeting of the American Educational Research Association, San Francisco, April 20–24, 1992.
34. Lowell Horton, *Mastery Learning*, Fastback 154 (Bloomington, IN: Phi Delta Kappa Educational Foundation, 1981), p. 9.
35. Adapted from Horton, *Mastery Learning*, pp. 15–18.
36. For an example of cross-age tutoring and the rationale as to why it is developmentally appropriate for use in middle school instruction, see Robert L. Gilstrap, et al. *Improving Instruction in Middle Schools*, Fastback 331 (Bloomington, IN: Phi Delta Kappa Educational Foundation, 1992), p. 22; and, for an account of sixth graders tutoring first graders, see Walter S. Smith and Cindy Burrichter, "Look Who's Teaching Science Today," *Science and Children* 30(7):20–23 (April 1993).
37. For examples of the use of learning centers and the rationale as to why the learning center is developmentally appropriate for use in middle school classrooms, see Gilstrap, *Improving Instruction in Middle Schools*, pp. 18–20.
38. Allan A. Glatthorn, *Developing A Quality Curriculum* (Alexandria, VA: Association for Supervision and Curriculum Development, 1994), p. 105.
39. See, for example, Spencer Kagan, "Group Grades Miss the Mark," *Educational Leadership* 52(8):68–71 (May 1995); Spencer Kagan, "Avoiding the Group-Grades Trip," *Learning* 24(4):56–58 (January/February 1996); and David W. Johnson and Roger T. Johnson, "The Role of Cooperative Learning in Assessing and Communicating Student Learning," Chapter 4 of Thomas R. Guskey (ed.), *Communicating Student Learning*, the ASCD 1996 Yearbook (Alexandria, VA: Association for Supervision and Curriculum Development, 1996).
40. See, for example, Kathy H. Barclay and Camille Breheny, "Letting the Children Take Over More of Their Own Learning: Collaborative Research in the Kindergarten Classroom," *Young Children* 49(6):33–39 (September 1994).
41. To read how one teacher uses the roundtable method, see Lyn Le Countryman, "Making Science Recent, Relevant, and Responsive," *Science Scope* 17(8):21–23 (May 1994).
42. See, for example, Barbara Means and Michael S. Knapp, "Cognitive Approaches to Teaching Advanced Skills to Educationally Disadvantaged Students," *Phi Delta Kappan* 73(4):282–289 (December 1991).
43. Betty Vetter, "Ferment: Yes; Progress: Maybe; Change: Slow," *Mosaic* 23(3):34–41 (Fall 1992).
44. Arthur N. Applebee et al., *The Writing Report Card: Writing Achievement in American Schools* (Princeton, NJ: National Assessment of Educational Progress, 1986).
45. See, for example, Arthur Whimbey, "Test Results from Teaching Thinking," in Arthur L. Costa (ed.), *Developing Minds: A Resource Book for Teaching Thinking* (Alexandria, VA: Association for Supervision and Curriculum Development, 1985), pp. 269–271; Children's Defense Fund, *Making the Middle Grades Work* (Washington, DC: Author, 1988), California State Department of Education, *Caught in the Middle* (Sacramento, CA: Author, 1987); and, Carnegie Council for Adolescent Development, *Turning Points: Preparing American Youth for the 21st Century* (Washington, DC: Author, 1989).
46. Barbara Z. Presseisen, *Implementing Thinking in the School's Curriculum*. Paper presented at the third Annual Meeting of the International Association for Cognitive Education, Riverside, California, February 9, 1992.
47. Costa, *The School as a Home for the Mind*, pp. 75–76.
48. Costa, *Developing Minds*, p. 312.
49. Reprinted from *National Science Education Standards* © 1996 National Academy of Sciences, p. 214. Courtesy of National Academy Press, Washington, DC.
50. Reprinted from *National Science Education Standards* © 1996 National Academy of Sciences National Academy Press, Washington, DC.
51. David W. Johnson and R. T. Johnson, *Learning Together and Alone*. 3d ed. (Boston: Allyn and Bacon, 1991).

52. Fran Lehr, "Instructional Scaffolding," *Language Arts* 62(1):667–672 (October 1985). See also theme issue "Thinking and Learning Across the Curriculum," *Journal of Reading* 34(7) (April 1991).
53. George Hillocks, Jr., *Research on Written Composition: New Directions for Teaching* (Urbana, IL: ERIC Clearinghouse on Reading and Communication Skills and the National Conference on Research in English, 1986).
54. For details on how to use Vee maps, see Wolff-Michael Roth and Guennadi Verechaka, "Plotting a Course with Vee Maps," *Science and Children* 30(4):24–27 (January 1993).
55. Each year, in January, the National Science Teachers Association publishes *NSTA Science Education Suppliers* as a supplement of *Science and Children, The Science Teacher,* and *Science and Scope.* The supplement provides a current list of publishers and descriptions of their products, including textbooks, program and resource materials, and trade books, as well as equipment, computer software, and other media. The supplement can be purchased directly from NSTA, 1840 Wilson Boulevard, Arlington, VA 22201-3000.
56. Twenty-four states use statewide textbook adoption review committees to review books and provide public school districts with lists of recommended books, from which a district may select its books and purchase them with stated-provided funds.
57. P. Young, C. Ruck, and B. Crocker, "Reading Science," *The Science Teacher* 58(2):46–49 (February 1991).
58. *Caught in the Middle* (Sacramento, CA: California State Department of Education, 1987), p. 30.
59. See H. J. Walberg, "Productive Teaching and Instruction: Assessing the Knowledge Base," *Phi Delta Kappan* 71(6):470–478 (February 1990).
60. *What Works: Research About Teaching and Learning* (Washington, DC: United States Department of Education, 1986), p. 42.
61. Reprinted from *National Science Education Standards* © 1996 National Academy of Sciences, p. 45. Courtesy of National Academy Press, Washington, DC.

SUGGESTED READINGS

Barman, C.R. "An Evaluation of the Use of a Technique Designed to Assist Prospective Elementary Teachers Use the Learning Cycle with Science Textbooks." *School Science and Mathematics* 92(2):59–63 (February 1992).

Beyer, B.K. *Critical Thinking.* Fastback 385. Bloomington, IN: Phi Delta Kappa Educational Foundation, 1995.

Blake, S. "Are You Turning Female and Minority Students Away from Science?" *Science and Children* 30(7):32–35 (April 1993).

Butts, D., et al. "Is Direct Experience Enough? A Study of Young Children's Views of Science." *Journal of Elementary Science Education* 6(1):1–16 (Winter 1994).

Caldwell, J.R. "String." *Science Activities* 31(1):8–10 (Spring 1994).

Cawley, J.F. "Science for Students with Disabilities." *Remedial and Special Education* 15(2):67–71 (March 1994).

Dean, R. A., M. M. Dean, J. A. Gerlovich, and V. Spiglanin. *Safety in the Elementary Science Classroom.* Arlington, VA: National Science Teachers Association, 1993.

Diamond, J. "Sex Differences in Science Museums: A Review." *Curator* 37(1):17–24 (March 1994).

Farivar, S. H., and N. M. Webb. "Are Your Students Prepared for Group Work?" *Middle School Journal* 25(3):29–30 (January 1994).

Feder-Feitel, L. "How to Avoid Gender Bias." *Creative Classroom* 7(5):56–63 (March 1993).

———. "How to Avoid Gender Bias: Part II." *Creative Classroom* 8(5):56–60, 64–66 (March 1994).

Feldkamp-Price, B., P. Rillero, and P. Brownstein. "A Teacher's Guide to Choosing the Best Hands-on Activities." *Science and Children* 31(6):16–19 (March 1994).

Freedman, R. L. H. *Open-ended Questioning.* Arlington, VA: National Science Teachers Association, 1994.

Hoff, P. B. "The Method of Knowing: Using Children's Questions in Elementary Science." *Hands-On* 48:28–31 (Summer 1994).

Holahan, G.G., et al. "Elementary School Science for Students with Disabilities." *Remedial and Special Education* 15(2):86–93 (March 1994).

Howe, A.C. "How Do You Manage?" *Science Activities* 31(1):11–13 (Spring 1994).

Iry, B.J., and R. Lara-Alecio. "High-Low Sponges." *Science and Children* 31(8):23–25 (May 1994).

Kaplan, J., and D. Aronson. "The Numbers Gap." *Teaching Tolerance* 3(1):21–27 (Spring 1994).

Keller, J. D., and P. Holden. "Science Guides Consumer Choices." *Science and Children* 32(3):20–23, 55 (November/December 1994).

Kennedy, C., et al. *The Pathfinder's Adventure Kit.* New York: Random House, 1993.

Keys, C. W. "Inquiring Minds Want to Know." *Science Scope* 19(5):17–19 (February 1996).

Knorr, S. "Consumer Fairs." *Science Scope* 18(4):28–31 (January 1995).

Kulas, L. L. "I Wonder . . ." *Science and Children* 32(4):16–18, 32 (January 1995).

Leach, L.S. "Sexism in the Classroom: A Self-Quiz for Teachers." *Science Scope* 17(6):54–59 (March 1994).

Nir, O. "A Model for the Development and Implementation of Field Trips as an Integral Part of the Science Curriculum." *School Science and Mathematics* 93(6):325–331 (October 1993).

Nix, M. "Groundbreaking Women." *The Science Teacher* 61(6):35–37 (September 1994).

Shelton, M. "Leaf Pals." *Science and Children* 32(1):37–39 (September 1994).

Sickbert, C. "Deer Me!" *Science Scope* 16(5):38–43 (February 1993).

Smith, W. S., and C. Burrichter. "Look Who's Teaching Science Today!" *Science and Children* 30(7):20–23 (April 1993).

Stanley, L. R. "A River Runs Through Science Learning." *Science and Children* 32(4):13–15, 58 (January 1995).

Wallach, C., and S. Callahan. "The 1st Grade Plant Museum." *Educational Leadership* 52(3):32–33 (November 1994).

Wilson, L.S. "Changing Our Ways: Teaching for a Different Future." *Journal of Science Education and Technology* 3(1):3–6 (March 1994).

Wolk, S. "Project-Based Learning: Pursuits with a Purpose." *Educational Leadership* 52(3):42–45 (November 1994).

Wood, K. D., and J. P. Jones. "Integrating Collaborative Learning Across the Curriculum." *Middle School Journal* 25(3):29–23 (January 1994).

Wynne, E.A. *Cooperation-Competition: An Instructional Strategy.* Fastback 378. Bloomington, IN: Phi Delta Kappa Educational Foundation, 1995.

CHAPTER 4

Selecting and Using Instructional Aids and Resources for Teaching Science

Teachers make the available science tools, materials, media, and technological resources accessible to students.[1]

Important to helping students construct their understandings, and to design their learning environment in a way that facilitates the construction of those understandings, are the cognitive tools available for their use. You will be delighted to know that there are a large variety of useful and effective educational materials, aids, and resources from which to draw as you plan your instructional experiences for science learning. On the other hand, you could also become overwhelmed by the sheer quantity of different materials available for teaching science—textbooks, pamphlets, encyclopedias, tests, supplementary texts, paperbacks, programmed instructional systems, dictionaries, reference books, classroom periodicals, newspapers, films, records and cassettes, computer software, transparencies, realia, games, filmstrips, audio- and videotapes, slides, globes, manipulatives, CD-ROMs and videodiscs, and graphics. You could spend a lot of time reviewing, sorting, selecting, and practicing with the materials and tools for your use. Although nobody can make the job easier for you, the information in this chapter can expedite the process. Guidelines are provided for the use of nonprojected and projected aids and materials, along with information about where to obtain additional resources.

NONPROJECTED INSTRUCTIONAL RESOURCES

Whereas projected aids are those that require electricity to project images onto screens, this first part of the chapter is about nonprojected materials—printed materials, three-dimensional objects, and flat materials on which to write or display. Historically, of all the nonprojected materials for science instruction, the printed textbook has had the greatest influence on teaching.

Print Resources

In selecting science textbooks and other printed materials, one item of concern to teachers is the reading level of the material. Sometimes the reading level is noted by the textbook publisher. If not, you get this information by applying selections to a readability formula or simply having students read selections from the book aloud. If they can read the selections without stumbling over many words and can tell you the gist of what has been said, you can be confident that the textbook is not too difficult.

READABILITY FORMULAS
To estimate the reading grade level of a student textbook, you can use a readability formula such as the Fry technique, which employs the following technique:

1. Determine the average number of syllables in three 100-word selections one taken from the beginning, one from the middle, and one from the end of the book.
2. Determine the average number of sentences in the three 100-word selections.
3. Plot the two values on the readability graph (Figure 4.1). Their intersection will give you an approximation of the text's reading level at the 50 to 75 percent comprehension level.

While learning science, children use a variety of printed material and other resources. Reading materials that are carefully selected and used appropriately can inspire students to read and facilitate student learning.

Because readability formulas give only the *technical reading level* of a book, you will have to interpret the results by subjectively estimating the *conceptual reading level*. To do so, consider your students' experience with the subject, the number of new ideas introduced, the abstraction of the ideas, and the author's external and internal cues. Then raise or lower the estimated level of difficulty.

To tell how well your students can read the text, use the Cloze technique or an informal reading inventory. Since first described by Bormuth in 1968, the Cloze technique has appeared in a number of versions.[2] The procedure is as follows. From the textbook select several typical passages so that you will have a total of 400 to 415 words. Delete every eighth word in the passage, except for the words in the first and last sentences, proper names, numbers, and initialed words in sentences. It will be helpful if you eliminate 50 words. Duplicate the passages with blank spaces replacing the eliminated words. Pass out these "mutilated" readings to the students. Ask them to fill in the blanks with the most appropriate words they can think

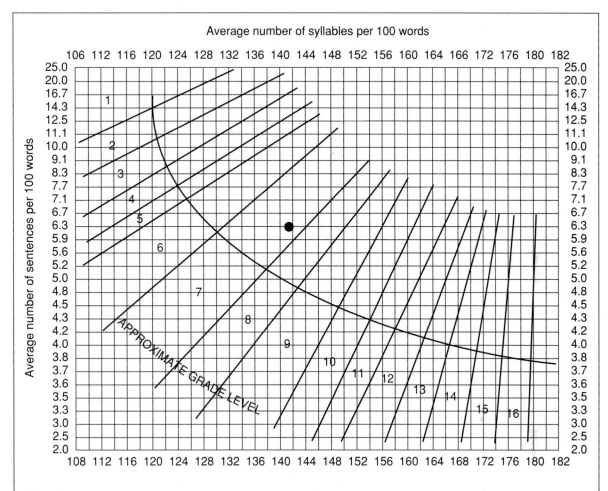

Average number of syllables per 100 words

Directions:
Randomly select 3 one hundred word passages from a book or an article. Plot average number of syllables and average number of sentences per 100 words on graph to determine the grade level of the material. Choose more passages per book if great variability is observed and conclude that the book has uneven readability. Few books will fall in gray area, but when they do, grade level scores are invalid.

Count proper nouns, numerals, and initializations as words. Count a syllable for each symbol. For example, *1945* is 1 word and 4 syllables and *IRA* is 1 word and 3 syllables.

Example:	Syllables	Sentences	
1st hundred words	124	6.6	
2nd hundred words	141	5.5	
3rd hundred words	158	6.8	
Average	141	6.3	Readability 7th grade (see dot plotted on graph)

FIGURE 4.1   Fry readability graph. (*Source:* Edward Fry, "A Readability Formula That Saves Time," *Journal of Reading* 11 (April 1968), p. 587. By permission.)

of. Collect the papers. Score them by counting all the words that are the exact words in the original text and dividing the number of correct responses by the number of possible correct responses. We suggest that you not count synonyms or verbs of different tense.[3] (Fifty blanks makes this division easy.)

$$\text{Score} = \frac{\text{Number of correct responses}}{\text{Number of possible}}$$

You can assume that students who score better than 50 percent can read the book quite well, students who score between 40 and 50 percent can read the book at the instructional level, and students who score below 40 percent will probably find the book difficult.

To conduct an informal silent reading inventory, ask your students to read four or five pages of the book, and then give them a 10-item quiz on what they read. You can consider the text too difficult for any student who scores less than 70 percent on the quiz. Similarly, to conduct an informal oral reading inventory, have a student read a 100-word passage. The text is too difficult if the student stumbles over and misses more than 5 percent of the words.[4]

MULTITEXT AND MULTIREADING APPROACHES

Expressing dissatisfaction with the single-textbook approach to teaching science, some teachers have substituted a multitext strategy, in which they use one set of books for one topic and another set for another topic. This strategy provides some flexibility, though it really is only a series of single texts.

Other teachers, especially those using an integrated thematic approach, use a strategy that incorporates many readings for a topic during the same unit. This multireading strategy gives students a certain amount of choice in what they read. The various readings allow for differences in reading ability and interest level. With the help of an additional study guide that you have developed, all the students can be directed toward specific information and concepts, even though they do not all have to read the same selections.

BEGINNING A RESOURCES FILE

Besides the student textbook, there are a vast array of other printed materials available for use in teaching, many of which are without cost (see "Sources of Free and Inexpensive Printed Materials" in the following section). It is a good idea to begin immediately a file of printed materials and other resources that you can use in your teaching. Figure 4.2 is offered to help you begin that process.

Printed materials include books, workbooks, pamphlets, magazines, brochures, newspapers, professional journals, periodicals, and duplicated materials. In reviewing these materials, be alert to the following factors:

- Appropriateness of the material in both content and reading level
- Articles in newspapers, magazines, and periodicals, related to the content your students will be studying, or to the skills they will be learning
- Assorted workbooks available from trade book publishers that emphasize thinking and problem solving rather than rote memorization
- Pamphlets, brochures, and other duplicated materials that students can read for specific information and viewpoints about particular topics
- Inexpensive paperback books that can provide multiple readings for your class, and that make it possible for students to read primary sources

Start now to build your own personal file of aids and resources for teaching, a file that will continue throughout your professional career. We advise you to begin your file on a computer database program, on file cards (color coded and perhaps preprinted), or in an accordion file, listing:

a. Name of resource
b. How to get the resource and when it is available
c. How to use
d. Evaluative comments, including grade level the resource is best for

Organize the file in whatever way that makes most sense to you. Cross-reference or color code your system to accommodate the following categories of aids and resources:

1. Articles from magazines, newspapers, journals, and periodicals
2. Assessment items
3. Compact disc sources
4. Computer software sources
5. Games and games sources
6. Guest speakers and other community resources
7. Manipulatives and other realia
8. Media catalogs
9. Motivational ideas
10. Multimedia program sources
11. Pictures, posters, and other stills
12. Sources of free and inexpensive items
13. Student laboratory work sheets
14. Supply catalogs
15. Thematic unit ideas
16. Unit and lesson plan ideas
17. Unit and lesson plans completed
18. Videocassette titles and sources
19. Videodisc titles and sources
20. Other or miscellaneous

FIGURE 4.2   Beginning a professional materials resource file.

A Guide to Print and Nonprint Materials Available from Organizations, Industry, Governmental Agencies, and Specialized Publishers. New York: Neal Schuman.
Bowman, L. *Freebies for Kids and Parents Too!* Chicago, IL: Probus, 1991.
Civil Aeronautics Administration, *Sources of Free and Low-Cost Materials.* Washington, DC: U.S. Department of Commerce.
Freebies editors. *Freebies for Teachers.* Los Angeles: Lowell House, 1994.
Freebies: The Magazine with Something for Nothing. P.O. Box 5025, Carpinteria, CA 93014-5025.
Index to Multi-Ethnic Teaching Materials and Teaching Resources. Washington DC: National Education Association.
National Committee for World Food Day. Teaching Materials, 1001 22nd St., NW, Washington, DC 20437.
Randolph, WI: Educators Progress Service. *Educator's Guide to Free Science Materials;* and *Educator's Guide to Free Teaching Aids.*
Scholastic Production, The Magic School Bus, 555 Broadway, New York, NY 10012. Write for free copy of teaching guide to PBS episodes of the Magic School Bus book series written by Joanna Cole and illustrated by Bruce Degen.

FIGURE 4.3   Resources for free and inexpensive printed materials.

The American Biology Teacher	Journal of Geography	The Middle School Journal	Science and Children
American Teacher	Journal of Reading	Phi Delta Kappan	Science Scope
The Computing Teacher	Language Arts	The Reading Teacher	Teacher Magazine
Creative Classroom	Learning	School Science and Mathematics	Teaching K–8

FIGURE 4.4   Professional periodicals for teachers.

SOURCES OF FREE AND INEXPENSIVE PRINTED MATERIALS

For free and inexpensive printed materials check your college, university, or public library, or the resource center of a local school district, for sources such as those listed in Figure 4.3.

PROFESSIONAL JOURNALS AND PERIODICALS

Figure 4.4 is a sample listing of the professional periodicals and journals that can provide useful teaching ideas for science teaching and that carry information about instructional materials and how to get them. Some of these may be in your university or college library. Check there for these and other titles of interest to you.

THE ERIC INFORMATION NETWORK

The Educational Resources Information Center (ERIC) system, established by the United States Office of Education, is a widely used network providing access to information and research in education. Although there are 16 clearinghouses providing information on specific subjects, the address of particular interest for science teaching is: *Science, Mathematics, and Environmental Education*, Ohio State University, 1200 Chambers Road, 3rd Floor, Columbus, OH 43212-1792.

COPYING PRINTED MATERIALS

You must be familiar with the laws governing the use of copyrighted materials both, printed and nonprinted. Although space prohibits full inclusion of the United States legal guidelines, your local school district should be able to provide a copy of current district policies for compliance with copyright laws. See also the suggested readings at the end of this chapter.

When preparing to make a copy, you must find out whether copying of the particular material is permitted by law under the category "permitted uses." If it is not allowed under "permitted uses," you must obtain written permission to reproduce the material from the holder of the copyright. In copying printed materials, adhere to the guidelines shown in Figure 4.5.

THE WRITING BOARD

Can you imagine trying to teach science in a classroom without a writing board? In times past teachers wrote on slate blackboards, but classrooms today may have either a blackboard or a board made of painted plywood (chalkboard), a magnetic chalkboard (plywood with a magnetic backing), or a white or colored (light green and light blue are common) multipurpose board on which you write with special marking pens. Multipurpose boards are important for classrooms where chalk dust would create problems—that is, aggravate allergies or interfere with computer maintenance. In addition to providing a surface on which you can write and draw, the multipurpose board can be used as a projection screen and as a surface to which figures cut from colored transparency film will stick. It may also have a magnetic backing.

Extending the uses of the multipurpose board is an electronic whiteboard that can transfer information written on it to a connected PC or Mac computer monitor, which in turn can save the material as a computer file. The board uses special dry-erase markers and erasers with optically encoded sleeves that enable the device to track their position on the board. The data are then converted into a display for the computer monitor, which may then be printed, cut and pasted into other applications, sent as e-mail or a fax message, or networked to other sites.[5]

Permitted Uses—You May Make:

1. A single copy of:
   - A chapter of a book
   - An article from a periodical, magazine, or newspaper
   - A short story, short essay, or short poem, whether or not from a collected work
   - A chart, graph, diagram, drawing, or cartoon
   - An illustration from a book, magazine, or newspaper
2. Multiple copies for classroom use (not to exceed one copy per student in a course) of:
   - A complete poem if less than 250 words
   - An excerpt from a longer poem, but not to exceed 250 words
   - A complete article, story, or essay of less than 2,500 words
   - An excerpt from a larger printed work (not to exceed 10 percent of the whole or 1,000 words)
   - One chart, graph, diagram, cartoon, or picture per book or magazine issue

Prohibited Uses—You May Not:

1. Copy more than one work or two excerpts from a single author during one class term (semester or year)
2. Copy more than three works from a collective work or periodical volume during one class term
3. Reproduce more than nine sets of multiple copies for distribution to students in one class term
4. Copy to create or replace or substitute for anthologies or collective works
5. Copy "consumable" works, e. g., workbooks, standardized tests, or answer sheets
6. Copy the same work year after year

FIGURE 4.5   Guidelines for copying printed materials that are copyrighted. (From section 107 of the 1976 Federal Omnibus Copyright Revision Act.)

Regardless of the type of writing board you have in your classroom—except for announcements that you place on the board—each day, each class, and even each new idea, should begin with a clean board. At the end of each class, clean the board, especially if another teacher follows you in that room—a simple professional courtesy.

Use colored chalk (or marking pens) to highlight your "board talk." This is especially helpful to students with learning difficulties. Beginning at the top left of the board, print or write neatly and clearly, with the writing intentionally positioned to indicate content relationships (e. g., causal, oppositional, numerical, comparative, and categorical).[6]

Use the writing board to acknowledge acceptance and to record student contributions. Print instructions for an activity on the board, rather than giving them orally. At the top of the board frame you may find clips for hanging posters, maps, and charts.

Learn to write on the board without having to entirely turn your back to students or blocking their view of the board. When you have a lot of material to put on the board, do it before class and cover it or, better yet, put the material on transparencies and use the overhead projector rather than the board—or use both. Be careful about not writing too much information at one time. When using the writing board to complement your teacher talk, write only key words and simple diagrams, thereby making it possible for the student's right brain hemisphere to process what is seen, while the left hemisphere processes the elaboration provided by your words.[7]

Visual Display Materials

Visual display materials include bulletin boards, charts, graphs, flip charts, magnetic boards, realia (real objects), pictures, and posters. As a new or visiting member of a school faculty, one of your first tasks is to find out what visual materials are available for your use and where they are kept. Guidelines for their use are presented in the following paragraphs.

The teacher creates a responsive classroom environment with meaningful and attractive visual displays.

THE CLASSROOM BULLETIN BOARD

Bulletin boards are found in nearly every classroom, and although sometimes poorly used or not used at all, they can be relatively inexpensively transformed into attractive and valuable instructional tools. In preparing a bulletin board, always keep in mind the importance of ensuring that the board display reflects gender and ethnic equity. For effective use of the classroom bulletin board, consider the following additional suggestions.

Making a C.A.S.E. for Bulletin Boards*

How can you use a classroom bulletin board effectively? Your classroom bulletin board will be most effective if you consider your "C.A.S.E.":

C, colorful constructions and captions
A, attractive arrangement
S, for simple and student prepared
E, enrichment and extensions of learning

*Adapted from Richard D. Kellough and Patricia L. Roberts, A *Resource Guide for Elementary School Teaching: Planning for Competence,* 3d ed. (New York: Macmillan, 1994), pp. 394–396. By permission of Prentice Hall.

C: *Colorful constructions and captions.* Take time to plan the colors you select for your board and, whenever possible, include different materials for the letters and the background of the board. For letter variety, consider patterns on bright cloth such as denim, felt, and corduroy. Search for special letters: they may be magnetic, ceramic, or precut letters of different sizes. Or make unique letters by cutting them from magazines, newspapers, posters, or stencils, or by printing the letters with rubber stamps, sponges, or vegetable prints. You may print out the shapes of letters by dabbing colors on ABC shapes with sponges, rubber stamps, or with vegetable slices that leave an imprint.

If this sounds to you like a lot of extra work that you may not want to take time for, consider having students help in preparation of your bulletin board. In doing so, they will learn and offer many creative ideas. Moreover, this is an excellent way of getting to know students better as people and of building rapport with them.

For the background of your board and the borders, consider gift-wrapping paper, wallpaper samples, shelf paper, remnants of fabric—flowers, polka dots, plaids, solids, or checks. Corrugated cardboard makes sturdy borders: cut out scallops, the shape of a picket fence, or jagged points for an icicle effect. Other colorful borders can be made with wide braid, wide rickrack, or a contrasting fabric or paper. Constructions for the board may be simple ones made of yarn, ribbon, braid, cardboard pointers, maps, scrolls, banners, pennants, wheels that turn, cardboard doors that open, shuttered windows to peek through, or flaps that pull down or up—to be peered under or over.

A: *Attractive arrangement.* Use your imagination to make the board attractive. Is your arrangement interesting? Did you use texture? Did you consider the shapes of the items selected? Are the colors attractive? Does your caption draw student attention?

S: *Simple and student prepared.* The bulletin board should be simple, emphasizing one main idea, concept, topic, or theme, and captions should be short and concise.

Are your students interested in preparing the bulletin board for your classroom? They often have great ideas.

- Students can help plan. Why not let them diagram their ideas and share them with each other?
- They can discuss. Is there a more meaningful way to begin to discuss an evaluation of what they see, to discuss the internal criteria that each student brings to class about a science topic, or to begin to talk about the different values that each student may have?
- They can arrange materials. Why not let them discover the concepts of balance and symmetry, of form and function?
- They can construct and contribute. Will they feel more actively involved and really participating if it is *their* bulletin board?
- When the bulletin board is finished, your students can get further involved by (1) reviewing the board during a class meeting, (2) discussing the materials used, and (3) discussing the information their bulletin board is emphasizing.

Additional class projects may be planned during this meeting. For instance, do the students want a bulletin board group or committee for their class? Do they want a permanent committee or one in which the membership changes from month to month? Or do they prefer that existing cooperative learning groups assume bulletin board responsibility, with periodic rotation of that responsibility? Do they want to meet on a regular basis? Can they work quietly and without disturbing other students who may still be completing their own learning tasks? Should they prepare the board, or should the committee ask everyone to contribute ideas and items for the weekly or monthly bulletin board? Does the committee want to keep a register, guest book, or guest file of students who contribute to the board? Should there be an honorary list of bulletin board illustrators? Should the authors of selected captions sign their names beneath each caption? Do they want to keep a file binder of all of the different diagrams of proposed bulletin boards? At each class meeting, should they discuss the proposed diagrams with the entire class? Should they ask the class to decide which idea would be an appropriate one for a particular study topic? What other records do they want to keep? Should there be a bulletin board medal or a classroom award?

E. *Enrichment and extensions of learning.* Illustrations on the bulletin board can accent learning topics; verbs can vitalize the captions; phrases can punctuate a student's thoughts; and alliteration can announce anything you wish on the board. For example,

Animals can accent! Pandas, panthers, and parrots can help to present punctuation symbols; a giant octopus can show students eight rules to remember, eight things to remember when preparing a book report, or eight activities to complete when academic work is finished early; a student can fish for anything—math facts, correctly spelled words, or the meanings of science words; a bear character helps students to "bear down" on errors of any kind; dinosaurs can begin a search for any topic; and pack rats can lead students into phrases, prose, or poetry.

Verbs can vitalize! Someone or something (your choice) can "swing into" any curriculum area. Verbs used often include *soar, win, buzz, rake, scurry,* and *race.*

Phrases point out! Short, concise phrases used as captions may include:

Roll into _____	All aboard for _____	Race into _____
Hop into _____	Peer into _____	Grow up with _____
Bone up on _____	Tune into _____	Monkey with _____
Looking good with _____	Fly high with _____	Get on track with _____

Alliteration announces! Some classroom bulletin boards show Viking ships or Voyages that guide a student to vocabulary words; Monsters Monitor Math Madness; other boards present Chameleon Condominiums, Surprises of Spring, Fantasies of Fall, and Wonders of Winter.

For a "touch me" bulletin board whereby fourth graders are challenged to "receive and interpret information about the natural world by relying on the sense they favor most naturally—touch," see Brian Heinz's article in *Science and Children* (4) (January 1989): 22–23.

CHARTS, POSTERS, AND GRAPHS

Charts, posters, and graphs can be used for displays just as bulletin boards are, but, as a rule, they are better suited for explaining, illustrating, clarifying, and reinforcing specific points in lessons. Charts, posters, and graphs might also be included in a bulletin board display. The previously discussed guidelines on the use of the writing board and bulletin board also apply to the use of charts, posters, and graphs. Clarity, simplicity, and attractiveness are essential considerations.

Most elementary and middle school students enjoy making charts, posters, and graphs. Involve them in these projects, in finding information, planning how to represent it, and making the chart or poster. Have the author(s) of the chart or poster sign it, then display it in the classroom. Students should credit their sources on the graphs and charts.

When making graphs, students may need help in keeping them proportional, and this provides an opportunity to help students develop mathematics and thinking skills.

Students can also enjoy designing flip charts, a series of charts or posters (may include graphs) to illustrate certain points or a series of related points. To make a large flip chart, they can use the large pads used by artists for sketching or small notepads to make mini-flip charts to use in dyads.

PROJECTED AND RECORDED INSTRUCTIONAL RESOURCES

Continuing with instructional resources available for use in science teaching, the following sections focus on equipment that depends on electricity to project light and sound and to focus images on screens. Included are projectors of various sorts, computers, CD-ROMs, sound recorders, video recorders, and laser videodisc players. The aim is *not* to teach you how to operate modern equipment but to help you develop a philosophy for using it and to provide strategies for incorporating these instructional tools in your teaching of science.

Media Resources

Certain instructional resources that rely on sight and sound fall into the category of media known as audiovisual aids. Included in this general category are such teaching tools as charts, models, pictures, graphs, maps, mock-ups, globes, flannel boards, and writing boards, as previously discussed. Also included in the general category of audiovisual aids are those devices that require electricity for their operation—projectors of various sorts, computers, sound recorders, video recorders, videodisc and compact disc players, and other technology. This section is about the selection and use of resources in this second group, those that require electricity to project sight and sound and that focus images onto screens.

It is important to remember that the role of these resources is to aid you in teaching science, not to teach it for you. You must still select the objectives, orchestrate the instructional plan, assess the results, and follow up the lessons. If you use media resources prudently, your teaching and students' learning will benefit.

USES OF AUDIOVISUAL AIDS

The main effort in instruction is to make the learning clear—to communicate the idea, capture the content, clarify the obscure for the students. Hence, teachers almost universally rely on the spoken word as their primary medium of communication. Most of the day is filled with explanation and discourse, to the point that the teaching profession has been accused of making words more important than reality—perpetuating a culture of verbalism and mimicry in the schools. Too many teachers use definitions, recitations, and rote memory in the quest of the goals for the day.

General Guidelines for Using Audiovisual Aids   Like any other boon to progress, audiovisual aids must be worked with if they are to yield what is expected. The mediocre teacher who is content to get by without expending additional effort will in all likelihood remain just that, a mediocre teacher, despite the excellent quality of whatever aids he or she chances to use. Because the mediocre teacher fails to rise to the occasion and hence presents poorly, that teacher's lesson results in being less effective and less impressive than it could have been. The effective teacher inquires about available audiovisual resources and expends the effort needed to implement them well for the benefit of the students. The effective teacher will capitalize on the drama made possible by the shift in interaction strategy and enhance the quest for knowledge by using vivid material. Such teaching involves four steps:

1. Selecting the proper audiovisual material
2. Preparing for using the material
3. Guiding the audiovisual activity
4. Following up the audiovisual activity

Selecting the Proper Audiovisual Material. Care must be exercised in the selection of an audiovisual aid for use in the classroom. A poor selection, inappropriate material, can turn an excellent lesson plan into a disappointing fiasco. An audiovisual aid that projects garbled sound, outdated pictures, or obscure or shaky images will not be met with delighted response from the students. Material that is too difficult or boring, or takes too long to set up, or is not suitable for students at the elementary or middle school age level will dampen students' enthusiasm.

In your selection of audiovisual materials, follow an inquiry routine similar to this:

1. Is the contemplated material suitable? Will it help to achieve the objective of the intended lesson? Will it present an accurate understanding of the facts in the case, or is it likely to lead to perpetuation of misconceptions? Will it highlight the important points? Will it work with the equipment available at the school?
2. Is the material within the level of understanding of the students? Is it too mature? too embarrassing? too dated?
3. Is the material lucid in its presentation? Are its images and sounds clear?
4. Is the material readily available? Will it be available when needed?

The answer to most of these questions is best arrived at after a careful preview of the material. Sometimes, because of various circumstances, this dry run is not possible. However, the best way to discover the inadequacy of catalogue descriptions of films, filmstrips, videotapes, videodiscs, computer software, and compact discs—or the condition in which a product has been left by previous users—is to try it out yourself under practice conditions.

Preparing for Using the Audiovisual Material. To use audiovisual aids with maximum effectiveness usually requires preparation of two types: psychological and physical. From the psychological standpoint, students have to be prepped for the use of the material and coached on how best to profit from its presentation. You will need to set the scene, make clear the purpose of the activity, suggest points to look for, present problems to solve, and, in general, clue your students about any potentially misleading content.

From the physical standpoint, preparation is needed pertaining to the machine to be used, the equipment involved, and the arrangement of the classroom furniture. Sometimes, as with the use of the writing board, preparation is minimal. All that is necessary may be the identification of the equipment and a brief recitation concerning how you intend to use it. At other times, however, as when the morning or afternoon sun affects classroom visibility, each section of the classroom will have to be checked, as well as the focusing dials of the apparatus (for the appropriate sharpness of images) and the amplitude dials (for clarity of voice sound). In the absence of preparation, bedlam can ensue. The missing chalk, the borrowing and lending of board erasers among the students, or the absence of an extension cord can spell defeat for even the best audiovisual aid. Double-checking the action-readiness of equipment is vital to success.

Guiding the Audiovisual Activity. The purpose of audiovisual materials is not to replace teaching but to make teaching more effective. Therefore, you cannot always expect the tool to do all the work. You should, however, make it work for your purposes. You will have to highlight in advance the presentation of those things you want to be remembered most completely. You may have to enumerate the concepts that are developed, or illustrate relationships or conclusions you wish to be drawn. You may have to prepare and distribute a study guide or a list of questions for students to respond to; you may have to stop the presentation periodically for hints or questions; or you may even have to repeat the entire performance to ensure a more thorough grasp of particulars. Student learning via the use of audiovisual materials can be enhanced by your coached guidance before, during, and after use of the materials.

Following Up the Audiovisual Activity. Audiovisual presentations that are allowed just to lie there upon completion squander valuable learning opportunities. Some activity and/or discussion should ensue that is pointed and directed toward closure. Time for such a postmortem should be a vital part of your lesson plan and preparation for the use of the material. Upon completion of the audiovisual presentation, students are now permitted to, and indeed expected to, respond to the sets of questions proposed in the preparation activity. Points that were fuzzily made should be clarified. Questions that were not answered should be pursued in depth. Deeper responses that go beyond the present scope of the inquiry should be noted and earmarked for further probing at some later date. Quizzes, reviews, practice, and discussions can all be used to tie loose ends together, to highlight the major concepts, to connect and clinch the essential learnings. The planned, efficient use of such an aid helps the understanding that audiovisual presentations are learning opportunities rather than recreational time outs.

WHEN EQUIPMENT MALFUNCTIONS

In using audiovisual equipment, it is nearly always best to set up the equipment and have it ready to go before students arrive. This helps to avoid problems in classroom management that can occur because of a delay. Of course, delays may be unavoidable when equipment malfunctions or a video tape breaks.

The "law" stating that *if anything can go wrong, it will*, is particularly relevant to the use of the equipment discussed in this section. The professional teacher is prepared for such emergencies. Effectively planning for and responding to this eventuality is part of your system of movement management. This preparation consists of a number of considerations.

When equipment malfunctions, three principles should be kept in mind: (1) You want to avoid dead time in the classroom; (2) You want to avoid causing permanent damage to equipment; (3) You want to avoid losing continuity of lesson content. What, then, do you do when equipment breaks down? The answer is, be prepared for the eventuality.

If a projector bulb goes out, quickly insert another. This means that you should have an extra bulb on hand. If a tape breaks, you can do a quick temporary splice with cellophane tape. This means that tape should be readily available. And, if you must make a temporary splice, do it on the film or videotape that has already run through the machine, rather than on the end yet to go through, so as not to mess up the machine or the film. Then, after class or after school, be sure to notify the person in charge of the tape that a temporary splice was made, so the tape can be permanently repaired before use again.

If a fuse blows, or for some other reason you lose power, or you can see that there is going to be too much dead time before the equipment is working again, this is the time to go to an alternate lesson plan. You have probably heard the expression, "Go to Plan B." It is a useful notion, which means that, without missing a beat in the lesson, to accomplish the same instructional objective or another objective, you immediately and smoothly switch to an alternate learning activity. For you, the beginning teacher, this doesn't mean that you must plan *two* lessons for every one, but when planning a lesson that utilizes audiovisual equipment, include an alternative activity, just in case. Thus, if necessary, you can move your students into the planned alternative activity quickly and smoothly.

Projectors

Projection machines are today lighter, more energy efficient, and easier to operate than they were a few years ago; they have been almost "defanged." Among the most common and useful to the classroom teacher are those discussed here: the overhead projector, the slide projector, the filmstrip projector, and, of course, the 16-mm film projector.

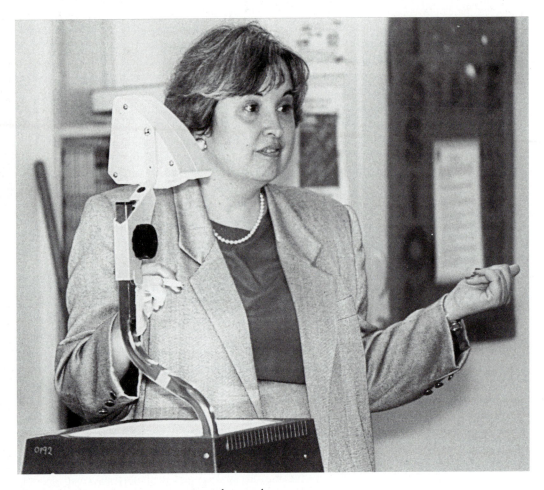

The overhead projector is an important teaching tool.

THE OVERHEAD PROJECTOR

The overhead projector is a versatile, effective, and reliable teaching tool. Except for the bulb burning out, not much can go wrong with an overhead projector. There is no film to break nor program to crash. And, along with a bulletin board and a writing board, nearly every classroom has one.

The overhead projector *projects* light through objects that are transparent (see Figure 4.6). An overhead projector usually works quite well in a fully or partially lit room. Truly portable overhead projectors are available that can be carried easily from place to place in their compact cases.

Other types of overhead projectors include rear-projection systems that allow the teacher to stand off to the side rather than between students and the screen, and overhead video projectors that use video cameras to send images that are projected by television monitors. Some schools use overhead video camera technology that focuses on an object, pages of a book, or a demonstration, while sending a clear image to a video monitor with a screen large enough for an entire class to see clearly.

In some respects, the overhead projector is more practical than the writing board, particularly for a beginning teacher who is nervous. Use of the overhead projector rather than the

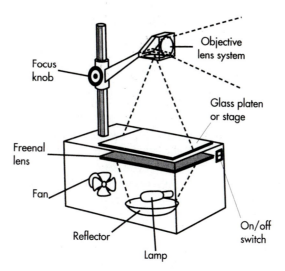

Focus knob

Objective lens system

Glass platen or stage

Freenal lens

Fan

Reflector

Lamp

On/off switch

FIGURE 4.6   Overhead projector, cutaway view.

writing board can help avoid tension by decreasing the need to pace back and forth to the board. And, by using an overhead projector, rather than a writing board, you can maintain eye contact and physical proximity with students, both of which are important for maintaining classroom control.

Guidelines for Using an Overhead Projector   Consider the following specific guidelines when using an overhead projector.

For writing, using an overhead projector, ordinary felt-tip pens are not satisfactory. Select a transparency marking pen available at office supply stores. The ink of these pens is water soluble, so keep the palm of your hand from resting on the transparency to avoid making smudges on the transparency and on your hand. Non-water-soluble pens—permanent markers—can be used, but then to reuse the transparency it must be cleaned with an alcohol solvent (ditto fluid works, but, for safety, be sure there is proper ventilation) or a plastic eraser. With a cleaning solvent you can clean and dry with paper toweling or a soft rag. To highlight the writing on a transparency and to organize student learning, use pens in a variety of colors. Transparency pens tend to dry out quickly, and they are relatively expensive, so the caps must be taken on and off frequently, which is something of a nuisance when working with several colors. Practice writing on a transparency, and also practice making overlays. You can use an acetate transparency roll or single sheets of flat transparencies. Flat sheets of transparency material come in different colors—clear, red, blue, yellow, and green, which can be useful in making overlays.

Some teachers prefer to prepare an outline of a lesson in advance on transparencies. This allows more careful preparation of the transparencies, and they are then ready for reuse at another time. Some teachers prefer to use an opaque material, such as 3″ × 5″ note cards, to block out prewritten material and then uncover it at the moment it is being discussed. For preparation of permanent transparencies you will probably want to use "permanent marker" pens, rather than those that are water soluble and can be easily smudged. Heavy paper frames are available for permanent transparencies; marginal notes can be written on the frames.

Other transparent materials can be shown on an overhead projector, such as transparent rulers, protractors, petri dishes, and even objects that are opaque if you simply want to show a silhouette.

Have you ever attended a presentation by someone using an overhead projector, who was using it improperly? It can be frustrating to members of an audience when the image is too small, out of focus, partially off the screen, or partially blocked from view by the presenter. To use this teaching tool in a professional manner: Turn on the projector, place the projector so that the projected white light covers the entire screen and hits the screen at a 90-degree angle, then focus the image to be projected. Face the students while using the projector. The fact that you do not lose eye contact with your students is a major advantage of using the overhead projector rather than a writing board. What you write, as you face your students, will show up perfectly (unless out of focus or off the screen). Rather than using your finger to point to detail (a finger can be distracting) or pointing to the screen (thereby turning away from your students), use a pencil by laying the pencil directly on the transparency with its tip pointing to the detail being emphasized. To lessen distraction, you may want to turn the overhead projector off when you want student attention to be shifted back to you, or when changing transparencies.

Personal computers with laser printers, and thermal processing (copy) machines, probably located in the teacher's workroom or in the school's main office, can be used to make permanent transparencies. If you have a personal computer and a laser printer at home, you can make transparencies easily; all you need are laser transparencies, which can be found in any office supply store. Commercial transparencies are available from science supply houses. For sources, check the catalogs available in your school office or at the audiovisual and resources centers in your school district. See Figure 4.7 for sample sources.

Calculators are available specifically for use on the overhead projector, as is a screen that fits onto the platform and is circuited to computers, so that whatever is displayed on the computer monitor is also projected onto the classroom screen.

Tracing transparent charts or drawings into larger drawings on paper or on the writing board is easily done with use of the overhead projector. The image projected on the screen can be made smaller or larger by moving the projector closer or farther away, respectively, and then traced when you have the size you want.

Addison-Wesley Publishing Co., 2725 Sand Hill Rd., Menlo Park, CA 94025

A-L-L Magnetics Inc., 930 S. Placentia, Placentia, CA 92670

American Educational Products, 3101 Iris Ave., #215, Boulder, CO 80301

Forestry Suppliers, Inc., P.O. Box 8397, Jackson, MS 39284-8397

Frey Scientific, 905 Hickory Lane, Mansfield, OH 44905

Harcourt Brace School Publishers, Orlando, FL 32887

Hubbard Scientific, 3101 Iris Ave., Ste. 215, Boulder, CO 80301

Instructional Video, P.O. Box 21, Maumee, OH 43537

Macmillan/McGraw Hill School Division, 1221 Avenue of the Americas, New York, NY 10020

Milliken Publishing Co., 1100 Research Blvd., P.O. Box 21579, St. Louis, MO 63132

Nasco, 901 Janesville Ave., P.O. Box 901, Fort Atkinson, WI 53538-0901

National School Products, 101 E. Broadway, Maryville, TN 37804

Sargent-Welch/VWR Scientific, 911 Commerce St., Buffalo Grove, IL 60089-2375

Schoolmasters Science, 745 State Circle, P.O. Box 1944, Ann Arbor, MI 48106

Scott, Foresman and Co., 1900 E. Lake Ave., Glenview, IL 60025

United Transparencies, Inc., 435 Main St., Johnson City, NY 13790

FIGURE 4.7   Sources of overhead transparencies.

SLIDES AND FILMSTRIPS

Slides and filmstrips are variations of the same medium, and most of what can be said about the use of one is true for the other. In fact, one projector may sometimes serve both functions. Filmstrips are, in effect, a series of slides connected on a roll of film. Slides can be made into filmstrips. Relatively inexpensive technology is now available that allows you to take slides or home movies and convert them into videocassettes. Because of their greater instructional flexibility, low cost, and hightened visual impact, videocassettes have replaced the earlier films and filmstrips once so popular for school use.

For teaching purposes, 35-mm slides are still quite useful and are available from school supply houses, and, of course, from your own collection and the collections of students and friends. Some schools have equipment for making slides from computer programs.

Films, Television, Videos, and Videodiscs

Because they are less expensive to make and offer greater instructional flexibility, videocassettes and videodiscs have replaced much of the earlier 16-mm films in popularity. Although there are still some effective and new 16-mm films available for science instruction, many others are old and sometimes include dated or incorrect information. As with filmstrips, you need to view films carefully and critically before showing them to your class.

Everyone knows that television, videos, and videodiscs represent a powerful medium. Their use as teaching aids, however, may present scheduling, curriculum, and physical problems that some school systems have been unable to handle adequately.

TELEVISION

For purposes of professional discussion, television programming can be divided into three categories: instructional television, educational television, and general commercial television. Instructional television refers to programs specifically designed as classroom instruction; educational television consists of programs of cable television and of public broadcasting designed to educate in general, but not aimed at classroom instruction; and general commercial television programs include the entertainment and public service programs of the television networks and local stations.

Watch for announcements for special educational programs in professional journals, such as *Science Scope,* and in the monthly issues of *National Geographic* magazine. And, of course, television program listings can be obtained from your local commercial, educational, and cable companies, or by writing directly to network stations. Addresses and phone numbers for the national networks are shown in Figure 4.8.

VIDEOS AND VIDEODISCS

Combined with a television monitor, the VCR (videocassette recorder) is one of the most popular and frequently used pieces of audiovisual equipment in today's classroom. Videotaped programs can do nearly everything that 16-mm films can do. In addition, the VCR combined with a video camera makes it possible to record student activities, practice, projects, experiments, demonstrations, and your own teaching. It gives students a marvelous opportunity to self-assess as they see and hear themselves in action.

Entire course packages, as well as supplements, are now available on videocassettes or on computer programs. The school where you student teach, and the school where you eventually are employed, may have a collection of such programs. Some teachers make their own.

Laser videodiscs and players for classroom use are reasonably priced, with an ever-increasing variety of disc topics for classroom use. There are two formats of laser videodisc: (1) freeze-frame format (CAV—Constant Angular Velocity, or Standard Play) and (2) non-freeze-frame format

American Broadcasting Company, Inc. (ABC), 77 West 66th St., New York, NY 10019; (212) 458-7777

Arts & Entertainment Network (A&E), 235 E. Forty Fifth Street, New York, NY 10017; (212) 661-4500

Black Entertainment Television, 1899 Ninth Street NE, Washington, DC 20018; (202) 636-2400

Cable News Network (WTBS), 1050 Techwood Drive, NW, Atlanta, GA 30318; (404) 827-1896

Columbia Broadcasting System, Inc. (CBS-TV), 51 West 52nd Street, New York, NY 10019; (212) 975-3166

C-Span, 400 North Capitol Street NW, Washington, DC 20001; (202) 737-3220

Discovery Channel, The, 7700 Wisconsin Ave., Bethesda, MD 20814-3522; (301) 986-1999

Disney Channel, The, 4111 West Alameda Ave., Burbank, CA 91505; (818) 569-7500

ESPN, ESPN Plaza, 935 Middle Street, Bristol, CT 06010; (203) 585-2000

Fox Broadcasting, 10201 W. Pico Blvd., Los Angeles, CA 90035; (310) 203-3553

Learning Channel, The, 7700 Wisconsin Ave., Bethesda, MD 20815-3579; (301) 986-0444

Lifetime, 36-12 35th Avenue, Astoria, NY 11106; (718) 482-4000

National Broadcasting Company (NBC-TV), RCA Building, 30 Rockefeller Plaza, New York, NY 10112; (212) 664-4444

Public Broadcasting Service (PBS), 1320 Braddock Place, Alexandria, VA; (703) 739-5068

Turner Broadcasting, One CNN Center, Atlanta, GA 30348-5366; (404) 827-1647

United Paramount Network, 5555 Melrose Ave., MOB 1200, Los Angeles, CA 90038; (213) 956-5000

USA Network, 1230 Avenue of the Americas, New York, NY 10020; (212) 408-9166

Warner Brothers Television Network, 4000 Warner Blvd., Bldg. 34R, Burbank, CA 91522; (818) 954-6000

FIGURE 4.8   Addressess and phone numbers for national television networks.

Combined with a television monitor, the VCR is a frequently used audio-visual tool in today's science classroom.

A.D.A.M. Software, Inc., 1600 River Edge Parkway, Ste. 800, Atlanta, GA 30328

AIMS Media, 9710 DeSoto Ave., Chatsworth, CA 91311-4409

American Educational products, 3101 Iris Avenue, #215, Boulder, CO 80301

Carolina Biological Supply, 2700 York Rd., Burlington, NC 27215

Central Scientific Co., 3300 CENCO Parkway, Franklin Park, IL 60131

Children's Television Workshop, School Services/RNSTA95, 1 Lincoln Plaza, New York, NY 10023

Churchill Media, 6901 Woodley Ave., Van Nuys, CA 91406

Coronet/MTI Film & Video, 108 Wilmot Road, 5th Floor, Deerfield, IL 60015

Educational Software Institute, 4213 South 94th Street, Omaha, NE 68127

Emerging Technology Consultants, Inc., 2819 Hamline Ave., North St. Paul, MN 55112

GPN, P.O. Box 80669, Lincoln, NE 68501-0669

The Learning Team, 10 Long Pond Road, Amonk, NY 10504

Let's Get Growing! 1900 Commercial Way, Santa Cruz, CA 95065

Miramar Productions, 200 Second Ave., W., Seattle, WA 98119-4204

National Geographic Society Education Services Division, 1145 17th St., NW, Washington, DC 20036

NYSTROM, 3333 Elston Ave., Chicago, IL 60618

Optical Data Corporation, 30 Technology Drive, Warren, NJ 07059

Optilearn, Inc., Park Ridge Dr., Ste. 200, Stevens Point, WI 54481

The Phoenix Learning Group, Inc., 2349 Chaffee Dr., St. Louis, MO 63146

Scholastic, Inc., 2931 E. McCarty St., Jefferson City, MO 65101

Science for Kids, P.O. Box 519, Lewisville, NC 27023

Sunburst Communications, 39 Washington Ave., P.O. Box 40, Pleasantville, NY 10570-0040

SVE, 6677 N. Northwest Highway, Chicago, IL 60631

Time-Life Education, P.O. Box 85026, Richmond, VA 23285-5026

Tom Snyder Productions, Inc., 80 Coolidge Hill Road, Watertown, MA 02172-2817

Videodiscovery, Inc., 1700 Westlake Ave., N, Suite 600, Seattle, WA 98109-3012

Workman Publishing Co., 708 Broadway, New York, NY 10003

Ztek Co., P.O. Box 1055, Louisville, KY 40201-1055

FIGURE 4.9   Sources of videodiscs and CD-ROMs.

(CLV—Constant Linear Velocity, or Extended Play). Both will play on all laser disc players. Laser videodisc players are quite similar to VCRs and just as easy to operate. The discs are visual archives, or visual databases, that contain large amounts of information that can be easily retrieved, reorganized, filed, and controlled by the user with the remote control that accompanies the player. Each side of a double-sided disc stores 54,000 separate still frames of information—pictures, printed text, diagrams, films, or any combination of these. Visuals, both still and motion sequences, can be stored and then selected for showing on a television monitor or programmed onto a computer disc for a special presentation. Thousands of videodisc titles are now available for educational use. Your school or district audiovisual or curriculum resource center probably has some titles already; for additional titles refer to the latest annual edition of *Videodisc Compendium*.[8]

Carefully selected programs, tapes, discs, films, and slides enhance student learning. For example, laser videodiscs offer quick and efficient accessibility to thousands of visuals, thus providing an appreciated boost to teachers of students with limited language proficiency. With the use of still-frame control, great programs such as *Ecology Treks*, *The Great Ocean Rescue*, *The Great Solar System Rescue* (Tom Snyder Productions), and *The Voyage of the Mimi* (Sunburst) allow students to visually observe phenomena that previous students only read about.

Check school supply catalogs for additional titles and sources for videodiscs and CD-ROM titles. Figure 4.9 lists sample addresses to which you can send for information.

Computers

As a science teacher of the twenty-first century you must understand and be able to use computers as well as you can read and write. To complete your teaching credential, your teacher education program and state teacher licensing commission probably require this expertise at some level of competency, or will soon.

The computer can be valuable to you in several ways. For example:

- The computer can be useful in managing instruction, by obtaining information, storing and preparing test materials, maintaining attendance and grade records, and preparing programs to aid in the academic development of individual students. This category of uses of the computer is referred to as computer-managed instruction, or CMI.
- The computer itself can be used for instruction with the use of various instructional software programs. In their analysis of research studies, Hancock and Betts report that "in some schools, computer-assisted instruction (CAI) using integrated learning systems (individualized academic tutorials) has shown impressive gains, especially in the early years and among under-achieving urban populations."[9] At Benjamin Banneker Computers Elementary School (Kansas City, Missouri), where students are expected to spend 50 percent of their daily learning time on a computer (and where, in their classrooms, they have one computer for every two students), their fourth and fifth graders now test at grades 5.4 and 5.8, respectively, on the Iowa Test of Basic Skills (ITBS), whereas when the fifth graders entered the program as third graders many of them were more than a year behind in grade level. Today, some of those fifth graders work at a tenth-grade level.[10]
- The computer can be used to teach about computers and to help students develop their skills in computer use.
- With the help of software programs about thinking, the computer can be used to teach about thinking and to help students develop their thinking skills.

Computers in science teaching can be used for practice and reinforcement, tutoring, simulations, games, and problem solving. With the computer, children can explore certain science phenomena in more accurate and graphic ways than are possible in traditional science teaching.

For a student, use of the computer is motivating, exciting, and effective as an instructional tool. Consider the following examples.

Computer programs can motivate. For example, one teacher motivated his students to write by sending their writing work to another class electronically. That was the beginning of the *kids2kids Writing Circle*, a national electronic writing project.[11]

Computer programs can activate. For example, a group of students in Maine prepare maps of local land and water resources from computer analyses of satellite images of the coastline, analyze the maps, and then advise local authorities on development. Mixing technology and environmental awareness, the students have learned that they can exercise some control over their environment and their future.[12]

Computer programs can excite. Especially exciting to students is the use of computers with telecommunications systems to connect with other students from around the world, providing, for example, format for comparing data, sharing ideas, and encouraging students to challenge each other toward better understandings of global environmental problems. For example, many elementary and middle school classrooms have joined the World School for Adventure Learning, one goal of which is to establish and sustain a global telecommunications network of schools for ongoing, interactive environmental studies. (For more information about World School, contact University of St. Thomas World School for Adventure Learning, 2115 Summit Avenue, St. Paul, MN 55105.) Similarly, the National Association of Secondary School Principals has joined the Global Learning Corporation to produce World Classroom, a telecommunications network involving K–12 students and teachers in global educational activities. (For further information, contact NASSP Partnerships International at 800-253-7746.)

THE PLACEMENT AND USE OF COMPUTERS AND MULTIMEDIA IN SCHOOLS

The way you use the computer for instruction is determined by your knowledge and skill in its use, the number of computers you have available, where computers are placed in the school, and the compatible hardware and software available. Despite tight budgets, schools continue to purchase computers.

Approximately 50 percent of the computers in schools are located in classrooms, and about 40 percent are in computer labs. The days of having a computer in every classroom have not yet arrived.[13] Considering the placement of computers, the following paragraphs describe some possible scenarios and how classroom teachers work within them.

Scenario 1. Many schools have one or more *computer labs* where a teacher may schedule time to take an entire class, or send a small group of students, for computer work. For example, at Skowhegan Area Middle School (Maine), computers have been integrated into the whole curriculum. In collaboration with members of the interdisciplinary teaching teams, the manager of the school's computer lab assists students in using computers as tools to build knowledge, to write stories with word processors, to illustrate diagrams with paint utilities, to create interactive reports with hypermedia, and to graph data they have gathered using spreadsheets.[14] In many instances, where schools have a computer lab, student computers are networked to the teacher's computer in the lab so that the teacher can control and monitor the work of each student.[15]

Scenario 2. In some schools students can take "computer" as an elective course. If students in your classes are simultaneously enrolled in a computer course, you may give them special computer assignments, which they can then share with the rest of the class.

Scenario 3. Some classrooms have one computer that is connected to a large-screen video monitor. The teacher, or a student, works the computer and the monitor screen can be seen by the entire class. As they view the screen, students can verbally respond and interact with what is happening on the computer.

Scenario 4. In your classroom, you may be fortunate to have one or more computers, a videodisc player, an overhead projector (one that has light projection from the base), and a LCD (liquid crystal display) projection system. Coupled with the overhead projector, the LCD projection system allows you to project onto your large wall screen (and TV monitor at the same time) any image from computer software or a videodisc. With this system, all students can see and verbally interact with the multimedia instruction.

Scenario 5. Many classrooms have one, or perhaps many, computers. If this is the case in your classroom, then you most likely will have one or two students working at the computer while others are engaged in other learning activities (an example of *multilevel teaching*). Computers can be an integral part of a learning activity center within the classroom and an important aid in your overall effort to individualize instruction within your classroom.

Telecommunications and the Online Classroom

Teachers seeking to make their classrooms more student centered, collaborative, and interactive are increasingly turning to telecommunications networks. Ranging in scale from local bulletin board systems (BBSs) to the Internet, these webs of connected computers allow teachers and students around the world to reach each other directly and gain access to quantities of information previously unimaginable. Unfortunately, still too few public school classrooms (estimated to be only about 3 percent) have access to telecommunications networks.

Students using networks learn new inquiry and analytical skills in a stimulating environment, and, as many people believe, they also gain an increased awareness of their role as world citizens. For example, Leisa Winrich, a teacher at North Middle School in Menomonee Falls, Wisconsin, connected her students to the *KidLink* network to share local weather data with distant classes. The Menomonee students compile the international data and send it back out over the network.[16]

There are many network service providers. Directories are available in most bookstores. Figure 4.10 shows a few examples.

EVALUATING AND SELECTING COMPUTER SOFTWARE PROGRAMS

There are a number of forms you can use in evaluating computer software programs and testing them for their compatibility with your science objectives. Evaluation forms are usually available from the local school district or state department of education and from professional associations.

When reviewing computer software, you should reject any software that:

- Gives an audible response to student errors. No student should be forced to advertise mistakes to the whole class.
- Rewards failure. Some programs make it more fun to fail than to succeed.
- Has sound that cannot be controlled. The teacher should be able to turn sound on and off easily.
- Has technical problems. Is the software written so that it will not crash if the user accidentally touches the wrong key? Incorrect responses should lead to software-initiated help comments.
- Has uncontrolled screen advance. Advancing to the next page should be under user control, not automatically timed.
- Gives inadequate on-screen instructions. All necessary instructions to run the program must be displayed on the screen (in a continuously displayed instruction window if possible).
- Has factual errors. Information displayed must be accurate in content, spelling, and grammar.

Classroom Connect. A monthly teacher's guide to Internet and commercial online services. For information, contact (800) 638-1639.

GALAXY Classroom. Schools connected to the GALAXY network are able to participate in interactive instructional programs by communicating via fax machines or through electronic mail (E-mail) on the Internet. Programs include Fixer-Uppers and S.N.O.O.P.S., interactive science programs for grades 1 and 5, respectively. For information contact GALAXY Institute for Education, 100 N. Sepulveda Blvd., Suite 1010, El Segundo, CA 90245, or phone (800) 33GALAXY.

Global SchoolNet. Develops collaborative electronic mail projects. For information, contact (619) 475-4852.

I*EARN. The International Education Resource Network, connecting students and teachers internationally with electronic mail, conferences, and travel exchanges. For information, contact (914) 962-5864.

International Society for Technology and Education. Promotes use of technology in schools. For information, contact (503) 346-4414.

K12Net. A network of bulletin board systems for teachers, students, and parents. For information, contact (503) 280-5280, ext. 450.

PBS Online's Learning Link. A network of BBSs based at locally public TV stations. For information, contact (703) 739-8464.

TERC. Devoted to math and science, network programs include Global Laboratory and LabNet. For information, contact (617) 547-0430.

FIGURE 4.10   Sample network science programs and service providers.

- Contains insults, sarcasm, and derogatory remarks. Students' character should not be compromised.
- Has poor documentation. Demand a teacher's guide that compares in quality with a textbook teacher's guide or other teaching aid.
- Does not come with a backup copy. Publishers should recognize the unique vulnerability of magnetic disks and offer low-cost replacements.[17]

When selecting software programs, you and your colleagues need, of course, to choose those that are compatible with your brand of computer(s) and with your instructional objectives. According to a recent study of computers in U.S. schools, about half are old computers for which software is no longer made, and for which multimedia software and computer networks are not available.[18] As budgets permit, schools will need to replace their old computers.

Like laser videodiscs and compact discs, computer software programs are continually being developed, and except for a selected sample list of tried and recommended software (Figure 4.11), are too many and varied to list in this book.

THE CD-ROM

For computers, there are three types of storage discs—the floppy disc, the hard disc, and the CD-ROM, which is an abbreviation for "compact disc—read only memory." Use of a CD-ROM disc requires a CD-ROM drive. Newer computers may have built-in CD-ROM drives, whereas older ones must be connected to them. As with floppy and hard discs, CD-ROMs are used for storing characters in a digital format, while images on a videodisc are stored in an analog format. The CD-ROM is capable of storing approximately 250,000 pages of text, or the equivalent of 1,520 360K floppy discs or eight 70M hard discs and are therefore ideal for storing large amounts of information, such as dictionaries, encyclopedias, and general reference works full of graphic images that can be copied and modified. Some CD-ROM discs contain information that cannot be erased, transferred to a computer, or modified in any way.

The same material is used for both videodiscs and laserdiscs, but the laserdisc platter is 12 inches across, whereas the CD-ROM disc is just 4.5 inches across. All CD-ROM discs require the use of a computer connected to, or that has a built-in, CD-ROM player. Newer CD-ROM discs include video segments, just like those of videodiscs.

Any information stored on a CD-ROM disc or a videodisc can be found and retrieved within a few seconds. CD-ROMs are available from the distributors of videodiscs. Sample CD-ROM

Program	Source	Computer	Grade Level
Bradford Discovery	William K. Bradford 310 School St. Acton, MA 01720	Macintosh	6–12
Dinosaur Dig	Mindscape	Apple, IBM, Tandy	K–8
GTV: Planet Manager	National Geographic	Apple IIGS with videodisc	5–12
Heat and Temperature	HRM 338 Commerce Dr. Fairfield, CT 06430	IBM PC	4–12
Motion	HRM 338 Commerce Dr. Fairfield, CT 06430	IBM PC	4–12
Project Water Works	American Water Works, 6666 W. Quincy, Denver, CO 80235	Apple	4–12
Rocket Factory	MECC	Apple	K–8
Simple Machines	Science for Kids, 9950 Concord Church Rd., Lewisville, NC 27023	Macintosh and CD-ROM	3–8
Small Blue Planet: The Electronic Atlas (CD-ROM)	Now What Software, 2303 Sacramento, San Francisco, CA 94115	MacIntosh with CD-ROM	K–12
The Amazon Trail	MECC	IBM/Tandy	3–7
Woolly's Garden	MECC	Apple	K–8
Zoo Keeper	Davidson	IBM, Tandy	K–8

FIGURE 4.11   Selected computer software for K–8 science.

multimedia programs appropriate for elementary and middle grade science students include *Cell″ebration, Forces & Motion,* and *Simple Machines,* available from Science for Kids, 9950 Concord Church Rd., Lewisville, NC 27023; *A Field Trip to the Rainforest,* available from Sunburst, 101 Castleton Street, P.O. Box 100, Pleasantville, NY 10570-100; and *Space Shuttle,* from The Follette Software Company, 800 N. Front St., McHendry, IL 60050. And, as a resource for teachers, there is *Science Helper K-8,* from The Learning Team, Armonk, NY. Two publications that focus on CD-ROM products are *CD-ROM Professional,* available from newstands, and the newsletter *Children's Software Revue,* available from 520 N. Adams St., Ypsilanti, MI 48197. A comprehensive listing of multimedia educational software (i. e., titles that have either a CD-ROM or a laser videodisc component) is available from the Educational Software Institute, 4213 South 94th Street, Omaha, NE 68127 (phone toll free 1-800-955-5570).

SOURCES OF FREE AND INEXPENSIVE AUDIOVISUAL MATERIALS
For free and inexpensive audiovisual materials, check your college or university library for the sources listed in Figure 4.12.

USING COPYRIGHTED VIDEO AND COMPUTER PROGRAMS
You must be knowledgeable about the laws on the use of videos and computer software materials that are copyrighted. Although space prohibits the full inclusion of United States legal guidelines here, your local school district undoubtedly can provide a copy of current district policies to ensure compliance with all copyright laws. As mentioned earlier in the discussion of the use of copyrighted print materials, when preparing to make any copy you must find out whether the copying is permitted by law under the category of "permitted use." If not allowed under "permitted

Professional periodicals and journals for teachers.
An Annotated Bibliography of Audiovisual Materials Related to Understanding and Teaching the Culturally Disadvantaged. Washington, DC: National Education Association.
Catalog of Audiovisual Materials: A Guide to Government Sources (ED 198 822). Arlington, VA: ERIC Documents Reproduction Service.

Catalog of Free-Loan Educational Films/Video. St. Petersburg, FL: Modern Talking Picture Service. From Educator's Progress Service, Randolph, WI.
Educator's Guide to Free Audio and Video Materials
Educator's Guide to Free Films
Educator's Guide to Free Filmstrips
Guide to Free Computer Materials

FIGURE 4.12 Resources for free and inexpensive audiovisual materials.

Permitted Uses—You May:

1. Request your media center or audiovisual coordinator to record a program for you if you cannot or if you lack the equipment.
2. Keep a videotaped copy of a broadcast (including cable transmission) for 45 calendar days, after which the program must be erased.
3. Use the program in class once during the first 10 school days of the 45 calendar days, and a second time if instruction has to be reinforced.
4. Have professional staff view the program several times for evaluation purposes during the full 45-day period.
5. Make a few copies to meet legitimate needs, but these copies must be erased when the original videotape is erased.

6. Use only a part of the program if instructional needs warrant (but see the next list.)
7. Enter into a licensing agreement with the copyright holder to continue use of the program.

Prohibited Uses—You May Not:

1. Videotape premium cable services such as HBO without express permission.
2. Alter the original content of the program.
3. Exclude the copyright notice on the program.
4. Videorecord before a request for use—the request to record must come from an instructor.
5. Keep the program, and any copies, after 45 days.

FIGURE 4.13 Copyright law for off-air videotaping. (*Source:* Robert Heinich, Michael Molenda, James D. Russell, and Sharon E. Smaldins. *Instructional Media and Technologies for Learning.* 5th ed. (Upper Saddle River, NJ: Merrill/Prentice Hall, 1996), p. 387. By permission of Prentice Hall.)

Permitted Uses—You May:

1. Make a single back-up or archival copy of the computer program.
2. Adapt the computer program to another language if the program is unavailable in the target language.
3. Add features to make better use of the computer program.

Prohibited Uses—You May Not:

1. Make multiple copies.
2. Make replacement copies from an archival or back-up copy.
3. Make copies of copyrighted programs to be sold, leased, loaned, transmitted, or given away.

FIGURE 4.14 Copyright law for use of computer software. (From the December 1980 Congressional amendment to the 1976 Copyright Act.)

use," then you must get written permission to reproduce the material from the copyright holder. Figures 4.13 and 4.14 present guidelines for copying videotapes and computer software. As of this writing there are no guidelines for fair use of films, filmstrips, and slides.

USING COPYRIGHTED CD-ROMS

Usually, when purchasing CD-ROMs and other multimedia software packages intended for use by schools, you are also paying for a license to modify and use their contents for instructional purposes. However, not all CD-ROMs include copyright permission, so always check the copyright notice on any disc you purchase and use. When in doubt, don't use it until you have inquired of your district media specialists about copyrights or have obtained necessary permissions from the original source.

To be effective as an environment for learning science, the school classroom must be adequately supplied with a variety of materials and resources.

SUMMARY

You have learned of the variety of resources available to supplement your science instruction. When used wisely, these tools will help you to reach more of your students more of the time. As you know, teachers must meet the needs of a diversity of students—many of whom are linguistically and culturally different. The material presented in this chapter should be of help in meeting these needs. The future will undoubtedly bring technological innovations that will be even more helpful—compact discs, computers, and telecommunications equipment have only marked the beginning of a revolution in teaching. Within the next decade, new instructional delivery systems made possible by microcomputers and multimedia workstations will likely alter the role of the classroom teacher fundamentally.

You should remain alert to developing technologies as they apply to your teaching. Laser videodiscs and CD-ROMs interfaced with computers (i. e., the use of multimedia) and telecommunications offer exciting possibilities for science teachers. New instructional technologies are advancing at an increasingly rapid rate. As a science teacher, you know the value of being a lifelong learner. As a lifelong learner, you must maintain vigilance in regard to new developments, constantly looking for those that will not only help make student learning meaningful and interesting, and your teaching effective, but that are cost-effective as well.

QUESTIONS FOR CLASS DISCUSSION

1. Research local and national newspapers for a week to find articles related to science. Identify those that can be used in your teaching and how they can be used. Identify those that you would not use and give reasons for your decisions.
2. Divide into teams, and have each team select a concept or theme common to elementary or middle school science. For that concept, design and build a bulletin board for use at a particular grade level. The board should integrate the concept with other disciplines. Have teams share their boards.
3. Historically, changing styles in language and dress frequently cause good films and film-strips to lose their educational impact for students. In addition, many of those films stereotyped scientists. Schools that bought these films and filmstrips may still be stuck with them. Will videocassettes and videodiscs be subject to the same problem? How are tapes, films, and slides discarded by a school or district? On what basis? Who decides? What is the expected life of a videotape? Of a videodisc? Can you generate a list of ways that old films and filmstrips could be made useful?
4. Browse among old science books, charts, workbooks, films, and other science teaching resources, looking for misconceptions, factual errors, and false and stereotypic depictions of science and scientists. Share your findings with others in your class, perhaps by building a bulletin board display of the materials.
5. Although a certain fourth-grade student will sit for four hours straight playing Nintendo, that same child must be prodded by his parents to spend just 20 minutes doing his home-work in the science workbook that accompanies his science textbook. How is this ex-plained? What does it tell us, if anything?
6. Is it important to you that some of your students come from homes rich in educational re-sources, while others do not? Explain.
7. Using the guidelines set forth in this chapter, start your science teaching resource file, and at the end of the term share its design and contents with others in your class.
8. Describe any concepts you held earlier that changed as a result of your experiences with this chapter. Describe the changes.
9. From your recent observations and field work as related to this teacher preparation pro-gram, clearly identify one specific example of educational practice that seems contradic-tory to exemplary practice or theory as presented in this chapter. Present your explana-tion for the discrepancy.
10. Do you have other questions generated by the contents of this chapter? If so, where might you find answers?

NOTES

1. Reprinted from *National Science Education Standards* © 1996 National Academy of Sciences, p. 44. Courtesy of National Academy Press, Washington DC.
2. J. Bormuth, "The Cloze Readability Procedure," *Elementary English* 45:429–436 (April 1968).
3. See N. McKenna, "Synonymic Versus Verbatim Scoring of the Cloze Procedure," *Journal of Reading* 20:141–143 (November 1976).

4. See M. S. Johnson and R. A. Kress, *Informal Reading Inventories* (Newark, DE: International Reading Association, 1965).

5. For information, contact Microfield Graphics, Inc., 9825 SW Sunshine Court, Beaverton, OR; (503) 626-9393.

6. Madeline Hunter, *Enhancing Teaching* (New York: Macmillan, 1994), p. 135.

7. Hunter, *Enhancing Teaching*, p. 133.

8. Published and sold by Emerging Technology Consultants Inc., 2819 Hamline Avenue North, St. Paul, MN 55113. Phone (612) 639-3973; Fax (612) 639-0110.

9. Vicki Hancock and Frank Betts, "From the Lagging to the Leading Edge," *Educational Leadership* 51(7):24–29 (April 1994).

10. Esther Richey, "Urban Success Stories," *Educational Leadership* 51(7):55–57 (April 1994).

11. For information on necessary equipment, how to participate, and how to register with the network, see Steven Pinney, "Long Distance Writing," *Instructor* 100(8):69–70 (April 1991).

12. See Lisa Wolcott, "The New Cartographers. In Maine, Students Are Helping Map the Future," *Teacher Magazine* 2(6):30–31 (March 1991).

13. National School Boards Association, "Education Vital Signs," *The American School Board Journal* 180(12):A22 (December 1993).

14. Mike Muir, "Putting Computer Projects at the Heart of the Curriculum," *Educational Leadership* 51(7):30–32 (April 1994).

15. For a discussion on how to use cooperative learning groups on computers and a recommended list of science software that works in a cooperative learning environment, see John S. Neal, "The Interpersonal Computer," *Science Scope* 17(4):24–27 (January 1994).

16. Philip Cohen, "The Online Classroom," *Association for Supervision and Curriculum Development Update* 36(10):1, 5–6 (December 1994).

17. Randall J. Souviney, *Learning to Teach Mathematics*. 2d ed. (New York: Merrill, 1994), p. 135.

18. Reported in National Science Teachers Association's *NSTA Reports!* (February/March 1994), p. 3.

SUGGESTED READINGS

Berge, L., and R. Hudson. "Newton's Apple Enters the Information Technology Age." *Science Scope* 18(1):42–43 (September 1994).

Bullock, M. "Technology Time." *Science Scope* 18(7):17–18 (April 1995).

Elliot, I. "Using Technology to Teach Science." *Teaching K-8* 24(5):38–41 (February 1994).

Etchison, C. "Tales from a Technology Teacher." *Science and Children* 32(7):19–21, 30 (April 1995).

Gauger, R. "Access the Internet: How to Use this Global Resource for Science Education." *The Science Teacher* 61(6):26–29 (September 1994).

Helisek, H., and Pratt, D. "Project Reconstruct." *Science and Children* 31(7):25–28 (April 1994).

Jackson, D. F., et al. "Implementing 'Real Science' Through Microcomputers and Telecommunciations in Project-Based Elementary Classrooms." *Journal of Science Education and Technology* 3(1):17–26 (March 1994).

Kanning, R. G. "What Multimedia Can Do in Our Classrooms." *Educational Leadership* 51(7):40–44 (April 1994).

Lehman, J. "Technology Use in the Teaching of Mathematics and Science in Elementary Schools." *School Science and Mathematics* 94(4):194–202 (April 1994).

Muir, M. "Putting Computer Projects at the Heart of the Curriculum." *Educational Leadership* 51(7):30–32 (April 1994).

Murray, K. T. "Copyright and the Educator." *Phi Delta Kappan* 75(7):552–555 (March 1994).

Osborn, S. *Free and Almost Free Things for Teachers*. New York: Putnam, 1993.

Riss, P. H. "We're Having a Seed Sale." *Science Activities* 30(4):29–31 (Winter 1994).

Tomecek, S. M. "3-2-1 Contact in the Classroom." *Science Scope* 16(5):33 (February 1993).

Walthall, B., ed. *IDEAAAS: Sourcebook for Science, Mathematics, and Technology Education*. Arlington, VA: National Science Teachers Association, 1995.

Wishnietsky, D. H. *Using Computer Technology to Create a Global Classroom*. Fastback 356. Bloomington, IN: Phi Delta Kappa Educational Foundation, 1993.

CHAPTER 5

Planning for Science Instruction

An effective program of science is planned to include these elements:

- *A set of clear goals and expectations for students.*
- *A curriculum framework is used to guide the selection and development of units and courses of study.*
- *Curriculum patterns that are developmentally appropriate, interesting, and relevant to students' lives.*
- *Inquiry is emphasized as a tool for learning.*
- *The curriculum connects to other school subjects.*[1]

As emphasized in the preceding chapters of this book, to be most effective in teaching important understandings to the diversity of students in today's classrooms, much of the learning in science can be made more effective and longer lasting when that learning is integrated with the whole curriculum and made meaningful to the lives of the students, rather than simply taught as an unrelated and separate discipline at the same time each day.

It is also quite clear that if learning is defined as being only the accumulation of bits and pieces of information, then we already know how that is learned and how to teach it. However, the accumulation of pieces of information is at the lowest end of a spectrum of types of learning and leads to what is sometimes referred to as *procedural knowledge*. For higher levels of thinking and for learning that is most meaningful and longest lasting, *conceptual knowledge*, the results of recent research—as exemplified by the National Science Education Standards (NSES)—supports the use of a curriculum whereby disciplines are integrated and the use of instructional techniques that involve the learners in social interactive learning, such as cooperative learning, peer tutoring, and cross-age teaching.

THE SPECTRUM OF INTEGRATED CURRICULUM

In learning about *integrated curriculum*, it is easy to become confused by the plethora of terms that are used, such as *thematic instruction*, *multidisciplinary teaching*, *integrated studies*, *interdisciplinary curriculum*, *interdisciplinary thematic instruction*, and *integrated curriculum*. In essence, regardless which of these terms is being used, the reference is to the same thing or idea.

Because it is not always easy to differentiate *curriculum* and *instruction*, to better understand the meaning of *integrated curriculum* let's assume for now that there is no difference between what constitutes *curriculum* and what constitutes *instruction*. In other words, for the intent of this discussion, there is no relevant difference between the two terms. Whether we use the term *integrated curriculum* or the term *integrated instruction* we will be referring to the same thing.

Definition of *Integrated Curriculum*

The term *integrated curriculum* (or any of its synonyms mentioned earlier), refers to *both a way of teaching and a way of planning and organizing the instructional program so that the discrete disciplines of subject matter are related to one another in a design that matches the developmental needs of the learners and that helps to connect their learning in ways that are meaningful to their current and past experiences.* In this respect, integrated curriculum is the antithesis of traditional disparate subject-matter-oriented teaching and curriculum designations.

The reason for the variety of terminology is, in part, that the concept of integrated curriculum is not new; it has had a roller coaster ride throughout most of the history of education in this country. Over time, efforts to integrate student learning have had varying labels, resulting in the plethora of terms.

The recent popularity of the integrated curriculum stems from (1) the late 1950s, with the National Science Foundation supported, inquiry-based, discovery-oriented, student-centered projects such as *Elementary Science Study* (ESS), an integrated and hands-on science program for grades K–6; *Man: A Course of Study* (MACOS), a hands-on, anthropology-based program for fifth graders; and *Environmental Studies* (name later changed to *ESSENCE*), an interdisciplinary program for use at all grades, K–12, regardless of subject matter orientation, (2) the "middle school movement," which began in the 1960s, and (3) the whole-language movement in language arts, which began in the 1980s.

Historically, there has been an understood need to develop a curriculum that considers the unique personal needs of learners as well as the challenges confronting them in the real world. Exemplary schools continue to work at integrating personal, social, and academic dimensions into a developmentally appropriate curriculum for their learners.

Today's renewed interest in the development and implementation of integrated curriculum and instruction has risen from at least three sources: (1) the success at curriculum integration enjoyed by exemplary middle level schools, (2) the literature-based movement in reading and language arts, and (3) recent research in cognitive science and neuroscience on how students learn (as discussed in Chapter 2).

As is true of traditional curriculum and instruction, an integrated curriculum approach is not without critics. As stated by Jarolimek, "Parents and teachers who find conventional schools too highly structured, too regimented, and too adult-dominated find the child-centered activities of the integrated curriculum mode attractive, [but] with its apparent lack of organization, its informality, and the permissiveness allowed, at a time when the nation seems to be calling for more fundamental approaches to education [and because school budgets are tighter], the integrated curriculum mode faces an uncertain future."[2]

A totally integrated curriculum approach may not necessarily be the best approach for every school, nor the best for all learning for every child, nor is it necessarily the manner by which every teacher should or must always plan and teach. As evidenced by practice, the truth of this statement becomes obvious.

Levels of Curriculum Integration

In attempts to connect students' learning with their experiences, efforts fall at various points on a spectrum, or continuum, from the least integrated instruction (Level 1) to the most integrated (Level 5), as illustrated in Figure 5.1.

This illustration is not meant to be interpreted as going from "worst case scenario" (far left) to "best case scenario" (far right), although some experts may interpret it exactly that way. It is meant solely to show how various efforts to integrate fall on a continuum of sophistication and complexity. The following are descriptions of each level of the continuum.

Level 1. This is the traditional organization of curriculum and classroom instruction, in which teachers plan and arrange the science scope and sequence in the format of topic outlines. If there is an attempt to help students connect their learning and their experiences, it is up to individual classroom teachers to do that. A sixth-grade student in a school and classroom that have subject-specific instruction at varying times of the day (e.g., reading and language arts at 8:00 A.M., mathematics at 9:00 A.M., social studies at 10:30 A.M., science at 2:00 P.M., and so on), and from one or more teachers, is likely learning within a Level 1 instructional environment, especially when what is being learned in one subject has little or no connection with the content being learned in another. This is also true of the junior high

Least Integrated				*Most Integrated*
Level 1	*Level 2*	*Level 3*	*Level 4*	*Level 5*
Subject-specific topic outline	Subject-specific	Multi-disciplinary	Interdisciplinary thematic	Integrated thematic
No student collaboration in planning	Minimal student input	Some student input	Considerable student input in selecting themes and in planning	Maximum student and teacher collaboration
Teacher solo	Solo or teams	Solo or teams	Solo or teams	Solo or teams
Student input into decision making very low		Student input into decision making moderate		Student input into decision making very high

FIGURE 5.1 Levels of curriculum integration.

school student who moves during the school day from classroom to classroom, teacher to teacher, subject to subject, from one topic to another. A topic in science, for example, might be "earthquakes." A related topic in social studies might be "the social consequences of natural disasters." Yet these two topics may or may not be studied by a student at the same time.

Level 2. If students are learning English/language arts, or social studies/history, or mathematics, or science, through a thematic approach rather than a topic outline, then they are learning at Level 2. At this level, themes for one discipline are not necessarily planned and coordinated to correspond or integrate with themes of another, or to be taught simultaneously. The difference between a topic and a theme is not always clear. For example, whereas "earthquakes" and "social consequences of natural disasters" are topics, "natural disasters" could be the theme, or umbrella, including these two topics. At this level, the students may have some input into the decision making involved in planning the themes and their content.

Level 3. When students are learning two or more of their core subjects (English/language arts, social studies/history, mathematics, and science) around a common theme, such as the theme "natural disasters," from one or more teachers, they are then learning at Level 3 integration. At this level, teachers agree on a common theme, then *separately* deal with that theme in their individual subject areas, usually at the same time during the school year. Thus, what a student is learning from a teacher in one class is related to and coordinated with what the student is concurrently learning in another or several other classes. Some authors refer to Levels 2 and 3 as *coordinated curriculum.* At Level 3, students may also be involved in selecting and planning themes and deciding on their content.

Level 4. When teachers and students collaborate on a common theme and its content, and when discipline boundaries begin to disappear as teachers teach toward understanding about this common theme, either solo or as an interdisciplinary teaching team (composed of several teachers working with a common group of students, such as in a school-within-a-school configuration), Level 4 integration is achieved. This is the level of integration at which many exemplary middle schools function. It is also the level at which many primary grade teachers in self-contained classrooms operate.

Level 5. When teachers and their students collaborate on a common theme and its content, and discipline boundaries are truly blurred during instruction, and teachers of several grade levels (e.g., grades 6, 7, and 8; or 2, 3, and 4) and of various subjects (e.g., core subjects and exploratories) teach toward student understanding of aspects of the common theme, the curriculum is operating at **Level 5,** within an integrated thematic approach.[3]

PLANNING THE SCIENCE CURRICULUM

In Chapter 2, you reviewed important historical and recent works of cognitive psychologists, works that have led to a modern view of teaching for meaningful understanding, and, in Chapter 3, a presentation of the relevant instructional methodology. As a science teacher, your instructional task is twofold: (1) to plan for and provide developmentally appropriate hands-on experiences, with useful materials and the supportive environment necessary for students' meaningful scientific exploration; and (2) to know how to facilitate the most meaningful and longest-lasting learning possible once the child's mind has been activated by the hands-on experience. This chapter is designed to help you complete these tasks.

For teachers of middle school in particular, the curriculum can present a unique challenge. Unlike the curricula of lower grades, which are usually developed for a single-grade-level teacher in a self-contained classroom, and unlike high school curricula developed for teachers of various subjects in departmentalized classrooms, the curricula of many middle schools, and of increasingly more elementary schools, are developed by a common group of teachers. They collectively plan special programs for specific cohorts of students.

The backbone of any effective instructional program is the curriculum. To learn how it is developed, you must first understand how the school is organized—that is, how teachers are assigned to subject matter and how students are grouped for instruction.

Planning for the Instruction

Planning for the instruction is a very large and important part of a teacher's job. Responsible for planning at three levels, you will participate in long-range planning, that is, (1) planning for a semester or academic year and (2) planning units of instruction, and you will do short-range planning, that is, (3) the preparation of lessons. Throughout your career you will be engaged almost continuously in planning at each of these three levels; planning for instruction is a steady and cyclic process that involves preactive and reflective thought processing. The importance of mastering the process at the very beginning of your career cannot be overemphasized.

Decision Making and the Thought-Processing Phases of Instruction

Teaching has been defined as "the process of making and implementing decisions before, during, and after instruction—decisions that, when implemented, increase the probability of learning."[4] The process of teaching is divided into four decision-making and thought-processing phases. These are the *preactive* (or planning) phase, the *interactive* (or instructional) phase, the *reflective* (analyzing and evaluating the instruction) phase, and the *projective* (application of that reflection) phase.[5] The preactive phase consists of all those intellectual functions and decisions you will make prior to actual instruction. The interactive phase includes all the decisions made during the immediacy and spontaneity of the teaching act. Decisions made during this phase are likely to be more intuitive, unconscious, and routine than those

- *Teachers develop a framework of yearlong and short-term goals for students.*
- *Teachers select science content and adapt and design curricula to meet the particular interests, knowledge, skills and experiences of students.*
- *Teachers work together as colleagues within and across disciplines and grade levels.*[6]

made during the planning phase. The reflective phase is the time you will take to reflect on, analyze, and judge the decisions and behaviors that occurred during the interactive phase. As a result of this reflection, decisions are made about how to use what was learned in subsequent teaching actions. At this point, you are in the projective phase, abstracting from your reflection and projecting your analysis into subsequent teaching actions.

REFLECTION AND THE LOCUS OF CONTROL

It is during the reflective phase that you have a choice of whether to assume full responsibility for the instructional outcomes or to assume responsibility for only the positive outcomes of the instruction, while placing blame for the negative outcomes on outside forces (e.g., parents and guardians, student peer pressure, other teachers, administrators, textbooks). Where responsibility for outcomes is placed is referred to as *locus of control*. It seems axiomatic that teachers who are professional and competent tend to assume full responsibility for the instructional outcomes, regardless of whether the outcomes are those that were intended in the planning phase.

PERSONAL STYLE OF TEACHING

Every teacher develops a personal style of teaching with which she or he feels most comfortable. This style develops from a combination of personal traits and the expertise of the teacher in methodology, subject matter, and instructional theory. The most effective teachers can vary their styles—that is, their styles are flexible enough to encompass a variety of strategies and are therefore readily available to the different types of situations that may develop. Teaching style is the way teachers teach, their distinctive mannerisms complemented by their choices of teaching behaviors and strategies.

There are other ways to label and describe teaching styles,[7] but here we present two contrasting styles—the traditional and the facilitating (see Figure 5.2). We emphasize that, although today's elementary and middle school science teachers must be eclectic, using the best elements from each style, they should lean heavily toward the facilitating style, which is con-

	Traditional Style	Facilitating Style
Teacher is	Autocratic	Democratic
	Confrontive	Supportive
	Curriculum centered	Student centered
	Direct	Indirect
	Dominative	Interactive
	Formal	Informal
	Informative	Inquiring
	Judgmental	Nonjudgmental
	Prescriptive	Reflective
Classroom is	Teacher centered	Student centered
	Linear (seats facing front)	Grouped or circular seating
	Barren, nondecorative	Stimulating
Instructional mode	Abstract learning	Concrete learning
	Teacher-centered discussions	Discussions
	Lectures	Peer and cross-age coaching
	Competitive learning	Cooperative learning
	Some problem solving	More problem solving
	Demonstration by teacher	Student inquiries
	Teaching moves from simple tasks to complex ones	Starts with complex tasks and uses instructional scaffolding and dialogue
	Transmission of information from teacher to students	Reciprocal teaching, using dialogue between teacher and a small group of students, and then among students

FIGURE 5.2   A contrast of two teaching styles.

sistent with the constructivist philosophy as presented in Chapter 2, and with the access mode as presented in Chapter 3.

Effective teachers can modify their styles by selecting and using the strategy that is most appropriate at the time for teaching specific content to a particular group of students, thus securing active student involvement and the greatest amount of student achievement. Researchers emphasize the importance of integrating traditional (or direct) instructional strategies with the facilitating (experiential) approaches.[8] Highly effective teaching of this sort requires both expertise in a wide variety of methods and a feeling for the appropriate situation in which to use each method, as well as a command of the subject matter and an understanding of the students being taught. This may sound like a large order, but many beginning teachers become adept at it surprisingly quickly.

Thus, to be an effective teacher you should: (1) develop a large repertoire of instructional strategies; (2) learn as much as you can about your students and their individual styles of learning; and (3) develop an eclectic style of teaching, one that is flexible and adaptable, that can function at many locations along the spectrum of integrated learning, as introduced at the beginning of this chapter.

Your teaching style will continue to emerge and develop; your selection and use of various behaviors and strategies will be a continuing consideration throughout your career.

Interdisciplinary Teaching and Teaching Teams Elementary and middle school teachers are members of a professional team. Usually, two to five teachers from the same grade level (elementary schools) or different subject areas (middle schools) work together as a team (grade-level team or interdisciplinary team) to plan the curriculum for a common group of students. (See Figure 5.3.) In middle schools, these teaching teams usually comprise one teacher each from English/language arts, mathematics, science, and history/social studies. These four subject areas constitute what is called the **core curriculum.** In addition to teachers of core subjects, specialty teachers—physical education, art, music, and so on—may be part of the teaching team.

Advantages of teaming are:

1. Teachers experience real collaboration within the workplace and become more satisfied professionally.

8:45–9:00	Whole school assembly (flag salute, birthdays, announcements, songs, and sharing)
9:00–9:20	Spelling in homeroom class
9:20–10:00	Music, art, and physical education (alternating every third day)
10:00–10:10	Bathroom break, change classes
10:10–11:10	Group 1: language arts; group 2: math; group 3: science and social studies
11:10–11:15	Class change
11:15–12:15	Group 1: math; group 2: science and social studies; group 3: language arts
12:15–12:20	Change back to homeroom classes
12:20–12:45	Oral and silent reading in homeroom class
12:45–1:10	Lunch
1:10–1:30	Recess
1:30–1:35	Change classes
1:35–2:35	Group 1: science and social studies; group 2: language arts; group 3: math
2:35–3:20	Reading in homeroom class
3:20–3:25	Clean up and dismissal

FIGURE 5.3 A fifth-grade schedule for a "house" of three teachers.[9]

2. Students feel less isolation and, therefore, greater social bonding with peers and individual teachers.
3. Teachers and students develop a strong sense of community and share a common rationale and mission for education.
4. The instructional program becomes highly coordinated across content areas in a way that encourages student creativity and critical thinking.[10]

One method shown to be successful in making learning meaningful for students is the use of interdisciplinary thematic units (ITU) (the specifics of this approach are presented later). The purpose of the thematic unit approach is to integrate various subject area content by finding a common thread or theme, thereby connecting the students' learning. Students need to know that the information being learned will be practical not only in school, but in the workplace and throughout life. In fact, the essence of today's concept of teaching is based on *connecting life with learning* and is often achieved through interdisciplinary thematic units. As explained at the opening of this chapter, integrated instruction is one step in that direction. When selecting science activities that integrate students' active learning, ask yourself the following questions:

- Does the activity involve more than one subject area?
- Does the activity involve the students in exploring a topic in depth and over an extended period of time?
- Does the activity provide interesting, meaningful, and accurate learning that relates to students' daily lives?
- Does the activity provide opportunity for students to work collaboratively and cooperatively while hypothesizing, making and recording observations, gathering and defending their own evidence, and to express their results in a variety of ways?
- Does the activity accomplish the objective(s) for which it is intended?
- Is the activity within the ability and developmental level of the students?
- Is the activity worth the time and cost needed to do it?
- Are the necessary materials available for doing the activity?
- Is the activity safe for students to do?

School-Within-a-School   In many schools an interdisciplinary team is a functioning instructional team of teachers within a "house" or "school-within-a-school" (also called, a "village," "pod," or "family"), which is assigned each day to the same group of about 125 students for a common block of time. Within this block of time, teachers on the team are responsible for the many professional decisions necessary, such as how to make school meaningful to students' lives, what specific responsibilities each teacher has to fulfill each day, which guidance activities are to be implemented, what sort of special attention is needed by individual students, and how students will be grouped for instruction.

The school-within-a-school concept helps students make important and meaningful connections between disciplines and provides them with peer and adult group identification that offers a significant and concomitant sense of belonging.[11] In middle schools, classes for a village's teachers and students are often clustered in rooms that are close to one another, thereby increasing teacher-teacher and student-teacher communication.

For an interdisciplinary team to plan a common curriculum, members must meet frequently. This is best accomplished by scheduling a shared preparation period to plan the curriculum and to discuss the progress and needs of individual students. A common planning time for members of the teaching team is critical to the success of interdisciplinary teaming.[12]

UNIT PLANNING

Organizing the entire year's content into units makes the teaching process manageable. Whether or not you are teaching in a self-contained classroom, the content you intend to present to students must be organized and carefully planned well in advance. The teaching unit is a major subdivision of a course (for one course or self-contained classroom there are several or many units of instruction), containing instruction planned around a central theme, topic, issue, or problem.

The teaching unit, whether an interdisciplinary thematic unit (known also as an integrated unit), or a stand-alone, standard, subject unit, is not unlike a chapter in a book, an act or scene in a play, or a phase of work in a project such as building a house. Breaking down information or actions into component parts and then grouping the related parts makes sense out of learning and doing. The unit brings a sense of cohesiveness and structure to student learning and avoids the piecemeal approach that might otherwise unfold. You can learn to articulate lessons within, between, and among unit plans and focus on important elements without ignoring significant tangential information. Students remember "chunks" of information, especially when those chunks are related to specific units.

Unit planning should include activities that allow children to work alone, in dyads, and in small groups. Grouping children and assigning roles facilitates science learning. When students have specific and understood tasks and responsibilities, they have more direction and will demonstrate a greater interest in learning.

Types of Units

Although the steps in developing any type of unit are essentially the same, a unit can be organized in a number of ways, basically differentiated and described as follows.

Conventional (or standard) unit. A conventional unit consists of a series of lessons centered on a topic, theme, major concept, or block of subject matter. In a standard unit each lesson builds on the previous lesson by contributing additional subject matter, supplying further illustrations, and providing more practice or added instruction, all of which are aimed at bringing about mastery of the knowledge and skills on which the unit is centered.

Integrated unit. When a conventional unit is centered on a theme, such as "Objects in the Sky," it may be referred to as a thematic unit. When, by design, a thematic unit integrates disciplines, such as one that combines the learning of science and mathematics, or social studies and language arts, or all four of these core disciplines, it is called an integrated (or interdisciplinary) thematic unit.

Self-instructional unit. A self-instructional unit (known also as a modular unit) is a unit of instruction that is designed for individualized or modularized self-instruction. Such a unit is designed for independent, individual study and, because it covers much less content than the units previously described, can generally be completed in a much shorter time, frequently in one class period. Many computer software programs use the self-instructional unit concept. The unit consists of instruction, references, exercises, problems, self-correcting materials, and all other information and materials that a student needs to complete the unit of work independently. Consequently, students can work on such units individually at their own speed, and different students can be working on different units at the same time. Students who successfully finish a modular unit can move on to another unit of work without waiting for others to catch up. These units are essential ingredients of continuous-progress courses. Whether for purposes of remediation, enrichment, or make-up, self-instructional units work especially well when done at and in conjunction with a learning activity center.

Contract unit. A contract unit is an individualized unit of instruction for which a student agrees (contracts) (and sometimes parents, too) to perform certain activities.[13] Some contract units have variables built in, such as variable time completion dates and variable letter grades, depending on the number and quality of activities completed.

Procedure for Planning and Developing Any Unit of Instruction

For the several types of unit plans—conventional unit, contract unit, self-instructional unit, and interdisciplinary thematic unit—steps in planning and development are the same. The procedure is as follows:

1. *Select a suitable topic or theme.* Topics or themes are often laid out in your science curriculum framework, course of study, or textbook, or have already been agreed to by members of the teaching team.
2. *Select the goals of the unit.* Goals are written as an overview or rationale, covering what the unit is about and what the students are to learn. In planning goals, you should:
   a. Become as familiar as possible with the topic and materials used.
   b. Consult curriculum documents, such as courses of study, state frameworks, and resource units, for ideas.
   c. Decide the content and procedures, i.e., what the students should learn about the topic and how.

When planning, it is important to select content that lends itself to manageable learning activities. A well-planned activity-based program of study benefits all types of learners and learning styles.

      d. Write the rationale or overview, summarizing what you hope the students will learn about the topic.

      e. Be sure your goals are congruent with those of the course.

3. *Select suitable specific learning objectives.*

      a. Include understandings, skills, attitudes, appreciations, and ideals.

      b. Be specific, avoiding vagueness and generalizations.

      c. Write the objectives in behavioral terms.

      d. Be as certain as possible that the objectives will contribute to the major learning described in the overview.

4. *Detail the instructional procedures.* These procedures include the subject content and the learning activities, established as a series of lessons. Proceed with the following steps in your initial planning of the instructional procedures:

      a. Gather ideas for learning activities that may be suitable for the unit. Refer to curriculum documents, resource units, and other teachers as resources.

      b. Check the learning activities to make sure that they will actually contribute to the learning designated in your objectives, discarding ideas that do not.

      c. Make sure that the learning activities are feasible. Can you afford the time, effort, or expense? Do you have the necessary materials and equipment? If not, can they be obtained? Are the activities suited to the intellectual and maturity levels of your students?

   d. Check resources available to be certain that they support the content and learning activities.

   e. Decide how to introduce the unit. Provide introductory activities, activities that:

     (1) Arouse student interest.

     (2) Inform students of what the unit is about.

     (3) Help you learn about your students—their interests, abilities, experiences, and present knowledge of the topic.

     (4) Provide transitions that bridge this topic with one that students have already learned.

     (5) Involve students in the planning.

   f. Plan developmental activities, activities that:

     (1) Sustain student interest.

     (2) Provide for individual student differences.

     (3) Promote the learning as cited in the specific objectives.

   g. Plan culminating activities, activities that:

     (1) Summarize what has been learned.

     (2) Bring together loose ends.

     (3) Apply what has been learned to new and meaningful situations.

     (4) Provide transfer to the unit that follows.

5. *Plan for preassessment and assessment of student learning.* Preassess what students already know, or think they know. Assessment of student progress in achievement of the learning objectives (formative evaluation) should permeate the entire unit. Plan to gather information in several ways, including informal observations, observation of student performance, portfolio assessment, and paper and pencil assessments. Assessment, as discussed in the next chapter, must be consistent with the specific learning objectives.

6. *Provide for the materials of instruction.* The unit cannot function without materials. Therefore, you must plan long before the unit begins for media equipment and materials, references, reading materials, reproduced materials, science equipment, and community resources. Material that is not available to the students is of no help to them.

These six steps are followed in developing any type of unit. There is, however, an additional point to keep in mind: there is no set duration for implementing a unit, although, for specific units, curriculum guides usually indicate a suggested time duration. Units may extend for a minimum of several days or, as in the case of interdisciplinary thematic units, for several weeks. However, be aware that when conventional units last more than two or three weeks, they tend to lose their identity as clearly identifiable units. The exact time duration will be dictated by several factors, including the topic or theme, the grade level, and the interests and abilities of the students.

- *Conducting scientific inquiry requires that students have easy and frequent opportunities to use a wide range of equipment, materials, supplies, and other resources for experimentation and direct investigation of phenomena.*
- *Good science programs require access to the world beyond the classroom.*[14]

THE INTERDISCIPLINARY THEMATIC UNIT (ITU)

As we have emphasized, interdisciplinary thematic teaching helps students to bridge the disciplines and to connect school learning with real-life experiences. (Sample ITUs are presented at the end of Chapters 10 and 14.) The six steps outlined earlier are essential in planning any type of teaching unit, including the interdisciplinary thematic (or integrated) unit. The interdisciplinary thematic unit is made up of smaller subject-specific units, developed according to the preceding guidelines.[15] For example, in 1991 at a school in Yorktown, Virginia, four teachers decided to make connections, for their students, between their disciplines—science, mathematics, geography, and English. Using a common planning period to collaborate, the teachers began modestly with an assignment to summarize earth science articles that strengthened students' knowledge of science as well as their writing skills. Later in the year,

Social interaction is an important component for learning science. While learning science, children can also learn reading and language arts, social studies, mathematics, and how to cooperate with and respect others.

the teachers launched an interdisciplinary project focused on the winter Olympics in Albertville, France. In small groups, students were presented with a problem related to one aspect of hosting the Olympics—providing transportation, food, lodging, entertainment, or security. The groups wrote proposals setting forth their solutions, drawing on what they had learned about the geography of the region and applying science knowledge and math skills. The English teacher taught vocabulary that students would encounter in their mathematics and earth science classes.[16]

At a junior high school in Concord, New Hampshire, a teaching team made up of five teachers (science, mathematics, English, social studies, and language arts) decided to build an ITU around the theme of animal behavior. Within that ITU they built a unit on the topic of wolves, because this topic provided a combination of images and issues for students to explore. Although wolves are sometimes perceived as friend and protector (as in the mythological tale of Romulus and Remus), more often they are viewed as dangerous and scary creatures. But today, in an effort to obtain balance in various ecosystems, wolves are being introduced by humans into environments where they had previously been extinct. The team felt that these issues suggested numerous opportunities for integrated learning. In science, the students combined textbook-based learning with the use of a variety of tradebooks and films, worked in cooperative groups to research topics, maintained individual journals, and followed up their study with a written report. In mathematics, "students analyzed population studies, predator/prey ratios, and territory/pack size projections, and then used data from those studies to practice their graphing, mapping, and computational skills." In social studies, the students studied the geographical aspects of wolf distribution and the interrelationship between humans and the reintroduction of wolf populations. In English and language arts, students "wrote letters to obtain information about wolves, analyzed the portrayal of wolves in literature, and considered the effects of animals in magazine advertisements."[17]

Some teaching teams develop one interdisciplinary thematic unit each year, semester, trimester, or quarter; that is, from one to four a year. Over time, then, the team develops several units that are available for implementation. However, the most effective units are often those that are most current or most meaningful to students. This means that ever-changing global, national, and local topics provide a veritable smorgasbord from which to choose, and teaching teams must constantly be aware of the changes in the world and society, as well as in the interests of students, to update old units and develop new and exciting ones.

One teaching team's unit should not conflict with another's at the same or another grade level. If a school has two or more seventh-grade teams, for example, the teams may want to develop units on different themes and share their products. Or a middle school team may want to share their units with high school teams and, perhaps, with feeder elementary schools. The lines of communication within, between, and among teams and schools is critical to the success of thematic teaching.

Because developing interdisciplinary thematic units increasingly is becoming an essential task for teachers, it behooves you to learn now the process that you may be practicing later as an employed teacher (as well as when student teaching). The following are steps for developing an interdisciplinary thematic unit.

1. *Agree on the nature or source of origin for the interdisciplinary thematic unit.* Team members should view the interdisciplinary approach as a collective effort in which all team members (and other faculty) participate somewhat equally. Discuss how the team wants students to profit from interdisciplinary instruction. Troubleshoot for possible stumbling blocks.

2. *Discuss subject-specific frameworks, goals and objectives, curriculum guidelines, textbooks and supplemental materials, and units already in place for the school year.* This discussion should focus on what each teacher must teach and should explain the scope and sequence so all team members share an understanding of perceived constraints and limitations.

3. *Choose a topic and develop a time line*. From the information provided by each subject specialist teacher regarding step 2, list possible topics that can be drawn from within the existing course outlines. Give and take is essential at this step, as some topics will fit certain subjects better than others. The chief goal here is to find a workable topic, that is, one that can be adapted to each subject without detracting from the educational plan already in place. This may require choosing and merging content from two or more other units previously planned. The theme is then drawn from the topic. In considering a theme, the team should consider these questions:

- Can this theme lead to a unit that is of proper duration, not too short and not too long?
- Is it worth the time needed to create and implement the theme? Do we have sufficient materials and resources to supply information we might need?
- Is the theme within the realm of understanding and experience of the teachers involved? Is the theme topic one with which teachers are not already too familiar, so they can share in the excitement of the learning? Will the theme be of interest to all members of the teaching team? Does it apply broadly to a wide range of subject areas?
- What is so important about this theme that it will promote future learning? Does it have substance and application to the real world? Does it lend itself to active learning? Will it be of interest to students; will it motivate them to do their best? Will it fascinate students once they are into it?

4. *Set two time lines*. The first time line is set for the team only and is set to ensure that given dates for specific work required in developing the unit will be met by each member. The second time line is for students and teachers and shows how long the unit will be, when it will start, and in which classes.

5. *Develop the scope and sequence for content and instruction*. Referring to the six steps for planning and developing a unit of instruction (listed earlier in this chapter), follow those steps for developing the interdisciplinary thematic unit. This should be done by team members individually, and as a group during common planning time, so team members can coordinate dates and activities in logical sequence and depth. This is an organic process that will generate ideas but can also produce some anxiety. Members of the team, under the guidance of the team leader, should strive to lower anxiety to a level conducive to learning, experimenting, and arriving at group consensus.

6. *Share goals and objectives*. Each team member should have a copy of the goals and objectives of every other member. This helps to refine the unit and lesson plans and to prevent unnecessary overlap and confusion.

7. *Give the unit its name*. The unit is based on a common topic and is unified by the theme you have chosen. Giving the theme a name and using that name lets the students know that this unit of study is integrated, important, and meaningful to school and to life.

8. *Share subject-specific units, lesson plans, print and nonprint materials*. After teachers have finalized their units, exchange them for review comments and suggestions. Keep a copy of each teacher's unit(s) and determine whether you could present a lesson from it for your own subject area. If you can, the plans are probably workable. If you can't, some modification may be necessary.

9. *Field-test the thematic unit*. Beginning at the agreed-upon time and date, and with the designated class(es), present the lessons. Team members may trade classes from time to time. Team teaching may take place when two or more classes can be combined for instruction, such as can be done with flexible and block scheduling. After field-testing, there is, of course, one final step, step 10. This is when the thematic unit is assessed and, perhaps, adjusted and revised. Team members discuss successes and failures during their common planning time and determine what needs to be changed, how, and when, to make the unit successful. Adjustments to the unit can be made along the way (by collecting data during

formative assessments), and revisions for future use can be made after the unit is completed (from data collected during summative assessment).

The preceding steps are not absolutes and should be viewed only as guides. Differing compositions of teaching teams and levels of teacher experience and knowledge make strict adherence to any procedural steps less productive than group-generated plans. In practice, the process that works for the team—one that results in meaningful student learning and in students' feeling good about themselves, about learning, and about school—is the appropriate process.

LESSON PLANNING

The emphasis in this chapter is on the importance and the details of planning your instruction. In this section you will be guided through the process of selecting content for a course, to preparing the specific learning outcomes expected as students learn that content. Then, from your knowledge of expected content to be taught and the related and specific learning outcomes, in the sections that follow you learn more on how to prepare daily lessons.

Although careful planning is a critical skill for a teacher, a well-developed plan for teaching will not guarantee the success of a lesson or unit or even the overall effectiveness of a course. However, the lack of a well-developed plan will almost certainly result in poor teaching. Like a good map, a good plan facilitates reaching the planned destination with greater confidence and with fewer wrong turns.

The heart of good planning is good decision making. For every plan, you must decide what your goals and objectives are, what specific subject matter should be taught, what materials of instruction are available and appropriate, and what methods and techniques should be employed to accomplish the objectives. Making these decisions is complicated because there are so many choices. Therefore, you must be knowledgeable about the principles that undergird effective planning. That the principles of all levels of educational planning are much the same makes mastering the necessary skills easier than you might now think.

Reasons for Planning

Thoughtful and thorough planning is vital if effective teaching is to occur. It helps to produce well-organized classes and a purposeful classroom atmosphere, and it reduces the likelihood of problems in classroom control. A teacher who has not planned or who has underprepared will have more problems than are imaginable. While planning, it is useful to keep in mind these two important teacher goals: (1) to not waste anyone's time and (2) to select strategies that keep students physically and mentally engaged on task and that assure student learning.

Thoughtful and thorough planning is likely to make your classes more lively, more interesting, more accurate, and more relevant, and your teaching more successful. Although good planning assures that you know the material well, have thought through the methods of instruction, and are less likely to have problems in classroom control, there are still other reasons for planning thoughtfully and thoroughly.

Careful planning helps to ensure program coherence. Daily plans are an integral part of a larger plan represented by the goals and objectives of the science curriculum. Students' learning experiences are thoughtfully planned in sequence, then orchestrated by a teacher who understands the rationale for their respective positions in the curriculum, not precluding, of course, an occasional diversion from planned activities.

There are prerequisites to what you want your students to learn, and there are learning objectives that follow and build on this learning. Good planning provides a mechanism for articulation of the scope (the content that is covered) and sequence (the order) of the content.

The diversity of students in today's classrooms demands that in planning you give consideration to students' individual differences—whether cultural experiences, different learning styles, various levels of proficiency in the use of the English language, special needs, or any other concerns.

Another reason for careful planning is to ensure program continuation. In your absence, a substitute teacher, or other members of the teaching team filling in, will use your plans to continue the program.

Thorough and thoughtful planning is also important for a teacher's self-assessment. After an activity, a lesson, a unit, and at the end of a semester and the school year, you will reflect on and assess what was done and the effect it had on student achievement. As discussed earlier, this is the reflective stage of the thought-processing phases of instruction.

Finally, administrators expect you to plan thoroughly and thoughtfully. Your plans represent a criterion recognized and evaluated by administrators, because with those experienced in such matters, it is aphoristic that inadequate attention to planning is a precursor to incompetent teaching.

COMPONENTS OF PLANNING

There are eight components to consider in instructional planning:

1. *Statement of Philosophy*. This is a general statement about why the plan is important and about how students will learn its content.

2. *Needs Assessment*. By its wording, the statement of philosophy should reflect an appreciation for the cultural plurality of the nation and of the school, with a corresponding perception of the needs of society and its students, and of the functions served by the school. The statement of philosophy and needs of the students should be consistent with the school's mission or philosophy statement. Every school or school district has such a statement, which can usually be found posted in the office, in classrooms, and written in the student and parent handbook. For example, the mission statement of Meyer Elementary School in Tempe, Arizona, reads as follows:

> Meyer School's mission is to nurture children to grow naturally and creatively as they develop connections across all areas of the curriculum. An integrated curriculum provides learning experiences which are designed to meet the individual and unique needs of each student. Learning flourishes in a stimulating and emotionally supportive environment. Interactive classrooms allow students to extend their knowledge and develop a strong academic foundation for success in present and future educational experiences.

3. *Aims, Goals, and Objectives*. The plan's stated aims, goals, and objectives (the difference in these terms is discussed later in this chapter) should be consistent with the school's mission or philosophy statement.

4. *Sequence*. Sometimes referred to as vertical articulation, sequence refers to the plan's relationship to the content learning that preceded and that follows, in the kindergarten through twelfth-grade curriculum.

5. *Integration*. Sometimes referred to as horizontal articulation, integration refers to the plan's connection with other curriculum and co-curriculum activities across the grade level. For example, the science program may be articulated with the mathematics program.

The science program should be coordinated with the mathematics program to enhance students use and understanding of mathematics in the study of science and to improve student understanding of mathematics overall.[18]

---

6. *Sequentially Planned Learning Activities.* This is the presentation of organized and sequential units and lessons appropriate for the subject and grade level, and for the age and diversity of the students.

7. *Resources Needed.* This is a listing of resources, such as books, speakers, field trips, and media materials.

8. *Assessment Strategies.* Consistent with the objectives, assessment strategies include procedures for diagnosing what students know or think they know (their misconceptions) *prior* to instruction (diagnostic assessment or preassessment), the evaluation of student achievement *during* instruction to find out what students are learning (formative assessment), and *after* instruction to find out what they have learned (summative assessment). Assessment is the topic of the next chapter.

When planning a science program, you must decide what is to be accomplished in that time period for which students are in your classroom, whether for an academic year, a semester, or some shorter time period. To help in deciding what is to be accomplished, you will probe, analyze, and translate your own convictions, knowledge, and skills into behaviors that foster the intellectual development of your students; review school and other public resource documents for mandates and guidelines; and talk with colleagues and learn of common expectations. In addition, as discussed later in this chapter, in many instances, to determine what exactly is to be accomplished and how it is to be done, many teachers plan collaboratively with their students.

Documents That Provide Guidance for Content Selection

Documents produced at the national level, state department of education curriculum frameworks, district courses of study, and school-adopted printed and nonprinted materials are the sources you will examine to obtain guidance for content selection. To examine such documents now, your college or university library may be a source. Others may be borrowed from or seen at local schools.

In about half of the states, middle schools and junior high schools are accredited by state or regional agencies. In other states, middle level schools can volunteer to be reviewed for improvement. To receive accreditation (which normally occurs every three to six years), schools are reviewed by an accreditation team. Prior to the team's visit, the schools prepare self-study reports, for which each department reviews and updates the curriculum guides that provide descriptive information about the objectives and content of each course and program offered. Elementary schools do not go through an accreditation process.

NATIONAL CURRICULUM STANDARDS

The National Council on Education Standards and Testing has recommended that national standards for subject matter content in education be developed for all core subjects—the arts, civics/social studies, English/language arts/reading, geography, history, mathematics, and science. Standards are definitions of what students should know and be able to do. For example,

---

A curriculum framework is used to guide the selection and development of units and courses of study. The goals for a science program provide the statements of philosophy and the vision that drive the program and the statements of purpose for which program is designed. The curriculum framework guides teachers as they select and design specific school and classroom work and ensures articulation and coherence for students as they move through their schooling.[19]

---

in 1989, the National Council of Teachers of Mathematics issued standards for mathematics for grades K–12. By 1992 more than 40 states, usually through state curriculum frameworks, were following those standards to guide what and how mathematics is taught and how student progress is assessed.

With a grant from the U.S. Department of Education, the National Research Council's National Committee on Science Education Standards and Assessment (with input from the American Association for the Advancement of Science and the National Science Teachers Association) developed standards for science education that were completed and published in 1996, and it is these standards that have provided guidance for this edition of our book.

COLLABORATIVE AND COOPERATIVE TEAM PLANNING

As you have learned, you need not do all your instructional planning from scratch, nor do you have to do all your planning alone. Planning for teaching can be thought of as rehearsing, both mentally and on paper, what will be done in the classroom. In science classrooms today, which tend to be more project-oriented, student- and group-centered, rather than tradition-ally teacher-centered, with the teacher as the primary provider of information, students more actively participate in their learning. The teacher provides some structure and assistance, but the collaborative approach requires that students inquire and interact, generate ideas, seriously listen and talk with one another, and recognize that their thoughts and experiences are valuable and essential to meaningful learning.

As discussed earlier, teachers often plan together in teams. Team members may plan together, or split the responsibilities and later share their individual planning, then cooperatively work their joint efforts into a final plan. Team planning works best when members of the teaching team have a common planning time.

Many teachers encourage students to participate in the planning of some phase of their learning; their involvement can range from planning an entire course of study, or units within that course of study, to specific learning activities within a unit of study. Such participation tends to give students a proprietary interest in the activities, thereby increasing their motivation for learning. That which students have contributed to the plan often seems more meaningful to them than what others have planned for them. And they like to see their own plans succeed. Thus, teacher-student collaboration in planning can be an effective motivational tool.

Preparing for the Year

Although some authors believe that the first step in preparing to teach is to write the objectives, others believe that a more logical first step is to prepare a sequential topic outline. The sequential course outline may be prepared by one teacher, by a team of teachers, or collaboratively with students. Whatever the case, from that outline, you can then prepare some of the important expected learning outcomes. Once you have decided on the content and anticipated outcomes, you are ready to divide this material into subdivisions or units of instruction and then prepare those units with their sequential lessons.

Most beginning teachers have the topic outlines and the instructional objectives presented to them (in the course of study or in the teacher's edition of the student textbook) with the expectation (often implied) that they will teach from them. For you, this may be the case, but someone had to have written these outlines and objectives, and that someone was one or several teachers. So, as a beginning teacher, you should know how this task is done, for some-day you will be concentrating on it in earnest.

A CAUTION ABOUT SELECTION AND SEQUENCING OF CONTENT

It is important to be aware that beginning teachers sometimes have unrealistic expectations about the amount of content a heterogeneous group of students can study, comprehend, and learn over a given period of time, considering that learning by these students is influenced by special needs and diverse cultural and language backgrounds. Reviewing school and other public documents and talking with experienced teachers in your school can be very helpful in choosing a realistic selection and sequencing of content, and the later development of a time frame for teaching that content. As Brooks and Brooks conclude,

> Constructivist teachers have discovered that the prescribed scope, sequence, and timeline often interferes with their ability to help students understand complex concepts. Rigid timelines are also at odds with research on how human beings form meaningful theories about the ways the world works, how students and teachers develop an appreciation of knowledge and understanding, and how one creates the disposition to inquire about phenomena not fully understood. Most curriculums simply pack too much information into too little time—at a significant cost to the learner.[20]

Once you have analyzed various curriculum documents and have prepared a content outline, you are ready to prepare the anticipated learning outcomes and write the specific instructional objectives, known also as behavioral (or performance) objectives—statements that describe what the student will be able to do upon completion of the instructional experience.

AIMS, GOALS, AND OBJECTIVES AND THEIR ROLES IN PLANNING

As discussed in Chapter 1, goals are general statements of intent, which are prepared early in course planning. Goals are useful when planned cooperatively with students and/or when shared with students as advance mental organizers. The students then know what to expect and can begin to prepare mentally to learn the subject matter. From the goals, specific objectives are prepared and written in behavioral terms.[21] Objectives are *not* intentions. They are the actual behaviors teachers intend to cause students to display. In short, objectives are what students *do*.

There is no standardization of terminology used for designating the various types of objectives. In the literature, the most general educational objectives are often called *aims*; the general objectives of schools, curricula, and courses are called *goals*; and the objectives of units and lessons are called *instructional objectives*.[22] Aims are more general than goals, goals are more general than objectives. Instructional (behavioral) objectives are quite specific.

As implied in the preceding paragraphs, goals guide the instructional methods; objectives drive student performance. Assessment (i.e., evaluation) of student achievement in learning should be an assessment of that performance. When the assessment procedure does match the instructional objectives, it is sometimes referred to as assessment that is aligned or authentic (discussed in Chapter 6).

Although instructional goals may not always be quantifiable, that is, readily measurable, instructional objectives should be measurable. Furthermore, those objectives then become the essence of what is measured in instruments designed to authentically assess student learning.

Consider the following examples of goals and objectives.

Goals   1. To learn about the properties of sound
              2. To provide opportunities for student inquiry

Objectives 1. The student will demonstrate that the pitch of the sound can be varied by changing the rate of vibration.
              2. The student will follow his or her own inquiry by asking a question, designing and completing an investigation about it, answering the question, and presenting the results to others.

Objectives and Their Relationship to Instruction and Assessment

One purpose for writing objectives in specific behavioral terms is to be able to assess with precision whether the instruction has resulted in the desired behavior. In many school districts the educational goals are established as competencies that the students are expected to achieve. This is known variously as *competency-based, performance-based,* or *outcome-based education.*[23] These goals are then divided into specific performance objectives, sometimes referred to as *goal indicators*. When students perform the competencies called for by these objectives, their education is considered successful. Expecting students to achieve one set of competencies before moving on to the next set is called *mastery learning* (discussed in Chapter 3). The success of school curricula, teacher performance, and student achievement may each be assessed according to these criteria.

Assessment is not difficult to accomplish when the desired performance is overt, that is, when it can be observed directly. Each of the two sample objectives of the preceding section is an example of an objective involving overt performance. Assessment is more difficult to accomplish when the desired behavior is covert, that is, when it is not directly observable. Although certainly no less important, behaviors that call for "appreciation," "discovery," or "understanding," for example, are not directly observable because they occur within a person, and so are covert behaviors. Because covert behavior cannot be observed directly, the only way to tell whether the objective has been achieved is to observe behavior that may be indicative of that achievement. The objective, then, must be written in overt language, and evaluators can only assume or trust that the observed behavior is, in fact, reasonably close to being indicative of the expected learning outcome.

Behaviorism and Constructivism: Are They Mutually Exclusive?

Whereas behaviorists (behaviorism) assume a definition of learning that deals only with changes in observable behavior (overt), constructivists (cognitivism), as discussed in Chapter 2, hold that learning entails the construction or reshaping of mental schemata and that mental processes mediate learning, and so are concerned with both overt and covert behaviors.[24]

Furthermore, in assessing whether an objective has been achieved, the assessment device must be consistent with the desired learning outcome; otherwise the assessment is invalid. When the measuring device and the learning objective are compatible, the assessment is referred to as being authentic. For example, a person's competency to teach fourth-grade students is best measured (i.e., with highest reliability) by directly observing that person *doing* that very thing—teaching fourth-grade students. Such assessment is referred to as being authentic. Using a standardized paper-and-pencil test to determine a person's ability to teach fourth graders is not.

Does this mean that you must be one or the other, a behaviorist or a constructivist? For teachers in the trenches, behaviorism and constructivism are not mutually exclusive. For now, the point is that when writing instructional objectives, you should write most or all of your basic expectations (minimal competency expectations) in overt terms (the topic of the next section), but, on the other hand, you cannot be expected to foresee all learning that occurs nor to translate all that is learned into behavioral terms—most certainly not before it occurs. We agree with those who argue that any effort to write all learning objectives in behavioral terms is, in effect, to neglect the individual learner for whom it purports to be concerned; such an approach does not allow for diversity among learners. Learning that is most meaningful to students is not so neatly nor easily predicted or isolated. Rather than teaching one objective at a time, much of the time you will be directing your teaching toward the simultaneous learning of multiple objectives, understandings, and appreciations. However, when you assess for learning, assessment is cleaner when objectives are assessed one at a time.

Preparing Instructional Objectives

When preparing instructional objectives, you must ask yourself: "How is the student to demonstrate that the objective has been reached?" For example, although "The student will enjoy science" may be an appropriate educational goal, it is not a behavioral objective. It is too ambiguous. The objective must include an action that demonstrates that the objective has been achieved, such as, "The student will demonstrate an enjoyment of science by volunteering to create a science display for the display case in the main building." We can only assume that volunteering to create a science display shows the expected achievement of enjoyment. That portion of the objective, in this case creating a display, is sometimes referred to as the terminal behavior, or the anticipated measurable performance, and is important in an outcome-based educational (OBE) program.

The example in the preceding paragraph represents a "responding" objective in the affective domain (see "Classification of Learning Objectives" on page 184). In assessment of learning, objectives of this domain are complicated because they represent attitudes, values, and feelings, behaviors that, although important, are difficult to measure objectively. Let's look at another example, one in the cognitive domain, the domain of knowledge.

Although the statement, "The student will know the order of the planets in our solar system," might be an appropriate educational goal, it, too, is not a behavioral objective. The primary reason it is not an acceptable statement of behavior is that it does not state how the student will demonstrate this knowledge.

Other examples will follow, but first let's consider the key components of a behaviorally stated objective.

FOUR KEY COMPONENTS TO WRITING OBJECTIVES

When completely written, an instructional objective has four key components. To aid in your understanding and remembering, you can refer to this as the ABCDs of writing behavioral objectives.

One of the components is the *audience*—the A of the ABCDs, that is, the student for whom the objective is intended. To address this audience, teachers sometimes begin their objectives with the phrase "The student will be able to . . ." or, to personalize the objective, "You will be able to . . ."

The second key component is the expected *behavior*—the B of the ABCDs. The expected behavior (or performance) should be written in terms that are measurable, that is, with action verbs. The reason for this is so it is measurable (directly observable) that an objective has been reached. As discussed earlier, some verbs (covert behaviors) are too vague, ambiguous, and not clearly measurable. When writing objectives, avoid verbs that are not clearly measurable, such as *appreciate, believe, comprehend, enjoy, know, learn, like,* and *understand* (see Figure 5.4).

appreciate
believe
comprehend
enjoy
familiarize
grasp
indicate
know
learn
like
realize
understand

FIGURE 5.4 Verbs to avoid when writing objectives.

The third ingredient is the *condition*—the C of the ABCDs—the setting in which the behavior will be demonstrated by the student and observed by the teacher.

The fourth ingredient, but not always included in objectives written by teachers, is the *degree (or level) of expected performance*—the D of the ABCDs. This is the ingredient that allows for the assessment of student learning. When mastery learning is expected (achievement of 85 to 100 percent), the level of expected performance is usually omitted (because it is understood). In teaching for mastery learning, the performance-level expectation is 100 percent. In reality, however, the performance level will most likely be between 85 and 95 percent, particularly in working with a group of students rather than with an individual student. The 5 to 15 percent difference reflects human error, as can occur with written and oral communication.

Performance level is used to assess student achievement, and it is sometimes used to evaluate the effectiveness of the teaching. Student grades may be based on performance levels; evaluation of teacher effectiveness may be based on the level of student performance. In recent years there has been a rekindling of interest in performance-based (or outcome-based, or competency-based) assessment.

Using one of our earlier examples, suppose your goal is to have your students be able to manipulate nine varying sizes of Styrofoam balls, each named for one of the planets of our solar system, by placing them on a table in the correct order starting from a basketball that represents the sun. The behavioral objective could read as follows: "When given nine Styrofoam

While learning science content, children can also develop their gross and fine motor skills.

balls, each labeled to represent a planet, and a basketball on the table to represent the sun (*the conditions*), the student (*the audience*) will correctly place the Styrofoam balls in order according to the distance of the planets from the sun (*the measurable performance*), with 80 percent accuracy (*the performance level*)." This means that the child's performance is acceptable if no more than two of the balls are out of sequence. (Including the basketball, there is a total of 10 balls). Or, if you desire that the objective be written to include the entire class's performance, you could write it as: "When given nine Styrofoam balls, each labeled to represent a planet, and a basketball on the table to represent the sun, the students will correctly place the balls in order according to the distance of the planets from the sun, with 80 percent accuracy." Or, if you have each student do the task separately, you might consider the class's performance acceptable if at least 80 percent of the students complete the task without error. Whereas the first objective is written specifically to determine a student's performance, the last two are not student-specific and so are more representative of teaching performance.

Classification of Learning Objectives

Useful in planning and assessing student learning are three domains for classifying learning objectives:

- Cognitive domain, the domain of learning that involves mental operations from the lowest level of simple recall of information to high-level and complex evaluative processes
- Affective domain, the domain of learning that involves feelings, attitudes, and values, from lower levels of acquisition to the highest level of internalization and action
- Psychomotor domain, the domain of learning that involves learning ranging from the low-level, simple manipulation of materials, to the higher level of communication of ideas, and finally to the highest level of creative performance

Exemplary schools attempt to provide learning experiences designed to meet the needs of the total child. Specifically, five areas of developmental needs are identified: (1) intellectual, (2) physical, (3) psychological, (4) social, and (5) moral and ethical. You should include learning objectives that address each of these developmental needs. In regard to the domains for classification of learning objectives, although the intellectual is primarily within the cognitive domain, and the physical is within the psychomotor, the others lie mostly within the affective domain.

Too frequently, teacher attention is directed to the cognitive, with the assumption that the psychomotor and affective will take care of themselves. Effective teachers direct their planning and sequence their teaching so students are guided from the lowest to the highest levels of operation within and across all of the three domains.

Following are the three developmental hierarchies to guide your understanding of how you can address each of the five areas of needs in teaching science. Notice the illustrative verbs within each hierarchy of each domain. These verbs help you to fashion your behavioral objectives for the lesson plans you will soon be developing.

COGNITIVE DOMAIN HIERARCHIES

In a taxonomy of objectives that is widely accepted, Benjamin Bloom and his associates arranged cognitive objectives into classifications according to the complexity of the skills and abilities embodied in the objectives.[25] The resulting taxonomy portrays a ladder ranging from the simplest to the most complex intellectual processes.[26] (*Note:* Within any of the domains, prerequisite to a student's ability to function at one level of the hierarchy is the student's ability to function at the preceding level or levels. In other words, when a student is functioning at the third level of the cognitive domain, that student is automatically also functioning at the first and second levels.)

The six major categories (or levels) in Bloom's taxonomy of cognitive objectives are:

Level 1. *Knowledge*. Recognizing and recalling information.
Level 2. *Comprehension*. Understanding the meaning of information.
Level 3. *Application*. Using information.
Level 4. *Analysis*. Ability to dissect information into component parts and see relationships.
Level 5. *Synthesis*. Putting components together to form new ideas.
Level 6. *Evaluation*. Judging the worth of an idea, notion, theory, thesis, proposition, information, or opinion.

Bloom's taxonomy includes various subcategories within each of these six major categories, but space does not allow such elaboration here. It is less important that an objective be absolutely classified than it is for you to be cognizant of hierarchies of levels of thinking and doing and to understand the importance of attending to student cognitive development and intellectual behavior from lower to higher levels of operation, in all three domains. A discussion of each of Bloom's six categories follows.

Knowledge The basic element in Bloom's taxonomy concerns the acquisition of knowledge—that is, the ability to recognize and recall information. Although this is the lowest level of the six categories, the information to be learned may not itself be of a low level. In fact, the information may be of an extremely high level. Bloom includes at this level knowledge of principles, generalizations, theories, structures, and methodology, as well as knowledge of facts and ways of dealing with facts.

Action verbs appropriate for this category include *choose, complete, define, describe, identify, indicate, list, locate, match, name, outline, recall, recognize, select*, and *state*. (Note that some verbs may be appropriately used at more than one cognitive level.)

The following is an illustrative example of objectives at this cognitive level.

- The student will state the chemical symbols for the elements hydrogen, oxygen, sulfur, and nitrogen.

Beyond the first category, knowledge, the remaining five categories of Bloom's taxonomy of the cognitive domain deal with the *use* of knowledge. They encompass the educational objectives aimed at developing cognitive skills and abilities, including comprehension, application, analysis, synthesis, and evaluation of knowledge. The last three—analysis, synthesis, and evaluation—are referred to as higher-order thinking skills.

Comprehension Comprehension includes the ability to translate or explain knowledge, to interpret that knowledge, and to extrapolate from it to address new situations.

Action verbs appropriate for this category include *change, classify, convert, defend, derive, describe, estimate, expand, explain, generalize, infer, interpret, paraphrase, predict, recognize, summarize*, and *translate*.

The following is an illustrative example of objectives at this cognitive level.

- When given the temperature in degrees Celsius, the student will correctly convert it to Fahrenheit.

Application Once students understand information, they should be able to apply it. This is the category of operation above comprehension.

Action verbs include *apply, compute, demonstrate, develop, discover, discuss, modify, operate, participate, perform, plan, predict, relate, show, solve,* and *use.*

The following is an illustrative example of objectives at this cognitive level.

- When given two coats on a cold winter day, a light-colored one and a dark-colored one, the student will correctly predict which would be warmest (assuming they are alike in all other respects).

Analysis   This category includes objectives that require students to use the skills of analysis.

Action verbs appropriate for this category include *analyze, break down, categorize, classify, compare, contrast, debate, deduce, diagram, differentiate, discriminate, identify, illustrate, infer, outline, relate, separate,* and *subdivide.*

The following is an illustrative example of objectives at this level.

- The student will detect discrepancies between advertising claims and actual nutritional quality of certain edible products.

Synthesis   This category includes objectives that involve such skills as designing a plan, proposing a set of operations, and deriving a series of abstract relations.

Action verbs appropriate for this category include *arrange, categorize, classify, combine, compile, constitute, create, design, develop, devise, document, explain, formulate, generate, modify, organize, originate, plan, produce, rearrange, reconstruct, revise, rewrite, summarize, synthesize, tell, transmit,* and *write.*

The following is an illustrative example of objectives at this cognitive level.

- From facts generated during a discussion of the controversy about the spotted owl and the cutting of forest trees in the Northwest, the student will summarize the environmental concerns raised by the issue.

Evaluation   The highest cognitive category of Bloom's taxonomy is evaluation. This includes offering opinions and making value judgments.

Action verbs appropriate for this category include *appraise, argue, assess, compare, conclude, consider, contrast, criticize, decide, discriminate, evaluate, explain, interpret, judge, justify, rank, rate, relate, standardize, support,* and *validate.*

The following is an illustrative example of objectives at this cognitive level.

- The student will write a critical appraisal of a magazine article about the use of nuclear power generating plants.

AFFECTIVE DOMAIN HIERARCHIES

Krathwohl, Bloom, and Masia developed a taxonomy for the affective domain.[27] The following are the major levels (or categories) they identified, ranging from least internalized to most internalized:

Level 1. *Receiving.* Awareness of an affective stimulus and the beginning of favorable feelings toward it.

Level 2. *Responding.* Taking an interest in the stimulus and viewing it favorably.

Level 3. *Valuing.* Showing a tentative belief in the value of the affective stimulus and becoming committed to it.

Level 4. *Organizing.* Organizing values into a system of dominant and supporting values.

Level 5. *Internalizing values.* Beliefs and behavior are consistent, and become a way of life.

The following paragraphs describe more fully the types of objectives that fit the categories of the affective domain. Although there is considerable overlap between one category and another, they do give a basis by which to judge the quality of objectives and the nature of learning within this domain.

Receiving   At this level, which is the least internalized, the student exhibits willingness to give attention to particular phenomena or stimuli, and the teacher is able to arouse, sustain, and direct that attention.

Action verbs appropriate for this category include *ask, choose, describe, differentiate, distinguish, hold, identify, locate, name, point to, recall, recognize, reply, select,* and *use*.

The following are examples of objectives in this category:

- The student pays close attention to the directions for the exploratory activities.
- The student listens attentively to the ideas of others.

Responding   Students respond to the stimulus they have received. They may do so because of some external pressure, or they may do so voluntarily because they find it interesting or because responding gives them satisfaction.

Action verbs appropriate for this category include *answer, applaud, approve, assist, comply, command, discuss, greet, help, label, perform, play, practice, present, read, recite, report, select, spend (leisure time in), tell,* and *write*.

The following are examples of objectives at this level:

- The student discusses what others have said.
- The student willingly cooperates with others during group activities.

Valuing   Objectives at the valuing level have to do with students' beliefs, attitudes, and appreciations. The simplest objectives concern a student's acceptance of beliefs and values. Higher-level objectives concern a student's learning to prefer certain values and finally becoming committed to them.

Action verbs appropriate for this level include *argue, assist, complete, describe, differentiate, explain, follow, form, initiate, invite, join, justify, propose, protest, read, report, select, share, study, support,* and *work*.

The following are examples of objectives at this level:

- The student supports actions against gender discrimination.
- The student argues in favor of or against a woman's right to abortion.

Organizing   This fourth level in the affective domain concerns the building a personal value system. At this level the student is conceptualizing values and arranging them to a value system that recognizes priorities and relative importance of various values faced in life.

Action verbs appropriate for this level include *adhere, alter, arrange, balance, combine, compare, defend, define, discuss, explain, form, generalize, identify, integrate, modify, order, organize, prepare, relate,* and *synthesize*.

The following are examples of objectives at this level:

- The student forms judgments concerning responsible ecological behavior in the classroom, school, and community.
- The student defends the important values of his or her own culture.

Internalizing Values   This is the highest level within the affective domain. At this level the student's behaviors are consistent with his or her beliefs.

Action verbs appropriate for this level include *act, complete, display, influence, listen, modify, perform, practice, propose, qualify, question, revise, serve, solve,* and *verify.*
The following are examples of objectives appropriate for this level:

- The student behaves according to a well-defined and ethical code of behavior.
- The student works independently and diligently.

PSYCHOMOTOR DOMAIN HIERARCHIES

Whereas identification and classification within the cognitive and affective domains is generally agreed upon, there is less agreement on the classification within the psychomotor domain. Originally, the goal of this domain was simply to develop and categorize proficiencies in skills, particularly those dealing with gross and fine muscle control. Today's classification of this domain, and as presented here, follows that lead but includes at its highest level the most creative and inventive behaviors, thus coordinating skills and knowledge from all three domains. Consequently, the objectives are arranged in a hierarchy from simple gross locomotor control to the most creative and complex, requiring originality and fine locomotor control—for example, from simply threading a needle to designing and making a piece of clothing.

Harrow has developed the following taxonomy of the psychomotor domain.[28] Included here are sample objectives, as well as a list of possible action verbs for each level of the psychomotor domain.

Level 1. *Movement.* This level involves gross motor coordination.
Action verbs appropriate for this level include *adjust, carry, clean, locate, obtain,* and *walk.*
The following is an illustrative example of objectives at this level:
- The student correctly grasps and carries the microscope to the workstation.

Level 2. *Manipulating.* This level involves fine motor coordination.
Action verbs appropriate for this level include *assemble, build, calibrate, connect,* and *thread.*
A sample objective for this level is:
- The student will adjust the microscope so that the object is in focus under high power.

Level 3. *Communicating.* This level involves the communication of ideas and feelings.
Action verbs appropriate for this level include *analyze, ask, describe, draw, explain,* and *write.*
A sample objective for this level is:
- The student will demonstrate the ability to listen to the ideas of others about an environmental issue.

Level 4. *Creating.* This is the highest level of the psychomotor domain, and of all domains, and represents the student's coordination of thinking, learning, and behaving in all three domains.
Action verbs appropriate for this level include *create, design,* and *invent.*
A sample objective for this level is:
- From his or her own data collecting and calculations, the student will design a more time-efficient and learning-effective way of moving people from one place to another on the school campus.

Using the Taxonomies

Theoretically, the taxonomies are so constructed that students achieve each lower level before being ready to move to the higher levels. But because categories and behaviors overlap, as they should, this theory does not always hold in practice. The taxonomies are important in that they emphasize the various levels to which instruction must aspire. For learning to be worthwhile, you must formulate and teach to objectives from the higher levels of the taxonomies as well as from the lower ones. Student thinking and behaving must be moved from the lowest to the highest levels of thinking and behavior. When all is said and done, it is, perhaps, the highest level of the psychomotor domain (creating) that we are striving for.

In using the taxonomies, remember that the point is to formulate the best objectives for the job to be done. The taxonomies provide the mechanism for assuring that you do not spend a disproportionate amount of time on science facts and other learning that is relatively trivial. Writing objectives is essential to the preparation of good items for the assessment of student learning. Clearly communicating your behavioral expectations to students and then specifically assessing student learning against those expectations makes the teaching most efficient and effective, and it makes the assessment of the learning closer to being authentic. This does not mean to imply that you will always write behavioral objectives for everything taught, nor will you always be able to accurately measure what students have learned. Learning that is meaningful to students is not as easily compartmentalized as the taxonomies of educational objectives would imply. As said by Caine and Caine, "The bottom line is that thoughts and feelings are inextricably interconnected—we 'think' with our feelings and 'feel' with our thoughts."[29]

THE LESSON PLAN

You may or may not notice that we have not referred to this section as the "daily lesson plan" but rather, simply, the "lesson plan." What you are going to be learning about now is how to prepare a lesson plan, and that plan may, in fact, be a "daily" plan, or it may not. In some instances, a single lesson plan may run for more than one class period, perhaps two or three. In other instances, the lesson plan is, in fact, a daily plan, and may run for an entire class period, or in instances of block scheduling, for less than an entire two-hour block of time. In the latter case, more than one lesson plan may be used during that block of time.

Effective teachers are always planning for their classes. For the long range, they plan the scope and sequence and develop the content. Within the long-range time frame they develop units, and within units they design the activities to be used and the assessments of learning to be done. They familiarize themselves with textbooks, materials, media, and innovations in science and science instruction. Yet—despite all this planning—the lesson plan remains pivotal to the planning process.

Assumptions About Lesson Planning

Not all teachers need elaborate written plans for every lesson. Sometimes effective and skilled teachers need only a sketchy outline. Sometimes they may not need written plans at all. Experienced teachers who have taught a particular science topic many times in the past may need only the presence of a classroom of students to stimulate a pattern of presentation that has often been successful. Frequent use of old patterns, however, may lead one into the rut of unimaginative teaching, and you probably do not need to be reminded that the obsolescence of many past classroom practices has been substantiated repeatedly by those researchers who have made serious and recent studies of educational practices.

Considering the diversity among elementary and middle school teachers, their instructional styles, and their students and noting what research has shown, certain assumptions can be made about lesson planning:

Good science teaching allows for, provides for, and indeed encourages coincidental learning.

1. Not all teachers need elaborate written plans for all lessons, but all effective teachers have a planned pattern of instruction for every lesson, whether or not that plan is written out.
2. Beginning teachers need to prepare detailed written lesson plans.
3. Some experienced teachers have clearly defined goals and objectives in mind even though they have not written them into lesson plans.
4. The depth of a teacher's knowledge on a topic in science influences the amount of planning necessary for the lessons.
5. A teacher's skill in following a trend of thought in the presence of distraction will influence the amount of detail necessary in planning learning activities.
6. A plan is more likely to be carefully plotted when it is written out.
7. The diversity of students within today's classroom necessitates careful and thoughtful consideration about individualizing the instruction; such concerns are best implemented when they have been thoughtfully written into lesson plans.
8. There is no particular pattern or format that all teachers need to follow in writing out plans. (Some teacher-preparation programs have agreed on certain lesson-plan formats for their student teachers; you need to know if this is the case in your program.)

Written Lesson Plans

Well-written lesson plans have many uses. They give a teacher an agenda or outline to follow in teaching a lesson. They give a substitute teacher a basis for presenting appropriate lessons to a class. They are certainly very useful when a teacher is planning to use the same or similar lesson again in the future. They provide the teacher with something to fall back on in case of a memory lapse, an interruption, or a distraction, such as a call from the office or a fire drill. Above all, careful lesson plans provide beginners security, because with a carefully prepared plan a beginning teacher can walk into a classroom with confidence gained from having developed a sensible framework for that day's instruction.

Thus, as a beginning teacher you should make considerably detailed lesson plans. Naturally, this will require a great deal of work for at least the first year or two, but the reward of knowing that you have prepared and presented effective lessons will compensate for that effort. Because most teachers plan their daily lessons only a day or two ahead, you can expect a busy first year of teaching.

Some prospective teachers are concerned with being seen using a written plan in class, thinking it may suggest that he or she has not mastered the subject. On the contrary, a lesson plan is a visible sign of preparation on the part of the teacher. A written lesson plan shows that thinking and planning have taken place and that the teacher has a road map to work through the lesson no matter what the distractions. Most experienced teachers agree that there is no excuse for appearing before a class without evidence of careful preparation.

A Continuous Process

Experienced teachers may not require plans as detailed as those necessary for beginning teachers. Yet lesson planning is a continuous process even for them, for there is always a need to keep materials and plans current and relevant. Because no two classrooms of students are ever exactly the same, today's lesson plan will have to be tailored to the peculiar needs of each classroom of students.

For these reasons, lesson plans should be in a constant state of revision. Once the basic framework is developed, however, the task of updating and modifying becomes minimal. If you maintain your plans on a computer, making necessary changes from time to time becomes even easier.

The lesson plan should provide a tentative outline of the teaching period but should always remain flexible. A carefully worked-out plan may have to be set aside because of an unpredictable, serendipitous "teachable moment," or because of unforeseen circumstances, such as a delayed school bus, an impromptu school assembly program, or a fire drill. A daily lesson planned to cover six aspects of a given topic may end with only three of the points having been considered, or a lesson plan designed to allow for five different kinds of learning activities may end with only three of them being done. These occurrences are natural in a school setting, and the teacher and the plans must be flexible enough to accommodate this reality.

The Problem of Time

A lesson plan should provide enough materials and activities to consume the entire class period or time allotted for instruction. It should be well understood that in planning for teaching, you need to plan for every minute of allotted instructional time. The "lesson plan," then, is more than a plan for a lesson to be taught, but a plan that accounts for the entire period of instructional time. Because planning is a skill that takes years of experience to master, especially when teaching a block of time that may extend for 90 minutes or more, a beginning teacher should overplan rather than run the risk of having too few activities to occupy the time students are in the classroom. One way of assuring that you overplan is to include alternate activities in your lesson plan.

When a lesson plan does not provide enough activity to occupy the entire time students are in the classroom, a beginning teacher often loses control of the class and behavior problems develop. Thus, it is best to prepare more than you are likely to accomplish in a given period of time. Students are very perceptive when it comes to a teacher who has finished the plan for the period and is attempting to bluff through the remaining minutes. If you ever get caught short—as most teachers do at one time or another—there are ways to avoid embarrassment. Spend the remaining time in a review of material that has been covered that day or in the past several days, or allow students time to begin work on a homework assignment or project.

Constructing a Lesson Plan

Each teacher should, perhaps, develop a personal system of lesson planning—the system that works best for that teacher. But a beginning teacher probably needs a more substantial framework from which to work. For that reason, this section provides several lesson plan formats. Nothing is sacred about any of these formats, however. Each has worked for some teachers in the past. As you review the formats, determine which appeals to your style of presentation and use it with your own modifications until you find or develop a better model. For many teachers, the lesson plan format changes according to the type of lesson; for example, the lesson plan format for a teacher-centered lesson will undoubtedly differ from that of a student-centered extended exploratory investigation.

Whatever the format, however, all plans should be written out in an intelligible style. There is good reason to question teachers who say they have no need for a written plan because they have their lessons planned "in their heads." The instructional time periods in a school day are from several to many, as may be the numbers of students a teacher encounters during one instructional day. When multiplied by the number of school days in a week, a semester, or a year, the task of keeping so many things in one's head becomes mind-boggling. Until you have considerable experience behind you, you will need to write and keep detailed daily plans for guidance and reference.

Components of a Lesson Plan

As a rule, your written lesson plan should contain the following basic elements: (1) descriptive course data, (2) materials, (3) goals and objectives, (4) rationale, (5) body of the lesson plan, (6) assignments and assignment reminders, and (7) assessment, reflection, and revision section. These components need not be present in every written lesson plan, nor must they be presented in any particular format. Nor are they inclusive or exclusive. You might choose to include additional components or subsections. You may not want to spend time developing a formal rationale, although you probably should. Figure 5.5 illustrates a format that includes the seven components and sample subsections of those components.

Following are descriptions of the seven major components with explanations of why each is essential and examples.

Descriptive Data

The descriptive data include the demographic and logistical information giving details about the class of students. Anyone reading this information should be able to know exactly when and where the class meets, who is teaching it, and what is being taught. Although as the

1. **Descriptive Data**
   Teacher _____ Class _____ Date _____
   Grade level _____ Room number _____ Period _____
   Unit _____
   Lesson Number and Topic _____

2. **Goals and Objectives**
   Instructional goals:

   Specific objectives:
   Cognitive:

   Affective:

   Psychomotor:

3. **Rationale**

4. **Procedure** (Procedure with time plan, modeling examples, transitions, guided practice experiences, etc.)
   Content:

   _____ minutes. Activity 1: Set (introduction)

   _____ minutes. Activity 2:

   _____ minutes. Activity 3: (the exact number of activities in the procedures will vary)

   _____ minutes. Final Activity or Closure:

   If time remains:

5. **Assignments and Reminders of Assignments**

   Special notes and reminders to myself:

6. **Materials and Equipment Needed**
   Audiovisual:

   Other:

7. **Assessment, Reflection, and Revision**
   Assessment of student learning:

   Reflective thoughts about lesson:

   Suggestions for revision:

FIGURE 5.5   Sample lesson plan format with seven components.

teacher you are familiar with this information, others may not be. Administrators, members of the teaching team, and substitute teachers—and, if you are a student teacher, your university supervisor and cooperating teacher—appreciate this information, especially when asked to fill in for you if even only for a few minutes during a class session. Most teachers find out which items of descriptive data are most beneficial in their situations and then develop their own identifiers.

Remember this: the mark of a well-prepared, clearly written lesson plan is *the ease with which someone else* (such as another member of your teaching team or a substitute teacher) *could implement it.*

As shown in the Sample Unit Plan (Figure 5.6), the descriptive data include:

1. *Name of course and grade level.* These serve as headings for the plan and facilitate orderly filing of plans. For example: Science 6.
2. *Name of the unit.* Inclusion of the unit name facilitates the orderly control of the hundreds of lesson plans a teacher constructs. For example: What's the Matter.
3. *Topic to be considered within the unit.* This is also useful for control and identification. For example: Density of Solids.

Goals and Objectives

In a lesson plan, the instructional goals are general statements of what students will learn from that lesson. Teachers and students need to know what the lesson is designed to accomplish. In clear, understandable language, the general goal statement provides that information. As taken from the Sample Unit Plan (Figure 5.5), examples of goals are:

- To understand that all matter is made of atoms
- To understand that matter stays constant; it is neither created nor destroyed
- To develop basic chemistry lab skills
- To develop a positive attitude about chemistry and to be prepared for subsequent science courses

The objectives of the lesson are included as specific statements detailing precisely what students will be able to do as a result of their learning the lesson. Teachers and students need to know these details. Behavioral objectives provide clear statements of what learning is to occur. In addition, from clearly written behavioral objectives, assessment items can be written to measure whether students have accomplished the objectives. The type of assessment items used (discussed in the next chapter) should not only measure *for* the instructional objective but should also be compatible *with* the objective being assessed. As discussed earlier, your specific objectives may be covert or overt or a combination of both. As illustrated in the Sample Unit Plan, examples include:

- List at least ten examples of matter.
- List the four states of matter with one example of each.
- Calculate the density of an object when given mass and volume.
- Describe the properties of solid, liquid, and gas.
- Demonstrate an understanding that matter is made of elements, and elements are made of atoms.

Setting specific objectives is a crucial step in the development of any lesson plan. It is at this point that many lessons go wrong. In writing specific objectives teachers sometimes mistakenly list what *they* intend to do—such as "cover the next five pages" or "do the next 10 problems"—and fail to focus on just what the learning objective in these activities truly is. When you approach this step in your lesson planning, ask yourself, "What do I want my students to learn from these lessons?" Your answer to that question is your objective!

Sample Unit Plan

Course: Science 6   Teacher: _____

Title of unit: What's the Matter   *Duration of unit:* 2 weeks

Purpose of unit: This unit is designed for sixth grade science students to develop their understanding of matter. At the completion of this unit, students should have a better understanding of properties and changes of properties in matter.

Rationale of unit: This unit is important in continuing to build a physical science foundation of knowledge for future science classes. This foundation can increase students' chances of success in later science courses, thereby increasing students' self-confidence and self-esteem. A basic understanding of matter and its properties is necessary for the sixth-grade student because of daily decisions that affect the manipulation of matter. It is more likely that students will make correct and safe decisions when they understand what matter is, how it changes form, and how its properties determine its use. (The unit topic is consistent with Content Standard B as recommended for grades 5–8 by the *National Science Education Standards* Washington, DC: National Academy of Sciences, 1996. See Figure 1.5.)

Goals of unit:
1. To understand that all matter is made of atoms.
2. To understand that matter stays constant; it is neither created nor destroyed.
3. To develop basic chemistry lab skills.
4. To develop a positive attitude about chemistry and to be prepared for subsequent science courses.

Objectives of unit: Upon completion of this unit of study, students should be able to
1. List at least 10 examples of matter.
2. List the three states of matter with one example of each.
3. Calculate the density of an object when given mass and volume.
4. Describe the properties of solid, liquid, and gas.
5. Demonstrate an understanding that matter is made of elements, and elements are made of atoms.

Overview of unit: Throughout this unit of study, students will be developing a concept map of matter. Information for the map will come from class and lab work, class discussions, lectures, and student readings and research. The overall instructional model is that of concept attainment.
1. What is matter and what are its properties? Students will develop the concept of matter by discovering the properties common to all matter (has mass and takes up space). Students will develop this concept through use of concept attainment model.
2. Students will continue to build on their concept of matter by organizing matter into its four major states (solid, liquid, gas, plasma). The concept development will be used to define the attributes of each state of matter, and students will gather information by participating in laboratory activities and discussions.
3. What are some of the physical properties of matter that make certain kinds of matter unique? Students will experiment with properties of matter such as elasticity, brittleness, and density. Lab activities will allow students to contribute their observations and information to the further development of their concept of matter. Density activities enable students to practice lab and math skills.
4. What are the basic units of matter and where did matter come from? Students will continue to develop their concept of matter by dissecting matter into mixtures, compounds, elements, and atoms.

Assessment of student achievement: Assessment of student achievement will be based on
1. Student participation as evidenced by completion of homework, classwork, lab activities, and class discussions.
2. Weekly quizzes.
3. Unit test.

Sample Lesson Plan

Lesson number: _____   *Time duration:* 1–2 hours

Unit title: What's the Matter   Teacher: _____

Lesson title: Mission Impossible

Lesson topic: Density of Solids

(continued)

FIGURE 5.6   Sample unit plan with one daily lesson plan. (Courtesy of William Hightower, Samuel Jackman Middle School, Elk Grove, California.)

Objectives of lesson: Upon completion of this lesson, students should be able to:
1. Determine the density of a solid cube.
2. Based on data gathered in class, develop their own definition of density.
3. Communicate the results of their experiments to others in the class.

Materials needed:
1. Two large boxes of cereal and two snack-size boxes of the same cereal
2. Four brownies (two whole and two cut in halves)
3. Four sandboxes (two large plastic boxes and two small boxes, each filled with sand)
4. Two scales or balances
5. Several rulers
6. Six hand-held calculators
7. Eighteen colored pencils (six sets with three different colors per set)
8. Copies of lab instructions, one for each student.

Procedure with approximate time line:
1. **Anticipatory set (10–15 minutes).** Begin class by brainstorming (preassessment) what students already know about density. Place the word *density* on the board or overhead, and ask students (using think-write-pair-share) to describe what the word means to them. As each pair shares what they have come up with, write down their definitions and examples.

   Hold up a large box of cereal in one hand and a snack-size box in the other. Ask students which is more dense. Allow them to explain their predictions. Then tell them that by the end of the lesson they will know the answer to the question. They will develop their own definition of density.

2. **Laboratory investigation (30–60 minutes).** Students are divided into teams of three or four students per team. Each team has eight minutes before switching stations. Each team completes three stations and then meets to do its graphs and discuss results. Each student has a role:

   Measure master: In charge of group's ruler and ruler measurements
   Weight master: Responsible for all weighing
   Engineer: In charge of the group's calculator and calculations
   Graph master: In charge of plotting data on graph paper

   STATION 1: *Cereal box density*
   Students calculate the density of large and small boxes of cereal brand A to determine if a larger and heavier object is more dense. The densities of the two boxes are plotted on graph paper (using one of the pencil colors).

   STATION 1: *Instructions*
   a. The density of any object is determined by dividing its mass (weight) by its volume. Density in grams divided by volume (cubic centimeters). Example: $20 \text{ g}/10 \text{ cm}^3 = 2 \text{ g/cm}^3$
   b. Measure the volume of the small cereal box (length $\times$ width $\times$ height), and use the balance to determine its weight in grams. The engineer can do the calculations on the calculator. The graph master should graph the results of each and connect the two points with a straight line.
   c. Repeat the procedure using the large box of cereal.
   d. The engineer computes the density of the cereal box with the calculator for both cereal boxes. Fill in the density spaces below the graph.

FIGURE 5.6 Continued.   *(continued)*

Rationale

The rationale is an explanation of why the lesson is important and why the instructional methods chosen will achieve the objectives. Parents, students, teachers, administrators, and others have the right to know why specific content is being taught and why the methods employed are being used. Teachers become reflective decision makers when they challenge themselves to think about what they are teaching, how they are teaching it, and why it must be taught. Sometimes teachers include the rationale statement in the beginning of the unit plan, but not in each daily lesson. Sometimes, as illustrated in the sample unit plan (Figure 5.5), the rationale is included within the unit introduction and goals.

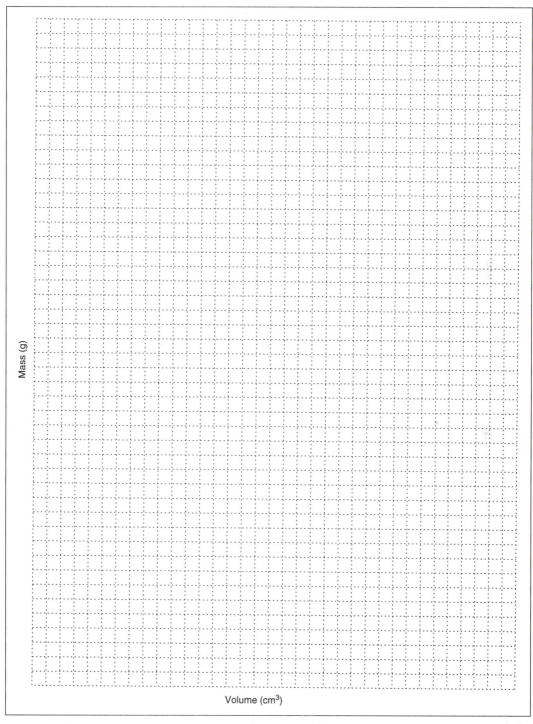

Mass (g)

Volume (cm³)

(continued)

FIGURE 5.6 Continued.

	Object	Density (g/cm^3)
1. Large box of cereal		
2. Small box of cereal		
3. Large brownie		
4. Small brownie		
5. Large sandbox		
6. Small sandbox		

STATION 2: *Brownie density*
Students calculate the density of a full-size brownie and of a half-size brownie. Results are plotted on the same graph, as in Station 1 (with a second color).

STATION 2: *Instructions*
a. The density of any object is determined by dividing its mass (weight) by its volume. Density in grams divided by volume (cubic centimeters). Example: 20 g/10 cm^3 = 2 g/cm^3.
b. Measure the volume of the small brownie (length × width × height), and use the balance to determine its weight in grams. The engineer can do the calculations on the calculator. The graph master should graph the results of each and connect the two points with a straight line.
c. Repeat the procedure using the large brownie.
d. The engineer computes the density of the brownie with the calculator for both sizes. Fill in the density spaces below the graph.

STATION 3: *Sandbox density*
Students calculate the density of a large and a small box of sand, each filled half full with sand. Results are plotted on the same graph (with a third color).

STATION 3: *Instructions*
a. The density of any object is determined by dividing its mass (weight) by its volume. Density in grams divided by volume (cubic centimeters). Example: 20 g/10 cm^3 = 2 g/cm^3.
b. Measure the volume of the small sandbox (length × width × height), and use the balance to determine its weight in grams. The engineer can do the calculations on the calculator. The graph master should graph the results of each and connect the two points with a straight line.
c. Repeat the procedure using the large sandbox.
d. The engineer computes the density of the boxes with the calculator for both sizes. Fill in the density spaces below the graph.

Lab work sheet
Teams return to their seats to do their graphing, to analyze their results, and to answer the following questions from their lab sheet.
a. Is a larger, heavier object always more dense than its smaller counterpart? Explain your evidence.
b. What is your definition of density?
c. Which is more dense, a pound of feathers or a pound of gold? Explain your answer.

3. **Closure.** When all teams are finished, teams should display their graphs, then share and discuss their results.

Reminder of week's assignments:

Concepts:
Density is one of the properties of matter.
Mass and volume are related.
Density is determined by dividing mass by volume.

Extension activities:
Use a density graph to calculate the mass and volume of a smaller piece of a brownie. Explore the story of Archimedes and the King's Crown.

Assessment, reflection, and revision:
Upon completion of this lesson and of the unit, on the basis of teacher observations and student achievement, this lesson may be revised.

FIGURE 5.6 Continued.

Procedure: The Body of the Lesson Plan

The procedure or body of the lesson plan consists of the following elements:

- *Content:* the substance of the lesson, the information to be presented, obtained, and learned. Appropriate information is selected to meet the learning objectives, the level of competence of the students, and the requirements of the course.

  To make sure your lesson actually covers what it should, you should write down exactly the content you intend to cover. This material may be placed in a separate section or combined with the procedure section. The important thing is to be sure that your information is written down so you can refer to it quickly and easily when you need to. If, for instance, you are going to introduce new material using a 10-minute lecture, you will want to outline the content of that lecture. The word *outline* is not used casually—you need not have pages of notes to sift through, nor should you ever read declarative statements to your students. You should be familiar enough with the content so that an outline (in detail, if necessary) will be sufficient to carry on the lesson.

- *Instruction:* the procedure or procedures to be used, sometimes referred to as the *instructional components*. Appropriate instructional methods are chosen to meet the objectives, to match the students' learning styles, and to ensure that all students have an equal opportunity to learn.

  The procedure section where you establish what you and your students will do during the lesson. Ordinarily, you should plan this section of your lesson as an organized entity having a beginning (an introduction or set), a middle, and an end (the closure) to be completed during the lesson. This structure is not always needed, because some lessons are simply parts of units or long-term plans and merely carry on activities spelled out in those long-term plans. Still, most lessons have to include in their procedure (1) an *introduction,* the process used to prepare the students mentally for the lesson, sometimes referred to as the *initiating activity,* (2) *lesson development,* the detailing of activities that occur between the beginning and the end of the lesson, (3) plans for *guided (or coached) practice,* ways in which you intend students to interact in the classroom, receiving guidance or coaching from each other and from you, (4) the *lesson conclusion* (or closure), the planned process of bringing the lesson to an end, thereby providing students with a sense of completeness and, with effective teaching, accomplishment and comprehension, through helping them to synthesize the information learned from the lesson, (5) a *timetable* that serves simply as a planning and implementation guide, and (6) *assignments,* that is, what students are instructed to do as follow-up to the lesson, either as homework or as in-class work, providing them an opportunity to learn further and to practice what is being learned. Let's now consider each of these procedural elements in further detail.

Introduction to the Lesson. Like any good performance, a lesson needs an effective beginning. In many respects the introduction sets the tone for the rest of the lesson by alerting the students that the business of learning is to begin. The introduction should be an attention getter. If it is exciting, interesting, or innovative, it can create a favorable mood for the lesson. In any case, a thoughtful introduction serves as a solid indicator that you are well prepared. Although it is difficult to develop an exciting introduction to every lesson taught each day, there are always a variety of options available to add interest to launching of a lesson. You might, for instance, begin by briefly reviewing the previous lesson, thereby helping students connect the learning. Another possibility is to review vocabulary words from previous lessons and to introduce new ones. Still another possibility is to use the key point of the day's lesson as an introduction and then again as a conclusion. Sometimes teachers begin a lesson by demonstrating a discrepant event (i.e., an event that is contrary to what one might expect).

Yet another possibility is to begin with a writing activity on a controversial aspect of the lesson content. An example of an introduction can be seen in the lesson shown in the sample unit plan (Figure 5.5): "Begin class by brainstorming (preassessment) what students already know about density. Place the word *density* on the board or overhead, and ask students (using think-write-pair-share) to describe what the word means to them. As each pair shares what they have come up with, write down their definitions and examples."

In short, you can use the introduction of the lesson to assess what students already know or think they know, review past learning, tie the new lesson to the previous lesson, introduce new material, point out the objectives of the new lesson, help students to connect their learning with other disciplines or with real life, or—by showing what will be learned and why the learning is important—induce in students a mindset favorable to the new lesson.

The Lesson Development. The developmental activities are the specifics by which you intend to achieve your lesson objectives. They include activities that present information, demonstrate skills, provide reinforcement of previously learned material, and provide other opportunities to develop understanding and skill. In addition, by actions and words, during lesson development the teacher models the behaviors expected of the students. Students need such modeling. By effective modeling, the teacher can exemplify the anticipated learning outcomes. Activities in this section of the lesson plan should be described in some detail so that you will know exactly what it is you plan to do, and during the stress of the class meeting you do not forget details of your plan and its subject content. It is for this reason you should note the answers to the questions you intend to ask and the solutions to problems you intend to have your students solve.

Lesson Conclusion. Having a clear-cut closure to the lesson (and to the unit) is as important as having a strong introduction. The closure complements the introduction. The concluding activity should summarize and bind together what has ensued in the developmental stage and should reinforce the principal points of the lesson. One way to accomplish these ends is to restate the key points of the lesson. Another is to briefly outline the major points. Still another is to repeat the major concept. In any case, the concluding activity is usually brief and to the point.

The Timetable. To estimate the time factors in any lesson can be very difficult. A good procedure is to gauge the amount of time needed for each learning activity and note that alongside the activity and strategy in your plan, as shown in the sample lesson plan. Placing too much faith in your time estimate may be foolish—an estimate is more for your guidance in planning than for anything else. Beginning teachers frequently find that their discussions and presentations do not last as long as expected. To avoid being embarrassed by running out of material, make sure you have planned enough work to consume the entire time allotted for instruction. Another important reason for including a time plan in your lesson is to give information to students about how much time they have for a particular activity, such as a laboratory or a cooperative learning group activity, so that you don't have to interrupt them once they are on task.

Materials and Equipment to Be Used

Materials of instruction include the textbook, supplementary readings, printed laboratory instructions and work sheets, media, science equipment, and other supplies necessary to accomplish the lesson objectives. Students cannot use what they do not have available. Teachers must be certain that the proper and necessary materials are available for the lesson, and to be certain takes planning.

Assignment

When an assignment is to be given, it should be noted in your lesson plan. When to present an assignment to the students is optional—with the exception that it should never be called out as an afterthought as the students are exiting the classroom. Whether the assignments are to be started and completed during classtime or done out of school, it is best to write them on the writing board, in a special place on the bulletin board, or on a handout, taking extra care to be sure that assignment specifications are clear to the students.

It is also important to remember that assignments and procedures are not the same thing. An assignment tells students *what* is to be done, whereas procedures explain *how* to do it. Although an assignment may include specific procedures, spelling out procedures only is not the same as giving an academic assignment. When students are given an assignment, they need to understand the reasons for doing it as well as having some notion as to ways the assignment might be done.

Homework assignments enhance student achievement from upper elementary grades through high school but research is not definitive about the value of homework for younger students. If homework is given to primary grade children the assignment should be short and simple work. For older students (grades 4–6) our recommendation is that homework assignments be given two to three times each week and that each assignment take 15 to 45 minutes of student time to do.

Many teachers give assignments to their students on a weekly basis, requiring that they maintain an assignment schedule in their portfolios. When given on a periodic basis, rather than daily, assignments should still be noted in your daily lesson plans so that you can remind students as necessary. Once assignment specifications are given, it is a good idea to not make major modifications to them, and it is especially important to not change assignment specifications several days after an assignment has been given. Last-minute changes in specifications can be very frustrating to students who have already begun or completed an assignment; to make such changes shows little respect for those students.

Benefits of Coached Practice. Allowing time in class for students to begin work on homework assignments and long-term projects is highly recommended; it provides opportunity for the teacher to give individual attention (guided or coached practice) to students. Being able to coach students *is the reason* for providing in-class time to begin assignments. The benefits of coached practice include the teacher's ability to (a) monitor student work so that a student doesn't go too far in a wrong direction, (b) help students to reflect on their thinking, (c) assess the progress of individual students, and (d) discover or create a "teachable moment." For example, while observing and monitoring student practice the teacher may discover a commonly shared misconception. The teacher then stops and discusses that misconception and attempts to clarify the point or, collaboratively with students, plans a subsequent investigatory activity centered on the common misconception.

Special Notes, Reminders, and Reflection. Many teachers provide a place in their lesson plan format for special notes and reminders. Most of the time you will not need such reminders, but when you do, it helps to have them in a regular location in your lesson plan so you can refer to them quickly. In that special section you can place reminders concerning such things as announcements to be made, school programs, makeup work for certain students, and so on. These things may vary in importance, but they do need to be remembered.

Assessment, Reflection, and Revision

You must include in your lesson plan details of how you will assess how well students are learning (formative assessment) and how well they have learned (summative assessment). Comprehension checks for formative assessment can be in the form of questions you ask and questions the students ask during the lesson. Questions you intend to ask (and possible answers) should be built into the developmental section.

For summative assessment, teachers typically use review questions at the end of a lesson or a unit (as a closure) or the beginning of the next lesson (as a review or transfer introduction), independent practice at the completion of a lesson, and a variety of tests. Again, questions for checking for comprehension should be detailed in your lesson plan.

In your lesson plan format, you should also include a section reserved for you to make notes or reflective comments about the lesson. Sample reflective questions you might ask yourself are:

- How did I feel about my teaching today?
- If I feel successful, what did I see the students saying and doing that make me feel that way?
- Would I do anything differently next time? If so, what and why?

CELEBRATING, PLANNING FOR, AND TEACHING STUDENTS OF DIVERSITY

Previously (Chapter 2), we emphasized that not all students learn and respond to learning situations in the same way. We know that students learn differently according to various elements of the situation, such as the time of day, the brightness of the classroom lighting, the amount of mobility allowed during their learning, whether the student is allowed to chew gum or take in food or drink while learning, the amount of peer interaction allowed and encouraged during the learning experience, and the student's ethnicity or socioeconomic status. Indeed, learning is an individual experience. We have mentioned the individuality of the learning experience, the cognitive differences in learning, differences in learning styles, and the learning strengths of individuals within a group. In addition, you must know about students' differences according to their socioeconomic backgrounds, ethnic and cultural backgrounds, and physical or learning disabilities. As a science teacher, you are placed in the difficult position of teaching 20 or more students as individuals, all at the same time. It seems an impossible expectation, and it is important that its difficulties are understood. The rest of this chapter is designed to help you to minimize failures and maximize successes. Specifically, you must understand

1. The challenges in teaching science to the diversity of students in today's classroom
2. General practices that are developmentally appropriate in meeting the needs of students in the science classroom
3. Developmentally appropriate practice for teaching science to specific learners

Developmentally Appropriate Practice (DAP)

Teachers must develop unit and lesson plans that provide instruction that is developmentally appropriate to meet the needs of their students. For teaching science to elementary and middle school students, developmentally appropriate practice includes the use of thematic units and interdisciplinary team teaching, with the students simultaneously involved in a variety of tasks at several levels of skill involvement (i.e., multilevel teaching). There are other developmentally appropriate practices, and guidelines for using them to meet the diversity of students in the classroom are offered in the discussions that follow.

Certain common past school practices are not very effective in working with elementary and middle school students today, especially those students who may be academically at risk. Such ineffective past practices include (1) failing underachieving students, (2) pulling students out of the regular classroom for part of the day for special instruction, and (3) placing special aides in the regular classroom.[30] As stated by Slavin and Madden, "Pullouts and in-class models are probably too limited a change in instructional strategy to make much of a difference."[31] Let's consider practices that do make a difference and that are developmentally appropriate.

The Challenge

To help you meet the challenge inherent in today's teaching, a wealth of information is available about teaching and working with young people. As a credentialed teacher you are expected to know, or at least to know where you can find, all necessary information—and to review it when needed. Certain information you have stored in long-term memory will surface and become useful at the most unexpected times. While concerned about all students' safety and physical well-being, you must remain sensitive to each student's attitudes, values, social adjustment, emotional well-being, and cognitive development. You must be prepared not only to teach science but also to do it effectively with students of different cultural backgrounds, diverse linguistic abilities, and different learning styles, as well as with students who have been identified as having special needs.

The following statistics make clear this challenge:

- Approximately one half of all U.S. children will spend some years being raised by a single parent. The traditional two-parent, two-child family now constitutes only 6 percent of U.S. households. Between one third and one fourth of U.S. children go home after school to places devoid of adult supervision. On any given day, it has been estimated that as many as 300,000 children have no place to call home.
- In the nation's largest school systems, minority enrollment levels range from 70 to 96 percent. By the year 2010, minority youths in the school-age population throughout the United States will average about 39 percent. By the year 2050, the nation's population is predicted to increase to 383 million (from today's 252 million). That population boom will be led by Hispanics and Asian Americans, with the nation's white population much less a factor. The average class size of elementary and middle school classrooms will likely increase during the next decade or so.
- In 1991 a quarter of all preschool students lived below the poverty level, the highest percentage in 20 years.
- The United States is truly a multilingual, multicultural country (see Figure 5.7). In 39 states and the District of Columbia, Spanish is now the second most common language, after English. The fastest growing language is Mon-Khmer, spoken by Cambodians. According to the 1990 U.S. census, since 1980 the number of residents speaking Mon-Khmer at home increased by more than 676 percent.

According to the 1990 census, about one of every thirteen U.S. residents was foreign born. About one of every six students aged 5 to 17 speak a language other than English at home. Many of these students have only limited proficiency in the English language (i.e., conversational speaking ability only). However, limited English proficiency is not always their only problem, albeit a huge one, in making adjustments to school. Before coming to the United States some of these children had never before even seen the inside of a school. For example, immigrant children from Asia, who statistically have tended to excel in school, are increasingly more apt to be from rural and impoverished areas. Therefore, as well as experiencing difficulty in language adjustment, these children are increasingly more apt to have many of the problems associated with poor, disadvantaged students.[32]

In just one school district, the Los Angeles Unified School District, more than 81 languages are represented, with as many as 20 different languages found in some classrooms. Yet

Language	Total Speakers Over 5 Years Old in 1990	Percentage Change Since 1980
Spanish	17,339,172	50
French	1,702,176	8
German	1,547,049	−4
Italian	1,308,648	−20
Chinese	1,249,213	98
Tagalog	843,251	87
Polish	723,483	−12
Korean	626,478	127
Vietnamese	507,069	150
Portuguese	429,860	19
Japanese	427,657	25
Greek	388,260	−5
Arabic	355,150	57
Hindi, Urdu, and related	331,484	155
Russian	241,798	39
Yiddish	213,064	−34
Thai	206,266	132
Persian	201,865	85
French Creole	187,658	654
Armenian	149,649	46
Navajo	148,530	21
Hungarian	147,902	−18
Hebrew	144,292	46
Dutch	142,684	−3
Mon-Khmer	127,441	676

FIGURE 5.7 Most common foreign languages spoken at home in the United States in 1990. (*Source:* U.S. Census Bureau survey report CPH-L-133, *Language Spoken at Home and Ability to Speak English for United States, Regions and States: 1990,* Population Division, Statistical Information Office, Census Bureau, Washington, DC.)

increasing ethnic and cultural diversity is no longer only a big-city problem. "Increasing cultural diversity is affecting schools across the country, from traditionally homogeneous suburbs to small-town America. Big city school districts in New York City and Houston, Texas, as well as smaller districts in Alexandria, Virginia, and Chattahochee County, Georgia, now have populations of ethnic minorities that equal or exceed non-Hispanic white students."[33]

By the time you read these words, the number of new immigrants is expected to rise to nearly 1,000,000 annually from the approximately 500,000 annually in 1990 (immigrant population in 1993 was 972,000), and birth rates among minority populations will continue to increase, while births to non-Hispanic whites will continue to decline. Nationwide, the number of students whose primary language is not English is expected to triple during the next quarter of a century.

The language diversity of our students poses special problems for teachers who use language as a major vehicle for the transmission of ideas. The overall picture that emerges is a rapidly changing, diverse student population that challenges the teaching skills of teachers. Teachers who traditionally have used direct instruction as the dominant mode of instruction did so with the assumption that their students were relatively homogeneous in terms of background, knowledge, motivation, and facility with the English language. However, no such assumption can be made today in classrooms of such cultural, ethnic, and linguistic diversity. As a science teacher for the twenty-first century, you must be knowledgeable and skilled in the use of teaching strategies that recognize, celebrate, and build upon that diversity; as stated in the 1991 Position Statement on Multicultural Science Education from the National Science Teachers Association (NSTA), teachers are urged to

- Provide access to high-quality science education experiences so that culturally diverse populations can become successful participants in our democratic society.
- Select and use curriculum materials and teaching strategies that reflect and incorporate diversity.
- Become aware of children's learning styles and instructional preferences.
- Expose culturally diverse children to career opportunities in science, engineering, and technology.[34]

Meeting the Challenge

A variety of instructional techniques that do make a difference have been recommended to teachers who wish to individualize the learning experience for their students. Some are forms of computer-assisted programs of instruction that have been designed by instructional systems designers rather than by classroom teachers. Here we present other less complex strategies for meeting the individual needs represented by the culturally diverse and rich classroom of students. First, consider the following rather general guidelines, many of which have been discussed previously in this book.

- Encourage cooperative learning and reciprocal peer and cross-age tutoring, with mixed-ability small group learning.
- Encourage the development of observation, generalization and other thinking and learning skills.
- Provide learning experiences that use all sensory modalities—verbal, visual, tactile, and kinesthetic.
- Establish multiple learning centers within the classroom.
- Identify individual student needs and teach to those needs using multilevel instruction.
- Provide a structured learning environment with regular routines so that children know what to expect.
- Provide independent and small group investigations and project-centered work.
- Provide frequent independent practice and comprehension checks to ensure that children are learning.
- Provide individualized learning plans and activities.
- Provide variations in assignments, with optional due dates, based on student abilities and interests.
- Teach in a step-by-step sequence from the concrete to the abstract.
- Use discovery and inquiry strategies.
- Use simulations and role-play.
- Utilize interactive computer programs designed for use by individual students or by students in pairs.

Developmentally Appropriate Practice for Specific Learners

Because social awareness is such an important and integral part of the young person's experience, many effective programs and much of their practices are geared toward some type of social interaction. Indeed, learning is a social enterprise among learners and their teachers. Although many exemplary instructional methods and modern programs for teaching science, such as Berkeley, California's Lawrence Hall of Science GEMS (Great Explorations in Math and Science) program, rely heavily on social learning activities and interpersonal relationships, each teacher must be aware of and sensitive to individual student differences. For working with specific learners, consider the guidelines that follow.

STUDENTS WITH SPECIAL NEEDS

Students with special needs include those in any of the following categories: autistic, deaf, deaf-blind, hard of hearing, mentally retarded, multihandicapped, orthopedically impaired, other health impaired, seriously emotionally disturbed, specific learning disabled, speech impaired, traumatically brain injured, and visually handicapped. These students must, to the extent possible, be educated with their peers in the regular classroom. Public Law 94-142, the Education of the Handicapped Act (EHA) of 1975, mandates that all students have the right to a full and free public education, as well as to nondiscriminatory assessment.[35] With emphasis on normalizing the educational environment for students with special needs, this legislation requires provision of the least-restrictive environment for these students. A least-restrictive environment is one that is as normal as possible.

Students who have been identified as having special needs may be placed in the regular classroom for the entire school day, a practice called *full inclusion* (as is the trend[36]). Such students may also be in a regular classroom the greater part of the school day, which is called *partial inclusion*, or only for designated periods. Although there is no single, universally accepted definition for *inclusion*, it is generally agreed that it involves a commitment to educate each special needs child in the school and, when appropriate, in the class that child would have attended had the child not had a disability. The underlying assumption "is that inclusion is a way of life, a way of living together, based on a belief that each individual is valued and does belong."[37] The term *inclusion* has largely replaced the use of an earlier and similar term, *mainstreaming*. As a classroom teacher you will need information and skills specific to teaching children with special needs.

Teaching science to students who have special needs because of their disabilities requires more care, better diagnosis, greater skill, more attention to individual needs, and an even greater understanding of the students. The challenges of teaching students with special needs in the regular classroom are great enough that to do it well you need additional specialized training beyond the general guidelines presented here. At some point in your teacher preparation you should, or may be required to, take one or more courses in working with the special needs learner in the regular classroom.

As a science teacher, you should keep this important fact in mind: When a student with special needs is placed in your regular educational classroom, your task should not be to make the student normal but, rather, to deal directly with the differences between this student and other students in your classroom. To deal directly with these differences, you should (1) develop an understanding of the general characteristics of different types of special needs learners, (2) identify the student's unique needs relative to your classroom, and (3) design lesson plans that teach to different needs at the same time (multilevel teaching, or multitasking).

Because of a concern for problems of the child with special needs, Congress stipulated in P.L. 94-142 that an *Individualized Educational Program* (IEP) be devised annually for each special needs child. According to that law, an IEP is developed for each student each year by a team that includes special education teachers, the child's parents, and the classroom teachers. The IEP contains (1) a statement of the child's present educational levels, (2) the educational goals for the year, (3) specifications for the services to be provided and the extent to which the child should be expected to take part in the regular education program, and (4) the evaluative criteria for the services to be provided. Consultation by special and skilled support personnel is essential in all mainstream IEP models. A consultant works directly with teachers or with students and parents. As a classroom teacher, you may have an active role in preparing the specifications for the students with special needs assigned to your classroom, as well as a major responsibility for implementing the program.

Guidelines for Working with Students with Special Needs in the Regular Classroom
The following are guidelines for working with special needs learners who are wholly or partially included in regular education classrooms. Although these guidelines are important in teaching all youngsters and helping them to develop their learning skills, they are especially necessary in working with students with special needs.

- *Adapt and modify materials and procedures to the special needs of each child.* For example, a student who has extreme difficulty sitting still for more than a few minutes will need planned changes in learning activities. When assigning student seating in the classroom, give preference to students according to their special needs. Try to incorporate into lessons activities that engage all learning modalities—visual, auditory, tactile, and kinesthetic. Be flexible in your classroom procedures; for example, allow the use of tape recorders for note taking and test taking when students have trouble with written language.
- *Break complex learning into simpler components, moving from the most concrete to the abstract, rather than the other way around.* Check frequently for student understanding of instructions, procedures, and comprehension of content. Use computers and other self-correcting materials for drill and practice and for provision of immediate feedback to the student without embarrassment.
- *Define the learning objectives in behavioral terms.* This helps to provide high structure and clear expectations.
- *Exercise your overlapping and withitness behaviors—that is, be aware of everything that is going on in the classroom, at all times, monitoring students for signs of restlessness, frustration, anxiety, and off-task behaviors.* Be ready to reassign individual learners to different activities as the situation warrants. *Have students maintain assignments for the week in a folder that is kept in their notebooks.* Post assignments for the week in a special place on the bulletin board and frequently remind students of deadlines.
- *Maintain consistency in your expectations and in your responses.* Special needs learners, particularly, can become frustrated when they do not understand a teacher's expectations and when they cannot depend on a teacher's reactions.
- *Plan interesting learning activities that help the students connect what is being learned with their real world.* Sometimes called "bridging" activities, learning that connects what is being learned with the real world helps to motivate students and to keep them on task.
- *Plan your questions and questioning sequences.* Plan the questions you will ask special needs learners, so that they are likely to answer them with confidence. Use signals to let students know that you are likely to call on them in class (e.g., prolonged eye contact or mentioning your intention to a student before class begins). After asking a question, give the child adequate time to think and respond. Then, after the child responds, build on his or her response to indicate that the child's contribution was important.
- *Provide for and teach toward student success.* Offer students activities and experiences that ensure success and mastery at some level. Use of student portfolios (discussed in Chapter 6) can give evidence of progress and help in building student confidence. To help build student self-esteem, make every effort to capitalize on students' strengths and to provide opportunities for success in a supportive classroom atmosphere.
- *Provide guided or coached practice.* Provide time in class for students to work on assignments and projects. During this time you can monitor the work of each child while looking for misconceptions, thus ensuring that students get started on the right track.
- *Provide help in the organization of students' learning.* For example, give instruction in the organization of notes and notebooks. Have a three-hole punch available in the

Although not all children learn in the same way, all can learn. Effective science teaching requires the planning and use of a variety of instructional strategies and teaching skills designed to match an appropriate plan with its set of anticipated outcomes. When suitable selection is made and the lesson is well implemented, children actively engage in the lesson and learn from it.

classroom so students can put papers into their notebooks immediately, thus avoiding disorganization and loss of papers. During class presentations use an overhead projector with transparencies; students who need more time can then copy material from the transparencies. Ask students to read their notes aloud to each other in small groups, thereby aiding their recall and understanding and encouraging them to take notes for meaning rather than for rote learning.

- *Teach (all) students the correct procedures for everything.*
- *Provide special science materials for students with special needs.* Special science programs are available, such as those shown in Figure 5.8.

STUDENTS OF DIVERSITY AND DIFFERENCES

A teaching credential authorizes you to teach in any public school throughout a state—in some instances, throughout a region that consists of several states. That means you could find yourself teaching in a school that is ethnically, culturally, linguistically, and socioeconomically diverse. As exemplified in Figure 5.7, the United States is a country of a variety of families, many with different ethnic heritages—African American, Cambodian American,

Chinese American, Cuban American, Filipino American, French Canadian American, Hungarian American, Iranian American, Italian American, Jewish American, Laotian American, Mexican American, Native American, Polish American, Puerto Rican American, Russian American, and Vietnamese American, to name but a few. Some schools have student bodies that represent 40 or more languages. It will be important for you to determine the language and nationality groups represented by the students in your classroom.

A major problem for recent immigrant students, as well as some ethnic groups, is learning a second language. As mentioned earlier, in many cities, and even in smaller communities today, it is not uncommon for more than half the students to come from homes where the native language is not English. Yet standard English is a necessity in most communities of this country if a person is to become vocationally successful and enjoy a full life. Learning to communicate reasonably well in English can take an immigrant student at least a year and probably longer; some authorities say three to seven years.

To be successful in teaching science to students who have limited proficiency in English (LEP) a teacher often includes the use of hands-on learning and cooperative learning. Some schools use a pull-out approach, whereby part of the student's school time is spent in special bilingual classes and the rest of the time in regular classrooms. In some schools, LEP students are placed in academic classrooms that use a sheltered English approach. For example, a section of science is established especially for students whose primary language is not English but who do have limited proficiency in English (i.e., conversational ability). The teacher of that class is one who is trained in techniques for teaching science to LEP students. Specific techniques include:

- Allowing more time for activities than usual.
- Allowing time for translation by a classroom aide or by a classmate, and allowing time for discussion to clarify meaning.
- Avoiding jargon and idioms that might be misunderstood.
- Dividing complex or extended language discourse into smaller, more manageable units.
- Giving directions in a variety of ways.
- Giving special attention to key words that convey meaning, and writing them on the board.
- Reading written directions aloud, and writing oral directions on the board.
- Speaking clearly and naturally but at a slower-than-normal pace, thereby simplifying information input.
- Using a variety of examples and observable models.
- Using a variety of contextual clues, such as dramatically acting out meaning, with facial expressions and body gesturing.
- Using simplified vocabulary, but without talking down to students.
- Frequent checking for understanding.[38]

Guidelines for Teaching Students with Limited Proficiency in English (LEP)   To work effectively with LEP students in your science classroom, there are additional guidelines. Although these guidelines are important for teaching all students and helping them to develop their learning skills, they are especially necessary for working with language minority students.

- *Avoid instruction that is abstract.* With LEP students you should use the most concrete (least abstract) forms of instruction.
- *Build on (or connect with) what the students already know.* As discussed in Chapter 2, building on what students already know, or think they know, helps them to connect their knowledge and construct their understandings.

- *Encourage student writing.* One way teachers encourage students to write is with the use of journals (discussed in Chapter 3).
- *Help students learn the vocabulary.* Assist the LEP student in learning two vocabulary sets: the regular English vocabulary needed for learning and the new vocabulary introduced by the science subject matter content.
- *Involve parents or guardians.* Parents (or guardians) of new immigrant students are usually truly concerned about the education of their children and may be quite interested in cooperating with you in any way possible. If their help is solicited, they may do all they can to help and perhaps can help you to facilitate their children's learning. Students whose primary language is not English may have other differences that you will also need to know about. These differences are related to culture, customs, family life, and expectations. To be most successful as a classroom teacher of LEP students, you should learn as much as possible about each child. To this end it can be valuable to solicit the help of the child's parent, guardian, or even an older sibling.

Effective science teachers plan activities that challenge and excite students. When planning science units, teachers should include many hands-on activities in which children actively participate. Investigations, field trips, and inquiry sessions can provide firsthand experiences for learning science content, developing process skills, and developing healthy attitudes about science, technology, and society.

- *Plan for and use all learning modalities.* In working with LEP students, you need to use multisensory approaches, learning activities that involve students in auditory, visual, tactile, and kinesthetic learning activities.
- *Use cooperative learning.* Use small-group, mixed-ability, cooperative learning groups, with individual rewards for students according to group achievement.
- *Use the benefits afforded by modern technology.* For example, use computer networking to allow language minority students to write and communicate with peers, as well as to publish their classroom work.

A teacher whose preparation is addressed exclusively to students whose backgrounds are similar to his or her own may not be adequately prepared to teach in a classroom of diversity. You will need to learn as much as you can about each student and to become aware of any child who has difficulties in adjusting or developing at school because of economic factors, racial insensitivity, home environmental conditions, or limited proficiency in English.

Guidelines for Teaching Students of Diverse Backgrounds   To be compatible with, and able to teach, science to students who come from backgrounds different from yours, you must believe that all students can learn—regardless of gender, social class, or ethnic or cultural characteristics. You also need to develop special skills that include those in the following guidelines, each of which has been discussed in detail in previous chapters. To work successfully and most effectively with students of diverse backgrounds, you should:

- *Build the learning around students' individual learning styles.*
- *Communicate positively with every student and with the student's parents or guardians, learning as much as you can about the student and his or her culture and encouraging family members to participate in the student's learning.* Involve parents, guardians, and other members of the community in the educational program so that all have a sense of ownership and responsibility and feel positive about the school program.
- *Establish a classroom climate in which each student feels he or she can learn and wants to learn.*
- *Set and maintain high expectations for each student.* However, you and your students must understand that intelligence is not a fixed entity, but a characteristic that—through a feeling of "I can" and with proper coaching—can be developed.
- *Involve students in understanding and in making important decisions about their own learning, so that they feel ownership* (i.e., a sense of empowerment and connectedness) *of that learning.*
- *Personalize learning for each student, much as is done in the use of the IEP for special needs learners, but perhaps less formally.*
- *Provide learning activities adapted to individual students' skill levels.*
- *Teach to individuals by using a variety of strategies to achieve an objective or by using a number of different objectives at the same time* (i.e., multilevel teaching).
- *Use techniques that emphasize cooperative learning and that deemphasize competitive learning* (such as the GEMS activities).

STUDENTS WHO ARE GIFTED AND TALENTED

Sometimes neglected in the regular classroom are the intellectually gifted students who have special talents. These are the students fortunate enough to have already developed a special intellectual gift or talent. There is no one accepted method for identification of these students. For placement in special classes or programs for the gifted and talented in elementary school and middle-level schools, most school districts have traditionally used standard intelligence quotient (IQ) testing.

Through evaluation of numerous studies, Rogers and Kimpston conclude that research indicates that bright students benefit academically from a more challenging learning environment and, contrary to popular opinion, that bright students are not harmed socially or psychologically when placed in an environment that is academically challenging.[39] Although grouping students in classes based on ability and achievement is still widely practiced, there is an overwhelming abundance of sources in the recent literature that adamantly opposes the tracking of students, that is, the homogeneous grouping of students according to ability.[40]

In attempting to diminish the discriminatory and damaging effects on students believe to be caused by traditional tracking and homogeneous ability grouping, although grouping by ability still remains common in some schools, educators in recent years have devised numerous other seemingly more productive ways of attending to student differences, of providing a more challenging learning environment, and of stimulating the talents of each student. These methods include interdisciplinary teaming, in-class projects, peer teaching, cooperative learning, individualized instruction, multiage grouping, allowing a student to skip a grade, nongraded classrooms, shortening the time it takes a student to pass through the grades, allowing students to attend an upper-grade class while still in a lower grade, and specialized magnet schools.

Guidelines for Working with Intellectually Gifted and Talented Students   Although the following guidelines are important for teaching science to all students, they are especially appropriate in working in the regular classroom with a student who has special intellectual gifts and talents.

- *Emphasize skills in critical thinking, problem solving, and inquiry.* For example, the gifted learner can be encouraged to pursue a special investigatory project.
- *Involve students in choosing and inviting guest speakers to class.*
- *Involve the students in selecting and planning field trips.*
- *Plan and provide optional and voluntary enrichment activities.* Self-instructional packages, learning activity centers, special projects, computer activities, and multimedia programs are excellent tools for provision of enrichment activities.
- *Plan assignments and activities that challenge the students to the fullest of their abilities.* This

Ball, D. W. *ESS/Special Education Teacher's Guide.* St. Louis: Webster/McGraw-Hill, 1978.

Brandwein, P. F., and H. A. Passow, eds. *Gifted Young in Science.* Arlington, VA: National Science Teachers Association, 1989.

Buffer, J. J., and M. L. Scott. *Special Needs Guide.* Reston, VA: International Technology Education Association, 1987.

Egbert, M., and K. Ricker. *Science for the Handicapped—An Annotated Bibliography.* Columbus, OH: Educational Resources Information Center, 1981.

Leitman, A. *Science for Deaf Students.* Washington, DC: Alexander Graham Bell Association for the Deaf, 1968.

McCormack, A. J. *Outdoor Areas as Learning Libraries: CESI Sourcebook.* Washington, DC: Council for Elementary Science, International, 1979.

Rakes, T. A., and J. S. Choate. *Science and Health: Detecting and Correcting Special Needs.* Boston, MA: Allyn and Bacon, 1990.

Schmidt, V. E., and V. N. Rockcastle. *Teaching Science with Everyday Things.* 2d ed. New York: McGraw-Hill, 1982.

McCoy, K., and H. Prehm. *Teaching Mainstreamed Students.* Denver, CO: Love Publishing, 1987.

Me Now (for intermediate grades) and *Me and My Environment* (for middle school grades), for educable mentally handicapped (EMH) children. Hubbard Scientific, Inc., 3101 Iris Ave., Ste. 215, Boulder, CO 80301.

Science Activities for the Visually Impaired (SAVI). Berkeley, CA: University of California, Lawrence Hall of Science.

Science Enrichment for Learners with Physical Handicaps (SELPH). Berkeley, CA: University of California, Lawrence Hall of Science.

FIGURE 5.8   Resources for teaching science to special learners.

does not mean overloading them with homework. Rather, carefully plan so that the students' time spent on assignments and activities is quality time.

- *Provide in-class seminars for students to discuss topics and problems that they are pursuing individually or as members of a learning team.*
- *Provide independent and dyad learning opportunities.* Gifted and talented students often prefer to work alone or with another gifted student.
- *Use preassessments (diagnostic evaluation) for reading level and subject achievement so that you are better able to prescribe objectives and activities for each student.*
- *Work with individual students in some planning of their own objectives and activities for science learning.*

SUMMARY

Theories about the intellectual, physical, and social-emotional development of young people directly affect the school science curriculum and instruction. Teachers must be aware of the developmental nature of each student and plan developmentally appropriate content and instruction to meet their students' diverse needs. Because learning is both a social and an individual process, teachers must be prepared to develop interactive and individual instruction for the students.

A concern to many teachers is how to find time to teach all of the required content areas of the elementary school curriculum. A very real problem in elementary schools is that many teachers give less attention to mathematics, science, and social science than they give to language arts instruction. Language arts is *not* more important than these other areas and does *not* deserve more extensive attention, although laws in your state may in fact dictate time requirements that imply the contrary. Many teachers effectively combine the teaching of language arts with mathematics, science, social science, or art, or with some combination of these, often by using interdisciplinary thematic units. When planned and implemented effectively, interdisciplinary thematic instruction can provide both interactive and individual instruction for the students.

We now turn your attention to the topic of assessment, discussed in Chapter 6.

QUESTIONS FOR CLASS DISCUSSION

1. Investigate the science programs used by local elementary and middle schools and discover their plans for science scope and sequence. Share your findings with those of others in your class.
2. Describe ways a science teacher can encourage serendipitous (incidental) learning. Should the teacher do this? Explain why or why not.
3. Form teams of four, and have each team develop one interdisciplinary thematic unit for use at a specific grade level.
4. From a variety of sources, obtain current samples of resource units, science teaching units, and interdisciplinary thematic units and review and share them with others in your class.
5. What are the characteristics of students who may be "at-risk" students? Describe what the classroom science teacher can do to minimize those students' being at academic risk. Is it possible that a student identified as being at risk is also one who is gifted and talented in science? Explain.
6. Explain what is meant by the term *developmentally appropriate practice*. Describe at least five instructional practices that are considered to be appropriate for teaching science to elementary and middle school students and why those practices are developmentally appropriate.

7. Why is it that failing underachieving students is not considered developmentally appropriate for elementary and middle school students? Do you agree? Explain why or why not.

8. Describe any concepts you held that changed as a result of your experiences with this chapter. Describe the changes.

9. From your recent observations and field work as related to this teacher preparation program, clearly identify one specific example of educational practice that seems contradictory to exemplary practice or theory as presented in this chapter. Present your explanation for the discrepancy.

10. Have other questions been generated by the contents of this chapter? If so, where might you find answers?

NOTES

1. Reprinted with permission from *National Science Education Standards*, pp. 210, 214. Copyright 1996 by the National Academy of Sciences. Courtesy of National Academy Press, Washington, D.C.

2. John Jarolimek and Clifford D. Foster, Sr., *Teaching and Learning in the Elementary School*. 5th ed. (New York: Macmillan, 1993), p. 149.

3. For detailed accounts of middle-grade teaching at this level of integration, see Chris Stevenson and Judy F. Carr (eds.), *Integrated Studies in the Middle Grades* (New York: Teachers College Press, 1993).

4. Madeline Hunter, *Enhancing Teaching* (New York: Macmillan, 1994).

5. Arthur L. Costa, *The School as a Home for the Mind* (Palatine, IL: Skylight Publishing, 1991).

6. Reprinted with permission from *National Science Education Standards*, p. 30. Copyright 1996 by the National Academy of Sciences. Courtesy of National Academy Press, Washington, D.C.

7. For example, see M. Ramirez and A. Castañeda, *Cultural Democracy, Bicognitive Development and Education* (New York: Academic Press, Inc., 1974), pp. 177–178; or Donna M. Gollnick and Philip C. Chinn, *Multicultural Education in a Pluralistic Society*. 3rd ed. (New York: Macmillan, 1990), pp. 286–287. Their descriptions of "field-independent" and "field-sensitive" teaching styles are similar to the "traditional" and "facilitating" teaching styles as described here.

8. See, for example, Janet Kierstead, "Direct Instruction and Experiential Approaches: Are They Really Mutually Exclusive?" *Educational Leadership* 42(8):25–30 (May 1985).

9. Courtesy of Stephanie Rice, Deana Romero, and Teri Catron, fifth-grade teachers at Hugh Bish Elementary, Lawton, Oklahoma. This schedule creates a unique learning environment involving the strengths of three teachers. Each teacher has a homeroom class for spelling and reading. For science and social studies, math, and language arts, the students are divided into three groups, each of which includes one-third of the children from each teacher's assigned class of fifth graders. These groups are changed each quarter, thus providing children the opportunity to work cooperatively with many different peers throughout the school year. This provides each student with the skills needed to work with and adjust to new situations, an important skill needed in life. The groups are created randomly, maintaining a balance of females and males. The three teachers maintain control of scheduling concerning students who attend special classes (learning disabled, speech, counseling, and tutoring). By changing the schedule every quarter, the teachers also have control in placing students with behavior problems and children with personality conflicts, thus creating a more effective learning environment for all.

10. Jerry W. Valentine et al., *Leadership in Middle Level Education* (Reston, VA: National Association of Secondary School Principals, 1993), p. 49.

11. For two significant reports about advantages to the organization of schools into small units, see Diana Oxley, "Organizing Schools into Small Units: Alternatives to Homogeneous Grouping," *Phi Delta Kappan* 75(7):521–526 (March 1994); and Edward A. Wynne and Herbert J. Walberg, "Persisting Group: An Overlooked Force for Learning," *Phi Delta Kappan* 75(7):527–528, 530 (March 1994).

12. Valentine et al., *Leadership in Middle Level Education*, p. 52.

13. See, for example, Irene Mafnas, Julie Calvo Flis, and Suzanne Dionio, "A Contract for Science," *Science Scope* 17(1):45–48 (September 1993).

14. Reprinted with permission from *National Science Education Standards*, p. 220. Copyright 1996 by the National Academy of Sciences. Courtesy of National Academy Press, Washington, D.C.

15. For additional sample interdisciplinary units, see the September 1993 issue of *Science and Children* 31(2).

16. Scott Willis, "Interdisciplinary Learning: Movement to Link Disciplines Gains Momentum," *Curriculum Update* (Alexandria, VA: Association for Supervision and Curriculum Development, November 1992), p. 1.

17. Edward J. Welch, Jr., "Animal Behavior: An Interdisciplinary Unit," *Science and Children* 32(3): (November/December 1994), p. 24.

18. Reprinted with permission from *National Science Education Standards*, p. 214. Copyright 1996 by the National Academy of Sciences. Courtesy of National Academy Press, Washington, D.C.

19. Reprinted with permission from *National Science Education Standards*, p. 210. Copyright 1996 by the National Academy of Sciences. Courtesy of National Academy Press, Washington, D.C.

20. Jacqueline Grennon Brooks and Martin G. Brooks, *In Search of Understanding: The Case for Constructivist Classrooms* (Alexandria, VA: Association for Supervision and Curriculum Development, 1993), p. 29.

21. The value of stating learning objectives in behavioral terms and in providing advance organizers is well documented by research. For example, see Thomas L. Good and Jere E. Brophy, *Looking in Classrooms*. 6th ed. (New York: HarperCollins, 1994), p. 244.

22. Whereas some authors distinguish between "instructional objectives" (hence referring to objectives that are *not* behavior specific) and "behavioral or performance objective" (objectives that *are* behavior specific), the terms are used here as if they are synonymous to stress the importance of writing objectives for instruction in terms that are measurable.

23. Depending on how it is interpreted, what is known as outcome-based education (OBE) has had major critics. For information and clarification, see the entire theme issue of *Educational Leadership* 51(6) (March 1994); see also Spence Rogers and Bonnie Dana, *Outcome-Based Education: Concerns and Responses*, (Fastback 388, Bloomington, IN: Phi Delta Kappa Educational Foundation, 1995).

24. See, for example, David Perkins and Tina Blythe, "Putting Understanding Up Front," *Educational Leadership* 51(5):4–7 (February 1994).

25. Benjamin S. Bloom (ed.), *Taxonomy of Educational Objectives, Book I: Cognitive Domain* (White Plains, NY: Longman, 1984).

26. Rather than an orderly progression from simple to complex mental operations as illustrated by Bloom's taxonomy, other researchers prefer an identification of cognitive abilities that range from simple information storage and retrieval, through a higher level of discrimination and concept attainment, to the highest cognitive ability to recognize and solve problems, as organized by Robert M. Gagné, Leslie Briggs, and Walter Wager in *Principles of Instructional Design*. 3d ed. (New York: Holt, Rinehart and Winston, 1988).

27. David R. Krathwohl, Benjamin S. Bloom, and Bertram B. Masia, *Taxonomy of Educational Goals, Handbook II: Affective Domain* (New York: David McKay, 1964).

28. A. J. Harrow, *Taxonomy of the Psychomotor Domain* (White Plains, NY: Longman, 1977).

29. Geoffrey Caine and Renate Nummela Caine, "The Critical Need for a Mental Model of Meaningful Learning," *California Catalyst* (Fall 1992), p. 19.

30. Robert E. Slavin and Nancy A. Madden, "What Works for Students at Risk: A Research Synthesis," *Educational Leadership* 46(5):4–13 (February 1989).

31. Ibid., p. 5.

32. William Dunn, "Educating Diversity," *American Demographics* (April 1993), p. 40.

33. Association for Supervision and Curriculum Development, *Program News* (Alexandria, VA: Author, May 1994), p. 4.

34. "An NSTA Position Statement: Multicultural Science Education," *NSTA Reports!* (October/November 1991), p. 7.

35. Public Law 94-142 was amended by P.L. 99-457 in 1986 and again in 1990 by P.L. 101-476, at which time its name was changed to Individuals with Disabilities Education Act (IDEA).

36. For a review of the history of special education reform, see Richard Schattman and Jeff Benay, "Inclusive Practices Transform Special Education in the 1990s," *School Administrator* 49(2):8–12 (February 1992). See also Special Education Group Weighs In on Full Inclusion," *Teacher Magazine* 4(9):9 (August 1993), Chapter 2 of Richard A. Villa and Jacqueline S. Thousand, Editors, *Creating*

an Inclusive School (Alexandria, VA: Association for Supervision and Curriculum Development, 1995), and the several articles about inclusion in the December 1995 issue of *Phi Delta Kappa*, volume 77, number 4.

37. Thomas P. Lombardi, *Responsible Inclusion of Students with Disabilities*, Fastback 373 (Bloomington, IN: Phi Delta Kappa Educational Foundation, 1994), p. 7.
38. Many of the suggestions on this list were adapted from Donovan R. Walling, *English as a Second Language: 25 Questions and Answers*. Fastback 347 (Bloomington, IN: Phi Delta Kappa Educational Foundation, 1993), p. 26.
39. Karen B. Rogers and Richard D. Kimpston, "Acceleration, What We Do vs. What We Know," *Educational Leadership* 50(2) (October 1992), p. 58.
40. See Jerry W. Valentine, et al., *Leadership in Middle Level Education. Volume 1: A National Survey of Middle Level Leaders and Schools* (Alexandria, VA: National Association of Secondary School Principals, 1993), pp. 56–60.

SUGGESTED READINGS

Allen, D. *Hands-on Science! One Hundred Twelve High-Interest Activities for Grades Four to Eight*. West Nyack, NY: The Center for Applied Research in Education, 1991.

Beane, J. A. "Curriculum Integration and the Disciplines of Knowledge." *Phi Delta Kappan* 76(8):616–622 (April 1995).

Berlin, D. F., and A. L. White. "The Berlin-White Integrated Science and Mathematics Model." *School Science and Mathematics* 94(1):2–4 (January 1994).

Brown, S. W. "Great Activities for the First Week." *Science Scope* 18(1):20–24 (September 1994).

Clough, M. P., R. J. Smasal, and D. R. Clough. "Managing Each Minute." *The Science Teacher* 61(6): 30–34 (September 1994).

Deal, D. "A Look at Project AIMS." *School Science and Mathematics* 94(1):11–14 (January 1994).

Dunn, R. *Strategies for Educating Diverse Learners*. Fastback 384. Bloomington, IN: Phi Delta Kappa Educational Foundation, 1995.

Fleming, D. L. "An Academic Field Day." *Science Scope* 18(5):24–29 (February 1995).

Kellough, R. D., et al. *Integrating Mathematics and Science for Intermediate and Middle School Students*. Columbus, OH: Prentice Hall, 1996.

———. *Integrating Mathematics and Science for Kindergarten and Primary Children*. Columbus, OH: Prentice Hall, 1996.

McDonald, J., and C. Czerniak. "Developing Interdisciplinary Units: Strategies and Examples." *School Science and Mathematics* 94(1):5–10 (January 1994).

Miller-Lachmann, L., and L. S. Taylor. *Schools for All: Educating Children in a Diverse Society*. Albany, NY: Delmar, 1995.

Moore, G. R. "Revisiting Science Concepts." *Science and Children* 32(3):31–32, 60 (November/December 1994).

Panaritis, P. "Beyond Brainstorming: Planning a Successful Interdisciplinary Program." *Phi Delta Kappan* 76(8):623–628 (April 1995).

Peters, T., K. Schubeck, and K. Hopkins. "A Thematic Approach." *Phi Delta Kappan* 76(8):633–636 (April 1995).

Roberts, P. L. *A Green Dinosaur Day: A Guide for Developing Thematic Units in Literature-Based Instruction, K–6*. Needham Heights, MA: Allyn and Bacon, 1993.

Roberts, P. L., and R. D. Kellough. *A Guide to Developing an Interdisciplinary Thematic Unit*. Columbus, OH: Prentice Hall, 1996.

Saul, W., et al. *Science Workshop: A Whole Language Approach*. New York: Heinemann, 1993.

Shaw, D. G., and Dybdahl, C. S. *Integrating Science and Language Arts: A Sourcebook for K-6 Teachers*. Boston: Allyn & Bacon, 1996.

Walling, D. R. *English as a Second Language: 25 Questions and Answers*. Fastback 347. Bloomington, IN: Phi Delta Kappa Educational Foundation, 1993.

Willis, S. "Teaching Language-Minority Students: Role of Native-Language Instruction Is Debated." *ASCD Update* 36(5):1, 4–5 (June 1994).

CHAPTER 6

Assessing and Reporting Student Achievement

Teachers of science engage in ongoing assessment of their teaching and of student learning.

■ *Teachers systematically gather data on students and their development.*

■ *Teachers analyze assessment data to guide teaching.*

■ *Teachers guide students in self-assessment.*[1]

Assessment (i.e., evaluation) is an integral part and an ongoing process of the educational scene. Curricula, buildings, materials, specific courses, teachers, supervisors, administrators, equipment—all must be periodically assessed in relation to student learning, the purpose of any school. When there are gaps between anticipated results and student achievement, efforts are made to eliminate those factors that seem to be limiting the educational output or, in some other way, to improve the situation. Thus, educational progress occurs.

To learn effectively, students need to know how they are doing. Similarly, to be an effective teacher, you must be informed about what a student knows, feels, and can do so that you can help the student build on her or his science skills, knowledge, and attitudes. Therefore you and your students need continuous feedback on their progress and problems in order to plan appropriate learning activities and to make adjustments to those already planned. If feedback indicates that progress is slow, you can provide alternative activities; if it indicates that some or all of the students have already mastered the desired learning, you can eliminate unnecessary activities and practice for some or all of the students. In short, assessment provides a key for both effective teaching and learning.

The importance of continuous assessment mandates that you know the principles and techniques of assessment. This chapter explains some of these and shows you how to construct and use assessment instruments, especially for science teaching, and to make sense from the data obtained. We define the terms related to assessment, consider what makes a good assessment instrument, suggest procedures to use in the construction of assessment items, point out the advantages and disadvantages of different types of assessment items and procedures, and explain the construction and use of alternative assessment devices.

In addition, this chapter discusses grading and reporting of student achievement, two responsibilities that can consume much of a teacher's valuable time. Grading is time-consuming and frustrating for many teachers. What should be graded? Should marks represent student growth, level of achievement in a group, effort, attitude, general behavior, or a combination of these? What should determine grades—homework, tests, projects, class participation and group work, or all of these? And what should be their relative weights? These are just a few of the questions that plague teachers, parents, and, indeed the teaching profession, when decisions about summative assessment and grades must be made.

In too many schools the grade progress report and final report card are about the only communication between the school and the student's home. Unless the teacher and the school have clearly determined what grades represent, and such understanding is periodically reviewed with each set of parents or guardians, these reports may create unrest and dissatisfaction on the part of parents, guardians, and students and prove to be alienating devices. The grading system and reporting scheme may then, instead of informing parents and guardians, separate even further the home and the school, which do have a common concern—the intellectual, physical, social, and emotional development of the child.

The development of the child encompasses growth in the cognitive, affective, and psychomotor domains. Traditional objective paper-and-pencil tests provide only a portion of the data needed to indicate student progress in these domains. Many experts today question the traditional sources of data and encourage the search for, development of, and use of alterna-

- *Assessment tasks must be reviewed for the use of stereotypes, for assumptions that reflect the perspectives or experiences of a particular group, for language that might be offensive to a particular group, and for other features that might distract students from the intended task.*
- *Assessment tasks must be modified appropriately to accommodate the needs of students with physical disabilities, learning disabilities, or limited English proficiency.*
- *Assessment tasks must be set in a variety of contexts, be engaging to students with different interests and experiences and must not assume the perspective or experience of a particular gender, racial, or ethnic group.[2]*

tive means to more authentically assess the student's development in thinking and higher-level learning. Although many questions remain, it is clear that various techniques of assessment must be used to determine how the student works, what the student is learning, and what the student can produce as a result of that learning. As a science teacher, you must develop a repertoire of means of assessing learner behavior and academic progress.

Assigning grades to students' work has been a part of school for about 100 years. Although it is clear that the conventional report card with marks or grades falls short of being a developmentally appropriate procedure for reporting the academic performance or progress of elementary and middle grade students, and although some schools are experimenting with other ways of reporting student achievement in learning, still letter grades seem to be firmly entrenched, especially in middle and junior high schools (see Table 6.1). Parents, students, colleges, and employers have come to expect grades as evaluations, and some critics suggest that the emphasis in our schools is on getting high grades rather than on learning, arguing that, as traditionally measured, the two do not necessarily go hand in hand. Today's interest is focused more on what the student can do (performance testing) as a result of learning than merely on what the student can recall (memory testing) from the experience.

In addition, there have been complaints about subjectivity and unfair practices. As a result of these concerns, a variety of systems of assessment and reporting have evolved and will likely continue to evolve throughout your professional career.

When teachers are aware of alternative systems, they may be able to develop assessment and reporting processes that are fair and effective for particular situations. So, after discussing assessment, this chapter considers today's principles and practices in grading and reporting student achievement.

PURPOSES OF ASSESSMENT

Assessment of achievement in student learning is designed to serve several purposes:

1. *To assess and improve student learning.* Assessment and improvement of student learning, the function usually first thought of when speaking of assessment, is the principal topic of this chapter.

2. *To identify students' strengths and weaknesses.* Identification and assessment of students' strengths and weaknesses are necessary for two purposes. First, data on student strengths and weaknesses in content and process skills are important in planning activities appropriate for both skill development and intellectual development. This is diagnostic assessment (also known as preassessment). Second, data on student strengths and weaknesses in content and skills are useful for making appropriate modifications to the curriculum.

3. *To assess the effectiveness of a particular instructional strategy.* It is important for you to know how well a particular strategy helped to accomplish a particular goal or objective. Competent teachers continually evaluate their strategy choices, using a number of sources: student achievement as measured by assessment instruments, their own intuition, informal feedback given by the students, and, sometimes, informal feedback given by colleagues, such as members of a teaching team.

4. *To assess and improve the effectiveness of curriculum programs.* Components of the curriculum are continually assessed by committees of teachers and administrators. The assessment is done while students are learning (i.e., formative assessment) and after (summative assessment).

5. *To assess and improve teaching effectiveness.* To improve student learning, teachers are periodically evaluated on the basis of (1) their commitment to working with students at a particular level, (2) their ability to cope with students at a particular age or grade level, and (3) their ability to show mastery of appropriate instructional techniques.

6. *To communicate with and involve parents and guardians in the learning of their children.* Parents, communities, and school boards all share in accountability for the effectiveness of the learning of the students. Today's schools are reaching out and engaging parents, guardians, and the community in their students' education. All teachers play an important role in the process of communicating with, reaching out to, and involving parents.

ASSESSING STUDENT LEARNING

Because the welfare and, indeed, the future of so many people depend on the outcomes of assessment, it is impossible to overemphasize its importance. For a learning endeavor to be successful, the learner must have answers to basic questions: Where am I going? Where am I now? How do I get where I am going? How will I know when I get there? Am I on the right track for getting there? These questions are integral to a good program of assessment. Of course, in the process of teaching and learning the answers may be ever-changing, and the teacher continues to assess and adjust plans as appropriate and necessary.

Principles That Guide the Assessment Program

Based on the preceding questions are the following principles that guide the assessment program.

- Teachers need to know how well they are doing.
- Students need to know how well they are doing.
- Evidence and input data for knowing how well the teacher and students are doing should come from a variety of sources.
- Assessment is an ongoing process. The selection and implementation of plans and activities require continuing monitoring and assessment to check on progress and to change or adopt strategies to promote desired behavior.
- Self-assessment is an important component of any successful assessment program. It involves helping students develop the skills necessary for them to assume increasingly greater ownership of their own learning.
- The program of assessment should help teaching effectiveness and contribute to the intellectual and psychological growth of students.
- Assessment is a reciprocal process, which includes assessment of teacher performance as well as student achievement.

- A teacher's responsibility is to facilitate student learning and to assess student progress in that learning, and for that, the teacher is, or should be, held accountable.

Terms Used in Assessment

In discussing the assessment component of teaching and learning it is easy to be confused by the terminology used. The following clarification of terms is offered to help in your reading and understanding.

ASSESSMENT AND EVALUATION

Although some authors distinguish between the terms *assessment* (i.e., the process of finding out what students are learning, a relatively neutral process) and *evaluation* (i.e., making sense of what was found out, a subjective process), in this text we do not—we find the difference too slight to matter; therefore, we consider the terms to be synonymous.

MEASUREMENT AND ASSESSMENT

Measurement refers to quantifiable data about specific behaviors. Examples of measurement are tests and the statistical procedures used to analyze their results. Measurement is a descriptive and objective process; that is, it is relatively free from human value judgments.

In science teaching, assessment includes objective data derived from measurement, as well as other types of information, some of which is more subjective, such as information from anecdotal records and teacher observations and ratings of student performance. Thus, in addition to the use of objective data (data from measurement), assessment also includes arriving at value judgments made on the basis of subjective information.

An example of the use of these terms is as follows. A teacher may share the information that Julie Jefferson received a score in only the 50th percentile on the eighth-grade statewide achievement test in science (a statement of measurement), but may add that "according to my assessment of her work in my science class, Julie has been an outstanding science student" (a statement of assessment).

VALIDITY AND RELIABILITY

The degree to which a measuring instrument actually measures that which it is intended to measure is called the instrument's *validity*. For example, when we ask if an instrument (such as a performance assessment instrument) has validity, key questions concerning that instrument are:

- Does the instrument adequately sample the intended content?
- Does it measure the cognitive, affective, and psychomotor knowledge and skills that are important to the unit of content being tested?
- Does it sample all the instructional objectives of that unit?

The accuracy with which a technique consistently measures that which it measures is called its *reliability*. If, for example, you know that you weigh 115 pounds and a scale consistently records 115 pounds when you stand on it, then that scale has reliability. However, if the same scale consistently records 100 pounds when you stand on it, we can still say the scale has reliability. Thus, it should be clear to you that an instrument can be reliable (produces similar results when used again and again), although not necessarily valid (in the second instance, the scale is not measuring what it is supposed to measure, so although it is reliable, it is not valid). Although a technique may be reliable but not valid, a technique must have reliability before it can have validity. The greater the number of test items or situations included in a particular content objective, the higher the reliability. The higher the reliability, the greater consistency there will be in students' scores measuring their understanding of that particular objective.

Approaches for Assessing Student Learning in Science

There are three general approaches for assessing a student's learning in science. You can assess:

1. What the student *says*—for example, the quantity and quality of a student's contributions to class discussions or to your questions
2. What the student *does*—for example, a student's performance in class—e.g., the amount and quality of a student's participation in class activities or in doing science exploratory activities
3. What the student *writes*—for example, as shown by items in the student's portfolio—e.g., homework assignments, checklists, written tests—and the student's journal writing.

Although your own situation and personal philosophy will dictate the levels of importance and weight you give to each avenue of assessment, you should have a strong rationale if you value and weigh the three categories differently than one third each.

Authentic Assessment

When assessing for student achievement, it is important that you use procedures that are compatible with the instructional objectives. This is referred to as *authentic assessment*. Other terms used for *authentic* (assessment) are *accurate*, *active*, *aligned*, *alternative*, and *direct*. Although the term *performance assessment* is sometimes used, it refers to the type of student response being assessed, whereas *authentic assessment* refers to the assessment situation. Although not all performance assessments are authentic, assessments that are authentic are most assuredly performance assessments.[3] In science, assessment that is authentic

> calls for exercises that closely approximate the intended outcomes of science education. Authentic assessment exercises require students to apply scientific information and reasoning to situations like those they will encounter in the world outside the classroom, as well as to situations that approximate how scientists do their work. . . . For instance, a student's ability to obtain and evaluate scientific information might be measured using a short-answer test to identify the sources of high-quality scientific information about toxic waste. An alternative and more authentic method is to ask the student to locate such information and develop an annotated bibliography and a judgment about the scientific quality of the information.[4]

In short, to authentically assess whether a student accurately understands the processes of scientific inquiry, the teacher observes the student doing inquiry. For the authentic assessment of the student's understanding of that which the student has been learning, you would use a performance-based assessment procedure. A paper-and-pencil test is not nearly so likely to accurately measure a student's understanding of the process of inquiry.

Assessment: A Three-Step Process

Assessing a student's achievement is a three-step process, involving:

1. *Diagnostic evaluation*—the assessment (sometimes called a preassessment) of the student's knowledge and skills *before* the new instruction;

2. *Formative evaluation*—the assessment of learning *during* the instruction; and
3. *Summative evaluation*—the assessment of learning *after* the instruction, ultimately represented by the student's term, semester, or year achievement grade.

Grades or marks shown on unit tests, progress reports, deficiency notices, and six-week or quarter grades (in a semester-based program) are examples of formative evaluation reports. However, an end-of-chapter test or a unit test is summative when the test represents the absolute end of the student's learning of material in that instructional unit.

ASSESSING WHAT A STUDENT SAYS AND DOES

When assessing what a student says, you should: (1) listen to the student's questions, responses, and interactions with others and (2) observe the student's attentiveness, involvement in class activities, and responses to challenges. Notice that we say you should *listen* and *observe*. While listening to what the student is saying, you should also be observing the student's nonverbal behaviors. For this purpose, teachers use checklists and rating scales, behavioral-growth record forms, observations of the student's performance in classroom activities and investigations, and periodic conferences with the student. Figure 6.1 illustrates a sample form for recording and evaluating teacher observations of a student's verbal and nonverbal behaviors. Figure 6.2 shows a checklist for recording students' sciencing process skills and attitudes development.

With each technique used, you must proceed from your awareness of anticipated learning outcomes (the instructional objectives) and you must evaluate a student's progress toward meeting those objectives. This is referred to as *criterion-referenced assessment*.

Guidelines for Assessing a Student's Verbal and Nonverbal Classroom Behaviors   Here are guidelines to follow in assessing a student's verbal and nonverbal behaviors in the classroom.

1. Maintain an anecdotal record book or folder, with a separate section for your records of each student.
2. For a specific activity, list the desirable behaviors.
3. Check the list against the specific instructional objectives.
4. Record your observations as quickly as possible following your observation. Audio or video recordings, and, of course, computer software programs, can help you check the accuracy of your memory, but if this is inconvenient, you should spend time during school, immediately after, or later that evening, recording your observations while they are still fresh in your memory.
5. Record your professional judgment about the student's progress toward the desired behavior, but think it through before transferring your statement to a permanent record.
6. Write comments that are reminders to yourself, such as:

   "Check validity of observation by further testing."
   "Discuss observations with Julie's parent."
   "Discuss observations with school counselor."
   "Discuss observations with other teachers on the teaching team."

ASSESSING WHAT A STUDENT WRITES

When assessing what a student writes, you can use laboratory work sheets, written assignments and homework, the student's journal writing and portfolio, and paper-and-pencil tests. In many schools, portfolios, work sheets, and homework assignments usually comprise the data used in the formative evaluation of each student's achievement. Tests, too, should be part

Student _____	Course _____	School _____
Observer _____	Date _____	Period _____

Objective for time period	Desired behavior	What student did, said, or wrote

Teacher's (observer's) comments:

FIGURE 6.1 Evaluating and recording student behaviors: sample form.

Activity Number _____ Date _____ Student _____

Skills Record

Observe	Classify	Communicate	Measure	Predict	Infer	Etc.	Teacher comments

Attitude Record

Curious	Persistent	Open-Minded	Cooperative	Withholds Judgment	Etc.	Teacher comments

FIGURE 6.2 Checklist for recording students' sciencing process skills and attitudes development: sample form.

of this evaluation, but tests are also used for summative evaluation at the end of a unit, and for diagnostic purposes as well.

Your summative evaluation of a student's achievement, and any other final judgment you make about a student, can have an impact on the emotional and intellectual development of that student. Special attention is given to this later, in "Recording Teacher Observations and Judgments."

Guidelines for Assessing What a Student Writes   When assessing what a student writes, use the following guidelines:

1. Laboratory worksheets, homework, and test items should correlate with and be compatible with specific instructional objectives; that is, they should be criterion-referenced.

2. Read everything a student writes. When an assignment is important for the student to do, then it is equally important that you give your professional attention to the product of the student's efforts.

3. Provide written or verbal comments about the student's work, and be positive in those comments. Rather than just writing "Good" on a student's paper, briefly state what made it good. Try to avoid negative comments. Rather than simply saying or pointing out that the student didn't do something correctly, tell or show the student acceptable results and how to get there. For reinforcement, use positive rewards and encouragement as frequently as possible.

4. Think before writing a comment on a student's paper, asking yourself how you think the student (or a parent or guardian) will interpret and react to the comment and whether that is the interpretation and reaction you intend or expect.

5. Avoid writing negative comments, marks, or grades in student journals. Student journals are for encouraging students to write, to think about their thinking, and to record their creative thoughts. In journal writing students should be encouraged to write about their experiences in school and out of school, and especially about their experiences related to what is being learned. They should be encouraged to record their feelings about what is being learned and about how they are learning it. Writing in journals gives them practice in expressing themselves in written form and in connecting their learning, and should provide freedom to do so. A teacher's comments and evaluations written in a journal may discourage creative and spontaneous expression. When reading student journals, talk individually with students to seek clarification about their expressions. Student journals are useful to the teacher in understanding the student's thought processes and writing skills (diagnostic evaluation), and journals should *not* be graded. For grading purposes, teachers may simply record whether the student is maintaining a journal and, perhaps, a judgment about the quantity of writing in it, but no judgment should be made about the quality.

6. When reviewing student portfolios, discuss with individual students the progress in their learning as shown by the materials in their portfolios. (See later in this chapter, "Using Portfolios for Student Self-Assessment.") As with student journals, a portfolio should *not* be graded or compared in any way with those of other students. Its purpose is for student self-assessment and to show progress in learning. To this end, students should keep in their portfolios all or major samples of papers related to the course.

Regardless of the avenues chosen and the relative weights you give them, you must evaluate against the instructional objectives. Any given objective may be checked by using more than one method, and by using more than one instrument. Subjectivity, inherent in the evaluation process, may be reduced as you check for validity, comparing results of one measuring technique against those of another.

ALTERNATIVE ASSESSMENT

Although evaluation of cognitive objectives lends itself to traditional written tests of achievement, evaluation of the affective and psychomotor domains requires the use of performance checklists whereby student behaviors can be observed in action. However, as indicated earlier, for cognitive learning as well, science educators today are encouraging the use of alternative assessment procedures; that is, alternatives to traditional paper-and-pencil written testing. Alternative assessment strategies include the use of projects, portfolios, skits, papers, oral presentations, and performance tests. Advantages claimed for the use of authentic assessment include the direct (performance-based; criterion-referenced; outcome-based) measurement of what students should know and can do, and an emphasis on higher-order thinking. On the other hand, disadvantages of authentic assessment include higher cost, difficulty in making results consistent and usable, and problems with validity, reliability, and comparability.

Unfortunately, because a teacher may never again see a particular student after a given school year is over, the effects he or she has had on the student's values and attitudes may never be observed by that teacher at all. However, in schools where groups or teams of teach-

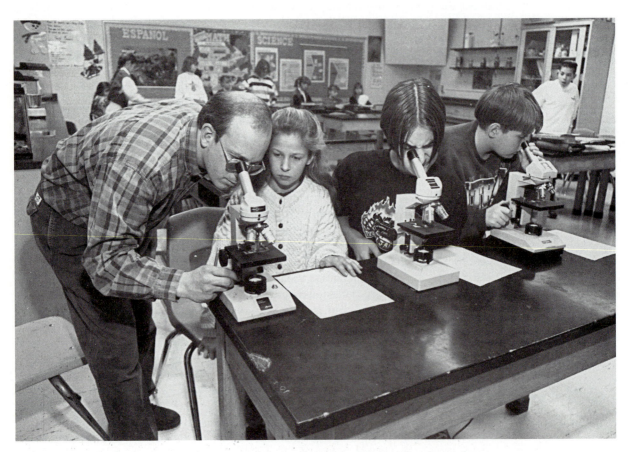

There are many alternative ways to assess student achievement. Children's developing abilities and skills in science can be assessed through direct observation made by the teacher to determine a child's thinking and how well the child can manipulate materials.

ers remain with the same cohort of students throughout several years of school (e.g., in "houses," or "villages"), those teachers often do have opportunity to observe the positive changes in their students' values and attitudes.[5]

COOPERATIVE LEARNING AND ASSESSMENT

The purpose of a cooperative learning group is for the *group* to learn, which means that *individuals* within the group must learn. Group achievement in learning, then, depends on the learning of individuals within the group. Rather than competing for rewards for achievement, members of the group cooperate by helping one another to learn so that the group reward will be a good one. As discussed in Chapter 3, when small groups of students of mixed backgrounds, skills, and capabilities work together toward a common goal, they increase their liking and respect for one another. As a result, there is an increase in each student's self-esteem *and* academic achievement.

When the achievement of a cooperative learning group is recognized, group achievement is rewarded and the individuals within the group are rewarded as well. Remembering that the emphasis must be on peer support, rather than peer pressure, you must be cautious about ever giving group grades.[6] Some teachers give bonus points to all members of a group to add to their individual scores when everyone in the group has met preset criteria. Preset standards can be different for individuals within a group, depending on each member's ability and past performance. It is important that each member of the group feel rewarded and successful. Some teachers also give subjective grades to individual students on their role performances within the group.

For determination of students' report card grades, individual student achievement is measured later through individual results on tests and other sources of data, and the final grade is based on these as well as on the student's performance in the group.

INVOLVING STUDENTS IN SELF-ASSESSMENT

In exemplary science programs, students' continuous self-assessment is an important component of the evaluation process. If students are to progress in their understanding of their own thinking (metacognition) and in their intellectual development, they must receive instruction and guidance in how to become more responsible for their own learning. During that empowerment process they learn to think better of themselves and of their individual capabilities. To achieve this self-understanding and improved self-esteem requires the experiences afforded by successes, along with guidance in self-understanding.

Using Portfolios for Student Self-Assessment

To meet the goals of self-assessment, teachers provide opportunities for students to think about what they are learning, about how they are learning it, and about how far they have progressed. One procedure is for students to maintain portfolios of their work, using rating scales or checklists periodically to assess their own progress. The student portfolio should be well organized and contain assignment sheets, laboratory work sheets, the results of homework, forms for student self-evaluation and reflection on their work, and other materials thought important by the students and teacher.

Although portfolio assessment as an alternative to traditional methods of evaluating student progress has gained momentum in recent years, setting standards is very difficult.

Thus far, research on the use of portfolios for assessment indicate that validity and reliability of teacher evaluation is quite low.[7] Before using portfolios as an alternative to traditional testing, teachers must consider and clearly understand the reasons for doing so, carefully decide on portfolio content, consider parent and guardian reactions, and anticipate grading problems.[8]

While emphasizing the criteria for evaluation, rating scales and checklists provide students with means of expressing their feelings and give the teacher still another source of input data for use in the total assessment of a student's learning in science. To provide students with reinforcement and guidance to improve their learning and development, teachers meet with individual students to discuss their self-evaluations. Such conferences should provide students with understandable and achievable short-term goals, as well as help them develop and maintain adequate self-esteem.

Although most any of the instruments used for evaluating student work can be used for student self-evaluation, in some cases it may be better for the teacher to construct specific instruments for it, keeping the student's understanding of the instrument in mind. Student self-evaluation and reflection should be done on a regular (perhaps biweekly or even weekly) and continuing basis, so comparisons can be made by the student from one time to the next. You will need to help students learn how to analyze these comparisons. Perhaps graphing would be useful, both as a means of analyzing a student's growth and to acquaint the student with skills in graphing. Comparisons should provide a student with information previously not recognized about his or her own progress and growth.

Among the items maintained by students in their portfolios is a series of self-evaluation checklists.

USING CHECKLISTS FOR ASSESSMENT

Items on a student's science learning self-assessment checklist and a teacher's checklist will vary depending on your purpose and grade level. (For a sample generic form of a self-assessment checklist for students in grades 2–6, see Figure 6.3. Sample checklists for assessing a student's oral report and kindergarten's attitudes in science can be found in Figures 6.4 and 6.5, respectively.) Checklist items can be used easily by a student for comparison with previous self-assessments; open-ended questions allow the student to give additional information and provide an opportunity to do some expressive writing. For nonreaders, the teacher or an aide can read the items individually to students.

A checklist similar to the one in Figure 6.4 can be constructed by the teacher to assess students' science attitudes (see Figure 6.5). After a student has demonstrated each of the skills satisfactorily, a check is made next to the student's name.

Guidelines for Using Student Portfolios in the Assessment of Science Learning   Here are general guidelines for using student portfolios in the assessment of student learning of science.

1. The contents of the portfolio should reflect your instructional aims and course objectives.
2. Date everything that goes into the portfolio.
3. Determine what materials should be kept in the portfolio and announce when, how, and according to what criteria portfolios will be reviewed by you; announce these specifications clearly.
4. Give students all responsibility for maintenance of portfolios.
5. Portfolios should be kept in the classroom.
6. A portfolio should not be graded or compared in any way with those of other students. Its purpose is for student self-assessment and to show progress in learning. To this end,

Student Self-Assessment Form
(*To be kept in student's portfolio*)

Student: _____ Date: _____

Teacher: _____ Number: _____

Circle one response for each of the first six items.

1. Since my last self-evaluation my assignments have been

    a. always on time.

    b. always late.

    c. sometimes late; sometimes on time.

    d.

2. Most of my classmates

    a. like me.

    b. don't like me.

    c. ignore me.

    d.

3. I think I am

    a. smart.

    b. the smartest in the class.

    c. the slowest in the class.

    d.

4. Since my last self-evaluation, I think I am

    a. doing better in the science experiments.

    b. doing worse in the science experiments.

    c. doing about the same in the science experiments.

    d.

5. In this class

    a. I am learning a lot.

    b. I am not learning very much.

    c. I am not learning anything.

    d.

6. In this class

    a. I am doing the best work I can.

    b. I am not doing as well as I can.

    c.

7. Describe what you have learned since your last self-evaluation that you have used outside of school. Tell how you used it. (You can refer to your previous self-evaluation.)

8. Describe anything that you have learned about yourself since you completed your last self-evaluation. (You can refer to your previous self-evaluation.)

FIGURE 6.3   Student self-assessment: Sample generic form for students in grades 2–6.

Oral Report Assessment Checklist

Did the student	Yes	No	Comments
1. Speak so that everyone could hear?	_____	_____	_____
			_____
2. Finish sentences?	_____	_____	_____
			_____
3. Seem comfortable in front of the group?	_____	_____	_____
			_____
4. Give a good introduction?	_____	_____	_____
			_____
5. Seem well informed about the topic?	_____	_____	_____
			_____
6. Explain ideas clearly?	_____	_____	_____
			_____
7. Stay on the topic?	_____	_____	_____
			_____
8. Give a good conclusion?	_____	_____	_____
			_____
9. Use science visuals effectively to make the presentation interesting?	_____	_____	_____
			_____
10. Give good answers to questions from the audience?	_____	_____	_____
			_____

FIGURE 6.4   Sample checklist: Assessing a student's oral report.

students should keep in their portfolio all papers, or major sample papers, related to the course. For grading purposes, teachers usually simply record whether or not the portfolio was maintained and whether it contains all materials it should.

MAINTAINING RECORDS OF STUDENT ACHIEVEMENT

You must maintain well-organized and complete records of student achievement. You may do this in a written record book or on an electronic record book (that is, a computer software program, either a commercially developed program[9] or one you develop yourself, perhaps by using a computer software program spreadsheet as the base). At the very least, the record book

---

Science Attitudes Checklist

Observation Period: _____
Check those attitudes by recording the number of times each child demonstrates the desired scientific attitude.

Student	Curiosity	Respect	Conservation	etc.
Mary	√	√√		
Bill	√√	√	√√	
Tia	√√√	√√√	√√√	
etc.				

FIGURE 6.5   Sample checklist: Kindergarten students' attitudes in science.

should include all records of attendance and scores on tests, homework, projects, and other assignments. A rather sophisticated high-tech record keeping and learner profile system is now available that uses a computer to help the teacher plan and customize assessment criteria and to observe and collect data anywhere without interrupting the learning process. The system uses the Apple Newton or a bar code scanner to make reports and to assist in student self-assessment.[10]

Anecdotal records can be maintained in alphabetical order in a separate binder, with a separate section for each student. Daily interactions and events that occur in the classroom may provide informative data about a student's intellectual, emotional, and physical development. Maintaining a dated record of your observations of these interactions and events can preserve important information that might otherwise be forgotten. At the end of a unit, and again at the conclusion of a grading term, you will want to review your records. During the course of the school year your anecdotal records (and those of other members of your teaching team) will provide important information about the intellectual, psychological, and physical development of each student, as well as ideas about attention that should be given to individual students.

Recording Teacher Observations and Judgments

You must think carefully about any written comments you intend to make about a student. Children can be quite sensitive to what others say about them, most particularly to comments made about them by a teacher.

In addition, we have seen anecdotal comments in students' permanent records that said more about the teachers who made the comments than about the subject students. Comments that have been made carelessly, hurriedly, or thoughtlessly can be detrimental to a student's welfare and progress in school. Teacher comments must be professional; that is, they must be diagnostically useful to the continued intellectual and psychological development of the student. This is true for any comment you make or write, whether on a student's paper or on the student's permanent school record, or in a note sent home to a student's parent or guardian.

That which separates the professional teacher from "anyone off the street" is the teacher's ability to go beyond mere description of a student's behavior. Keep this in mind always when you write comments that will be read by students, parents or guardians, or other teachers.

GRADING AND MARKING

If conditions were ideal (which they are not), and if teachers did their job perfectly well (which many of us do not), then all students would receive top marks (the ultimate in mastery learning) and there would be less need to talk about grading. Mastery learning implies that some end point of learning is attainable, but there probably is no end point. In any case, because conditions for teaching are never ideal, and we teachers are mere humans, let us continue with this topic (of grading) that is undoubtedly of special interest to you, to your students, to their parents or guardians, and to school counselors, administrators, and school boards.

We have frequently used the term *achievement*. Achievement means accomplishment, but in this context does it mean accomplishment of instructional objectives as measured against preset standards, or simply accomplishment? Most teachers probably choose the former definition whereby the teacher subjectively establishes a standard that must be met in order for a student to receive a certain grade for an assignment or a test, or a quarter, a semester, or a course. Achievement, then, is decided by degrees of accomplishment.

Preset standards are usually expressed in percentages (degrees of accomplishment) needed for marks or ABC grades. If no student achieves the standard required for a top mark, for example, then no student receives that top mark. On the other hand, if all students meet the preset standard for the top mark, then all receive it. Determining student grades on the basis of preset standards is referred to as *criterion-referenced grading*.

Criterion-Referenced Vs. Norm-Referenced Grading

As stated in the preceding paragraph, criterion-referenced grading is grading that is based on preset standards. Norm-referenced grading, on the other hand, is based on the relative accomplishment of individuals in a group (e.g., one classroom of seventh-grade science students) or in a larger group (e.g., all students enrolled in seventh-grade science), by comparing and ranking students, and is commonly known as "grading on a curve." Because it encourages competition and discourages cooperative learning, *norm-referenced grading is not recommended* for the determination of student grades. Norm-referenced grading is educationally dysfunctional.[11] After all, each student is an individual and should not be converted to a statistic on a frequency-distribution curve. For your own information, after several years of teaching, you can produce frequency-distribution studies of grades you have given in a course you have been teaching, but do *not* grade students on a curve. *Grades for student achievement should be tied to performance levels and determined on the basis of each student's achievement toward preset standards.*

In criterion-referenced grading the aim is to communicate information about an individual student's progress in knowledge and work skills in comparison with that student's previous attainment or in the pursuit of an absolute, such as content mastery. Criterion-referenced grading is featured in continuous-progress curricula, competency-based (outcome-based education) curricula, and other programs that focus on individualized education.

Criterion-referenced or competency-based grading is based on the level at which each student meets the specified objectives (standards) for the subject. The objectives must be clearly stated to represent important student learning outcomes. This approach implies that effective teaching and learning result in high grades or top marks for most students. In fact, when a mastery concept is used, the student must accomplish the objectives before being allowed to proceed to the next learning task. The philosophy of teachers who favor criterion-referenced procedures recognizes individual potential. Such teachers accept the challenge of finding teaching/learning strategies and situations to help students progress from where they are to the next designated level. Instead of wondering how Julie compares with Juanita, the comparison is between what Julie could do yesterday and what she can do today, and how well these performances compare to the preset standard.

Most school systems use some combination of norm-referenced and criterion-referenced data. Sometimes both kinds of information are useful. For example, a report card for a student in the eighth grade might indicate how that student is meeting certain criteria, such as through an A grade for addition of fractions. Another entry might show that this mastery is expected, however, at the sixth grade. Another entry might show how the student compares with the statewide norm of students of that grade level in mathematics. Both criterion- and norm-referenced data may be communicated to the parents or guardians, and to students. Appropriate procedures should be used: a criterion-referenced approach to show whether or not the student can accomplish the task, and a norm-referenced approach to show how well that student performs as compared with the larger group to which the student belongs.

Determining Grades or Marks

Determining achievement grades (or marks) for student performance is serious business, for which you must make several important and professional decisions. Although in many elementary schools and in a few middle and upper-grade schools, and for certain classes or assignments, only marks such as "S/U" or "pass/no pass," are used; for most courses taught in grade 5–8, percentages of accomplishment and ABC grades are used (see Table 6.1).

Guidelines for Determining Grades or Achievement Marks   For the determination of marks or grades as designators of student achievement in science, consider the following guidelines.

1. At the start of the school term, explain your marking and grading policies *first to yourself*, then to your students and to their parents or guardians at "back-to-school night," or in a written explanation that is sent home, or both.

2. When converting your interpretation of a student's accomplishments to a mark or letter grade, be as objective as possible.

3. Build your grading policy around accomplishment rather than failure, whereby students proceed from one accomplishment to the next. This is continuous promotion, not necessarily from one grade to the next, but within the classroom. (However, some schools have done away with grade-level designations and, in its place, use the concept of continuous promotion—or multigrade classrooms—from the time of a student's entry into the school through the student's graduation or exit from the school.)

4. For the selection of criteria for marks or ABC grades, select a percentage standard, such as 92 percent for an A, 85 percent for a B, 75 percent for a C, and 65 percent for a D. Cutoff percentages used are your decision, although the district, school, or program area may have established guidelines to which you are expected to adhere.

TABLE 6.1   Grade reporting procedures used by grades 5–8[*]

	% Used by Grade Level			
	5	6	7	8
Letter scale	70	78	81	79
Word scale, e.g., *excellent, good*	13	16	14	14
Number scale	3	10	10	10
Satisfactory/unsatisfactory; pass/fail	30	32	28	25
Informal written notes	30	36	31	30
Percentage marks	27	25	21	22
Progress in relation to potential	17	16	11	10
Other	7	7	7	7

Source: Jerry W. Valentine et al. *Leadership in Middle Level Education. Volume 1: A National Survey of Middle Level Leaders and Schools* (Reston, VA: National Association of Secondary School Principals, 1993), p. 61. By permission of the National Association of Secondary School Principals.

5. *Evaluation* and *grading* are *not* synonymous. As you learned earlier, evaluation implies the collection of information from a variety of sources, including measurement techniques and subjective observations. These data then become the basis for arriving at a final grade, which in effect is a final value judgment. Grades are one aspect of evaluation and are intended to communicate educational progress to students and to their parents or guardians. For it to be valid as an indicator of that progress, you *must* use a variety of sources of data for determination of a student's final grade.

6. For the determination of students' final grades, in the upper grades, we recommend using a point system, whereby things that students write, say, and do are given points (but not for journals or portfolios, except, perhaps, simply whether or not the student maintains one); then the possible point total is the factor for grade determination. For example, if 92 percent is the cutoff for an A, and 500 points are possible, then any student with 460 points or more (500 $\times$ .92) has achieved an A. Likewise, for a test or any other assignment, if the value is 100 points, the cutoff for an A is 92 (100 $\times$ .92). With a point system and preset standards, the teacher and students, at any time during the year, always know the current points possible and can easily calculate a student's current grade standing. Then, as far as a current grade is concerned, older students should know always where they stand in the subject or course.

7. Students will be absent and will miss assignments and tests, and it is best that you decide beforehand your policy about makeup work. Your policies about late assignments and missed tests must be clearly communicated to students and to their parents or guardians. For makeup work, consider the following.

- *Homework assignments.* For homework assignments, our recommendation is that after due dates have been negotiated or set, you strictly adhere to them, giving no credit or reduced credit for work that is turned in late, except in unusual situations. You may think this is harsh and rigid, but experience has shown it to be a good policy to which students can and should adjust. It is much like the world of work (and of college) to which they must become accustomed, and it is a policy that is sensible for a teacher who deals with many papers each day. Of course, to work well, students must be given their assignments, not at the last minute, but long before the due dates. And, of course, the teacher must be flexible and sensitive to the fact that many students have problems that make it impossible for them to do any schoolwork at home. This is one reason that an increasing number of schools and teachers are encouraging the use of class time to do all or most homework.
- *Tests.* Sometimes students are absent when tests are given. In this situation you have several options. Some teachers allow students to miss or discount one test per grading period. Another technique is to allow each student to substitute a written homework assignment or project for one missed test. Still another option is to give the absent student a choice of either taking a makeup test or having the next test count double. A makeup test should be taken within a week of the regular test unless there is a compelling reason (e.g., medical or family problem) that this is not possible.

Some students miss a testing period, not because of being absent from school, but because of their involvement in other school activities. In those instances, the student may be able to arrange to attend another of your class periods, on the day of the test or the next, and take the test.

If a student is absent during performance testing, the possible diminished reliability of the test and the logistics of having to readminister the test for one student may necessitate giving the student an alternate written test.

TESTING FOR STUDENT ACHIEVEMENT IN SCIENCE

One source of information used in determining grades are data obtained from testing for student achievement.

Standardized and Non-Standardized Tests

There are two kinds of tests, those that are standardized and those that are not. Standardized tests are those that have been constructed and published by commercial testing bureaus and used by states and districts to determine and compare student achievement, principally in the core subjects of reading, science, social studies, and math. Standardized norm-referenced tests are best for diagnostic purposes and should *not* be used for determining student marks and grades. Space in this textbook does not allow discussion of standardized achievement testing. For that you can refer to resources found in the readings at the end of this chapter. The focus here is on tests designed by the classroom teacher for his or her own unique group of children. Although textbook publisher's tests, test item pools, and standardized tests are available from a variety of sources, because schools are different, teachers are different, and children are different, most of the time you will (or should) be designing and preparing tests for your purposes for your distinct group of children.

Competent planning, preparing, administering, and scoring of tests is an important professional skill, for which you will gain valuable practical experience during your student teaching. Here are guidelines that you will want to refer to while you are student teaching and again, occasionally, during your first few years as a credentialed teacher.

Purposes for Testing

Tests can be designed for several purposes, and a variety of kinds of tests and alternate test items will keep your testing program interesting, useful, and reliable. As a university student, you are probably most experienced with testing for measuring achievement, but when teaching science to elementary and middle school youngsters, you will use tests for other reasons as well, such as to:

- Assess and aid in curriculum development
- Help determine teaching effectiveness
- Help students develop positive attitudes, appreciations, and values
- Help students increase their understanding and retention of science facts, principles, skills, and concepts
- Motivate students
- Provide diagnostic (preassessment) information for planning for instruction
- Provide review and drill to enhance teaching and learning
- Serve as a source of information for students and parents

When and How Often to Test Students for Achievement

First of all, assessment for student learning should be continual, that is, it should be going on every minute of every class day. For grading or marking purposes, it is difficult to generalize about how often to formally test for student achievement in science for grades K–8, but we believe that testing should be continuous, frequent, and cumulative, that is, the items for each assessment should measure for the student's understanding of previously learned material as well as for the current unit of study. Advantages of cumulative assessment include the review, reinforcement, and articulation of old material with the recent. Advantages of continual and frequent assessment include a reduction in student anxiety over tests and an increase in the validity of final grades or marks.

CONSTRUCTION OF TEACHER-MADE TESTS

After determining the reasons for which you are designing and administering a test, you need to identify the specific instructional objectives the test is being designed to measure. As you learned in Chapter 5, your written instructional objectives must be specific so that you can write assessment items to measure against them, that is, so you can perform criterion-referenced assessment. The first step in test construction, therefore, is the identification of the purpose(s) for the test (from those listed in the preceding discussion). The second step is to identify the objectives (including performance objectives, as well as science content and attitudinal objectives) to be measured, and the third step is to prepare the test items. The best time to prepare draft items is after you have prepared your instructional objectives, that is, while the objectives are still fresh in your mind, which means *before* the instruction. After the instructional activity you will then rework your first draft of the test items to make any modifications as a result of the actual instructional activity that occurred while it is still clear in your mind.

Administering Tests

For many students, test taking can be a time of high anxiety. To more accurately measure achievement you will want to take steps to reduce students' anxiety. Students demonstrate test anxiety in various ways. Just before and during testing some are quiet and thoughtful, whereas others are noisy and disruptive. To control or reduce students' anxieties, consider the following discussion as guidelines for administering tests.

Because students respond best to familiar routine, plan your program so that tests are given at regular intervals (e.g., same day each week) and administered at the same time and in the same way.

Avoid making up tests that are too long and that will take too much time. Beginning teachers sometimes have unreasonable expectations of young people in regard to their attention spans during testing. Frequent testing with frequent sampling of student achievement is preferred over infrequent and long tests that attempt to cover everything.

When giving paper-and-pencil tests, try to arrange the classroom so that it is well ventilated, the temperature is comfortable, and the seats are well spaced. If spacing is a problem, consider using alternate forms of the test, in which students seated adjacent to one another have different forms of the same test, for instance, multiple-choice answer alternatives that are arranged in different order.

Before starting the test, explain to students what they are to do when finished, such as begin a homework or reading assignment for this or another class. Not all of the students will finish at the same time, and it is unreasonable to expect young people to sit quietly after finishing a test; they need something to do.

When ready to test, don't drag it out. Start the testing quickly and efficiently. Once testing has begun, avoid interrupting the students. Items or announcements of important information can be written on the board or held until all are finished with the test. During testing, remain in the room and visually monitor the students. If the test is not going to take an entire class period (and most shouldn't), and it's a major test, then give it at the beginning of the period, if possible, unless you are planning a test review just prior to testing. It is improbable that any teacher can teach a lesson just prior to or immediately after a major test, that evokes a high degree of student interest.

CHEATING

Cheating on tests does occur, but there are steps you can take to discourage it or to reduce the opportunity and pressure that cause students to cheat. Consider the following:

1. Space students, or, as mentioned earlier, use alternate forms of the test.

2. Frequent testing, and not allowing a single test to count too much toward a quarter or semester grade, reduces test anxiety and the pressure that can cause cheating and increases student learning by "stimulating greater effort and providing intermittent feedback" to the student.[12]

3. Prepare tests that are clear, that are not ambiguous, thereby reducing student's frustration caused by a question or instructions that they do not understand.

4. As mentioned earlier, avoid tests that are too long and that will take too much time. During long tests, some students get discouraged and restless, and that is a time when some students begin looking around and when classroom management problems can occur.

5. Performance tests, by their nature, can cause even greater pressure on students, and can also provide greater opportunity for cheating. When administering performance tests to an entire class it is best to have several monitors, such as members of your teaching team. If that isn't possible, consider testing groups of students, such as cooperative learning groups, rather than individuals. Evaluation of test performance, would then be based on group, rather than individual, achievement.

6. Consider using open-text and open-notebook tests, even during performance testing. Allowing students to use their books and pages of notes not only reduces anxiety, but also helps them with the organization and retention of what has been learned.

If you suspect cheating *is* occurring, move and stand in the area of the suspected student. Usually that will stop it. When you suspect cheating *has* occurred, you are faced with a dilemma. Unless your suspicion is backed by solid proof you are advised to forget it, but keep a close watch on the student during the next testing time to prevent the possibility of cheating. Your job is not to catch students being dishonest, but to prevent their dishonesty. If you have absolute proof that a student has cheated, then you are obligated to proceed with school policy on student cheating, which may call for a session with the counselor, or with the student and the student's parent or guardian, and perhaps an automatic F grade on the test.

TIME NEEDED TO TAKE A TEST

Again, avoid giving tests that are too long and that will take too much time. Preparing and administering good tests is a skill you will develop over time. In the meantime, it is best to test frequently and to use tests that sample student achievement rather than try for a comprehensive measure of that achievement.

Some students take more time on a test than do others. You should also avoid giving too much time, or classroom management problems will result. On the other hand, you don't want to cut short the time needed by students who can do well but need more time to think and to write. As a guide, use the following table of time needed for different types of test items (Table 6.2). As actual time will vary according to grade level and student maturity, this is merely a guide for determining the approximate amount of time to allow students to complete a test. For example, for a test made up of 10 multiple-choice items, 5 arrangement items, and 2 short-explanation items, you should plan about 30 minutes for students to complete the test.

TABLE 6.2   Time to allow for testing as determined by the types of assessment items

Type of Test Item	Time Needed per Item[*]
Matching	1 minute per matching item
Multiple-choice	1 minute per item
Completion	1 minute per item
Completion drawing	2 to 3 minutes
Arrangement	2 to 3 minutes
Identification	2 to 3 minutes
Short explanation	2 to 3 minutes
Essay and performance	10 or more minutes

[*]Actual time will vary greatly according to grade level and student maturity.

PREPARING ASSESSMENT ITEMS

Preparing and writing good assessment items is yet another professional skill, and to become proficient at it takes study, time, practice, and reflection. Because of the recognized importance of an assessment program, please assume this professional charge seriously and responsibly. Although poorly prepared items take no time at all to construct, they will cause you more trouble than you can imagine. As a professional you should take time to study different types of assessment items that can be used and how best to write them, and then practice writing them. Although it has already been said many times in this book, because it is very important, we stress once again: in preparing assessment items, you should ensure that they match and sufficiently cover the instructional objectives. In addition, you should prepare each item carefully enough to be reasonably confident that it will be understood by the student as you intend it to be understood. With the diversity of children in today's classroom, especially in respect to English language proficiency, this is an especially important point. Finally, after administering a test you must take time to analyze the results and reflect on the value of each item before ever using that item again.

Classification of Assessment Items

Assessment items can be classified as verbal (oral or written words), visual (pictures and diagrams), and performance (handling of materials and equipment). Written verbal items are those that have traditionally been most frequently used in testing. However, visual tests are useful, for example, when working with students who lack fluency with the written word or when testing for the knowledge of students who have limited or no proficiency in English. Performance items are recommended as often as time and materials will allow.

PERFORMANCE AND ALTERNATIVE ASSESSMENT
Performance items and tests are useful in measuring for psychomotor skill development; for example, in performance testing of locomotor skills, such as a student's ability to manipulate a compass, to carry a microscope (gross motor skill), or to focus a microscope (fine motor skill). Performance testing should also be a part of a wider testing program that includes testing for higher-level skills and knowledge, such as

- When a student or small group of students are given the task (objective) of creating from discarded materials a habitat for an imaginary animal, then displaying and describing their product to the rest of the class.

- When groups are assigned the task, using a sheet of aluminum foil, to design a river-going vessel to transport building materials from a supply house to a construction site on a river island. Using identical sizes of aluminum foil, the group that designs a vessel with the greatest load capacity "gets the construction contract."[13]
- Where a fourth-grade class studying a unit on the plant life cycle is given the performance task of creating a children's book explaining the subject (plant life cycle) to third graders.[14]

Educators today have a rekindled interest in performance testing as a means of assessing learning that is closer to measuring for the real thing (i.e., that is authentic). In a program for teacher preparation, micro peer teaching (see Chapter 7) and the student teaching experience are examples of performance assessment, that is, assessment practices used to assess the teacher candidate's ability to teach. It seems probable that most of us would agree that assessment of student teaching is a more authentic assessment of a candidate's ability to teach science to third graders than a written (paper-and-pencil test) or verbal (oral test) form of assessment. In other words, if you want to determine how well someone can teach science to third graders, the best way to do that is to observe (and analyze the observation data) that person doing it, preferably over some long time period. By the same token, if you want to determine a third grader's ability to do science, then you set up a situation in which the student does science and you observe (and analyze) that student's sciencing behaviors.

As should be obvious to you by now, performance testing is usually more expensive and time-consuming than verbal testing, and verbal testing is more time demanding and expensive than is written testing. However, a good program of assessment in science achievement will use alternate forms of assessment, not relying solely on one form (such as written) and on only one type of written item (such as multiple-choice).

The type of test and items you use depends on your purpose and objectives. Carefully consider the alternatives within that framework. To provide validity checks and to account for the individual differences of students, a good assessment program should include items from all three types—what the student says, does, and writes. That is what writers of articles in professional journals are referring to when they talk about *alternative assessment*. They encourage the use of multiple assessment items, as opposed to the traditional heavy reliance on written objective items such as multiple-choice questions.

GENERAL GUIDELINES FOR PREPARING ASSESSMENT ITEMS
In summary, when preparing assessment items you should adhere to these guidelines:

1. Include several kinds of items (see sample types included in "Specific Guidelines for Preparing Assessment Items," page 24).
2. Assure that content coverage is complete, that is, that all objectives are being measured.
3. Assure that each item of the test is reliable, that it measures the intended objective. One way to check item reliability is to have more than one test item measuring for the same objective.
4. Assure that each item is clear and unambiguous.
5. Plan the item to be difficult enough for the poorly prepared student, but easy enough for the student who is well prepared.
6. Because it is time-consuming to write good assessment items, you are advised to maintain a bank of items, with each item coded according to its matching instructional objective and according to its domain (cognitive, affective, or psychomotor), whether it requires low-level recall, processing, or application, and perhaps according to its level within the hierarchy of that particular domain. Computer software programs are avail-

able for doing this task. Ready-made test item banks are available on computer discs and usually accompany science programs and textbooks. If you use them, be certain that the items match your objectives and that they are well written. It doesn't follow that because they were published they are well written. Some state departments of education have made efforts to develop test banks for teachers.[15] When preparing items for your test bank, use your best creative writing skills—prepare items that match your objectives, put them aside, think about them, share them with colleagues, then work them over again.

Every test you administer to your students should represent your best professional effort—clean, without spelling or grammatical errors, and easily read if it is a written test. A quickly and poorly prepared test can cause you more grief than you can imagine. One that is obviously prepared hurriedly and filled with spelling and grammatical errors, or run off on a duplicating machine that is about out of duplicating fluid, will quickly be frowned upon by discerning parents or guardians. If you are a student teacher, such poor presentation will certainly bring about an admonishment from your university supervisor and, should the sloppiness continue, your speedy dismissal from the teacher preparation program.

ATTAINING CONTENT VALIDITY

To ensure that your test measures what it is supposed to measure, you can construct a table of specifications, such as that shown in Figure 6.6. This two-way grid indicates behavior in one dimension and content in the other. In this grid, "behaviors" refer to the three domains: cognitive, affective, and psychomotor. In this sample grid the cognitive domain is divided, according to Bloom's taxonomy (Chapter 5), into six categories: (1) knowledge, (2) comprehension, (3) application, (4) analysis, (5) synthesis, and (6) evaluation. This sample does not specify levels within the affective and psychomotor domains.

To use a table of specifications, the teacher examining objectives for the unit decides the emphasis that should be given to the behavior and to the content. In this sample, four content areas are represented: vocabulary, concepts, technological applications, and inquiry skills. For instance, if vocabulary development is a concern for this sixth-grade study of the density of solids, then probably 12 percent of the test on vocabulary may be appropriate, but 50 percent would be unsuitable. This planning enables the teacher to design a test to fit the situation, rather than a haphazard test that does not correspond to the objectives in either content or behavior emphasis. Because knowledge questions are easy to write, science tests too often fail to go beyond this level even though the objectives state that the student will

Content	Behaviors								
Science (Grade 6)	Cognitive								
Density	Knowledge	Comprehension	Application	Analysis	Synthesis	Evaluation	Affective	Psychomotor	TOTAL
I. Vocabulary development		2 (1, 2)	3 (2)						
II. Concepts		2 (3, 4)	1 (4)	1 (5)					
III. Applications	1 (5)	1 (5)		1 (5)		1 (5)			
IV. Inquiry skills	1 (6)	1 (6)			1 (6)	1 (6)			
Total	2	6	4	2	1	2			17
Percentage	11.7	35	23.5	11.7	6	11.7			100%

FIGURE 6.6 Table of specifications: Sample I.

Content	Behaviors							Total
	Cognitive		Affective		Psychomotor			
	Input	Processing	Application	Low	High	Low	High	
I.								
II.								
III.								
IV.								
Total								

FIGURE 6.7   Table of specifications: Sample II.

analyze and evaluate. This sample table of specifications for a sixth-grade science unit on density indicates a distribution of questions on a test (the test item numbers are the numbers *not* in parentheses). The teacher could also show the objectives tested, as indicated within parentheses. Then, a check on inclusion of all objectives would be easy.

Preferred by some teachers is the alternative table shown in Figure 6.7. Rather than differentiating between all six of Bloom's cognitive levels, this table separates cognitive objectives into just three levels, those that require simple low-level recall of knowledge, those that require information processing, and those that require application of the new knowledge—analogous to the three levels of thinking as discussed in Chapter 3. In addition, in this table the affective and psychomotor domains are each divided into low- and high-level behaviors. Another alternative, not illustrated here, is a table of specifications that shows all levels of each of the three domains.

Specific Guidelines for Preparing Assessment Items

This section presents the advantages, disadvantages, and guidelines for use of 12 types of assessment items. In reading the advantages and disadvantages of each, note that some types are appropriate for use in performance assessment, whereas others are not.

ARRANGEMENT

Description: Terms or real objects (realia) are to be arranged in a specified order.

Example 1: From the following list of planets in our solar system, arrange the planets in order beginning with the one that is closest to our sun.

Example 2: The assortment of balls on the table represents the planets in our solar system. (Note: The balls are of various sizes, such as marbles, tennis balls, basketballs, and so on, and are labeled with their appropriate planetary names, with a large sphere in the center representing the sun.) Arrange the balls in their proper order around the sun.

Advantages: This type of item tests for knowledge of sequence and order and is good for review, for starting discussions, and for performance assessment. Example 2 is an example of a performance test item.

Disadvantages: Scoring may be difficult, so be cautious and meticulous when using items of this type for grading purposes.

Guideline for use: To enhance reliability, you may need to include instructions for students to include the rationale for their arrangement, making it a combined arrangement and short-explanation type, allowing space for explanations on an answer sheet.

COMPLETION DRAWING

Description: An incomplete drawing is presented, and the student is to complete it.

Example 1: Connect the following items with arrow lines to show the stages from the planting of cotton to the distribution of wearing apparel to consumers.

Example 2: Draw a line connecting the sun, the owl, the corn grains, and the field mice to show the direction in which energy travels through the food web.

Advantages: This type requires less time than needed for a complete drawing, as may be required in an essay item. Scoring is relatively easy.

Disadvantages: The instructions must be given with care so that students do not misinterpret the expectation.

Guidelines for use: Use occasionally for diversion, but take care in preparing. Example 1 is typical of this type when used in integrated thematic teaching. Consider making the item a combined completion-drawing, short-explanation type by having students include their rationales for their drawings. Be sure to allow space for their explanations.

COMPLETION STATEMENT

Description: An incomplete sentence is presented, and the student is to complete it by filling in the blank space(s).

Example 1: The point around which a lever turns is called a _____.

Example 2: To test their hypotheses, scientists conduct _____.

Advantages: This type is easy to devise, to take, and to score.

Disadvantages: In using this type, there is a tendency to emphasize rote memory. It is difficult to write this type of item to measure for higher levels of cognition. You must be alert for a correct response that is different from the expected. For example, in Example 2, although the teacher's key has *experiments* as the correct answer, a student might answer the question with *investigations*, or *tests*, or some other response that is equally correct.

Guideline for use: Use occasionally for review or for preassessment of student knowledge. Avoid using this type for grading unless you can write quality items that extend student thinking beyond mere recall. In all instances, avoid copying items verbatim from the student book. As with all types, be sure to provide adequate space for students' answers.

CORRECTION

Description: Similar to the completion type, except that sentences or paragraphs are complete but with italicized or underlined words that can be changed to make the sentence correct.

Example 1: Photosynthesis in *Arkansas* is the breakdown of *children* into hydrogen and oxygen, the release of *minerals*, and then the combining of *arms* with carbon dioxide to make *Legos*.

Example 2: 1, 1, 2, 3, 5, 8, *12*, <u>21</u>, 34, <u>92</u>

Advantages: Writing this type can be fun for the teacher for the purpose of preassessment of student knowledge or for review. Students may enjoy this type for the relief of tension afforded by the incorrect absurdities. It can also be useful for introducing words with multiple meanings.

Disadvantages: Like the completion type, the correction type tends to measure for low-level recall and rote memory (although this is not the case in Example 2, which is a relatively high-level question). The underlined or italicized incorrect items could be so whimsical that they might cause more classroom disturbance than you want.

Guidelines for use: Use occasionally for diversion and discussion. Try to write items that measure for higher-level cognition. Consider making it a combined correction, short-explanation type. Be sure to allow space for student explanations.

ESSAY

Description: A question or problem is presented, and the student is to compose a response in the form of sustained prose, using the student's own words, phrases, and ideas within the limits of the question or problem.

Example 1: Explain the major steps in purifying water for drinking in our city. Describe each step, from original source to faucet, explaining its function.

Example 2: Describe the relationship and the difference between these two processes that occur in flowering plants—pollination, fertilization.

Advantages: Measures higher mental processes, such as ability to synthesize material and to express ideas in clear and precise written language. Especially useful in integrated thematic teaching. Provides practice in written expression.

Disadvantages: Essay items require a good deal of time to read and to score. They tend to provide an unreliable sampling of achievement and are vulnerable to teacher subjectivity and unreliable scoring. Furthermore, they tend to punish the student who writes slowly and laboriously, who has limited proficiency in the written language, but who may have achieved as well as a student who writes faster and is more proficient in the language. Essay items tend to favor students who have fluency with words but whose achievement may not necessarily be better. In addition, unless the students have been given instruction in their meaning and how to respond to them, the teacher should not assume that all students understand key directive verbs, such as *explain* in the first example.

Guidelines for use:

1. In preparing an essay-only test, many questions, each requiring a relatively short prose response (see short-explanation type), are preferable to a smaller number of questions requiring long prose responses. Briefer answers tend to be more precise, and including many items provides a more reliable sampling of student achievement. In preparing short-prose-response-type questions, be sure to avoid using words verbatim from the student textbook.

2. Allow students adequate test time for a full response.

3. Different qualities of achievement are more likely comparable when all students must answer the same questions, as opposed to providing a list of essay items from which students may select those they will answer.

4. After preparing essay items, make a tentative scoring key, deciding on the key ideas you expect students to identify and how many points will be allotted to each.

5. Students should be informed about the relative test value for each essay item. Point values, if different for each item, can be listed in the margin of the test next to each item.

6. When reading student essay responses, read all student papers for one item at a time and, while doing that, make notes to yourself; then return and, while reading that item again, score each student's paper for that item. Repeat the process for the next item. While scoring essay responses, keep in mind the nature of the objective being measured, which may or may not include the qualities of handwriting, grammar, spelling, and neatness.

7. To nullify the "halo effect," some teachers use a number code rather than having students write their names on essay papers, so that while reading the papers the teacher is unaware of whose paper is being read.

8. Although having some understanding of a concept, many students are not yet facile with written expression, so you must remember to be patient, tolerant, positive, and helpful. Mark papers with positive and constructive comments, showing students how they could have explained or responded better.

9. Prior to using this type of test item, give students instruction and practice in responding to the key directive verbs that will be used. For example, see Figure 6.8.

Compare asks for an analysis of similarity and difference, but with a greater emphasis on similarities or likenesses.
Contrast asks more for differences than for similarities.
Criticize asks for the good and bad of an idea or situation.
Define means to express clearly and concisely the meaning of a term, as from a dictionary or in the student's own words.
Diagram means to put quantities or numerical values into the form of a chart, graph, or drawing.
Discuss means to explain or argue, presenting various sides of events, ideas, or situations.
Enumerate means to name or list one after another, which is different from "explain briefly," or "tell in a few words."
Evaluate means to express worth, value, and judgment.
Explain means to describe, with emphasis on cause and effect.
Illustrate means to describe by means of examples, figures, pictures, or diagrams.

Interpret means to describe or explain a given fact, theory, principle, or doctrine within a specific context.
Justify means to show reasons, with an emphasis on the correct, positive, and advantageous.
List means just that, to simply name items in a category or to include them in a list, without much description.
Outline means to give a short summary with headings and subheadings.
Prove means to present materials as witnesses, proof, and evidence.
Relate means to tell how specified things are connected or brought into some kind of relationship.
Summarize means to recapitulate the main points without examples or illustrations.
Trace means to follow a history or series of events, step by step, by going backward over the evidence.

FIGURE 6.8　Meaning of key directive verbs for essay item responses.

GROUPING

Description: Several items are presented, and the student is to select and group those that are in some way related.

Example 1: Separate the following list of animals into two groups, one that consists of those that are mammals, the other of those that are not mammals.

Example 2: Circle the animal that is least like the others: snake, alligator, rhinoceros, turtle.

Advantages: This type of item tests knowledge of grouping and can be used to measure for higher levels of cognition. Students like this type of question. It can stimulate discussion. As in Example 2, it can be similar to a multiple-choice type item.

Disadvantage: Remain alert for the student who has a valid alternative rationale for grouping; for instance, in Example 2, a snake does not have legs.

Guidelines for use: To allow for an alternative correct response, consider making the item a combination grouping, short-explanation type, being certain to allow adequate space for student explanations.

IDENTIFICATION

Description: Unknown "specimens" are to be identified by name or some other criterion.

Example 1: Identify by type each of the rocks on the table.

Example 2: With your dichotomous key to leaves of trees on our campus, proceed outdoors and use the key to identify five different trees. The trees are marked with numbers; use those numbers to reference the name of each tree you identify.

Advantages: Verbalization (i.e., the use of abstract symbolization) is less significant, as the student is working with real objects. Should be measuring for higher-level learning than simple recall. The item can also be written to measure for procedural understanding, such as for identification of steps in booting up a computer program.

Disadvantages: To be fair, "specimens" used should be equally familiar or unfamiliar to all students. Adequate materials must be provided.

Guideline for use: If equipment, photographs, drawings, photocopies, and recordings are used, they must be clear, familiar to all or to none of the students, and not confusing.

MATCHING

Description: Match related items from a list of numbered items to a list of lettered choices, or in some way connect those items that are the same or are related. Or, to eliminate the paper-and-pencil aspect and make the item more direct, use an item such as, "Of the materials on the table, pair up those that are most alike."

Example 1: Match pictures of (Column A) of the following weather instruments with the weather conditions they measure (Column B):

Column A	Column B
thermometer	used to measure wind direction
weather vane	used to measure temperature
barometer	used to measure wind speed
wind gauge	used to measure moisture in the air
hygrometer	used to measure air pressure
	used to measure depth of precipitation

Example 2: Match items in Column A (stem column) to those of Column B (answer column) by drawing lines to the matched pairs.

Column A	Column B
snake	worm
eagle	mammal
whale	reptile
praying mantis	insect
	bird

Advantages: Can measure for ability to judge relationships and to differentiate between similar ideas, facts, definitions, and concepts. Easy to score. Can test a broad range of content. Reduces guessing, especially if one group contains more items than the other. Interesting to students. Adaptable for performance assessment.

Disadvantages: Although this item type is adaptable for performance assessment, items are not easily adapted to measuring for higher cognition. Because all parts must be homogeneous, it is possible that clues will be given, thus reducing item validity. A student might have a legitimate rationale for an "incorrect" response.

Guidelines for use: The number of items in the answer column should exceed the number in the stem column. The number of items to be matched should not exceed twelve. Matching sets should have high homogeneity, that is, items in both columns (or groups) should be of the same general category. If answers can be used more than once, the directions should so state. Be prepared for the student who can legitimately defend an "incorrect" response. If pictures or photographs are used, they should be clear and familiar to all students.

MULTIPLE-CHOICE

Description: This type is similar to the completion type in that statements are presented, sometimes in incomplete form, with several options, requiring recognition, or even higher cognitive processes, rather than mere recall.

Example 1: Using the map shown above, if you were to go from where you are now (marked on the map) to New York City, in what direction must you travel?

a. East
b. West
c. North
d. South

Example 2: If all four strings were equally tight, the one that would make the lowest-pitched sound would be

a. short and thick
b. short and thin

    c. long and thick
    d. long and thin

Advantages: Items can be answered and scored quickly. A wide range of content and higher levels of cognition can be tested in a relatively short time. Excellent for all testing purposes—motivation, review, and assessment of learning.

Disadvantages: Unfortunately, because multiple-choice items are relatively easy to write, there is a tendency to include items measuring only for low levels of cognition. Multiple-choice items are excellent for major testing, but it takes care and time to write quality questions that measure higher levels of learning.

Guidelines for use:

1. If the item is in the form of an incomplete statement, it should be meaningful in itself and imply a direct question rather than merely lead into a collection of unrelated true and false statements.
2. Use a level of language that is easy enough for even the poorest readers and those with limited proficiency in English to understand; avoid unnecessary wordiness.
3. If there is much variation in the length of alternatives, arrange the alternatives in order from shortest to longest, i.e., first alternative is the shortest, last alternative is the longest.
4. For single word alternatives, consistent alphabetical arrangement of alternatives is recommended.
5. Incorrect responses (distracters) should be plausible and related to the same concept as the correct alternative. Although an occasional humorous distracter helps to relieve test anxiety, the inclusion of absurd distracters should be avoided as they offer no measuring value.
6. Arrangement of alternatives should be uniform throughout the test and listed in vertical (column) form rather than in horizontal (paragraph) form.
7. Every item should be grammatically consistent; e.g., if the stem is in the form of an incomplete sentence, it should be possible to complete the sentence by attaching any of the alternatives to it.
8. It is not necessary to maintain a fixed number of alternatives for every item, but the use of less than three is not recommended. The use of four or five reduces chance responses and guessing, thereby increasing the item's reliability.
9. The item should be expressed in positive form. A negative form presents a psychological disadvantage to students. Negative items are those that ask what is *not* characteristic of something, or what is the *least* useful. Discard the item if you cannot express it in positive terminology.
10. Responses such as "all of these" or "none of these" should be used only when they will contribute more than another plausible distracter. Care must be taken that such responses answer or complete the item. "All of the above" is a poorer alternative than "none of the above," because items that use it as a correct response must have four or five correct answers; in addition, if it is the right answer, knowledge of any two of the distracters will cue it.
11. There must be only one correct or best response. However, this is easier said than done (refer to guideline 19).
12. The stem must mean the same thing to every student.
13. Measuring for understanding of definitions is better tested by furnishing the name or word and requiring a choice between alternative definitions than by presenting the definition and requiring a choice between alternative words.
14. The stem should state a single and specific point.

15. The stem must not include clues that cue the correct alternative. For example, "A four-sided figure whose opposite sides are parallel is called ___. (a) an octagon, (b) a parallelogram, (c) a trapezoid, (d) a triangle." The use of the word *parallel* cues the answer.
16. Avoid using alternatives that include absolute terms such as *never* and *always*.
17. Multiple-choice items need not be entirely verbal. Consider the use of realia, charts, diagrams, and other visuals. They can make the test more interesting, especially to students who have low verbal abilities or limited proficiency in English, and, consequently, make the assessment more direct (authentic).
18. Once you have composed a multiple-choice test, tally the position of answers to be sure they are evenly distributed, to avoid the common psychological mistake (when there are four alternatives) of having the correct alternative in the third position. In other words, when alternative choices are A, B, C, and D, or 1, 2, 3, and 4, unless the test maker is aware and avoids it, more correct answers will be in the "C" or "3" position than in any other.
19. Consider providing space between test items for students to include their rationales for their response selections, thus making the test a combination multiple-choice and short-explanation type. This provides for the student who can rationalize an alternative you had not considered plausible. It also provides for the measurement of higher levels of cognition and encourages student writing.
20. While scoring, on a blank copy of the test, for each item tally the incorrect responses. Analyze incorrect responses for each item to discover potential errors in your scoring key. If, for example, many students select "B" for an item which your key says "A" is the correct answer, you may have made a mistake on your scoring key or in teaching the lesson.

PERFORMANCE

Description: Provided with certain conditions or materials, the student solves a problem, makes a prediction, or accomplishes some other action involving sciencing or science content.

Example 1: (As a culminating project for a unit on sound, groups of students were challenged to design and make their own musical instruments.) The performance assessment included:

1. Play your instrument for the class.
2. Show us the part of the instrument that makes the sound.
3. Describe the function of other parts of your instrument.
4. Demonstrate how you change the pitch of the sound.
5. Share with us how you made your instrument.

Example 2: On the table is a jar containing a healthy, young green bean plant that was planted this morning in fertile, moist soil. If we screw the jar's lid on tightly and place the jar in a window where it receives sunlight and the temperature will be maintained between 60°F and 80°F, how long do you predict the plant will live? Write (or tell me) your scientific explanation supporting your prediction.

Advantages: Performance test item types come closer to direct measurement (authentic assessment) of certain expected outcomes than do most other types. However, as indicated in discussions of the preceding question types, other types of questions can actually be prepared as performance-type items, that is, for which the student actually does what he or she is being tested for. Example 2 is both a performance type and a short-explanation type.

Disadvantages: Can be difficult and time-consuming to administer to a group of students. Scoring may tend to be subjective. For instance, in Example 1, it may be difficult to give makeup tests to students who are absent.

Guidelines for use: Use your creativity to design and use performance tests, as they tend to measure important objectives. To reduce subjectivity in scoring, prepare distinct scoring guidelines (rubric) (see below), as discussed in regard to scoring essay-type questions. To set up a performance test situation you should:

a. Specify the performance objective.
b. Specify the test situation or conditions.
c. Establish the criteria (scoring rubric) for judging the excellence of the process and/or product.
d. Make a checklist by which to score the performance or product. This checklist is simply a listing of the criteria you established in step c.
e. Prepare directions in writing, outlining the situation, with instructions for the students to follow.

For example, here is a checklist and scoring rubric for an exploratory activities work sheet assessment:

Check each item if the work sheet comes up to standard in this particular category. Value of each item is 20 percent of total.

_____ 1. Adequate number of trials
_____ 2. Sufficient data to draw a conclusion
_____ 3. Accuracy of methodology
_____ 4. Demonstration of proper skills
_____ 5. Attention to details

Here is a sample rubric for assessing a student's skill in listening.

A. Strong listener: characteristics

Responds immediately to oral directions
Focuses on speaker
Maintains appropriate attention span
Listens to what others are saying
Is interactive

B. Capable listener: characteristics

Follows oral directions
Usually attentive to speaker and to discussions
Listens to others without interrupting

C. Developing listener: characteristics

Has difficulty following directions
Relies on repetition
Often inattentive
Short attention span
Often interrupts the speaker

SHORT-EXPLANATION

Description: The short-explanation question is an essay-type but requires a shorter answer.

Example 1: Briefly explain in a paragraph why piano wires vary in length.

Example 2: Explain what is wrong with the science implied in the following drawing.

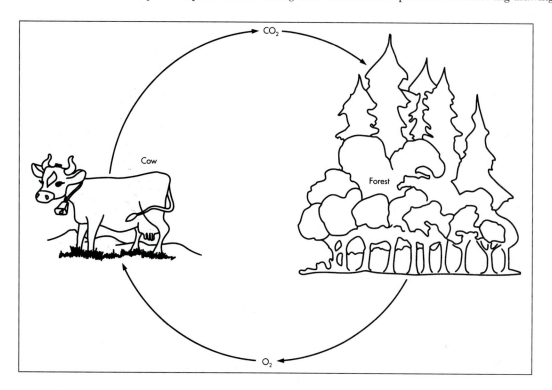

Advantages: Like the essay type, the short-explanation type measures the student's understanding, but takes less time for the teacher to read and to score. In Example 2, for instance, the diagram of the cow and the forest, similar to drawings we have seen in some science textbooks, represents a misconception about our own place in nature. The intent of the authors of such a diagram is to illustrate the interdependence of animals and plants; the lesson frequently learned is that plants use carbon dioxide produced by animals and that animals use oxygen produced by plants. Following such a study, we interviewed teachers and their students, asking, "Do plants use oxygen?" The majority said no. A misconception was learned: the teachers and students did not understand that all living organisms need oxygen. The focus was on what humans gain from "interdependence," rather than on the nature of "interdependence." *Artificialism* is the term used by Piaget to represent the tendency to believe that everything here on earth is for the benefit of humans. Although natural for students in early grades, it does represent a selfish, prejudiced, nonobjective misconcept that should be corrected and avoided in teaching. Science teachers have an obligation, and an opportunity, to correct such misconceptions, providing they have correct understandings themselves.

By using several questions of this type, a greater amount of content can be covered than with a lesser number of essay questions. This type of question provides good practice for students in learning to express themselves succinctly in writing.

Disadvantages: Some students will have difficulty expressing themselves in a limited fashion, or in writing. They need practice, coaching, and time to do so.

Guidelines for use: Useful for occasional reviews and quizzes, and as an alternative to other types of questions. For scoring, establish a scoring rubric and follow the same guidelines as for the essay-type item.

TRUE-FALSE AND MODIFIED TRUE-FALSE

Description: A statement is presented that students are to judge as being accurate or not.

Example 1: Photosynthesis occurs only in green plants. T or F?

Example 2: Spiders have six legs. T or F?

Advantages: Many items can be answered in a relatively short time, making broad content coverage possible. Scoring is quick and simple. True-false items are good for starting discussions, for review, and for diagnostic evaluation.

Disadvantages: As illustrated by the first example, it is difficult in science to write true-false items that are strictly true or false without qualifying them in such a way that cues the answer. Much of the content that most easily lends itself to this type of test item is relatively unimportant. Students have a 50 percent chance of guessing the correct answer, thus giving this type of item poor validity and reliability. Scoring and grading give no clue about why the student missed an item. The disadvantages of true-false items far outweigh their advantages, and true-false items should *not* be used for arriving at grades. To determine student grades, you may use modified true-false items, where space is provided between items for students to write in explanations, thus making each item a combined true-false, short-explanation type.

Guidelines for use:

1. First write the statement as a true statement, then make it false by changing a word or phrase.
2. Avoid using negative statements, as they tend to confuse students.
3. A true-false statement should include only one idea. For more than one reason Example 1 is a poor item. One reason is that it measures two ideas: that photosynthesis goes on in plants (which is true), and that it does so only in plants that are green in color (which is false).
4. Use close to an equal number of true and false items.
5. Avoid specific determiners, which may be a clue that the statement is false; e.g., *always, all,* or *none.*
6. Avoid words that may be a clue that the statement is true, words such as *often, probably,* and *sometimes.*
7. Avoid words that may have different meanings for different students.
8. Avoid using language verbatim from the student textbook.
9. Avoid trick items.
10. As stated earlier, for grading purposes, you may use modified true-false items, where space is provided between items for students to write their explanations, thus making the item a combined true-false, short-explanation type. Another form of modified true-false item is the use of "sometimes-always-never," whereby a third alternative, "sometimes," is introduced to reduce chances for guessing.

REPORTING STUDENT ACHIEVEMENT

As a teacher, one of your responsibilities is to report student progress in achievement to parents or guardians. In some schools student progress and effort are reported as well as achievement. Reporting is done in at least two, and sometimes three ways, described as follows.

The Grade Report

Every six to nine weeks a grade report (report card) is issued (from four to six times a year, depending on the school district). This grade report represents an achievement grade (formative evaluation) and the second or third one of the semester is also the semester grade; for courses that are only one semester long, it also is the final grade (summative evaluation). In essence, the first, and sometimes second, report is a progress notice, the semester grade being the one that is transferred to the student's transcript of records. In some schools the traditional report card is marked and sent home either with the student or by mail. In some schools reporting is done by computer printouts often sent by mail directly to the student's home address.

Whichever reporting form is used, you must separate your assessments of a student's social behaviors (classroom conduct) from the student's academic achievement in science. Academic achievement (or accomplishment) is represented by a letter (sometimes a number) grade (A through E or F; or E, S, and U; or 1 to 5, and sometimes with minuses and pluses). Social behavior is indicated by a "Satisfactory" or "Unsatisfactory," or by more specific items, or supplemented by teacher-written or computer-generated comments. In some instances there may be a place on the reporting form for a teacher to check whether basic grade-level standards have been met in language arts, mathematics, science, and social studies.

Direct Contact with Parents

Although not always obligatory, some teachers make a point to contact parents or guardians by telephone, especially when a student has shown a sudden turn for either the worse or the better in academic achievement or in classroom behavior. That initiative and contact by the teacher is usually welcomed by parents and can lead to private and productive conferences between teacher and parents. A telephone conversation saves valuable time for both the teacher and the parent.

Another way of contacting parents is by letter. Contacting a parent by letter gives you time to think and to make clear your thoughts and concerns to that parent, and to invite the parent to respond at his or her convenience by letter, by phone, or by arranging to have a conference with you.

Conferences and Meetings with Parents

You will meet many parents or guardians early in the school year during "Back to School Night" and throughout the year in individual parent conferences. For the beginning teacher these meetings with parents can be anxious times. Here are some guidelines to help you with these experiences.

Back-to-School Night is an evening early in the school year when parents (and guardians) can come to the school and meet their students' teachers. The parents arrive at the student's home base and then proceed through a simulation of their child's school day as a group, meeting each class and each teacher for a few minutes. Later, in the spring, there is an "Open House," where parents may have more time to talk individually with teachers, but Open House is usually a time for the school and teachers to show off the work and progress of the students for the year. Throughout the school year there will be opportunities for you and parents to meet and talk about individual students.

AT BACK-TO-SCHOOL NIGHT

On the evening of Back-to-School Night parents are anxious to learn as much as they can about their student's new teachers. You will meet each group of parents for about 10 minutes.

During that brief meeting you will make some straightforward remarks about yourself and then briefly discuss your expectations of the students.

Although there will be precious little time for questions from parents, during your introduction they will be delighted to learn that you (1) have your program well planned, (2) are a "task master," and (3) will communicate with them. The parents and guardians will be pleased to know that you are from the school of the three Fs—firm, friendly, and fair.

Specifically, parents will expect to learn about your curriculum—goals and objectives, long-term projects, when tests will be given and whether given on a regular basis, and your grading procedures. They will need to know what you expect of them: will there be homework, and if so, should they help their students with it? How can they contact you? Try to anticipate other questions. Your principal and colleagues can help you to anticipate and prepare for these questions. Of course, you can never prepare for the question that comes from left field. Just stay calm and don't get flustered. Ten minutes will fly by quickly, and parents will be reassured to know you are an in-control person.

As parents who have attended many Back-to-School Nights at the schools our students have attended and are attending, we continue to be both surprised and dismayed that so few teachers seem well prepared for the few minutes they have with the parents; that considering how often we hear about teachers wanting more involvement of parents, so few seem delighted that parents have indeed come; and that so few teachers take full advantage of this time with parents to truly celebrate their programs.

PARENT-TEACHER CONFERENCE

When meeting parents (or guardians) for conferences, you should be as specific as possible when explaining to a parent the progress of that parent's child in your class. Be helpful to their understanding, and don't saturate the parent with more information than he or she needs. Resist the tendency to talk too much. Allow time for the parent to ask questions. Keep your answers succinct. Avoid comparing one student with another or with the rest of the class. If the parent asks a question for which you do not have an answer, tell the parent you will try to find an answer and will phone him or her as quickly as you can. And do it. Have the student's portfolio and other work with you during parent conferences so you can show the parent examples of what is being discussed. Have your grade book on hand as well, or a computer print out of it, but be prepared to protect from the parent the names and records of the other students.

Sometimes it is helpful to have a three-way conference with the parent, the student, and you, or a conference with the parent, the principal or counselor, and several or all of the student's teachers.

Ideas for Teacher-Parent Collaboration

Parents often ask how they may help in the students' learning. Here are a number of suggestions you may offer:

- As needed, plan short family meetings after dinner, but while you are still seated at the table. Ask for a "tableside" report on "What's happening in school?" Ask, "How can I help?" When your child expresses a concern, emphasize ways to solve problems that occur. Help your child develop his or her problem-solving skills.
- Ask your child to share with you one specific thing learned in science that day.
- Helping students become critical thinkers is one of the aims of science education and one that parents can help with by reinforcing the strategies used in the classroom; for example, asking "what if" questions; thinking aloud as a model for your student's think-

Assessment of student learning is an ongoing process that involves children in their own self-assessment.

ing development; encouraging the student's own metacognition by asking questions such as, "What evidence caused you to arrive at that conclusion?" or "How do you feel about your conclusion now?"; asking these questions about the student's everyday social interactions, topics that are important to the student; asking your child to elaborate on his or her ideas; allowing your child to make mistakes and encouraging the child to learn from them.

- Limit and control the child's television pleasure viewing.
- Several books are available for parents to use at home. For example, the United States government offers a variety of free or low-cost booklets. For information, contact the Consumer Information Center, Department TH, Pueblo, CO 81109. You can also encourage a parent to go to the neighborhood public library and ask for a librarian's assistance in locating helpful resources.

SUMMARY

Whereas preceding chapters of this text addressed the *why*, *what*, and *how* components of science teaching, this chapter has focused your attention on the fourth and final component—

the *how well* component—and on the first of two aspects of that component. Assessment is an integral factor in the teaching-learning process; consequently, this chapter has emphasized a number of components that are important to your teaching performance, which are summarized in the following sentences.

- Use a variety of instruments that focus on the individual development of students to assess their learning.
- Use assessment procedures continuously so as to contribute to the positive development of the individual child.
- Adapt the grading system of the school to your situation.
- Consider your assessment and grading procedures carefully, plan them, and explain them to the students.
- Explain any ambiguities that result from the terminology used and base assessments on the material that has been taught.
- Strive for objective and impartial assessment as you put your assessment plan into operation.
- Try to minimize arguments about grades, cheating, and teacher subjectivity by involving students in the planning, reinforcing individual student development, and providing an accepting, stimulating learning environment.
- Maintain accurate and clear records of assessment results so that you will have an adequate supply of data on which to base your judgmental decisions about achievement.

Because teaching and learning work hand-in-hand, and because they are reciprocal processes whereby one depends on and affects the other, the *how well* component deals with the assessment of both how well the students are learning and how well the teacher is teaching. This chapter deals with the first consideration. In the next and final chapter of Part I of this text, your attention is directed to techniques designed to help you develop your teaching skills and to assess that development, a process that will continue throughout your teaching career.

QUESTIONS FOR CLASS DISCUSSION

1. Other than a paper-and-pencil test, identify three alternative techniques for assessing student learning during or at completion of an instructional unit.
2. Investigate various ways schools are experimenting today with assessing and reporting student achievement, especially, but not exclusively, in science. Share what you find with your classmates. Analyze the pros and cons of various systems of assessing and reporting.
3. In using a point system for determining student grades for a class of students, is it educationally defensible to give a student a higher grade than that student's points call for? a lower grade? Give your rationale for your answers.
4. Explain the dangers in using true-false and completion-type items in assessing student learning in science and using the results for grade determination.
5. Describe any student learning activities or situations in science that should *not* be graded but should or could be used for assessment of student learning.
6. Explain the value of, and give a specific example of, a performance test item that you would use for a specific concept or skill in science at a particular grade level.
7. Do you believe that a teacher's evaluation of students should be based on their performances according to individual abilities or on their performances as compared with the rest of the students? Explain why.

8. As a teacher, what you will say when you meet the parents of your students for the first time at Back-to-School Night? Try it out on your classmates.

9. At schools you have visited, what standardized tests in science achievement are administered? What are their purposes? How are their results used?

10. Describe any concepts you held that changed as a result of the experiences of this chapter. Describe the changes.

11. From your recent observations and field work as related to this teacher preparation program, clearly identify one specific example of educational practice that seems contradictory to exemplary practice or theory as presented in this chapter. Present your explanation for the discrepancy.

12. Do you have other questions generated by the contents of this chapter? If so, where might you find answers?

Notes

1. Reprinted with permission from *National Science Education Standards*, pp. 37–38. Copyright 1996 by the National Academy of Sciences. Courtesy of the National Academy Press, Washington, D.C.

2. Reprinted with permission from *National Science Education Standards*, pp. 85, 86. Copyright 1996 by the National Academy of Sciences. Courtesy of National Academy Press, Washington, D.C.

3. For further elaboration, see Carol A. Meyer, "What's the Difference Between 'Authentic' and 'Performance' Assessment?" *Educational Leadership* 49(8):39–40 (May 1992).

4. Reprinted with permission from *National Science Education Standards*, pp. 78, 84. Copyright 1996 by the National Academy of Sciences. Courtesy of National Academy of Sciences, Washington, D.C.

5. See, for example, Edward A. Wynne and Herbert J. Walberg, "Persisting Groups: An Overlooked Force for Learning," *Phi Delta Kappan* 75(7):527–528, 530 (March 1994).

6. See, for example, Spencer Kagan, "Group Grades Miss the Mark," *Educational Leadership* 52(8):68–71 (May 1995); Spencer Kagan, "Avoiding the Group-Grades Trip," *Learning* 24(4):56–58 (January/February 1996); and, David W. Johnson and Roger T. Johnson, "The Role of Cooperative Learning in Assessing and Communicating Student Learning," Chapter 4 of Thomas R. Guskey, ed., *Communicating Student Learning,* the ASCD 1996 Yearbook (Alexandria, VA: Association for Supervision and Curriculum Development, 1996).

7. John O'Neil, "Portfolio Assessment Bears the Burden of Popularity," *ASCD Update* 35(8):3, 8 (October 1993).

8. Susan Black, "Portfolio Assessment," *Executive Educator* 15(1):28–31 (February 1993).

9. One such program is the *Grade Machine*, available from Misty City Software, 13625 NE 126th Place, Suite 430, Kirkland, WA 98034. For a review of several computer software programs for use in classroom recordkeeping, see Carol S. Holzberg, "Classroom Management at Your Fingertips," *Learning,* pp. 57–59 (January/February 1995).

10. For information about *Learner Profile: The Assessment Tool,* contact Sunburst, 101 Castleton Street, P.O. Box 100, Pleasantville, NY 10570-0100. Phone 1-800-321-7511.

11. For further discussion of the detrimental effects of grading on a curve to both teaching and learning, see Thomas R. Guskey, "Reporting on Student Learning: Lessons from the Past—Prescriptions for the Future," Chapter 3 of Thomas R. Guskey, ed., *Communicating Student Learning,* the ASCD 1996 Yearbook (Alexandria, VA: Association for Supervision and Curriculum Development, 1996).

12. Herbert J. Walberg, "Productive Teaching and Instruction: Assessing the Knowledge Base," *Phi Delta Kappan* 71(6): (February 1990), p. 472.

13. The buoyancy and flotation performance project idea is from Kenneth V. Adams, Drew H. Gitomer, and Richard A. Duschl, "Rethinking Teaching for Student Success," *Science Scope* 18(7):18–21 (April 1995).

14. The plant life cycle example is from Philip Cohen, "Designing Performance Assessment Tasks," *Education Update* 37(6):1, 45, 8 (August 1995).

15. For example, see John A. Willis, "Learning Outcome Testing Program: Standardized Classroom Testing in West Virginia Through Item Banking, Test Generation, and Curricular Management Software," *Educational Measurement: Issues and Practices* 9(2):11–14 (Summer 1990).

SUGGESTED READINGS

Bakunas, B. "Putting the Lid on Test Anxiety." *Learning 93* 22(2):64–65 (September 1993).

Black, S. "Portfolio Assessment." *Executive Educator* 15(1):28–31 (February 1993).

Bracey, G. W. "Assessing the New Assessments." *Principal* 72(3):34–36 (January 1993).

Chambers, D. L. "Standardized Testing Impedes Reform." *Educational Leadership* 50(5):80–81 (February 1993).

Daisey, P., and M. G. Shroyer. "Parents Speak Up: Examining Parent and Teacher Roles in Elementary Science Instruction." *Science and Children* 33(3):24–26 (November/December 1995).

Davis, S. J. "Teaching Practices That Encourage or Eliminate Student Plagiarism." *Middle School Journal* 25(3):55–58 (January 1994).

Feuer, M. J., and K. Fulton. "The Many Faces of Performance Assessment." *Phi Delta Kappan* 74(6):478 (February 1993).

Finson, K. D., and J. B. Beaver. "Performance Assessment: Getting Started." *Science Scope* 18(1):44–49 (September 1994).

Funk, H. J. *Learning and Assessing Science Process Skills.* Arlington, VA: National Science Teachers Association, 1995.

Hart, D. *Authentic Assessment.* Arlington, VA: National Science Teachers Association, 1994.

Hein, G., and S. Price. *Active Assessment for Active Science.* Arlington, VA: National Science Teachers Association, 1994.

Laidlaw, E. N., et al. "The Effects of Notetaking and Self-Questioning on Quiz Performance." *Science Education* 77(1):75–82 (January 1993).

Ostlund, K. L. *Science Process Skills: Assessing Hands-on Student Performance.* Arlington, VA: National Science Teachers Association, 1992.

Simmons, R. "The Horse Before the Cart: Assessing for Understanding." *Educational Leadership* 51(5):22–23 (February 1994).

Continuing Professional Development as a Science Teacher

- *Opportunities are provided for teachers to receive feedback about their teaching and to understand, analyze, and apply that feedback to improve their practice.*
- *Experiences provide opportunities for teachers to learn and use various tools and techniques for self and collegial reflection.*
- *Sharing of teacher expertise is supported by preparing and using mentors, teacher advisors, coaches, lead teachers, and resource teachers.[1]*

The evaluation and development of your effectiveness as a science teacher is a process that continues throughout your professional career. Elementary and middle school science teaching is such an electrifying profession that you may have difficulty in remaining energetic and staying abreast of changes and trends that result from research and practice. To remain an alert and effective science teacher you will need to make a continuous and determined effort—the exemplary science teacher is a lifelong learner.

One way to collect data and to improve effectiveness is through periodic evaluation of your teaching performance, either by an evaluation of your teaching in the real classroom or by a technique called micro peer teaching. The latter is the focus of the first section of this final chapter of Part I.

MICRO PEER TEACHING

Micro peer teaching (MPT) is a skill-development strategy, useful for professional development by both preservice and inservice teachers. In some states new teachers must have a certain number of hours of inservice work within their first three years of teaching (before receiving tenure in some cases). In many school systems, micro peer teaching is one way that inservice work is done.

Micro peer teaching is a scaled-down teaching experience involving a limited objective, a brief interval for teaching a lesson, a lesson taught to a few (8–10) peers as your students, and a science lesson that focuses on the use of one or several instructional strategies.

Micro peer teaching can be a predictor of later teacher effectiveness in a regular classroom, but more important, it provides opportunity to develop and improve specific teaching behaviors. A videotaped MPT allows you to see yourself in action for self-assessment and diagnosis. Evaluation of a micro peer teaching session is based on the quality of the teacher's preparation and lesson implementation, the quality of the planned and implemented student involvement, whether or not the instructional objective(s) was reached, and the appropriateness of the cognitive level of the lesson to the students.

Whether a preservice or inservice teacher, you are urged to participate in one or more micro peer teaching experiences. Instructions will be provided by your instructor.

CLASSROOM OBSERVATIONS AND MENTORING

You can also continue your professional development as a science teacher by (1) observing other science teachers and (2) having other professionals observe and evaluate your teaching. Like MPT, these procedures, too, are often used in mentoring programs for probationary teachers.

For self-improvement, and for personnel decisions on retention and tenure, probationary teachers are periodically reviewed. Of course, the ultimate purpose of such reviews is to provide the most effective service to students. Essentially, in considering your reemployment, the school district wants to be assured of two things—that, as a classroom teacher, you can work effectively with and manage youngsters and that you can effectively teach science (and any other subject you are expected to teach).

For these reviews, data from several sources are collected, and although from school to school, even within the same district, forms will vary in wording and in format, there remains a common set of criteria of competencies, which are those that have been presented and discussed in this book.

Data on a teacher's effectiveness are collected from two sources—teacher self-evaluation and evaluations performed by administrators (usually the principal).

Mentoring, one teacher facilitating the learning of another teacher, is sometimes called peer coaching. A mentor teacher volunteers or is selected by the teacher who wishes to improve, or is selected by a school administrator, formally or informally, to observe the teaching and to coach the teacher to enable that teacher's improvement in science teaching. Sometimes the teacher simply wants to learn a new skill, such as inquiry. Other times, the teacher being coached remains with the mentor teacher for an entire school year, developing and improving new and old skills or learning how to teach with a new program. In many districts, new teachers are automatically assigned to mentor teachers for their first year.

During mentoring, the mentor teacher and the teacher being coached meet in a preobservation conference and discuss the skill or skills to be observed. Then the teacher is observed, and, following the observation, joins the mentor in a postobservation conference to discuss the observation and plan for the next one. The cycle continues until the desired skills have been acquired.

INSERVICE AND GRADUATE STUDY

Inservice workshops and programs are offered for science teachers at the school level, by the district, and by other agencies such as a county office of education, a local museum or zoo, or a nearby college or university. Inservice workshops and programs are usually designed for specific purposes, such as to train teachers in science skills, to update their knowledge in content, and to introduce them to new science teaching materials or programs. Inservice workshops and programs are often led by science teachers, sometimes by scientists and college professors.

Inservice programs are offered when science teachers are available, which means on minimum days (short school days), in the late afternoon or evening, on weekends, and during vacation periods.

University graduate study is yet another way of continuing your professional development. Some teachers pursue master's degrees in a field of science, and many others pursue master's degrees in science curriculum and methods of instruction. Some universities offer a master of arts degree in teaching, a program of courses in science and science education especially designed for teachers. School districts encourage teachers to pursue graduate work by providing pay raise incentives according to units earned and degrees granted.

PARTICIPATION IN SCIENCE TEACHER ORGANIZATIONS

For the teacher interested in science there are many professional organizations, beginning with a local science teachers' organization. In most states there is a statewide science teachers' organization, probably affiliated with the National Science Teachers Association. Local, district, state, and national organizations have annual meetings that include guest speakers, workshops, and publishers' displays. Professional meetings of science teachers are educational, enriching, and fulfilling to those who attend.

In addition, many other professional associations, such as those for reading teachers, offer speakers and articles in their journals that are often of interest to science teachers as well as to reading teachers.

Professional organizations publish newsletters and journals for their members, and these journals are likely to be found in your college or university library. Journals of particular interest to elementary and middle school science teachers include *Journal of Research in Science Teaching*; *School Science and Mathematics*; *Science*; *Science and Children*; and *Science Scope*.

COMMUNICATIONS WITH OTHER TEACHERS

Valuable experiences may be gained from visiting teachers at other schools; attending inservice workshops, graduate seminars and programs, and meetings of professional organizations for science teachers; and sharing with teachers by means of electronic bulletin boards. Meeting and talking with teachers from other locations includes sharing, not only "war stories," but also ideas and descriptions of new science programs, books, materials, and techniques that work.

As is true for the other science process skills, the science teacher practices and models skill in communication, in and out of the classroom. This includes communicating with other science teachers to improve one's own repertoire of strategies and knowledge about science teaching, and to share one's experiences with others. Teaching other teachers about your own special skills, and sharing your experiences, are important components of the communication and professional development processes.

SUMMER AND OFF-TEACHING WORK EXPERIENCE

Whether your school is a year-round school or one that follows the traditional late-August-through-the-middle-of-June plan, in many areas of the country there are special programs of short-term employment available to interested science teachers, offered by private industry, foundations, and research institutes. The interest of these sources includes the dissemination of information and the provision of opportunities for teachers to update their skills and knowledge, with the desire to create a society of people who are science and technology literate, and an ultimate hope that the teachers will stimulate in more children an interest to consider careers in science and technology. Participating industries, foundations, and institutes provide on-the-job training with salaries or stipends to teachers who are selected to participate. During the program of employment, teachers, scientists, technicians, and, sometimes, university educators meet, usually weekly, to discuss and share experiences, to talk about what is being learned and its implications for teaching and science curriculum development. Sometimes the part-time work experience becomes a continuing part-time job, available to the same teacher year after year.

There are also NSF-sponsored summer programs for teachers. These programs are field centered and content specific. For example, one program may concentrate on geology, and at another location the program focus may be on teaching, using a specific science program. These programs are located around the country and may have university affiliation, which means that university credit may be available. Room and board, travel, and a stipend are sometimes granted to participating teachers.

Sources of information about the availability of these programs include professional journals such as *Science and Children* and *Science Scope, NSTA Report,* your local chamber of commerce, and meetings of the local or regional science teachers' organization. In areas where there are no organized programs of science-related part-time work experience for teachers, some teachers have succeeded in initiating their own by establishing contact with management personnel of a local industrial or research company.

SUMMARY

Because teaching and learning go hand in hand, and the effectiveness of one affects that of the other, the final two chapters of Part I of this book have dealt with both aspects of the "how well" component of elementary and middle school science teacher preparation—how well the students are learning and how well the teacher is teaching. In addition, you have been presented with guidelines on how to continue your professional development. Although you have not been told everything you will ever need to know about the assessment of teaching and learning, or about other aspects of elementary and middle school teaching, or about continuing your professional development, it is hoped that we have addressed the essentials. Throughout your teaching career you will continue improving your knowledge and skills in all aspects of teaching and learning.

You have arrived at the end of this part of the text. We thank you for allowing us to be a part of your journey to become a competent science teacher. We hope your quest has been and continues to be enjoyable and profitable, and we wish you the very best in your new career. Be the very best science teacher that you can be. The nation and its youth need you.

QUESTIONS FOR CLASS DISCUSSION

1. Attend a regional or national meeting of a professional science teacher's association. Then report to your class on the meeting, telling what you learned, and share with your class any free or inexpensive materials you obtained.
2. Talk with experienced science teachers to find out how they stay current. Share what you find with others in your class.
3. In addition to their professional publications, many professional organizations have benefits available to members, such as group purchasing power and inexpensive liability insurance coverage. Invite representatives from professional organizations to your class to discuss their organizations and the benefits of joining them.
4. Some predictions indicate that education will be quite different in the twenty-first century. Education will continue to be viewed as a lifelong process (the early years will remain critically important in human development), with experimental education increasing. More technologies (voice-recognition systems, videos, discs, computer programs) will be used, and more individualization of instruction will be planned, with some students doing schoolwork at home (called distance learning). Further, the next century may see some public schools going private, other schools facing lawsuits when students fail to meet minimum competency standards, and still others increasing the length of sessions or changing to year-round schedules. There is also the possibility of a technology gap as well-to-do parents purchase computers and other educational equipment for their children. These children may have a technological edge and develop much faster than children in poorer homes. Discuss with your colleagues what these predictions mean for you as you consider teaching children in the twenty-first century.
5. Do you believe teaching effectiveness can be measured? Explain why or why not. If so, then explain how.

6. Identify and describe the experiences that have been most helpful to your professional development as an elementary school science teacher.

7. What academic college preparation in science do you think a prospective elementary or middle school teacher should have? Explain why. Has your post-high-school education in science prepared you to teach elementary or middle school science? Explain why or why not.

8. Talk with experienced science teachers and find out how much out-of-pocket money they spend for their own science classrooms and teaching, and what funds are provided by their school district. Share what you discover with others in your class.

9. Describe any concepts you held that changed as a result of the experiences of this chapter. Describe the changes.

10. You have reached the end of Part I of this book, but there may be questions lingering in your mind. As before, identify them and try to find answers.

NOTE

1. Reprinted with the permission of *National Science Education Standards*, p. 68. Copyright 1996 by the National Academy of Sciences. Courtesy of National Academy of Sciences, Washington, D.C.

SUGGESTED READINGS

Barringer, M. "How the National Board Builds Professionalism." *Educational Leadership* 50(6):18–22 (March 1993).

Cutler, A. B., and F. N. Ruopp. "Buying Time for Teachers' Professional Development." *Educational Leadership* 50(6):34–37 (March 1993).

Darling-Hammond, L., and A. L. Goodwin. "Progress Toward Professionalism in Teaching." In *Challenges and Achievements of American Education,* edited by Gordon Cawelti. 1993 ASCD Yearbook. Alexandria, VA: Association for Supervision and Curriculum Development, 1993.

DiMauro, V., and S. Gal. "Use of Telecommunication for Reflective Discourse of Science Teacher Leaders." *Journal of Science Education and Technology* 3(2):123–135 (June 1994).

Duke, D. L. "Removing Barriers to Professional Growth." *Phi Delta Kappan* 74(9):702–704, 710–712 (May 1993).

Fullan, M. G. "Why Teachers Must Become Change Agents." *Educational Leadership* 50(6):12–17 (March 1993).

Goodlad, J. I. *Educational Renewal: Better Teachers, Better Schools.* San Francisco: Jossey-Bass, 1994.

Havens, B. "Teaching 'Cadet' Teachers." *Educational Leadership* 50(6):50–51 (March 1993).

Latham, G. I., and K. Fifield. "The Hidden Costs of Teaching." *Educational Leadership* 50(6):44–45 (March 1993).

Lieberman, A. "Practices That Support Teacher Development." *Phi Delta Kappan* 76(8):591–596 (April 1995).

Moryan, J. "The Corporate Connection." *Science and Children* 31(8):18–19, 38 (May 1994).

Nettles, D.H., and P.B. Petrick. *Portfolio Development for Preservice Teachers.* Fastback 379. Bloomington, IN: Phi Delta Kappa Educational Foundation, 1995.

Poda, J. H. "The Teacher-in-Residence Program." *Educational Leadership* 50(6):52 (March 1993).

Raizen, S., and A. Michelsohn. *The Future of Science in Elementary Schools: Educating Prospective Teachers.* San Francisco: Jossey-Bass, 1994.

Wakshul, B. "Partnerships in Education." *Winds of Change* 8(1):32–33 (Winter 1994).

BASIC SCIENCE INFORMATION, DEMONSTRATIONS, EXPLORATORY ACTIVITIES, AND OTHER RESOURCES

EARTH AND THE UNIVERSE

Chapter 8: The Universe
Chapter 9: The Earth
Chapter 10: Water, Weather, and Climate
Chapter 11: Air, Aircraft, and Space Travel

*Students in **grades K–4** should develop an understanding of*
- *Properties of earth materials*
- *Objects in the sky*
- *Changes in earth and sky*

*Students in **grades 5–8** should develop an understanding of*
- *Structure of the earth system*
- *Earth's history*
- *Earth in the solar system*

CHAPTER 8

The Universe

THE SUN

I. THE NATURE OF THE SUN

  A. The stars that scientists formerly could study only with the aid of a telescope are no longer so mysterious. Massive computer programs now simulate the nuclear reactions at the stars' cores and follow the flow of energy by convection and radiation to the visible surfaces. These computer programs help scientists to understand and explain both the present appearance of stars and how they have evolved.

  B. The sun is a star.
    1. It is only one of billions of stars in the universe, but it is the star that is closest to earth.
    2. It is not a large star. It looks larger than the other stars because it is relatively close to us on earth, although it still is about 150 million kilometers (93 million mi) from the earth.

  C. The sun is much larger than the earth and contains about 99 percent of the mass of our entire solar system.
    1. The diameter of the sun at its equator is about 1,380,000 kilometers (860,000 mi), about 109 times larger than the diameter of the earth. If the sun were a hollow ball, it could hold more than a million earths.

  D. Like all other stars, the sun gives off a vast amount of radiant energy, including light energy and solar wind.
    1. The sun's energy comes from a series of nuclear reactions taking place inside the sun. Hydrogen atoms in the sun keep combining to form helium atoms. While the helium is being formed, some of the hydrogen is converted into tremendous amounts of energy.
    2. The nuclear reaction causes the sun to be very hot. Its surface temperature is about 6,000° Celsius (10,800° Fahrenheit), and the temperature at its center is estimated to be about 15,000,000° Celsius (27,000,000° F).

II. THE PARTS OF THE SUN

  A. The sun is not a solid body like the earth, but a huge ball of very hot gases. Three layers of gases, called the sun's atmosphere, surround the main body of the sun. These layers are called the photosphere, the chromosphere, and the corona.

  B. The innermost layer is the **photosphere.** It is approximately 400 kilometers (250 mi) thick. The photosphere glows brilliantly and is the source of most of the sun's light.
    1. Energy from the photosphere travels to earth in the form of electromagnetic wave energy, in tiny units called **photons.**

  C. Outside the photosphere is a second layer of gas called the **chromosphere.** The chromosphere is pinkish red and can be seen only when the sun is blotted out in total eclipse. It rises about 3,200 kilometers (2,000 mi) above the photosphere.

  D. A silvery halo of gases, called the **corona,** surrounds the chromosphere. The corona also can be seen only during a total solar eclipse. The corona glows with a weak light that reaches far in all directions from the sun.

DEMONSTRATION 8.1
Comparing the Size of the Sun and the Earth

Draw two circles, one with a diameter of 54 1/2 centimeters (21 4/5 in) and the other with a diameter of 1/2 centimeter (1/5 in). The larger circle, labeled *sun,* will be 109 times larger than the smaller circle, labeled *earth.* Place the circles 150 centimeters (93 in) apart. By letting 1 centimeter equal 1 million kilometers (or 1 in equal 1 million mi), then the 150 centimeters (or 93 in) would indicate the distance from the sun.

III. SUNSPOTS, SOLAR PROMINENCES, AND SOLAR FLARE ACTIVITY

A. The sun has violent storms that sometimes protrude from its surface. These storms are called **solar flares.**
 1. A solar flare is a bright cloud of gas leaping from the sun's surface, emitting an extreme amount of ultraviolet and X-ray radiation.
 2. A flare may cover an area of a billion square kilometers and shoot up as high as 480,000 kilometers (300,000 mi).
 3. A flare becomes 20 to 30 times brighter than other areas of the sun, and then fades away in a few hours.
B. Solar storms are related to the presence of **sunspots** on the sun's surface.
 1. Sunspots are dark spots that *seem* to move slowly from east to west across the sun's surface. Actually, sunspots stand still while the sun turns on its axis. The spots look dark because they are cooler than the surrounding glowing gases.
 2. The spots most often appear in the photosphere near the sun's equator, often as pairs, but sometimes in large groups.
 3. Their size can vary from 800 kilometers (500 mi) in diameter to more than 80,000 kilometers (50,000 mi).
 4. Sunspots usually appear in 11-year cycles; that is, they reach their greatest number every 11 years.
 5. Sunspots are evidence of magnetic storms within the sun.
 6. These magnetic storms send out electrified particles, called the **solar wind,** that affect the earth.
 7. When the particles strike the earth's ionosphere, they interfere with radio, television, and telecommunication signals.
 8. The particles also strike the earth's lower atmosphere and produce the brilliant show of colored lights near the north pole (**northern lights** or aurora borealis) and south pole (the **southern lights,** or aurora australis).

C. When the sun's rotation on its axis carries a sunspot to the "edge" of the sun, **solar prominences** are sometimes formed. Prominences are not as violent as flares, and they appear to move more gracefully.
 1. Prominences send great streamers of bright gas far out into the sun's atmosphere. Some prominences suddenly rush back to the sun, whereas others seem to be blown off the sun.
D. Because the sun provides the energy that drives all weather systems, scientists have long believed that solar variations likely affect weather on earth, although little is yet known about the mechanisms linking our sun with earth's weather.
 1. Scientists have been able to demonstrate that winter storms follow an 11-year pattern of low-pressure systems over the North Atlantic Ocean, a pattern that matches the 11-year cycle of sunspots.
 2. Evidence indicates that our troposphere, the dense bottom layer of the earth's atmosphere, grows hotter and cooler in step with the solar cycle in regions near the tropics.
E. Although it is obvious that great disturbances happen within the sun, scientists do not yet know the exact reason for the appearance, or the exact effects here on earth, of sunspots, solar flares, and prominences.
 1. In 1992, the National Aeronautics and Space Administration (NASA) launched its Extreme Ultraviolet Explorer (EUVE) satellite. An hour after the launch the EUVE was in orbit 550 kilometers (340 mi) above the earth, where it is expected to remain until at least the year 1999.
 2. The satellite has four telescopes that in six months can map the entire sky above the earth.
 3. High above the earth's atmosphere, the telescopes are capable of detecting and measuring ultrahigh-frequency radiation (extreme ultraviolet), undetectable by earth-bound telescopes.

DEMONSTRATION 8.2
Solar Eclipse and Sunspots

Arrange a telescope or binoculars (at least six-power) so that it is pointing directly at the sun (Figure 8.1). This arrangement can be made by getting a long, rectangular cardboard carton from the supermarket. One side of the carton should be open to allow the sunspots to be easily seen. Prop the carton on a box or another carton in such a way that the rear end is facing the sun's rays directly. In the front end of the carton make a hole large enough for the eyepiece end of the telescope or binoculars to be inserted.

If a telescope is used, make just one hole, and also make a large cardboard sunshade for the barrel of the telescope. If binoculars are used, make two holes and fasten the binoculars securely with tape to the box. Cover one of the outer binocular lenses with dark paper so that only one image of the sun will be produced inside the carton. A sunshade is not necessary when binoculars are used.

Now adjust the eyepiece of the telescope or binoculars until there is a sharp, clear image of the sun on the inside rear end of the carton. A sheet of white paper taped on the rear end will make the image more easily visible. The sunspots will appear on the sun's image as small, dark marks near the equator. Observe the sunspots every day at the same time. They will slowly move across the sun as the sun rotates. Note that they appear only on or near the sun's equator and never at the poles. If the sunspots seem to be moving from west to east (instead of east to west), this is because of the way the astronomical telescope operates. Moreover, the sunspots will be upside down.

(Note: Do not look directly at the sun through the telescope or binoculars! You can permanently damage your vision in this way.)

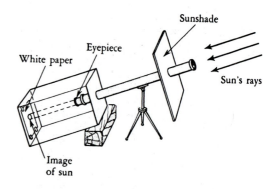

FIGURE 8.1   Arrangement for observing sunspots.

---

4. Extreme ultraviolet radiation is emitted by stars and planetary objects from both within and outside our solar system. With new technology such as the new extreme ultraviolet sensing telescopes and NASA's EUVE satellite, scientists are still learning about our sun, planets, interstellar media, and other celestial bodies.

IV. THE LIFE SPAN OF THE SUN

A. Like many other systems, stars have a life span, a beginning and a death.
B. Evidence indicates that matter, energy, space, and time had a beginning in a violent explosion, called the "**big bang**," about 15 billion years ago.
   1. The sun resulted from the emergence of hydrogen and helium.
   2. Scientists believe that a star that burns hydrogen, such as the sun, has enough energy for a "lifetime" of about 10 billion years.
   3. Astrophysicists believe that the sun has been producing energy for at least five billion years, which means the sun will continue to produce energy for many billions of years to come.
C. It is believed that, eventually, when about 15 percent of its hydrogen atoms have been used up, the nuclear reaction inside the sun will speed up, slowly at first, then faster and faster.
   1. The inside of the sun will get hotter, and the sun will expand to about 100 times its size.
   2. Meanwhile, the surface of the sun will become cooler, and its color will change to orange and then to red (a **red star**).
   3. When enough of the hydrogen has been consumed, the sun will suddenly collapse and become so small (called a **white dwarf**) that both its size and its light will be only a small fraction of what they are today.
   4. The sun will become cooler and fainter until it becomes completely dark and cannot be seen at all.

5. Sometimes a neighboring star is a source of gas that streams onto a white dwarf, forming a type of **supernova,** and a sudden synthesis of new elements, thereby enriching the universe with a new supply of chemical elements.

6. The composition of the earth is the natural by-product of energy generation in stars and successive waves of star birth and death in our galaxy.

THE SOLAR SYSTEM

I. THE MEMBERS OF THE SOLAR SYSTEM

A. What is referred to as our solar system is a group of bodies, called **satellites,** that move around our sun. A satellite is any body that travels around another body. The principal members of the solar system are nine satellites called **planets.**
   1. The word *planet* means "wanderer." Collectively, the planets were given this name because they seemed to wander over the sky instead of appearing to stay in a fixed position like the stars.
   2. The names of the planets, in order of their increasing distance from our sun, are Mercury, Venus, Earth, Mars, Jupiter, Saturn, Uranus, Neptune, and Pluto (although there is still some question as to whether Pluto is truly a planet. Because of the extreme elliptical shape of their orbits, as their orbits cross each other, Pluto and Neptune change in their relative positions from the sun.
   3. Some astronomers believe there could be other planets in our solar system yet unconfirmed.
   4. Alexander Wolszczan discovered the first known planets *outside* our own solar system, three planets in the constellation Virgo. Although these planets are 7,000 trillion miles from earth, this is nearby by astronomical standards.
   5. Between Mars and Jupiter there is a belt of several thousand satellite bodies of different sizes, called **asteroids** or **planetoids,** which also move around the sun.
B. Planets are not stars and stars are not planets.
   1. Stars shine because they give off light, but planets shine because they reflect the light of the sun or other stars.
   2. Planets are much smaller than the sun and are smaller than most of the other stars.
   3. Unlike stars, planets do not appear to twinkle (see page 286).

C. The planets travel in an elliptical (oval) path around the sun.
   1. The invisible, noncircular path followed by orbiting planets (and moons, comets, and asteroids, as well) is called an ellipse or orbit.
   2. Johann Kepler, in 1605, was the first to arrive at the conclusion that planets orbit the sun in elliptical paths. Galileo was the first to use a telescope (several years later, at about 1610), so Kepler, nearly blind himself, drew his conclusion from studying the reports made by naked-eye astronomer Thcho Brahe, to whom Kepler was an assistant.
   3. All the planets revolve in a counterclockwise elliptical path around the sun.
   4. In 1619, Kepler, through his study of data recorded by other naked-eye astronomers, concluded that the distance planets are from the sun precisely determines how long they take to orbit the sun. That conclusion helped to separate astronomy from astrology by showing that there are distinct mathematical relationships that bind the solar system together.
   5. The time needed for a planet to complete one revolution around the sun is called the planet's **year.**
D. The planets also spin like tops, or rotate, as they travel around the sun. They rotate around an imaginary line, called an **axis,** which runs through the north and south poles of the planet. The time needed for a planet to make one complete rotation on its axis is called the planet's **day.**
E. Most planets have their own smaller satellites that revolve around them. These satellites are called **moons.** There at least 61 moons: 1 for Earth, 2 for Mars, at least 16 for Jupiter, at least 18 for Saturn, 15 for Uranus, 8 for Neptune, and 1 for Pluto.
F. The planets are alike in certain ways.
   1. They are satellites of the sun.
   2. They rotate on their axis.

DEMONSTRATION 8.3
Planets Shine as the Result of Reflected Light

Use a playground ball, basketball, or globe to represent a planet. The "planet" can barely be seen in a darkened room. In a closet or completely darkened room it can not be seen at all. If you use a flashlight (or a 35 mm projec- tor, which will give a much brighter light) to represent the sun, and shine the light on the "planet," the "planet" can now be seen because the light from the "sun" is reflected off the "planet" to your eyes.

3. They obtain energy from the sun.
4. Although the proportions differ, they all contain the same basic chemical elements.
G. The planets differ in many ways.
  1. They differ in their distance from the sun.
  2. They differ in their size and mass.
  3. They differ in their atmospheres.
  4. They differ in the time it takes them to re-volve around the sun, the planetary year.
  5. They differ in the time it takes them to ro-tate once on their axis, the planetary day.
  6. They differ in the number of moons they have.
  7. They differ in their chemical makeup.
H. In the solar system there are also bodies called **comets,** which have long oval-shaped orbits that bring the comets close to the sun and then take them far out into the solar system.
I. In the solar system there are billions of fast-moving rocks of all sizes, called **meteors.**

5. Eventually a huge ball of material was formed, with its particles packed closely together.
6. Hydrogen atoms in the center of the ball began to collide, causing a nuclear reac-tion, along with the formation of helium and the release of radiant energy, includ-ing light.
7. In this way, our sun, a star, was formed.
8. Part of the cloud of dust and gases, from which the sun was formed, remained around this new star and slowly rotated.
9. Later, huge whirlpools formed in the ro-tating cloud, creating smaller globes of gases and dust.
10. Each globe eventually cooled into a planet, which still revolves around the sun because of the original motion of the rotating cloud of gases and dust.
11. Planetary satellites were formed from this rotating cloud in the same way.

II. How the Solar System Was Formed

A. Over the centuries, many theories have been proposed to explain how the solar system formed. Because it seems to be able to explain not only the formation of the sun and the so-lar system, but also the formation of the stars and their satellites, the theory that is most widely acceptable by scientists today is the **dust cloud theory.**
  1. According to the dust cloud theory, the solar system was formed from huge clouds of gases and dust.
  2. Atoms in these gases and dust were pushed toward one another by the light from the stars, and formed larger particles.
  3. These larger particles were attracted to each other by their respective gravita-tional pulls and began to crowd together.
  4. Large numbers of these particles came to-gether, shrank, and grew heavier.

III. The Cause of the Planets' Revolving Around the Sun

A. Two simultaneous conditions keep planets in orbit around the sun—inertia of the moving planet, and the sun's gravitational pull.
  1. According to Newton's (Isaac Newton, 1643–1727) **first law of motion,** a body at rest will remain at rest unless some force starts it moving, and a body that is moving will continue to move in the same direc-tion and at the same speed unless some force acts on that body to change it's direc-tion and speed. We have all experienced inertia as passengers in a moving vehicle when brakes are applied. We continue to move forward as the vehicle stops. This is why seat belts are necessary. All planets would continue moving straight into space and away from the sun if they were not af-fected by another force, gravity.

DEMONSTRATION 8.4
Ellipitical Orbit

An elliptical orbit can be demonstrated by using a lighted lamp (without its shade) in a stationary position to represent the sun. While walking an earth globe counter-clockwise (west to east) and elliptically (noncircularly) around the "sun," point out that it takes the earth 365.25 days to make this orbit. That is the earth's year.

2. According to Newton's **law of gravitation,** every body in the universe attracts or pulls on every other body. The more mass a body has, the greater its pull on another body. Because the sun has more mass than any of its planets, its gravitational pull on any given planet is much more powerful than the planet's gravitational pull on the sun. If only gravity were acting on the sun and each planet, the more powerful pull of the sun's gravity would cause the planet to rush into the sun and burn up.

3. Both inertia and gravity, however, affect each planet at the same time and in such a way that the planet travels neither straight into space nor toward the sun; instead, it travels in orbit around the sun.

IV. MERCURY

A. Mercury is the planet nearest the sun, about 58 million kilometers (36 million mi) from the sun.
1. Because it can be seen near the horizon shortly after sunset or just before sunrise, it is sometimes called an "evening" or "morning star," even though it is not a star but a planet.
2. Mercury revolves around the sun once every 88 days, so its year is much shorter than Earth's year.
3. When viewed closely, Mercury looks much like Earth's moon, heavily cratered.
4. Mercury has no atmosphere or water.
B. With a diameter of about 4,800 kilometers (3,000 mi) it is the smallest planet.
1. It rotates on its axis once in 59 days, so it has long days and nights.
C. The side of Mercury that is facing the sun is hot, as hot as 430° Celsius (775° F), and the side that faces away from the sun is quite cold, as cold as −170° Celsius (−275° F).

V. VENUS

A. Venus is the next closest planet to the sun, about 108 million kilometers (67 million mi) from the sun.
1. Venus also can be seen near the horizon as an "evening star" just after sunset, and as a "morning star" just before sunrise.
2. Venus revolves around the sun once every 224 Earth days, and it rotates on its axis only once in about 243 Earth days. Consequently, its day is longer than Earth's 365-day year.
B. With a diameter of about 12,200 kilometers (7,900 mi), Venus is slightly smaller than Earth.
C. The hottest part of the sunlit side of Venus is 500° Celsius (900° F), hot enough to melt lead, while the cool or dark side, the side facing away from the sun, is about 200° Celsius (360° F). The rocks on the surface of Venus are as hot as those of Earth buried deep beneath Earth's surface.
1. Strong winds on Venus transfer heat from the hot side (sunlit side) to the dark side; seasons are absent on Venus.
D. Venus is surrounded by thick, reflective clouds. Because of the thick cloud covering, traditional optical telescopes are not able to penetrate through to the surface. Using the technology afforded by microwave radar when Venus is closest to Earth, visitations and probes by orbiting spacecrafts, and the dropping of instrument probes onto Venus, scientists are now beginning to understand more clearly our nearest planet neighbor.
1. Next to the sun and the moon, Venus is the brightest body in the sky, because of its highly reflective cloud cover.
2. The clouds are made of tiny droplets of sulfuric acid.

DEMONSTRATION 8.5

Planetary Spin on an Axis

If you do not have a large earth globe, you can demonstrate this with a knitting needle and a grapefruit (or other large fruit), or a Styrofoam ball and skewer. Push the knitting needle through the grapefruit. The knitting needle represents the axis, or imaginary line, running through the earth's north and south poles. Tilt the needle slightly and make the grapefruit, which represents the earth, spin or rotate. Draw a line on the grapefruit with a felt-tip marker, from top to bottom, to show the spin more clearly.

---

    3. Venus's barometric pressure is about 100 times higher than Earth's.
    4. Small impact craters are missing on the surface of Venus, probably because only large bodies can penetrate its dense atmosphere to reach its surface.

VI. EARTH

    A. Earth, the next planet from the sun after Venus, is about 150 million kilometers (93 million mi) from the sun.
        1. It revolves around the sun once every 365.25 days.
    B. Earth has a diameter of about 12,600 kilometers (7,900 mi).
        1. It rotates on its axis once every 24 hours and a few seconds.
        2. At its equator Earth rotates at a speed of about 1,600 kilometers (1,000 mi) an hour, but the speed decreases as you move from the equator toward the poles, because the distance decreases.
    C. Earth has one moon.
    D. Earth is the only planet whose surface temperature is usually between the boiling and freezing points of water. Consequently, much of the water on Earth is found in the liquid state, rather than in the solid (ice) or gaseous (water vapor) state.
        1. This temperature stability has probably lasted for nearly 4 billion years.
        2. Earth is biologically active, having a vast variety of life forms spread widely over its surface.

VII. MARS

    A. Mars, the next planet after Earth, is about 228 million kilometers (141 million mi) from the sun.
        1. Every 15 years the paths of Mars and Earth come close, to a point where there are only about 56 million kilometers (35 million mi) between them.
    B. Mars is a small planet, with a diameter of about 6,700 kilometers (4,160 mi) about one-half the diameter of Earth.
        1. Although its diameter is only about one-half that of Earth, because of its rugged terrain, Mars has a surface area equal to that of all of Earth's continents combined.
        2. On Mars, you would weigh only one-third as much as on Earth.
    C. Mars revolves around the sun once every 687 days, so its year is almost twice that of Earth.
    D. With rotation on its axis of once every 24.5 hours, its day is about the same as Earth's.
    E. Mars has two small moons.
    F. Like Earth, but unlike Venus, Mars has seasons.
        1. Frozen caps of carbon dioxide at its poles grow smaller in summer and larger in winter.
        2. Sometimes Mars is obscured beneath a dusty shroud, usually when it is nearest the sun.
        3. Approximately three fourths of Mars's surface is covered with bright reddish or yellowish patches, which may be deserts.
    G. Although Mars has an atmosphere, that atmosphere is much thinner than that of Earth, so there is likely very little oxygen and water vapor in its atmosphere.
        1. The Martian atmosphere contains mostly carbon dioxide.
    H. The average temperature on Mars is about −50° Celsius (−58° F). Compare this to an average temperature of about 15° Celsius (59° F) on Earth.
        1. During the day the temperature at the Martian equator may be as warm as 20° Celsius (68° F), but it drops to about −70° Celsius (−94° F) at night.
    I. Scientists believe that 4.5 billion years ago, both Earth and Mars were warm and wet, with thick atmospheres and heavy volcanic

DEMONSTRATION 8.6
Effects of Inertia and Gravity

Attach a string that is 1 meter (3 ft) long to a ball or a chalkboard eraser and, while holding one end of the string in your hand, whirl the ball around your head; then let go of the string suddenly and you will observe how the ball travels out in a straight line as it obeys Newton's first law of motion. Whirl the ball around your

ahead again. Note how your hand must pull inward on the string so that the ball will travel around in a circle and not fly out. This pull corresponds to the pull or force of gravity, whereas the tendency of the ball to fly out and travel in a straight line corresponds to the movement due to inertia.

---

activity. While life formed on Earth, Mars cooled to a frozen planet. Scientists wonder whether life exists on Mars beneath its frozen surface.

VIII. THE ASTEROIDS (OR PLANETOIDS)

A. The asteroids (or planetoids) are a belt of about 25,000 bodies that circle the sun between Mars and the next planet, Jupiter.
B. They are called *asteroids* because they look like small stars, and *planetoids* because they are really small planets.
   1. In 1994, while studying images taken from telescopes aboard the Galileo spacecraft, scientists discovered that the asteroid Ida, a chunk of rock just 50 kilometers (31 mi) across, has a small moon.
C. All asteroids revolve around the sun in the same direction as the larger planets, although some may leave their orbits and cross the paths of planets or moons—and even crash into those bodies.
D. The asteroids are irregular lumps of rock, perhaps mixed with metal, that differ in size and brightness.
   1. Only a few are larger than 160 kilometers (100 mi) in diameter.
   2. Ceres, the largest yet discovered, is more than 1,000 kilometers (600 mi) in diameter, about one fourth the size of our moon.
   3. A few hundred are 16 to 160 kilometers (10 to 100 mi) in diameter, and the rest are less than 16 kilometers, some perhaps only about the size of a basketball.
E. Scientists are not sure how asteroids were formed. They may have come from a planet that exploded, or from two planets that collided and exploded, or they may be from a part of the solar system that never grew large enough to form one or more larger planets.

IX. JUPITER

A. Jupiter is the next planet after Mars. It is about 778 million kilometers (484 million mi) from the sun.
   1. To the naked eye, it appears in the sky as a very large "star."
B. Jupiter is the largest planet, with a diameter of about 143,000 kilometers (89,000 mi), about 11 times that of Earth.
   1. It revolves around the sun once in about 12 Earth years.
C. It rotates on its axis once in about 10 hours, so it has a very short day.
   1. Its speed of rotation is very fast, that is, about 40,000 kilometers (25,000 mi) an hour at its equator, or about 25 times faster than Earth's speed of rotation at the equator.
   2. This rapid rotation causes Jupiter to flatten at its poles and bulge at its equator, even more than Earth does.
D. Jupiter has at least 16 moons.
E. Rather than a solid surface, Jupiter seems to consist of shifting belts of ammonia clouds that run parallel to its equator and are spread out in colored bands which, when observed by telescopes, keep changing their patterns and colors.
   1. Evidence indicates that Jupiter is a giant ball of gas with an atmosphere of nearly 90 percent hydrogen, 10 percent helium, and a trace amount of water.
F. Jupiter has a large red spot, which appears to be slowly growing smaller.
   1. The red spot rotates counterclockwise in Jupiter's southern hemisphere.
   2. The red spot moves about irregularly as it rotates.
G. Three thin, flat, faintly visible rings, one of which contains large boulder-size debris, encircle Jupiter.

H. In 1994 scientists were able to predict and observe the crashing of a comet, Shoemaker-Levy 9, into Jupiter, the impact of which left an initial hole in Jupiter's atmosphere that is estimated to be about the size of Texas.
   1. Astronomers have yet not been able to explain the appearance of vast, dark splotches that appeared on Jupiter after the comet crash.
   2. One hypothesis about these splotches is that they were caused by carbon compounds derived from organic molecules in the comet.
   3. With the hubble space telescope, scientists detected yet unexplained bright flashes and large plumes that rose about 3,000 kilometers (1,863 mi) above the top of Jupiter's cloud cover.
   4. From further study of the impact of this comet on Jupiter, scientists expect to learn more about how energy spreads after huge impacts such as this, including those that may have caused mass extinctions of life on Earth. From these studies, scientists also expect to learn more about the frequency at which large comets crash into Jupiter, and, by extension, into Earth. It has been hypothesized that such impacts on Jupiter or its moons occur about every 150 years.

X. SATURN

A. Saturn, the next planet after Jupiter, is about 1,430 million kilometers (890 million mi) from the sun.
B. Saturn has a diameter of about 120,000 kilometers (75,000 mi).
   1. It revolves once around the sun in about 29.5 Earth years.
   2. It rotates on its axis once in about 10 hours.
C. Saturn has at least 18 moons.
D. It is also surrounded by seven broad rings that revolve at different speeds around the planet. These are composed of ice and rock that range in size from tiny particles to boulders as large as tall buildings. There are thousands of ringlets making an orbit within these rings.

XI. URANUS

A. Uranus is the next planet after Saturn, and is about 2,900 million kilometers (1,800 million mi) from the sun.

B. Uranus has a diameter of about 50,000 kilometers (31,000 mi).
   1. It revolves once around the sun in about 84 Earth years.
   2. It rotates on its axis once every 17 hours, but in a different position from all other planets. Whereas the other planets rotate on a vertical axis, like a top spinning upright, Uranus rotates on an almost horizontal axis, like a top spinning on its side.
C. Uranus has at least 15 moons; it also has at least 11 rings that surround it, but the rings are narrow and quite faint.
D. Uranus seems to have a solid core that is surrounded by an icy layer, and a thick atmosphere of gases.

XII. NEPTUNE

A. Neptune is usually the next planet after Uranus, and is about 4,500 million kilometers (2,800 million mi) from the sun.
B. From 1990 to 2007, however, Neptune will be in the part of its orbit that is farthest from the sun, while Pluto will be closer than usual to the sun.
C. Neptune has a diameter of about 49,000 kilometers (30,000 mi).
   1. Neptune revolves around the sun once every 165 Earth years.
   2. It rotates on its axis once in about 18 hours.
D. Neptune has eight known moons, and two narrow and two broader rings surrounding it.
E. Neptune has a very dynamic atmosphere, showing bright cloudlike covers and high-pressure systems appearing and disappearing in a matter of hours.

XIII. PLUTO

A. Pluto is about 5,900 million kilometers (3,700 million mi) from the sun.
   1. As discussed earlier, because of Pluto's and Neptune's elliptical orbits, Pluto is not always the planet that is farthest from the sun.
B. Pluto's diameter is estimated to be about 2,300 kilometers (1,400 mi).
   1. Pluto revolves around the sun once in about 248 Earth years.
   2. It rotates on its axis once in about every six days.
C. Pluto is known to have at least one moon.

XIV. COMETS

A. Comets are bodies that revolve around the sun in long, oval-shaped orbits (see Figure 8.2).
   1. The sun is at one far end of the comet's orbit.
   2. The comet's orbit cuts across the paths of the planets' orbits.
B. A comet has a head and, as it nears the sun, a tail.
   1. The head is made of small rocks and dust, mixed with frozen gases, believed to contain ice.
   2. A comet does not have a tail until it nears the sun, at which time the solid frozen gases in the comet begin to vaporize. The tail is actually a thin stream of vapors. The tail may be millions of kilometers long and so thin that stars can be seen through it. As the comet travels away from the sun, the gases condense and freeze again and the tail disappears.

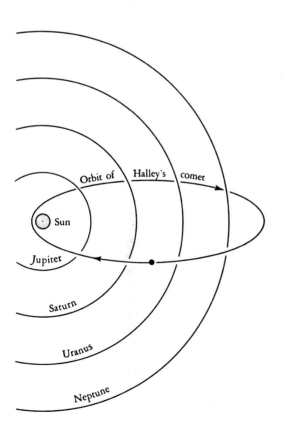

FIGURE 8.2   Orbit of Halley's comet.

3. The comet and its tail reflect the light of the sun. The pressure of this light makes the tail point away from the sun both when the comet approaches and leaves the sun.
C. As a comet approaches the sun it gains speed, and the sun's pull of gravity on it becomes stronger; then it slows down again as it travels away from the sun.
D. Some comets return to our view rather quickly, but others take much longer.
   1. Encke's comet returns every 3.5 years, whereas Halley's comet returns every 76 years.
   2. Some comets never return, because they either waste away as material is forced out of the head into the tail or are destroyed as they approach a large body. An example of a comet that was destroyed is the Shoemaker-Levy 9 comet that crashed into Jupiter in July 1994.
E. It is not known how comets are formed.

XV. METEOROIDS, METEORS, AND METEORITES

A. **Meteoroids** are chunks of rock and metal in space. When they pass through earth's atmosphere and begin to burn, they are called **meteors.**
   1. Meteors greatly range in size; they can be as small as tiny grains of sand or as big as very large boulders.
   2. Some meteors are metallic, containing iron and nickel. Others are stony and contain silicates.
B. Billions of meteors enter the earth's atmosphere each year, traveling about 160,000 kilometers (100,000 mi) an hour.
   1. When within about 80 kilometers (50 mi) above the earth's surface, the friction caused by air rubbing against the meteors makes them white hot and they begin to burn, creating a streak of light as they travel through our atmosphere. These bright streaks are sometimes referred to as "shooting stars."
   2. Most meteors burn up before they reach the earth's surface.
   3. Those meteors that strike the earth's surface before they completely burn up are called **meteorites.**
C. A large meteorite can form a large crater when it strikes the earth's surface.
   1. Meteor Crater in Arizona and Chubb Crater in Canada were caused by meteorites.

2. One meteorite, weighing about 55,000 kilograms (60 tons), was found in Africa and is still in the spot where it struck the earth. Another, weighing about 32,000 kilograms (35 tons), is in the American Museum of Natural History in New York City. It was found in Greenland in 1894.

3. Another large impact crater is the Chicxulub Crater, discovered in 1981 but completely hidden by sediments that formed the Yucatan Peninsula. That crater is 300 kilometers (186 mi) in diameter and is about 65 million years old. Large impacts, such as made by the projectile (whether a meteorite or not is still uncertain) that caused the Chicxulub Crater, have been hypothesized to be the cause of major extinctions of life on earth. This hypothesis is especially well documented for the time in the earth's history that resulted in the end of half of the living species on earth, including the dinosaurs, about 65 million years ago.

D. Meteorites that reach the earth today seem to come from two sources.
   1. Most are small bits of rocks, like those in the belt of asteroids between Mars and Jupiter, that are traveling through space.
   2. Some seem to come from comets, because swarms of meteors, called **meteor showers,** are seen whenever the earth crosses the path of a comet.
   3. There are some meteor showers that return to the earth annually. These meteor showers are named after the constellations from whose direction they seem to come. Common among these are the Perseid shower that arrives at about August 10 to 14, the Orionid shower at about October 20 to 24, the Leonid shower at about November 15 to 19, and the Geminid shower at about December 10 to 14.

THE EFFECTS OF THE SUN ON THE EARTH

I. THE SUN CAUSES THE YEAR ON EARTH

A. The earth travels in an elliptical (oval) path, called an **ellipse** or orbit, around the sun.
   1. It revolves in this orbit in a counterclockwise direction (from west to east).
   2. The time needed for the earth to make one complete turn, or revolution, around the sun is 365.25 days, and is called the earth's **year.**

II. THE EARTH'S SPIN CAUSES DAY AND NIGHT ON EARTH

A. The earth also spins like a top, or rotates, as it revolves around the sun.
   1. It spins around an imaginary line, called an **axis,** which runs through the earth's north and south poles.
   2. It rotates on its axis in a counterclockwise direction (from west to east).
   3. The time needed for the earth to make one complete turn on its axis is 24 hours, and is called the earth's **day.**

B. At the equator the earth rotates at a speed of about 1,600 kilometers (1,000 mi) an hour, but this speed diminishes as we move farther away from the equator toward the north and south poles. Halfway between the equator and the north pole the speed is about 1,280 kilometers (800 mi) an hour.

C. The earth gets its light from the sun.
   1. Because the earth is shaped like a ball, only one half can be lighted at one time. When one half is lighted by the sun it is in daylight; the other half is in darkness (nighttime).
   2. Every 24 hours, as the earth rotates once on its axis, one part of the earth will have had one period of daytime and one period of nighttime.
   3. Because the earth turns from west to east, the sun *seems* to move across the sky from east to west. The sun is said to "rise" in the east and "set" in the west.

D. When the sun (or the moon) is just "rising" or just "setting," it looks bigger.
   1. This phenomenon is an optical illusion resulting from viewing the sun (or moon) in relation to buildings or trees when it is lower in the horizon than when it is higher in the horizon and there are no structures with which to compare it (see Figure 8.3).

E. Also at sunrise and at sunset, the sun looks orange or reddish.
   1. This phenomenon happens because rays of red light can pass through a greater distance of the earth's atmosphere more easily than rays of blue light, which are bent and scattered more than the red (see Figure 8.3).
   2. When the sun is low on the horizon, as at sunrise or sunset, the light from the sun must

DEMONSTRATION 8.7
Day and Night

Use a globe of the earth that rotates and a flashlight (or slide projector or a lamp). Have a student find and mark on the globe with chalk or piece of tape where you live. Darken the classroom and turn on the light source (which represents the sun). Half the globe will be lighted (daytime) and half will be in darkness (nighttime). Now spin the globe slowly from west to east (counterclockwise when looking down from the north pole). Show the students how where they live goes from day to night and back to day again. Show also how the east will receive sunlight before the west, so that when it is dawn in New York, it is still dark in Chicago, Los Angeles, and Hawaii.

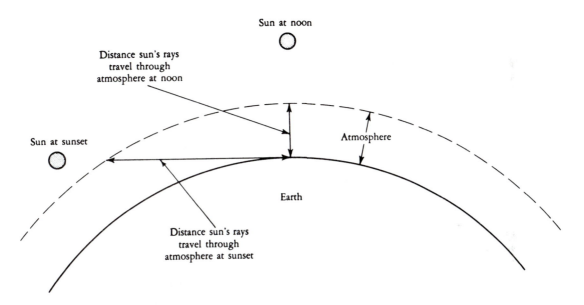

FIGURE 8.3   The distance that sunlight passes through the atmosphere at sunrise or sunset is greater than at noon.

travel a much greater distance through the thicker part of the earth's atmosphere than when the sun is overhead.

3. The blue rays in sunlight cannot get through this greater distance of air, and they are reflected and scattered by the dust particles in the air.
4. The reflection and scattering of the blue light by the dust particles is what makes the sky appear blue.
5. However, the red rays in sunlight can still pass through; the sunlight now has less blue in it, so the sun looks orange or reddish.
6. When the sun is overhead, all the rays of light can get through this thinner and shorter distance of atmosphere, so the sun

appears more white. Its rays are more concentrated, as demonstrated in Figure 8.4.

III. THE SUN CAUSES THE SEASONS ON EARTH

A. The earth's axis is tilted at an angle of 23.5 degrees, and is always pointed toward Polaris, the North Star.
B. Because of this tilt and because of the earth's revolution around the sun, the earth has different seasons of the year (see Figure 8.5).
   1. It is *not* the closeness of the Earth to the sun that causes the seasons.
C. When the northern hemisphere is tilted toward the sun, the northern hemisphere has summer.
   1. Summer begins on June 21, which is called the **summer solstice.**

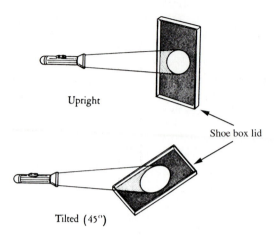

Upright

Shoe box lid

Tilted (45")

FIGURE 8.4   Direct rays are more concentrated than slanted rays.

2. In the summer the sun's rays are shining directly on the northern hemisphere.
3. The stronger, direct rays cover a smaller amount of the earth's surface, and that surface becomes quite hot.
4. Because of the tilt of the earth's axis, the northern hemisphere also gets more daylight than darkness in the summer, so the days are longer than the nights.

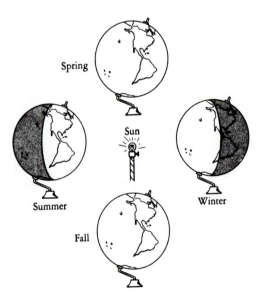

FIGURE 8.5   The tilt of the earth's axis and the revolution of the earth around the sun together

5. More daylight means that the northern hemisphere gets the sun for a longer time, which also helps the northern hemisphere become warmer in the summer.
6. When it is summer in the northern hemisphere, the north pole has daylight all 24 hours.

D. When the northern hemisphere is tilted away from the sun, the northern hemisphere has winter.
   1. Winter begins on December 22, which is called the **winter solstice.**
   2. In winter the sun's rays are shining at a slant on the northern hemisphere.
   3. The weaker, slanted rays now cover a larger amount of the earth's surface, and the surface is not heated as much as it was during the summer.
   4. Because of the tilt of the earth's axis, the northern hemisphere gets more darkness than daylight in the winter, so the nights are longer than the days.
   5. Longer nights mean that the northern hemisphere gets the sun's rays for a shorter time, which also helps the northern hemisphere become much colder in the winter.
   6. When it is winter in the northern hemisphere, the north pole is in darkness all 24 hours.

E. When it is summer in the northern hemisphere, the southern hemisphere is tilted away from the sun and the southern hemisphere has winter; when it is winter in the northern hemisphere, the southern hemisphere is tilted toward the sun and the southern hemisphere has summer.

F. In the spring and fall, the earth is tilted neither toward nor away from the sun.
  1. Neither hemisphere receives strong rays of sunlight, and it is not summer or winter in either hemisphere, but rather somewhere between.
  2. At the same time, the days and nights are of equal length.
  3. The northern hemisphere spring begins March 21, the **vernal equinox;** fall begins September 23, the **autumnal equinox.**

IV. THE SUN IS A SOURCE OF ENERGY FOR THE EARTH

  A. The sun sends out radiant energy in all directions, but only a fraction of the sun's energy reaches the earth. This energy heats the earth and gives it light. Without the energy of sunlight, the earth would be a frozen and lifeless wasteland.
  B. The sun's energy makes it possible for some organisms to manufacture food by the process known as photosynthesis (see Chapter 12).
  C. From the bodies of organisms that have died, the sun's energy is stored in natural fuels such as wood, coal, oil, and gas.
  1. Coal is what remains of fernlike plants that died millions of years ago, were buried under masses of rock and soil, and were then subjected to tremendous pressure and heat.
  2. Oil and gas are what remain of tiny animals and plants that died, were buried under layers of mud and sand, and were then subjected to tremendous pressure and heat.
  3. When natural fuels are burned, they give off energy in the form of heat and light—the same energy that originally came from the sun and was stored in plants through photosynthesis.

V. THE SUN CAUSES THE WEATHER

  A. The sun does not heat all parts of the earth equally.

  1. The parts of the earth near the equator are heated more than the parts of the earth away from the equator, because the rays of light become more slanted farther away from the equator (see Figure 8.4).
  2. Because the sun's rays heat only one half of the earth at one time, during daytime, a daily heating and cooling cycle results.
  3. The land on the earth is heated and cooled more quickly than water.
  4. Dark-colored bodies of land absorb more heat than light-colored land bodies.
  B. This unequal heating causes movements of great masses of air.
  1. Some air masses are cold, and others are warm.
  2. Cold air masses originate from the polar regions of the earth, whereas warm air masses originate from the tropical or equatorial regions.
  3. The warmer, lighter air from the equator rises and moves toward the poles, and the colder, heavier air from the poles moves toward the equator.
  4. Because gas expands when warm and contracts when cold, colder, heavier air masses have greater pressure than warmer, lighter air masses.
  C. The heat of the sun also causes some of the water on the earth to evaporate into the air and become a gas called **water vapor.**
  1. Warm air, because of the greater energy in its molecules, can hold more water vapor than cold air.
  D. When a warm air mass and a cold air mass meet, the warm air mass is cooled and some of the water vapor falls out of the air, or **condenses,** in some form of **precipitation.**
  E. The combination of moving air masses, differences in air pressure, and changing amounts of water vapor in the air—all caused by the sun—are responsible for the different kinds of weather and changes in weather throughout the earth.

EARTH'S MOON

I. THE NATURE OF THE EARTH'S MOON
  A. The earth's moon is a large ball of rocky material that revolves around the earth.

  1. It is about 3,500 kilometers (2,160 mi) in diameter, that is, about one fourth the diameter of the Earth.

2. The volume of the moon is about one fiftieth that of the earth.

3. Its weight is about one eightieth that of the earth.

B. The moon's pull of gravity is only one sixth that of the earth.

   1. A broad jumper who can jump 7 meters (23 ft) on earth would jump 42 meters (138 ft) on the moon; a high jumper who can jump 2 meters (6.5 ft) on earth would jump 12 meters (39 ft) on the moon.

   2. The high jumper would not fall any harder from the greater height, because the jumper's *mass* remains the same, but the jumper's *weight* would be only one sixth as much on the moon as on earth.

C. The moon has no atmosphere or water.

   1. Without an atmosphere, there is no wind on the moon, nor can sounds travel in that void.

   2. The moon has no water or water vapor, so there are no brooks, rivers, lakes, or oceans, nor are there clouds or weather.

D. The temperature on the moon's surface varies greatly, depending on whether it is day or night, from as high as 104° Celsius (220° F) during the day and as low as −70° Celsius (−94° F) at night.

E. The surface of the moon consists of smooth plains or basins, jagged mountains, and many craters.

   1. The basins cover about half the surface of the side we see; they are shaped like rough circles and appear dark because they do not reflect as much sunlight as do the mountains. The basins are what create the dark features in what some call "the man in the moon."

   2. The basins were caused by vast lava flows that leaked out onto the moon's surface billions of years ago.

   3. The largest basin is about 2,500 kilometers (about 1,500 mi) in diameter, about half the distance across the continental United States.

   4. The surface of the moon is covered with a layer of dust particles, pebbles, and stones, the moon's version of soil, called **regolith.** The regolith covers most of the moon's surface at depths up to 20 meters (approximately 66 ft). Samples of the lunar regolith were brought back to earth by U.S. astronauts Neil Armstrong and Buzz Aldrin upon their return from the voyage of the Eagle

spaceship (flight of Apollo 11—see Figure 11.12), which landed on the moon's surface in 1969 in a large basin called the Sea of Tranquillity.

   5. A person walking on the moon kicks up a cloud of loose dust; the dust falls back to the surface just as quickly as heavy pieces of stone or iron, because there is no atmosphere of air to slow down the falling dust particles.

F. There are many mountain ranges, most of which are concentrated in the moon's southern hemisphere.

   1. Some of these mountains soar 7,500 meters high (25,000 ft). The altitudes of the mountains are determined through measuring the length of the shadows they throw on the moon's surface.

   2. The mountains are very jagged, because there are no forces of wind or water to wear them down to a smoother form.

G. There are also many rounded depressions called **craters,** spread over the moon's surface. Evidence indicates that the vast majority of the lunar craters were formed by impacts that occurred during formation of the moon about 3.9 billion years ago.

   1. It is estimated that in any one area of the moon, within a radius of 100 kilometers (62 mi) there will be about 500 craters wider than one kilometer each (0.6 mi).

   2. There are about 5,000 craters each larger than five kilometers (3 mi) in diameter.

   3. More than 30,000 craters have been identified, the largest being about 240 kilometers (150 mi) in diameter.

   4. In most craters the floor is above the level of the surrounding basin.

   5. Some craters have smooth floors, and others have rough floors, often with smaller craters in them.

   6. Some craters have light-colored streaks or rays radiating beyond them in all directions. The most conspicuous rays come from the crater Tycho. It is believed that the rays were created by a lava flow that spread out over the moon's surface, caused by the impact of the object that made the crater.

H. The lunar surface is also covered with many cracks, called rills, usually about 1 kilometer (0.6 mi) wide and of unknown depth. Some rills are crooked and others run in a straight line.

II. THE MOTION OF THE MOON AROUND THE EARTH
 A. The moon revolves around the earth in an elliptical orbit, in a counterclockwise direction (from west to east), the same direction in which the earth revolves around the sun.
  1. Because the moon's orbit is elliptical, the moon comes a little closer to the earth on one side of its orbit.
  2. The point of the moon's orbit nearest the earth is called its **perigee,** and the point farthest from the earth is called its **apogee.**
  3. Although the moon's average distance from the earth is 384,000 kilometers (240,000 mi), at perigee it is about 350,000 kilometers (220,000 mi) from earth and at apogee it is about 400,000 kilometers (250,000 mi) from earth.
 B. The conditions that keep the moon orbiting the earth are the same ones that keep the planets in orbit around the sun, as discussed earlier.
  1. One condition is the **pull of gravity,** in this case the earth's pull on the moon. If this were the only condition, then the earth's pull of gravity on the moon would cause the moon to be pulled to the earth.
  2. The other condition, that which keeps the moon from crashing into the earth (and the planets from crashing into the sun) is **inertia,** in this case the moon's own motion and tendency to continue in motion in a straight line. The moon's inertia would cause the moon to travel away from the earth were it not for the earth's pull of gravity.
  3. Because of the "balance" between inertia and gravity, the moon travels neither straight into space nor toward the earth, but rather in an orbit around the earth.
 C. The moon revolves around the earth at a speed of about 3,500 kilometers (2,200 mi) an hour. It takes about 27.3 days for the moon to make one complete orbit around the earth. This is called a **lunar month.**
  1. However, because the earth is revolving around the sun at the same time, it takes 29.5 days for the moon to go from one full moon (see "Phases of the Moon") to the next. Calendars use 29.5 days as the time for one lunar month.
 D. The moon "rises" about 50 minutes later each day. The difference in rising time happens because the moon moves in its orbit in the same direction (counterclockwise) as the earth rotates. Therefore, it takes the earth a little longer

each day to turn around so that the moon can next be seen as the earth moves farther along its orbit.
 E. The moon rotates on its axis in a counterclockwise direction (west to east).
  1. It takes the moon just as long to rotate once on its axis as it does to revolve once around the earth, which means that the moon's day is the same length as its month. Thus, the moon has about two weeks of daylight at one time, followed by about two weeks of nighttime at another.
  2. Because the earth rotates in a counterclockwise direction, the moon seems to rise in the east, move across the sky, and set in the west. As with the sun, an optical illusion causes the moon to appear bigger when it is rising or setting (see Figure 8.6).
 F. Because of the moon's rotation on its axis only once in a lunar month, all we see from the earth is about one half of the moon's surface.
  1. Actually, we see about 59 percent of the moon's surface. Because it's orbit is slightly tilted, we can look a little over the moon's top and under its lower edge as it travels around.
  2. We can also see a little more of each side of the moon, because the moon moves faster at perigee than at apogee. At perigee, when the moon increases its speed, the earth lags behind and we see a little more of one side of the moon. At apogee, when the moon decreases its speed, the earth moves ahead and we see a little more of the other side of the moon.
  3. Lunar space flights and earth satellite pictures taken of the other side of the moon indicate that it is not much different from the side we can see.

III. PHASES OF THE MOON
 A. The moon does not give off its own light. It reflects the light of the sun, just as do the planets.
  1. Because the moon is so close to the earth, to us on earth it is the second brightest object in the sky.
 B. The side of the moon that faces the sun is always brightly lighted, but the side that is turned away from the sun is always in darkness.
  1. Because the sun's light is very bright and because the earth's atmosphere scatters the sunlight in all directions, the lighted side of the moon is sometimes difficult to see in the daytime except in early morning and late afternoon.

DEMONSTRATION 8.9
Optical Illusion of Moon's Size

To show the optical illusion of the size of the moon (and sun) during rising and setting, bend a paper clip so that it fits a meter stick snugly, as shown in Figure 8.6. When there is a full moon on the horizon, sight the moon so that it fits exactly within the two ends of the paper clip, pinching or widening the ends if necessary. Look at the moon again through the paper clip later when the moon is higher in the sky. Its size will not have changed at all.

Historically, the illusion of the size of the moon (and sun) has inspired novelists, songwriters, artists, and the invention of myths and words (harvest moon, lunatic). Have your students research examples and share those with the class.

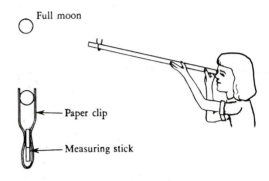

FIGURE 8.6   The apparent change in the moon's size when it is rising or setting is an optical illusion.

C. As the moon travels in its orbit around the earth, we see different amounts of the moon's lighted surface, as shown in Figure 8.7.
   1. These changes in the amount of lighted surface that we see are called the **phases** of the moon (see Figure 8.7).
   2. During the calendar lunar month, when the moon makes one complete revolution around the earth in 29.5 days, the moon passes through each of its phases, going from completely dark to completely bright and then back to completely dark again.
   3. When the moon is between the earth and the sun, the dark side of the moon is turned toward the earth and we cannot see the moon. This phase is called the **new moon.**
   4. Sometimes the new moon can be seen only faintly because it is lighted by sunlight reflected from the earth onto the moon (earthshine).
   5. One or two days later, as the moon continues to revolve from west to east around the earth, a little of the lighted side of the moon can be seen from earth. The part that can be seen is shaped like a thin **crescent.** The rest of the dark part can be seen faintly because of earthshine.
   6. About one week after the new moon, one half of the lighted side of the moon is visible from earth. This phase is called the **first quarter,** or **half moon.**
   7. The first quarter rises at noon and sets at midnight.
   8. A few days later almost all of the moon's lighted side is visible from earth, a phase called the **gibbous moon.**
   9. About two weeks after the new moon, all of the lighted side is visible; this phase is called the **full moon.**
   10. During full moon the earth is between the moon and the sun.

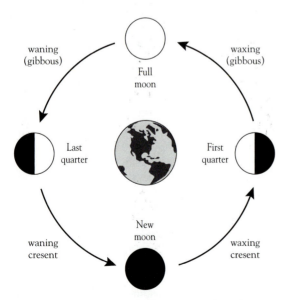

FIGURE 8.7   Phases of the moon as seen from the earth.

DEMONSTRATION 8.9
We See Only Half the Moon's Surface

To demonstrate this to students, make an *X* with chalk on a large ball that represents the moon. Let one child represent the earth and sit in the center of the classroom. Have a second child hold the ball and walk counterclockwise around the first child in a wide circle, always keeping the *X* facing the first moonchild's head. It should be apparent to the students that the moon rotates just once as it makes one revolution around the earth. Therefore the moon shows only one side to the earth at all times.

---

11. At full moon, the moon has made one half of one complete revolution around the earth.
12. The full moon appears to rise at sunset and set at sunrise.
13. When the moon goes from full moon to new moon and the amount of lighted surface we see grows larger, we say the moon is **waxing.**
14. When the moon goes from full moon to new moon and the amount of lighted surface we see grows smaller, we say the moon is **waning.**
15. One or two days after the full moon, the amount of the lighted side that is visible from earth grows smaller, or wanes, and we see a gibbous moon again.
16. About one week after the full moon, only one half of the moon's lighted side is visible from earth. This phase is called the **last quarter, or half moon.**
17. The last quarter rises at midnight and sets at noon.
18. After the last quarter, the moon wanes even more until it is again crescent shaped.
19. About one week after the last quarter, the moon has completed one revolution around the earth and is back in its original position as a new moon. The phases then start again, with the moon waxing until it becomes a full moon and then waning until it is a new moon again.

IV. THE MOON CAUSES TIDES ON EARTH
   A. **Tides** are the rise and fall of the oceans, caused mainly by the moon's gravitational pull on earth.
      1. The earth has a gravitational pull on the moon, and at the same time the moon has a pull of gravity on the earth.
      2. Because the earth is larger and heavier than the moon, its pull of gravity on the moon is greater than the moon's pull of gravity on the earth.
      3. The earth's stronger pull of gravity helps keep the moon revolving around the earth, from going out into space away from earth.
      4. The moon's weaker pull of gravity affects the earth in the form of tides.
   B. Tides are formed because the moon's pull of gravity on the side of the earth facing the moon makes the easily movable waters of the earth on that side bulge out toward the moon. This watery bulge is called a **high tide** or **flood tide.** Because this tide is on the side of the earth facing the moon, it is also called a **direct tide.**
   C. At the same time, another high tide is formed on the opposite side of the earth. This pull leaves the water on the opposite and farthest side, where the moon's pull of gravity is weaker, bulging out behind to form another high tide. Because this tide is on the opposite side of the earth, away from the moon, it is called the **opposite tide.**
   D. The water that is drawn in to make bulges at these two points on earth comes from the remaining water at the opposite two points on earth. The water at the opposite two points now flattens out and forms lower levels, and these lower levels are called **low tides.**
   E. Because the earth rotates on its axis once every 24 hours, the earth has two high tides and two low tides every 24 hours at different points on the earth.
      1. The tide rises for about six hours; then it falls or ebbs for about six hours.
      2. Because the moon rises about 50 minutes later each day, high tide and low tide also are approximately 50 minutes later each day, but with considerable variation.
      3. Knowing when tides will be high and low can be very useful information. For example, in some channels, ships arrive and leave only at high tide, when these channels are at their deepest, allowing ships to come and go

safely. Ship captains prefer to leave port when the tide is going out so that the ship does not have to fight an incoming tide. At low tide, people dig for clams.

F. At its perigee, about 48,000 kilometers (30,000 mi) closer to the earth than at apogee, the moon's pull of gravity on the earth becomes greater, so the tides are higher and lower than usual.

G. The sun's pull of gravity on the earth also causes tides on earth. However, because the sun is so much farther away from the earth, the sun-caused tides are less than half as strong as those caused by the moon.

H. When the sun is in line with the moon, very high and very low tides are formed. These tides occur because the sun and moon combine their pull of gravity on the earth. The sun and moon are in line with each other twice a month, at new moon and at full moon. These very high tides and very low tides are called **spring tides,** from the German word *springen,* which means "to jump."

I. When the sun and moon are at a right angle to each other, tides that are not as high or as low as usual are formed, because the sun's pull of gravity and the moon's pull of gravity are now working against each other. The sun and moon are at a right angle to each other twice a month, at first quarter and at last quarter. These smaller high and low tides are called **neap tides.**

J. The rise in tides differs at different parts of the earth, depending on the nature of the shoreline and ocean floor at each location. For example, on the open sea the rise in tides is only about 1 meter (3 ft). At Cape Cod Bay the rise in tides may be 3 meters (10 ft) at times. At the Bay of Fundy, the narrow bay can have tides that rise more than 15 meters (50 ft).

V. ECLIPSES

A. As the sun shines on the earth and the moon, both throw a long shadow into space. Earth's shadow is about 1,400,000 kilometers (866,000 mi) long. The moon's shadow is about 384,000 kilometers (240,000 mi) long.

B. We experience night on earth because we are carried by the earth's rotation into the earth's own shadow.

C. At certain times the moon passes between the earth and the sun in such a way that people on earth cannot see the sun. This phenomenon is called an **eclipse** of the sun, or a **solar eclipse.** A solar eclipse happens only when there is a new moon and the moon is between the earth and the sun, blocking the sun's light to earth (see Figure 8.8).

1. In a solar eclipse the moon's shadow falls on the earth.

2. The moon's shadow on the earth has two parts: a cone-shaped inner part called the **umbra,** which is completely dark; and a broader outer part, called the **penumbra,** in which the light is only partially blocked.

3. The tip of the umbra covers only a small part of the earth's surface, so only this small part of the earth's surface is in complete shadow.

4. People within the umbra see the sun become completely covered and blotted from view.

5. When the sun's light is completely cut off, we say that a **total eclipse** of the sun is taking place.

6. At any given spot on earth a total eclipse lasts only about eight minutes.

7. During a total eclipse, the sun's corona can be seen without the use of special instruments, although one still needs to protect

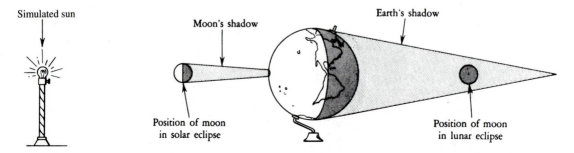

Simulated sun

Moon's shadow

Earth's shadow

Position of moon in solar eclipse

Position of moon in lunar eclipse

FIGURE 8.8 Solar and lunar eclipses.

the eyes from damage. Even during a total solar eclipse, people should *not* look directly at the sun.

8. The penumbra covers a larger part of the earth's surface.
9. People within the penumbra see only part of the sun covered and blotted from view.
10. When the sun's light is only partially blocked from view, we say a **partial eclipse** of the sun is taking place.
11. Sometimes, especially if the moon is near apogee and the moon is in position to produce a solar eclipse, the moon's umbra may be too short to reach the earth's surface.
12. When this phenomenon occurs, the sun is still eclipsed, but not completely; it shows a thin ring of light around the edges. This kind of eclipse is called an **annular** or **ring eclipse.**
13. Total eclipses of the sun do not happen often. For a total eclipse of the sun, the moon must be in an exact line between the sun and the earth when the moon reaches the new moon phase.
14. This position is not reached often, because the moon's orbit is tilted a little. Consequently, the moon usually passes between the earth and the sun either too high or too low for its shadow to fall on the earth. Therefore, we don't have an eclipse each month.

D. Sometimes the earth passes between the sun and the moon in a way that the earth blocks the sunlight that the moon reflects, and the moon cannot be seen.
  1. This phenomenon is called an **eclipse** of the moon, or a **lunar eclipse.**
  2. An eclipse of the moon occurs only when there is a full moon, when the earth is between the moon and the sun.
  3. In a lunar eclipse the earth's shadow falls on the moon.
  4. The moon frequently passes through the earth's rather large penumbra, so that a partial lunar eclipse happens rather often.
  5. However, because the moon's orbit is tilted, the moon does not pass through the earth's umbra very often and a total lunar eclipse is rare.
  6. Again, because the moon's orbit is tilted a little, the earth's shadow doesn't always fall on the moon and we don't have an eclipse monthly.

Beyond The Solar System

I. The Stars

A. Stars are suns in space; they produce their own light.
B. There are countless stars in the sky; about 3,000 are visible with the naked eye.
C. Stars are not in a fixed position, but are actually moving rapidly in various directions through space.
D. Stars vary in size. Small stars, like our sun, are called **dwarfs.** Large stars, such as Aldebaran and Pegasi, are called **giants.** Tremendously large stars, like Antares and Betelgeuse, are called **supergiants.**
E. Depending on their age and temperature, stars vary in color.
  1. As stars grow older, their surfaces become cooler and they change color.
  2. The youngest stars are blue-white to white, and their surface temperatures range from about 7,500° to 30,000° Celsius (13,500° to 54,000° Fahrenheit).
  3. Yellow star surfaces are about 6,000° Celsius (10,800° F).
  4. Orange star surfaces are about 4,000° Celsius (7,200° F).
  5. Red stars are the oldest stars, having surface temperatures of about 3,000° Celsius (5,400° F).
  6. Our sun is a yellow star.

F. Star brightness (luminosity) as observed from here on earth depends on the star's temperature, size, and distance from earth.
  1. Astronomers call the apparent brightness of a star, as seen from earth, its **magnitude.** The brighter the star, the lower its magnitude number.
  2. **First-magnitude** stars are the brightest.
  3. A first-magnitude star is two and a half times brighter than a second-magnitude star; a second-magnitude star is two and a half times brighter than a third-magnitude star, and so on. The faintest stars the eye can see are **sixth-magnitude** stars. Stars of the **twenty-third magnitude** have been discovered with telescopes.

G. **Double** stars, also called **binary** stars, are two stars that are held closely together by their pull of gravity on each other.

H. **Variable** stars are stars that flare up and become brighter, then grow dimmer again.
   1. For some stars, this happens because the star has exploded.
   2. For others, this change in brightness occurs when they grow larger and shrink at intervals.
   3. Astronomers can accurately measure distances to galaxies by monitoring a type of star referred to as a **Cepheid variable.** Cepheid variable stars are about 10,000 times brighter than our sun.
   4. Over time, a Cepheid variable star changes in brightness in a periodic and distinctive way.
   5. During the first part of its cycle, its luminosity increases very rapidly, whereas during the rest of the cycle, the luminosity of the Cepheid decreases slowly.
   6. The distance to a Cepheid can be calculated from its period (the length of its cycle) and its average brightness. In 1908, Henrietta S. Leavitt discovered that the longer the period, the brighter the Cepheid, because the brightness of a Cepheid is proportional to its surface area.
   7. In the 1920s, using measurements taken by observing Cepheids, Edwin P. Hubble established that other galaxies exist beyond our own Milky Way galaxy.
   8. To observe and to calculate distances in the galaxy, astronomers use two devices together, light-measuring devices coupled to large reflecting telescopes such as those at Mauna Kea in Hawaii, Las Campanas in Chile, and Mount Palomar in California.

I. A **nova,** or "new star," is a dim star that suddenly becomes thousands of times more brilliant than it had been previously.
   1. A nova is not really a new star; it only seems to be new because it has suddenly become so conspicuously bright.
   2. Scientists do not know the exact cause of a nova.
   3. Occasionally, an unusually bright nova, in this case called a **supernova,** appears in the sky. A supernova is a catastrophic explosion that marks the death of certain kinds of stars.
   4. One type of supernova is believed to occur in double star (binary) systems in which one of the stars is a very dense object known as a white dwarf. The explosion is triggered when mass from the companion star is transferred to the white dwarf.
   5. A white dwarf packs a mass roughly equal to the sun's within a volume equal to the earth's and therefore produces tremendous gravitational forces at its surfaces, typically 100,000 times the force of gravity on earth.
   6. Because supernovas release tremendous amounts of radiation, astronomers are hoping to be able to observe supernovas as far away as five billion light-years.

J. Star **clusters** are groups of stars held together by their gravitational pull on one another.
   1. Some star clusters are made up of a few stars that are moving in parallel paths. Other star clusters are loose collections of stars called **open clusters.**
   2. **Globular clusters** are shaped like a ball or globe and may contain as many as 100,000 stars.
   3. Clusters that are so large and thick with stars that they look like shining clouds are called **star clouds.**

K. Although stars seem to **twinkle,** they really do not.
   1. Stars are so far away from the earth that they appear only as small dots of light when we look at them with the naked eye.
   2. Movements of the earth's atmosphere caused by heat make the thin rays of light from these distant stars seem to twinkle.

L. Planets do not twinkle either.
   1. Planets are not point sources of light as are stars, but rather reflect light at an angle.
   2. Movements of the earth's atmosphere do not affect these thicker reflected rays of light, so there is no appearance of a twinkle when one is observing a planet with the naked eye.

M. **Pulsars,** first discovered in 1967, are believed to be the dense remnants of collapsed stars, sometimes called **neutron stars.**
   1. Pulsars have very strong magnetic fields.
   2. A pulsar spins on its axis very rapidly, up to 1,000 revolutions per second.
   3. Because of a pulsar's rapid spin, the wave energy emitted by the pulsar is received on earth as a pulsating beacon of energy.

N. **Black holes,** first discovered in 1972, are also believed to be the remnants of stars that have collapsed to a very dense state, with a resultant very strong gravitational field. The gravitational force of a black hole is so strong that no object or form of energy radiation can escape it.

DEMONSTRATION 8.10
Twinkling

To demonstrate the cause of the twinkling effect of stars, you can set up a demonstration similar to that shown in Figure 8.9, as follows. Establish a light image on a screen. This can be done by placing a light source on a pile of books. Place the handle of a magnifying glass (convex lens) in a small lump of clay so that the magnifying glass remains fixed in an upright position. Adjust the height of the magnifying glass so that the center of the lens is at the same height as the bulb. Place the magnifying glass in front of the bulb, between the bulb and the screen, and adjust the position of the glass and screen until a clear image of the bulb appears on the screen. Darken the room. Note that the image is fixed and does not move or twinkle. Now place a hot plate or other heat source close to the lens and below it. The image will tremble or twinkle, just as a star does, because heat energy from the heat source makes the air above move. This movement makes the light rays shift back and forth, or twinkle, as well.

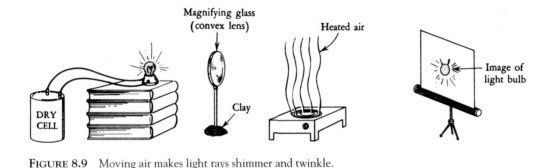

FIGURE 8.9   Moving air makes light rays shimmer and twinkle.

O. **Quasars,** first discovered in 1963, are very distant objects that emit tremendous amounts of light.
   1. Quasars are from 10 to 1,000 times more luminous than our entire galaxy.
   2. It is thought that a quasar represents the vast energy that is given off as matter spirals violently into a massive black hole.
   3. The objects providing fuel for the quasars appear to be giant galaxies.
   4. Discovered in 1992, Quasar PC1247+3406 is the most distant object known in the universe.
   5. One of the many mysteries of quasars is the blobs bursting out of them, seemingly going faster than the speed of light, which is faster than is supposed to be possible.
II. CONSTELLATIONS
   A. Long ago astronomers divided the stars into groups, called **constellations,** which made it easier to describe the location of a given heavenly body. These constellations were named after gods, legendary heroes and heroines, animals, and objects. (Today celestial naming is controlled by the International Astronomical Union.)
   B. The movement of the earth as it turns on its axis makes the constellations seem to move through the sky as if they were on a transparent globe surrounding the earth.
   1. If the earth's axis were extended into space, it would also become the axis for this imaginary globe.
   2. In the earth's northern hemisphere all the constellations seem to move around a point, called the **celestial north pole,** that is directly above the earth's north pole.
   3. In the southern hemisphere all the constellations seem to move around a point called the **celestial south pole,** which is directly above the earth's south pole.
   4. A star located directly on the celestial north or south pole would not seem to move, thus it would serve as an excellent signpost for navigation.
   5. The North Star, called **Polaris,** is so close to the celestial north pole that it does not seem to move at all; thus Polaris has historically

been used as a signpost for navigators. Polaris is the end star in the handle of the constellation known as the **Little Dipper** (see Figure 8.10). Constellations in the northern hemisphere appear to revolve around Polaris.

C. Because the earth is in different positions as it revolves around the sun, different constellations are seen at different times of the year and in varying positions. Moreover, persons living in the northern hemisphere see constellations that are different from those seen by persons living in the southern hemisphere.

D. The sun's path among the constellations during one earth-year is called the **ecliptic.** A strip of sky slightly above and below the sun's path, or ecliptic, is called the **zodiac.** Special names, known as the "signs of the zodiac," one for each month of the year, were given to 12 star formations in the zodiac.

III. GALAXIES

A. A **galaxy** is a large collection of stars, dust, and gas, held together in a group by the pull of gravity. The sun and the solar system are part of one galaxy called the **Milky Way galaxy.**
   1. There are several hundred billion stars in the Milky Way, and their light gives the appearance of a milky band in the sky. Part of the Milky Way galaxy can be seen any clear night as a broad band of light stretching across the sky.

B. With its billions of stars, the Milky Way galaxy forms a spiral shape that is somewhat like a flattened wheel.
   1. The distance across the wheel is about 100,000 **light-years.** That is the distance

light would travel in 100,000 years.
   2. Three spiral arms curve out from the center of the galaxy.
   3. The entire galaxy is rotating around its center at a tremendous speed. The galaxy rotates once around its center in about 250 million years. All stars in the galaxy rotate in the same direction, but at different speeds.
   4. The sun and our solar system are about 26,000 light-years from the center of the Milky Way galaxy, about halfway between the center of the galaxy and its outer edge. The sun and the solar system are moving at a speed of about 225 kilometers (140 mi) a second (504,000 mph) in a circular orbit around the center of the galaxy.
   5. The stars at the outer edge of the galaxy are moving about four times as fast as our solar system.

C. A **nebula** is a great cloud of dust in a galaxy. In each galaxy there are many nebulae.
   1. Nebulae do not give off any light of their own.
   2. Some nebulae are easily seen because they reflect the light from nearby stars. Others are dark because they either cut off the light from stars behind them or because there are no stars nearby to light them.

D. Beyond the Milky Way galaxy there are more than a billion galaxies, all rotating at tremendous speeds.

E. Galaxies are usually found in three shapes: irregular, spiral, and elliptical.
   1. Irregular galaxies have many blue-white stars in them and are probably young galaxies.
   2. Spiral galaxies have a number of spiral arms extending from their centers. In spiral galaxies, there are blue-white giant stars in the arms and red stars toward the center. Many astronomers believe that a spiral galaxy later becomes an irregular one. As the galaxy rotates, spiral arms form and direct the younger blue-white stars toward the center.
   3. Elliptical galaxies are shaped like an oval or ellipse and are smaller than spiral galaxies. Most of the stars of elliptical galaxies are older yellow and red stars. Many astronomers believe that an elliptical galaxy forms from a spiral one, when all the stars in the spiral arms have gathered into the main body of the galaxy.

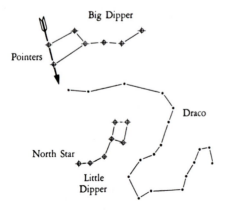

FIGURE 8.10   Finding the North Star.

IV. EXPANDING UNIVERSE

   A. The universe seems to be a tremendous expanse of space that is at least 10 billion light-years across. Scattered over this expanse of space are more than a billion galaxies.
1. Most galaxies are separated from their neighbors by millions of light-years of space.
2. Evidence indicates that galaxies are moving away from each other at great speed. It is believed that the galaxies are moving away from one another as a result of the big bang, the fiery birth of the universe.
3. Galaxies that are farther away from us seem to be traveling faster than those nearer to us.
4. Some galaxies are moving through space at a speed of more than 48,000 kilometers (30,000 mi) a second.
5. This high speed means that the space between galaxies is steadily increasing, while the galaxies themselves remain the same size.
6. Present evidence indicates that the universe is about 15 billion years old, and that its expansion may continue indefinitely.

V. HOW DISTANCES IN THE UNIVERSE ARE MEASURED

   A. Until recently, scientists measured the vast distances in the universe by using a unit of measurement called the **light-year.** Today they speak of the **parsec.**
1. Light travels through space at a speed of about 300,000 kilometers (186,000 mi) a second.
2. A light-year is the distance that light travels in one year.
3. A light-year is about 9,600 billion kilometers (6,000 billion mi). The distance light travels in one year is found by multiplying 300,000 kilometers by 60 seconds, then by 60 minutes, then by 24 hours, and then by 365.25 days. By multiplying this answer by 3.55, the distance traveled in a parsec is obtained. A **parsec** is about 3.33 light-years, or 31,000 trillion kilometers (19 trillion mi).
4. A **megaparsec** is the distance light travels in 3.26 million years.

VI. HOW THE UNIVERSE IS STUDIED

   A. The oldest instruments used in studying the universe are the ocular telescopes—the **refracting** and the **reflecting telescopes.**

   B. Sophisticated electronic telescopes on spacecraft, such as the Space Radar Laboratory that flew on the space shuttle Endeavor in 1994 and the radar system on board the Magellan spacecraft that mapped Venus, and satellites, such as NASA's Extreme Ultraviolet Explorer (EUVE) satellite and the satellite COBE (Cosmic Background Explorer), are providing ever more data about our earth, solar system, galaxy, and universe. For example, in 1995 the ultraviolet telescopes aboard the spaceship Endeavor filmed what is thought to have been the collision of two galaxies that are approximately 90 million light-years away from the earth. These two colliding galaxies involve as many as 20 billion stars, and their diameter is approximately 100,000 light-years.
1. It is believed that galaxy collisions today are less common than they were billions of years ago.
2. A collision, in regard to galaxies, is an event that occurs over millions of years.
3. It will take several years for scientists to scan and analyze all the pictures taken of the collision recorded in 1995.

   C. The **radio telescope** is able to study distant objects by detecting the radio waves given off by these objects.
1. A large radio telescope built by the United States Navy in Sugar Grove, West Virginia, is about 185 meters (600 ft) across.
2. The **Very Large Array** (VLA) radio telescope network in New Mexico is equal to a single radio telescope about 30 kilometers (19 mi) in diameter.
3. At Mauna Kea, in Hawaii, scientists and technicians put together one end of one of the largest radio telescopes in the world, one that is more than 8,000 kilometers (5,000 mi) wide and is called the **Very Long Baseline Array** (VLBA). Like an ant's eye, the VLBA isn't just one viewer, but many. It consists of a string of 10 large antennas that extend from Hawaii to the Virgin Islands, and across the mainland in Washington, California, Arizona, New Mexico, Iowa, Texas, and New Hampshire.
4. The VLBA system is able to view detail of an area 1,000 times greater than any previous optical telescope, and certain chemical compounds will become visible that have never before been seen with other telescopes.
5. Ultimately, the VLBA may be linked up with a European system. The linking of multiple, distant telescopes is called **Very Long Baseline Interferometry** (VLBI).

EXPLORATORY ACTIVITIES FOR "THE UNIVERSE"

1. *A WALK THROUGH THE SOLAR SYSTEM** (GRADES 3 AND UP)

Overview. If the sun were the size of a bowling ball, Neptune would be a peanut, Jupiter would be a chestnut, Mars would be a pinhead, and earth would be a small berry such as the peppercorn (berry of the pepper plant, which is the pepper used in unground pepper). Using this 1:6,336,000,000 scale, the distance from the sun to Pluto would be about 1,000 meters or 1 kilometer.

This model uses everyday objects with which students are familiar to represent the solar system. The sun is a 23 cm sphere, about the size of a bowling ball or beach ball, and Pluto, the smallest planet, is a tiny pin head. Beginning with the sun, your class of students will set off on a walk to pace off the relative distances to each planet and place a representative object where the planet would be located.

Purpose of Model. The purpose of this model is to demonstrate the vast size of the solar system, the relative smallness of the planets, the great distance between planets, and the overall emptiness of space.

Length of Activity and Subject Integration. This activity integrates the student learning of mathematics and science and could take place over several days.

Nature of Learning Activities. While participating in this activity, students work in cooperative groups and engage their verbal, visual, psychomotor, and kinesthetic learning modalities.

Materials Needed
- meter stick, or metric measuring tape, or rolling measuring wheel
- fluorescent paint or chalk or some other type of marker
- balls of various sizes, assorted balloons, peas, peanuts, filberts, walnuts, a bowling ball, straight pins with colored plastic heads of different sizes, almonds, steel shot or bearings of various sizes, and other spherical objects (It doesn't matter if some of the objects are not exactly spherical; see Figure 8.11)
- glue
- golf tees or blocks of wood

*Adapted from Kenneth M. Uslabar, "A Stroll Through the Solar System," *Science Scope* 17(2):41–43 (October 1993), by permission of Kenneth M. Uslabar and the National Science Teachers Association.

Body	Object	Approximate Diameter
Sun	Bowling ball	23 cm
Mercury	Pin head	0.08 cm
Venus	Peppercorn	0.2 cm
Earth	Peppercorn	0.2 cm
Moon	Pin head	0.06 cm
Mars	Pin head	0.1 cm
Jupiter	Chestnut or pecan	2.4 cm
Saturn	Filbert or acorn	2.0 cm
Uranus	Peanut or coffee bean	0.9 cm
Neptune	Peanut or coffee bean	0.8 cm
Pluto	Pin head	0.04 cm

FIGURE 8.11   Objects suggested for a model of the universe.

Preparation.   Before doing anything else, you and a student should pace off the distances, either with a meter stick or tape, or with a rolling measuring wheel. The scale of this model is 1:6,336,000,000, rounded off to 1:6,000,000,000. Thus, each meter-long distance represents 6,000,000 m, each centimeter represents 60,000 km, and the entire model solar system occupies a distance of about 1,000 m.

Select an area for the walk where the class can safely cover a 1,000-meter, relatively straight course, such as a long sidewalk or a field. As you and your student helper measure off the distances, at each planet location, place a marker (water-soluble paint or chalk if you are using a paved surface) and the first letter of the planet's name. Figure 8.12 gives the relative distances of the planets' orbits from one another and their overall distance from the sun.

Body	Distance	Total Distance
Sun	0 m	0 m
Mercury	10 m	10 m
Venus	8 m	18 m
Earth	7 m	25 m
Mars	13 m	38 m
Jupiter	92 m	130 m
Saturn	108 m	238 m
Uranus	240 m	478 m
Neptune	271 m	749 m
Pluto	234 m	983 m

FIGURE 8.12   Planet distance table.

Initiating activity: Before the walk

1. The day before the actual walk, put a number of different spherical objects on a table, such as balls of various sizes, assorted balloons, peas, peanuts, filberts, walnuts, a bowling ball, straight pins with colored plastic heads of different sizes, almonds, steel shot of various sizes, and other spherical objects. Explain that the bowling ball will represent the sun; ask students to choose appropriately sized objects to represent the planets.

2. Have groups of students glue or press the selected objects onto blocks of wood or golf tees and mark each with the planet's name. Affix the pin head representing the moon to Earth's block approximately 6.4 cm from Earth, to show its relative distance.

3. Several days in advance of the walk, assign groups of students to research planets and then report their findings as "expert" astronomers to other groups in mini-workshops during the walk.

Day of the walk

4. On the day of the walk, hand out a worksheet (see Figure 8.13) to each student, similar to the planet-distance table, but with blank spaces where the distances between planets and total distances are given and another column for students to record information given during the mini-workshops. Instruct students to count the number of paces it takes them to get to each planet during the walk, so that they can relate the size of the solar system to the length of their individual pace. When groups of students give their planetary or solar reports, students can make notes on their work sheets in the "Characteristics" column. The work sheets help students keep track of their paces, to organize and record information, and keeps them on task during the long walks from planet to planet.

The walk should begin at the sun. You may want to stagger the start of small groups of students, perhaps beginning with the Pluto astronomers.

You can assign various students to carry the sun and planet models, perhaps as groups responsible for a particular body, and to place them in their appropriate locations. Normally, the entire walk takes about 45 minutes, depending on the amount of discussion and explanation.

Here are some additional comments and focus questions that may be brought up by you or the workshop groups during the walk:

- *Sun:* The sun is the source of heat and light for the entire solar system. Keep the size of the bowling ball in mind throughout the walk and mentally compare it with the sizes of the planets.

- *Mercury:* With Mercury's orbit so close to the sun, what do you suppose it would be like to visit Mercury?

- *Venus:* Can you see the sun from Venus? Can you see Mercury from Venus?

- *Earth:* This little peppercorn is our home. It is the only place we know of in the solar system where life exists.

- *Moon:* The moon is the only body in the solar system that humans have visited directly. Compare the distance from Earth to the moon with the distance from Earth to other planets.

- *Mars:* Standing at the Red Planet, look back toward the sun. Can you see it? Can you see Earth? You can also remind the students that between Mars and Jupiter there are thousands of asteroids.

- *Jupiter:* Did you get through the asteroid belt OK? (In the model, Jupiter is about a city block from its nearest neighbor.) Think of all the empty space we have traveled.

- *Saturn:* Herschel's discovery of Uranus in 1781 effectively doubled the size of the solar system as we knew it, but we are still only halfway to Pluto.

- *Uranus:* This was the last of the planets known to the ancients. Think of all the space we have come through to arrive here. What is the total number of your paces now? We are about to walk that entire distance *again* just to get to the next planet, Neptune.

- *Neptune:* Neptune was discovered in 1846. Can you see the sun from here? Can you see any other planet in our model?

- *Pluto:* This is the last known planet in the solar system. Pluto's eccentric orbit and rocky composition lead some to believe it is a captured body that was not formed with the rest of our solar system. Right now (if you are doing this activity prior to 1999), Pluto actually isn't the outermost planet in the solar system. Because of Pluto's highly eccentric orbit, Neptune will be the outermost planet until 1999. Can you see the sun from here?

Once your students reach Pluto, ask if anyone knows how far they would have to walk to get to the nearest star, other than the sun. The answer: 6,700 km. You can reinforce the reason that planets *rarely* align with one another and discuss the fact that the planets all move at different speeds.

Body	Distance	Total Distance	Characteristics
Sun			
Mercury			
Venus			
Earth			
Mars			
Jupiter			
Saturn			
Uranus			
Neptune			
Pluto			

FIGURE 8.13   Student worksheet for the walk.

After the walk

When back in the classroom, you can review the amazing observations made about the size of the solar system. Students will probably be surprised to find, for example, that it is difficult to see Earth, even from Mars, and they will wonder how sunlight can reach the outer planets inasmuch as they could not even see the sun from there. Compare the number of paces of different students and help them understand that no matter how long or short their paces, they all walked a great distance. Students know that the solar system is vast, but until they experience this model, many never realize just how vast and empty the solar system really is.

2. STUDYING THE ELLIPTICAL SHAPE OF A PLANET'S ORBIT* (GRADES 3 AND UP)

Overview. Science and mathematics are partners in making discoveries about the universe. Orbiting planets, moons, comets, and asteroids follow invisible non-

*From Michael B. Leyden, "Three Big Ideas Going Around and Around," *Teaching K–8*, 23(5):34–35 (February 1993). Reprinted with permission of the publisher, *Teaching K–8*, Norwalk, CT 06854.

circular paths, called ellipses. Students can construct and examine the ellipse. A good way to begin studying the ellipse is for you to diagram one at the writing board while the students follow along with smaller versions at their desks.

Materials Needed. Students: one set of two pushpins, string, paper, and cardboard for every pair of students Teacher: two small sink plungers (suction cups sometimes known as "plumbers' helpers") and some string

Activity. Wet the edge of one suction cup to form a seal and then "whap" it to the middle of the writing board—hard. From the handle, hang a loop of string that's shorter than the top and bottom limits of the board. Put a piece of chalk at the end of the loop and draw a circle on the board.

Then "whap" the other suction cup to the board, about 20 to 40 cm to the left or right of the first plunger. Stretch the string over the other handle and ask the students to guess what the "circle" will look like this time. Make the drawing with the chalk, but hold off naming the resultant figure. Students may call it "an egg," "a circle that got sat on" (see Figure 8.14).

Pairs of students can then make smaller ovals at their desks. See Figure 8.15. What happens to the oval if the pins are moved farther apart? closer together?

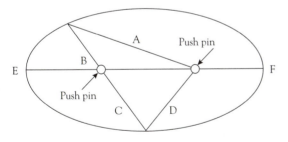

FIGURE 8.14 This diagram, which shows the A + B = C + D = EF, is a visual definition of an ellipse.

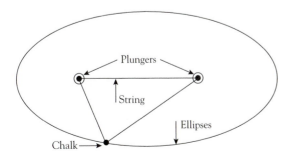

FIGURE 8.15 Two small plungers, string, chalk, and a chalkboard are all you need to draw an ellipse.

Concept Introduction—Student Activity. This shape is called an ellipse. Ellipses have a unique property that students can discover with a ruler. Have them make a new ellipse on a separate sheet of paper, then measure the line that passes through both push pins (line EF in Figure 8.14). This is the major axis, the longest line that can be drawn in an ellipse. Next ask the students to draw lines from any spot on the ellipse to each of the holes left by the pushpins. When they add the lengths of these two lines together, they'll find that the sum equals the length of the major axis. Have them try it again with two lines drawn from another point on the ellipse.

This discovery leads to the definition of an ellipse: a curved figure in which the sum of two lines, drawn from a point on the curve to the two points used to draw the ellipse, is a constant number.

Concept Application. Ellipses, not circles, are the curved figures most commonly seen by people every day. Whenever a circle is viewed off-center, an ellipse is seen. Once a person has been trained to look for noncircles, they see ellipses everywhere—even in cylindrical drinking glasses. Pour some water in a glass and have students tip the glass as if they were going to take a drink. The water's surface in a tipped cylindrical glass has an elliptical shape.

When the next space shuttle is launched, look in the newspaper for its orbital data. You'll find the astronaut's distance from the earth reported as being anywhere from 356 to 563 km (221 to 350 mi). The distance varies because even the shuttle's orbit is elliptical. If it were a circular orbit, the distance would be constant.

3. EXPLORING SHADOWS (ANY GRADE LEVEL)

Overview. Incorporating several process skills (e.g., observing, measuring, recording, graphing) and integrating their learning of mathematics and science, the study of shadows is always of interest to students. Take students out on the school grounds to study their own shadows.

Procedure. Have the students, working in pairs, stand with their backs to the sun and observe their shadows. Have them do this three times during the day: once in the early morning, again at noon, and once again in the late afternoon.

- Young children can discover the kinds of shadows they can make with their bodies at these different times of the day; make shadows with different objects, such as umbrellas and boxes; outline shadows at different times of the day and compare their outlines; and play shadow tag.

■ Older students can measure, record, and graph their own height, the lengths of their own shadows, and the direction in which their shadows are pointing (N, S, E, or W) for each of these three periods of time. Use record sheets as shown in Figure 8.16.

Have students share their record sheets, first in their working pairs, then in groups of four, then as a whole class.

Students will note that the lengths of their shadows vary according to whether the sun's light is striking their bodies at a slant or vertically. They will also note that the direction in which the top (head) of a shadow is pointing changes from morning to afternoon.

Follow-up and Application. Students can then be led into a discussion of what value this information might be. Could their body heights be calculated according to the lengths of their shadows? Could the height of a tall object (tree or building or pole in the play yard) be determined as well? Is more heat generated from the more direct rays? Could the time of day be determined according to the lengths of their shadows? If lost in the wilderness, could a hiker determine direction and time of day by examining shadows? Would that information be of help to the hiker? Perhaps students would like to make a sundial to be used on the school grounds, or individual sundials so that each child can take one home to share with family members.

Name _____

My height _____

	Length of shadow	*Direction the top is pointing*
Morning	_____	_____
Noon	_____	_____
Afternoon	_____	_____

My conclusions from this experiment:

My conclusions after sharing the results with others:

Questions I have as a result of this experiment and the sharing:

FIGURE 8.16   Student record sheet for the study of shadows.

STUDENT BOOKS AND OTHER RESOURCES FOR "THE UNIVERSE"

Banks, D. A. Earth, Sun, and Moon: A Moving Experience."
Science Scope 17(4):36–41 (January 1994).

Bulla, C. R. *What Makes a Shadow?* New York: HarperCollins,
1994.

Jay, J. " 'Interactive' Display Case." *Science Activities* 31(1):34–35
(Spring 1994).

Kennedy, A. "Your Guide to the Stars." *Teaching Pre K–8*
24(5):60 (February 1994).

Kindersley, D. *The Visual Dictionary of the Universe*. New York:
Dorling Kindersley, 1993.

Lebofsky, N. R. "A Skunk Is in the Sky (or Is It a Plow?)."
Science Scope 17(6):26–30 (March 1994).

Moore, G. R. "Revisiting Science Concepts." *Science and
Children* 32(3):31–32, 60. (November/December 1994).

National Science and Technology Week. "The View from
Here." *Science Scope* 18(7):Instructional Foldout (April
1995).

Newcott, W. "Venus Revealed." *National Geographic*
183(2):36–59 (February 1993).

Reston, J., Jr., "Orim: Where Stars Are Born." *National
Geographic* 188(6):90–101 (December 1995).

Schatz, D. *Astronomy Activity Book.* Arlington, VA: National
Science Teachers Association, 1991.

Simon, S. *Comets, Meteors, and Asteroids.* New York: Morrow,
1994.

Smith, B. "New Eyes on the Universe." *National Geographic*
185(1):2–41 (January 1994).

Smith, P. S. *Project Earth Science: Astronomy.* Arlington, VA:
National Science Teachers Association, 1992.

Sorge, C. "Capturing the Sun's Energy." *Science Scope*
18(8):27–29 (May 1995).

Weissman, D. B., and Tremper, C. B. "A Conversation with
Constellations." *Science and Children* 31(4):16–19, 44
(January 1994).

Whitney, D. E. "The Case of the Misplaced Planets." *Science
and Children* 32(5):12–14, 46 (February 1995).

CHAPTER 9

The Earth

The Composition of the Earth

I. How and When the Earth Was Formed

A. Evidence indicates that the earth was formed from the same materials and in the same way as the sun. Evidence indicates that the beginning, referred to as the "big bang," occurred about 15 billion years ago.
   1. From an accumulation of materials that resulted from the big bang, the earth's beginning occurred about 4.5 billion years ago.
   2. Prior to the Apollo space program in the 1960s, it was thought that Earth and the other rocky planets, Mercury, Venus, and Mars, were created by the rapid collapse of a dust cloud.
B. The Apollo's space program studies of moon craters revealed that the craters were caused by the impact of objects that were in great abundance about 4.5 billion years ago, after which the number of impacts quickly diminished.
   1. In 1944, the Russian geophysicist Otto Schmidt postulated that planets grew in size gradually, by **accretion.**
   2. According to the accretion theory, cosmic dust that resulted from the big bang lumped together over time to form fine particles called **particulates.**
   3. Particulates became gravel, gravel became small balls, then big balls, then tiny planets, meteorites, or **planetesimals,** and, finally, what began as dust became the size of the moon.
   4. As the planetesimals became larger, their numbers became fewer and the number of collisions between planetesimals diminished.
C. Large meteorites, however, continued to slam into the new earth, causing immense heat in the earth's interior.
   1. This heat caused a furnace effect deep in the earth's interior, creating molten material, what is referred to as a **magma ocean.**
   2. The magma ocean was active for millions of years, giving rise to volcanic eruptions.
   3. Heat at the surface, caused by volcanism and lava flows from the interior of the earth, was supplemented by a continuing bombardment of large meteorites, some of them thought to be as large as our moon or even as large as Mars.
   4. **Isotope geology,** the study of the radioisotopes found in rocks, is the primary tool that has permitted scientists to determine that the accretion of the earth culminated in the differentiation of the earth: the creation of the core, the source of the earth's magnetic field, and the beginning of the earth's atmosphere.
   5. Claire Patterson, in 1953, used the uranium-lead clock to establish an age of approximately 4.5 billion years for the earth and many of the meteorites that formed it.
   6. More recently, scientists have concluded that the bombardment by meteorites continued for up to 150 million years; then, about 4.4 billion years ago, the earth began to retain its atmosphere and create its core.

D. The emergence of **continents,** large land masses, came later, perhaps about 4.2 billion years ago.
   1. In Greenland, rock was found that is about 3.75 billion years old; rock was found in North America that is nearly 4 billion years old; and rock found in Western Australia is about 4.2 billion years old, the oldest rock discovered yet.
   2. Although records of early life would have been destroyed by early geologic activity, the earliest evidence of life on earth consists of fossils of a blue-green bacterium, found in Australia and South Africa. These bacteria lived about 3.5 billion years ago.

II. EVOLUTION OF THE EARTH'S ATMOSPHERE

A. Evidence indicates that the earth's terrestrial atmosphere was created by gases emerging from the planet's interior, similar to volcanic gases escaping today.
   1. The earth's early atmosphere was mostly carbon dioxide, with nitrogen as the second most abundant gas.
   2. The early atmosphere also contained sufficient quantities of ammonia and methane to give rise to organic matter, which in turn evolved into the earliest life forms on earth.
   3. Scientists are undecided as to our sun's energy output during the earth's early life, a problem important to resolve so as to more fully understand the evolution of the earth. Evidence indicates that between 4.5 and 2.5 billion years ago, the sun's power output was only 75 percent of what it is today.
   4. Many theories have been put forth to explain how life developed on earth in this early cold atmosphere that was rich in carbon dioxide but lacking in oxygen.
   5. Although some aquatic microorganisms, such as chemosynthetic bacteria, can thrive in a carbon-dioxide-rich and oxygen-poor environment, the presence of oxygen in the atmosphere was necessary before life could begin to flourish on land. Evidence indicates that oxygen reached its present level in the earth's atmosphere less than 2 billion years ago.
B. The presence of atmospheric oxygen allows the formation of **ozone.**
   1. Ozone forms when the sun's ultraviolet (UV) radiation, which is deadly to life forms on land, splits oxygen molecules into the unstable atomic form O, which can combine back into O_2 and into the very special molecule O_3, or ozone.
   2. Ozone absorbs ultraviolet radiation, making possible life on land.
C. Although a fairly stable level of oxygen in the atmosphere was reached about 1 to 2 billion years ago, the earth's climate was not uniform.
   1. There were long stages of relative warmth and coolness.
   2. The composition of fossilized shells of plankton that lived near the ocean floor indicates that over the past 100 million years, bottom waters of the oceans have cooled by nearly 15° Celsius.
   3. Sea levels dropped by hundreds of meters, and continents drifted apart.
   4. Inland seas mostly disappeared, and the climate cooled an average of 10° to 15° Celsius.
   5. Approximately 20 million years ago permanent ice built up on Antarctica.
   6. Approximately 2 to 3 million years ago there were significant expansions and contractions of warm and cold periods in cycles of about 40,000 years. The 40,000-year cycle or periodicity corresponds to the time it takes the earth to complete an oscillation of the tilt of its axis of rotation.
   7. This change in the earth's orbital geometry could alter the amount of sunlight in winter versus summer and could be responsible for starting or ending ice ages.
   8. Between 600,000 and 800,000 years ago this periodicity switched from 40,000-year periods to 100,000-year intervals between fluctuations.
   9. The last major phase of glaciation ended about 10,000 years ago.
   10. At its peak, 20,000 years ago, ice sheets a mile thick covered much of northern Europe and North America. These massive ice sheets revamped the face of the earth, which was 5° Celsius cooler that it is today.
D. In terms of where life is found today, scientists divide the earth into **spheres.** The **atmosphere** is the sphere of gases that surround the earth. The **hydrosphere** is the sphere that consists of the bodies of water. The **lithosphere** is the sphere consisting of the earth's solid surface mass. These three spheres make up the parts of the earth where life is found, called the **biosphere.**

III. THE LITHOSPHERE AND BELOW

A. The earth's crust, or lithosphere, is a very thin outer layer of rock, mostly granite and basalt.
   1. The raised parts of the rock form the earth's continents, and the low parts form the oceans' floors.
   2. The crust is thickest beneath the continents, as much as 48 kilometers (30 mi) thick. It is thinnest beneath the oceans, as thin as 11 kilometers (7 mi).
B. Tremendous forces inside the earth continue to act on the crust, causing it to bend and crack, producing mountains, earthquakes, and volcanic activity.
C. In the earth's crust are found soil, water, coal, oil, gas, and minerals.
D. Except for hydrogen and helium, which escape from the earth's gravitational pull, the elements of the earth are the elements of the universe, formed by stars and dispersed throughout the galaxy.
E. Although there are at least 90 chemical elements found in the earth's crust, just 5 of these elements make up about 92 percent of the crust's weight.
   1. Oxygen makes up about 47 percent of the crust's weight. It is found in air, water, sand, quartz, limestone, clay, and other materials.
   2. Silicon makes up about 28 percent of the crust's weight. It is found in sand, quartz, clay, and other materials.
   3. Aluminum is the earth's most abundant metal, making up 8 percent of the crust's weight. It is found in clay and other materials.
   4. Iron makes up about 5 percent of the crust's weight. It is usually found combined with oxygen and sulfur.
   5. Calcium makes up about 4 percent of the crust's weight. It is usually found in limestone and other materials.
F. Beneath the lithosphere is the mantle, or middle layer of the earth's solid mass, known as the **asthenosphere** (see Figure 9.1).
   1. The boundary between the crust and the mantle is called the **Moho.**
   2. The mantle extends to a depth of about 2,900 kilometers (1,800 mi).
   3. The mantle is made up of rock, called **peridotite,** which is heavier than the basalt and granite of the crust.
   4. The mantle is very hot, but the rock in it is solid rather than liquid because of the high pressures exerted on it.

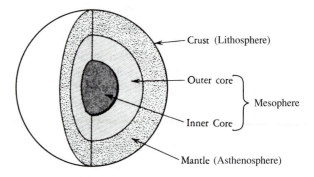

FIGURE 9.1   Model of the earth's layers.

   5. When deep cracks are formed in the earth's crust, the pressure on the mantle is reduced, and the solid rock then turns into liquid.
G. Beneath the earth's mantle is the third and final layer, the earth's core or **mesosphere.**
   1. The core is about 7,000 kilometers (4,400 mi) in diameter. That is, it goes down about 3,500 kilometers (2,200 mi) to the center of the earth.
   2. The core is a mixture of about 90 percent iron and 10 percent nickel.
   3. The core is divided into the outer and the inner cores. The inner core extends about 1,280 kilometers (800 mi) from the center of the earth and is solid. The outer core is about 2160 kilometers (1350 mi) thick and is plastic; that is, it is less solid.
   4. The deeper we go toward the center of the earth, the higher the temperature. In mines and oil wells, for example, the temperature rises about 1° Celsius (2° F) for every 36 meters (120 ft) of depth. The temperature of the mantle may be as high as 1,600° Celsius (2,880° F). The temperature of the core may be as high as 4,500° C (8,100° F).

IV. ROCK

A. The earth's crust is made up of great masses of hard material called rock. Rock is a natural combination of two or more minerals into a solid mass called an **aggregate.** Large rock masses can be several miles thick. Smaller rocks and boulders are simply pieces that were broken off from the larger masses.
   1. Much of the rock on the earth's surface is covered by soil.
B. Although there are many different kinds of rocks, they can be divided into three major groups, according to the way in which they

formed. These are **igneous, sedimentary,** and **metamorphic.**

C. **Igneous** (which means "formed from fire") **rock** is formed from molten material (magma) in or below the earth's crust.

1. Magma forms when pressure below the earth's crust changes. When the pressure is reduced, the solid material in the earth's mantle becomes liquid magma, which may then work its way upward through cracks or breaks in the layers of rock lying above it, and flow out. Flowing magma is called **lava.**

2. The heat and pressure of the flowing magma may also cause the rock above it to move, break up, or even melt, which makes room for the magma to rise.

3. Rock formed from magma that reaches the earth's surface and then cools is called **extrusive rock.** Extrusive rocks are either glassy or made up of very fine crystals. The lava cools so quickly that large crystals do not have opportunity to form.

4. Rock formed from magma that could not reach the earth's surface and therefore cooled below the surface is called **intrusive rock.** It is coarser than is extrusive rock and may have large crystals, because the magma cooled more slowly.

D. **Granite** is the most common igneous intrusive rock and is used in the construction of roads, buildings, and monuments.

1. It is easily recognized by its speckled appearance, caused by the presence of three minerals—quartz, feldspar, and mica.

2. Quartz has glasslike crystals that are usually colorless or milky.

3. Feldspar can be most any color, but most often is white.

4. Mica can also be any color, but most often is shiny brown or black.

E. **Basalt** is an igneous extrusive rock. It is dark colored and heavier than granite.

1. The earth's continents consist of huge masses of lighter granite lying on a foundation of heavier basalt.

F. **Pumice** and **obsidian** are igneous extrusive rocks formed from magma or lava given off by erupting volcanoes.

1. Pumice comes from lava that comprised many hot gases. The lava cooled so quickly that the gases did not have time to escape and were trapped inside the cooled lava, thus forming a light-colored spongy rock.

2. Because of the many trapped gases, some samples of pumice are so light they can float on water.

3. Obsidian, black and glassy with a chemical composition similar to that of glass, is another form of lava that cooled very quickly.

G. **Sedimentary rocks** were formed from different sediments that accumulated for thousands of years and then cemented tightly together.

1. One kind of sediment that forms sedimentary rocks includes such materials as sand, clay, silt, pebbles, and gravel.

2. Streams and rivers carry these sedimentary materials to lakes or oceans, where they settle to the bottom.

3. As the sediment accumulates, layers are formed which slowly change to solid rock as the weight of the upper layers presses the sediment of the lower layers tightly together.

4. At the same time, chemicals that are already dissolved in the water begin to deposit out again on and between the particles of sediment, filling in the tiny spaces between particles and cementing them firmly together.

5. Conglomerate, sandstone, and shale are examples of sedimentary rock.

6. **Conglomerate** is made of pebbles and gravel that cemented together.

7. **Sandstone** is made of grains of sand that cemented together.

8. The material that cemented the sand determines the color and hardness of the sandstone. Sandstone may be red, brown, yellow, or very light colored. It can be very soft, or it can be hard enough to use as a building material.

9. **Shale** is clay or mud that became sedimentary rock.

10. Because clay is made of fine, flaky material, shale usually can be split easily into flat, thin pieces. Shale is often gray or green, but may also be red, blue, purple, or black.

11. Another kind of sediment that forms sedimentary rock includes the remains of organisms that live in the oceans and form shells or skeletons of calcium carbonate. As these organisms die, their shells and skeletons accumulate and then harden to form great beds of calcium carbonate, commonly called **limestone.** Limestone formed from the remains of coral and

DEMONSTRATION 9.1
Extrusive and Intrusive Crystals

Obtain alum in a drugstore. Dissolve as much alum as possible in each of two beakers almost full of hot water. Place one beaker in the refrigerator or surround it with ice so that the solution cools as quickly as possible. Place the other beaker in a quiet corner of the room and allow it to stand overnight. Examine the crystals from both solutions the next day. The crystals from the alum solution that was cooled quickly are rather fine and small, like extrusive crystals, because the solution was cooled so quickly that large crystals were unable to form. The crystals from the alum solution that was allowed to cool slowly are much coarser and larger, like intrusive crystals, because the solution cooled gradually and allowed large crystals to form.

---

other tiny organisms that live in clear, warm, shallow water is fine, nearly pure, calcium carbonate.

12. Limestone has also formed from the shells of larger animals such as clams, oysters, and mussels, in which case the limestone is much coarser and may contain pieces of shell. This type of limestone may also have sand and clay mixed in it.

13. **Chalk** is a soft, porous form of limestone, made of the shells of tiny organisms that lived millions of years ago.

14. Another kind of material that forms sedimentary rock includes chemicals that are dissolved in the ocean water, such as salt and calcium carbonate. Conditions in the oceans often change so that the water in certain parts of the ocean can no longer hold these chemicals; therefore, they deposit out and form accumulations that later harden into rock. **Rock salt** is formed from salt that once was dissolved in ocean water. A very pure and fine form of limestone is formed from calcium carbonate that deposited out of ocean water.

15. Sedimentary rocks often have the fossil remains of early organisms embedded in them.

16. Iron and other metal ores sometimes accumulate as sediment and are then found in sedimentary rock.

17. **Soft coal** is sedimentary rock formed from the remains of plants that died long ago and accumulated in a swamp. They were covered by other sediment to form layers, which were then changed by heat and pressure into a rocky material.

H. **Metamorphic** (which means "change in form") **rocks** are igneous and sedimentary rocks that were changed by heat and pressure.

1. Some changes were physical, whereby the original materials in the rock were only rearranged. Other changes were chemical, whereby new materials were formed.

2. Common metamorphic rocks are gneiss, quartzite, slate, marble, and hard coal.

3. **Gneiss,** a coarse rock that contains parallel streaks or bands of minerals, is commonly formed from igneous granite and from many other kinds of igneous or sedimentary rocks.

4. **Quartzite** is a very hard rock formed from sedimentary sandstone.

5. Formed from sedimentary shale, **slate** is a fine-grained rock that splits easily into thin sheets.

6. **Marble** is a large-crystal rock formed from sedimentary limestone.

7. **Hard coal**, formed from soft coal, contains much more carbon than soft coal.

8. Hard coal is also changed by further heat and pressure to **graphite.** Graphite is pure carbon.

I. Although geologic activity, erosion, and metamorphism have destroyed most all of the most ancient rocks, continents and their rock formations still provide much valuable data regarding the earth's earliest history.

1. Dating rocks using **radioactive clocks** allows isotope geochemists to study the most ancient rocks, those without fossil evidence.

2. The "hands" of a radioactive clock are isotopes, atoms of the same element that have different atomic weights. Geologic time is measured by the rate of decay of one isotope into another (see Figure 16.2).

V. Minerals

A. Rocks are made up of two or more minerals. Minerals are solid materials made of one or more chemical elements, having an orderly arrangement of atoms and therefore a definite crystal structure.

B. Minerals are *not* made of organisms, nor do they come from organisms.

 1. For this reason, a **pearl,** even though it is a chemical compound, is not considered a mineral, because it was produced by an organism—the oyster.

 2. For the same reason, coal is not a mineral because it was formed from plant materials.

D. **Ore** is rock that contains enough of a particular mineral to make it economically worthwhile to mine.

E. Minerals are classified into groups according to the kinds of chemicals they contain and the structure of their crystals.

 1. One group of minerals includes those that contain the chemical element silicon, and makes up about 40 percent of the minerals on earth. Members of this group, called the **silicate minerals,** include quartz, feldspar, mica, hornblende, augite, garnet, olivine, and talc. The minerals found in granite rock, which makes up 90 percent of the earth's crust, are found in this group. **Olivine,** the most abundant mineral of the earth's upper mantle, is playing a significant role today in the study of earthquakes.

 2. Another group of minerals includes those considered to be nonmetallic, the **nonmetallic minerals,** although some members of this group contain chemical elements, such as calcium and magnesium, which, chemically, are metals. Examples of nonmetallic minerals are calcite, dolomite, sulfur, rock salt, gypsum, apatite, fluorite, and graphite.

 3. A third group of minerals includes those that contain the common metal ores, and this group is called the **metal ore minerals.** It includes gold, silver, iron, copper, lead, zinc, tin, aluminum, mercury, titanium, and uranium.

 4. A fourth group of minerals includes those that are made into precious and semiprecious stones. These minerals, called the **gem minerals,** include opal, jade, garnet, topaz, tourmaline, emerald, aquamarine, ruby, amethyst, sapphire, zircon, and diamond. Because zircon is not dissolved during erosion but is deposited as sediment, it can survive for billions of years. In recent years, as a signpost for better understanding the age of rocks and for determining when life first appeared on earth, scientists have been searching for the mineral zircon and studying the continental rocks where it is found.

VI. **IDENTIFICATION OF MINERALS**

A. Many tests are used to absolutely identify a mineral. Only rarely can a mineral be identified by a single test.

 1. The mineral is scratched, and the color of a fresh surface of the mineral is examined. Rather than a dull or tarnished surface that has been exposed to the air and soil, a fresh surface is more likely to display the true color of the mineral. This is the **color test.**

 2. A **streak test** is done by examining the color produced when the mineral is rubbed against a piece of unglazed porcelain tile, called a streak plate. Nonmetallic minerals usually produce a colorless or a light-colored streak, whereas metallic minerals often produce a dark streak that may differ from the visible color of the mineral.

 3. Another test has to do with the **luster** of the mineral, that is the shine the mineral has when light strikes it. Such terms as *dull, pearly, silky, metallic, glassy,* and *brilliant* or *diamondlike* are commonly used to describe the luster of a mineral.

 4. Scientists also examine the **crystal form** of the mineral. Most minerals are made of crystals, showing that the atoms in the minerals are arranged in regular or definite patterns. These crystals have distinct forms, such as square, double triangle, cube, and pyramid.

 5. Minerals are examined also according to how they split or break when struck. This is referred to as the **cleavage test.** For example, some minerals may split into thin sheets (as does mica), into cubes (as does galena), or into an eight-sided cleavage (as does fluorite).

 6. Another test for minerals is the **hardness test.** Because there is such a wide difference in the hardness of minerals, certain minerals are used as standards of hardness. All others are then compared with these standards. The standard minerals are arranged in a scale, in which they are listed in the order of their hardness, with the softest listed first.

 7. A commonly used scale of hardness is the **Mohs' scale of hardness.** Mohs' scale lists 10 minerals, arranged in the order of hardness, with each mineral being harder than those with lower numbers that come before it. See Figure 9.2. Talc, one of the softest minerals, is first in the scale, and diamond, the hardest

Test	Hardness Number	Sample Mineral
Mineral is scratched by fingernail	1	Talc
Mineral is scratched by fingernail	2	Gypsum
Mineral is scratched by a copper penny	3	Calcite
Mineral is scratched easily by a knife blade	4	Fluorite
Mineral is scratched by a knife blade	5	Apatite
Mineral will easily scratch glass	6	Orthoclase
Mineral will scratch glass	7	Quartz
Mineral will scratch most other minerals	8	Topaz
Mineral will scratch topaz	9	Corundum
Mineral will scratch all other minerals	10	Diamond

FIGURE 9.2   Classifying minerals by Moh's hardness scale.

of all minerals, is last. Mineral hardness is determined by using one mineral to make scratches on another. For example, apatite, 5, is harder than fluorite, 4, but softer than orthoclase, 6. Any mineral that scratches apatite, but not orthoclase, is said to have a Mohs' scale hardness of between 5 and 6. The mineral would also scratch all minerals with hardness numbers lower than apatite, but none of those with hardness numbers higher than orthoclase.

    8. Minerals can also be determined by testing their **specific gravity,** or density. This is done by weighing a mineral in the air and then suspended in water. The weight in the air, divided by the difference in weight while in water, is called the specific gravity.

B. There are many other tests that are used for mineral identification.

    1. Some minerals, such as lodestone or magnetite, are magnetic and will be attracted by a magnet.

    2. Some minerals, such as sulfur, will become electrically charged when rubbed or squeezed.

    3. When exposed to ultraviolet light, some minerals give off a fluorescent glow.

    4. Many fluorescent minerals are also phosphorescent, and will give off light after an ultraviolet light has been turned off.

    5. Some minerals, such as uranium, are radioactive, which is detected with a Geiger counter.

    6. When a drop of dilute hydrochloric acid is placed on a mineral containing calcium carbonate, a chemical reaction occurs and bubbles of carbon dioxide gas are given off.

    7. Some minerals give a special color to a flame when a bit of such a powdered mineral, which has first been moistened with hydrochloric acid, is placed on one end of a clean platinum wire and thrust into a Bunsen burner flame.

    8. Certain minerals will give a special color to powdered borax that has been put on one end of a clean platinum wire and heated to form a small glassy bead; the color changes when some of the powdered mineral is put on the bead and the bead is thrust into a flame that has been made hotter with a blowpipe.

VII. CONSERVATION OF MINERAL RESOURCES

A. For economic reasons, mineral resources are grouped in three categories: metals, nonmetals, and fossil fuels.

    1. Metals include such materials as iron, aluminum, lead, zinc, copper, and silver.

    2. Nonmetals include limestone, marble, quartz, slate, and phosphates.

    3. Fossil fuels include coal, oil, and natural gas.

B. Minerals are fixed resources; that is, once removed from the earth, they are gone forever except when meteorites hit the earth's surface. Because minerals can hardly be replaced and because we use more minerals each year, the problem of conserving our mineral resources becomes increasingly important.

    1. Metals must be used wisely and efficiently.

    2. Alternate materials must be developed.

    3. Economically effective ways are being found to extract metals from low-grade ores.

    4. New deposits of minerals are being searched for on earth and eventually will be searched for on other celestial bodies.

5. We must continue to improve efforts at recycling reclaimable materials such as glass and aluminum.
6. Coal is still in ample supply to last many years, but alternate and cleaner fuels must be developed and used. Supplies of coal, oil, and natural gas will not last forever.

C. Coal is our nation's primary energy source, accounting for one-third of total energy production.
   1. From 1970 through 1990, coal mining in the United States increased 72 percent and has more than doubled since 1980.
   2. The electric utility industry uses 80 percent of all coal mined.

3. Satellites and the NAVSTAR Global Positioning System help locate potential coal-mining sites. With refined sensors and computers, satellites can measure distances of up to 25 miles to within an inch or less accuracy.
4. Coal mining today relies heavily on the use of sophisticated machinery, including robotics, lasers, and computers.
5. Surface mining accounts for more than half of U.S. coal mining.
6. Restoring the land that has been surface mined is an important component of the surface mining industries.
7. Today's coal mining and use relies heavily on the concept of clean coal technology.

Forces That Shape and Change the Earth's Surface

I. Plate Tectonics
   A. Above the earth's metallic core lies a slowly churning mantle of rock kept in a plastic state by heat and pressure.
      1. The mantle is topped by the cold, rigid crust of continents and ocean floors.
      2. Mantle rock continuously rises toward the crust, cools, and then sinks.
      3. This continuous motion has cracked the earth's thick crust into about 20 rocky slabs, or plates.
      4. These plates slowly drift on the mantle, causing the movement of continents.
      5. Plates separate at **rifts,** where the plastic rock of the mantle, freed of overlying pressure, liquefies into magma and rises to the surface as lava.
      6. Plates collide at **subduction zones,** where the heavier plate is forced down into the mantle. It is the collision of plates that causes earthquakes.
      7. This movement of plates, called **plate tectonics,** offers a theory about how continents have moved together and apart several times during earth's history, and why similar fossils and related organisms can be found on continents that are today widely separated.

II. Earthquakes
   A. Earthquakes occur at subduction zones when faulting, and sometimes folding, takes place. (See **folded mountains** and **fault-block mountains** in part IV that follows.)

1. The great plates of rock that lie next to a fault are pressed tightly together.
2. These plates are under great stress because one is usually being pushed in one direction while the other is pushed in the opposite direction.
3. After many years of increasing strain there is a sudden movement as the plates slide and then come to rest in a new position that eases the pressure.
4. The plates may move up and down, sideways, or up and over each other, or they may even pull away from each other.
5. With this sudden movement a series of violent vibrations occurs that can shake large land masses for a period of many seconds.
6. The movement may be very slight, but it may set up earthquake vibrations that can destroy a city, as in the 1976 earthquake that killed a half million people and devastated the city of Tangshan in China.
7. The point on the earth's surface above the place where the shifting takes place is called the earthquake's **epicenter.**

   B. Sometimes earthquakes occur just below the surface, and sometimes they occur inside the earth.
      1. Most earthquakes occur within 70 kilometers (43 mi) of the earth's surface as a result of the fracturing and sliding motions of plates.
      2. The San Andreas fault in California is a very long fault, but not a deep one. Earthquakes caused by it are within the upper 15 kilometers (9 mi) of the earth's crust.

3. In 1994 a great earthquake rumbled through the earth's mantle more than 600 kilometers (373 mi) below Bolivia. It was the largest earthquake ever recorded at such depths. The tremors of the Bolivian earthquake were felt as far away as Toronto, Canada. No other earthquake in history is known to have shaken the earth at such a great distance from its epicenter.

4. So-called deep-focus earthquakes, those occurring 300 or more kilometers (186 mi) below the earth's surface, may be caused by a different mechanism than those earthquakes that are closer to the surface, as described earlier.

C. Although earthquakes may occur anywhere on earth, they happen most often along two large areas of the earth called **earthquake belts.**

1. Earthquake belts usually occur where tall mountain ranges are near deep ocean floors. These are zones where huge plates of the lithosphere are shearing past each other.

2. The largest earthquake belt circles the Pacific Ocean, from Chile northward to Peru, Central America, Mexico, California, Puget Sound, to the Aleutian Islands and Japan, and southward to the Philippines, Indonesia, and New Zealand. The other large earthquake belt includes the mountainous areas next to the Mediterranean Sea, a section of northern Africa, Asia Minor, and southern Asia.

D. Earthquakes that begin under the ocean set up huge seismic sea waves, called **tsunamis,** sometimes mistakenly called "tidal waves." Tsunamis may travel as fast as 800 kilometers (500 mi) an hour and may be more than 30 meters (100 ft) high when they reach the seashore.

E. Earthquakes are detected by an instrument called a **seismograph.**

1. Slippage along a fault that produces an earthquake radiates waves (called seismic waves) that travel through the earth's crust.

2. The seismograph detects and records these waves, and from the data it collects we can tell where an earthquake occurred and how strong it was.

F. The most widely recognized measure of the strength of an earthquake at its source is the scale of magnitudes developed in 1935 by Charles F. Richter and Beno Gutenberg, the **Richter scale.**

1. Although the Richter scale has no limits, it is usually thought of in terms of numbers 1 to 10, each higher number representing an earthquake 10 times stronger than that of the preceding number. For example, an earthquake of magnitude 8 is 10 times stronger than one of magnitude 7.

2. An earthquake registering 2 on the Richter Scale is just strong enough to be felt. An earthquake with a rating of 5 can cause considerable damage, and an earthquake with a rating of 7 or higher is a **major earthquake.** The 1906 San Francisco earthquake was an 8.3 quake. The 1971 earthquake in San Fernando in the Los Angeles area had a Richter rating of 6.5.

3. The smallest quakes recorded using the Richter scale have been at about minus 2. The largest have been between 8 and 9. Earthquakes of an 8 or 9 rating occur somewhere on earth about every five years.

4. There are several other magnitude scales in common use. One of the most recent measures of strength of an earthquake is a measure of the quake's **seismic moment,** rather than of its seismic magnitude.

5. Seismic moment is a measurement of the seismic energy emitted from the entire fault rather than from its epicenter. Using a scale based on a quake's seismic energy, rather than its strength at its epicenter, is thought to be a more useful and fundamental measure of the strength of an earthquake.

G. Many scientists are focusing their research on ways to reduce the hazards of earthquakes by learning how to predict their consequences.

1. Equally important to the ability to predict the time, place, and magnitude of future earthquakes, is the ability to determine how the ground is likely to vibrate during a quake, how strong the quake will be, and how long it will last.

2. Knowledge of the ground motion that can be expected during an earthquake makes it possible to design structures that are not unnecessarily strong, and thus uneconomical, but are still able to survive the shaking.

3. To predict both the occurrence of an earthquake and its consequences, it is essential to understand the characteristics of the earthquake source. That is the direction of the research of many of today's seismologists.

III. MOUNTAINS
  A. Mountains are great masses of rock pushed high by forces inside the earth.
  B. Mountains are formed in various ways, depending on whether the masses of rock have been folded, tilted, shaped into domes, built up from volcanic activity, or formed when the earth material around a great mass of rock is eroded by wind and water.
     1. **Folded mountains** are formed when plates of rock are pushed into a series of wavelike folds by tremendous sideward forces that are produced by great pressure within the earth.
     2. The **anticlines,** or crests of these waves, become mountain peaks; the **synclines,** or troughs of these waves, become valleys.
     3. Folded rocks can be uplifted many times over a long period of time, producing an entire region of long ridges that curve back and forth on each other.
     4. Part of the Appalachian Mountains are folded mountains. The Himalayan range is a folded mountain that is still growing today.
     5. **Fault-block mountains** are formed when layers of rock break or crack, producing a fault.
     6. When faulting occurs, the layers of rock on one side of the fault are pushed up higher than those on the other side.
     7. The layers of rock often tilt to one side after they have been pushed up.
     8. Mountains formed in this way are called block mountains because they look like huge blocks.
     9. The Sierra Nevadas are fault-block mountains.
     10. In some areas these mountains are called **hogbacks,** because one side of the mountain is steep and nearly vertical and the other side has a more gentle slope.
     11. **Domed mountains** are formed either by folding or when magma (molten rock) flows up and between two layers of rock.
     12. As the molten rock accumulates, it pushes up the layers of rock above it to form a large dome.
     13. The Black Hills of South Dakota and Wyoming and the Adirondack Mountains of New York are domed mountains.
     14. **Volcanic mountains** are formed by the gradual and periodic accumulation of lava and other materials that are thrown up when a volcano erupts.
     15. Mount Lassen, Mount St. Helens, and Mount Ranier in the United States, Mount Popocatepetl in Mexico, Mount Vesuvius in Italy, and Mount Fuji in Japan are volcanic mountains.
     16. Volcanic activity, occurring in the ocean floor near the Aleutian Islands and the Hawaiian Islands, is building up a series of volcanic mountains at the bottom of the ocean around both of these areas.
  C. Mountains are often grouped together to form a mountain range, with a series of peaks of different heights. Ranges that are side by side, or parallel, are referred to as a chain of mountain ranges.
  D. Like most systems, mountains have a life history, passing from youth to maturity to old age.
     1. During their youth mountains are still growing. Young mountains, such as the Tetons of Wyoming, are high and rugged, with steep slopes, rushing streams, and narrow valleys. Many young mountains have snow on their tops at all times. Snowslides and avalanches are common. The Rocky Mountains, Andes Mountains, Alps, and Himalaya Mountains are also examples of young mountains.
     2. At maturity, the mountains have stopped growing, and the action of water, ice, wind, and other elements of weather wears away the mountains, gradually lowering their peaks and making their slopes more gentle. Sometimes mature mountains become so much lower that trees grow to their very tops. Streams flow more slowly, and the valleys become wider. The Appalachian Mountains, the Adirondack Mountains, and the White Mountains are mature mountains.
     3. At old age the mountains have been worn down until almost level. The flat surface that is left is called a **peneplane,** which means "almost a level plane." Southern New England and the areas of Manhattan and Weschester County of New York are examples of peneplanes.
     4. Sometimes a peneplane has low, rolling hills with an occasional high hill, called a **monadnock,** which is made of hard igneous rock that has resisted wearing and so remains. Monadnock Mountain in New Hampshire and Pikes Peak in Colorado are monadnocks. Rivers of old mountain areas move very slowly and have low banks.

5. When mountains have passed through their life history and have been worn away, the process of mountain building will eventually begin again.

IV. PLAINS AND PLATEAUS

A. Plains and plateaus are different from mountains because they are made of rock layers that are in the very same horizontal position in which the layers originally formed.

B. Plains are low-level flat surfaces and plateaus are high-level flat surfaces, as compared with the land around them.

1. **Coastal plains** are made of pieces of rock that either were worn away from rocks along the seashore, by ocean waves, or were carried by rivers to the ocean. The wave motion of the ocean spread out the pieces of rock until a smooth, flat surface formed. Some coastal plains are very narrow, and others are quite broad.

2. A coastal plain extends into the ocean, sometimes for a great distance, forming what is called a **continental shelf.**

3. Sometimes forces inside the earth will lift up all or part of a continental shelf so that it too becomes a coastal plain.

4. **Interior plains** were formed from large, shallow inland seas. Sediments filled these shallow seas until the water disappeared and flat plains formed. The Great Plains of the interior United States, and the Argentine pampas, are examples of interior marine plains.

5. **Lake plains** were formed from the bottom of large lakes.

6. Some lake plains formed when forces inside the earth caused the lake floors to lift, and other lake plains formed when conditions caused all the water in the lakes to drain away.

7. The largest lake plain in North America includes a large part of Minnesota, North Dakota, and the provinces of Saskatchewan and Manitoba in Canada.

C. Most plateaus formed from forces beneath the earth's surface that raised horizontal layers of rock straight up.

1. Some plateaus formed by lava flowing out of cracks in the earth, spreading out over large areas, and forming level regions of layers of volcanic rock.

2. Like mountains, plateaus also have a life history, passing from youth to maturity, to old age.

3. Young plateaus are very high and flat and have not been worn away much by rivers flowing through them.

4. Mature plateaus are frequently called mountains, even though they are not truly mountains, because many rivers and streams have cut wide valleys through their broad surfaces, giving the effect of a series of mountains.

5. The tops of these mountainlike plateaus are usually flat; the Catskill Mountains are an example of a mature plateau.

6. At old age, plateaus are worn almost level, with only a few parts of the original plateau still standing.

7. In dry areas the parts that remain have high walls and flat tops.

8. Large plateaus with broad tops are called **mesas,** and smaller plateaus with tops that are more rounded are called **buttes.**

9. Both mesas and buttes are found in New Mexico, Utah, and Arizona, but most of the plateaus in North Dakota, South Dakota, Montana, and Wyoming are buttes.

10. In humid areas the remaining parts of a plateau are more rounded and look more like hills.

V. VOLCANOES

A. A volcano is a mountain, a hill, or vent formed around a crack in the earth's crust, where tectonic plates have pulled apart, through which molten rock and other hot materials exude.

1. The rock inside the earth's mantle is very hot, but it is solid because of the great pressures on it.

2. When the pressure is reduced, as when a crack or fault forms in the earth's crust, such as when tectonic plates move apart, the rock becomes liquid, or molten rock called **magma.**

3. The magma flows upward to the earth's surface, either through a crack or through a weak spot in the earth's crust.

4. The initial opening at the top of the volcano is called a **vent,** which later may become a **crater.**

5. Volcanic activity occurs in the oceans as well as on land. Thousands of active deep-sea vents exist in the Pacific Ocean, such as those off the coasts of Mexico and California, adding new sea floor to the area caused by the separation of tectonic plates.

6. A crater is usually rather narrow, but sometimes it blows apart or collapses, forming a wide basinlike hollow, called a **caldera.** A caldera may fill with water and become a lake, such as Crater Lake in Oregon. The volcanoes of Yellowstone National Park are caldera volcanoes.

B. Some volcanoes, like those in Iceland, Yellowstone National Park, and the Pacific Ocean, erupt slowly and quietly, whereas others, like those in the East Indies and the Mediterranean area, erupt violently because of tremendous pressures inside. Some, like Stromboli in Italy, alternate between being quiet and being explosive. Depending on their eruption cycles, individual volcanoes are considered to be active, dormant, or extinct.

1. Active volcanoes are erupting or have recently erupted.

2. Dormant volcanoes have not erupted for some time but show signs of underground activity.

3. Extinct volcanoes have not erupted for a long time and show no signs of underground activity.

C. When magma reaches the earth's surface, it is called **lava.**

1. Sometimes lava hardens to form a rough and jagged surface. Other times it forms a smooth, ropy surface.

2. The tiniest drops of lava spray form fine **volcanic dust** that spreads out high into the atmosphere and is distributed in locations far from the volcano.

3. Larger drops of lava become **volcanic cinders** (coarse) and **volcanic ash** (fine), which fall relatively close to the volcano.

4. **Obsidian** is a dark glassy rock that forms from lava that cools quickly.

5. **Pumice** and **scoria** are light-weight rocks, with holes in them, that form from lava that hardens while steam and other gases are still bubbling from it.

6. **Tuff** is volcanic ash that becomes cemented to form a rock.

D. There are three categories or types of volcanoes: shield, cinder cone, and composite.

1. **Shield volcanoes** are usually formed from quiet eruptions, whereby the lava spreads out to form a broad base with gentle slopes. Mauna Loa and Kilauea in Hawaii are shield volcanoes.

2. **Cinder cone volcanoes** form from explosive eruptions, which create a fairly narrow base with steep slopes. Paricutin in Mexico is a cinder cone volcano.

3. The difference between oozing and explosive volcanoes lies in the viscosity and gas content of the magma. Explosive volcanoes hold magma that is thick and sticky, with the gases under great pressure, so the magma explodes rather than oozes when released.

4. **Composite volcanoes** usually form as a result of alternating explosive and quiet periods, which create alternate layers of lava and cinders or ash. Composite volcanoes have slopes that are steeper than those of shield volcanoes, but gentler than those of cinder cone volcanoes. Fujiyama in Japan and Rainier in the United States are composite volcanoes.

E. Most volcanoes on earth are located in the two earthquake belts.

1. One belt circles the Pacific Ocean, and the other extends from the Mediterranean area eastward across southern Asia.

2. In the areas around the Aleutian Islands and in the Pacific Ocean, volcanic mountain chains are being formed on the floor of the ocean.

3. Most of the islands of the South Pacific are the tops of submerged and extinct volcanoes. The Philippines originated as huge volcanoes built up from the ocean floor. The island of Luzon alone has 13 active volcanoes.

4. The pattern of volcanoes around the entire rim of the Pacific Ocean is called the Ring of Fire.

5. Volcanoes are also found in Iceland, the Azores, and some islands in the West Indies.

F. One of the most destructive forms of volcanic activity is the collapse of volcanic cones. The 1980 explosion of Mount St. Helens in Washington State is an example.

1. Earthquake activity often accompanies volcanic eruption; after centuries of sporadic eruptions of the lava and ash that built its cone, Mount St. Helens was jarred by earthquakes caused by magma moving upward. The north flank of its cone collapsed, and volcanic debris was scattered far in all directions.

G. The effects of a single volcanic eruption can be felt and seen around the world.

1. The lighter sulfur dioxides emitted can circle the earth for years, lowering earth's surface temperatures and damaging its ozone layer.

2. Clouds of ash can pose a threat to aircraft, because the small pieces of volcanic glass can be sucked into jet engines, fuse into clumps, and destroy engine thrust.
3. Volcanic eruptions beneath glaciers can melt the ice and cause flooding.

VI. HOT SPRINGS, GEYSERS, AND GEOTHERMAL ENERGY

A. Hot springs and geysers are common wherever hot rock is present beneath the earth's surface.
B. The earth continuously produces heat, primarily by the decay of naturally radioactive chemical elements that occur in small amounts in all rocks.
1. The annual heat loss from the earth is enormous—equivalent to 10 times the annual energy consumption of the United States and more than that needed to power all nations of the world, if it could be fully harnessed.
2. If only 1 percent of the thermal energy contained within the uppermost 10 kilometers (62 mi) of the earth's crust could be harnessed, this amount could replace 500 times that contained in all oil and natural gas resources of the world.
3. The earth's natural heat energy is cleaner than coal, oil, and gas, and there is less environmental impact associated with its use.
4. Scientists and engineers are working at finding ways to utilize more fully the earth's abundant thermal energy—commonly called **geothermal energy.**
C. Hot springs are formed when underground water is heated by hot rock and gases beneath the earth's surface, and the hot water then flows to the surface.
1. The passageway along which the hot water travels is wide and open, so the water reaches the surface quickly and easily.
2. The temperature of the water may range from just warm to boiling.
3. On its way to the surface the hot water dissolves large amounts of minerals.
4. These minerals, deposited around the mouth of the hot spring as the water evaporates, tend to build up colored layers or terraces.
D. A geyser is a hot spring that sprays its water high into the air at intervals.

1. The eruption of water occurs because the geyser has to travel a narrow, twisted pathway to reach the earth's surface, rather than a wide pathway.
2. Heated water is often trapped in the passageway, where it continues to be heated far above its boiling point of 100° Celsius (212°F) without being changed into steam.
3. This occurs because the water on top presses down on the water below, and this water under pressure can be superheated without boiling.
4. The superheated water expands and causes some of the water above it to overflow onto the earth's surface.
5. The loss of water on top eases the pressure on the superheated water on the bottom, so that some of it is suddenly changed to steam, which blows all the water above it high into the air as a geyser.
6. After the geyser erupts, some of the water flows back into the passageway, where it meets more underground water coming up, and the process repeats itself.
7. Some geysers, like Old Faithful in Yellowstone National Park, erupt at nearly regular intervals, whereas others erupt at irregular intervals.
8. Most geysers are found in three places in the world: Yellowstone National Park, Iceland, and New Zealand. However, geysers have also been found bursting through the ocean floor in the Atlantic and Pacific Oceans.
E. In 1992, The Geysers, a hydrothermal system in northern California, became the world's largest development that uses geothermal energy to move large turbines to produce electricity.
1. Actually, The Geysers is not a spouting geyser or system of geysers but a field of slow erupting vents, warm springs, and fumaroles.
2. Pipes set deep into ground wells carry steam to turbine generators that in turn generate electricity.
F. Other places using geothermal energy to create electrical energy are El Salvador and Nicaragua, since the 1970s, and Costa Rica, since 1994. In Iceland and in some areas around Paris, France, geothermal energy is used for heating water and as a source of heat for buildings.

DEMONSTRATION 9.2
A Geyser

Put a funnel in a Pyrex beaker and add water until the bowl of the funnel is covered and the water is level with the beginning of the stem (Figure 9.3). Heat the beaker on a hot plate. When the water begins to boil, the bubbles of steam expand and rise, pushing the water up the stem and making it spout like a geyser.

SAFETY NOTE: Use extreme caution for this demonstration.

1. Use extra caution whenever using a hotplate (or any heat source) in the classroom, keeping curious or careless students protected from touching it.
2. Protect students from possible glass breakage (even when using a Pyrex beaker) and spattering of glass and boiling water by placing the beaker into a baking pan (not shown here) that is in turn placed directly onto the hotplate.
3. If you use a glass funnel (a plastic funnel will work, too), the largest diameter of the funnel should be somewhat less than the diameter of the bottom of the inside of the beaker (as shown in the figure), and small enough that the funnel does not fit so snug into the beaker that troubles are caused if the glass expands during heating and contracting when cool.
4. As with all demonstrations, practice this one in the absence of children. During the demonstration the children should be protected from the hot water that spouts and sprays from the end of the funnel.

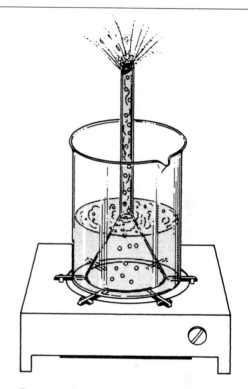

FIGURE 9.3   A funnel geyser.

FORCES THAT WEAR AWAY THE EARTH'S SURFACE

I. THE EARTH'S SURFACE IS IN A CONSTANT STATE OF CHANGE

   A. Although the surface of the earth appears solid and permanent, it is always changing.
   B. Rocks that make up the earth's surface are always being broken up and carried away, by the process known as **weathering.**
      1. Weathering is caused by the action of the sun, wind, and water.
      2. There are two types of weathering. Mechanical or physical weathering is the breakdown of rock into smaller pieces without causing any change in the chemical makeup of the rock. The process is called chemical weathering when a change occurs in the chemical makeup of the rock.
      3. The process whereby the products of weathering are carried away is called **erosion,** and it is effected by water, ice, and wind.
      4. While the forces of weathering and erosion are constantly at work on the earth's surface, the forces inside the earth continuously rebuild the surface.
   C. **Mechanical weathering** is caused in a variety of ways.
      1. Mechanical weathering can be caused by water seeping into cracks and pores of rocks and then freezing. When the water freezes it

expands, putting pressure on the rock and causing small pieces of rock to break off.

2. Another type of mechanical weathering is caused by water that has seeped into cracks and pores of rock when the temperature remains above freezing. When rocks are heated by sunlight during the day, the minerals in the rocks combine with the water and expand, causing cracks to occur in the rocks. At night the rocks cool and contract, and this eventually causes the outside of the rocks to peel off in thick layers or sheets, a process known as **exfoliation.**

3. Plants can also cause mechanical weathering. As shrubs and trees grow, their roots work into small cracks in rock, eventually causing the rock to split or crumble.

4. Animals also play a part in mechanical weathering. Burrowing animals, such as gophers and prairie dogs, dig into the ground and expose rock surfaces to weathering. Earthworms bring fine particles of rock to the surface; then also make tiny passageways in the earth, which let air and water enter the soil and expose the rock surfaces to weathering.

5. Wind carries fine rock particles which, over time, can create friction on rock surfaces and erode them away.

D. **Chemical weathering,** whereby there is a chemical change in the rock's composition, is most likely to occur in damp areas.

1. Carbon dioxide in the air can produce chemical weathering. When dissolved in water, carbon dioxide forms **carbonic acid,** a relatively weak acid that can react with rocks such as limestone, breaking down the rock into materials that easily dissolve and are then carried away by water and wind erosion.

2. Many rocks contain at least one mineral that is affected by carbonic acid, and when that mineral is removed, the rest of the rock is exposed, making it easier for other forms of weathering to occur.

3. Oxygen in the air combines directly with many minerals in rocks, forming materials that crumble more easily.

4. Water, either in the air or on the ground, combines with many minerals, causing them to swell and form cracks in rock, making it easier then for mechanical weathering to continue the process of breaking down the rock.

5. Lichens can grow on rocks, using the minerals of the rocks for their growth, by giving off an acid that causes the rock to break down and release its minerals, thereby causing chemical weathering.

6. When organisms die and decay, acids released in the decay process attack and break down rock material.

II. Erosion by Water

A. Water is the greatest of all forces that produce erosion.

1. Each year great quantities of water fall on the earth's surface.

2. Some of this water evaporates back into the air, some seeps into the land and remains as groundwater, and the rest flows over the earth's surface in a huge number of streams and rivers.

3. This running water carrys with it the materials formed by weathering, and it carries them to lakes and oceans where they are deposited and accumulate.

B. Groundwater causes erosion below the earth's surface.

1. Carbon dioxide in the air combines with water to form weak carbonic acid, which attacks limestone and forms materials that dissolve in the water and are eventually carried away.

2. Where a great amount of limestone is present, large underground caves may be formed by the action of carbonic acid on limestone.

3. At times, the underground water, which has limestone dissolved in it, forms solid deposits inside the caves.

4. The underground water forms these deposits by dripping so slowly through the roof of the cave that some of the water evaporates and the limestone deposits out again, forming limestone "icicles," called **stalactites,** hanging from the cave ceiling, and columns of limestone, called **stalagmites,** may build upward on the cave floor.

5. The Carlsbad Caverns in New Mexico and Mammoth Cave in Kentucky are caves with stalactites and stalagmites.

C. Running water causes erosion of the earth's surface.

1. As rainwater runs off to join streams and rivers, it carries particles of soil, rocks, and minerals with it.

DEMONSTRATION 9.3
Formation of Carbonic Acid

Obtain some distilled water or fresh rainwater. Test the pure water with litmus paper for acidity. Now blow for quite some time through a straw into a glass of this water. Test again with litmus paper. This time the litmus paper will turn red, showing the presence of carbonic acid that was formed when the carbon dioxide from the air in your lungs dissolved in the water.

2. As the water flows in the streams and rivers, it wears away the stream beds and causes the sides to cave, making the streams and rivers wider.
3. Particles of rock in the water also act as weathering forces to wear away more of the earth's rock, carrying it to the lakes and oceans.
4. Many large rivers move very slowly as they near a lake or ocean, dropping the materials they are carrying, forming deposits called **deltas.**

D. Oceans both erode and build up the earth's surface.
1. Waves, pounding against rocks and soil along a shore, wear them away and carry off particles of the rock and soil; at Cape Cod, for example, 1 to 2 meters (3 to 6 ft) of shoreline are worn away by the ocean each year.
2. Current and waves also carry materials, such as sand and pebbles, to the shore and make beaches; sometimes, however, storms and strong undercurrents carry beach materials away faster than the waves can deposit them.
3. Sometimes waves deposit materials just off shore, forming sandbars and sandy islands.

III. EROSION BY ICE

A. Glaciers are huge masses of moving ice, formed where climate and weather are quite cold.
1. In these places much snow falls each year, more than can melt or evaporate. Some of the snow remains year after year, accumulating layers that pile up into deep masses.
2. The great weight of the snow presses on the layers beneath, causing these layers of snow to melt and refreeze as ice grains or pellets, called **neve.**

3. In the deepest layers the pressure is so great that the neve is recrystallized to form one solid mass of ice.
4. Each winter more layers are added to the top, forming more ice below.
5. Eventually the weight of this huge mass of snow and ice becomes so great that the whole mass slowly begins to move. This moving mass of ice is called a glacier.

B. **Valley glaciers** are those that are formed in mountain valleys.
1. Some valley glaciers are small, and others are quite large.
2. As the valley glacier begins to move to lower levels, it gouges out the rock beneath it and carries the broken pieces along with it.
3. As it moves forward, it picks up more rock that it wears away from the sides of the valley.
4. These rocks, embedded in the ice, act as a huge file to wear away the earth over which the glacier moves.
5. This movement of the valley glacier tends to smooth out the valley floor.
6. As the same time, the glacier grinds away the valley walls and straightens sharp bends, changing the V-shape of the valley to a broader U-shape.
7. As the glacier moves, big cracks, called **crevasses,** form at the top and sides of the glacier.
8. When the glacier meets warmer temperatures, it begins to melt and to drop the material it has been carrying or pushing along in front. The material that it drops is called **moraine.**

C. **Continental glaciers** are found today only in the earth's polar regions.
1. In the polar regions the average temperature is below freezing. Most of the snow that falls remains from year to year, although the

south pole gets less than 6 inches of new snow each year.

2. The coldest temperature ever recorded on earth was −88° Celsius (−127° F), recorded in 1960 in Antarctica.

3. The continental glacier at the north pole, which also covers most of Greenland, is more than 2,440 meters (8,000 ft) thick. The glacier that covers the south pole is more than 4,270 meters (14,000 ft) thick, deep enough to fit 14 Empire State Buildings on top of each other.

4. These continental glaciers, covering Greenland and Antarctica, move outward toward the sea where the rise and fall of the ocean tides eventually snap off large pieces of the glaciers, which float off as **icebergs.**

5. Continental glaciers smooth the surfaces over which they pass by grinding down the higher elevations and filling in the valleys.

6. Where parts of the earth's surface are softer, a glacier may gouge out huge depressions or basins.

7. When the climate becomes warmer and the glacier retreats, these basins remain, filled with melted ice, as lakes. In summer the continent of Antarctica is only half the size it is in winter when its ice pack includes more of the frozen surrounding sea.

D. The earth has gone through four glacial periods, in which large parts of the earth were covered by glaciers.

1. These glacial periods followed a cycle.

2. First the earth's climate became colder and huge glaciers formed at the poles, then the growing glaciers moved out from the poles in all directions to cover large parts of the earth.

3. Then the climate warmed, whereupon the glaciers melted and retreated back toward the poles.

4. The retreating glaciers left behind the moraines they brought, and also the grinding changes they made to the earth's surface.

5. The first glacial period occurred about 800 million years ago, followed by a warm period of about 3 million years. The second period came about 500 million years ago, followed by a warm period of about 300 million years. The third period came about 200 million years ago, and the fourth period about 1 million years ago.

6. The last major phase of glaciation ended about 10,000 years ago.

7. At its height 20,000 years ago, ice sheets a mile thick covered much of northern Europe and North America.

8. Enough ice was formed on land to cause sea levels to drop to more than 100 meters (nearly 330 ft) below where they are today.

9. Evidence indicates that at present the earth is in a period of glacial retreat.

IV. EROSION BY WIND

A. The chief work of wind is to carry away loose bits of soil and rock.

1. This erosion by wind is quite common in dry areas where there are few plants, shrubs, or trees to cover the ground and protect it.

2. Even mild winds move fine particles of dust and rock, but strong winds create tremendous dust storms.

3. Over a long time, wind can blow away all loose material from a desert floor, leaving behind only a floor of bare rock.

B. Wind also deposits material.

1. Hills of sand, called **dunes,** are wind deposits.

2. Dunes are formed when there is something in the way of the wind, slowing it down and causing it to deposit the particles.

3. As a mound of sand grows it helps to slow the wind even more, allowing even more material to be deposited and the dune to grow even larger.

4. Winds often move sand dunes from one place to another, unless grass and shrubs cover the sand sufficiently to hold it in place or fences are erected, which is often done to prevent dunes from covering highways, railroads, airplane runways, or even buildings.

C. Another type of wind deposit is a fine sediment called **loess,** which is composed of particles of earth. It is deposited over large areas of land and can become very thick. When water is available, loess makes very fertile soil.

D. As well as an erosion agent, wind is also a weathering agent.

1. As wind blows against solid rock, the particles of rock carried by the wind rub against the solid rock; this causes friction that wears the rock away.

2. Beach cliffs and rocks are often made smooth in this way, as are desert rocks and boulders.

SOIL

I. THE FORMATION OF SOIL

  A. Although forces of mechanical and chemical weathering act on rock very slowly, over millions of years these forces have broken up almost all the rock on or near the earth's surface.
   1. This is the reason the earth's surface has a layer of pieces of rock on it.
   2. These pieces are all of sizes, ranging from microscopic pieces to massive boulders. This layer of pieces of rock is called **mantle rock.**
  B. The forces of weathering continue to act on the mantle rock until a layer of soil is formed.
   1. Soil is made of tiny grains of rock and minerals.
   2. Soil that has not moved from the original mantle rock from which it was formed is called **residual soil.**
   3. Soil that has been carried by erosion from one place to another is called **transported soil.**
  C. Soil becomes fertile, that is, things will grow in it, when **humus** is added to it. Humus is the remains of dead organisms.
  D. Because humus is added only to the top portion of soil, there is a difference in the quality of soil layers.
   1. The first 20 centimeters (8 in) of soil is called the **topsoil** or **A horizon.**
   2. The top of the A horizon, when rich in humus, is called **O horizon,** which is the most fertile soil and the soil that helps crops grow.
   3. Topsoil has spaces filled with air or water or both.
   4. It takes about 500 years for the earth's weathering and erosion process to make 2.5 centimeters (1 in) of topsoil.
   5. Beneath the A horizon is the **E horizon,** which is mostly sand and silt.
   6. Beneath the E horizon is the **subsoil** or **B horizon.**
   7. The subsoil is a much thicker layer than the topsoil.
   8. Subsoil has little or no humus, but mostly minerals and clay.
   9. Beneath the subsoil is partially weathered bedrock (**C horizon**), then solid bedrock (the **R horizon**).

II. KINDS OF SOIL

  A. Soil contains different sizes and kinds of rocks and minerals, which include large pebbles or gravel, smaller particles of sand, tiny particles of clay, and sometimes particles of silt (which are smaller than grains of sand but larger than clay particles), and is classified according to the predominant kind of material in it.
   1. **Sandy soil** is made mostly of sand, together with a little clay, but almost no humus.
   2. Sandy soil does not hold water well and contains very few minerals that plants can use to grow.
   3. **Clay soil** contains mostly clay, with a little sand and a little humus.
   4. Clay soil holds water well, but becomes sticky when wet, almost as hard as rock when dry.
   5. **Loam soil** is a mixture of gravel, sand, clay, and humus, is dark in color, and is the best soil for most crops.
   6. For growing crops, soil is cultivated; that is, the large clumps are broken up and the earth around the plant roots is loosened so the roots can grow and more easily obtain air and water.

III. SOIL EROSION, THE LOSS OF FERTILE TOPSOIL

  A. In areas of the earth untroubled by humans, loss of fertile topsoil by erosion is a slow process.
   1. Shrubs and trees above the ground level, and roots below ground level, help prevent soil from being washed away by water and wind.
   2. What little soil is lost is replaced by new soil formed over the years in the natural weathering processes.
  B. When humans use soil to grow crops, erosion can occur very quickly, especially if the shrubs and trees that prevent soil loss have been removed.
  C. The most powerful force causing soil erosion is the force of running water.
   1. Raindrops hit the soil and loosen it, causing it to be splashed away; this type of erosion is called **splash erosion.**
   2. When rain falls steadily, soil absorbs water until it is saturated and cannot hold any more; then the water runs off in broad sheets, carrying soil away with it, causing a type of erosion called **sheet erosion.**
   3. Sheet erosion can remove all the topsoil, leaving behind only the subsoil or even bare bedrock.
   4. As water runs off the soil it eventually collects into small streams that flow to lower ground.

DEMONSTRATION 9.4
Composition of Soil

Obtain a tall cylindrical jar, and fill half of it with garden soil. Add water until the jar is almost full and screw the cap on tightly. Shake the jar vigorously for a minute and then set it down. The soil will begin to settle in layers. The fine gravel sinks to the bottom immediately, followed by sand, and then by clay and silt. Particles of humus may float on top of the water. The muddy water may take days to become clear, because it takes time for the very fine particles of silt and clay to settle.

5. As a stream flows, it may wash out some of the ground and form a small channel, called a **rill.**
6. A rill is often formed when crops have been planted in rows that run up and down a sloping field.
7. A rill can become deeper and wider with each rainfall, as the running water carries more soil away each time, eventually forming a larger channel, called a **gully.**
8. This type of erosion is called gill or gully erosion.
9. The small streams flow into larger streams, each taking away soil from the bottom and sides of the stream bed.

IV. PREVENTING SOIL EROSION

A. There are many ways to slow the erosion of top-soil.
1. Farmers use **contour plowing** and planting on sloping land.
2. This form of cultivation means that on hills the rows run sideways rather than up and down, thereby slowing soil runoff caused by rain.
3. **Terrace plowing** and planting is used when slopes are steep.
4. The terraces follow the contours of the hill and run sideways, as in contour cultivation.
5. **Alternate strip cropping** is used on gentle slopes.
6. In strip cropping different crops are grown on the same piece of land, in alternating plots.
7. One plot may contain row crops such as corn, and the adjacent plot may contain a ground-covering plant such as alfalfa or hay.
8. The covering crops catch and prevent soil from being washed away.
9. The following year the same crops are planted, but in opposite plots from the prior year; the covering crop is grown where the row crop was grown before, and vice versa.
10. Bare land, unsuitable for growing crops, is planted with trees and grass to help replenish lost soil.
11. In rather open land, or land bordering crop fields, trees can be planted in rows to provide a shelter belt to slow erosion caused by wind.
12. Construction of catchment ponds to deter loss of soil into streams, maintenance of vegetation on agricultural lands and stream banks, and revegetation of construction and mining sites can also decrease the loss of fertile soils through erosion.

V. ENRICHING THE SOIL

A. There are many minerals in soil that plants need in order to grow and to make food through photosynthesis.
1. The most important of the needed minerals are those that contain nitrogen, phosphorus, potassium, calcium, and magnesium.
2. Plants remove large amounts of these minerals from soil, and the minerals must be replaced if the soil is to remain fertile.
3. One way to replace minerals is by the use of natural fertilizer, such as animal manure, which adds both minerals and humus to the soil.
4. Another way is to use commercial fertilizers that contain minerals in various quantities, depending on which minerals have been most depleted.
5. Yet another way is to rotate the kind of crop grown in a field from one year to the next. For example, if a field becomes low in nitrogen because of using it to grow corn (which uses a lot of nitrogen), it might be planted next with clover, alfalfa, beans, or peas, plants that help return nitrogen to the soil.

6. These plants have nodules on their roots, tiny but visible bumps in which live **nitrogen-fixing bacteria.**
7. Although 78 percent of air is nitrogen, crop plants cannot use this nitrogen in its gaseous state as found in the atmosphere; nitrogen-fixing bacteria, on the other hand, can use this nitrogen, and they convert it to a form of nitrogen in the soil that crop plants can use.

B. Soil can be tested to see how it can be improved to grow better crops. It can be tested for moisture content and for its ability to retain water, for mineral content, to determine whether it is too acid or too alkaline, and for its humus content.

GEOLOGIC HISTORY OF THE EARTH

I. HOW SCIENTISTS LEARN ABOUT THE EARTH'S HISTORY

A. The history of the earth is recorded in the rocks.
   1. From earth's rocks we can learn about changes that have occurred in the earth's surface, we can find evidence of changes in the earth's climate, and we can find evidence of organisms of long ago.
B. **Stratigraphy** is the study of rock layers.
   1. The order in which rocks are layered is an important clue to the earth's history.
   2. Layers are usually formed horizontally, with the oldest rock strata on the bottom and the youngest on top.
   3. Even when folding, faulting, and metamorphosis have changed rock formations, scientists can still identify them.
   4. Rock layers reveal data about the locations of earlier oceans, mountains, plains, and plateaus.
C. **Petrology** is the study of rocks themselves.
   1. Petrologists study rocks to learn how they were formed, what changes occurred, and what kinds of minerals they contain.
   2. Every rock tells a story through its structure, texture, physical and chemical makeup, and traces of former life embedded in it.
   3. A piece of old sandstone may have ripple or wave marks, or it may contain seashells, indicating that the sandstone was formed in the ocean.
   4. A conglomerate rock may show evidence that it was made by a swiftly moving stream or by heavy ocean waves.
   5. The earlier existence of shallow seas, lakes, deserts, glaciers, and other forms of the earth's surface can be learned from the sediments left behind.
   6. Sediments can also reveal what kinds of rocks there were, the climate at the time, and other conditions on earth a long time ago.
D. **Paleontology** is the study of fossils, the remains or traces in rock of early life forms.
   1. The remains may be skeletons, or they may be complete organisms.
   2. The traces may be footprints or body and tail marks.
   3. Fossils are rarely found in igneous rock.
   4. Fossils can be found in sedimentary rock that was changed to metamorphic rock, but most fossils were destroyed or damaged when the sedimentary rock changed.
   5. From sedimentary rock scientists can learn many things about organisms of long ago, such as their development, body structure, habits, and the climate in which they lived.
   6. Fossils are formed in many different ways. Some were formed when life remains were covered by sediment. Animals that lived in or near bodies of water were sometimes buried by the mud, dirt, and gravel; then the sediment hardened into rock and the hard parts of the animals' bodies were preserved in their original form.
   7. Some animals fell into tar pits, swamps, or quicksand, which later hardened, preserving their bones and teeth.
   8. Some fossils were formed when animals were frozen in ice or mud and were preserved whole.
   9. Some insects became fossils when they became trapped by the sticky sap of trees, which then hardened. Then, later, oceans and their sediments covered the remains of the trees, changing the sap to a material called **amber.** While the insects dried inside the amber, their bristles, wing scales, and thin exoskeletons were preserved.

10. Some organisms formed fossils by leaving behind a cast of their remains. When organisms were covered by sediment, water of the sediment dissolved the organisms' hard parts, leaving behind a hollow space that filled with minerals from the water, which hardened, forming a cast of the original organism.

11. Many organisms were preserved in great detail as fossils when they were petrified, or "turned into stone." This does not mean that the original material of the organism was really changed into stone, but rather, when the organism died and was buried by sediment, its body was replaced, particle by particle, with minerals, sometimes with such perfection that exceptionally clear and complete fossil specimens have been found.

12. Animals without hard parts, such as jellyfish and worms, and plants without woody parts often left fossil prints. When these soft living creatures were covered with sediment and the sediment hardened into rock, their parts were chemically changed into carbon, forming a detailed outline of the original organisms. Even the delicate outlines of fish scales and leaf veins can often be seen in these prints.

13. Fossils of footprints, body and tail marks, outline and vein patterns of leaves, and imprints of stems and flowers have been found. These marks were first made in soft mud, then soil or silt may have been blown or washed into the print, more layers of sediment were added, and eventually the sediment hardened into rock, preserving the marks and imprints in the original mud.

14. Fossils are often found in coal, especially soft coal. Coal itself is the fossil remains of plants that lived long ago in swampy land. The organisms were buried under layers of sediment and then, under heat and pressure, were changed and hardened into coal, with some of the original plant material found as fossils in the coal.

II. CALCULATING THE AGE OF THE EARTH

A. Radioactivity is used to calculate the age of rocks and the age of the earth.
   1. Dating rocks using so-called **radioactive clocks** allows scientists to study the most ancient rocks, those without fossil evidence.
   2. The hands of a radioactive clock are isotopes, atoms of the same element that have different atomic weights.
   3. Geologic time is measured by the rate of decay of one isotope into another.
   4. One technique involves the study of the uranium found in igneous and metamorphic rocks.
   5. Uranium is a radioactive element that breaks down slowly to form radium, which in turn breaks down into a number of other elements and finally becomes lead.
   6. Because uranium breaks down at a slow and steady rate that is not altered by changes in temperature or pressure, it provides a reliable clock.
   7. It takes 5 billion years for half of the atoms of a piece of uranium to become lead.
   8. By examining a piece of rock that contains uranium and comparing the amount of uranium still present with the amount of lead that has formed from the uranium, scientists can calculate the age of the rock, and even the earth, with considerable accuracy.
   9. By using this method, the earth is estimated to be about 4.5 billion years old.
   10. Another radioactive method involves the study of radioactive carbon-14, which is found in sedimentary rocks.
   11. All living things contain carbon-14, but when an organism dies no more carbon-14 is produced; instead, the carbon-14 begins to break down at a slow and steady rate, just as uranium does.
   12. It takes about 5,600 years for half of the atoms of a piece of carbon-14 to break down.
   13. By examining a piece of rock that has fossil remains and comparing the amount of carbon-14 in it with the amount of other elements that have been formed from the carbon-14, it is possible to calculate the age of the rock.
   14. The carbon-14 method is used to find the age of rocks to 15,000 years, and the uranium method is used to find the age of rocks that are older.

III. THE GEOLOGIC TIMETABLE AND LIFE ON EARTH

A. Because the history of the earth involves such a long period of time, when studying the earth's history scientists refer to a geologic timetable.

B. The longest division of time in the timetable is an **eon.** The timetable is divided into three eons.
   1. The **Archean eon** and the **Proterozoic eon** are sometimes referred to as **Precambrian** time, the time from the earth's formation 4.5 billion years ago until about 570 million years ago. Precambrian time, representing about four-fifths of the earth's history, is the time of the earth before complex life forms existed on it.
   2. The third eon is the **Phanerozoic.**
C. Each eon is divided into smaller units of time called **eras.** The earliest era is the **Azoic.** The most recent is the **Cenozoic.**
   1. Specific geologic changes took place on earth during each era.
   2. New mountain ranges formed, shapes of continents changed, and shallow seas within the continents were either formed or drained.
   3. Changes occurred in the atmosphere and in the oceans' circulations.
   4. These changes brought about changes in climate, which in turn caused changes in the forms of life on earth.
   5. Some forms of life disappeared, while new forms developed that were better adapted to the new climate.
   6. Each era usually had its own distinctive kinds of organisms.
D. Each era is subdivided into units called **periods.** Periods are further divided into units of time called **epochs.** There were geologic changes characteristic of periods and of epochs, but these changes were not as great as those of eras.

IV. THE ARCHEAN EON

A. Beginning with the formation of the earth about 4.5 billion years ago, the Archean eon lasted until 2 billion years ago.
   1. At the end of the Archean eon there was nothing on earth but rocks, water, and air.
   2. The **Azoic** era is the only era attributed to this eon.

V. THE PROTEROZOIC EON

A. Lasting from about 2.5 billion years ago until 570 million years ago, the **Proterozoic eon** is divided into two eras, the Archeozoic and the Proterozoic.
B. Lasting for 1 billion years, the **Archeozoic era** began about 2.5 billion years ago.

   1. During the Archeozoic era there was much volcanic activity, great mountain ranges formed, and the oceans alternated between covering the land areas and withdrawing.
   2. Some Archeozoic rocks contain much graphite, a pure form of carbon.
   3. Simple life forms may have existed, such as bacteria and algae.
C. The **Proterozoic era** began about 1 billion years ago and lasted for approximately 450 million years.
   1. During the Proterozoic era the basic shapes of the earth's continents as we know them to be today developed, vast masses of igneous rock formed, and glaciers may have been present.
   2. It was during this era that **invertebrates** (animals without backbones) first appeared. These organisms included the sponges, jellyfish, coral, and wormlike animals, and the more complex invertebrates, such as crabs, spiders, and insects.
   3. Nonanimal life of this era was limited to the simplest forms of **protists,** including protozoa, bacteria, and algae.
   4. Most life forms of this era were marine, that is, lived in the oceans.

VI. THE PHANEROZOIC EON

A. Starting about 570 million years ago, the Phanerozoic eon continues today. The Phanerozoic eon is divided into three eras, the Paleozoic, the Mesozoic, and the Cenozoic.
B. Beginning about 570 million years ago, the **Paleozoic era** lasted for about 330 million years.
   1. Many geological developments occurred during this era, especially the movement and merging of great land masses, the continents.
   2. The Paleozoic era was the age of the invertebrates, fishes, and amphibians.
   3. The Paleozoic era is divided into six periods, the Cambrian, Ordovician, Silurian, Devonian, Carboniferous, and the Permian (see Figure 9.4).
C. The **Cambrian period** lasted for about 70 million years.
   1. Large parts of the North American continent were covered by shallow seas, and the earth's climate was warm and wet.
   2. Prevalent forms of life were blue-green bacteria, jellyfish, and **trilobites.**

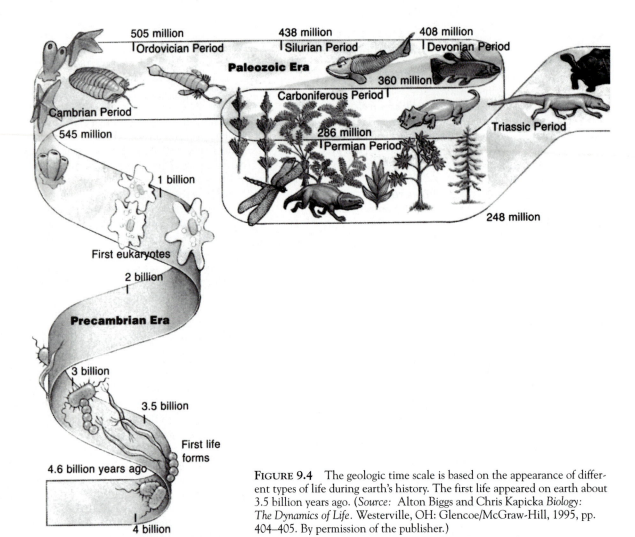

FIGURE 9.4   The geologic time scale is based on the appearance of different types of life during earth's history. The first life appeared on earth about 3.5 billion years ago. (*Source:* Alton Biggs and Chris Kapicka *Biology: The Dynamics of Life*. Westerville, OH: Glencoe/McGraw-Hill, 1995, pp. 404–405. By permission of the publisher.)

3. An early ancestor of modern crabs and lobsters, the trilobite had a shell that was divided lengthwise in three clearly notched sections.

4. Trilobites had jointed legs that were used for walking on the ocean floor; some had eyes and feelers that helped them to find food, which was probably small organisms and decaying plants and animals.

5. Although some trilobites were more than 60 centimeters (2 ft) long and weighed as much as 7 kilograms (15 lb), most were less than 7.5 centimeters (3 in) long.

6. By the end of the Paleozoic era trilobites had died out and become extinct.

D. Beginning about 500 million years ago, the second period of the Paleozoic era, the **Ordovician period,** lasted about 65 million years.

1. During the Ordovician period, the continents of North America and Europe moved toward each other. As a result of that continental movement, the **Appalachian Mountains** appeared.

2. During the Ordovician, a great mass of ice covered South America, South Africa, India, and Australia.

3. Algae and invertebrate life flourished.

E. Beginning about 435 million years ago, the third period of the Paleozoic era, the **Silurian period,** lasted about 25 million years.

1. During this time the continents of Europe and North America were one.

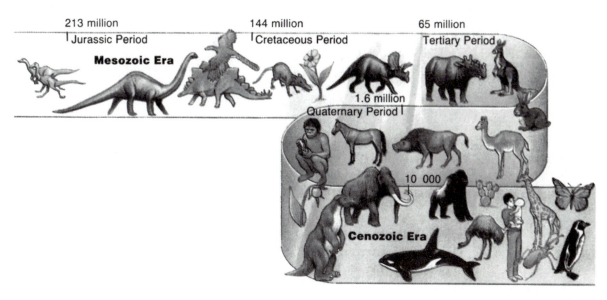

FIGURE 9.4   *continued*

2. The earth's climate was warm.
3. The first land plants appeared during this period, first beside oceans and lakes and then further inland. These earliest land plants were mosses, ferns, and early seed plants. Some fernlike trees grew to heights of 12 meters (40 ft).
4. The first fish with jaws appeared, which included armored fish, the ancestors of modern-day sharks, and fish with lungs called lungfish.
F. Beginning about 410 million years ago, the fourth period of the Paleozoic era, the **Devonian period,** lasted for about 50 million years.
   1. During the Devonian, the earth had three large continents, called Euramerica, Asia, and Gondwana.
   2. Earth's climate continued to be warm and dry. Forests appeared, and with the appearance of large plants on land, animals also began to live on land. These earliest land animals included amphibians and insects.
G. Beginning about 360 million years ago, the fifth period of the Paleozoic era, the **Carboniferous period,** lasted for about 70 million years.
   1. During this period, the North American and African continents collided.
   2. Swampy forest of giant mosses and ferns were abundant. Much of today's coal was formed during this period. Land in some of

the forested areas sank slowly and gradually. Huge piles of dead plants accumulated.
   3. The piles of plants were slowly covered by water, which helped to preserve them. The land areas continued to sink until they were far below sea level and eventually were covered by thick layers of sediment.
   4. The weight of these layers produced much pressure and heat, which caused the plant material to change into coal.
   5. The coal was soft coal, but because of the continued heat and pressure caused by the forces inside the earth, some of it later became hard coal.
   6. Insects and amphibians flourished during the Carboniferous period. It was also when the first reptiles appeared.
H. The sixth and final period of the Paleozoic, the **Permian period,** lasted for about 50 million years.
   1. During this period, continents had merged. There was now only one large supercontinent, called the **Pangaea.** Climate was variable.
   2. Many invertebrates became extinct, while reptiles flourished.
   3. Mammal-like reptiles, which had teeth and skulls similar to those of today's mammals, were probably the ancestors of mammals that appeared later.

4. Seed plants appeared during this final period of the Paleozoic era.

I. The second era of the Phanerozoic eon, the **Mesozoic era** began about 240 million years ago and lasted about 140 million years. The Mesozoic era, often called the **Age of Reptiles,** is divided into three periods: the Triassic, the Jurassic, and the Cretaceous.

1. It was during the **Triassic period** that dinosaurs and mammals first appeared.
2. The Triassic period lasted about 35 million years, during which the large Pangaea continent broke apart and the Atlantic Ocean formed.
3. Birds first appeared during the Triassic period, a time when dinosaurs were the dominant animals.

J. During the **Jurassic period,** lasting about 65 million years, dinosaurs and birds flourished.

K. The **Cretaceous period** lasted about 138 million years, ending about 63 million years ago.

1. It was during the Cretaceous period that the first snakes, marsupials, and flowering plants appeared.
2. It was toward the end of the Cretaceous period that dinosaurs became extinct.
3. Several theories have been proposed to explain the rather sudden extinction of dinosaurs. One theory and strong possibility is that a large comet crashed into the earth causing cataclysmic damage, including the extinction of dinosaurs and many other life species. Another, but perhaps related, theory is that dinosaurs and many other organisms could not survive in the cold climate that occured at the end of this era.

VII. THE MESOZOIC ERA: THE AGE OF REPTILES

A. Many land and water changes occurred during the Mesozoic era.

1. The shape of North America became much as we know it today. For the most part, the land was high and dry.
2. The Palisades Mountains were formed along the Hudson River, but have been worn down over the many years since then.
3. The Sierra Nevada Mountains and the Rocky Mountains in North America and the Andes Mountains of South America were formed during this era.
4. The Appalachian Mountains, an older mountain range that had formed millions of years earlier, during the Paleozoic era,

were wearing down to a fairly level peneplane, but toward the end of the Mesozoic they again were lifted by activity in the earth, although not to their earlier height.

B. Marked changes in plants occurred during the Mesozoic era.

1. Initially, in this era, land was covered with cycads, palmlike seed plants that produced flowerlike structures, although not true flowers.
2. Conifer trees were common in this era, including pine, cedar, spruce, juniper, and cypress.
3. Also common were ginkgo trees, trees with seeds but not flowers.
4. During the Mesozoic, the giant mosses and ferns became extinct and were replaced by flowering plants, including oak, elm, maple, birch, and beech trees.
5. Grasses and grain plants also made their appearance during the Mesozoic.

C. It was during the Mesozoic that reptiles flourished and became highly specialized. The most well known of these were the huge **dinosaurs,** meaning "terrible lizards."

1. They left behind many fossilized bones, teeth, and feces, which is why we have been able to learn so much about them.
2. Approximately half of the 350 known dinosaur species have been identified only since 1970.

D. Over a period of 165 million years all kinds of reptiles developed. They lived on land, in oceans, swamps, and in the air. Some were very large, and others were quite small. Some ate only plants (herbivorous), and others were meat eaters (carnivorous).

1. **Eoraptor** is the oldest and one of the smallest known dinosaurs. It dates back to the beginning of the dinosaur age, about 225 million years ago. It grew to about 40 inches and 25 pounds, walked on two legs, and was a predator. Its remains have been found at the foot of the Andes in northwestern Argentina.
2. **Plateosaurus** is the earliest known large dinosaur, measuring up to 8 meters (26 feet) from head to tail. It had a long neck and a long tail and browsed either on all fours or on hind legs. It lived in Europe and Greenland.
3. **Baronyx** was a large swamp-dwelling, fish-eating dinosaur that could rear up on its hind legs and use its front, curved, 12-

inch claws as hands, perhaps for grabbing fish. It had a long neck and a head that resembled a crocodile's head. Its standing height was 4.6 meters (15 feet). Its length was 9 meters (30 feet), and it weighed approximately 2 tons. It lived in England about 120 million years ago.

4. **Apatosaurus** (formerly called **Brontosaurus**) was about 20 meters (65 ft) long and weighed about 27,000 kilograms (30 tons). It had a long, thin neck and a tiny head. Its legs were the size of thick tree trunks, and it had a very long tail. It had a very small brain. It was amphibious, living both on land and in water where it fed on plants, and walked on all four feet. It lived in western North America.

5. **Diplodocus** resembled Apatosaurus, but was longer. Its length was about 27 meters (88 feet), and it weighed about 88,000 kilograms (88 tons). It lived in western North America.

6. **Stegosaurus** had a double row of triangular bony plates that ran from its small head almost to the end of its tail. The bony plates may have helped regulate body temperature. Its length was about 8 meters (25 ft). Near the end of its tail were two pairs of large, sharp, bony spikes. It had a heavy body with short, thick front legs. It was herbivorous and lived in western North America.

7. **Allosaurus** was a large predator with sharp, curved claws and long, serrated teeth. Evidence indicates that it hunted and killed in packs. Its length was about 9 meters (30 ft). It lived in western North America.

8. **Iguanodon** was a swamp dweller with teeth like an iguana's and a large thumb spike. Its length was about 10 meters (33 ft). It lived in western North America, northern Africa, and Asia.

9. **Sauropelta** was a broad-bodied plant eater with bony studs, pebbly plates, and fringes of spikes. It lived in western North America, where it grew to a length of about 5 meters (17 ft).

10. **Deinonychus** was an agile predator that may also have traveled and killed in packs. It had sickle-like claws. It grew to a length of about 3 meters (9 ft) and lived in western North America.

11. **Triceratops** was a plant eater with two sharp horns on top of its head and a third on its nose. Over its neck there was a frill of strong bony plates connected to its head. Its length was about 9 meters (30 ft), and it lived in western North America.

12. **Quetzalcoatlus** is believed to be the largest animal ever to fly. It had a standing height of about 3 meters (10 ft) and a wingspan of about 12 meters (40 ft.). It was of light weight (about 150 lbs, or 68 kg), warm blooded, and covered with fur. Its remains have been found in Texas, where it lived about 75 million years ago. It fed on fish.

13. **Giganotosaurus** is believed to be the largest of the carnivorous dinosaurs. It was approximately 12.5 meters (38 feet) long and weighed approximately 7.5 U.S. tons (6.9 metric tons). Its remains were discovered in 1993 in western Argentina, where it lived 100 million years ago. It had short front legs and could stand erect. Similar to Tyrannosaurus, which evolved approximately 35 million years later in North America, it had a large head filled with many short teeth set in powerful jaws.

14. **Tyrannosaurus** was about 11 meters (35 ft) long and weighed approximately 5 U.S. tons (4.6 metric tons). Although some scientists believe that it could move at a speed up to 65 kph (40 mph), others believe that because of its heavy build it was too slow to catch live prey and thus was a scavenger. It lived during the close of the dinosaur age, the late Cretaceous era, about 65 million years ago. It had short front legs and could stand erect, using its tail for balance. It had a large head that was roughly 1.2 meters (4 ft) long, filled with short teeth that were approximately 15 centimeters (6 in) long. With its powerful jaws set with large saw-edged teeth, it tore apart its prey. It lived in western North America.

15. **Parasaurolophus** was a plant-eating reptile with a crest on its head that may have been used to resonate mating calls. It grew to a length of about 10 meters (33 ft) and lived in western North America.

E. In the sea there were crocodiles, turtles, and other kinds of reptiles.

1. The **Ichthyosaurs** were long fishlike reptiles that used their feet and tails as paddles for swimming.
2. The **Plesiosaurs** were long, slender reptiles with necks that looked like snakes.

F. **Pterodactyls** were a group of carnivorous reptiles that glided, rather than flew, in the air. They were not true birds.
  1. They had a wide piece of skin connected from the very long joints of the fourth finger of each front leg to the body near the hip.
  3. They were of many sizes, some as small as a sparrow, and others with a wingspread of 6 meters (20 ft).

G. The first birds appeared during this era and were about the size of the modern-day pigeon.
  1. Birds developed from a branch of reptiles other than the Pterodactyls.
  2. Although their skeletons and teeth were similar to these of reptiles, their wings and bodies were partly covered with feathers.
  3. These birds had fingers with claws at the end of each wing, jaws without bills, and teeth.

H. Toward the end of this era mammals appeared.
  1. The earliest mammals were small, about the size of modern rats, with a rodentlike similarity.
  2. Although they bore a resemblance to reptiles, they were true mammals. They were warm-blooded, were covered with hair, and had mammary glands to suckle their young.

I. At the end of the Mesozoic era dinosaurs and many other species of organisms became extinct.

VIII. THE CENOZOIC ERA: THE AGE OF MAMMALS

A. Having its beginning about 60 million years ago, the Cenozoic era continues today. It is called the **Age of Mammals.**

B. Land changes took place during this era, giving rise to the land masses we know today.
  1. The fourth and most recent glacial period carried over into this era. During this fourth glacial period there were four separate ice ages.
  2. Areas along the Atlantic coast, the Gulf of Mexico, and parts of the Pacific coast, which had been under water, gradually became dry land during this era.
  3. Much volcanic activity took place in North America.
  4. The Colorado Plateau was lifted, and the Colorado River began cutting through to form the Grand Canyon.
  5. The Rocky Mountains and the Appalachian Mountains lifted, and forces of erosion began working on them. As erosion continued, great amounts of sediment were formed and deposited.
  6. The remains of many plants and animals were embedded in these sedimentary layers and became fossils.

C. Plants continued to evolve into the kinds we see today.

D. There was a tremendous increase in the number and species of insects.

E. Fishes developed into those we see today.

F. Reptiles left over from the Mesozoic era included crocodiles, alligators, turtles, lizards, and snakes.

G. Modern toothless birds with beaks appeared and grew in number and species.

H. Mammals became larger and flourished to cover the earth.
  1. At first there were two kinds of mammals—those that laid eggs from which their young were born and those that give birth to their young alive, without laying eggs.
  2. Today only a few mammals, such as the duckbill and the spiny anteater, lay eggs.

I. Some mammals, called **marsupials,** developed pouches for their young. The kangaroo and opossum are marsupials. Young marsupials are born prematurely but remain in the mother's pouch where they get warmth, shelter, and milk.

J. One group of mammals returned to the sea to spend all their lives in the water. This group includes whales, porpoises, and dolphins. They have no hind legs, their forelegs are shaped into paddles, and their tails are like those of fish. Their young are born alive (not in egg shells) and are fed by their mother's milk, just like the young of land mammals.

K. Some mammals spend most of their lives in the water, such as the seal and the sea lion.

L. Some mammals, such as the bat, developed flaps between their very long finger bones and are able to fly.

M. Many mammals of the early part of Cenozoic era became extinct.
  1. The **Smilodon,** or saber-tooth tiger, had two large teeth, or fangs, in its upper jaw.
  2. The **Megatherium** was a giant sloth that stood about 6 meters (20 ft) high on its hind legs.
  3. The **Mastodon** looked like a large elephant, with woolly and coarse hair and large tusks.

4. The **Mammoth** also looked like an elephant, but had such big teeth that there were never more than eight teeth in its mouth at a time.
5. The **Canis Diris** looked like a wolf, but was about 2 meters (6 ft) long.

N. Mammals of this era that did not become extinct gradually developed into the mammals we see today. The horse is an example of a present-day mammal that developed from an earlier version in the Cenozoic era.

1. The first horse was **Eohippus,** which appeared early in the Cenozoic era. Eohippus was about the size of a small dog, with a short neck, a few stiff hairs instead of a mane, and a short tail. Its teeth were not suited for eating grass, so it ate leaves and shrubs instead. Eohippus had four toes on each front foot and three toes on each hind foot.
2. Eohippus evolved into **Mesohippus,** which was larger, about the size of a large dog. Mesohippus had a slightly longer neck, the beginning of a mane, and a longer tail. It had just three toes on each foot, with the middle toe larger than either the other two, but when it walked or ran all three toes of each foot touched ground.
3. Following Mesohippus was **Meryohippus,** which was still larger, with an even longer neck, mane, and tail. Meryohippus also had three toes on each foot, but only the longer middle toe touched ground.
4. From Meryohippus evolved **Pliohippus.** Pliohippus was quite tall, with a good-sized mane and a long, flowing tail. Its teeth were specialized for biting and grinding the tough grass it ate. It had just one large toe on each foot, which helped it run more swiftly than its predecessors. The other two toes on each foot had become quite small, vestigial, and could no longer be seen because they were inside the foot. The nail of the large toe became the hoof. From Pliohippus evolved the modern-day horse, **Equus.**

IX. THE AGE OF HUMANS

A. Although some scientists place the history of humans as beginning in the Cenozoic era, others prefer to put humans in an era called the **Psychozoic.** Whichever the case, the **Age of Humans** began more than a million years ago, perhaps as far back as 3 or 4 million years.

1. From petrified bones, primitive tools, fossil pollen, the study of other animals, their biochemistry, and their behavior, and many other sources of evidence, scientists are gaining in their knowledge of early humans.
2. The evolution of humans appears to have begun in Africa. Tools, such as stone hand axes, have been found in Africa that date back about one and a half million years.
3. Evidence indicates that the branch of the animal kingdom that gave rise to humans emerged about eight million years ago in eastern Africa. It indicates that hominids (chimps, gorillas, and humans) all descended from a single unknown species that lived 5 to 7 million years ago (see Figure 9.5).
4. The earth's changing climate is believed to have played a role in two key events that led

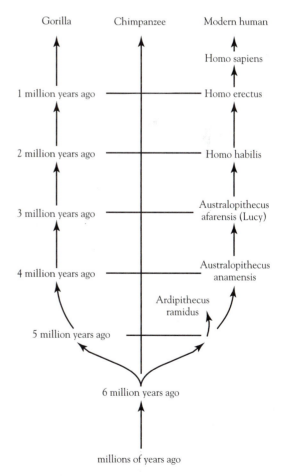

FIGURE 9.5 Common origin and parallel evolution of the hominids.

to the evolution of modern apes and humans (the hominids). The key events were a shift from living in trees to living on the ground and an increasing reliance on brain power.

5. Although apes and humans share a similar body structure, each species has developed different adaptations in response to its environment. Genetically, chimpanzees and bonobos are closest to humans. In fact, their DNA is so similar to that of humans that some scientists look at those two species for clues to the origin, evolution, and behavior of early humans.

B. A subfamily developed, the **australopithecines,** about three or four million years ago, and moved from eastern toward southern Africa as the forests retreated and they were forced to adapt to dry and open land and to find other sources of food.

1. As determined by the analysis of geographic strata where fossil remains have been found, evolution of the australopithecines begins with the *Australopithecus afarensis*, remains of which are found in the lower strata, evolving to several species in the upper strata, including *A. aethiopicus* and *Homo habilis*.

2. In 1995 scientists unearthed 4-million-year-old bones that are believed to be of a previously unknown prehuman species, named *Australopithecus anamensis*, that lived between 3.9 and 4.2 million years ago in Kenya.

3. *A. anamensis* is believed to be an intermediate step between the oldest known prehuman ancestor, called *Ardipithecus ramidus*, which lived 4.4 million years ago, and the short, apelike human ancestor called *Australopithecus afarensis*, whose most famous representative is a partial skeleton known as "Lucy."

4. Found in Ethiopia in 1974, fossil remains of the three-million-year old hominid Lucy indicate that she was as adept at upright walking as people are today.

C. Beginning about three million years ago, the evolution continued with the emergence of another subfamily, the **hominines,** who moved extensively from eastern Africa around the entire planet. There is only one genus of hominines, and that is the genus *Homo*.

1. It is believed that the last of the australopithecines coexisted for about two million years with the first of these hominines, *Homo habilis*.

2. The remains of *Homo habilis* have been found in Africa in strata of the earth that date back between 3.0 and 2.5 million years ago.

3. Fossils remains of *Homo erectus* have been found in Africa that date back about 2 million years.

4. *Homo erectus* is believed to have begun wandering off the African continent and to other parts of the world about a million years ago.

D. **Neanderthals,** descendants of *Homo erectus*, flourished from western Europe to Central Asia between 75,000 and 35,000 years ago.

1. Neanderthals lived in caves, hunted animals, used fire for cooking, and made fine tools.

2. Neanderthals became extinct, and it is not known why, although it is known that some Neanderthals coexisted with early Cro-Magnon people.

3. The differences between Neanderthal and early Cro-Magnon people was not as great as was once thought.

E. The **Cro-Magnon** is believed to be the immediate ancestor of *Homo sapiens*.

1. Cro-Magnon lived during the Late Ice Age, from 40,000 to 12,000 years ago.

2. Five skeletons of Cro-Magnon were discovered at about 1868 in the Cro-Magnon Cave in southern France. Since then, many more fossils have been found in caves in France, Spain, Italy, and other parts of southern Europe.

3. Cro-Magnon did not have the low brow, thick brow ridges, protruding chin, and receding jaw of earlier species that are characteristic of the great apes.

4. Cro-Magnon was tall, stood perfectly upright, and had a brain as large as that of modern humans.

5. Cro-Magnon made excellent tools and stone weapons, hunted with a bow and arrow, and used animal skins for clothing.

F. The **Neolithic,** called the Recent Stone Age humans, followed the Cro-Magnon.

1. Neolithic humans knew how to grind and polish stone and bone to make smooth, sharp tools.

2. They tamed wild animals and kept them in herds to be used for work, food, and clothing.

3. They built their own shelters and joined with others in villages as protection from enemies and wild animals.

EXPLORATORY ACTIVITIES FOR "THE EARTH"

1. *EXPLORING CRYSTAL FORMATION (ANY GRADE LEVEL)*

Students are fascinated by crystal formation. Here is the procedure for the formation of various crystals.

Materials needed

sugar   hot water
alum   beakers or tumblers (plastic is OK)
borax   string
salt   saucer
hand lens, magnifying glass, or microscope

Procedure. Dissolve as much sugar as possible in a tumbler half-filled with hot water, stirring vigorously as you add more sugar, a little at a time until no more will dissolve. Pour the sugar solution into a small, deep saucer and put a string into the solution (see Figure 9.6). Place the saucer in a quiet corner of the room and allow it to evaporate for a day or two. Crystals will form on the string and at the bottom of the saucer. Pour off any solution that remains, allow the crystals to dry, and examine the crystal structure with a magnifying glass or through the low-powered lens of a microscope.

You can divide your class into groups and have them repeat the experiment. Instead of sugar, one group uses salt, another uses borax, and another uses alum.

Closure and Application. Once crystals have been formed, have the students sketch and compare the crystal structures of each type. Discuss the location and formation of earth's crystals.

2. *FORCES THAT SHAPE AND CHANGE THE EARTH'S SURFACE* * (GRADES 3–9)

The continents are moving. To give students a sense of this almost imperceptible movement, use the following

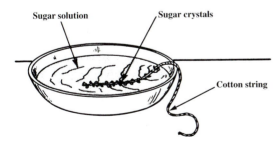

FIGURE 9.6   Forming sugar crystals.

*William J. Boone, "Continents on the Go," *Science Scope* 17(1):30–35 (September 1993). Permission granted by William J. Boone and the publishers of *Science Scope*.

trio of activities. These activities allow students to experience the wonder of the earth's dynamic processes and can be used to introduce earth science, physics, mathematics, and geography.

- The Puzzling Plates activity helps students understand and visualize plate motion better by acting as the earth's crystal plates, moving about to simulate plate motion over the past 200 million years.
- The Predicting Plate Motion activity connects mathematics to science by having students calculate the distance plates will move for specific time periods, given the current speeds of the plates.
- The What Makes Plates Move? activity is a simple demonstration of convection. Students are exposed to the big picture as they learn about one of the major forces at work in plate tectonics.

The three activities lead to excellent opportunities for further study. As a wrap-up and assessment, ask students these questions:

Where will the plates go in the future?
How could one figure out where plates were in the past?
What other plate speed calculations could be made?
What are some real-life examples of convection?
Do tectonic plates exist and move on other planets?
Why might earthquakes take place at the edge of plates?

Many students may have noticed the apparent "fitting together" of South America and Africa on the world map. As you create lessons to explain the motion of the continents (plate tectonics), an initial teaching goal should be to have students *experience* tectonic plate motion. A fun way to achieve this goal is to have students assume the roles of the major plates and act out past plate motion (Figure 9.7).

2.1 Puzzling Plates

Visual aids help to dramatize this activity and make it easier to follow. Start by having students create a time line spanning 200 million years by taping eight pieces of paper end-to-end. Students should label a point near the right-hand edge of the paper "Today." Then they should mark the time line in 1/2-meter increments, labeling the marks "50 million years ago," "100 million years ago," "150 million years ago," and "200 million years ago." For another visual aid, students can create posterboard or cardboard cutouts in the shapes of the continents. Place one or two globes or world maps at the front of the classroom and

FIGURE 9.7   Students can experience tectonic plate motion by pretending to be major plates and acting out past plate motion.

draw plate locations (shown in Figures 9.8–9.11) on the blackboard before the lesson.

Procedure

1. Have students make labels with the names of the plates shown in Figure 9.8. Then have students tape or pin these labels to their shirts. Students should hold the cutouts of the continents they represent.

2. With the aid of the labeled students, the past and present configurations of the world's plates can easily be shown. Align students (plates) at each time period shown in Figures 9.8 to 9.11. Make sure you have one student point to the appropriate part of the time line as each configuration of plates is set up. To help you make the movement of students, ask them to hold up their cutouts and look at the figures on the blackboard portraying plate locations. Try to let students find their spots, but if necessary, you can act as plate traffic director.

How long should students stay in one location before they move? It is best to keep students in place for enough time to discuss the changes in plate location. The plate motion should be shown twice, once with a thorough discussion at each time shown in the figures, and once more quickly so that the plates stay in one

place for only a minute; then move to another orientation. By moving more quickly, students can get a motion-picture feel for the continuous movement of the earth's plates.

3. Spice up your presentation by mentioning a few interesting results of plate motion. One group of students' favorite fun fact was that the ramming of the Indian plate into the Asian plate caused the Himalayas (and thus Mount Everest) to be created! This lesson can serve as a great "name that continent" geography lesson.

It should be noted that the earth's plates are *not* simply the continental land masses highlighted in Figure 9.8. However, we have found that considering only continents is the best tactic for this basic lesson. Most geologic texts provide the additional details needed for a more thorough presentation.

2.2 Predicting Plate Motion

Following the first demonstration, present students with some of the speeds at which the earth's plates are currently moving. One way of bringing the speed of each plate into perspective is to have students make some simple calculations. This exercise not only introduces

FIGURE 9.8   Continental land masses 200 million years ago.

FIGURE 9.9   Continental land masses 150 million years ago.

FIGURE 9.10   Continental land masses 100 million years ago.

FIGURE 9.11   Continental land masses 50 million years ago.

new geologic topics, but also highlights the interdisciplinary nature of science and math. Conduct this activity after the previous one because students will have a clearer idea why they are making the plate speed calculations—they have actually seen the plates moving.

How to present the lesson? The best example to use is the African plate because of its central location in the figures. The African plate moves about 31 cm per year.

Procedure

1. Supply each student with a ruler and show the class the distance the African plate moves in 1, 10, and 100 years.

2. Help students use basic multiplication to calculate how far the African plate will travel in 1, 10 and 100 years. The following formula can be used:

(Plate Speed × Number of Years = Distance)
Sample Calculation:
Q: *Calculate the distance the African plate will move in 10 years.*
A: (31 cm/yr)(10yr) = 310 cm

3. After students carry out these three calculations, supply them with masking tape. Have groups of two or three students measure and mark on the classroom floor the distances the plate moves in 1, 10, and 100 years. Starting with the floor adjacent to the wall works best. Because students will discover that the African plate will move more than 30 m in 100 years, it is probably a good idea to either ask students to measure and calculate outdoors, or ask them to calculate smaller time periods. If possible, try to stick with the large time periods because the plate motions will then really come to life.

4. After the groups have completed step 3, ask them to calculate and mark out the distance the African plate will move for additional time periods, for example, 15 years, 100 years, 350 years. Pick any time frame you wish. There are two ways in which the plate motion can be calculated: (1) using the multiplication formula, and (2) using the first step of tape markings and a ruler.

If students have calculated and marked the distance the plate will move in 10 years, they can calculate the distance the plate will move in 30 years by measuring the 10-year distance three times. For example, if the 10-year distance is 310 cm, students will measure this distance and mark the distance from the wall (or whatever starting point they have selected).

Then they will measure another 310 cm, but this time they will begin at the endpoint of their first measurement. The new distance from the wall is 620 cm. For the final measurement students will measure 310 cm from the endpoint of their second measurement. With this final measurement they will have marked out a final 30-year distance of 930 cm without having done any

paper-and-pencil calculations. Ask students to do their calculation both ways. Stress that they are predicting the future location of the plate much as a professional earth scientist would.

5. Have groups share their data on the blackboard. Stress that there will always be error in measurements, which is why different groups' floor measurements will vary.

6. The speeds of other plates can be used so that students can mark the distances many different plates move. Some plate speeds reported by Le Pichon and others are as follows:

- The Indian plate is moving into the Eurasian plate at 35 cm per year.
- The Nazca plate is moving into the American plate at 16 cm per year.
- The Indian plate is moving into the Pacific plate at 10 cm per year near New Zealand.
- In the Atlantic ocean two plates (the American and Eurasian) are separating at 29 cm per year, each moving at about 14.5 cm per year.[*]

If time permits, this lesson can also be expanded into an introduction to or review of basic metric conversions. For example, ask students to determine the distance in kilometers that a plate will move for different periods of time.

2.3 What Makes Plates Move?

To complete your lesson on plate tectonics, a demonstration can help students understand the forces that move tectonic plates.

First, divide students into discussion groups of four or so and request that each group suggest a hypothesis as to why the earth's plates move. After the brainstorming session, ask students to present their ideas to the class. Next, tell students that you are going to present a demonstration that will allow them to visualize the mechanism scientists think drives plate motion.

To create the convection demonstration, simply heat a glass coffeepot about half full of water until the water is hot, but not boiling. A hot plate or stove burner works well. Then set a jar filled with water into the pot so the bottom of the jar sits on the base of the pot and so the water of the pot and of the glass do not mix. (Two containers are used so the water in the jar will be more uniformly heated. If only the coffeepot is used to hold the water, then most of the heat from the hot plate will affect only the water at the base of the coffeepot.)

[*]X. Le Pichon, J. Francheteau, and J. Bonnin. Developments in Geotectonics. Vol. 6. Plate Tectonics (New York: Elsevier Scientific Publishing Company, 1973).

Then add unground peppercorns to the water in the smaller jar. As the water heats up, you will be able to point out to students that the peppercorns move up and down in a circular pattern. The reason for the distinctive pepper motion is *convection*, the mechanism that moves plates. If the peppercorns do not work, try adding ground pepper. Peppercorns are easier to see, but ground pepper needs less heat to be set in motion.

How does convection work? As the water in the jar is heated, gravity pulls water from the top of the jar to the bottom (this motion is marked by the peppercorns that get carried downward by the water). The reason the cold water sinks to the bottom is that it is denser than the water being heated at the bottom, which becomes less dense as it warms. As the cool water sinks, it displaces the hot water, which is forced upward. Rising water can be detected whenever a pepper grain is carried to the top of the jar. A circular pattern develops because a continuous cycle is formed of cold water sinking and heating up and hot water being pushed upward and cooling off. To avoid confusion, remind students that the peppercorns just mark the motion of the water in the jar. At this point, stress that the circulation pattern of the peppercorns (both up and down) is taking place *throughout* the jar of water.

Only now, after this explanation of what convection looks like in the real world, should you point out to students that the earth's plates are moved by the same sort of forces that move the peppercorns in the water. Explain that within the earth, radioactive decay toward the center heats magma. The heated magma is pushed toward the earth's surface by the sinking, cooler magma from above. Because of the limited amount of room at the earth's surface for magma, the cool magma at the surface is pushed aside by the rising currents of hot magma and sinks into the earth, just as cool water at the surface of the heated water sinks to the bottom of the jar. Many students will ask why the cool magma sinks. Remind students that cool magma is denser than hot magma (just as cool water is denser than hot water).

Following the demonstration, ask students how close their hypothesis was to that suggested by scientists. In concluding, point out that the Puzzling Plates activity shows what is happening at the surface of the earth, whereas the moving peppercorns display the force within the earth that moves the plates.

3. HISTORY OF THE EARTH: MAKING A LEAF OR A SHELL IMPRINT*

3.1 Make a Leaf or a Shell Imprint

Obtain a pie tin and coat the bottom and sides with a thin layer of petroleum jelly. Cover a leaf with petroleum jelly and place it on the bottom of the pie tin (Figure 9.12). Prepare a mixture of plaster of paris in a large tin can by adding water to the plaster of paris according to instructions on the package. Stir the mixture gently with a flat stick until it is smooth and has the consistency of pancake batter. Now pour the plaster of paris slowly into the pie tin over the leaf until you have a layer 13 millimeters (1/2 in) thick. Let the plaster of paris set for 30 minutes and then remove the cast carefully. Wash the petroleum jelly off with soap and warm water the next day after the cast has become very hard. Dry the cast with a soft cloth.

Repeat this activity, using a small seashell such as a clam or oyster shell. The cast you obtain will be a negative cast with a hollow imprint of the shell. To make a positive cast with a raised imprint, cover the negative cast with a thin coat of petroleum jelly. Coat one side of a strip of cardboard, 7.5 centimeters (3 in) wide, with petroleum jelly, and wrap the cardboard around the cast, holding it firmly in place with a rubber band (Figure 9.13). Pour more plaster of paris over the negative cast until you have a layer at least 2.5 centimeters (1 in) thick. Let it set for 1 hour. Now remove the cardboard and, inserting a knife gently between the positive and negative casts, separate the two casts. Smooth the sides of the positive cast with sandpaper. The next day wash off the petroleum jelly with soap and warm water. Preserve the cast by giving it a coat of shellac.

---

*To conserve space in this book, the activities that follow are written only as instructions on how to make leaf and shell imprints and not as detailed lessons. However, to the extent that materials and the maturity of your students allow, we encourage you to incorporate the activities into your own lesson plans in a way that your students are doing as much of the activity as possible, individually or in groups, rather than to do them as teacher demonstrations.

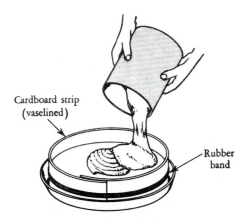

Cardboard strip (vaselined)

Rubber band

FIGURE 9.12   A plaster of paris leaf imprint.

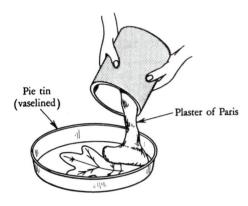

Pie tin
(vaselined)

Plaster of Paris

FIGURE 9.13   Making a negative and positive cast of an imprint.

3.2 Make a Carbon Imprint of a Leaf

Coat a leaf with a very thin layer of petroleum jelly, making sure to coat the side of the leaf where the veins are raised. Place the leaf, jellied side up, on some newspaper. Place a sheet of carbon paper, carbon side down, on the leaf. Cover the carbon paper with a sheet of white paper and rub the side of a round pencil or dowel back and forth many times on the white paper. The leaf will now be coated with carbon. Now place the leaf, carbon side down, between two fresh pieces of white paper, and rub the pencil or dowel back and forth on the top sheet several times. Remove the top sheet and the leaf. The bottom sheet will have a carbon imprint of the leaf, showing the size, shape, and vein formation. Draw in any gaps in the leaf's shape and vein pattern. Point out that you made an artificial coating of carbon on the leaf. What actually happens in nature is that the leaf itself carbonizes and forms an imprint on the top and underside of the rock.

STUDENT BOOKS AND OTHER RESOURCES FOR "THE EARTH"

Boone, W. J. "Continents on the Go." *Science Scope* 17(1):30–35 (September 1993).

Brendzel, S. "Schoolyard Erosion and Terrain Studies." *Science Scope* 17(7):36–38 (April 1994).

Brook, R., and M. Tisdale. "Mystery of the Mesa: A Science Detective Story." *Science and Children* 31(2):33–40 (October 1993).

Cherif, A. H., and G. E. Adams. "Planet Earth: Can Other Planets Tell Us Where We Are Going?" *American Biology Teacher* 56(1):26–37 (January 1994).

Chrichton, M. *Jurassic Park: The Junior Novelization.* New York: Grosset and Dunlap, 1993.

Colegate, C., and J. Smith. "A Cave of Our Own." *Science and Children* 33(1):21–23, 65 (September 1995).

Cook, N. *Measuring Earthquakes.* Menlo Park, CA: Addison-Wesley, 1994.

Crossland, C. *Ten Tall Oaktrees.* New York: Tambourine, 1993.

Czerniak, C. M. "The Jurassic Spark." *Science and Children* 31(2):19–22 (September 1993).

Daugherty, B. "The Great Bone Search." *Science and Children* 31(2):14–16 (September 1993).

Davidson, K, and A. R. Williams. "Under Our Skin: Hot Theories on the Center of the Earth." *National Geographic* 189(1):100–111 (January 1996).

Dixon, D. *Dougal Dixon's Dinosaurs.* Honesdale, PA:Boyds Mills, 1993.

Fields, S. F. "Life in a Teaspoon of Soil." *Science Scope* 16(5):16–18 (February 1993).

Ford, B. A. *Project Earth Science: Geology.* Arlington, VA: National Science Teachers Association, 1996.

Gamlin, L. *Eyewitness Science: Evolution.* New York: Dorling Kindersley, 1993.

Getz, D. *Frozen Man.* New York: Holt, 1994.

Gibbons, G. *Caves and Caverns.* New York: Harcourt Brace, 1993.

Gore, R. "The Cambrian Period Explosion of Life." *National Geographic* 184(4):120–136 (October 1993).

———. "Dinosaurs." *National Geographic* 183(1):2–52 (January 1993).

———. "Living with California's Faults." *National Geographic* 187(4):2–35 (April 1995).

———. "The Dawn of Humans: Neanderthals." *National Geographic* 189(1):2–35 (January 1996).

Jam, T. *The Year of Fire.* New York: McElderry, 1993.

Johansen, D. C. "The Dawn of Humans: Face-to-Face with Lucy's Family." *National Geographic* 189(3):96–117 (March, 1996).

Johnson, R. L. *Investigating the Ozone Hole.* Minneapolis: Lerner, 1993.

Kindersley, D. *The Visual Dictionary of Dinosaurs.* New York: Author, 1993.

———. *The Visual Dictionary of the Earth.* New York: Author, 1993.

Larson, W. *The Dinosaurs of Jurassic Park.* New York: Grossett and Dunlap, 1993.

Leakey, M. "The Dawn of Humans: The Farthest Horizon." *National Geographic* 188(3):38–51 (September 1995).

Lessem, D. *The Iceman.* New York: Crown, 1994.

Lewington, A. *Antonio's Rain Forest.* Minneapolis: Carolrhoda, 1993.

Lowder, C. C. "Spelunking in the Classroom." *Science and Children* 31(3):19–22 (November/December 1993).

McVey, V. *The Sierra Club Kid's Guide to Planet Care and Repair*. San Francisco: Sierra Club, 1993.

Munsart, C. A. *Investigating Science with Dinosaurs*. Arlington, VA: National Science Teachers Association, 1993.

National Energy Foundation and the U.S. Bureau of Mines. *Out of the Rock*. Arlington, VA: National Science Teachers Association, 1994.

Pringle, L. *Oil Spills: Damage, Recovery, and Prevention*. New York: Morrow, 1993.

Riesser, S., and L. Airey. "Will My Fossil Float?" *Science and Children* 31(2):42–43 (October 1993).

Rigby, S. *Our Planet: Caves*. Mahwah, NJ: Troll, 1994.

Roberts, P. L. *A Green Dinosaur Day: A Guide for Developing Thematic Units in Literature-Based Instruction, K–6*. Needham Heights, MA: Allyn and Bacon, 1993.

Saters, J. F. *Deep-Sea Vents: Living Worlds Without Sunshine*. New York: Cobblehill, 1994.

Seymour, S. *Mountains*. New York: Morrow, 1994.

Shewell, J. "Focus on the Rock." *Science and Children* 31(6):28–29 (March 1994).

———. "Technology and 'Buried Sunshine'." *Science Scope* 18(5):35–36 (February 1995).

Silver, D. M. *One Small Square: Seashore*. New York: Freeman, 1993.

———. *One Small Square: Cave*. New York: Freeman, 1993.

Skurzynski, G. *Zero Gravity*. Old Tappan, NJ: Simon & Schuster, 1994.

Stetsko, D. "Exploring Erosion." *Teaching Pre K–8* 24(5):60 (February 1994).

Tattersall, I. *The Human Odyssey: Four Million Years of Human Evolution*. New York: Prentice Hall, 1993.

Teitelbaum, M. *Welcome to Jurassic Park*. Racine, WI: Golden Book, 1993.

Thompson, S. A., and K. S. Thompson. "Volcanoes in the Classroom—An Explosive Learning Experience." *Science and Children* 33(6):16–19, 44 (March, 1996).

Van Burgh, D., E. N. Lyons, and M. Boyington. *How to Teach with Topographic Maps*. Arlington, VA: National Science Teachers Association, 1994.

Wiggers, R. *The Amateur Geologist*. Arlington, VA: National Science Teachers Association, 1993.

Water, Weather, and Climate

WATER

I. THE WATER TABLE

A. When water falls to earth as rain or other forms of precipitation, some of the water sinks into the earth, sinking deeper until it reaches the solid rock beneath the soil.

1. This solid rock may be porous or nonporous.

2. Porous rock, or **permeable** rock, is either loose (like gravel) or has spaces in it (like sandstone), and it allows the water to enter and pass through it.

3. Water will continue to sink deeper into the earth until it is stopped by a layer of nonporous or impermeable rock. **Impermeable** rock is firm and solid (like granite) and stops the water from sinking any deeper.

4. The soil and rock above this nonporous layer then become soaked or saturated with water, which is then called **groundwater.**

5. The upper level of the groundwater in the soaked soil and rock is called the **water table.**

6. The level or depth of this water table depends on how much rain has fallen recently, how porous the soil and rock are, and how far down the porous layer goes until it meets a layer of nonporous rock that will not let the water sink any deeper. During dry weather the level of the water table decreases. During rainy weather the depth increases.

7. As a rule, the level of the water table follows the general contour of the land, sloping where the surface of the land slopes and rising where the surface rises.

8. Groundwater can flow through a porous layer of soil and rock; thus it is possible for water to enter the ground at one place and to appear in another place later.

9. Whenever the land surface dips below the water table, the groundwater flows out to the surface of the land, forming a spring, joining with a river, or helping to feed a pond or lake.

II. WELLS

A. A well is a hole that is dug or drilled deep enough into the ground to reach the water table.

1. Water then flows into the hole, filling it with water and forming a well. When water is taken out of the well, it is replaced by the water that is flowing underground. A well must be dug deep enough so that when the level of the water table drops during dry weather, the well will not run dry.

B. An **artesian well** is a well that is sunk deep into the earth's surface. The water is obtained from a layer of porous rock, called an **aquifer.** The aquifer is sandwiched between two layers of nonporous rock.

1. This layer of porous rock originally began at the earth's surface and then slanted

downward into the earth. Water entering this layer can travel only through this porous layer. It cannot move up or down through the nonporous layers of rock above and below it.

2. When a well is drilled deep enough to reach this porous layer, the water in it rises again, either to the land surface or to just below the surface, depending on the contour of the land. The water rises because the water at the beginning of the aquifer is higher and exerts pressure on water below it. Water in an artesian well is under pressure in exactly the same way as the water at the bottom of a long, slanting pipe would be under pressure.

3. Water from artesian wells is usually pure, because it comes straight up the walls of the well and does not dissolve any minerals in other layers of rocks on its way up.

III. SPRINGS

A. When the water table meets the earth's surface, a spring is formed.
1. Springs may also form on hillsides where the water table cuts across the earth's surface.
2. Spring water usually has minerals dissolved in it. Spring water that comes from deep below the earth's surface may have so many minerals dissolved in it that the water is not suitable for drinking.

B. **Hot springs** form when the groundwater is heated because of volcanic activity going on below the earth's surface.
1. Hot springs are common in regions where there is volcanic activity because the heated rocks are very near the earth's surface in these areas.
2. The water is heated either by contact with the hot, melted rock (magma), or by mixing with steam and hot gases that are escaping from the magma.
3. Because hot water dissolves minerals better than cold water, most hot springs have a high mineral content.

IV. LAKES, SWAMPS, BOGS, MARSHES, AND WETLANDS

A. **Lakes** are large bodies of water found on many parts of the earth's surface, usually made up of a depression, called a basin, that is filled with water.

1. Some lake basins were formed by faulting, in which layers of rock inside the earth slipped over other layers of rock and were pushed up to form a hollow in the earth's surface.
2. Some basins were formed when forces within the earth, acting in a sideways direction, pushed layers of rock and into wavelike folds with crests and hollow troughs.
3. Glaciers often gouged out deep hollows as they moved across the earth's surface, leaving these hollows to fill with water as the glaciers later retreated.
4. In some cases, a basin was formed when lava from a volcano created a dam across a valley.
5. Lakes were often formed from rivers when trees, brush, and other debris clogged up the rivers, making them back up to form a lake.

B. Lakes obtain their water in many ways.
1. Rain and other forms of precipitation fall directly into the lake.
2. Rain that falls on land around the lake runs off into the lake.
3. Rivers flow into the lake.
4. When the water table is above the surface of the lake basin, groundwater flows into the lake in the form of a spring.

C. Lakes do not remain on earth as long as hills or mountains.
1. Some lakes become filled with sediment carried by streams.
2. Sometimes plants growing at the edge of a lake advance farther and farther into the lake until the lake becomes filled and disappears.
3. Some lakes disappear because the springs in their basins, or the rivers that feed the lakes, dry up and disappear.

D. **Swamps** and **marshes** are lake basins that are filled by small streams and that partly or completely filled with live plants, dead plants, sediment, and water.
1. The plant life of a swamp consists largely of trees, and that of a marsh consists primarily of grasses.
2. Some swamps and marshes are just beginning to become lakes, whereas others are slowly becoming dry land.
3. When swamps and marshes are drained, the land makes very fertile farmland; however, the draining of a swamp or marsh re-

moves the habitat of many species of wildlife.

E. A **bog** is like a swamp, but smaller, and the water of a bog is nearly completely covered by live plants, decaying plants, and sediment, so much so that a person could walk on a bog. To do that is very dangerous, however, because the "ground" is plant life and sediment that is actually covering a small lake basin, and a person could sink in too far to get out.

    1. Unlike marshes and swamps, bogs receive rainwater as their primary source of water. The water of bogs has far fewer dissolved minerals.

    2. The plants of a bog are often mosses, which can live in a less nourishing habitat than that of the mineral-rich swamps and marshes.

    3. Over time a bog completely fills in and becomes land that can support grasses, shrubs, and trees.

F. **Wetlands** is a term used for any natural land area that is wet for a portion of the year. This includes bogs, swamps, sloughs, flood plains, marshes, prairie potholes, and river bottom lands.

    1. Wetlands are producers of life, some being equal in output to the same amount of tropical rain forest.

    2. Wetlands provide feeding, spawning, and nursery grounds for more than half the saltwater finfish and shellfish harvested annually in the United States, and for most of our freshwater game fish.

    3. Wetlands are a habitat for a third of the country's resident bird species, more than half of its migratory bird species, and for one of three plants and animals currently listed on the federal registry of endangered and threatened species.

    4. Wetlands absorb and filter pollutants that would otherwise degrade lakes, rivers, reservoirs, and aquifers.

    5. Wetlands provide flood control, recharge groundwater aquifers, and help to stabilize shorelines and riverbanks.

    6. Wetlands are found in every region and climate of the United States.

    7. Alaska contains 170 million acres of wetlands, and Hawaii has 52,000 acres of wetlands sheltering four endangered species of birds.

    8. Through photosynthesizing organisms, wetlands bind large amounts of carbon, preventing it from entering the atmosphere as carbon dioxide.

    9. Wetlands are the special habitats for unique species of life.

    10. Because of their ecological value, it is illegal to drain wetlands to make more land available for farming and building construction.

V. IMPURITIES IN WATER

A. As rain begins to fall from the clouds, it is quite pure.

    1. As rain falls through the air, it dissolves some of the gases in the air and picks up bits of dust and bacteria that are in the air.

    2. In some heavily industrialized areas the rain picks up sulfur and nitrogen compounds from industrial wastes and forms sulfuric acid and nitric acid, which then pollute bodies of water and kill plants. This form of contaminated rain is called **acid rain.**

B. When rain reaches the ground, it picks up many other impurities. Many kinds of minerals dissolve in the water. Some sand, silt, mud, and other sediments are not dissolved but remain suspended in the water as very fine particles. The water also comes in contact with various kinds of bacteria that are found in the wastes of organisms. Some of the impurities in water are harmless to humans, plants, and animals, whereas others can be very harmful.

    1. Small amounts of minerals and gases in water make it taste better, because the water would taste "flat" without them.

    2. The mineral salt content of many bodies of water is nearly poisonous to humans and other organisms. To be usable, the salts must be removed.

    3. Some impurities in water make the water toxic to fish and other wildlife.

    4. Many bacteria in water cause diseases in humans and must be removed or killed before the water is suitable for drinking.

VI. PURIFICATION OF WATER

A. In the home, harmful bacteria in the water can be killed by boiling, and suspended material and gases that give the water a bad taste can be removed by passing the water through charcoal.

B. In the laboratory, water can be purified by **distillation.**

1. In distillation the water is boiled, which drives off the gases that are dissolved in the water, and the water vapor that forms is led through a tube that is surrounded by cold water, which condenses the water vapor back into water.
2. The hot, boiling water kills the bacteria, which are left behind when the water is changed into water vapor.
3. Minerals and suspended materials are also left behind when the water is changed into water vapor.

C. Cities go through several steps to purify water for drinking.
1. First, the water is run into large basins, where the suspended particles of sediment settle to the bottom.
2. Because the very tiny particles settle very slowly, two chemicals—alum and lime—are added to the water, forming a jellylike material. The very fine particles of sediment stick to this material and settle to the bottom.
3. Some of the bacteria in the water are also trapped by the material and are removed when the material settles.
4. The water is then passed to another basin containing layers of sand and gravel. The water passes through these layers, which remove the rest of the suspended particles along with more of the bacteria.
5. Sometimes a layer of charcoal is placed between the sand and gravel to remove coloring matter and bad-tasting gases from the water.
6. To remove the remaining bacteria, the water is treated by spraying it into the air, a process called *aeration*. Aeration allows the oxygen in the air to kill the bacteria and, at the same time, puts oxygen into the water to improve its taste. If there is a large amount of bacteria present, the water is treated with chlorine, which kills all the bacteria.
7. Most cities also add fluorides to the water. Fluorides help reduce tooth decay by limiting the acid production of bacteria in the mouth.

VII. SOFT AND HARD WATER

A. Water that has certain minerals dissolved in it, in the form of calcium and magnesium salts, is called hard water.
1. Rainwater that has not touched the ground is very soft water. It is excellent for washing purposes; however, once rainwater has hit the ground it begins to dissolve ground minerals with which it comes in contact and becomes harder.
2. Hard water is difficult to use for washing because it will not produce a lather when used with soap. Instead, it forms a scum, which is the product formed when the dissolved calcium and magnesium salts react with the soap.
3. We call it hard water because it is "hard" to make a lather or wash with this water. It also leaves mineral deposits inside steam furnaces, hot water heaters, hot water pipes, and tea and coffee pots.

B. Hard water can be made into soft water in several ways.
1. One way to soften hard water is to add certain chemicals, such as ammonia, washing soda, borax, or trisodium phosphate, which remove the calcium and magnesium from the water by precipitating them out of the water. This process of softening hard water is called the lime-soda process.
2. Another way is to use a chemical called zeolite, which removes the calcium and magnesium when hard water is passed through it, and replaces these minerals with sodium, which does not affect soap. When the zeolite is used up and does not work any longer, it can be restored by soaking it overnight in a strong saltwater solution therefore replenishing the sodium.

   Zeolite is a group of more than 30 silicon containing minerals naturally occurring in cavities and veins of volcanic and sedimentary rocks of arid regions and on the ocean floor. Zeolites have unusual properties that make them valuable as filtering agents. Synthetic zeolites have been developed.
3. Another way to soften hard water is to use certain resins that are able to remove calcium and magnesium from the water.
4. Today, many people use detergents instead of soap. Although detergents are not soap, they are made of chemicals that have a cleaning action similar to that of soap. The chemicals in solid and liquid detergents are not affected by the calcium and magnesium salts in hard water, so they lather easily in hard water and do not form a scum.
5. However, when detergents come in contact with the water of streams and lakes, they can form so many suds that the sur-

DEMONSTRATION 10.1
Making Water Potable (Fit to Drink)

A. By Distillation

Fill a glass jar half full with water. To the water add some food coloring, a tablespoon of salt, and some soil. Shake the mixture well, then pour it into a tea kettle. Obtain a long piece of rubber tubing. Place one end of the rubber tubing inside the spout of the tea kettle and use modeling clay in and around the spout to hold the rubber tubing in place and to make sure that the steam will pass out only through the tubing (Figure 10.1). Put the other end of the rubber tubing into a glass tumbler that has been placed in a pan filled with ice cubes. Now place the tea kettle on a hot plate. When the water boils, drops of water will condense in the tumbler or drip from the hose into the tumbler. This water will be clear and pure, and it will not taste salty. When the water in the tea kettle boiled and changed into water vapor or steam, the impurities were left in the tea kettle. Only pure, clean water condensed as the steam was cooled in the tumbler.

B. By Settling

Fill a glass jar about three quarters full of water. Add a mixture of coarse and fine soil to the jar, shake the contents thoroughly, and then set the jar down, cover it, and allow the soil to settle. The coarse soil will quickly settle to the bottom, but it may take many days for the fine soil to settle completely, leaving the water free of sand and soil.

C. By Filtering

In a large plastic or glass funnel, place a layer of small pebbles, then a layer of gravel or coarse sand, and finally a layer of fine sand (Figure 10.2). First pour some clean water through the funnel to allow the layers to settle and pack together. Then place the funnel in a narrow-mouth glass jar and pour some muddy water into the funnel. The layers will filter the mud, and clear water will pass into the jar.

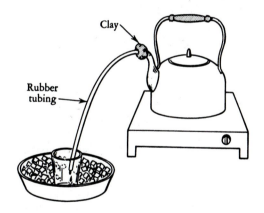

FIGURE 10.1   Distillation purifies water.

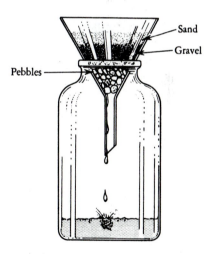

FIGURE 10.2   Filtering helps purify water.

---

face of the body of water becomes covered with suds and the normal oxygen and gas exchange cannot take place at the surface of the water. Fish and other aquatic organisms then die because of the lack of dissolved oxygen that they need.

VIII. WATER PRESSURE

    A. Water has weight and exerts a pressure because of its weight.

        1. At any given point in an amount of water, the water will exert pressure downward, upward, and sideways, and the pressure is the same in all directions.

        2. At a deeper point in the water, the pressure will be greater, but this new and greater pressure will again be the same in all directions.

    B. When water is placed in a container, its pressure is greatest at the bottom.

DEMONSTRATION 10.2

Hard and Soft Water: Action of a Detergent

A. Make and Soften Temporary Hard Water

Obtain some limewater from the drugstore. Pour lime-water into a test tube until it is half full and, using a soda straw, bubble carbon dioxide from your breath through the limewater. At first the limewater will become milky, but continue the bubbling until the milkiness disappears. Pour an equal amount of distilled water or rainwater into a second test tube. Make a soap solution by dissolving soap shavings in warm water. Now add an equal number of drops of soap solution to each of the test tubes and, while holding a thumb over the mouth of each test tube, shake them vigorously. The soft water will make lots of suds, but the temporary hard water will make very few suds and form curds instead.

Make some more temporary hard water and boil it for a few minutes to remove the hardness. Add the same amount of soap solution you added to the other two test tubes, and note how the boiled water now makes lots of suds.

B. Make and Soften Permanent Hard Water

To a test tube half full of water, add a small amount of Epsom salts (magnesium sulfate), shaking the test tube until the salt dissolves. Pour the same number of drops of soap solution (as prepared above) into the test tube containing the freshly prepared permanent hard water and into a test tube containing an equal amount of distilled water or rainwater. Shake both test tubes vigorously and note the difference in amount of suds produced.

Soften the permanent hard water by adding some washing soda, borax, or ammonia. Now add the same number of drops of soap solution you added to the other test tubes and compare the increased amount of suds formed.

C. Action of Detergents

Obtain some high-sudsing detergent. Prepare samples of temporary and permanent hard water (described in demonstrations A and B). Obtain three test tubes. Pour some temporary hard water into one test tube, an equal amount of permanent hard water into the second test tube, and an equal amount of distilled water or rainwater into the third test tube. Now add the same amount of detergent to each test tube and shake them vigorously. Note that all three test tubes have lots of suds, showing that the sudsing (and cleaning) action of detergents is not affected by water hardness.

---

1. The shape of the container does not affect the water pressure on the bottom, but the height of the container does.
2. The higher the container, the deeper the water, and the greater the water pressure will be at the bottom.

C. When water is in a closed container, any pressure on the water will be sent or transmitted in all directions through the container.
   1. This pressure occurs because the molecules of water are so close together that the pressure is passed unchanged from molecule to molecule.
   2. Special machines, called **hydraulic machines,** make use of this property of water in a closed container, being able to send a small force elsewhere and, at the same time, change the small force into a much larger force.
   3. Hydraulic machines include the hydraulic press for baling cotton, the hydraulic lift for raising automobiles at service stations, and hydraulic brakes in a car or truck.

IX. WATER CAN BE USED TO DO WORK
   A. When water moves from a higher level to a lower level, because of the earth's pull of gravity on the water, it has a great deal of energy. This energy of motion is called **kinetic energy.**
      1. Because of kinetic energy, water can exert a great amount of pressure and force. The faster the water moves, the greater kinetic energy it will have.
      2. Moving water can be used to turn water-wheels. Waterwheels are used to grind grain or run machines in factories. Waterwheels, called **turbines,** in dams, for example, are used to run large electric generators to produce electricity.
   B. When water is heated to a high enough temperature, it will boil, changing from a liquid to a gas, called steam, that expands tremendously and can exert a great deal of pressure and force.
      1. Steam can be used to run machines and engines and to turn large turbines, which can then run giant electric generators.

DEMONSTRATION 10.3
Water Pressure

A. Demonstrate Water Pressure

Obtain a tall can. Place a piece of two-by-four wood, or any other wood of suitable thickness, in the can. Use a hammer and a large nail to punch a hole in one side of the can near the bottom (Figure 10.3).

Now take the can to a sink and, while keeping one finger over the hole, fill the can with water. Release your finger, and a stream of water will shoot out some distance from the hole, showing that water exerts pressure.

B. Water Pressure Is the Same in All Directions

Use a hammer and large nail to punch holes around the sides of a tall can near the bottom (Figure 10.4). It may help to use a block of wood (as described in demonstration A) when making the holes. Take the can to the sink and run water into it rapidly so that it stays full while water is escaping through the holes. Note how the water shoots out exactly the same distance from all the holes.

C. The Effect of Depth on Water Pressure

Use a hammer and large nail to punch three holes in one side of a tall can, using a block of wood (as described in demonstration A) if necessary. One hole should be near the top of the can, another hole in the middle, and the third hole near the bottom (Figure 10.5). Take the can to the sink and run water into it rapidly so that it stays full while the water is escaping through the holes. The greater the depth of the water, the farther it will shoot out of the hole.

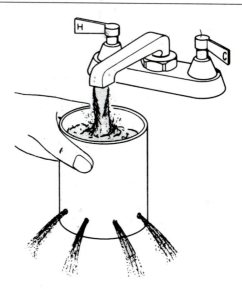

FIGURE 10.4   Water exerts the same pressure in all directions.

FIGURE 10.5   The deeper the water, the greater the water pressure will be.

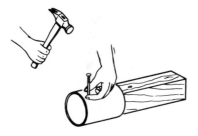

FIGURE 10.3   Using a piece of wood to punch a hole in one side of a can.

X. SINKING AND FLOATING

A. When a body is placed in water, two forces act on the body—the earth's pull of gravity and the upward force of the water being displaced.
  1. The first force, the earth's pull of gravity, pulls downward on the body. The weight of the body determines the amount of downward force acting on it—the heavier the body, the greater the earth's pull of gravity on it and the larger the downward force will be.
  2. The second force is the upward force of the water that has been displaced, or pushed out of the water. The size of the body determines the amount of upward force of the displaced water—the larger the body, the more water it can displace, and the greater the upward force.
B. A small, heavy body usually sinks in water.
  1. Because it is small, such a body will displace a small amount of water, and a small, upward force will act on the body.
  2. Because the body is heavy, the downward force resulting from the pull of gravity will be great. Because the downward force acting on the body is greater than the upward force acting on the body, the body will sink.
C. A large, light body usually floats in water.
  1. Because it is large, such a body will displace a large amount of water, and a large, upward force will act on the body.
  2. Because the body is light, the downward force resulting from the pull of gravity will be small.
  3. A large, light body will sink in water only until the upward force of the displaced water equals the downward force of the object's weight, and then the object will float.
D. Although iron and steel are quite heavy, a **ship** made of iron or steel can float.
  1. The iron or steel is spread out over a large area to form a hollow shell so that it will displace a large amount of water and a large upward force will act on the metal.
  2. The downward force, caused by the combined weight of metal, air, equipment, passengers, and cargo, is still less than the upward force caused by the displaced water, so the ship floats.
  3. When a ship is set afloat, it sinks until it displaces just enough water to create an upward force that equals the downward force produced by the ship's weight.

  4. When the ship is loaded, it sinks deeper until enough water is displaced to produce an additional upward force to support the weight of the cargo.
E. A **submarine** floats for the same reason that an iron or steel ship floats.
  1. The submarine is able to sink because it has tanks that let in water and make it heavy enough (or increase the downward force) to sink.
  2. When the water is pumped out of the tanks, the submarine becomes lighter and rises to the surface.
F. A body floats more easily in saltwater than in freshwater.
  1. The same downward force of gravity acts on a body, whether it is in saltwater or freshwater.
  2. However, saltwater is heavier than freshwater because it has more minerals dissolved in it, and, as a result, displaced saltwater has a greater upward force than displaced freshwater.
  3. If a ship sails from freshwater into saltwater, it rises farther out of the water, because the salt water has a greater upward force than the freshwater.
  4. If a ship sails from saltwater into freshwater, it sinks farther into the water, because the freshwater has a smaller upward force than the saltwater.

XI. WATER CONSERVATION

A. Every year the need for freshwater becomes greater.
  1. Today, each person in the United States uses more than 58,000 liters (15,000 gal) of water a year for drinking, washing, laundry, cooking, heating, and air-conditioning purposes.
  2. Industry uses approximately 606,000 liters (160,000 gal) of water a year for each person living in the United States.
  3. Agriculture also uses large amounts of water to irrigate the land.
  4. Only a small percentage of the earth's freshwater is available for immediate use. The earth's total water distribution is as follows:

Rivers, lakes, and shallow groundwater	0.3%
Deep groundwater	0.3%
Saltwater lakes, soil, atmospheric moisture, and glaciers	0.1%
Polar ice	2.2%
Oceans (saltwater)	97.1%

DEMONSTRATION 10.4
Buoyancy and Displacement

A. A Body's Apparent Loss of Weight in Water

Tie a string around a stone, connect it to a spring balance, and note the weight of the stone in air (Figure 10.6). Now lower the stone into a large, wide-mouthed jar half filled with water. Observe the loss of weight caused by the upward buoyant force of the displaced water.

B. A Floating Body Displaces Its Own Weight of Water

Make an overflow cup. Obtain a large Styrofoam cup, and use a hole puncher to punch a hole near the top of the cup. Get a plastic straw with a diameter slightly larger than the hole, cut off a 5-centimeter (2-in) piece of straw, and insert it into the hole (Figure 10.7). Seal the outside spot where the straw enters the cup with glue or chewing gum. Coat the underside of the end of the straw lightly with petroleum jelly. Pour water into the cup until the water is just level with the straw. Get a block of wood that will fit inside the cup. Weigh the block. Get a small can and weigh it. Now place the can so that its center is beneath the end of the straw. Lower the block of wood gently into the cup of water. The displaced water will overflow into the empty can. When the water stops overflowing, weigh the can again. Subtract the weight of the can from the combined weight of the overflow water and the can. The difference will be the weight of the overflow water. Compare the weight of the overflow water with the weight of the block of wood. The weights should be just about the same.

C. A Steel Ship Floats

Cut out two pieces of aluminum foil 15 centimeters (6 in) long and 10 centimeters (4 in) wide. Fold one piece in half again and again, flattening the foil each time with your fingers to remove any trapped air, until you have a small, flat wad. Drop this wad into a pie tin full of water, and it will sink to the bottom because it displaces very little water, thus producing a small upward force. Fold the second piece of foil lengthwise and shape with your fingers until you have a figure similar to a rectangular boat. Place this boat in the water. As with a steel ship, it will float because it displaces a large amount of water, producing a large upward buoyant force.

D. The Effect of More Cargo on a Ship

Place a small rectangular cake pan in a rectangular glass aquarium almost full of water. Measure how much of the sides of the pan sink below the level of the water. Now spread a few stones evenly along the bottom of the pan. Again measure how much of the sides of the pan sink. The pan sinks more deeply in the water, displacing enough water to support the added weight of the stones.

E. Comparing the Buoyancy of Saltwater and Freshwater

Fill two identical large, wide-mouthed jars about three quarters full of water. Add salt to the water in one jar, a tablespoon at a time and stirring vigorously, until no more salt will dissolve. Now place an egg first in the freshwater and then in the saltwater (Figure 10.8). The egg will float in the heavier, more buoyant, salt water. Get two large ice cubes of the same size, put one into each jar, and note which ice cube protrudes the most from the water.

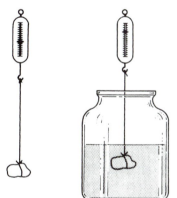

FIGURE 10.6   When lowered into water, the rock seems to lose weight.

FIGURE 10.7
An overflow cup.

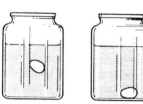

FIGURE 10.8   An egg will sink in freshwater and float in saltwater.

B. As the population in the United States increases, the need for water could become greater than the supply, so we must continue to take steps to conserve water.
   1. We should avoid needless use and waste of water.
   2. Soil and forest conservation practices helps prevent water from running off quickly before it can be used.
   3. Dams holds back river water that is rushing to the sea.
   4. Scientists and engineers continue to explore economical ways to change seawater into usable freshwater.
C. Our water is also being polluted.
   1. Some factories still pour into rivers large amounts of waste materials that pollute the water.
   2. Wastes and sewage from homes in some cities are also dumped into rivers without

first being treated so that the water will not be polluted.
   3. This means that those cities and factories that are located downstream from the pollution sources must purify the water before they can use it.
   4. Sometimes waste materials accumulate or are so foul that, even after all regular methods of purifying water are used, the water is still unfit to use.
D. Because they consist of frozen freshwater and not ocean saltwater, icebergs and polar ice-caps could become a future source of freshwater.
   1. Scientists and engineers have hypothesized ways of transporting icebergs to regions where they could be utilized as a freshwater source. So far no technique has been successfully tested.

THE OCEANS

I. OCEANS OF THE EARTH
   A. Although we think of the oceans as separate bodies of water, all the oceans are part of one great sea that covers almost 71 percent of the earth to an average depth of about 4,250 meters (14,000 ft). The Mariana Trench in the Pacific Ocean is the deepest point ever measured—11,022 meters (36,163 ft).
      1. The earth's sea is divided into three great oceans: the **Pacific Ocean,** the largest and the deepest, with an average depth of about 4,250 meters (14,000 ft); the **Atlantic Ocean,** the second largest with an average depth of about 4,000 meters (13,000 ft); and the **Indian Ocean,** with the average depth yet to be agreed on. Other oceans or seas are actually extensions of these three great oceans.
      2. Marginal to the Atlantic Ocean are the Arctic Ocean, the Scotia Sea, the North Sea, the Labrador Sea, the Weddell Sea, the Norwegian Sea, the Greenland Sea, the Mediterranean and Caribbean Seas, and the Gulf of Mexico.
      3. Marginal to the Pacific Ocean are the Bering Sea, the Coral Sea, the East and South China Seas, the Sea of Okhotsk, the Sea of Japan, the Yellow Sea, and the Philippine Sea.
      4. Marginal to the Indian Ocean are the Arabian Sea, the Red Sea, and the Bay of Bengal.
      5. The Antarctic Ocean, a region of the south geographic pole that surrounds the Antarctic continent, is actually the southernmost extension of each of the three great oceans. In contrast to the Antarctic continent, where a bitter climate supports only a few species of life, the Antarctic Ocean is rich with organisms, especially where the cold Antarctic waters meet the warmer waters from northern latitudes, an area called the **Antarctic Convergence.**

II. THE OCEAN FLOOR
   A. The lower parts of the earth's surface, where the oceans are located, are called ocean basins.
      1. **Ocean basins** are the true surface of the earth, whereas the continents are really huge islands that were raised above the ocean basins by forces acting inside the earth.
   B. Depths of the oceans vary
      1. Over the **continental shelf,** which is really the edge of a continent under water, the ocean is shallow and rarely more than 180 meters (590 ft) deep.

2. Beyond the continental shelf, however, the ocean becomes much deeper very quickly, as the edge of the continent drops off sharply to the bottom of the ocean, forming a slope called the **continental slope.**

3. The deep **ocean floor** begins at the end of the continental slope.

C. The ocean floor is made up of many mountains and valleys.

1. In the Atlantic Ocean floor there is a tremendous mountain chain, called the **Mid-Atlantic Ridge,** that is about 320 kilometers (200 mi) wide, 3,050 meters (10,000 ft) high, and stretches along the entire Atlantic Ocean to the southern tip of Africa.

2. Here the mountain chain joins with a similar mountain chain that runs through the Indian Ocean. This Indian Ocean chain then joins with many chains of mountains that stretch across the Pacific Ocean.

3. The tops of these Mid-Atlantic mountains are higher than those found on the continents, yet most of them are at least a mile below the surface of the ocean.

4. The Azores in the North Atlantic and Ascension Island in the South Atlantic are tops of the very high mountains in this chain. These mountains are believed to have formed from volcanic activity that took place millions of years ago.

D. Volcanic activity has also been responsible for forming mountains in other parts of the ocean floor. The islands in the oceans are the tops of these mountains extending above the surface of the oceans.

1. The Aleutian Islands, West Indies, and South Sea Islands are tops of volcanic mountains on the ocean floor.

2. Near these islands are huge trenches and troughs, which are very deep. These trenches and troughs may be as long as 1,600 kilometers (1,000 mi) and as wide as 160 kilometers (100 mi).

3. They have been formed by cracks in the earth's crust, called **faults,** where the volcanic action that formed these islands took place.

4. The deepest parts of the ocean are found in these trenches and troughs.

E. In the continental slopes are deep canyons, some of which are larger than the Grand Canyon and are believed to have been carved out of the slope by underwater ocean currents.

F. The entire ocean floor is covered with a large layer of sediment.

1. The continental shelf is covered with gravel, sand, clay, and shells.

2. The ocean floor itself is covered with a soft, fine ooze or mud, made up of volcanic dust and the remains of tiny marine organisms.

III. EXPLORING THE OCEAN

A. Oceanographers use a variety of instruments to study the ocean.

1. The deep-sea thermometer measures the temperature at different depths.

2. The bottom sampler, called the Nansen bottle, collects samples of material at the bottom of the ocean. The Spilhaus sampler collects samples from upper levels of ocean water.

3. The current meter measures the speed and direction of the ocean currents.

4. Satellite imaging systems can depict large features in the deepest parts of the ocean.

5. The deep-sea camera can take pictures of sea life in the deep parts of the ocean and of the materials on the ocean floor.

6. Ocean depth measurements are taken with various instruments.

7. Wave data and sea temperatures are collected from aircraft, satellites, and buoys.

8. Corers and grabs bring sediments up from ocean bottoms.

9. Underwater vessels allow scientists to explore the ocean and its bottom.

IV. SEAWATER

A. The composition of seawater today is not the same as that of millions of years ago.

1. In the earth's early history, the waters of the oceans were fresh, with no salts in them.

2. As rain fell on the land, many minerals were dissolved and carried to the oceans by the rivers and streams. Each year the oceans become saltier.

3. Today, every 45 kilograms (100 lb) of seawater contains about 1 kilogram (3 lb) of dissolved minerals. About three fourths of this mineral material is common salt, or sodium chloride, while the rest is made up of salts of magnesium, calcium, and potassium.

4. Each cubic kilometer of seawater includes 1 million tons of magnesium, a metallic element that is used in making planes and for

other purposes. Almost all the world's supply of magnesium is obtained from seawater.

5. Bromine is also obtained from seawater. It is used in making high-test gasoline and photographic film.

6. Common salt, or sodium chloride, is obtained from seawater as well.

7. Although a cubic kilometer of seawater has about $50 million worth of gold in it, with today's technology it would cost more than $50 million to recover that amount of gold.

B. The temperature of seawater varies. It is warmest, of course, at its surface.

1. The warmest surface water is found in oceans near the equator.

2. In the tropics, surface water is about 21° Celsius (70° F), although in the Persian Gulf it has been as high as 35° Celsius (95° F).

3. In the polar regions, the average temperature of the surface water is about −2° Celsius (28° F), which is the freezing point of salt water.

4. Many marine vertebrate animals that live in polar waters have special body fluids, a kind of built-in "antifreeze," that keep them from freezing in the freezing waters.

5. Most parts of the sea have surface temperatures between those of the tropical oceans and the polar oceans, depending on their location and on weather conditions.

6. Deeper down in the ocean, the temperature of the water becomes colder, and even at the equator the temperature of the deep ocean may be 2° to 4° Celsius (35° to 40° F).

C. Two kinds of ice are found floating in the sea—icebergs and floes.

1. **Icebergs** are large blocks of glaciers that break off and float in the sea.

2. Icebergs are freshwater ice.

3. Icebergs are dangerous to ships, because about nine tenths of an iceberg is below the surface of the water and the part below the surface is often spread far out in all directions.

4. The larger icebergs in the Northern Hemisphere may be 1.6 kilometers (1 mi) long, with 90 meters (295 ft) of ice showing above the water.

5. The icebergs that break off the Antarctic glaciers are huge and may be more than 64 kilometers (40 mi) long.

6. **Floes** are large pieces of frozen seawater that drift away from the Arctic Ocean.

7. In the Arctic Ocean, the temperature is cold enough for the surface water to freeze, so the Arctic Ocean is always covered with an ice pack about 4 meters (13 ft) thick.

8. During the summer, some of this ice pack melts and breaks up, sending large pieces of ice floating southward.

9. These floes are different from icebergs in that they are smaller, have a flat shape, and are saltwater ice.

V. WAVE ACTION

A. Ocean waves are caused by winds. As the wind blows across the ocean, there is friction between the moving air and the surface of the water. This friction makes the water rise and fall in a regular rhythmic movement, called a wave.

1. A wave has two parts: the highest point to which the water rises is called the **crest** of the wave; the lowest point to which the water falls is called the **trough** of the wave.

2. The height of a wave is the vertical distance between its crest and its trough.

3. The length of a wave is the horizontal distance from one crest to another, or from one trough to another.

4. The stronger the wind and the greater the distance over which the wind blows, the greater the waves will be. During a storm, waves may be more than 20 meters (65 ft) high and 150 meters (490 ft) long, and they may travel through the water at speeds of 96 kilometers (60 mi) an hour.

5. On very windy days, waves may have foamy white tops, called **white caps.** White caps occur when strong winds push water off the tops of waves; they can be formed close to shore or far out at sea.

6. When waves reach the shore, **breakers** are formed.

7. A wave approaching the shore travels smoothly until its trough hits the bottom of the seashore.

8. The trough of the wave is slowed down as it rubs against the bottom of the sea shore.

9. At the same time, the water in the wave piles up and the wave becomes higher and higher.

DEMONSTRATION 10.5
Water Displacement of an Iceberg

Place a square ice cube in a tumbler of water. Note how much (about nine tenths) of the ice cube is below the surface of the water. Point out that although icebergs are huge, only about one tenth of an iceberg can be seen above the surface of the water.

10. Finally, the wave crest falls forward, and the wave breaks to form a breaker.
11. At beaches where the seashore is steep, breakers form close to shore and do not last long. At beaches where the seashore is shallow, breakers form far out and can last for as long as a mile.

B. When a wave strikes the beach, the water immediately begins to move back along the ocean bottom as an **undertow.**
   1. The returning undertow moves beneath the waves that are coming in to shore.
   2. The stronger the waves, the more water they throw up on the beach and the stronger the returning undertows become.
   3. Undertows carry away sand from the beach to the deeper sea.

C. Giant waves, called **tsunamis,** are produced by earthquakes or volcanic explosions at the bottom of the ocean. Tsunamis are often mistakenly called "tidal waves."
   1. Tsunamis are different from regular waves because they can be more than 160 kilometers (100 mi) long and can travel at speeds of 800 kilometers (500 mi) an hour.
   2. In midocean tsunamis are only a few meters or feet high, but close to shore they may be more than 30 meters (100 ft) high and cause great shoreline damage.

VI. OCEAN CURRENTS

A. The surface waters of the oceans are constantly moving in the form of currents.
   1. The movement of these surface waters is mainly caused by the force of the winds blowing across the surface of the water.
   2. If the earth were completely covered with water and the winds always blew with the same force and from the same direction, the surface currents of the sea would move in a great circle around the earth.
   3. However, there are many factors that affect the direction these currents follow;

consequently, the winds on earth actually blow with different force and from different directions.
   4. Because the earth rotates, the waters in the Northern Hemisphere move to their right and the waters in the Southern Hemisphere move to their left.
   5. The outlines of the earth's continents cause the currents to turn and change direction.
   6. The depth and shape of the ocean floor also affects the direction of currents.
   7. Currents that flow away from the equator are warm currents, and currents that flow toward the equator are cold currents.

B. In the oceans that lie along the equator, there are powerful currents just above and below the equator, called the **equatorial currents.**
   1. The equatorial currents move toward the west, driven by the steady winds that are present in these regions.
   2. If there were no continents, these currents would move in a continuous circle around the earth.
   3. However, the continents make these currents turn to the north or the south, and they even make the currents turn back on themselves as well.
   4. The current flowing just above the equator is called the North Equatorial Current, and the current flowing just below the equator is called the South Equatorial Current.
   5. The North Equatorial Current moves westward to the West Indies, then at the West Indies this current branches.
   6. One branch moves north along the east coast of the United States as the **Gulf Stream,** while the other branch goes into and around the Gulf of Mexico, where it becomes enlarged and warmer. Then it passes through the Straits of Florida and flows north, rejoining the first branch at

DEMONSTRATION 10.6
Ocean Currents and the Earth's Rotation

Obtain a globe that can spin. Spin the globe very slowly in a counterclockwise direction (from west to east). At the same time pour a small amount of fairly thick blue washable paint in a thin stream onto the north pole. As the stream flows down the Northern Hemisphere, it is deflected to its right (to the west) by the earth's rotation. When the stream crosses the equator and enters the Southern Hemisphere, it is now deflected to its left (to the east). It can be made equally obvious that ocean currents moving to the north pole are deflected to their right, and currents moving to the south pole are deflected to their left. This demonstration will help to show students why the ocean currents have a clockwise circulation in the Northern Hemisphere and a counterclockwise circulation in the Southern Hemisphere.

Cape Hatteras and becoming part of the Gulf Stream.

7. The Gulf Stream is one of the strongest water currents on earth, moving about 6 kilometers (4 mi) an hour in a path that is about 160 kilometers (100 mi) wide.

8. Because of the earth's rotation, the Gulf Stream moves to the right, northeast toward Europe.

9. When the Gulf Stream reaches the North Atlantic Ocean, it branches into two weaker currents.

10. The first branch moves directly toward Europe, where it warms the shores of Iceland, the British Isles, Norway, and Sweden, and the second branch turns south, as the **Canary Current,** and returns to the North Equatorial Current.

11. Thus there is a complete circle of current in the North Atlantic Ocean.

12. In the center of this circle is a very large, quiet area of water called the **Sargasso Sea,** where great masses of sargassum seaweed accumulate, sometimes remembered as the legendary graveyard of lost ships.

13. The **Labrador Current** flows out of the Arctic Ocean into the North Atlantic, carrying very cold water southward to the northeast coast of the United States as far as Cape Cod, where it then sinks below the surface.

14. The South Atlantic Currents are similar to the North Atlantic Currents, but they flow in the opposite direction, moving from the equatorial zone westward, to the northern part of South America, where they turn south.

15. They then move along the South American coast as the **Brazil Current,** then move east as the **South Atlantic Current** to Africa, where they move north as the **Benguela Current,** and finally return to the South Equatorial Current.

16. In the Pacific area, the North Equatorial Current moves westward to the Philippines, where most of it turns northward as the **Japan Current** (the equivalent of the Atlantic Ocean's Gulf Stream).

17. The warm Japan Current then turns to the northeast as the **North Pacific Current,** which heads toward the Pacific coast of the United States and divides into two branches, the **Alaska Current,** which flows northward and warms the southern coast of Alaska, and the **California Current,** which flows southward, carrying cooler waters down the west coast of the United States, and rejoins the North Equatorial Current off the coast of Mexico.

18. The South Equatorial Current of the Pacific moves westward across the Pacific Ocean.

19. Because of the many islands in the South Pacific, it is rather difficult to follow the direction of this current as it nears Asia and is turned to the south. These islands weaken the current by dividing it into a number of smaller currents that go off in different directions.

20. The only strong current in the South Pacific is the **Peru Current,** which carries cold water from the south polar region to the coast of South America and then rejoins the South Equatorial Current of the Pacific.

21. Generated by winds that are blowing to the west, the **Antarctic Current** is formed in the southernmost parts of the Atlantic and Pacific Oceans. Because there are no land masses in this area, this current completely circles the Antarctic region.

C. In addition to surface currents that are driven by the wind, there are also powerful currents that flow deep below the surface of the sea. These are called **deep-sea currents.**

1. Some deep-sea currents are caused by the slow movement of cold water from the polar regions to the equator. Because cold water is heavier than warm water, the cold waters around the polar regions sink and travel along the ocean bottom to the equator.

2. In 1959 scientists found a deep current 2,750 meters (9,000 ft) below the Gulf Stream, going in the opposite direction from the Gulf Stream surface current with a speed of about 13 kilometers (8 mi) a day.

3. Other deep currents, also traveling in opposite directions from the surface currents, have been discovered in the South Atlantic Ocean and the Pacific Ocean.

4. Some deep currents are caused by a difference in concentration of salt in the seawater. The more salt in the seawater, the heavier the water is.

5. Inasmuch as the **Mediterranean Sea** is shallow as compared with the large oceans, a large amount of its water is exposed at its surface. As a result, the waters of the Mediterranean Sea evaporate more quickly than the waters of the larger Atlantic Ocean. For that reason the waters of the Mediterranean Sea (as in the case of the **Great Salt Lake** in Utah) become saltier and heavier.

6. At Gibraltar, where the Atlantic Ocean and the Mediterranean Sea meet, there is a strong, deep current of saltier and heavier water that runs along the sea bottom past Gibraltar and into the Atlantic Ocean.

VII. LIFE IN THE OCEANS

A. Ocean water has all the necessary conditions to support a wide variety of life.

1. It has a tremendous amount of oxygen, minerals, and other chemicals dissolved in it.

B. Most organisms that live in the ocean are found either near the shore or in the surface waters.

C. The ocean also contains tiny organisms, called **plankton,** which are the basic food for sea life.

1. Plankton grow in tremendous numbers in the upper layers of the ocean, where sunlight is plentiful.

2. All forms of sea life either feed directly on plankton or eat animals that feed on plankton.

D. In the middle and deepest parts of the ocean there are also living things, but like the **coelacanth** fish, they often do not look at all like the living things found nearer the surface.

E. Small sea animals, called **corals** (see Chapter 14), affect shorelines in warm waters.

1. Corals live in colonies in warm, shallow water that must be 20° Celsius (68°) or higher.

2. The animals swim around freely when they are young, but when they mature, they permanently fasten to the rocky sea floor, where they then depend on the waves and currents to deliver food to them.

3. Corals also remove lime from the seawater to make the shells in which they live. When the corals die, their shells remain. New colonies of corals grow on top of these shells. Eventually, the accumulation of shells forms a **coral reef,** which is separated from the mainland by a broad lagoon of calm water. The coral reef is the ecological habitat for many other organisms as well as coral.

4. Sometimes when there is a sunken volcanic cone not too far below the surface of the water, the corals form in a narrow, circular ring around that cone, called an **atoll.**

VIII. ECONOMIC IMPORTANCE OF OCEANS

A. Oceans are like huge highways, which ships use to bring food and supplies to all parts of the world. The oceans supply a large amount of the food we eat. The farming and cultivation of materials from the ocean is called **mariculture.**

B. The oceans contain chemicals that industries remove and use.
C. The ocean makes it possible for us to grow things on land.
 1. Water evaporates in tremendous amounts from the surface of the oceans, forming water vapor that rises into the air.
 2. The air then moves across the land, and eventually the water vapor condenses into rain and other forms of precipitation, providing water for the soil.

D. Because our demand for freshwater may eventually become greater than the supply, scientists and engineers continue to look for inexpensive ways of changing salt seawater into freshwater.
E. Ocean waves and tides can be harnessed to power turbines to generate electricity.
F. The oceans are more delicate than people once believed, so today's scientists worldwide are cooperating to find ways to preserve and protect this vast natural resource.

WINDS

I. THE EARTH AND ITS ATMOSPHERE ARE HEATED BY THE SUN

A. The radiant energy from the sun passes through the air without heating it very much. Most of the sun's radiant energy passes through the atmosphere and strikes the earth's surface, which absorbs this energy and changes it into heat.
 1. The heated earth's surface then warms the air above it. It does this in two ways.
 2. The warm earth radiates some of its heat energy back into the air, which absorbs much of this heat energy and becomes warmer.
 3. Although air is a poor conductor of heat, some of the earth's heat is conducted into the air just above the earth.
 4. At the same time, as the sun's radiant energy passes through the air, a small amount of this energy is absorbed by the air nearest the earth and is changed into heat.
B. Every day the air goes through a cycle of heating and cooling.
 1. When the sun shines on the earth, the air becomes warmer as the heated earth radiates heat energy.
 2. At night the earth cools and the air becomes cooler.
 3. The air becomes much warmer in the summer, when the days are longer, than in the winter, when the nights are longer.
 4. Cloudy nights are warmer than clear nights because the clouds act as a blanket to reflect and absorb the radiant energy given off by the earth, and in this way they keep the heat within the air next to the earth.

II. THE EARTH IS HEATED UNEQUALLY

A. The earth is heated unequally because of its shape.

 1. Because the earth's surface is curved, the sun's rays strike different parts of the earth at different angles.
 2. At the equator, the sun's rays strike the earth's surface directly or at right angles.
 3. Away from the equator, the sun's rays strike the earth's surface at a slant.
 4. The closer we get to the polar regions, the more the earth is curved, and the greater is the slant of the sun's rays striking the earth's surface.
 5. Direct rays are warmer than slanted rays, because with direct rays the sun's energy is concentrated over a smaller area of the earth's surface, whereas with slanted rays the same amount of energy is now spread out over a large area, making the energy less concentrated.
 6. Because the earth's surface that receives direct rays of the sun becomes warmer than the surface that receives slanted rays, the air above this warmer surface becomes warmer as well.
 7. When one part of the earth has summer, this part is tilted so that the sun's rays shine directly on its surface, and this part of the earth becomes warmer. When the same part of the earth has winter, this part is now tilted so that the sun's rays shine at a slant on its surface, and this part of the earth now becomes cooler.
B. The different surfaces of the earth are heated unequally.
 1. Some surfaces of the earth absorb and radiate heat faster than others.
 2. Dark and rough land surfaces, such as rocks and soil, absorb heat quickly and radiate it just as quickly.
 3. Bodies of water have clear, smooth surfaces. They absorb and radiate heat more slowly.

DEMONSTRATION 10.7
Absorption of Radiant Energy by Dark and Light Surfaces

Obtain two cans exactly the same size. Paint the outside of one can with flat, black paint, and paint the outside of the other can with white paint. Now put equal amounts of water into each can so that the cans are about one half to three quarters full. Place a thermometer in each can (the thermometers must have the same reading), and place both cans in the sunlight (Figure 10.9). Record the temperature reading every 15 minutes for one hour. The water in the black can will become warmer than the water in the white can.

FIGURE 10.9   A black surface absorbs radiant energy more quickly than a white surface.

4. As a result, when the sun shines directly on land and water surfaces, the land surfaces become warmer than the water surfaces, and the air above the land surfaces becomes warmer as well.

III. UNEQUAL HEATING OF THE EARTH'S SURFACE CAUSES WINDS

A. Wind is the movement of air caused by the unequal heating of the earth's surface by the sun.
   1. When air directly above the earth's surface is heated, it expands and becomes lighter. This warmer, lighter air is pushed up by the colder, heavier air that surrounds it.
   2. The colder, heavier air now is heated and becomes lighter, being pushed up in turn by more cold, heavy air that surrounds it. This process continues as a steady flow of air, called a **convection current,** with warm air rising and cold air falling.
B. Cold air is heavier than warm air, and so it exerts a greater pressure than warm air.
   1. Winds are formed when cold air from high-pressure areas moves to low-pressure areas where the air is warmer.

IV. THE EARTH'S WIND BELTS

A. There is a constant movement of air over the entire earth in the form of wind belts.
   1. If the earth did not rotate on its axis, the movement of the air over the earth would be simpler. At the equator the heated air would rise and flow toward the north and south poles, and at the north and south poles the colder air would move toward the equator. However, because the earth does rotate, the movement of air over the earth is more complicated.
   2. Winds in the Northern Hemisphere are deflected to their right. Winds in the Southern Hemisphere are deflected to their left. As a result, a series of wind belts is produced around the earth, with the winds in each belt moving in a definite direction (see Figure 10.10).
   3. The sun's rays shine differently on the Northern and Southern Hemispheres in the summer and winter, causing the wind belts to shift with the seasons.
B. The **doldrums** is an area of low pressure at the equator. Most of the air movement in the doldrums is upward, as the heated air rises. There are mostly calms in the doldrums, with occasional light breezes.
C. The heated air above the equator rises and moves toward the north and south poles, cooling as it moves higher into the atmosphere. At about one third of the distance from the equator to the poles (30 degrees latitude), the air has cooled enough to sink down toward the earth's surface again. This belt of descending, high-pressure air is called the **horse latitudes.** The air is still warm, but not as warm as the air in the doldrums. There are also mostly calms in the horse latitudes, with occasional light, changeable winds.
D. The air sinking at the horse latitudes forms two wind belts. One flows back toward the equator, and the other flows toward the poles.

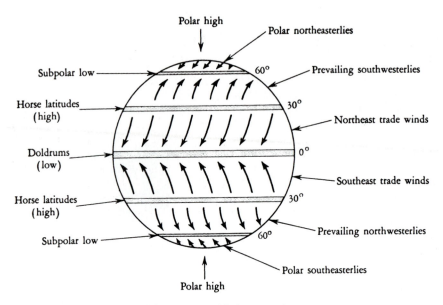

FIGURE 10.10   Diagram of the major wind belts on earth.

1. The winds flowing back to the equator are called the **trade winds.**
2. Because of the earth's rotation, in the Northern Hemisphere the trade winds are deflected, or turned, to their right and become the northeast trade winds, and, in the Southern Hemisphere the trade winds are deflected to their left and become the southeast trade winds. The tradewinds blow very steadily in respect to direction and speed.
3. Winds that flow from the horse latitudes toward the poles are called the **prevailing westerlies.**
4. Because of the earth's rotation, in the Northern Hemisphere the prevailing westerlies are deflected to their right and become the southwesterlies, and in the Southern Hemisphere the prevailing westerlies are deflected to their left and become the northwesterlies.
5. The prevailing westerlies are not as steady as the trade winds and vary more, both in direction and in speed.

E. At a little more than two thirds of the distance from the equator to the poles (65 degrees latitude), there is a second belt of low-pressure area, called the **subpolar lows.** At this point, the warmer air that is still moving toward the poles is pushed up by the cold air moving down from the poles toward the equator. The upward movement of this warm air produces an area of low pressure.

F. At the poles, masses of cold air move down toward the equator, forming **polar easterlies.** They move to their right in the Northern Hemisphere to become the polar northeasterlies, and to their left in the Southern Hemisphere to become the polar southeasterlies. The polar easterlies move in the same direction as the trade winds, but they are very cold and violent.

G. In the Northern Hemisphere, there is a narrow band or river of high-speed winds, called the **jet stream,** that separates cold and warm air masses.
1. These winds are located in the prevailing westerlies, but they are 8 to 16 kilometers (5 to 10 mi) above the surface of the earth and travel at speeds as high as 640 kilometers (400 mi) an hour.
2. They move eastward around the earth, but with some variation.
3. The position and speed of the jet stream vary with the seasons, moving closer to the north pole in the summer, and farther south in the winter.
4. The jet stream is about 13 to 16 kilometers (8 to 10 mi) high (above the earth) in the summer, and 8 to 11 kilometers (5 to 7 mi) high in the winter.

5. Its winds move faster in the summer.
6. Besides the northern jet stream, there is a jet stream in the Southern Hemisphere that is exactly like the stream in the Northern Hemisphere, another in the lower stratosphere of the Arctic Circle, and yet another in the lower stratosphere of the Antarctic Circle.
7. In the winter, when traveling in the same direction, jet planes take advantage of the jet stream, using it as a strong tailwind to cut down flying time and fuel consumption.

H. A **monsoon** is a seasonal wind that changes its direction in the summer and in the winter. A monsoon wind is produced by the difference in heating between continents and oceans during the summer and winter.
1. In summer the land is heated more than the ocean, so the cooler air over the ocean moves in across the land.
2. In winter the land becomes colder than the ocean, so the cooler air over the land moves out toward the ocean.
3. The best example of a monsoon is found in India. In summer the Indian Ocean is cooler than the hot land. The air above the hot land becomes hot and light, forming a low-pressure area, and the cooler, moist air from the Indian Ocean blows across the land. This summer monsoon, also called a **wet monsoon,** brings India its rainy season from May through October. In winter northern India becomes much colder than the Indian Ocean. The air above the cold land becomes cold and heavy, forming a high-pressure area, and the cold, dry air blows from the land to the Indian Ocean. This winter monsoon, also called a **dry monsoon,** brings dry weather to India from November through April. Australia, Spain, and Portugal also have monsoons.

I. Similar to the conditions that create the monsoons are those that cause **land and sea breezes.**
1. Land and sea breezes are winds at the seashore that blow in one direction in the daytime and in the opposite direction at night.
2. During the day, the land and sea receive the same amount of heat from the sun. But, absorbing rather than reflecting the sun's heat energy, land heats more quickly and becomes warmer than the sea.
3. The air over the land becomes warmer and lighter than the air over the sea. The warmer air over the land is forced upward by the cooler air coming from the sea to produce a sea breeze.
4. At the seashore a sea breeze usually begins before noon and dies down at sunset.
5. At night the land loses its heat more quickly than the water, and the air over the land becomes cooler and heavier than the air over the water. The cooler, heavier land air moves out to sea, forming a land breeze.
6. Land breezes blow during the night and die down at sunrise.
7. Land breezes are weaker than sea breezes.
8. Land and sea breezes can also be formed at large lakes.

J. **Mountain and valley breezes** are also a kind of daily monsoon.
1. During the day, the sunny, exposed mountain heats up more quickly than the sheltered, shady valley.
2. The air over the mountain becomes warmer and lighter than the air in the valley.
3. A cool valley breeze then blows up the mountain, and it pushes the warmer, lighter mountain air up and away.
4. At night the mountain cools more quickly than the valley, so the air over the mountain becomes cooler than the air in the valley and a cool mountain breeze then blows down the mountain into the valley, pushing the warmer, lighter valley air up and away.
5. The narrower the valley, the stronger the mountain and valley breezes are. Because a valley breeze has to travel uphill, its speed is not as great as that of a mountain breeze.

WATER IN THE AIR

I. EVAPORATION

A. When water changes from a liquid into an invisible gas, called **water vapor,** this change is called **evaporation.** Evaporation takes place because of molecular motion within the water. Evaporation always takes place at the surface of the water.
1. Water is made up of molecules that are constantly moving. Some of these molecules have more energy and move faster than others.

2. The faster-moving molecules near the surface of the water leave the surface and go off into the air, becoming molecules of water vapor.
3. Some solids, like moth balls and solid air deodorizers, can evaporate directly as a solid without first becoming a liquid.

B. Several factors affect the speed of the evaporation of water.
1. Heat makes water evaporate more quickly. Heat makes the molecules move faster. As a result, more molecules can leave the water at one time.
2. The larger the surface, the more quickly evaporation will take place because more molecules can leave the water at one time.
3. The amount of water vapor already in the air affects the speed of evaporation. If the air already contains a lot of water vapor, there is less room in the air for more molecules of water vapor to enter, and the speed of evaporation is slow. If the air contains only a little water vapor, there is plenty of room in the air for more molecules to enter, and evaporation takes place more quickly.
4. Wind helps water evaporate more quickly. As molecules leave the water and become water vapor, the air above the water eventually becomes filled, or saturated, with water vapor. This saturation slows evaporation because there is no more room in the air for more molecules of water vapor to enter. Wind blows away the air that is saturated with water vapor and provides new air that can hold a fresh supply of water vapor.
5. The lower the air pressure above the surface of the water, the faster evaporation takes place. Lower air pressure means that the air is not pressing down as hard on the surface of the water. This lower air pressure makes it easier for the molecules to leave the water and go into the air as water vapor.
6. Warm, dry air can hold more water vapor than cold, moist air. Consequently, the warmer and drier the air above the water, the faster the water evaporates.

C. Liquids other than water also evaporate. At a given temperature some liquids evaporate faster than others because their molecules are moving faster initially.

D. Evaporation is a cooling process.
1. When a liquid evaporates, it takes in, or absorbs, heat from materials around it.

2. When a drop of liquid is placed on a person's skin, the liquid begins to evaporate, and because the evaporating liquid gets its heat from the skin, the skin becomes cooler. The quicker the liquid evaporates, the more heat it needs and the cooler the skin becomes.
3. This is the reason that the evaporation of perspiration, or water, on the skin cools the body.
4. When a liquid evaporates, the liquid itself becomes cooler.
5. The faster-moving molecules in the liquid have a higher temperature than the slower-moving molecules.
6. When the faster-moving molecules leave a liquid and become a vapor, the cooler, slower-moving molecules are left behind, making the liquid cooler.

II. HUMIDITY

A. Humidity refers to the water vapor content of the air.
1. **Absolute humidity** is the actual amount of water vapor present in the air at a certain temperature.
2. **Relative humidity** is the ratio between the actual amount of water vapor in the air (absolute humidity) at a certain temperature and the maximum amount of water vapor the air can hold at that temperature.
3. Relative humidity is usually multiplied by 100 to give the result in percentages. When the air contains as much water vapor as it can hold at a certain temperature, the air is said to be saturated, and the relative humidity is 100 percent.

III. CONDENSATION

A. Condensation is the change of water from a vapor to a liquid.
1. Condensation takes place because of a change in the molecular motion of the molecules of water vapor in the air. When air containing water vapor is cooled, the water vapor molecules move more slowly and come closer together, and if the air is cooled enough, the molecules come together closely enough to become liquid water.
2. Condensation also takes place because air contracts, or becomes smaller, when cooled. As air containing water vapor is cooled, the air will keep on contracting until it is saturated with water vapor and can hold no

DEMONSTRATION 10.8
Evaporation of Water[*]

A. The Effect of Heat on Evaporation

Put 10 drops of water in each of two pie tins the same size. Put one on the window sill where the sun can shine on it. Put the other tin in the coolest place in the classroom. The water will evaporate more quickly in the heated tin because the water molecules move faster, and thus more molecules can leave the water at one time.

B. The Effect of Surface Area on Evaporation

Using a measuring cup, put equal amounts of water in a pie tin, a water tumbler, and a bottle. Set all three containers on a table where conditions such as temperature and air currents will be the same for each container. The next day pour any water remaining in the containers back into the measuring cup, one at a time for each container. In each case measure the amount of water that remains. The most water will have evaporated from the pie tin, which has the largest surface area, because more water molecules were able to leave the water at one time.

C. The Effect of Wind on Evaporation

Obtain two sponges of the same size and wet them. Make two spots of equal wetness on the chalkboard. Fan one of the spots vigorously with a piece of cardboard. The

[*]To conserve space in this book, the activities that follow are written only as instructions for studying the evaporation of water. To the extent that safety, availability of materials, and the maturity of your students allow, we encourage you to incorporate these activities into your own lesson plans in a way that your students are doing as much of the activity as possible, individually or in groups, rather than as teacher demonstrations.

moisture on the fanned spot will evaporate more quickly because the fanning blows away the saturated air above the spot and provides a fresh supply of unsaturated air.

D. The Effect of Humidity on Evaporation

Compare the time it will take for water in a wet cloth (or in a pie tin) to evaporate on a dry day when the humidity is low, and on a damp or rainy day when the humidity is high. The greater the humidity, the more water vapor there will be in the air, and the less opportunity there will be for more molecules of water to go off into the air.

E. The Cooling Effect of Evaporation

Dip your forefinger into a tumbler of water. Keeping the wet forefinger and dry middle finger a slight distance apart, blow on both fingers at the same time. As the water evaporates from the forefinger, the heat needed for evaporation is taken from the finger, leaving the finger cooler. The middle finger, which serves as a control, does not become cooler.

F. The Rate of Evaporation of Different Liquids

Have a student extend both hands, palms down. Put one drop of rubbing alcohol on the back of one hand and a drop of water on the back of the other hand. The alcohol will evaporate more quickly because its molecules are moving faster from the beginning at the same temperature. In addition, because the rubbing alcohol evaporates more quickly, it takes heat away from the hand more quickly, and the spot with the alcohol on it will feel cooler as well.

---

more. Any further cooling will make the air contract even more and cause some of the water vapor to liquify.

B. The temperature below which air must be cooled for condensation to take place is called the **dew point.**

C. The same factors that affect the speed of evaporation also affect the speed of condensation, but in reverse, so that the condition that speeds evaporation slows the process of condensation, and vice versa.

D. **Dew and frost** are forms of condensation that take place on surfaces at or near the earth at night.

1. At night the earth's surface and solid objects on it give up their heat rather quickly and become cool. The air coming in contact with these surfaces is also cooled.

2. If the air is cooled below its dew point, the water vapor in the air condenses on these surfaces as water droplets, called dew.

3. If the dew point is below freezing (which is 0° Celsius or 32° Fahrenheit), the water vapor condenses directly as crystals of ice, called frost. Frost is not frozen dew.

4. Dew and frost condense on any surface that has a temperature lower than the dew point of the air that touches this surface.

DEMONSTRATION 10.9
Condensation of Water*

A. Condensing Water Vapor

Add water to a shiny can until the can is half full. Add ice cubes and stir. Soon a thin film of tiny droplets of water will form on the sides of the can, as the air containing water vapor is cooled and the molecules of water vapor move more slowly and come close enough together to become water again. The thin film will gradually form large droplets. In summer the humidity may be so high that the water vapor condenses without ice cubes being added. In winter the humidity may be so low that salt has to be added to the cold water and ice cubes to get the water vapor to condense.

*To conserve space in this book, the activities that follow are written only as instructions for studying condensation of water. To the extent that safety, availability of materials, and the maturity of your students allow, we encourage you to incorporate these activities into your own lesson plans in a way that your students are doing as much of the activity as possible, individually or in groups, rather than as teacher demonstrations.

B. Factors Affecting Condensation

The same factors affecting the speed of evaporation also affect the speed of condensation, but in reverse. Repeat demonstration A in (1) a cold and a warm location, (2) a windy and a calm location, and (3) a dry and a humid location.

C. Find the Dew Point

Repeat demonstration A, and relate the results to the formation of dew and rain. Find the dew point by slowly adding small pieces of ice to a can half filled with water, stirring regularly with a thermometer. Measure the temperature at which a thin film of water appears on the sides of the can. Be careful not to breathe on the sides of the can when watching for dew to form. Otherwise, the water vapor in your breath will condense on the cold sides of the can and produce inaccurate results.

---

5. Dew and frost form more easily on a clear night, when the surfaces can radiate their heat away more quickly through the air, whereas clouds act like a blanket to prevent the heat from radiating away.

6. Dew and frost form more easily on a calm night, because winds blow the air around and prevent the air next to the earth from getting cold enough to cause condensation.

IV. FOGS AND CLOUDS

A. When a sizable layer of air next to the earth's surface is cooled below its dew point, the water vapor in this layer condenses into tiny water droplets to form a fog.

1. The water droplets are heavier than air, but they are so small and fall so slowly that the slightest air movement is enough to keep them floating in the air.

2. A fog is really a cloud at or near ground level.

3. **Ground fog** forms under exactly the same conditions as dew and frost form.

4. Ground fogs often form in valleys, which fill with cold, heavy air.

5. In the morning the sun warms the air, which expands and can then hold more water vapor, and the water droplets in the fog evaporate and the fog disappears.

6. An **advection fog** is formed when warm, moist air from one region blows over a cool surface.

7. Advection fogs are quite common along the seacoast when warm, moist air from the sea blows over the cooler land. In the Grand Banks of Newfoundland, fogs are very common because the warm, moist air from the Gulf Stream blows constantly over the cold Labrador Current.

B. **Clouds,** like fogs, are formed when a mass of air is cooled.

1. When warm air containing water vapor rises high in the air, it becomes colder.

2. The warm, rising air reaches levels where the air pressure is less, and the air expands.

3. When air expands by itself, it uses up some of its heat energy to make it expand, and the air becomes colder.

4. If the air is cooled below its dew point, the water vapor in the air condenses as tiny droplets of water to form a cloud.

5. The water vapor usually condenses around tiny bits of dust or other particles in the air.

6. If the air is below freezing (0° Celsius or 32° Fahrenheit), the water vapor condenses directly as tiny ice crystals.

7. Just as with fog, the droplets of water or ice crystals in the cloud are heavier than air, but

DEMONSTRATION 10.10
Fog

Fill a clean, dry soda bottle (or any narrow-necked bottle) with very hot water, adding the water slowly to prevent the glass from cracking. Now pour out most of the water, leaving about 5 centimeters (2 in) at the bottom. Put an ice cube on the mouth of the bottle (Figure 10.11) and hold the bottle between you and the sunlight or the light of a lamp. A fog will form in the bottle as the warm, humid air is cooled by the ice cube and the cool air below the ice cube, and the water vapor condenses in tiny droplets that float in the air.

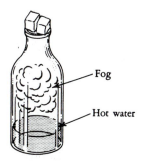

Figure 10.11
Condensation produces a fog in a bottle.

they are so small and fall so slowly that the slightest air movement is enough to keep them floating in the air.

8. A cloud on earth would look like fog, and a fog high in the air would look like a cloud.

C. The shapes of clouds are determined by how they are formed.
　1. If the movement of the cooling air is vertical, clouds form in large, billowy masses.
　2. If the movement of the cooling air is horizontal, clouds form in layers.

D. The three basic types of clouds are cirrus, cumulus, and stratus.
　1. **Cirrus (meaning "curl") clouds** are the highest clouds, from 6 to 13 kilometers (4 to 8 mi) high in the sky.
　2. They look like thin wisps of curls or like thin feathers.
　3. Because they are so high in the sky, they contain tiny ice crystals.
　4. **Cumulus (meaning "heap") clouds** look like large fluffs of cotton or wool and are below 1.8 km (approximately 1 mile) in the sky.
　5. Although they are flat on the bottom, they can pile up very high.
　6. They most often form in the afternoon, and they usually disappear toward evening.
　7. They are usually associated with fair weather.
　8. On hot summer days, cumulus clouds may grow very large and black, causing thunderstorms with heavy rain and sometimes hail.

9. **Stratus (meaning "layer") clouds** are made up of low layers of clouds and are the clouds nearest (below 1.8 km, about 1 mile) to the earth.
10. They usually cover the whole sky and blot out the sun.
11. They are usually associated with stormy weather.
12. Sometimes a cloud is given two names because it has the characteristics of two different cloud types.
13. **Cirrostratus clouds** are high, thin, feathery layers of ice-crystal clouds that often produce the appearance of a halo or "ring" around the moon or sun, indicating the coming rain or snow.
14. **Stratocumulus clouds** are layers of cumulus clouds (below 3 km or 3.3 mi) that cover the whole sky, especially in winter.
15. **Cirrocumulus clouds** are a large group of small, round, high (above 5.5 km or 3.5 mi) fluffy clouds that are made up of ice crystals.
16. Scientists also add prefixes to the names of clouds, which help them describe the clouds more accurately, prefixes such as *alto* (meaning "high"), *nimbus* or *nimbo* (meaning "rain"), and *fracto* (meaning "broken").
　　Altostratus clouds are high (1.8 to 6 km, 1 to approximately 4 mi) stratus clouds, and **altocumulus clouds,** high (1.8 to 6 km, 1 to approximately 4 mi) cumulus clouds.

DEMONSTRATION 10.11
A Cloud

Obtain a gallon jug and a one-hole rubber stopper to fit the mouth of the jug tightly. Insert a short piece of glass or plastic tubing into the hole of the stopper. Add enough water at room temperature to cover the bottom of the jug. Allow the water to stay in the jug for about 20 minutes to allow some of it to evaporate into the air inside the jug. Shake a little chalk dust into the jug. Now fit the stopper tightly into the jug and connect the rubber tubing of a bicycle pump securely to the glass tubing (Figure 10.12). Pump air into the jug for no more than five or six strokes, then remove the stopper quickly. A cloud will form in the jug, which can best be seen by holding the jug between you and the sunlight or the light of a lamp. If a cloud does not form, repeat the experiment, but add a little rubbing alcohol to the water this time.

When more air is pumped into the jug, the air inside the jug is compressed. When the stopper is removed, the air will expand. When a gas expands it becomes cooler. The air is cooled below the dew point by the sudden expansion, and the water vapor in the air condenses on the par-

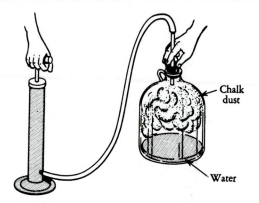

FIGURE 10.12   Condensation produces a cloud in a jug.

ticles of chalk dust, forming a cloud. Real clouds are formed the same way, being cooled because of the expansion of the warm, rising air.

Nimbostratus clouds are rain clouds.
Cumulonimbus clouds are thundershower clouds, also called thunderheads.
Fractocumulus clouds are cumulus clouds that have been broken up into smaller masses.

V. PRECIPITATION

A. *Precipitation* refers to all forms of moisture that fall from the atmosphere.
   1. Rain, drizzle, sleet, snow, and hail are forms of precipitation because they fall from the atmosphere.
   2. Dew, frost, fog, and clouds are not forms of precipitation. They are forms of condensation.
B. **Rain** is water that falls from a cloud. The droplets of water in a cloud are so small that the slightest air movement is enough to keep them floating in the air. These droplets come together and form larger drops, which in turn come together to form even larger drops. When the drops of water are large and heavy enough, they fall to the earth as rain.
C. **Drizzle** is the only other form of precipitation that falls as a liquid. Drizzle is made up of very fine cloud (or fog) droplets that fall very slowly. Ordinarily, these water droplets would stay in

the cloud or fog, but sometimes the air is so still that they fall to earth.
D. **Snow** is the most common form of solid precipitation.
   1. Snow forms from water vapor that condenses when the temperature of the air is below freezing.
   2. The water vapor condenses directly into ice crystals, or snow.
   3. Snow, therefore, is frozen water vapor, not frozen rain.
   4. Every snow crystal has six sides to it, but no two snowflakes are exactly alike.
   5. When the air near the ground is cold, the snowflakes fall separately.
   6. When the air near the ground is warmer, the snowflakes melt together to form large clots of wet, sticky snow.
E. **Sleet** is frozen rain, and it is usually formed during the winter when raindrops fall through a below-freezing layer of air that is near the ground.
F. **Glaze** is a coating of ice that forms when rain freezes after it reaches the ground.
   1. The rain forms a thick coating of ice on streets, trees, telephone and electric wires, and other objects.
   2. When this phenomenon occurs, it is called an ice storm.

DEMONSTRATION 10.12
Frost, Snow, Sleet, and Glaze

Fill a tall can with alternate layers of cracked ice and table salt. Make each ice layer twice as thick as the salt layer. Pack the mixture down firmly. Put some drops of water on a piece of wax paper, and set the can on top of the water (Figure 10.13).

Use enough water to make one large drop high enough to touch the bottom of the can. Some dew may form on the sides of the can and then freeze, but frost will also form as the temperature of the air beside the can falls to below freezing.

After the sides of the can are well covered with frost, remove the can from the wax paper. The large drop of water will have frozen into ice. Point out that frost and snow are formed when water vapor condenses directly

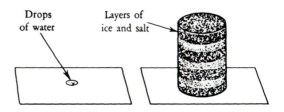

FIGURE 10.13 Frost, snow, sleet, and glaze are formed at temperatures that are below freezing.

into ice crystals, whereas sleet and glaze are formed when raindrops freeze.

---

3. The coating of ice often becomes so heavy that it makes bushes and tree branches collapse, breaks telephone and electric wires, and makes traveling on highways dangerous or impossible.

G. **Hail** is formed mostly in the summer during a thunderstorm, when there are strong upward currents of air within a thundercloud.
   1. These currents carry the raindrops high into a layer of below-freezing air.
   2. The raindrops freeze and become pellets of ice.
   3. These pellets of ice then fall into warmer air, where they pick up another coating of water.
   4. Then the pellets, now coated with water, are blown up again into the colder air, where the coating of water freezes to form a second layer of ice.
   5. This process is repeated until the pellets of ice, now called hailstones, become too heavy for the upward air currents to lift, and the hailstones fall to earth.
   6. A hailstone is formed somewhat like an onion, with an ice pellet as its center and many layers of ice around this center.
   7. Each layer shows one complete movement up into cold air and back down again into warmer air.
   8. The more violent the thunderstorm, the more times the hailstones move up and down between the layers of cold and warm air and the larger the hailstones become, sometimes as large as a softball. When hailstones are large enough, they can cause great damage to

crops and can even hurt small animals. The largest hailstone ever recorded in the United States fell on Coffeyville, Kansas, in September 1970. It weighed 757 g (1.7 lb) and had a diameter of over 14 cm (5.5 in).

VI. THE WATER, OR HYDROLOGIC, CYCLE

A. All the water on earth is constantly evaporating to form water vapor.
   1. This evaporation takes place from the surfaces of the oceans, lakes, ponds, reservoirs, and rivers. Water also evaporates from the soil, and plants give off water vapor during transpiration.
   2. This water vapor is constantly condensing back into water again.
   3. On or near the ground water vapor condenses as dew, frost, and fog.
   4. High in the air water vapor condenses as clouds, rain, and snow.
   5. This process of evaporation and condensation goes on in a continuous cycle, called the water cycle or hydrologic cycle.

B. Oceans are the basic source of all the water that the land surfaces receive because practically all the water that falls on the land surfaces eventually goes back to the oceans in some way.
   1. Some of the water runs off into rivers and streams and is carried to the oceans.
   2. Some of the water sinks into the ground, where it flows underground through roundabout paths either directly to the sea or to streams and lakes on the earth's surface.

DEMONSTRATION 10.13
Model of the Hydrologic Cycle

Fill a Pyrex pot with water and heat it on a hot plate until the water is boiling. Fill a frying pan with ice cubes and hold the pan about 10 centimeters (4 in) above the pot (Figure 10.14). A miniature water cycle will be produced as the water vapor from the boiling water is cooled by the cold bottom of the frying pan, causing droplets of water to condense on the bottom of the pan and then drop back into the water.

FIGURE 10.14 A model water cycle.

3. Most of the water that falls on land surfaces evaporates directly into the air from bodies of water on land, and from the soil.
4. This evaporated water is carried by air currents to the oceans, where it falls as rain or snow.

5. The water then evaporates from the surfaces of the oceans, and the moist air is carried by air currents across the land, where it meets conditions that make the water vapor condense back to water again.

WEATHER CHANGES

I. CONDITIONS AND CHANGES IN THE WEATHER

A. When describing the weather at a certain time and place, a forecaster usually lists the conditions of the air at that time and place.
  1. These conditions include the temperature of the air, the air pressure, the amount of moisture in the air (humidity), and the direction and speed of the wind.
B. When predicting or forecasting the weather, the weather forecaster looks at the kinds of air masses that are moving across the earth.
  1. These air masses are responsible for changes in the weather.

II. AIR MASSES

A. An air mass is a huge body of air that may cover a vast portion of the earth's surface and may be very wide and quite high.
  1. In any air mass the temperature and the humidity are about the same throughout.
  2. Air masses differ greatly from each other, and the weather an air mass will bring depends mostly on its particular temperature and humidity.
  3. An air mass is formed when the atmosphere remains quietly over a certain part of the earth's surface until it picks up the temperature and humidity of that part of the earth's surface.
  4. An air mass formed over Canada is cold and dry. An air mass formed over the Gulf of Mexico is warm and moist.
B. Air masses are named according to the part of the earth's surface over which they are formed.
  1. Those that are formed in the tropics are called **tropical** (T) and are warm.
  2. Those that are formed in the polar regions are called **polar** (P) and are cold.
  3. Air masses also come from continents and oceans. Air masses from continents are called **continental** (c) and are dry.
  4. Air masses from oceans are called **maritime** (m) and are moist and humid.
  5. Consequently, there are four possible kinds of air masses (see Figure 10.15).

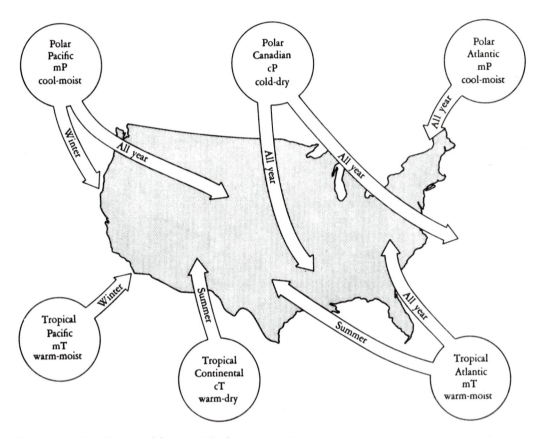

FIGURE 10.15   Diagram of the major North American air masses.

The **continental tropical** (cT) air mass is dry and warm.

The **maritime tropical** (mT) air mass is moist and warm.

The **continental polar** (cP) air mass is dry and cold.

The **maritime polar** (mP) air mass is moist and cold.

6. Once an air mass is formed, it is usually carried to another place by the general movements of the atmosphere.

7. Air masses often change their conditions when they move from one place to another.

8. A dry air mass can move out over the ocean and become moist.

9. When a cold air mass moves over a warmer surface, the lower part of the air mass becomes warmer and rises, producing clouds and possibly precipitation.

10. A warm air mass can become a cold air mass automatically, just by moving over a part of the earth's surface that is warmer than the air mass.

11. In the same way, a cold air mass can become a warm air mass if it moves over a colder part of the earth's surface.

C. The air masses that affect the weather in North America come from six different areas.

1. **Polar Canadian** (cP) air masses are formed over north-central Canada and move in a southeasterly direction across Canada and the northern United States. They are cold and dry, and in the winter they bring the cold waves that sweep across the United States and sometimes move as far south as the Gulf coast, while in the summer they bring cool, dry weather.

2. **Polar Atlantic** (mP) air masses are formed over the northern Atlantic Ocean, and although they generally move eastward toward Europe, they can also move southward to affect the northeastern part of the United States. They are cold and moist,

and in the winter they bring cold, cloudy weather and some form of light precipitation; in summer they bring cool weather with clouds and fogs.

3. **Polar Pacific** (mP) air masses are formed over the northern Pacific Ocean, and although they usually travel southward along the Pacific coast, they sometimes move eastward across the United States. They are cool rather than cold and are very moist. In winter they bring rain and snow, and in summer they bring cool, foggy weather.

4. **Tropical Continental** (cT) air masses are formed over Mexico and the southwestern United States and usually move in a northeasterly direction over the central part of the United States. They are warm and dry and affect North America only in the summer, bringing dry, clear, and very hot weather.

5. **Tropical Atlantic** (mT) air masses are formed over the tropical part of the Atlantic Ocean and the Gulf of Mexico and usually move in a northeasterly direction over the eastern part of the United States. They are warm and moist; in winter they bring mild weather, and in summer they bring hot, humid weather, thunderstorms, and hurricanes.

6. **Tropical Pacific** (mT) air masses are formed over the tropical part of the Pacific Ocean and usually move in a northeasterly direction across the Pacific coast. They are warm and moist and affect the Pacific coast only in winter, bringing cool, foggy weather.

III. WEATHER FRONTS

A. When two air masses meet, the boundary between them is called a **front.** Along the front there is almost always some form of precipitation. This precipitation occurs because a very large amount of warm, moist air is rising to great heights along the front, and rising, moist air means precipitation.

B. There are two common kinds of fronts—warm fronts and cold fronts.

1. If warm air is pushing colder air ahead of it, the front is called a **warm front.** Because masses of warm tropical air usually come from the southwest, warm fronts in the United States generally move toward the northeast.

2. If cold air is pushing warmer air ahead of it, the front is called a **cold front.** Because masses of cold polar air usually come from the northwest, cold fronts in the United States generally move toward the southeast.

C. In the Temperate Zones of both North and South America, the principal changes in weather are brought about by the passage of warm and cold fronts.

1. When a warm front advances, warm air moves up over the retreating cold air. The slope of the warm front is very gradual, and the warm air may have to travel as much as 1,600 kilometers (1,000 mi) to rise 8 kilometers (5 mi).

2. When the warm air rises, it becomes cooler and the water vapor in the air condenses to form large masses of clouds along the entire warm front.

3. Where the level of the warm air is highest, cirrus clouds form.

4. Behind the cirrus clouds are different forms of stratus clouds, each kind floating lower and lower, with nimbostratus or "rain" clouds last and nearest the ground.

5. The rains produced by a warm front cover a wide area, are usually steady, and last until the warm front passes.

6. When a cold front advances, the cold air pushes under the warm air that is retreating and lifts up this warm air.

7. A cold front moves more quickly than a warm front because the air in a cold front is colder and heavier. Heavy, cold air can push light, warm air out of the way more quickly than light, warm air can push heavy, cold air.

8. As the warm air is lifted up very quickly, it cools, and the water vapor in the air condenses to form different kinds of clouds, most typically cumulonimbus (or thundershower) clouds.

9. The rains produced by a cold front cover a smaller area, are rather violent, and last only a short time as the front passes.

D. A **stationary front** is the boundary line between a cold air mass and a warm air mass when both air masses stop and do not move for several days.

1. When this stoppage occurs, the boundary between the two air masses becomes a slope that is as gentle as that of a warm front.

2. As a result, the weather produced by a stationary front is about the same as that produced by a warm front.

E. Sometimes an **occluded front** is formed when a warm air mass, which lies between two cold

air masses, is lifted up by the cold air mass behind it.

1. To create an occluded front, both cold air
   masses and the warm air mass between them
   must all be moving in the same direction.
2. Because cold fronts move faster than warm
   fronts, sometimes the second cold air mass
   at the rear catches up with the first cold air
   mass in front, and at the same time lifts the
   warm air mass completely off the ground.
3. This condition, called an occluded front,
   brings a combination of warm and cold
   front weather.
4. Moreover, as the occluded front passes,
   there is no change in the temperature of the
   air, because there is only a change from one
   mass of cold air to another.

IV. LOWS AND HIGHS

A. The air masses that move across the earth differ in air pressure.
   1. Cold air masses have higher pressures than
      warm air masses.
   2. This difference occurs because cold air is
      heavier than warm air, and it can exert
      more pressure than warm air.
B. An area of low pressure is called a **low,** or a **cyclone.**
   1. The lowest air pressure in a low is at its
      center.
   2. As a result, air of higher pressure blows in-
      ward toward the center of the low.
   3. Because of the earth's rotation, the air in
      the northern hemisphere is deflected to the
      right. In the southern hemisphere it is de-
      flected to the left.
   4. This deflection makes the air blowing to-
      ward the center of the low travel in a circu-
      lar, counterclockwise direction in the
      northern hemisphere (see Figure 10.16).
   5. Lows, or cyclones, usually bring bad weather.
      This weather occurs because the warmer,
      lighter air in a low-pressure area is pushed up
      by the colder, heavier air around it.
   6. The warmer, lighter air rises and becomes
      colder, so clouds and precipitation are
      formed.
   7. The bad weather caused by lows usually
      covers a wide area. The lows in the United
      States start in the northwest, southwest,
      southeast, then move toward the northeast
      and end in New England, bringing all kinds
      of weather changes. They travel about

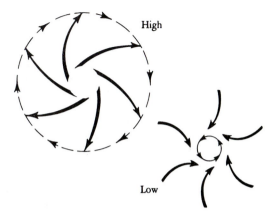

FIGURE 10.16   Highs travel in a clockwise direction, and lows travel in a counterclockwise direction.

1,100 kilometers (700 mi) a day in winter
and 800 kilometers (500 mi) a day in summer.

C. An area of high pressure is called a **high** or an
   anticyclone.
   1. The highest air pressure in a high is at its
      center. As a result, air blows outward from
      the center of the high.
   2. Because of the earth's rotation, the air blow-
      ing outward from the center of a high trav-
      els in a circular, clockwise direction in the
      northern hemisphere (see Figure 10.16).
   3. Highs, or anticyclones, usually bring good
      weather. This weather occurs because the
      colder, heavier air in a high-pressure area is
      falling toward the earth. As the air falls, it
      becomes warmer.
   4. Because warm air can hold more moisture,
      or water vapor, than cold air, no precipita-
      tion takes place and the weather is bright
      and clear.
   5. Highs in the United States can start in ei-
      ther polar or tropical regions.
   6. They also travel eastward across the United
      States, but more slowly than lows.
   7. Highs from the polar regions bring extreme
      cold waves in winter and cool, clear weather
      in summer. Highs from the tropical regions
      bring mild weather in winter and hot, dry
      spells in the summer.

V. HURRICANES

A. Hurricanes develop from small thunderstorms
   that develop over ocean waters.

1. Ocean thunderstorms form as warm, moist air of late summer rises and hits cold air.
2. The thunderstorms begin to merge into a cluster, which may reach from 161 to 483 kilometers (100 to 300 mi) in diameter.
3. The thunderstorm cluster forms a center of low pressure, which is then classified as a **tropical depression.**
4. Surface winds of a tropical depression reach 32 to 61 kilometers per hour (20 to 38 mph) as the storm drifts and begins to rotate.
5. As evaporation and condensation intensify, rising warm air is trapped and spreads out in all directions, forming rain bands.
6. Spinning, as a result of the earth's rotation, increases, and winds reach 63 kilometers per hour (39 mph), and the storm is now classified as a **tropical storm.**
7. Billions of gallons of water evaporate and condense, fueling the storm.
8. Warm air in the center loses its moisture, forming an **eye.**
9. In the Pacific Ocean, when winds reach 119 kilometers per hour (74 mph), with an average diameter of 483 kilometers (300 mi), a tropical storm is technically known as a **tropical cyclone.**
10. A tropical cyclone formed west of the international date line—the 180th meridian—is called a **typhoon.** If east of the line, it is called a **hurricane.**
11. All hurricanes formed in the western Atlantic Ocean are called hurricanes. All hurricane-force storms formed in the Indian Ocean are known as **cyclones.**

B. According to the strength of their winds and their barometric pressure, there are five classes of hurricanes as designated by the **Saffir-Simpson scale.**
1. A **Class 1** hurricane produces winds of 119 to 154 kph (74 to 95 mph); barometric pressure of 28.94 or more. A Class 1 hurricane can blow down signs, power lines, and tree branches, but is unlikely to cause structural damage to buildings.
2. A **Class 2** hurricane produces winds of 155 to 177 kph (96 to 110 mph) and is likely to cause greater damage to signs and trees; barometric pressure of 28.50 to 28.93.
3. A **Class 3** hurricane produces winds of 178 to 209 kph (111 to 130 mph) and can cause damage to signs, trees, and some buildings; barometric pressure of 27.91 to 28.49.
4. With winds of 210 to 250 kph (131 to 155 mph), a **Class 4** hurricane can cause great destruction to doors, windows, and roofs of buildings, and to utility poles, trees, and crops; barometric pressure of 27.17 to 27.90. In 1992, hurricane Andrew, which devastated south Florida, and hurricane Iniki, which hit the Hawaiian island of Kauai, were both classified as Category 4 hurricanes.
5. With winds of more than 250 kph (155 mph) a **Class 5** hurricane, the strongest type, causes catastrophic damage to buildings, trees, crops, utility poles, and anything else in its wide path; barometric pressure of less than 27.17. According to the National Hurricane Center in Coral Gables, Florida, only two Category 5 hurricanes have hit upon United States soil during the modern era of record keeping: one in Florida in 1935 and one on Mississippi's Gulf Coast in 1969. However, it is possible that hurricanes Andrew and Iniki, in 1992, may have developed Category 5 winds. The sheer strength of the winds of Category 4 and 5 hurricanes makes wind measurements very difficult. Wind speed measuring instruments often are literally blown away.

VI. TORNADOES

A. Tornadoes, also called twisters, are the smallest, most violent, and most short-lived of all storms. They occur almost exclusively in the United States, chiefly in the Mississippi Valley and the eastern half of the Great Plains.
1. The states where tornadoes commonly form are Iowa, Kansas, Texas, Arkansas, Oklahoma, Mississippi, Illinois, Indiana, Ohio, and Missouri.
2. However, tornadoes may also occur in any level land area.
3. They are most frequent during the spring and early summer, and they usually occur during the afternoon.
4. There are between 700 and 1,000 tornadoes a year in the United States.

B. Tornadoes are formed under special conditions.
1. Ordinarily cold, heavy air moves under warm, light air.
2. When a tornado is formed, a layer of cold, dry air is pushed over a layer of warm, moist air. The warm, moist air then quickly forces its way in a spiral movement through the layer of cold air.

3. Strong, whirling winds are formed around a center of low pressure, producing a tornado.
C. A tornado looks like a narrow, funnel-shaped, whirling cloud that is very thick and dark.
   1. The funnel reaches down toward the earth, and its tip may touch the earth as it moves along. Sometimes the funnel rises for a while, and then it comes down again a short distance away.
   2. The vortex or tip of the funnel acts like a big vaccuum cleaner, sucking in air from near the ground. The tornado funnel is usually dark because of dirt and debris that has been sucked up from the ground. Strong tornadoes can lift an automobile.
   3. Tornadoes vary in size but can be as much as 1 kilometer (1 mi) wide.
   4. Although the tornado itself moves in a wandering path at a speed of about 40 to 64 kilometers (25 to 40 mi) an hour, the winds spin around like a top and can reach a speed of 800 kilometers (500 mi) an hour. When a tornado passes a particular point, there is a deafening roar heard. Many people report it as sounding like a train passing through.
   5. A tornado is usually accompanied by lightning, thunder, and heavy rain.
   6. The tornado lasts usually about 8 minutes and travels about 24 kilometers (15 mi).
D. A tornado that passes over a body of water is called a **waterspout.**
   1. In a waterspout the bottom part of the funnel is made of spray instead of the dust and other materials found in a tornado over land.
   2. A waterspout has very little water in it. Most of its lower part is a fine mist or spray, with perhaps a few feet of water at the bottom.
E. A tornado can cause a tremendous amount of damage.
   1. The strong winds blow away almost everything in their path.
   2. The center of the tornado is also very destructive, because the air pressure within the funnel is very low.
   3. Buildings within the center of the funnel often explode, because the normal air pressure inside a building becomes so much greater than the suddenly reduced air pressure outside.

VII. THUNDERSTORMS

A. Thunderstorms are strong, local storms formed from cumulonimbus clouds, which involve heavy rain, accompanied by lightning, thunder, and strong gusts of wind.
   1. Sometimes hail falls at the beginning of a thunderstorm.
   2. A thunderstorm is short, rarely lasting more than two hours, but it is possible to have many thunderstorms in a day.
B. Thunderstorms are formed whenever warm, moist air is pushed upward rapidly, accompanied by equally rapid downdrafts of cool air.
C. An **air-mass thunderstorm,** usually called a **summer thunderstorm,** is formed within an air mass during hot, summer afternoons.
   1. This happens when hot, moist air above the earth's surface rises, forming first cumulus and then cumulonimbus clouds.
   2. Summer thunderstorms are local storms, and they form over scattered areas.
D. A **frontal thunderstorm** is formed when a cold front arrives, pushing warmer air ahead of it.
   1. This air movement forms a series or line of thunderstorms, which may be hundreds of miles long and up to 80 kilometers (50 mi) wide.
   2. Frontal thunderstorms can occur at any time of day or year.
E. **Lightning** is a huge electrical spark produced during a thunderstorm.
   1. Lightning heats air to more than 24,000° C (46,000° F), hotter than the surface of the sun, which is about 6,000° C (14,000° F).
   2. The fast-rising air rubs against the water droplets in the cloud and charges them electrically.
   3. The top of the cloud becomes positively charged, while the bottom of the cloud becomes negatively charged.
   4. Sometimes the fast-rising air is strong enough to rip the cloud in two, so that each half has a different electrical charge.
   5. When the force of attraction between the positively and negatively charged parts of a cloud becomes great enough, a huge spark of electricity, called lightning, flows from the negatively charged part to the positively charged part.
   6. Lightning can flow between the bottom and top of the same cloud, between two clouds of different charges, from a cloud to the earth, and sometimes even from the earth to a cloud.
F. **Thunder** is the sound produced by the rapid heating and expansion of the air through which lightning passes.

1. The rumbling of thunder is a series of echoes produced when thunder is reflected many times by clouds.
2. Lightning is seen first and thunder is heard next.
3. This order occurs because lightning travels with the speed of light, which is about 300,000 kilometers (186,000 mi) a second, whereas thunder travels with the speed of sound, which is about 1/3 kilometer (1/5 mi) a second.
4. Because it takes thunder about 3 seconds to travel 1 kilometer (5 seconds to travel 1 mi) and lightning is seen almost instantaneously, we can calculate how far away we are from the lightning of a thunderstorm. If a person counts the number of seconds that pass from the time the lightning is seen and the thunder is heard, and divides this number by 3, the answer will be the number of kilometers the person is away from the lightning. (If you divide the number of seconds by 5, the answer will be the number of miles away from the lightning.)

G. **Heat lightning** is the lightning from a thunderstorm too far away to be heard.
H. **Sheet (heat) lightning** is lightning that takes place within the same cloud. The lightning cannot be seen, but part or all of the cloud lights up.

WEATHER MEASUREMENTS

I. METEOROLOGY

A. **Meteorology** is the science that deals with the study of the weather, which is the condition of the atmosphere at a particular time and place. (**Climatology** is the science that deals with climates over long periods of time.) A meteorologist is a professional who studies and forecasts the weather. Meteorologists can make fairly accurate weather forecasts by collecting data about the temperature, the air pressure, the direction and speed of the wind, the humidity, the kind and amount of precipitation, and the condition of the sky. To collect this information, the meteorologist uses a wide variety of weather instruments.

II. MEASURING THE TEMPERATURE OF THE AIR

A. A **thermometer** is used to measure the temperature of the air.
B. One kind of thermometer that meteorologists use is the **liquid thermometer.**
  1. It consists of a hollow glass tube with a liquid in it. The liquid expands and rises when heated, and it contracts and falls when cooled.
  2. The temperature scale on the weather thermometer is either the Fahrenheit (F) scale or the Celsius (C) scale, which is the scale used in science laboratories. Although the United States still uses the Fahrenheit scale, the rest of the world uses the Celsius scale.

C. Meteorologists also use a **metal thermometer.**
  1. This thermometer does not have a liquid in it, but it uses a strip of metal made up of two different heat-sensitive metals that have been welded together.
  2. The two metals expand and contract differently when heated and cooled, and the unequal expansion and contraction make the metal strip bend or twist.
  3. The metal strip is wound into a coil, and a pointer is attached to the outside free end of the coil.
  4. When the metal strip bends or twists, a pointer moves across the temperature scale and shows the temperature.
D. A **thermograph** is a metal thermometer that records the temperature continuously all day.
  1. In the thermograph is a sheet of paper marked with the temperature scale, and this paper turns on a cylinder.
  2. A pen at the end of a pointer makes it possible for the pointer to draw a line on the paper and produce a permanent record of the temperature all day.
  3. Today's meteorologists use electronic computers rather than the mechanical thermograph to make the continuous and permanent recordings.
  4. This permanent record also shows the maximum, or highest, temperature and minimum, or lowest, temperature for that day.
E. Because metal thermometers are not as accurate as liquid thermometers, a special liquid **maximum and minimum thermometer** is

used to record the highest and lowest temperatures during a day.

1. Like a regular liquid thermometer, this special thermometer shows the temperature of the air at any particular time.
2. However, it also has special indicators, which stay at the highest and lowest temperatures for that day.

III.   MEASURING AIR PRESSURE

A. The **barometer** is the tool used to measure atmospheric pressure, the most difficult weather element to sense without an instrument. Two kinds of barometer are commonly used: the mercury barometer and the aneroid barometer.
B. The **mercury barometer** is a narrow glass tube about 92 centimeters (36 in) long, sealed at one end, that has been filled with mercury and then turned upside down into a dish of mercury.
   1. Some of the mercury runs out of the tube until the pressure of the air on the mercury in the dish just supports a column of about 76 centimeters (30 in) of mercury in the tube.
   2. When the air pressure becomes greater, or increases, the air pushes harder on the mercury in the dish, making the mercury in the tube rise.
   3. The mercury moves easily up the tube because there is no air in the space above the level of the mercury, so there is nothing to slow or stop the upward movement of the mercury.
   4. When the air pressure lessons, or decreases, the mercury moves down the tube.
   5. The height of the mercury in the tube is a measure of the pressure of the air at the time.
C. The **aneroid** (meaning "without liquid") **barometer** does not use mercury. It is sturdier, safer, and less awkward to use than the mercury barometer.
   1. It has a thin, hollow disc from which some of the air has been removed.
   2. The removal of air makes the disc very sensitive to changes in air pressure.
   3. When the air pressure increases, the disc is squeezed in a little; when the air pressure decreases, the disc expands a little.
   4. This change in thickness of the disc is passed on to a pointer that moves across an air-pressure scale.
   5. A **barograph** is an aneroid barometer that has a pen at the end of the pointer and uses a revolving sheet of paper with an air-pressure scale on it so that there is a continuous record of the changes in air pressure during the day. To make permanent and continuous records, today's meteorologists use computers rather than the mechanical barograph.
D. Air pressure can be expressed in two ways: in inches or **millimeters of mercury,** showing the height of a column of mercury that could be supported by a particular air pressure; and in **millibars,** which are the international air-pressure units.
E. On a weather map, air pressure is shown by **isobars,** which are solid, curving lines that join points throughout the United States or other parts of the world where the air pressure is the same.
F. Falling air pressure means a low is coming, bringing bad weather with it, whereas rising air pressure means a high is coming, bringing good weather with it.

IV.   MEASURING WIND DIRECTION AND SPEED

A. A **wind vane** is used to measure wind direction.
   1. The wind vane that is commonly used looks like an arrow. This arrow is mounted on a pole in such a way that it can swing freely when the wind blows on it.
   2. The arrow has a broad tail, and the wind strikes this tail, making the arrow swing so that the head points to the direction from which the wind comes.
   3. Winds are named according to the direction from which they come, so a south wind is one that comes from the south. A south wind strikes the tail of the wind vane and makes the head point toward the south.
B. An **anemometer** is used to measure wind speed, or velocity. Wind speed is measured in kilometers or miles per hour. The most common type of anemometer has three hollow cups, all facing the same way, that catch the wind and begin to move. The stronger the wind, the faster the cups move, recording the speed of movement on a meter.
C. The wind vane and anemometer are often combined into one instrument.

V.   MEASURING THE RELATIVE HUMIDITY

A. Relative humidity is determined by dividing the actual amount of water vapor in the air (absolute humidity) by the maximum amount of water vapor the air can hold at a certain temperature, and multiplying the result by 100 to express the relative humidity in a percentage.

B. A **hygrometer** is used to measure relative humidity.
1. One common form of hygrometer is the **psychrometer,** or wet-and-dry-bulb thermometer.
2. The psychrometer has two thermometers that are the same, except that one of them has a water-soaked cotton cloth or wick wrapped around its bulb.
3. Air is made to pass across both thermometer bulbs, either by whirling the thermometers around or by fanning them with an electric fan.
4. The moving air does not affect the dry thermometer bulb, and that thermometer shows the temperature of the air around it.
5. However, the water in the wet cloth evaporates, taking from the thermometer bulb inside the cloth the heat it needs to evaporate.
6. This evaporation cools the thermometer bulb and makes the temperature fall.
7. The drier the air, the faster the water in the cloth evaporates, the cooler the bulb becomes, and the lower the reading of the "wet" thermometer.
8. When the temperature of the wet thermometer has reached its lowest point, the meteorologist finds the difference in temperature between the wet thermometer and dry thermometer, using this difference to find the relative humidity by consulting a **relative humidity table.**
9. Another type of hygrometer, the **hair hygrometer,** uses a bundle of human hairs to find the relative humidity.
10. Human hair is very sensitive to moisture, becoming longer when the air is humid and shorter when the air is dry.
11. This change in the length of the bundle of human hairs makes a pointer move across a scale, from which the relative humidity can be read directly in percentages.

VI. MEASURING RAINFALL AND SNOWFALL

A. The **rain gauge** is the tool used to measure the amount of rainwater or melted snow.
1. The most common form of rain gauge is a narrow cylinder with a funnel on top.
2. The area of the mouth of the funnel is exactly 10 times larger than the area of the mouth of the cylinder, therefore, the cylin-

der receives 10 times as much water when the funnel is in it than it would receive alone.
3. This larger amount of water is easier to measure, but the amount must be divided by 10 to find the correct amount of rainfall.
4. To measure the amount of rain collected in the cylinder, a marked stick is dipped into the cylinder.
5. Rainfall and snowfall are measured in centimeters or inches, and in tenths or hundredths of a centimeter or inch.

B. Snowfall can be measured either with a rain gauge or by measuring the depth of snow in an open location.
1. Meteorologists are also interested in how much rain a snowfall might have produced.
2. To determine this amount, they melt and weigh a certain number of centimeters or inches of snow.
3. Because snow can be light and fluffy, or heavy and wet, the amount of rainfall that snow may have produced varies.
4. A light, fluffy snow may produce 2 centimeters (1 in) of rain for every 50 centimeters (20 in) of snow, but a heavy, wet snow may produce 2 centimeters (1 in) of rain for every 15 centimeters (6 in) of snow. As an average, 25 centimeters (10 in) of snow will make 2 centimeters (1 in) of rain.

VII. MEASURING WEATHER CONDITIONS AT HIGH ALTITUDES

A. The **radiosonde** is an instrument used to measure weather conditions at upper levels of the earth's atmosphere.
1. It contains a small thermometer, a barometer, and a hygrometer. It also has a small radio transmitter that automatically sends out signals showing the temperature, pressure, and relative humidity of the air through which the radiosonde is passing.
2. The 1-kilogram (2-lb) radiosonde is attached to a 2-meter (6-ft) balloon filled with helium. This balloon can travel 16 to 24 kilometers (10 to 15 mi) into the stratosphere before the balloon bursts. A parachute opens when the balloon bursts. This allows the radiosonde to return undamaged to earth.

B. **Radar** is also used to measure conditions and predict weather.

1. Cloud droplets and raindrops reflect the radar waves and show up on the radar screen.
2. Radar can also locate storms and show the extent of the areas they are covering.
3. It can detect how a storm forms and moves across the earth.
4. It can measure the speed of high-altitude winds by tracking a balloon as it moves through the air at high levels.
5. It can track hurricanes, locate the "eye" of a hurricane, follow the movement of the hurricane, and predict its path.

C. Artificial **satellites** are also used to measure conditions and predict global weather, to send back radar pictures to earth that are then analyzed by meteorologists.
1. Because the atmosphere's density is altered by the air's temperature, pressure, and humidity, scientists use microsatellites and radio signals beamed from one satellite to another to measure atmospheric density.

Orbiting pairs of weather surveillance satellites make it possible to detect weather systems the moment they begin.

VIII. ARTIFICIAL WEATHER

A. Scientists are constantly trying to have some control of the weather.
1. In some cases supercooled clouds high in the sky have been made to give up their moisture. By dropping small particles of dry ice, silver iodide, or other crystals into these clouds, scientists have caused some of the cloud droplets to become ice crystals, which grow larger as the water vapor in the cloud condenses on them. When the ice crystals are large enough, they fall as precipitation.
2. Scientists have also invented devices that are able to reduce or eliminate fog on airport landing fields.

CLIMATE

I. WEATHER AND CLIMATE

A. **Weather** is the condition of the atmosphere at a particular time and place, whereas **climate** is the average weather of a place over a period of years.
B. Climatologists have discovered many factors that affect the kinds of climate found in different parts of the earth. These factors of climate can be divided into two classes. One class consists of those factors that control the yearly temperature of a particular place. Another class consists of those factors that control the yearly rainfall of that place.

II. FACTORS THAT CONTROL YEARLY TEMPERATURE

A. **Latitude** influences temperature more than any other factor. Latitude is the distance of a region or place from the equator.
1. A region near the equator is said to have a low latitude, and a region near the poles is said to have a high latitude.
2. The higher the latitude, the colder the climate.
3. Near the equator, where the sun's rays are direct almost all year and the days and nights are equally long, there is the same hot climate throughout the year.

4. Halfway between the equator and the north pole, during the summer the sun's rays are direct and the days are much longer than the nights, so the summers are hot. However, during the winter the sun's rays are slanted and the nights are longer than the days, so the winters are cold.
5. Near the poles, the sun's rays are always slanted. During the summer near the poles, the sun shines all 24 hours of the day for months. The weather is still cold, but mild in comparison with the winter. During the winter near the poles, the sun does not shine for months and the weather is bitterly cold.

B. The higher the **altitude** of a place, that is, its height above sea level, the colder its climate. Even near the equator, a city that is located at a high altitude experiences much cooler weather and climate than a city located at sea level.
C. **Land and water masses** affect the climate of a place. Land masses heat up and cool down more quickly than water masses. As a result, land regions are more likely to have hot summers and cold winters. Sea regions in the same latitude are more likely to have cooler summers and milder winters.

D. The **direction of the prevailing winds** affects the climate of a continent's seacoasts.
  1. On the northwest coast of the United States the prevailing westerlies blow in from the warm Pacific Ocean, so the northwest coast has a cool summer and a mild winter.
  2. On the northeast coast of the United States the prevailing westerlies blow from the land out to the ocean, so the northeast coast has a hot summer and a cold winter.
E. **Mountain ranges and plains** determine the extent to which faraway winds affect a region's climate.
  1. The high Rocky Mountains stop the mild west coast climate from extending any farther into the Great Plains.
  2. At the same time, the level Great Plains allow very cold winds to speed from the poles all the way to the Gulf of Mexico and allow hot winds from the south to move north, thereby giving the Great Plains hot summers and cold winters.
F. **Ocean currents** can make the climate of a region much warmer or colder than normal for the region's latitude.
  1. The prevailing westerlies, blowing from the warm Gulf Stream, give the British Isles and northwestern Europe climates just as warm as those of regions that are nearer the equator.
  2. At the same time, winds from the cold Labrador Current give northern Labrador a climate much colder than that of a region, such as southern Sweden, which has the same latitude.
G. During the past two centuries carbon dioxide in the atmosphere has increased, and there is worldwide concern that this increase may be warming the earth's atmosphere.
  1. The increase in carbon dioxide is caused mostly by the burning of fossil fuels and the clearing and burning of forests.
  2. An increase in carbon dioxide allows solar radiation to penetrate the earth's atmosphere but prevents part of the heat reflected or reradiated by land and bodies of water from escaping into space.
  3. As carbon dioxide increases, enough heat may be trapped to cause an increased warming of the earth's atmosphere, much like heat trapped in a greenhouse; thus, this effect is called the **greenhouse effect.**
  4. Researchers hypothesize that at the present rate of increase in the amount of atmospheric carbon dioxide, the earth's mean temperature could rise from 1.5° to 4.5° Celsius (35° to 45° F) centigrade by about the year 2050, making the earth's atmosphere warmer than at any time during the past 100,000 years.
  5. The impact of such a change could include the following:
    a. Global shifts in rainfall patterns, bringing heavy rains to previously arid areas.
    b. Droughts to currently productive farmlands, such as those of the United States Midwest.
    c. Mass flooding of coastal cities and farmlands as a result of a melting of part of the Antarctic ice sheet.

III. FACTORS THAT CONTROL YEARLY RAINFALL
  A. Latitude also affects the amount of rainfall a region receives.
    1. The latitude determines in which wind belt a region will be located during the year.
    2. Places where warm, moist wind is rising will have rainy weather, and places where cool, dry air is falling will have dry weather.
    3. Places in the doldrums will have heavy rains all through the year.
    4. Places in the trade winds and horse latitudes will be mostly dry during the year.
    5. Places in the prevailing westerlies will have moderate rainfall all year.
    6. Places in the polar easterlies will have light snow all year.
  B. Because wind belts shift during the year as the earth revolves around the sun, some places may be in a rainy belt for part of the year and in a dry belt for the other part of the year.
  C. Sometimes seasonal wind changes give a region a dry season and a wet season, such as with the monsoons of India (see the earlier discussion of monsoons).
  D. Mountains affect the amount of rainfall a region will receive.
    1. When warm, moist wind strikes the windward side of a mountain and rises, there is much rainfall on this side.
    2. However, the leeward or protected side will now have very little rain, because most of the water vapor will have already condensed from the air before the air passes over the mountain to the leeward side.
  E. When winds blow in from the ocean, the regions nearest the ocean get the most rainfall.

1. This distribution occurs because the moisture condenses out of the ocean air as it blows across the land.
2. The warmer the ocean, the heavier the rainfall will be.

F. When ocean currents are much warmer or colder than the land or water around them, much fog is formed.
1. The warm Gulf Stream air striking the cold British Isles causes a great amount of fog.
2. In summer New England has a lot of fog when the warm winds coming up from the south are cooled by the cold waters of the New England coast.
3. When the warm Gulf Stream air blows over the cold Labrador Current in the Grand Banks, thick fogs are formed.

IV. CLASSIFICATION OF CLIMATES

A. Climatologists divide the earth into **tropical, middle latitude,** and **polar** climates.
1. Each of these climates is subdivided into various types of climates, depending on their temperature and rainfall.

B. Three different types of climates are included under the classification of **tropical climates:** the **tropical rainforest,** the **savanna,** and the **desert climates,** all of which are located within 30 degrees latitude above and below the equator.
1. They all have an average yearly temperature of at least 20° Celsius (68° F), but they differ in the amount of rainfall they get.

C. The **tropical rainforest climate** is found encircling the earth in regions at or close to the equator. Central Africa, the Amazon Valley, the east coast of Central America, Madagascar, and Indonesia have this climate.
1. The regions with this climate have heavy rainfall all year, averaging 200 centimeters (80 in) per year.
2. The temperature is always high, averaging 27° Celsius (80° F).
3. Because of the high temperature and heavy rainfall, there is a dense growth of plants, often forming a jungle.
4. The relative humidity is always high, and there is usually a thundershower each afternoon.
5. Although home to nearly half the earth's plant and animal species, today the tropical rainforest covers less than 7 percent of the earth's land surface. There is international concern today about the rapid destruction

of tropical rainforest land for wood, farming, and development.

D. The **savanna climate** is found farther away from the equator. The Sudan of North Africa, the veldt of South Africa, the campos of Brazil, the llanos of Venezuela, the downes of Australia, and parts of India and Burma all have a savanna climate.
1. The regions with this climate have wet and dry seasons as the wind belts shift during the year. Mostly coarse grasses, spiny plants, and a few trees grow in the savanna climate.
2. During the doldrums, there is heavy rainfall. When the wind belts shift, the regions then are subjected to the trade winds and have little to no rain.

E. The **desert climate** is even farther away from the equator. The Sahara, Arabian, American, Kalahari (south Africa), Australian, and Peruvian Deserts are found in the desert climate. These are sandy deserts.
1. The regions in this climate are always in the wind belt of the trade winds, so they get practically little to no rainfall. As a result, only a few plants grow in these regions.
2. When rain does come, it falls as a thundershower or cloudburst.
3. Because there is very little moisture in the air, the days are very warm and the nights are quite cool.

F. Six different types of climate are included under the classification of **middle latitude climates: Mediterranean, humid subtropical, marine west coast, humid continental, dry continental,** and **subarctic.** All are all located between 30 and 65 degrees latitude.
1. Although there is a wide range of temperature in these climates, they all have at least 1 month where the average temperature is 10° Celsius (50° F) or higher.
2. The regions in these climates lie mostly in the wind belt of the prevailing westerlies, which produces all kinds of weather.

G. The regions in the **Mediterranean climate** lie between 30 and 40 degrees latitude in both the Northern and Southern hemispheres. Southern California, southern Australia, central Chile, and the areas around the Mediterranean Sea have the Mediterranean climate.
1. These regions are all found on the western side of the continents.
2. They lie in the path of trade winds or horse latitudes in the summer, and in path of the prevailing westerlies in the winter.

3. Summers are warm or hot and almost completely dry. Winters are mild and have some rainy months.

4. Because the rainfall is only about 40 to 65 centimeters (16 to 26 in) a year, this climate is also called the **dry subtropical climate.** Fruits, olives, grapes, and nuts grow well in this climate.

H. The regions in the **humid subtropical climate** also lie between 30 and 40 degrees latitude, but on the eastern side of the continents. The southeastern United States, eastern and southern Asia, northern Argentina, and southern Brazil have a humid subtropical climate.

1. There is no dry season. Annual rainfall is between 90 and 150 centimeters (36 and 60 in). Tall grasses and pine forests grow in this climate.

2. Summers are warm and winters are mild, although there are often cold waves and frosts during the winter.

3. The humidity is very high in the summer and can become uncomfortable.

I. The regions in the **marine west coast climate** lie between 40 degrees latitude and the edges of the polar regions. They lie on the western side of the continents. The northwest coast of the United States, the British Isles, Norway, western Australia, New Zealand, and southern Chile have a marine west coast climate.

1. Regions with a marine west coast climate are in the prevailing westerlies most of the year, so they get a good supply of rain all year. Hardwood and evergreen trees grow well in these regions.

2. Where mountains block the movement of the winds, the rainfall is heavy on the windward side of the mountains.

3. Because the westerlies blow in from the ocean, summers are cool and winters are mild in these regions.

4. They get more rain and fog in winter than in summer.

J. Regions with a **humid continental climate** are in the same latitude as those with a marine west coast climate, but on the east side of continents. The eastern United States, from the Great Plains to the coast, eastern Europe, and eastern Asia have this humid continental climate.

1. These regions have hot summers and cold winters.

2. The weather changes are sharp. These regions experience blizzards, very cold spells, heat waves, high humidity, thunderstorms, and tornadoes.

3. More rain falls in the summer than in the winter, and is heavier at the coast. Where the rainfall is more than 76 centimeters (30 in) a year, both deciduous and evergreen trees grow.

4. Where the rainfall is less than 76 centimeters (30 in) a year, tall grasses grow, forming prairies.

K. The regions with a **dry continental climate** are also in the same latitude as the humid continental and marine west coast climates, but in the interior of the continents.

1. These regions have hot summers and very cold winters.

2. Rainfall is light, and usually heavier in summer than in winter.

3. Regions of the dry continental climate where the rainfall is 25 to 50 centimeters (10 to 20 in) a year are called **steppes.** Steppes are found in the midwestern states of the United States, in Argentina, and in Russia. Low grasses and sagebrush grow in the steppes.

4. Regions where the rainfall is less than 25 centimeters (10 in) a year are called **middle latitude deserts.** Middle latitude deserts are found in the western United States, western Argentina, and the interior of Asia. The prevalent plants growing in the middle latitude deserts are sagebrush and cactus.

L. Most of the regions in the **subarctic climate** lie between 50 and 65 degrees latitude. Most of northern Canada, Europe, north of 60 degrees latitude, and most all of Siberia have a subarctic climate. Mostly small evergreen trees grow in this climate.

1. These regions have very long, cold winters and short, mildly warm summers.

2. They have less than 40 centimeters (15 in) of precipitation a year, most of which falls in the summer.

3. In summer the days are very long, and in winter the nights are very long.

M. Two different types are included under the classification of **polar climates:** the **tundra** and the **icecap climates.** These climates begin where the middle latitude climates end and extend to the poles.

1. These climates have no summer at all, because the sun's rays are so slanted that they give very little heat.

2. There is very little precipitation, because the air is too cold to hold much water vapor.
3. The **tundra climate** is a cold climate, beginning where the subarctic climate ends. The tundra climate exists only in the Northern Hemisphere, as there are no land areas in this latitude at the Antarctic.
4. The average temperature of the warmest month is between 0° and 10° Celsius (32°–50° F). The average temperature of the coldest month is −40° Celsius (−40° F).

5. The light summer rains permit mosses and lichens to grow.
6. The **icecap climate** is found near the poles, where the temperature is never higher than 0° Celsius (32° F). There are always icecaps or glaciers in this climate. Precipitation is light and falls only as light snow.
7. The average yearly temperature is between −24° and −35° Celsius (−10° and −30° F). The lowest temperature ever recorded was −88° Celsius (−126° F), in 1960, on the Antarctic icecap.

EXPLORATORY ACTIVITIES FOR "WATER, WEATHER, AND CLIMATE"

1. WEATHER STATION PROJECT (GRADES 3 AND UP)

Overview Weather is always an area of interest for student project work in science. After an initial period of data collection from newspaper and television weather reporting, ask the students whether they would like to build a weather station as a class project. Instructions for building the various data collection instruments follow. If they choose to do this, divide the class into groups of three or four students. Each group assumes partial responsibility for the class weather station project. Depending on the evolution of this project, the final product of the students' work can take many forms, such as the following:

- The class makes daily weather forecasts that are announced each day to the entire school.
- Groups assume partial responsibility for aspects of weather study, predicting, and reporting.
- Students post a chart comparing the accuracy of their predictions with those of official weather forecasts.

1.1 Initial Activity

Have the students cut out weather maps from the newspaper for a period of two weeks. You can also obtain official weather maps by consulting your local weather station or by writing to the United States Weather Service at Asheville, North Carolina. Examine the weather maps closely. Note the presence and movement of cold and warm fronts across the country. List the kinds of weather changes the appearance of each front might bring, and check your list with the actual weather conditions that took place in your locality. Note the location of highs and lows on the weather map. Compare the kinds of weather found in those parts of the country that had highs with those that had lows.

Watch for the appearance of fronts, using the weather forecast as a guide, such as found in the newspaper, on Cable TV's Weather Channel, or the Blue Skies service of Internet. When a front begins to move in, have the students keep a record of the weather conditions, continuing this record until the front has passed.

On the chalkboard, draw diagrams of the movement of a cold front and a warm front, showing the kinds of clouds and precipitation that are formed in each case (Figure 10.17).

1.2 Keep a Record of the Weather

Have the students keep a daily weather chart for a month. Make seven columns on a sheet of paper. In the first column write the date and time the weather observations were made. The weather should be observed at about the same time each day. In the other columns record the following information: temperature outdoors, air pressure, humidity, direction and speed of the wind, condition of the sky, and kind and amount of precipitation, if any. In the column describing the condition of the sky, make a small circle. Show how much of the sky is covered with clouds by filling in all, part, or none of the circle. While the students are keeping this chart, have them clip the weather forecast from the newspaper each day of the month. Then have them compare the actual weather for each day with the weather predicted for that day, to see how often the weather forecaster was correct.

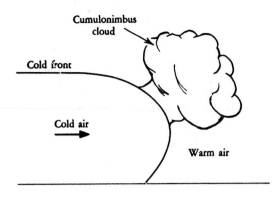

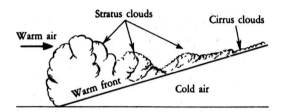

FIGURE 10.17   Diagrams of a cold front and a warm front.

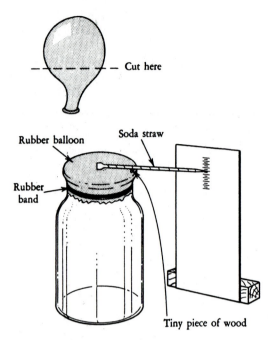

FIGURE 10.18   A homemade barometer.

1.3 Make a Barometer

Obtain a milk bottle or a glass jar with a medium-to-narrow mouth. Cut out the dome-shaped end of a rubber balloon and stretch the rubber tightly across the mouth of the balloon, fastening the rubber sheet securely with a rubber band (Figure 10.18). Flatten both ends of a soda straw and cut one of the ends to a sharp point. Place rubber cement or glue on the flattened end of the straw and attach the flattened end to the middle of the rubber sheet. Cut a tiny piece of wood from a match and glue it at the edge of the rubber sheet so that the straw rests on top of the wood.

When the air pressure in the room increases, the rubber sheet is pushed down, making the straw move up. When the air pressure in the room decreases, the greater air pressure inside the bottle now pushes the rubber sheet up, making the straw move down. A cardboard scale can help the students see the change in air pressure. Calibrate the marks on the cardboard scale with the readings on a standard barometer. Keep the homemade barometer in a place as free from temperature changes as possible. Otherwise, the air inside the bottle will expand and contract, pushing the rubber sheet in and out. Have the students take barometer readings each day for two weeks or a month and predict the weather on the basis of rising or falling air pressure.

1.4 Make a Thermometer

Pour water that has been colored dark red with food coloring into a Pyrex flask until the flask is almost full. Insert a long glass or plastic tube into a one-hole rubber stopper and fit the stopper tightly into the mouth of the flask (Figure 10.19). The amount of water in the flask will have to be adjusted so that when the stopper is inserted, the colored water will rise about one third to one half of the distance of the part of the tube above the stopper. Make two slits in an unlined index card and slide the card over the tube. Mark the original height of the water in the tube.

When the temperature of the room becomes warmer, the water is heated, expands, and rises up the tube. When the temperature drops, the water is cooled, contracts, and falls down the tube. Calibrate the marks on the scale of the index card with the readings on a standard thermometer. Have the students take daily readings outdoors on a standard thermometer (placed away from direct sunlight) for an extended period of time. Keep a record of these readings and make a chart showing the changes in temperature during the year.

1.5 Make an Anemometer

Obtain two pieces of wood about 40 centimeters (16 in) long, 2 centimeters (3/4 in) wide, and 7 millimeters (1/4 in) thick. Place one piece on top of the other so that they form four right angles. At the center, where the

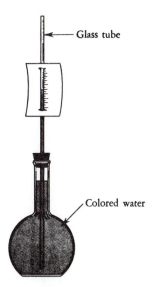

FIGURE 10.19   A home-made thermometer.

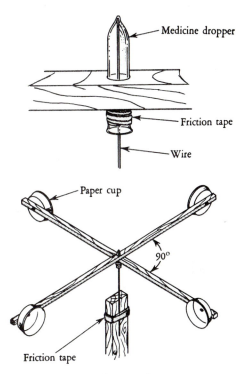

FIGURE 10.20   A homemade anemometer.

pieces meet, bore a hole just large enough for the glass part of a medicine dropper to pass through, so that both pieces of wood will rest on the lip of the medicine dropper (Figure 10.20). Now use small screws or nails to fasten the two pieces of wood together, leaving the hole free. Obtain four paper cups, paint one cup red, and tack a cup horizontally to each end of the pieces of wood.

Hold the medicine dropper by the rubber bulb and place the tip of the dropper in the edge of a gas flame or the flame of an alcohol lamp. Rotate the dropper slowly but steadily as you heat it, and continue heating until the tip of the dropper melts and the opening is closed. Make sure that the tip is completely closed before you remove it from the flame. Set the dropper to one side and allow the tip to cool for at least 5 minutes.

Use wire cutters to cut a straight piece of wire from a coat hanger. File one end of the wire to a sharp point. Fasten the wire upright with friction tape to a sturdy piece of wood. Now remove the rubber bulb from the medicine dropper and insert the dropper into the center hole of the two fastened pieces of wood. Use friction tape above and below the hole, if necessary, to prevent the pieces of wood from slipping off the medicine dropper. Place the medicine dropper over the sharp point of the wire; the anemometer is now ready to operate with a minimum of friction.

To calibrate the anemometer, hold it outside the window of a moving car on a calm day when there is no traffic and the road is smooth and level. With the car moving at a steady speed of 8 kilometers (5 mi) an hour, use a watch with a second hand to count the number of turns the anemometer makes in one minute. The col-

ored cup will make it easier to count the number of turns. Repeat the count at 16 kilometers (10 mi) an hour and again at 24 kilometers (15 mi) an hour. From these three counts you can make a graph that will enable you to calculate the wind speed at any time. (A quick but rough method for finding the wind speed is to count the number of turns in one minute and then divide by 10. The result will be the wind speed in miles per hour.)

1.6 Make a Wind Vane

Cut two large identical arrows from a piece of heavy cardboard, making sure the tails are much larger than the heads. Staple or paper clip the two arrows together at the edges of the head and the tail (Figure 10.21). Seal the tip of a medicine dropper, as in activity 1.4. Place the arrow across the edge of a ruler and find the point where it best balances. Insert the medicine dropper between the two pieces of cardboard at this balancing point, and staple together the edges of the body of the arrow.

Use wire cutters to cut a straight piece of wire from a coat hanger, and file one end of the wire to a sharp point. Fasten the wire upright with friction tape to a sturdy piece of wood, and place the medicine dropper over the sharp point of the wire. Use a compass when

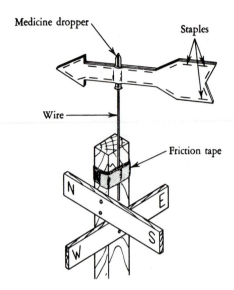

FIGURE 10.21   A homemade wind vane.

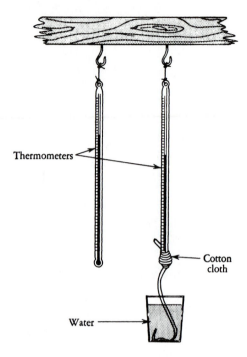

FIGURE 10.22   A wet-and-dry-bulb thermometer.

mounting the wind vane to fix the direction of the wind vane properly. If small strips of wood with the compass directions on them are nailed onto the vane, the students will be able to determine the wind direction more quickly and easily.

Because the tail is larger than the head, it will catch more wind. As a result, when the wind blows, the vane will swing around until it points into the wind toward the direction from which the wind is blowing.

1.7 Make a Wet-and-Dry-Bulb Thermometer

Obtain two chemical thermometers with Fahrenheit scales and suspend them so that they hang side by side a few inches apart. If chemical thermometers are not available, use two identical wall thermometers, either suspended or strapped to a cardboard box with rubber bands.

Obtain a white woven cotton shoelace or a piece of soft cotton cloth. Fit a section of the shoelace snugly around one of the thermometer bulbs and insert the end of the shoelace into a tumbler of water (Figure 10.22). Now fan both thermometers, either by hand or with an electric fan, for a few minutes to blow away the air next to the cloth and keep it from being surrounded by a layer of saturated air.

To find the relative humidity, read both thermometers and find the difference between the two tempera-

tures. Use this temperature difference and the temperature of the dry-bulb thermometer to find the relative humidity (in percentages) in Table 10.1.

1.8 Make a Hair Hygrometer

Obtain a blond human hair about 20 centimeters (8 in) long. Wash it in hot, soapy water, rinse it in cold water, and let it dry. Obtain a piece of two-by-four lumber about 30 centimeters (12 in) long. Use a razor blade to cut a piece about 2 centimeters (1 in) long from a soda straw, making sure to preserve its round form. Obtain a broom straw 10 centimeters (4 in) long, and glue one end to the piece of soda straw (Figure 10.23).

Obtain a long, narrow nail, put it through the piece of soda straw, and drive it into the center of the two-by-four lumber near one end. Fasten one end of the hair to a piece of cellophane tape 5 centimeters (2 in) long, and glue the other end of the hair to the soda straw. When the glue has dried, turn the soda straw a few times to wrap the hair around the soda straw. Now attach the cellophane tape to the two-by-four lumber so that the hair is tight and the broom straw is in a horizontal position. Press the cellophane tape down firmly on top of

TABLE 10.1   Relative humidity index

Dry-Bulb Reading ↓	Difference Between Wet- and Dry-Bulb Readings																													
	1	2	3	4	5	6	7	8	9	10	11	12	13	14	15	16	17	18	19	20	21	22	23	24	25	26	27...		
65	95	90	85	80	75	70	66	62	57	53	48	44	40	36	32	28	25	21	17	13	10	7	3							
66	95	90	85	80	76	71	66	62	58	53	49	45	41	37	33	29	26	22	18	15	11	8	5	1						
67	95	90	85	80	76	71	67	62	58	54	50	46	42	38	34	30	27	23	20	16	13	9	6	3						
68	95	90	85	81	76	72	67	63	59	55	51	47	43	39	35	31	28	24	21	17	14	11	8	4	1					
69	95	90	86	81	77	72	68	64	59	55	51	47	44	40	36	32	29	25	22	19	15	12	9	6	3					
70	95	90	86	81	77	72	68	64	60	56	52	48	44	40	37	33	30	26	23	20	17	13	10	7	4	1				
71	95	90	86	82	77	73	69	64	60	56	53	49	45	41	38	34	31	27	24	21	18	15	11	8	5	3				
72	95	91	86	82	78	73	69	65	61	57	53	49	46	42	39	35	32	28	25	22	19	16	13	10	7	4	1			
73	95	91	86	82	78	73	69	65	61	58	54	50	46	43	40	36	33	29	26	23	20	17	14	11	8	5	2			
74	95	91	86	82	78	74	70	66	62	58	54	51	47	44	40	37	34	30	27	24	21	18	15	12	9	7	4			
75	96	91	87	82	78	74	70	66	63	59	55	52	48	44	41	38	34	31	28	25	22	19	16	13	11	8	5			
76	96	91	87	83	78	74	70	67	63	59	55	52	48	45	42	38	35	32	29	26	23	20	17	14	12	9	6			
77	96	91	87	83	79	75	71	67	63	60	56	52	49	46	42	39	36	33	30	27	24	21	18	15	13	10	7			
78	96	91	87	83	79	75	71	67	64	60	57	53	50	46	43	40	37	34	31	28	25	22	19	16	14	11	9			
79	96	91	87	83	79	75	71	68	64	60	57	54	50	47	44	41	37	34	31	29	26	23	20	17	15	12	10			
80	96	91	87	83	79	76	72	68	64	61	57	54	51	47	44	42	38	35	32	29	27	24	21	18	16	13	11			
82	96	92	88	84	80	76	72	69	65	62	58	55	52	49	46	43	40	37	34	31	28	25	23	20	18	15	13	10		
84	96	92	88	84	80	77	73	70	66	63	59	56	53	50	47	44	41	38	35	32	30	27	25	22	20	17	15	12		
86	96	92	88	85	81	77	74	70	67	63	60	57	54	51	48	45	42	39	37	34	31	29	26	24	21	19	17	14		
88	96	92	88	85	81	78	74	71	67	64	61	58	55	52	49	46	43	41	38	35	33	30	28	25	23	21	18	16		
90	96	92	89	85	81	78	75	71	68	65	62	59	56	53	50	47	44	42	39	37	34	32	29	27	24	22	20	18		
92	96	92	89	85	82	78	75	72	69	65	62	59	57	54	51	48	45	43	40	38	35	33	30	28	26	24	22	19		
94	96	93	89	86	82	79	75	72	69	66	63	60	57	54	52	49	46	44	41	39	36	34	32	29	27	25	23	21	19	17
96	96	93	89	86	82	79	76	73	70	67	64	61	58	55	53	50	47	45	42	40	37	35	33	31	29	26	24	22	20	18
98	96	93	89	86	83	79	76	73	70	67	64	61	59	56	53	51	48	46	43	41	39	36	34	32	30	28	26	24	22	20
100	96	93	90	86	83	80	77	74	71	68	65	62	59	57	54	52	49	47	44	42	40	37	35	33	31	29	27	25	23	21

the two-by-four lumber, inserting thumb tacks to prevent the tape from loosening. However, let the rest of the cellophane dangle loosely over the side to keep the hair from rubbing against the wood. Tack an index card to the two-by-four lumber on the side nearer to the broom straw.

When the air is dry, the hair contracts and the broom straw moves up. When the air is humid, the hair becomes moist and expands, making the broom straw move down. Calibrate the hygrometer by putting it into a pail and covering the pail with a towel that has been soaked in very hot water. The relative humidity in the pail will quickly reach 100 percent, and the broom straw will move down as the hair stretches. After 15 minutes, remove the hygrometer and mark the position of the broom straw as 100 percent relative humidity. Allow some time for the pointer to move back to a normal position, then calibrate other positions on the index card by using either a commercial hygrometer or a wet-and-dry-bulb thermometer.

1.9 Make a Rain Gauge

Obtain a large kitchen funnel and a glass jar whose mouth has exactly the same diameter as the rim of the funnel. Pour exactly 1 centimeter (or 1 inch) of water into the jar, using a ruler to get the exact depth (Figure 10.24). Pour this water into a narrow bottle, such as an olive jar. Place a strip of paper about 12 millimeters (or 1⁄2 inches) wide against the side of the narrow bottle, using strips of cellophane tape to hold the paper in place. With non-water soluble ink, make a mark on the strip of paper to indicate the centimeter or inch of water, and label this mark "1 centimeter" or "1 inch." Measure the distance from this mark

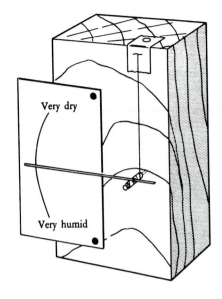

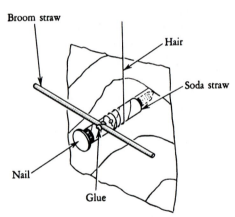

FIGURE 10.23 A homemade hair hygrometer.

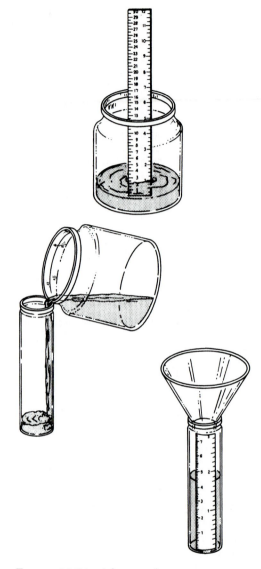

FIGURE 10.24 A homemade rain gauge.

to the bottom of the water in the jar, and use this distance to make additional marks on the paper, each mark accounting for another centimeter or inch of water. Now divide the space between each mark into 10 smaller marks so that each smaller mark represents 1/10 centimeter or 1/10 inch of water. Empty the narrow bottle.

Put the narrow bottle in a large can so that the wind will not blow the bottle over during a rainstorm. Put the funnel in the neck of the narrow bottle, and place the can in an open area. The funnel will collect rain and send it into the narrow bottle, where the amount of rainfall can be measured.

2. OPENING THE OCEAN: AN INTERDISCIPLINARY THEMATIC UNIT (GRADE 5)[1]

Opening the Ocean is a five-day unit designed for a fifth-grade classroom. For each day, the students focus on one aspect of the ocean: Water and Sound, Marine Life, People and the Ocean, and the Sandy Beach. For a culminating activity, we have suggested a field trip to the ocean. We have also included an anticipatory set for the unit—designing a class mural.

To help you out, we have included an additional reference list to provide more activities and to individualize the unit for class. Good luck and enjoy "Opening the Ocean" with your starved-for-knowledge students!

Opening the Ocean: Class Mural

1. Have the class brainstorm things that are needed for an ocean mural. Record the class suggestions on the overhead.
2. Your class may suggest sand, seaweed, boat, treasure chest, octopus, coral, fish, etc. If not, try to ask questions to stimulate discussion toward these ideas.
3. Have students select the items they would like to make. (Make sure you have at least two or three of each.)
4. Staple a 6' × 5' piece of dark blue butcher paper to the wall.
5. Have students, by groups, place their items on the wall. Because there are no specific instructions for where items should be placed, the mural will be very creative. (If you would rather give instructions, designate a "building engineer" to direct the placement of student work on the mural.)

2.1 Water and Sound

This section of the unit combines water and sound, two vital influences in the ocean. Each lesson relates sound in some way to the study of the water of the ocean. Four lessons are represented in this section of an interdisciplinary unit. Specific materials as well as adjustments for needs of special and multicultural students are included in each lesson. This section can be taught as an entire day, as there are lessons involving language arts, science, math, and social studies. It may, however, be divided into separate days if desired, as the lessons do not directly depend on one another.

- Lesson 1: Language Arts. The Ocean: What Does It Say?
- Lesson 2: Math. Water and Sound: A Group Activity to Determine the Speed of Sound
- Lesson 3: Social Studies. The Ocean: A Newfound Planet
- Lesson 4: Science. Why Is the Ocean Salty? Myth and Fact

The Ocean: What Does It Say?

Objective Having read the children's book *Fish Eyes*, a counting book, the students may be inspired by the brilliant colors of the fish to be curious about the wonders and creatures of the ocean. Students will create an artistic representation of a sea creature. They may research the means by which this animal communicates or imagine how the fish or mammal sounds. Students will then write on the back of their creations how this animal contributes to the sounds of the ocean.

Materials *Fish Eyes* by Lois Ehlert, or any book that displays the brilliance and variety of sea life. Construction paper of various colors, colored pens, pencils, white lined paper for the backs of the creatures, a set of encyclopedias for researchers, a list of ocean dwellers as possible art projects, and a tape of whale or ocean sounds. *Interludes* is a great CD of ocean sounds and can be ordered through Great American Audio, 33 Portman Rd., New Rochelle, NY 10801.

Anticipatory Set Guide the students in their project somewhat like this: As you can hear, there is music of the ocean playing in the background. Close your eyes for a minute and listen to the sounds of the ocean. As we have been studying marine life, you now know about the many types of creatures that inhabit the ocean. What do you know about how they sound and communicate? Imagine that you are a fish swimming through the waters of the ocean. What do you hear? You see the sea horses. What are they saying? How do they communicate with one another? I am going to show you the pictures in this book, *Fish Eyes*. Look at them and notice their colors. We are now going to pick an inhabitant of the ocean. You are each responsible for creating a sea dweller. We will then write about how you think the animal communicates, and this will be attached to your creation. You may be creative or you may use the encyclopedia or books from the library. These creations will be hanging in our classroom for everyone to enjoy and admire.

Procedures

1. Allow the students sufficient time to brainstorm and share ideas as well as ask questions. This assignment asks a lot of their creative juices.
2. Model both the creative choice as well as the factual.
3. Encourage the students to enjoy the art project and spend time designing their sea creatures. The writing will mean more to the students if they have a personal attachment to the creations.
4. Limit the time for creation and encourage writing.
5. Do one yourself to model procedure.

Closure Ask the students to share their writings or their creations or both. Have the students talk about whether they think that the ocean is quiet or loud.

Collect the creatures and hang them from the ceiling or utilize them as part of a bulletin board.

Evaluation To determine the level of the children's thinking, study the outcomes. Also compare the number of students who selected the creative option and those who selected the research option. Does this tell you anything about the individuals or your class? Special-needs students may need individual attention with this assignment. Match these students with a buddy in the class.

Assessment Ask the children what they learned and how they learned it. Use this as a quick writing assignment in a journal.

Water and Sound: A Group Activity to Determine the Speed of Sound

Objective Students will create mathematical problems using the equations for the speed of sound in water. This is a group activity in which the groups work together to create and solve math problems involving water and sound.

Materials Paper, pencils, at least one calculator per group, a chart with the equations and steps, and a map with mileage measurements.

Anticipatory Set Do you think sound travels faster in water or in air? Did you know that if you were a sound wave, you could travel five times faster in water than in air. That means if you were whispering to your friend in class and all our classes were underwater, your friend would hear you five times faster than he or she would as you sit where you are right now. We are going to get into groups and create our own math problems using these equations. You may use any distance in the world you wish, as long as the distance is provided in your problem.

Procedures
1. Teach the math lesson that explains that the speed of sound is 5,000 feet per second in the water. One mile is equal to 5,280 feet. Thus, to compute the amount of time it would take for sound to travel underwater, from one town to another, assuming the distance is 30 miles, one would use the following procedure: 30 miles (the distance) times 5,280 ft (1 mile) = the distance in feet, which is 158,400 feet. You know that sound travels 5,000 feet each second; thus, divide the 158,400 feet by 5,000 to reach the time in seconds. Answer: 31.68, or 32 seconds.
2. You will need a step-by-step chart for the students.

3. Have the students work in groups (incorporate strong math students).
4. Each student picks a distance for which he or she wants to measure the speed of sound underwater.
5. Each group writes its problem as a word problem on one paper and puts the solution on another.
6. The teacher then collects the groups' problems and passes out the problems for another group to solve.
7. Groups check their answers with the original group.
8. If a discrepancy exists, the class may work together, facilitated by the teacher, to solve the problem.
9. Each problem must include the distance from one location to a desired destination.

Conclusion Have students go over procedures for solving the problems with the teacher. Talk about problem solving and group work.

Evaluation Collect problems and work to see how solutions were attempted and found.

Assessment Have the students write the steps needed to solve this equation, to be handed in to the teacher. Include why each step is necessary.

(Because this activity is group oriented, special-needs students should be able to participate without any problem.)

The Ocean: A Newfound Planet

Objective After discussing the combined size of the oceans, students will realize the vastness of the sea. Pose the question, Why not call this Planet Ocean inasmuch as 75 percent of our Earth is covered by water? Students will create posters displaying the new Planet Ocean.

Materials Posterboard or construction paper, pens, glue, and magazines if you wish.

Anticipatory Set Why do we call our planet "Earth" when 75 percent of it is covered with water? You have just been assigned to the committee to change the name of Earth to Planet Ocean. Your assignment is to create a poster, with a partner, which encourages us to change the name to Planet Ocean. The posters will be judged and given various prizes.

Procedures
1. Explain how the earth is 75 percent water.
2. Have students work in pairs to create their posters.

3. Have other teachers and the principal select the most creative and influential poster (tell students the judging criteria beforehand).
4. Award all posters a prize if you wish!

Closure Allow students to share posters and explain them to the class. Display them in the classroom.

Evaluation Check for understanding of surface area covered by water by evaluating posters.

(Multicultural and special-needs students should have no problem with this activity if it is explained thoroughly.)

Why Is the Ocean Salty? Myth and Fact

Objective Students will discover why the ocean is salty. First, in groups, they will create their own myths to explain the salt in the ocean. Second, students will research and present the facts about the salt in the ocean.

Materials Paper, pencils, encyclopedia or science book that includes information on the ocean and a myth, such as that of Johnny Appleseed.

Anticipatory Set I am going to tell you why the ocean is salty today, class. In 1332, a gigantic ship was traveling from a faraway land carrying salt to sell to another nation. The ship hit a glacier and all the salt spilled into the ocean. The ship was so big that it made all the oceans in the world salty. Is that a fact or a myth? What do you think? Today you will be in groups to create your own myths about why the ocean is salty. We will then work together as a class to find out the facts about why the ocean is salty.

Procedures
1. Read a myth to the students so that they are clear as to what a myth is. Johnny Appleseed is a popular myth.
2. Place students in groups and ask them to brainstorm and create a reason or myth about why the ocean is salty.
3. Give the students ample time to work, and let them know their myths will be read aloud.
4. Have the students read their myths to the class.
5. Work together under teacher instruction to find the real answer. (Do you know? Work with your class to find out!)

Closure Ask the students what they learned about myths as well as about the ocean and its salt. Place their myths on the wall in your classroom.

Evaluate Read students' work. Determine whether they mastered the concept of *myth*. Because this is a group activity, all students should be able to participate.

Assessment Ask students the following day to define *myth* and explain the facts about why the ocean is salty.

BOOKS

Language Arts
Fish Eyes by Lois Ehlert. Tein Wah Press, 1992.

Math
Equations for sound from *Whales in the Classroom, Vol. 11: Oceanography* by Lary Wade, illustrated by Stephen Bolles. Singing Rock Press, 1992.

Social Studies
M.A.R.E.: A teacher's guide to the ocean. (These are ideas for the study of the ocean published by the University of California at Berkeley.)

Science
Johnny Appleseed, author unknown.

2.2 Marine Life

The following lessons surround the kings of the ocean—the whales. The disciplines covered are art, language arts (writing), science, physical education, and mathematics. Each lesson's time will vary from class to class, but here are some estimations:

- Lesson 1: The Art of Scrimshaw (art and social science) 90 minutes. This activity requires drying time for the artwork. It may be beneficial to time this during a recess or natural scheduling break.
- Lesson 2: A Whale Story (language arts) 60 minutes. This activity should follow the Art of Scrimshaw lesson because there can be a natural transition from one to the other.
- Lesson 3: Blubber Is Beautiful (science) 45–75 minutes. Hands-on science. This activity may require a few mintues' setup by the instructor.
- Lesson 4: Migration Graph (math and physical education) 90 minutes. Time to exercise and think. Always a great wakening activity on distance; can also spruce up a slow afternoon.

Have a whale of a time!

The Art of Scrimshaw

Objective After gathering information about scrimshaw art (history, examples), students will create their own artwork and distinguish its history.

Materials

Large, smooth white seashells	Linseed oil
Polish (light, clear cover-spray or paint)	Nails
Superfine sandpaper	Ink or watercolor

Anticipatory Set Show students scrimshaw art. Can they figure out what materials it would take to create such beauty? What do they figure the art means to the artist? Provide students with prompts. Could the artist be a recycler?

Procedures Share with students the history of the art of scrimshaw.

Provide students with the materials and necessary steps for their artwork: sand and polish the shell to be inscribed. Scratch, with a nail, a marine-oriented scene, using a nautical theme (for example, a whaler scene, harpooners, a battle scene, mermaids, or pirates). Cover the shell with ink and wipe with linseed oil. The inscribed design will be filled with ink.

Closure Explain to students that this art activity is going to be a transition to their language arts later in the day. During language arts they will be writing or dictating their art's history. Discuss as a whole class their thoughts about scrimshaw.

Evaluation What was scrimshaw art used for? (trade)

Why don't we see much scrimshaw anymore? (Few whales and even fewer whales' teeth are available.)

A Whale Story

Objective Students will analyze and support their Art of Scrimshaw work through writing its history in the American whalers' setting.

Materials

Completed student scrimshaw work
Writing instruments
Sand, seashells, other materials
Paper cut in whale shapes
Historical vocabulary journals
Glue

Anticipatory Set Read students a teacher written history of your scrimshaw work. Be creative here—depending on your comfort level, try turning your history piece into a reader's theater or other dramatic presentation.

Procedure Remind students of the historical and cultural importance of scrimshaw art. Provide them with whale-shaped paper and materials for authentic writings. Have students write their short historical fiction (extensions for able students: dictate history into a tape recorder, do share-pair, write poetry, provide historical vocabulary journals). After writing, provide students with marine materials (sand, shells) for writing decoration.

Closure In groups, have students share their historical fiction along with their scrimshaw artwork. Ask each

group to choose one piece they thought was historically accurate, interesting, funny, exciting, and/or had a strong correspondence with the artwork. The chosen piece will then be shared with the entire class.

Evaluation After students have displayed their writing and artwork, evaluate their work based on their ability to connect the art and history. Did the students place their writing in American whaling history as asked to do?

Blubber Is Beautiful

Objective Students will investigate the beauty of whale blubber and compare and contrast blubber with plain body heat.

Materials
plastic gloves (2 pairs for every two students)
crushed ice/ice cubes
laboratory thermometers (1 for every two students)
buckets (1 for every two students)
water
shortening
clock with second hand
recording sheet

Anticipatory Set BLUBBER. "Blubber Is Beautiful"—today on (your name) talk show. Many in the United States are lean and slick. Few in the world are blubbers and beautiful. It is a personal choice for some but a genetic makeup for others. Join us today on (your name) talk show to hear from and examine the truth—blubber or not?

Procedures Students are now the scientists testing the two opinions about blubber. In groups of two they will:

1. Fill a bucket with ice water. Measure and record the water temperature.
2. One student will put on a pair of gloves. The other student will spread a thick layer of shortening over student 1's right hand. Then the first student will put the second pair of gloves over the first.
3. Have student 1 put both hands in the ice water, being sure that hands are not deeply immersed so no water enters from the top of the gloves.
4. Student will keep hands immersed, sharing feelings with student 2 (recorder).
5. Student will remove each hand as soon as it become uncomfortable. Recorder will note how long he or she was able to keep each hand in the water.
6. Repeat the activity, changing roles of students. (Be sure to measure water temperature to ensure that it is the same each time.)

7. Each student-scientist pair will then answer the discussion questions on a record sheet (Fig. 10.25) and report their findings to the class summary wall chart.

Closure Class discussion—review the class summary wall chart. Ask the following questions of (your name) talk show guests: Explain the scientific experiment to our audience. Which hand stayed in the water longer? Why? Discuss why shortening insulated these hands. How does shortening compare with blubber? Why do marine animals need blubber to keep warm? Close as host of the talk show: "As I promised, we have an answer to the Is Blubber Beautiful? debate. For the lean, slick fish, blubber is not so important. Yet for the survival of whales in our world's ocean, BLUBBER IS BEAUTIFUL!

Related Activities To demonstrate how blubber helps prevent the loss of body heat, have students take their palm temperatures under the gloves directly before putting their hands in the water. For best results, use laboratory thermometers. After one minute, have them remove their hands from the ice water and immediately take their palm temperatures again. Subtract the end temperature from the start temperature. Repeat with other students. Compare temperature loss between the "blubber" and "plain" hands and analyze the results. What was the average heat loss for each hand?

Migration Graph

Objective Students will develop an appreciation and understanding of the gray whales' migration (problem solving, graphing, physical education).

Materials
Example graphs
Materials for graph making
Exercise area for runner, swimmers, wheelchairs

Anticipatory Set Challenge students to make predictions on how many days it would take them to finish the 5,000-mile migration of the gray whale. Display various types of graphs and how predictions can be made from graphs.

Procedures Students will make their own predictions for the amount of time it would take them to complete a 5,000-mile migration. Then they will create their own unique graphs to illustrate their prediction and amount of distance per day using an equation: for example, 20 miles a day times number of days = migration distance.
Students will walk, run, or wheelchair a mile to determine the time. Then they will return to their graphs to reestimate the distance and days. (Students will realize the distance and most likely adjust their prediction for days.) Redo estimated graphs and equations for distance.

Closure Hold a class discussion, sharing original estimations of distance and migration time. Graph student time estimates.

Evaluation Did the students finish the activity with a stronger sense of distance? Were the equations generated acceptable for finding solutions? Have the students write their final estimation of time needed to complete the distance.

RESOURCES FOR MARINE LIFE
The following resources provide ideas, guidelines, and information for these lessons.

Is Blubber Beautiful?

Water Temperature:

Which hand was removed first?

How long were you able to keep hands in the bucket?

On a separate piece of paper, answer the following:
Which hand stayed in the bucket longer?
Why?
Did the shortening make a difference?
Share your findings and conclusions.

Names: _____

	#1		#2	
	R	L	R	L

FIGURE 10.25   Record sheet.

The Art of Scrimshaw

The art of scrimshaw has been considered a very important indigenous folk art of the Indians and, later, early Americans. It involved the carving and decorating of whales' teeth, walrus tusks, or bone (usually whales' teeth). Whalers had a considerable amount of time on their hands and, with scant tools, etched whales' teeth to pass the time. A trophy of a whale hunt—a large tooth—was the measure of the whaler's success, and the carefully etched pictures expressed great individuality.

> C. Kiorpes, Elk. *Teacher's Guide to the Whales of the Gulf of Maine.*
> *Insulation Investigation.* Sea World Materials, Inc., 1987.
> *Los Marineros Curriculum Guide.* NOAA and Santa Barbara Superintendant of Schools.
> *M.A.R.E. Teacher Guide.* UC-Berkeley, California.
> *Wet and Wild.* USC Sea Grant Program, Institute for Marine and Coastal Studies, University of Southern California, 1983.

2.3 People and the Ocean

On this day, we will discuss how people use the oceans and how people affect the oceans. For a culminating activity, we will cook seafood recipes from different countries, utilizing at least one of our senses—taste.

The day is divided by the different disciplines: math, language arts, social studies, and science. An approximate time line for each discipline and a day's schedule follow, for your use in completing all activities in one day.

Time line

- Lesson 1: Gone Fishing (Sharing of Common Resources) (math)
  45 minutes
- Lesson 2: Mini-Paper (language arts)
  1 hour

- Lesson 3: Globetrotters (social studies)
  45 minutes
- Lesson 4: Plastic in the Sea (science)
  1 hour
- Lesson 5: Cooking
  1 hour, 20 minutes

Sample day's schedule

   8:00–8:45 Lesson 1
   8:50–9:50 Lesson 2
   10:05–10:50 Lesson 3
   11:10–12:40 Lesson 5
   11:45–12:45 Lesson 4
   12:50–1:40 Eating

Most of the following activities contain cooperative group work, so you might want to preassign the groups to have some variety.

Gone Fishing

Objective After simulation, students will be able to discuss the different scenarios that could occur with a large group of people fishing in the same waters.

Materials 600 paper clips, poster board, 50 square meters of area, marking pens, and small magnets

Procedures

1. Randomly scatter paper clips within the 50 square meters.
2. Duplicate the chart in Figure 10.26 on poster board.
3. Divide the class into four groups, and have each group choose a name for its country.
4. Explain to students that they will be fishing in common waters, and each country depends on fishing for survival.

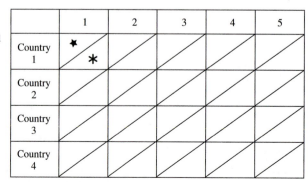

FIGURE 10.26 Gone Fishing chart.

5. Each group is allowed one boat (one person) and one year (1 minute) to fish.
6. Each country sends out one boat, and he or she fishes for one year using a magnet as a fishing pole. After one minute is up, have each group divide its fish into piles of 10.
7. Each group must have at least 10 fish a year to survive. Any extra fish can be used for profit.
8. Every 10 fish after the first 10 are worth $2. Groups can use the profit to purchase more boats for $20 each.
9. Have countries record their catch on the chart on poster board (Figure 10.27).
10. Have groups do their buying at this time. Each group should also choose another person to be the boat.
11. After a round, have students figure out how many fish are left from the original 600.
    - If 400 or more remain, you can collect all the fish that were caught and replenish the ocean.
    - If 300–399 remain, only 150 may be returned.
    - If less than 299 remain, then the ocean is left as is.
12. Continue the same steps for the four countries for five rounds, or until the fish are caught.

Closure   Ask the class to consider the following questions:

- Which country was most profitable in its fishing excursions?
- What happened to the number of paper clips students collected as fishing continued?
- If the goal was not to make money, but to sustain themselves on earth for the longest time, did anyone win?
- What could the students have done to sustain the fish population?

Evaluation   Listen to discussion of closure questions to check for understanding of the topic: the positive and negative effects of sharing an area of water for fishing.

Mini-Papers[2]

Objective   After discussion about how people have different uses for what the ocean provides, students will be able to research and write mini-papers about these uses in cooperative groups.

Materials   Encyclopedia set, library access, poster board, construction paper, and markers

Anticipatory Set   Activate prior knowledge by brainstorming what uses we have for the ocean. Record the ideas on the overhead, chalkboard, or a large piece of butcher paper (the latter is suggested because it's mo-

bile). Students will likely describe uses very close to those on which they will write their papers.

Procedures

1. Have the class divide into six groups and choose which cooperative group jobs they want (i.e., recorder, speaker, editor, reader, illustrator, and runner).
2. Have runners come to the front of the class and draw their topics out of a container.
3. Following is the list of topics students need to cover:
   - Mariculture (ocean agriculture): History of; uses and practices of; used in future—how? and drawbacks and consequences of.
   - Desalinization (getting freshwater from the sea): How can freshwater be obtained from the sea? How could people benefit? Why isn't this a big industry? How can this be more effective? Possible environmental consequences.
   - Ocean fishing: Foods we get from the sea; Name several countries where ocean fishing is a major industry; Describe methods for catching ocean fish; Negative effects of ocean fishing.
   - Mining at Sea: Which minerals (if any) do we get from the sea? What kind of minerals could we get? Problems with ocean mining.
   - Ocean energy: Discuss ocean tides; ocean waves; thermal energy in the ocean.
   - Ocean pollution: Name different kinds of ocean pollution. How is this pollution affecting the sea, animals, and plants? What's being done to help? What people can do to help.
4. You need to explain that there are only 45 minutes to research and write about the topics, so students need to have a plan that utilizes all group members to complete the assignment.
5. The runners will also go to library to get books for the group. Make sure you have this time slot reserved, so that the runners will have access during the 45 minutes.

Closure   Have a speaker from each group share a brief summary of its topic.

Evaluation   Read mini-papers and make sure every area that needed to be covered was completed.

Globetrotters[3]

Objective   After playing a team game, students will know facts about important historical ocean explorations and will be able to read the longitude and latitude lines on a map.

Materials   Fact sheet, "Chart a New Course" and *Magellan* and *Challenger* ships (Figure 10.27), straight

Chart a New Course

Exploration Clues

1000: Many people believe the Vikings discovered America long before Columbus did. We know that Eric the Red got as far as what large island? (70°N, 40°W)

1492: Christopher Columbus reached the New World—now called the Americas—by sailing west across the Atlantic Ocean in search of a new route to Asia. The first island he landed on is in what island chain? (24°N, 74°W)

1513: The first European to see the Pacific Ocean was Vasco de Balboa. What country did he cross to see it? (8°N, 80°W)

1773: Captain James Cook sailed in search of a "southern continent." He never saw it, but while searching, he became the first person to cross what major latitude line? (66°S)

1786: Ben Franklin published the first map of the Gulf Stream to help sailors cross the ocean. The Gulf Stream originates in what body of water? (25°N, 90°W)

1831: Starting from England, naturalist Charles Darwin went on a worldwide research voyage aboard the HMS *Beagle*. He discovered fossil seashells 12,000 feet high in what mountain range? (33°S, 72°W)

1840: Charles Wilkes of the U.S. Navy proved the existence of a seventh continent by leading an expedition there. What is the seventh continent? (70°S, 135°E)

1866: The first successful transatlantic cable was laid across the ocean floor. Depth charts developed by Matthew Maury helped people know where to lay the cable. It stretched from Ireland to what Canadian province? (48°N, 56°W)

1872: Anton Dohm founded the first marine biological station. This research laboratory is in what country? (42°N, 14°E)

1892: Louis Boutan took the first underwater photographs. What country was Boutan from? (42°N, 4°E)

1905: Scripps Institution of Oceanography was founded. Many ocean research scientists work here. What state is Scripps in? (35°N, 120°W)

1925: A research ship named the *Meteor* crisscrossed the South Atlantic Ocean to survey it with echo sounding. What country did the *Meteor* belong to? (50°N, 10°E)

1930: Woods Hole Oceanographic Institute was founded. Many ocean research scientists work here. What state is Woods Hole in? (43°N, 71°W)

1934: William Beebe descended a half-mile into the ocean depths in a steel ball called a *bathysphere*. This deep-sea dive took place near what island? (32°N, 65°W)

1943: Jacques Cousteau developed the *aqualung*. The aqualung enables divers to carry their own air supply underwater. In what sea was this new invention tested? (40°N, 5°E)

1960: Jacques Piccard descended to the deepest known spot in the ocean in a submarinelike ship called the *Trieste*. This spot is nearly seven miles below the surface in the Mariana Trench. It's located at the bottom of the ocean near what island? (14°N, 145°E)

1969: Thor Heyerdahl sailed across the Atlantic Ocean in a reed raft called *Ra II* to show that sailors from ancient Africa also could have done so. What African country did he sail from? (33°N, 7°W)

1970: Sylvia Earle led the first all-woman team of U.S. aquanauts. (Aquanauts are divers who live in an undersea laboratory and study the ocean while scientists on the surface study the divers' ability to live and work underwater.) Earle's team spent two weeks in the underwater station called *Tektite II* near a group of islands in what sea? (15°N, 65°W)

1974: Robert Ballard explored a volcanic mid-ocean ridge in a small submersible called *Alvin*. He saw lava oozing from an area where two plates of the Earth's crust are spreading apart. In which ocean was this discovery made? (38°N, 32°W)

1975: The United States established the first National Marine Sanctuary to protect the wreck of a Civil War ship that sank in an 1862 storm. The ship, called the *Monitor*, was discovered off the barrier islands of what state? (36°N, 76°W)

1977: Robert Ballard explored a mid-ocean ridge in a small submersible called *Alvin* and discovered an unusual community in the dark ocean depths. This community lives where heat from the Earth's core is released through vents. Giant tube worms and other strange creatures are part of this community. Near what group of islands was the community first discovered? (1°S, 91°W)

1979: Sylvia Earle dove to the ocean floor inside an armored suit called a Jim suit. The Jim suit is like a one-person submersible. Earle went to a depth of 1,250 feet—the deepest any person has ever been without being connected to a boat with a line. Near what islands did she make this historic dive? (20°N, 155°W)

1985: An undersea robot called *Argo* located the wreck of the *Titanic* at the bottom of the ocean. (The *Titanic* was a luxury ocean liner that hit an iceberg and sank in 1912.) In what ocean was the wreck found? (42°N, 50°W)

1985: A treasure hunter located millions of dollars' worth of silver, gold, and gems from the wreck of a Spanish galleon. The ship sank in a 1622 storm off the coast of what state? (25°N, 82°W)

FIGURE 10.27   Globetrotters fact sheet and game pieces. (Answers are given on page 385.)

Answers to the Fact Sheet (Chart a New Course)

1000: Greenland	**1930:** Massachusetts
1492: Bahamas	**1934:** Bermuda
1513: Panama	**1943:** Mediterranean
1773: Antarctic Circle	**1960:** Guam
1786: Gulf of Mexico	**1969:** Morocco
1831: Andes	**1970:** Caribbean
1840: Antarctica	**1974:** Atlantic
1866: Newfoundland	**1975:** North Carolina
1872: Italy	**1977:** Galapagos
1892: France	**1979:** Hawaiian
1905: California	**1985:** Atlantic
1925: Germany	**1985:** Florida

pins, class set of small world maps (Figure 10.28), large world map (all maps need longitude and latitude lines), container for fact sheet, overhead projector, overhead pens, and transparency of each handout

Procedure
Before students arrive

- Place a large map on a wall where straight pins can be used.
- Cut up a fact sheet and place the facts in a container.
- Color the two ships.

1. Instruct the class on how to use longitude and latitude lines.
2. Divide the class into two groups.
3. Have a student volunteer (or you) plot the starting point for each ship (Figure 10.29). Use a transparency of the small map each individual student has to demonstrate the plotting on the overhead.
4. Explain the rules of the game:
   - Have two members from the *Magellan* group come up to the map. Have one student draw a fact from the fact can, and the other student read the fact.
   - Have the two members answer the question by finding the location on the map from the longitude and latitude clues (30-second time limit).
   - If their answer is *correct*, they attach the fact at the point, then move their ship to the next stop on their route. If their answer is *incorrect*, they put the fact back into the can and leave their ship where it is.
   - Now it is the *Challenger* team's turn.
   - Continue taking turns until one team completes its round-the-world voyage. (Answers to the fact sheet questions and map with approximate routes plotted are included.)

Closure Ask students to recall what longitude and latitude are and some of the places both ships explored.

Evaluation Make sure every student understands what longitude and latitude are. To check this, you can collect the small maps that each individual student worked on and make sure the exact points were marked.

Plastic in the Sea[4]

Objective After discussion about plastic dumping in the ocean, students will be able to complete a graph-reading work sheet, explain how harmful dumping is to wildlife, and graph their own plastic use.

Materials Graph paper, Plastic in the Sea fact sheet, graphs, and "Graphing Activity" questions (see below), overhead projector, overhead pens, and transparencies for all handouts

Anticipatory Set Have students work in groups to answer the following questions:
- What types of trash have you seen wash up on beaches?
- How do you think the trash got there?
- How do you think this could harm wildlife?
- How do you use plastics at home?

Procedure
1. Show class statistics of what was collected on the Texas coast in 1986 (page 388).
2. Have students graph these results on graph paper using a bar graph.
3. Have students read the fact sheet as a class.
4. You can include the following facts in addition to the fact sheet:
   - Trash is disposed of in the following ways: burned in an incinerator, put into landfills, or dumped into the oceans.

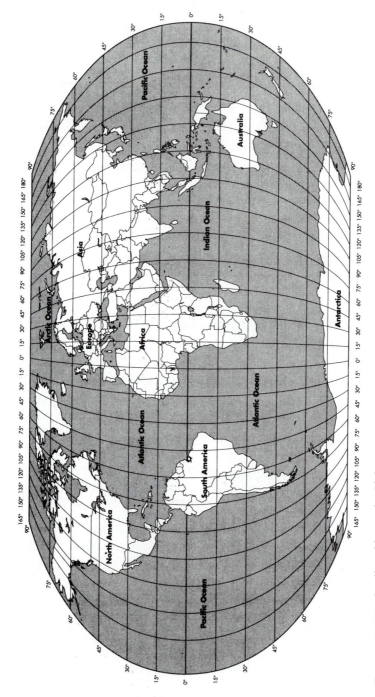

FIGURE 10.28 Small world maps for Globetrotters game.

386

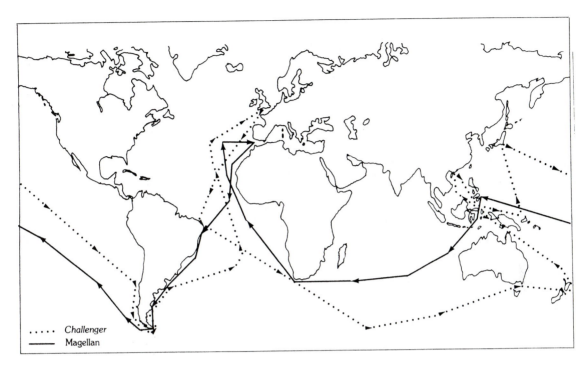

FIGURE 10.29 Approximate routes of *Magellan* and *Challenger*.

Magellan's Route	**Route of the Challenger**
start: 37°N, 6°W	start: 51°N, 1°W
1: 5°N, 15°W	1: 5°S, 35°W
2: 8°S, 35°W	2: 35°S, 20°E
3: 52°S, 68°W	3: 65°S, 80°E
4: 40°S, 80°W	4: 40°S, 174°E
5: 24°S, 100°W	5: 20°N, 112°E
6: 2°N, 170°W	6: 3°S, 145°E
7: 10°N, 124°E	7: 35°N, 140°E
8: 3°S, 126°E	8: 20°N, 155°W
9: 30°S, 90°E	9: 35°S, 75°W
10: 35°S, 20°E	10: 52°S, 68°W
11: 40°N, 30°W	11: 35°S, 57°W
end: 37°N, 6°W	end: 51°N, 1°W

Enlarge and place near large world map.

Items Collected in 1986 Texas Coast Cleanup

Material	Number of Items	% of Total
Plastics	95,560	56%
Rubber	20	0.01%
Glass	20,040	12%
Styrofoam	19,280	11%
Metal	22,100	13%
Paper	10,340	6%
Wood	4,160	2%

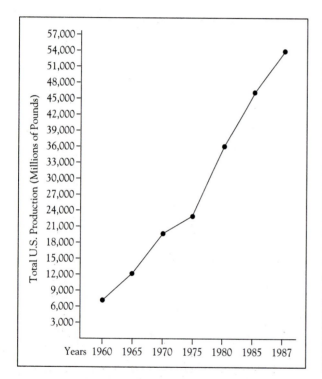

FIGURE 10.30   Increase in U.S. plastic production.

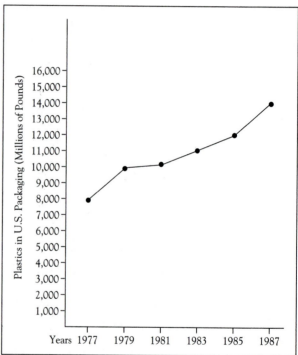

FIGURE 10.31   Increase in use of plastics in U.S. packaging.

- Plastic, metal, chemicals, paper, food, and other materials are dumped into the ocean.
- Ocean dumping is harmful to wildlife. Poison in toxic chemicals kills fish, shellfish, and other creatures. Plastic cuts, tangles, poisons, and strangles turtles, seabirds, and sea mammals.

5. Have students record their own use of plastics for one day.
6. Have students complete the graphing activity (included) and graph their use of plastic, in groups.

Closure Discuss ways that students themselves can help with the plastic problem.

Evaluation Students should be able to complete the activities with at least 90 percent accuracy because they are done in groups.

GRAPHING ACTIVITY QUESTIONS (FIGURES 10.30 AND 10.31)

1. During which five-year period did the greatest increase in plastic production occur?
2. Compare the plastic production in 1987 and 1960. How much higher or lower was it in 1987?
3. How much did plastic production increase from 1975 to 1987?

Fact Sheet: Plastic in the Sea

- Young seals often play with plastic six-pack rings and get the bands caught around their necks. These bands can strangle them as they grow.
- More than 14 billion pounds of trash are dumped into the ocean every year. A large percentage of this trash is plastic.
- Small pellets, beads, cylinders, and other types of raw plastic are dumped or spilled into the ocean. Seabirds often mistake this plastic for fish eggs, fish eyes, or plankton and sometimes die from eating it.
- Some states have banned nonbiodegradable plastic six-pack rings.
- Some plastics contain PCBs—chemicals that cause some birds to lay thin-shelled eggs that break easily.
- Every year, millions of pounds of plastic fishing nets, buoys, lines, and other gear are lost at sea.
- Sea turtles often feed on plastic bags, mistaking them for jellyfish. Many of these turtles eventually starve to death because the plastic clogs their digestive systems.
- More than 30,000 northern fur seals die each year after becoming entangled in plastic nets and plastic six-pack rings. They die of strangulation, starvation, drowning, or exhaustion.
- Most plastic is not biodegradable. That means it takes many years for the plastic to break down, or disintegrate.
- Scientists have developed some biodegradable plastics. However, not enough research has been done to know whether these biodegradable plastics break down into safe substances.
- In late 1988 an international treaty took effect that restricts plastic ocean dumping by the nations that ratified it—including the United States.

---

4. Compare the graphs in Figures 10.30 and 10.31. Between the years of 1977 and 1987, which graph shows a greater increase? Can you explain why the rate of increase is different between the two graphs?
5. How many millions of pounds of plastic were used to make nonpackaging plastic in 1987? Name some other types of plastic products.
6. Given the trends you see in the two graphs, predict what each group will look like 10 years from now. What are some factors that might affect plastic production and packaging?

Cooking

1. Start cooking after you have finished three of your lessons.
2. Recipes have been included.
3. *Caution:* Seafood can be lethal if not stored or cooked properly.
4. Students can help by cutting the vegetables and putting together all the ingredients that are needed.
5. If you can obtain a crockpot and skillet, you can cook inside your classroom.
6. If timed properly, the food will be ready to eat after you finish your last lesson.

Note: You will need at least two parent volunteers to watch the food while it cooks and to help serve when it's finished.

REFERENCES

Carter, K. (1958). *The True Book of Oceans.* Chicago: Children's Press.

"Diving into Oceans." *Ranger Rick's Nature Scope* 4(2) (1988).

Investigations in Oceanography. (1976). Bellevue, WA: Bellevue Public Schools.

Lambert, D., and A. McConnell. *Seas and Oceans.* New York: Facts on File Publications.

Parfit, M. "Diminishing Returns: Exploiting the Ocean's Bounty." *National Geographic* 188(5): 2–37 (November 1995).

Sund, R., and D. Adams. (1985). *Accent on Science.* Ohio: Bill and Howell Company.

Water Wisdom. (1990). Oakland, CA: Alameda County Office of Education.

2.4 The Sandy Beach

This unit introduces the sandy beach. It contains activities and information on sand and other related aspects

---

Recipes[*]

Portugal
Fisherman's Stew

3 onions, peeled and sliced
2 cloves garlic, peeled and mashed
3 green bell peppers, seeded and diced
2 bay leaves
1/4 cup olive oil
1 pound tomatoes, peeled and diced
1/3 cup tomato paste
1 T. salt
1/2 tsp. white pepper
1/8 tsp. dried basil
1/8 tsp. dried thyme
6 pounds of varied fish slices—preferably snapper, cod, bass, perch, and flounder

Have fish prepared ahead of time. Students can prepare the vegetables and add them to the crockpot. Add 1 cup of water to the crockpot. Bring the vegetables and spices to a boil. After all vegetables are soft, add the fish, and stir until cooked (approximately 30 minutes).

Brazil
Broiled Salmon with Bearnaise Sauce

Salmon steaks
1 1/2 tsp. salt
1/2 tsp. pepper
1/2 cup melted butter

Have salmon steaks prepared. All the students will need to do is baste the steaks. Have parent fry them in a skillet (10 minutes). Students can help parents prepare the Bearnaise sauce.

Shrimp Cocktail

Baby cooked shrimp
Cocktail sauce

Fill paper cups with baby shrimp and top with cocktail sauce. Students can do this right before the class is about to eat because this shrimp is already cooked when you purchase it at the store.
   You can also buy dried cuttlefish at any Asian market. This is usually eaten for dessert.

[*]Be sure none of your students are allergic to seafood.

---

of the beach. Each lesson, along with its incorporated discipline, follows. The time required for each lesson is specified.

- Lesson 1: The Facts About Sand (social studies)
  Time needed: approximately 1 to 1 1/2 hours
- Lesson 2: Sand Weight (math)
  Time needed: 45–60 minutes
- Lesson 3: Strange Beginnings—A Creative Writing Activity (language arts)
  Time needed: 40 minutes
- Lesson 4: What Is a Food Chain? (science)
  Time needed: approximately 1 hour

The Facts About Sand

Key Concept Sand grains can be make of many things and come in many different shapes, sizes, and colors. These differences can be clues about the material makeup and origin of sand.

Objective Students, using magnifiers and working in small groups, compare the color, size, and shape of several sand samples to determine their material makeup and origin.

Materials Magnifiers; zip-lock bags, each containing a different type of sand; question work sheet; world map

Background Information Nearly all solid materials in the world, both living and nonliving, will eventually be eroded into sand. Rocks, shells, corals, bones, metals, and glass are all worn over time by wind, waves, rivers, earthquakes, and other forces into smaller and smaller particles. For this reason, sand is often said to be the earth in miniature.

The sand of every beach has its own unique history. Detailed observations combined with some good detective work, however, often allow us to make some reasonable hypotheses about the material makeup and origin of the sand. Sand from the remains of plants or animals is referred to as "biogenic," and sand from non-living sources is called "abiogenic." A closer look at sand through a hand lens or microscope also reveals a lot about the sand's individual grains.

Some sand is produced right at the shore, where waves crash on rocks, headlands, and reefs. For example, black or red sand beaches in Hawaii and the Galapagos are found directly next to or on top of lava flows of the same color. White sand beaches in Florida and in the Caribbean are primarily made of eroded coral reefs. Parrot fish, which eat coral polyps, grind up the corals with their sharp teeth and can excrete up to 100 pounds of coral sand per year. Pink sand may be full of coralline algae fragments. Other sand comes from far inland. Mountains are weathered by freezing, wind, rain, and streams, and their fragments are carried down streams and rivers to the seashore. Quartz, a glasslike mineral, is often the most common component of these transported sands. Quartz is the most common mineral on earth, and it is nearly insoluble in water. Most light-colored sand beaches contain large amounts of quartz.

Anticipatory Set Today we will be working as geologists. We are going to try to figure out what sand is made of and where it came from. We will be doing some very interesting investigating.

Procedure

1. Divide students into groups of four. Give each group two bags of sand and a magnifier.
2. Each group selects a recorder to record the answers to the questions on the work sheet.
3. Each group will be given five minutes to inspect its two sand bags and record its observations. When time is called, groups will switch sand bags until all sand bags have been rotated around the room.
4. When all types of sand have been observed by each group, distribute and allow about 10 minutes completion of the work sheet.
   Work sheet questions
   ■ What material do you think your sand is made of?

(Small rocks? Shells? Wood? Glass? Plant material?)
   ■ What do you think the source of your sand is? (A coral reef? A mountain? A lava flow? Clams or snail shells?)
   ■ Do you think the material makeup of sand or its color can tell us anything about where it was produced? If yes, how?
5. Discuss the work sheets. Encourage students to share their answers.
6. Tell students that sand's makeup/color does give clues as to where it came from. For example, black or red sandy beaches in Hawaii and the Galapagos are found directly next to or on top of lava flows of the same color. White sand beaches in Florida and in the Caribbean are primarily made up of eroded coral reefs.
7. Prepare an index card for each location mentioned in question 6. Draw the color of sand likely to be found there on each card.
8. Call on volunteers to locate each place on the map. Tape each index card on its proper location.
9. Collect all work sheets.

Closure Review the information about sand. Inform students that these were only a few of the many interesting facts to be learned about sand.

Evaluation Review the students' work sheets. The students' work should demonstrate an understanding of the task assigned.

Sand Weight

Key Concepts and Processes Measurement, patterns, functions, statistics, and probability

Objective After being introduced to sand and weight, students will work cooperatively in centers to estimate the weight of sand. Their results will be recorded and mapped out on a graph.

Materials Scale, teaspoon, weights, small cup, 1 cup of sand, and graph paper.

Demonstration

1. Show students 1/2 teaspoon of sand.
2. Students estimate the weight of the sand in grams.
3. Place 1/2 teaspoon of sand in a small cup. Place the cup on a scale.
4. Place the smallest gram weight on opposite side of the scale. Increase the weight until the scale is even.
5. Then tell students that they will be weighing sand in the same manner.

Procedure Tell each student which sand learning station he or she will be working at. List the following steps at each station.

1. Estimate what 1 teaspoon of sand will weigh, and record your estimate on paper.
2. Put 1 teaspoon of sand in the cup and place it on the scale.
3. Put the smallest weight on the scale. Increase the weight until you discover the actual weight of the sand.
4. Record the weight on your paper.
5. Estimate what 2 teaspoons of sand will weigh.
6. Weigh and record the weight of 2 teaspoons of sand.
7. Repeat for 3 teaspoons and 4 teaspoons.
8. Look for a pattern. Then estimate the weight of 10 teaspoons of sand.
9. Make a graph of your results.

Closure Review findings, asking students to share their results. Ask whether they had accurate estimations of how much the sand would weigh.

Evaluation Collect graphs. Check each graph for accuracy. The results of the graphs will determine the success or understanding of the lesson.

Strange Beginnings—A Creative Writing Activity

Objective After becoming familiar with animals from the beach and the ocean, students will practice creative writing skills by selecting one of the following questions and answering it as they choose.

Materials Paper, questions (included), pencils, drawing paper, and markers/crayons

Anticipatory Set Today we will be having some fun with creative writing. I want everyone to get in a creative mood. On the board, I have written three questions. It is your job to choose the one you would like best to write on and go with it. Remember, creativity makes the most interesting reading.

Questions
- How did the octopus get its tentacles?
- How did the sea urchin get its spines?
- How did the eel get its electricity?

Procedure
1. Have students select a question to write about.
2. Inform them of the amount of time they'll have to answer their questions.
3. Set expectations (at least one page).
4. Inform students when it is time to start wrapping up their writing.

5. Give students the opportunity to share their stories if they so choose.
6. (Optional) Have students draw a picture that corresponds with their stories.
7. Collect stories and drawings.
8. Display works on a bulletin board.

Closure Ask students if they enjoyed this assignment.

Evaluation Collect all writings and drawings, then determine by the outcome whether or not the assignment was a success.

Other Options
1. The class can vote on the best or most interesting creative writing/drawing. The winner's work can be displayed in a special place.
2. Rather than do this lesson on one given day, it can be spread out over a period of a week. This can be done by assigning one question a day.

   For example, writing journals can be used. Time can be set aside (1/2 hour each day after lunch) for each question. The day's question may be on the board when students return from lunch. They are then given time to answer the question. Journals can be collected at the end of the week.

What Is a Food Chain?

Objective After reading *Life in the Oceans*, students should understand what a food chain is. To demonstrate understanding of a food chain, each student will complete a handout and construct her or his own food chain.

Materials Work sheet (not included), *Life in the Oceans* by Lucy Baker, and pencils

Anticipatory Set Today we will be learning about food chains. First you will hear some important information about food chains, and then you will design your own food chain.

Procedure
1. Read *Life in the Oceans*.
2. Discuss the book and encourage students to ask questions.
3. Hand out a food chain work sheet and provide an example of a food chain.
4. Allow time needed for students to complete their food chain worksheets.
5. Encourage students to share their work.
6. Point out the importance of knowing how a food chain works.
7. Collect the students' work.

Closure Today we have learned that living things depend on each other for food and energy.

Evaluation Collect and assess students' work. Their food chains will reflect whether or not they grasped the concept.

BIBLIOGRAPHY

Baker, Lucy. (1990). *Life in the Oceans.* New York: Watts.
Lambert, D. (1984). *The Oceans.* New York: The Bookwright Press.
Parfit, M. "Diminishing Returns: Exploiting the Ocean's Bounty." *National Geographic* 188(5) 2–37 (November 1995).
Parker, S. (1989). *Seashore.* New York: Alfred A. Knopf.
Wood, J. M. (1985). *Nature Hide and Seek Oceans.* New York: Alfred A. Knopf.

Opening the Ocean: Culminating Activity Field Trip
For a culminating activity, your students will enjoy a hands-on experience: a trip to the ocean. They can relate and apply everything they have acquired during the week to the real thing.

All you need to do is contact your local Department of Parks and Recreation or the tourist information bureau for an oceanside city near you. If an ocean is not available, an aquarium is also a worthwhile experience.

We hope you enjoy the ocean with your class!

Opening the Ocean: Informal Student Assessment

How did you like the activities you did this week? Mark an X where it is appropriate and explain.

Loved Them   Thought They Were Ok
Explain: _____

_____

_____

What would you have included in or deleted from your Opening the Ocean unit? Please take your time and share your expertise and knowledge.

Formal Student Assessment

Write about five things that made the greatest impact on you in this study. Be sure to explain your statements thoroughly.
1. _____
_____
2. _____
_____
3. _____
_____
4. _____
_____
5. _____
_____

Notes

1. Courtesy of Chris Harrigan, Erika Yee, Deanne Sacchi, and Shannon Zundel.
2. Reprinted with the permission of the National Wildlife Foundation from the "Diving Into Oceans" issue of *Nature Scope*. For more information on National Wildlife Foundation educational programs, please contact us at 1-800-432-6564.
3. Reprinted with the permission of the National Wildlife Foundation from the "Diving Into Oceans" issue of *Nature Scope*. For more information on National Wildlife Foundation educational programs, please contact us at 1-800-432-6564.
4. Reprinted with the permission of the National Wildlife Foundation from the "Diving Into Oceans" issue of *Nature Scope*. For more information on National Wildlife Foundation educational programs, please contact us at 1-800-432-6564.

STUDENT BOOKS AND OTHER RESOURCES FOR "WATER, WEATHER, AND CLIMATE"

Bellipanni, L. J., and N. Hazen. "A Wave Tank for Elementary Science." *Science and Children* 31(5):23–25 (February 1994).

Brendzel, S. "Keeping Your Classroom Current: A Mariculture Model." *Science Scope* 18(1):33–35 (September 1994).

De Larramendi, R. H. "Perilous Journey: Three Years Across the Arctic." *National Geographic* 187(1):120–138 (January 1995).

Domel, R. "You Can Teach About Acid Rain." *Science and Children* 31(2):25–28 (September 1993).

Fisher, M., and J. Lane. "Navigation: Traveling the Water Highways." *Science and Children* 32(7):16–18 (April 1995).

Fisher, M., and D. Ayres. "Navigation . . . What Would We Do Without It?" *Science Scope* 18(8):30–33 (May 1995).

Ford, B. A., and P. S. Smith. *Project Earth Science: Physical Oceanography*. Arlington, VA: National Science Teachers Association, 1995.

Hiscock, B. *The Big Storm*. New York: Atheneum, 1993.

Jewett, J. "Protecting Our Water Resources." *Science Scope* 19(7)26–27 (April 1996).

Jones, M. G., and G. Carter. "Weather Folklore: Fact or Fiction." *Science and Children* 33(1):19–20, 51 (September 1995).

Koziel, K. "The Water Cycler." *Science and Children* 32(1):42–43 (September 1994).

Lambert, D. *Seas and Oceans*. Milwaukee: Raintree, 1994.

Luenn, N. *Squish! A Wetland Walk*. New York: Atheneum/Simon & Schuster, 1994.

Mogil, H. M., and B. G. Levine. *The Amateur Meteorologist: Explorations and Investigations*. New York: Franklin Watts, 1993.

Oppenheim, J. *Oceanarium*. New York: Bantam, 1994.

Roychoudhury, A. "Weather Data: Variable Sunshine." *Science Scope* 18(5):21–23 (February 1995).

Schipper, A. L. Schipper, and A. Hornsby. "Going Underground." *Science and Children* 31(3):16–18, 71 (November/December 1993).

Simon, S. *Winter Across America*. New York: Hyperion, 1994.

Smith, S., R. Brook, and M. Tisdale. "Understanding Ecosystem Management." *Science and Children* 32(3):33–40 (November/December 1994).

Smith P. S. and B. A. Ford. *Project Earth Science: Meterology*. Arlington, VA: National Science Teachers Association, 1994.

Stanley, L. R. "A River Runs Through Science Learning." *Science and Children* 32(4):13–15, 58 (January 1995).

Strycker, J. A. "Science First." *Science and Children* 32(7):26–29 (April 1995).

Turkall, S. F. "Student-Designed River Study." *Science Scope* 19(7):22–25 (April 1996).

Tripp, N. *Thunderstorm!* New York: Dial, 1994.

United States Department of the Interior. *Global Change* (a packet of teaching activities for use with grades 4–6). Reston, VA: U. S. Geological Survey, 1993.

Vandas, S. "Ground Water: The Hidden Resource." *Science and Children* 31(3): 36–37, 71 (November/December 1993).

———. "Investigating Water Quality." *Science and Children* 32(1):44–45, 78 (September 1994).

CHAPTER 11

Air, Aircraft, and Space Travel

AIR

I. WHERE AIR IS FOUND

  A. Air occupies the space all around the earth. We live at the bottom of an ocean of air.

  B. Air is also found in all the tiny spaces between particles of materials, in soil, in water, and in such porous materials as sponges, bricks, wood, and bread.

II. THE COMPOSITION OF AIR

  A. Air is a mixture of many gases, but the two principal gases in the air are oxygen and nitrogen, making up about 99 percent of the air we breathe.

  B. About one fifth (21 percent) of air is oxygen.

    1. Oxygen is a very active gas and combines easily with many materials.

    2. Animals and plants need oxygen for breathing and digesting their food.

    3. Homes and industries need oxygen to burn fuels.

  C. The most abundant gas in the air is nitrogen, making up nearly four fifths (about 78 percent).

    1. Nitrogen is not an active gas and does not help things burn, nor does it combine with other materials easily.

    2. If there were only oxygen in the air, without nitrogen, all burning would be very rapid and impossible to control. Nitrogen helps dilute the oxygen in the air and in this way controls burning.

    3. Nitrogen is needed by plants and animals as food, but they cannot use nitrogen directly from the air.

    4. Certain bacteria are able to change the nitrogen in the air into materials that plants and animals can use as food.

  D. The remaining 1 percent of the air is made up of carbon dioxide gas, hydrogen gas, and a group of rare and inactive gases: helium, neon, argon, krypton, and xenon.

    1. Even though carbon dioxide is present in the air in only small quantities, it is a very important gas.

    2. Through **photosynthesis,** plants with chlorophyll use carbon dioxide to make food, which is used not only by the plants themselves but by animals as well.

    3. If by human or natural means, large quantities of plants are removed from the earth, the amount of carbon dioxide in the air would increase, creating a thicker atmosphere, which would hold in the sun's heat energy that is normally reflected outward into the atmosphere, causing a **greenhouse effect** and resulting in a **global warming.** Such a global warming could have cataclysmic effects on the earth, including the melting of the polar ice caps and worldwide flooding.

    4. Carbon dioxide is used in making "soda water" and "dry ice."

    5. The action of the yeast or baking powder in bread or cake dough releases bubbles of carbon dioxide gas, which expand and make the bread or cake rise.

  E. Air also contains water in the form of an invisible gas called **water vapor.**

DEMONSTRATION 11.1
Percentage of Oxygen in Air

Obtain two test tubes of the same size. Insert a wad of steel wool into one of the test tubes and push it down to the bottom. Pour some water into each test tube, shake well, and then pour off the water. Put each test tube, mouth down, into a wide-mouthed jar or beaker of water and fasten each test tube with a clamp (Figure 11.1). Have the mouths of the test tubes the same distance (about 13 millimeters or 0.5 inch) below the surface of the water. Let the test tubes stand this way for 24 hours.

After 24 hours, water will have risen up the test tube containing the steel wool. Nothing will have happened in the empty test tube (the control). Measure the length of the test tube above the surface of the water, and then measure how high the water rose in the test tube. Compare these lengths: the water will have risen about one fifth, or 20 percent of the way up the test tube. Note the rusty appearance of the steel wool. The steel combined with the oxygen in the air inside the test tube to form iron oxide (rust). Because the water rose one fifth of the way up the tube to replace the oxygen, it means that about one fifth, or 20 percent, of the air in the tube was oxygen.

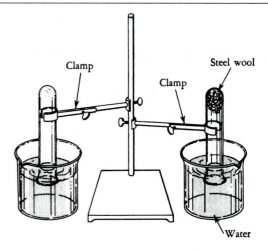

FIGURE 11.1   About 20 percent of the air in the test tube is oxygen.

1. Water vapor becomes part of the air through the evaporation of water from the bodies of water on the earth's surface.
2. The amount of water vapor in the air differs from day to day and from place to place.
F. Air also carries changing amounts of dust, pollen, living spores, and waste gases given off by factories and the exhausts of vehicles.
G. The relative amounts of oxygen and carbon dioxide in the air remain nearly the same because of the **carbon dioxide–oxygen cycle.**
   1. In **photosynthesis,** plants that contain chlorophyll take in carbon dioxide from the air and combine it with hydrogen taken from water to make food, such as carbohydrates; oxygen is given off by these plants as a by-product of photosynthesis.
   2. Most organisms use oxygen to burn food in **cellular respiration,** the body building and maintenance process. Carbon dioxide is released as a waste product of this respiration.
H. The amount of nitrogen in the air remains constant because of the **nitrogen cycle** (see Figure 11.2).
   1. A kind of bacteria, called **nitrogen-fixing bacteria** (also known as nitrifying bacteria), living in soil and in the roots of certain legu-

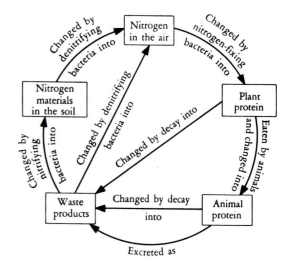

FIGURE 11.2   Diagram of the nitrogen cycle.

minous plants (beans, alfalfa, peas, and clover) can change the nitrogen of the air, which plants cannot use, into a form of nitrogen that plants can use to live and grow.
   2. Animals eat plants and give off waste materials that contain nitrogen.

3. Decay bacteria in the soil act on these materials and on dead plants and animals, break them down, and return the nitrogen to the soil.
4. Nitrifying bacteria then change the nitrogen from these waste materials and the dead plants and animals into forms of nitrogen that plants can use.
5. At the same time other bacteria, called **denitrifying bacteria,** change some of the nitrogen materials to free nitrogen, which returns to the air to continue the nitrogen cycle.

I. The present composition of the earth's air is much different from its composition when the earth was first developing (see Chapter 9).

III. AIR POLLUTION

A. Every day our air is polluted by large quantities of gases and solids.
1. These materials are given off by industrial furnaces, chemical plants, motor vehicles, and other sources.
2. Some impurities in the air are emitted directly from identifiable sources, and others are formed indirectly through photochemical reactions in the air.
3. Major air pollutants, their sources, and the problems they can cause in humans are illustrated in Table 11.1.
4. In addition to causing human health problems, pollutants in the air also cause damage and death to plants, as well as irreversible damage from oxidation and acid erosion to cultural treasures of the world, such as the Parthenon of Athens, the Roman Coliseum, Westminster Abbey, the Taj Mahal, the famous stained-glass windows of Chartres, and others throughout the cities of Europe.
5. As an example of the irreversibility of such effects, sulfur oxides in the smog over Athens, Greece, chemically transform marble (of which the Parthenon is built) into gypsum, which in turn cracks and flakes off.
B. Air pollution becomes a serious problem when weather conditions are formed in which the polluted air cannot be blown away.
1. Such a condition occurs when there is a layer of cold air next to the ground and a layer of warm air lies on top of the cold air.
2. The upper layer of warm air acts as a cover and stops the cold air from being carried away.
3. This condition is called a **temperature inversion.**
C. In most parts of the United States, attempts are being made to control air pollution.

1. Factories install equipment to remove the poisonous gases and smoke particles from their exhaust gases before they can escape into the air.
2. Automobiles now come equipped with anti-smog devices to trap or burn the exhaust pollutants.

IV. THE EARTH'S ATMOSPHERE

A. The ocean of air around the earth is called the **atmosphere.**
1. The earth's pull of gravity holds the atmosphere close to the earth's surface.
2. The atmosphere is important because all animals and most plants need air to live. The atmosphere also acts as a protective blanket to reduce the sun's heat and to shield us from harmful rays that come from the sun and from outer space.
B. The atmosphere is divided into five principal layers: the troposphere, stratosphere, mesophere, thermosphere (or ionosphere), and exosphere.
1. The **troposphere** is the lowest layer of the atmosphere, the layer at the earth's solid surface. It extends upward to a height of 6 kilometers (4 mi) at the poles and 16 kilometers (10 mi) at the equator, with an average of about 10 kilometers (6 mi) in the areas between these two. Because almost all water vapor in the atmosphere is in this layer, most weather conditions such as clouds and storms occur in the troposphere.
2. The **stratosphere** is the layer above the troposphere. It extends upward from the top of the troposphere to a height of about 50 kilometers (30 mi). Air is much thinner in the stratosphere. The stratosphere is clear and cloudless and has little or no weather conditions. For this reason, pilots of commercial planes prefer flying in the stratosphere.
3. A special form of oxygen, called **ozone,** is found in the stratosphere. Ozone absorbs most of the ultraviolet rays coming from the sun, protecting organisms on earth from severe burning.
4. Evidence indicates that a hole in the ozone layer forms seasonally over the southern pole, and may be getting larger each year, and that the ozone layer over the Northern Hemisphere may be getting thinner.
5. Chemicals known as **chlorofluorocarbons** react with ozone and break it down; they have been banned from use in this country. For 50 years these ozone-depleting chemicals were ubiquitous—used in car air condi-

TABLE 11.1   Major Air Pollutants, Their Sources, and Problems They Can Cause

Pollutant	Source	Problems Pollutants Can Cause
Arsenic	Fossil fuel furnaces and glass manufacturing	Lung and skin cancer
Benzene	Refineries; motor vehicles	Leukemia
Cadmium	Smelters; burning waste; fossil fuel furnaces	Kidney and lung damage; weakened bones
Carbon monoxide	Motor vehicles; fossil fuel burning; smelters and steel plants	Prevents body from obtaining oxygen; damages heart
Chlorine	Chemical industries	Forms hydrochloric acid; irritates mucous membranes
Fluoride ions	Smelters; steel plants	Can mottle teeth
Formaldehyde	Motor vehicles; chemical plants	Irritates eyes and nose
Hydrocarbons	Unburned gasoline vapor	Combines with oxides of nitrogen to form smog.
Hydrogen chloride	Incinerators	Irritates eyes and nose
Hydrogen fluoride	Fertilizer plants; smelters	Irritates skin, eyes, and mucous linings.
Hydrogen sulfide	Refineries; sewage plants; pulp mills	Nausea; eye irritation
Hydroxyl ion	Formed in sunlight from hydrocarbons and nitrogen oxides	Reacts with other gases to form acid droplets
Lead	Motor vehicles; smelters	Brain damage; high blood pressure; impaired growth
Manganese	Steel and power plants	May contribute to Parkinson's disease
Mercury	Fossil fuel furnaces; smelters	Causes nerve disorders
Nickel	Smelters and fossil-fuel-burning furnaces	May cause lung cancer
Nitric acid	Forms from nitrous oxide a major component of acid rain	Respiratory problems
Nitric oxide	Motor vehicles; fossil fuel burning	Oxidizes to form nitrogen dioxide
Nitrogen dioxide	Formed in sunlight from nitrogen oxide	Produces ozone; causes bronchitis; lowers resistance to influenza
Nitrous acid	Forms from nitrous oxide and water vapor	Respiratory problems
Ozone	Formed in sunlight from nitrogen oxides and hydrocarbons	Irritates eyes; aggravates asthma
Peroxyacetyl nitrate	Formed in sunlight from nitrogen oxides and hydrocarbons	Irritates eyes; aggravates asthma
Silicon tetrafluoride	Chemical plants	Irritates lungs
Sulfur dioxide	Fossil fuel burning	Restricts breathing; irritates eyes
Sulfuric acid	Forms in sunlight from sulfur dioxide and hydroxyl ions (from water vapor in air)	Respiratory ailments

tioners, foam cups and plates, coolers and refrigerators, rocket missiles, manufacture of cleaning compounds, and medical sterilizing equipment.

6. The **mesosphere,** above the stratosphere, extends to a height of about 80 kilometers (50 mi). The coldest temperatures of the earth's atmosphere are in the mesosphere. The mesosphere also has the highest clouds.

7. The fourth layer of the atmosphere, the **thermosphere** (or ionosphere), extends to a height of about 640 to 800 kilometers (400 to 500 mi).

8. Powerful ultraviolet rays from the sun strike the particles of air in the thermosphere, causing them to be electrically charged. These electrically charged particles of air are called **ions.** It is the ionic (charged) particles

of the thermosphere that makes possible worldwide radio reception.

9. When radio waves, which travel in straight lines, travel out into space and reach the thermosphere, the waves bounce off the ions and are reflected back to a different place on earth.

10. The northern lights (**aurora borealis**) and the southern lights (**aurora australis**) occur in the ionosphere (see Chapter 8).

11. The fifth and final layer, the **exosphere,** begins at the outer limit of the ionosphere and extends upward, until it cannot be distinguished from outer space, about 500 kilometers (310 mi). There is almost no air at all in the exosphere.

12. The exosphere contains an area of very intense radiation, called the **Van Allen radiation belt.** It is thought to be shaped like a doughnut within a doughnut. The inner ring or belt begins about 1,280 kilometers (800 mi) above the earth and extends to about 4,800 kilometers (3,000 mi). The outer belt begins about 12,800 kilometers (8,000 mi) above the earth and extends to about 64,000 kilometers (40,000 mi).

V. THE PROPERTIES OF AIR

A. The gases that make up air are colorless, odorless, and tasteless.

B. Like all gases, air has no shape of its own; it assumes the shape of the container it fills.
   1. Although air is invisible, it is real; it takes up space and has weight. One liter of air weighs about 1 1/5 grams (1 cu ft weighs about 1 1/4 oz).

C. Air has weight, and anything that has weight pushes or presses against other things.
   1. We live at the bottom of an ocean of air hundreds of kilometers or miles high.
   2. This air presses down on the earth's surface and creates pressure on it; the pressure on the earth's surface is called **air pressure,** or **atmospheric pressure.**
   3. As we go higher into the atmosphere, there is less air pressing down and thus the air pressure decreases.
   4. Air presses in all directions—downward, upward, and sideways—on any exposed surface, and it presses just as hard upward and sideways as it does downward.
   5. Air presses on every square inch of the surface of our bodies, but we do not feel this pressure because air within our bodies pushes outward with the same pressure.

D. Moving air exerts pressure.
   1. When air moves, it pushes harder against other things.
   2. Wind is moving air, and the harder the wind blows, the greater its pressure.
   3. At sea level the weight of the air pressing on 1 square centimeter of the earth's surface is about 1 kilogram (or on 1 square inch it is about 15 lb).
   4. Air pressure is constantly changing from day to day.
   5. An instrument called a **barometer** is used to measure air pressure (see Chapter 10).

E. An **altimeter** is an aneroid barometer that measures altitude, or height, above sea level.
   1. The higher in the atmosphere we go, the less air pressure there is and the lower the barometer reading.
   2. For every 305 meters (1,000 ft) up we go, atmospheric air pressure falls about 2 centimeters (1 in).
   3. The dial of an altimeter is marked so that instead of giving the air pressure in centimeters or inches of mercury, they give the number of meters or feet above sea level.

F. Air in a container pushes, or exerts pressure, on the walls of the container.
   1. Gases in the air are made up of tiny particles called **molecules,** which are moving rapidly.
   2. When fast-moving molecules hit the walls of a container, they push against the walls and exert pressure on them.
   3. The air pressure in a closed container can be changed by adding or taking away more air.
   4. If more air is added to the container, the air pressure inside increases because more molecules of air are now striking and pushing against the walls of the container; if air is removed from the container, the air pressure inside decreases because fewer molecules of air are now striking and pushing against the walls of the container.
   5. If all the air is removed from a container, there will be no air pressure at all inside the container because there are no molecules of air inside to strike the walls.
   6. An absence of all air inside a container is called a **vacuum.**
   7. When only part of the air is removed from the container, there is only a partial vacuum present.
   8. The air pressure inside a closed container can be changed by making the size of the container larger or smaller.

DEMONSTRATION 11.2
Air Takes Up Space, Has Weight, and Exerts Pressure

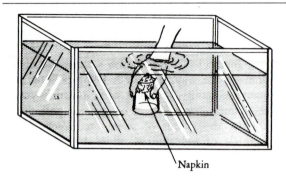

FIGURE 11.3   Because air occupies space, the napkin does not get wet.

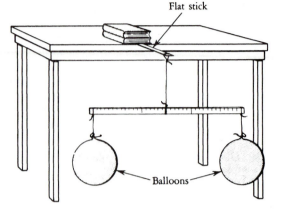

FIGURE 11.4   Air has weight.

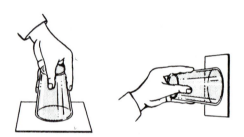

FIGURE 11.5   Air exerts pressure in all directions.

A. Air Takes Up Space

Crumple a dry paper napkin and stuff it into a tumbler so that it will not fall out when the tumbler is held upside down. Now, while holding the tumbler upside down, push the tumbler straight down to the bottom of an aquarium or large glass jar that is filled with water (Figure 11.3). Note that the water does not fill the tumbler. The space in the tumbler is occupied by air. Tilt the tumbler slightly, and you will be able to see air escaping from the tumbler in the form of bubbles. Now lift the tumbler straight out of the water. Remove the paper napkin and note that it is still dry.

B. Air Has Weight

Place a pile of books at the edge of a table. Insert a flat stick about 30 centimeters (12 in) long between the books and the table top. Tie one end of a string about 25 centimeters (10 in) long to the stick, tie the other end to the middle of a meter stick or yardstick, and slide the meter stick back and forth until it balances (Figure 11.4). Obtain two large, round balloons of the same size, and blow them up so they are the same size when inflated. Tie a string about 15 centimeters (6 in) long around the end of each balloon and hang the balloons near the ends of the meter stick at the same distance from the ends. Slide the balloons back and forth until the meter stick balances evenly. Puncture one balloon with a pin. The deflated balloon will not weigh as much as the balloon that still has air in it, and the meter stick will become unbalanced. (*Note:* When the balloon bursts, a piece or two of the rubber may be blown off. Be sure to collect these pieces and drape them around the deflated balloon. Otherwise the results will be inaccurate.)

If a sensitive balance is available, weigh a basketball when it is deflated. Fill the ball with air and weigh it again. The difference in weights is the weight of the air in the ball.

C. Air Exerts Pressure

Fill a tumbler with water. Put a piece of cardboard on top of the tumbler and hold it firmly against the tumbler with the palm of one hand. Grasp the base of the tumbler with the other hand and quickly turn the tumbler upside down (Figure 11.5). Remove the palm of your hand carefully from below the cardboard, being careful not to jar the cardboard or the tumbler. The cardboard and the water will remain in place. Point out that the water stays in the tumbler because air is exerting a pressure on the cardboard. The pressure of the air against the cardboard is greater than the pressure of the water against the cardboard.

Ask the students to predict what will happen when you turn the tumbler sideways. Turn the tumbler sideways and to many other positions. The water will still stay in the tumbler, showing that air exerts pressure in all directions.

DEMONSTRATION 11.3

The Effect of Heating and Cooling on the Air Pressure in a Container

A. Inflating a Balloon

Snap a balloon over a Pyrex flask or bottle. Place the flask on a hot plate and heat it for 1 minute (Figure 11.6). The air inside the flask and balloon expand when heated. This expanded air exerts pressure against the sides of the balloon and begins to inflate it. Now place the Pyrex flask into a pan of cold water containing ice cubes. The air inside the flask and balloon contract when cooled and exert less pressure. As a result, the balloon deflates, and it may even be drawn inside the flask because the decreased pressure inside the balloon is now so much less than the normal pressure of the air around the balloon.

B. Collapsing a Can

Pour into an empty soda can enough water to cover the bottom. Place the can on a hot plate and heat it until steam rises from its top. With a glove or hot pad, grasp the hot can and quickly invert it, inserting its top into a pan of water. You do not need to submerge the entire can. Under the force of atmospheric pressure the thin sides of the can will quickly collapse. Try to blow the can up again.
SAFETY NOTE: Use extreme caution for this demonstration.

1. Use extreme caution whenever using a hotplate (or any heat source) in the classroom, keeping curious or careless students protected from touching it.
2. Protect children from possible glass breakage (even when using Pyrex glassware) and from spattering of glass and boiling water.

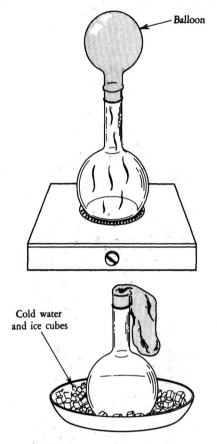

FIGURE 11.6   Air expands when heated and contracts when cooled.

9. If the size of a container is increased, air pressure inside becomes smaller. Because the air has spread out into a larger space, there are fewer molecules striking and pushing against each part of the container. If the size of a container is decreased, air pressure inside becomes greater. Because the molecules of air have been squeezed into a smaller space, there are more of them striking and pushing against each part of the container.
10. Air pressure inside a container can be changed by heating or cooling the container.
11. If a container is heated, the air pressure inside increases. Because the molecules of air inside the container gain more energy and move faster, they strike and push harder against the walls of the container.
12. If a container is cooled, air pressure inside the container decreases. Because the molecules of air inside the container loose energy and move more slowly, they strike and push less strongly against the walls of the container.

VI. PRACTICAL APPLICATIONS OF AIR PRESSURE

A. The use of a soda straw depends on decreasing the air pressure inside the straw.
1. When a straw is placed in a tumbler of soda, the soda rises up the straw to the level of the soda in the tumbler.

2. The soda in the straw does not rise any higher because the air pressure on the soda inside the straw and the air pressure on the soda outside the straw are equal.
3. When the movement of the cheek muscles sucks some air out of the straw, there is a partial vacuum inside the straw, as the air pressure inside the straw is decreased.
4. Normal or regular air pressure on the soda outside the straw is now greater than the air pressure on the soda inside the straw.
5. The outside air pressure, because it is greater, forces the soda up the straw and into the mouth.

B. Filling a medicine dropper depends on decreasing the air pressure inside the dropper.
1. When the bulb is pressed, some of the air is forced out of the dropper, forming a partial vacuum and decreasing air pressure inside the dropper.
2. The regular air pressure on the liquid outside the dropper is now greater than the air pressure on the liquid inside the dropper.
3. When the dropper end is inserted in liquid, the outside air pressure, because it is greater, forces the liquid up into the dropper.

C. The use of a suction cup depends on decreasing the air pressure inside the cup.
1. When a suction cup is pressed against a surface, some of the air is forced out of the cup, forming a partial vacuum and decreasing air pressure inside the cup.
2. The outside air pressure is now greater and holds the cup firmly in place.
3. If the cup is moistened first, a tighter seal is made, so outside air cannot get inside the cup and remove the partial vacuum.

D. The operation of a vacuum cleaner depends on decreasing the air pressure inside the cleaner.
1. An electrically driven fan drives air out of a compartment in the machine, forming a partial vacuum and decreasing air pressure inside the compartment.

2. The outside air pressure is now greater than the air pressure inside the compartment, and the air rushes in through the nozzle, carrying dirt and lint with it.
3. The dirt and lint are caught by a bag or screen, while the air passes through and out of the machine.

E. When a great deal of air is pumped into a container, the air is compressed and the air pressure inside the container is increased.
1. The molecules of air are squeezed, or compressed, very close together, so there are many more of them striking and pushing against the walls of the container.
2. The molecules are now striking with more force against the walls of the container, so the air pressure inside the container becomes greater.

F. Many devices make use of the increased pressure of compressed air.
1. An **air brake** uses compressed air to stop trains, streetcars, buses, and heavy trucks. A motor-driven pump in the vehicle compresses the air, which is stored in a tank. When the brakes are applied, the compressed air passes into a cylinder, where the compressed air exerts pressure against a piston. The piston then forces the brake shoes tightly against a drum that is connected to the wheels, making the vehicle come to a stop.
2. A deep-sea diver uses compressed gases in a diving suit to descend hundreds of feet in water.
3. A submarine sinks when tanks let in seawater and rises when compressed air forces the water out of the tanks.
4. Pneumatic drills and riveters operate with compressed air.
5. Automobile tires, footballs, basketballs, and volleyballs contain compressed air.
6. Many paint and garden spray machines are operated with compressed air.
7. Jet engines operate with compressed air.

Aircraft and Rockets

I. Forces Involved in Flying an Aircraft

A. When a plane is flying, there are four forces acting on it: gravity, lift, thrust, and drag.
1. The pull of the earth's gravity on the aircraft, which becomes the weight of the aircraft, is a downward force.
2. *Lift* is an upward force that acts against gravity, caused by the action of the air on the wings, lifting the aircraft into the air and keeping it there while it is flying.
3. *Thrust* is the force that pulls or pushes the aircraft forward; it is produced by a propeller, a jet engine, a rocket, or any combination of these.
4. *Drag* is the resistance that the air offers; caused by the friction created when the aircraft moves through it; drag is a backward force that works against thrust.

DEMONSTRATION 11.4
Applications of Air Pressure

Paper bag

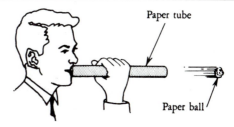

Paper tube

Paper ball

FIGURE 11.8   How an air gun works.

FIGURE 11.7   Using increased air pressure to lift a book.

A. Lifting with Air Pressure

Place a paper bag on a table so that its mouth extends beyond the table's edge. Put a book on top of at least half of the paper bag. Now hold the mouth of the bag closely against your mouth without letting in any air and blow hard into the bag (Figure 11.7). The increased air pressure will

lift the book easily. Repeat the experiment, this time using two books.

B. Force of Compressed Air

Roll up a sheet of paper so that it forms a tube. Crumple a piece of paper into a round ball, whose size is such that it just fits inside the tube. Place the ball into one end of the tube and blow hard into this end (Figure 11.8). The ball will be shot out of the tube by the compressed air you created. Air guns and air hammers are common examples of this method of using compressed air.

B. For an aircraft to take off, the lift must be greater than the force of gravity, and the thrust must be greater than the drag.
  1. The aircraft is lifted chiefly because of the flow of air passing over the wing. A scientific principle, called **Bernoulli's principle,** explains the reason for this lifting effect. This principle states that when air moves faster across the top surface of a material than across the bottom surface, the pressure of the air pushing down on the top surface is less than the pressure of the air pushing up on the bottom surface.
  2. The shape of a wing is designed to make use of Bernoulli's principle. The front edge of the wing is thicker than the back edge, and the upper surface of the wing is curved whereas the bottom surface is straight.
  3. As the wing moves through the air, some air flows over the wing and some flows under the wing.
  4. Because the upper surface of the wing is curved, air flowing over the upper surface must travel a longer distance than air flowing along the bottom surface.

  5. All of the air flowing over and under the wing reaches the end of the wing at the same time. Consequently, air flowing over the curved top surface of the wing must move faster than air flowing along the shorter bottom surface, to reach the end of the wing at the same time.
  6. According to Bernoulli's principle, because the air is moving faster across the top surface of the wing than across the bottom surface, the air pressure pushing down on the top surface is less than the air pressure pushing up on the bottom surface. The greater air pressure beneath the wing pushes up on the wing and produces lift.
  7. The greater the wingspread, the more air passes over and under the wing, and the greater the lift will be.
  8. The faster the aircraft moves, the faster the air will flow over the wing, the less the air pressure pushing down on top of the wing will be, and the greater the lift will become.
C. A wing's **angle of attack** also helps to lift the aircraft.
  1. The wing is set so that it tilts a little and meets the air at a slight slant, or angle, called the angle of attack.

DEMONSTRATION 11.5
Effects of Drag

Have a student hold a large piece of cardboard in front of him- or herself and run into the wind. The resistance of the air against the cardboard will cause drag and slow the student's forward motion.

2. Because the wing is slanted, the air strikes the underside of the wing and pushes up on it.
3. When greater lift is needed, the wing can be made to slant even more, so that the air will push up harder on the wing.
D. **Thrust** is the force that pulls or pushes the aircraft forward and, at the same time, makes air flow above and below the wings.

1. Thrust is explained by **Newton's third law of motion,** which states that for every action, there is an equal but opposite reaction.
2. To produce thrust, some airplanes use a motor-driven propeller. The propeller is made to turn at a very high speed by an engine that uses gasoline as fuel.

DEMONSTRATION 11.6
Bernoulli's Principle

Have a student place one end of a sheet of paper inside a book so that the paper hangs downward. Now hold the top of the book level with your lips and blow over the top of the paper (Figure 11.9). The sheet of paper will rise, because the fast-moving stream of air across the top of the paper causes the air pressure on the top surface of the paper to be less than the air pressure beneath the paper.

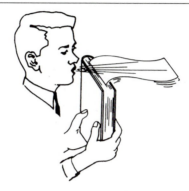

FIGURE 11.9   Using Bernoulli's principle to make the paper rise.

3. The propeller bores into the air somewhat like a screw going into wood or a boat propeller going through water.
4. The whirling blades of the propeller are adjusted so that they will strike as much air as possible in order to produce the greatest thrust.
5. The faster the propeller is turned by the engine, the greater the forward thrust.
E. Jet airplanes get their thrust from **jet engines,** which are simpler than the engines in propeller-driven planes.
   1. The jet engine is a hollow cylinder, open at both ends.
   2. Air entering the front end of the cylinder is compressed; then a fuel such as kerosene is sprayed into the cylinder.
   3. The mixture of kerosene and compressed air burns with intense heat, giving off hot gases that expand and shoot out of the rear of the cylinder with great force and speed, pushing the aircraft forward.
   4. As the hot gases shoot out with a backward force, there is an equal but opposite force, or thrust, that pushes the aircraft forward at great speed.
   5. The faster the fuel burns, the greater the backward push of the hot escaping gases and the greater the forward push on the plane.
   6. Three common types of jet engines are the ramjet engine, the turbojet engine, and the turboprop engine.
F. The **ramjet engine** is the simplest type of jet engine. It has no moving parts.

   1. It is a hollow tube with nozzles inside to spray the fuel.
   2. When the ramjet travels forward at great speed, air is packed or "rammed" into the front of the engine. The ramming of the air into the engine helps to compress it.
   3. Fuel is sprayed into the compressed air by the nozzles and burns, and the hot gases expand and rush out through the rear of the engine with great speed.
   4. These hot gases, escaping from the rear of the engine, produce the forward thrust needed to move the plane.
   5. The ramjet plane cannot start from the ground, but must be moving at high speed in order to ram air into the engine. Usually a ramjet plane is carried into the air under another plane, which cuts the ramjet loose when it has achieved enough speed.
G. The **turbojet engine** is the engine used most often by commercial and military aircraft.
   1. The turbojet engine has three main parts: a compressor, a combustion chamber, and a turbine.
   2. The compressor compresses the air that enters the engine, then feeds the compressed air to the combustion chamber.
   3. In the combustion chamber a fuel such as kerosene is sprayed into the compressed air.
   4. The mixture of kerosene and compressed air burns, giving off hot gases that expand and shoot out of the rear of the engine.
   5. Before the gases can leave the engine, they must first turn the blades of the turbine.

DEMONSTRATION 11.7
Newton's Law of Action and Reaction

Obtain a plastic bottle, preferably a flat one, and a cork to fit the bottle. Fill the bottle about one third full of vinegar. Place a teaspoon of baking soda on a small piece of cleansing tissue, wrap the tissue into a roll, and twist the ends. Drop the roll into the bottle, give the bottle one good shake to break up the roll, and push the cork into the bottle firmly, but not too firmly. Immediately place the bottle on three or four round pencils, in the position shown in Figure 11.10. In a very short time the cork will blow out of the bottle, and the bottle itself will move in the direction opposite to that of the cork, demonstrating Newton's third law—action and reaction.

The baking soda reacts with the vinegar to form carbon dioxide gas, which pushes in all directions. When the force is strong enough, the gas blows the cork out of the

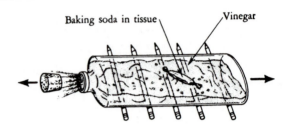

FIGURE 11.10   Action and reaction in a corked bottle.

bottle. As the gas shoots out of the bottle in one direction, there is an equal but opposite force that moves the bottle in the opposite direction. The bottle moves a shorter distance than the cork because it is heavier than the cork.

---

6. A shaft connects the turbine to the compressor so that the escaping gases turn the turbine, which then operates the compressor.
7. When the turbojet plane is on the ground, a small engine starts the shaft turning and operates the compressor.
8. After the aircraft has reached sufficient speed, the jet engine itself takes over and operates the turbine and the compressor.

H. The **turboprop engine** is like a turbojet engine except that it has a propeller in front of it.
   1. The propeller is attached to the same shaft that connects the turbine and the compressor.
   2. Thus, both the propeller and the escaping gases from the rear of the engine produce the thrust that moves the turboprop aircraft forward.
   3. The turboprop aircraft operates very well at low speeds or low altitudes because of the added thrust from the propeller, but the turbojet aircraft does not.

I. The friction of air rubbing against a moving aircraft causes the air to resist the aircraft's forward motion, in effect, slowing the aircraft, causing a **drag** on the aircraft.
   1. At high speeds this air resistance, or drag, can be very great and slow down the aircraft—or car, bus, train, or any other vehicle that travels at a fairly high speed.
   2. To overcome drag, the vehicle is streamlined. Streamlining means that the vehicle is designed in such a way (like the streamlined shapes of fish, birds, and teardrops) that the air flows past the vehicle smoothly.

II. Parts of An Airplane and Their Functions
   A. The **fuselage** is the body of an aircraft, and it carries the cargo, passengers, crew, and fuel.
   B. The **engine** provides the power or thrust to move the plane forward by turning a propeller or, in a jet or rocket-driven aircraft, by the action of the engine itself.
   C. The **wings** are attached to the sides of the fuselage and provide the lift for the aircraft. Vehicles designed for flight outside the earth's atmosphere do not have wings because there is no air to provide lift.
   D. The **ailerons** are long, narrow movable flaps located near the wing tips at the rear of the wings.
      1. Ailerons move up and down, but, when one aileron moves up, the other must move down.
      2. Ailerons are used to steer the aircraft to the right or left.
      3. There are also movable flaps at the rear of the wings, between the ailerons and fuselage, that help the plane take off and land.
   E. The tail of the airplane has many parts.
      1. The **fin,** or vertical stabilizer, does not move, helping to keep the plane flying straight.
      2. A movable **rudder** is connected to the back of the fin, which helps to turn the plane to the right or left.
      3. **Horizontal stabilizers** on each side of the fin keep the plane from rising and falling while it is flying level.
      4. **Elevators** are movable flaps connected in pairs to the horizontal stabilizers, and both

DEMONSTRATION 11.8
A Jet-Propelled Balloon

Inflate a narrow balloon and tie a string in a bow around the neck of the balloon. Attach the balloon to a soda straw, using cellophane tape, as shown in Figure 11.11. Run a long wire through the soda straw and attach both ends of the wire to opposite parts of the room, keeping the wire horizontal. Now untie the string so that the air can escape. The balloon will be "jet-propelled" across the room.

When the balloon is filled with air and the string is tied around its neck, it does not move because the air pressure inside the balloon is equal in all directions. When the string is untied and air begins to escape from the balloon, the air pressures inside the balloon becomes unequal. The air pressure is now greater on the surface opposite the neck of the balloon, because the air pressure on the

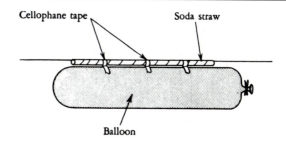

FIGURE 11.11   Making a balloon act like a jet plane.

neck decreases as the air escapes. Therefore, the balloon moves in a direction opposite to that of the escaping air.

---

elevators move up or down at the same time to enable the plane to climb or dive.
- F. The landing gear is beneath the plane and is used for taking off and landing.
  1. Wheels are used for planes that take off or land on hard surfaces.
  2. In most planes the wheels fold up into the body of the plane after the plane is off the ground, to reduce the effects of drag while the plane is flying.
  3. Long, hollow floats, called pontoons, are used for planes that take off or land in water, and skis are used for planes that take off or land in snow.

III. AIRCRAFT INSTRUMENTATION

- A. A **radio altimeter** measures how high a plane is above the ground. It sends out a radio beam that hits the ground and bounces back. The time it takes for the beam to reach the ground and return to the plane is calculated by the radio altimeter as feet above the ground.
- B. A **compass** helps the pilot keep the plane flying in the right direction.
- C. An **air-speed indicator** shows the flying speed of the plane, but the actual speed is less if the plane is heading into the wind, or greater if the wind is at the plane's tail.
- D. A **bank indicator** lets the pilot know whether the plane is tilting, or banking, properly when making a turn.

- E. A **turn indicator** lets the pilot know whether the plane is turning properly and how fast the turn is being made.
- F. A variety of gauges complete the aircraft's instrumentation panel.
  1. A fuel gauge shows the amount of fuel in the tank.
  2. Pressure gauges show the oil pressure, fuel pressure, and cabin pressure.
  3. Engine temperature gauges show the temperatures in different parts of the engines.
  4. A tachometer shows how fast the shaft in each engine is turning.
- G. A two-way radio helps the pilot stay on course when the plane is flying and gives instructions for taking off or landing.
- H. An automatic pilot control, which uses spinning gyroscope wheels, takes over the controls and keeps the plane on the course set by the pilot.

IV. CONTROLLING THE AIRCRAFT IN FLIGHT

- A. The takeoff
  1. To take off, an aircraft must be going fast enough to rise in the air.
  2. Planes take off into the wind because the wind makes the air flow faster over the surface of the wings and provides greater lift.
  3. The plane increases speed until it reaches its take-off speed, at which point the lift is great enough to make the plane rise.

4. The pilot then pulls the control wheel back just a little, which makes the elevators in the tail tilt upward a little.
5. The rushing air strikes these elevators, which forces the tail down.
6. This action swings the nose of the plane up, and the plane takes off into the air.
7. As the plane rises, the landing gear is pulled back into the plane.
8. The plane climbs until it reaches the height at which the pilot wants to fly. The elevators are then lowered until they are even again, and the plane flies level.

B. Changing Altitude
1. To climb, the pilot pulls the control wheel back, making the elevators in the tail tilt upward.
2. The air strikes these elevators and forces the tail down, which swings the nose of the plane up so that the plane climbs.
3. The plane needs more power when it is climbing and moving against gravity, so the engines are given more fuel and, consequently, speed up.
4. To dive, the pilot pushes the control wheel away, making the elevators tilt downward.
5. The air striking the elevators forces the tail up, which swings the nose down so that the plane dives.
6. The plane needs less power when it is diving because gravity helps pull the plane down, so the engines are given less fuel and, consequently, slow down.

C. Turning to the right and left
1. To make a turn the pilot must tilt, or bank, the plane's wings in the desired direction, in much the same way that we tilt a bicycle when going around a curve.
2. To turn to the right, the pilot turns the control wheel to the right.
3. This turning of the wheel makes the right aileron in the wing go up and the left aileron go down.
4. When the rushing air strikes the ailerons, it causes the right wing to fall and the left wing to rise. This action makes the plane roll on its side and turn, or bank, to the right.
5. At the same time, the pilot pushes the right foot pedal and makes the rudder in the tail swing to the right. The air strikes the rudder, making the tail swing to the left and the nose of the plane move to the right.
6. This action helps the plane turn to the right and also helps to prevent the plane from yawing, or skidding sidewise, in the turn.

7. To make a left turn, the pilot turns the control wheel to the left, making the right aileron go down and the left aileron go up.
8. Air strikes the ailerons, making the right wing rise and the left wing fall, and the plane turns, or banks, to the left. At the same time, the pilot pushes the left foot pedal, making the rudder swing to the left.
9. Air strikes the rudder, pushing the tail to the right and the nose to the left.

D. Landing
1. To land, the pilot dives by making the elevators tilt downward.
2. As the plane dives, the pilot lowers the landing gear.
3. The plane moves into the wind so that the resistance of the air striking the plane will cut down the landing speed.
4. When the plane nears the runway, the pilot moves the elevators up to make a level landing.
5. When the plane is ready to land, the pilot lowers the flaps in the wings between the ailerons and the fuselage.
6. These flaps act as air brakes.

V. THE SOUND BARRIER

A. The speed of sound is about 336 meters (1,100 ft) per second, or about 1,220 kilometers (760 mi) per hour.
B. As an aircraft moves through the air, it produces sound, which travels out in waves.
1. These sound waves are compressed, and then expanded, as they travel.
2. When a plane travels slower than the speed of sound, the sound waves travel away from the plane faster than the plane is moving.
3. But when a plane travels at the speed of sound, these compressed sound waves cannot travel away from the plane because both the plane and the waves are now traveling at the same speed.
4. The sound waves then pile up in front of the plane and form a huge wall of air, called the **sound barrier.**
5. This wall of piled-up, compressed air pushes along at the speed of sound and becomes a **shock wave,** which causes a loud noise, like a giant clap of thunder, so strong that it can rattle—even break—dishes and windows in homes far below.
C. Aircraft that can fly through, or break, the sound barrier are designed in a special way. The nose of the aircraft is made longer and

more needle-like. The wings are thin, with sharp edges in front, and sweep back at an angle so that they look like large triangles.

VI. THE HEAT BARRIER

   A. The friction of the air as it moves across an aircraft produces heat. The faster the plane moves, the greater the air friction and the more heat is produced.

   B. The temperature at which the heat weakens and begins to melt parts of the aircraft is called the **heat barrier.**

      1. The kinds of materials that make up an aircraft are more important in overcoming the heat barrier than the speed of the aircraft itself. Heat-shielding tiles made of a silicon material successfully protect the space shuttle Columbia during its flights.

VII. THE HELICOPTER

   A. The helicopter has a large wing or rotor that spins above the plane.

      1. As the rotor spins rapidly, it provides both the lift to raise the helicopter in the air and the thrust to move the helicopter forward.

      2. By changing the tilt of the rotor, the helicopter can go straight up or down, forward or backward, or sideways, or just hover in the air.

      3. As the rotor spins, it tends to twist the rest of the helicopter.

      4. To stop this twisting effect, a smaller propeller or rotor, placed on the helicopter's tail, spins in the opposite direction to that of the large rotor.

      5. The smaller rotor is also used to steer the helicopter.

   B. The helicopter has many valuable uses. It can be used to rescue persons at sea or to remove injured persons from places difficult to reach in other ways. It can carry mail or persons for short distances to airports. It can patrol the waterfront or supervise automobile traffic on highways. It can be used to spot forest fires or persons lost in a forest.

VIII. ROCKETS

   A. Rocket engines, like jet engines, make use of Newton's third law of motion, which is concerned with action and reaction.

   B. As in a jet engine, burning fuels in the rocket produce hot, expanding gases that blast from the tail of the rocket and give it the thrust required to go up into space.

      1. The main difference between a rocket and a jet is in the source of oxygen needed to burn the fuel.

      2. Whereas a jet engine gets its oxygen from the air, a rocket carries its own oxygen supply, called the **oxidizer,** either as liquid oxygen (LOX) or as a solid or liquid fuel chemical that contains oxygen and gives it up readily.

      3. The fuel and oxidizer together are called the **propellant.**

      4. Because a rocket carries its own oxygen, its flight is not limited to the earth's atmosphere; it can travel in space where there is little or no oxygen.

   C. The simplest rockets are the solid fuel, or **solid propellant,** rockets.

      1. The solid fuel is really a mixture of a fuel and a chemical that contains oxygen.

      2. These rockets are used to help launch planes, and they are also used in fireworks and as signal rockets.

   D. **High-altitude rockets** are usually liquid fuel, or **liquid propellant,** rockets.

      1. These rockets use both a liquid fuel and liquid oxygen.

      2. These two liquids are stored in separate tanks in the rocket and are pumped into the combustion, or burning, chamber at the same time.

      3. High-altitude rockets do not have wings because they travel where there is no air to provide lift.

      4. The intercontinental ballistic missile (ICBM) is a high-altitude rocket.

      5. In the head of the rocket there is an atomic or hydrogen bomb.

      6. The missile can travel far into outer space and then return to earth a great distance away from the point where it was launched.

   E. Rockets can be made to travel faster and farther when rockets are connected together to form a **multistage rocket.**

      1. A three-stage rocket has three rockets, one mounted on top of the other, each with its own fuel and combustion chamber.

      2. The first stage is the largest rocket, at the bottom.

      3. When the first stage is fired, it launches all three rockets.

      4. The three-stage rocket climbs until all the fuel in the first stage is depleted.

      5. Then the first stage drops off, and the second stage is fired; the second and third stages together climb faster and higher until all the fuel

in the second stage is depleted, then the second stage falls off, and the third stage is ignited.

6. The third stage holds the instruments and any people that may be aboard.

7. The third stage climbs even higher and faster, then returns to earth, goes into orbit around the earth as a satellite, or goes farther into outer space.

SPACE TRAVEL

I. EARLY SPACE EXPLORATION WITH ROCKETS

A. During and after World War II, scientists made great advances in the study of rockets.
1. They improved rocket design and were able to send rockets up to greater heights than had ever before been reached.
2. Rockets containing instruments, cameras, and recording devices were sent up as high as 400 kilometers (250 mi).
3. However, these rockets were fired almost straight up, reached their greatest height in minutes, and then fell back to earth.
4. These early rockets were at different levels of the air for only a very short time, and very little could be found out about space during that time.
5. Moreover, because the rockets went straight up, only the space above just one part of the earth's surface could be explored.

II. ARTIFICIAL SATELLITES

A. After scientists had experimented with rockets that went straight up, they decided to try something different; they tried the idea of a rocket's going high above the earth's surface and staying there for some time.
1. The only way this could be done was to make the rocket travel around the earth in an orbit, just as the moon makes an orbit around the earth.
2. Because the moon is called a satellite (a body revolving around a planet), this orbiting rocket was called a satellite too.
3. On October 4, 1957, the Soviet Union sent up Sputnik I, the first earth satellite.
4. A month later the Soviet Union sent up Sputnik II with a dog in it.
5. On January 31, 1958, the United States sent up its first satellite, Explorer I.
6. Today there are thousands of orbiting satellites, some of which are launched by the government and many others owned by private corporations.

B. Very high speeds and powerful thrusts are necessary to get a satellite or a spaceship high into the air and then to either send the satellite sideways in an orbit around the earth or let the spaceship escape the earth's pull of gravity.
1. To accomplish this, three or even more rockets are put together, one on top of the other with the biggest rocket at the bottom, to form a multistage rocket.
2. Each rocket is called a stage, and each stage has its own fuel and combustion chamber.
3. The stages are not all fired together, but one after the other as the fuel from one stage is depleted; when one stage uses up its fuel, it drops off, and the next stage takes over.
4. The satellite or spaceship is on top of the last rocket, and it contains the instruments and astronauts.

C. The satellite or spaceship is the smallest part of the rocket.
1. It is covered with a nose cone to protect it from the heat produced by friction as the rocket moves through the air.
2. It is often called the **pay load** of the rocket.

D. When the first stage of a three-stage rocket is fired, the rocket goes straight into the air.
1. The rocket goes up slowly at first because it must overcome the pull of gravity and because the heavier air in the lower atmosphere would batter the rocket into pieces if it were traveling at high speed.
2. The rocket begins to pick up speed and then is made to tilt so that it travels at an angle.
3. By the time the rocket is in the outer limits of the stratosphere, the fuel in the first stage burns out, and that stage drops off.
4. The second stage takes over and lifts the rocket higher and faster into space.
5. The rocket keeps tilting until its path is more in a line with the direction in which the spaceship or satellite is intended to go.
6. The fuel in the second stage burns out, and that stage drops off. Then the third stage either sends the spaceship beyond the earth's pull of gravity or puts the satellite into orbit.
7. To put the satellite into orbit, the third stage fires at the proper height and tilts the satellite in a path as close to parallel to the earth's surface as the instruments will allow.

8. The third stage then drops off, leaving the satellite in orbit.
9. The protective nose cone drops off the satellite at the same time.
E. Rockets are often launched toward the east because east is the direction of the earth's rotation.
   1. The earth rotates at a speed of about 1,600 kilometers (1,000 mi) per hour.
   2. The earth's speed gives the rocket an extra push, which helps it to reach the speed it needs to go into orbit.
F. The speeding satellite stays in orbit around the earth because there are two conditions affecting it.
   1. One condition is earth's pull of gravity on the satellite, which tries to pull the satellite down to earth.
   2. The second condition is inertia, which tends to make the satellite move in a straight line out into space. Inertia is defined by a scientific principle, **Newton's first law of motion,** which says that a body at rest tends to stay at rest and a body in motion tends to continue in motion in a straight line at the same speed, unless some outside force acts on the body to change this condition.
   3. These conditions, gravity and inertia, act against each other.
   4. If only gravity were affecting a satellite, it would fall to the earth; if only inertia were affecting the satellite, it would fly off into space.
   5. The third stage of the rocket gives the satellite exactly the proper sideways speed, called the **orbital velocity,** so that the force of gravity and the effect of inertia balance each other, and the satellite neither falls to earth nor flies off into space but instead moves in an orbit around the earth.
G. Most artificial satellites travel in an elliptical, or oval-shaped, orbit rather than a circular orbit because it is very hard to launch a satellite at just the right angle and speed to achieve a perfect circular orbit.
   1. Some satellites are purposely made to travel in an elliptical orbit so that they can give information about conditions in space both near the earth and much farther away.
   2. In an elliptical orbit a satellite comes closer to the earth at one part of its trip around earth and then goes farther away at another part of its trip.
   3. The point in the orbit where the satellite is nearest the earth is called the **perigee;** the point where the satellite is farthest away from the earth is called the **apogee.**

4. The satellite needs a sideways speed, called orbital velocity, to stay in orbit around the earth.
5. The farther the orbit is away from the earth, the smaller the earth's pull of gravity on the satellite becomes and the less sideways speed the satellite needs.
6. To travel in an orbit at a height of 480 kilometers (300 mi), a satellite needs an orbital velocity of about 29,000 kilometers (18,000 mi) per hour; at 3,200 kilometers (2,000 mi) the orbital velocity must be about 23,000 kilometers (14,400 mi) per hour; at 16,000 kilometers (10,000 mi) the orbital velocity must be about 11,500 kilometers (7,200 mi) per hour; at 35,000 kilometers (22,000 mi) the orbital velocity must be about 10,900 kilometers (6,800 mi) per hour, and the satellite travels around the earth once every 24 hours.
7. At 35,000 kilometers (22,000 mi) such a satellite seems stationary in the sky, as it travels in the same direction as the earth (west to east).
8. Eventually, most satellites orbiting the earth fall back to earth.
9. At the perigee of its orbit, the heavier air slows the satellite a little, especially if it started with a perigee fairly close to earth.
10. Each time the satellite enters its perigee, it is slowed more, so its orbit gets rounder and smaller and the earth's gravity pulls harder and harder on it.
11. When the satellite is slowed to the point where it cannot keep its orbit any longer, it falls.
12. A falling satellite gets very hot because of the friction of the air rubbing against it, and it will burn up unless it is protected from the heat.
13. Some satellites have stayed up as little as 3 months, but one satellite is expected to remain in orbit for about 200 years.
H. Scientists follow the path, or track, of a satellite by radar, telescope, and radio transmission.
   1. Direction-finding antennas, set up at special receiving stations, are used to fix the position of a satellite.
   2. By telescope, satellites are seen best at early dawn or at twilight.
   3. In the daytime a satellite cannot be seen against the bright, sunlit sky.
   4. At night the satellite is often in the shadow of the Earth.
   5. At early dawn and twilight, the satellite is in sunshine, while on earth we still have a dark sky and are thus able to see the satellite, sometimes with the naked eye.

I. A satellite is filled with automatic instruments and recording devices that get the electrical energy needed to operate them from any one of three sources: chemical batteries, which change chemical energy into electrical energy; solar energy batteries, which change solar energy into electrical energy; and nuclear energy batteries, which use radioactive isotopes to change nuclear energy into electrical energy.

   1. Satellite instruments have already discovered, studied, and measured many things: they have measured X-ray, ultraviolet, and infrared radiation; how strongly the earth is being bombarded by tiny meteors coming into the atmosphere from outer space; the size and shape of the earth's magnetic field; and the earth's force of gravity at high altitudes; they have discovered that the earth is not round like an orange, but more pear-shaped or egg-shaped; they have studied the height of the earth's atmosphere, and the atmosphere's temperature, pressure, and composition at high altitudes; they have taken pictures of cloud patterns to be used in predicting the weather; they have measured the magnetic field, temperature, and pressure near the moon and have taken pictures of the side of the moon that we cannot see; they have reflected radio, radar, and television signals back to earth; and they have been used to detect fossil strata in the earth's crust.

III. Space Programs

  A. History of United States and Soviet Union space exploration programs

    1. For a summary of space exploration programs, from the first person in orbit around the earth until 1995, see Figure 11.12.

  B. The National Aeronautics and Space Administration (NASA) describes its spacecraft by groups or series, depending on their design and what they are supposed to do or find out.

    1. **Scientific satellites** such as Explorer, Vanguard, Discoverer, Landsat, Lageos, Orbiting Astronomical Observatory, Orbiting Solar Observatory, and Orbiting Geophysical Observatory, all built and launched by the United States, carry instruments that supply information about radiation, the earth's magnetic field, earth's shape, temperatures in space, micrometeoroids, and other conditions in the upper parts of the atmosphere and in outer space.

    2. There are also joint projects between the United States and other countries: the Ariel with England, the Alouette with Canada, the San Marco with Italy, the French–U.S. project, and the international Isis project.

    3. **Weather satellites** such as the Tiros and the Nimbus series make weather observations, help scientists forecast the weather more accurately, and contribute a better understanding of what causes weather.

    4. **Communications satellites** such as Echo, Telstar, Relay, Syncom, Intelsat, Oscar, and ATS-6 are used to send and reflect radio and television signals, telephotos, and telephone calls to all parts of the world.

    5. **Navigation satellites** such as the Transit series help to guide aircraft and ships by transmitting special radio signals to them.

    6. **Lunar and interplanetary spacecraft** are used to explore the moon and the planets.

    7. The **Pioneer series** investigates interplanetary space to learn more about solar radiation, interplanetary magnetic fields, and micrometeoroids.

    8. The **Ranger series** gathers information about the moon to help pave the way for landing on the moon.

    9. The **Surveyor series** was designed to land gently on the moon, send television pictures back to earth, find suitable landing sites, analyze the moon's crust, check the moon's surface for strength and stability, and measure the bombardment of the moon by meteorites.

    10. The **Lunar Orbiter series** is designed to photograph suitable landing sites on the moon and to learn more about the moon's gravitational pull.

    11. The **Mariner series** is designed to fly near Venus and Mars and to send back information about these planets.

    12. The **Voyager series** is designed to fly near the planets beyond Mars and to send back information about them.

    13. The purpose of **Project Mercury** was to investigate human reactions and abilities during space flight and to recover both personnel and spacecraft safely.

    14. The purpose of **Project Gemini** was to determine human performance and behavior during prolonged space flight, develop techniques that would enable two or more spacecraft to rendezvous and couple together while in orbit, carry out space investigations that need human presence in the spacecraft, and demonstrate both controlled reentry

- April 12, 1961: First person in earth's orbit, Soviet cosmonaut Y. A. Gagarin in the Soviet Union's Vostok 1 mission.
- May 5, 1961: First United States astronaut into space, A. B. Shepard, Jr., in Mercury 3 mission.
- February 20, 1962: First U.S. astronaut in earth's orbit, J. H. Glenn, Jr., in Mercury 6 mission.
- June 16, 1963: First woman in space, cosmonaut V. Tereshkova, in the Vostok 6 mission.
- March 18, 1965: First U.S. two-person space flight, V. I. "Gus" Grissom and J. W. Young, in the Gemini 3 mission.
- June 3, 1965: First U.S. spacewalk, E. H. White II, in Gemini 4 mission with astronaut J. McDivitt.
- January 27, 1967: After astronauts Gus Grissom, E. White and R. Chaffee died in a launch-pad fire during a countdown dress rehearsal, the aborted mission of the Apollo 204 spacecraft was later renamed Apollo 1.
- July 5, 1967: Unmanned Apollo 2 mission.
- August 26, 1967: Unmanned Apollo 3 Saturn 1-B booster mission.
- November 9, 1967: First launch of 363-foot Saturn V launch vehicle, the unmanned Apollo 4 mission.
- January 22, 1968: Apollo 5, the first earth-orbit flight test of an unmanned lunar module.
- April 4, 1968: Apollo 6, an unmanned mission; engines of Saturn V either failed to ignite or shut down too early.
- October 11–21, 1968: Apollo 7. W. Schirra, D. Eisele, and W. Cunningham on board for the first test in orbit of a command module.
- December 21–27, 1968: Apollo 8, first manned flight to orbit the moon. U.S. astronauts W. A. Anders, F. Borman, and J. A. Lovell, Jr., completed 10 lunar orbits.
- March 3–13, 1969: Apollo 9. Astronauts J. A. McDivitt, D. Scott and R. Schweickart conduct first combined earth-orbit test of the command and lunar modules.
- May 18–26, 1969: Apollo 10. Astronauts T. Stafford, J. Young, and G. Cernan are first to test both the command and lunar modules in orbit around the moon.
- July 16–24, 1969: Apollo 11, first manned landing on the moon. On July 20, U.S. astronauts N. A. Armstrong and E. E. "Buzz" Aldrin, Jr., land the lunar module Eagle on the moon's surface and collect 48 pounds of lunar rock and soil samples while M. Collins orbits in the command module Columbia.
- November 14–24, 1969: Apollo 12, a second lunar landing. Astronauts C. "Pete" Conrad, Jr., and A. Bean collect rocks while R. F. Gordon, Jr., orbits in the command module Yankee Clipper.
- April 11–17, 1970: Apollo 13. Plans for a third lunar landing are aborted when a cryogenic tank explodes. Astronauts J. Lovell, J. Swigert, and F. Haise are forced to use the lunar module Aquarius as a lifeboat.
- January 31–February 9, 1971: Apollo 14. A lunar landing in which A. Shephard and E. D. Mitchell touch down while S. Roosa orbits in the command module.
- June 7, 1971: First manned orbiting space station, cosmonauts G. T. Dobrovolsky, V. I. Patsayev, and V. N. Volkov.
- July 26–August 7, 1971: Apollo 15. Astronauts D. Scott and J. Irwin log 17.5 miles on the moon's surface in the Lunar Rover on July 30 and collect approximately 170 pounds of lunar materials, while A. Worden orbits in the command module.
- April 16–27, 1972: Astronauts J. Young and C. Duke drive the Lunar Rover and collect 200 pounds of lunar samples, while K. Mattingly pilots the command module in orbit for this Apollo 16 mission.
- December 7–19, 1972: Apollo 17 mission. Astronaut G. Cernan returns to the moon with H. Schmitt, collecting 250 pounds of lunar materials, then rejoins command module pilot R. Evans after leaving behind a plaque on the moon that reads, "Here man completed his first explorations of the moon."
- May 25, 1973: First manned U.S. space station, astronauts C. Conrad, Jr., J. P. Kerwin, and P. J. Weitz.
- July 15, 1975: First international space mission (Apollo-Soyuz Test Project), V. D. Brand, D. K. "Deke" Slayton, and T. P. Stafford of the U.S. and A. A. Leonov and V. N. Kubasov of the Soviet Union.
- April 12, 1981: First space shuttle flight, U. S. astronauts J. W. Young and R. L. Crippen.
- June 18, 1983: First U. S. woman in space, Sally K. Ride.
- August 30, 1983: First African American astronaut in space, Guion S. Bluford, Jr.
- January 28, 1986: First loss of a U.S. spacecraft while in flight. The Challenger explodes 73 seconds after lift-off, killing all persons aboard—F. Scobee, M. Smith, E. Onizuka, S. C. McAuliffe, G. Jarvis, and R. McNair.
- December 21, 1988: Longest time spent in space, 366 days in a space station, cosmonauts M. Manarov and V. Titov.
- March 14, 1995: Norman Thagard becomes the first U.S. astronaut shot into space by the Russians, orbiting the earth with two cosmonauts and then docking with the Russian space station Mir, then returning to earth on the U.S. space shuttle Atlantis.

FIGURE 11.12 Chronological history of selected United States and Russian space exploration programs.

into the atmosphere and controlled landing at a specific site.

15. The purpose of **Project Apollo** was to land astronauts on the moon and then return them to earth.

16. Apollo 11 landed astronauts on the moon on July 20, 1969, and safely returned them to earth.

17. After several successful Apollo missions, NASA's focus was on development of the space shuttle and an orbiting space station.

18. The shuttles carry into orbit such items as government and private communications satellites, military and weather surveillance hardware, scientific research laboratories, and a huge telescope for exploring space.

19. Project shuttles in the space shuttle program are the *Challenger, Discovery,* and *Atlantis.*

20. Project shuttles are now fairly commonplace, with as many as 50 flights planned and orbiting the earth each year.

C. A large satellite spinning around the earth can be a **space station.**

1. The orbit of the satellite can be almost circular, and the satellite can be well outside the earth's atmosphere.

2. Because there is no air resistance at this altitude, the station can stay in orbit for hundreds of years.

3. Supplies can be sent to the station by rockets acting as freight cars.

4. A space station can have many valuable uses.

5. It can collect a vast amount of knowledge about the earth, its atmosphere, its weather, and its fields of gravity and magnetism.

6. It can be used to reflect and send back radio, radar, and television signals all over the earth.

7. During war it can watch for enemy troops and planes and discover industrial targets.

8. It can be used to launch rockets easily into outer space, because the rockets will not have to overcome the earth's pull of gravity to take off.

9. There are plans for a permanently inhabited space station by about the year 2002.

10. Shuttle flights are used to ferry the materials for building the station and to deliver supplies needed by the crew of astronauts who will live and work on the station.

IV. PROBLEMS OF ASTRONAUTS DURING SPACE FLIGHT

A. The force of acceleration.

1. An astronaut must be able to endure the tremendous force acting on the body as a rocket accelerates (speeds up). This force is the same kind of force you feel when you go up quickly in an elevator.

2. You feel heavier, and it seems as if you are being pushed downward to the floor of the elevator car.

3. This force of acceleration really does make you heavier when you are speeding faster and faster and going against gravity. At the surface of the earth, the earth's pull of gravity on you is the weight of your body. This pull, which is your weight, is called 1 g. At a point during the first part of a flight, the astronaut feels a force of about 6 g's.

4. At this point, the astronaut's weight is six times what it is on the ground.

5. At 3 g's a person cannot walk, and it is very hard even to move. When seated, a person "blacks out" at 6 g's because the heart cannot pump blood to the brain against this great force of acceleration.

6. Tests show, however, that a person can endure this force without too much trouble while lying down on his or her back.

7. The astronaut must be able to endure the same force again when the rocket decelerates (slows down) quickly.

B. Zero gravity or weightlessness.

1. When acceleration stops and the spacecraft is in space, the astronaut and all the materials inside the ship have no weight. Earth's gravity has been left behind, and everything is weightless.

2. The astronaut loses the feeling of what is "up" and what is "down."

3. The astronaut must use special shoes to be able to walk rather than float across the spacecraft.

4. If the things inside the spaceship were not fastened, they would float about in the ship. Because of weightlessness, food and water can be a problem: it is impossible to pour water from a bottle. If an astronaut lifts food toward his or her mouth, the food continues to move to the roof of the ship. The astronaut must use food and water stored in tubes, like toothpaste.

5. A large amount of dehydrated food can be stored in tubes or as compressed wafers.

6. The water problem can be solved only by recycling all water.

7. A space biology mission aboard the shuttle *Columbia,* in 1994, revealed that the zero gravity (weightlessness) caused dramatic and unexpected effects on the human body. These effects include severe loss of muscle tone, blood pressure irregularities, and reduced ability to burn stored fat for energy. The findings suggest that extended space travel could be more difficult for humans than had been previously thought.

C. Oxygen and carbon dioxide.
   1. The astronaut needs a steady supply of oxygen. The carbon dioxide that is exhaled must be removed.
   2. One way of supplying oxygen is to use tanks of liquid oxygen, which can be mixed with helium gas, also in tanks, to give the astronaut the right proportion of oxygen for breathing. Chemicals can remove the carbon dioxide that the astronaut exhales.

D. Temperature.
   1. A chief problem in an airtight spaceship is to maintain body temperature.
   2. Most of a spaceship's travel is in direct sunlight, and the sun's rays strike at least one side of the ship all the time. As a result, the ship could become too hot inside.
   3. One way to keep the ship cool is to have the outside of the ship smooth and silvery so that the sun's rays are reflected.

4. If the spaceship travels far from the sun, where it is very cold, the outside of the ship can be painted black to absorb the sun's rays and warm the ship.

5. Another way of controlling temperature inside a spaceship is to paint one side of the ship silver and the other side black. The ship can then be turned as necessary to adjust the temperature.

6. Space suits can be heated or cooled by electricity.

E. Radiation.
   1. Cosmic rays can pass directly through the metal walls into the spaceship.
   2. Although short-term exposure to these rays shows no harmful effects, it may be that the astronaut will have to be protected from long-term exposure to cosmic rays.

F. Meteors.
   1. Meteors of all sizes are always traveling through space.
   2. If a meteor should strike a spaceship and puncture a hole in it, the air in the spaceship would quickly rush out and the astronauts would die.
   3. Double walls can protect the ship from small meteors. Most meteors are very small, so it is not likely that a ship would be struck by a large meteor.

Exploratory Activities for "Air, Aircraft, and Space Travel"

1. *A PLACE IN SPACE*[1] (GRADES 4–9)

Overview Without technology, the exploration of space would be impossible. As we increase the possibility that humans will one day live and work in space, we also increase the need for more sophisticated technology. In this activity, the students identify the basic needs of living things, examine a variety of self-contained biospheres designed to support life, and construct a simple model of a space station. Through these experiences, the students will realize some of the challenges that scientists and engineers face when exploring the frontier of space.

Scientific Principles

- The basic needs of living things include oxygen, carbon dioxide, water, light, food, and protection from extreme heat and cold.
- Artificial biospheres rely on technology to provide the basic needs of resident organisms.
- Engineers use scale models to help them in the design of complex systems.
- A closed system is an isolated system; neither energy nor material can pass through its boundaries.

Student Outcomes Upon completion of this activity, students will be able to

- Identify the basic needs of a living organism
- Construct a biosphere for a simple organism such as a plant
- Recognize different models of complex biospheres
- Use scale models to design larger objects

Skills Analyzing, discussing, constructing models

Related Disciplines Life science, Earth science, Physical science, Mathematics

Time Frame

Life under Glass	45 minutes
A Human Terrarium?	45 minutes
Little Plans for Big Ideas	45 minutes

Materials and Advance Preparation for:

Life Under Glass

Materials

- Large potted plant
- 2-liter soft-drink bottles
- 1 small plant, no more than 8″ tall, for the demonstration terrarium
- Large scissors, 1 pair per lab group
- Potting soil, 10-pound bag
- Newspaper, enough to cover desk
- Seeds, 5 per student (suggested seeds: radish, marigold, alfalfa)
- 500 ml beaker of water, 1 per lab group
- Duct or electrical tape, 15 cm per lab group
- Masking tape, 30 cm per lab group

Before Class

- A week in advance, ask the students to bring in empty, rinsed, clear 2-liter soft-drink bottles. You will need one per student.
- Organize materials for lab groups.
- Make a soft-drink bottle terrarium using a small plant instead of seeds. This will serve as the demonstration terrarium. (See Life under Glass, step 3.)

A Human Terrarium?

Materials

- Terrarium with small plant (from Life under Glass)
- Overhead projector

Before Class

- Make transparencies of Figures 11.13 and 11.14.

Little Plans for Big Ideas

Materials

- Meter stick or metric tape measure
- Graph paper with metric divisions, 1 sheet per student
- Scissors, 1 per lab group
- Metric rulers, 1 per student
- Masking tape

Before Class

- Write the dimensions of the space module on the chalkboard. (See Little Plans for Big Ideas, step 2.)

Life Under Glass

1. Display a large plant and ask the students to explain what this organism needs to stay alive. List the students' responses on the chalkboard, and assist them in identifying needs that are basic to the plant's survival: minerals, water, air, and light.
2. Display the demonstration terrarium containing a small plant. Review the students' lists of basic needs. Will this plant stay alive? Why or why not? Have the class explain how each basic need of the plant is being met.
3. Divide the students into lab groups and distribute materials so students can construct terraria by doing the following:
   a. Use the large scissors to cut off the top of each plastic bottle.
   b. Separate the colored base from the rest of the bottle by tugging on it vigorously.
   c. Use the duct or electrical tape to seal the holes in the base from the inside. Do this carefully to make the base watertight.
   d. Fill the base with soil.
   e. Add 50 ml of water to moisten the soil. *Do not overwater.* Stir the soil.
   f. Use a pencil to poke five holes in the soil, and then plant a seed in each hole. Gently cover each seed with soil.
   g. Invert the clear plastic part of the bottle to create a dome to cover the base. Use masking tape to seal the base and dome. Record names on the tape.
4. Keep the students' terraria in a warm place until the seeds germinate (two or three days), and then place the terraria in sunlight. After the majority of the seedlings are well sprouted, ask the students to evaluate the varying success of individual terraria. Have the students discuss how the basic needs of the plants are, or are not, being met. Your students may want to design and conduct experiments to test the relative importance of different factors on plant life in a terrarium.

A Human Terrarium?

1. Instruct the students to reexamine the terrarium containing the small plant. Ask the students if they think humans could live in a terrarium. Discuss the needs of humans and list these needs on the chalkboard. Ask the students to decide which of the items listed are biological needs that are basic to the survival of humans (oxygen, light, water, food, protection from heat and cold) and which are psychological needs (companionship, entertainment, recreation). Have the class discuss how the biological needs could be met in a closed system like a terrarium.

2. Define a closed system for your students. In a closed system, the total amount of water and air remains constant. In addition, no new food or nutrients can enter the system, so food and nutrients must cycle through the system for plants and animals to use them again. The earth is a closed system; energy is the only resource that reaches the system from the outside. Sunlight is necessary to heat air and supply energy for various cycles.

3. In the Arizona desert, scientists built an artificial, closed biosphere—or a human terrarium—called Biosphere II (Figure 11.13). Modeled after the biosphere of the earth (Biosphere I), Biosphere II is a self-supporting ecosystem containing five biomes: a savanna, a marsh, a desert, a tropical rain forest, and an ocean 35 feet deep. A group of eight men and women inhabited the two-acre structure. The $30 million project could serve as a prototype for orbiting space stations or planetary outposts, and as a model for improved resource management.
Use a transparency of Figure 11.13 to present the Biosphere II project in Arizona, and discuss the project, asking the students to consider the following:
   a. What are the objectives of the project? (According to the planners, there are two: to develop technology for settlements on the moon and Mars, and to improve human stewardship of earth by learning how to manage such things as human wastes.)
   b. What problems require solutions if Biosphere II is to become self-sustaining? (Some suggestions are how to seal the glass roof so that no air can escape or enter; how to cool the air temperatures, which could peak at 156°F, without using conventional methods that draw air from the outside; how to handle water purification and air quality; how to make sure there is adequate vegetation to sustain all life forms; and how to make sure that none of the selected life forms will be a hazard to the ecosystem.)
   c. What would it be like to live in Biosphere II? What kind of people would be appropriate to include in the group of eight Biosphereans? What skills should they have?
   d. What were the likely social dynamics of the Biosphereans? What strains do you imagine the Biosphereans encountered during their two-year stay in Biosphere II? Would the students like living for two years with seven other people in a closed system?

4. Another life-supporting biosphere model is the extravehicular mobility unit (EMU) used by astronauts in space (Figure 11.14). NASA developed the EMU to enable astronauts to work in space without the support of a spacecraft. An attachable manned maneuvering unit (MMU) allows astronauts to work untethered in space and return safely to the spacecraft. By providing the atmospheric pressure and oxygen necessary for human life as well as insulation from the sun's heat, the EMU protects the astronaut from the hostile environment of space. The technology involved in the EMU is complex; astronauts preparing to work in space must carry all of their life-support systems with them. Use a transparency of Figure 11.14 to illustrate an EMU. Have the students identify the basic needs of an astronaut and describe how the EMU meets those needs.

Little Plans for Big Ideas

As we push back the frontiers of space, we must create self-supporting biospheres. Most people call these artificial biospheres *space stations*. In 1984, President Ronald Reagan directed NASA to develop a permanently occupied space station. Scientists once envisioned a collection of modules that would form huge, spoked wheels that would spin through space. Current U.S. plans for the station, however, describe a structure that includes four pressurized, cylindrical modules in the center of a huge supportive structure. Two of these modules will provide living space, and the other two will provide a working area. The space station will house a crew of six, with replacement crews arriving every 90 days.

1. If space is available, have the students measure the dimensions of one module on the classroom floor. Instruct six people to stand within the boundaries of the module, and ask the students to imagine living in that space for 90 days at a time. Remind the students that they would have only two modules available for sleeping, eating, recreation, and relaxation.

2. Currently, plans for the space station are only on paper. Because something as large as a space sta-

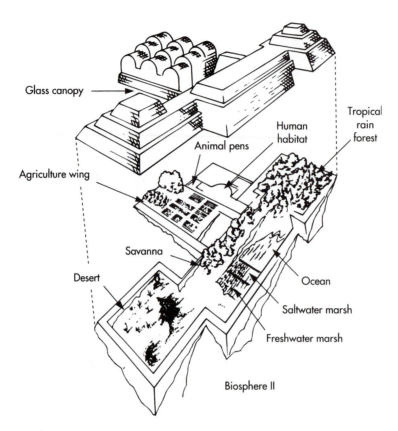

FIGURE 11.13   Biosphere II.

tion is difficult to design, engineers use scale models. Scale models are small two- or three-dimensional renderings of a large object (Figure 11.15). With the advent of sophisticated computers, computer modeling has replaced paper-and-pencil drafting in the design of complex objects. In a scale model, the relative sizes of the parts of the model are the same as those of the larger object; all the proportions are identical. Introduce the students to the concept of a scale model. Use familiar examples, such as airplane models and architectural plans. Ask the students to make a three-dimensional scale model of one of the cylindrical modules:

a. Review the dimensions with students:
   Diameter of module = 4.2 meters
   Length of module = 12.1 meters

   Optional: The module is cylindrical. In order to draw the module two-dimensionally and then roll it into a correctly scaled cylinder, ask the students to calculate the circumference of

the module. Review with the students the formula for calculating the circumference of a circle from its diameter: circumference = $\pi\, d$. If students are not familiar with the formula for calculating the circumference, include the circumference (13.2 meters) in the dimensions.

b. Ask the students to convert the measurements of the module from meters to centimeters, using the scale of 1 cm = 1 m. In this way, one centimeter on paper will be equivalent to one meter on the module.

c. Supply each student with one sheet of graph paper with metric divisions. Ask the students to draw on the graph paper the scale dimension they had calculated (length × circumference). The finished drawing will be a rectangle.

d. Instruct students to cut out the rectangle with scissors and tape the two short sides together to form a cylinder. This cylinder is proportionally accurate and resembles the proposed module. Each dimension is 1/100 of the size of

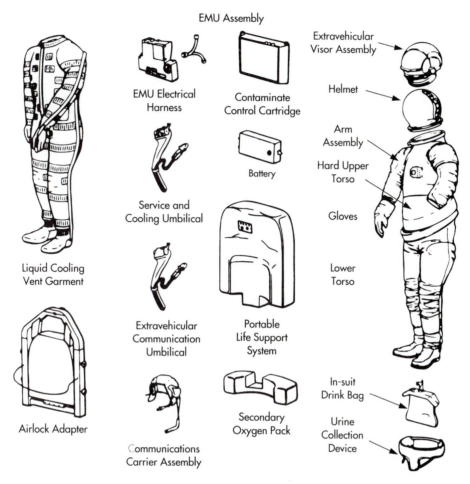

FIGURE 11.14   Extravehicular mobility unit (EMU). Assembly instructions: 1. Put on urine collection device, cooling and ventilation garment, in-suit drink bag, communications carrier assembly, biomedical instrumentation subsystem, boot inserts; 2. Don space suit: hard upper torso, lower torso, gloves, helmet, extravehicular visor assembly.

the real module, making the scale model, with its three dimensions, 1/1,000,000 of the size of the real module.

e. The students can use a metric ruler to check their model by measuring the diameter of the cylinder. Being careful to maintain the cylindrical form, the students should measure the diameter as approximately 4.2 cm.

Going Further

- Have the students write a letter from space, describing where they live, what they do, and how they feel about living on a space station.

- Ask the students to search their school or local libraries for science fiction that includes predictions of how humans will live in space.

- Have the students conduct research on plans for the industrialization of space. Ask the students to find out the results of various projects on shuttle flights and what industrial applications may be suited for a space station.

- Have the students draw a scale model of one room of their house. Ask them to measure the room's size and the furniture and to draw a two-dimensional plan with all parts of the room in relative proportion.

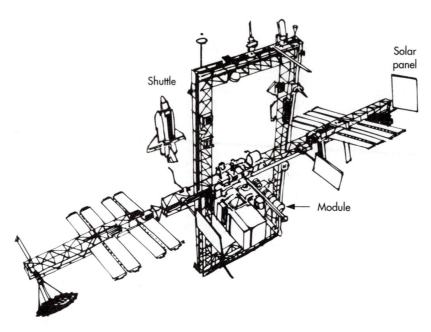

FIGURE 11.15   A scale model of a space station.

- Have the students investigate the numerous spin-offs produced by the space program, such as Teflon, Velcro, and Temperfoam. Information on the products is available in the library or from the U.S. Government Printing Office (address listed under "Resources for the Classroom").
- Encourage the students to study the history of space exploration. What happened when? How did the explorations benefit life on earth? When did the first animal, man, or woman orbit the earth, walk on another planet, or travel past the moon?
- Let the students explore the accomplishments of the U.S. and Russia in space. Why is there so much competition between these nations? When have they cooperated? What other nations have active space programs?

RESOURCES FOR THE CLASSROOM

Freundlich, N. J. (1986). "Biosphere." *Popular Science* 229 (6), 54–56.

Maranto, G. (1987). Earth's First Visitors to Mars. *Discover* 8 (5), 28–43.

NASA. (undated). *NASA Facts: Waste Management.* JSC-09696 (rev. ed.). Washington, DC: USGPO.

NASA (1984). *NASA Facts: A Wardrobe for Space.* JSC-09378 (rev. ed.). Washington, DC: USGPO.

Scobee, J and D. Scobee. (1986). "An Astronaut Speaks." *Science and Children* 23 (6), reprint.

Taylor, P. (1982). *The Kid's Whole Future Catalog.* New York: Random House.

Government documents can be ordered from the Superintendent of Documents, U.S. Government Printing Office, Washington, DC 20402. Many fliers are free, even in bulk quantities.

A *Teacher's Companion to the Space Station: A Multidisciplinary Resource,* as well as other materials, is available at the NASA Teacher Resource Centers listed below:

NASA Ames Research Center, Moffett Field, CA 94035-1000. Serves Alaska, Arizona, California, Hawaii, Idaho, Montana, Nevada, Oregon, Utah, Washington, and Wyoming.

NASA Goddard Space Flight Center, Greenbelt, MD 20711-0001. Serves Connecticut, Delaware, District of Columbia, Maine, Maryland, Massachusetts, New Hampshire, New Jersey, New York, Pennsylvania, Rhode Island, and Vermont.

NASA Jet Propulsion Laboratory, 4800 Oak Grove Drive, Pasadena, CA 91109-8099. Serves inquiries related to space exploration and other JPL activities.

NASA Johnson Space Center, Houston, TX 77058-3696. Serves Colorado, Kansas, Nebraska,

New Mexico, North Dakota, Oklahoma, South Dakota, and Texas.

NASA Kennedy Space Center, Kennedy Space Center, FL 32899-0001. Serves Florida, Georgia, Puerto Rico, and the Virgin Islands.

NASA Langley Research Center, Hampton, VA 23681-0001. Serves Kentucky, North Carolina, South Carolina, Virginia, and West Virginia.

NASA Lewis Research Center, Cleveland, OH 44135-3191. Serves Illinois, Indiana, Michigan, Minnesota, Ohio, and Wisconsin.

NASA Marshall Space Flight Center, Tranquillity Base, Huntsville, AL 35807-7015. Serves Alabama, Arkansas, Iowa, Louisiana, Missouri, and Tennessee.

National Space Technology Laboratories, NSTL, MS 39529. Serves Mississippi.

The United States Space Foundation, 1522 Vapor Trail Drive, Colorado Springs, CO 80916, also has many teacher and student resource materials.

BACKGROUND FOR THE TEACHER
Space stations orbiting earth, space travellers living in artificial, enclosed biospheres, and shuttles transporting people between Earth and Mars—are these just science fiction images, or is the space program bringing us to the reality of settlements beyond Earth?

NASA has been working toward the settlement of space for many years. With President Ronald Reagan's directive in 1984 to "develop a permanently manned space station—and do it within a decade" (Anderson, undated, p. ii) NASA has been able to put form to its concepts and deadlines to its timetable. An occupied space station requires a self-supporting biosphere—a closed, complex system in which organisms support and maintain themselves. Because human survival in space requires oxygen, water, food, light, protection from temperature extremes, and a shield from cosmic and solar radiation, scientists and technologists have several complex problems to solve.

The *Challenger* disaster in January 1986 changed NASA's schedule for launching a space station. Originally, NASA planned to build a station in space over the course of 18 months, taking up materials with 12 shuttle flights (National Commission on Space, 1986, p. 120). Because of the problems with *Challenger*, NASA decided to reduce each shuttle's cargo capacity from 65,000 pounds per launch to 40,000 pounds, thus changing the timetable for building the station. Current plans call for construction of a modest station, which NASA can enlarge later. Shuttle flights will ferry the modules for living and working, and, after 11 flights, a crew of four will occupy the station. The station originally scheduled for

completion in 1996 will have required a total of 32 flights (Biddle, 1987).

For centuries, humans have been curious about the worlds beyond our planet. Why do we want to explore beyond the confines of Earth? Why do we need to? What do we hope to accomplish?

Research in space will help answer numerous scientific questions. Aboard the space station, specialists will conduct astronomical studies, such as mapping Venus with the Magellan probe, which has high-resolution radar equipment. There is widespread interest in manufacturing in space, because the microgravity environment eliminates heat convection, hydrostatic pressure, sedimentation, and buoyancy, and enables the fusion of mixed particles into homogeneous composites that are impossible to make on earth (*The Futurist,* 1987). Private industries hope to use the space station to purify pharmaceutical and biological products, such as erythropoietin, a kidney hormone that controls the production of red blood cells. Other products include nearly flawless glasslike linings for artificial hearts that would prevent clotting, and membranes coated with antibodies that could filter the blood of an AIDS patient (Biddle, p. 45). The computer industry hopes to improve high-speed computers by growing high-quality gallium arsenide crystals in space. Researchers also would like to develop new polymers and catalysts, to process improved fiber optics, and to create new metal alloys not produced on earth.

The scientific purpose of space travel is the pursuit of new knowledge. Scientists, however, are not the only people interested in space travel. Others also see space as an avenue to pursue their goals. The National Commission on Space has said, in its rationale for exploring and settling the solar system, that exploring the universe is a goal that will encourage increased world cooperation and will be a peaceful mission with respect for the integrity of planetary bodies and alien life forms (1986, p. 4). The ratio of funding for space projects, however, is tipped heavily in favor of the armed services. The defense budget helps to build technological infrastructures and underwrites expensive high-tech science (Biddle, p. 45). The existence of the Strategic Defense Initiative (SDI) as an impetus for space research underscores that there may not be unity of purpose in space exploration. Space is a large frontier; how and why the United States ventures into it will determine the benefits derived from its exploration.

Consultant
Victoria Duca
Director of Special Projects
U.S. Space Foundation
Colorado Springs, CO

REFERENCES

Anderson, D. A. (undated). "Space Station." EP-211. Washington, DC: U.S.G.P.O.

Biddle, W. (1987). "NASA: What's Needed to Put It on Its Feet?" *Discover* 8 (1), 31–49.

National Commission on Space. (1986). *Pioneering the Space Frontier*. New York: Bantam Books, Inc.

Space Industries. (1987) "Manufacturing Facilities in Space," cited in *The Futurist* 21 (3), 33.

NOTE

1. Adapted from Leslie W. Trowbridge and Rodger W. Bybee, *Becoming a Secondary School Science Teacher*. 5th ed. (Columbus, OH: Prentice Hall/Merrill, 1990), 482–488. By permission of Prentice Hall.

STUDENT BOOKS AND OTHER RESOURCES FOR "AIR, AIRCRAFT, AND SPACE TRAVEL"

Brinks, V. L., and R. L. Brinks. "Taking the Hot Air Out of Balloons." *Science Scope* 17(7):22–24 (April 1994).

Burns, G. "Flight: Floating, Gliding, and Flying." *Creative Classroom* 7(5):44–46, 48, 50 (March 1993).

Fowler, B. "More 'Space' in the Classroom." *Science and Children* 32(1):40–41, 55 (September 1994).

Griffith, E. F. "Go Fly a (Micro) Kite." *Science Scope* 17(7):25–28 (April 1994).

Hanson, K., and L. U. Scott. "A Design for Life . . . In Space!" *Science Scope* 17(1):18–21 (September 1993).

Heiligman, D. *Barbara McClintock: Alone in Her Field*. New York: Scientific American, 1994.

Leyden, M. B. "Teaching Science: Air Pressure 'Eggs-periments.'" *Teaching Pre K–8* 24(6):28–31 (March 1994).

Martirano, M. J. "My Beautiful Balloons." *Science Scope* 17(7):16–20 (April 1994).

———. "Come Fly with Me!" *Science Scope* 18(8):19–21 (May 1995).

Morehouse, P. "The Building of an Airplane (With a Little Help from Friends.)" *Educational Leadership* 52(8):56–57 (May 1995).

Moser, B. *Fly! A Brief History of Flight Illustrated*. New York: HarperCollins, 1993.

Mulane, R. M. *Liftoff! An Astronaut's Dream*. Minneapolis: Carolrhoda, 1994.

Nicholson, J. H. "Children with a Mission." *National Geographic* 186(2):54–69 (August 1994).

Richardson, J. "Scoring Points for Physics." *Science and Scope* 18(4):25–27 (January 1995).

Riss, P. H., and E. C. Niccum. "I've Been Shot by a Rocket." *Science Scope* 17(7):29–32 (April 1994).

Rowley, J. B. "Catch a Rising Star." *Science and Children* 30(4):19–21 (January 1993).

Siebert, D. *Plane Song*. New York: HarperCollins, 1993.

Tanaka, S. *The Disaster of the Hindenburg: The Last Flight of the Greatest Airship Ever Built*. New York: Scholastic, 1993.

LIVING THINGS

*Students in **grades K–4** should develop an understanding of*
- *The characteristics of organisms*
- *Life cycles of organisms*
- *Organisms and environments*
- *Personal health*
- *Characteristics and changes in populations*
- *Types of resources*
- *Changes in environments*
- *Science and technology in local challenges*

*Students in **grades 5–8** should develop an understanding of*
- *Structure and function in living systems*
- *Reproduction and heredity*
- *Regulation and behavior*
- *Populations and ecosystems*
- *Diversity and adaptations of organisms*
- *Personal health*
- *Populations, resources, and environments*
- *Natural hazards*
- *Risks and benefits*
- *Science and technology in society*

CHAPTER 12

Plants

CLASSIFICATION AND COMPOSITION OF LIVING THINGS

I. CLASSIFICATION OF LIVING THINGS

A. All living things, called organisms, are grouped into main divisions, called **kingdoms.** Biologists place organisms into five or six kingdoms. For this book we use a simpler classification: **plants, animals,** and those that are **neither plant nor animal.**

1. Kingdoms are subdivided into very large groups of organisms called **phyla.** The further the phyla are subdivided into smaller groups, the greater the similarity there is among members of each group.

2. Phyla are first subdivided into **classes.** Classes are subdivided into **orders,** orders into **families,** families into **genera** (plural of *genus*), genera into **species,** and species into **varieties** or **hybrids** (see Table 12.1).

3. A species is a group of closely related organisms that can interbreed.

4. A variety or hybrid is an individual of a species that varies slightly from other individuals in the same species, but not enough to be considered a separate species.

5. The "neither plant nor animal" group, discussed in Chapter 13, is divided into several kingdoms:

   a. The **Protista kingdom** (most algae and protozoans), which contains 15 phyla and up to 200,000 species;

   b. The **Monera kingdom** (including blue-green algae and bacteria), comprising 9 phyla and more than 40,000 species;

   c. The **Fungi kingdom,** which includes 4 phyla and approximately 100,000 species; and

   d. The **viruses,** which are not included in any kingdom.

6. The plant kingdom, called the **Metaphytae kingdom,** contains more than 265,000 species and is divided into eight phyla, but for the purposes of this book we divide the plants into simply two groups, the **bryophytes** and the **tracheophytes.**

7. The animal kingdom (Chapter 14), called the **Animalia kingdom,** is divided into 16 phyla and contains more than one million species.

B. When classifying organisms, scientists give each phylum and its subgroups **scientific names** made of Latin words or words that have been Latinized.

1. Because Latin is a universal and unchanging language, the names have the same and continuing meaning to scientists worldwide.

2. This scientific naming makes the classification of organisms definite, so that there can be no duplication.

3. The scientific name describes the organism well enough so that it can be readily identified.

4. The scientific name also helps show relationships between the different organsims.

II. COMPOSITION AND LIFE PROCESSES OF ORGANISMS

A. All organisms have **life cycles** that include being born, developing into adults, reproducing,

TABLE 12.1 Classification Tables for Cocker Spaniel and Red Delicious Apple Tree

Classification of the Cocker Spaniel Dog		*Classification of Red Delicious Apple Tree*	
Kingdom:	Animalia	Kingdom:	Plantae (Metaphytae)
Phylum:	Chordata (have a notochord)	Phylum:	Tracheophyta (have system of tubes)
Subphylum:	Vertebrata (have a backbone)	Class:	Angiospermae (flowering plants with seeds inside the fruits)
Class:	Mammalia (are mammals)		
Order:	Carnivora (the flesh-eating mammals)	Subclass:	Dicotyledoneae (seeds have two cotyledons)
Family:	Canidae (including the foxes and the wolves)	Order:	Rosales (roses and their relatives)
		Family:	Rosaceae (produce roselike flowers)
Genus:	Canis (includes the wolf, coyote, and dog)	Genus:	Pyrus (produce apple fruits)
		Species:	malus (cultivated apple trees)
Species:	familiaris (domestic dog)	Variety:	Red Delicious
Variety:	Cocker Spaniel		

and dying. The details of this life cycle vary for different organisms.

B. The basic unit of structure and function for all organisms is the **cell.** This is known as the **cell theory.** The cell theory consists of three main ideas.

1. All organisms are composed of one or more cells.
2. The cell is the basic unit of organization of organisms.
3. All cells come from preexisting cells.

C. Depending on their internal organization, cells are of two types—prokaryotic and eukaryotic.

1. A **prokaryote** is an organism with a cell that lacks internal structures surrounded by membranes. Most prokaryotes are single-celled (unicellular) organisms.
2. A **eukaryote** is an organism that has cells containing internal membrane-bound structures, called **organelles.** The largest organelle is a membrane-bound **nucleus,** which contains the cell's DNA and manages the cell's functions. Eukaryotes are either unicellular or made of many cells (multicellular).

D. All cells have an external boundary, called the **cell** (or **plasma**) **membrane,** which separates the cell from its external environment.

1. This cell membrane controls what enters and exits the cell.
2. Food and oxygen needed by the cell enter the cell through this membrane.
3. Carbon dioxide and waste materials exit the cell through this membrane.

E. In addition to the cell membrane, some cells have an outer rigid protective covering called the **cell wall.** It is made of different substances in different organisms. The cells of plants, fungi, most bacteria, and some protists have cell walls. Animal cells do not have cell walls.

F. The activities of a cell are controlled by the **nucleus.** Although often found in its center, the nucleus may be anywhere inside the cell.

1. The nucleus is surrounded and held together by a **nuclear membrane,** which controls what materials enter and leave the nucleus.
2. The nucleus contains the cell's genetic material, called **deoxyribonucleic acid (DNA).**

G. The fluid part of the cell outside the nucleus and inside the cell membrane is called **cytoplasm** (meaning cell fluid), whereas the fluid part of the nucleus is called the **nucleoplasm.**

1. The cytoplasm of eukaryotes contains many specialized structures called **organelles.** Each organelle has a role in the cell's functions.
2. Much of the cytoplasm is occupied by a folded system of interconnected membranes, called the **endoplasmic reticulum (ER).**
3. This system of membranes provides a large surface area on which chemical reactions can take place. For example, the ER contains the enzymes for almost all of the cell's lipid (fats and oils) synthesis, so they serve as the site of lipid synthesis in the cell.
4. Some of the ER is coated with **ribosomes,** which are the sites of protein synthesis. In some cells, ribosomes may also be found free in the cytoplasm.
5. **Vacuoles**—sacs of fluid surrounded by a membrane—store food, enzymes, water, and other materials needed by the cell, and, in

DEMONSTRATION 12.1
Examine Plant Cells

Slice an onion into rings. Discard the first two outer layers. Tear off the thinnest possible piece of skin from the third layer. Have students place a portion of this skin on a microscope slide, add a drop of water and a drop of tincture of iodine, and cover with a cover glass. Soak up any excess liquid by placing the tip of a blotter against the edges of the cover glass. The iodine stains the onion cells and makes them stand out very clearly. Examine the onion cells under the microscope. The tip of the aquarium plant elodea can also be used to observe plant cells.

some instances, vacuoles store waste products.

6. Cytoplasm contains many other structures, each with important cellular functions, such as **mitochondria** (which play an important role in cellular respiration, including the generation of energy from the breakdown of food) and **chloroplasts**—in plant cells only (which play an important role in photosynthesis).

H. Not all cells are alike.
   1. Many cells, especially those in the more complex plants and animals, have special functions. Consequently, they differ in size, shape, and cellular makeup.
   2. In more complex animals, examples of specialized cells are bone, muscle, and red blood cells; in more complex plants, examples of specialized cells are root tip cells and cambium cells.

I. A group of cells that work together for the same function are called a **tissue.**
   1. Examples of human tissues include muscle and nerve.
   2. Examples of tissues in trees are those of the stem and root.

J. A group of two or more tissues working together for a common function make up what is called an **organ.**
   1. Examples of human organs are the skin, heart, and brain. The skin, for example, contains more than one kind of tissue: connective and nervous.
   2. Examples of organs of a tree are root, stem, and leaf. The stem, for example, contains more than one kind of tissue: xylem, phloem, and cambium.

K. A group of organs that work together for a common function are called an **organ system.**
   1. An organ system in humans, for example, is the digestive system, which includes several organs: the esophagus, stomach, liver, and intestines.

   2. The flower is an example of an organ system in some plants. It contains organs necessary for reproduction and other organs that are necessary for transport of materials from one part of the plant to another.

L. Systems working together make up an organism.
   1. **Ecology** is the study of organisms in their environment.

M. Cells exhibit the characteristic activities of life.
   1. These activities are called **life processes.**
   2. Life processes specific to plants include photosynthesis, transpiration, respiration, digestion, circulation, assimilation, growth, excretion, reproduction, and tropisms.
   3. Disease can cause a breakdown in one or more of the life processes. Some diseases are the result of intrinsic failures of the system, whereas others are caused by infection by other organisms.

N. **Cellular respiration** is the breakdown of molecules of food to release energy used for building new cells.
   1. Cellular respiration is a biochemical process; it should not be confused with the mechanical process that occurs in animals, called breathing.
   2. Cellular respiration is generally represented as the breakdown of carbohydrates into water and carbon dioxide. Some of the energy released during this process is captured by the cell in a molecule called **adenosine triphosphate (ATP).**
   3. The water and carbon dioxide are released by the cell as waste products, and the captured energy is used to carry on the activities of assimilation (building and repair of cells) and other processes (e.g., movement and osmosis).

O. **Digestion** is the mechanical and biochemical breakdown of food into molecules small enough for the body to absorb. These molecules are then used for cellular respiration and assimilation.

1. Plants, like animals, digest their food so that it can be absorbed by the cells.
2. In the more complex plants, such as trees and flowering plants, the food is broken up into smaller molecules and then dissolved in the plant fluid, which is called **sap,** and transported through the plant to the various cells where it is used to build new cells.
3. In higher plants, digestion takes place mostly in the leaf.

P. **Assimilation** is the process of using the products of digestion and the energy released from respiration to build new cells (growth) and to repair others (maintenance).

Q. At the cellular level, **excretion** is the process of eliminating waste products, and it usually takes place as these substances are collected in vacuoles.

1. In some unicellular organisms, a specialized vacuole collects excess water and pumps it out of the cell. A plant cell has a single large vacuole that stores water and other substances.
2. Some waste products are expelled from cells by **exocytosis** when vesicles or vacuoles fuse with the cell membranes and their contents are released outside the cell. Exocytosis is also the method used by cells to secrete substances produced by the cell, such as hormones. (Exocytosis is the opposite of **endocytosis.** Endocytosis is a process in which a cell surrounds and takes in material from its environment. Instead of passing directly through the cell membrane, the material is engulfed and enclosed by a portion of the cell's membrane. That portion of the membrane then breaks away, and the resulting vacuole with its contents moves to the inside of the cell. Both endocytosis and exocytosis require energy and are therefore called **active transport** processes. Some substances, such as water and lipids, can pass directly through cell membranes by diffusion, and because the cell expends no energy for this to occur, it is referred to as **passive transport.** Active transport is an important means for the cell to expel or take in large molecules or substances that, for one reason or another, cannot pass through the cell membrane by simple diffusion.)

R. **Motion** is the process of movement, either from one place to another or within a stationary location. Examples of the first include humans walking, fish swimming, birds flying, and protozoans swimming. Many other organisms move without changing location. Leaves of plants move during the day with respect to the sun's location. Although sea anemones become stationary as adults, they still move their tentacles in search of food, and when food is found the tentacles bring it to their mouth openings.

1. Although plants cannot move from place to place, as many animals and protists do, they can and do move. When an organism is affected by such things as light, water, heat, or gravity, it responds by moving either toward or away from the stimulus. This movement is called a **tropism.** If the movement is toward the stimulus, it is called a **positive tropism.** If the organism moves away from the stimulus, the movement is called a **negative tropism.**
2. The response of an organism to light is called **phototropism.** Leaves and stems move toward light, a positive tropism, whereas roots move away from light, a negative tropism. The movement of a stem toward light is due to a more rapid growth of cells on the side of the stem that is away from the light source.
3. The response of an organism to gravity is called **geotropism.** Roots grow downward because of the pull of gravity, and this movement is a positive geotropism. Primary stems grow upward against the pull of gravity. This movement is a negative geotropism.
4. The response of organisms to water is called **hydrotropism.** Roots turn in any direction toward water. They even grow upward against the force of gravity because of this strong hydrotropism.
5. The response of organisms to touch is called **thigmatropism.** The Venus flytrap has a leaf that quickly folds in half when touched by a fly or other insect. This is an example of thigmatropism. The leaves of the mimosa plant turn away from a tactile stimulus. As the result of thigmatropism, some vines, peas, and other climbing plants curl around any firm support.
6. The response of organisms to heat is called **thermotropism.** The leaves of certain plants, like the mimosa, turn away from strong heat.
7. The response of organisms to chemicals is called **chemotropism.** Most roots turn toward soil that has a good supply of the minerals that the plant needs.

S. **Reproduction** is the process of creating new individuals from existing ones.

DEMONSTRATION 12.2
Tropisms

A. Hydrotropism

Cut off one side of a waxed carton, such as a milk carton, to make a trough for holding soil. Cut a rectangular
hole from another side of the carton and tape a piece of
glass or some clear plastic wrap over the hole on the inside of the carton to produce a window (Figure 12.1).
Punch a few holes in the bottom of the carton for drainage,
cover the holes with flat rocks, and fill the carton with soil.
Get some lima beans from a seed store and place them
2 or 5 centimeters (1 or 2 in) in the soil beside the plastic wrap so that their germination and root growth will be
visible. Place the carton in a shallow pan and water the
soil regularly until the beans have germinated into growing plants. Now water the soil at one end of the carton
only. In a week or two you will see the roots turned toward the direction of the water.

B. Climbing Plants Twist in a Counterclockwise Direction

Grow two twining plants, such as a morning glory or a
pole bean plant. Insert a long, thin, round stick or dowel
into each of the pots for the plants to twine around.
Allow only one tendril in each plant to twine around the
stick. The tendrils will twine in a counterclockwise direction. Try twining one of the tendrils around the stick
in a clockwise direction. In a few hours the tendril will
unwind itself.

C. Plants Sensitive to Touch and Heat

Obtain some mimosa seeds from a seed order house, a
scientific supply house, or from someone that teaches in
the South. Plant the seeds and cultivate them until they
grow 15 centimeters (6 in) high. Now pinch one of the top
leaves, or stroke it gently a few times. The leaf will droop
and will not regain its original shape for several hours.

Next, strike a match and let it burn for a second or two.
Blow out the match and touch one of the leaves with the
warm tip of the match. The leaf will droop and will not regain its original shape for several hours.

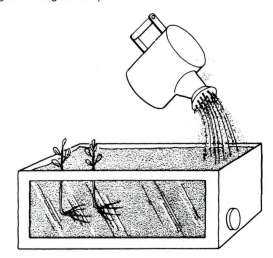

FIGURE 12.1   Roots turn toward water.

1. At the cellular level this process is usually
   done by cell division.
T. All cells experience a cycle of growth and division. This cycle is called the **cell cycle.**
   1. The growth period of the cell cycle is
      known as the **interphase,** during which
      time the cell grows in size, makes ATP, car-
      ries on metabolism, gets rid of wastes, and
      duplicates its chromosomes in preparation
      for the period of cell division.
   2. Following interphase, the cell enters its pe-
      riod of **cell division,** in which its nucleus
      and then its cytoplasm divide to form two
      daughter cells, each containing a complete
      set of chromosomes. The process of nuclear
      division followed by division of the cyto-

plasm, when chromosomes are distributed
equally to daughter cells, is known as **mitosis.**
3. Interphase and mitosis together make up
   the cell cycle (see Figure 12.2).
4. In cell division, the cell divides to form two
   daughter cells, each exactly like the original
   parent cell.
5. This process involves four phases or stages:
   the prophase, metaphase, anaphase, and
   telophase.
6. **Prophase** is the visible beginning and
   longest lasting phase of mitosis. During
   prophase, the long stringy chromosome material (called chromatin) coils up into visible chromosomes, which were duplicated

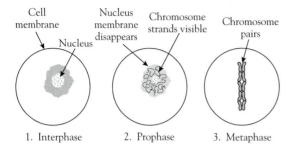

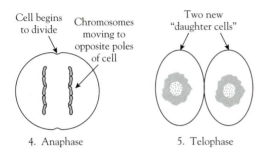

FIGURE 12.2   Mitosis, or cell division.

during interphase. Each duplicated chromosome is made up of two halves, called **sister chromatids.** Sister chromatids and the DNA they contain are exact copies of each other and are formed when DNA is copied during interphase. The sister chromatids are held together by a structure called a **centromere.**

7. **Metaphase** is characterized by the alignment of the chromosomes in the center of the cell.

8. **Anaphase** is characterized by the separation of sister chromatids toward opposite poles of the cell.

9. The fourth and final stage of mitosis is **telophase.** It is characterized by the formation of nuclear membranes around the two new daughter nuclei and the division of the original parent cytoplasm. Each daughter cell has its own cell membrane and the same number of chromosomes as in the original parent cell.

10. In plants, division of the cell cytoplasm usually begins when membrane vesicles fuse to form an equatorial plate, whereas in animals division of the cell cytoplasm is usually by formation of a cleavage furrow, which constricts the cell around the outside cell membrane and pinches it in two.

11. The **resting stage** (or **interphase**) of the cell cycle is between telophase and the beginning of the next prophase. Although chromosomes are not visible during interphase, it is during interphase that duplication of DNA in the chromosomes takes place.

U. Cell division, as described earlier, involves one parent cell giving rise to two new daughter cells. This type of reproduction is **asexual;** that is, it does not involve the union of cells but simply the division of a cell into two new ones. Another type of reproduction involves the union of cells to create a new individual. This is called **sexual reproduction.** Important to sexual reproduction is a unique process of cell division called **meiosis.**

1. It is through meiosis that sex cells, or **gametes**—egg and sperm cells—are produced.

2. Meiosis occurs in specialized body cells that produce gametes.

3. Meiosis consists of two separate divisions, called meiosis I and meiosis II. Meiosis I begins with one cell with the normal (called **diploid**) chromosome number. But by the end of meiosis II, there are four cells, each with one half of the original chromosome number (called **haploid** cells).

4. In animals and most plants, these haploid cells are called sex cells, or gametes.

5. When gametes unite, in a process called **fertilization,** the cell that results from their union, called a **zygote,** is diploid (2N); that is, it has the same chromosome number as the original parent cells. In humans, for example, the diploid chromosome number is 46, but when meiosis occurs, each daughter cell receives only 23 chromosomes. This is referred to as the haploid or 1N number. When the egg and sperm unite, the 46 chromosomes (diploid number) characteristic of humans is maintained.

6. Mitotic cell division is the process by which organisms increase their number of cells for growth, healing, and maintenance.

7. Mitotic cell division is also the asexual method used to produce new organisms, such as in **budding,** which occurs both in plants and in some animals.

8. An unusually rapid rate of mitotic cell division can cause an enlargment of tissue, a **tumor,** which occurs in plants as well as animals. These abnormal growths in plants may be caused by the action of viruses, bacteria, or chemicals produced by insects that live in the plant's tissues.

THE PLANT KINGDOM

I. THE PLANT KINGDOM, SCIENTIFICALLY CALLED THE PLANTAE KINGDOM OR METAPHYTAE KINGDOM, IS DIVIDED INTO AS MANY AS 10 DIVISIONS OR PHYLA:

Bryophyta, the mosses and liverworts
Psilophyta, the whisk ferns
Lycophyta, the club mosses
Sphenophyta, the horsetails
Pterophyta, the ferns
Cycadophyta, the cydads
Gnetophyta, certain highly specialized trees, shrubs, and climbing vines

Ginkgophyta, with only one living species, *Ginkgo biloba.*
Coniferophyta, the conifers
Anthophyta, the flowering plants

A. Members of the plant kingdom have chlorophyll and manufacture their own food by photosynthesis; that is, they are **autotrophic.**

B. The plant kingdom can be divided into two broad groups: the plants that have no vascular tissue (vessels for transport)—the **bryophytes,** and plants that do have vascular tissue—the **tracheophytes.**

THE BRYOPHYTES

I. THE BRYOPHYTES ARE MEMBERS OF THE PLANT PHYLUM BRYOPHYTA THAT INCLUDES THE MOSSES AND LIVERWORTS. (LIVERWORTS ARE ALSO KNOWN AS HEPATICS BECAUSE OF THEIR LIVER-SHAPED LEAF STRUCTURES.)

A. Members of the Bryophyta have simple leaves (that is, without the transport system of the tracheophytes), and although they do have rootlike and stemlike parts, again, these are without the complex transportation system of tissues (xylem and phloem) of the tracheophytes.

B. Bryophytes do not produce flowers, fruits, or seeds.

C. Bryophytes reproduce both sexually (by the union of gametes) and asexually (by the production of spores).

1. In mosses, spores are produced in tall structures called the spore capsules. These usually extend high above the miniature leaves of the moss.

2. Liverwort spores are produced in capsules that resemble little pits in their "leaves."

D. Bryophytes are small but ubiquitous plants; that is, they are found all over the world, although always on land areas and where it is damp with fresh water.

1. There are no marine (saltwater) bryophyte species, and very few that are aquatic. (Green, slimy plants frequently found growing on rocks in streams or along ocean shores are algae, not bryophytes.)

2. Mosses commonly grow in sidewalk cracks, on wood shingle roofs that stay moist, on the sides of trees (especially the northernmost sides, which remain moist because they get less direct sunlight), on the soil and clay pots of damp greenhouses, and on soil that remains moist much of the time.

E. Liverworts are flat, with broader "leaves." They are commonly found on the soil of moist and seldom-used pathways.

F. The term *moss* is frequently used incorrectly for plants that have no affiliation with a true bryophyte.

1. Some plants are referred to incorrectly as moss. Spanish moss, for example, is actually a member of the pineapple family of tracheophytes. The mossback turtle is one with an alga, not a moss, growing on its carapace. Mossy-looking plants that hang from the limbs of trees in forests are more likely lichens. A lichen is a plant that combines an alga and a fungus growing together in a symbiotic relationship.

G. Moss plants have cells that are capable of retaining large amounts of water. For that reason, **sphagnum moss** (peat moss) is used by plant nurseries for wrapping the roots of trees and shrubs for transplanting.

1. Sphagnum moss grows in small lakes and ponds. It forms floating masses that eventually cover the water and form a **bog.**

2. The bog may thicken, as grass, shrubs, and small trees become established and grow in it. Eventually the bog becomes solid land.

3. Sphagnum moss, and perhaps other bryophytes as well, have an antibiotic property. In certain cases, a moss wrapped around an injury can both absorb fluids from the injury and speed up the healing process.

H. Bryophytes play an important role in making soil. Like lichens, bryophytes can grow in areas that have very little soil or minerals, and where more complex plants cannot become established. The metabolic activity of bryophytes (and lichens) growing on rock begins the breakdown of the rock into what ultimately will become soil.

1. Because they can grow where more complex plants cannot, bryophtes are among the first organisms to inhabit an area that was devastated of plant life by fire or volcanic activity. They are important in initiating the rebuilding of the habitat that was destroyed. Bryophytes and other simple plants help to make and bind the soil so that larger and more complex plants can establish themselves and continue the process of rebuilding.

I. Bryophytes are of special interest to botanists, cellular biologists, and geneticists. In bryophytes the dominant generation (that is, for example, the moss plant that we are familiar with, that we see growing on a tree or ground) is the gamete-producing generation (known as the **gametophyte**). It is the generation with the **haploid** (1N) chromosome number in each cell. (Refer to p. 429). However, in humans, other animals, flowering plants, trees, and other tracheophytes, the dominant generation is that with the **diploid** (2N) chromosome number in its cells. (When referring to plants, the diploid generation is referred to as the **sporophyte.**)

1. Sex cells (called **gametes** which are the egg or sperm cells) always have the haploid (1N) number.
2. Cells of the bryophyte plant that we see growing and are familiar with are haploid.
3. Where the dominant generation in bryophytes is the gametophyte (the haploid or 1N generation), in higher plants and animals the dominant generation is sporophyte (the diploid or 2N generation).

The Tracheophytes: Vascular Plants

I. THE TRACHEOPHYTES ARE PLANTS THAT CONTAIN VASCULAR TISSUE IN THEIR ROOTS, STEMS, AND LEAVES.

A. Tracheophytes have vascular tissue, in which cells are specialized for the transport of materials throughout the organism. Tracheophytes have a continuous system of tubes running through their roots, stems, and leaves, hence the name *tracheo* (tube) *phyte* (plant).

B. They usually have chlorophyll and are green in color. Most are **autotrophic;** that is, they can make their own food. (In the course of their evolution, a few species have lost their ability to manufacture food and thus have become parasitic to other plants.)

C. The tracheophytes are divided into two groups: those that have seeds and those that do not.

D. Ferns, horsetails, and club mosses are tracheophytes, and although they have roots, stems, and leaves, they have no flowers, fruits, or seeds.

E. Unlike that of bryophytes, the dominant generation of the reproductive cycle of tracheophytes is diploid in chromosome number. It is the plant organism we see and is the sporophyte rather than the gametophyte generation.

F. Seed plants, which produce flowers, fruits, and seeds, include all trees, shrubs, crop plants and vegetables, garden and wild flowers, and grasses.

1. Seed plants grow in soil and in fresh water.
2. The smallest seed plants are floating duckweeds, which grow in ponds and slow-moving streams. They are about 1 centimeter (0.3 in) across.
3. The largest are the giant sequoias and the redwoods of California, which can be more than 90 meters (300 ft) tall.

G. Depending on whether their seeds are covered or unprotected, scientists divide seed plants into two groups. **Angiosperms** have seed coverings. **Gymnosperms,** which means "naked seed," are those without seed coverings.

1. The seeds of angiosperms are enclosed in a protective coat, called a fruit. The seeds of gymnosperms are unprotected.

H. In evolutionary history, gymnosperms are older seed plants than the angiosperms.

1. They are also called **conifers,** because they produce woody cones.
2. Examples of conifers include pine, spruce, fir, cedar, bald cypress, redwood, hemlock, yew, and larch trees.
3. The cone, the "fruit" of the conifers, is made up of scales, wherein lie the "naked" or unprotected seeds.
4. Conifer leaves are in the form of either needles or flat scales.

5. Conifers keep their needles or scales for two to five years. The bald cypress and larch trees are exceptions because they lose their needles each autumn.

6. Because their "leaves" stay green all winter, conifers are also called evergreen trees.

7. When new needles or scales grow, they appear in the spring.

8. The trunk of a conifer does not divide. It grows tall and straight, and most of the branches are usually found nearer the top of the trunk.

9. Characteristic of conifers is a sticky substance they produce called **resin.**

10. The wood of conifers is usually soft. It is widely used for lumber and making paper.

11. Conifers, planted in particular locations, are also used to stop the force of the wind around farms. In addition, they are used as decorative trees in parks and yards.

I. Angiosperms are seed plants that produce flowers that form fruits with seeds. They include all garden and wild flowers, plants that produce crops and vegetables, grasses, cereal grains, and trees and shrubs that lose their leaves in the autumn.

1. Angiosperms have broad, flat leaves, which most species lose each year. For this reason they are called **deciduous** (from the Latin *decidere*, "to fall off") plants, rather than evergreens.

2. Angiosperm trees have a main trunk that may divide in two. Branching begins rather low on the trunk.

3. Depending on the nature of their seed coverings, the angiosperms are divided into two groups: the monocotyledons (meaning one cotyledon), or **monocots,** and the dicotyledons (meaning two cotyledons), or **dicots.**

4. A **cotyledon** is a special kind of leaf found in the seed. It contains stored food that nourishes the tiny embryo plant inside the seed when the seed sprouts and grows into a new plant. Monocotyledon plants produce seeds that have just one leaf, and dicotyledon plants produce seeds with two seed leaves.

5. Most of the monocotyledons are relatively small plants. They include the lily, tulip, iris, onion, grasses and the cereal grains, and coconut and date palms.

6. The dicotyledons include most flowers, vegetables, shrubs, and flowering trees.

J. Botanists also divide plants into two broad groups: **herbaceous,** or weedy, and **woody** plants.

1. A herbaceous plant is any plant with a soft stem. The stem may or may not be green.

2. This soft stem lasts for only one growing season and then dies to the ground.

3. Flowers, garden vegetables, grasses, and the cereal grains are all herbaceous plants.

4. A woody plant has a hard stem, usually colored brown when it gets older.

5. This hard stem does not die at the end of a season. It continues year after year, growing both longer and wider each year.

6. Examples of woody plants include trees, shrubs, and such vines as the wild grape and poison ivy.

K. The major parts of a flowering seed plant include the root, stem, leaves, and flowers. Each part has special functions (discussed later in this chapter).

FERNS, HORSETAILS, AND CLUB MOSSES

I. THE NATURE OF FERNS, HORSETAILS, AND CLUB MOSSES

A. Ferns, horsetails, and club mosses are vascular plants (tracheophytes) without seeds. Their size ranges from that of small moss-sized plants to that of a good-sized tree.

1. Although they all have true roots, stems, and leaves, they do not produce flowers, fruits, or seeds.

2. They are mostly land plants and grow best in cool, damp, shaded places where the soil is rich in humus.

3. Some grow in the cracks of rocks and cliffs, and others grow in fields and open woods.

4. They all have chlorophyll, are colored green, and are autotrophic.

II. FERNS

A. Ferns were very numerous millions of years ago, forming large forests in the wet and marshy land that was common at that time.

1. Giant ferns as large as trees were quite common.

2. Smaller ferns, much like those found today, also lived during that period.

3. Today tree ferns are found only in the tropics, where they can be as much as 15 meters (49 ft) tall with leaves 4 meters (13 ft) long.

4. Ferns are much smaller in the temperate zones.

B. The stems of ferns are underground, growing horizontally just below the surface.
   1. Such underground stems are called **rhizomes.**
   2. Each year these stems put up new leaves.
   3. Fine roots also grow from these stems.

C. In most ferns, the leaves, sometimes called **fronds,** are the only parts of the plant that appear above the ground.
   1. They are called "compound" leaves because they have many tiny leaflets arranged along one main vein, called the **midrib.**
   2. The veins of fern leaves are forked, a characteristic of ferns.
   3. When the leaves appear in the spring, they are rolled up tight and are covered with a hairy growth at their base. This hairy covering is lost when the leaves unroll.

D. Ferns go through a reproductive cycle, having both a spore stage and a sexual stage.
   1. When the fern leaves are fully grown, spore cases form on their underside.
   2. There are many tiny spores in each spore case.
   3. When the spores become ripe, the spore case bursts open, and the spores are carried away by the wind, water, or animals.
   4. When a spore falls on a moist place where conditions are right for growth, the spore develops into a threadlike chain or filament of cells.
   5. This chain or filament thickens and then broadens at the tip, which becomes a flat, heart-shaped green body, called a **prothallus,** that is notched on its upper side.
   6. On its underside the prothallus has hairlike threads, called **rhizoids,** similar to the rootlike hairs of mosses and liverworts. The prothallus stage of the fern's life cycle is physically (in appearance) reminiscent of mosses.
   7. The rhizoids hold the prothallus to the ground and absorb moisture from the soil.
   8. Male sexual organs, each containing several sperm cells, develop among the rhizoids.
   9. Female sexual organs, each containing one egg cell, develop on the underside of the prothallus near the notch.
   10. When the male organ is fully grown, it opens up and allows the sperm cells to escape.
   11. The sperm cells swim to the female organs after a rain or when the plant is covered with dew.
   12. A sperm cell enters a female organ and unites with the egg to form a fertilized egg, called a **zygote.**
   13. The zygote then grows into a fern plant with roots, stem, and leaves.

E. Ferns can also reproduce asexually.
   1. The leaves of some ferns form tiny buds, which break off and form new ferns.
   2. Some ferns can form new ferns from their leaves if the leaves bend down and touch the ground. When the tip of the leaf touches the ground, roots form at the tip. These roots then develop stems and leaves to become a new fern plant. The tip of the leaf dies, which separates the new plant from the parent plant.

F. Many ferns are used to make Christmas wreaths and flower arrangements.

G. Coal comes from the ferns that lived and died millions of years ago. Large masses of dead ferns accumulated in layers in the swampy areas where they grew; these layers turned into coal under the influence of great heat and pressure that were produced by strong upheavals and movements of the earth's crust.

III. HORSETAILS AND CLUB MOSSES

A. Horsetails and club mosses are similar to ferns, especially in the way they reproduce.

B. Also like ferns, they were very numerous millions of years ago.
   1. At that time they were the size of trees.
   2. Most of them are now extinct, and their remains can be seen as leaf and stem imprints.

C. They have horizontal stems, underground for horsetails and just above or below the ground for club mosses, and upright branches grow from these stems.
   1. Some of their upright branches have bushy side branches.
   2. Other upright branches produce spores in cones that develop at their tips. There are small scalelike leaves in a circular pattern farther down the branches below the cones.

D. There is only one living group of horsetails today, but they can be found nearly everywhere, especially in wet places such as drainage ditches and at the edges of lakes, ponds, and bogs.

E. Club mosses are small, low-growing evergreen plants.

1. They grow on the ground in temperate regions, and on tree trunks in tropical regions.
2. They grow best in damp places.
3. Their upright branches look like the leaves of fir and spruce trees.
4. They produce spores in cones (some of which are club-shaped) that grow at the tip of some of their branches.
5. Because some club mosses are dainty and beautiful, they are commonly used in making Christmas decorations and other ornamental arrangements.

ROOTS

I. DEFINITION AND KINDS OF ROOTS AND ROOT SYSTEMS

A. Roots are the part of a plant that anchors the plant by growing downward and outward in the ground.
   1. When a seed first begins to grow, the first root, called the **primary root,** grows rapidly and pushes its way into the soil.
   2. After a while, **secondary roots** branch out from the primary root, first near the top of the primary root and then farther down. The carrot is a good example.
   3. The roots keep branching and rebranching until a complete root system is formed.

B. There are two main kinds of root systems: the **taproot system** (like that of a carrot or dandelion) and the **diffuse root system** (like that of corn or grass).
   1. In the taproot system, the primary root (the taproot) grows until it is the largest root in the root system. Smaller secondary roots grow from this large taproot.
   2. In the diffuse root system, the primary root lives only for a short time, while the secondary roots continue to grow as a cluster at the base of the stem. All of these secondary roots are thin, have the same size, and are called **fibrous roots.** Dahlias and sweet potatoes are examples of plants with fleshy fibrous roots.
   3. Some taproots and fibrous roots become quite large, because of stored food, and are called **fleshy roots.** Beets, carrots, and radishes are examples.

C. In some plants, roots grow from the stems or leaves of the plant; these are called **adventitious roots.**
   1. Tomato, cucumber, potato, and squash plants have adventitious roots.
   2. Leaves of the begonia, sedum, and sansevieria plants form adventitious roots when placed in soil.
   3. Some plants send out roots from their stems just above the ground. These roots are a special kind of adventitious root, called **prop roots** (as they help to prop or hold up the plant) or **brace roots.** They grow into the ground and help hold the plant upright. The corn plant is an example.
   4. Climbing plants, such as English ivy, poison ivy, and tropical orchids, send out roots from their stems. These roots are another special kind of adventitious root, called **aerial roots.** Aerial roots grow in the air, clinging to a wall or tree and hold the stem firmly in place.

II. THE STRUCTURE AND GROWTH OF A ROOT

A. A short distance behind the tip of each root are many tiny, nearly microscopic, delicate **root hairs,** which add immensely to the total surface area of the root system.
   1. In addition to helping to anchor the plant, by adding to the total surface area of the root system root hairs play a major role in absorbing water and dissolved minerals from the soil.
   2. As the root grows in the soil, new root hairs form near the tip, while the older root hairs wither and die.

B. At the tip of the root is the **root cap,** which not only protects the delicate end of the root but also contains most of the cells that, by dividing (mitotic cell division), add length and width to the root.
   1. The primary growth of a root occurs within this root cap.
   2. Although other root cells may grow in size, it is from the cell division within the root cap that new cells are added.

C. The length of a root varies, depending on the species of plant and the conditions of the environment. For example, the taproot of the

DEMONSTRATION 12.3
Young Roots

Soak some radish seeds overnight. Put a dark-colored blotter on the bottom of a large saucer. Wet the blotter thoroughly with water, but do not have any excess water on the blotter. Scatter the seeds on the wet blotter and cover the saucer with a square, flat glass plate. Place the saucer in a darkened part of the room. The radish seeds will germinate in two or three days. Keep the blotter moist constantly. Examine the seeds each day. Note the primary root that grows directly from the seed, and the secondary roots that branch out from the primary root. Using hand lenses, have the students look closely at the fuzzy outgrowths at the tips of the primary and secondary roots. These are the root hairs, which absorb water and dissolved minerals from the soil.

DEMONSTRATION 12.4
Taproot and Diffuse Root Systems

Dig up a dandelion from a yard,—get the complete root if possible. Also dig up a small clump of grass. Show students the long taproot of the dandelion and the many shorter diffuse roots of the clump of grass.

---

mesquite plant can grow 12 meters (40 ft) down into the desert sand to reach a water supply, but the diffuse roots of a cactus plant cover large areas just beneath the surface of the ground to absorb quickly the water from infrequent rains. Roots of the eggplant and squash grow downward about 2 meters (7 ft) and then spread sideways from 1 to 6 meters (3 to 20 ft).
  D. To say that roots grow *down* is incorrect.
    1. Although it is true that roots tend to grow toward gravity, their primary response is to grow toward water. In other words, a root's positive hydrotropism (movement toward water) is stronger than its positive geotropism (movement toward gravity).
  E. A root grows toward water because of the biochemical reactions taking place inside the root cells that cause cells of one side of the root to divide and to grow faster than cells on the other side of the root. Thus, the root bends toward or away from something.
    1. Because of a root's positive hydrotropism, the cells on the side away from the water source divide and grow faster than those on the side closest to the water source, thus bending the root toward the water.
    2. The same cause-and-effect relationship applies to the movements of stems, leaves, and flowers.

III. THE FUNCTIONS OF ROOTS

  A. Roots absorb water and dissolved minerals from the soil, sending these materials to the stem and leaves.
    1. The water and dissolved minerals are absorbed by the root hairs.
    2. Root hairs give off an acid that helps dissolve minerals in the soil.
  B. Roots also help to anchor the plant.
  C. Through a history of genetic adaptation, roots of different species of plants have become specialized to the conditions of their environments.
    1. Some roots, such as the beet, carrot, and sweet potato store food for the plant.
    2. By asexual reproduction (rather than union of gametes) some roots, such as those of the sweet potato and dahlia, can produce new plants.

IV. USE OF ROOTS BY HUMANS

  A. Some roots, such as the carrot, turnip, parsnip, radish, beet, and sweet potato, are used for food.
  B. Some roots, such as the horseradish, are used for food seasoning.
  C. Some roots, such as sassafras, ginger, licorice, and mandrake, are used for making medicines.
  D. Some roots, such as licorice and ginger, are used in making candy.
  E. The roots of the madder and yellowwood trees are used to make dyes.

STEMS

I. DEFINITION AND KINDS OF STEMS

A. A stem of a plant is the part of the plant located between the roots and the leaves.
   1. Stems may be found above the ground, below the ground, or both above and below the ground.
   2. The trunk of a tree is actually the stem of the plant.
   3. The trunk of the palm tree is an example of a giant monocotyledon stem; the trunk of the oak or the elm tree is an example of a large dicotyledon stem.
   4. Some stems are woody, and others are herbaceous (weedy).
   5. **Herbaceous stems** are usually soft and green. As they grow, they become longer, but not thicker, and they live for only one season. The stems of tomatoes, beans, peas, corn, grasses, and most annual flowers are herbaceous stems.
   6. **Woody stems** are brown and stiff and have woody tissue (stem tissue that contains dead and hardened cells). As they grow, they become both longer and thicker and form branches; they live season after season. The stems of trees and most shrubs are woody stems.

B. A stem that grows above the ground is called an **aerial stem.** Aerial stems vary in length, ranging from less than 2 centimeters (1 in) to more than 30 meters (98 ft).
   1. There are four main groups of aerial stems: shortened stems, creeping stems, climbing stems, and erect stems.
   2. **Shortened stems** are very short stems, sometimes so short that they seem to be missing from the plant. Dandelion, primrose, and carrot all have shortened stems. Their very short, flat, circular stems can be seen growing just above the roots. Plants with shortened stems need open places to grow, where they can get lots of light.
   3. **Creeping stems,** also called runners or stolons, are long and slender and stay close to the ground, as exemplified by strawberry and bent grass. These stems do not have woody tissues and are weak, so they grow along the surface of the ground. Plants with creeping stems also need open places to grow, where they can get lots of light.
   4. **Climbing stems** are thin and very long, as exemplified by ivy, morning glory, and sweet

potato. They do not have woody tissues and are weak, so they grow by wrapping themselves around a tall object.
   5. **Erect stems** stand above the ground by themselves, tall and erect, as exemplified by trees, shrubs, and many garden flowers. They may be either a few centimeters tall or very many meters high, and they may be either herbaceous or woody.

C. A stem that grows below the ground is called an **underground stem.** Because they are located underground, most persons do not usually think of them as stems.
   1. There are four main groups of underground stems: rhizomes, tubers, bulbs, and corms.
   2. **Rhizomes** are long underground stems that grow horizontally, close to the surface of the ground. Some rhizomes are thick and fleshy and filled with food. Examples are the rhizomes of the iris, the lily of the valley, and the trillium. Other rhizomes are thin, such as those of the grasses.
   3. **Tubers** are the enlarged tips of rhizomes, with food stored in them, such as the white potato. The "eyes" of the potato are really buds on the stem from which new growth develops.
   4. A **bulb** is made up of a stem shortened to the size of a disk, surrounded by thick, fleshy, scalelike leaves that have food stored in them, as exemplified by the hyacinth, tulip, daffodil, and onion.
   5. A **corm** is different from a bulb only in that most of it is stem surrounded by thin scalelike leaves, as exemplified by the crocus and gladiolus.

II. STRUCTURE AND GROWTH OF STEMS

A. The bare winter branch of a tree is an excellent example of a woody stem.
   1. The branch has buds on it.
   2. Each bud is a place on the branch where a new stem, leaves, and flowers can grow.
   3. In cold climates the delicate buds are protected by overlapping bud scales.
   4. Each branch usually has a **terminal bud** at its tip.
   5. As with the tips of roots, growth in length of a branch occurs because of rapid mitotic division of cells within the bud.
   6. Along the sides of a branch are **lateral buds**, from which other branches may grow.

DEMONSTRATION 12.5

Which Is Greater, a Root's Positive Hydrotropism or Its Positive Geotropism?

Experiment to discover the answer to this question. Obtain two plates of glass (each about 4 inches square), and place one on top of the other with about one-half inch of fertile but dry soil between them. Place a bean seed in the middle of the "sandwich" so that the bean is visible through the glass when looking at it from either side. Tape all the way around the two plates with the soil between, but leave about a one-inch opening in the tape at one side near a corner, where you will add a bit of water each day. Keep the soil fairly moist by adding water every day until the seed germinates (the embryo plant

emerges from the seed). From the time that the embryo emerges keep the setup in a well-lit place in the room and turn it clockwise 90 degrees each day. Water a bit each day, but the soil should not be kept completely moist as before the seed germinated. As the young plant grows, its roots will likely move toward the water source and its young stem will likely grow in a circular pattern because of the 90° turning each day.

Following this demonstration, have your students hypothesize and explore other seeds by devising a similar experimental setup.

---

7. Along the branch there are also oval, circular, or shield-shaped **leaf scars,** which mark the spots where leaf stalks were attached during previous seasons.
8. A node is a point on the leaf scar where leaves or branches were produced by the stem.
9. Also along the branch are rings circling the branch, called **bud-scale scars,** which show the exact locations of the terminal buds during previous seasons.
10. By starting at the present terminal bud and counting the number of bud-scale scars along the branch, one can find out the exact age of the twig.
11. Some branches have thorns, which help to protect the plant. Some thorns are short and broad, some are long and pointed, and others are branched.

B. There are four distinct regions inside the branch or trunk of a **woody tree:** the bark, the cambium, the wood, and the pith in the center.
1. The **bark** is the outer covering of the stem and consists of two layers, an outer layer, which is mostly dead cells, and an inner layer made of mostly living cells. The outer bark protects the stem from injury, from disease, and from losing water. The inner part of the bark conducts the food made by the leaves downward to the roots, through the **phloem tissue.**
2. Sometimes humans and bark-chewing animals, such as beavers, porcupines, deer, and horses, remove a circular section of the bark all the way around a tree, a removal called

girdling, which will kill a tree because the tree's food transport system has been disrupted.
3. The **wood** of the stem is made up of hollow tubes of specialized cells, the **xylem tissue,** which conduct water and dissolved minerals upward from the roots to the leaves.
4. In an old stem there are often two kinds of wood: the **sapwood,** which is the living xylem tissue, and the **hardwood,** which is dead tissue and whose only function is to provide support for the tree. Hardwood is the part of the tree that people use to make furniture.
5. The **pith** is in the center of the stem.
6. In an old, woody stem the pith is hardly noticeable, but in a young stem, because there is still little wood in it, the pith seems to be quite large and serves as a place to store food. However, the size of the pith is the same in both cases because the pith never grows beyond the size it was during the first year of the stem's growth.
7. Between the bark and the wood of a stem there is a fourth region, called the **cambium,** which is made up of a very thin layer of delicate tissue. It is the cambium tissue that is made of cells that continue to divide to create new cells, adding to the diameter of the stem.
8. Each spring and summer the cambium forms new wood and new inner bark for the stem. As a result, each year a new layer of wood is added to the stem. This new layer of wood forms a circle or ring, called an **annual ring,**

DEMONSTRATION 12.6
Roots Absorb Water and Dissolved Minerals

Dig up a complete dandelion plant with its roots, and gently wash the soil from the roots. If dandelions are unavailable, use plants grown from bean, radish, or tomato seeds instead. Place the roots in a glass jar containing water that has been colored a very deep red with food coloring. In a few hours, or by the next day, the veins of the dandelion leaves will be colored red, because the water and dissolved food coloring will have been absorbed by the roots and then traveled up to the leaves.

inside the stem. This formation of layers makes it possible to estimate the age of a tree by counting the number of annual rings in a cross section of the tree's trunk.

C. A monocotyledon **herbaceous stem** has a hard outer covering called a rind, and a dicotyledon herbaceous stem has a thin skin called an epidermis.

1. The monocotyledon herbaceous stem does not have a cambium, but the dicotyledon herbaceous stem does have a cambium.
2. Because both of these stems live only one year, they are usually long and thin.
3. The bundles of hollow tubes (xylem and phloem tissues) inside a monocotyledon herbaceous stem are scattered at random inside the stem; however, in a dicotyledon herbaceous stem, the bundles of hollow tubes are arranged regularly in a circle.

III. THE FUNCTIONS OF STEMS

A. Stems serve several functions.
1. They conduct water and dissolved minerals upward from the roots to the leaves through the xylem tissue.
2. They conduct food from the leaves downward to the roots through the phloem tissue.
3. A stem produces and displays the leaves so that they receive the sunlight they need.
4. Most stems support the plant and hold it erect.
5. Green herbaceous stems (that is, those with chlorophyll) can make food for the plant.
6. Some stems, like the potato, store food for the plant.
7. Some aerial stems, such as the coleus, philodendron, strawberry, and black raspberry, can grow new plants.
8. Most underground stems can generate new plants.
9. Some stems have adaptations that help protect the plant from animals or from dehydration during drought.

IV. HUMAN USES OF STEMS

A. Humans have made numerous uses of plant stems.
1. For many plant species, such as the potato, asparagus, and celery, the stem of the plant is used as a food source. The sap of the maple tree and the juice of the sugar cane are a source of sugar. Cinnamon bark is used to make spice for flavoring.
2. Rubber is made from the sap of the rubber tree.
3. The stem of the flax plant is used to make linen.
4. The cinchona bark produces quinine, which is used to treat malaria. The bark of the Pacific yew produces a cancer-fighting drug. The bark of the cherry tree is used for cough syrups. Camphor comes from the laurel tree, and witch hazel comes from the witch hazel shrub.
5. Ropes and all kinds of string are made from the fibers of hemp and other plants.
6. The bark of many trees is used to make dyes.
7. Turpentine from the pine tree is used in paint and varnish.
8. The wood of trees is used for making lumber, furniture, paper, telephone poles, piles for piers, parts of machines, and wooden boxes, baskets, and barrels. In addition, many people use wood for heating and cooking.

DEMONSTRATION 12.7
Stem Growth Occurs at the Tip, Not at the Bottom

Plant some zinnia seeds. When the plants are about 5 centimeters (2 in) high, mark the stems with nail polish 2 centimeters (1 in) from the soil. Have students check the height of the marks periodically.

LEAVES

I. LEAF STRUCTURE

  A. The main parts of a leaf are the blade, the petiole, and the leaf veins.
    1. The **blade** is the flat, thin, green part of the leaf, with veins running through it.
    2. The **petiole** is the stem of the leaf and is attached to the stem of the plant at a node. In some plants the leaves do not have a petiole but are fastened directly to the plant's stem.
    3. The **leaf veins** are tiny, hollow tubes, continuations of the xylem and phloem tissues that carry water, dissolved minerals, and food between the leaf and the stem. The veins also help to strengthen the leaf and make it firm.
  B. There are three main patterns in which the veins of a leaf are arranged. These are called palmate, pinnate, and parallel patterns. The size and shape of a leaf are related to the arrangement of its veins.
    1. In the **palmate** pattern, there are a few large veins that start at the tip of the petiole and spread out very much like the outstretched fingers of your hand. Smaller veins, called veinlets, then branch out from these large veins. Leaves with palmate veins are usually broad. Examples are the leaves of geranium, maple, and sycamore plants.
    2. In the **pinnate** pattern, there is just one large vein, called a midrib, with smaller veins (veinlets) branching out on each side of the midrib, giving the same effect or appearance as the arrangement in a feather. Leaves with pinnate veins are shorter and wider than those with parallel veins. Elm and willow are examples of plants whose leaves display pinnate vein patterns.
    3. In the **parallel** pattern, there are many large veins running parallel, or side by side, from the bottom of the leaf to its tip. Parallel veins are found mostly in the leaves of monocotyledon plants, whose seeds have only one seed leaf (cotyledon). Leaves with parallel veins are long and thin. Examples are the leaves of the lily, iris, and the grasses.
  C. Leaves have different kinds of edges.
    1. Some edges are smooth, like the leaves of the willow, redbud, and magnolia.
    2. Some edges are toothed, or serrated, like the leaves of the elm.
    3. Some leaves have lobes, or fingerlike projections, like the leaves of the maple.
    4. If the blade of a leaf is all in one piece, it is called a **simple leaf,** but if the blade is divided into three or more separate parts, called leaflets, the leaf is called a **compound leaf.**
    5. A leaf is still a simple leaf, even if it is lobed or greatly indented. Maple, oak, elm, and apple leaves are simple leaves. Clover, horse chestnut, locust, ash, and strawberry leaves are compound leaves.
    6. When the leaflets spread out or radiate from a single common point, as in the horse chestnut and the clover, the leaf is called a **palmately compound** leaf. When the leaflets are arranged on each side of the midrib, or opposite each other, as in the ash and the pea, the leaf is called a **pinnately compound** leaf.
  D. Leaves of the evergreens are different from those of other seed plants. In some evergreens the leaves are thin and needle-like, such as the pine and the spruce. In others, such as the cedar, the leaves are overlapping scales.

II. LEAF FUNCTIONS

  A. The main function of a leaf is to make food for the plant. An important by-product of that manufacturing of food is the release of oxygen into the atmosphere. Photosynthesizing plants are the major source of oxygen for all living organisms on earth.
    1. Chlorophyll gives the leaf its green color and makes it possible for the plant to make food by the process known as **photosynthesis.**

DEMONSTRATION 12.8
Stems Carry Water

A. Celery Stalk

Obtain a stalk of celery with some leaves still on it, and put it in a glass of water that has been colored a deep red with food coloring (Figure 12.3). With a sharp knife cut 2 centimeters (1 in) off the bottom of the stalk while the stalk is under the colored water. Allow the celery stalk to stand overnight. Note that the colored water has moved up the stalk and into the leaves. Remove the stalk from the colored water and cut off a section of stalk from the bottom. Note the red color of the hollow tubes in the stem.

B. Make a Two-Colored Carnation

Obtain a white carnation with a long, thick stem. Split the stem in two parts for a distance of about 3 inches. Place one part in a test tube or glass of water that has been colored with red food coloring, and the other part in a test tube that has been colored with blue or green food coloring (Figure 12.4). Allow the carnation to stand overnight. The flower will have two colors, the color of the various petals depending on which colored liquid reached them.

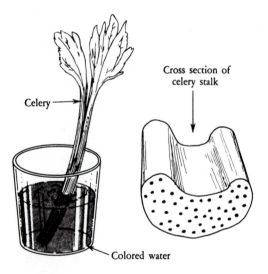

FIGURE 12.3   Colored water rises up the celery stalk.

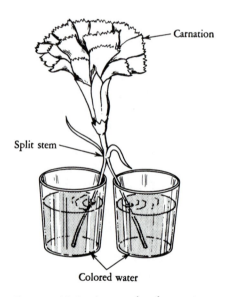

FIGURE 12.4   A two-colored carnation.

Photo means "light," and *synthesis* means "putting together."

2. A plant part, such as a leaf, may still contain chlorophyll but not be green in color because of the predominance of some other pigment, such as the carotenoid pigments, which are yellow and orange. These other pigments trap certain rays of sunlight and transfer that energy to help in the manufacture of food, usually in the form of carbohydrates.

3. Chlorophyll and the other pigments are located in the cytoplasm of leaf cells in organelles called **chloroplasts.**
4. Chloroplasts use two raw materials to manufacture carbohydrates: water and carbon dioxide.
5. Water comes from the ground, together with dissolved minerals, passing into roots, up the stem, and into the leaf.
6. Chloroplasts trap the energy of sunlight, convert it to chemical energy, and then store it.

DEMONSTRATION 12.9
Leaves, Chlorophyll, and Photosynthesis

A. Examining Chloroplasts

Obtain the water plant elodea from a store that sells aquarium supplies. Have students examine a leaf of elodea under the microscope and note the green chloroplasts that are present.

B. Extracting Chlorophyll from Leaves

You can extract chlorophyll from any green leaf by first boiling the leaf in water for several minutes to break down the plant cell walls. Frozen or fresh spinach leaves work nicely. Prepare a double boiler with water in the bottom section and rubbing alcohol in the upper section. Place the leaf in the alcohol and heat the double boiler until the water boils, then continue to boil for 10 to 15 minutes. The hot alcohol will extract the chlorophyll from the leaf and become dark green.

C. Leaves need Carbon Dioxide for Photosynthesis

Obtain a geranium plant. Coat the top and bottom surfaces of one leaf with a thin layer of petroleum jelly. Keep the plant in a sunny location. In a few days the jelly-coated leaf will begin to turn yellow. Point out that the petroleum jelly prevented carbon dioxide in the air from entering the leaf's stomata, and this lack of carbon dioxide stopped the process of photosynthesis in the leaf.

D. Leaves Need Sunlight for Photosynthesis

Repeat demonstration C, but now cover one leaf completely with aluminum foil instead of petroleum jelly. The leaf will turn yellow because the aluminum foil prevents sunlight from reaching the leaf, and this failure to receive sunlight stops the process of photosynthesis.

E. Leaves Produce Starch During Photosynthesis

Put a plant, such as a geranium, in the sun for several hours so that photosynthesis can take place. Pluck one of the leaves and boil it in water for several minutes to break down the cell walls in the leaf. Prepare a double boiler with water in the bottom section and rubbing alcohol in the top section. Place the leaf in the alcohol, heat the double boiler until the water boils, and continue to boil for 10 to 15 minutes (or longer if necessary) until the alcohol extracts most of the chlorophyll from the leaf.

Remove the leaf and rinse it in hot water. Place the leaf in a large, shallow saucer and dry it by blotting gently with cleansing tissue. Place a few drops of tincture of iodine on the leaf. A dark blue or purple color will appear after a few minutes, indicating the presence of starch in the leaf. Show that the blue color is a test for starch by adding a few drops of iodine to cornstarch or to a slice of potato. If you use a coleus leaf, only the green sections will test for starch.

F. Leaves Give off Oxygen During Photosynthesis

Obtain a water plant, such as elodea or sagittaria, from an aquarium supply store. Put the plant in an aquarium filled with water and set a short-stemmed transparent funnel over the plant. Fill a test tube with water making sure that there are no air bubbles in the water, then invert the test tube, still full of water, over the stem of the funnel (Figure 12.5). Now put the aquarium in a sunny place for several days. The plant will give off bubbles of oxygen, which will displace the water in the test tube. After most of the water is displaced, remove the test tube and hold it mouth upward. Blow out a burning wood splint and quickly put the glowing splint inside the test tube. The oxygen in the test tube makes the splint either glow more brightly or burst into flame.

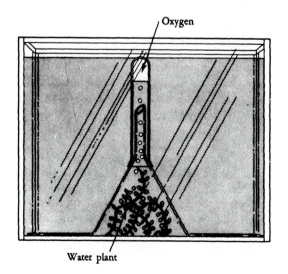

FIGURE 12.5   The water plant gives off bubbles of oxygen during photosynthesis.

(continued)

DEMONSTRATION 12.9
Continued

G. Leaves Give Off Water

Obtain a potted geranium plant and a wooden stick about the same length as the flowerpot and plant combined. Place the stick in the soil of the pot so that the top of the stick extends slightly above the plant. Cover the soil and the sides of the flower pot with aluminum foil. Now place a plastic bag over the plant and tie the mouth of the bag securely around the stem (Figure 12.6). Prepare a control by duplicating every condition except the presence of the geranium plant. Such a control involves having the same size flower pot, same amount of soil and moisture in the soil, same size wooden stick, aluminum foil over the soil and sides of the pot, and the same size plastic bag over the stick and tied around the stick.

Now place both flowerpots in the sun for a few hours. A large number of water droplets will appear on the inside of the plastic bag covering the geranium plant. Point out that covering the soil and the sides of the flowerpot eliminated the possibility of the water coming from the soil or through the porous pot. Because no water droplets appear in the control, the water cannot have come from the air, which usually contains water vapor. Therefore, the water droplets can only have come from the plant itself.

H. Leaves Change Color in the Fall

Observe the changes in the color of leaves of various trees in the fall, and associate the change in color with the kind of tree. The colors appear when the leaves stop

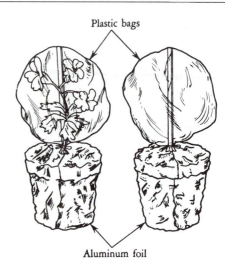

Plastic bags

Aluminum foil

FIGURE 12.6   A controlled experiment to show that leaves give off water.

making chlorophyll. Obtain two plants of the same kind and size. Allow one plant to stay in the sunlight all day. Keep the other plant in a dark closet for half the day. After a few days note the yellowish appearance of the leaves that had less sunlight. These leaves now have less chlorophyll in them as well, and the yellow pigment in the leaves has begun to show.

7. The process of photosynthesis includes two main groups of reactions. These are the **light reactions** and the **Calvin cycle.**

8. The light reactions are the reactions in which light energy is converted to chemical energy. They represent the "photo" part of *photosynthesis*. These reactions result in the splitting of water molecules, providing hydrogen and an energy source for the Calvin cycle.

9. The Calvin cycle is the series of reactions that forms carbohydrates (usually glucose) using carbon dioxide and the hydrogen that was released from water in the light reaction. The Calvin cycle is the "synthesis" part of *photosynthesis*.

10. Carbon dioxide is a gas in the atmosphere that enters the leaf through its many tiny

openings, called **stomata,** which are on the surface of the leaf—especially on the underside, which is more protected from sunlight.

11. Whereas the water-splitting reaction (called **photolysis**) constitutes the first series of reactions in photosynthesis and requires light energy, the Calvin cycle, that is, the union of carbon dioxide with the hydrogen from water, is the second series of reactions (sometimes called **catalysis**), and does not require light energy. For this reason it is sometimes known as the *dark reaction*, although it occurs all the time, day or night.

12. Oxygen gas, released as a result of the light reactions, exits back into the surrounding atmosphere through the same stomata that allowed the carbon dioxide to enter.

DEMONSTRATION 12.10
Function of a Leaf and Its Stomata

A. Air Enters a Plant Through the Leaf

Fit a flask or jar with a two-hole rubber stopper. Into one hole insert a leaf with a long stem, such as the leaf of an African violet. Into the other hole insert a piece of glass tubing bent at a right angle or a plastic soda straw bent at an angle (Figure 12.7). Add enough water to the flask so that the stem of the leaf is below the level of the water when the cork is inserted. Now fit the stopper very tightly into the neck of the flask. Use drops of melted paraffin from a burning candle to seal the holes of the stopper containing the glass tubing and the stem of the leaf. Suck air from the glass tubing. Air bubbles will come from the end of the leaf stem, showing that air entered the leaf and traveled down its stem.

B. Observe Stomata and Guard Cells

Select a leaf from a plant that has soft, tender leaves. *Geranium* and *Coleus* work well. If those are unavailable, fresh spinach leaves also work well. Tear a leaf at an angle to expose a thin section of epidermis. The epidermis will appear as a clear strip of leaf tissue at the jagged torn edge. Use tap water to make wet slide mounts of both the upper and lower epidermis sections. Cover each epidermis section with a cover glass. Have students observe both slides under a microscope and look for stomata and the surrounding guard cells. Notice that chloroplasts are seen only in guard cells. Epidermal cells contain no chloroplasts and are irregular shaped while guard cells are sausage shaped. Also observe if there are more, fewer, or the same number of stomata on the upper and lower epidermis sections.

C. Opened and Closed Stomata

Make another wet slide mount of the lower epidermis of a leaf but rather than using tap water for the mount use a 5% saltwater solution (5 grams of table salt in a graduated cylinder; then add water until the level reaches 100 ml). Have students observe this slide under a microscope and explain what they see and how it differs from the epidermal tissue in the tapwater mount. In the saltwater solution the guard cells will close because a higher water

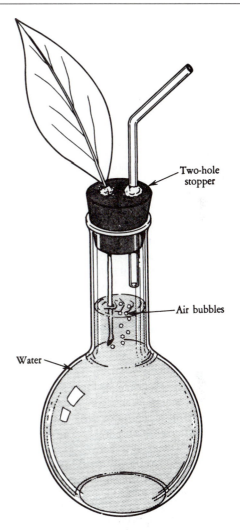

FIGURE 12.7   Air bubbles show that air enters the leaf and travels down the stem.

concentration inside cells compared to outside cells resulted in water moving out of guard cells causing them to collapse and close the stomata.

13. The leaf changes the sugar (glucose) to starch, either immediately or soon after photosynthesis has occurred. The leaf also changes some of the sugar into fats and proteins.
14. Food made by the leaf may then be carried to the stem and the roots for use or for storage.
15. Any part of the plant that has chlorophyll can make food for the plant, but it is the plant's leaf that predominates in photosynthesis.
16. Many factors influence the rate at which plants photosynthesize. These include the availability and quality of the light source,

the availability of the raw materials water and carbon dioxide, and the environmental temperature.

B. Another important function of the leaf is that known as **transpiration.** Transpiration is the loss of water from the leaf's surface by evaporation.

1. Although the plant needs water to make food and for other purposes, it usually takes in more water than it uses. Excess water passes through the stomata, where it evaporates into the atmosphere as water vapor. This evaporation provides a cooling effect on the leaf.

2. Typically, plants give off a great amount of water by transpiration. A sunflower, for example, gives off 1 liter (approximately 1 qt) of water a day. During the summer months, an average size tree can give off as much as 47 liters (50 qt) of water a day.

3. Specialized leaf cells, called **guard cells,** control the amount of water that passes out of the leaf. Each **stoma** (singular of *stomata*) is surrounded by two guard cells.

4. Guard cells usually keep the stomata wide open, allowing water to leave the leaves freely. However, when the plant does not have enough water and is wilting, the guard cells make the stomata smaller, which slows the loss of water from the leaf.

5. Through transpiration, plants of the **tropical rain forests** that encircle the earth near the equator play an important role in replenishing the earth's freshwater supply. By 1990 the destruction of the world's tropical rain forests, for timber, farming, and development, was at a rate of 55,000 square miles a year, an area larger than the state of Florida. Today, there is worldwide concern among scientists and environmentalists about the effects of this destruction on the global ecosystem if it is allowed to continue. For example, it is estimated that because the rain forests hold approximately 10 million species of plants and animals, the destruction of these forests is causing the extinction of about 50,000 species a year, many of which have not even been identified.

C. Other functions of the leaf are as follows.

1. The leaf helps the plant digest food and change the food into the energy it needs to live and grow.

2. The leaf helps the plant remove waste materials.

3. Some leaves, such as those of sedum, sansevieria, and African violet, can grow new plants by budding.

III. SOME LEAVES CHANGE COLOR, ESPECIALLY IN THE FALL

A. During the late spring and summer the leaves keep making chlorophyll and stay green, but in the fall, when it becomes colder, leaves of many plants stop making chlorophyll and the green color in the leaves disappears.

1. The hidden yellow and orange pigments in some of the leaves may then appear.

2. The cool weather and the increase in the amount of moisture in the air also reveal red colors in other leaves.

3. When the weather becomes still colder, the leaves die, turn brown, and fall to the ground.

IV. USE OF LEAVES BY HUMANS

A. Some leaves are used for human food, such as the leaves of the lettuce, cabbage, spinach, endive, parsley, and kale plants.

B. Tea leaves are used to make a beverage.

C. The leaves of spearmint, peppermint, sage, and thyme are used for spices and flavoring.

D. Tobacco leaves are used for smoking.

E. Leaves such as palm and grass are sometimes used to cover the roofs of their homes by people in the tropics.

FLOWERS

I. DEFINITION AND FLOWER STRUCTURE

A. The flower is a special part of a plant that produces new plants by sexual reproduction, that is, by the union of sex cells.

1. The flower lives for a short time only, and then parts of the flower become a fruit.

2. The fruit contains seeds, and the seeds produce the new plants.

3. The fruit serves the function of dispersing or scattering the seeds, which helps to prevent overcrowding of individual plants.

B. The large, flattened part of the stalk that holds the flower is called the **receptacle.**

C. Most flowers have four kinds of organs: sepals, petals, stamens, and pistils.

1. **Sepals** are the thin, usually green, leaflike parts on the outside of the flower. They cover and protect the young flower bud and the flowers that close at night. When the bud opens, the sepals separate and fold back in support and protection for the open flower. Collectively, the sepals are called the **calyx.**

2. Inside the calyx are the **petals.** Petals are usually larger than the sepals, are often brightly colored, and attract insects. Collectively, the petals are called the **corolla.**

3. At the base of the petals there are usually little pockets or cups of a sweet liquid, called **nectar,** which is attractive to hummingbirds, bees, and other insects. (Flowers that are pollinated by beetles and flies are often those flowers that lack colorful petals and nectar but produce a strong scent. Examples include magnolias and skunk cabbage.)

4. In some flowers, such as the tulip and the lily, both the sepals and the petals are the same color.

5. The calyx and the corolla comprise what are referred to as the **accessory parts** of the flower, because they are not entirely needed for reproduction.

6. Inside the petals are the organs that are necessary for reproduction, the stamens and the pistil, which are the **essential parts.**

7. Inside the petals, and usually grouped in a ring around the center of the flower, are the **stamens,** which constitute the male part of the flower.

8. Each stamen has two parts: the filament and the anther. The **filament** is the thin stalk or stem of the stamen. The **anther** is on top of the filament, and is usually knobby or boxlike.

9. The anther produces a yellow or reddish powder called **pollen.** Inside the pollen are the **male gametes,** or sperm cells.

10. In the center of the flower, usually surrounded by the stamens, is the female organ, the **pistil.** There are three parts to a pistil: the stigma, the style, and the ovary.

11. The **stigma** is the sticky top of the pistil, the **style** is the thin stalk or stem of the pistil, and the **ovary** is the large or swollen base of the pistil, usually positioned on top of the receptacle.

12. Inside the ovary are one or more **ovules,** which will develop into **seeds.**

D. There is such a variation in shapes, sizes, colors, and configurations of flower parts that these flower features are often used in plant identification.

1. A flower, such as the rose or the lily, that has all four parts (sepals, petals, stamens, and pistil) is called a **complete** flower. A flower, such as the willow or the oat, that has one or more parts missing, is called an **incomplete flower.**

2. If a flower, such as the oat or wild ginger, has both stamens and a pistil, even if its sepals and petals are missing, it is called a **perfect flower,** but if a flower, such as the pussy willow or cottonwood, has either the stamens or the pistil missing, it is called an **imperfect flower.**

3. Some flowers are not really a single flower but are a whole cluster of individual flowers. Such flowers are called **composite flowers.** Examples include the zinnia, aster, daisy, chrysanthemum, marigold, and dandelion.

E. Flowers of monocotyledon plants are different from the flowers of dicotyledon plants.

1. Monocotyledon flowers, such as the tulip and the lily, have their flower parts in threes or in multiples of three, such as six or nine. The tulip has three sepals and three petals (both the same color), six stamens, and a pistil with three parts to its ovary.

2. Dicotyledon flowers, such as the rose, buttercup, and columbine, usually have their flower parts in fours or fives, or in multiples of fours or fives.

II. Pollination and Fertilization

A. For seeds to be formed, the pollen from the anther of a stamen must be carried to the sticky stigma of the pistil. This transfer of pollen is called **pollination.**

1. When the pollen is carried from the anther to the stigma in the same flower, or to the stigma of another flower on the same plant, it is called **self-pollination.**

2. The process of self-pollination does not occur often. In some flowers the stamens are too short for the pollen to fall on the pistil. In other flowers the stamens lose their pollen before the pistil is mature enough to receive it. Imperfect flowers are lacking either stamens or a pistil.

DEMONSTRATION 12.11
Flowers and Pollen

A. Flower

Obtain a large simple flower, such as a tulip, lily, gladiolus, petunia, or sweet pea. Examine the flower closely (Figure 12.8). Observe the flower stalk and its upper larger part, the receptacle. At the base of the receptacle note the sepals that surround the petals. In the tulip and the lily the sepals are the same color as the petals. Use tweezers to remove the sepals and petals and place them on separate pieces of paper, appropriately labeled. Count the number of sepals and petals.

Observe the stamens surrounding the pistil in the center of the flower. Count the number of stamens, remove them with the tweezers, and place them on a labeled piece of paper. Examine the stamens with a magnifying glass. Locate the filament and anther, and observe the pollen that may be present on the anther. Remove the pistil and observe the stigma, style, and ovary under the magnifying glass. With a razor blade or sharp knife cut through the ovary lengthwise. Observe the ovules with the magnifying glass and try to count the number present.

Have the students make a large drawing or diagram of the whole flower and its individual parts. Label the parts of the flower and the parts of the pistil and stamen.

B. Compare Kinds of Flowers

Have the students observe examples of different kinds of flowers. Note the basic difference between complete and incomplete flowers, perfect and imperfect flowers, and monocotyledon and dicotyledon flowers. Point out that the flower parts of monocotyledon plants are in threes or multiples of three, whereas the flower parts of dicotyledon plants are in fours and fives or their multiples. Note also, that the sepals and petals of monocotyledon flowers are often the same color.

Obtain a composite flower such as a daisy, dandelion, chrysanthemum, zinnia, marigold, sunflower, or aster. Pull out a ray flower (petal) and a disk flower (little tube in the center), and examine them with a magnifying glass. Do the ray flower and disk flower have all the parts of a perfect flower? What parts, if any, are missing?

C. Germinate Pollen Grains

Place a drop of water on a microscope slide. Shake pollen from a flower onto the drop and cover with a cover glass. Examine the pollen under a microscope.

Pollen will germinate in a solution containing the right proportions of sugar in water. Fill three cups with boiled water. Add 1 teaspoon of sugar to one cup, 2 teaspoons of sugar to the second cup, and 3 teaspoons of sugar to the third cup. Stir the water in each cup until all the sugar is dissolved. Now pour a portion of the sugar solutions into shallow saucers. Shake the pollen of different kinds of flowers onto the surfaces of the sugar solutions. Cover each saucer with a piece of glass and let the solutions stand at room temperature for several hours. Examine the pollen grains with a magnifying glass to see whether tubes are growing from them. If nothing is visible, place a drop of the sugar solution on a microscope, cover with a cover glass, and examine under the microscope.

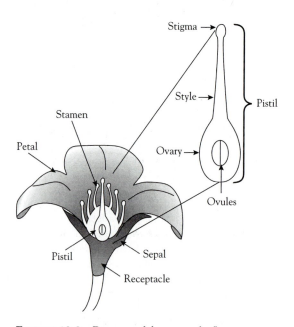

FIGURE 12.8 Diagram of the parts of a flower.

DEMONSTRATION 12.12

Exploring Developing Ovaries

Collect flowers at different stages in their growth, ranging from freshly opened buds to those where all the petals have fallen off. Cut open the ovary of each and observe the changes that have taken place. Two excellent flowers to observe are the iris, which has hundreds of ovules in its ovary, and the rose, which forms a sizable fruit after it has been fertilized.

Obtain a quantity of fresh string beans or peas, and open some of the pods that do not seem to be completely filled. The tiny, seedlike parts are the remains of ovules that were not fertilized by pollen and so did not develop into beans or peas.

3. When the pollen is carried from the anther of one flower on one plant to the stigma of a flower on another plant, it is called **cross-pollination.**

4. Cross-pollination can take place in many ways. Wind may blow pollen from flower to flower. Gymnosperms and many flowering plants depend only on the wind for pollination. Water may carry pollen from flower to flower of plants that live in the water. As insects, like the bee, crawl into flowers to find nectar, they pick up pollen on their hairy bodies and coincidentally carry the pollen from flower to flower. Some flowers lack attractive coloration or nectar, but produce strong scents that attract certain insects such as beetles and flies, which, while looking for a place to deposit their eggs, inadvertently collect pollen on their bodies and transfer it to another flower. Hummingbirds carry pollen from flower to flower on their beaks and long tongues. Humans carry on pollination, called **artificial pollination,** to develop new kinds of flowers, fruits, vegetables, corn, and wheat.

B. The control of pollination by humans is also called **selective breeding.**

1. Very often plant breeders try to produce certain kinds of flowers. They produce these new flowers by controlling the pollination of flowers through artificial pollination.

2. In artificial pollination, pollen from one flower is transferred carefully by hand to the stigma of another flower of the same kind.

3. Usually, the flower with the stigma has had its stamens removed before the pollen was mature to ensure that no other pollen could be transferred to that stigma.

4. After the flower has been artificially pollinated, it must be protected from visits by insects, which may transfer pollen from their hairy bodies.

5. In selective breeding, scientists try to combine different qualities of two varieties of a flower into one new variety of the same flower. For example, the breeder may try to combine a large flower that has little fragrance with a small but fragrant flower to produce a large, fragrant flower.

6. Many new varieties of flowers, especially roses and corn, have been produced by selective breeding. A new variety of flower is called a **hybrid.**

C. When a grain of pollen from the right kind of flower falls on the stigma, it starts to form a **pollen tube,** which extends down the stigma and the style and into the ovary.

1. From the pollen grain emerge sperm cells that swim down the pollen tube and enter the ovule through a small opening, called the **micropyle.** One sperm will unite with the egg that is in the ovule.

2. The joining of the sperm cell with the egg cell in an ovule is called **fertilization.**

3. For fertilization to take place, a flower's stigma must receive pollen that comes from the same kind of flower.

4. After fertilization, the ovule develops into a **seed.** Seeds are formed only if fertilization takes place. If an ovule is not fertilized, a seed will not be formed in that ovule.

5. Pollination starts the development of the ovary into a **fruit.** A fruit is a ripened ovary.

6. Fertilization starts the development of the seed. A seed is a matured ovule.

7. Pollination without fertilization results in a seedless fruit.

III. USE OF FLOWERS BY HUMANS
  A. Because of their beauty, flowers are used everywhere for decorative purposes.
  B. The buds of the cauliflower are used for food.
  C. Cloves are the dried flower buds of the myrtle tree, which grows in the tropics.
    1. The buds are used as a seasoning or spice.
    2. The buds also produce an oil that is used in medicines.
  D. Saffron, a yellow dye, comes from the stigmas of the saffron crocus.
  E. Flowers are used in making dyes and perfumes.

FRUITS

I. DEFINITION AND FUNCTION OF FRUITS

  A. After the ovule in the ovary of a flower has been fertilized, seeds form and the ovary enlarges and ripens.
    1. A fruit is the ripened ovary of the flower, with or without the presence of other parts of the flower. It is the part of the plant that contains the seeds.
    2. To many persons the word *fruit* means only tree fruits, such as the apple, pear, peach, orange, grape, and banana. To a botanist, however, *fruit* means the ripened ovary from any flowering plant.
    3. Garden flowers, wild flowers, grasses, shrubs, and flowering trees all produce fruits.
    4. Cereal grains, such as corn, oats, and wheat, are fruits. Nuts are fruits.
    5. Many "vegetables," like the pea, bean, tomato, cucumber, pumpkin, and squash, are really fruits, not vegetables. True vegetables come from roots, stems, or leaves of plants.
  B. A fruit has two main functions. One function is to protect the seeds inside it. The other is to help to scatter or disperse the seeds.
  C. Fruits are classified in two main groups: fleshy fruits and dry fruits. Fleshy fruits, like the peach, are soft and fleshy when ripe. Dry fruits, like nuts, are dry when ripe.

II. FLESHY FRUITS

  A. Fleshy fruits are classified in three main groups: pomes, drupes, and berries.
    1. In a **pome,** the fleshy part is formed by the sepals (calyx) and the large flattened end of the receptacle.
    2. The papery core of the pome is really the ovary, which contains the seeds.
    3. The apple, pear, and quince are examples of pomes.
    4. The strawberry is a pome in which many tiny, hard fruits (ripened ovaries) are embedded in one fleshy receptacle. A strawberry is formed this way because its flower has many pistils inside it.
    5. Pomes usually contain many seeds.
    6. In a **drupe,** the ovary wall ripens into two layers. The outer layer becomes soft and fleshy, and the inner layer becomes very hard, usually containing one or two seeds.
    7. The plum, peach, apricot, cherry, and olive are examples of drupes.
    8. The almond comes from a drupe. We throw away the fleshy outer part and eat the seed of the hard inner part.
    9. The raspberry and blackberry are really collections of many tiny drupes clustered on one receptacle. The raspberry and blackberry are formed this way because their flowers have many pistils inside them.
    10. In the **berry,** the whole ovary becomes fleshy.
    11. Some berries, such as the tomato, grape, and gooseberry, have rather soft, thin skins, whereas some other berries, such as the cantaloupe, watermelon, and cucumber, have hard skins, and still other berries, such as the orange, lemon, and grapefruit, have leathery skins.
    12. Berries usually contain many seeds.
    13. The pineapple is a fleshy fruit that is really made up of many fruits joined together, which is a kind of fruit called a **multiple fruit.** A multiple fruit forms from many flowers that are clustered together. The mulberry is another example of a multiple fruit.

III. DRY FRUITS

  A. Dry fruits are classified as either dehiscent or indehiscent.
    1. **Dehiscent fruits** are further divided into pod fruits and capsule fruits.
    2. **Pod fruits,** such as the bean, pea, and milkweed, split open along definite seams when ripe.

3. **Capsule fruits,** such as the poppy, iris, and lily, crack open when they are ripe.
4. Both pod and capsule fruits contain many seeds.
5. **Indehiscent fruits** do not split open along definite seams and do not open when they are ripe.
6. Indehiscent fruits usually contain just one or two seeds.
7. Some indehiscent fruits, such as the acorn, hazel nut, and chestnut, have a hard ovary wall covering the seed, while others, such as corn, wheat, and oat, have a thin ovary wall fastened to the seed.
8. In some indehiscent fruits, such as the sunflower, buttercup, and dandelion, the seed is not fastened to the ovary wall but is separated from it.
9. In some other indehiscent fruits, such as the elm, maple, and ash, the seed is separated from the wall, but there are winglike growths attached to the ovary wall.

IV. FRUITS WITHOUT SEEDS

A. Some fruits develop from the flower without forming seeds.

1. The banana is a seedless fruit. What looks like seeds in the banana are really unfertilized ovules. Banana trees do not ordinarily produce seeds. Instead, new sprouts grow from the roots each season, and their flowers produce more bananas without being fertilized.
B. Seedless oranges, grapefruits, and grapes are produced by grafting parts of seedless plants onto the roots and stems of ordinary plants that produce these fruits with seeds in them.
C. Through selective breeding, plant scientists are always trying to improve the kinds of fruit we eat.
1. For example, scientists may try to make a fruit larger, give the fruit more flavor, make the skin smooth instead of hairy, get more seeds in the fruit, eliminate seeds from a fruit, make fruit mature earlier, or make a fruit sturdier and more resistant to disease.
2. Sometimes scientists create new fruits by transferring the pollen from a flower that produces one kind of fruit to the stigma of a flower that produces another kind of fruit. The tangelo is a fruit that is produced by crossing a tangerine with a grapefruit. The plumcot is a fruit produced by crossing a plum with an apricot.

SEEDS

I. DEFINITION AND STRUCTURE OF A SEED

A. A seed is a matured ovule whose egg cells have been fertilized by sperm cells from pollen grains. The seed then can grow into a new plant of the same kind as the parent plants.
B. Seeds typically have three parts: a seed coat, stored food, and a tiny young plant, called the embryo.
1. The **seed coat** is the covering of the seed that protects the embryo.
2. Most seeds have two seed coats, but some seeds have only one.
3. The outer coat is usually thick and tough, and the inner coat is much thinner.
4. The **stored food** helps the young plant grow until it can make its own food by photosynthesis.
5. Some seeds store their food in thick seed leaves, called **cotyledons.**
6. These seed leaves (cotyledons) are not true leaves, but part of the seed.

7. Monocotyledon plants, such as the corn plant, have only one seed leaf (cotyledon) in their seeds.
8. Dicotyledon plants, such as the bean plant, have two seed leaves (cotyledons) in their seeds.
9. The **embryo** is a tiny, young plant inside the seed that developed from the fertilized egg, the **zygote.**
10. When mature, the embryo has tiny roots, stem, and leaves that will become the new plant.
11. When the embryo begins to grow, it lives on the stored food inside the cotyledon(s) until its own leaves are able to make food for the plant.

II. CONDITIONS NECESSARY FOR SEEDS TO GROW

A. Seeds need water to grow. Water makes a seed swell and softens its outer coat.

DEMONSTRATION 12.13

Testing Seeds for Stored Food

A. Test Seeds for Food Used During Germination

Soak lima beans, peas, and kernels of corn in water overnight; remove the seed coats and mash the seeds thoroughly. If you like, you may grind the dried seeds, then add a little water to the flour and stir to form a paste.

Add a few drops of tincture of iodine to some of the ground seeds. The seeds will turn a deep purple, showing the presence of **starch.**

Put some of the mashed seeds in a test tube. Add a small amount of nitric acid, boil for a few seconds, and then add enough ammonia to neutralize the nitric acid. If **protein** is present, the nitric acid will turn the solution a bright yellow, and the ammonia will change the yellow color to orange.

Rub a piece of walnut meat vigorously on a piece of white or brown paper. Warm the paper over a hot plate, but be careful not to set the paper on fire. Then hold the paper up to the light and note the grease spot, showing the presence of **fat.**

When seeds sprout, the starch is changed to **sugar.** Mash some sprouting seeds, add a small amount of water, stir, and transfer to a test tube. From the drugstore obtain Tes-Tape or Clinitest Tablets, which are used to test for presence of sugar. Follow their instructions carefully, and note the change in color that shows the presence of sugar.

B. Seeds need the right temperature to grow. Most seeds grow best when the temperature ranges between 16° and 27° C (60° and 80° F).

C. Seeds need oxygen to grow, and this is the reason that the soil in a garden must be loose and the seeds must be planted close to the surface of the soil.

D. Seeds need room to grow, and they grow best then they are scattered away from the plant that produced them.

E. Seeds do *not* need sunlight when they first begin to grow. At first they live off the food stored within each seed. When the new plant grows leaves, it then needs sunlight to make its own food.

III. HOW SEEDS GROW

A. When a seed begins to grow, we say that it is sprouting or **germinating.** First, the seed absorbs water. Water makes the seed swell and softens the seed coat. This softening of the seed coat allows the tiny plant (embryo) inside the seed to grow out through the seed coat.

B. In most seeds, the roots are the first part to grow; next, the primary stem grows upward; then the tiny leaves unfold, forming the first true leaves of the plant.

1. While the roots, stem, and true leaves are forming, the young plant lives on the stored food inside the seed. At this time it is called a **seedling.**

2. In the bean seed, which is a dicotyledon plant, the two cotyledons (seed leaves) grow with the stem above the ground; in the corn seed, which is a monocotyledon plant, the single cotyledon (seed leaf) stays below the ground.

3. By the time the young plant is able to make its own food and no longer needs the stored food in the cotyledons, the cotyledons have shriveled up and will drop off.

4. The true leaves of the plant then supply food for the plant through photosynthesis.

IV. HOW SEEDS DISPERSE

A. Seedlings grow best when they are scattered far away from the parent plant. If seeds fell to the ground only beside and beneath the parent plant, there would be overcrowding of the young plants, all struggling to live and grow. The large number of seedlings would use up the minerals in the soil and make the soil poor for growing. If there is a condition unfavorable for growing, the seedlings will die, thus endangering the survival of that species. Many adaptations have occurred in the dispersal of seeds, which help to ensure species survival.

B. Some fruits scatter their own seeds.

1. Some fruits that grow in pods, such as the bean and the pea, twist when they ripen, so the pods break open and scatter the seeds.

2. Some pods, such as those of the balsam and the touch-me-not, burst open at the slightest touch and propel their seeds some distance away.
3. Tiny holes open in the fruit of the poppy, and, as the poppy stem moves back and forth in the wind, the seeds fly out through the holes.
4. The witch hazel, pansy, and violet plants also scatter their own seeds.

C. The wind scatters many seeds.
1. Some seeds, such as those of the milkweed, cottonwood, and dandelion, have fine hairs or tufts that act like parachutes and are carried far away by the wind.
2. Some seeds, such as those of the maple, ash, elm, and pine, have wings that act like tiny propellers or sails and are also carried away by the wind.
3. The tumbleweed scatters its seeds as the wind rolls it across the ground.

D. Some seeds, such as the coconut, are carried away by water.

E. Birds and other animals help to scatter seeds.
1. Mud on a bird's feet may contain seeds, which are then deposited elsewhere.
2. Seeds may stick to a bird's bill or feathers and be carried far away.
3. Some birds eat fleshy fruits, such as the cherry, and then drop the seeds to the ground.
4. Sometimes birds eat the whole fruit and pass the seeds as waste products, which fall to the ground.
5. Squirrels bury nuts, such as the hickory and acorn, in the ground and sometimes don't dig them up.
6. Many plants, such as the thistle and burdock, produce fruits with stickers that cling

to the fur of animals and later come loose far from the parent plants.

F. People help scatter seeds.
1. If a vehicle passes through mud that has seeds in it, some of the mud may stick to the wheels and the seeds may be carried away.
2. Burrs of the thistle and cocklebur cling to clothes and so are carried away.
3. Seed companies ship seeds to all parts of the world.

V. USE OF SEEDS BY HUMANS

A. Seeds are used for food.
1. One of the most valuable sources of food in the world comes from the fruits and seeds of the grasses, such as wheat, corn, oats, rice, and barley.
2. Peas and beans are used throughout the world for food.
3. The peanut is used as food, and its oil is used for cooking.
4. Chocolate and cocoa are made from the cacao bean, and coffee is made from the coffee bean.
5. The seeds of pepper, mustard, nutmeg, and celery are used as spices.

B. Cotton seeds are used to make cooking oil, and the fibers that stick to the seeds are used to make cotton cloth.

C. Oil from the seeds of the coconut tree is used to make soap, candles, and butter substitutes.

D. Seeds from the flax plant produce linseed oil, which is used to make paint, varnish, and other materials.

E. Soybeans are used as food and have many industrial uses as well.

CARING FOR AND GROWING PLANTS

I. CONDITIONS NECESSARY FOR PLANT GROWTH

A. Like all organisms, plants need oxygen.
1. Plants use carbon dioxide to make food through the process of photosynthesis.
2. They use oxygen to burn their food and set energy free by the process of respiration.

B. Like all organisms, plants need water.
1. They use water to make food through the process of photosynthesis.

2. Water also contains dissolved minerals that plants need for making new plant parts and for growing taller.
3. Plants also use water to dissolve waste materials and to eliminate those materials.

C. Plants need the proper temperature to grow.
1. For each kind of plant there is a certain temperature at which it grows best, and temperature limits beyond which it cannot live.

2. Plants may die if the temperature rises and falls too quickly.

D. Plants need the energy of sunlight to make food and grow.

E. Land plants need soil to grow.
   1. Most plants grow best in loam, which is a mixture of sand, clay, and humus (decayed animal and vegetable matter).
   2. Some plants grow better in sandy soil, and others grow better in clay soil.

F. Plants need minerals in the soil to grow well.
   1. Plants need nitrogen, phosphorus, potassium, calcium, magnesium, and other chemical elements.
   2. Some plants grow better when the soil is acid, but most plants grow best when the soil is neutral or slightly alkaline.

G. The cutting or trimming of dead or dying branches from trees and shrubs helps keep the trees and shrubs healthy.
   1. This cutting and trimming is called **pruning.**
   2. In nature, pruning occurs naturally from natural forces such as wind and fire.
   3. Live branches are often pruned by humans to give a tree a certain shape or to make a tree produce more fruit and fewer leaves.

II. EFFECT OF CLIMATE ON PLANTS

A. The climate has a great deal to do with the kinds and amounts of plants that will grow in a certain region.

B. In the tropics there is an abundance of plants because of the favorable temperature and great amount of rainfall.
   1. The foliage is dense, and the leaves are broad.
   2. Plants grow continuously the whole year around.
   3. Such plants as banana trees, date palms, bamboo, orchids, and large ferns grow in the tropics.
   4. A greater number and variety of plants grow in the tropics than anywhere else on earth.
   5. Although the tropical rain forests cover less than 7 percent of the earth's land surface, they contain about half of all the earth's plant and animal species.

C. Very few plants grow in the cold Arctic and Antarctic regions. There are almost no trees in these regions. A few dwarf willow trees can sometimes be found. Ferns, mosses, lichens, some flowering plants, and grass grow in the very short summer of these regions. Many of the plants are covered with a sort of hair, and the plants have thick seed coats.

D. A wide variety of plants grow in the temperate climate regions.
   1. Oranges, lemons, limes, grapefruit, and cotton grow in regions where the climate is mild and there is little or no frost.
   2. All kinds of trees, shrubs, fruits, flowers, and cereal grasses grow in the moderate temperate regions.
   3. Evergreens and hardy trees, shrubs, flowers, and grasses grow in cold temperate regions.

E. Not many plants grow in warm desert regions because there is so little rainfall.
   1. Desert plants have fewer leaves than other plants; consequently, the loss of water from such a plant is decreased.
   2. The leaves have a thick covering and are often relatively narrow, which also helps to prevent water loss.
   3. The mesquite plant sends long roots down to the water table many feet below the surface.
   4. The cactus plant has roots that cover a wide area just below the surface, and these roots can quickly take up any rain that falls.
   5. Desert plants bloom very quickly; their flowers have brilliant colors, which immediately attract insects for pollination before the flowers die soon from the hot sun.

III. EFFECT OF SEASONS ON PLANTS

A. Because it is warm all year in the tropics, plants grow year round.

B. Most plants in the temperate regions grow only in the warm weather of the spring, summer, and fall.
   1. Leafy trees, such as the oak and the maple, lose their leaves in the fall and are inactive during the winter.
   2. Evergreen trees, such as the pine and the spruce, do not lose their leaves in the fall; they stay green all winter, but most of the activity in the tree stops.
   3. Some nonwoody plants, such as the peony and chrysanthemum, die to the ground in the winter, but their roots stay alive and produce new growth in the spring.
   4. Other nonwoody plants, such as the balsam and zinnia, die completely in the winter, but the seeds they produce grow new plants in the spring.

C. Plants in the polar regions have a very short growing season, because there may be no more than 10 weeks when the temperature is above freezing.

CONSERVATION OF EARTH'S PLANT RESOURCES

I. EARTH IS LOSING ITS PRECIOUS FORESTS

  A. The earth has lost one half of its original acreage of tropical rain forests.

  B. The United States has already lost three fourths of its original forests.

  C. Human-caused forest fires destroy much of our forests.

  D. Fungi and insects destroy certain trees.

  E. Grazing and gnawing animals also destroy our trees.

II. FOREST CONSERVATION EFFORTS

  A. Many efforts are now being made to conserve the forests that are left.

    1. Lumbering companies are now managing trees more wisely.

    2. They are removing weed trees, crowded trees, crooked trees, damaged trees, and diseased trees so that the trees to be used for timber can grow bigger and healthier.

    3. They are removing only part of the forest, then planting new trees that will eventually take the place of those cut down.

    4. Spraying diseased trees will stop, or at least check, the spread of the disease.

    5. The United States Forest Service, established in 1905, fights and controls forest fires, develops and recommends better lumbering practices, and finds ways of controlling harmful fungi and insects.

    6. Education programs have been developed to lessen our carelessness in starting forest fires and to better our understanding of the importance of natural wild fires.

III. OUR WILD FLOWERS ARE DISAPPEARING

  A. Persons destroy wild flowers by picking them carelessly.

  B. Some people destroy the trailing arbutus by pulling up the long trailing stem or pulling up the whole plant instead of just picking the flower.

  C. Wildflowers disappear when their habitats are taken for building homes, suburbs, and industries.

  D. Wildflower conservation efforts include the following.

    1. States are trying to protect their wild flowers by passing laws that forbid the picking of wild flowers.

    2. Individuals and organizations are protecting endangered species of plants by maintaining populations and growing new plants.

    3. There are many ways of growing plants: all plants can be grown from the seeds they produce; some plants can be grown from roots; some stems can grow new plants; some plants can be grown from rhizomes, tubers, bulbs, corms, and from cuttings.

EXPLORATORY ACTIVITIES FOR "PLANTS"

1. *EXPLORING A BRYOPHYTE MICROHABITAT* (ANY GRADE)

Overview Small clumps of moss plants growing on the ground or at the base of a tree represent a habitat for many small organisms. To teach the concept of a microhabitat, an appreciation for the world of small organisms, and about bryophytes, the following activities can provide an interesting, motivating, and valuable science learning experience for students. The steps that follow are only suggestions and can be modified according to the maturity and interests of your students.

Initiating Activity Begin by putting on the board the word *habitat* and, using the think-pair-write-share technique (discussed in Chapter 3), have students share their understanding of the meaning of the word.

After there is a consensus of understanding of the meaning of the term, ask the students what they hypothesize are factors that determine an organism's habitat. Record on the board all the factors that students offer. During this brainstorming session, note these key factors: food source, shelter and protection, the organism's size and its mobility.

After students have an understanding of habitat and some of the factors that determine an organism's habitat, talk about types of habitats, leading students to understand that for very small creatures, a habitat may be quite small as well.

Exploratory Activity Show the students a clump of moss that you have collected (a fairly good-sized clump, perhaps nearly a foot square) from a damp area beneath a tree in a forest. Ask students if they know what the green plant is called and whether it would represent a habitat. Guide them to understand that this might well represent a habitat for some very small creatures.

Ask students to predict what kinds of creatures they think would make this clump of moss their habitat for all or a great portion of their lives, and which of these they think would dominate in numbers. Record their predictions on the writing board.

Divide the class into groups of three or four students. Give each group a portion of the moss clump on a paper towel and have them explore the moss for (1) moss plant structures (as noted in the preceding section "The Bryophytes") and (2) small animals that spend all of or a great portion of their lives in moss (spiders, mites, insects). Each team should make its own prediction of the percentages of different kinds of creatures that make the moss their habitat; their predictions may differ from that made initially by the entire class.

For this exploratory portion of the study, each member of a group should be given a special task. For example, one student might be the official recorder and graphing specialist; another, the procurer of the scientific equipment needed, such as a hand lens and forceps; another, the chief scientist whose responsibility it is to identify the procedure and creatures found; and another, the reporter whose responsibility it will be to report the group's findings to the entire class.

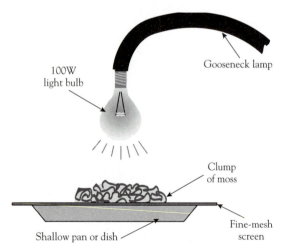

100W light bulb

Gooseneck lamp

Clump of moss

Fine-mesh screen

Shallow pan or dish

Figure 12.9 Forcing animals from their bryophyte microhabitat.

One of the decisions that the groups must make is how they are going to find the creatures that are living in their clumps of moss. One way to do this may be to shake the clump onto a white paper towel. Another is to place the moss clump upside down on a fine mesh screen that is laid on top of a shallow pan and then shine a very bright and hot lamp above and down on the moss—the heat from the lamp will force tiny animals away from the heat and down through the screen, where they will be caught in the shallow pan (see Figure 12.9).

Members of each team record all organisms found and then plot their numbers on a graph. This graph is compared with their initial predictions and with the class prediction. A final report is made to the entire class regarding their findings and what they learned about their exploratory study of this microhabitat.

Application or Follow-up Activity A class discussion of group findings is held to discuss the features of habitats, factors that determine an organism's habitat, and what happens when habitats change or are modified.

2. EXPLORING LEAVES BY CLASSIFYING THEM, AND BY MAKING LEAF COLLECTIONS AND LEAF PRINTS (ANY GRADE)

Overview The following three exploratory activities may lead to students' questions and further study, as determined by the interest they generate.

2.1 Comparing Leaves

Have students collect a large variety of leaves (that have fallen from plants) to examine their parts, structure, similarities, and differences. Compare their sizes, shapes, edges, and different kinds of vein formation. Also distinguish between simple and compound leaves. Representative leaves may be preserved by placing them on a large piece of blotting paper, arranging them so that they do not touch. Cover the leaves with another piece of blotting paper, then place a board on top of the blotting paper. Weight the board down with heavy books or stones, and let the leaves stay this way until they have dried out thoroughly. The leaves may then be removed and either placed in albums or taped to pieces of construction paper.

2.2 Classifying Leaves

Have the students collect autumn leaves and classify them by color. Let them explore other ways to classify the leaves. It may be appropriate for older students to practice using a key to classify the names of the plants from which the leaves come.

2.3 Making Blueprints of Leaves

From leaves that have been gathered, allow each student to select one, then proceed with the following directions. Cut a piece of blueprint paper larger than the leaf and put the paper, sensitive side up, on a piece of cardboard. Put the leaf on the blueprint paper and cover it with a pane of glass. Expose the leaf to sunlight for a few minutes until the paper darkens and turns blue. Dip the paper in a pan of cold water, rinse it well, then set it on a flat surface to dry. The paper will show a white print of the leaf's shape against a blue background.

3. *EXPLORING SEED GERMINATION AND SEEDLING GROWTH (ANY GRADE)*

Overview The following exploratory activities may generate student's interest, leading to further questions and study. The procedures given here are only suggestions. After being given the initial idea, students should be allowed to hypothesize and design their own experimental procedures.

3.1 Germinating Seeds

Obtain lima beans and kernels of corn from a seed store. Do not use grocery store seeds because they may be immature or heat-treated, and so may not germinate. Line a water tumbler with a rectangular piece of dark-colored blotter, and stuff absorbent cotton or peat moss into it to keep the blotter tight against its sides (Figure 12.10). Soak the lima beans and corn

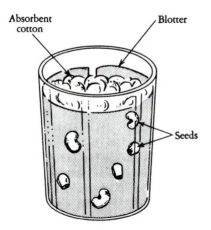

FIGURE 12.10 A tumbler seed germinator.

kernels overnight, then slip a few of each between the blotter and the sides of the tumbler. Moisten the cotton and keep it moist throughout the experiment to make sure the blotter is always moist. Place the tumbler in a warm place away from direct sunlight. Observe the tumbler each day and note the way the seeds germinate. Continue the germination until the seeds are well sprouted.

3.2 Exploring Conditions Necessary for Germination

Prepare eight tumbler germinators. Put one tumbler in the dark and one in the light (but not in direct sunlight). The seeds will germinate just as well in the dark as in the light. Students will learn that light is not necessary for germination and, in some cases, may even be harmful. However, once the plant has germinated and forms leaves, it needs light to grow.

Keep one tumbler watered regularly, and refrain from giving the other tumbler any water at all. The seeds in the dry tumbler will not germinate.

Cover one tumbler tightly with plastic wrap and keep the other tumbler continually exposed to the air. The seeds in the covered tumbler will not sprout because they need air to germinate.

Place one tumbler in a refrigerator and keep the other tumbler at room temperature. The seeds in the cold tumbler will not germinate because they need warmth to germinate.

Obtain three flowerpots of the same size. Fill one pot with sand, the second with clay, and the third with rich soil containing humus. Soak some lima beans or radish seeds overnight, then plant two or three seeds in each pot. Keep all three pots at the same temperature and give all of them the same amount of water. Although the seeds in all three pots may germinate, the plants in the pot containing the rich soil will eventually be taller and sturdier.

3.3 Test Seeds for Percentage of Germination

Obtain radish seeds from a seed store and soak 50 of them overnight. Obtain a piece of cotton flannel 30 centimeters (12 in) square. Moisten the flannel cloth and place the radish seeds on the flannel. Roll the flannel into a loose roll and place it in a shallow pan. Keep the flannel moist and warm for a week, then unroll the flannel carefully and count the number of seeds that have germinated. The number of germinated seeds divided by the total number of seeds (50), multiplied by 100, will give you the percentage of germination. Repeat the experiment using bean, corn, and tomato seeds.

3.4 Testing for Carbon Dioxide Given Off by Germinating Seeds (a Teacher or Student Demonstration)

Obtain 20 to 30 lima beans from a seed store and soak them overnight. Put the seeds into a flask or jar and add enough water to cover about half the seeds. Fit the flask with a two-hole rubber stopper. Into one hole insert a thistle tube and let the tube extend to just above the bottom of the flask. Into the other hole insert a glass tube that leads to a water tumbler (Figure 12.11). Allow the beans to stay in the flask for a day or two. Then pour fresh limewater, which can be obtained from a drugstore, into the tumbler. Pour water slowly into the thistle tube until the flask is half filled. The water will force the carbon dioxide, which is now above the seeds, through the glass tubing and into the limewater, making the limewater turn milky. You can first show that carbon dioxide turns limewater milky by bubbling air from your lungs into limewater through a soda straw.

3.5 Exploring the Rate of Seed Growth

Obtain some radish seeds from a seed store, soak them overnight, and then plant them in a flowerpot filled with soil. Water the pot regularly and wait until the tiny plants begin to appear above the soil. Obtain two pieces of glass about 30 centimeters (12 in) square, and insert a wet piece of dark-colored blotter between them. Each day, for 10 to 14 days, carefully remove one entire radish plant from the soil and place it on the moist blotter. You can keep the panes of glass together with string or rubber bands. Keep the blotter moist at all times. At the end of 2 weeks you will have a clear-cut record of the daily growth of the radish seeds.

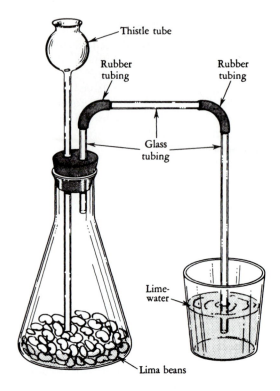

FIGURE 12.11   When seeds germinate, the carbon dioxide gas they give off causes limewater to become milky.

STUDENT BOOKS AND OTHER RESOURCES FOR "PLANTS"

Beals, J. "See Spot Run: Elementary Lessons on Chromatography." *Science and Children* 31(4):28–30 (January 1994).

Borer, L. C. Magnusson, and B. Fendall. "Citrus Chemistry." *Science Scope* 18(5):28–29 (February 1995).

Brown, H. "Lemon-Lime Science Time." *Science and Children* 32(4):23–25 (January 1995).

Cohen, M. R., and C. R. Barman, "Did You Notice the Color of Trees in the Spring?" *Science and Children* 31(5):20–22 (February 1994).

Demchik, M. L. "Calling Attention to Common Weeds." *Science Scope* 17(7):41–44 (April 1994).

Faulkner, S. P., and R. V. Hairston. "Supermarket Cytology: Reinforcing Cell Concepts with Single Models." *Science Scope* 19(3):22–25 (November/December 1995).

Fleagle, G. "Herbs Will Grow on You." *Science and Children* 31(4):12–15 (January 1994).

Goh, N., Y. Wan, and L. Chia. "Simply Photosynthesis." *Science and Children* 31(1):32–34 (September 1993).

Goldenberg, J. *Weird Things You Can Grow.* New York: Random House, 1994.

Hampton, C., C. Hampton, and D. Kramer. *Classroom Creature Culture: Algae to Anoles.* Arlington, VA: National Science Teachers Association, 1994.

Hardy, G. R., and M. N. Tolman. "How to Bend a Plant Out of Shape." *Science and Children* 30(7):24–25 (April 1993).

Holmes, A. *Flowers for You: Blooms for Every Month.* New York: Bradbury, 1993.

Hunken, J. "Trees and the Seasons." *Science Activities* 31(1):15–18 (Spring 1994).

King, E. *Backyard Sunflower*. New York: Dutton, 1993.

Marturano, A. "Horticulture and Human Culture." *Science and Children* 32(5):26–29, 50 (February 1995).

McBride, J. W. "Acid Tests and Basic Fun." *Science and Children* 32(4):26–27 (January 1995).

Moseley, C. "The Continuing Adventures of the Truffala Tree Company." *Science Scope* 18(8):22–25 (May 1995).

Nelson, D. "Sizing Up Trees." *Science and Children* 32(8):16–18 (May 1995).

Shelton, M. "Leaf Pals." *Science and Children*. 32(1):37–39 (September 1994).

Shimabukuro, M. A., and V. Fearing. "How Does Your Garlic Grow?" *Science and Children* 30(8):8–11 (May 1993).

Squires, F. H. "Is the Grass Always Greener?" *Science Scope* 17(7):46–49 (April 1994).

Wadsworth, G. *Giant Sequoia Trees*. Minneapolis, Lerner, 1995.

Wexler, J. *Jack-in-the-Pulpit*. New York: Dutton, 1993.

CHAPTER 13

Neither Plant nor Animal

CLASSIFICATION OF ORGANISMS THAT ARE NEITHER PLANT NOR ANIMAL

I. THE NATURE OF SCIENCE AND ORGANISMS THAT ARE NEITHER PLANT NOR ANIMAL

   A. Not all organisms fit neatly into schemes designed by humans to classify them.

      1. Schemes for classifying organisms are developed by scientists to help their understanding of, organization of, and communication about those organisms in an attempt to make order out of the millions of living things.

      2. Making sense and order out of what first often appears to be chaos is the nature of science. Specifically, in learning about and attempting to make sense out of the nature of organisms, scientists are always playing "catch up." That is, nature leads and our understanding always lags behind.

      3. Organisms continue to adapt and change within their environments, thus systems that have been created in the past may not always accommodate all organisms that exist in the present or that will exist in the future.

      4. Human attempts to classify organisms are never perfect. As organisms change, new discoveries are made. Likewise, as the tools for learning become ever more sophisticated, more is learned about any group of organisms and about their unique characteristics. Classification systems are continually modified and changed by scientists.

   B. As scientists learn more about the complexity of the living world, the system for classifying organisms increases in complexity.

      1. When we review ancient classification schemes, those systems appear to be quite simple. For example, depending on their size, plants were either trees, shrubs, or weedy. If an insect flew, it was probably called a fly. If not, it was likely called a bug. If an animal lived in the ocean, it was probably called a fish, and if it flew in the air, it was probably called a bird. For the time, such a simple system worked.

      2. Later, as tools for learning about creatures became more sophisticated and as what was learned revealed greater detail, classification systems became more extensive and detailed.

      3. For a long time organisms were divided into just two kingdoms—plant and animal.

      4. As biologists learned more about the similarities and differences between organisms, it became obvious that this two-kingdom approach did not always work. Certain organisms classified as plants did not fit well in the plant kingdom because of their own unique characteristics; likewise, certain organisms classified as animals didn't fit well in the animal kingdom.

      5. Biologists invented a third kingdom, **Protista**, which has included anywhere from nine to thirteen phyla.

   C. The protists included the following groups: **algae, bacteria, fungi, slime molds, mildew,** and **protozoans**. Some of these groups are now considered in neither plant nor animal sciences.

      1. The taxonomy (classification) of organisms is important to taxonomists (persons who study

classification) but may not be very important to scientists who specialize in the study of certain groups of organisms.

2. Students of **botany** (the study of plants), for example, probably include the algae and even fungi. A general course in **zoology** (the study of animals) may include protozoans.

3. **Virologists** investigate viruses, and **bacteriologists** study bacteria, without much concern as to where these organisms most logically fit in today's overall scheme for the classification of living things.

D. Today both bacteria and the blue-green algae are usually classified in a separate kingdom, **Monera.** This kingdom, which may include both spirochetes and rickettsiae, includes more than 40,000 species.

E. Our study of organisms in this chapter begins with still another group, the **viruses**, which don't always fit into the generally accepted concept of what constitutes a living thing; that is, what an organism is.

VIRUSES

I. WHAT VIRUSES ARE

A. Before viruses were discovered, it was easy to classify objects into living things and nonliving things.
   1. When scientists began to study viruses, they discovered that viruses seemed to be both living and nonliving things.
   2. By themselves, viruses do not seem to be alive. Within cells, they appear to be very much alive.

B. We usually think of a virus as something that has to do with a disease. As a matter of fact, the word *virus* comes from the Latin word meaning "poison."
   1. There are hundreds of viruses that can produce diseases in different kinds of organisms, but there are also many viruses that appear quite harmless.

C. Scientists classify viruses into four groups, based on the host cells they infect: **bacterial viruses** live in bacteria cells; **plant viruses** live in the cells of seed plants, especially flowering plants; **animal viruses** live in the cells of animals; and **human viruses** live in the cells of humans; however, humans are also susceptible to some animal viruses.
   1. It seems that unless a mutation occurs, each kind of virus enters only certain kinds of living cells. For example, a bacterial virus enters only a certain kind of bacterial cell; a plant virus may enter only the cells of the flowers or leaves or stem of a certain plant; a human or animal virus may enter the cells of the nervous system or skin or lungs of a human or animal.

II. CHARACTERISTICS OF VIRUSES

A. Viruses are particles of protein and nucleic acid, about one half to one hundredth the size of the smallest bacterium, which can be seen only with an electron microscope.
   1. One million of the smallest viruses can sit side by side and occupy only 2 ½ centimeters (one inch) of space.

B. Unlike plants, animals, and protists, viruses are not composed of cells. They are **acellular.**
   1. They are particles of **nucleic acid** (DNA or RNA, but never both) surrounded by one or two protein coats. (Viroids, the smallest known agents of infectious disease, are merely short strands of ribonucleic acid, or RNA. Viroids cause several plant diseases and have been implicated in certain diseases of humans and other animals.)
   2. The nucleic acid consists of genes that contain coded instructions for making copies of the virus. They code for nothing else.
   3. Viruses exist in a variety of shapes: some are round and look like tiny golf balls, some are shaped like bricks or cubes, and some resemble needle-like rods. These shapes play a role in the infection process.

C. Viruses cannot manufacture their own food.
   1. Viruses live and grow only inside living cells.
   2. A virus is **parasitic**, living in an organism, which is called its **host**.

D. When outside living cells, viruses do not have characteristics of living things.
   1. Scientists have been able to isolate viruses from living cells and obtain them in the form of crystals, similar to salt or sugar crystals. Virus crystals can be stored in a jar for long periods of time.
   2. When virus crystals are rubbed against or put inside living cells, the virus begins to live and grow.

III. BACTERIAL VIRUSES OR BACTERIOPHAGES
   A. Much of what we know about viruses comes from the study of bacterial viruses, called bacteriophages or phage viruses.
      1. These viruses somewhat resemble a miniature lunar landing module.
   B. From the study of the action of these viruses on bacteria, scientists have learned how viruses reproduce to make new viruses.
      1. When a virus attaches to a bacterial cell, part of the virus enters the cell.
      2. Attachment is a very specific process. Most viruses can attach, enter, and reproduce in only a few kinds of host cells.
      3. Once attached, the virus must enter the host cell and take over that cell's metabolism.
      4. The method of entry varies, depending on the shape and structure of the virus. Some viruses are shaped so that they inject their nucleic acid into the host cell. Others make an indentation in the host cell's membrane and burst into the cell.
      5. Once inside, the virus quickly takes over the metabolic activity of the bacterial cell, destroys the host's DNA, and reprograms the cell to copy the viral genes and make new viruses.
      6. In a short time the bacterial cell bursts, allowing 200 to 300 newly formed viruses to escape.
      7. The new viruses are now free to enter and destroy other bacterial cells.
      8. If a bacterial cell survives the onslaught of a virus, the DNA of the original bacterial host may be mutated to a new form or strain of bacterium, which some microbiologists hypothesize as the cause of new outbreaks of certain types of bacterial infections in humans and other organisms.

IV. PLANT VIRUSES
   A. Plant viruses are often named after the plant they enter, the special part of the plant they damage, or the appearance they produce in the plant.
   B. Many plant viruses damage and even kill plants, especially flowering plants, when they enter the plant cells.
      1. Plant viruses cause diseases in tomato, lettuce, potato, bean, cucumber, beet, tulip, and aster plants.
      2. They also cause diseases in the American elm and the peach tree.

C. Plant viruses can be spread in many ways.
   1. Most plant viruses are spread by insects, such as the aphid and the leaf hopper, which suck juices from leaves.
   2. Some viruses are spread when a leaf of one plant rubs against the leaf of another.
   3. Some are spread when the roots of an infected plant grow and touch the roots of a healthy plant.
   4. Sometimes they are spread by gardeners when handling diseased plants.
   5. Sometimes a virus can be spread in multiple ways, such as by infected insects that feed on a plant, and then by roots that are infected, which in turn infect roots of other nearby trees or plants.

V. HUMAN AND ANIMAL VIRUSES
   A. Viruses cause many diseases in humans and animals.
   B. Some well-known viral diseases are the common cold, influenza, viral pneumonia, polio, smallpox, cowpox, chicken pox, measles, German measles, warts, cold sores and fever blisters, shingles, mumps, rabies, infectious mononucleosis, infectious hepatitis, yellow fever, parrot fever, acquired immune deficiency syndrome (AIDS), and the hantavirus pulmonary syndrome, which had an outbreak in 1993 in the area of the four corners of New Mexico, Arizona, Utah, and Colorado.
   C. The virus that causes hantavirus pulmonary syndrome was first detected in the United States in a non-disease related form more than 10 years before its virulent outbreak in 1993.
      1. By 1994 cases of hantavirus pulmonary syndrome had been reported in people in more than 20 states.
      2. Victims can become ill by simply inhaling dried urine or feces of infected deer mice, which are the primary vectors of the virus.
   D. Human and animal viral diseases are spread in a number of ways.
      1. Virus-caused diseases that infect the respiratory system, such as the common cold and influenza, are spread by coughing and sneezing.
      2. Diseases that produce sores on the skin, such as chicken pox and cold sores, are spread by touching the sores.
      3. Viruses of diseases such as polio and infectious hepatitis are passed out in feces, which may then be touched by flies and carried to food and water that is consumed by humans.
      4. The human immunodeficiency virus (HIV) that causes acquired immune deficiency syn-

drome (AIDS) is passed from one victim to another in body fluids that contain the virus. Body fluids of an infected person that can have a high concentration of the HIV virus are blood, semen, vaginal fluids, and the breast milk of an infected mother.

E. Humans and animals often become immune to certain diseases after they have had those diseases.

1. Becoming immune to a disease means never getting that disease again.

2. When a person gets a viral disease, the body starts to make special proteins or molecules, called **antibodies**.

3. Antibodies try to neutralize the viruses that have entered the body by covering the viruses and making them harmless.

4. Sometimes a virus reproduces too fast and gets the best of the antibodies; the victim's immune system begins to break down and the person is then susceptible to even more diseases.

5. The body makes a different kind of antibody for each virus.

6. Normally, the body makes more antibodies than it needs, and these extra antibodies float around in the blood.

7. Some antibodies stay in the blood for the rest of a person's life. This means that the antibodies will destroy a certain virus if it should ever enter the body again.

VI. HOW HARMFUL VIRUS DISEASES MAY BE CONTROLLED

A. Antibiotics such as penicillin cannot be used to stop virus infections, because they work only against bacterial infections.

B. Some viral diseases can be controlled by using a **vaccine**.

1. A vaccine has a small amount of weakened or dead viral particles in it.

2. Some vaccines, such as smallpox and flu vaccine, are either scratched or injected into the arm or another part of the body. Giving a vaccine this way is called **vaccination**.

3. Other vaccines, such as the polio vaccine, are given by mouth.

C. When a person is vaccinated, the body begins to make antibodies immediately.

1. The antibodies remain in the blood for a long time.

2. Now the person becomes immune to the viral disease.

3. If new viruses for the same disease should get into the body, the antibodies will destroy the viruses.

D. Some plant, animal, and human viruses mutate so rapidly that finding drugs that are effective as treatment against them is a never-ending task.

E. By manipulating plant genes, genetic engineers were able to transfer into potato plants a gene that expresses a hepatitis B antigen. Mice eating these potatoes developed antibodies against the hepatitis virus.

F. Meanwhile, we can stop virus diseases from spreading by covering our mouths when coughing or sneezing, by not touching virus-caused sores, by disinfecting or burning things that have been touched by people who are sick with a viral disease, by being very careful when getting rid of body wastes from people who have the disease, by not touching dead or wild animals or their droppings, by protecting ourselves from inhaling dust particles that may carry a virus, and generally by being knowledgeable about how particular viral infections are spread and avoiding or taking precautions in situations where we may become exposed or might expose others.

BACTERIA

I. BACTERIA: THEIR CLASSIFICATION, STRUCTURE, AND VARIETY

A. Bacteria can be found everywhere—in the air; in the waters of streams, ponds, lakes, and oceans; in ice on the surface of ponds and lakes; in the soil; in other organisms; in dead plants and animals; on our skin and throughout our intestines; and in garbage.

1. Because fossil remains of bacteria have been found in rock dating more than 3.5 billion years old, bacteria represent the oldest form of life that is still found on earth today.

2. The study of both viruses and bacteria has been important to scientists in their formation of theories of how life began on earth.

B. In order to live and thrive, bacteria need a suitable temperature, which varies among different bacteria.

1. Some bacteria grow well in high temperatures, and others grow well in low temperatures, but

most bacteria grow best at temperatures ranging from 25° to 40° Celsius (77° to 104° F).

2. Although very high temperatures kill many bacteria, low temperatures do not usually kill bacteria but slow their metabolic activity and growth.

3. Some species, however, thrive at extreme temperatures. For example, certain bacteria thrive on the ocean floor where deep-sea volcanic vents release very hot fluids (with temperatures as high as 757° F or 400° C), where the water pressure may be as high as 250 tons per square inch, and where there is little to no oxygen. Around such deep-sea vents bacteria form the base of a food chain in that unusual environment, where energy is supplied not by sunlight but by hydrogen sulfide discharged from deep within the earth. The bacteria are able to oxidize the hydrogen sulfide and convert carbon dioxide from seawater into organic compounds.

4. Some bacteria thrive both at high temperatures and in acidic environments, such as those that live in the hot sulfur springs at Yellowstone National Park.

5. Colonies of cold-thriving bacteria have been found growing in a frozen pond near the geographic south pole.

C. Bacteria need water or moisture for growth.

1. Although lack of water does not kill most bacteria, it does stop or slow their activity and growth. That is why dehydrated foods can be stored for long periods of time without spoiling.

D. Bacteria are classified in two groups, the archaebacteria and eubacteria. The **archaebacteria** include three types of bacteria that are found in oxygen-free habitats where little else will live.

1. One type lives in oxygen-free environments and produces methane gas. Some members of this group live in the stomachs of cows, where the bacteria help to break down cellulose in the grass eaten by cows. Methane-producing bacteria are also found in sewage treatment plants, freshwater swamps, and deep-sea habitats. They get their energy from carbon dioxide and hydrogen gas, producing methane as a waste product.

2. Another group lives only in bodies of concentrated saltwater, such as the Great Salt Lake in Utah and the Dead Sea in the Middle East. These bacteria produce a purple pigment that allows them to photosynthesize.

3. A third group is found in the hot, acidic waters of sulfur springs such as those in Yellowstone National Park. These bacteria grow best at temperatures of about 60° Celsius (140° F) and a pH of 1 to 2, which is the pH of concentrated sulfuric acid.

E. The **eubacteria** are the most diverse group in terms of habitat and metabolism.

1. One group of eubacteria, the heterotrophs, are found everywhere. Heterotrophic bacteria need organic molecules as an energy source but are not adapted for trapping the food that contains these molecules. Thus, some live as **parasites**, absorbing nutrients from other living organisms. Others live as **saprobes**, organisms that feed on dead organisms or organic wastes. Saprobes help to recycle the nutrients contained in decomposing organisms.

2. A second group of eubacteria are **photosynthetic autotrophs**. They obtain their energy from light. These bacteria have a photosynthetic pigment that allows them to trap sunlight. Some are blue-green in color and others are red or yellow. The cyanobacteria are in this group. They are common in ponds, streams, and moist land areas. They are composed of chains of cells, rather than of single cells. Cyanobacteria are often one component of lichens. The other component is a fungus.

3. A third group of eubacteria are **chemosynthetic autotrophs**. These bacteria obtain their energy from the breakdown of inorganic substances such as sulfur and nitrogen compounds. Some of these bacteria are important in converting nitrogen in the atmosphere to forms that can be used readily by plants.

F. Bacteria are the smallest and simplest of living things, falling in complexity between the viruses and the cellular organisms.

1. Their cells have no membrane-bound organelles such as a nucleus, mitochondria, or chloroplasts.

2. Their cytoplasm is bound by a plasma membrane which regulates what enters and exits the cell.

3. Around that is a cell wall that gives the cell its shape.

4. In addition to the plasma membrane and the cell wall, some bacteria are coated with a gelatinous capsule and still others have yet another but thinner coating called a slime layer. These coatings help such bacteria to stick to the surface of a food supply, prevent them from drying out, and protect them from predators such as white blood cells.

DEMONSTRATION 13.1
The Exponential Growth of Bacteria*

Demonstration

Bring a checkerboard and $21.00 in pennies to class. Ask students to calculate how many squares you can cover on the board if you put one penny in the first square, two in the second, four in the third, and so on until you run out of pennies. (Eleven squares will be completely covered and $0.53 will remain.) Relate this demonstration to the way in which large populations of bacteria can be produced in just a few generations.

Problem

When living in a favorable environment, bacteria can reproduce every 20 minutes or so. As conditions become less ideal, the rate of cell division slows. Suppose you begin with a single bacterium, and it and its progeny reproduce once an hour. Ask students to set up a table to de-

termine how many bacteria there would be at the end of one day (24 hours). To do this, they should set up a table listing hours 0 to 24. At hour 0, there would be one bacterium. After one hour, the bacterium will have reproduced once, so there will be two bacteria. At hour 2, each of these bacteria will have reproduced once, giving a total of four. To find the number of bacteria after 24 hours, continue this doubling 24 times, once for each time the bacteria reproduce. (After 24 hours there will be 2^{24}, or 16,777,216 bacteria). Remind students that bacteria in food may double in number every 20 minutes. Food poisoning often results when foods are not properly refrigerated.

*Adapted from Alton Biggs, Chris Kapicka, et al., *Biology: The Dynamics of Life* (Westerville, OH: Glencoe/McGraw-Hill, 1995), p. 524. By permission of the publisher.

5. Their inherited information (DNA) is contained in a region in the cytoplasm called a nucleoid. There is extrachromosomal nucleic acid outside the nucleoid in circular arrangements called plasmids.
6. Although larger than viruses, which can be seen only with an electron microscope, bacteria appear tiny under a light microscope. They are so small that hundreds of thousands of them can be placed on the period at the end of this sentence. Their size range is from 0.5 to 2.0 micrometers in diameter (in spherical bacteria) to 60 micrometers in length (in some spiral bacteria).
G. Bacteria are often classified by shapes and arrangements of their cells.
   1. The three most common shapes are spherical (coccus), rods (bacillus), and spirals (called spirillum).
   2. In addition, there are comma-shaped bacteria called vibria and flexible wavy-shaped bacteria called spirochetes.
   3. Although some bacterial cells live singly, others are typically grouped together. When arranged in pairs of cells, the prefix *diplo-* is used. A diplococcus bacterium is one that exists as pairs of spherical cells. When cells are arranged in grapelike clusters, the prefix *staphylo-* is used. A staphylococcus bacterium is one that exists as grapelike clusters of spherical cells. The prefix *strepto-* refers to

long chains of cells. A streptococcus bacterium is one with long chains of spherical cells, like a necklace.
   4. Many bacilli and spirilli have tiny, threadlike structures called flagella protruding from their cells. Some have flagellae at one or both ends of the cell, and others have these structures distributed throughout the surface of the cell. These structures have a whiplike movement, which makes it possible for the bacteria to move about in water, blood, and other liquids. Because these bacteria are mobile, they were once thought to be tiny animals.

II. HOW BACTERIA REPRODUCE

A. Bacteria cannot reproduce by mitosis or meiosis because they have no nuclei. Instead, they have evolved different methods of reproduction.
B. Bacteria usually reproduce **asexually** by **binary fission**, in which (1) a cell grows in size, (2) the cell duplicates its single chromosome, (3) the pair of chromosomes split apart and move to opposite sides of the enlarged cell, and (4) the cell then divides into two new daughter cells, each of which is genetically identical to the original parent cell.
   1. In some cases the two new cells break apart, and in other cases they stay connected to form a chain of cells.
   2. When conditions for growth are just right, cells can mature in 20 to 30 minutes and start

the process all over again. Under the right conditions, a few hundred bacteria can become millions in a very short time.

3. Their ability to grow and reproduce quickly is what makes bacteria so important and what makes **pathogenic** (disease-causing) bacteria so dangerous.

4. When conditions are unfavorable for growth, bacteria protect themselves by producing an **endospore.** An endospore is produced within a bacterial cell. Endospores have a hard outer covering and are resistant to drying out, boiling, and many chemicals. While in the endospore form, the bacterium is in a state of slow metabolism, and it does not reproduce. When it encounters more favorable conditions, the endospore germinates and gives rise to a bacterial cell that resumes growing and reproducing. Some endospores have been found to germinate after thousands of years. Because endospores can survive boiling, canned foods and medical instruments must be sterilized under high pressure. The greater degree of heat can kill endospores.

5. Endospore formation is especially common with bacilli, the rod-shaped bacteria.

6. Some bacteria, such as the *E. coli* bacterium, have a simple form of **sexual reproduction** called conjugation. During conjugation, one bacterium cell transfers all or part of its chromosome material to another cell through a bridge formed to connect temporarily the two conjugating cells.

III. HELPFUL AND HARMFUL BACTERIA

A. Most bacteria are harmless, living in air, soil, and water, on our skin, and even in our bodies, without doing any harm.

1. Even bacteria that are potentially pathogenic may not always cause disease.

2. The coccus bacterium that causes **meningitis** is often found in people who are healthy, never causing them harm. The meningitis-causing bacterium is found in the throat. Normally, the throat's epithelial lining is a barrier to the bacterium, keeping it from getting into the bloodstream and moving to the meninges, the membranes that surround the brain and spinal cord. But if the normal lining is broken down and the bacterium gains access to the bloodstream and finds its way to the cerebrospinal fluid that bathes the central nervous system, it can cause the disease meningitis, which is fatal if untreated.

3. Recent studies indicate that an infection by one kind of nonpathogenic bacteria may sometimes protect against invasion by a similar but pathogenic strain, which might be one reason that some people seem more susceptible to certain diseases (both bacterial and viral diseases) than others. Exposure to a strain of a similar but nonpathogenic bacteria or virus may provide immunity to a person later exposed to pathogenic strains.

B. Many bacteria have long been known to be quite helpful to humans.

1. One group of bacteria sours milk, which is important in the making of butter and cheese.

2. Certain kinds of cheeses, such as Swiss cheese, get their flavor from the metabolic activity of bacteria.

3. Another group of bacteria changes alcohol into vinegar.

4. The action of bacteria on the stems of the flax plant loosens the plant fibers, which are then stripped and woven into linen.

5. Bacteria are used in curing tobacco, giving the tobacco a special flavor.

6. Bacteria live on our skin, the "good" ones preventing pathogenic bacteria and fungi from occupying space and causing skin diseases, unless we overwash.

7. Bacteria help to separate the flesh from animal skins and, in a process called tanning, change the skin into soft leather.

8. Bacteria are used in septic tanks and sewage treatment plants to get rid of sewage by changing the solid wastes into easily removable liquids.

9. Bacteria act quickly on dead plant and animal matter, changing it into humus, which enriches the soil.

10. Nitrogen-fixing bacteria take nitrogen gas from the air and change it into nitrogen materials that plants need to grow.

11. A relatively newly discovered anaerobic bacterium that lives in the digestive tract of bowhead whales may eventually be used to help clean up oil spills by degrading key oil spill components, PCBs, and other carcinogenic compounds. Further study of this bacterium may also explain how whales can consume high levels of toxic compounds without getting cancer, as other animals would.

C. Some bacteria are harmful to humans.

1. Some bacteria make food spoil, producing poisonous materials, called toxins, which can cause illness and even death.

DEMONSTRATION 13.2
Some Bacteria are Helpful to Humans*

Bring to class a bag full of groceries containing food items that could not be made without bacteria. Include Swiss cheese, pickles, vinegar, sauerkraut, yogurt, peas, beans, soybeans, peanuts, milk, and sour cream. Explain the importance of bacteria to the development of each product,

including the role of nitrogen-fixing bacteria to the growth of certain kinds of plants.

*Source: Alton Biggs, Chris Kapicka, et al., *Biology: The Dynamics of Life* (Westerville, OH: Glencoe/McGraw-Hill, 1995), p. 524. By permission of the publisher.

TABLE 13.1 Diseases in Humans Caused by Bacteria

Bacterial pneumonia	Gonorrhea	Scarlet fever	Tuberculosis
Botulism	Leptospirosis	Staph infections	Typhoid fever
Boils	Lyme disease	Strep throat	
Diphtheria	Meningitis	Syphilis	
Ear infections	Rocky Mountain spotted fever	Tetanus	

    2. Some bacteria are pathogens; that is, they cause disease (see Table 13.1).

IV. HOW HARMFUL BACTERIA MAY BE CONTROLLED

  A. Ultraviolet rays can kill bacteria.

  B. Antibiotics can destroy many kinds of bacteria that are parasitic and disease causing in the human body. (Antibiotics can also kill nonpathogenic bacteria.)

  C. Disinfectants, germicides, heat, filters, heavy metals, changes in pH, ionizing radiation, changes in osmotic pressure—all can kill bacteria outside the body.

  D. Heat, cold, and certain chemicals can stop the growth of many bacteria.

    1. The growth of harmful bacteria in raw milk is stopped by heating the milk at 60° Celsius (140° F) 20 to 30 minutes. Milk treated this way is said to be pasteurized.

    2. When food is canned, it is heated to stop the growth of harmful bacteria in the food and then sealed in airtight containers to prevent other harmful bacteria from getting into the containers.

    3. Antiseptics can stop bacteria from growing.

    4. Cold temperatures and quick-freezing can slow or stop the growth of bacteria.

    5. The removal of water, called dehydration, from foods stops the growth of bacteria.

    6. Salting, sugar curing, and pickling all preserve foods. Both the salt and sugar remove moisture from the bacteria cells and stop their growth. Smoking foods also removes moisture and stops the growth of bacteria.

FUNGI

I. FUNGI: THEIR CHARACTERISTICS, STRUCTURE, AND VARIETY

  A. Fungi resemble viruses and bacteria in that they lack chlorophyll and cannot make their own food; that is, they are not autotrophic. Instead, fungi are **heterotrophic.**

    1. There are more than 77,000 kinds of fungi, including molds, mildews, yeasts, rusts, smuts, and mushrooms.

    2. Fungi vary in size. Some are so tiny that they can be seen only under a microscope; others combine to form large masses that make up mushrooms and puffballs. A mushroom is only an above-ground portion of an individual fungus that can be larger than a whale. In 1992 an enormous fungus specimen of *Armillaria bulbosa* was found on the border of Wisconsin and Michigan. It is estimated to weigh at least 220,000 pounds, to spread over more than 37 acres, and to be 1,500 years old, which makes it one of the largest and oldest of all living organisms.

  B. Most fungi are made up of threads, or filaments, called **hyphae.**

1. Each hypha is made up of many cells, some with cell walls and some without cell walls.
2. The whole mass of hyphae that make up the fungus is called the **mycelium**.
3. The hyphae themselves are white or gray, but many fungi have red, orange, yellow, green, blue, or black pigments that give the fungi a special color.

C. Fungi grow best in darkness under conditions of moisture and warm temperatures.

D. Because fungi have no chlorophyll and consequently cannot produce their own food, they must get their food from other sources.
1. Some fungi are **parasites**, getting their food from other organisms.
2. Other fungi are **saprophytes**, getting their food from dead plants and animals, or from materials made from plants and animals, such as food products.
3. Still other fungi live in a **mutual symbiotic relationship** with other organisms. For example, Douglas fir and western hemlock trees, in old-growth forests of the Pacific northwest, depend on a fungus that lives on the logs of fallen trees. The fungus provides a shield around the trees' roots and secretes antibiotics into the soil that helps to prevent infection in the trees' roots. The fungus, in turn, depends on the sugar provided by the photosynthesis occurring in the trees.

E. Nearly all fungi are **aerobic**, being able to use the free oxygen in the air.

F. All fungi can reproduce asexually through cell division by forming tiny, round bodies called **spores**.
1. Fungi produce tremendous numbers of spores.
2. Each spore is surrounded by a protective cover or wall.
3. The spores are carried off in all directions by the wind and through other means.
4. When they land on objects, if conditions are favorable for growth (moisture, warmth, darkness, suitable food supply), the spores grow into fungi.
5. When conditions are unfavorable, the spores can live quietly without growing for long periods of time until conditions become favorable for growth.

G. Some fungi can reproduce sexually by forming sexual cells, called gametes, through meiosis.
1. The male haploid cell is called a sperm, and the female cell is called an egg.
2. The male and female cells unite (fertilization) to form a diploid cell, called a zygote.
3. The zygotes form new fungi, which can then reproduce either asexually, by forming spores, or sexually, by forming gametes that unite to form new zygotes.

II. Molds

A. Although most molds grow best in places that are dark, damp, and warm, some grow well at temperatures near freezing.

B. Molds can grow on most foods, as well as on paper, leather, wood, and human skin.

C. Most molds are made up of tubular threads, or filaments, called **hyphae**.
1. Some molds, such as bread mold, have three kinds of hyphae.
2. Tiny, rootlike hyphae, called **rhizoids**, grow downward into the bread, digest the food materials, and then take in, or absorb, the digested food.
3. Other hyphae, called **stolons**, spread out horizontally over the surface of the bread and then grow downward to form more rhizoids.
4. Some hyphae grow upright, and their purpose is to form spores.
5. After a few days, round bodies or knobs appear on the ends of these hyphae.
6. Each knob is a spore case, called a **sporangium**, containing thousands of spores.
7. These spores, which are colored, give the molds their characteristic colors; for example, black bread mold has black spores.
8. When the spore cases (sporangia) are ripe, they split open and the spores float away in the air.
9. Each spore can form a new hyphae, which will soon become a complete mold made up of many hyphae.

D. All molds reproduce asexually by forming spores, but some can also reproduce sexually by forming sexual cells (gametes).
1. Sometimes two hyphae of the same mold develop connecting branches, which join together.
2. Where the branches join together, a cell from each branch acts as a sexual cell, and these cells unite to form a zygote.
3. The zygote then begins to form a new mold.

E. Some molds are parasitic, and others are saprophytic.
1. Molds may be harmful: many molds spoil foods; molds growing on fruit trees damage the fruit; and some parasitic water molds kill fish and other sea animals.

2. Molds can also be helpful: molds are used in making such cheeses as Roquefort, Camembert, and Limburger; antibiotics, such as penicillin, streptomycin, and aureomycin, are obtained from molds.

III. MILDEWS

A. Mildews are whitish or dark-colored fungi and are closely related to molds.
B. Most mildews are parasites.
  1. Some mildews have a downy texture and attack such plants as radishes, potatoes, cereal grains, sugar cane, and tobacco.
  2. Some mildews are powdery and attack such plants as lilacs, roses, phlox, clover, grapes, and apples.
C. Black mildew is often found on clothes and shower stalls that have been exposed to dampness for a long time.
D. Mildews reproduce through spores.

IV. YEASTS

A. Yeasts are microscopic, one-celled fungi, usually oval in shape, that reproduce in a special way called **budding.**
  1. When conditions are favorable, a little knob or bud pushes out from one side of the yeast cell, and breaks away to form a new yeast cell.
  2. Sometimes many buds stay attached to the same yeast cell and form a chain.
B. When conditions are unfavorable, a yeast cell may produce a spore case, usually containing four spores.
C. Yeast is important to humans because of its action on sugar.
  1. It breaks down sugar to form alcohol and carbon dioxide gas.
  2. This action is called **fermentation**.
  3. In making alcohol by using yeast, the alcohol is saved, but the carbon dioxide is usually allowed to escape.
D. Yeast is used in making bread.
  1. Bubbles of carbon dioxide gas are formed, which swell and make the dough rise.
  2. This bubbling leaves many small spaces and makes the bread light and fluffy.
  3. As the bread is baked, the heat drives off the carbon dioxide and the alcohol that have been formed.
E. Fruits, such as grapes and apples, ferment when they are crushed.
  1. Their skins usually have wild yeast on them.

2. When the skin of these fruits is broken, the yeasts act on the sugar in the fruit, turning the juice into wine or cider.
F. Yeasts are also helpful to humans as a source of vitamin B_2, which they produce in their cells.
G. Some yeasts cause infections in humans.

V. RUSTS AND SMUTS

A. Rusts and smuts are parasitic fungi that thrive under moist, dark, and warm conditions.
B. Rusts produce reddish brown spores, which look like rust, and can destroy such plants as wheat, apple trees, white pine trees, roses, oranges, and melons.
C. Smuts produce blackish spores and can destroy cereal grains, such as corn, oats, barley, and wheat.

VI. MUSHROOMS

A. Mushrooms are the largest fungi.
B. They are saprophytes, living on dead plant and animal matter in the soil.
C. They may grow underground for years, producing a large mass of tangled threads (hyphae), that eventually come together just below the surface of the ground to form a small cap.
D. When the weather is damp, especially in the spring or the fall, this closely packed mass pushes its way above the ground and the cap opens to form a mushroom.
  1. The mushroom stalk is called the **stipe**.
  2. The umbrella-shaped top of the mushroom is called the cap or **pileus**.
  3. On the underside of the cap are fleshy plates, called **gills**, which contain the spores of the mushroom.
E. Some mushrooms have a ring around their stalk (stipe), which is the point where the cap was attached to the stalk before the mushroom moved above the ground and the cap spread open.
  1. Each fleshy gill contains hundreds of spore cases.
  2. Each spore case contains four spores.
  3. The spores may be black, white, pink, yellow, or brown.
F. Some mushrooms are good to eat, but others are very poisonous.
  1. Only experts should pick wild mushrooms for food. Some mushrooms that are deadly to humans look very much like the edible kinds, and eating just one could be fatal.
G. Puffballs are like mushrooms, except that they are not umbrella shaped.

1. They are either round or pear-shaped balls, usually white in color.
2. When the puffballs are fully grown, they dry up and split open, sending all their spores out into the air.
3. Puffballs can be as large as 1 meter (3 ft) across when fully grown.

4. They can be eaten when they are young and before their spores have ripened, *but collecting edible puffballs and mushrooms in the wild should clearly be left to the professionals.*

H. Mycologists (biologists who specialize in fungi) are concerned about a possible worldwide decline in mushroom populations, possibly caused by air pollution.

Slime Molds

I. The Characteristics of Slime Molds

A. Slime molds are different from fungi molds. They are not true molds.
B. Slime molds usually grow on damp, decaying leaves and other dead plant material. Their colonies can be orange, yellow, blue, violet, white, black, or colorless.
C. During the slime mold's life cycle, it is both animal-like and plant-like.

1. Slime molds reproduce from spores.
2. At first they are one-celled, have threadlike hairs, termed **flagella**, and move about as they feed and grow.
3. Individuals join to form a very large colony, which also moves as it feeds on bacteria, other protists, and dead plant or animal matter.
4. Later the colony moves to a drier place, stops moving, and produces spore cases.

Lichens

I. Characteristics of Lichens

A. Although lichens are often grouped with fungi, a lichen is really two organisms—either a green alga or a cyanobacterium, and a fungus—living together in a special form of **symbiosis**, called **mutualism**. Each benefits from the association. In the case of lichens, two organisms live as one organism.
   1. In this mutualistic relationship, both organisms benefit from the association. In other forms of symbiosis, such as parasitism, only one benefits.
   2. The fungus gets its food from the algal or the cyanobacterial component, which contains chlorophyll and makes food through photosynthesis. The fungus protects the photosynthesizing component with its hyphae (threads) and supplies it with the moisture needed for photosynthesis.
   3. Some evidence indicates that the fungus component actually consumes some of the algae or bacteria for food energy. This, then, would be a more parasitic than mutualistic relationship.
B. Lichens are usually green because of the green algae they contain. Some have other pigments too, which make them appear red, orange, yellow, or brown.

C. Lichens grow on the bark of trees, on the ground, and on rocks.
   1. Lichens that grow on rock eventually cause the rock to crumble. The lichen gives off carbon dioxide gas, which combines with water to form carbonic acid. The acid causes the rock to become soft and crumbly, changing it eventually into soil.
D. Lichens can grow anywhere. Some even grow in desert regions and others near the north and south poles.
   1. Lichens grow very slowly. Very large lichens may be thousands of years old.
   2. Sometimes lichens are erroneously referred to as moss, but lichens can grow in a much drier habitat than can moss plants.
   3. Reindeer moss and Iceland moss, for example, are not mosses, but lichens. Spanish moss is neither a lichen nor a moss, but a flowering plant, a member of the pineapple family.
   4. The lichens commonly called reindeer moss and Iceland moss are used by reindeer and other mountain animals as a source of winter food.
E. Lichens have been used in making dyes, in tanning hides for leather, and in making perfumes. Litmus paper, used to test acidity, can be made with a lichen dye. In China, Japan, and Iceland, some lichens are used as food.

Algae

I. The Classification of Algae

A. The cells of all algae contain chlorophyll. Algae are **autotrophs,** that are able capable of making their own food through photosynthesis.
   1. Although all algae contain green-colored chlorophyll, many algae also have other pigments that dominate or mask their green color.
B. Algae are classified according to their dominant pigments.
   1. Algae are classified into five (or six when euglenoids are included) phyla.
   2. Euglenoids, diatoms, and dinoflagellates are composed of only unicellular species. The green, red, and brown algae may contain some unicellular members, but most are multicellular.

II. Structure of Algae

A. Already indicated, some algae have only one cell (unicellular) and others have many cells (multicellular). The multicellular forms live together in colonies.
   1. Algae that form colonies are not truly multicellular organisms, but are made up of many one-celled organisms living together. The algae that make up a colony are attached to each other, yet each lives independently and does not have to depend on other algae.
B. Many algae are mobile. All algae are aquatic or semiaquatic (living in very moist habitats).
   1. Some algae seem to swim about like animals, whereas others float in the water or settle to the bottom.
C. Many algae are shaped like threads and are called filaments. These may be attached to each other to form colonies.
D. Many kinds of algae have a jellylike cell covering.
   1. This covering protects the cell from dehydration and from unfavorable conditions, such as occur when a pond dries up.
   2. These coverings make the algal colony feel slimy and hard to grasp when in the water.

III. How Algae Reproduce

A. Algae can reproduce in many ways.
B. All algae can reproduce asexually through fission or simple cell division (mitosis). An algal cell divides into two new algae cells.
   1. When the algae in a colony reproduce by fission, the colony becomes larger, because all the new algae are connected to the older ones and to each other.
C. Many algae reproduce asexually by forming small bodies, called spores.
   1. At first the spores swim around freely like tiny animals.
   2. Later, they settle against an object such as a pebble or rock in the stream or pond.
   3. Some spores form new algae immediately. Other spores remain dormant for weeks or months until environmental conditions are right, and then they develop into new algae.
D. Some algae reproduce sexually through meiosis, which produces sex cells or gametes.
   1. The male gamete is called a sperm, and the female cell is called an egg. The gametes unite to form the new diploid cell, called a zygote.
   2. Some zygotes grow into new algae immediately. Others remain dormant for a time before forming new algae.

IV. The Euglenoids

A. Euglenoids are unicellular, aquatic, green-colored, autotrophic/heterotrophic organisms that display traits of both plants and animals. Euglena is likely to be studied both in general botany and in general zoology.
   1. Euglenoids belong to the phylum **Euglenophyta**. A commonly studied genus is *Euglena* (see Figure 13.1).
   2. They lack a cellulose wall that is characteristic of plant cells, but they do contain chlorophyll and can produce their own food through photosynthesis. They are autotrophic.
   3. Euglena has a bright red spot, called an eyespot, which is sensitive to light and may help direct the cell toward sunlight.
   4. When light is unavailable for photosynthesis, the euglenoid can ingest food from its surroundings, much in the same way that protozoans do. They can be heterotrophic.
   5. Euglena is commonly found in freshwater ponds and streams. It is shaped like a pear, with one end rounded and the other pointed. It seems to be flexible and can change its shape, such as into a ball.
   6. Euglena is quite mobile, moving about by the use of one or two flagella that are lo-

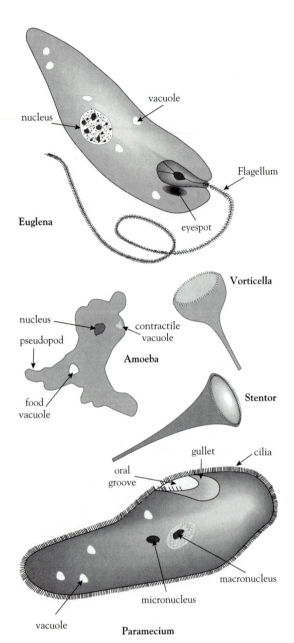

nucleus
vacuole
Flagellum
Euglena
eyespot

Vorticella

nucleus
contractile vacuole
pseudopod
Amoeba
food vacuole

Stentor

gullet
cilia
oral groove
macronucleus
micronucleus
vacuole
Paramecium

FIGURE 13.1   Some common protozoans (not to scale).

cated at one end of the cell, which turn in a spiral motion and drive the euglena through the water.

7. When environmental conditions become unfavorable, such as during a drying out period, euglena forms a protective coating, called a cyst, around its cell and loses it flagellum. Inside this cyst the euglena can live through periods of drought. When condi-

tions are once again favorable, the cyst breaks open and the euglena again becomes an active organism. Many protozoans have this same ability to form cysts when environmental conditions are unfavorable.

V. DIATOMS: THE GOLDEN-BROWN ALGAE

A. Diatoms are unicellular algae that are usually golden-brown in color, although some are yellow-green. Although they contain chlorophyll, their dominant pigments are carotenoids, which give the diatoms their characteristic coloring.
   1. They belong to the phylum **Bacillariophyta,** unicellular organisms with cell walls that create a shell made of silica.
B. Diatoms are photosynthetic autotrophs and are abundant in both marine and freshwater ecosystems, where they make up a large component of the phytoplankton.
   1. Diatoms are major players in the food chain of marine animals. They are the principal food of whales and other marine life.
   2. The food they manufacture photosynthetically is stored in the form of oils rather than starch. It is these oils that give fish and other animals that feed on them the familiar "fishy" or oily taste.
C. Diatoms have distinctive shapes. They can be round, oval, triangular, rectangular, spindle-shaped, or boat-shaped.
   1. Because of their geometric shapes, intricate patterns, and interesting designs, diatoms have long been the fascination of artists and mathematicians.
D. They have cell walls that are filled with a glasslike material called silica.
   1. The cell wall is composed of two parts that fit together, one over the other, like the halves of a shoe box.
E. Diatoms reproduce both asexually, by cell division, and sexually, by the production of gametes.
F. When diatoms die, their shell-like walls fall to the bottom of the ocean or pond and, over a long period of time, pile up into masses.
   1. These masses, called **diatomaceous earth,** are scooped up, cleaned, and refined.
   2. They are then used in toothpastes and powders, scouring powders, blackboard chalk, pool filters, and other materials.

VI. THE DINOFLAGELLATES

A. The dinoflagellates belong to the phylum **Dinoflagellata**.

1. They are unicellular and have cell walls made of thick cellulose plates.
2. Dinoflagellates have two flagella. When these flagella beat, the cells spin. The group is commonly referred to as the "spinning algae."
3. They are autotrophic and contain chlorophyll, carotenoids, and red pigments.
4. They typically reproduce by cell division.

B. The dinoflagellates are found mostly in oceans, in saltwater.
1. Many species live symbiotically with jellyfish, mollusks, and corals, giving those animals vivid colorations.
2. Some free-living species are bioluminescent.
3. Several species of dinoflagellates produce very poisonous toxins. In the warm waters of the summer, they can reproduce in great numbers, causing the phenomenon known as the "red tide."

VII. THE RED ALGAE

A. The red algae belong to the phylum **Rhodophyta.**
1. All members of this group are marine algae. These are the red seaweeds, all of which are multicellular.
2. They produce new individuals by sexual reproduction.
3. Red algae grow attached to rocks along shorelines in both tropical and colder waters. Some species live in deep water.
4. Some cells of a colony have become specialized to attach the colony to rocks by structures known as holdfasts.

VIII. THE BROWN ALGAE

A. Brown algae constitute the phylum **Phaeophyta.**
1. Almost all of the brown algae live in saltwater along rocky coasts in cool seas.
2. Some are very small, but others can grow in colonies as long as 46 meters (150 ft). The larger brown algae, attached to rocks along the seacoast, are commonly called **kelp**. Kelp is used as packing around lobsters, crabs, oysters, and clams for shipping.

B. Some cells of the colonial forms of brown algae have become specialized.
1. Some cells have formed air bladders that help keep the colony afloat so that it is exposed to fresh oxygen and sunlight.
2. A cuplike part, called a holdfast, holds some cells tightly to a rock, similar to those of the red algae.

C. Some of the larger brown algae float freely in water.
1. Some cells of the colony have specialized to become air bladders that keep the plants afloat.
2. Sometimes these algae cover vast areas of water, as in the Sargasso Sea, the legendary graveyard of lost ships, in the North Atlantic Ocean.

D. The smaller forms of brown algae usually reproduce asexually by fission or by spores. The larger forms reproduce sexually (gametes).

IX. THE GREEN ALGAE

A. Although most species of green algae live in freshwater, some live in oceans, some on land on moist soil, and others on tree trunks, in snow, and even on the carapace of turtles and the fur of sloths. They belong to the phylum **Chlorophyta.**
1. Of all the algae types, the green algae are the most diverse, with more than 7,000 species worldwide.
2. Although their dominant pigment is chlorophyll, their color ranges from bluish- to yellowish-green.
3. Some green algae are one-celled, whereas others form large colonies comprised of single-cell individuals.

B. Some green algae reproduce asexually by fission or by spores, and still others reproduce sexually (by union of gametes).

C. Because they have a high protein content (higher in percentage than fish meal), unicellular forms of green algae, especially a genus known as *Chlorella*, have been grown hydroponically (in controlled liquid solutions) as a potential food source for humans either on earth or in space. For example, *Chlorella* can be grown on rooftops of buildings in large, shallow hydroponic containers, harvested, dried, and made into a high-protein powder that can then be used as a dough for baking.

X. USES OF ALGAE

A. Algae are the chief source of food for many aquatic animals.

B. Because of their ability to photosynthesize and their large numbers, algae are a also major source of the earth's atmospheric oxygen.

They are the primary source of oxygen needed by aquatic animals to live.

C. Seaweeds are used by farmers for fertilizing the soil. Brown algae are rich in potassium. In some parts of the world algae are used to make soups, gelatins, and a variety of other foods. Algae are used to make some ice creams smooth, and salad dressings thick.

D. One kind of algae is used to make agar-agar, which forms a jellylike material good for growing bacteria (in agar plates) in hospitals and laboratories.

E. Algae, especially the Chlorophyta, may eventually be used in space stations.

   1. Because algae carry on photosynthesis, they are able to use the carbon dioxide that human passengers give off and produce fresh oxygen.

   2. Because they grow so rapidly, there can always be a fresh supply to be strained, dried, and then prepared for use as food.

   3. As food, algae are high in protein.

PROTOZOANS

I. CLASSIFICATION OF PROTOZOANS

A. Protozoans are tiny, one-celled, animal-like protists.

B. Most are so small that they can be seen only with a light microscope or hand lens.

   1. At least two kinds of sessile (attached to an object in the water) protozoans, *Vorticella* and *Stentor*, are large enough to be seen with the unaided eye.

C. Because they can eat, breathe, move, and reproduce, just as animals do, they used to be considered members of the animal kingdom.

   1. Because they are unicellular, some classification schemes separate protozoans from the animal kingdom, which consists of multicellular animals.

D. Although most protozoans live independently, some live together in colonies; however, each colony member usually lives independently of other members, as is the case with colonial forms of algae.

E. Protozoans live either in water or where conditions are moist.

   1. Aquatic protozoans are found in either freshwater or saltwater.

   2. Some protozoans live in damp soil, and others live in decaying animal or plant matter.

   3. Some protozoans even live in the intestines of insects. Protozoans living in the termite are able to break down cellulose material, which permits the termite to feed on wood and other materials that have a high cellulose content.

F. Most protozoans are not autotrophic and cannot manufacture their own food.

G. Examples of well-studied and well-known protozoan genera include the *Amoeba, Paramecium, Vorticella, Stentor*, and *Euglena* (see Figure 13.1).

II. THE AMOEBA

A. The amoeba is one of the simplest protozoans. It belongs to the phylum **Sarcodina**.

B. Most of the hundreds of species in this phylum are marine amoebas, but there are freshwater amoebas that live in the slime on the bottom of ponds and rivers, in backyard puddles, in wet clumps of moss, and on the surface of the leaves of aquatic plants.

   1. Two forms of sarcodines have shells. These are marine amoebas that have a hard, outer shell of either calcium carbonate or silica. These sarcodines are so abundant that much of the bottom ooze that covers the sea floor is made up of their tiny shells.

C. Under a light microscope an amoeba looks like a blob of grayish jelly with no definite shape.

   1. Because they are nearly colorless, amoebas are located most readily under low power using minimum light levels. One species of amoeba, *Chaos chaos*, is almost large enough to be seen with the unaided eye.

   2. The shape of the amoeba keeps changing as it moves. Movement speeds up when the temperature is warm and slows down when the temperature is cool.

   3. As it moves, the amoeba sends out finger-like projections called **pseudopodia** (false feet). The rest of the amoeba's body then flows in the direction of the false feet.

   4. As the amoeba moves, it engulfs bits of food by flowing around and over them.

   5. There are tiny spaces or cavities, called vacuoles, in the cell of the amoeba. Some vacuoles contain food. Freshwater amoebas must constantly take in water because of living in a hypotonic environment (where the concentra-

tion of dissolved substances in the water in which they live is less than that of their cytoplasm). To counter this problem, they have contractile vacuoles that collect and pump out excess water from the cell.

    6. Oxygen in the water enters the amoeba by diffusion through the cell membrane, and carbon dioxide produced by cell's metabolism leaves in the same manner.

D. The amoeba reproduces asexually by simple cell division. It divides into two equal parts, forming two new cells.

III. THE PARAMECIUM

A. Paramecia are also unicellular. They are larger generally than the amoeba.

    1. Unlike the amoeba, the paramecium has a definite shape, somewhat like a slipper or the sole of a shoe (see Figure 13.1).

B. Paramecia belong to the phylum **Ciliophora**, known as ciliates.

    1. Paramecia move by the synchronized beating of the thousands of tiny hairlike cilia that emerge from their tough cell membranes to cover their bodies. By coordinated movement of these cilia, paramecia can move forward or backward and can change directions quickly.

C. Paramecia can be found in every kind of aquatic habitat, from backyard ponds to streams, lakes, oceans, and sulfur springs.

    1. The paramecium feeds primarily on bacteria that are swept into the cell through an opening known as the oral groove, located on the side of the paramecium's cell.

    2. The food then passes into a narrow tube, called the gullet, which leads into the cytoplasm of the cell.

    3. The food is held in vacuoles (cavities), where it is digested.

    4. The paramecium also has two vacuoles, one at each end of the cell, that get rid of excess water and some of the waste products.

    5. Oxygen from the water enters by diffusion through the cell membrane, and carbon dioxide produced by metabolism leaves the same way.

D. There are two kinds of nuclei in the paramecium: large and small.

    1. The large nucleus controls and directs the regular activities of the cell.

    2. The small nucleus functions in reproduction.

E. The paramecium reproduces as the amoeba does; that is, it splits in two.

    1. First the small nucleus splits, and each half moves to an end of the cell.

    2. Then the large nucleus splits.

    3. The cell narrows in the middle and separates, forming two new paramecia.

F. Occasionally, two paramecia come together and exchange nuclear material.

    1. This process of coming together is called conjugation.

    2. In conjugation no new paramecia are formed as in true sexual reproduction, but from the exchange of nuclear material, the paramecia are given a new genetic makeup; they then continue reproducing asexually through cell division.

IV. SPORE-FORMING PROTOZOANS

A. Some protozoans reproduce by forming tiny, round bodies, called spores. These belong to the phylum **Sporozoa**. They are all parasitic, nonmotile protozoans.

    1. They have no structures for moving, but are carried along in water or in the blood of their host.

B. A **spore** is a reproductive cell that can produce a new organism asexually, that is, without fertilization or the union of gametes.

    1. The nucleus of the cell divides into many small nuclei.

    2. Parts of the cytoplasm around the nucleus then surround each of the new nuclei to form spores.

    3. Finally, the whole protozoan breaks up and releases these spores.

    4. The spores then become new protozoans.

C. Living as internal parasites in one or more hosts, sporozoans have complex life cycles.

    1. The life cycle includes a sexual stage, during which gametes are produced and fuse to form a zygote.

    2. The zygote then divides many times (asexual reproduction) to form spores.

    3. Once inside a second host, each spore can then divide many times to produce many more spores.

D. Among the best known sporozoans are members of the genus *Plasmodium*.

    1. Different species of *Plasmodium* cause the disease malaria in humans, some mammals, and birds.

    2. Malaria is caused by sporozoans that are spread from host to host by female *Anopheles* mosquitoes.

3. In humans, the malaria cycle begins when a female mosquito bites an infected person.
4. It takes in the *Plasmodium* reproductive cells with its blood meal. Inside the mosquito those cells fuse to form a zygote, which, in turn, divides many times to form many spore fragments. Eventually the zygote breaks open, releasing the spores.
5. These spores invade the mosquito's salivary glands, from where they will be injected into a new host when the mosquito bites again. When the mosquito bites another human host, these spores are released into the victim's bloodstream. Through the bloodstream, the spores reach the victim's liver, where they form a second type of spore cell.
6. From the liver, these new spores reenter the bloodstream, invade red blood cells, and mul-

tiply rapidly inside those red blood cells. Eventually, the blood cells rupture, releasing great numbers of spores, and the process of invading and destroying red blood cells continues.
7. If untreated, the victim can become anemic and die. Worldwide, several million people each year die from malaria.

V. PROTOZOANS CAN BE BOTH HELPFUL AND HARMFUL

A. Protozoans serve as food for fish and other aquatic animals. Protozoans are helpful because they eat large amounts of bacteria that may be harmful.
B. Some protozoans cause serious diseases, such as malaria, African sleeping sickness, giardia, and amoebic dysentery.

EXPLORATORY ACTIVITIES FOR "NEITHER PLANT NOR ANIMAL"

1. *EXPLORING FOR ALGAE AND PROTOZOANS* (ANY GRADE LEVEL)

The following activities for exploring algae and protozoans contain general guidelines; specific procedures for student investigations will vary according to student maturity, grade level, availability of equipment and materials, and the interest that develops from these initiating activities.

Have students collect samples of pond water and water from backyard puddles to explore for living algae and protozoans. This activity can continue all year long.

1.1 Exploring Algae

Algae are easiest to collect during the spring and summer. They may be found as a greenish scum in shallow or stagnant pools and lakes, as a greenish coating on moist stones and walkways, or on the damp bark of the shaded side of a tree. Collect the algae from pools and lakes in large wide-mouthed jars, taking along a good amount of the water in which the algae were found. Do not put too many algae in one jar. Collect algae from bark by prying off a few small pieces of the bark and soaking it in tap water that has been allowed to stand for 24 hours in a large, wide-mouthed, open jar (to allow any chlorine in the water to escape). Algae found on stones may be scraped off and placed in jars containing tap water that also has been allowed to stand for 24 hours. In addition, collect water from standing puddles, ditches, and so on.

Because algae and protozoans kept in containers die rather quickly, they should be examined as soon as possible. Keep the containers in strong light, but not in direct sunlight. Place a drop of the green material on a microscope slide, cover with a cover glass, examine the algae under both the low and high powers of a microscope, and watch for protozoans too. In the cells of algae and euglena, look for the tiny bodies (chloroplasts) containing chlorophyll. See whether you can find examples of algae in different stages of reproduction. Find pictures of the common algae and use these to identify the specimens you have collected.

1.2 Investigating Conditions for Growth of Algae

Divide your class of students into investigatory teams. Have students hypothesize about the conditions necessary for algae to thrive. Place samples of algae in darkness, in medium to strong light, and in sunlight. Also keep samples of algae in the refrigerator, on or near a heated radiator, and at room temperature. This variation of conditions will help the students learn the optimum conditions of light and heat for the growth of algae.

1.3 Exploring Kelp

Look for rockweed, seaweed, or kelp along the seashore. If you live inland, obtain some from a fish store. Ask for the kind of seaweed or kelp that is used to pack lobsters, clams, and oysters that are flown or shipped from the sea-

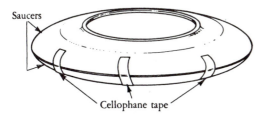

Saucers

Cellophane tape

FIGURE 13.2   A homemade petri dish.

coast to your city or town. Examine and cut open the air bladders. Look for and examine the cuplike holdfasts. The larger specimens will have divisions that look like stems and leaves. Look for protozoans and other creatures that inhabit the kelp. Have the students read about and report on the Sargasso Sea and the sargassum floating in it. During the days of the early explorations, the Sargasso Sea was the legendary graveyard of lost ships.

2. EXPLORING BACTERIA* (UPPER GRADES)

The following activities for exploring bacteria are general guidelines; specific procedures for student investigations will vary according to student maturity, grade level, availability of equipment and materials, and the interest that develops from these initiating activities.

2.1   Preparing Agar for Growing Bacteria

Boil a pint of water and add 4 tablespoons of nutrient agar. If nutrient agar is unavailable, use 4 tablespoons of gelatin, one beef bouillon cube, a teaspoon of sugar, and a pinch of baking soda. Boil the mixture for about 15 minutes. Let the culture liquid cool a few minutes until it is quite warm, but not hot. An alternate and much simpler culture material may be prepared by boiling a potato in water to which a pinch of baking soda has been added. Slices of the boiled potato will also grow bacteria, but not as well as the nutrient solutions.

Obtain four or five petri dishes that have been sterilized in an oven for one hour at 107° to 121° Celsius (225° to 250° F). If petri dishes are unavailable, use saucers instead. Place one saucer on top of another and hold them in place by taping their edges at two or three places (Figure 13.2). Stack four or five pairs of saucers in the oven and heat as directed. After one hour, remove the petri dishes or saucers and allow them to cool to room temperature, keeping them covered at all times. These containers will be used to hold the nutrient solution for collecting and growing bacteria.

Pour about 6 millimeters ($\frac{1}{4}$ in) of nutrient agar or gelatin mixture into each dish and cover the dishes. If a boiled potato is used as a culture material, cut off thin

*Note: When working with bacteria, it is advisable to wear a mask and plastic gloves.

slices with a sterilized knife and transfer them to the culture dishes with sterilized forceps or tweezers.

2.2   Collect and Grow Bacteria

Collect and grow bacteria in several different ways, perhaps by dividing your class of students into investigatory teams. Expose the culture material by lifting the top of a culture dish quickly; then have a child cough over the culture materials. Another child can stroke a dirty finger across the culture material or drop some dirt that has collected under his or her fingernails. Expose the culture material to the air in the classroom or elsewhere for about 15 minutes. Keep one dish sterile and closed at all times so that it can serve as a control. Keep the dishes in a warm, dark place. In a few days different colored spots will appear in the exposed dishes, showing the presence of colonies of bacteria.

2.3   Examine Bacteria Under a Microscope

Make a transfer needle by pushing the sharp point of a needle well into a small cork stopper. Use the cork stopper as a handle and sterilize the eye of the needle in a flame. Use the eye of the needle to transfer the bacteria to a microscope slide. Add a coloring agent, such as methylene blue or eosin, which can be obtained from the drugstore. The coloring agent should be very dilute, and the proper dilution can be prepared for you by a pharmacist. Although they are very small, some of the larger ones can be seen by focusing the microscope very carefully and experimenting with the angle and amount of light entering the microscope. Look for examples of the three different kinds of bacteria.

If the variety of bacteria is limited, try growing others by placing a handful of dead or decaying grass and leaves in a large, wide-mouthed jar of water. First expose the jar to air for one or two days, then cover the jar and let it stand for a few days more. The water should now contain a good supply of bacteria. Place a drop of the water on a microscope slide, then a drop of the coloring agent, as described earlier. Cover with a cover glass, blot up the excess liquid around the edges of the cover glass with the tip of a blotter, and examine the bacteria under the high power of a microscope.

2.4   Investigate Conditions for Growth of Bacteria

Prepare six sterile culture dishes of nutrient culture material, as described in activity 2.1. Grow bacteria in each dish by touching a sterile needle, prepared as described in activity 2.3, to a bacteria colony growing in another dish and smearing the bacteria on the needle across the culture material in the dishes.

Place one dish in a dark, warm place and another in the refrigerator, where it is dark and cold, and examine the dishes after a few days. Repeat the experiment, using a dark, warm place and a bright, sunny, warm place. Repeat the experiment, using a dark, warm, moist place and a dark, warm, dry place. Create a dark, warm, dry place by placing the dish on a radiator or a hot plate set at low heat, then covering the dish by putting a tin can over it. The experiments will show that bacteria grow best under dark, warm, moist conditions.

2.5 Explore Ways of Controlling Harmful Bacteria

Prepare and inoculate five sterile dishes containing nutrient culture, as described in the preceding activities. Place one dish in direct sunlight and a second dish in the oven, where it is both hot and dry. To the third dish add some disinfectant, such as Lysol or Creosol. To the fourth dish add some antiseptic, such as tincture of iodine or Metaphen. To the fifth dish add an antibiotic, such as a tablet or capsule of penicillin that has been dissolved or mixed in water. An antibiotic can be obtained from the drugstore or a doctor. Note that bacteria colonies fail to grow in each dish. Have the students read about and report on the work of Pasteur, Koch, and Lister in controlling harmful bacteria.

3. EXPLORING WITH FUNGI[*] (ANY GRADE LEVEL)

The following activities for exploring fungi are general guidelines; specific procedures for student investigations will vary according to student maturity, grade level, availability of equipment and materials, and the interest that develops from these initiating activities.

3.1 Growing Mold

Rub a piece of bread across a dusty surface, then moisten the bread. Place the bread in a closed container and put it in a warm, dark place. After a few days a white, cottonlike mold will form. Then black spots, which are spore cases, will appear as well. Molds can also be formed by placing cheese, jam, or a wet orange in a closed container and keeping the container in a warm, dark place for several days.

New items or more of the same items can now be inoculated if some of the mold is transferred to them. An orange or an apple can be inoculated simply by picking up some mold from one fruit with a sterilized pin or needle, plunging the mold into a fresh fruit, and then keeping the fruit in a warm, moist place.

Investigate conditions for control of molds. Have the students try growing molds, as described here, under moist and dry, warm and cold, and light and dark conditions. Then have the students draw conclusions as to which are the most favorable conditions for growing and for controlling molds.

3.2 Examining Molds with a Hand Lens and a Microscope

A magnifying glass will show the threads and black spore cases of molds quite clearly. To see the spores themselves, place a bit of the mold on a microscope slide and then add a drop of water and a drop of coloring agent, such as methylene blue, prepared and properly diluted by a pharmacist. Cover with a cover glass and examine under the high power of a microscope. Move the slide until a spore case can be clearly seen; then examine the spores inside.

3.3 Look for and Examine Mildew with a Hand Lens and a Microscope

Mildew will often form when old shoes, pieces of leather, or books are placed in a dark, moist, warm place. This mildew is usually black. A white mildew will often form on the leaves of flowering plants when the air is hot and humid and the weather has been rainy. Examine the mildew both under a magnifying glass and under a microscope.

3.4 Grow and Examine Yeast Cells

Dissolve one teaspoon of sugar in a tumbler of warm (not hot) water. Add a quarter of a yeast cake or a package of dried yeast, then let the tumbler stand for 24 hours in a warm place. Place a drop of the yeast culture that has formed on a microscope slide, cover with a cover glass, and observe the yeast plants under both the low and high powers of a microscope. Look for cell shapes, special features of yeast cells, and evidence of budding.

3.5 Observe the Action of Yeast on Dough

Mix flour, water, and sugar in the proper proportions to make bread dough. Divide the dough into two equal parts, and mix one part with half of a yeast cake or package of dry yeast that has been stirred in some water. Place each dough sample in a pan and set in a warm place for a few hours. The dough with the yeast will rise as the action of the yeast produces bubbles of carbon dioxide that expand in the dough.

[*]*Note:* When working with molds, it is advisable to wear a mask and plastic gloves.

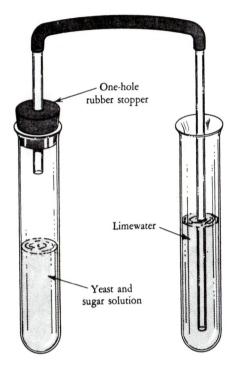

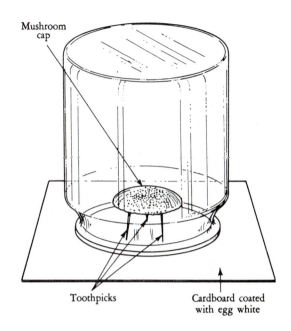

FIGURE 13.4 Obtaining spore prints from a mushroom.

FIGURE 13.3 When yeast ferments, the carbon dioxide it gives off causes limewater to become milky.

3.6 Investigate the Effect of Temperature on Yeast

Prepare a batch of bread dough and yeast, as described in the preceding activity. Divide the dough into three equal parts and place each part in a pan. Put one pan in the refrigerator, another sample in a warm place, and the third sample in a hot place. Examine all three batches of dough after a few hours. The dough in the warm place will show the greatest action of the yeast.

3.7 Yeast Causes Fermentation

Dissolve a full tablespoon of sugar in a tumbler of warm water. Add a quarter of a yeast cake or package of dried yeast, and let the tumbler stand for several days in a warm place. Smell the yeast culture and note the odor of ethyl alcohol. Point out that the yeast causes the sugar solution to ferment, producing ethyl alcohol and carbon dioxide.

3.8 Fermentation Produces Carbon Dioxide (Teacher Demonstration)

Prepare a yeast and sugar solution, as described in activity 3.7. Pour some solution into a test tube or narrow-necked glass jar and fit tightly with a one-hole rubber stopper, or modeling clay. Insert a small glass or plastic tube into the hole of the stopper, and connect this tube to another tube with rubber tubing (Figure 13.3). Insert the second tube into a test tube or jar containing clear limewater, which can be obtained from a drugstore. Place the apparatus in a warm place. In a few hours the limewater will turn milky, showing the presence of carbon dioxide. Show that limewater is a test for carbon dioxide by bubbling your breath through a straw into a test tube containing a little limewater.

3.9 Exploring Mushrooms and Making Spore Prints

Collect full-grown mushrooms and examine the stalks, caps, and gills. Carefully and gently cut away the stalk of a mushroom. Coat a piece of smooth or shiny cardboard with egg white. If the gills of a mushroom are covered with light-colored spores, use dark cardboard. If the spores are dark, use light cardboard. Push three toothpicks vertically into the sides of the mushroom cap so that they hold the cap 13 millimeters ($\frac{1}{2}$ in) above the cardboard (Figure 13.4). Place the cap on the cardboard and cover it with a wide-mouthed glass jar to prevent air currents from disturbing the spores. After 24 hours remove the jar carefully, then remove the cap. The gills of the mushroom will be permanently outlined on the cardboard by the spores that have fallen upon it.

STUDENT BOOKS AND OTHER RESOURCES FOR "NEITHER PLANT NOR ANIMAL"

Cobb, V. *Lots of Rot: Molds and Bacteria.* Philadelphia: J.B. Lippincott, 1984.

Fox, C. H. *AIDS and HIV Diseases.* Gladstone, Oregon: Carolina Biological Supply Co., 1991.

Hubbell, S. "How Taxonomy Helps Us Make Sense Out of the Natural World." *Smithsonian* 27(2): 140–151 (May 1996).

Jaret, P. "Viruses." *National Geographic* 186(1):58–91 (July 1994).

———. "The Disease Detectives." *National Geographic* 179(1):114–140 (January 1991).

Landau, E. *Rabies.* New York: Lodestar, 1993.

Shimkanin, J. "What Makes the Fizz?" *Science and Children* 32(7):12–15 (April 1995).

Silverstein, A., and V. B. Silverstein. *AIDS: Deadly Threat.* New York: Enslow, 1991.

Steinheimer, M. "The Moneran Museum." *Science Scope* 18(8):38 (May 1995).

CHAPTER 14

Animals

CLASSIFICATION OF ANIMALS

I. THE ANIMAL KINGDOM
   A. The animal kingdom, scientifically called the **Kingdom Animalia** (or the **metazoan kingdom**) is divided into 16 phyla that contain more than 1,200,000 species. The animal kingdom comprises two broad groups: animals with backbones (**vertebrates**) and animals without backbones (**invertebrates**). Members of phylum Chordata are vertebrates. All other phyla consist of invertebrates.
   B. Animal cells differ from plant cells in several ways. Animal cells do not have chlorophyll nor walls made of cellulose.
   C. All animals are **multicellular** organisms. Their bodies are made of many cells with different functions.

SPONGES AND COELENTERATES

I. THE PORIFERANS—SPONGE ANIMALS
   A. Poriferans are the simplest animals. Phylum Porifera includes the saltwater and freshwater sponges.
      1. The body of a poriferan is a hollow tube with many pores, or openings, in it. Water flows through the hollow tube, bringing in food and dissolved oxygen to the sponge cells, and taking away carbon dioxide and other waste products.
      2. The body wall is made up of two layers of cells, each of which is composed of cells with special functions.
      3. Many sponges have irregularly shaped bodies. They are **asymmetrical** (without symmetry).
      4. Asymmetrical animals are often sessile organisms. *Sessile* means that they are fastened to something and generally do not move from place to place. Long ago sponges were thought to be plants because they resembled plants and were attached to rocks and other objects in the water and did not seem to move from place to place.
   B. Sponges may be white, red, orange, yellow, brown, purple, black, or green.
      1. Some sponges look green because they are living together with algae. The algae have chlorophyll and make their own food through photosynthesis, giving off oxygen which the sponges use.
      2. The sponges give off carbon dioxide as a waste product of metabolism, and the algae use the carbon dioxide for photosynthesis.
      3. This arrangement, whereby two organisms live together and help each other, is a form of **symbiosis** called **mutualism.** It is similar to the relationship of fungi and algae, or fungi and cyanobacteria, in lichen.
   C. Sponges can live singly or in colonies; they feed on tiny floating plants and animals.

DEMONSTRATION 14.1
Examining Animal Cells

Obtain a toothpick with a blunt end. Gently scrape the inside of your cheek a few times with the blunt end of the toothpick. Spread the accumulated material on a microscope slide. Add a drop of water, stain with a drop of tincture of iodine, then cover the material with a cover glass. Examine the material carefully under the microscope until you find a clearly defined cell (that is, one that is very flat, polyhedral, and containing some small dark structures). Look for and identify the different parts of the cell. Compare this animal cell with a plant cell, such as an onion cell. Note both the similarities and differences between the plant and animal cells.

DEMONSTRATION 14.2
Comparing a Natural Sponge with an Artificial Sponge

Obtain a natural sponge and have the students observe the many holes in it. Let them feel the sponge; then point out that this soft, flexible material is the skeleton of the sponge. Compare a natural sponge and an artificial sponge.

D. Sponges have skeletons made of various kinds of materials. Poriferans are subdivided into classes based on their types of skeleton. Skeletons are made of calcium carbonate, silicon, or a soft and flexible material called spongin.
  1. The natural sponges that people use are the spongin skeletons of large sponges that live in warm parts of the oceans, especially the Mediterranean Sea, the Red Sea, the waters around the West Indies, and parts of the Gulf Coast of Florida. In deep waters the sponges are collected by divers; in shallow waters they are collected with hooks attached to the ends of long poles. The sponges are hung on the collectors' boats or piled on the shore and left there until the living cells die; the spongin skeleton parts that are left are then washed, dried, and sorted according to size.
E. Sponges can reproduce sexually by producing gametes through meiosis.
  1. The gametes are either male cells, called sperm, or female cells, called eggs.
  2. A sperm cell unites with, or fertilizes, an egg cell, producing a **zygote** that develops into a young sponge. The zygote can swim freely in the water by means of long whiplike threads called flagella. As young sponges grow older, they settle to the bottom of the sea and finally attach to a rock or another object.
F. Sponges can also reproduce asexually by **budding.**
  1. A bud develops near the base of the sponge and grows into a new sponge.
  2. Some grown buds stay attached to the parent sponge, but others break off, attach to an object, and live independently.

  3. As is true with many of the simpler animals, when a live sponge is cut up into many pieces, each piece can grow into a new sponge by **regenerating** the lost parts.

II. THE COELENTERATA—HYDRA, JELLYFISH, SEA ANEMONE, AND CORAL

  A. The general characteristics of the coelenterates, also called **cnidarians,** are as follows:
    1. Coelenterates have body walls that are two cells thick.
    2. They all have tentacles that surround their mouths, radiating out regularly like the spokes of a wheel. Some coelenterates have as few as six tentacles, but others may have hundreds.
    3. Circulation and digestion take place inside their hollow bodies.
    4. Their bodies have only one opening.
    5. A coelenterate body demonstrates **radial symmetry.** This means that a line drawn through the body along *any* plane would divide the animal into roughly equal halves. Radial symmetry is an adaptation that enables the animal to detect and capture prey coming toward it from any direction.
    6. Coelenterates display two basic body forms at different stages of their life cycle, **polyp** and **medusa.** Polyps are typically sessile (attached), whereas medusa forms are free-swimming.
    7. Coelenterates can reproduce both sexually and asexually. Polyp forms reproduce asexually by budding. Medusa forms reproduce sexually to form polyps. Polyps, in turn, reproduce asexually to form new medusae.

DEMONSTRATION 14.3
Exploring Live Hydra

Hydras can be found attached to the submerged stems or undersides of floating leaves of water plants in ponds. They are large enough to be seen with the naked eye. Tear off bits of plants to which hydras are attached and place them in glass jars together with some of the pond water. In the classroom keep the jars in semidarkness and feed the hydras a few tiny bits of lean meat once or twice a week.

Transfer one or two hydras to a saucer by using a medicine dropper with a wide tip. If necessary, break off part of the tip to make it wide enough to pick up a hydra without harming it. Place the tip of the medicine dropper directly over the hydra when sucking it up. After the hydra is in the saucer, add enough pond water to keep it covered.

Wait until the hydra has relaxed and stretched; then examine it with a magnifying glass. Note the movement of the tentacles. Tap the saucer with your finger. The startled hydra will contract to a tiny ball. The hydra will also contract if you touch it gently with a pin. Place one or two tiny bits of lean meat near the hydra and observe how the tentacles take the meat and bring it to the hydra's mouth. The tentacles will sting live tiny animals, such as water fleas or mosquito wigglers, that are placed near them. Look to see whether any of the hydras are reproducing by forming buds. Cut a hydra into two or more pieces with a razor blade and place the pieces and some pond water in a glass jar. In two or three weeks each piece will have become a new hydra.

B. **Hydra** is a member of phylum Coelenterata.
1. The name *Hydra* is a generic name. There may be several species of Hydra, but here the name will be used as if speaking of one organism, just as was done previously with other organisms such as Euglena, Paramecium, and Amoeba.
2. The hydra is found only in fresh water and is 3 to 6 millimeters (1/8 to 1/4 in) long.
3. A hydra may be white, brown, or green. Like some sponges, some hydras are green because they are living in symbiosis with green algae.
4. A hydra has a round, tubular body with a mouth at one end.
5. Surrounding the mouth are six to ten tentacles, which radiate outward like wheel spokes.
6. The tentacles contain specialized stinging cells, called **nematocysts.**
7. When small animals touch the tentacles, the stinging cells shoot out tiny threads with poison that paralyzes or kills the prey. The tentacles bend inward and push these captured animals through the hydra's mouth and into its body cavity.
8. Cells inside the hollow body digest the animals, and any waste products pass out through the mouth.
9. The polyp form attaches itself to rocks or aquatic plants at its closed, base end. It can move, however, by leaving the point where it is attached, floating in the water, then attaching itself at another point.
10. It can also move by turning "cartwheels": the body bends over, the tentacles touch the

ground, then the body releases the attachment and swings up and over.
11. When the hydra is disturbed or irritated, its tentacles and body quickly contract.
12. Similar to poriferans, hydras can reproduce asexually by budding. A bud develops on the side of the body to form a new hydra, which separates from its parent to live independently.
13. The hydra can also reproduce sexually. Sexual reproduction usually occurs in the autumn. The hydra develops a swelling, called a **testis,** in which sperm cells form. Another hydra, or sometimes the same individual, produces a different swelling, called an **ovary,** in which an egg cell forms. Sperm cells leave the testis and swim toward the ovary. When a sperm cell unites with the egg in an ovary, the fertilized egg (**zygote**) grows into a new hydra.
14. Like the sponge, when the hydra is cut up into pieces, each piece can regenerate cells and grow into a new hydra.
15. Some forms of hydrozoans form colonies. The Portuguese man-of-war is a well-known colonial hydroid. Individual cells of colonial forms carry on specialized functions, such as reproduction, feeding, or keeping the colony afloat.
C. The **jellyfish** is also a member of the phylum Coelenterata.
1. *Jellyfish* is the common name for a large number of species. All live in seawater and live their lives predominately as medusa forms.

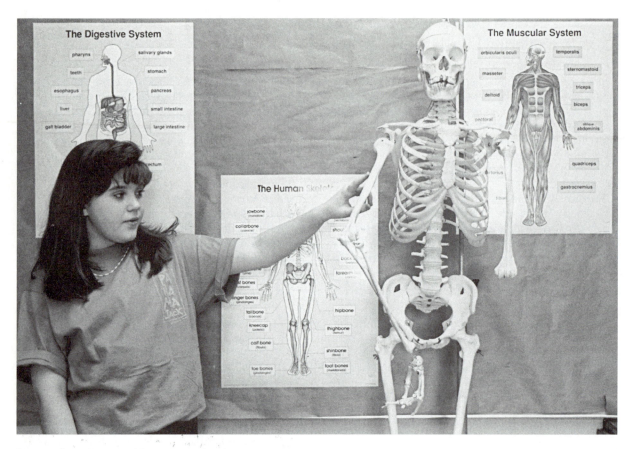

Peer coaching is a powerful instructional tool.

2. Many are transparent and hard to see in the water.

3. Some jellyfish are only about 0.2 (0.5 cm) inches across, whereas others can be as wide as 2 meters (6 ft).

4. The body of the medusa form is shaped like an open umbrella.

5. Between the two cell layers of the body there is a gelatinous, or jellylike, material, which gives the jellyfish its name. In the evolutionary development of more complex body systems, this gelatinous material represents the beginning of what in higher animals is a third layer of cells in the body wall.

6. The mouth of the jellyfish is on the underside of the body and is usually surrounded by tentacles. Each tentacle has thousands of stinging cells.

7. In large jellyfish the tentacles can be more than 15 meters (49 ft) long and can entrap a swimmer or sea animal because of their sheer number and length.

8. Large jellyfish catch small fish and other sea animals, which swim within range of its tentacles and are stung and either paralyzed or killed by the poison secreted by the nematocysts. When the tentacles of a jellyfish touch a swimmer's skin, the stinging cells can produce painful blisters—and even death. The **Australian box jelly** is one of the most poisonous of all ocean animals.

9. Jellyfish are usually found close to the surface of the water. The animal swims by taking some water into its umbrella-like body, then forcing the water out again. As the water is forced out, it makes the jellyfish move up and down with a jerking motion.

D. The **sea anemone** (of which there are many species) is also a coelenterate. Sea anemones attach to rocks and look like king-sized hydras. Their dominant stage is the polyp stage, as in the hydra. They have hundreds of short tentacles around their mouths. Many are brightly colored and can often be seen alone or in great numbers along some seacoasts at low tide. Like all other coelenterates, sea anemones reproduce both asexually and sexually.

E. **Coral** (of which there are many species) is a coelenterate that lives in large colonies.

1. Corals live in seawater, most often where the water is warm and shallow.
2. A coral looks like a hydra, but is larger.
3. Each coral animal builds a skeleton of limestone around itself. It extracts the limestone from seawater. Each skeleton is connected firmly to the skeletons around it, making one large colony. When the coral dies, its skeleton remains.
4. The coral's body and tentacles usually extend beyond the skeleton, but when the coral is disturbed, it can withdraw its tentacles and shorten its body so that the entire body is contained inside its skeleton.
5. Corals can reproduce by budding, but unlike new hydras, the new corals stay connected to the parents. This results in a mass of skeletons that becomes higher and wider over a long time until it forms a rocky ridge, called a **reef.**

6. Reefs are usually under water, but some protrude above water, either temporarily at low tide or permanently. Permanent protrusions occur if changes take place either in the earth's climate (such as a colder world climate resulting in larger polar ice masses) or inside the earth (resulting in deeper oceans or higher continental land masses). Both changes result in a lowering of the sea level.
7. Coral reefs are commonly formed near islands, where the water is shallow; some reefs even circle small islands. Sometimes a circular reef is formed, with open water in the center. This kind of reef is called an **atoll.** Atolls accumulate soil and other particles from the air, eventually becoming islands.
8. Corals can also reproduce sexually. The zygote forms a young coral, which swims freely. When it gets older, it becomes attached to the sea bottom or to an object and no longer moves.
9. Coral skeleton is made into jewelry and is also used for decoration in homes and stores. Crushed coral is sometimes used as paving for roads.

WORMS

I. PLATYHELMINTHS—THE NONSEGMENTED FLATWORMS

A. To many people the word *worm* means something that is long, has a soft, ringed body, and wiggles when it moves. However, all worms are not the same.

1. Zoologists have divided worms into three large groups: flatworms, roundworms, and segmented worms. These three groups of worms are members of separate phyla and are quite different from one another.
2. The members of the phylum **Plathyhelminthes** are the flatworms.

B. Flatworms have certain common characteristics.

1. Platyhelminths are flat and ribbonlike, with lengthwise (bilateral) symmetry, but no rings or body divisions (segments).
2. Bilateral symmetry is a body plan in which the right and left halves form mirror images when divided down the animal's length.
3. In animals with bilateral symmetry, there is a distinct **anterior,** or head end, and a distinctly different **posterior,** or tail end. Moreover, the **dorsal,** or back side, looks different from the **ventral,** or belly side.

4. Animals with bilateral symmetry have a major advantage over those that are radially symmetrical: they can find food and mates and avoid predators more efficiently because they have more muscular control.
5. Like the coelenterates, flatworms have a digestive tube with an opening only at one end. Unlike the sponges and coelenterates, their body walls are three cell layers thick.
6. They have simple digestive and nervous systems.
7. Some flatworms move about freely in water and get their food from the water. Others live as parasites in larger animals, getting their food from the host animal.
8. The planarian, tapeworm, and fluke are members of this phylum.

C. The **planarian** (a generic name, which includes several species) is a flatworm that is free-living (not parasitic) in freshwater or very damp soil.

1. Planaria is usually found under stones in ponds and streams.
2. It is 3 to 13 millimeters (⅛ to ½ in) long, and may be brown, black, or white.
3. Planaria's head is triangular. There are two light-sensitive eyespots on the head, which

DEMONSTRATION 14.4
Exploring Live Planarians

Planarians can be found in quiet ponds, either clinging to reeds or on the undersides of stones. You will have to look carefully, because they are only 3 to 13 millimeters (1/8 to 1/2 in) long and they blend so well with their surroundings that they are difficult to see. Suck up the planarians with a medicine dropper and keep them in jars filled with pond water. Be sure to obtain an extra supply of pond water.

Planarians may also be obtained from scientific supply houses. Feed the planarians twice a week with a few tiny bits of lean beef or boiled egg yolk. It is wise to change the water shortly after each feeding, using either the additional pond water you collected or tap water that has been allowed to stand for two or three days.

Observe the planarians with a magnifying glass or under the low power of a microscope. Note their triangular heads and two dark eyespots.

Animals with very simple nervous systems have amazing regenerative abilities. Observe how planarians regenerate. Suck up three planarians with a medicine dropper and place them on a wet paper towel. With a sharp razor blade, cut one planarian horizontally in half, the sec-

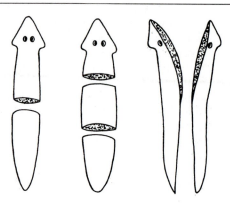

FIGURE 14.1   When planarians are cut into segments, they regenerate.

ond planarian horizontally in thirds, and the third planarian vertically in half (Figure 14.1). After each planarian is cut, wash the pieces in a saucer of pond water. Keep the saucers covered with glass squares to prevent evaporation. Feed and add water regularly. In about two weeks each piece will have become a new planarian.

give the animal the appearance of being cross-eyed. These eyespots permit the planarian to move away from strong light.

4. Planaria's mouth is on the ventral side in the middle of its body. A tube sometimes sticks out of the mouth when the planarian is looking for food or is feeding.

5. The planarian has a simple digestive system that is open at only one end. It is similar to coelenterates in that food enters and waste materials pass out from the same opening.

6. The planarian lives on tiny water animals and on dead plant and animal matter.

7. It moves both by means of muscles and by using many tiny hairlike cellular projections, called **cilia,** on its underside.

8. The planarian can reproduce asexually by splitting in two. It can also reproduce sexually, each planarian having both male sex cells (sperm) and female sex cells (eggs). Planaria are **hermaphroditic.**

9. When a planarian is cut into many pieces, each piece can regenerate cells by cell division to form a new planarian.

D. The **tapeworm** is a well-known flatworm.

1. All tapeworms are parasitic, living off a host organism. Actually, during its life cycle the tapeworm has two hosts. The host for the adult tapeworm is called the **primary host,** and the host for the young tapeworm is called the **secondary host.**

2. People are sometimes infected with a tapeworm from meat that has not been cooked thoroughly.

3. A tapeworm has a knob-shaped head that has suckers and, sometimes, hooks. The suckers and hooks help the tapeworm clamp itself to the wall of a host animal's intestine.

4. The tapeworm is a highly evolved and specialized parasite. It has no mouth or intestine. The digested food from the host's intestine diffuses directly into the tapeworm's head. The tapeworm has no eyes, and as an adult it does not move.

5. Sections keep forming just behind the tapeworm's head. As new sections form, older sections are pushed farther away from the head. As a result, the worm eventually looks like a long piece of flat measuring tape.

Sometimes there are more than 200 sections to a tapeworm's body, and the tapeworm can be more than 15 meters (50 feet) long. Each section behind the head of the tapeworm is specialized for reproduction.

6. The end sections of the tapeworm's body grow larger and older and then drop off and pass out of the primary host's body. These sections are filled with egg cells that have already been fertilized, because each section of the tapeworm is able to produce both male sex cells (sperm) and female sex cells (eggs). The tapeworm is hermaphroditic.

7. Sections that drop off soon decay, but the fertilized eggs remain alive.

8. When eggs are eaten accidentally by an animal, such as a cow or pig, the eggs develop into tiny young tapeworms. They remain in the cow or pig, the tapeworm's secondary host animal. They worm their way into tissue, such as that of the muscle or the liver. Once inside the tissue each young tapeworm forms a capsule, called a **cyst,** around itself.

9. Inside the cyst the tiny tapeworm forms a head (with suckers) and a few sections, then waits until the meat of the animal is eaten by a primary host.

10. If the cow or pig meat is not thoroughly cooked, a young tapeworm that is still alive can come out of its cyst, clamp onto the host's intestine, and grow into an adult tapeworm, living off the nutrients inside the intestines of the new primary host.

11. A host with a tapeworm can become anemic, develop an ulcer, and lose weight, but the condition is curable and not usually fatal.

12. Tapeworms are very successful parasites. While in the primary host, each tapeworm produces thousands of fertile eggs. When segments from the new tapeworm drop off and pass out of the primary host's body, the whole life cycle of the tapeworm starts again.

E. The **fluke** is another well-known and successful parasitic flatworm.

1. Flukes are very dangerous to many animals, including humans. Fluke infections in humans are most common in Africa and Asia.

2. They live in organs such as the stomach, intestine, liver, or lung, where they damage or destroy the lining tissues of these organs and cause loss of blood and ulcers.

3. Many flukes resemble the planaria in size and shape.

4. Almost all of the flukes have more than one host during their life cycle. One of the fluke's secondary hosts is always a snail.

II. THE NEMATODES—NONSEGMENTED ROUNDWORMS

A. Members of the phylum Nematoda include a number of common characteristics.

1. Each has a round, unsegmented body.

2. A definite digestive system extends the length of the body. There is an opening at each end. This is the first group of animals in our phylogenetic listing to have a **complete digestive tract.** At the head end is the worm's **mouth;** at the rear end is the worm's **anus.**

3. Although some roundworms are free-living (nonparasitic), many others are parasites in animals, including humans, and in plants. These include the **hookworm, pinworm,** and **trichinella.** Parasitic roundworms currently infect about one third of the people on earth. Some nematodes parasitize plants, especially the roots of plants. They feed on the plant tissues and cause damage to crops and horticultured plants.

4. Some parasitic roundworms can be up to 1 meter (3 ft) long.

5. Free-living roundworms are very small and are harmless.

6. Roundworms can be found in soil, freshwater, and ocean water.

B. A common parasitic roundworm is the **ascaris.**

1. This is a large worm, which lives in the intestine of larger animals, such as the dog, pig, and horse, and sometimes in humans. It feeds on the partly digested food in the intestine.

2. Ascaris worms lay millions of eggs, which pass out of the body with the waste products.

3. In regions where there is no sanitary sewage disposal, these eggs are deposited in water, soil, and food grown on that soil. The eggs then enter and infect other animal and human bodies through the contaminated food or water. In places that may be contaminated with ascarids, water should be boiled or purified before drinking. Vegetables should be washed thoroughly before they are eaten.

4. Although most infections caused by ascaris worms are not serious, sometimes such large masses of these worms form that they block the intestine and death can result. Sometimes the adult worms bore through the intestine, travel through the body, and go into

vital organs, such as the liver or heart, where they can cause the host's death.

C. The **hookworm** is a parasitic roundworm that in some parts of the world is a serious health menace to humans. It is found in all tropical and semitropical regions lacking in sanitary sewage disposal.

   1. Hookworms are quite small, less than 1/2 inch (1.25 centimeters) in length. Thousands can live in the host's intestine at one time.

   2. Adult hookworms attach themselves to the wall of the intestine by their hooklike teeth and suck the blood from the intestine wall. This steady loss of blood makes the host tired and anemic.

   3. In the intestines the worms reproduce and lay eggs, which pass out of the body with the waste products. The eggs hatch in the soil and grow into young hookworms.

   4. Young hookworms enter the bodies of animals and humans by boring through the skin, usually at the feet. This is a reason for not going barefoot in areas where the soil could be contaminated with hookworms.

   5. Once they enter the body, they travel in the blood to the lungs. In the lungs they pass through the air passages and move up the windpipe into the throat. In the throat they are swallowed and pass through the stomach into the intestine, where they attach themselves and grow into adult hookworms, producing more eggs to continue their life cycle.

D. **Trichinella** is a parasitic roundworm that causes the disesase **trichinosis,** which can cripple and kill a human.

   1. Trichinella lives in the intestine of its host, which can be an animal or a human.

   2. Each trichinella can produce as many as 2,000 eggs. These eggs hatch into young worms, which travel in the blood or lymph vessels to muscles and other organs. The young worms bore into the muscles, where they surround themselves with tiny capsules, called **cysts.**

   3. The young worms stay inside these cysts and cannot grow into adults until the flesh of the host is eaten by another animal or by a human. When animals or people eat infected meat, the young worms come out of their cysts, become adult worms, and start producing their own young worms, to continue their life cycle.

   4. People become infected with trichinella from eating undercooked meat of an animal (usually pork) that is host to the trichinella.

   5. Pigs get the trichinella by eating garbage that has scraps of raw meat containing trichinella worm cysts.

   6. When a human is infected with trichinella, the muscles become inflamed and painful as the young worms bore their way into the muscles and form cysts. If too many worms find their way into the muscles, the person may become crippled or even die. Once the worms find their way into the muscles, there is no way to remove them because they are so small.

III. THE ANNELIDS—SEGMENTED ROUNDWORMS

A. Segmented worms are members of the phylum **Annelida.** The earthworm, sandworm, and leech belong to this phylum.

   1. Annelids have bodies that are divided into rings or body divisions, called segments.

   2. Of all the worms, annelids are the most highly developed. They have many well-developed **organ systems,** including digestive, circulatory, excretory, reproductive, and nervous systems.

   3. Annelids can be found in saltwater, freshwater, and soil.

B. The **earthworm** is a common segmented worm that lives in the soil. Approximately 3 million worms can live in one acre of fertile soil.

   1. Earthworms range in size. They may be as small as 1 mm ($\frac{1}{25}$ in) long or as large as the **Giant South African earthworm,** which can reach a length of more than 7 m (22 feet).

   2. The earthworm's head end is darker and more pointed than its tail.

   3. Four pairs of bristles, called **setae,** stick out from the sides and underside of each body segment, except the first and the last segments. Setae help the earthworm to anchor itself as it moves through the soil.

   4. The earthworm is able to move because it has two sets of muscles. One set (circular muscles) are used to stretch the earthworm so it is long and thin. The other set (longitudinal muscles) are used to make the earthworm short and thick.

   5. The earthworm has no respiratory system. It absorbs oxygen and gives off carbon dioxide directly through its thin skin. To allow for this gaseous transfer, the worm must stay moist. Too much water, however, will drown it.

DEMONSTRATION 14.5
Exploring Live Earthworms

The best place to find earthworms is in rich garden soil. Either dig them up or wait until after a heavy rain, when the worms come to the surface at night. Try to collect the large "night crawlers." Keep the worms in a box containing equal parts of peat moss and rich garden soil. Cover the box with a damp piece of thick cloth towel. Keep the earth and towel damp, but not wet, at all times. About once a week feed the worms a quarter cup of oatmeal or bread that has been softened in water.

Place an earthworm on a damp paper towel and see how it crawls by lengthening and then contracting its body. Find the head of the earthworm by watching closely for the lip or pharynx that the worm pushes out as it moves along. Touch the head and note how the worm contracts the front part of its body; it may even crawl backward.

Pass your fingertips gently along the underside of the earthworm and feel the bristle feet (setae). Observe these feet through a magnifying glass. See what happens when you place the earthworm on a damp, smooth glass surface, where there is nothing for these bristle feet to grip.

Place an earthworm on a piece of damp paper towel and cover the earthworm with a saucer so that it cannot escape. Keep the worm in a dark room for about an hour, then shine a flashlight on the worm's head. Note how the worm quickly pulls its head away from the bright light.

---

6. The earthworm has as many as 10 simple "hearts" in its closed circulatory system.
7. The digestive system has a pharynx, an esophagus, a crop, a gizzard for grinding food, and an intestine.
8. Each earthworm forms both sperm and eggs (it is hermaphroditic). To cross-fertilize or mate with another, two earthworms come together (copulate) and exchange sperm so that the eggs in each worm can be fertilized. The earthworm lays a batch of fertilized eggs in the soil within a special mucous cocoon secreted by a specialized area, the clitellum. Eggs hatch and become young earthworms.
9. If cut across in half, each half can regenerate into a new earthworm. If cut, but not in halves, only the portion or portions containing the vital organs will live and grow the lost portions.
10. The earthworm eats soil, digesting the decayed plant and animal matter from the soil and eliminating the rest. Earthworms are valuable to humans because they bore holes and loosen and turn the soil, thus allowing air and water to enter the soil and help plant roots grow. One common earthworm can till, fertilize, drain, and aerate 0.2 Kilogram (½ lb) of soil per day.
C. The **sandworm** is a segmented roundworm that lives in the ocean near the shore.
   1. It is more active than the earthworm.
   2. It has four light-sensitive eyespots and a group of tentacles on its head.
   3. Sometimes the sandworm burrows into the sand, with only its head exposed to the water. The sandworm can also swim about in the water, helped by little projections on each side of its body.
   4. The sandworm feeds on tiny marine animals.
D. The **leech** is a segmented roundworm that is parasitic.
   1. Most leeches are found in freshwater, but a few live in the ocean.
   2. They are commonly called "bloodsuckers" because they live by sucking the blood of larger animals, such as fish and turtles—or even humans if they venture where leeches live.
   3. A leech has two suckers, one at each end of its body, which provide a means of clinging to its host.
   4. It uses the rear sucker to attach itself to the animal's body, then it attaches the front sucker to another part of the animal's body. It breaks the skin of the host animal with sharp little jaws in its mouth. A chemical substance in the saliva of the leech prevents the animal's blood from clotting while the leech is sucking the blood of its victim.
   5. When leeches mate, the one playing the male role clings to the body of the one playing the female role and deposits a sac of sperm on her skin. The sac produces flesh-deteriorating enzymes that eat a hole through the skin and fertilize the eggs within the body.
   6. Because of their unusual abilities and behavior, leeches have played various roles in medical treatment and research.

ECHINODERMS AND MOLLUSKS

I. THE ECHINODERMS—SPINY-SKINNED ANIMALS

  A. The starfish, sea urchin, sand dollar, and sea cucumber are members of the phylum **Echinodermata.**

    1. They have endoskeletons (internal skeletons) of hard calcareous plates, covered by a thin skin with bumps and spines.

    2. The parts of their bodies usually radiate out regularly from the center like the spokes of a wheel, a kind of symmetry known as **radial symmetry,** as opposed to the bilateral symmetry present in planarians, earthworms, humans, and many other animal groups.

    3. All echinoderms are marine animals.

    4. Members of this phylum include the starfish, brittle star, sea urchin, sand dollar, and sea cucumber.

  B. The **starfish** is not a fish.

    1. It has no head, but is made up of a circle of arms that come together at a central body disc, forming a star shape.

    2. Most starfish have five arms, but some have six or more.

    3. There are spines all over the body and arms.

    4. The stomach of the starfish is at the center of the body. Its mouth is on the ventral or underside.

    5. A starfish feeds on clams and oysters.

    6. On the underside of each arm there are hundreds of little tubes, called **tube feet.** Each tube foot acts as a vacuum or suction cup that can stick firmly to any object on which it is pressed.

    7. The starfish crawls over the top of a clam and presses its tube feet firmly on both sides of the shell. It then pulls on the clam shell until the clam tires and relaxes its muscles and its shell opens. Then the starfish turns its stomach inside out, so that the stomach extends through the mouth and into the opening in the clam shell, where it digests the clam's body.

    8. A starfish can crawl in any direction. An eyespot at the end of each arm is sensitive to light. The starfish moves about mostly at night.

    9. Starfish are either male or female; the **sexes are separate.** They discharge their sperm and eggs into the water, where fertilization takes place externally. A female starfish may lay more than 100 million eggs in one season.

    10. Starfish can regenerate lost parts. If a starfish loses an arm, it can grow a new one. If a starfish is chopped into three or four pieces, and if each piece has at least one arm and part of the central disc as well, each piece may grow into a new starfish.

  C. The **brittle star** is a starfish that has very thin arms.

    1. Brittle stars live and hide among sponges. They feed on the plankton swept in by the sponges.

    2. Before they knew how well brittle stars could regenerate, sponge fishermen would capture the brittle stars that prey on sponges, cut them into pieces, and throw them back into the ocean, thinking they had reduced the animal's population and saved their sponges. They didn't realize that by doing this they were increasing the population of brittle stars.

  D. The **sea urchin** is a globe-shaped echinoderm with very long spines. The **sand dollar** is a flat echinoderm with short spines. The **sea cucumber** is long and soft-bodied, with very short spines.

II. THE MOLLUSKS—THE SHELLFISH

  A. The phylum **Mollusca** comprises a large and varied group of animals, including the oyster, snail, and octopus. Some mollusks live on land, and many others are found in aquatic habitats.

    1. Mollusks have soft, fleshy bodies that are not segmented.

    2. Most mollusks have a protective shell made of calcium carbonate, hence the name shellfish. Like most common names, shellfish is a poor name for the mollusks. They are not fish and not all have shells.

    3. A mollusk has a muscular **foot** and a special sheet of tissue, called the **mantle,** which produces the shell.

    4. Within the large phylum there are seven classes. The three classes that include the most common and well-known species are the bivalvia, gastropoda, and cephalopoda.

    5. **Bivalved** mollusks live inside two shells hinged at the mid-dorsal line. Powerful muscles hold the shell parts together.

    6. **Gastropods** have just one spiral shell and seem to be moving on their bellies, carrying their shells on their backs.

    7. **Cephalopods** have a definite head, surrounded by many arms, called tentacles.

  B. The bivalved mollusks include the **clam, oyster, scallop,** and **mussel.** They all live in the ocean, but some clams and mussels can also be found in freshwater.

1. Bivalves never shed their shells. The shells become larger and larger. Lines on the outside of a shell tell roughly the age of the animal, each line representing a year's growth.
2. They all have a tough muscular foot, shaped somewhat like a hatchet, which sticks out from the shells and is used for digging or anchoring. This class is sometimes referred to as the **hatchet-footed** mollusks.
3. Two tubes, called siphons, direct the water flow through the animal. Water carrying oxygen and food flows into the animal through one siphon. Water carrying carbon dioxide and waste products flows out of the other siphon.
4. Bivalves' respiratory organs, called gills, allow oxygen in the water to diffuse into the blood in the body and allow carbon dioxide to leave.
5. Both the gills and the siphons are lined with cilia that beat to draw water in and to direct its flow. Cilia lining the gills filter and push food particles to the stomach.
6. Bivalves have a well-developed digestive system, an exretory system, a nervous system, a reproductive system, and a circulatory system with a heart, blood, and blood vessels.
7. They reproduce sexually, and the sexes are separate.
8. In the ocean the oyster and many kinds of clams do not move about at all, but permanently attach to a rock or some other object.
9. Bivalves exhibit a range of sizes. Some are less than 1 mm (the thickness of a U.S. dime) long, and others, such as the giant clams found in the South Pacific Ocean, are as large as 2 meters (6 ft) across.
C. Most of the **gastropods** are univalves; that is, they have one shell or valve, which is usually spiral shaped. These mollusks include the **snail, slug, periwinkle, conch,** and **abalone.** The slug does not have a shell. It looks like a snail that has lost its shell. Rather than a shell for protection, land slugs are protected by their secretion of a thick layer of mucus. Sea slugs, or **nudibranchs,** protect themselves in other ways. Some incorporate into their own bodies the poisonous nematocysts from jellyfish. Others secrete mucus that has a strong, unpleasant odor and may even be poisonous.
   1. Univalves have the same vital body organs as bivalves, except that land snails have lungs instead of gills for breathing.
   2. Univalves also have a much larger foot than the bivalves. This large foot looks like part of the univalve's body, causing it to appear to be crawling on its belly and carrying its shell on its back. Hence the common name sometimes used for this class—**stomach-footed** mollusks.
   3. When a univalve is attacked, it pulls its foot and head up inside its shell.
   4. The snail has two tentacles on its head. Some snails have an eye on the tip of each tentacle. When the snail is touched, it draws in its tentacles.
   5. The foot of a land snail or slugs gives off a lubricating slime, and these animals move only on this slime.
   6. Snails and slugs also have a straplike rasping organ called a radula, which acts as a file to scrape or rasp off bits of food on the suface of objects. Water snails help keep an aquarium clean by using their radulas to eat algae, bacteria, and dead or decaying materials that collect on the glass sides of the aquarium.
D. The **cephalopods** (meaning "head-footed") include the **chambered nautilus, octopus, cuttlefish,** and **squid.** They live only in the ocean.
   1. Cephalopods have mostly the same parts as the other mollusks, but arranged differently. The chambered nautilus, however, is the only cephalopod that has an external shell.
   2. When attacking, attacked, or frightened, the squid and octopus shoot out an inky material that clouds the water and hides them. This expulsion of ink is accompanied by the secretion of another substance that dulls an attacker's sense of smell. The first ink used in writing came from the octopus's ink sac.
   3. Squids, octopuses, and cuttlefish have beaklike jaws used to bite and to get into the hard shells of their prey.
   4. They can also escape from predators by shooting a jet of water through their bodies to create a burst of jetlike speed.
   5. Most cephalopods can change their skin coloration to camouflage themselves.
E. The **squid** has a long, narrow, torpedolike body and no external shell.
   1. Its foot is divided into two long and eight short tentacles, which have double rows of suction cups for grasping objects.
   2. It has a large eye on each side of its head.
   3. Most squids are no more than 1 meter (3 ft) in length, although there are giant squids at least 18 meters (59 ft) long.

F. The **octopus** is built much like the squid, but with a shorter, more rounded, bag-shaped body, which is the animal's mantle.
   1. It has only eight tentacles, all the same size, which it uses for swimming, crawling, fighting, nest building, holding prey, and mating.
   2. The octopus is a night and bottom feeder. During the day it stays hidden in its nest, which is usually a hole or rock crevice or a nest dug in the sand, usually in fairly shallow waters.
   3. Its tentacles have nerve endings that help the octopus sense its surroundings. The tentacles also have many suction cups that help to hold prey.
   4. After catching its prey, the octopus paralyzes its victim with a secretion of nerve poison.
   5. The octopus has a well-developed brain and nervous system, making it a surprisingly intelligent animal. It is considered to be the most intelligent of all the invertebrates. Octopuses have been trained to distinguish between shapes and to recognize objects by touch. They are very clever and effective predators.
   6. Inside its body, the octopus has the remnants of a shell.
   7. Like the squid, it has eyes that can change position to focus and a sharp beak.
   8. Some octopuses have tentacles 15 centimeters (6 in) long, but others may have tentacles 4 meters (13 ft) long. If a tentacle is lost, the octopus can regenerate and grow a new one.
   9. An octopus can grow to approximately 3 meters (10 ft) long, and up to 55 lb, although most are smaller.
   10. When mating, the male sends sperm cells down one of its tentacles (called the hectocotylus) into the female to fertilize her eggs.
   11. At maturity, about age 2, the female lays up to 150,000 eggs. Most are eaten by other animals before or soon after hatching into small larva, which look like small octopuses. The female octopus stays with her eggs to protect them and may even starve to death while doing so.

G. Mollusks are an important group of animals.
   1. Clams, oysters, scallops, snails, octopus, squid, and abalone are eaten by humans.
   2. Clam and oyster shells are used to make buttons and mother-of-pearl.
   3. Shells are also ground up and sold to farmers for chicken feed to provide the calcium carbonate needed by chickens for making egg shells.
   4. Certain oysters make pearls. A pearl is formed when an irritating object, such as a parasitic worm, gets inside the flesh of an oyster and forms a tiny round capsule, called a cyst. The mantle (shell-producing tissue) forms layers of shell material around the cyst, producing the pearl. The Japanese discovered a way of making a pearl from an oyster. They take a small round bead made from shell, cover the bead with living mantle cells, and push the bead inside the oyster. The oyster is then put into the ocean for a few years, and a pearl forms around the bead. This pearl, which is called a cultured pearl, looks just like a natural pearl.

ARTHROPODS

I. THE ARTHROPODS—ANIMALS WITH JOINTED APPENDAGES

   A. Members of the large phylum Arthropoda have a number of general characteristics.
      1. Their bodies are covered by the cuticle, an **exoskeleton** (external skeleton), made of a tough material called **chitin.** The cuticle is thick, hard armor over some parts of the body and thin and flexible over other parts, such as joints that can bend.
      2. The muscles of the body are attached to the inside of the skeleton.
      3. Arthropods' bodies are segmented and organized into distinct body regions.
      4. Their legs and other attached body parts are called **appendages.** The appendages are jointed and can bend.
      5. All appendages are paired. They are arranged on the right and left sides of the body in such a way that one side of the body is a mirror image of the other. This is bilateral symmetry.

II. THE CRUSTACEANS

   A. The crayfish, the lobster, the crab, the shrimp, the tiny water flea, the sow bug, and the pill bug are members of the class **Crustacea,** one class within the phylum Arthropoda.

DEMONSTRATION 14.6
Exploring Live Snails

A. Water Snails

Obtain some water snails from a pet shop or scientific supply house. Snails can also be found among the water plants of a pond that has a muddy bottom. Place two or three snails in an aquarium or large glass jar of tap water that has been allowed to stand for two or three days, making sure that there is a good supply of water plants in the container.

Note how the snail uses its foot to move along a surface. Use a magnifying glass to watch the snail's rough "tongue" scrape the algae from the aquarium walls. Touch the snails and see how they withdraw into their shells and fall to the bottom of the aquarium. The snails may lay masses of transparent eggs on the walls of the container. Examine these eggs periodically for two or three weeks and see them hatch.

B. Land Snails

Land snails are often found early in the morning feeding on plants in the garden. They can be kept in an aquarium or in a large glass jar containing damp garden soil. If you use a glass jar, keep the mouth covered, either with a wire screen or with a screw top that has been perforated several times by a nail. Keep the snail well supplied with soft, green leaves or lettuce.

Note how the snail's foot leaves a trail of slime, along which it travels. See how the snail quickly shreds the leaves and lettuce with its "tongue." Look for the eyes at the ends of the larger pair of feelers. Touch the feelers gently with a pencil and see how they retract. Touch the feelers more forcibly and make the snail withdraw into its shell. A snail mates only once in its entire life, but the act of copulation may last as long as 12 hours.

1. In addition to having the general characteristics of arthropods, the crustaceans have unique characteristics that distinguish them as a class within the phylum Arthropoda.
2. They have two pairs of feelers, called antennae.
3. Their outer skeletons contain calcium carbonate.
4. They have two distinct body regions—the cephalothorax and the abdomen.
5. Most crustaceans are aquatic, living in saltwater or freshwater.
6. Many have special breathing organs, called gills, which allow oxygen to enter their bodies and carbon dioxide to leave.
7. The class Crustacea is sometimes called Decapoda, because they have five pairs of legs (ten legs).
B. The **crayfish** exemplifies a typical crustacean.
   1. It has a dark outer skeleton containing calcium carbonate.
   2. It has two distinct body regions—the cephalothorax and the abdomen.
   3. The cephalothorax is really made up of two regions: the head and the thorax, grown together to look like one region.
   4. The cephalothorax is covered by a hard, thick cuticle, called the **carapace,** which gives the crayfish extra protection.
   5. The abdomen, commonly called the tail, consists of seven movable segments.

6. The crayfish has two eyes, each on the end of a short, movable stalk on each side of the front end of the cephalothorax. Each eye consists of many lenses and, for this reason, is called a compound eye.
7. The crayfish has two pairs of long feelers, called antennae, and several smaller feelers, called antennules.
8. It has six pairs of mouth parts. Three pairs are connected to the head, and three pairs are connected to the thorax. All are used for holding food, cutting and grinding it, and pushing it into the mouth.
9. It has five pairs of legs, all connected to the thorax. The first pair, called the chelipeds, are much larger than the other four pairs.
10. The chelipeds have large pincers, used for grabbing and holding food. One cheliped is always larger than the other.
11. The remaining four pairs of legs are used mostly for walking. Two pairs of these walking legs end in tiny pincers, and two pairs end in tiny claws.
12. On its abdomen are six pairs of appendages, called swimmerets. Each segment of the abdomen has a pair of swimmerets, except for the last segment, which has none.
13. The first five pairs of swimmerets are quite small and are used by the female for carrying her eggs until they are hatched. Both males

DEMONSTRATION 14.7

Exploring Live Crustaceans: Crayfish or Lobsters

The freshwater crayfish and the ocean lobster are highly similar, and either is quite suitable for the study of crustaceans. Crayfish are found in ponds and streams, hiding under rocks and logs. You can catch one by tying one end of a string around a small piece of meat and dangling the meat near a rock at the bottom of the pond or stream. When the crayfish seizes the meat with its claws, pull up the string with a slow steady movement. If you are quick, you can also catch a crayfish by lifting up its rock and grabbing it as it swims backward. Keep the crayfish you collect in large glass jars filled with pond water or tap water that has been allowed to stand for two or three days to allow any chlorine in the water to escape.

Observe the crayfish carefully. Note how the outside skeleton forms a hard, protective shield for the crayfish, especially over the head and chest area. Note the segments of the abdomen and the paddles of the tail. Count the number of jointed walking legs and examine the large pair of front claws. Feed the crayfish earthworms or small pieces of raw meat and see how it uses its claws and mouth parts. Locate the feelers and count them. Observe the eyes and see how they move around on their stalks.

Put a crayfish on its back. Lift up the free, lower edge of the skeleton that covers the chest region and observe the gills. Find the mouth parts. Examine the swimmerets and see how the crayfish uses them. Note how the crayfish uses its abdomen to swim backward quickly.

and females use these pairs for slow, forward swimming.

14. The sixth pair of swimmerets is large and paddle-like. These swimmerets are called uropods. The uropods and the seventh segment of the abdomen, called the telson, together make up the tail fan of the crayfish.

15. The crayfish usually moves backward, using its sixth and seventh abdominal segments and its four walking legs. The crayfish also uses its four walking legs to travel forward and sideways.

16. The crayfish breathes through feathery organs called gills, which are attached to the five pairs of legs and the three pairs of mouth parts that are connected to the thorax. The gills allow oxygen in the water to diffuse into blood in the body of the crayfish, and carbon dioxide to diffuse out.

17. The crayfish is a freshwater animal, living at the bottom of lakes, ponds, and streams, where it eats plants and any live or dead animal material it can grasp.

18. Crayfish breed once a year, usually in autumn. In spring the female lays about 100 eggs, which are attached to the first five pairs of swimmerets on her abdomen, where they are carried until they hatch.

19. The young crayfish stay attached to the swimmerets for about two weeks, holding onto the hairs of the swimmerets with their pincers. During this time the young crayfish feed on the yolk in the eggs.

20. After two weeks the young crayfish let go of the swimmerets and are now independent.

21. Crayfish grow larger by shedding their exoskeletons, a process called **molting.** Most crayfish molt about seven times the first year and once or twice a year thereafter. While a crayfish is molting, it is defenseless, so it usually goes into hiding until the new skeleton is formed. The term "soft-shell" is used when referring to crayfish (and lobsters and crabs) just after they have molted and before they have grown a new hard exoskeleton.

22. If the crayfish should lose one or more of its appendages during molting or in a battle, new appendages can be regenerated to replace the lost ones.

C. The **lobster** is built like the crayfish, but the lobster lives in saltwater and is much larger. One kind is found in the North Atlantic Ocean. Another kind of lobster, found in the coastal waters of Florida, California, and the West Indies, does not have the first pair of large legs (chelipeds).

D. The body of a **crab** is wide and round, rather than long and narrow like that of the crayfish and the lobster. The crab's abdomen is very small and folds under the broad shell (cephalothorax). Crabs move by walking sideways.

E. **Shrimp** have five pairs of walking legs and a large, muscular abdomen. They can swim very fast, moving backward like the crayfish and the lobster. When the shrimp is threatened, it buries itself in the sand, with only its antennae and eyes exposed.

F. Crustaceans are useful as scavengers because they eat dead animals. Many varieties are used by humans as food.

DEMONSTRATION 14.8
Exploring Live Crustaceans: Water Fleas (Daphnia)

Water fleas are tiny, transparent crustaceans that can be found during the spring and summer in almost any quiet pool or stream. Because they eat algae, water fleas are easiest to find in ponds that are covered with green scum. A good way to catch them is to use a sieve or tea strainer that has been lined with cheesecloth. Use needle and thread to hold the cheesecloth against the sides of the sieve or strainer. Place the water fleas in glass jars containing pond water and a good supply of green algae, and keep the jars in sunlight. When you finish examining the

water fleas, use them as food for fish, tadpoles, and hydra. They can also be placed in aquariums to remove excessive algae in the water.

Use a medicine dropper to suck up a water flea, then place it on a microscope slide and examine it under the low power of a microscope. Because it is transparent, you will see not only the outer skeleton and the appendages, but also the inner organs. Notice the rapidly beating heart. Look for the intestine and trace it from the mouth to the anus.

III. THE INSECTS

  A. Insects form a separate class of arthropods called **Insecta** (or **Hexapoda**). This is the largest single class of animals, in terms of number of species, number of individuals, and total biomass. There are about 700,000 known species of insects, which may be less than half the total number of insect species on earth.

  B. The characteristics of the class Insecta are as follows.
    1. Insects have three separate and distinct body regions—head, thorax, and abdomen.
    2. They have one pair of feelers, called antennae, attached to their heads.
    3. They have three pairs of legs, all attached to the thorax. The class Insecta is sometimes called Hexapoda, referring to the fact that insects all have three pairs of legs (six legs).
    4. Most insects have one or two pairs of wings, also attached to the thorax.
    5. Most adult insects have both simple eyes, which are made up of just one lens, and compound eyes, which are made up of many single lenses.
    6. In their adult stage, most insects live on land.
    7. They breathe through branching tubes, called tracheae, which are connected to tiny outside openings, called spiracles, located on each side of the abdomen and thorax.
    8. Insects are able to adjust to their environment well. They have been very successful in their struggle for existence and have lived on earth for a long time.

  C. From the time their eggs hatch until the young insects become fully grown adults, most insects pass through a series of forms or stages, a process called **metamorphosis.**
    1. There are three kinds of metamorphosis: gradual metamorphosis, incomplete metamorphosis, and complete metamorphosis.
    2. Insects such as the grasshopper, cricket, dragonfly, true bug, aphid, and termite undergo gradual metamorphosis. **Gradual metamorphosis** has three stages: **egg, nymph,** and **adult.**
    3. The nymph hatches from the egg and looks just like the adult, except that it does not have wings or mature sex organs. When it hatches, the nymph is only as large as the egg and its head is much larger than its body.
    4. The nymph eats and grows, but its exoskeleton does not grow as fast as the nymph itself. As a result, from time to time the nymph rests, splits and sheds its skeleton, and then continues to grow a new, larger skeleton.
    5. The shedding of the skeleton is called **molting,** which usually takes place about five times before the nymph becomes an adult insect. After each molting the nymph looks and becomes more like the adult insect. After the final molting, the nymph is a fully grown adult.
    6. The metamorphosis of the dragonfly and the damselfly is similar to gradual metamorphosis, except that the second stage, called a **naiad,** is an aquatic stage in the insect's life cycle. The naiad looks nothing like the adult. This is called **incomplete metamorphosis,** and includes three states: egg, naiad; and adult. Naiads are sometimes used as bait for freshwater fishing.
    7. Insects such as the butterfly, moth, bee, ant, beetle, fly, and mosquito undergo **complete metamorphosis,** in which there are four stages—**egg, larva, pupa,** and **adult.**

DEMONSTRATION 14.9
Exploring Live Insects: Grasshoppers

A. Observing the Grasshopper's Habits

Catch a live grasshopper and put it in a large glass jar along with some twigs, leaves, and blades of grass. Keep the jar covered with a lid that has several holes punched in it. Notice the division of the body into three regions. Locate and identify the parts attached to the head and the thorax. Point out the difference in size of the legs. Watch the grasshopper eat and observe how it chews its food. See how the color of the grasshopper blends in with the color of the leaves and grass. When you hold the grasshopper between your finger and thumb, it will "spit molasses." This brown liquid is partially digested food from the grasshopper's crop. Examine the grasshopper with a magnifying glass. Look at the eyes and the an-

tennae. Find out how many mouth parts it has. Spread out and observe the outer and inner wings. Examine the sides of the abdomen and find the holes that are the openings of the grasshopper's breathing tubes. Trace the life cycle of the grasshopper, using appropriate pictures or drawings. Note that the very young grasshopper has no wings, but develops them after it has molted a few times.

B. Have a Grasshopper Jumping Contest

Divide your class of students into groups, and give each group an adult grasshopper. Hold a grasshopper jumping contest. Have groups predict, observe, measure, and graph how far their grasshoppers jump.

---

8. The larva hatches from the egg and looks like a segmented worm. It eats and grows, stopping from time to time to shed its skin (to molt). After each molting the larva does not change in form, but continues to eat and become larger.
9. After several moltings the larva enters the pupa stage. Although there is no apparent changes during the pupa stage, a remarkable transformation is taking place. During the pupa stage all the tissues of the larva change into those of an adult insect. When the change is complete, a fully grown adult insect emerges by biting its way out of the pupa case.
10. In many insects that undergo complete metamorphosis, the larva has a voracious appetite, whereas the adult form may not have complete mouth parts and may not eat at all.
D. Entomologists (biologists who specialize in the study of insects) divide the class of insects into about 26 orders, based largely on the types of metamorphosis and the kinds of mouth parts and wings of the adults.
  1. Eight orders that are common, and perhaps most relevant to elementary and middle school children, are grasshoppers, dragonflies, beetles, true bugs, aphids, butterflies and moths, flies and mosquitoes, and bees, termites, and ants.
E. The grasshopper, cricket, praying mantis, katydid, walking stick, locust, and cockroach belong to the order **Orthoptera** (which means "straightwinged").

1. All orthopterans undergo gradual metamorphosis.
2. Orthopterans have mouth parts designed for chewing, with hard jaws that move from side to side instead of up and down.
3. They have two pairs of wings. The front wings are long, narrow, and like stiff paper, and the hind wings look like cellophane and are wide, thin, and veined. When not in use, the hind wings fold up lengthwise like a fan and are protected under the front leathery wings.
4. In some orthopterans, such as the grasshopper, the rear legs are large and developed for jumping. For its size, the grasshopper has the greatest jumping ability of any animal on earth. It can leap over obstacles 500 times its own height or horizontal distances 20 times its own length.
5. The grasshopper makes sounds by rubbing a row of spines on its rear leg against a wing vein.
6. The grasshopper and cricket are very destructive insects, eating pasture and grain crops. The praying mantis is beneficial to humans. It eats other insects (even its own kind), many of which are harmful in some way to humans.
F. The dragonfly and damselfly belong to the order **Odonata.**
  1. They have long, very thin bodies.
  2. They have chewing mouth parts.
  3. They have two pairs of wings; both pairs are thin, like cellophane. The wings do not fold but stick straight out from the body.

4. Odonates undergo incomplete metamorphosis. The larval form is aquatic and feeds on the aquatic larvae of other insects.

5. The adult dragonfly and damselfly eat mosquitoes, gnats, and other insects.

6. One of the largest members of this order is the **Borneo dragonfly,** which can measure nearly 10 cm (4.24 in) long and have a wingspan of about 20 cm (7.5 in).

G. The Japanese beetle, bark beetle, potato beetle, wood boring beetle, boll weevil, ladybug (ladybeetle would be a better common name for this insect), and carrion beetle belong to the order **Coleoptera,** the order of insects known as beetles.

1. Adult beetles have chewing or sucking mouth parts.

2. The name Coleoptera means "sheath-winged." Beetles have two pairs of wings. The front wings are very hard and meet in a straight line down the back, fitting closely over the body and looking very much like a shell. The rear wings are thin or membranous, and fold beneath the front wings when the insect is not in flight. Because of their hard front wings, these insects make a whirring sound when flying.

3. Beetles undergo complete metamorphosis, and their larvae are called **grubs.**

4. The potato beetle destroys potato plants, the boll weevil destroys grain and cotton, and the Japanese beetle destroys the fruit and leaves of trees, shrubs, and grasses.

5. The ladybird beetle (sometimes called the "ladybug") feeds on many harmful insects, such as aphids. The carrion beetle acts as a scavenger by feeding on dead animals.

6. The European elm bark beetle is the carrier of a fungus that can kill elm trees (the Dutch elm disease). The fungus blocks the water transfer system of the tree. Once the fungus infects the elm tree, the tree will die. Another beetle lives on the leaves of elm trees, and when not checked by chemical treatment, will quickly defoliate and eventually kill a tree. Other beetles infect yet other kinds of trees.

H. Many people use the word *bug* to mean almost any insect, but to entomologists *bug* refers to just one order of insects, the **Hemiptera.**

1. The bedbug, stinkbug, squash bug, and water bug belong to this order, but the ladybug does not.

2. In their adult stage true bugs, the hemipterans, have sucking mouth parts and feed by sticking these parts into plants and sucking the plant juices. Many of them are troublesome pests. The bedbug sucks the blood of humans and is a carrier of disease as well.

3. Although a few kinds of bugs have no wings, most have two pairs of wings. Both the front and back wings are thin. The edges of the wings overlap, and one half of the wing is thicker than the other. The name Hemiptera means "half-winged."

4. Members of this order undergo gradual metamorphosis.

I. The aphid or plant louse, scale insect, mealy bug, leaf hopper, and cicada belong to the order **Homoptera.**

1. They have sucking mouth parts and feed on the juice of plants.

2. Some have two pairs of wings, but others are wingless. Those that have wings hold them over their bodies like an upside down V. Both pairs of wings are thin. The name Homoptera means "like-wing."

3. Homopterans undergo gradual metamorphosis.

4. Many do great damage to plants; some carry disease. The lac insect, however, is a source of shellac, which is used in lacquers and wood finishes.

J. Moths and butterflies belong to the order **Lepidoptera.**

1. Lepidopterans have sucking mouth parts, although some adult moths have no mouth parts at all. Other moths and all butterflies have a long, coiled tube, which they use to sip nectar from inside flowers.

2. They have two pairs of wings that are covered with tiny scales. The name Lepidoptera means "scale-wing." These scales produce the often brilliant and beautiful colors in their wings. Most butterflies and some moths have colorful wings, but the wings of many moths are more subdued in hue.

3. Butterflies and moths undergo complete metamorphosis. Their larvae are called **caterpillars** or worms, such as the tomato worm and tent worm. The moth larva usually spins a strong silk case, called a **cocoon,** when it goes into the pupa stage. The butterfly pupa, however, rests in a hardened case called a **chrysalis.**

4. Many people find it difficult to distinguish between butterflies and moths, especially if both have colorful wings. Here are some ways to distinguish between butterflies and moths.

DEMONSTRATION 14.10
Caterpillars, Chrysalids, and Cocoons

Collect a number of caterpillars and place them in glass jars containing moist soil and some of the leaves upon which they were found. Each jar should also have a twig to support the chrysalids or cocoons when they are formed. Cover the mouth of each jar with either fine screen wire or with the jar's lid after it has been perforated several times with a small nail. Put only one caterpillar in a jar to determine whether the caterpillar is a butterfly or moth larva. Continue feeding the caterpillar until it passes into the pupa stage. If the caterpillar is a butterfly larva, it will form the hardened case called a chrysalis. If the caterpillar is a moth, it will spin a cocoon.

Additional chrysalids and cocoons may be collected in the garden and woods. You will have to look carefully, because they often resemble dead leaves or twigs. Place each chrysalis or cocoon in a glass jar with a perforated cover or fine screen wire over the mouth. Each jar should contain some moist soil and a twig for the adult moth or butterfly to stand on when it comes out of its container. Keep the jars in a warm place and examine the chrysalides and cocoons regularly until the adult moths and butterflies emerge. Eventually, turn them loose quickly.

Butterfly Characteristics	Moth Characteristics
Thin abdomen	Thicker abdomen
Antennae usually with knobs at their ends	Antennae usually feathery
Flies more commonly during the day	Flies more commonly at night
Wings usually vertical when at rest	Wings horizontal when at rest
Pupa in a hard chrysalis	Pupa usually in a spun cocoon

5. Some butterflies and moths migrate, traveling to different parts of the country or world during different seasons of the year. For example, monarch butterflies live in the northern United States during the summer. In late summer they fly away in very large groups, some going to the Gulf states and others going to the Pacific Coast, where they remain quietly until the winter is over. In spring they fly northward again.

6. The larvae of butterflies and, especially, moths are very destructive. The apple worm, tomato worm, corn borer, cabbage worm, cotton boll weevil, and tobacco worm all eat and destroy vegetables and crops. The larvae of the gypsy moth and browntail moth destroy forest and orchard trees by eating their leaves. The larvae of the clothes moth feed on clothing, especially wool.

7. The silkworm moth is helpful; its larva spins a cocoon of silk threads, which people use to make silk cloth.

8. All butterflies and many moths help in the cross-pollination of flowers as they travel from flower to flower in their search for nectar.

K. The housefly, tsetse fly, stable fly, and mosquito belong to the order **Diptera.**

1. Diptera usually have mouth parts specialized for sucking. Mosquitoes, for example, do not bite. They stab their hosts and then suck up as much as three times their own weight in blood in one feeding.

2. Except for some fruit flies that have only short vestigial or rudimentary wings and cannot fly, members of this order have just one pair of thin but highly developed wings with veins. The name Diptera means "two-wing."

3. Members of this order undergo complete metamorphosis.

4. The **housefly** has large eyes, short antennae, and a baseball-bat-shaped sucking tube. The housefly does not bite. Other flies, such as the horsefly and the tsetse fly, do bite.

5. The housefly's feet have suction pads and sticky hairs, which help it attach securely to walls, windows, and ceilings. The sticky hairs work well only if they are free from dust. The fly seems to always be cleaning its feet by rubbing one foot against the other.

6. The female housefly lays its eggs in manure or other similar matter. Its larvae that hatch are commonly called **maggots.**

7. The fly carries many kinds of bacteria on its hairy feet and body. When a fly lands on food, it can leave bacteria that cause typhoid fever, dysentery, and cholera, all of which are dangerous to humans.

8. The female **mosquito** lays its eggs in water. Larvae that hatch are commonly called wigglers. The pupa stage of the mosquito is dif-

ferent from most insect pupa stages in that mosquito pupae are mobile.

9. The adult mosquito has mouth parts that are designed for stabbing and sucking. The mosquito (only the female) usually feeds on the blood of people and other animals. To make the sucking of blood easier and to prevent the blood from clotting, the mosquito injects a little of its saliva into the host. The saliva contains a chemical that prevents blood clotting and causes the irritation and swelling that we know as a "mosquito bite."

10. Some mosquitoes carry diseases, such as malaria and yellow fever, and spread these diseases from person to person as they bite and suck blood.

L. Bees, hornets, wasps, and ants belong to the order **Hymenoptera.**

1. Although most insects live alone, some live together in large groups or communities, called colonies. These insects are called **social insects** because different members of the colony have special jobs that help the colony. Most hymenopterans are social insects.

2. Hymenopterans usually have two pairs of thin, veined wings, with the front pair much larger than the back pair. The name Hymenoptera means "membrane-wing."

3. They have biting, sucking, or lapping mouth parts.

4. They undergo complete metamorphosis.

5. There is a definite narrowing, or constriction, between the thorax and the abdomen.

M. In a **bee colony** there are three kinds of bees—the queen, the drones, and the workers.

1. The **queen** is the only egg-laying bee. Although one colony may contain 50,000 individual bees, there is only one queen.

2. The queen is the largest bee in the colony. She has a long, pointed abdomen with an egg-laying organ at the tip of the last abdominal segment. Her only function is to lay eggs so that the colony can continue to exist. She can lay about 1,500 eggs a day. She usually lives five or six years, although some queen bees have been known to live for ten years.

3. She can lay both fertilized and unfertilized eggs. Fertilized eggs develop into non-egg-laying females, which become the **workers.** Unfertilized eggs develop into males, which are called **drones.**

4. The queen is mated just once by a drone, while in flight. From that mating she will receive several million sperm cells, which she keeps in a pouch in her body and uses to fertilize eggs for the rest of her life.

5. Drones are smaller than the queen bee, but larger than the female workers. There are hundreds of drones in a colony. They have fat bodies, large eyes, and powerful wings, but no stinger.

6. Drones do no work. They are cared for by worker bees. Their mouth parts are not long enough to suck up nectar, so they must be fed by the workers. The drones' only function is to mate with the queen. Their big eyes help them to find her as she flies.

7. During the summer there are usually a few hundred drones around the beehive, but only one of them mates with the queen. Soon after mating with the queen, the drone dies. In the fall, when the supply of honey is low, the workers refuse to feed the drones and sting them to death.

8. The **workers** are infertile female bees, developed from fertilized eggs. Workers are the smallest bees in the colony and the most numerous. There are thousands of workers in each colony.

9. Worker bees have a "stinger" at the tip of their last abdominal segment, which is connected to a gland that produces a poison. Drones do not have stingers. When a worker bee stings a person or animal, usually the stinger and parts of the bee's internal organs are pulled out and the bee dies.

10. Although workers are infertile and, therefore, cannot lay eggs, they carry on all the other duties of the colony. They bring in the nectar and pollen from flowers. It is the worker bee that we usually see flying around.

11. Workers prepare the materials and build the honeycomb that make up the hive. They collect and prepare food for members of the colony. Some feed and groom the queen, others feed the drones, and still others nurse feeding larvae that hatch from the eggs laid by the queen.

12. Some workers guard the hive and keep it clean. Others fan the hive, either to keep it airy and cool or to help the watery nectar evaporate more quickly. Indeed, worker bees are "busy little bees" during their brief six-week life in the summer working season. In the fall or winter, however, workers may live for as long as six months.

13. Worker bees learn by early adulthood to recognize certain scents carried by bees of their

colony. They reject or accept other bees depending on their scents.

14. Their mouth parts form a long proboscis (a tube or tongue), which makes it possible for the bee to suck up **nectar** from flowers. The nectar is sucked into the bee's honey stomach, or crop, where the nectar remains until it is taken to the hive to be used as food.

15. Although **pollen** collects on all parts of a bee's hairy body and legs, much of it is deposited in a hairy cavity, called a pollen basket, located on its hind legs. Pollen brought back to the hive is made into food.

16. The workers make three kinds of material for use in the hive: **wax, honey,** and **propolis.** The wax oozes out of the segments of a worker's abdomen. It usually is produced after the worker has eaten a lot of honey. Other workers remove the wax that forms, chew it to make it soft, and then bring it to yet other workers, who use the wax to make the **honeycomb** of the hive, a structure made of six-sided cells.

17. The honeycomb is used for storing honey and a special food, called beebread, which is made by the bees from pollen and bee saliva.

18. Eggs are also put into the honeycomb, one to a cell, by the queen, where they hatch into larvae which, in turn, are cared for by the worker bees.

19. **Honey** is made from flower nectar, which the bees have collected in their stomachs (crops). In their stomachs, the nectar is changed into honey, which is then emptied into the cells of the honeycomb. The honey thickens as the water it contains evaporates. By fanning their wings, workers speed up this evaporation. When the honey is thick enough, the cell is sealed by the bees.

20. **Propolis** is a bee glue. It is a brown material collected from the sticky leaf buds of certain plants. The workers use propolis to hold the honeycomb together, to patch up holes and cracks, to make the inside of the cells smooth, and sometimes to cover the body of small, dead animals that have died inside the hive.

21. A bee can handle 300 times its own weight, the equivalent of a human moving a 10-ton object.

22. Bees communicate with each other by doing different kinds of dances. In this way, they are able to tell other workers of their colony where they have found pollen and nectar.

23. Occasionally, during early spring or summer, a large group of bees may **swarm;** that is, they leave the hive to look for another location to start a new home. Bees may swarm because the colony has become too big or because food in the vicinity has become scarce. Sometimes they leave if another queen is developed in the colony.

24. A queen develops when the workers give a fertilized egg special treatment. The workers make one cell of the honeycomb larger, and when the egg hatches, the workers feed the larva a substance called **royal jelly,** which is a special mixture of honey and pollen. The larva is fed this royal jelly until it spins a cocoon and enters the pupa stage. Later, when it emerges from this pupa stage, it is an adult queen bee.

25. The new queen bee will try to kill the old one. If workers prevent this action, the new queen bee, many workers, and some drones swarm from the hive.

26. After a new colony is established, the queen bee flies into the air and is followed by the drones. One drone mates with the queen, after which the drone dies and the queen returns to the hive to lay eggs for the rest of her life.

N. **Ants,** too, are social insects.

1. There are many different kinds of ants, some large and others quite small.

2. It has been estimated that ants constitute a greater biomass than any other single group of organisms on earth.

3. Some ant species live in tunnels in the ground. Others build large mounds, called anthills. Some live in decaying trees.

4. Ants cannot sting like bees, but they have a strong bite and powerful jaws.

5. As compared with a bee colony, an ant colony also has many workers but relatively fewer males. An ant colony also has many queens, living peacefully together.

6. Both queens and males have wings, but workers do not.

7. During the mating season the females fly high into the air, followed by the males.

8. The males mate with the females, depositing a huge number of sperm cells. The males die soon after mating with the females.

9. The females return to earth, bite off their own wings, and begin laying eggs.

10. Many species of ants also have **soldiers** in their colonies. Soldiers do the fighting for a colony. They have larger heads and powerful biting jaws.

DEMONSTRATION 14.11
Fruit Flies

You can easily collect fruit flies most of the year. Peel a ripe banana and leave the skin, soft side up, on a saucer. Tiny fruit flies will soon gather on the skin. Collect some of the flies and put them in a glass or plastic jar. Put a small piece of banana peel or a thin slice of ripe banana in the jar to keep the fruit flies alive. Plug the mouth of the jar with a wad of cotton. The cotton will keep the fruit flies from escaping but still supply them with air.

Study the behavior of the flies and observe them with a magnifying glass. If the flies mate and lay tiny eggs, observe their life cycle as larvae, pupae, and then adult flies appear. How long does it take for the rapid life cycle to occur? Try to distinguish the male from the female flies. The male fruit fly is a little smaller than the female, and its abdomen tends to be more strongly colored than the female's.

---

11. Soldier ants sometimes attack another ant colony. If they defeat the other colony, they carry away the larvae and pupae of the conquered ants. When these captured larvae and pupae become mature ants, they become slave workers for the colony.
12. All ants undergo complete metamorphosis. Their eggs are tiny and generally can be seen only with the aid of a magnifying glass. Their larvae are usually white and have no legs.
13. When the larvae go into the pupa stage, they usually spin white cocoons, sometimes mistakenly called "ant eggs."
14. With an ability to lift 50 times their own body weight, the workers in an ant colony have many duties. They take care of and protect the larvae and pupae, gather food for the colony, build the anthill, and keep the colony clean.
15. Many species of ants keep their own "cows," which are aphids. During the winter the ants carry these aphids into their colony and care for them. In spring the ants set the aphids on plants, where the aphids feed. The ants then stroke the bodies of the aphids with their antennae, which causes the aphids to give off a sweet liquid that the ants drink.

O. Many insects are camouflaged, which protects them from their enemies.
1. Some insects have **protective coloration,** which causes them to blend with their environment. The grasshopper's wings and upper parts are green, blending with the grass so that the grasshopper is not easily seen. The praying mantis is the same color as a green leaf and thus is not easily detected.
2. Some insects have adapted their appearances and look like objects on which they rest. The walking stick, a relative of the grasshopper and member of the order Orthoptera, looks like a small twig. The walking-leaf butterfly

looks like a large green leaf. The dead-leaf butterfly looks like a dead leaf.
3. Some insects look like other, more annoying, insects. The robber fly looks like a bumble bee, but it is a fly, not a bee. The viceroy butterfly looks very much like the monarch, butterfly, which tastes bad to birds.

P. Insects can be helpful to humans, but some are harmful.
1. Some insects are beneficial to humans. Many insects, such as bees, wasps, butterflies, moths, beetles, bugs, and certain kinds of flies, play an important part in the pollination of plants. Bees produce honey and beeswax. The silk moth gives us silk. The lac insect gives us shellac. The bodies of some insects, such as the cochineal insect, are ground up to produce dyes. Some insects, like the dragonfly, praying mantis, and ladybug, prey on harmful insects. Others, such as the carrion beetle, are scavengers and feed on the dead bodies of animals.
2. Some insects are detrimental to human interests. Many insects, like the grasshopper, cricket, boll weevil, fruit fly, and Japanese beetle, destroy grain crops, vegetables, and fruits. Some insects, especially certain kinds of moths and beetles, destroy entire forests of trees. Other insects, such as the termite, damage wooden buildings and foundations. Certain moths and beetles destroy clothes and carpets. Others, like the mosquito, flea, louse, and fly, carry disease germs to humans and animals. Some insects, like the flea, louse, and bedbug, are parasites on humans and pet animals.

Q. Various methods are used to control insects.
1. One method of controlling harmful insects is to destroy the environment in which they live. The draining of ditches and ponds, where mosquitoes breed, will break the life

cycle of these insects. Changing or rotating crops that harmful insects use for food will take away their food supply.

2. Another method of controlling harmful insects is to use quarantine laws to prevent the importing of insects into a state or country. Sometimes the eggs or larvae of insects are brought into an area unknowingly because they are hidden on plants or fruit. These insects can then destroy the "balance of nature" in that area if there are no natural predators of the insects to hold them in check, and the insects can quickly become numerous and highly destructive. Agricultural inspectors at seaports, state lines, and airline terminals inspect plants and fruit coming into the area and take away and destroy those suspected of carrying harmful insects.

3. Yet another method of controlling harmful insects is to use chemical controls. Stomach poisons can be sprayed on plants that are attacked by chewing insects. Contact poisons, sprayed on plants that are attacked by insects that suck rather than chew leaves, kill as they come in contact with an insect's body. Poison gases, which enter an insect's body through the tiny openings (spiracles) on each side of the thorax and abdomen, kill insects instantly. Some gases, like the vapor used for controlling the clothes moth, do not kill adult insects but destroy the larvae.

4. Many people, scientists included, are very much concerned about the use of chemicals to kill insects. These chemicals may have several detrimental effects: their entering plants and being eaten by humans; the pollution of streams and the killing of life in the streams; and the killing of valuable birds, animals, and insects.

5. Many insects build up a resistance to chemical poisons, and their offspring inherit this resistance. This renders these insecticides ineffective, unless their concentrations of poisonous ingredients are increased.

6. Perhaps a more ecologically correct method of controlling harmful insects is to import natural enemies of the insects or to make use of local natural enemies. This is called **biological control.** Birds are the best natural enemies of insects. Other good natural enemies are spiders, frogs, toads, and snakes. Importing a natural enemy may become a problem if the "balance of nature" is upset and the natural enemy becomes too numerous and itself destructive.

7. Another method of controlling harmful insects is sterilization. In this method, a large number of male insects are exposed to X-rays or radioactive materials that make them sterile so that they cannot fertilize the female insects' eggs. The sterile male insects are then released, and they mate with the female insects. However, because the eggs are not fertilized by the sterile males, no offspring develop. As a result, the number of harmful insects is greatly reduced. With repeated treatments, the harmful insects could be eradicated completely.

IV. SPIDERS, TICKS, MITES, AND SCORPIONS

A. **Arachnida** is the class of arthropods that consists of spiders and their close relatives, the ticks, mites, and scorpions. Arachnids are not insects. They have characteristics different from those of insects and other arthropods, which place them in their separate class.
  1. Whereas most arthropods have three body regions—head, thorax, and abdomen—arachnids have no distinct thorax.
  2. Arachnids have six pairs of jointed appendages. The first pair, called chelicerae, are located near the mouth. In arachnids, chelicerae are usually modified as pincers to hold food, or as fangs that can inject prey with poison.
  3. Arachnids do not have antennae. Their second pair of appendages, called the pedipalps, are adapted for handling food and for sensing.
  4. The two remaining pairs of appendages are legs used for locomotion.

B. A **spider** has its head and thorax joined together, whereas an insect has a head and a thorax separate from each other.
  1. Spiders have only simple eyes, each made of just one lens. Nearly all insects have compound eyes, made up of many lenses.
  2. Spiders have two pairs of appendages attached to their heads. One pair, the chelicerae, are hollow and have small openings in their tips, through which poison from glands in the spider's head can be injected into a victim. The other pair, the pedipalps, are used as feelers. They also are used by the male spider to hold sperm cells during union with a female.
  3. A spider usually has eight eyes, arranged in a definite pattern on its head. This pattern varies among different kinds of spiders and is used in classifying spiders.

4. The breathing organs of spiders are called book lungs, because of their folds that look like pages of a book. Spiders usually have either two or four of these book lungs. Air enters the book lungs from a slit in the spider's abdomen.

5. Many spiders have three pairs of appendages, called spinnerets, on the tip of the underside of the abdomen. Each spinneret contains hundreds of tubes. Liquid silk from the spider's silk glands flows through these tubes out into the air, where it hardens to form a thread. This thread is used to spin a web and to build cocoons or nests for eggs.

6. In the fall, the young of some spiders spin long threads. When wind catches the thread, it carries the young far away.

7. Spiders bite but do not sting. When they bite, they inject poison into the victim. In humans, this can cause pain and swelling.

8. Spiders usually mate in late summer or early fall. The female spider is usually larger than the male. In many species, the female eats the male after mating.

9. The female lays a large batch of eggs, around which she spins a cocoon or nest. Some females die soon after laying their eggs. The eggs hatch in the winter, and the young stay inside the cocoon or nest. Young spiders often eat each other. In spring the spiders that remain leave the cocoon or nest.

10. Spiders feed mostly on insects. Those that feed on insects that are pests to humans are beneficial animals. They do not eat the insects, but suck the juices from them.

C. The **tarantula,** or banana spider, can measure as much as 15 to 20 centimeters (6 to 8 in) across when its legs are spread. The **cane spider,** which lives in sugar fields, is similar in size.

1. The tarantula and the cane spider live in the tropics but are sometimes transported to other areas in shipments of bananas.

2. They eat insects, but sometimes can attack small mammals and birds.

3. Their bite is painful, but not deadly, to humans.

4. One of the largest spiders is the **South American bird-eating spider,** which has a body about 9 cm (3.5 in) long and a leg span up to 25 cm (10 in).

D. The **black widow** spider is found mostly in warm climates but can sometimes be seen in temperate climates.

1. It has a round, black abdomen with a red hourglass-shaped spot on the underside.

2. The female is vicious. After mating, she kills the male unless he is able to bind her with web silk.

3. To humans, a black widow bite is painful and poisonous, sometimes causing death. This is especially true of the **Australian black widow spider.**

4. The thread of the black widow spider is so fine and strong that it has been used in marking lenses of gunsights, bombsights, and surveying instruments.

E. The **brown recluse spider** has a violin-shaped figure on the underside of its abdomen. It is found in temperate climates and has a poison that can be fatal to humans.

F. **Trap-door spiders** are found in the southeastern and western United States. Instead of spinning webs to catch insects, they build a kind of trap-door. They dig a tubelike hole in the ground, line it with silk, and fasten a hinged "door" over the hole. When an insect prey comes into the hole, the open door is shut tight, trapping the insect.

G. The **scorpion** is an arachnid found in all tropical countries and in the southern and southwestern United States. It has many abdominal segments and quite large pincers.

1. In addition to its four pairs of walking legs, a scorpion has a large pair of appendages attached to its head, with a large pincer at the end of each appendage.

2. It has a long, segmented abdomen that forms a tail at the end. At the tip of the tail is a poisonous stinger, which the scorpion uses to kill insects and spiders. The scorpion's sting is very painful, but seldom fatal, to humans.

3. Related to the scorpion is the **horseshoe crab.** This marine animal is considered to be a living fossil, because it has remained relatively unchanged since it first appeared on earth some 500 million years ago. The horseshoe crab has an extensive exoskeleton and lives on the sea floor.

H. The **harvestman,** or daddy longlegs, looks very much like a long-legged spider, but with its long, segmented abdomen, it is not a spider. It is very useful to gardeners because it feeds mostly on aphids. It is found in gardens, fields, woods, and sometimes in the home, where it feeds on mites.

I. **Mites** and **ticks** are small arachnids with only a single body section. The head, thorax, and abdomen are completely fused.

1. They live mostly as parasites on the bodies of humans, chickens, cattle, dogs, and other animals. They are dangerous because they carry germs from one animal to another.

2. Mites carry such diseases as sheep scab and dog mange. Chiggers are mites that bore into the skin, causing itchiness and pain. The "red spider" that harms apple leaves and fruit is a mite, not a spider.
3. Ticks carry Rocky Mountain spotted fever, Texas cattle fever, and Lyme disease. Lyme disease, so-called because it was first discovered in Lyme, Connecticut, in 1975, is a disease caused by a corkscrew-shaped bacterium that is transmitted to humans through the bite of certain ticks. The ticks pick up the bacteria by sucking the blood of infected deer and white-footed mice. Lyme disease is a crippling disease but can be arrested with antibiotics if diagnosed and treated early.

V. CENTIPEDES AND MILLIPEDES

A. Centipedes and millipedes are two arthropods grouped together in a special class, **Myriapoda,** which means "many feet."

1. They both have bodies composed of many segments.
2. The centipede's head has its antennae and mouth parts.
3. Its first body segment has a pair of poison claws. Centipedes are dangerous because of their poison.
4. All other segments, except the last two, have one pair of legs each.
5. The centipede moves fast and is hard to capture.
6. The millipede's head also has its antennae and mouth parts.
7. All of its body segments, except the last two, have two pairs of legs each.
8. It moves slowly and may curl up when disturbed.
9. Millipedes are not poisonous.

THE VERTEBRATES

I. PHYLUM CHORDATA

A. Characteristics of this phylum are as follows.
1. All chordates have a dorsal hollow nerve cord.
2. In their embryonic state, they have an anterior-posterior axis that provides a support structure. This structure is called the **notochord.**
3. Most adult chordates have a backbone, which develops around the notochord. These chordates comprise the subphylum called **vertebrata**–the vertebrates.

4. At some point during their development, chordates have pharyngeal gill slits and a muscular post-anal tail.
5. Most chordates have an internal skeleton, called an **endoskeloton.**
6. Most have two pairs of limbs attached to their bodies.

B. The major classes of chordates are: Osteichthyes and Chondrichthyes (collectively referred to as fish), Amphibia, Reptilia, Aves (the birds), and Mammalia.

FISH

I. CLASSIFICATION OF FISH

A. Fish are members of the phylum Chordata and share the characteristics common to that phylum. Fish are grouped into three broad classes: the **bony fish (Osteichthyes),** the **lampreys (Agnatha),** and the **sharks** and **rays (Chondrichthyes).**
1. The skeletons of bony fish are made of **bone,** but the skeletons of the other two classes are made of a tough tissue, called **cartilage.**
2. On the basis of both numbers and economic importance, bony fish make up the most significant group.

II. WHERE FISH ARE FOUND

A. Fish live only in water.
1. Most fish are found in the ocean, but there are also many fish in lakes, ponds, rivers, and brooks.
2. Some live near the surface of the water; others live closer to the bottom.
3. Some fish live alone, whereas others travel in large groups, called schools.

III. PHYSICAL CHARACTERISTICS OF FISH

A. Fish range in size from less than 2 centimeters (1 in) long to as much as 15 meters (49 ft) long. Most fish are less than 1 meter (3 ft) long.

B. There are three parts to the body of a fish—head, body, and tail.
   1. The head has no neck and is attached directly to the body.
   2. The body is the largest part of a fish.
   3. The tail is narrow and immediately behind the body. It is often confused with the tail fin.
   4. The body of a fish is streamlined and tapers at both ends.
C. The bodies of most fish are covered with scales, which grow from pockets in the skin and overlap one another like the shingles on the roof of a house.
   1. The skin of a fish gives off a slime, which oozes between the scales and covers the body, lubricating the body and making it easier for the fish to swim.
   2. The slime also protects the fish from being attacked by tiny parasites in the water.
D. Some fish are brightly colored, either partially or completely, with the colors often arranged in spots, lines, or bars.
   1. Many fish are dark-colored on top and light-colored beneath. This pattern helps them to avoid being seen by their enemies from either above or below.
E. Most fish have large eyes that are partially movable. They have no eyelids.
   1. The pupil of the eye is large, as compared with pupils in other vertebrates. It can admit a great deal of light.
F. The body of a fish has a number of appendages, called fins.
   1. Each fin is made of many bony spines called rays, which are covered by a thin fold of skin.
   2. A pair of fins, called the pectoral fins, are located near the head, corresponding to the front legs of land vertebrates.
   3. Posterior to the pectoral fins is a second pair of fins, called the pelvic fins, which correspond to the rear legs of land vertebrates.
   4. Along the dorsal (back) side of the body are one or two dorsal fins.
   5. Along the ventral (front) side of the body, toward the tail, there is a caudal fin, which is the end of the fish's tail.
G. Fish are **ectothermic** animals. The temperature of their blood is approximately the same as that of the surrounding water, and this temperature changes with the seasons.

IV. HOW FISH OBTAIN OXYGEN

A. Fish have respiratory organs, called gills, located on each side of the head.
   1. The gills are made of many small, thread-like filaments, giving them a feathery appearance.
   2. Each filament contains tiny, thin-walled blood vessels.
   3. Most fish obtain oxygen from water by opening and closing their mouths. When a fish opens its mouth, water rushes in. When the fish closes its mouth, the water is forced out through two openings on each side of the back of the head. Each opening is covered by an operculum, a movable external flap.
   4. There are four or five gills in each gill chamber located just prior to the opening. As water is forced out over the gills, dissolved oxygen in the water passes through the thin walls of the blood vessels and is picked up by the blood. The blood gets rid of its carbon dioxide as it picks up fresh oxygen.
   5. Because cold water holds more oxygen than warm water, fish are more active in cool water than in warm water.

V. HOW FISH SWIM

A. A fish swims forward rapidly by moving its tail and tail fin from side to side.
B. Dorsal and caudal fins, used mostly for balance, help to keep the fish from tipping over.
C. The paired pectoral and pelvic fins have several functions.
   1. They help a fish keep its balance when the fish is resting.
   2. They act as oars when the fish is swimming slowly.
   3. They help the fish steer to the right or left.
   4. When spread out at right angles, they act as brakes to help the fish come to a stop.
   5. The fish also uses their fins to swim backward.
D. Most fish have a swim bladder inside their bodies, located beneath the backbone and surrounded by the ribs.
   1. The swim bladder makes it possible for the fish to rise, sink, or stay at a particular depth.
   2. Fish sink as more air is taken into the swim bladder and rise as air is released from it. The overall volume of the fish remains fairly

constant while the amount of air taken into the swim bladder from the gills increases or decreases. As the swim bladder takes in more air, the overall density (specific gravity) of the fish increases to more than 1 (the specific gravity of freshwater is approximately 1) and the fish sinks in the water.

VI. WHAT FISH EAT

   A. Some fish eat only algae and other water plants.

   B. Some fish eat animals, such as insects, worms, crayfish, snails, and other fish.

      1. Fish that eat other animals have many sharp teeth. These teeth slant backward toward the throat, making it easy for a fish to swallow the prey and making it hard for the animal to escape.

      2. Fish can use their teeth to seize, tear, and hold food, but not to chew.

VII. HOW FISH REPRODUCE

   A. Most fish develop from eggs that the female lays outside her body.

      1. At a certain time of the year a female fish lays a large number of eggs. This process of laying eggs is called **spawning.**

   B. Shortly after spawning, the male swims over the eggs and gives off a liquid, called **milt,** which contains large numbers of sperm cells.

   C. The sperm cells swim to the eggs and fertilize the eggs by uniting with them.

      1. When fertilization takes place outside the female's body, it is called external fertilization **(oviparous).**

   D. The fertilized eggs develop and hatch into tiny fish, usually from 10 to 40 days later, depending on the kind of fish and the temperature of the water.

      1. While the fish are developing from the egg, they are fed by the yolk of the egg.

      2. The yolk is contained within the yolk sac, which remains attached to the newborn fish for some time after they hatch, supplying them with food.

   E. The young of some freshwater tropical fish, like the guppy, molly, and swordtail, develop inside the female's body and are born alive.

      1. The female of these fish keeps her eggs inside her body and receives the sperm of the male when he mates with her, in a process called internal fertilization **(ovoviviparous).**

      2. The sperm fertilize the eggs, which develop inside the female's body and then are brought forth alive.

   F. As a rule, most freshwater fish either spawn where they live or travel a short distance to shallower water for spawning.

      1. The **eel** has an unusual spawning habit.

      2. Eels live in rivers and streams that flow into the ocean.

      3. At spawning time the eels that live in rivers flowing into the Atlantic Ocean and the Gulf of Mexico swim far out into the Atlantic Ocean.

      4. The female lays her eggs and the male deposits his sperm on the eggs. Then both adult eels die.

      5. When the young eels that hatch are about 5 centimeters (2 in) long, they return to the rivers and streams from which their parents came.

      6. After three to eight years the adult eels return again to the same part of the Atlantic Ocean for spawning.

      7. Although both American and European eels spawn in the same part of the Atlantic Ocean, the young eels never make a mistake and go to the wrong continent.

      8. The **Pacific salmon** also has unusual spawning habits.

      9. The adult fish live in the ocean along the north Pacific coast.

     10. At spawning time they swim up the Columbia River to the same streams where they had hatched three or four years earlier.

     11. The females spawn, and the males deposit their sperm to fertilize the eggs. Then both adults soon die.

     12. The young salmon that hatch from the eggs swim to the ocean and live there for three or four years until it is time for them to spawn.

VIII. THE ECONOMIC IMPORTANCE AND CONSERVATION OF FISH

   A. Fish are a valuable source of food for humans.

      1. Common saltwater food fish include tuna, herring, sardine, swordfish, halibut, mackerel, haddock, sole, flounder, cod, and sea perch.

      2. Common freshwater food fish include trout, salmon, pike, whitefish, perch, buffalo carp, and catfish.

      3. The eggs of both the sturgeon, commonly called caviar, and the shad are eaten as food.

      4. Oil from the liver of the codfish, halibut, and shark is rich in vitamins A and D.

B. Ground fish, called fish meal, is used in making foods for cats, dogs, and chickens.

C. Many people catch fish for sport and recreation, as well as for food.

D. Fish oil is used in making certain paints.

E. The bones and other body parts of fish are used to make glue.

F. Fish are sometimes wastefully lost from bodies of water for many reasons.
   1. The water level of a lake may become lower during hot, dry spells or because of unwise treatment of the land around the lake. This lowering of the water level may destroy spawning areas or areas where the food supply is rich.
   2. Sometimes humans straighten river channels, which discourages the breeding of fish; fish live better in rivers that have bends, rapids, and quiet pools.
   3. Dams across rivers prevent fish from traveling upstream to spawn.
   4. Lakes and streams are sometimes contaminated by sewage and chemical wastes, which can poison and kill the fish.
   5. Sometimes too many adult fish are caught during the spawning season, or too many young fish are caught before they can become adults and have the opportunity to breed new fish.

G. To protect and conserve fish, states have passed many laws.
   1. There are restrictions regarding the catching of fish. Fish under a certain length cannot be kept, but must be thrown back. Only a certain number of fish may be caught by one person in one day. Certain fish may not be caught during their spawning season. Fish must not be caught by using explosives in the water.
   2. Sewage and chemical wastes cannot be dumped in certain lakes and streams that have been set aside for fishing.
   3. Dams that interfere with the travel of fish upstream to spawn must have fish ladders beside them, a series of small pools, one higher than the other, connected by small waterfalls that can be leaped by the fish.

H. Both the federal and the state governments have established fish hatcheries to breed and raise fish for lakes and streams. In a hatchery, eggs are taken from the female and put into a tank; then milt, containing the sperm of the male, is poured over the eggs. In this way almost all the eggs are fertilized and hatch. When the young fish are old enough to take care of themselves, they are released into lakes and streams.

I. Scientists constantly investigate diseases, fungus infections, and natural enemies of fish in an effort to maintain a balance in nature.

IX. RELATIVES OF THE BONY FISH

A. The **lamprey** is a primitive kind of fish. It belongs to the class **Agnatha.**
   1. Some kinds of lampreys live in saltwater, and others live in freshwater.
   2. The lamprey has a long, thin body and looks much like an eel.
   3. Its skeleton is made of cartilage instead of bone.
   4. It has a soft, slimy skin.
   5. Its only fins are two fins along its back and a tail fin.
   6. It has no jaws, but it does have a round sucking mouth lined with sharp teeth.
   7. Its rasping tongue is hard and rough, with teeth on it, so it can act like a coarse file.
   8. The lamprey is a parasite, living on the blood of other fish. Its sucking mouth clamps onto the side of a fish, and its teeth and tongue rip through the scales and flesh of the victim. The lamprey then sucks out the blood, and sometimes even the internal organs.

B. Although the **shark** is similar to bony fish, it has characteristics that place it in its own class, **Chondrichthyes.**
   1. Sharks live only in saltwater.
   2. Some sharks are about two thirds of a meter (2 ft) long, but others can be 15 meters (49 ft) or longer.
   3. The shark's skeleton is made of cartilage instead of bone.
   4. A shark's placoid scales do not overlap, like those of bony fish, but instead lie side by side.
   5. Its fins are very much like those of a bony fish, but the upper part of its tail fin is longer than the lower part.
   6. Its mouth is on the lower side of its head and is lined with many rows of very sharp teeth.
   7. Sharks feed on other fish and sea animals, dead or alive.
   8. The **tiger shark** is a deadly predator that will eat anything whether it is dead or alive.
   9. Tiger sharks average about 4 meters (13 ft) in length, but can be as large as twice that.

DEMONSTRATION 14.12
The Classroom Aquarium

A rectangular tank that holds 23 liters (6 gal) is an excellent size for classrooms. Clean the tank thoroughly with detergent and water and rinse it several times. Obtain enough aquarium gravel from a pet shop to cover the bottom of the tank 5 centimeters (2 in) deep. Before adding it to the tank, place the gravel in a large pan, tilt the pan to one side, and allow running water to flow in and overflow the pan. Continue running the water into the pan until the gravel is quite clean.

Place the gravel evenly in the tank, add one or two colored rocks, and put a few clam or oyster shells in the gravel. The shells will slowly dissolve in the water and provide the calcium that the growing snails will need for their shells.

Lay a piece of paper over the gravel so that when water is poured into the tank, the water will not become cloudy (cloudiness usually lasts a long time). Use either clear pond water or tap water that has been allowed to stand for two days so that the chlorine dissolved in it can escape. Pour the water into the tank almost to the top.

Place the tank in north or east light, but not in direct sunlight. From the pet shop obtain some rooted plants, such as sagittaria or valisneria, and some floating plants, such as elodea or cabomba. Place the plants toward the back of the tank so you will have a clear view of the fish. The water plants will take in the carbon dioxide given off by the fish and give off oxygen that the fish will need. Do not include too many plants, as they will grow and spread. Remove any dead leaves. Allow the aquarium to stand for about a week until the water is clear and the plants are growing.

Now you are ready to add the fish. Do not overcrowd the aquarium. About one-2 centimeter (¾ in) fish to 3 liters (1 gal) of water is recommended. The 23-liter (6-gal) tank will then hold either six 2-centimeter (1-in) fish or three 5-centimeter (2-in) fish. Obtain small, active fish, such as guppies, rather than sluggish goldfish.

Add about six to twelve snails, also obtained from the pet shop, and then place a glass cover over the tank. Do not overfeed the fish; uneaten food causes the water to become foul, and the fish may die. Fish will eat prepared fish food, bread crumbs, bits of egg yolk, and oatmeal. Occasionally, give them small amounts of chopped earthworms or meal worms.

Observe the fish in your aquarium. Compare shapes and sizes of the head, trunk, and tail regions. Identify the fins, and see which fins are paired. Observe how the fish use their fins and tails. Watch the eyes and see whether they move. Note how the fish take in water through their mouths and then force the water out through their gill covers. See how easily the fish can rise or sink in the water without using their fins very much. This movement is made possible by the inflation or deflation of the air bladder inside the fish.

Remove a small fish from the aquarium and wrap it in wet absorbent cotton, leaving only the tail exposed. Place the fish on a flat glass dish and observe the tail under the low power of the microscope. If the fish flaps its tail, place a microscope slide on the tail. You will see the arteries, veins, and capillaries. Note the blood cells moving through the blood vessels, quickly through the arteries and slowly through the veins. In the small capillaries, the blood cells move almost in single file. Switch to the high power of the microscope and observe the blood cells. Do not keep the fish out of water this way for more than 15 minutes.

---

10. Tiger sharks live mainly in tropical, coastal waters throughout the world. They spread north and south during summer months, frequently inhabiting deep waters on the fringe of reefs. Here they occasionally move into the channels of the reef looking for prey.
11. The wedge-shaped head of the tiger shark gives it minimum side resistance in the water, allowing the shark to make quick turns.
12. Small pits on each side of its head are electrical sensors that allow the tiger shark to sense even the tiniest muscle movement of other animals, so it can find prey even in dark waters.
13. In addition, the tiger shark has an acute sense of smell, which enables it to sense even the faintest traces of blood in the water and follow them to their source.
14. Its pectoral fins act like wings, providing lift as the shark swims.
15. The long upper lobe on its tail fin provides thrust for sudden bursts of speed.
C. The **ray,** which belongs to the same group of fish as the shark, is also called the **devilfish, sting ray,** or **blanket fish.**
    1. It has a large, flat body that looks like a blanket.
    2. When it swims, the sides of its body look somewhat like moving wings.
    3. It has a long, whiplike tail with a sharp spine that can penetrate its victim and cause tissue damage, swelling, and severe pain.

4. The ray's spine is a skin-covered cartilage bone located at the base of the tail, near the anus, not at the end of its tail. There is no poisonous secretion, but the skin covering the spine is covered with bacteria that can cause an infection in the punctured victim.

5. It uses this spine to wound the fish and other sea animals it preys on.
6. The ray lives only in saltwater and often lies half buried in the sand.

AMPHIBIANS

I. THE CLASSIFICATION OF AMPHIBIANS

  A. Amphibians are members of the animal phylum **Chordata** and share the characteristics of this phylum with other classes of chordates.

    1. Common amphibians include **frogs, toads, and salamanders.**

    2. They are all rather small vertebrates: most frogs and toads are from 5 to 15 centimeters (2 to 6 in) long, although the African frog is about 30 centimeters (12 in) long; salamanders are 5 centimeters (2 in) to $\frac{2}{3}$ meter (2 ft) long, and there is a giant salamander in Japan that is $1\frac{1}{2}$ meters (5 ft) long.

  B. Amphibians also have their own special characteristics which separates them from other groups in the phylum and places them in their own class, **Amphibia.**

    1. Their bodies are covered with a thin, loose skin that is usually moist.

    2. Their feet are often webbed, and they have no claws on their toes.

    3. Their eggs are fertilized externally (outside the female's body).

    4. Young amphibians live in water, but adult amphibians live mostly on land (*amphibia* means "two lives").

    5. Young amphibians look different from adult amphibians, which means that a change, or **metamorphosis,** takes place as the young amphibian becomes an adult.

    6. Like fish, amphibians are ectothermic. Their body temperature is nearly the same as that of their external environment. However, through muscular contractions and increased breathing, they can raise their body temperature above their surroundings for short periods of time.

II. THE FROG, TOAD, AND SALAMANDER

  A. Frogs and toads are members of the order **Anura.** Worldwide, they exhibit an extensive variety of sizes and colors and can be found in many different types of habitats.

1. The frog has a short, broad body covered by a thin, loose, moist skin that is colored very much like the surroundings the frog lives in. Glands in the skin give off a slimy mucus, which makes the skin slippery. The glands of some frogs secrete toxic chemicals, making these frog poisonous. Some of the most colorful frogs in the world are found in South and Central America, including more than 130 species that are poisonous.

2. The frog has large, bulging eyes, which have upper and lower lids. There is also a third eye lid, called the nictitating membrane, joined to the lower eyelid. This extra lid protects the eye when the frog is under water and keeps the eye moist when the frog is on land.

3. The frog has a large mouth with a long, sticky tongue that is attached anteriorly and lies on the floor of the mouth.

4. When a frog catches its prey, the mouth opens wide and the sticky tongue shoots out and catches the prey, throwing the prey against the roof of the mouth.

5. The frog has two short, weak front legs, each with four toes. The front legs are used to support the frog and to break the force of its fall after it has made a leap.

6. The frog has two highly developed hind legs, which are used for swimming and leaping, each with five long toes with webbing between them. When the frog is resting on land, the rear legs fold together along the body in a position that makes it possible for the frog to make a sudden leap.

7. On land the adult frog breathes through its lungs; in water it breathes through its skin.

8. Oxygen dissolved in the water passes directly through the skin into the blood, while carbon dioxide leaves the blood and passes out through the skin. This breathing through the skin makes it possible for the frog to stay under water or to bury itself in mud for long periods of time.

9. The heart of the frog is three-chambered; it mixes oxygen-rich with oxygen-poor blood.

10. Frogs and toads have vocal cords capable of producing a wide range of sounds. In many male frogs, air passes over the vocal cords, then into a pair of vocal sacs lying beneath the throat. Male frogs use their distinct sounds to attract female frogs. Females make sounds to indicate whether they are willing to mate.

11. Most frogs breed in water. The female lays her eggs, which are usually black and white in color. As the eggs pass out of the female, the male immediately spreads sperm over them. The sperm enter the eggs and fertilizes them.

12. The white part of an egg is the yolk, which contains stored food for the young frog when it first hatches from the egg. The black part of the frog egg is the living embryo, which will develop into a young frog. The young frog that hatches from the egg is called a **tadpole.**

13. At first the tadpole is a tiny animal with a short body, which immediately attaches itself to water plants and feeds on the yolk of the egg and on the jellylike material that surrounds the egg.

14. A mouth and horny jaws soon develop, and the tadpole begins to feed on tiny plants.

15. The body begins to lengthen, gills form at the sides of the head, but enclosed in an atrial chamber, and the tail becomes longer. The tadpole is now a fishlike animal and swims about freely in the water.

16. The tadpole eventually metamorphoses into an adult frog and lives on land. Depending on the species, development and metamorphosis to an adult frog can take from three weeks up to several years.

17. First the hind legs appear, and then the front legs form. As the legs develop, the tail is absorbed into the body and disappears.

18. Changes take place inside the body, gills are reabsorbed, and lungs form. The tadpole is now completely changed, or has undergone metamorphosis, into a frog.

19. Frogs are ectothermic. In temperate climates, as winter approaches the body temperature of the frog becomes so low that the frog cannot remain active. The frog buries itself in the mud at the bottom of a pond and stays quiet all winter; this is a period of inactivity called **hibernation.** In spring the days become warmer, and the frog becomes active again.

20. When it is very hot in summer, the frog may bury itself in the cool mud and again become inactive. This period of summer inactivity is called **estivation.**

B. The **leopard frog** is the most common frog in the United States, living in damp places near ponds, marshes, and ditches. It feeds on insects, worms, and crayfish.
   1. Its back is covered with dark spots surrounded by white or yellow rings, and it blends in with the grass and rocks among which it lives.
   2. Its underside is a creamy white.
   3. With a favorable water temperature, the tadpoles of leopard frogs become adults in a single summer.

C. The **bullfrog,** a large frog with legs as much as 25 centimeters (10 in) long, lives mostly in water. Bullfrogs feed on insects, worms, crayfish, and small fish.
   1. Most bullfrogs are a greenish brown, although their color may range from green to yellow.
   2. Their undersides are a grayish white mixed with dark splotches.
   3. With favorable water temperatures, it takes two summers for the tadpole of a common North American bullfrog to develop into an adult.
   4. The large legs of the bullfrog are eaten by people as food.
   5. The **African bullfrog** takes nearly 28 years to reach full adult size. Canine-like projections on this bullfrog's lower jaw enable it to catch and feed on larger animals, such as mice.

D. The **tree frog** is a very small frog, about 2.5 centimeters (1 in) long, that spends most of its life in trees.
   1. Its body looks very much like the bark of a tree.
   2. Its toes have sticky pads that make it possible for this frog to climb trees easily.
   3. It makes a very loud sound for its size.

E. All members of the order Anura are called frogs. However, some frogs bear the common name **toad.** Frogs that are called toads usually have a drier skin that is covered with bumps. Other characteristics of "toads" include the following:
   1. The toad has shorter legs than the frog.
   2. The toad lives on land all the time, returning to the water only to lay eggs.
   3. The toad's eggs are laid in strings instead of masses.
   4. The toad has no teeth.
   5. The toad cannot swim as well as the frog.
   6. The rounded bumps on its back, sides, and legs contain poison glands, which help protect the toad from some of its enemies.

7. The toad sleeps most of the day under rocks and logs and becomes active at night.
8. It feeds on insects and slugs.
F. The **salamander** looks more like a lizard than a frog or toad.
  1. It has a long and slender body and a long tail.
  2. Its short legs are all about the same size. Some salamanders do not have legs at all.
  3. Its skin is soft and moist, and its legs have no claws.
  4. Some salamanders live in water, and others live on land in damp places.
  5. The **mudpuppy** or necturus, common in the Midwest, has a pair of red gills around its head just above its front legs, and it keeps these gills all its life.
  6. The **tiger salamander** has yellow bars on a brown body, whereas the **spotted salamander** has yellow spots on a black body. The tiger salamander has a flat tail, and the spotted salamander has a round tail. Both live in water the first three months of their lives, then on land the rest of their lives.
  7. The **newt** is a salamander with a "triple life." For the first two months of its life it lives in the water and breathes only through its gills. During the next year or two it lives on land and breathes through lungs. Then it returns to the water for the rest of its life, breathing through its lungs when on the surface of the water and through its skin when under water.

REPTILES

I. THE CHARACTERISTICS OF REPTILES

A. Reptiles are members of the animal phylum called **Chordata** with characteristics common to all members of that phylum, and together with fish, amphibians, birds, and mammals, they make up a special group of animals called **vertebrates.**
  1. As vertebrates, reptiles have a backbone, their skeletons are inside their bodies, and most of them have two pairs of appendages attached to their bodies at the shoulder and hip.
B. Reptiles also have their own special characteristics, which gives them their own class, **Reptilia.** This class that includes snakes, turtles, lizards, and alligators is a very diverse group of animals.
  1. Reptiles have a rough, thick, dry skin covered with scales, unlike salamanders with their moist skin. It is this scaly skin that has provided a key to the success of reptiles on earth.
  2. Reptiles that have feet have claws on their toes.
  3. Both young and adult reptiles breathe only through lungs.
  4. Reptiles have a breastbone, called the sternum, which protects the heart and lungs.
  5. The female's eggs are fertilized by the male's sperm inside her body (internal fertilization).
  6. The eggs that are laid on the ground (not in water, as with amphibians) have a protective shell or membrane around them, another key to the success of reptiles on earth.
  7. Like fish and amphibians, reptiles are ectothermal. However, by regulating their behavioral activity (such as sunning to get warm on a cool morning or lying in the shade of a rock during a hot afternoon), snakes and lizards can maintain body temperatures very different from those of their surrounding environments. However, because they are still dependent on the temperatures of their environment, reptiles do not inhabit extremely cold climates.
  8. Most reptiles, like amphibians, have three-chambered hearts. The crocodile and alligator, however, have a four-chambered heart that completely separates the supply of oxygen-enriched blood from oxygen-depleted blood.
  9. At one time reptiles were the most numerous and most powerful animals on earth.

II. THE TURTLE

A. Turtles are a relatively small group within the class Reptilia. Some turtles live in salt water, others live in fresh water, and still others live on land. Land turtles are often called **tortoises.**
  1. Some turtles are quite small, but others, especially the sea turtles and the tortoises found on the Galapagos Islands off the coast of Ecuador, can be 2 meters (7 ft) long and weigh 450 kilograms (1000 lb).
B. All turtles have an upper and lower shell; the body is located between these shells.
  1. The shells protect the turtle. Most turtles can withdraw into their shells.

The Classroom Terrarium

Set up a terrarium as a home for frogs, toads, salamanders, turtles, and lizards.

A. Observe and compare frogs and toads

Frogs and toads live very well in a terrarium. Put a frog and a toad in separate cartons and watch them closely. Compare their appearance, skin, and color. Touch their skin to see if it is wet or dry. Compare the way they hop. Count the number of toes on each foot and see if the frog and toad have the same amount of webbing between their toes. Bring your finger very near their eyes and see if they can wink. Locate their large tympanic membranes, which correspond to a human's eardrum.

Place the frog and toad in separate, covered glass jars for a few minutes. Introduce some live houseflies or fruit flies into each jar and see how the frog and toad use their tongues to catch and eat the flies. Note how the eyes move inward to help the frog and toad swallow their food. Frogs and toads eat living insects only, such as flies, grasshoppers, caterpillars, June beetles, roaches, and meal worms. They can also be trained to eat bits of lean beef and liver if the meat is dangled in front of them with a string.

Place a frog in a large aquarium containing about 15 centimeters (6 in) of water. Watch how the frog swims. Note that when the frog is resting, it keeps its eyes and nostrils above the water. If you hold the frog under water and gently rub its sides, it will usually croak. Replace the water in the aquarium with very cold water, and see how the frog becomes motionless, as if it is ready to go into hibernation.

B. Raise tadpoles

Frogs and toads lay their eggs in spring. The eggs are found in shallow, quiet pond water, floating at or just beneath the surface near water plants. Frogs' eggs are found in clumps, whereas toads' eggs are found in strings. Both kinds of eggs are embedded in a jellylike material. Collect the eggs with a cup and pour them into a glass jar containing some of the pond water.

Place the eggs in an aquarium or in a terrarium pond that has water plants growing in it. If possible, add some of the green scum (algae) that is often found floating on top of ponds. Have the aquarium only partly full of water, and put a large rock in the aquarium that juts above the water. This rock will allow the tadpoles to leave the water and crawl around.

Watch the eggs each day with a magnifying glass. After a few days, tiny tadpoles will appear. Observe their growth and accompanying changes. Note that the toad's tadpole stage does not last as long as the frog's tadpole stage. Feed the tadpoles algae (green pond scum), small living insects, and dried fish food.

C. Keep and observe salamanders

Land salamanders can be kept very well in a woodland terrarium. Water salamanders can be kept in your classroom aquarium. They both can be fed earthworms, meal worms, ground lean beef, and liver cut into small pieces. It is better to feed the water salamander in a shallow pan of water outside the aquarium, so as to avoid contamination of the water in the aquarium.

Observe the salamander closely. Although it may look like a reptile, it is really an amphibian and has all the characteristics of an amphibian. Touch the salamander's body gently with the palm of your hand and see how smooth and moist the skin is. Observe how small and weak the legs are. Count the number of toes on the front and hind legs, and see whether the toes are webbed and have claws. Watch how the water salamander uses its tail for swimming. See how the salamander seizes and eats its food. Find out whether salamanders are attracted or repelled by strong light. Compare the salamander with other amphibians, such as the frog and toad, and note the similarities and differences. Contrast their living, feeding, and breeding habits as well.

D. Keep and observe turtles

The box turtle, which is mostly a land turtle, can be kept in a classroom terrarium. Water turtles can be kept in an aquarium tank containing about 7 centimeters (3 in) of water, with a few flat stones jutting above the water. Feed the turtles earthworms, meal worms, tadpoles, snails, bits of raw hamburger, slices of apple and banana, berries, and small pieces of lettuce. Because water turtles eat only under water, be sure to throw the food directly into the water. Do not become alarmed if water or land turtles refuse to eat for long periods of time and become sluggish. This inactivity is quite usual, so let them alone.

Observe the turtle closely. Examine the top and bottom shells and see how the shells form an excellent means of protecting the turtle from enemies and injury. Poke the turtle's head gently with a stick and watch the turtle pull its head, neck, legs, and tail inside its shell. Bring the stick near the turtle's eyes and see whether they can blink. Observe how the turtle seizes and eats its food. Try to find out if the mouth contains any teeth. Also note how the flexible neck can turn in all directions. Examine the short legs and count the number of toes on the front and hind legs. See whether the toes are webbed and have claws. Observe how the water turtle swims. Review the characteristics of a reptile and see whether the turtle has all these characteristics. Have the students find out how to distinguish between a turtle, tortoise, and terrapin. Compare the turtle with other reptiles, such as the lizard and snake, and note the similarities and differences. Contrast their living, feeding, and breeding habits as well.

2. Some turtles can even close their shells tightly.
3. The shells have plates that are of different colors and markings, and this difference helps biologists identify the turtles.

C. A turtle has either a pointed or triangular head.

D. It has no teeth, but it does have horny jaws that form a sharp beak, which the turtle uses to bite off pieces of food.

E. It has well-developed eyes and eyesight, with upper and lower eyelids.
  1. There is also a third eyelid, called the nictitating membrane, which is transparent and moves from the front corner of the eye to cover the eyeball.

F. A turtle's legs are quite short, and it walks slowly.
  1. The skin on a turtle's legs is scaly and tough.
  2. Most turtles have five toes on each leg, and the toes have claws.
  3. Some turtles have completely webbed toes, but others have very little webbing between the toes. Aquatic turtles use their webbed feet for swimming.

G. Some turtles have good-sized tails, but others have little or no tails.

H. All turtles, even sea turtles, lay their eggs on land.
  1. They lay their eggs in shallow holes and cover them with sand or dirt.
  2. The heat of the sun helps the eggs hatch.

I. Land turtles eat insects, earthworms, and plants. Water turtles eat fish, frogs, and birds that live near the water.

J. The greatest economic benefit of turtles to humans is as a source of food. Turtles constitute a major protein source, and in every region where they occur, they are eaten by humans.

III. The Lizard

A. Lizards have adapted to many types of habitats and can be found all over the world, except in polar regions.

B. Some lizards, like the **skink** or **swift,** are small, but the **Komodo dragon lizard** of the East Indies is 4 meters (15 ft) long and weighs almost 115 kilograms (250 lb). The Komodo dragon can prey on animals as large as water buffalo.

C. Most lizards have four legs; some can run quite swiftly. A few lizards, such as the **glass "snake,"** have no legs and are sometimes mistaken for snakes.

D. Many lizards that have their tails broken off, between the caudal vertebrae, can regenerate new ones.

E. **Chameleons** are tree-dwelling lizards that can change their color, not just once, but many times. They change color in response to light, heat, and emotional states. There are approximately 80 species of chameleon, most of which live in Africa. One species lives in Hawaii.

F. The **horned "toad"** is really a lizard and is found in the western United States.
  1. It has scales of different lengths, which give it a horny appearance.
  2. Some horned "toads" lay their eggs, but others keep the eggs inside their bodies and bear their young alive, especially in the colder climates.

G. The **Gila monster** and the **beaded lizard** of Mexico are poisonous lizards.
  1. The Gila monster is two thirds of a meter (2 ft) long and is found in Arizona, New Mexico, and Mexico.
  2. Its skin is brown or black and covered with blotches of orange or pink.
  3. It bites very hard, by twisting its head from side to side.
  4. It has poison glands at the rear of its lower jaw. Its poison is painful but seldom fatal to humans.

H. **Iguanas** are a large family of lizards. They live primarily in the tropics.
  1. The **green iguana** of Central America lives in the treetops of tropical rainforests. It is considered a delicacy and has been hunted by humans for many years. Today it faces extinction.

I. **Geckos** are small nocturnal lizards that live in warm, tropical climates. The toe pads of some geckos enable them to walk across walls and ceilings.

IV. The Snake

A. Snakes have long, round bodies that are covered with scales, many of which are beautifully colored.

B. Snakes shed their outer layer of scales (called molting) many times during a single season. When the thin layer becomes loose, the snake hooks a loose part over a twig or stone edge and then works its way out of this old layer of "skin."

C. A snake has no legs. It moves by using the broad scales, called scutes, on the underside of its body and by using a large number of muscles.
  1. Snakes commonly move by winding from side to side and forming curves.
  2. Some snakes move up and down slowly in a straight line, like a caterpillar.

3. Some snakes that live in the desert have a side-winding movement, whereby the body is raised and twisted into S-shaped loops, touching the ground only at two or three points, the snake moving across the ground only at these points.

4. Most snakes move slowly, and even the fastest cannot travel faster than 5 kilometers (3 mi) an hour. Some snakes can swim and climb trees.

D. Snakes have no outer ear, only an inner ear. Sound is detected only by vibrations that reach the bone of that inner ear. Snakes have developed other specialized sense organs that enable them to detect prey or danger in their environment.

1. Rattlesnakes have heat-sensitive pits below their eyes that enable them to detect prey, and the exact distance and direction of the prey, even in total darkness.

2. Snakes (and lizards) have a specialized sense organ in the roof of the mouth for detecting airborne chemicals.

E. The snake has a large mouth with a double row of teeth on each side of its upper jaw and a single row of teeth in its lower jaw.

1. The teeth all slant backward toward the throat.

2. The snake swallows its food whole, using its teeth only to hold and pull the food while it is swallowing.

3. The snake's jaws are flexible and can dislocate, allowing it to swallow animals thicker than its own body.

4. There is a long, forked tongue in the snake's (and in the lizard's) mouth, which the snake thrusts out to capture airborne molecules that it then transfers to the organ in the roof of its mouth for analysis.

5. Snakes can go for long periods, sometimes up to a year, without eating.

F. The snake has no eyelids, which makes it different from other reptiles. There is a protective transparent scale, however, that covers the eye.

G. All snakes eat only animals, and they use different methods for getting their food.

1. Most snakes just grab an animal with their mouths and swallow it alive. These snakes eat insects, frogs, toads, lizards, rats, mice, squirrels, and other small animals. Snakes that use this method of getting food include the garter snake, hog-nosed snake, and milk snake.

2. Some snakes first wrap their bodies around an animal's chest and squeeze hard so that the animal cannot breathe and it dies. Usually, these snakes are quite long and have fairly thick bodies. Snakes that kill by this squeezing method include the boa, python, king snake, and bull snake. The king snake eats other snakes, even the poisonous ones.

3. Some snakes first poison their prey quickly and then swallow it. Such a snake has poison fangs in the roof of its mouths The fangs are hollow, and when the snake strikes the animal, poison from poison glands flows through the fangs into the animal and kills it. Snakes that kill by poisoning include the rattlesnake, water moccasin, copperhead, coral snake, and cobra.

4. A **spitting cobra** spits its poison into the eye of its victim.

5. The most poisonous snake in the United States is the coral snake of the southeast.

H. Most snakes lay eggs that have a tough, leathery white shell.

1. Each egg contains stored food for the young snake that is developing within.

2. The heat of the sun helps the egg hatch.

3. A few snakes, like the garter snake, rattlesnake, and copperhead, keep the eggs inside their bodies, and the young snakes are born alive.

V. THE ALLIGATOR AND THE CROCODILE

A. The alligator and the crocodile are large reptiles that live mostly in tropical and semitropical climates, usually in swamps and along the banks of rivers. With a true cerebral cortex and a four-chambered heart, they are the most advanced of all living reptiles.

1. Alligators are found in the southeastern United States, mainly in Alabama, Florida, and Georgia.

2. Crocodiles are found largely in Africa and India, but there are also some crocodiles in the southeastern United States and in South America.

B. These reptiles are covered with large, bony scales, and their legs have toes that are partly webbed.

C. The American alligator and the American crocodile are similar, but with distinct differences.

1. The crocodile has a narrower and more triangular head, and its snout is more pointed.

DEMONSTRATION 14.14
Keep and Observe Nonpoisonous Snakes

Garter snakes are easily found and are very safe to keep and observe. When lifting the snake, hold it just behind the head with one hand and support the rest of the body with the other hand. When first captured, the frightened garter snake may void feces and expel musk from its anal scent glands. This expelled material is not harmful and washes off easily. Take the snake back to the classroom in a cloth bag or pillow case with the mouth of the bag or pillow case tied securely.

Keep the snake in a large aquarium tank covered by zinc mesh (hardware cloth), which can be obtained from a hardware store. Get enough zinc mesh so that you can bend the edges down snugly against the sides of the tank (Figure 14.2). Then place at least two heavy bricks cater-cornered on the top frame of the tank. The mesh and the bricks will ensure that the snake does not escape. Place some rocks, one or two forked branches, and a pan of water in the aquarium. Clean the cage once a week by flushing the cage well with water. Wash the snake with water at the same time. Feed the snake small living animals, such as frogs, mice, lizards, tadpoles, earthworms, and other large insects. Snakes are especially hungry after they shed their skins, so have plenty of food on hand at that time.

Observe the snake closely. Note how it moves. Locate the eyes and see whether they blink. See whether you can find any ears. Watch how and for what reason the

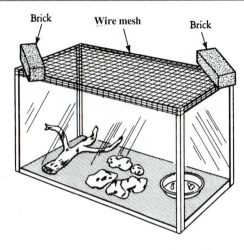

FIGURE 14.2   A prepared cage for a snake.

snake uses its forked tongue. Observe how the snake seizes and eats its food. See whether the snake has all the general characteristics of a reptile. Compare the snake with other reptiles, such as the lizard and the turtle, and note the similarities and differences. Contrast their living, feeding, and breeding habits as well.

---

2. The crocodile is slightly smaller than the alligator, and less bulky.
3. The alligator is brown, whereas the crocodile is a grayish green.
4. The alligator is sluggish, especially on land; the crocodile is more active.
5. In the alligator, all teeth in the upper jaw overlap with those in the lower jaw, whereas the crocodile has a pair of enlarged teeth in the lower jaw that fit into a notch on each side of its snout, and those enlarged teeth can be seen even when the crocodile's mouth is closed.
6. The crocodile spends more time in the water than the alligator.
D. The alligator and the crocodile eat fish and any land animals that come near them.
1. They do not chew food but swallow it whole. Small stones in their stomachs help in grinding the food. Similarly, birds, lacking teeth,

routinely swallow gravel which, when agitated in the bird's stomach, grinds food.
2. Alligators and crocodiles do attack humans, although the crocodile, especially the African crocodile, is more likely to do so than the alligator.
E. Adult alligators and crocodiles mate at night in shallow water during the spring.
1. The male (bull) roars loudly to attract females and to warn off other males.
2. After choosing a mate, the bull swims around her in circles a few times before mating.
3. The female lays her eggs in a nest of mud and vegetation.
4. The young hatch a few months later and are protected for a while by the mother. The young hatchlings, only about 8 inches (20 cm) long, are completely independent at birth and grow to maturity in about six years.

BIRDS

I. CHARACTERISTICS OF BIRDS

A. As members of the phylum Chordata, birds demonstrate the characteristics of members of that phylum. They belong to the subphylum **Vertebrata,** along with fish, amphibians, reptiles, and mammals. As vertebrates, birds have the following general characteristics in addition to those common to all chordates.
   1. A vertebral column
   2. An endoskeleton
   3. Two pairs of limbs, or appendages, attached to their bodies at the shoulder and hip
   4. One pair of eyes
   5. Separate sexes
   6. Cranial brain development
   7. A ventral heart and a dorsal aorta
   8. Paired kidneys

B. Birds have their own special characteristics that place them in the class **Aves.**
   1. Their bodies are covered with feathers.
   2. They have light, compact skeletons with porous or hollow bones containing air spaces. This characteristic of their skeletons makes it easier for birds to fly.
   3. Instead of front legs, birds have wings, which they use only for flying.
   4. They stand and perch on two legs.
   5. They have horny beaks and no teeth in their mouths.
   6. The female's eggs are fertilized by the male's sperm inside her body.
   7. The females lay eggs that have a protective shell.
   8. Birds are **endothermic,** which means that they can regulate their body temperature to keep it constant, regardless of the temperature of their environment.

C. Birds vary greatly in size and shape. The smallest bird is the hummingbird, which is a little more than 5 centimeters (2 in) long and weighs about 3 grams (1/10 oz). The largest bird is the ostrich, which can be as much as 2 meters (6 ft) tall and weigh more than 115 kilograms (250 lb).

D. The feathers of birds are modified scales. Their form has changed through the course of evolution.
   1. The feathers grow from little pits in the skin.
   2. They grow only on certain parts of the skin, but they spread out to cover those parts that are featherless.
   3. There are four kinds of feathers.
      a. Soft down feathers, plainly seen on young birds, are close to the skin and help keep both young and adult birds warm. Baby birds have mostly down feathers, which helps to make them look different from their parents.
      b. Filoplumes are thin, almost hairlike, feathers with a tuft on their ends.
      c. Contour feathers cover and protect the body and also give the adult bird its characteristic color.
      d. The large, strong quill feathers are in the wings and tails and are used mostly for flying.
   4. The feathers of birds are widely different in color. In some species, the males have brilliantly colored feathers, whereas the females have little color in their feathers. In other species, the feathers of both the male and female are of the same colors.
   5. Birds shed, or molt, their feathers at least once a year. New feathers replace those that have fallen out or have been broken.

E. Birds have large eyes that not only give them sharp eyesight but also make it possible for them to judge distances.

F. Birds possess a keen sense of hearing.

G. Most birds have a small, horny tongue, which they use to touch things.

H. Most birds have a voice. Some birds can sing beautifully.

II. WHERE BIRDS LIVE

A. Birds live in all parts of the world, from the polar regions to the tropics. Many species of birds live in woodlands and in open fields and meadows. Many species live near oceans, lakes, swamps, and marshlands. Some, such as the pigeon and the starling, live in the city.

B. Many birds migrate, or move from one home to another, during the spring and fall of the year.
   1. Scientists offer various reasons to explain why birds migrate. Birds may migrate because (a) the climate changes, (b) their food supply is gone, or (c) they are accustomed to breed in certain parts of the world.
   2. Most birds that live in the north fly south for the winter. For example, the bobolink spends its winter in Argentina, the wood

thrush in southern Mexico, and the house wren in Florida.

3. Some birds have very long migration flights. The arctic tern holds the record for distance—22,000 miles per year for its seasonal round trip from the Arctic to the Antarctic. The golden plover summers in northern Canada and winters in Brazil and Argentina. The ruddy turnstone summers in Alaska and winters in Hawaii. Despite its small size, the ruby-throated hummingbird migrates more than 1,850 miles from the eastern United States, crossing 600 miles of the Gulf of Mexico, to spend the winter in Central America. Before embarking on its migration, this hummingbird stores food as a layer of fat equal to half its body weight.

III. WHAT BIRDS EAT

A. Birds are so active that they need large amounts of food. They seem to eat all the time, which helps maintain their internal body temperature.
1. The hummingbird uses so much energy that it must eat twice its body weight in food every day. Humans, by contrast, consume about 1/50 their body weight in food each day.

B. Two main foods of birds are insects and seeds. However, many birds eat different foods.
1. Some birds, like the crow, bluejay, and red-winged blackbird, also eat corn, grain, rice, and peas.
2. Some birds, such as the bluebird, robin, cedar waxwing, and wren, also eat fruit and berries.
3. Some large birds, for example, the owl and the hawk, eat small animals, such as the rat, field mouse, and rabbit.
4. Other birds, like the pelican, kingfisher, and loon, eat mostly fish.
5. Some birds, such as the vulture and buzzard, eat dead animals.
6. Although flower nectar is its main food, the hummingbird also eats small insects and spiders.

C. Most birds drink by taking a beakfull of water, tilting their heads back, and letting the water run down their throats.

IV. HOW BIRDS REPRODUCE

A. Birds display elaborate premating courtship rituals and patterns.

B. When the male and female bird finally mate, the male deposits sperm inside the female so that the female's egg cells are fertilized internally.
1. The female lays a number of eggs with hard shells around them.
2. Each egg contains a tiny fertilized egg cell.
3. The egg also contains yolk, which serves as a food source for the young bird developing inside the egg.
4. Some birds, like the owl and hawk, may lay just one egg. Others, such as the chicken, duck, goose, and turkey, may lay two or more eggs at a time.
5. As soon as the female bird lays her eggs, she sits on them to keep them warm so that they will develop into birds. Most birds have a patch of bare skin, called **brooding patch,** that serves to transmit heat from the bird's body to the eggs. This process of sitting on the eggs and keeping them warm until they hatch is called **incubation.** The time needed to incubate the eggs varies from about 10 days for smaller birds to as much as 50 days for large birds.
6. Usually the female sits on the eggs while the male gets food, but the habit of some birds, like the ostrich, is for the male bird to take turns with the female bird in sitting on the eggs.
7. When the egg is ready to hatch, the baby bird pecks the shell until it splits open, and then works its way out of the shell.

C. Baby robins and cardinals, which hatch in 10 days to 2 weeks, are quite helpless.
1. They are weak, almost blind, and covered with very few down feathers.
2. They must be fed and attended for many days before they become feathered, are able to fly, and can get food for themselves.
3. Other birds, for example, the chicken and the quail, which hatch in 3 to 6 weeks, are well formed and can run around and look for food within a few hours after hatching.

V. THE NESTING HABITS OF BIRDS

A. Birds build nests to provide a place for incubating and hatching their eggs and for protecting the young birds when they are newly born.
1. Birds choose sites for their nests that provide the greatest protection possible from their enemies and from heavy rains and strong winds.

B. Nests vary in a number of characteristics: size and shape, the materials used to build them, and how well they are constructed. All birds within a certain species build their nests in the same way, with the same kinds of materials, and in the same sort of location.

1. Birds use such materials as soil, clay, twigs, grass, stems, leaves, bark, hair, feathers, and even string to build their nests.

2. Some birds build large nests, with materials only loosely put together. Other birds build small nests that are beautifully constructed with twigs and other rough materials, and then lined with leaves, grass, and other soft materials.

3. Shore birds, like the penguin and the Arctic tern, lay their eggs on rocks or pebbles that are arranged on the ground in such a way as to keep the eggs from rolling.

4. The whippoorwill lays its eggs on dead leaves in a small hole in the ground.

5. The kingfisher lays its eggs in a hole that has been dug in a clay bank, and the eggs rest either on the bare ground or on feathers.

6. A duck builds a very simple grass nest.

7. The oriole builds a long, baglike nest, made of grass, string, and hair, on the branch of a tree.

8. The owl and woodpecker live in holes cut out of hollow or dead trees.

9. The bluejay builds a bulky, rough nest on a tree branch.

10. The robin builds a heavy, bulky nest either on a tree branch or in the crotch of a tree. The nest is made of twigs and mud and then lined with grass.

11. The meadowlark and quail build grassy nests in underbrush.

12. The barn swallow builds its nest in hollow trees or in the eaves of a house. It uses straw and mud and lines the nest with hay or feathers.

13. The hummingbird builds a tiny, basketlike nest on the branches of a tree.

14. Some hawks and eagles build their nests up high in very tall trees.

15. Flamingoes build nests of mud shaped into volcano-like cones.

VI. BIRD BILLS, FEET, WINGS, AND TAILS

A. Over the course of time much adaptation of the feet, bills, wings, and tails of birds has occurred. As a result, various forms and structures have developed for special functions, such as perching, swimming, catching food, eating, and flying.

B. Birds have developed different kinds of feet, depending on whether they are adapted for perching, climbing, swimming, wading, or grasping.

1. Seed-eating birds, like the robin and bluebird, have three toes in front and one in back, which are used for perching on branches.

2. The duck and the goose have long, webbed toes for swimming.

3. The crane and the heron have long legs and toes for wading.

4. The duck and the loon have short legs, set far back on their bodies, for diving.

5. The woodpecker has two toes in front and two toes in back, an arrangement that helps it when climbing tree trunks.

6. The owl, hawk, and eagle have powerful claws, called talons, on their toes, which are used for grabbing and holding small animals.

C. Birds have bills that are adapted for gathering food and eating.

1. The duck has a wide, flat, and notched bill, used for scooping and straining food.

2. The booby has a tapered, pointed bill with serrated edges, ideal for grasping fish out of ocean water.

3. The owl, hawk, and eagle have the upper jaw curved over the lower jaw, making the bill hooked so that it is easy to tear flesh.

4. The heron and snipe have a long, pointed bill for searching for food in mud.

5. The sparrow and finch have a short, straight, stout bill for crushing seeds and other hard foods.

6. The hummingbird has a long, thin bill, curved in some cases, for reaching deep into flowers and obtaining nectar. In addition, the ability of the hummingbird to hover and to fly backward and upside down is unique.

D. The shape of a bird's wing is adapted for the kind of flying the bird does.

1. Soaring birds, like the hawk, have long, broad wings.

2. Sailing or gliding birds, such as the gull, have long, slender wings.

3. Birds that maneuver quickly, like the robin, have short, broad wings.

4. Ground birds, like the pheasant and the partridge, have short wings that can furnish only short, quick flights.

5. Domesticated chickens do not fly much and have underdeveloped wings.

6. The penguin has wings that are paddle-shaped for swimming.

E. A bird's tail acts as a rudder in flying and as a balance in perching.

1. The woodpecker has a stiff tail, which supports the bird when it is climbing a tree trunk.
2. The bluejay has a long tail for balancing itself on tree branches.

VII. CONSERVATION AND PROTECTION OF BIRDS

A. Most birds are beneficial to humans. Some feed on insect or rodent pests. Some help to clean the environment by eating garbage and dead animals. Some are used as human food. Others are treated as pets.

B. Some birds can be pests to humans. Some eat fruits and vegetables grown by humans. Some birds prey on other birds.

C. Large numbers of song birds and game birds have been wantonly destroyed by human civilizations.

1. The destruction of nesting sites occurs when forests are cut, underbrush is cleared, and fields are burned.
2. The unnecessary drainage of marshes and wetlands and the lowering of the water level in lakes and ponds take away the food supply and nesting sites of both water birds and wading birds.
3. Vast numbers of birds continue to be killed for sport or for food.

D. Both state and national governments have laws to protect and conserve our bird wildlife.

1. Song birds cannot be killed at any time, nor can their eggs be collected.
2. Game birds can be hunted only at certain times of the year.
3. Feathers of wild birds cannot be brought into the United States.
4. Agreements have been made between Canada, the United States, and Mexico to protect migrating and endangered species.

MAMMALS

I. CHARACTERISTICS OF MAMMALS

A. As members of the phylum **Chordata,** mammals demonstrate the characteristics of members of that phylum. They belong to the subphylum **Vertebrata,** along with fish, amphibians, reptiles, and birds. As vertebrates, mammals have the general characteristics of vertebrates in addition to the characteristics common to all chordates (see page 502).

B. Mammals also have their own special characteristics that distinguish their class, **Mammalia.**

C. All mammals have **hair** on their bodies. Hair grows from follicles, tiny epidermal pits in the skin.

1. Most mammals have much hair on their bodies. Whales have almost no body hair, only a few bristles.
2. Some mammals, like the mink, seal, beaver, and muskrat, grow thick coats of hair in the winter.
3. The hair of some mammals, such as the weasel, arctic fox, and snowshoe rabbit, changes color in different seasons of the year. In late spring, summer, and early fall the hair of these animals is brown. In late fall, they shed their brown coats of hair and grow white coats, which stay white all winter.

4. Some mammals have hair that has changed in form and structure. The porcupine's hair is in the form of quills. The armadillo's hair has changed into horny plates that overlap and act like a coat of armor. The horns of the rhinoceros are made of masses of hair.

D. Many mammals have fingernails and toenails growing from their skin.

E. All mammals have lungs for breathing.

F. All mammals are endothermic. They regulate their body temperature to keep it constant, regardless of the temperature of their environment.

G. All mammals have **seven neck bones (cervical vertebrae),** although these are not the same size for all mammals.

H. Most mammals have two pairs of limbs.

1. The whale and the manatee have lost their hind limbs, and their front limbs look like fins.
2. The seal and the walrus have limbs in the form of flippers.
3. The front limbs of the bat have long finger bones with webbed skin between them, enabling the bat to fly.

I. Mammals have different numbers of toes on their legs, but there are rarely more than five toes on one leg.

1. The horse walks and runs on one toe that has developed into a hoof.
2. The cow walks on a hoof that formed from two toes.
3. Most smaller animals have separate toes, which help them walk and run.
4. Some animals, like the lion and tiger, have powerful nails or claws on their toes, which are used for catching and injuring smaller animals.
5. Some animals, like the squirrel and raccoon, have claws that can bend and are used for climbing trees.

J. The young of mammals are, with a very few exceptions, born alive. They are *not* born from shelled eggs.
1. When mammals mate, the male deposits sperm inside the female to fertilize the female's eggs.
2. The female's eggs are very small and do not have enough yolk to feed the developing baby mammals.
3. As a result, each egg attaches to the wall of the **uterus** in the female reproductive system.
4. In the uterus the developing mammal receives food and oxygen from the mother's blood until it is born.
5. It takes various periods of time for different mammals to develop from a fertilized egg to birth. The time from fertilization of an egg to birth is called **gestation.** Gestation is about 21 days for a mouse, 30 days for a rabbit, 63 days for a cat or dog, 40 weeks for a human, 48 weeks for a horse, and 20 to 22 months for an elephant.

K. All mammals care for their young after birth. The female parent nurses the young by giving them milk that comes from special glands called **mammary glands.** The presence of mammary glands, in both males and females, gives this class of animals its name, Mammalia.

L. Mammals vary in size.
1. Some mice and shrews are about 5 centimeters (2 in) long and weigh less than 28 grams (1 oz). In contrast, the largest mammal, the blue whale, can be more than 30 meters (100 ft) long and weigh more than 136,000 kilograms (150 tons).

M. Mammals are ubiquitous, living all over the world. Many mammals live on land. Whales and porpoises live in the ocean. Seals and walruses live in saltwater and on land. The beaver, muskrat, and hippopotamus live in freshwater and on land. The mole and shrew live mostly underground. The monkey and squirrel live mostly in trees. Mountain sheep and mountain goats live on high mountains. Bats live in caves and cavelike places. Polar bears and reindeer live in polar climates. The lion and tiger live in hot, dry climates. A large number of mammals live in the temperate climates.

N. Mammals eat plants and other animals.
1. Some mammals, like the cow and the horse, eat only plants and are called **herbivorous.**
2. Some mammals, such as the lion and the tiger, eat only animals and are called **carnivorous.**
3. Other mammals, like the bear and the raccoon, eat both plants and animals and are called **omnivorous.**

O. Some mammals move to different locations, or **migrate,** at different seasons of the year.
1. Seals spend the winter in the Pacific Ocean between Alaska and California. In spring they travel to the Pribilof Islands, which are north of the Aleutian Islands. Here, the adult seals breed and new seals are born.
2. Elk live high in the mountains during the summer and in the valleys in the winter.

P. Some mammals, like the woodchuck and ground squirrel, are inactive all winter. This inactivity is termed **hibernation.** During hibernation the animal's heartbeat slows, the body temperature drops, breathing slows to as little as once in five minutes, and the animal cannot be wakened.

Q. Some mammals, such as the bear, skunk, and raccoon, have a long **winter sleep.** During this time, the heartbeat and breathing rate slow and the mammal lives on food stored in its body. This winter sleep is different from hibernation, because in winter sleep mammals can wake up on mild days and then go back to sleep again. Animals in true hibernation do not waken until spring.

R. Mammals that share some similar characteristics are grouped in many categories called orders.

II. EGG-LAYING MAMMALS

A. The Australian duck-billed platypus and the spiny anteater are mammals that lay eggs instead of giving birth to their young alive.
1. The **duck-billed platypus** has fur like a beaver's, webbed feet like a muskrat's, and a horny bill like a duck's. It lays two or three

DEMONSTRATION 14.15
Keep and Observe Small Mammals

White mice, guinea pigs, gerbils, and hamsters are excellent small mammals to observe in the classroom. Although different kinds of homemade animal cages can be built, it may be more expedient to purchase sturdy, well-built animal cages made of metal and of the proper size. The animals, along with suitable food and books on their care, can be obtained at a pet shop. There are also many reference books available on the care of pet mammals. When purchasing these animals, try to get young ones. They quickly become used to being around students and to being handled by them. Faithfully follow instructions for the care of these animals. Have the students note the physical characteristics and the living and feeding habits of each animal.

eggs that resemble reptile eggs. When the eggs hatch, the young lap up a kind of milk given off by mammary glands on the mother's abdomen.
2. The **spiny anteater** is covered with long spines that resemble porcupine quills. It has a tubelike bill and a long tongue, which it uses to catch ants. It lays two eggs, which it places into a special pouch on its ventral side.

III. POUCHED MAMMALS

A. This group includes the kangaroo, the opossum, the koala or "teddy bear," and the wallaby. These animals are known collectively as **marsupials.** Most marsupials live in Australia.
1. Their young are helpless when they are born. Immediately after birth they enter into a special body pouch near the mother's mammary glands, which have nipples.
2. The young feed on milk from the mammary glands until they are developed enough to leave the pouch.

IV. "TOOTHLESS MAMMALS"

A. The sloth, armadillo, and great anteater are members of this group. These animals are not completely toothless, but have no teeth at all in front.
1. The **sloth** is a bearlike animal that hangs upside down from trees and moves slowly. It feeds chiefly on leaves. The hair of some kinds of sloths appears to be green because of green algae growing in it.
2. The **armadillo** has a body covered with heavy, overlapping, bony scales. It feeds chiefly on insects. Its young are born either as identical twins or quadruplets.

V. INSECT-EATING MAMMALS

A. This group includes the mole, the shrew, and the hedgehog.
B. The mole and the shrew eat large numbers of grubs and worms.
C. The **mole** has soft, fine fur, used in making coats and capes.
1. It uses its sharp front legs to dig long burrows just beneath the surface of the ground. It lives underground.
2. It has a long, sharp nose, which it uses for digging grubs and worms out of the soil.
3. It has eyes that are blind.
D. **Moles** are pests in lawns and golf courses.
E. The tiny **shrew** looks both like a mouse and like a mole.
1. It eats not only grubs and worms, but also mice and other shrews.
F. The **hedgehog** has long, quill-like hair, looks like a porcupine, and eats only insects.

VI. FLESH-EATING MAMMALS

A. All members in this group have large, well-developed canine teeth located near the corners of the mouth. In addition, they have strong jaws for tearing flesh. They are referred to as the carnivores.
B. Their other teeth are pointed and help cut up the flesh.
C. Sea members of this group include the seal, walrus, and sea lion.
D. Land members of this group are divided into three subgroups, according to how they walk.
1. One subgroup includes the bear and raccoon. These animals walk flat-footed on the soles of their feet.
2. The second subgroup includes the cat, dog, lion, tiger, wolf, and coyote. They walk only on their toes.

3. The third subgroup includes the skunk, weasel, mink, and otter. They walk partly on their toes and partly on the soles of their feet.

E. The **polar bear,** one of the largest carnivores, lives at the edge of the Arctic ice cap.

1. The polar bear is the largest member of the bear family, which includes the North American grizzly, the black bear, and the Kodiak bear.

2. When on all fours, the polar bear is about 5 feet (1.5 m) tall, but when standing on its hind legs, it measures up to 11 feet (3.3 m).

3. Males weigh nearly 1,000 pounds. Females weigh about 750 pounds.

4. The polar bear preys on seals and their young pups. It also feeds on vegetation.

5. Recent conservation projects and regulated hunting have allowed the world population of polar bears to increase to about 40,000 animals. A few years ago the population had declined to only about 5,000.

F. The largest living cat is the **Siberian tiger.** Today it is found in Siberia, China, and Korea.

1. The Siberian tiger is an endangered species. It is estimated that only about 200 animals are left in the wild today.

2. The Siberian tiger is much larger than its relative, the **Bengal tiger.**

3. The male Siberian tiger can measure up to 12 feet (3.7 m) from its head to the tip of its tail and can weigh more than 600 pounds (270 kg).

4. It feeds on deer, boar, elk, bear, fish, and rabbit, and can live for about 25 years.

G. Another large cat in danger of extinction is the **jaguar,** a close relative of the leopard. The greatest threats to the jaguar's extinction are humans hunting the cat for its fur and the loss of its habitat as a result of clearing land for farming. Jaguars are found in Central and South America. The jaguar is the only large cat that does not roar.

VII. GNAWING MAMMALS

A. This group includes the rat, mouse, squirrel, chipmunk, prairie dog, woodchuck, rabbit, hare, muskrat, and beaver. They are commonly referred to as rodents.

B. All but the rabbit and the hare have two large, chisel-like front incisor teeth on each jaw. The rabbit and hare have four of these teeth on each jaw.

1. These incisor teeth have sharp edges, which stay sharp because the front edge is harder than the back edge so that the biting surface always wears out at an angle. The teeth themselves do not wear out because they keep growing.

2. All gnawing animals have strong grinding teeth behind their sharp front incisors.

3. Most members of this group do a great deal of damage by eating grain and crops. The rat spreads disease as well.

VIII. HOOFED MAMMALS

A. This group includes most of the domesticated mammals used for food, clothing, work, and transportation. It is divided into two large subgroups: the odd-toed and the even-toed hoofed animals.

B. The odd-toed hoofed group includes such animals as the horse and the rhinoceros; the even-toed group is further divided into two smaller groups: the cud-chewers and the non-cud-chewers.

C. The even-toed cud-chewers include the cow, sheep, goat, camel, giraffe, and deer.

1. These animals' stomachs have four divisions.

2. They usually swallow large amounts of food quickly. This food passes into the first stomach division, where it is stored for chewing later.

3. Later, the food is forced back into the mouth and chewed thoroughly as a cud.

4. The cud then passes into the second stomach division, where it begins to be digested.

D. The even-toed non-cud-chewers include the pig and the hippopotamus.

E. Some hoofed mammals have horns.

1. The cow, ox, and bison have hollow horns, which are never shed.

2. The deer, elk, caribou, and moose have solid horns with many branches. These horns are shed each year.

F. Some hoofed mammals can survive a long time without drinking water.

1. Water is essential to all living organisms. Humans cannot survive if water is withheld for about 10 days.

2. The camel can survive without drinking water during a two-week period. However, it then may drink at much as 106 liters (28 gal) in 10 minutes.

3. A giraffe can go without water even longer than a camel, for up to several weeks.

G. The **giraffe** is the tallest animal on earth; males may be as tall as 6 m (20 ft). Its habitat is limited to the tropical grasslands (the savannas) of Africa.
   1. Because it is so tall, the giraffe must spread its forelegs very wide and then bend its knees in order to drink from a watering hole. When doing this, the giraffe is especially vulnerable to its predators, such as the lion.
   2. To keep out dust, giraffes can close their nostrils completely.
   3. The giraffe uses its long upper lip and its dark gray tongue, which can extend outward more than 54 cm (21 in), to forage food from tall trees.
   4. The giraffe's tongue has a built-in sunscreen that protects it from the hot African sun.
   5. Because the giraffe cannot swim, rivers are barriers to its roaming.
   6. Much of the habitat of giraffes has become land for cattle farms. People have hunted the giraffe for food, used the hide for making sandals and the tail to make ornaments, string, and fly swatters.

IX. TRUNK-NOSED MAMMALS

A. The African and the Asian elephants are the only trunk-nosed animals alive today.
   1. As recently as 10,000 years ago, however, the **hairy mammoth** roamed the earth in large numbers.
   2. It was the ancestor to today's elephants.
   3. Many remains of the hairy mammoth have been found in Siberia, northern Europe, northern Eurasia, and North America.
   4. Complete specimens have been discovered deep-frozen in the ice of the Arctic tundra.
   5. With no tusks or trunks, predecessors of the hairy mammoth and today's elephants were more like hippopotamuses than like today's elephants.
B. Elephants are the largest land mammals today and can weigh more than 6,350 kilograms (7 tons).
C. The elephant's trunk is a stretched-out upper lip and nose.
D. Because of their heavy exploitation by humans and our encroachment upon their habitats, the few remaining herds of elephants today are protected by most of the nations party to the Convention on International Trade in Endangered Species.

E. At present there are two kinds of elephants.
   1. The **Asian elephant** is found only in India, Sri Lanka, and Southeast Asia.
   2. The Asian elephant has an arched back, an enormous domed head with relatively small ears, and a single protuberance, or "finger," at the tip of its trunk.
   3. Only the male has tusks.
   4. Today there may be fewer than 50,000 individual Asian elephants in the wild.
   5. The **African elephant** is found south of the Sahara Desert in Africa only. It is slightly larger than the Asian elephant. The total population of African elephants is less than 600,000.
   6. The African elephant has a swayed back, a tapering head with large ears, and two trunk "fingers."
   7. Its large ears are used as fans to cool the body. Heat loss in animals occurs mainly through surface area, whereas heat production occurs in all cells and varies in proportion to an animal's volume. Because volume (proportional to the cube of average length) increases faster than surface area (proportional to the square of average length), as the size of an animal decreases, heat loss increases. In proportion to body weight, small animals lose more heat than humans and so need extra calories to maintain body temperature. This is the reason that the hummingbird, for example, consumes such a large quantity of food daily. However, the African elephant, living in a hot climate, needs the larger surface area provided by its large ears to get rid of extra body heat through radiation and evaporation.
   8. In the African elephant, both sexes have tusks, which are elongated incisor teeth, that continue to grow throughout the elephant's lifetime, about 70 years.
   9. Elephants are entirely vegetarian, eating a wide range of grasses, foliage, and fruit.
   10. Elephants are intelligent animals with elaborate means for communicating with one another.

X. FLYING MAMMALS

A. Bats are mammals that fly.
   1. The toe bones of their front legs are very long and have skin stretched over and between them.

2. The skin is also attached to the side of the body, the back legs, and the tail.
3. This gives the bat a large wingspread.

B. Because skin covers both the bat's front and back legs, bats cannot walk very well. They usually drink and feed while in flight.

C. The bat flies at night. During the day it stays in a cave or another dark place, where it hangs upside down by the claws of its back legs.

D. Most bats eat insects, but the vampire bat feeds exclusively on the blood of large animals, such as cows, pigs, and horses.
1. The **vampire bat** is found in Central and South America. Its range includes tropical and subtropical regions from Mexico to northern Chile and Argentina.
2. The vampire bat does not suck blood like a mosquito, but laps it up with its long tongue. It can take up to its own weight (about 28 g) in one feeding.
3. Although no larger than a mouse, the vampire bat is a threat to domestic animals because it can infect its host with disease organisms, such as the virus that causes rabies.

E. Contrary to the myths about bats, bats are not blind, they will not tangle in people's hair, and they do not usually carry rabies. Bats can fly in complete darkness without bumping into things.
1. Because of the myths about bats, they have been extensively killed by humans and many of their habitats have been destroyed. In some locations today, their habitats are protected.
2. Bats can hear very well; they listen to the echoes of their own very high-pitched voices as the echos bounce back from objects around them.
3. Bats can also see very well and often fly without engaging their echolocation signals.

F. Bats are very beneficial animals.
1. Bats in the deserts of the southwestern United States play an important role in pollinating cactus plants and dispersing their seeds. The desert-inhabiting bats feed on the plant's nectar and transfer pollen from plant to plant. They also feed on the cactus fruits, thereby dispersing seeds.
2. Bats also feed on countless mosquitoes and on beetles and moths that can destroy farm crops and forest trees. Some farmers have built bat houses and placed them strategically on their farms to attract and keep bats, in order to eradicate destructive crop-eating insects.

G. Most North American bats use caves to hibernate in winter and to raise their young during the summer. Hibernating and nursing bats should not be awakened or disturbed. If awakened from hibernation, a bat can quickly lose its stored food and may then not survive until spring.

XI. MARINE MAMMALS

A. The whale, dolphin, and porpoise are mammals that resemble fish.
1. Although they have lungs and breathe air, they inhabit the ocean.
2. They use their tails for swimming and their finlike front limbs for balance.
3. They usually have one or two young at a time, which are fed by their milk just like other mammals.
4. They eat plankton, fish, and other sea life.

B. At 30 m (100 ft) and 138 metric tons (154 short or U.S. tons), the **blue whale** is the largest animal ever to live on earth.
1. In comparison, a full grown African elephant is about the same weight as a newborn baby blue whale.
2. The blue whale has a very slow metabolism, with a heart beat of only about nine times a minute. It feeds on some of the smallest organisms, sea plankton.
3. Like the dinosaurs before them, both the blue whale and the African elephant are threatened by extinction. Unlike that of the dinosaurs, however, their extinction is human-induced.

C. Because the whale, dolphin, and porpoise have been exploited in the past, the endangered populations of these intelligent animals are now protected by international agreements, although enforcement of these agreements is a continuing problem.

XII. FLEXIBLE-FINGERED MAMMALS

A. Members of this group include the lemur, monkey, gibbon, orangutan, bonobo, chimpanzee, and gorilla. Humans are also included in this group, but in a separate family. The group is referred to as the primates. Despite their diversity of sizes and shapes, all primates share certain characteristics.

1. A distinctive characteristic of primates is the shape of the head. It is relatively rounded and the face is flattened. This is due, in part, to the size of the brain in primates. Only marine mammals have larger brains. However, the brains of primates are much more complex than those of other animals. This complexity is reflected in their diverse behaviors and social interactions.
2. All primates have a highly developed sense of vision. The position of their eyes on their heads permits them to perceive depth and to gauge distance. They also have color vision.
3. Most primates are tree dwellers. Primates have thumbs that enable them to grasp objects, and many have feet that are also constructed for grasping.
4. Both hands and feet have flexible joints, and nails rather than claws.
5. The ability to oppose the thumb with the fingers allows primates to make finer manipulations with their hands.
6. The shoulder and hip joints of primates are adapted for flexible movement in varying directions.
7. Primates can walk on just their hind legs or move about on all four legs.

B. Many members of this group are endangered or potentially endangered animals.

1. Their habitats have become highly limited, primarily to Africa and Southeast Asia. Many members of this group have been and continue to be killed by humans—for sport, for trophy, and for food. Many suffer from habitat destruction.
2. Some are now being protected by national parks and preserves and through international agreements. Money for upkeep of these parks and preserves, the education of people, and enforcement of international agreements continue to be problems.
3. The rare **bonobo** (known also as the pygmy chimpanzee) has almost no pro-

tected habitat. This animal's total population in the wild is estimated at only 10,000 to 20,000 individuals, all living within the country of Zaire.
4. The worldwide chimpanzee population is at about 200,000 animals.
5. The **mountain gorilla,** first seen in 1901, is now in serious danger of extinction. Today there are only about 300 mountain gorillas living in the wild in central Africa, near Lake Victoria.
6. In Nigeria, more western **lowland gorillas** are killed each year than are born. Today's population of lowland gorillas is about 50,000 individuals, found in several countries of central Africa, including Zaire, Gabon, Congo, and Nigeria.
7. Central African people, who do little cattle farming, depend on ape meat as a primary source of protein.
8. With their habitats suffering from deforestation, **orangutans** are found only in Southeast Asia, in Sumatra and Borneo, and number no more than 20,000 individuals.
9. The chimpanzee and the bonobo have genetic makeups nearly identical to that of humans. For this reason they are often used for testing by scientific and medical researchers.

XIII. CONSERVATION OF OUR WILD MAMMALS

A. Historically, many mammals have been killed without any thought given to protecting and conserving them.

1. Fur-bearing animals have been tortured and slaughtered in huge numbers.
2. The bison of the Great Plains were nearly made extinct because of the earlier demand for their fur and meat.
3. In the West, the elk, antelope, and mule deer were killed in large numbers for their meat and horns.

B. State, federal, and international laws are now in force for the purpose of protecting and conserving wildlife.

C. Mammals are among the world's great natural resources and, like our forests, deserve to be protected and preserved by the world community.

Exploratory Activities for "Animals"

1. *EXPLORING THE QUESTION: WHAT IS AN ANIMAL?* (ANY GRADE LEVEL)[*]

Overview The object of this exploration is to facilitate students' understanding of the common characteristics of animals. During this study students will hypothesize, design an experiment, compare and contrast, observe and infer, and older students should be expected to make and use tables.

Materials Needed Live animals (e.g., mouse, earthworm, crayfish, frog, crab, sea urchin, cricket, lizard, planaria, snail, starfish, spider, beetle, etc.) that are safe and common to your location; suitable containers for each animal; rulers

Procedure

WHOLE CLASS

1. Display a large goldfish in a bowl. Ask students how they can tell that the goldfish is an animal. (Most suggestions will deal with moving and breathing.)
2. Feed the goldfish. Instruct students to time how long it takes the fish to swim to the food. As they watch the fish eat, ask how this behavior is important in identifying the goldfish as an animal. (All animals obtain food from their environments.)
3. Ask students what the fish does with the food. (It uses the food for energy or as raw material for building tissue.)
4. Ask how the fish is different from a protist that might move around to get food. (The fish is multicellular and has tissues and organs.)
5. Ask how they can tell the animal is a fish. (Swimming, backbone, scales and gills.)

SMALL GROUP EXPLORATORY INVESTIGATIONS—PART I
Students should wash their hands before and after handling the animals.

6. Divide the students into groups of four, and give each group its own animal to observe and study. Explain to the students that they are to develop ways of identifying their organisms first as animals, and next as part of a particular animal group. It is not important that their answers are

correct, but it is important that students think critically about their animals and their unique traits. As in previous explorations, each member of a group should assume certain responsibilities, such as those of chief scientist, recorder, materials engineer, and so forth.

7. First, in their groups students brainstorm a list of possible characteristics that could be used to categorize and identify their animal.
8. Students next construct a data table for the features that identify the organism as an animal.
9. They then give reasons for constructing their table as they did.
10. Ask, what data do you plan to collect? (The students' tables may include the following types of data: type of movement toward food, reaction to touch stimulus, structural adaptations that enable the animal to get food or escape predators, time spent in lighted part of container. The tables should also include some quantitative data, structural features, and behavioral data.)
11. At this point each group's data table should be checked by the teacher before the group continues with its exploration.
12. The group then is allowed to carry out its investigation.
13. Each group records measurements and observations in its data table.

SMALL GROUP EXPLORATORY INVESTIGATIONS—PART II

14. After Part I of the investigation has been done, have groups trade animals and repeat steps 6–13.

CULMINATING ACTIVITY AND ASSESSMENT

15. As a conclusion to this activity, have groups share and compare their completed data tables and summarize what they learned about how organisms are identified as animals and how animals are classified. The following are questions that groups should address (science process skills are given in parenthesis):
    a. On what basis did you identify your animals generally and specifically? (identifying variables)
    b. Did your results confirm your hypothesis? Why or why not? (checking a hypothesis)
    c. When you compared your table with that of another group, how were the tables the same, and how were they different? (comparing and contrasting)

[*]Adapted from Alton Biggs et al. *Biology: The Dynamics of Life* (Westerville, OH: Glencoe/McGraw-Hill, 1995), 696–697. By permission of Glencoe/ McGraw-Hill.

d. What did you learn in this exploration about animals that you did not know before? (drawing conclusions)

e. How are animals identified? (thinking critically)

2. OUR FRIEND, OUR HOME: THE EARTH ECOLOGY—AN INTERDISCIPLINARY THEMATIC UNIT (GRADE 3)[1]

Notes to the Teacher

This 10-day unit includes a wide variety of activities involving language arts, math, science, social studies, art, and games. The daily lessons can be expected to take about an hour each, with the exceptions of Day 5 (*Fern Gully*), which will take 1 1/2 hours, and the culminating activity, Day 10, which will take a half day. Extension activities are listed at the end of the unit should you wish to lengthen the unit to three weeks.

This unit is planned to accommodate a full class of 34 students but is suitable for use with any number of students. Because most, if not all, classrooms include students with diverse needs and abilities, these lessons are suitable for all children, with only minor accommodations necessary for some mainstreamed students. In addition, you will find strategies to promote the social integration of mainstreamed students and suggestions with respect to support staff and services.

Several lessons in the unit involve cooperative learning activities. If your students have not had prior experience working in cooperative groups, the unit should be preceded by a discussion of expected behavior and perhaps a practice activity during which the students are divided into groups and assigned roles to complete a task.

Days 2–5 of the unit focus primarily on the rain forest. Students can be greatly motivated through the creation of an arranged environment. During the week before the unit, have your students make paper-ring vines that can be hung from the ceiling. Add some rubber snakes, potted plants, a tape of rain forest sounds, and a humidifier to create your own simulated rain forest.

A letter to parents is included, which can be sent home with students prior to the start of the unit. The letter outlines ways in which parents can help their children during the unit and invites parents to lend theme-related items to the class, thus helping you to establish an arranged environment for the unit.

We urge you to take anecdotal notes on your students throughout this unit and to use these in addition to portfolio assessment and formal assessment when evaluating your students.

Additional Suggestions

1. Display books on ecology around the room for students' independent reading.
2. Set up a seasonal display, using objects from nature. Encourage students to add to the display.
3. Create a participatory bulletin board as ecology problems are discussed and solutions are proposed. (See Persuasive Poster extension activity.)
4. Ask students to bring in newspaper and/or magazine articles concerning the environment that can be read and discussed. These can be posted on an "Earth News" bulletin board.
5. Conduct an ongoing newspaper recycling project.
6. Present awards to students at the completion of the unit (see certificate).

This is to Certify That

_____

_____
Student's Name

has successfully completed the unit on Ecology. Thank you for your participation, and remember, we all have a part in making our planet a safe and healthy place to live!

_____   _____
School Principal   **Classroom Teacher**

Date _____

Dear Parent,

We are ready to start a theme study on ecology. Throuth a wide variety of activities involving math, science, art, social studies, and language arts, we will learn how all living things are dependent on their environment.

You can help your child in the following ways:

1. Visit the library. Help your child find books that focus on ecology, the rain forest, and/or the environment.
2. Look over and comment on the school projects and activities your child brings home.
3. Ask your child to share with you what he/she is learning.

If you have any theme-related items that could be displayed in our classroom during this unit, please tag them with your name and send them in with your child. They will be returned upon completion of the unit.

Our study of ecology will be both fun and rewarding as we learn how to make our world a clean, healthy place for living things.

_____

Teacher

---

7. Use recycling funds to purchase a tree for the school grounds.
8. Give students a letter-writing resource list that has sources of further information for children and encourages active social participation.

Strategies to Promote Social Integration

1. Read books in class that focus on accepting and valuing differences.
2. Discuss the causes and characteristics of disabilities.
3. Establish a cross-age buddy system with a kindergarten class.
4. Encourage students to volunteer their services as tutors for special-education students.
5. Have students participate in an obstacle course that simulates vision, hearing, and physical disabilities.
6. Encourage cooperative friendships to develop through small-group assignments and activities.

Scope and Sequence

Ecology

A. Diminishing rain forests
B. Living versus nonliving things
C. Our interdependent ecosystem
D. Endangered species

E. Landfills/biodegradable materials
F. Water pollution/water treatment plants

Unit Goals and Objectives

Goals of the unit

1. To understand the negative effects of humans on the rain forest.
2. To understand the interdependence of the living and nonliving things in the ecosystem.
3. To be able to differentiate between living and nonliving things.
4. To understand the importance of preserving threatened species.
5. To develop proactive strategies, such as recycling and avoidance of nonbiodegradable materials, to alleviate our dependence on landfills.
6. To develop water conservation strategies.
7. To develop a positive, politically active, aggressive attitude toward environmental preservation.
8. To understand what the term *ecology* encompasses.

Objectives

Upon completion of this unit of study, students should be able to

1. Give four reasons why the rain forest should be preserved.

2. List three causes of animal extinction.
3. Identify biodegradable versus nonbiodegradable materials.
4. List four ways people can conserve water.
5. Participate in a hike and contrast living and nonliving things, using specific criteria.
6. Demonstrate an understanding that the living and nonliving things in an ecosystem are interdependent.

Unit Assessment   Students will keep all papers relevant to this study in their ongoing individual portfolios. During and at the completion of this unit the student and teacher will assess the student's work by using the following (or a similar) assessment checklist.

	Point Value	
1. Vocabulary Scribble	5	____
2. Ecology Math Worksheet	10	____
3. Rain Forest Multiplication	10	____
4. Cooperative Group Project	10	____
5. Kapok Tree Creative Writing	10	____
6. Scavenger Hunt Categorization	5	____
7. *Fern Gully* Questions	10	____
8. Food Web Activity	10	____
9. Endangered Species Report	20	____
10. Landfill Chart and Predictions	5	____
11. Good Ways to Save Water	5	____
	100	

Materials List

Day 1   Vocabulary scribble, crayons, markers
Ecology math work sheet (class set)
Day 2   Large piece of butcher paper with kapok tree and animals drawn on it
Rain forest multiplication (class set)
Day 3   12 2-ft × 3-ft butcher paper, cooperative group, job cards, drawing materials (i.e., markers, crayons)
Day 4   17 small brown paper bags, 17 scavenger hunt checklists, writing paper, drawing paper, drawing materials
Day 5   *Fern Gully* questions (class set)
Day 6   Ball of string, organism cards, animal-shaped paper (class set)
Day 7   Endangered species cards, endangered animal report (class set)
Day 8   Large plastic container, heavy plastic liner, soil, Styrofoam, aluminum foil, plastic, banana peel, lettuce

Day 9   Large piece of chart paper, marker, writing resource list, stationery, envelope
Day 10   "Good Ways to Save Water???" handout; flour sifter; clean gravel; coarse, clean sand; large glass jar; cotton; muddy water for each group

Day 1   Introduction to Ecology (spelling, language arts)

Objective   After discussing what students already know about ecology, they will complete a correlating vocabulary scribble.

Materials   Class copies of the vocabulary scribble, (Figure 14.3) crayons, pens

Anticipatory Set   Begin by asking your students these questions: Can anyone tell me what is meant by the term *ecology*? How does the environment affect living things? How do living things affect the environment? What should we do to keep our environment healthy and clean?

Procedures
1. Explain to the class that they are now going to do a vocabulary scribble with the words from the class discussion. Explain the directions. (They are to color the word with its matching definition in the same crayon color.)
2. Pass out materials and read each word and definition for the class to hear.
3. Monitor students as they work. (Have those who need extra assistance work with a partner.)

Closure   Review the words in the vocabulary scribble with the class.

Evaluation   To determine students' understanding of the assignment, look over the scribbles to see whether students were able to comprehend the words and their definitions.

Answers to Vocabulary Scribble

atmosphere—the air surrounding the earth
ecology—the pattern of relations between organisms and their environment
environment—our surroundings
habitat—the place where a plant or animal lives
marsh—where land joins water
pollution—man-made waste
rain forest—a tropical woodland
species—a kind or a sort of animal
wilderness—an area untouched by humans
zoology—the study of animals

Name: _____

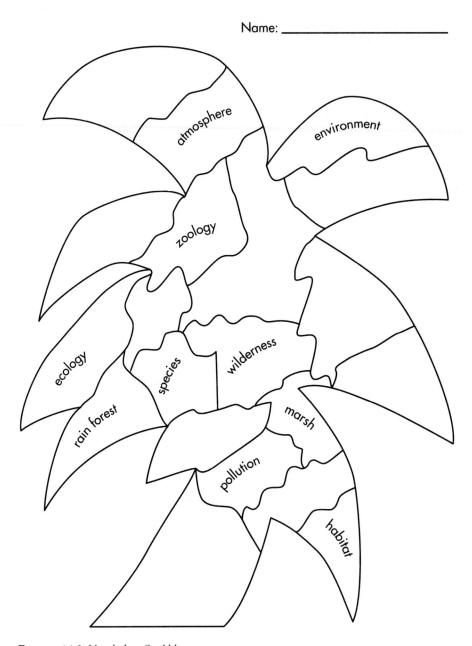

FIGURE 14.3 Vocabulary Scribble.

Day 1   The Importance of Recycling (math, language arts)

Objective After a discussion of the importance of trees, students will complete a correlating math work sheet.

Materials Class copies of the sheet, "Ecology Math: The Importance of Recycling," pencils

Anticipatory Set Begin by asking the students these questions: Why do we need trees? (They provide shade, provide homes for animals, add beauty to the environment, make carbon dioxide.) Does anyone know how much wood is used for 4 sq feet of paper? (One whole tree!) Now, can you imagine how many trees are cut down just to create newspapers for this city (area)

Name: _____

Ecology Math: The Importance of Recycling

Directions: Read problems and show all your work.

1. If we lose one tree for every 4 square feet of paper made, how many trees would we lose if 5,624 feet of paper were made? _____
   If 10,000 feet of paper were made? _____
   If 20,500 feet of paper were made? _____
2. If every person in the United States recycled his or her Sunday newspaper just one time, we would save 500,000 trees! How many trees would be saved if everyone recycled the Sunday paper for three Sundays? _____
   Write two ways you can use less paper.
   1. _____
   2. _____
3. Every American throws away 60 pounds of plastic trash every year.
   How many people are in your family? _____
   How many pounds of plastic does your family throw away in a year? _____
4. List four items you can recycle at home or school.
   1.
   2.
   3.
   4.
5. If you turn off the water while brushing your teeth, you will save about 2 gallons of water each time. How many times a day do you brush your teeth? _____
   How much water can you save in 1 day? _____
   How much water can you save in 1 week? _____
   Write one other way you can save water. _____

---

alone? What are some ways that we can save the trees and not have to cut down so many? This is just one thing in our environment that can be recycled. What else can be recycled?

Procedures
1. Now that you understand the importance of recycling, we are going to figure out some math calculations that relate to recyling. (Pass out the "Ecology Math" sheets.)
2. Read each problem aloud with the students so that everyone can comprehend the problems. (Review basic math skills if necessary.)
3. Explain that some of the problems have to be done at home and that parents can get involved if they would like to.
4. Allow students to work quietly at their desks, and provide assistance where needed.

Closure Review the importance of recycling.

Evaluation Look over the worksheet to see whether students comprehended not only the math part, but also the questions relating to the importance of recycling.

Day 2 Rain Forest Multiplication (math, language arts, science)

Objective After listening to and discussing *Great Kapok Tree: A Tale of the Amazon Rain Forest* by Lynn Cherry (Harcourt, Brace, Jovanovich, 1990) and reviewing the concept of multiplication as repeated addition, students will solve four word problems correctly, using both addition and subtraction.

Materials *Great Kapok Tree* by Lynn Cherry, butcher paper with kapok tree and animals drawn on it (Figure 14.4), "Multiplication in the Rain Forest" work sheets

Anticipatory Set Begin with these words: Every time a tree is cut down in a rain forest, many animals lose their

This Kapok tree

is home to...

6 morpho butterflies

5 spider monkeys

4 arrow poison frogs

3 emerald tree boas

2 tarantulas

FIGURE 14.4   Kapok tree.

homes. Today I'm going to read you a story about a kapok tree in a rain forest and what happens when a man tries to cut it down. After that, we will use multiplication to figure out how many animals lose their homes when trees are cut down in a rain forest.

Procedures
1. Read *Great Kapok Tree* aloud to the class.
2. Ask students what they thought was the main idea of the book.
3. Introduce the illustration of the kapok tree (on butcher paper). Discuss how many of each animal live in one kapok tree.
4. Ask students how many of each animal will lose their home if one kapok tree is cut down.
5. Put the following word problem on the board. "If three kapok trees are cut down, how many spider monkeys will lose their homes?"
6. Model how to solve the problem using both addition and multiplication: $5 + 5 + 5 = 15$; $3 \times 5 = 15$
7. Explain that multiplication is really a shorter way of writing out a long repeated addition problem.
8. With the class, go through a few problems. Have students explain answers.
9. Have students complete the work sheet.

Closure   Ask students to explain how addition and multiplication are related. Discuss the fact that the more trees that are cut down, the more animals lose their homes.

Evaluation   Assess whether the four word problems were correctly solved.

Day 3   Rain Forest Multiplication—Cooperative Groups (math, language arts, science)

Objective   After reviewing the rain forest multiplication activities of Day 2, students will work in cooperative groups to form their own word problems, correctly using an addition and multiplication problem, writing a sentence to go along with their problem, and illustrating their problem.

Materials   Kapok tree illustration, a large piece of butcher paper (3 ft $\times$ 3 ft) for each cooperative group, crayons

Anticipatory Set   Begin with: Today you're going to be working in cooperative groups to create your own word problems about the kapok tree.

Procedures
1. Review the rain forest multiplication activity of Day 2. Go through a few problems together. Make sure students explain their answers.
2. Have students help to "create" a word problem about the kapok tree (have them decide how many trees will be cut down, and which animal will be in the problem).
3. Tell students that they'll be working in cooperative groups to form their own problems. Go through the following directions with them (post directions on the board):
   a. Decide how many trees will be cut down in your problem.
   b. Chose the animal that will be in your problem.
   c. Do the addition and multiplication problems for your word problem.
   d. Create a sentence for your problem.
   e. Illustrate your problem.
4. Give each cooperative group a sheet of butcher paper. Tell groups that when they have finished, each will present its problem to the class.

Closure   Have each group present its word problem and illustration.

Evaluation   Groups will be evaluated on:
1. Their ability to work productively as a cooperative group.
2. A completed word problem, including a sentence, addition and multiplication, and an illustration.

Name: _____

Multiplication in the Rain Forest

In each kapok tree in the rain forest, there are:

6 morpho butterflies
5 spider monkeys
4 arrow poison frogs
3 emerald tree boas
2 tarantulas.

For each problem, show an addition and a multiplication problem.
Example: If 4 kapok trees are cut down, how many spider monkeys will lose their homes? 20

$$5 + 5 + 5 + 5 = 20 \quad 4 \times 5 = 20$$

1. If 3 kapok trees are cut down, how many morpho butterflies will lose their homes?
_____

2. If 6 kapok trees are cut down, how many emerald tree boas will lose their homes?
_____

3. If 5 kapok trees are cut down, how many tarantulas will lose their homes?
_____

4. If 4 kapok trees are cut down, how many arrow poison frogs will lose their homes?
_____

Day 4   Great Kapok Tree—Creative Writing (language arts, science, art)

Objective After discussing the events in *Great Kapok Tree* and listing various rain forest creatures, students will pretend that they are rain forest creatures and will write what they would say to someone in the rain forest who was chopping down trees—using at least four sentences.

Materials *Great Kapok Tree* by Lynn Cherry, butcher paper, paper that is half blank and half lined, crayons, and pencils

Anticipatory Set Begin the lesson with: A couple of days ago, I read you *Great Kapok Tree*. What I want you to do right now is think about what the main idea in that story was.

Procedures

1. Discuss the story and what the main idea might be (the creatures of the rain forest were telling the man why he shouldn't be chopping trees down).
2. Have students name various creatures that live in a rain forest. Record on a large piece of butcher paper.
3. Ask students to choose one rain forest animal. Each student will pretend to be that animal while doing some writing. Using at least four sentences, they are to write what they would say to someone who was chopping down trees.
4. Once they finish their writing, have students illustrate what they wrote.
5. Finished illustrations and writings can be mounted on construction paper and posted around the room.

Closure Have students volunteer to share what they wrote. Discuss how all creatures of the rain forest are affected when trees are cut down.

Evaluation Students' writings should be from the viewpoints of the rain forest creatures they chose to be. Their writing should contain at least four sentences, and an illustration should accompany the writing.

Day 4   Scavenger Hunt (physical education, language arts, science)

Objective After learning how to differentiate living from nonliving material, students will participate in a

---

Scavenger Hunt Checklist

Here are the things you will be looking for on your scavenger hunt. Remember to be nice to nature!

- Find two kinds of seeds.
- Find four kinds of leaves.
- Find three objects with different textures.
- Find five shades of green.
- Find three different colors of rock.

---

nature scavenger hunt and will correctly distinguish living from nonliving material.

Materials 17 small brown paper bags, 17 copies of the "Scavenger Hunt Checklist," 34 pieces of writing paper

Anticipatory Set This week we've been learning about the environment and how important it is that we do our part to preserve our planet. Today we're going to go on a scavenger hunt, and we'll learn how to tell whether something is living or nonliving.

Procedures

1. Discuss some of the criteria for an item to be living.
2. Give students examples of both living and non-living items, and have them give suggestions.
3. Put students in pairs. Make sure that students with special needs or limited English are paired with those who can help them.
4. Pass out one checklist and one paper bag to each pair. Remind students that when gathering the items on their checklist, they should not be destructive to the environment.
5. Give students approximately 20 minutes for their scavenger hunt.
6. On a piece of paper, have each student make a column for living items and a column for nonliving items they find. Have them list their finds in the appropriate columns.

Closure Ask each pair to explain the criteria they used to classify their living and nonliving items.

Evaluation Students will be evaluated according to the criteria they established for living and nonliving items and whether they followed these criteria when categorizing their items.

Day 5 *Fern Gully* (language arts/social studies)

Objective Having learned about the rain forest on Days 2 and 3, students will now watch *Fern Gully* and respond to five written questions that require higher-order, evaluative responses.

Materials *Fern Gully* video, "*Fern Gully* Questions" handouts

Anticipatory Set This week we've been learning about the wide variety of plant and animal life found in the rain forest. Raise your hand if you can tell me one reason that the rain forest is important. (Make a list of students' responses on the board.) Today we are going to watch a movie, *Fern Gully*, which will give us a better understanding of what it is like to live in the rain forest. We will also see how devastating it is when parts of this habitat are destroyed.

Procedures

1. Distribute the *Fern Gully* Questions, and explain that the students should think about the questions and jot down ideas as they watch the film.
2. Read the questions aloud to aid the special-needs students and the slow readers.
3. Ask for volunteers to restate the questions.
4. Watch *Fern Gully*.
5. Give the students time to complete their answers and illustrations.

Closure Let's share some of our responses to the movie. If you were one of the characters, what would you have done to help save the rain forest? What can *you* do today and in the future to preserve the existing rain forests?

Evaluation Take anecdotal notes as the students respond to questions that require analysis and synthesis of information. Ask students to add the *Fern Gully* handout to their portfolios.

Day 6 A Food Web (language arts)

Objective After participating in an activity that shows how living things interact, students will write about how the extinction of one organism would affect the environment.

Name: _____

Fern Gully Questions
_____

1. Characters:

   _____   _____
   _____   _____
   _____   _____

2. Imagine that all of the characters are in the room. Write down *two* questions that you would like to ask each one.

   _____
   _____
   _____

3. If you were one of the characters, what would you have done to help save the rain forest? Illustrate how you would have saved the forest.

   _____
   _____
   _____

4. What would you tell the students of the future to do to save the rain forest?

   _____
   _____
   _____

5. What changes would you make in the movie if you could? Why would you make those changes?

   _____
   _____
   _____

   Draw a picture showing the changes that you would make.

Sample Organisms for Food Web Activity

Write each of these on a 3 × 5 card and give one to each student. (You may create two of the same organisms to accommodate a larger class.)

Sun	Bird	Butterfly
Oak tree	Rabbit	Fly
Mouse	Spider	Deer
Frog	Lion	Whale
Mosquito	Fish	Plant
Pine tree	Bear	Tiger
Flower	Bee	Grasshopper
Lizard	Vulture	Fox
Turtle	Ant	Jellyfish
Snake	Minnow	Oyster
Starfish	Shark	Grass

My Endangered Animal Report
By _____

1. Name of animal: _____
   _____

2. Where does this animal live?
   _____
   _____

3. Why is this animal endangered?
   _____
   _____

4. What is being done to protect the animal?
   _____
   _____

5. Can you think of another way to protect this animal?
   _____
   _____

6. Use the back of this page to illustrate your animal in its natural habitat.

Materials Ball of string, cards with different organisms printed on them, pencils

Anticipatory Set Can anyone tell me what is meant by the phrase "food web"? Now we are going to participate in a little simulation of the food web. Everyone will get a card with the name of an organism on it, and that will be who you are. Now, I will be the sun, and every organism who is directly dependent on me will take hold of the string. Each student then passes the string to someone who is dependent upon him or her in some way, until everyone has part of the string. (When everyone has the string, it should look like a web.) Now, let's say that someone cut down a tree. The student who is the tree has to tug on his or her string. When you feel the tug, you tug on the string, until everyone can feel the tug—the effect. (Introduce a couple of different problems, such as pollution or a forest fire, and let students see how one problem can affect many organisms.)

Procedures

1. After the activity, discuss with the students the importance of interaction and the dependency of one organism on another. Ask how they felt about the different things being destroyed.
2. Explain to the class that they are now to write how the extinction of the organism on their card would affect the environment, both positively and negatively.
3. Monitor students as they work to make sure they stay on task.

Closure Review the effects that organisms have on one another. Have students share their writings.

Evaluation To check for understanding, study students' writings of how living things are interconnected and the reasons they give in discussion.

Day 7   Endangered Species (social studies/language arts)

Objective After discussing/researching endangered animals, students will write endangered animal reports.

Materials Illustrated endangered species cards (must be obtained or teacher created), copies of "My Endangered Animal Report" form, world map

Anticipatory Set What are some problems wild animals face? (obtaining food and shelter, predators, hunters) There are some groups of animals—species—that have only a few members left. They are in danger of disappearing from the earth forever.

Procedures

1. Discuss some of the reasons for the extinction of animals (e.g., habitat destruction, illegal hunting).
2. Randomly pass out the endangered species cards so that each student has one card.
3. Distribute and explain "My Endangered Animal Report."
   a. Each student researchers his or her animal using classroom, library, and/or home resources.

b. Each student places his or her animal card on the world map to indicate the animal's natural habitat.

c. Students needing help may be paired with another child or an assistant, if available.

4. Students begin their research.

Closure Discuss: What can we do to prevent further extinction of animals?

Evaluation Circulate among students as they research their endangered animals. Anecdotal notes can be taken during observations. Reports will be collected for evaluation and can be displayed in the classroom.

Day 8   Landfill (science/social studies/art)

Objective After discussing the problems of waste disposal and the benefits of recycling, students will help to create a mini-landfill, make predictions about which items will decompose, and create a collage or sculpture with recycled materials.

Materials Large plastic container, heavy plastic liner, soil, Styrofoam, aluminum, paper, plastic, banana peel, lettuce

Anticipatory Set Where does your garbage go after it is picked up from your house? Do you recycle items? Why do you think it is important to recycle?

Procedures

1. Discuss landfills and the fact that many are rapidly reaching maximum capacity, with few new sites available.
2. Discuss the term *decompose*.
3. Students help to create a class mini-landfill.

DIRECTIONS

a. Line a large plastic container with a heavy plastic liner.
b. Place a layer of soil on the bottom.
c. Call teams of 4 or 5 at a time to add waste materials to the container.
d. Layer waste materials and soil until the container is full.
e. Put the container in a warm, dark place and keep the soil moist.

4. Students, working in pairs, each create a chart listing the trash items buried in the mini-landfill. They then make predictions as to whether each item will decompose.

Closure Which items will decompose? (Students share their ideas.) In about three weeks, we will empty out the contents of our landfill. What should we do with the items that we discover do not decompose?

Evaluation Student charts and predictions will be added to their portfolios. As a home project, students create a collage or sculpture using only items recycled from the family trash. Make a classroom display of these creations.

Day 9   Class Letter (language arts, social studies)

Objective After discussing how they might help to save the rain forests, students will write a class letter to request more information on how they can do this.

Materials Large piece of chart paper, marker, copies of the "Letter-Writing Resource List," stationery, envelope

Anticipatory Set There are many things that you can do to help save the rain forest. Today we're going to write a letter to a group that will give us more information on how we can help save the rain forest.

Procedures

1. Review with the students which is happening as a result of destruction of the rain forests.
2. Lead a class discussion on some of the things that can be done by the students to help save the rain forests.
3. Tell the students that they can, as a class, purchase an acre of rain forest to protect from destruction. Tell them that today they will be writing a class letter to request more information about buying the acre.
4. Using student suggestions, compose a letter on chart paper stating why the class would like to help and requesting more information.
5. Once the letter is complete and meets with class approval, have a volunteer copy the letter on stationery. Send the letter to:

    The Children's Rainforest
    P.O. Box 936
    Lewiston, Maine 04240

Closure Tell students that the destruction of the rain forest is not the only environmental issue facing the world today. There are many endangered species, there is much pollution in the atmosphere, and we are using up our limited resources, just to name a few issues. Provide students with a copy of the "Letter-Writing Resource List," and encourage them to write on their own and get involved with environmental issues.

Evaluation Assess the completed class-composed letter.

Day 10   Water: Treatment and Conservation (science, language arts/social studies)

Objective After reading *The Magic School Bus at the Waterworks* and discussing water treatment and conser-

Letter-Writing Resource List

1. To learn more about aluminum recycling, write and ask for a free *Michael Recycle* comic book.
   Public Relations Department
   Reynolds Metals Company
   P.O. Box 27003
   Richmond, VA 23261-7003

2. "Don't You Dare Breathe That Air" is a booklet filled with information on air pollution, its causes, and what we can do about it. This booklet is free from:
   New York Lung Association
   432 Park Avenue South
   New York, NY 10016

3. "You Can Do It!," a kid's guide to helping the environment, is available from:
   National Wildlife Federation
   1412 Sixteenth St., NW
   Washington, DC 20036-2266

4. If you would like to receive a "Letter from a Whale" and a whale poster, write to:
   Animal Welfare Institute
   P.O. Box 3650
   Washington, DC 20007

5. The World Wildlife Fund has two excellent posters with fact sheets entitled "Save the Rain Forest" and "Save the African Elephant."
   World Wildlife Fund
   1250 24th Street NW
   Washington, DC 20037

6. To find out how your class can buy an acre of rain forest to protect from destruction, write to:
   The Children's Rainforest
   P.O. Box 936
   Lewiston, Maine 04240

7. The Cousteau Society will update you on the ecology of our oceans. Ask for "The Dolphin Log."
   Cousteau Society
   930 W. 21st Street
   Norfolk, VA 23517

Good Ways to Save Water???

Directions: Circle the numbers of the good ways to save water.

1. Water the grass while it's raining.
2. Take showers instead of baths.
3. Turn off the water while brushing your teeth.
4. Leave the hose running while washing the car.
5. Fix leaky faucets.
6. Stop drinking water.
7. In the summer, water the lawn during the hottest time of the day.

Name: _____

Unit Self-Evaluation

1. Name three things that you learned in this unit that you did not know before.

   _____

   _____

2. How are you going to use what you learned in this unit in your own life?

   _____

   _____

3. What was your favorite activity? Why?

   _____

   _____

4. What activity did you like least? Why?

   _____

   _____

5. What else would you like to learn about ecology?

   _____

   _____

6. Have you shared what you learned with anyone else? Why or why not?

   _____

   _____

---

vation, students will make mini–water-treatment plants and demonstrate an understanding of water conservation strategies.

Materials *The Magic School Bus at the Waterworks* by Joanna Cole (Scholastic, 1986); copies of the "Good Ways to Save Water???" handout

For each group:

flour sifter	course, clean sand	cotton
clean gravel	large glass jar	muddy water

Anticipatory Set Begin with statements similar to the following (as relevant to your area): Today we're going to talk about water. When I was in elementary school, we were taught that water is a renewable resource and that we would never run out of water. Recently, however, we have had years with little rainfall, which we call a drought, and there hasn't been enough water for all of our wants and needs. Raise your hand if you can tell me why water is important to us. (List student ideas on the board.)

Procedures

1. Read *The Magic School Bus at the Waterworks*.
2. Have students brainstorm ways in which water can become polluted (through dumping trash, insecticides, industrial waste, oil spills, etc.).
3. Working in cooperative groups of four, have students make a mini–water-treatment plant. Assign the following cooperative group roles: runner, thinker, assembler, recorder.

Directions

   a. Place a layer of cotton at the boom of a sifter.
   b. Add 1 inch of coarse sand, then 1 inch of gravel.
   c. Set the sifter over a jar and slowly pour muddy water into the container. *Don't drink the water, as it may contain bacteria!*
4. Have students record the results.

Closure How is your treatment plant like the one in the book? How is it different? Why is it important that we conserve water?

Evaluation   Students will complete the handout "Good Ways to Save Water???" Responses will be discussed as a class, and students will be encouraged to add their own ideas. This will be a required element to include in their portfolios.

Culminating Activity

Objective   Given a tour of a recyling plant, students will have a firsthand view of what their efforts in recycling are accomplishing and will write a one-page summary of their feelings about recycling.

Materials   Permission slips, principal approval, coordination with the recycling plant

Anticipatory Set   This will be the grand finale in the thematic unit. Recycling will already have been discussed.

Procedures

1. Contact a local recycling plant for tour information.
2. Get principal's approval.
3. Send home permission slips.
4. Review ways that students can recycle and the items they can recycle.
5. Go on field trip.

Closure   In discussing the events of the day, ask students to recall what they have learned.

CHILDRENS LITERATURE SELECTIONS

Fiction

Baker, J. (1988). *Where the Forest Meets the Sea*. New York: Greenwillow.

Cooney, B. (1982). *Miss Rumphius*. New York: Viking Children's Books.

Peet, B. (1966). *Farewell to Shady Glade*. Boston: Houghton Mifflin.

Peet, B. (1981). *Wump World*. Boston: Houghton Mifflin.

Seuss, Dr. (1971). *The Lorax*. New York: Random.

Udry, J. M. (1987). *A Tree Is Nice*. New York: Harper Collins Children's Books.

Van Allsburg, C. (1990). *Just a Dream*. Boston: Houghton Mifflin.

Nonfiction

Bellamy, D. (1988). *Our Changing World: The Forest*. New York: Crown.

Bellamy, D. (1988). *Our Changing World: The River*. New York: Crown.

Bellamy, D. (1988). *Our Changing World: The Roadside*. New York: Crown.

Dehr, R., and R. Bazar. (1990). *Good Planets Are Hard to Find: An Environmental Information Guide for Kids*. Buffalo, NY: Firefly Books Ltd.

Fitzsimons, C. (1990). *The Modern Ark*. Hudson, NY: Dial Books for Young Readers.

Greenberg, J. E., and H. H. Carey. (1990). *The Rain Forest*. Milwaukee, WI: Raintree Publishers.

Hane, T. (1991). *Vanishing Habitats*. New York: Gloucester Press.

Resource Book

MacEachern, D. (1990). *Save Our Planet: Seven Hundred & Fifty Everyday Ways You Can Help Clean Up the Earth*. New York: Dell.

Publication
Ranger Rick
National Wildlife Federation
1400 16th Street NW
Washington, DC 20036-2266

EXTENSION ACTIVITIES

1. Recycled Paper

Materials

newspaper
plastic tub
cornstarch
whisk or blender
plastic wrap
piece of window screen
rolling pin

Procedure

1. Fill the tub half full with small pieces of newspaper. Add enough water to wet the newspaper, and let it soak for several hours.
2. Beat the newspaper mixture into a creamy pulp.
3. Dissolve 3 tablespoons of cornstarch in 1 cup of water and add it to the mixture. Stir.
4. Lower a piece of window screen into the tub repeatedly until it is covered with a layer of the mixture about 1/8 inch thick.
5. Place the screen on a thick layer of newspaper. Cover with plastic wrap and press out the extra moisture with a rolling pin.
6. Prop the pulp-covered screen where it can dry. After the fibers dry, peel the recycled paper away from the screen.

2. Persuasive Poster

Students, working in cooperative pairs, develop a poster to convince people to conserve water, save the rain forests, recycle, or save endangered species. They can choose any topic related to the ecology theme. A participatory bulletin board can be created with student posters.

3. Endangered Species Bingo

Students create their own game cards with their favorite endangered animals.

4. Ecology News Report

Students select an article from an "Earth News" bulletin board and write a summary of the key ideas. The teacher guides students through a process of responding to who, what, when, where, why/how questions.

5. Miniature Rain Forest

Materials:

clear plastic 2-liter bottle with a black bottom section

potting soil

gravel

several small plants (Philodendron and pothos with roots attached work well.)

Procedure

1. Separate the black bottom from the clear portion of the bottle, and cut away the top of the bottle.
2. Spread ¾ inch of gravel in the black bottom, then spread 1 ½ inches of potting soil over the gravel.
3. Plant and water the plants.
4. Invert the clear portion of the bottle and place it over the plants so that it fits tightly into the bottom.
5. Put the bottle in a sunny spot.
6. As the days go by, ask students to observe the transformation.
7. After it begins to "rain" in your bottle, ask your students to explain what's happening. (The sunlight causes the water to evaporate from the potting soil. The mist rises to the top, cools, and turns into droplets like rain.)

3. EXPLORING AN OWL PELLET (ADAPTABLE TO ANY GRADE)[2]

Rationale

Owl pellets can be collected from around the nests of owls or purchased from science supply companies.[3] Careful opening and sorting of material in the pellets reveals interesting information about the eating habits of owls. The contents of the pellets can be the inspiration for an interesting discussion and informative study of

- how aspects of the environment are interrelated and that changes to one aspect affect other aspects,
- the concept of interdependence,

- food chains,
- skeletal anatomy.

Disciplines Involved in This Study

Science and mathematics.

Skills Involved

Fine locomotor control, sketching, comparing and contrasting, observing, calculating, writing, sorting and classifying, basic calculations.

Instructional Procedures

Read the entire exploration and then adapt it according to your own needs, or present it to your class of students as it is here.

Background Information

Owls, as birds of prey, eat small rodents (such as mice and shrews) as a major part of their diet. They do not rip the prey apart, they swallow them whole. Since the stomach muscles and stomach acid in an owl are not very strong, all of the bones and fur of a mouse or shrew cannot be completely digested. If a bone were to accidentally start to move through the intestine, it could poke a hole in the intestine and cause serious problems for the owl. Faced with this problem, nature has supplied the owl with a solution that allows the owl to continue its regular diet of rodents without worrying about the weak stomach or the possibility of intestinal poking. The solution is the owl pellet.

Owl pellets are balls of fur and bones that the owl regurgitates (spits up) after the meat is digested from its prey. This process is similar to the way a cat makes fur balls to keep the fur it licks off its own coat from clogging its intestines. An owl will produce one pellet about every 12 hours. (Have students now answer questions 1 and 2 shown at the end of this exploration.)

Investigatory Procedures

1. Divide your class of students into groups of four. One person in each group is the "materials manager," and will obtain the pellet and other materials needed by the group. From each group, children are to select two people to be "hunters." The hunters will divide the pellet in half, locate bones, and place the bones in the team's Petri dish. The fourth person is the "sorter."
2. *Materials needed:* The materials manager should now obtain the following materials for the group exploration: owl pellet, Petri dish, sheet of plain white paper, pair of scissors,

metric ruler, tweezers, dissecting needles, bone sorting sheet (showing major types of rodent bones).

3. The sorter will outline the bottom (small half) of the Petri dish on a sheet of paper, cut out the circle, write the names of the four group members on the paper, and push the paper in up into the top of the Petri dish with the names showing. Later, the sorter will take each of the bones placed in the Petri dish bottom by the hunters, decide what kind of bone it is, and place it on the bone sorting sheet provided with the team owl pellet.

4. Students are now to answer questions 3 and 4.

5. Place the owl pellet on the table in front of you. Unwrap it. Using the metric ruler, measure the length and width of the pellet.

6. Very carefully use the tweezers and dissecting needles to split the pellet into two approximately equal parts. Give one part to each of the hunters.

7. Hunters now use the tweezers and needles to gently pull the pellet apart and locate bones. Remove fur from the bone (if necessary) to be sure that each bone has as little fur on it as possible before placing it into the Petri dish.

8. The sorter will take the bones, check them against the bone sorting sheet, and place them on the correct space on the sorting sheet.

9. Continue to locate, clean, identify, and sort bones until all of the bones are removed from the pellet. Each group member is responsible for checking the accuracy of the sorting.

10. Now answer questions 5, 6, 7, and 8.

11. The entire group will now take their completed chart (question 6) to the teacher. The teacher will give the sorter a "skeleton page" and a bottle of glue. Both hunters will copy the group data onto the Entire Class Bone Chart either on the board or the overhead projector.

12. Glue the bones on the skeleton page to form your own rodent skeleton.

13. Copy down the class data from the Entire Class Bone Chart onto your own chart.

14. Turn in your group skeleton page.

15. Take your own chart and answer sheet home. Total the number of bones of each type from the entire class data.

16. Now answer questions 9–12.

Question (to be duplicated for students)

1. How many pellets would an owl produce in each of the following lengths of time? Show your work.

   a. 1 day
   b. 1 week
   c. 1 month
   d. 1 year

2. Pretend that you live on a farm. You clean your barn each Saturday, picking up everything on the concrete floor of the barn and washing the floor off with water from a hose. When you clean one week you find 42 owl pellets. How many owls are living in your barn?

3. Who is your group's materials manager? Sorter? Hunters?

4. Why does the sorter need a sheet of paper?

5. How long was your pellet (in millimeters)? How wide was it?

6. Make a chart on your paper. Put the type of bone across the top and the number of bones your pellet contained under each type of bone.

7. What type of bone did you have the most of?
   a. How many were there?
   b. Why do you think there were so many?

8. What type of bone did you have the least of?
   a. How many were there?
   b. Is this type of bone the same as your group's highest number? If it is not, why do you believe this to be so?

9. What type of bone did the class have the most of?
   a. How many were there?
   b. Is this type of bone the same as your group's highest number? If it is not, why do you think this is so?

10. What type of bone did the class have the least number of?
    a. How many were there?
    b. Is this type of bone the same as your group's lowest number? If it is not, why not?

11. What is the total number of rodent skulls in your class?
    a. How many femurs should the class have? Did they have that many? If not, why not?
    b. How many humerus bones should the class have? Did they have that many? If not, why not?

12. Assume that all the rodent skulls in your class were from the pellets of a single owl.
    a. How many days of eating did this sample cover?
    b. If the number of rodents eaten in one day equals 0.5% of the total rodent population, what is the rodent population in this owl's hunting territory?

Notes

1. Courtesy of Lisa Caruso, Cathleen Gilbert, Nancy Mortham, and Lori Venkus.
2. Portions of this investigation were provided by Charles R. Downing. © 1993–1994 by Charles R. Downing. By permission of Charles R. Downing.
3. For owl pellet kits, contact, for example, Etgen's Science Stuff, 3600 Whitney Avenue, Sacramento, CA 95821, (916) 972-1871; Genesis Inc., P.O. Box 2242, Mt. Vernon, WA 98273, (800) 4-PELLET; Hawks, Owls & Wildlife, R.D. 1, Box 293, Buskirk, NY 12028, (518) 686-4080; and Owls, Etc., 15 Riviera Court, Great River, NY 11739, (516) 581-1905.

Student Books and Other Resources for "Animals"

Andersen, C. "A Walk-in Butterfly Vivarium." *Science and Children* 31(1):25–27 (September 1994).

Arnosky, J. *All About Alligators*. New York: Scholastic, 1994.

Bavendam, F. "The Giant Cuttlefish: Chameleon of the Reef." *National Geographic* 188(3):94–107 (September 1995).

Berg, C. *Chameleon Condos: Critters & Critical Thinking*. Arlington, VA: National Science Teachers Association, 1994.

Bombaugh, R. "Praying Mantises and Whole Language Learning." *Science Scope* 18(8):12–15 (May 1995).

Bonners, S. *Hunter in the Snow: The Lynx*. Boston, MA: Little, Brown, 1994.

Booth, J. *Big Bugs*. Orlando, FL: Harcourt Brace Jovanovich, 1994.

Cerullo, M. M. *Lobsters: Gangsters of the Sea*. New York: Cobblehill, 1994.

———. *Sharks: Challengers of the Deep*. New York: Cobblehill, 1993.

Chadwick, D. H. "On the Edge of Earth and Sky." *National Geographic* 187(4):102–121 (April 1995).

Clark, M. G. *The Endangered Florida Panther*. New York: Cobblehill, 1993.

Crain, D. "Close-up: Red Squirrels." *Creative Classroom* 8(5):29 (March 1994).

D'Agostino, J. B. et al. "Dancing for Food: The Language of the Honeybees." *Science and Children* 31(8):15–17, 50 (May 1994).

Darling, K. *Kangaroos: On Location*. New York: Lothrop, 1993.

Demuth, P. B. *Those Amazing Ants*. New York: Macmillan/Simon & Schuster, 1994.

Emory, J. *Nightprowlers: Everyday Creatures Under Every Night Sky*. New York: Harcourt Brace, 1994.

Esbensen, B. J. *Playful Slider: The North American River Otter*. Boston, MA: Little, Brown, 1993.

Godkin, C. *Wolf Island*. New York: Freeman, 1993.

Gowell, E. T. *Sea Jellies: Rainbows in the Sea*. New York: Watts, 1993.

Grace, E. S. *Snakes*. San Francisco: Sierra Club, 1994.

Grace, E. S. *Apes*. San Francisco: Sierra Club, 1995.

Grambo, G. "Raising Butterflies in Your Classroom." *Science Scope* 18(8):16–18 (May 1995).

Hamner, W. M. "Australia's Box Jellyfish: A Killer Down Under." *National Geographic* 186(2):116–130 (August 1994).

Hatch, L. "Animal Care, Day by Day." *Science and Children* 32(1):30–33 (September 1994).

Hinshaw, D. *Killer Whales*. New York: Holiday House, 1993.

Hirschi, R. *A Time for Babies*. New York: Cobblehill, 1993.

Holley, D. *Animals Alive: An Ecological Guide to Animal Activities*. Arlington, VA: National Science Teachers Association, 1994.

Hosoume, K. and J. Barber. *Terrarium Habitats*. Arlington, VA: National Science Teachers Association, 1994.

Johnson, S. A. *A Beekeeper's Year*. Boston, MA: Little, Brown, 1994.

Joubert, D. "Lions of Darkness." *National Geographic* 186(2):34–53 (August 1994).

Kneidel, S. S. *Creepy Crawlies and the Scientific Method*. Arlington, VA: National Science Teachers Association, 1993.

Kyle, J. "The Opal Winskin Show: A Script, Activities, and Facts About Wolves." *Creative Classroom* 8(5):46–48 (March 1994).

Lauber, P. *Earthworms*. New York: Henry Holt, 1994.

Leakey, M. "The Dawn of Humans: The Farthest Horizon." *National Geographic* 188(3):38–51 (September 1995).

Livo, L., McGlathery, G., and Livo, N. *Of Bugs and Beasts*. Arlington, VA: National Science Teachers Association, 1995.

Markle, S. *Outside and Inside Birds*. New York: Bradbury/Simon & Schuster, 1994.

———. *Outside and Inside Spiders*. New York: Bradbury/Simon & Schuster, 1994.

Martin, L. *Watch Them Grow*. New York: Dorling Kindersley, 1994.

McLeod, J. "From Caterpillar to Butterfly." *Science and Children* 32(1):22–24 (September 1994).

Miller, D. S. *A Caribou Journey*. Boston, MA: Little, Brown, 1994.

Moffett, M. W. "Poison-Dart Frogs: Lurid and Lethal." *National Geographic* 187(5): 98–111 (May 1995).

Morris, D. *The World of Animals*. New York: Viking, 1993.

Nabors, M. L., et al. "Webbing with Spiders." *Science and Children* 31(8):33–35 (May 1994).

Nicklin, F. "Bowhead Whales." *National Geographic* 188(2):114–129 (August 1995).

Parfit, M. "Diminishing Returns: Exploiting the Ocean's Bounty." *National Geographic* 188(5):2–37 (November 1995).

Patent, D. H. *Deer and Elk*. New York: Clarion, 1994.

Payne. O "Kaolas Out on a Limb." *National Geographic* 187(4):36–59 (April 1995).

Peters, L. W. *This Way Home*. New York: Holt, 1994.

Riley: L. C. *Elephants Swim*. Boston: Houghton-Mifflin, 1995.

Rodenberg, B. "Urban Bird-Watching." *Science Scope* 18(7):12–17 (April 1995).

Rudloe, A., and Rudloe, J. "Sea Turtles: In a Race for Survival." *National Geographic* 185(2):94–121 (February 1994).

Ryden, H. *Your Dog's Wild Cousins*. New York: Lodestar, 1994.

Sanner, S H. "How Did Those Bugs Get There?" *Science and Children* 32(1):28–29 (September 1994).

Sattler, H. R. *The Book of North American Owls*. New York: Clarion, 1995.

Savage, S. *Frog*. Fresno, CA: Thomson, 1995.

Simon, S. *Sharks*. New York: Harper Collins, 1995.

Smith, J. G. "Beauty and the Butterflies." *Science and Children* 32(4):29–32 (January 1995).

Smith, K. R., and A. H. Bush. *Investigating Science Through Bears*. Arlington, VA: National Science Teachers Association, 1994.

Snedden, R. *What Is a Reptile?* San Francisco: Sierra Club, 1995.

Sobol, R. *Seal Journey*. New York: Cobblehill, 1993.

Stone, L. M. *Vultures*. Minneapolis: Carolrhoda, 1993.

Stuart, D. *The Astonishing Armadillo*. Minneapolis: Carolrhoda, 1993.

Taylor, B. D., and R. D. Fell. "What a Surprise—They're Flies!" *Science and Children* 33(2):16–19 (October 1995).

Trebonaik, L., and M. Jaworski. "Science—It's for the Birds!" *Science and Children* 33(3):16–19 (November/December 1995).

Tuttle, M. D. "Saving North America's Beleagured Bats." *National Geographic* 188(2): 36–57 (August 1995).

Vincent, A. "The Improbable Seahorse." *National Geographic* 186(4):126–140 (October 1994).

Wade, L. *Getting to Know the Whales*. Arlington, VA: National Science Teachers Association, 1995.

Welch, E. J., Jr. "Animal Behavior: An Interdisciplinary Unit." *Science and Children* 32(3):24–26 (November/December 1994).

Wilkinson, V. *Flies Are Fascinating*. Chicago: Children's Press, 1994.

Woelflein, L. Metamorphoris: *Animals That Change*. Alburquerque: Lodestar, 1995.

CHAPTER 15

The Human Body

THE MAKEUP OF THE HUMAN BODY

I. THE HUMAN BODY IS MADE OF CELLS

   A. The human body is made up of millions of tiny cells. They have the same parts and characteristics as other animal cells. Many cells have specific functions and thus differ in size and shape and may even contain special materials, all of which makes it possible for them to perform their particular kinds of work. Examples of specialized cells include blood, epithelial, muscle, nerve, and bone cells.

   B. A group of the same kind of cells that carry on the same activity or work is called a **tissue.** There are five main kinds of tissue in the human body: muscle tissue makes up the muscles in the body; nerve tissue makes up the nerves and the brain; epithelial tissue includes the outer skin and the linings of such parts as the mouth, nose, throat, heart, stomach, liver, and intestines; connective tissue helps hold the body parts together and includes tendons, ligaments, cartilage, and bone; blood is a liquid tissue that distributes oxygen to cells and carries away wastes.

   C. A group of different tissues, working together in a common function, is called an **organ.** An organ carries out a special activity or group of activities in the body. Examples of organs are the heart, lungs, liver, stomach, eyes, and brain.

   D. A group of organs working together in a special body activity is called a **system.** There are ten systems in the human body:

1. The skin system covers and protects the body and helps maintain body temperature. It includes the skin, hair, and nails.
2. The skeletal system supports the body. It includes the bones.
3. The muscular system makes it possible for the body and its parts to move.
4. The digestive system digests the food we eat and includes the mouth, stomach, pancreas, intestines, and liver.
5. The circulatory system moves materials needed by cells and carries away wastes. It includes the heart, arteries, veins, and tiny blood vessels called capillaries.
6. The respiratory system is the system that takes in oxygen and eliminates carbon dioxide; it includes the nose, windpipe (trachea), bronchi, and lungs.
7. The excretory system helps to eliminate the waste products formed in the body. It includes the kidneys and bladder.
8. The nervous system makes it possible for the body to respond to stimuli. It includes the nerves, brain, sensory organs, and spinal cord.
9. The reproductive system includes those organs that affect sex characteristics and allow the body to produce offspring. It includes the male penis and testes and the female vagina, uterus, and ovaries.
10. The endocrine system consists of various glands that produce chemicals that control and regulate body functions.

DEMONSTRATION 15.1
Compare Fingerprints

Have the students make and compare fingerprints. Obtain an ink stamp pad. Let each student pick up ink on his or her right forefinger by pressing the right side of the fingertip against the pad and rolling the finger from right to left. Then have the student roll the inked fingertip from right to left on a small piece of white paper with the student's name on it. Let the students compare fingerprints, using a magnifying glass, and note that no two prints are exactly the same. Common patterns, however, are the arch, the whorl, the loop, and combinations of these.

II. THE REGIONS OF THE BODY
   A. The human body is divided into three regions: the head, the trunk, and the limbs (arms and legs). The trunk region is subdivided into two smaller regions: the chest, or thorax, and the abdomen.

   B. There are three important cavities in the body: the cranial cavity, which contains the brain; the thoracic cavity, which contains the heart, esophagus, and lungs; and the abdominal cavity, which contains the stomach, intestines, liver, pancreas, kidneys, and bladder.

THE SKIN

I. THE SKIN AND ITS PARTS

   A. The skin is an organ, about 3 millimeters (1/8 inch) thick, that covers the body.
      1. It is an organ because it consists of tissues joined together to perform specific functions.
      2. The skin is the largest organ of the body. The average adult's skin occupies approximately 7 square meters (approximately 23 square ft).
      3. The skin has two layers: a thin outer layer, called the epidermis; and a thicker inner layer, called the dermis.
   B. The **epidermis** is made up of many layers of cells.
      1. The outer cells are flat, scaly, and horny, and are constantly being shed or rubbed off as dead cells. As these dead cells are lost, new living cells from the living layers beneath push up and take their place. As these new cells come closer to the surface of the skin, they become harder and flatter.
      2. If a spot on the skin, such as the side of the large toe, is rubbed extensively, a large number of living cells may push up quickly and form an extra, thick layer of dead cells, called a **callus.**
      3. When minor injuries occur to the epidermis, living epidermal cells divide by mitosis to quickly replace the damaged cells. If damage occurs to dermal cells, the body takes longer to repair the damage.
      4. The living cells of the epidermis contain a colored pigment, called **melanin,** which gives the skin its characteristic color. Differences in skin color are due to the amount of melanin produced by the cells. Exposure to sunlight causes an increase in melanin production, and the skin becomes darker. Changes in melanin is what allows animals like the chameleon and the cuttle fish to change their colors.
   C. The much thicker dermis lies beneath the epidermis.
      1. It is made up of tough connective tissues that allow the skin to stretch (such as when injured) and then return to its original shape.
      2. In the dermis are blood vessels, nerves, oil glands, sweat glands, muscles, and cells that produce hair.
   D. Beneath the dermis is a layer of fatty tissue that attaches the skin to the rest of the body. This is referred to as the subcutaneous layer.

II. HAIR AND NAILS

   A. Hair is a thread of horny material produced by special cells in the dermis. Hair is made of the same material as that found in the dead cells of the epidermis.
      1. Newly formed hair grows, passing up a tube through both the dermis and epidermis, and then moves out beyond the surface of the skin.
      2. Although the root of the hair is alive, the rest of the hair is dead. Hair can be coarse or fine, straight, or curly.
      3. The hair grows until it reaches a certain length and then falls out. The length of a

DEMONSTRATION 15.2
Exploring Human Hair and Nails

A. Study Different Colored Human Hairs under a Microscope

See whether you can find three layers of cells. The middle layer is the one that contains the color. Note any difference in appearance and quality of the hairs.

B. Measure the Rate of Growth of Nails

Place a tiny drop of dilute nitric acid close to the base of one fingernail and one toenail. The nitric acid will produce a permanent yellow stain on the nail. Measure the distance between the edge of each nail and the nitric acid spot. Repeat the measurement each week until the yellow spot is cut off. Determine and compare the rates of growth of the nails.

---

hair depends on whether it is body, head, eyebrow, or eyelash hair.

4. When a hair falls out, a new one may grow in its place.

5. Inside the hair is a pigment that gives it its special color. When people become older, the hair pigment disappears and the hair becomes white.

B. Nails are also made of a horny material produced in the skin. This material is the same as that found in the dead cells of the epidermis. The root of the nail is alive, but the rest of the nail is dead. Fingernails grow about three times as fast as toenails.

III. FUNCTIONS OF SKIN

A. The skin has many important functions.
1. It acts as a protective covering to prevent harmful bacteria from entering the body.
2. It forms a waterproof covering, preventing water and other liquids from leaving the inner tissues.
3. It protects the inner parts of the body from such injuries as scratches, bruises, bumps, and cuts.
B. When the skin is injured, many of its cells are damaged or killed. However, the skin is able to repair itself and regenerate new skin.
C. The pigment, melanin, in the skin helps protect the skin from the sun's rays. A person with a large amount of melanin pigment (whose skin is dark) is better protected from the sun's ultraviolet rays than a person whose skin is much lighter or an albino person (one who has no melanin).
D. The skin has many nerve endings, which make it sensitive to touch, pressure, pain, heat, and cold.
E. Sweat glands in the skin help the body to get rid of some of its waste materials and help regulate body temperature.

1. The sweat glands open through pores on the surface of the skin, allowing the escape of body wastes (sweat). Sweat is a mixture of water, salt, sugar, lactic and ascorbic acids, and small amounts of organic wastes.
2. Each sweat gland has a tiny tube leading from the surface of the skin to the lower part of the dermis, where the tube winds around and around to form a coil.
3. Tiny blood vessels surround the cells of the sweat glands. The cells of the sweat glands take saltwater, minerals, and other waste products from the blood, and the sweat then flows up the tube and out onto the skin, where it evaporates.
4. There are more than a million sweat glands in the skin. These are spread out over the entire body, but are most numerous in the palm of the hand, the sole of the foot, and the armpit.
5. In very warm environments, sweat glands give off large amounts of sweat, which evaporates on the surface of the skin.
6. Water needs heat to evaporate; it takes this heat from the surface of the skin, thus cooling the body.
7. In cold environments, sweat glands give off very little sweat; thus less evaporation and cooling of the body occur.
F. Blood vessels in the skin also help to control or regulate body temperature.
1. When the body is warmer than normal, blood vessels in the dermis open wider (dilate) and body heat is lost by radiation through the skin. When the body is colder than normal, the vessels constrict and heat is conserved. In addition, when the body is warmer than normal, body heat is lost during the evaporation of sweat from the skin's surface. In these ways the skin helps maintain body temperature.

DEMONSTRATION 15.3
Skin Helps Regulate Body Temperature

Have students wet a finger and blow on it. The finger feels cool as the moisture evaporates, as heat energy is taken away from the finger to produce evaporation. Point out that the evaporation of perspiration produces the same cooling effect.

Have the students recall how flushed their faces become when they are hot. Point out that this flushing oc-curs because the blood vessels expand and allow more of the heated blood to flow into the skin. Now have the students recall the "goose bumps" that form on their arms when they become cold. The reason for this phenomenon is that the blood vessels contract and the pores close tightly to prevent body heat from escaping. As a result, tiny bumps are formed all over the surface of the skin.

G. Oil glands are connected to the cells that produce hair. Oil that is secreted by these glands help keep hair from drying out, keeps the skin elastic, and retards the growth of certain bacteria found on skin.

H. When exposed to ultraviolet rays from sunlight, dermis cells produce vitamin D, a nutrient that aids the absorption of calcium into the bloodstream.

THE SKELETAL SYSTEM

I. THE STRUCTURE OF THE SKELETON

A. The approximately 206 bones that make up the human skeleton can be divided into two groups. The **axial skeleton** includes the skull and the bones that support it, such as the vertebral column, the ribs, and the sternum. The **appendicular skeleton** includes the bones of the arms and legs and the structures associated with them, such as the shoulders and the pelvic girdles.

B. **Skull bones** form a case that surrounds the brain.
1. In children the joints between these bones are movable, allowing the bones to grow. In adults the bones have grown together to form a solid case, and the joints cannot move.
2. Other important bones in the skull are the cheek, nose, and jaw bones.

C. The **vertebral** (or spinal) **column** consists of 33 blocklike bones, called **vertebrae,** one stacked on top of the other with discs of cartilage between them.
1. These vertebrae make it possible for the head and trunk of the body to turn and bend in different directions.
2. They form a strong support for the weight of the body and the head.
3. The spinal column also protects a large bundle or network of nerves, called the spinal cord.

D. The skeleton has 12 pairs of ribs, forming a **rib cage** that protects the heart and lungs. All 12 pairs are connected in back, by hinge joints, to the vertebrae of the spinal column. The upper 7 pairs of ribs are connected in front to the breastbone, or sternum, by cartilage.

E. The arm is made up of a long bone that runs from the shoulder to the elbow, the two bones of the forearm, the wrist bones, the hand bones, and the finger bones.

F. A pair of bones join each arm at the shoulder. A long, narrow collarbone connects the upper end of the breastbone with each shoulder. A large, flat shoulder blade is at the back of each shoulder.

G. The leg is made up of a long bone that runs from the hip to the knee, a kneecap that protects the knee joint, the two bones that go from the knee to the ankle, the ankle bones, the foot bones, and the toe bones.

H. Several hip bones together form the pelvis and are connected to the vertebrae near the bottom (above the coccyx) of the spinal column.
1. The pelvis provides a firm circular support, called the pelvic girdle, for the body.
2. It also allows the legs to move freely.
3. In females the pelvic girdle can expand at its joints to allow for childbirth.

II. THE MATERIALS IN THE SKELETON

A. The skeleton is made of two kinds of connective tissue—**bone** and **cartilage.**
1. In bone a large amount of hard mineral matter, especially calcium phosphate, is deposited between the cells, making the outer part of bone quite hard.

2. Cartilage has a soft, smooth material, which is tough and flexible, between its cells.

3. When a baby first begins to form inside its mother's womb, its skeleton is mostly cartilage. Soon after, bone cells begin to replace the cartilage cells.

4. Long bones in young people have cartilage **growth plates** near each end of the bones. This is the growth plate where bone cells are produced. Eventually, the growth plates fill in with bone cells and growth in size ceases.

5. The change from cartilage to bone continues until the child grows into an adult, a major reason that a child needs milk. Milk supplies the calcium necessary to make bone tissue.

6. The adult skeleton still contains some cartilage. The ears and the end of the nose are made of cartilage. There is also a disc of cartilage between each of the vertebrae of the spinal column, and the ends of the long bones are covered with cartilage. Ribs are connected to the breastbone by strips of cartilage.

B. Many bones have a soft, spongy tissue, called **marrow,** within them. Bones that contain this center cavity of marrow include the ribs, sternum, vertebrae, skull, and the long bones of the arms and legs. There are two kinds of marrow—red and yellow.

1. **Red marrow** is found in the ends of long bones, in the vertebrae, and in flat bones such as the ribs, breastbone, and shoulder bones. Red and white blood cells are made in the red marrow, giving red marrow its reddish color and name.

2. **Yellow marrow** is found in the shafts of the long bones. Yellow marrow stores fat for energy, which gives the marrow a yellowish color; hence its name.

III. THE SKELETAL JOINTS

A. The place where two bones meet is called a **joint.**

B. Some joints do not allow movement at all. This lack of mobility occurs because the bones have grown together to form one solid mass. Examples of immovable joints include the cranial bones of the skull, the breastbone, and the tailbone.

C. Some joints, like the joint between the ribs and the backbone, as well as the female pelvis, are partially movable.

D. Some joints can move quite freely. One type is called a **hinge joint.** Similar to a door hinge that allows a door to swing back and forth easily, a hinge joint allows a bone to move back and forth easily. Joints of the elbows, knees, fingers, and toes are examples of hinge joints.

E. Another type of movable joint is the **ball-and-socket joint.** In this kind of joint the end of one bone forms a ball that fits into a hollow, or socket, of another bone. A ball-and-socket joint makes it possible for a bone to move in many directions. The shoulder and hip joints are examples of ball-and-socket joints.

F. Another type of movable joint is called the **pivot joint.** This joint works like a pivot to allow the bones to move around and back. The lower arm bones and the head on the spine move around on pivot joints.

G. Bones that come together at movable joints are all held together by strong bands of connective tissue called **ligaments.**

IV. FUNCTIONS OF THE SKELETON

A. The skeleton holds the body erect and gives the body its shape.

B. It provides a place for the muscles to be attached, thus making it possible for the body to walk, breathe, and eat.

C. It protects delicate organs in the body.

D. Bones are responsible for producing blood cells and storing fat and minerals.

E. Specialized bones of the middle ear function in hearing.

THE MUSCULAR SYSTEM

I. KINDS OF MUSCLES

A. There are more than 400 muscles in the human body. Their function is to provide movement. The muscles contract and cause other parts of the body to move. Every movement the body makes is caused by muscles.

B. There are two types of muscles—**voluntary** and **involuntary.** Both are controlled by the nervous system.

C. **Voluntary muscles** are muscles we can consciously control.

1. These muscles move whenever we want them to move.

2. The muscles that move the bones of the skeleton are voluntary muscles.
3. Some voluntary muscles, like the arm muscles, are connected to bones by tough white cords of connective tissue, called **tendons.**
4. Other voluntary muscles are connected directly to the bones.
5. Some voluntary muscles, such as the lip muscles, are connected to other muscles.
6. The cells of voluntary muscles are long and round and are bound together by connective tissue into small bundles.
7. These voluntary muscle cells have cross-stripes, and such muscles are called **striated** muscles.
   D. **Involuntary muscles** are muscles that we cannot consciously control.
1. The action of these muscles is controlled by the nervous system.
2. These muscles produce the movements needed to keep us alive, by moving food through the digestive system, by moving blood through the body, and by controlling breathing.
3. The cells of involuntary muscles are spindle-shaped and are found in layers in the walls of the digestive system, blood vessels, and other organs.
4. These cells do not have any cross-stripes, and the involuntary muscles are called **smooth muscles.**
5. Contraction of smooth muscle is slower and more prolonged than that of heart or skeletal muscle.

E. The **heart muscles** consist of a special kind of involuntary muscle that is branched. Heart muscles are found only in the heart.
F. Some muscles are both voluntary and involuntary. They operate automatically without our control, but can also partially be controlled. Muscles that operate the eyelid and the diaphragm are both voluntary and involuntary. We can consciously control the action of those muscles, but not forever.

II. HOW MUSCLES WORK

A. Muscles work in only one way: by tightening or contracting. When muscles contract, they become shorter and thicker and in this way exert a pull. Muscles can exert only a pull, never a push.
B. Voluntary skeletal muscles that move joints always work in pairs.
1. When one muscle contracts, the other muscle relaxes.
2. The muscle that bends a joint is called a **flexor,** and the muscle that straightens the joint is called an **extensor.**
3. The flexor **biceps muscle** on the top of your upper arm makes the forearm move upward, and the extensor **triceps muscle** beneath your upper arm makes the forearm move down again. When the biceps contracts and works, the triceps rests and relaxes.
C. Voluntary muscles usually work singly. They either contract or relax.

NUTRIENTS

I. THE BODY NEEDS NUTRIENTS

A. The body needs nutrients to live and grow. In the foods we eat, there are materials that give the body energy, materials that are used to repair and build tissues, and materials that are used to help regulate body functions.
1. These materials, called nutrients, are divided into six kinds: **carbohydrates, fats, proteins, minerals, vitamins,** and **water.**
B. **Carbohydrates** are used in the body to supply energy. They include sugar and starches. They are digested in the body to produce heat for warmth and energy for movement.
1. Honey, sugar, candy, ice cream, and pastry are foods that are rich in sugar.
2. Bread, potatoes, rice, cereals, spaghetti, and macaroni are rich in starches.

3. When a person eats more carbohydrates than the body needs, the extra carbohydrates are changed into fat and stored in the body.
C. **Fats** are also used in the body to supply energy. Fats produce more than twice as much energy as carbohydrates, as compared with a portion of equal weight. Fats are also necessary for building cell membranes, in the synthesis of hormones, for protecting the body against injury, and for insulating the body against cold.
1. Butter, shortening, oils, salad dressing, bacon, and nuts are rich in fats.
2. Unused fats are stored as fat deposits throughout the body.
D. **Proteins** help to repair and build muscles and other tissues. In addition to nutrient proteins, there are other proteins: enzymes, antibodies,

Exploring Bones, Joints, Muscles, Ligaments, and Tendons

A. Examine an Animal Bone

Obtain the leg bone of a lamb, calf, or pig from a meat market. Ask for a bone that has the end of a joint still on it, and have the bone split lengthwise in half. Examine the joint and distinguish between the cartilage and the bone. Identify the ligaments holding the joint together. Look for bits of tendon tissue that serve to hold the muscles to the bone. Locate the yellow, fatty marrow in the center of the long part of the bone.

B. Determine the Composition of Bone

Put a chicken bone in a metal pie tin and heat it over a hot plate or in the oven until the bone is covered with a grayish-white ash. Let the bone cool, and note how light and brittle the bone is now. Point out that the heat has burned away all the animal matter in the bone, leaving only the mineral matter. If you have an accurate balance, weigh the bone both before and after heating, and determine the percentages of animal and mineral matter in the bone.

Soak the leg or thigh bone from a chicken in a jar of strong vinegar for four or five days. Remove the bone and wash it in water. Now bend the bone. The vinegar has dissolved and removed the mineral matter from the bone, leaving the soft, flexible animal matter. Although the bone still has its original shape and appearance, it will now be soft and flexible enough that you can very easily tie it into a knot.

C. Examine a Ligament

Obtain the joint from a calf, lamb, or pig shoulder from a meat market. Move the joint and examine the ligament that holds the ends of the bones together.

D. Examine X-Rays of Broken Bones

Obtain X-rays of broken bones and point out the different kinds of breaks. Point out the need for a cast or splint in helping a broken bone to mend. Discuss what might happen if an unqualified person moves a person who may have broken bones in an accident.

E. Locate Body Tendons

Have students move the fingers of both hands up and down rapidly, as if they were playing the piano. Notice the movement of the tendons on the back of the hand. The tendons are being moved by muscles in the forearm. Continue the movement for a full minute or two, and notice the forearm muscles becoming tired.

Place the fingers of the left hand on the inside of the elbow of the right hand, just above the joint, and flex the right forearm a few times. You will feel the tendons moving. Grasp the back of one ankle and move your foot up and down. The large tendon that you feel moving is the Achilles tendon.

F. Explore the Tendons of a Chicken's Foot

Obtain a chicken's foot from a meat market. Cut away some of the skin and flesh to expose the strong, white tendons. Pull the tendons one at a time. Some tendons will make the toes bend, whereas others will straighten the toes. Because the tendons are attached to muscles, note that the muscles only pull, and never push, regardless of how the toes move.

G. Observe how Voluntary Muscles Work

Double your arm and feel your "muscle." This "muscle" is the biceps muscle. Now grasp the outside of your upper arm near the elbow and straighten the arm. You will feel the pull of your triceps muscle. Note that muscles work in pairs. When you bend your arm, the biceps muscle contracts while the triceps muscle relaxes. When you straighten your arm, the biceps muscle relaxes and the triceps muscle contracts. Point out that when a muscle contracts, it becomes shorter and thicker, producing a pull on the bones.

Grip the back of your thigh and bend your leg at the knee, bringing your heel up toward the thigh. Note how the thigh muscle thickens as it contracts and pulls on the bone.

H. See the Action of Involuntary Muscles

Look in a mirror. Watch your eyelid close automatically. This demonstration shows that involuntary muslces are working. Now use voluntary muscles to close the eyelid yourself. This phenomenon can also be observed in the movement of your diaphragm. Note how involuntary muscles make the diaphragm move automatically as you breathe. Now use voluntary muscles to raise and lower the diaphragm muscles yourself.

I. Observe the Action of the Lip Muscles

Purse your lips tightly, just as if you were whistling, and feel the ring of muscles around the lips. Point out that these lip muscles are unusual in that they are attached to other muscles rather than to tendons or bones.

many hormones, and chemicals that help in blood clotting.

1. Proteins contain nitrogen, which the body needs to repair and grow cells, tissues, and organs.
2. Children need proteins for growing.
3. Lean meat, fish, eggs, milk, cheese, whole wheat, beans, peas, and nuts are foods rich in proteins.

E. **Minerals** are needed in small quantities for body growth, for the repair of body tissues, and for regulating some activities of the body.

1. **Calcium** and **phosphorus** are two important minerals. Together with oxygen they make the hard material found in the bones and teeth. Foods rich in calcium include milk, cheese, eggs, and leafy vegetables. Foods rich in phosphorous include liver, nuts, peas, whole-grain cereals, milk, cheese, eggs, and leafy vegetables.
2. **Iron** is another important mineral in the body. It is present in the chemical compound that makes the blood red, hemoglobin. Foods rich in iron include liver, lean meats, egg yolk, peas, and certain dried fruits such as prunes and raisins.
3. Another important mineral is **iodine**, present in a gland in the neck called the **thyroid gland,** an important regulator of body activities. The thyroid gland controls the burning of food in the body (it is a regulator of metabolism). Iodine is found in seafood, eggs, milk, and in iodized salt.
4. Other minerals considered vital to the human body include the following: **sodium** (for regulation of body pH and for the transmission of nerve impulses; found in bacon, butter, table salt, and vegetables), **potassium** (for muscle and nerve function, bone formation, and enzyme function; found in vegetables and bananas), **magnesium** (for muscle and nerve function, bone formation, and enzyme function; found in potatoes, fruits, whole-grain cereals, and vegetables), **fluorine** (for protection of teeth; found in treated water), **manganese** (enzyme activator; important in cartilage and bone growth; found in nuts, bran, leafy green vegetables), **copper** (for enzyme action and formation of red blood cells; found in liver, beans, whole-grain flour), and **sulfur** (component of insulin; builds hair, nails, and skin; found in nuts, dried fruits, barley, oatmeal, eggs, beans, and cheese).

F. **Vitamins** are complex chemical compounds that are found in foods. They control or regulate certain activities in the body and are important for body growth.

1. **Vitamin A** keeps the lining of the nose, throat, and eyelids healthy. A deficiency of vitamin A makes it difficult for people to see clearly in dim light or at night and can cut down the body's resistance to colds and other infections. A severe lack of vitamin A causes a serious eye disease that may result in blindness. This vitamin is also necessary for the growth of bones and teeth. Vitamin A is found in the oils of fish livers and in milk, butter, eggs, tomatoes, and nearly all yellow and green vegetables.
2. **Vitamin B_1** (also called **thiamine**) helps to control the digestion and use of carbohydrates in the body and plays an important role in the transmission of nerve impulses. A mild deficiency of vitamin B_1 causes loss of appetite, poor digestion, headaches, tiredness, and irritability. A severe lack of vitamin B_1 causes a serious nerve disorder called **beriberi.** Vitamin B_1 is found in whole grain foods and cereals, chicken and seafood, ham, milk, eggs, and leafy green vegetables.
3. **Vitamin B_2** (also called **riboflavin**) is needed to help the cells in the body function properly, to keep the skin healthy, and to help control the digestion and use of carbohydrates in the body. A deficiency in vitamin B_2 causes stunted growth, a disease of the mouth whereby the lips and tongue become cracked, and a scaly skin disease. Vitamin B_2 is found in green vegetables, meats, yeast, and eggs.
4. **Vitamin B_3** (also called **niacin**) helps the digestive and nervous systems function properly and is needed for the digestion and use of fats. A deficiency of vitamin B_3 causes a disease called **pellagra,** which results in skin rashes, a smooth tongue, digestive disturbances, mental disturbances, and paralysis. Vitamin B_3 is found in yeast, meats, liver, fish, whole-grain cereals, and nuts.
5. **Vitamin C** (also called **ascorbic acid**) regulates the use of calcium and phosphorus, helps build and maintain healthy teeth and gums, and functions in protein metabolism and in wound healing. A mild lack of vitamin C produces sore gums, soft teeth, and weak blood vessels. A severe lack results in a disease called **scurvy,** which causes bleeding gums, a swollen tongue, a tendency to bruise easily, bleeding around the bones, and sometimes teeth falling out. Vitamin C is found in citrus fruits, tomatoes,

green peppers, potatoes, and leafy green vegetables.

6. **Vitamin D** helps in the absorption of calcium and phosphorus in the digestive tract. A deficiency in vitamin D can result in soft bones and poor teeth. Children who do not get enough vitamin D may develop a disease called **rickets,** whereby the bones grow out of shape and "bow legs" or "knock knees" form. Vitamin D is found in shrimp, liver, egg yolk, and fortified milk. It is also produced by the skin when exposed to ultraviolet rays in sunlight.

7. **Vitamin K** (also called **menadione**) helps the blood to clot. Vitamin K is found in tomatoes and green vegetables. It is also produced by bacteria that live in the intestines.

8. **Vitamin E** is important to the formation of chromosome material and red blood cells. It is found in leafy vegetables, milk, and butter.

9. **Vitamin B_6**, important in the metabolism of fats, is found in salmon, yeast, tomatoes, corn, spinach, liver, yogurt, wheat bran, and whole-grain cereals.

10. **Vitamin B_{12}**, important in the development of red blood cells and in the metabolism of amino acids, is found in liver, milk, cheese, eggs, and meats.

11. **Pantothenic acid,** important in metabolism and in the synthesis of hormones, is found in milk, liver, yeast, green vegetables, and whole-grain cereals.

12. **Folic acid,** important in the synthesis of chromosome material and in the production of blood cells, is found in liver, leafy green vegetables, nuts, and orange juice.

13. **Biotin,** important in metabolism, is found in yeast, liver, and egg yolks.

G. **Water** is the most abundant substance in the body. It makes up 60 percent of red blood cells and 75 percent of muscle cells. It is so important to the body that a person will die more quickly from lack of water than from lack of any other nutrient. All cells in the body need water to function properly.

1. The body needs water to digest food, absorb it, carry it to all parts of the body, and get rid of the waste materials that are formed.

2. The body loses about 2.5 liters of water per day through exhalation during breathing, and through sweat and urine. Consequently, water must be replaced constantly.

3. There are three sources of water for the human body: most foods contain water; some water is formed when the food is burned in the body; and water is taken into the body as drinking water or in milk and other liquids.

II. THE AMOUNT OF ENERGY THE BODY NEEDS

A. The human body uses food to produce energy. The amount of energy a person needs depends on many factors. Larger people need more energy than smaller people. People who are very active need more energy than those who are less active. Young people use more energy than older people. Some people have bodies that use up energy more quickly than those of other people; that is, they have higher metabolic rates.

1. The amount of energy a food produces when it is metabolized in the body is measured in units called **calories.** Every bit of food you eat produces a certain number of calories. Some foods are richer in calories than others.

2. The calorie is defined as the amount of heat needed to raise the temperature of one milliliter (one gram, or about 0.03 ounce by weight) of water 1 degree Celsius.

3. The amount of heat energy available in foods is represented in Calories, which is *calories* spelled with a capital C. A Calorie (spelled with a capital C) is equal to 1,000 (small *c*) calories.

4. If a person takes in more Calories a day than the body can use, the extra energy is stored in the body as fat, and the person gains weight. If a person takes in fewer Calories a day than the body needs, the body uses the stored fat, and the person loses weight.

III. THE BASIC FOOD GROUPS

A. A balanced diet is one that gives the body all the nutrients it needs and in the proper amounts.

1. About four sixths of the diet should be carbohydrates, one sixth fats, and one sixth proteins.

2. The diet should also contain the proper amounts of minerals and vitamins the body needs.

B. Food experts have divided the foods we need to keep healthy into five food groups. A person who eats the proper amounts of food from each food group every day has a balanced diet (see Exploratory Activity 1).

C. A balanced diet is helpful in many ways.

1. It helps a person grow normally.

2. It helps keep the body free of excessive and harmful fat.

3. It gives the body the energy it needs.

THE DIGESTIVE SYSTEM

I. DIGESTION

   A. The changing of foods into a simpler, dissolved form that can enter and be used by the cells is called **digestion.**

     1. For food to be used by the body, it must enter the bloodstream, where it is carried to all the cells in the body.

     2. The food we eat is too complicated, and in pieces too large, to be sent directly into the bloodstream for use by the cells.

     3. Moreover, some of the foods we eat do not dissolve in water and could not enter the cells even if it reached the cells.

     4. Therefore, the foods have to be broken down, simplified, and changed into dissolved forms that the cells can use.

     5. Digestion is carried on by special organs that make up the digestive system in the body.

     6. There are two parts to the digestive system: the **alimentary canal** and the **digestive glands.**

   B. The **alimentary canal** is the food tube, or digestive tract or passageway, through which the food moves in the body.

     1. About 9 meters long (nearly 30 ft), it includes all the organs that act on the food and digest it, the **mouth, throat** or pharynx, gullet or **esophagus, stomach, small intestine, large intestine, rectum,** and **anus.**

   C. The digestive glands include the **salivary glands, the liver, the pancreas,** the **gastric glands** of the stomach, and the **intestinal glands** of the small intestine.

     1. These glands give off juices that enter the alimentary canal through small tubes, called ducts.

     2. These juices contain powerful chemicals, called **enzymes,** that act on the foods and break them up into simpler, dissolved forms, which can then be digested.

II. DIGESTION IN THE MOUTH

   A. The function of the mouth is to start the preparation of food for digestion.

   B. The teeth break up the food into smaller pieces.

     1. There are different kinds of teeth in the mouth.

     2. A child first gets a temporary set of 20 baby teeth, 10 in each jaw.

     3. As the jaws grow larger, the child loses these baby teeth and grows a permanent set of 32 teeth, 16 in each jaw.

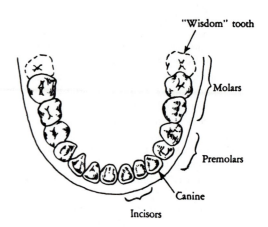

FIGURE 15.1   Diagram of the teeth in a jaw.

     4. The four flat, sharp-edged front teeth in each jaw are called **incisors** and are used for biting and cutting (see Figure 15.1).

     5. The two long, pointed teeth, one on each side of the incisors, are called **canine** teeth and are used for tearing.

     6. On each side of the canine teeth are two **premolars** and three **molars** (10 in each jaw), which have large surfaces and are used for grinding and chewing.

   C. Most of the tooth is made of a hard, bonelike material, called **dentine.**

     1. The part of the tooth beyond the gum is called the **crown** and is covered with a very hard white material, called **enamel.**

     2. The root of the tooth fits into a socket in the jawbone.

     3. Incisor and canine teeth usually have one root, and premolar and molar teeth have two, three, or even four roots.

     4. Blood vessels and nerves run from the root into the hollow center of the tooth.

   D. While food is being chewed, it is mixed with a liquid called **saliva.**

     1. Saliva comes from three pairs of **salivary glands,** located in the sides of the face and under the jaw.

     2. Saliva moistens and softens the food, making it easier to swallow.

     3. Saliva also contains an enzyme (amylase) that digests starch, changing it into sugars that can dissolve in water.

DEMONSTRATION 15.5
Digestion in the Mouth

Have the students chew a soda cracker or saltine and note how the cracker tastes sweeter after it has been chewed for some time and the saliva has had a chance to act on the starch in the cracker. Place some of this chewed cracker-saliva mixture in a test tube and test with Benedict's solution (available from a pharmacy or scientific supply house) for the presence of simple sugars. As a control, test some saliva alone for the presence of simple sugars.

E. The tongue helps in chewing the food by keeping it between the teeth, and helps in swallowing by pushing the food to the back of the mouth.

F. Food stays in the mouth for a short time, is swallowed, and then is moved by muscles down the throat and esophagus into the stomach.
1. The action of involuntary muscles moving food in one direction down the esophagus is called **peristalsis.**

III. Digestion in the Stomach

A. The stomach is a pear-shaped pouch located on the left side of the body under the lower ribs.
1. It is elastic and can expand to hold large amounts of food.
2. The stomach's main function is to hold food while it is being prepared for digestion in the small intestine.
3. Food usually stays in the stomach for two to four hours.

B. The lining of the stomach has many glands, called **gastric glands**.
1. These glands secrete **gastric juice**, which flows through tiny tubes (ducts) into the stomach where it mixes with food.
2. Gastric juice contains an enzyme (pepsin) that breaks some proteins down into simpler materials.
3. Gastric juice also contains a strong acid, called **hydrochloric acid,** that dissolves minerals in the food and kills many bacteria that enter the stomach with the food.

C. To prevent the stomach from digesting itself, which it does to some extent, the lining of the stomach secretes a protective layer of mucus.
1. Stomach lining cells that are damaged by digestion are constantly regenerated or replaced with new cells.

D. The stomach has powerful muscles that keep contracting and relaxing, churning the food.
1. This churning action breaks the food into small pieces and mixes these tiny pieces thoroughly with the gastric juice.

E. The food then passes into the small intestine, a little at a time, through a valve at the intestinal end, which opens and closes regularly.
1. By the time the digested food leaves the stomach and enters the small intestine, it is in the form of a thin liquid.

IV. Digestion in the Small Intestine

A. The small intestine is the main organ for digesting food in the body. It is about 6 meters (20 ft) long and 2 centimeters (1 in) in diameter.
1. Because it is so long, it coils back and forth many times inside the body.
2. It is called "small" because of its small diameter.

B. Food stays in the small intestine much longer than in the stomach. While food is in the small intestine, juices from three digestive glands pour into the small intestine: **intestinal juice, pancreatic juice,** and **bile.**
1. Intestinal juice is produced by glands in the lining of the small intestine.
2. Pancreatic juice is produced by the pancreas, a long gland that lies just behind the stomach. The juice flows through a duct (tube) into the upper end of the small intestine, called the **duodenum.**
3. Bile is a brownish green liquid produced in the liver, a large gland located in the upper right part of the abdomen.
4. From the liver, bile flows into a sac, called the **gallbladder,** where it is stored until needed.
5. When food leaves the stomach and enters the small intestine, the bile flows into the bile duct, which joins with the pancreatic duct just as they both reach the duodenum.
6. Bile and pancreatic juice enter the small intestine at the same time.
7. An enzyme in bile breaks the fat into simpler materials, and at the same time the bile separates the fat into tiny droplets, which can be more easily attacked by enzymes from the pancreatic juice.

8. Both pancreatic and intestinal juices have many enzymes that together digest carbohydrates, fats, and proteins, changing them into simpler dissolved forms that can be used by the cells in the body.
C. After food has been digested in the small intestine, it is absorbed through the walls of the small intestine into the bloodstream.
   1. The inside of the small intestine has many ridges and fingerlike projections or bulges, called **villi**, which absorb the simple, dissolved forms of digested food.
   2. The ridges and villi contain blood vessels that absorb the dissolved food, and the bloodstream carries the food away to cells in all parts of the body.
   3. **Osmosis** is the movement of water molecules through a cell membrane, either out of a cell or into a cell. The movement of dissolved materials into or out of a cell (any living cell) is partly due to this process of osmosis. Water will diffuse through a cell membrane from an area of higher water concentration to an area of lower water concentration. Sometimes materials dissolved in the water pass through the membrane with the water. This process, which requires no consumption of cellular energy, is referred to as **passive transport.**
   4. For other nutrients, such as minerals, to move across a cell membrane, the cell may have to expend energy. This is **active transport.** In this process a cell protein binds with the particle of the substance to be transported, and chemical energy from the cell is then used to change the shape of the proteins

so that the particle to be moved is released on the other side of the cell membrane. Once the particle is released, the protein's original shape is restored. Thus, a substance can be transported into or out of a cell, moving from an area where there is less of the substance (a lesser concentration) to a region where there is more of it (greater concentration).
   5. The process of changing digested food into cellular material is called **assimilation.**

V. THE LARGE INTESTINE
A. The large intestine, about 1.5 meters (5 ft) long and 6.5 centimeters (2.5 in) in diameter, begins below the small intestine.
B. Food that cannot be digested or used by the body passes from the small intestine into the large intestine as waste material.
C. Waste materials also contain large amounts of bacteria that normally live in the large intestine.
D. Initially, the waste materials are quite watery.
   1. They pass through the large intestine very slowly while the water is absorbed back into the bloodstream through the walls of the large intestine.
   2. This removal of the water gives the waste material a more solid form, called **feces.**
E. The feces pass into the lower part of the large intestine, called the rectum, where they are temporarily stored, for 18 to 24 hours, and then out through an opening, called the anus. This act of eliminating feces is called **defecation.**
F. The entire journey from the time food enters the mouth until defecation of waste materials takes from 24 to 33 hours.

THE CIRCULATORY (CARDIOVASCULAR) SYSTEM

I. THE FUNCTION OF THE CIRCULATORY SYSTEM
A. The circulatory system, made up of the heart, blood, and blood vessels, has four main functions.
   1. It carries digested and dissolved food to the cells of the body.
   2. It brings oxygen to the cells for burning the food and producing heat and energy.
   3. It takes away the waste materials produced by the cells and carries the materials to organs that remove them from the body.
   4. It carries germ-fighting blood cells.

II. THE BLOOD
A. Blood is a liquid tissue.
B. There are about 5 liters (6 qt) of blood in the human body.
C. The liquid part of blood is called **plasma**.
   1. Plasma is mostly water with salts, such as table salt (sodium chloride) and calcium salts, dissolved in it.
   2. It contains a special protein, called **fibrinogen,** which helps the blood clot when there is an injury to the body and danger of losing blood from that injury.

DEMONSTRATION 15.6
Blood

(Caution: This is a teacher demonstration only. Students should not handle body fluids, such as blood, without wearing disposable gloves.)

Wash your hands thoroughly and then rub a piece of cotton dipped in alcohol over one fingertip. Prick the fingertip with a sterilized needle and squeeze out a drop of blood. Press the blood against a clean microscope slide and cover with a cover glass. Let students observe your blood under the high power of a microscope. They will see many disc-shaped red blood cells and perhaps one or two of the larger white cells. Note that the red blood cells have no nuclei.

---

    3. It contains special materials, called antibodies, which fight disease.

    4. It contains special materials, called **hormones,** which are given off by ductless (tubeless) glands in the body and help control the activities of the body.

    5. Plasma also brings dissolved food particles to the cells and carries away waste materials.

D. There are three kinds of solid materials in blood: red cells (or red corpuscles), white cells (or white corpuscles), and platelets.

E. The **red blood cells** are the most numerous cells in the body, looking from a side view something like dumbbells.

    1. They look like very small discs that have had both sides pushed in.

    2. Red cells have no nucleus.

    3. They contain an iron compound, called **hemoglobin,** which gives them their red color.

    4. Red cells pick up oxygen from the lungs and carry it to the cells in the body.

    5. The cells use the oxygen to burn food, and carbon dioxide is produced as a waste material.

    6. The red cells pick up the carbon dioxide and carry it to the lungs, where the carbon dioxide is given off.

F. **White blood cells** are larger than red cells, but are less numerous: there is about one white cell to every 600 red cells.

    1. White blood cells are clear, colorless, and have no special shape, but they do have a nucleus.

    2. They can leave the walls of the blood vessels and move around among the cells in the body.

    3. Their purpose is to destroy bacteria and other disease-causing germs.

G. **Platelets** are much smaller than the red blood cells, and they are not cells.

    1. They are irregularly shaped and colorless.

    2. Their function is to help blood clot when the body is injured and bleeds.

    3. Clotting helps prevent the body from losing too much blood and thus bleeding to death.

    4. When a blood vessel breaks and bleeds, platelets stick to the edges of the wound and begin to contract.

    5. Platelets give off a chemical that unites with the calcium salts and fibrinogen in the plasma to form threadlike fibers.

    6. The fibers form a net that slows the flow of blood, traps the corpuscles, and forms a clot that prevents the blood from escaping.

H. The normal temperature of an adult's blood is about 37° Celsius (98.6° F).

    1. Some persons have a normal temperature a little above or below this average.

    2. When a person is ill, the blood temperature is usually elevated.

I. Harmful bacteria, disease germs, and worn-out blood cells in the blood are filtered and removed by the **liver** and the **spleen.**

    1. The liver is a large organ, located in the upper right part of the abdomen.

    2. The spleen is much smaller and is located in the upper left part of the abdomen behind the stomach.

    3. The spleen also stores a reserve of red blood cells.

III. The Blood Vessels

A. The blood moves throughout the body in closed tubes called blood vessels. There are three kinds of blood vessels in the body: arteries, veins, and capillaries.

B. **Arteries** are blood vessels that carry blood away from the heart.

    1. A large artery leaves the heart and keeps branching into smaller and smaller arteries (called arterioles) that spread throughout the body.

    2. The smallest branches lead to every part of the body.

DEMONSTRATION 15.7

Valves in the Veins

Ask students to stand; then ask each to let an arm hang down until the large veins on the hand become quite visible. Give the following instructions: Make a fist, place a fingertip on one vein, and push firmly downward toward the knuckles. While holding the finger in place, note how

smooth the vein becomes as your finger presses on the valve and prevents blood from flowing into that portion of the vein. Now take away your finger. The vein will fill up with blood again.

---

    3. The walls of arteries are made of involuntary muscle, which contracts much in the same manner as the heart muscle contracts.

C. **Veins** are blood vessels that carry blood back to the heart.
    1. There are tiny veins (called venules) throughout the body.
    2. These tiny veins come together, joining to form larger and larger veins, until a large vein that enters the heart is formed.
    3. Veins are wider than arteries, and their walls are thinner and less elastic, so the flow of blood in the veins is slower than the flow in the arteries.
    4. The larger veins have cuplike valves that keep the blood from flowing backward.
    5. Veins do not contract as do the large arteries.

D. **Capillaries** are very tiny blood vessels connecting the smallest arteries (arterioles) and the smallest veins (venules).
    1. Some are so small that blood cells must go through them in single file.
    2. Blood from the smallest arteries (arterioles) flows into the capillaries, travels through the capillaries, and then flows into the smallest veins (venules).
    3. All cells in the body are adjacent to a capillary.
    4. Capillaries are the blood vessels that actually supply the cells of the body with the materials they need.
    5. The walls of the capillaries are so thin that molecules of materials in the blood can pass into the cells, and molecules of materials in the cells can pass into the blood of the capillaries.
    6. The blood gives the cells food, oxygen, and minerals, whereas the cell gives the blood carbon dioxide and other waste materials.

IV. THE HEART

A. The heart is a strong muscle, shaped like a pear and about as big as a human fist.

B. It slants downward and is located to the left of the middle of the chest.

C. It acts as a pump by contracting and relaxing.
    1. When it contracts, blood is pumped out of it into the arteries, which also contract somewhat.
    2. When it relaxes, blood flows into it from the veins.

D. The heart pumps the blood, which moves through blood vessels, to every part of the body and back again in about 30 seconds.

E. The heart has two sides: a right side and a left side.
    1. The two sides are completely separated by a wall called the **septum.**
    2. Each side pumps blood separately from the other.
    3. The blood in the two sides does not mix while it is in the heart.

F. The heart is also divided into four chambers, or compartments.
    1. The top two chambers are called **atria,** and the bottom two chambers are called **ventricles.**
    2. Thus the heart has a right atria and a left atria at the top, separated from each other by the septum, and a right ventricle and a left ventricle at the bottom, also separated by the septum.
    3. The atria receive blood from the veins in the body and pump it down into the ventricles.
    4. The ventricles pump the blood into the arteries in the body.
    5. Both atria contract or pump at the same time, followed quickly by both ventricles contracting or pumping at the same time.

G. The heart has valves that prevent the blood from flowing back into the atria when the ventricles are contracting.
    1. There is a flap of connective tissue between the opening of the right atrium and right ventricle, and between the opening of the left atrium and left ventricle.

DEMONSTRATION 15.8
Examine an Animal Heart

Obtain the heart of a calf, sheep, or pig from a meat market. Pare away any fatty material present, and note how muscular the heart walls are. Try to identify the ventricles and atria before you begin to cut the heart open. Make incisions on either side of the lower narrow end of the wall. When you enter the ventricle, cut away more material so that you may see the cavities more clearly. Note how thick the walls are, especially those of the left ventricle.

Use a probe to find the main artery leading from the left ventricle to the body, and the pulmonary artery leading from the right ventricle to the lungs. Also probe for the flabbier veins entering the right and left atria. Look for the valves between the atria and ventricles. Slit the artery walls lengthwise and look for the valves that prevent blood from flowing back into the heart.

2. These flaps act like valves, in that they can move only one way.
3. When an atrium contracts, the flap is pushed aside, allowing the blood to move down into the ventricle.
4. When a ventricle contracts, the flap is pushed upward and closes the opening so that the blood cannot flow up into the atrium.
H. The large arteries also have valves, located where the arteries leave the heart.
   1. These valves are made of tissue and are pushed aside when the blood leaves the heart and goes through the arteries.
   2. When the blood tries to flow back into the heart, it pushes the valve shut, and this action stops the blood from flowing back.
I. Veins also have valves located all through the body, which prevent the blood from flowing back, and in this way force the blood to move toward the heart.
J. The sound of the heart beating is made by the closing of the valves between the atria and ventricles of the heart and by the closing of valves in the large arteries near the heart.
K. The contracting of the heart also makes the tip of the heart move back and forth. You can feel the tip beating.
L. A **pulse** is the beat that can be felt in the arteries every time the heart beats.
   1. The surge of blood through the arteries makes the artery walls expand and also produce a beat.
   2. This pulse can be felt by placing the finger over an artery in the wrist or neck.
   3. By counting the number of pulse beats in a minute, we can find out how fast the heart is beating, or contracting.

V. THE CIRCULATION OF THE BLOOD
   A. There are really two large circulatory systems in the body, connected to and controlled by the heart.
      1. In one system (called pulmonary circulation) the blood flows from the heart to the lungs and returns.
      2. In the other system (called systemic circulation) the blood flows from the heart through the body and returns.
   B. In the system that sends blood to the lungs, blood coming from all over the body enters the right atrium of the heart.
      1. The right atrium pumps the blood down to the right ventricle.
      2. The right ventricle then pumps the blood to the lungs.
      3. In this system the blood contains carbon dioxide, and when the blood is sent to the lungs, it gives up the carbon dioxide and picks up oxygen.
   C. In the system that sends blood to the body, blood coming from the lungs enters the left atrium of the heart.
      1. The left atrium pumps the blood down to the left ventricle.
      2. The left ventricle then pumps the blood to the body.
      3. In this system the blood brings fresh oxygen to the cells in the body, gives up the oxygen to the cells, and at the same time picks up carbon dioxide, which it brings back to the heart.
   D. Each ventricle has one artery leading from it.
      1. The artery leading to the lungs branches at about 1 inch above the heart, each branch going to one of the lungs.

DEMONSTRATION 15.9
Exploring Heartbeat and Pulse Rate

A. Explore with a Stethoscope

Make a stethoscope from three funnels, a glass Y-tube or T-tube, and two long plus one short pieces of rubber or plastic tubing (Figure 15.2). Let the students take turns listening to heartbeats. Compare the heartbeats when they are quiet with their heartbeats after they have jumped up and down 15 to 20 times or exercised vigorously.

B. Explore Your Pulse

Using the first two fingers of the right hand, feel for the pulse on the left hand at the base of the thumb where the left hand joins the wrist (Figure 15.3). Count the number of pulse beats in 1 minute. Now jump up and down 15 to 20 times, or exercise vigorously, and take your pulse beat for 1 minute again. Note how much stronger and faster the pulse beat has become.

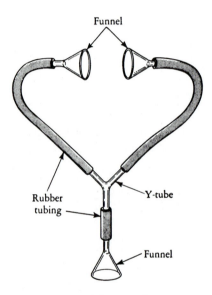

FIGURE 15.2   A homemade stethoscope.

FIGURE 15.3   Taking a pulse beat.

---

  2. The other large artery passes to various parts of the body, with branches going to the brain, arms, rib areas, body organs, and legs.
 E. More than one vein comes back to the atria.
  1. Four veins return the blood from the lungs to the left atrium.
  2. Two veins return blood from the body, one vein coming from the head and arms, and the other vein coming from the lower part of the body.
 F. In each system the large arteries branching again and again into smaller arteries and finally lead into capillaries; then the capillaries lead into small veins that come together again and again to form the large veins.

VI. LYMPH
 A. As blood flows through the capillaries, some of the plasma passes through the thin capillary walls and fills the spaces between the cells of the body.
  1. This liquid, called **lymph,** is the clear liquid that fills blisters and appears when the skin is scraped and bruised.
 B. Lymph contains digested food, water, salts, and other materials.
 C. The lymph bathes the cells and gives them food, and the cells give the lymph the waste products that have been formed in the cells.
 D. The lymph returns to the bloodstream through special lymph vessels.

1. The lymph collects in tiny tubes that join again and again to form larger tubes.
2. These lymph vessels have valves, just as veins do.
3. Exercise moves the lymph through the lymph vessels.
4. The lymph finally collects in two large vessels that open into two large veins just above the heart.

E. Occasionally, the lymph vessels enlarge to form swellings called **lymph nodes.**
   1. In the lymph nodes the lymph tubes break up into many smaller tubes again.
   2. The nodes contain large numbers of special white blood cells that kill bacteria and other disease germs that may have entered the lymph from the cells in the body.
   3. The function of the lymph nodes, then, is to filter and purify the lymph before it returns to the blood.
   4. There are many lymph nodes concentrated in the neck, armpit, and groin.
   5. These lymph nodes may swell and become painful when there is an infection in the part of the body where the nodes are located.

THE RESPIRATORY SYSTEM

I. PARTS OF THE RESPIRATORY SYSTEM

A. The breakdown of carbohydrates in the cells that produces energy is called **respiration.** In respiration the cells of the body take in oxygen, use the oxygen to burn the digested food and produce heat and energy, and then give off carbon dioxide.

B. The function of the respiratory system is to bring oxygen into the body and to get rid of waste carbon dioxide.

C. The parts of the respiratory system include the **nose** and nasal passages, the throat or **pharynx,** the windpipe or **trachea,** the voice box or **larynx,** the **bronchi,** the **bronchial tubes,** and the **lungs.**

D. Air enters the nose through two nostrils, which are separated by a wall called the septum.

E. The air then passes through the nasal passages, which are spaces that lie above the mouth.
   1. In the nostrils and the front part of the nasal passages are hairs that trap dust and germs.
   2. In the rear part of the nasal passages are hairlike projections, called **cilia,** which are always beating back and forth.
   3. The cilia trap dust and other materials and carry them toward the mouth, where they are either swallowed or coughed up.
   4. The nasal passages have a soft lining, which gives off a liquid called **mucus,** that also helps trap dust and germs.
   5. As the air passes through the nasal passages, it becomes warm and moist.

F. The air passes from the nasal passages to the throat, or pharynx.

G. In the back of the throat are two tubes. The gullet, or esophagus, leads to the stomach. The windpipe, or trachea, which is in front of the esophagus, leads to the lungs.

H. At the top of the windpipe is a flap or lid of tissue called the **epiglottis.**
   1. The epiglottis covers and closes the windpipe when food and water are being swallowed because otherwise the food and water would go down the windpipe and cause choking.
   2. The epiglottis is raised during breathing, allowing air to enter the windpipe freely.

I. At the top of the windpipe is the voice box, or larynx. The voice box, which is really like a box, is made of cartilage.
   1. The "Adam's apple" is a strip of cartilage that sticks out in front of the voice box.
   2. Inside the voice box are two strips of elastic tissue called the vocal cords. Tiny muscles can stretch these vocal cords and make them tight.
   3. When the vocal cords are tight and air passes between them, they vibrate, thereby producing sound.
   4. The tighter the vocal cords, the faster the cords vibrate and the higher is the pitch of the sound produced. The looser the vocal cords, the slower they vibrate, and the lower the pitch of the sound.
   5. Men have larger voice boxes than women and their vocal cords are longer and thicker, so their vocal cords vibrate more slowly and their voices are lower.

J. This arrangement of the trachea, esophagus, and larnyx in humans is different from that of any other animal or primate, and this difference is what allowed humans to develop speech. It is also this particular arrangement that disallows human to speak, breathe, and eat (or drink) simultaneously (or causes them to choke when trying to do so).

K. The bottom of the windpipe divides into two branches, called bronchi, and each branch enters one of the lungs. Each bronchus divides into smaller branches called bronchial tubes.

1. The bronchial tubes branch again and again until the smallest tubes end in clusters of little air sacs called **alveoli** (plural for *alveolus*). The alveoli look like tiny clusters of grapes. Each lung is one great mass of these clusters of air sacs.

II. HOW WE BREATHE

A. Breathing is different from respiration.

1. Breathing is the mechanical process of getting air containing oxygen into the lungs and getting air containing carbon dioxide out of the lungs. Although breathing is a function of what is known as our "respiratory system," it is only one function.

2. The actual exchange of these two gases takes place at the cellular level. The chemical process of breaking down food to release energy is called **cellular respiration** (discussed in the section that follows).

3. What is commonly referred to as *artificial respiration* would be more correctly called *artificial breathing*.

B. Many persons think that in breathing the lungs draw in air, expand, and make the chest bulge, but this is not true.

1. Air is breathed in (inhaled) by being forced into the lungs because of changes in the size of the chest cavity and changes in the air pressure of the chest cavity.

2. The **diaphragm**, a strong sheet of muscle between the chest and the abdomen, plays an important function in breathing.

3. When muscles in the diaphragm contract, the diaphragm is pulled downward.

4. At the same time, the rib muscles contract and lift the ribs upward and outward.

5. This action of the diaphragm and ribs increases the size of the chest cavity, and the elastic lungs expand and become larger.

6. The increased lung size reduces the pressure of the air already in the lungs.

7. The air outside the body now exerts greater pressure than the air inside the lungs, and so it rushes into the nose, nasal passage, windpipe, and lungs to these areas of lesser pressure.

C. Air is breathed out (exhaled) when the chest cavity becomes smaller.

1. The muscles in the diaphragm relax, and the diaphragm moves upward again.

2. The muscles in the ribs relax, and the ribs move downward and inward.

3. The chest cavity now becomes smaller, making the lungs smaller, so that air is forced out of the lungs and the body.

D. Breathing is an activity of the body that can take place involuntarily or voluntarily. In involuntary breathing, nerves in the brain control the muscles of the diaphragm and the ribs so that breathing takes place automatically. Although we can hold our breath and stop breathing, we can not do it for very long before the involuntary action takes over and we breathe again.

III. THE PROCESS OF GAS EXCHANGE

A. The air sacs (alveoli) in the lungs are surrounded by millions of capillaries.

B. The oxygen that comes with the air into the lungs passes through the thin walls of the air sacs and through the thin walls of the capillaries into the blood.

C. Red blood cells pick up the oxygen by osmotic diffusion of oxygen into the cells, and the blood becomes bright red because of the oxygenated hemoglobin.

D. The blood passes from the lungs to the heart, which pumps it through the arteries and capillaries to every part of the body.

E. The cells in the body use the oxygen to burn nutrients (or glucose), producing heat and energy and giving off carbon dioxide.

1. The chemical process of breaking down food to release energy is called **cellular respiration**.

2. Oxygen is required for this process to occur; oxygen is the catalyst that speeds up the chemical reaction.

3. The breakdown of a carbohydrate, for example, in the presence of oxygen, is shown by the following chemical equation:

$$O_2 + CH_2O \rightarrow H_2O + CO_2 + energy.$$

4. The products of this breakdown of a carbohydrate are water, carbon dioxide, and energy.

5. The energy is in the form of heat energy and chemical energy; the chemical energy is a compound called **adenosine triphosphate (ATP)**.

6. Some water is released with the exhaled air, and some of it is recycled by the blood and used elsewhere in the body.

7. The rate at which cellular respiration occurs is referred to as the **metabolic rate**. It is de-

DEMONSTRATION 15.9
Exploring the Respiratory System

A. Examining Animal Lung Tissue

Obtain a portion of the lung of a calf, sheep, or pig from a meat market. Note how spongy the lung tissue is. Examine a section of this lung tissue under the low power of a microscope and locate a cluster of the many air sacs that are found throughout the tissue. Note that each air sac is surrounded by a fleshy wall. Change to the high power of the microscope, and you will be able to see capillaries in the wall.

B. Exploring How We Breathe

Obtain a lamp chimney and a one-hole rubber stopper to fit the top opening of the chimney. Insert a glass or plastic tube through the hole of the stopper. Use a rubber band to fasten a small rubber balloon to the bottom end of the glass tubing, then insert the stopper into the top of the chimney (Figure 15.4). Cut a piece of rubber from a large rubber balloon and use a rubber band to fasten this piece of rubber firmly to the bottom opening of the chimney. The chimney will represent the chest cavity, the balloon will represent one of your lungs, and the large piece of rubber will represent your diaphragm.

Pull the piece of rubber (diaphragm) downward. The air in the chimney (chest cavity) expands, reducing the air pressure in the chimney. Air from outside the chimney is forced in, inflating the balloon (lung). Now push the piece of rubber (diaphragm) upward. The air in the chimney (chest cavity) is compressed and contracts, increasing the air pressure in the chimney. Air will be forced out of the chimney through the glass tubing, causing the balloon (lung) to deflate. Repeat this procedure several times to simulate the steady action of inhaling and exhaling.

C. Exploring the Effect of Exercise on the Rate of Breathing

Have one student place a hand on another student's chest and count the number of times the student is breathing in 1 minute. Let one inhalation and one exhalation together count as just one breath. Now have the second student jump up and down or exercise until he or she is breathing quite heavily; then let the first student count the number of breaths in 1 minute again.

FIGURE 15.4   Simulating the operation of the diaphragm and lungs during breathing.

fined as the amount of energy (Calories) burned per hour per body surface area. Metabolic rate is affected by gender (males have a higher rate than females), age (rate decreases with age), and level of activity.

8. The **basal metabolic rate** (BMR) is a person's metabolic rate when at rest.

F. The red blood cells pick up the carbon dioxide, and the blood becomes dark red.

G. The blood passes through the capillaries and veins back to the heart.

H. The heart sends the blood containing the carbon dioxide to the lungs.

DEMONSTRATION 15.10
Products of Respiration

A. Excretion of Carbon Dioxide

Obtain some limewater from a drugstore and pour a little into a test tube. Have one or all of the students bubble the limewater with a soda straw until the limewater becomes milky, showing the presence of carbon dioxide. The carbon dioxide comes from the air inside the students' lungs.

B. Excretion of Mineral Salts

Have the students lick their wrists after they return from a recess period where they have been playing actively. Point out that the salty taste is caused by the presence of mineral salts, which were dissolved in their perspiration and were left behind when the perspiration evaporated.

I. In the lungs the carbon dioxide leaves the blood by passing through the thin walls of the capillaries and through the thin walls of the air sacs into the lungs.

J. The air containing carbon dioxide is forced out of the lungs, and fresh air containing oxygen is forced in the lungs.

K. This action—getting oxygen into the body, using oxygen to produce heat and energy, and getting waste carbon dioxide out of the body—goes on all the time.

L. People **yawn** when the brain has received the message that the carbon dioxide content of the blood is getting too high. A yawn, then, is the body's way of inhaling a larger than normal quantity of fresh air to exchange oxygen for the carbon dioxide.

M. At higher altitudes there is less oxygen than there is at sea level. To compensate, people who live at very high altitudes have larger lungs and more red blood cells per cubic centimeter of blood.

IV. THE CELL ENERGY CYCLE

A. Cells get the energy to do work through a special energy process.

B. All cells—plant, animal, and human—contain high-energy ATP (adenosine triphosphate) molecules that result from the breakdown of food.

C. The cell breaks the ATP down into ADP (adenosine diphosphate) and P (phosphate), and energy is given off for the cell to do its work.

D. The ATP is replenished when the cell receives glucose (a simple sugar) from digested food.
   1. The glucose combines with oxygen, giving off energy.
   2. This energy changes ADP and P back into ATP again.

E. Thus there is a continuous cycle, called the **cell energy cycle**, whereby ATP is broken down into ADP and P to provide energy, then energy obtained from glucose and oxygen changes the ADP and P back to ATP again.

THE EXCRETORY SYSTEM

I. EXCRETION

A. The removal of waste materials from the body is called **excretion**.

B. The human body produces various kinds of waste materials.
   1. Carbon dioxide and water, produced by the cells, are waste materials, although some of the water may be used elsewhere in the body.
   2. The used digestive juices that remain after digestion are waste materials.
   3. When cells, tissues, and muscles wear out or break down, mineral salts and nitrogen compounds are formed as waste materials.
   4. Undigested and unused food are waste materials.

II. HOW WASTE MATERIALS ARE REMOVED

A. The body gets rid of the various waste materials in different ways.
   1. The lungs give off carbon dioxide and some water in the form of water vapor.
   2. The skin gives off perspiration, which contains water and dissolved mineral salts.
   3. Solid undigested wastes are passed through the digestive tract and eliminated as feces during defecation.
   4. Some liquid and dissolved wastes are eliminated by way of the kidneys and the urinary tract.

B. The **kidneys** play an important part in the removal of waste materials.

DEMONSTRATION 15.11

Examine an Animal's Kidney

Obtain the kidney of a calf, sheep, or pig from a meat market. Note the size and shape of the kidney. Observe where a large artery and a large vein enter the kidney. Cut the kidney lengthwise in half with a sharp knife. Note the many tubes in the tissue near the surface of the kidney and the large chamber where the urine collects. Point out that the urine leaves this chamber and travels through a duct that empties into the bladder.

1. The kidneys are two dark red, bean-shaped organs located in the lower part of the back.
2. Each kidney is packed with millions of tiny tubes, called **nephrons,** which are the functioning filtering units of kidneys.
3. These nephrons filter from the blood such waste materials as mineral salts and protein compounds.
4. These wastes, together with excess water, form a liquid called **urine**.
5. The urine flows from each kidney through a tube, called a **ureter**, to a storage organ called the **urinary bladder**.
6. From the urinary bladder urine passes out of the body through a tube called the **urethra**, located in the penis of males and in front of the vagina in females.

THE NERVOUS SYSTEM

I. THE FUNCTION AND PARTS OF THE NERVOUS SYSTEM

   A. The nervous system has several functions. It controls the action of the muscles and other tissues; it controls the actions of the organs, sensations such as smell, taste, touch, pressure, sight, hearing, heat, cold, and pain; it controls thinking, learning, memory, and many human behaviors.

   B. The central part of the nervous system consists of the brain and the spinal cord.

   C. The rest of the nervous system is made up of **nerves**, which spread out from the brain and spinal cord through the body.

II. THE BRAIN

   A. The brain, located inside the skull, is the most highly specialized organ in the human body. It is the control center of the body, receiving messages from all parts of the body and sending out orders in return. It has a wrinkled appearance because its surface has many folds. There are three main parts to the brain: the cerebrum, the cerebellum, and the medulla.

   B. The **cerebrum,** the largest part of the brain, located at the front and top, is made up of two halves that are firmly joined together. The cerebrum has many functions.

     1. It is the part of the brain that controls thinking, reasoning, learning, memory, and imagination.

     2. It receives messages from the sense organs and recognizes them as smell, taste, touch, pressure, sight, hearing, heat, cold, and pain.

     3. It also controls the voluntary movement of the muscles in the body.

     4. The left side of the cerebrum controls movement of the right side of the body, and the right side of the cerebrum controls movement of the left side of the body.

   C. The much smaller **cerebellum** is located below and behind the cerebrum. It coordinates the movements of the muscles so that they operate together smoothly, as in walking. It also helps the body to keep its sense of balance.

   D. The **medulla** is located at the bottom of the brain, where it joins the top of the spinal cord. It controls the operation of the involuntary muscles in the body. This means that it controls such vital functions as heart action, breathing, digestion, coughing, and sneezing.

III. THE SPINAL CORD

   A. Connecting with the brain's medulla, the spinal cord is a long rod of nerve tissue going down almost the whole length of the backbone.

   B. Thirty-one pairs of nerves branch off the spinal cord and connect the brain with the rest of the body.

   C. If the spinal cord is cut, all nerves below the point of the cut do not operate, and all parts of the body controlled by these nerves are paralyzed.

DEMONSTRATION 15.12
Examine an Animal's Brain

Obtain a fresh, undamaged brain of a calf, sheep, or pig from a meat market. Locate and identify the cerebrum, cerebellum, and medulla. Note how large the cerebrum is and how its surface is folded in many places. Cut into the gray matter of the cerebrum and note the white matter beneath. See how the cerebellum is attached to the rest of the brain. Observe how the medulla connects with the other parts of the brain and with the spinal cord.

IV. THE NERVES

A. The cells of the nervous system are called **neurons**. Neurons vary in size and shape, but all are designed to carry messages, called **nerve impulses**, through the body.

B. Every neuron has a cell body and many fine threads, called nerve fibers, which spread out through the body.
1. One of these nerve fibers, called an **axon**, is very long, and carries messages away from the cell body.
2. All the other nerve fibers, called **dendrites**, are much shorter, and carry messages to the cell body.
3. The axon and dendrites branch many times at their tips, making the tips look like tiny brushes.

C. The bodies of the nerve cells usually lie in the brain and spinal cord, and the nerve fibers run to the head, body, feet, and other parts of the body.

D. There are three kinds of neurons: sensory neurons, motor neurons, and associative neurons.

E. Sensory neurons have to do with feelings or sensations.
1. Their cell bodies usually lie in the brain and spinal cord, and their nerve fibers spread out to sense organs all over the body.
2. The nerve fibers carry messages (nerve impulses) from the sense organs to the cell bodies.
3. Nerve impulses flow somewhat as an electrical current does, but are actually biochemical reactions.

F. Motor neurons carry impulses that produce motion in the body.
1. Their cell bodies also usually lie in the brain and spinal cord, and their nerve fibers spread out to the muscles, tissues, and organs of the body.
2. The nerve fibers carry messages from the cell bodies to the muscles, tissues, and organs.

G. Associative neurons, sometimes also called central neurons, are located between the cell bodies of the sensory and motor neurons.
1. Both the cell bodies and the nerve fibers of associative neurons are usually located in the brain and the spinal cord.
2. The associative neurons act as "go-betweens" in receiving and sending messages.

H. All three kinds of neurons are involved in receiving and sending messages (nerve impulses).
1. Nerve fibers in the sense organs all over the body carry messages to the cell bodies of the sensory neurons.
2. The sensory neurons send these messages through nerve fibers to the cell bodies of the associative neurons, which immediately transfer these messages through nerve fibers to the cell bodies of the motor neurons.
3. The cell bodies of the motor neurons then send messages through nerve fibers to the muscles, tissues, and organs of the body.

I. Bundles of nerve fibers are called **nerves**.
1. In most nerves the fibers carry messages in one direction only.
2. Nerves that carry messages only toward the brain and spinal cord are called sensory (**afferent**) nerves.
3. Nerves that carry messages only away from the brain and spinal cord are called motor (**efferent**) nerves.
4. A few nerves, called mixed nerves, can carry messages both toward and away from the brain and spinal cord.

V. REFLEX ACTION

A. An action of the body that takes place automatically or involuntarily, without a person's thinking about it, is called a reflex action.

B. In most reflex actions the messages (nerve impulses) travel only to the spinal cord and then back to the area involved, without going to the brain.

DEMONSTRATION 15.13
Exploring a Reflex Action

Have one student sit with his or her legs crossed so that one leg swings freely. Strike the leg just below the knee with the side of your hand. The leg will kick out immediately in a simple reflex action. Other simple reflex actions include a person blinking their eyes when an object suddenly comes near them, laughing when tickled, turning pale when frightened, blushing when embarrassed, coughing, yawning, sneezing, and shivering.

C. An example of a simple reflex action is the behavior that takes place when a person touches something hot.
  1. The person pulls the fingers away almost immediately, even before pain is felt.
  2. This action occurs because the skin sends a message to sensory nerve cells in the spinal cord.
  3. The sensory nerve cells transfer the message to nearby associative nerve cells, which transfer the message to motor nerve cells.
  4. The motor nerve cells then send a message to the muscles in the person's arm, and the muscles contract, pulling the arm and fingers away.
  5. Meanwhile, the spinal cord also sends a message to the brain, which then recognizes the sensations of both heat and pain.
  6. The extra time saved by the reflex action, which takes place before the brain is able to learn what is happening, prevents the finger from becoming badly burned.

D. Other examples of reflex action include a person jumping when frightened, blinking their eyes when objects suddenly come near them, and laughing when tickled.

E. The medulla of the brain controls such reflex actions as swallowing, coughing, and sneezing.

THE SENSE ORGANS

I. THE SPECIAL SENSES

A. The nervous system makes it possible for the human body to have many sensations.
B. Different sensory nerves located in special sense organs send nerve impulses (messages to the brain, which recognizes these impulses as sensations).
C. Such sensations include touch, pressure, heat, cold, pain, smell, taste, sight, hearing, and balance.
D. These sensations come from five sense organs: skin, nose, tongue, eyes, and ears.

II. THE SKIN

A. The skin has five kinds of sensory nerve endings, each responsible for a different type of sensation. These sensations are **touch, pressure, heat, cold,** and **pain.** Each kind of nerve ending can produce only one special sensation.
B. The sensory nerves are not spread out evenly over the skin.
  1. As a result, the skin is more sensitive in some places than in others.
  2. The fingertips and the forehead have a great many nerve endings that are sensitive to touch.
  3. The nerve endings sensitive to touch are near the surface of the skin, those sensitive to pressure are located deeper inside the skin.

III. THE NOSE

A. The sense of smell is located in the nose, and in humans the sense of smell is poor as compared with that of many animals, such as the deer and the dog.
B. Nerve endings in the nose are sensitive to chemicals in the air that are inhaled.
  1. These chemicals then dissolve in the liquid (mucus) that covers the lining of the nasal passages.
  2. When the nose smells the same odor for a long time, the nerve endings become accustomed to that particular odor, and then there is no more sensation of smell for that odor.

DEMONSTRATION 15.14
Exploring the Senses of Touch, Taste, and Smell

A. The Sense of Touch

Touch the point of a thin, sharp nail to different spots, front and back, of a student's fingers. In some spots the student will feel only a sense of pressure. In other spots, which are more sensitive, there will also be a feeling of pain.

Spread a hairpin or paper clip until the points are about 5 centimeters (2 in) apart. Blindfold a student and touch the palm of the student's hand with both ends of the hairpin. The student will feel both points. Repeat the procedure several times, bringing the points a little closer each time. Eventually the student will say that she feels just one point. At this stage, both points of the hairpin are touching just one nerve ending.

B. Sense of Touch in Hand Versus Upper Arm

Spread points of the paper clip (or hairpin) and begin on the back of the hand, moving gradually up the forearm, to the back of the neck, touching with one and sometimes two points, asking each time for the student to tell you how many points he feels. As you do this, hold one or two fingers up to let the rest of the class know how many points are actually touching the skin each time. As you move upward, the student's skin will show less sensitivity to the touch of the points, and the student will be less able to tell how many points his skin is being touched with. Have the rest of the class keep data as to correct/incorrect responses as you move up the student's arm.

C. Diffusion and the Sense of Smell

Have the students sit quietly in various parts of the classroom. Pour some inexpensive strong perfume on a hand-

kerchief and wave the handkerchief in the air. Ask the students to raise their hands as soon as they smell the perfume. Call their attention to the way the odor diffuses progressively to all parts of the classroom.

D. The Sense of Taste

Blindfold a student and have her stick out her tongue. Dip an absorbent cotton stick into a solution of sugar and water. Touch the cotton to the tip, sides, and back of the tongue. Have the student identify the taste as sweet, sour, salty, or bitter in each case. Make sure the student's tongue is moist with saliva. Repeat, using salt solution, lemon juice, and a bitter solution of an aspirin tablet in a small amount of water, rinsing the mouth after each test. The student will detect sweet flavors mostly at the tip of her tongue, salt flavors at the tip, sour flavors along the sides, and bitter flavors at the back of the tongue.

Have students repeat the experiments in groups of two or four.

E. Smell and Taste

Point out that smell has a lot to do with taste. Blindfold a student and have the student hold her nose tightly. Give the student a raw mashed apple, pear, and potato to eat and have the student try to identify which she is eating. Now let the student eat a piece of apple while you hold a piece of pear under the student's nose. The student will think she is eating a pear. Reverse the procedure, and the student will now think she is eating an apple. After the demonstration, you may want to have groups of students repeat the experiments.

IV. THE TONGUE

A. The sensation of taste is located in clusters of cells, called taste buds, that are spread unevenly over the tongue. Inside these cells are nerve endings that are sensitive to taste. The taste comes from chemicals in the food, which must first be dissolved in the saliva before the taste can be sensed.

B. The taste buds can recognize four flavors: sweet, sour, salty, and bitter.
   1. The taste buds at the tip of the tongue are sensitive to sweet and salty flavors.
   2. The taste buds along the sides of the tongue are sensitive to sour flavors.

   3. The taste buds at the back of the tongue are sensitive to bitter flavors.
C. Many foods include more than one flavor.
D. Much of what we may think is taste is really smell. While a food is being chewed, odors are given off that enter the nasal passages and reach the nerve endings sensitive to smell. The combination of taste and smell gives the food its complete flavor.

V. THE EYE

A. The sense of sight is located in the eye. The eye is protected by the bones of the skull on all sides except the front.

B. The front of the eye is protected by eyelids.
   1. They close, or blink, to protect the front of the eye.
   2. They help spread a watery liquid across the surface of the eye that keeps the eye surface moist, protects the eyes against germs, and washes out dirt.
   3. When drops of this watery liquid come out of the eye, they are called tears.
C. Because the entire human eye is shaped similarly to a ball, it is called the eyeball.
   1. Most of the eyeball has a tight, white cover around it. The part of that covering we can see is called the white of the eye. A small part of this cover is transparent, and light can pass through it. That part is called the **cornea.**
   2. The cornea covers a dark opening in the eye, called the **pupil**, which appears black because of the darkness from inside of the eyeball. The pupil allows light to pass into the eyeball.
   3. The colored circle around the pupil is the **iris**. The iris protects the eye by controlling the amount of light that enters the eyeball. Muscles of the iris change the size of the pupil, depending on the intensity of light reaching the eye. When the light is bright, the iris enlarges, making the opening of the pupil smaller, thereby reducing the amount of light that enters the eyeball. When the light is dim, the iris narrows making the pupil larger to allow more light to enter the eyeball.
   4. Inside the eyeball is a **convex lens** and two liquids. A watery liquid in front of the lens is called **aqueous humor**. A jellylike liquid behind the lens is called **vitreous humor**.
   5. The lens, with the help of these two liquids, bends the rays of light as they enter the eyeball and causes the rays of light to come together to focus on the sensitive lining at the back of the eyeball, called the **retina**. The retina has tiny, sensitive nerve endings, leading to the **optic nerve**.
   6. When light strikes the retina, the tiny nerves send impulses (messages) through the optic nerve to the brain, where the impulses are interpreted as the sensation of sight.
   7. In the retina there are two types of neurons, called the **cones** and the **rods**. The cones allow us to see objects in bright light and to recognize colors. The rods allow us to see objects in dim light, to detect brightness, not color.
   8. Many animals see better than humans at night because there are more rods in their retinas. Squirrels and deer, for example, see only in black and white.
D. Because of the round shape of the eyeball, adjustments must be made for clear focus for varying distances.
   1. Muscles attached to the lens can make the lens more convex or less convex.
   2. These muscles allow the rays of light reflected from objects to come together, that is, to focus, at the retina.
   3. When an object is far away, the lens becomes thinner or less convex because the rays of light from the distant object do not have to be bent as much in order to focus at the retina. When an object is near, the lens becomes thicker or more convex because the rays of light from the nearer object must be bent more to focus at the retina.
   4. In humans, the eye must make adjustments for clear focus at varying distances, but this is not the case with all animals. Squirrels and many birds of prey, for example, have perfect focus for their entire field of vision.
E. Because the lens of the eye is a convex lens, the image formed on the retina is upside down, yet, in some way, the brain is able to invert the image or to interpret this message as right side up.
   1. Furthermore, because we have two eyes, we get two images, which the brain is able to put together as one image.
   2. The advantage of having two eyes is the provision of depth perception.
F. The eye is able to retain the image of an object for a little while after light from the object is no longer entering the eye. This effect is called **persistence of vision**.
   1. Motion pictures use persistence of vision to give a series of still pictures the effect of motion. A series of still pictures, each a little different from the last, is shown on a screen quickly so that we continue to see one picture while the next is being shown. Persistence of vision allows the series of still pictures to blend together, and our brain creates the impression of movement.

VI. DEFECTS OF THE EYE

A. Many persons suffer from one or more defects of the eye and cannot see properly. Four common defects of the eye are nearsightedness, farsightedness, astigmatism, and color blindness.

DEMONSTRATION 15.15
Exploring Vision

A. Examine an Animal's Eye

Obtain the eye of a cow, sheep, or pig from a meat market. Use a single-edge razor to slice the eye in half lengthwise. The aqueous and vitreous humors will flow out. Examine the rest of the eye closely and identify each of the parts. If you can obtain another eye, dissect it carefully and remove the lens. Note that the lens is convex.

B. A Convex Lens Produces an Image

Tape a sheet of paper on a wall opposite a window. Draw the shades on all the windows in the room except for the window facing the paper. Hold a magnifying glass close to the paper, and move the glass back and forth until you see a clear image on the paper (Figure 15.5). The convex lens of the magnifying glass will form a smaller inverted image of the window, of whatever is on the window sill, and of objects that are outside the window at the time.

C. Effect of Light on the Size of the Pupil

Have a student sit in a dark part of the room for five minutes. Let the other students note how large the pupil of the eye has become to admit as much light as possible into the eye. Now shine a flashlight into the student's eye. Note how quickly the pupil becomes smaller to cut down the amount of light entering the eye.

D. The Blind Spot

Make a square and a circle 10 centimeters (4 in) apart on a white card (Figure 15.6). Hold the card at arm's length. Close your left eye and look at the square with your right eye. Slowly bring the card toward you, staring at the square, and yet looking at the circle from the corner of your eye. At a certain position the circle will disappear. Point out that the image of the circle has fallen on that spot of the retina where all the nerves come together and go to the brain through the optic nerve. No image can form at this spot, making it a blind spot for the eye. When you continue to bring the card closer, the circle reappears.

E. Each Eye Produces a Separate Image

Bring the forefingers of both hands together 30 centimeters (12 in) in front of you, at eye level (Figure 15.7). First look at both fingertips, then look just over the fingertips at the wall across the room. You will see a tiny third finger appear between your two fingers. Point out that each eye sees both fingers, but the images from both eyes overlap to produce the third finger.

F. The Retina Holds an Image for a Short Time

Obtain a sturdy piece of white cardboard about 7 centimeters (3 in) long and 5 centimeters (2 in) wide. Draw

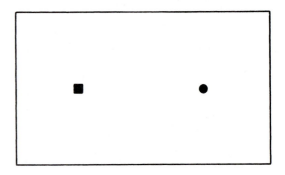

FIGURE 15.6   Find the blind spot of your eye.

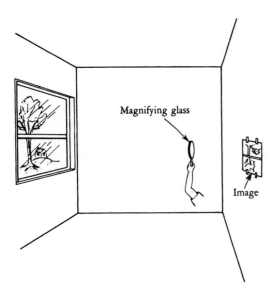

FIGURE 15.5   A convex lens produces a small inverted image.

FIGURE 15.7   Images from both eyes overlap to produce a tiny third finger.

DEMONSTRATION 15.15
Continued

a fish bowl on one side and a goldfish on the other side (Figure 15.8). Make a small hole at each corner of the cardboard and thread a 30-centimeter (12-in) piece of fine, strong string through two holes on each side of the card, as shown in Figure 15.8. Twist each string as much as you can, then insert a finger in each of the loops and twirl the card rapidly by pulling the two loops hard sideways. When the card twirls, the goldfish will seem to be inside the bowl. Point out that the eye holds an image for a short time after the object has disappeared. When the card twirls, the pictures follow each other so rapidly that you see one picture before the image of the other has had time to disappear. As a result, you see both pictures at the same time.

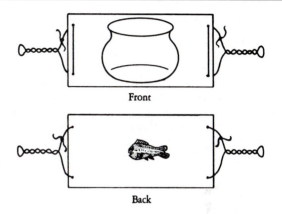

FIGURE 15.8   Persistence of vision puts the goldfish inside the bowl.

Except for color blindness, these defects can be corrected with the help of lenses.
B. In **nearsightedness**, nearby objects can be seen clearly, but distant objects seem blurred and fuzzy.
 1. Nearsightedness occurs if the eyeball is too long, or if the eye muscles make the lens too thick, so that the rays of light come together, or focus, in front of the retina.
 2. Nearsightedness is corrected by glasses with concave lenses, which spread the rays of light before they enter the eye; in this way the rays come together farther back and form sharp, clear images on the retina.
C. In **farsightedness**, distant objects can be seen clearly, but nearby objects seem blurred and fuzzy.
 1. Farsightedness occurs if the eyeball is too short, or if the eye muscles do not make the lens thick enough, so that the rays of light still have not come together when they reach the retina.
 2. Farsightedness is corrected by glasses with convex lenses, which bend the rays of light inward before they enter the eye; in this way the rays come together sooner and form sharp, clear images on the retina.
D. In **astigmatism**, lines of light rays running in one direction may seem clear, but those running in another direction may seem blurred.
 1. Astigmatism occurs if the cornea or the lens is not curved properly; this defect makes the lines of light rays curve either too much or too little in one direction.
 2. Astigmatism is corrected by glasses with specially ground lenses, which have exactly the opposite curve to the defect in the cornea or lens.
E. In color blindness, the eye is unable to recognize the difference in colors, especially red and green.
 1. Color blindness occurs if the retina does not have enough cones or if the cones are defective.
 2. Scientists have not discovered a way to correct color blindness.
F. **Cataracts**, the leading cause of blindness, is the result of lens opacities that prevent light from reaching the retina.

VII. THE EAR

A. Most animals, including humans, can hear a much broader frequency range than they can produce. For example, humans can receive between 20 and 20,000 Hz (cycles per second) but can emit sounds ranging only from 80 to 1,100 Hz. Dolphins can receive from 150 to 150,000 Hz but can emit only 7,000 to 120,000 Hz. Bats can receive 1,000 to 120,000 Hz but

DEMONSTRATION 15.16
The Ear

A. Locating the Direction of Sounds

Blindfold a student and have that student sit in the center of the room. Stand at different locations in the room and strike two pencils together. The student will be able to tell from what direction the sound is coming because sound usually reaches one ear sooner than the other. Now have the student place a wad of cotton in one ear. Repeat the procedure. This time the student will have difficulty telling the direction from which the sound is coming.

B. The Sense of Balance

Have a student spin around for a short while. After stopping, the student will continue to have a spinning sensation because the liquid in the semicircular canals of the inner ear is still whirling around.

can emit only 10,000 to 120,000 Hz. A wider range of hearing likely has a survival advantage in the wild.

B. For humans, the sense of hearing is located in the ear, of which there are three parts: the outer ear, the middle ear, and the inner ear.

C. The **outer ear** collects the sound waves and sends them through a tube to the middle ear.
1. A thin piece of tissue (membrane), commonly called the **tympanum** or **eardrum**, is stretched across the end of the tube.
2. When sound waves strike the eardrum, they make it move back and forth rapidly, or vibrate.
3. The higher the sounds, the faster the eardrum vibrates.
4. The louder the sound's frequency, the more strongly the eardrum vibrates.

D. The **middle ear** passes the vibrations of the eardrum to the inner ear.
1. The middle ear has three small bones that are joined together. Because of their shapes, they are called the **hammer,** the **anvil**, and the **stirrup**.
2. The first bone, the hammer, is connected to the eardrum.
3. The second bone, the anvil, connects the hammer to the stirrup.
4. The third bone, the stirrup, is connected to the inner ear by another membrane, called the oval window.
5. As these three bones vibrate, they cause the oval window to vibrate.

E. The inner ear consists of a spiral passage, called the **cochlea**, that is shaped like a snail's shell and is filled with a liquid.
1. Inside the liquid, and attached to the cochlea, are thousands of tiny nerve endings.
2. When the oval window of the inner ear vibrates, the liquid inside the cochlea also begins to vibrate.
3. The tiny nerve endings receive the vibrations of the liquid and send nerve impulses to the **auditory nerve**, which, in turn, relays these to the brain where they are translated as sounds.

F. The ear helps to control our sense of balance.
1. The inner ear also contains three tubes that curve around in half circles, which are called the **semicircular canals**.
2. The semicircular canals are laid out in the three directions in which the head can move: up, down, and sideways.
3. The canals are filled with a watery liquid that moves every time the head moves.
4. Nerve endings line the walls of the canals, and when the head moves, the liquid in one of the canals rushes to one end and presses on the nerve endings.
5. This pressure on the nerve endings causes nerve impulses to travel through a branch of the auditory nerve to the **cerebellum** of the brain.
6. The cerebellum then sends a message to the muscles that help us keep our balance.
7. Any whirling movement, or a steady up and down movement like that produced in a boat, makes the liquid in the canals move continuously from one side to the other, which can cause dizziness and sometimes a feeling of nausea.

THE REPRODUCTIVE SYSTEM

I. THE FUNCTION AND PARTS OF THE
REPRODUCTIVE SYSTEM

A. The primary function of the reproductive system is to continue the species by producing new organisms.

B. The **male reproductive system** has two functions. It produces sperm and delivers these cells to the reproductive tract of the female, and it produces the male sex hormones, called **androgens**.

1. The androgens are responsible for the development of the male secondary sex characteristics, which are facial axillary and pubic hair, lower voice, broad shoulders, narrow hips, penile growth, and testicular growth.

2. The sperm cells, or **spermatozoa**, are produced continuously in the tiny coiled tubules in the two **testes**, or male sex organs.

3. The testes lie outside the pelivic cavity in a sac of skin called the **scrotum**.

4. Upon leaving the testes, the sperm cells pass through a sperm duct, the **vas deferens**.

5. In the vas deferens, secretions are added to the sperm cells from four glands—the **seminal vesicles,** the **prostate,** the **ampulla**, and the **bulbourethral gland.**

6. This fluid makes up what is known as **semen**.

7. Semen is conducted through the urethra and out of the body through the **penis**.

8. Mucous membranes line the urethral canal, adding lubricant to the semen.

C. The **female reproductive system** has three functions. It produces egg cells, called **ova**. It secretes the female sex hormones, called **estrogens** and **progesterones**. It protects and nourishes the developing embryo from fertilization (union of egg and sperm that results in a zygote) until birth.

1. The egg cells are developed in the **ovaries**, one of which is located on each side of the lower part of the abdominal cavity.

2. The ovaries are surrounded by funnel-like extensions of the oviducts, or **fallopian tubes**.

3. If fertilization occurs, it usually takes place in the upper portion of an oviduct.

4. The oviducts are connected posteriorly to a pear-shaped organ called the **uterus**.

5. It is in the uterus that the embryo attaches to the uterine wall and grows.

6. The lower part of the uterus is a thick muscular ring called the **cervix**.

7. The cervix extends partially into the birth canal, the **vagina**.

8. The vagina opens to the exterior of the body.

D. Beginning with puberty, eggs are released from the ovaries, usually one egg from one ovary about every 28 days. This release of eggs continues for about 35 years.

1. At the onset of release of an egg the uterine lining thickens, readying for an egg, if fertilized, to implant and grow. If no egg implants, the uterine lining sheds.

2. This pattern is known as the **menstrual cycle**, which is interrupted if pregnancy occurs.

E. The release of an egg cell from the ovary is controlled by hormones released from the **pituitary gland** in the brain.

1. The pituitary hormones also control the release of other hormones by the ovary.

2. In turn, the hormones released by the ovary regulate the release of pituitary gland hormones.

3. The pituitary gland secretes **follicle-stimulating hormone** (FSH), which is carried to the ovary in the blood.

4. FSH causes cells around the egg to develop a fluid-filled sac or follicle.

5. The follicle then begins to produce **estrogen**.

6. FSH is also produced in males, where it stimulates the formation of sperm in the testes.

F. Estrogen serves several functions.

1. It causes the development of the primary and secondary female sex characteristics. The primary sex characteristics are the sex organs.

2. In females, the secondary sex characteristics are a wider pelvis, smoother skin, breasts, and a thicker layer of fat beneath the skin.

3. Estrogen also regulates FSH production by the pituitary.

4. Another function of estrogen is to stimulate the pituitary to release **luteinizing hormone** (LH), which helps to break the follicle and release the egg, a process called **ovulation**.

5. At ovulation, the remaining cells of the broken follicle develop into a new and temporary gland, the **corpus luteum**.

6. The corpus luteum produces another female hormone called **progesterone**, which helps to prepare the lining of the uterus for the embryo if the egg is fertilized.

7. If fertilization does not occur, the corpus luteum breaks down after about 10 days. This causes a drop in the level of progesterone and the beginning of the menstrual flow, the discarding of the lining of the uterus.

8. Menstrual flow lasts about five days, at which time estrogen levels are high enough to stimulate rebuilding of the uterine lining.

G. Fertilization usually takes place in the upper third of the oviduct.

1. Sperm cells are deposited by the penis into the vagina.

2. They swim to the oviduct and are helped along by contractions of the uterus and oviduct.

3. Sperm cells move along quite quickly, entering the oviducts within 15 minutes after ejaculation of semen into the vagina.

4. The egg cell lives for only about one day after emerging from the ovaries.

5. Sperm cells may live for two days or so while in the oviducts.

6. If fertilized, the egg, now called a **zygote**, moves down the oviduct to the uterus, where it attaches to the uterine lining and becomes a developing embryo.

7. Once it is attached, a new organ, the **placenta,** forms.

8. The placenta is composed of tissue from both the mother and the embryo. The placenta allows for the exchange of nutrients and wastes between the mother and the baby.

9. The placenta produces several hormones, including **human chorionic gonadotropin (HCG)**, which stimulates the production of progesterone to keep the lining of the uterus from being shed. HCG will appear in the blood and urine of the mother. Its detection in the urine is a sign of pregnancy.

II. OUR INHERITANCE

A. Like other members of the plant and animal world, we resemble our parents in many ways.

1. Many of our characteristics (both physical and behavioral) are inherited from our parents, but other characteristics (such as our learning to play a musical instrument) result from our interactions with our environment.

2. Inherited characteristics include the color of our skin and eyes.

B. Reproduction is characteristic of all living organisms. Because no individual organism lives forever, reproduction is essential to the continuation of the species.

1. In many species of plants and animals, including humans, females produce eggs and males produce sperm.

2. An egg and sperm unite, beginning the development of a new individual, the **zygote.** (**Meiosis**, the cell division process that results in egg and sperm cells, with haploid chromosome numbers, is discussed in Chapter 12.)

3. The zygote has an equal contribution of genetic information from each of its parents (via the egg and the sperm).

4. Sexually produced offspring are never identical to either parent.

C. Each organism requires a set of instructions for specifying its traits.

1. **Heredity** is the passage of these instructions from one generation to the next.

2. Hereditary (genetic) information is contained in **genes**, located in the chromosomes of each cell (discussed in Chapter 12).

3. Each gene carries a single unit of instruction, and an inherited trait of an individual can be determined by either one or many genes.

4. A human cell contains many thousands of different genes.

5. Genes are small sections of **deoxyribonucleic acid (DNA)**, which itself is a large molecule.

6. A mutation is a change in the DNA code. Mutations may affect one gene or entire chromosomes.

D. Sex is determined by just two chromosomes, named for their shapes—the X chromosome and the Y chromosome.

1. A female contains a pair of X chromosomes, one inherited from each parent, whereas a male contains an X chromosome and a Y chromosome, again, each one inherited from the parents.

2. If the zygote receives an X chromosome from the egg and an X chromosome from the sperm, then the offspring is a female. If, however, an X chromosome is inherited from the egg and a Y chromosome from the sperm, then it is a male.

3. The mathematical probability of the offspring being a male or a female is 50 percent.

E. Some inherited traits are dominant and others are recessive. This means that if a trait is dominant, the offspring needs only one chromosome to inherit that trait. To inherit a recessive trait, the offspring needs two chromosomes, one from each parent.

1. Some dominant traits in humans are tongue curling, free-hanging earlobes (which is dominant over attached earlobes) and Huntington's disease (a lethal genetic disorder caused by a rare dominant chromosome).

2. Unlike Huntington's disease, most genetic disorders are recessive traits, meaning that genes for the disease must be inherited from both parents.
3. Cystic fibrosis is a common recessive disorder among white Americans. Although 1 in 20 white Americans carries the trait, only about 1 in 2,000 children born to white Americans inherits the disorder.
4. Sickle-cell anemia, a blood disorder, is another recessive inherited disease. Sickle-cell anemia is most common in African Americans, affecting about 1 (or less) in 40 African Americans. About 1 in 12 persons are heterozygous carriers.

F. The international Human Genome Project is in the process of mapping the genetic makeup of human chromosomes.
   1. Its researchers have already located more than 3,000 of the estimated 100,000 genes carried on human chromosomes.
   2. The identification of genes and genetic tests for disease susceptibility offer a chance for preventive action, which can extend life expectancy.
G. Concerns for civil rights in regard to today's genetic research have prompted new state and national laws to protect individual privacy.

THE ENDOCRINE SYSTEM

I. DUCT AND DUCTLESS GLANDS

A. Glands are organs whose cells give off secretions that have special uses in the body. There are two kinds of glands: those with ducts (tubes) and those without (ductless).
B. Glands with ducts, called **duct glands**, give off secretions that travel through the ducts to the body parts they affect.
   1. Examples of duct glands are the salivary glands in the mouth and the sweat and oil glands in the skin.
   2. The digestive juices that help digest food in the body are given off by duct glands in the stomach, the intestine, the pancreas, and the liver.
C. Glands without ducts are called ductless glands, or **endocrine glands**.
   1. These glands give off secretions containing chemicals called **hormones**.
   2. Hormones pass directly through the walls of the capillaries (tiny blood vessels) into the blood and travel to different parts of the body.
   3. Their function is to regulate the body's activities.
   4. Some hormones affect every part of the body, but others affect only certain parts.
D. Six important endocrine glands in the body are the pituitary gland, the thyroid gland, the parathyroid glands, the islets of Langerhans in the pancreas, the adrenal glands, and the reproductive glands.

II. THE PITUITARY GLAND

A. The pituitary gland is a tiny gland, about the size of a cherry, attached to the base of the brain. It secretes at least 10 different hormones and is called the master gland.
   1. Some of these hormones affect or regulate the activity of almost all the other ductless glands.
   2. Other hormones affect the activity of the kidneys and blood vessels.
   3. One hormone, commonly called growth hormone, regulates the growth of the skeleton and the body.
   4. If the pituitary gland is overactive during childhood, the child will grow up to be a giant; if the pituitary gland is overactive in an adult, the adult's jaws, nose, hands, and fingers will become very large; if the pituitary gland is underactive during childhood, the child will become a midget.

III. THE THYROID GLAND

A. The thyroid gland looks like a butterfly with its wings spread out and is located below the voice box on the windpipe. It gives off a hormone, called **thyroxine**, which controls the speed or rate at which the body burns and uses food.
   1. Thyroxine contains iodine. A lack of iodine in the diet can cause the thyroid gland to swell and the neck to bulge out, forming a goiter.
   2. In parts of the country where there is little iodine in the soil and in the food, specially prepared iodized salt is used.
   3. If the thyroid gland is overactive, making the cells in the body speed up their activities, a person can become restless, nervous, and easily excited; the heart will beat faster and the hands may shake.

4. Although hyperthyroid people can be obese, it is possible that a person with a hyperactive thyroid may eat a lot and not get fat, and may even lose weight. This overactivity can be corrected medically by removal of part of the thyroid gland, by giving radioactive iodine to destroy part of the thyroid, or by medication that blocks the gland's activity.

5. If the thyroid gland is not active enough, a person will not have any energy; the cells in the body slow down their activities. The person with a hypoactive thyroid may not eat much, but may still gain weight. Thyroxine medication can usually take care of this problem.

IV. THE PARATHYROID GLANDS

A. The parathyroids are four small glands on the back of the thyroid gland. They secrete **parathormone**, which controls the use of calcium in the body.

1. Too much parathormone takes calcium from the bones, making the bones soft. Too little of the hormone in the body causes painful muscle cramps.

V. THE ISLETS OF LANGERHANS

A. The pancreas is both a duct gland and a ductless gland and is located just behind the stomach, adjacent to the duodenum.

1. As a duct gland it gives off pancreatic juice, which helps in the digestion of food in the small intestine.

2. Scattered throughout the pancreas are small groups of cells called the islets of Langerhans, which are ductless glands that produce the hormone insulin.

B. Insulin regulates the use and storage of sugar in the body.

1. When the body digests food, the carbohydrates are broken down into simple sugars, mainly one called glucose.

2. The cells in the body use oxygen to burn some of this glucose, producing heat and energy in the form of a chemical known as adenosine triphosphate (ATP).

3. Whatever glucose the body does not use at the moment is stored in the liver until needed by the cells.

4. When the pancreas does not produce enough insulin, a person develops a disease called **diabetes**.

5. The liver then cannot store the sugar, and the cells cannot use it efficiently.

6. The muscles and tissues cannot get the sugar they need, and the blood becomes flooded with sugar.

7. The person loses weight, urinates very often, and is very thirsty.

8. Some of the excess sugar in the blood passes out through the urine.

9. Persons with diabetes are given insulin regularly by injection or are given pills to help their bodies release more of their own insulin if their pancreas is still producing it. They are also put on a special healthful diet.

C. Diabetes can occur in young children.

1. When it does, it is probably due to a viral infection or to an autoimmune reaction in a person with a genetic predisposition.

2. An autoimmune reaction is one in which the body's immune system attacks its own tissue, in this case the islet cells of the pancreas, as if they were a foreign substance.

D. Diabetes can also affect adults in their middle years.

1. In the adult form of diabetes, unlike childhood diabetes, the adult has a higher than normal amount of insulin as well as sugar in the blood because the pancreas is producing insulin normally, but the body cells are resistant to the insulin.

VI. THE ADRENAL GLANDS

A. The adrenal glands are two small glands located on top of the kidneys.

B. The outer layer of the adrenal glands gives off many hormones, which control the digestion of food and regulate the balance of salt and water in the body.

C. The inner layer gives off a hormone called **adrenaline**.

1. When a person becomes angry or frightened, the adrenal glands respond quickly and pour adrenaline into the blood.

2. Adrenaline makes the heart beat faster, blood pressure rise, and digestion slow down. Adrenaline also causes breathing to become faster and deeper, it causes the liver to send more of its stored sugar to the blood; and it drives more blood into vessels in the deeper muscles.

3. In addition, adrenaline makes blood clot more easily and quickly.

4. When doctors are concerned that the heart may stop beating, they may give the patient adrenaline.

Exploratory Activities for "The Human Body"

1. EXPLORING THE CONTENT OF FOODS: BEING A NUTRITION DETECTIVE (ANY GRADE LEVEL)

Overview   Students enjoy and learn when they are active participants in learning. In this series of exploratory studies, students participate as chemists and nutrition detectives, exploring (by hypothesizing and testing their hypotheses) various foods for their sugar, starch, fat, protein, mineral, water, and energy content.

Connections with Other Disciplines   Students will do reporting, writing, and graphing. Art activities include the creation of posters and charts. Extension activities may include the study of food marketing and supermarket shelving practices. Students may want to investigate careers in nutrition, chemistry, and others, as related to this study.

Initiating Activity   Have students keep a record of what they eat each day for a week, being quite specific about the size of the portions and the number of helpings. Have them put their records on individual poster charts that they each create. At the end of the week of record keeping, either as a whole class or in groups of four, have students select sample foods from the charts, foods that are most prevalent in their weekly diets.

Student Exploratory Learning Activities   Have students bring in sample foods that represent their weekly diets as shown by their records. Divide the class into groups of four, assign responsibilities to the members of each group, and then have the groups test the food samples. In all tests, students should hypothesize about the content of material being tested for in each food and plot their results on a table of their own making.

Individual titles and roles within each group might include the following:

Materials, Equipment, and Safety Manager: monitors group safety and sees that the group has the materials needed for the test
Record keeper: maintains records of the experiment
Chief chemist: performs the actual test
Reporter: works with the record keeper and prepares a group report on the results of the test

Classroom Management Suggestions   Ten exploratory activities follow. All groups could do each of the 10 activities, or groups could be divided so that all activities are completed, but not by all groups. Because of safety hazards and depending on the maturity of your students,

as noted in the individual activities, some of the tests that follow might better be done as demonstrations by the teacher.

1.1   Testing Foods for the Presence of Simple Sugars

Materials   Test tubes, corn syrup, water, Tes-Tape or Clinitest tablets (available from drug stores), assorted fruit juices, various solid foods, soda crackers, table sugar, raisins, onion.

Control Test   Obtain corn syrup from a supermarket and pour 10 drops into a test tube. Add water until the test tube is half full, then shake to dissolve the syrup in the water. From a drugstore obtain Tes-Tape, Clinitest tablets, or another similar material used to test for the presence of sugar. Follow instructions carefully and observe the change in color that shows the presence of sugar.

Exploratory Tests   Repeat the test, using different amounts of syrup. Repeat the test, using various fruit juices. Try using small amounts of solid foods, first mixed with water, including soda crackers or saltines, raisins, table sugar, and a bit of onion. Students should hypothesize about the content of simple sugar in each food and plot their results on a table that they devise. (The students will be surprised to learn that the onion is rich in simple sugars, whereas the table sugar is not. In this test, students are testing for simple sugars, or monosaccharides; sucrose (found in table sugar) is a complex sugar, a disaccharide.)

1.2   Testing Foods for the Presence of Starch

Materials   Test tubes, cornstarch, water, tincture of iodine, various foods.
   Safety note: tincture of iodine is poisonous so should be handled only by the teacher or by mature students under the careful guidance of the teacher.

Control Test   Place a small amount of cornstarch in a test tube half filled with water. Add one or two drops of tincture of iodine to the solution and stir. A blue-black color will form, showing the presence of starch. Place a drop or two of the iodine on a slice of raw potato and on a slice of bread. The blue-black color will again show the presence of starch.

Exploratory Tests   Repeat the test, using a variety of both starchy and nonstarchy foods, such as soda crackers or saltines, boiled macaroni or spaghetti, boiled rice, a lump of table sugar, cooked egg white, cheese, bacon, and meat. Students should hypothesize about the content of starch in each food and plot their results on a table that they devise.

1.3 Testing Foods for the Presence of Fats

Materials   Butter, brown wrapping paper or lunch bag paper, hot plate, water.
   Safety note: The hot plate should be used only by the teacher or by mature students under the careful guidance of the teacher.

Control Test   Rub a bit of butter on a piece of brown paper bag, and warm the paper gently over a hot plate (*use caution*). Put two or three drops of water on a second piece of brown paper. Now hold both pieces of paper up to sunlight or a bright light. Both spots will be translucent and allow light to pass through. However, the water spot will become dry and no longer translucent, but the "grease" spot will continue to be translucent.

Exploratory Tests   Try this test for the presence of fats with such foods as bacon, nuts, the white and the yolk of a boiled egg, olive oil, mayonnaise, beef, bread, and leafy vegetables. Note which foods produce a permanent grease spot on the brown paper. Students should hypothesize about the content of fat in each food and plot their results on a table that they devise.

1.4 Testing Foods for the Presence of Proteins

Materials   Test tube, hard-boiled eggs, dilute nitric acid, alcohol burner, test tube clamp or holder, household ammonia, various foods.
   Safety note: This testing should be done as a demonstration by the teacher if students are not mature enough to work with heat and nitric acid.

Control Test   Place a small piece of the white of a boiled egg in a test tube. Add enough nitric acid to cover the piece of egg white. Holding the test tube with a test tube holder, heat the test tube gently over the flame of an alcohol lamp, shaking the test tube to keep the egg white moving, at the same time keeping the mouth of the test tube pointed away from yourself and others. Remove the test tube as soon as the nitric acid begins to boil. Pour off the nitric acid into a plastic tub (to be discarded later). Note that the egg white has turned yellow. Now pour a little ammonia into the test tube. An orange color will form on the egg white, showing the presence of proteins.

Exploratory Tests   Repeat the test, using a variety of foods, such as bread, cheese, boiled spaghetti or macaroni, lean meat, and lima beans.

1.5 Testing Foods for the Presence of Minerals

Materials   Alcohol burner, bread, metal spoon, burner mitt, various foods.
   Safety note: This testing should be done as a demonstration by the teacher if students are not mature enough to work with an alcohol burner.

Control Test   Place a small piece of bread on an old metal spoon and, holding the spoon with a mitt, heat well over an alcohol burner flame. The bread will burn, turn black, and finally become a small amount of gray-white ash. This ash shows the presence of minerals.

Exploratory Tests   Repeat the test, using a variety of foods.

1.6 Testing Foods for the Presence of Water

Materials   Bread, test tubes, alcohol burner, various foods.
   Safety note: This testing should be done as a demonstration by the teacher if students are not mature enough to work with an alcohol burner.

Control Test   Place a few small pieces of bread in a dry test tube and heat the tube gently over the flame of an alcohol lamp. Tiny droplets of water will appear on the upper part of the test tube. The water was driven out of the heated bread in the form of steam, and it then condensed on the cool upper part of the test tube.

Exploratory Tests   Repeat the test, using a variety of foods.

1.7 Investigating the Vitamin Content of Foods

Have the students make a chart listing foods that are good sources of vitamins. Let them check the foods in their daily diets to see whether they appear on the chart. There are more than 25 vitamins that our bodies need. Have the students read about and report on the diseases caused by vitamin deficiencies.

1.8 Discovering That Foods Release Heat Energy When Digested

Materials   Paper clip, peanut, brazil nut, or cashew, matches, butter or cooking oil, saucer, string
Safety note: This test should be done as a demonstration by the teacher.

Demonstration   Put a straightened paper clip through a peanut, brazil nut, or cashew. Apply a lighted match to the nut. The nut will burn, giving off heat energy.
   Pour some melted butter or cooking oil into a small saucer and place a piece of soft string in the butter or oil,

with one end of the string protruding above the liquid and hanging over the side of the saucer. After the string has become saturated with the butter or oil, apply a lighted match to the end of the string. The string will act as a wick, and the butter or oil will burn for some time. Point out that when foods are digested in the body, they give off heat energy.

1.9 Investigating the Calorie Value of Food

Using their individual records of their diets for a week, have the students consult a chart of the calorie values for common foods, to find out how many calories they took in each day, and then find an average for the week. Let them compare their average daily caloric intake with the value suggested in the calorie chart. (Most life insurance companies have booklets available including calorie charts and other pertinent information.)

1.10 Checking Diets for the Five Basic Food Groups

Using their individual records of their diets for a week, have the students check each day's diet to see whether all five basic food groups were represented and whether the recommended number of servings for each group was consumed.

Food groups:

Milk group: provides carbohydrate, calcium, vitamin B_2, protein, fat

Meat group: provides protein, niacin, iron, vitamin B_1, fat

Vegetable group: provides vitamins A and C, carbohydrate, fiber

Fruit group: provides vitamins A and C, carbohydrate, fiber

Grain group: provides carbohydrate, vitamin B_1, iron, niacin

Conclusion of Study and Assessment of Student Learning Groups should make their reports to the entire class about their findings on the nutritional content of the various foods and of their diets for the week. The following key questions should be answered:

a. What did you learn from this study?
b. What conclusions have you made about your diet for the week?
c. Will you make any changes in what you eat as a result of what you have learned? Why?
d. What did you learn about scientific research?

STUDENT BOOKS AND OTHER RESOURCES FOR "THE HUMAN BODY"

Bryan, J. *Genetic Engineering*. Fresno: Thomson, 1995.

Butler, L. A. "Designer Anatomy." *Science and Children* 32(5):19–21, 33 (February 1995).

Ford, M. T. *The Voices of Aids*. New York: Morrow, 1995.

Larsen, J. "Slam Dunk Science." *Science Scope* 18(4):15–24 (January 1995).

Long, M. E. "The Sense of Sight." *National Geographic* 182(5):2–41 (November 1992).

———. "What Is This Thing Called Sleep?" *National Geographic* 172(6):786–821 (December 1987).

Miller, M. *My Five Senses*. New York: Simon & Schuster, 1994.

Misiti, F. L. "A Sense of Science." *Science and Children* 30(4):28–29 (January 1993).

Owtwald, T. "An Eye for Learning." *Science and Children* 33(2):25–26 (October 1995).

Parker, S. *The Body Atlas*. New York: Dorling Kindersley, 1993.

———. *How the Body Works*. New York: Reader's Digest Books for Children, 1994.

Pluckrose, H., and C. Fairclough. *Exploring Our Senses Series: Seeing, Hearing, Smelling, Tasting, Touching*. Milwaukee: Gareth Stevens, 1995.

Sylwester, R. *A Celebration of Neurons: An Educator's Guide to the Human Brain*. Alexandria, VA: Association for Supervision and Curriculum Development, 1995.

Thompson, S. "Super Ears." *Science and Children* 32(8)19–21, 50 (May 1995).

VanCleave, J. *The Human Body for Every Kid*. Arlington, VA: National Science Teachers Association, 1995.

Westheimer, R. *Dr. Ruth Talks to Kids: Where You Came From, How Your Body Changes, and What Sex Is All About*. New York: Macmillan, 1993.

MATTER, ENERGY, AND TECHNOLOGY

*Students in **grades K–4** should develop an understanding of*
- *Properties of objects and materials*
- *Position and motion of objects*
- *Light, heat, electricity, and magnetism*
- *Types of resources*
- *Changes in environments*
- *Science and technology in local challenges*

*Students in **grades 5–8** should develop an understanding of*
- *Properties and changes of properties in matter*
- *Motions and forces*
- *Transformations of energy*
- *Natural hazards*
- *Risks and benefits*
- *Science and technology in society*

CHAPTER 16

Changes in Matter and Energy

The Structure of Matter

I. Matter

  A. Matter is anything that occupies space and has weight. Air, water, wood, stones, and metals are examples of matter. People, plants, animals, the sun, stars, and the planets are also examples of matter.

  B. Some materials are made up of only one particular kind of matter, and others are made up of more than one kind of matter.

    1. A material that is made up of only one particular kind of matter is called a pure substance. Water, salt, sugar, silver, and oxygen are examples of pure substances.

    2. Air is an example of matter that is made up of many substances. Air consists of oxygen, nitrogen, carbon dioxide, and other substances.

  C. Matter is found in four states: **solid, liquid, gas,** and **plasma.**

    1. A solid has a definite size and shape. Wood, iron, glass, ice, rubber, wool, and butter are examples of solids. Solids can be hard or soft.

    2. A liquid has a definite size, but it does not have a definite shape. Water, milk, alcohol, oil, and gasoline are examples of liquids. A liquid's shape depends on the shape of the container into which it is poured.

    3. A gas has neither a definite size nor a definite shape. When a gas is poured into a container, it spreads out until it has the same size as the container, and it also takes the shape of the container. Air, oxygen, carbon dioxide, and ammonia are examples of gases.

  D. If a gas is heated to many thousands of degrees or if it is bombarded by other forms of energy, such as ultraviolet or gamma rays, electrons are knocked free from the atoms and the gas is then said to be in a highly ionized state (it consists of positively charged ions and free, negatively charged electrons), the gas is called a **plasma.** Plasma is a fourth state of matter.

    1. It is estimated that 99 percent of the matter in the universe is in the plasma state. This is the material in and around the stars and throughout interstellar space.

  E. Matter can be changed from one state to another by heating or cooling it, that is, by adding or removing energy.

    1. For example, when liquid water is cooled until it freezes, it becomes solid ice. When liquid water is heated until it boils, it becomes a gas called steam.

  F. **Chemistry** is the science that deals with the different kinds of matter around us, what they are made of, and the changes that happen to them.

II. Gravity, Weight, and Mass

  A. Every body in the universe attracts, or pulls, on every other body. This attraction or pull that each body has for another is called **gravity.**

    1. The more massive a body, the greater its pull of gravity.

    2. The farther away two bodies are from each other, the smaller their pull of gravity on each other.

DEMONSTRATION 16.1

The Definition of Matter

Show that solids, liquids, and gases are matter because they occupy space and have weight. A book or block of wood is a solid that can be measured and weighed eas-

ily. Pouring water into a glass jar can show that a liquid occupies space, and weighing the jar before and after pouring can show that the liquid has weight.

B. The earth's gravity pulls on every body at or near the earth's surface. This pull is always directed down toward the center, no matter where on the earth the body is located. This downward pull of the earth's gravity keeps people from falling off the earth, and holds the air and water on the earth as well.
1. The measure of the earth's pull of gravity on a body is called the **weight** of that body.
2. The weight of a body changes, depending on its distance from the center of the earth. The nearer a body is to the center of the earth, the greater the downward pull of the earth's gravity on the body, and the more the body will weigh.

C. Every body has a **center of gravity,** the point at which all of the weight of the body seems to be located.

D. The actual amount of matter in a body is called its **mass.** Mass has nothing to do with the earth's pull of gravity. A body has the same mass whether it is on the earth's surface or far out in space.
1. The mass of a body is also a measure of the body's **inertia.** All objects have inertia. The tendency of a body to stay at rest if it is at rest or to stay in motion if it is in motion is called inertia.
2. An outside force is needed to overcome or change the inertia of a body.
3. The greater a body's mass, the more force is needed to overcome its inertia.
4. Mass, then, is defined in terms of the force needed to overcome or change a body's inertia.

III. PHYSICAL AND CHEMICAL PROPERTIES OF MATTER

A. All matter has certain qualities or characteristics, called properties. The properties of a substance help us to distinguish one substance from another and also to determine the purposes for which various substances can be used. These properties are divided into two

main groups: physical properties and chemical properties.
1. The **physical properties** of a substance are those qualities or characteristics that we can readily observe with our five senses. Physical properties include the characteristics of color, odor, taste, heaviness, hardness, brittleness, elasticity, melting and boiling temperatures, solubility in water and other liquids, conductivity of heat and electricity, ductility, and malleability.
2. The **chemical properties** of a substance are those qualities or characteristics that have to do with the activity of the substance with other substances. We observe chemical properties when we see air and moisture act on iron to make iron rust, vinegar act on baking soda to produce bubbles of carbon dioxide gas, and a fuel use the oxygen of air to burn. In each case a new substance is formed.
3. A substance that acts readily with other substances is called **chemically active,** and a substance that does not act readily with other substances is called **chemically inert.**

IV. PHYSICAL AND CHEMICAL CHANGES

A. There are two kinds of changes that can happen to matter: physical changes and chemical changes.
1. In a **physical change,** only the physical properties or characteristics of a substance are changed. It remains the same substance. A physical change takes place when a substance changes in size or shape, such as when wood is chopped, paper is torn, or glass is broken. A physical change takes place when a substance is heated and expands, or is cooled and contracts. A physical change takes place when a substance changes its form, or state, such as when a solid is changed into a liquid, or a liquid is changed into a gas. In most physical changes the substance can be changed back into its original size, shape, or appearance.

DEMONSTRATION 16.2
The Center of Gravity

Have a student balance a uniform object, such as a meterstick or a yardstick, on the end of one finger. The point at which the meterstick balances is where the center of gravity is located. Now make the meterstick unsymmet-

rical by putting some modeling clay at one end. Balance the meterstick again, and note that the center of gravity has shifted toward the thicker, and heavier, part of the meterstick.

---

2. In a **chemical change,** the chemical properties or characteristics of the substance are changed so that a new substance is formed, with properties that are different from the original substance. Examples of chemical change include the burning of wood, rusting of iron, tarnishing of silver, souring of milk, and digestion of food. For a chemical change to occur, energy such as heat, light, or electricity—is either needed, given off, or both.

V. MOLECULES

A. Substances are made up of tiny particles called molecules. A molecule is the smallest particle of a substance that is still that substance, having all the properties of that substance.
   1. Molecules are so small that only the largest of them can be seen by an electron microscope. One drop of water is made up of billions of molecules.
   2. A lump of sugar can be crushed and broken up into many particles of sugar. These particles can be ground into a fine powder, but each tiny particle of powder is still a particle of sugar. If we could keep breaking up a particle of sugar again and again into smaller and smaller particles, we would finally end up with the smallest possible particle of sugar. This smallest possible particle of sugar would be one molecule of sugar.
B. All the molecules of a substance are alike, but the molecules of one substance are different from the molecules of another substance. For example, all the molecules of table salt in a container are alike, but molecules of salt are different from molecules of a sugar.
C. Molecules are always moving rapidly, striking other molecules and then bouncing off in different directions.
   1. In a gas, the molecules move very fast and are far apart.

2. In a liquid, the molecules move more slowly and are closer together.
3. In a solid, the molecules are very close together, and each molecule seems to be moving back and forth, or vibrating, in one fixed position rather than moving about freely.
D. Molecules attract each other. The attraction that molecules of the same substance have for each other is called **cohesion.** The attraction that molecules of different substances have for each other is called **adhesion.**
E. Cohesion makes it possible for molecules to come together and form the physical states of matter.
   1. In a solid, the attraction between molecules is very strong, so the solid holds its shape.
   2. In a liquid, the attraction between molecules is weaker, and although the molecules still stick together, the liquid does not hold its shape but takes the shape of its container.
   3. In a gas, there is practically no attraction between molecules, so the molecules move away from each other, and in this way the gas spreads throughout its container.
F. Adhesion makes it possible for two different substances to stick together.
   1. Because of the attraction of molecules of different substances for each other, paint sticks to wood.
   2. Because of adhesion, water sticks to other materials, making them wet.
   3. The action of glue, cement, and paste also depends on adhesion.
   4. The adhesive and cohesive properties of water in a drinking glass make it possible to "overfill" a glass of water without the water overflowing the sides of the glass.

VI. ATOMS

A. Molecules are made up of even smaller particles called **atoms.**

DEMONSTRATION 16.3
Cohesion and Adhesion

Using a medicine dropper, allow a drop of water to fall on a penny. Point out that the drop of water remains intact because of the cohesion of the water molecules, and that the water adheres to the coin because of adhesion.

Ask students to predict how many drops of water they think the penny will hold before the water overflows the sides of the penny. Write their guesses on the board and then test. They will be surprised at the number of drops that it will hold.

Follow with questions as to how the principles of cohesion and adhesion are used in nature and in technology.

1. In some cases a molecule is made up of just one atom. For example, a molecule of neon is made up of just one atom of neon.
2. In most cases a molecule is made up of more than one atom. A molecule of oxygen is made up of two atoms of oxygen that are close together. A molecule of water is made up of two atoms of hydrogen and one atom of oxygen.
B. Atoms are made up of even smaller particles: electrons, protons, and neutrons.
   1. The particle of an atom with a negative electrical charge ($-$) is called an **electron.** Although an electron has a very small mass, it usually has a great deal of energy and moves around quickly. Because all electrons have the same negative charge, they repel each other.
   2. The particle of an atom with a positive electrical charge ($+$) is called a **proton.** A proton has a mass about 1,836 times greater than that of an electron. A proton has about the same amount of energy as an electron, but because its mass is greater, it moves more slowly than an electron.
   3. Because the electrical charges of the proton and the electron are opposite, these two particles attract each other.
   4. The **neutron** is a particle of the atom that has neither a positive nor a negative electrical charge. As a result, the neutron does not attract or repel other neutrons.
   5. The energy of a neutron is slightly greater than the combined energies of one electron and one proton. Evidence indicates that a neutron is made up of an electron and a proton held together by a small particle of energy, called a **neutrino,** which has no mass or electrical charge.

C. In an atom the protons and neutrons, which are heavier than electrons, are closely packed together in the center of the atom, which is called the **nucleus.**
   1. Because protons all have the same positive ($+$) charge, and because like charges always repel each other, the protons in the nucleus should also repel each other rather than stay close together.
   2. Evidence indicates that there is a strong force that holds or binds the protons and neutrons closely together in the nucleus of an atom. This is called the **binding energy** of the nucleus.
D. Electrons are spaced around the nucleus in rather definite regions, called shells or **energy levels.**
   1. Some electrons in any given energy level move about the nucleus like bees swarming about their hive.
   2. In this way the electrons occupy the empty space around the nucleus, forming a sort of hazy "electron cloud."
   3. Sometimes the electrons are near the nucleus and sometimes they are farther away, depending on how much energy they have at the moment.
E. Because every atom is made up of electrons, protons, and neutrons, matter is electrical in nature. Typically, an atom is electrically neutral because it contains the same number of electrons and protons.
F. The difference between the atoms of different substances lies principally in the number of electrons, protons, and neutrons contained in the atoms of these substances.
G. Although an atom may have many electrons, protons, and neutrons, an atom is mostly empty space.

DEMONSTRATION 16.4
Models of Atoms

Tape a sheet of paper on a piece of corrugated cardboard. Draw a small circle to represent the nucleus of an atom. Draw concentric circles to represent the shells or energy levels of the electrons outside the nucleus. Now use thumbtacks of three different colors to represent the number of electrons, protons, and neutrons in an atom of aluminum (Figure 16.1). Place 13 protons and 14 neutrons in the nucleus, and position 13 electrons in the concentric circles as shown in the diagram.

Have the students make similar representations for other common atoms. Point out that an atom is really three-dimensional.

Have the students look at a table that provides the atomic numbers and atomic weights of several or all of the elements. Let the students use these values to determine the number of electrons, protons, and neutrons in atoms of some of the well-known elements.

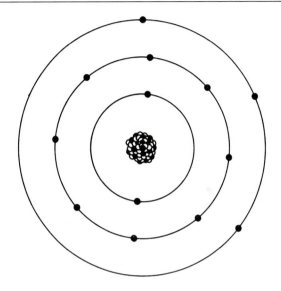

FIGURE 16.1   Atomic structure of an aluminum atom.

1. The nucleus is small as compared with the rest of the atom, and all the protons and neutrons in the nucleus are packed very tightly together.
2. The electrons, however, in their different shells or energy levels, are spread out so that there is a vast amount of space between the nucleus and the electrons.

VII. ELEMENTS
    A. Although all atoms are made up of electrons, protons, and neutrons, atoms are not all alike. Atoms differ in their number of electrons, protons, and neutrons, and because of this difference, there are different kinds of atoms.
    B. There are 92 naturally occurring kinds of atoms found in or on earth. Each different kind of atom is called an **element.** Each element has its own particular number of protons in the nucleus and number of electrons outside the nucleus.

1. Chemists define an element as the simplest form of a substance that cannot be broken up into anything simpler by ordinary chemical reactions.
2. Elements are often called the building blocks of matter.
3. Elements can combine with each other to form new substances.
4. All the substances on earth are made up of different combinations of these 92 natural elements.
5. In addition to the 92 natural elements, scientists have made at least 13 other elements, bringing the total number of known elements to at least 105.
    C. According to certain properties shared by the elements, they can be divided into two main groups—**metals** and **nonmetals.**
       1. Most metals have a special shiny surface, called a metallic luster, and they conduct electricity and heat very well. Many metals are **ductile,** which means they can be drawn out into wire, and are also **malleable,** which

means they can be hammered into thin sheets. Examples of metals are gold, silver, copper, iron, and aluminum.

2. Most nonmetals conduct electricity and heat very poorly, and the solid nonmetals cannot be drawn into wire or hammered into sheets. Examples of nonmetals are sulfur, carbon, oxygen, hydrogen, and nitrogen.

3. Some elements have certain properties of both metals and nonmetals. These elements are called **metalloids.** Examples of metalloids are arsenic and silicon.

VIII. SYMBOLS OF THE CHEMICAL ELEMENTS

A. Instead of writing the whole word, chemists use a symbol for the name of an element.
   1. Sometimes the symbol is just one letter of the alphabet. In this case we use the first letter of the name of the element as the symbol. Examples of symbols using one letter are C for carbon and H for hydrogen.
   2. Two letters are used when we have two or more elements whose names begin with the same first letter. In this case the symbol is made up of the first letter of the name of the element together with another letter that helps identify the element. Examples of symbols with two letters are Ca for calcium, Co for cobalt, and Cr for chromium. The first letter of a symbol is always a capital letter, and the second letter, if needed, is always a small letter.

B. In many cases, a symbol is taken from the Latin name for the element. For example, the symbol for iron is Fe, from the Latin word *ferrum.* Some common elements and their symbols are shown in Table 16.1.

IX. THE ATOMIC STRUCTURE OF THE ELEMENTS

A. The difference between the atoms of the various elements is in the number of electrons, protons, and neutrons contained in the atoms of these elements.

B. There is also a definite arrangement of all the electrons, protons, and neutrons in the atoms of every single element.

C. In all atoms the protons and neutrons are located in the nucleus, and the electrons are lo-

TABLE 16.1   Some common elements and their symbols

Element	Symbol	Element	Symbol
Aluminum	Al	Nickel	Ni
Arsenic	As	Nitrogen	N
Calcium	Ca	Oxygen	O
Carbon	C	Phosphorus	P
Chlorine	Cl	Platinum	Pt
Copper	Cu	Potassium	K
Fluorine	F	Selenium	Se
Gold	Au	Silicon	Si
Helium	He	Silver	Ag
Hydrogen	H	Sodium	Na
Iodine	I	Sulfur	S
Iron	Fe	Tin	Sn
Lead	Pb	Tungsten	W
Magnesium	Mg	Radium	Ra
Mercury	Hg	Uranium	U
Neon	Ne	Zinc	Zn

cated in shells or energy levels outside the nucleus.

D. The number of protons in the nucleus of an atom of an element is called the **atomic number** of the element. This number of protons in the nucleus is distinct for the atoms of each element. For example, an atom of the element oxygen has 8 protons in its nucleus and its atomic number is 8. An atom of iron has 26 protons in its nucleus and its atomic number is 26. The atomic number of an element identifies the element and determines its chemical properties as well.

E. It is possible to arrange all 105 elements in a table of atomic numbers that range from 1 to 105.
   1. In this table the first element has an atomic number of 1, the next element has an atomic number of 2, the third element an atomic number of 3, and so on until the last element, which has an atomic number of 105.
   2. Each element in the table has an atomic number that is one number higher (one more proton) than the element before it, and one number lower (one less proton) than the element after it.

F. When atoms are electrically neutral, there are the same number of negatively charged (−) electrons outside the nucleus as there are positively charged (+) protons inside the nucleus. An atom of hydrogen, for example, with an atomic number of 1, has one proton in its nucleus and one electron outside the nucleus. An atom of uranium, with an atomic number of 92, has 92 protons in its nucleus and 92 electrons outside the nucleus.

G. Electrons are spaced around the nucleus in shells or **energy levels.**
   1. There are seven shells or energy levels that electrons may occupy.
   2. There is a definite limit to the number of electrons that can occupy each shell or energy level. There can be no more than 2 electrons in the first shell, the one nearest the nucleus, 8 electrons in the second shell, 18 electrons in the third shell, and 32 electrons in the fourth shell or energy level.
   3. Generally, the farther away the shells or energy levels are from the nucleus, the more energy the electrons in these shells will demonstrate.
   4. When **chemical changes** take place, it is because of the action between the electrons in the outermost shells of the atoms of two or more different elements.

H. The mass of an atom is called its **atomic mass,** or its **atomic weight.** It is the mass of all the electrons, protons, and neutrons in the atom.
   1. Because electrons have so little weight, for all practical purposes the weight of the atom can be said to be the weight of the protons and neutrons in the nucleus.
   2. A neutron has a weight of one atomic mass unit.
   3. A proton, which weighs about the same as a neutron, also has a weight of one atomic mass unit.
   4. Because a proton and a neutron have just about the same atomic weight, the number of neutrons in a nucleus can be found by subtracting the atomic number from the atomic weight. For example, if the atomic number of the element aluminum is 13 and its atomic weight is 27 mass units, this means that there are 13 protons and 27 minus 13, or 14, neutrons in the nucleus.
   5. In general, as the atomic numbers of the various atoms increase, the atomic weights increase as well.

I. The atomic structure of the simplest element, hydrogen, is as follows.
   1. The hydrogen atom has an atomic number of 1 and an atomic weight of 1.
   2. The atomic number of 1 means that there is one proton in the nucleus and one electron in the first shell or energy level outside the nucleus.
   3. The one proton in the nucleus makes up the atomic weight of 1.

J. The atomic structure of the next simplest element, helium, is as follows.
   1. The helium atom has an atomic number of 2 and an atomic weight of 4.
   2. The atomic number of 2 means that there are two protons in the nucleus and two electrons in the first shell or energy level outside the nucleus.
   3. There are 4 minus 2, or two, neutrons in the nucleus, which together with the two protons make up the atomic weight of 4.

K. The atomic structure for the first 24 elements is given in Table 16.2.

L. Not all atoms of the same element have the same weight. Atoms of an element that have the same atomic number but a different atomic weight are called **isotopes** of that element. Isotopes can occur naturally or they can be produced artificially.
   1. Some atoms of an element have a slightly different number of neutrons from other atoms of the same element.
   2. Because of this difference in the number of neutrons, some atoms of an element have a different atomic weight than other atoms of the same element.
   3. This explains why atomic weights are not expressed as whole numbers only.
   4. However, even though these atoms of the same element differ in atomic weight, they all still have the same atomic number, so they are all part of the same element and have the same chemical properties of that element.
   5. Isotopes of the same element have the same number of protons and electrons but have a slightly different number of neutrons.

M. The element hydrogen has three known isotopes.
   1. Hydrogen has an atomic number of 1, which means that all three isotopes have one proton in the nucleus and one electron outside the nucleus.
   2. The most common isotope has just one proton in the nucleus, so its atomic weight is 1. A second isotope, called **deuterium,** has a neutron in the nucleus, as well as one

TABLE 16.2 Atomic structure of the first 24 elements

Element	Atomic Number	Atomic Weight	Number of Protons	Number of Neutrons	Arrangement of Electrons by Energy Levels
Hydrogen	1	1	1	0	1
Helium	2	4	2	2	2
Lithium	3	7	3	4	2,1
Beryllium	4	9	4	5	2,2
Boron	5	11	5	6	2,3
Carbon	6	12	6	6	2,4
Nitrogen	7	14	7	7	2,5
Oxygen	8	16	8	8	2,6
Fluorine	9	19	9	10	2,7
Neon	10	20	10	10	2,8
Sodium	11	23	11	12	2,8,1
Magnesium	12	24	12	12	2,8,2
Aluminum	13	27	13	14	2,8,3
Silicon	14	28	14	14	2,8,4
Phosphorus	15	31	15	16	2,8,5
Sulfur	16	32	16	16	2,8,6
Chlorine	17	35	17	18	2,8,7
Argon	18	40	18	22	2,8,8
Potassium	19	39	19	20	2,8,8,1
Calcium	20	40	20	20	2,8,8,2
Scandium	21	45	21	24	2,8,9,2
Titanium	22	48	22	26	2,8,10,2
Vanadium	23	51	23	28	2,8,11,2
Chromium	24	52	24	28	2,8,13,1

proton, so its atomic weight is 2. A third isotope, called **tritium,** has two neutrons in the nucleus, as well as one proton, so its atomic weight is 3.

3. Because all three isotopes have different weights, the average atomic weight of hydrogen is 1.0078.

N. A **radioactive isotope** of the element carbon is used to estimate the age of rocks, fossils, and minerals.

1. Carbon has an atomic number of 6, which means that all isotopes of carbon have six protons in the nucleus and six electrons outside the nucleus.
2. The common isotope of carbon has an atomic weight of 12, so there are 12 minus 6, or six, neutrons in the carbon-12 atom.
3. The radioactive isotope of carbon has an atomic weight of 14, so there are 14 minus 6, or eight, neutrons in the carbon-14 atom.

O. Two of the element uranium's many isotopes have atomic weights of 238 and 235.

1. Both these isotopes have the same atomic number of 92, so there are 92 protons in the nucleus and 92 electrons outside the nucleus.
2. In the uranium-238 isotope there are 238 minus 92, or 146, neutrons in the nucleus.
3. In the uranium-235 isotope there are 235 minus 92, or 143, neutrons in the nucleus.

P. Only a few of the 92 elements found on earth are naturally radioactive. However, scientists discovered that when they bombarded the other natural elements with neutrons or deuterons (the nuclei of hydrogen atoms containing a proton and a neutron), radioactive isotopes of these elements are formed.

1. Through the use of a nuclear reactor, a cyclotron, or other "atom smashers," radioactive isotopes of practically all the elements have now been prepared.

TABLE 16.3   Some artificial elements

Name	Symbol	Atomic Number	Source of Name
Neptunium	Np	93	The planet Neptune
Plutonium	Pu	94	The planet Pluto
Americum	Am	95	America
Curium	Cm	96	Marie Curie
Berkelium	Bk	97	University of California at Berkeley
Californium	Cf	98	University and State of California
Einsteinium	Es	99	Albert Einstein
Fermium	Fm	100	Enrico Fermi, Italian nuclear physicist
Mendelevium	Md	101	Dmitri Mendeleyev, Russian chemist
Nobelium	No	102	Alfred B. Nobel
Lawrencium	Lw	103	Ernest O. Lawrence, inventor of the cyclotron

2. These artificial radioactive isotopes are more commonly called radioisotopes.

Q. Radioisotopes have been most helpful in medicine, industry, agriculture, and research.

1. Because they all give off radiations that can be detected by instruments, they can be used as tracers in many different ways.
2. They can be traced as they move through pipelines, to detect leaks in the pipes; they can be used to study the wear of machine parts or automobile treads; they can also be used to study refining processes in oil refineries, to detect flaws in metal parts, and to gauge the thickness of sheets of metal, rubber, plastic, cloth, and paper.
3. Radioactive carbon can be used to show how the leaves of green plants make food for a plant by photosynthesis.
4. Radioisotopes are used to tell how well a plant is making use of fertilizers that have been added to the soil.
5. The exposure of seeds and plants to radiations from radioisotopes is producing new and better varieties of plants.
6. Radioactive cobalt is used to treat cancer instead of radium because it is easily made, cheaper, and more satisfactory.
7. Radioactive phosphorus and arsenic are used to detect brain tumors.
8. Another radioisotope, radioactive boron, is used to treat brain tumors.
9. Radioactive iodine is used to detect and treat diseases of the thyroid gland.
10. Radioisotopes are used by chemists to discover how chemical changes take place

and to learn more about the structure and properties of matter.

R. Scientists have also been able to use the nuclear reactor and the "atom smasher" to create entirely new elements as well.

1. All of these new elements have a higher atomic number than uranium, the 92nd natural element (see Table 16.3).
2. They are all radioactive, and some of them have a long half-life, but others have a half-life that lasts for just a few seconds or considerably less. (Half-life is the time required for one-half of the atoms in a piece of radioactive element to break into simpler atoms, a new element.) (See Figure 16.2 and section II, p. 595.)

X. COMPOUNDS AND MIXTURES

A. All substances that make up matter can be divided into three main classes: **elements, compounds,** and **mixtures.**

1. Because there are only 92 naturally occurring elements on earth, most substances are either compounds or mixtures.

B. A **compound** is a substance that is made up of two or more elements that have combined in such a way that each element has lost its own special physical and chemical properties.

1. As a result, the compound is a new substance with physical and chemical properties different from those of the elements that formed the compound.
2. This means that a chemical change takes place when a compound is formed, with energy either given off or required.

3. Every compound has its own special properties. Thus it is possible to tell one compound from another.

4. A compound is always made up of the same elements, and the number of atoms of each element that combine to form one molecule of the compound is always the same. For example, water is a compound made from the elements hydrogen and oxygen; there are always two atoms of hydrogen and one atom of oxygen in a molecule of water. Ammonia is a gaseous compound made of the elements nitrogen and hydrogen; there always are one atom of nitrogen and three atoms of hydrogen in a molecule of ammonia.

5. The elements in a compound cannot be separated easily, and some form of energy, such as electricity or heat, is needed to cause the separation to take place.

6. Because there are 92 natural elements, it is possible to make hundreds of thousands of compounds by using different combinations of elements.

7. Some elements, such as gold and platinum, do not combine very easily to form compounds. There are a few elements, like helium and neon, that rarely combine to form compounds.

C. A **mixture** is a substance made up of two or more elements or compounds that have combined in such a way that each element or compound has *not* lost its own special physical and chemical properties. As a result, no new substance has been formed.

1. Energy, such as heat or electricity, is not given off or required when a mixture is formed.

2. The amounts of the different substances that make up a mixture are not fixed. In a mixture, any amount of one substance can be combined with any amount of other substances.

3. The air we breathe is an example of a mixture. Air is made up of many gases, including oxygen, nitrogen, carbon dioxide, and water vapor. None of these gases has combined with the others, and each gas still retains its own special physical and chemical properties. The amounts of the gases in the air are not fixed, therefore they change from time to time.

4. The substances in a mixture can usually be separated very simply. Such separation is usually achieved by making use of the physical properties of the materials, such as their size, weight, color, and solubility in water or other liquids. For example, when a strong magnet is stirred in a mixture of iron powder and sulfur powder, the magnet picks up all the iron powder, thus separating the iron from the sulfur.

XI. FORUMULAS

A. Chemists use a combination of symbols and, where necessary, small numbers beside the symbols to show the makeup of a compound. This combination of symbols and small numbers is called a **formula.** A chemical formula tells us two things.

1. It tells us what elements are in the compound.

2. It tells us how many atoms of each element are in a molecule of the compound. For example, the formula for water is H_2O, illustrating that water is made up of the elements hydrogen and oxygen and that a molecule of water contains two atoms of hydrogen and one atom of water. The formula for cane sugar is $C_{12}H_{22}O_{11}$, illustrating that sugar is made up of the elements carbon, hydrogen, and oxygen and that a molecule of cane sugar contains 12 atoms of carbon, 22 atoms of hydrogen, and 11 atoms of oxygen. A list of some common compounds and their formulas is shown in Table 16.4.

XII. TYPES OF CHEMICAL CHANGES OR REACTIONS

A. Chemical changes are also called chemical reactions. All chemical changes or reactions can be grouped according to four types: combination, decomposition, simple replacement, and double replacement reactions.

B. In **combination reactions,** two or more elements or compounds combine to form a larger and more complicated compound.

1. For example, the elements carbon and oxygen combine to form carbon dioxide, and the compounds water and carbon dioxide combine to form carbonic acid.

C. **Equations** describe what happens during a chemical change or reaction.

1. Equations use formulas to show what materials take part in the chemical change or reaction and what new materials are formed.

2. For the two combination reactions described in section B, the equations are as follows:

TABLE 16.4　Some common compounds and their formulas

Compounds	Formulas
Ammonia	NH_3
Baking soda (sodium bicarbonate)	$NaHCO_3$
Carbon dioxide	CO_2
Carbon monoxide	CO
Lime (calcium oxide)	CaO
Limestone (calcium carbonate)	$CaCO_3$
Salt (sodium chloride)	$NaCl$
Sand (silicon dioxide)	SiO_2
Sugar (sucrose)	$C_{12}H_{22}O_{11}$
Sulfuric acid	H_2SO_4
Vinegar (acetic acid)	$HC_2H_3O_2$
Water	H_2O

$$C + O_2 \rightarrow CO_2$$
$$H_2O + CO_2 \rightarrow H_2CO_3$$

D. In **decomposition reactions,** a compound is broken up into the elements that formed it, or into simpler compounds.

   1. For example, the breakdown of iron sulfide into iron and sulfur is shown by this equation:

$$FeS \rightarrow Fe + S$$

   2. The breakdown of limestone (calcium carbonate) into lime (calcium oxide) and carbon dioxide is shown by this equation:

$$CaCO_3 \rightarrow CaO + CO_2$$

E. In **simple replacement reactions,** a free element replaces another element from a compound.

   1. For example, free iron replaces copper sulfate to form free copper and the compound iron sulfate, shown in this equation:

$$Fe + CuSO_4 \rightarrow Cu + FeSO_4$$

   2. Free zinc replace hydrogens from sulfuric acid to form free hydrogen gas and the compound zinc sulfate. That replacement reaction is shown by this equation:

$$Zn + H_2SO_4 \rightarrow H_2 + ZnSO_4$$

F. In **double replacement reactions,** an element in one compound trades places with an element in another compound, and the result is two new compounds.

   1. For example, silver in silver nitrate trades places with sodium in sodium chloride when both chemicals are first dissolved in water and then mixed together. Two new compounds, silver chloride and sodium nitrate, are formed. The equation for this reaction is as follows:

$$AgNO_3 + NaCl \rightarrow AgCl + NaNO_3$$

   2. In another example, when equal amounts of hydrochloric acid (a strong acid) and sodium hydroxide (a strong base) are mixed, the hydrogen in the hydrochloric acid trades places with the sodium in the sodium hydroxide, and common table salt ($NaCl$) and water are formed, as shown in the following equation:

$$HCl + NaOH \rightarrow H_2O + NaCl$$

XIII. SOLUTIONS

A. When a lump of sugar is added to a glass of water, the sugar gradually disappears. By tasting the water, however, we can tell that there is still sugar in the water even though we no longer may see it.

   1. What has happened is that the molecules of sugar have spread out and spaced themselves among the molecules of water.

   2. The water has the same amount of sweetness throughout, because the molecules of sugar have spread evenly and equally among the water molecules.

   3. We say that the sugar has **dissolved** in the water to form a **solution.**

   4. A solution is any mixture of two substances or materials in which the molecules of one substance are spread evenly and equally between the molecules of the other substance.

   5. The substance that dissolves is called the **solute,** which, in our example, is the sugar. The solute can be either a solid, a liquid, or a gas.

   6. The substance that does the dissolving, which in our example is the water, is called the **solvent.**

   7. A solvent is usually a liquid, such as water, although it can also be a gas or a solid.

   8. So many substances can dissolve in water that water is referred to as the **universal solvent.**

B. A **dilute solution** is one in which only a small amount of solute is dissolved in the solvent.

C. A **concentrated solution** is one in which a large amount of solute is dissolved in the solvent.

DEMONSTRATION 16.5
Types of Chemical Reactions

A. To Demonstrate Combination

Place some steel wool in water and allow it to rust. Remove the steel wool and examine the rust under a magnifying glass. Notice how the dark, metallic iron threads have been changed into the reddish orange, powdery iron oxide. Soak another wad of steel wool in water and leave it exposed to the air for a few days until it has become quite rusty. Scrape off some of the rust and see if it can be attracted by a magnet.

B. To Demonstrate Decomposition

Pour some 3 percent hydrogen peroxide (available from a drugstore) into a glass jar. Add a piece of liver the size of a half dollar, then cover the jar with a piece of cardboard. (Keep the liver cool, but do not freeze, until one hour before using.) The bubbling shows that a liver enzyme, called catalase, decomposes the hydrogen peroxide into water and oxygen gas. When the bubbling subsides, insert a glowing wood splint into the jar. The splint will burst into flame, showing the presence of oxygen.

C. To Demonstrate Simple Replacement

Dissolve some copper sulfate crystals (available from a plant nursery) in a tumbler of water and stir until the crystals dissolve completely. Place one or two iron nails, which are free of grease coating, into the solution and allow them to remain there overnight. Remove the nails and examine the coating of copper that has formed on them. Note that some iron from the nails has replaced the copper from the solution of copper sulfate.

D. To Demonstrate Double Replacement

Obtain a small amount of dilute silver nitrate solution from a drugstore. Dissolve some table salt (sodium chloride) in a glass tumbler or beaker half filled with water. Pour the clear silver nitrate solution into the equally clear salt solution. A white solid, or precipitate, forms immediately. Point out that the silver nitrate and sodium chloride interact to form silver chloride and sodium nitrate. The sodium nitrate remains in solution, whereas the silver chloride comes out of solution as the insoluble white solid.

D. A **saturated solution** is one in which as much solute as possible is dissolved in the solvent at a certain temperature and pressure.

E. The most common type of solution is one in which a solid dissolves in a liquid. Other common types of solutions are:
1. A solution of a gas in a liquid, such as carbon dioxide gas dissolved under pressure in water to form soda water.
2. A solution of a gas in a gas, such as air, for example, where the several gases in the air are spread evenly and equally among one another.
3. A solution of a liquid in a liquid, such as a solution of alcohol and water.

F. Special words are used to describe substances that will or will not dissolve.
1. For example, when a solid can dissolve in a liquid, we say that the solid is **soluble** in the liquid.
2. A solid that does not dissolve in a liquid is said to be **insoluble.**
3. When two liquids mix to form a solution, we say that the two liquids are **miscible.**
4. Two liquids that will not mix to form a solution are said to be immiscible or **nonmiscible.**

G. Usually, solids dissolve better in hot liquids than in cold liquids. Consequently, more of a solid will dissolve in a liquid when it is hot than when it is cold.
1. More sugar can dissolve in hot water than in cold water.
2. Some solids, such as salt, are almost as soluble in cold liquids as in hot liquids. Almost as much salt will dissolve in cold water as in hot water.
3. Some solids, such as calcium sulfate, are less soluble in hot liquids than in cold liquids, which means that less calcium sulfate will dissolve in hot water than in cold water.

H. Gases usually dissolve better in cold liquids than in hot liquids. Consequently, less of a gas will dissolve in a hot liquid than in a cold liquid.
1. When a glass of cold water is allowed to stand in a warm room for a while, bubbles of air collect on the sides of the glass.
2. What happens is that as the water becomes warmer, it cannot hold as much of the air dissolved in it, so some of the air comes out of the water.

I. An increase in pressure usually makes a gas more soluble in a liquid.

1. Soda water is water in which much carbon dioxide has been made to dissolve by using great pressure.
2. When the cap is removed from a bottle of soda water, the pressure is now lessened or reduced, and carbon dioxide escapes from the solution in the form of gas bubbles.
J. There are three ways to make solids dissolve more quickly in a liquid.
   1. Stirring can help the molecules of the solid spread quickly throughout the molecules of the liquid and, at the same time, bring fresh parts of the liquid in contact with particles of the solid that have not yet dissolved.
   2. Powdering the solid can allow more of the liquid to come in contact with the solid at one time, and this increased contact will help the solid dissolve more quickly.
   3. Heating the liquid will make the molecules of the liquid move more quickly so that the particles are spread more quickly throughout the molecules of the liquid, and at the same time fresh parts of the liquid will come in contact more quickly with particles of still undissolved solid.

XIV. THE LAW OF CONSERVATION OF MATTER
   A. In many chemical changes, such as when hydrogen gas and oxygen gas combine to form water, it seems as if new matter has been created. In other chemical changes, such as when a candle burns, matter seems to disappear, and we get the impression that matter has been destroyed. However, the law of conservation of matter tells us that, in ordinary chemical reactions, matter is neither created nor destroyed but only changed from one form to another.
      1. When wood is burned in air, gases are formed and ashes are left, and it be shown that the combined weight of the wood and the air that was used to burn the wood are exactly equal to the combined weight of the ashes and gases that are formed.
      2. So, in this chemical change, the matter changes from one form to another, but the amount of matter itself does not change.

ENERGY

I. DEFINITION OF ENERGY
   A. Energy is the ability of matter to move other matter or to produce a chemical change in other matter.
      1. Scientists also define energy as the ability to do work, usually when they are talking about machines.
      2. Work is done only when a force, which is a push or a pull, is moved through a distance.
   B. There are two kinds of energy: kinetic energy and potential energy.
   C. **Kinetic energy** is the energy a body has when it is in motion. Kinetic energy, therefore, is the energy of motion, an active energy. A moving automobile, falling water, a strong wind, and expanding gas are all examples of kinetic energy.
   D. **Potential energy** is the energy a body has because of its position or condition. Potential energy is stored-up energy, which will not do any work until it is set free or released.
      1. A rock balanced on a cliff has potential energy because it is in a position to do work when it is released, and water at the top of a dam or waterfall also has potential energy because of its position.
      2. A stretched rubber band and a wound-up spring both have potential energy because they are in a condition to do work when they are released.
      3. A chemical, such as gunpowder, also has potential energy because it is in a condition to do work when it ignites and explodes.
      4. The chemicals in a dry cell battery have potential energy because they are in a condition to do work when the dry cell is connected to an appliance.
      5. When potential energy is set free, it is changed to kinetic energy.
      6. When water at the top of a dam or waterfall is released, it moves faster and faster, gaining more and more kinetic energy, and when the water hits the bottom, its potential energy has been changed to kinetic energy.
      7. The potential energy of a stretched rubber band or wound-up spring is changed to kinetic energy when the band or the spring is released.
      8. The potential energy of gunpowder is changed to kinetic energy when the gunpowder explodes.

II. FORMS OF ENERGY

   A. There are six major forms of energy: mechanical, kinetic, electrical, wave, chemical, and nuclear.
   B. **Mechanical energy** is the form we see most often around us, the energy of machinery in motion. All moving bodies produce mechanical energy. The energy produced from most kinds of machines is mechanical energy.
   C. **Kinetic energy** is the energy produced by the moving molecules in a substance and is measured as **heat energy.** The faster its molecules move, the more energy a substance has and the hotter it becomes. Kinetic energy heats our homes, dries our clothes, cooks our food, and runs power plants.
   D. **Electrical energy** is the energy of electrons as they transfer energy through a substance. A transfer of energy of from one electron to the next through a substance is called an **electric current**. Electrical energy lights our homes, runs motors, and makes our telephones, radios, and television sets operable.
   E. **Wave energy** is energy that travels in waves.
      1. One kind of wave energy is **sound energy,** which is produced when matter moves back and forth, or vibrates, rapidly.
      2. Another kind of wave energy is **radiant energy.** There are many different forms of radiant energy, including light rays, X-rays, radio waves, infrared rays, ultraviolet rays, and radiant heat.
   F. **Chemical energy** is really a form of potential energy, because the energy is stored in substances. Chemical energy is released when a chemical reaction takes place and new substances are formed. The new substances are formed because of the action between the electrons in the outermost shells or energy levels in atoms of the different substances.
   G. **Nuclear energy** comes from the nucleus of an atom when the atom splits in two or when the nuclei of atoms fuse together.

III. THE TRANFORMATION AND CONSERVATION OF ENERGY

   A. Energy can be changed from one form to another.
      1. The production of electricity in a power plant illustrates how energy can be changed from one form to another.
      2. When coal or another fuel is burned, the chemical energy in the fuel is released and changed into heat energy.
      3. The heat energy is used to change water into steam, and the steam then turns a turbine to produce mechanical energy.
      4. The turbine runs an electric generator, or dynamo, that changes mechanical energy into electrical energy.
      5. The electrical energy may then be changed in a light bulb into light energy, or it may be changed in a doorbell to sound energy.
   B. In all these changes, energy is not destroyed, but changed in form. The **law of conservation of energy** says that energy is neither created nor destroyed, but only changed from one form to another. When energy is changed from one form to another, other forms of energy are produced. Usually these other forms of energy are not wanted and are wasted because we have no use or have found no use for them. For example, when we get light energy from an electric light bulb, unwanted and unused heat energy is also produced at the same time.

IV. THE LAW OF CONSERVATION OF MATTER AND ENERGY

   A. In 1905, Albert Einstein proposed his famous theory, which says that matter and energy are related to each other. According to Einstein, matter can be changed into energy, and energy can be changed into matter. Matter can be destroyed, but it reappears as newly created energy. Energy can be destroyed, but it reappears as newly created matter.
      1. Einstein's theory is usually expressed by the mathematical formula $e = mc^2$, where e represents the amount of energy, m represents the mass (amount of matter) and c represents the speed of light in a vacuum; c^2 means that this value for the speed of light is multiplied by itself. Thus, the formula reads: energy equals mass times the speed of light times the speed of light.
   B. Einstein's theory was verified when scientists began to study the atom.
      1. It was discovered that when certain atoms break up into simpler atoms, the simpler atoms all together weigh less than the original atom from which they came.
      2. However, when atoms do break up into simpler atoms, a tremendous amount of energy is also given off, which means that some of the matter in the atoms turns into energy.
   C. Scientists also found that when energy is used to make an electron move faster, the mass of the electron becomes greater. Supplying energy to

the electron increases not only its speed, but its mass as well. Some of that added energy turns into matter.

D. These findings showed that the law of conservation of matter and the law of conservation of energy do not always hold true. Now both laws are combined into a single law, the law of conserva-

tion of matter and energy. According to this law, neither matter nor energy can be destroyed, but either can be changed into other forms of matter or energy. Matter can be changed into energy, and energy can be changed into matter. As a result, the total amount of matter and energy in the universe stays constant.

NUCLEAR ENERGY

I. NATURAL RADIOACTIVITY

A. Certain elements, such as radium and uranium, give off invisible radiations, or rays, and these radiations have peculiar properties.
1. They can penetrate solid materials, such as paper, wood, thin sheets of metal, and flesh.
2. They affect a photographic negative in exactly the same way as visible light affects the negative when it is exposed to light.
3. They can stop seeds from germinating, kill bacteria, and destroy small animals.
4. A person exposed to these rays for some time will receive severe burns, which take a long time to heal or may even be fatal.
5. When compounds of these elements are added to certain other compounds, the mixture will become fluorescent, or glow in the dark.

B. These elements and their compounds also give off heat and visible light, as well as invisible radiations.

C. Elements that give off these invisible radiations are said to be radioactive, and this highly unusual property is called **radioactivity.** Elements that are naturally radioactive include uranium, thorium, carbon, potassium, radon, and radium.

D. These radiations are produced because the radioactive elements are breaking up, that is, they are giving up matter and energy.
1. In all cases it has been found that the breakup takes place in the nucleus.
2. While the breakup is going on, three different kinds of invisible radiations are given off.
3. Two of these radiation types are really particles of matter, called alpha particles and beta particles. The third radiation type is an energy wave, called a gamma ray.

E. **Alpha particles** are the nuclei of helium atoms.
1. Each helium nucleus has two protons and two neutrons and is about four times as heavy as a hydrogen atom.

2. Because of the positively charged protons in the helium nucleus, an alpha particle is positively charged.
3. When an alpha particle, or helium nucleus, gains two electrons, it becomes a helium atom.
4. Alpha particles have a speed of about 16,000 to 32,000 kilometers (10,000 to 20,000 mi) a second.
5. They have the smallest penetrating power of the three invisible radiation types given off by radioactive elements and can be stopped by a thin sheet of paper.

F. **Beta particles** are electrons traveling at high speeds.
1. These electrons are given off by the neutrons in the nucleus of the radioactive element.
2. They are negatively charged, and travel 96,000 to 256,000 kilometers (60,000 to 160,000 mi) a second.
3. Because of their high speed, beta particles have high penetrating power. A fairly thick sheet of aluminum metal is needed to stop them.

G. **Gamma rays** are high-energy X-rays.
1. They have more penetrating power than the other two radiation types.
2. Very thick layers of lead or concrete are required to stop them.

H. Radioactive elements break up because the nuclei of their atoms are unstable.
1. These unstable atoms are known as **radionuclides.**
2. The nuclei of radionuclides give off either alpha or beta particles.
3. New nuclei are formed, which are a little lighter and more stable than the original nuclei.
4. Gamma rays are produced because changes in energy levels take place in the nucleus when the new nuclei are formed.
5. At the same time, while the radioactive elements are breaking up, a small amount of

their matter is changed into tremendous amounts of energy.

I. When the unstable nuclei of radioactive elements give off alpha particles, new elements are formed.

1. An alpha particle is a helium nucleus, containing two protons and two neutrons.

2. When an atom of a radioactive element loses an alpha particle from its nucleus, this means that the nucleus has lost two protons, so the atomic number (number of protons in the nucleus) is now two less than it was previously.

3. Because the atomic number has changed, an atom of a new element has now been formed.

4. Moreover, because the two protons and two neutrons in the alpha particle give it an atomic weight of four, the loss of an alpha particle from the nucleus means that the atomic weight of the new element is four less than the atomic weight of the original element. An example of how the loss of an alpha particle produces a change in atomic number and atomic weight is shown by the radioactive element **radium,** which has an atomic number of 86 and an atomic weight of 222. When the nucleus of a radium atom loses an alpha particle, an atom of the gaseous element **radon** is formed, with an atomic number of 84 and an atomic weight of 218.

5. Radon is an odorless, colorless, and tasteless radioactive gas formed by the natural radioactive decay of uranium, which is found in minute amounts throughout the earth's crust. From the earth, radon seeps into homes and other buildings through fissures in foundations and can accumulate in homes in concentrations much higher than those measured outdoors. Radon can also enter homes through groundwater supplies.

6. Radon itself is radioactive because it also decays, losing an alpha particle and forming the element **polonium** (see Figure 16.2). Polonium, produced by the decay of radon in the air and in people's lungs, can cause lung cancer.

J. When the unstable nuclei of radioactive elements give off **beta particles,** new elements are also formed.

1. A beta particle is an electron given off by a neutron in a nucleus.

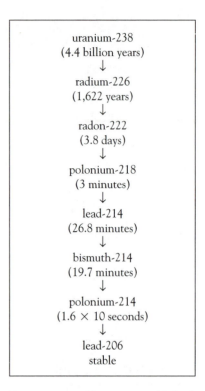

uranium-238
(4.4 billion years)
↓
radium-226
(1,622 years)
↓
radon-222
(3.8 days)
↓
polonium-218
(3 minutes)
↓
lead-214
(26.8 minutes)
↓
bismuth-214
(19.7 minutes)
↓
polonium-214
(1.6 × 10 seconds)
↓
lead-206
stable

FIGURE 16.2   Uranium to stable lead decay series, showing half-lives.

2. When a neutron gives off an electron, the neutron becomes a proton.

3. As a result, there is now one more proton in the nucleus than there was previously, so the atomic number has been increased by 1, which means that a new element has been formed.

4. Because an electron has little or no weight, the loss of a beta particle does not change the weight (mass) of the new element that has been formed. An example of how the loss of a beta particle produces a change in atomic number but not in atomic weight is shown by the radioactive element **thorium,** which has an atomic number of 90 and an atomic weight of 234. When an atom of thorium loses a beta particle, an atom of the element **protoactinium** is formed, with an atomic number of 91 and an atomic weight of 234.

K. The unstable nucleus of a radioactive element continues to give off either alpha or beta particles, accompanied by gamma rays in each case, forming lighter and more stable nuclei until a nucleus is finally formed that is completely stable.

1. When this condition results, radioactivity stops and no more alpha or beta particles and gamma rays are given off.
2. For example, the radioactive element **uranium** goes through a series of breakups, giving off either alpha or beta particles and forming new radioactive elements with each breakup, until it finally becomes **lead,** which is nonradioactive and stable (see Figure 16.2).

II.   THE LIFE OF RADIOACTIVE ELEMENTS

A. Radioactivity is much different from ordinary chemical changes.
   1. Ordinary changes can be speeded up or slowed down by changes in heat or pressure or by other means.
   2. Radioactive elements, on the other hand, break up at a steady rate of speed that cannot be changed.
B. The life of radioactive elements varies.
   1. Some elements take billions of years to break up into simpler elements, whereas others take days, hours, minutes, seconds, or fractions of seconds to break up.
   2. The time required for one half of the atoms in a piece of radioactive element to break up into simpler atoms is called the **half-life** of that element. Each radioactive element has its own half-life. (See Figure 16.2.)
   3. Radium, for example, has a half-life of 1,622 years, which means that half the atoms in a piece of radium will break up into simpler atoms in 1,622 years. Half of the radium atoms that remain, or one fourth of the original number, will break up in the next 1,622 years. Half of the remaining radium atoms, or one eighth of the original number, will breakup in the next 1,622 years. The radium atoms will keep on breaking up this way as long as there are radium atoms present. The half-life of uranium-238 is about 4.5 billion years.

III.   DETECTING AND MEASURING RADIOACTIVITY

A. Because radiations from radioactive elements are invisible, special instruments are necessary to detect and measure these radiations.
B. One simple method of detecting radiations is to observe their action on special, highly sensitive photographic film.
   1. Radiations from radioactive materials affect photographic film even though the film has not been exposed to ordinary light.

2. For safety, persons who work with or near radiations wear **film badges** to detect the amount of radiation present.
3. Each of these badges contain a small piece of special, highly sensitive photographic film, which is removed and developed to show the amount of radiation that has been absorbed by the person.
C. Another instrument used to detect and measure radiation is the electroscope.
   1. An electroscope is an instrument that is commonly used to detect and measure small electrical charges.
   2. When radiations from radioactive materials pass through air, they cause the particles of air to become electrically charged.
   3. The electroscope detects and measures these electrically charged particles of air, and in this way also detects and measures radiations.
   4. A type of electroscope, called a **dosimeter,** looks like a pencil and is clipped to a person's lapel or breast pocket.
D. Another instrument used to detect and measure radiations is the **Geiger counter.**
   1. This instrument is a cigar-shaped tube made of glass and metal, with a wire running through it, connected to a storage battery and a loudspeaker or amplifier.
   2. When a Geiger counter is brought near a radioactive material, the radiations cause a small pulselike flow of electricity to take place inside the tube.
   3. This tiny electric current is amplified and either produces a series of "clicks" or makes a bulb flash on and off.
   4. Normally, a Geiger counter produces 25 to 50 clicks a minute even without being near a radioactive material.
   5. These clicks come from cosmic rays passing through the air and from natural radioactivity in the ground.
   6. However, when a radioactive material is present, a Geiger counter clicks very rapidly and produces a "machine gun" effect.
   7. Geiger counters are used by prospectors when hunting uranium ore and are also used in laboratories where radioactivity is being studied.
E. The particles that make up radiations are invisible, but their paths can be seen and photographed in a **cloud chamber.**
   1. The cloud chamber is filled with air that is saturated with water vapor.
   2. When the particles pass through the chamber, the water vapor condenses.

3. Although the particles themselves are still invisible, the paths of the condensed moisture, called fog tracks, are visible and can be photographed.
4. A fog track is very much like the vapor trail made by a jet plane flying so high that it is invisible to the unaided eye.

IV. NUCLEAR FISSION

A. As a result of learning how uranium, radium, and other radioactive elements break up naturally to form new, lighter elements, scientists decided to try to break up atoms.
   1. They began by bombarding atoms of simpler elements with all kinds of high-speed particles, including protons, electrons, alpha particles (the nuclei of helium atoms), and deuterons (the nuclei of hydrogen atoms containing a proton and a neutron).
   2. With the exception of the electrons, all these high-speed particles are positively charged.
   3. The high speeds are given to these particles by instruments commonly called "atom smashers" or atomic accelerators.
   4. Atomic accelerators are able to give the particles speeds as high as 240,000 kilometers (150,000 mi) a second and tremendous amounts of energy.
   5. In the atomic accelerator called the **cyclotron**, protons or deuterons are made to whirl around faster and faster in a spiral path until they finally shoot out of the cyclotron at tremendous speed. Other accelerators that are used to give high speeds to positively charged particles include the cosmotron, the synchrotron, and the linear speed accelerator.
B. When scientists bombarded the nuclei of atoms of simple elements with the high-speed particles, new elements were formed.
   1. A particle entered the nucleus of an atom and made the nucleus unstable.
   2. The unstable nucleus then rearranged itself by giving off a proton or a neutron, forming a new element, and releasing much energy.
   3. This nuclear energy is produced when a small amount of an element's matter is changed into large amounts of energy, in accordance with Einstein's formula $e = mc^2$.
   4. When scientists bombarded nitrogen with high-speed alpha particles (helium nuclei), oxygen and neutrons were formed.
   5. When lithium was bombarded with high-speed protons, two alpha particles (helium nuclei) were formed.
   6. When beryllium was bombarded with high-speed alpha particles, carbon and neutrons were formed.
   7. Scientists had finally found a way to change one element into another.
C. However, scientists were not completely satisfied with these high-speed particles.
   1. The protons, deuterons, and alpha particles had to be given tremendous amounts of energy before they could enter the nucleus of an atom.
   2. This high energy was necessary because these particles were all positively charged, and when they came near the nucleus of an atom, they were repelled by the same kind of positive charges that the protons in the nucleus had.
   3. On the other hand, although the electrons were negatively charged and were attracted to the positively charged protons in the nucleus, the electrons were so light that it was hard for them to break up the atom.
D. As a result, as soon as scientists learned how to obtain neutrons by bombarding beryllium with high-speed alpha particles, they began to use neutrons to bombard the nuclei of atoms of other elements.
   1. The neutrons were much better particles to use, because they were neutral and would not be repelled by the positively charged nucleus of an atom.
   2. At first scientists used high-speed neutrons.
   3. However, they soon learned that because atoms were mostly empty space and because the nucleus is very small as compared with the rest of an atom, too often these high-speed neutrons went right through the atom without striking the tiny nucleus.
   4. They discovered that when they slowed the neutrons, the slowed-down neutrons were more likely to hit and be captured by the nucleus.
   5. In fact, the slowed-down neutrons seemed to behave as if they were attracted to the nucleus, going straight to the nucleus.
   6. One of the ways commonly used to slow neutrons is to allow them to pass through graphite, a pure form of carbon. The graphite in this case is called a moderator, because it slows or moderates the speed of the neutrons.

E. When scientists began to bombard the atoms of heavy elements with neutrons, a surprise occurred.

1. When they bombarded uranium with slowed-down neutrons, it did not break up as did the lighter elements, giving off a proton or a neutron and forming a new element.

2. Sometimes the uranium atom split into two parts, forming an atom of barium and an atom of krypton, both having medium-high atomic weights.

3. Two or three slow-moving neutrons were also given off, together with radiations in the form of gamma rays.

4. In addition, more energy was given off than had ever before been released.

5. This energy was formed when a small amount of the matter in the nucleus of the uranium atom was changed into large amounts of energy.

6. Scientists called this splitting of the nucleus of the atom **nuclear fission.**

F. The products of uranium fission are not always barium and krypton. Sometimes they are strontium and xenon, and still other elements can also be produced.

G. Because the uranium atom released two or three slow-moving neutrons, scientists hoped that a continuous splitting up of uranium atoms would be possible.

1. These slow-moving neutrons could split more uranium atoms, which would release more neutrons, which could split even more uranium atoms.

2. In this way a continuous splitting, called a **chain reaction**, would take place, continuing until all the atoms split.

H. However, the scientists found that only a few uranium atoms would split.

1. One reason for the failure to produce a chain reaction was the nature of uranium itself.

2. The uranium used had two isotopes: uranium-235, with 143 neutrons in its nucleus; and uranium-238, with 146 neutrons in its nucleus.

3. The uranium-235 isotope splits very easily, but the uranium-238 isotope does not.

4. More than 99 percent of the element uranium is made up of the uranium-238 isotope, and less than 1 percent is made up of the uranium-235 isotope.

5. So, for a chain reaction to take place, the uranium-235 isotope must be separated from the uranium-238 isotope, and only the uranium-235 isotope used.

6. A second reason for the failure of a chain reaction to take place had to do with the amount of uranium being used in the reaction.

7. If too small an amount of uranium is used, the released neutrons from the fission of one of the uranium atoms will be emitted without striking any other uranium atoms, and the reaction stops.

8. Enough uranium must be present to allow the neutrons to strike other uranium atoms and keep the chain reaction going.

9. The smallest amount of uranium needed to keep a chain reaction going is called the **critical size.**

10. Because so little uranium-235 is available, scientists began looking for other, more easily available elements that could be split by neutrons.

11. They discovered that they could change the more common uranium-238 isotope into a new element that could be split by neutrons.

12. When uranium-238 atoms were bombarded with neutrons, each nucleus kept a neutron and became unstable, giving off a beta particle (an electron) and forming a new artificial element, called **neptunium**, with an atomic number of 93.

13. Neptunium is an unstable element. It gives off a beta particle too, forming a second artificial element, called **plutonium,** with an atomic number of 94.

14. Plutonium is comparatively stable, but when bombarded by neutrons it splits up just as easily as uranium-235 to produce a chain reaction.

V. CONTROLLING AND USING NUCLEAR ENERGY

A. It is possible to control nuclear energy with a device called a nuclear reactor, which is sometimes also called an **atomic pile.**

1. A nuclear reactor helps to keep a chain reaction under control and makes use of the energy produced as a result of this reaction.

2. The reactor acts somewhat like a large oven or furnace.

3. In the reactor there is a large block of graphite serving as a moderator to slow down the neutrons so that they can enter the nuclei of the uranium-235 and produce a chain reaction.

4. Rods of uranium-235, sealed in aluminum cans for protection, are put into holes running horizontally through the graphite block from one end to the other.

5. Boron-steel or cadmium-steel rods are inserted into holes at the top of the reactor and run vertically through the graphite block.

6. These steel rods, called control rods, can be moved in and out of the reactor, and in this way can control the speed of the chain reaction.

7. The control rods absorb any neutrons that hit them.

8. If the chain reaction is going too fast, the control rods are lowered farther into the reactor so that they can absorb more neutrons and thus slow down the reaction; or if the reaction is going too slow, the rods are lifted farther out of the reactor so that fewer neutrons are now absorbed and the reaction can accelerate.

9. In some reactors the tremendous amount of heat that is produced is removed by blowing air through circulating tubes in the reactor; in other reactors the heat is removed by water or another liquid passing through the circulation tubes in the reactor.

10. The entire reactor is enclosed in a thick layer of solid concrete, which absorbs any dangerous radiations and therefore helps to protect the people operating the nuclear reactor.

B. The heat produced from the nuclear reaction is used to boil water and to change the water into steam.

1. The steam then turns a turbine, which runs an electric generator that produces electricity.

2. After the steam passes through the turbines, it is condensed and returned to the boilers to be changed back into steam again.

C. Nuclear reactors are used to run submarines and ships.

1. Vessels driven by the power from nuclear reactors can sail for long distances without the need to refuel.

2. The first nuclear submarine, the *Nautilus*, traveled almost 96,000 kilometers (60,000 mi) before it had to refuel.

D. Disposal of nuclear waste material is an environmental problem that has not been satisfactorily resolved.

E. On April 26, 1986, in what was then the Soviet Union, a nuclear power plant at Chernobyl, said to be one of the most powerful in the world, exploded and became the worst accident reported in the history of controlled nuclear reactions.

1. The cause of this explosion was a series of errors by the power plant operators that caused a power surge.

2. Thrown into the air were tons of the uranium dioxide fuel and fission products such as cesium-137 and iodine-131.

3. Explosion and heat sent up a 5-kilometer (3-mi) plume full of radioactive contaminants.

4. Although the complete toll of damage and deaths resulting from the accident at Chernobyl is yet unclear, of the 116,000 people immediately evacuated, 24,000 received serious radiation doses of 45 rem. Five rem is considered acceptable for a nuclear power plant employee for one year.

5. Children of the village of Lelev, 9 kilometers (5.6 mi) away, have been found to have thyroid radiation as high as 250 rem, the result of ingesting iodine-131.

6. Scientists have estimated that as a result of the accident at Chernobyl, there ultimately may be as many as 5,000 to 280,000 deaths.

7. Soil and water contamination may make the immediate area uninhabitable for a long time.

8. In 1995 it was reported that the sarcophagus that had been built over the explosion site to encase the high radiation was decaying, cracking, and leaking. It is likely that the environmental, health, and economic effects of the accident at Chernobyl will be experienced for decades to come.

EXPLORATORY ACTIVITIES FOR "CHANGES IN MATTER AND ENERGY"

1. *EXPLORING THE PROPERTIES OF MIXTURES AND COMPOUNDS* (GRADES 3 AND UP)

The activities of this exploration should be performed by the teacher, but with student input, responding to teacher questioning.

Overview   These activities designed to facilitate student understanding of the nature of the properties of mixtures and compounds.

1.1 Exploring the Properties of Mixtures
Mix fine sand, sugar, iron filings, bits of cork filed from a stopper, and small marbles. Now ask students to hy-

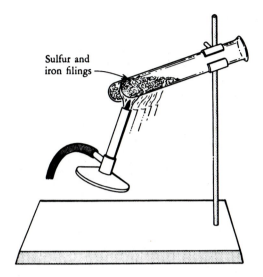

Sulfur and
iron filings

FIGURE 16.3   Heating sulfur and iron will produce a compound.

pothesize about ways of separating the components of the mixture. Then test their hypotheses. Conclusions should be something like the following. The marbles can be removed by hand or by pouring the mixture through a kitchen strainer. The iron filings can be removed with a strong magnet. Adding water to the remaining part of the mixture and then stirring causes the sugar to dissolve and the bits of cork to float on top of the solution. The bits of cork can be removed with a large spoon. The solution can then be poured off, leaving the sand behind. The solution can be allowed to evaporate in a pie tin or other shallow container; this action causes the sugar to be left behind.

1.2   Exploring the Properties of Compounds

Physical change only: Mix three parts sulfur powder and one part iron powder by weight. Stir until the mixture is uniform and the ingredients are indistinguishable. Ask students to hypothesize ways of separating the substances that you mixed together. Test their hypotheses. Conclusions should be as follows.

Place one half of the mixture in a shallow dish, and use a strong magnet to separate the iron from the sulfur, thus showing that the materials in a mixture retain their own special properties and can usually be separated by very simple means. Pass the magnet over the sulfur several times to pick up all the iron powder.

Chemical change: Now pour the second half of this mixture of sulfur and iron powder into a Pyrex tube that is supported on a ring stand with a clamp (Figure 16.3). Heat the test tube with a Bunsen burner, first gently and

then strongly. Keep moving the flame up and down the lower half of the test tube to make sure the contents are being heated uniformly. Soon the contents will begin to glow, showing that a chemical change is taking place. Remove the flame and observe that the chemical change continues to take place, with the contents glowing strongly. Allow the test tube to cool to room temperature, wrap it in a piece of cloth or toweling, and break the end of the test tube gently with a hammer. Remove the contents with tweezers and place the material in a shallow dish. Try to separate the iron powder with a magnet. Ask students to hypothesize about what has happened. Nothing will happen because a new substance, called iron sulfide, has been formed, and it is not magnetic.

2. *WHAT'S THE MATTER? EXPLORING THE PROPERTIES OF DENSITY* (GRADES 5–9)

(See page 195 of Chapter 5.)

3. *EXPLORING THE PROPERTIES OF SOLUTIONS* (GRADES 4–9)

Set up six stations, with instructions at each station as follows.

3.1   Exploring Solutions

Obtain three tumblers the same size. Fill each tumbler three-quarters full of tap water of the same temperature. To one tumbler add ¼ teaspoon of sugar and stir until all the sugar is dissolved. To the second tumbler add 2 teaspoons of sugar and stir until all the sugar is dissolved. This can be set up as a blind test for students. Let them taste both solutions and predict which is dilute and which is concentrated.

To the third tumbler add ½ teaspoon of sugar and stir until all the sugar is dissolved. Continue adding sugar, a teaspoon at a time and stirring after each addition, until no more sugar will dissolve and a small pile of undissolved sugar remains at the bottom of the tumbler. Total the number of teaspoons of sugar you added to obtain a saturated sugar solution. Graph the results.

3.2   Some Substances Are More Soluble in Water Than Others

Add equal amounts of water at room temperature to three test tubes. Add a level teaspoon of sugar to one test tube, a level teaspoon of salt to the second test tube, and a level teaspoon of sodium bicarbonate to the third test tube. Placing your thumb over its mouth, shake each test tube vigorously 10 times; then place the test tubes upright and allow any undissolved material to settle. Record your conclusions about the degree of solubility of the three different materials.

3.3 Some Substances Are Insoluble in Water

Place a small stone in a test tube of water. Place your thumb over the mouth of the test tube and shake the tube vigorously. Record your conclusion. (No dissolving will take place.)

Add a few drops of oil to a test tube containing water. Record what happens. (The oil floats on top of the water.) Shake the test tube vigorously. Although the oil may break up into small drops, the drops will reassemble and the oil will continue to float undissolved on top of the water. Repeat the experiment, using a commercial "spot remover" instead of water. Record your conclusion. (The oil will be dissolved.)

3.4 The Effect of Temperature on the Solubility of Solids in Liquids

Pour a measured amount of water at room temperature into a tumbler. Add sugar, a teaspoon at a time, stirring after each addition until no more will dissolve. Repeat the experiment, using an equal amount of hot water this time. Compare the number of teaspoons of sugar that dissolved in the cold and hot water, respectively. Repeat the experiment, graphing the results of each trial. Write your conclusions.

3.5 The Effect of Pressure on the Solubility of Gases in Liquids

(Possibly as a teacher demonstration.) Obtain two identical bottles of soda. Put one in the refrigerator and allow it to stand overnight. Keep the other bottle at room temperature. The next day remove the caps from both bottles. Place the cold, open bottle back in the refrigerator, and let the warm, open bottle stand again at room temperature. At the end of an hour pour the contents of each bottle into a tumbler. Observe and record your conclusion. (The soda from the cold bottle will fizz fairly vigorously, showing the presence of dissolved gas. The soda from the warm bottle will fizz weakly, if at all, showing that most of the dissolved gas has been driven from the soda at the warmer temperature.)

3.6 Making Solids Dissolve More Quickly in Water

Pour equal amounts of water at the same temperature in two tumblers. Record the temperature of each. Obtain two cubes of sugar and crush one of the cubes into small crystals. Put the lump of sugar into one tumbler and the crushed sugar into the second tumbler. Stir the water in each tumbler vigorously. Observe and record your conclusion. (The crushed sugar dissolves more quickly, because more of the water can come in contact with the sugar at one time.)

Pour equal amounts of water at the same temperature into two tumblers. Record the temperature of each. Add a level teaspoon of sugar to each of the tumblers. Stir the water in one of the tumblers, but not the other. Observe and note the result. (The sugar in the stirred water dissolves more quickly, because the stirring helps spread the sugar more quickly throughout the water and at the same time brings fresh parts of the water in contact with particles of sugar that have not yet dissolved.)

Pour a measured amount of water at room temperature into a tumbler. Pour an equal amount of hot water into a second tumbler. Record the temperature of each. Drop a sugar cube into each tumbler and note the results. (The sugar dissolves in the hot water more quickly.)

STUDENTS BOOKS AND OTHER RESOURCES FOR "CHANGES IN MATTER AND ENERGY"

Belcher, D. C. "Balancing Chemical Equations." *Science Scope* 19(3):37–39 (November 1995).

Crow, L. W., and B. G. Aldridge. *Middle Level Energy Series*. Arlington, VA: National Science Teachers Association, 1995.

Eimer, T. "The Politics of Plutonium." *Science Scope* 18(1):39–41 (September 1994).

Harris, R. L., and F. Roberts. "How Sweet It Is." *Science Scope* 19(3):34–35 (November 1995).

League of Women Voters, The. *The Nuclear Waste Primer: A Handbook for Citizens*. Washington, DC: The League of Women Voters Education Fund, 1993.

Otton, J. K., L. Gundersen, and R. R. Schumann. *The Geology of Radon*. Washington, DC: U. S. Government Printing Office, 1993.

Pflaum, R. *Marie Curie and Her Daughter Irène*. Minneapolis: Lerner, 1993.

Runyan, T., and S. Gertz. "The Chemistry of Corrosion." *Science Scope* 16(5):20–26 (February 1993).

Sarquis, J., M. Sarquis, and J. Williams. *Teaching Chemistry with Toys*. Arlington, VA: National Science Teachers Association, 1995.

Shaw, M. I., and G. F. Smith. "Double Bubble? No Trouble!" *Science and Children* 33(1):24–27 (September 1995).

Strain, J. "Moving Molecules and Mothball Madness." *Science Scope* 17(1):25–28 (September 1993).

CHAPTER 17

Friction and Machines

FRICTION

I. THE NATURE OF FRICTION

  A. Whenever the surfaces of two materials rub against each other, friction is produced. Friction is the force that resists the movement of one material over another material.

    1. Friction is caused by irregularities in the surfaces of materials.

    2. Every surface contains little bumps and hollows.

    3. On rough surfaces these bumps and hollows can be seen or felt, but on smooth surfaces the bumps and hollows can be seen only through a magnifying glass or microscope.

    4. When two surfaces are rubbed together, the bumps and hollows catch and stick and resist the movement of the surfaces over each other.

    5. Friction can make it difficult to push one material across another material.

    6. Friction is also caused by the attraction of the molecules of one surface to the molecules of another surface as the surfaces rub against each other.

  B. Friction produces heat.

    1. The greater the friction, the more heat will be produced.

II. FACTORS AFFECTING FRICTION

  A. The nature of the materials used affects friction.

    1. Firm, hard materials produce less friction than soft, sticky materials.

  B. The nature of the surfaces affects friction.

    1. Smooth surfaces produce less friction than rough surfaces.

  C. For a given force, an increase or decrease in area of contact affects friction. For example, the larger the area of disc pads on automobile brakes, the greater the friction and the braking force.

  D. The force of the two surfaces against each other affects friction.

    1. The greater the force pressing the surfaces against each other, the greater the friction will be.

  E. **Sliding friction** is less than **starting friction**.

    1. More force is needed to start an object sliding than to keep it sliding.

  F. **Rolling friction** is less than sliding friction.

    1. In sliding friction, the bumps and hollows catch against each other.

    2. In rolling friction, the roller or wheel lifts up over the bumps and hollows instead of sliding and catching against them.

III. METHODS OF REDUCING FRICTION

  A. Making surfaces smoother levels out the bumps and hollows and reduces the friction between them.

  B. A slippery material, called a **lubricant**, can be applied to reduce friction.

    1. The lubricant is placed between the two surfaces, filling up the hollows and covering the bumps, in effect, making the surfaces seem smoother.

DEMONSTRATION 17.1
Friction Produces Heat

Have the students rub the palms of their hands together briskly and note the heat produced by the resulting fric-tion. The more briskly the hands are rubbed, the greater the friction and the hotter the hands become.

DEMONSTRATION 17.2
Sliding, Rolling, and Starting Friction

A. Comparing starting friction and sliding friction

Slip a loop of string inside a large book and place the book on a table. Attach the string to a spring balance (Figure 17.1). Pull on the scale (making sure to hold it horizon-tally) until the book begins to move. Note the reading on the scale just before the book moves. Now pull the scale and book together along the table and note the reduced reading on the scale while the book is moving.

B. Comparing rolling friction and starting friction

Slip a loop of string inside a large book and attach the string to a spring balance, as described in demonstration A. Pull the scale and book together along the table and note the reading on the scale while the book is moving. Now place about a dozen round pencils beneath and be-side the book, and pull the book along the table again (Figure 17.2). Note the reduced reading on the scale as the book moves along the rollers.

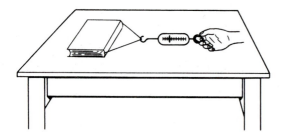

FIGURE 17.1 Sliding friction is less than starting friction.

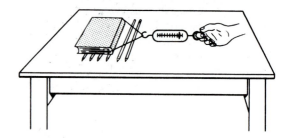

FIGURE 17.2 Rollers can reduce friction.

2. In this way the lubricant prevents the two surfaces from rubbing directly against each other.
3. Oil is a lubricant used to reduce friction be-tween parts of machines; grease is used to lu-bricate parts of an automobile; glycerine and water can be used as lubricants to reduce the friction between rubber and glass; soap and candle wax are used as lubricants to reduce friction between two pieces of wood, or be-tween wood and metal; graphite (a form of pure carbon) can be used to reduce friction between two metals, or between wood and metal.

C. Rollers, wheels, and ball bearings reduce friction by changing sliding friction to rolling friction.
D. Streamlining reduces the friction of autos and planes moving through air, as well as the fric-tion of a boat moving through water.
   1. At high speeds air resistance can be great, resisting the forward motion of an auto or plane and slowing it down.

IV. BENEFICIAL AND HARMFUL EFFECTS OF FRICTION
   A. Friction can be useful.
      1. Without friction, we could not walk, be-cause our feet would slip, and we could not

DEMONSTRATION 17.3

Lubricants Reduce Friction

Rub two pieces of dry toast together. Note the amount of friction and the wearing away of bits of toast. Now spread some jam thickly across each piece of toast and rub the pieces together again. The pieces will now slide smoothly over each other because the jam has filled the hollows and covered the bumps, thus reducing the friction.

write with a pencil, pen, or chalk, or hold a baseball and bat.

2. Sand or cinders are dropped in front of an automobile's rear wheels to increase friction and stop the wheels from spinning on icy roads.

3. Auto brakes use friction to slow or stop a moving auto.

4. Friction helps hold nails and screws in wood, and helps us to unscrew the tops of bottles or jars, and to open cans.

5. In industry, friction helps a conveyor belt to move things along.

6. Friction is useful in making things smoother, as in sanding wood or grinding lenses.

7. The heat caused by friction causes a match to burst into flame.

B. Friction can be harmful.

1. Friction wears away materials, such as automobile tires, shoes, and clothing.

2. The moving parts of machines rub against each other and wear away.

3. Friction makes work harder, because extra force must be used to overcome friction.

4. Friction resists the movement of objects, making sliding parts stick.

5. Friction between air and moving objects hinders the speed of these objects.

6. Friction produces heat, which can start a fire or cause machine parts to melt or bend. At high speed, the friction between the air and a plane, spacecraft, or rocket may cause parts of the craft to become so hot that it will burn up, melt, or bend.

7. If a person falls and slides across a gymnasium floor, the heat produced by the friction between a part of the body and the floor may cause a painful and easily infected burn.

MACHINES

I. WHAT MACHINES DO

A. Machines are devices that help make our work easier.

B. A **force**, which is a push or a pull, must be applied to make a machine work.

C. A force may be produced by any of the following: earth's gravity; electricity; falling water; gasoline; muscles; springs and weights; steam; sun's rays; and wind.

D. Machines can help us in four ways.

1. Machines can transfer a force from one place to another.

2. Some machines can increase the amount of a force so that we can lift heavier things or exert more force with the machine than we can alone.

3. Some machines can change the direction of a force so that we can make things move in different directions.

4. Some machines can increase the distance and speed of a force so that we can move things farther or faster.

E. No machine can increase both force and distance moved at the same time.

1. If only a small force is needed to move or lift a heavy object, there is a gain in force; however, the heavy object will now move or be lifted through a shorter distance. So, although there is a gain in force, there is a loss in distance.

II. THE SIX SIMPLE MACHINES.

A. No matter how many parts they have, all machines are made up of one or more of six simple machines: the lever, the wheel-and-axle, the pulley, the inclined plane, the wedge, and the screw.

1. The wheel-and-axle and the pulley are different forms of the lever.

DEMONSTRATION 17.4

Machines Can Increase the Distance and Speed of a Force

Let a student sweep with a kitchen broom. As the student sweeps, point out that the upper part of the broom handle is moving just a short distance back and forth. How-ever, the lower and bottom parts of the broom are moving faster and farther.

---

2. The wedge and the screw are different forms of the inclined plane.

III. WORK

A. Machines help make work easier, but machines do *not* save work.
B. Work is done only when an effort or a resistance moves through a distance.
   1. The force exerted on a machine is called the **effort**.
   2. The force that the machine exerts, or the object that the machine lifts or moves, is called the **resistance**.
   3. No matter how much effort or resistance is exerted, if they have not moved through a distance, no work has been done. For example, if you are standing and pushing on a brick wall but the wall is not moving, then you are doing no work (although your muscles may be using up energy and will tire).
   4. To find out how much work has been done, the force is multiplied by the distance through which the force moves, which can be stated as a formula.

   Work = (force used) × (distance moved)

   5. In the **English system** of measurement, force is usually stated in pounds, distance in feet, and work done in **foot-pounds**.
   6. To calculate the work that is put into a machine, multiply the effort times the distance the effort moves. For example, if an effort of 2 pounds is exerted over a distance of 5 feet, 2 × 5, or 10, foot-pounds of work is done.
   7. To calculate the work that a machine does, or puts out, multiply the resistance times the distance the resistance moves. For example, if a machine lifts an object weighing 5 pounds through a distance of 2 feet, the machine has done 2 × 5, or 10, foot-pounds of work.
   8. In the **metric system,** force is stated in newtons, distance in meters, and work done in **newton-meters** (more commonly called

joules). For example, if you move a body 5 meters with a force of 2 newtons, you do 10 joules (or newton-meters) of work.
C. The speed with which the effort or resistance moves will make no difference in the amount of work done.
D. No machine can produce more work than the work that was put into the machine.
E. If there were no friction, the amount of work a machine could do, or put out, would be equal to the amount of work put into the machine.
   1. This concept is the **principle of work**.
   2. The principle of work helps explain why a small force must move through a longer distance to make a heavy object move through a shorter distance.
   3. Because of friction, however, the amount of work put out by a machine is less than the work put into the machine.
   4. Extra effort, which means more work, must be used to overcome friction; the amount of extra effort involved in overcoming friction makes a difference in the efficiency of a machine.

IV. MECHANICAL ADVANTAGE

A. When we apply a small force on a machine and the machine gives us more force, or lifts or moves a heavy object, we say that we get a mechanical advantage (M.A.) of force.
   1. If a machine produces a force that is five times as great as the force that is acting on the machine, the mechanical advantage of force is 5.
B. There are two ways of finding the mechanical advantage of a simple machine.
   1. One way is to divide the resistance, or weight, by the effort that is exerted; this expression can be stated as a formula:

   $$\text{M.A.} = \frac{\text{Resistance}}{\text{Effort}}$$

   2. If the effort is 2 pounds, and the resistance 8 pounds, the mechanical advantage is ⅘, or 4.

3. This mechanical advantage is called the **actual mechanical advantage** (A.M.A.) because extra effort had to be exerted in overcoming friction, so this mechanical advantage is the advantage of force that you actually get when you use the machine.
4. The second way is to divide the distance the effort moves by the distance the resistance moves; this expression can be stated as a formula too:

$$\text{M.A.} = \frac{\text{Effort distance}}{\text{Resistance distance}}$$

5. If the effort moves 10 feet while the resistance moves 2 feet, the mechanical advantage is $^{10}\!/_2$, or 5.
6. This mechanical advantage is called the **ideal mechanical advantage** (I.M.A.), because friction is not involved in this calculation.
7. For many simple machines there are also special, and usually easier, ways to find the ideal mechanical advantage.
8. If extra effort were not needed to overcome friction, the A.M.A. and the I.M.A. would be exactly the same.
9. However, because extra effort is needed to overcome friction, the A.M.A. is smaller than the I.M.A.
10. The I.M.A. then tells us the highest possible mechanical advantage we can get from a machine, whereas the A.M.A. tells us the actual or real mechanical advantage we get when we use the machine.
C. A machine can also give us a mechanical advantage of speed.
 1. When a machine makes an object move faster, we get a mechanical advantage of speed. If, for example, a machine makes an object move five times as fast as the force that is acting on the machine, the mechanical advantage of speed is 5.

V. THE LEVER
 A. A lever is a rigid bar, straight or curved, that rests on a fixed point called the **fulcrum**.
 B. The force exerted on the lever is called the **effort**.
 C. The force that the lever exerts, or the object that the lever lifts or moves, is called the **resistance**.
 D. The distance from the fulcrum to the point where the effort is exerted is called the **effort arm**, and the distance from the fulcrum to the

point where the resistance is exerted or lifted is called the **resistance arm**.
E. The closer the fulcrum is to the resistance, the less effort will be needed to move or lift the resistance; the effort, however, will move a longer distance and the resistance will move a shorter distance.
 1. There will be a gain in force, but a loss in distance and speed.
 2. This action follows the principle of work.
F. The closer the fulcrum to the effort, the greater the force needed to move or lift the resistance; but now the effort will move a shorter distance and the resistance will move a longer distance.
 1. There will be a loss in force, but a gain in distance and speed.
 2. This action also follows the principle of work.
G. The actual mechanical advantage (A.M.A.) of the lever is found by dividing the resistance or weight by the effort.
H. The ideal mechanical advantage (I.M.A.) can be found in two ways:
 1. Dividing the distance the effort moves by the distance the resistance moves.
 2. Dividing the length of the effort arm by the length of the resistance arm.
I. Levers are divided into three classes, depending on the positions of the effort, resistance, and fulcrum.
J. A **first-class lever** is one in which the fulcrum is located anywhere between the effort (or force) and the resistance (or weight) (see Figure 17.3).
 1. Examples of first-class levers include the crowbar, scissors, pliers, tin snips, tack puller, pry bar, oar of a rowboat, and seesaw.
 2. A first-class lever changes the direction of a force, so the effort pushes in one direction while the resistance moves in the opposite direction (see Figure 17.4).
 3. When the fulcrum is closer to the resistance than to the effort, we gain in force, but get less speed and distance (see Figure 17.5).
 4. When the fulcrum is closer to the effort than to the resistance, we get more speed and distance, but lose in force.
 5. When the fulcrum is exactly between the effort and the resistance, there is no change in force, speed, or distance, but there is a change in direction.
K. A **second-class lever** is one in which the resistance is between the effort and the fulcrum (see Figure 17.6).

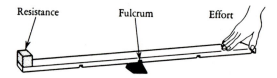

FIGURE 17.3   A first-class lever.

1. Examples of second-class levers include the wheelbarrow, nutcracker, crowbar, and bottle opener (see Figure 17.7).
2. A second-class lever does not change the direction of a force, so the effort and resistance move in the same direction.
3. In a second-class lever the fulcrum is usually closer to the resistance, so there is a gain in force.

L. A **third-class lever** is one in which the effort is between the resistance and the fulcrum (see Figure 17.8).
   1. Examples of third-class levers include the broom, shovel, sugar tongs, tweezers, and fishing pole.
   2. A third-class lever does not change the direction of the force.
   3. In a third-class lever there is always a gain in speed and distance and a loss in force.

VI. THE WHEEL-AND-AXLE

   A. A simple wheel-and-axle machine is one in which a large wheel is connected to a smaller wheel or shaft, called an axle (see Figure 17.9).
   1. When either the wheel or the axle turns, the other part also turns.
   2. One complete turn of the wheel produces one complete turn of the axle.

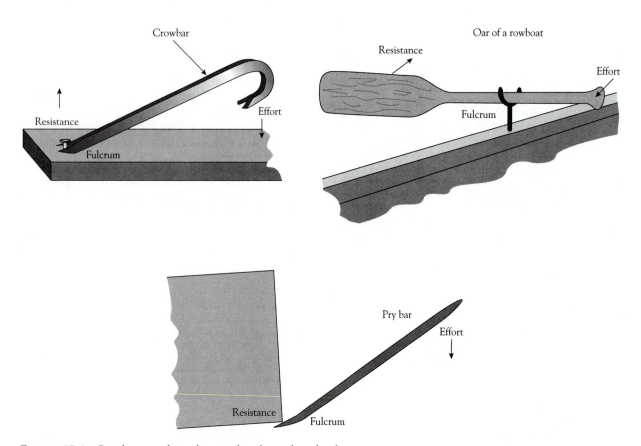

FIGURE 17.4   Crowbar, oar of a rowboat, and pry bar as first-class levers.

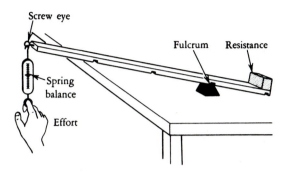

FIGURE 17.5   Less effort is needed when the fulcrum is nearer the resistance.

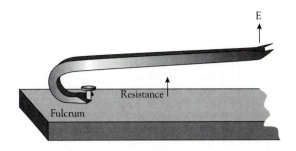

FIGURE 17.7   A crowbar used as a second-class lever.

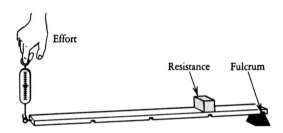

FIGURE 17.6   A second-class lever.

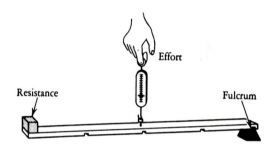

FIGURE 17.8   A third-class lever.

3. If the wheel turns but the axle does not, the device is not a wheel-and-axle machine.
4. The wheel does not have to be a complete wheel; instead, there may be a crank that turns.
5. When the crank is turned, it makes a complete circle, just as though it were a complete wheel.

B. A wheel-and-axle is really a form of the lever; it is a rotating lever.
   1. The spinning lever can be seen very clearly when a crank is used instead of a wheel.
   2. The fulcrum is at the center of the axle and the wheel (or crank).
   3. The radius of the wheel is the effort arm, and the radius of the axle the resistance arm, of the lever.

C. A wheel-and-axle can change the direction of a force.

D. When the wheel turns the axle, there is a gain in force.
   1. A smaller force, or effort, at the wheel will move a larger weight, or resistance, at the axle.

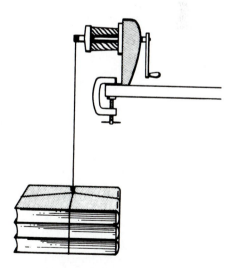

FIGURE 17.9   The pencil sharpener acts as a wheel-and-axle.

   2. But the weight, or resistance, will not move as far or as fast as the force, or effort, because the wheel is larger than the axle.

3. The larger the wheel, as compared with the axle, the greater the gain in force will be.

E. When the axle turns the wheel, there is a loss in force and a gain in distance and speed.

1. With a larger force exerted at the axle, the wheel (the resistance) will turn faster and farther.

2. The smaller the axle, as compared with the wheel, the greater the gain in speed and distance.

F. The actual mechanical advantage (A.M.A.) of the wheel-and-axle is found by dividing the weight or resistance lifted by the effort exerted.

G. The ideal mechanical advantage (I.M.A.) can be found in the following ways:

1. Divide the distance the effort moves by the distance the weight or resistance moves.

2. Divide the circumference of the wheel by the circumference of the axle.

3. Divide the diameter of the wheel by the diameter of the axle.

4. Divide the radius of the wheel by the radius of the axle.

H. Examples of wheel-and-axle machines containing complete wheels include an automobile steering wheel, the gear wheels of a bicycle, a door knob, and a screwdriver.

I. Examples of wheel-and-axle machines containing a crank instead of a complete wheel can be found in a pencil sharpener, a meat grinder, and an egg beater.

VII. The Pulley

A. A pulley is a wheel that turns around a stationary axle.

1. Usually there is a groove in the rim of the pulley so that the rope around it will not slip off.

2. Sometimes two or more wheels are placed side by side on the same axle.

B. There are two types of pulley: the fixed pulley and the movable pulley.

1. A **fixed pulley** does not move from its location but will rotate.

2. It helps by changing the direction of the force.

3. It gives no gain in force, speed, or distance.

4. Fixed pulleys are used with flag poles, clothes lines, curtain rods, and venetian blinds.

5. The fixed pulley acts like a turning first-

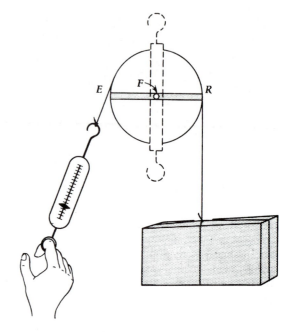

FIGURE 17.10   A fixed pulley is a spinning first-class lever.

class lever, with the fulcrum at the center of the axle, the effort at one rim of the pulley wheel, and the resistance at the other rim (see Figure 17.10).

6. A **movable pulley** moves along a rope.

7. It helps us gain in force, but we lose in distance.

8. In a single movable pulley, two sections of rope support the pulley so that only half as much effort is needed to raise a resistance.

9. However, the effort must now move about twice as far as the resistance.

10. A movable pulley does not change the direction of the force.

11. A movable pulley acts like a turning second-class lever, with the fulcrum at one rim of the pulley wheel, the resistance at the center of the axle, and the effort at the other rim of the pulley wheel (see Figure 17.11).

C. A single pulley may be combined with a movable pulley to change direction and gain force at the same time (see Figure 17.12).

1. Such a combination is called a **block and tackle**.

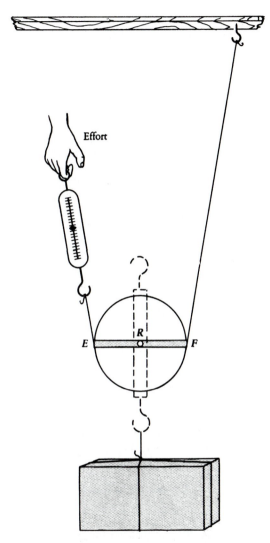

FIGURE 17.11   A movable pulley is a spinning second-class lever.

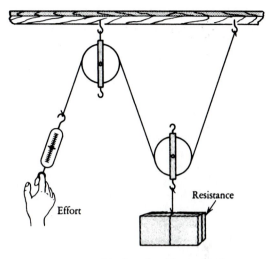

FIGURE 17.12   A block and tackle is a combination of a fixed and a movable pulley.

1. Divide the distance the effort moves by the distance the resistance moves.
2. Count the number of sections of rope that support the movable pulleys.

VIII. THE INCLINED PLANE

  A. An inclined plane is a slanting surface that connects one level to a higher level, thereby requiring less force to lift an object.

    1. By moving an object up an inclined plane, we use less effort in getting the object to the higher level than if we had to lift the object directly from the lower to the higher level.

    2. We gain lifting power at the expense of distance. The object must be moved a longer distance as it travels up the inclined plane to reach the desired higher level.

    3. The longer the inclined plane, the more gradual the slope becomes, and the less effort will be needed to move the body up the incline. The shorter the inclined plane, the steeper the slope becomes, and the more effort will be needed to move the body up the inclined plane.

  B. The actual mechanical advantage (A.M.A.) of an inclined plane is found by dividing the resistance by the effort. The ideal mechanical advantage (I.M.A.) is found by dividing the length of the inclined plane by the height.

  C. Examples of the inclined plane include a plank, ramp, sloping floor of a theater or au-

2. Several fixed and movable pulleys can be used in a block and tackle.
3. Each fixed pulley changes the direction of the force, and each movable pulley changes the amount of the force.
4. The more movable pulleys used, the less force will be needed.
5. A block and tackle is used in scaffolds for painters and for billboard workers.

  D. The actual mechanical advantage (A.M.A.) of a pulley, or set of pulleys, is found by dividing the resistance by the effort.

  E. The ideal mechanical advantage (I.M.A.) can be found in two ways:

ditorium, straight road up a hill, escalator, and stairway.

IX. THE WEDGE

A. A wedge is a simple machine used either to spread an object apart or to raise an object. A wedge has a sloping or slanting side, like an inclined plane.
 1. A single wedge looks like an inclined plane and has one sloping side.
 2. A double wedge looks like two inclined planes that have been joined together with their sloping sides facing outward.

B. A wedge is a form of inclined plane with only one difference.
 1. With the use of an inclined plane an object moves up the incline, but with use of a wedge the incline moves into or under the object.
 2. The gain in effort is obtained at the expense of distance, because the effort moves over a longer distance than the resistance.
 3. The farthest the resistance can be moved is the thickness of the large end of the wedge.

C. The actual mechanical advantage (A.M.A.) of a wedge is found by dividing the resistance by the effort. The ideal mechanical advantage (I.M.A.) is found by dividing the length of the wedge by the thickness of its large end.
 1. The actual mechanical advantage of a wedge is always much less than the ideal mechanical advantage because of the friction between the wedge and the object.
 2. Friction is helpful in this case, because it keeps the wedge from slipping out.

D. Examples of the wedge include an ax, knife blade, scissors blade, chisel, pin, nail, and plow.

X. THE SCREW

A. A screw is an inclined plane that winds around and around in a spiral.
 1. The spiral ridge of the screw is called the **thread**.
 2. One complete turn of the screw moves the screw into the object the distance from one thread to another.
 3. The distance between two threads is called the **pitch** of the screw.
 4. The screw gives a gain in force, but at the expense of distance.
 5. The effort distance of one complete turn of the screw is larger than the resistance distance of one pitch.

 6. The closer the threads are together, the smaller the pitch becomes and the greater the gain in force.

B. The actual mechanical advantage (A.M.A.) of the screw is found by dividing the resistance by the effort. The ideal mechanical advantage (I.M.A.) is found by dividing the circumference of the screw (distance of one complete turn) by the pitch.

C. Because of friction the actual mechanical advantage is very much less than the ideal mechanical advantage. However, friction helps keep the screw from turning backward or pulling out.
 1. We can make up for the loss of effort caused by friction by using another machine, such as the lever or wheel-and-axle, to turn the head of the screw.
 2. Using another machine to turn the head of the screw produces a large gain in effort.

D. Examples of the screw are found in a wood screw, bolt, cap of a jar or bottle, base of an electric light bulb, monkey wrench, clamp, and vise.

XI. EFFICIENCY OF MACHINES

A. There are two ways of finding how efficient a machine is.
 1. One way is to divide the actual mechanical advantage by the ideal mechanical advantage, then multiplying by 100. This can be stated as a formula:

$$\text{Efficiency} = \frac{\text{A.M.A.}}{\text{I.M.A.}} \times 100$$

 2. We multiply by 100 so that we can describe the efficiency of a machine in a percentage.
 3. If the A.M.A. of a machine is 4, and its I.M.A. is 5, the efficiency of the machine is $(4/5) \times 100$, or 80 percent.
 4. The second way to find the efficiency is to divide the amount of work put out by the machine by the amount of work put into the machine, then multiply by 100. This can be stated as a formula:

$$\text{Efficiency} = \frac{\text{Work put out}}{\text{Work put in}} \times 100$$

 5. The work put out can be found by multiplying the resistance by the distance the resistance moves, and the work put in can be found by multiplying the effort by the distance the effort moves.
 6. If a machine puts out 30 foot-pounds of work and the work put into the machine is

50 foot-pounds, the efficiency of the machine is (30/50) × 100, or 60 percent.

B. Because extra force, or effort, is needed to overcome friction, the A.M.A. is always less than the I.M.A. and the work put out is always less than the work put in, so the efficiency of a machine is always less than 100 percent.

XII. Power

A. When one machine can do the same or more work than another in a shorter time, we say that the first machine provides more power than the second machine.

1. Power is the rate of doing work.

2. The unit of power is the **horsepower**, which is 33,000 foot-pounds of work in one minute (or 550 foot-pounds of work in one second).

3. To find the horsepower of a machine, the foot-pounds of work done is divided by 33,000 times the number of minutes it takes to do the work. This can be stated as a formula:

$$\text{Horsepower} = \frac{\text{Work done (in foot-pounds)}}{33{,}000 \times \text{number of minutes}}$$

XIII. Compound Machines and Gears

A. Most machines used in daily life are made up of two or more simple machines.

1. A machine that is a combination of two or more simple machines is called a compound machine.

B. There are many examples of compound machines.

1. The handle of an ax is a lever, and the blade is a wedge; a pair of scissors has two levers with blades that are wedges; the handle of a pencil sharpener is part of a wheel-and-axle that turns two screws with sharp wedge-shaped edges that act like blades to sharpen a pencil; a rotary can opener is made up of a wheel-and-axle and a circular wedge.

C. Sometimes, in compound machines, one wheel is used to turn another wheel.

1. Each wheel is connected to an axle that also turns, making a wheel-and-axle machine.

2. One way of causing a wheel to turn another wheel is by putting a tight belt around both wheels. When one wheel is turned, it makes the belt move and turn the other wheel. The second wheel moves in the same direction as the first wheel.

3. If we want the second wheel to turn in the opposite direction to the first wheel, we cross (in a figure 8) the belt that goes around both wheels.

4. When the first wheel, the driving wheel, is larger than the second wheel, the driven wheel, we get a gain in speed, but we lose in force. When the driving wheel is smaller than the driven wheel, we get a gain in force and a loss in speed.

5. A second way to cause wheels to turn is to put teeth on the wheels and slip a chain around both wheels. The teeth fit into the open places in the chain, and the cross-pieces of the chain fit into the notches between the teeth. The teeth and notches of the wheels stop the chain from slipping.

6. Wheels with teeth and notches in them are called **gears** or gear wheels.

7. A bicycle is a machine that uses gears and a chain. The gears are part of a wheel-and-axle machine. The pedal turns a crank that turns a large gear. A chain connected from the large gear to the smaller gear on the rear wheel turns the smaller gear. The smaller gear then turns the rear wheel, which drives the bicycle forward. Each time the pedals turn the larger gear around once, the smaller gear turns the rear wheel around many times. In this way the gears of a bicycle give up force but gain in speed and distance.

8. A third way to make wheels turn is to fit two gears together without a chain. The teeth of one gear fit into the notches of the second gear and make the second gear turn. Each gear is part of a wheel and axle. When one gear makes another gear move this way, the second gear moves in a direction opposite to the first gear. If a large gear turns a small gear, there is a gain in speed and distance but a loss in force. If a small gear turns a larger gear, there is a gain in force but a loss in speed and distance.

9. To get two gears to move in the same direction, a third gear must be placed between them.

10. The actual mechanical advantage of two gears may be found by comparing the forces that both gears exert.

11. The ideal mechanical advantage can be found by either comparing the number of teeth that each gear has or comparing the speeds of both gears.

XIV. COMPLEX MACHINES

A. The **windmill** is a machine that uses the wind as the force to run the machine and do the work.
   1. The windmill has blades, or propellers, connected to a shaft that runs through the center of the blades.
   2. The blades are set at an angle and slope backward so that when the wind hits the blades, it makes the blades turn around and around.
   3. The turning blades make the shaft turn so that together they act like a wheel-and-axle machine.
   4. A windmill can be used to pump water and to run an electric generator to produce electricity.
   5. A windmill runs only as long as the wind blows hard enough to turn the blades, so it works best in windy places.
B. The **water wheel** uses the force of falling or moving water to run machines.
   1. It has many blades that make the wheel turn quickly when the water strikes them.
   2. A shaft in the center of the wheel turns as the wheel turns, forming a wheel-and-axle machine.
   3. Water wheels called **turbines** use the tremendous force of falling or moving water from huge dams, such as the Grand Coulee Dam on the Columbia River or the Norris Dam on the Tennessee River. Turbines are used to run giant electric generators, producing large amounts of electricity.
C. The **steam engine** uses the heat of burning fuels to run machines.
   1. The heat of the burning fuel changes water into steam.
   2. When water changes into steam, it expands about 1,700 times, and the expanding steam provides the energy to operate the engine.
   3. The steam engine is called an **external combustion machine,** because the fuel is burned outside the engine.
   4. Steam is produced by making water boil in a boiler outside the engine.
   5. The steam then passes through a pipe into a cylinder inside the engine.
   6. In the cylinder the expanding steam pushes a sliding piston back and forth.
   7. The piston is attached to a wheel with a lever called a connecting rod.
   8. As the piston moves back and forth in the cylinder, the attached connecting rod makes the wheel turn.
   9. Every movement of the piston is useful, producing power that makes the wheel turn.
   10. The steam engine has been used to pull trains, push boats, saw wood, spin thread, and weave cloth.
   11. The **steam turbine** also uses steam to run machines.
   12. It works very much like the water turbine, except that it is run by steam that comes from a boiler.
   13. Most steam turbines have many curved blades arranged in rows so that a row of movable blades is followed by a row of fixed blades.
   14. The expanding steam is shot through nozzles at a slant or angle against the movable blades, making the blades spin at a very high speed.
   15. After the steam has passed a row of movable blades, it is then directed by a row of fixed blades to the next row of movable blades.
   16. Each row of movable blades is larger than the row before it, because the steam expands as it travels through the turbine and can make good use of the larger space to get more power from the turbine.
   17. The spinning movable blades turn a long rod that can run a large electric generator or turn the propellers of a large ship.
D. **Gasoline** and **alcohol engines** use hot, expanding gases, produced by burning gasoline or alcohol, to run machines.
   1. These are called **internal combustion engines,** because the fuel is burned inside the cylinder of the engine.
   2. Outside the engine a device called a carburetor or a fuel injector changes the liquid fuel into a vapor and mixes this vapor with the right amount of air to make the fuel burn properly.
   3. Fitted into the top or head of the cylinder is a spark plug, which has a small space or gap between its two metal tips so that at the right moment a hot electric spark can

jump across the gap and make the mixture of fuel vapor and air in the cylinder burn.

4. A piston in the cylinder moves up and down when the engine is running.

5. In the most common gasoline engine, used by automobiles, the piston has to move four times, or make four strokes, inside the cylinder to get just one stroke that will produce power to run the machine.

6. In the first stroke or movement, called the intake stroke, the piston moves down, allowing a valve at the top of the cylinder to open and let the mixture of gasoline vapor and air enter the cylinder.

7. Then the piston moves up for its second stroke, called the compression stroke, compressing or squeezing the mixture of gasoline and air into a very small space.

8. Just when the mixture of gasoline and air is compressed the right amount, an electric spark from the spark plug sets the mixture on fire.

9. The mixture burns quickly, almost explosively, and produces very hot, expanding gases, which give the piston a tremendous downward push.

10. This third downward stroke, called the power stroke, provides the power that runs the machine.

11. The piston then moves up again for its fourth stroke, called the exhaust stroke, pushing out the waste gases through another valve at the top of the cylinder.

12. Now the same series, or cycle, of four strokes starts all over again and continues in this way as long as the engine is running.

13. The piston is attached to a connecting rod, which turns the crankshaft of the engine.

14. The crankshaft is connected to the drive shaft, which is then connected to the axle of the machine (for example, in an automobile) and makes the machine run.

15. Because only one piston stroke in every four is a power stroke, the more cylinders a gasoline engine has, the more smoothly it will run.

16. An automobile has at least four cylinders in its engine so that there will be one power stroke taking place at all times.

17. Compact automobiles usually have four-cylinder gasoline engines, but larger automobiles may have six, eight, or more cylinders.

18. Gasoline engines are also used to run small airplanes, motorcycles, motorbikes, outboard motors, lawn mowers, and power saws.

E. The **diesel engine** also uses hot, expanding gases to run machines.

1. Machines that use diesel engines do not use a carburetor or spark plugs.

2. They use a special fuel oil that is usually cheaper than gasoline.

3. A simple diesel engine uses a cycle of two strokes to produce one power stroke.

4. The first stroke is a combustion intake-compression-exhaust stroke.

5. During the first stroke, air is blown in at one side of the cylinder while waste gases are being forced out through two valves at the top of the cylinder.

6. Then the piston moves up, compressing the air a great deal more than in the cylinder of a gasoline engine, making the air very hot.

7. When the piston nears the top of the cylinder, the fuel oil is sprayed into the cylinder through a nozzle at the top, and the hot air makes the oil catch fire immediately and burn very quickly.

8. The hot, expanding gases push the piston down with great force for its second, or power, stroke.

9. When the piston nears the bottom of the cylinder, the waste gases are pushed out through the valves and more air enters the cylinder.

10. Great pressure is produced in the cylinders, so they must be made of thick metal.

11. Because the diesel engine is so much more powerful and efficient than the gasoline engine, it is commonly used to drive trucks, buses, tractors, power shovels and bulldozers, locomotives, ships, submarines, and electric generators.

F. The **electric motor** (discussed in Chapter 21) uses electricity to run machines and do work, and the **rocket engine** (discussed in Chapter 11) uses solid or liquid fuels.

Exploratory Activities For "Friction and Machines"

1. EXPLORING WITH SIMPLE MACHINES (ANY GRADE LEVEL)

Overview   As stated by James Kirkwood, "Children are intrigued by the functions of objects, but they're not much interested in the abstract construct of 'simple machines.' "[1] Professor Kirkwood suggests that the study of simple machines begin with asking students questions such as, Why is a steering wheel round? How does it steer the car? How does a teeter-totter work? Where do you sit on a teeter-totter when you try to balance with an adult? Why is there no curb at a driveway? or why is it not as tall? How can it be possible to pull down to lift something up? The following set of 14 separate exploratory activities supply the basics for making and scientifically exploring simple machines. Depending on the age and maturity of your students, you may want to supplement these activities with student-found and student-built simple machines.

1.1 Exploring with the First-Class Lever

Obtain a piece of wood 92 centimeters (36 in) long, 7 ½ centimeters (3 in) wide, and about 13 millimeters (½ in) thick. Use a triangular block of wood about 5 centimeters (2 in) wide and 2 ½ centimeters (1 in) high as a fulcrum. Cut grooves on the underside of the board at each end and at the quarter, midway, and three-quarters marks.

For all students. Rest the center of the board (at the midway groove) on the fulcrum. Put a weight or brick at one end of the board and push down at the other end (see Figure 17.3). Note the force you have to exert to lift the weight. Also note that you push down while the weight moves up, so that there is a change in direction, and your hand moves just as far down as the weight moves up.

Move the fulcrum nearer the weight and push down on the board again. This time less force is needed to lift the weight, but now the weight moves up a little, while your hand moves down a lot. Now move the fulcrum so that it is near your hand. You will have to use a lot of force to lift the weight, but the weight will now move up a lot while your hand moves down just a little.

For older students. Repeat this activity, this time using quantitative techniques. Insert a screw eye into one end of the board and have this end extend a little beyond the edge of the table (see Figure 17.5). For the resistance, use a known weight or a brick whose weight you have determined. Attach a spring balance to the screw eye to measure the effort needed to lift the weight. Now place the fulcrum at different positions under the board and measure the force necessary to lift the weight in each case.

Measure the lengths of the effort arm and the resistance arm. Also measure the distances that both the resistance and the effort move. Find the ideal and actual mechanical advantage. (Refer to page 605). Calculate the amount of work done, both input and output, and determine the efficiency of the lever. (Keep in mind that you will obtain only approximate results, because the weight of the board will not have been taken into consideration in the calculations. Moreover, when the spring balance is held upside down, its position affects the reading of the balance.)

1.2 Exploring with the Second-Class Lever

Repeat activity 1.1, but now position the board as a second-class lever, with the resistance between the effort and the fulcrum (see Figure 17.6), as in a wheelbarrow or bottle opener). Depending on the age and maturity of your students, conduct both qualitative and quantitative measurements. (Note that the second-class lever does not change the direction of the force, because both the effort and the resistance move upward.)

1.3 Exploring with Third-Class Levers

Repeat activity 1.1, now positioning the board as a third-class lever, with the effort between the resistance and the fulcrum (see Figure 17.8), as exemplified by a hammer and a fishing pole. You will have to insert a second screw eye into the board, this time into the top surface. In addition, you will have to press down on the board to keep it from being lifted into the air when you pull up on the spring balance. Depending on the age and maturity of your students conduct both qualitative and quantitative measurements. (Note that the third-class lever does not change the direction of the force, because both the effort and the resistance move upward.)

For all students. Ask students to enlist parents or guardians in locating and identifying other examples of levers at home. Ask them to bring their finds to class, if permitted. Repeat these exploratory activities using some of their examples.

1.4 Exploring the Wheel-and-Axle

Clamp a pencil sharpener, with its cover removed, to the edge of a table, as shown in Figure 17.9. Turn the handle of the sharpener and point out that when the handle is turned, it makes a complete circle, just as though it were a complete wheel. The shaft of the sharpener is the axle. When the handle (wheel) is turned, the shaft (axle) is turned.

Tie three books together with a string and have the students lift the books by the string, noting the force needed to do this. Tie the other end of the string firmly around the shaft of the sharpener, using cellophane tape, if necessary, to keep the string from slipping. Now turn the handle and lift the books. (Holding your fore-finger lightly against the string while you turn the han-dle will keep the string from slipping off the shaft.)

Note that much less force is needed to lift the books, using the handle. This gain in force is accompanied by a loss in distance and speed, because the handle must move many times to raise the books a short distance. Older students can find the ideal mechanical advantage of the pencil sharpener. (The radius of the wheel is the length of the handle, and the radius of the axle is one half the diameter of the shaft.)

Turn the handle of the pencil sharpener until the books are close to the shaft, then let go of the handle and allow the books to move downward. Now the axle is turning the wheel. Note the loss in force, but the large gain in distance and speed, as the handle spins rapidly.

Draw a diagram to show that the wheel-and-axle is a form of spinning first-class lever (Figure 17.13). Its ful-crum is always at the center of the axle and the wheel. The radius of the wheel and the radius of the axle are the two arms of the lever. Have the students locate and identify other examples of wheel-and-axle machines. Let them re-peat the experiment, using some of their examples.

1.5 Exploring the Fixed Pulley

Screw two cup hooks about 10 centimeters (4 in) apart into a long, rectangular wood board about 13 millime-ters (1/2 in) thick. Rest the board on the backs of two chairs placed a short distance apart (Figure 17.14). Tie a string around a brick or book and weigh it with a spring balance. Attach a pulley to one cup hook and pass a string around the groove of the pulley. Connect one end of the string to the brick and the other end to a spring balance.

Pull down on the spring balance. Note that the force needed to raise the brick is just about equal to the weight of the brick, so all you have done is to change the direction of your force. Older students can calcu-late the amount of work done, both input and output. Find the mechanical advantage and determine the ef-ficiency of the fixed pulley.

Draw a diagram to show that the fixed pulley is a form of spinning first-class lever (Figure 17.15). Its fulcrum is at the center of the axle, with the effort and resistance at opposite ends of the wheel. Note that the effort arm and the resistance arm are equal.

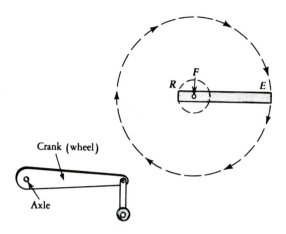

FIGURE 17.13   The wheel-and-axle is a spinning first-class lever.

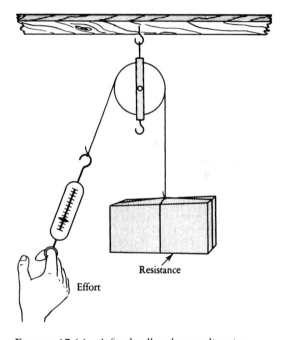

FIGURE 17.14   A fixed pulley changes direction.

1.6 Exploring the Movable Pulley

For older students: Rearrange the pulley as shown in the diagram (Figure 17.16). Pull up on the balance and note that only half the force is needed as with the fixed pul-ley. However, your effort must move twice as far as the distance the brick is lifted. Note that there is now no change in the direction of your force. Calculate the amount of work done, both input and output. Find the ideal and actual mechanical advantage, and determine the efficiency of the movable pulley.

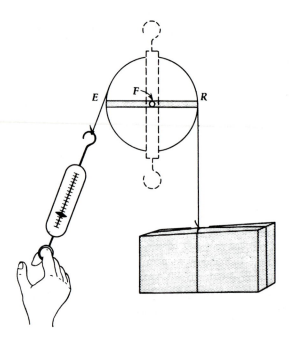

FIGURE 17.15   A fixed pulley is a spinning first-class lever.

Draw a diagram to show that the movable pulley is a form of spinning second-class lever (Figure 17.17). Its fulcrum is at one end of the wheel, the effort at the opposite end, and the resistance at the center of the axle. The effort arm is twice as long as the resistance arm.

1.7 Exploring the Block and Tackle

Use two pulleys to form a combination fixed and movable pulley, as shown in the diagram (Figure 17.18). Note that there is no difference between this block and tackle and the movable pulley shown in Figure 17.17, as to increase in force, work done, mechanical advantage, and efficiency. The block and tackle allows increasing force and changing direction at the same time. If possible, repeat, using a double fixed and a double movable pulley.

1.8 Exploring the Inclined Plane

Rest one end of a long wood board at least 13 millimeters (0.5 in) thick on a pile of books so that the board makes an inclined plane. Obtain a toy cart and place some stones in it to give added weight. Tape the stones to the cart so they will not fall out, and then weigh the cart and stones with a spring balance.

Now attach the spring balance to the cart and pull it slowly up the board, keeping the balance horizontal with the board while you are pulling (Figure 17.19). Note that much less force is needed to pull the cart up the incline than to lift it straight up into the air, but the

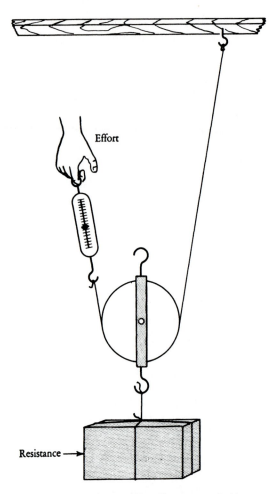

FIGURE 17.16   A movable pulley requires half as much force as a fixed pulley.

cart must now be moved a longer distance to reach the same height. Find the height of the inclined plane by measuring the vertical distance from the higher end of the board to the surface upon which the books are resting. Calculate the amount of work done, both input and output. Find the ideal and actual mechanical advantage, and determine the efficiency of the inclined plane.

Make the slope of the inclined plane steeper, either by using a shorter board or by adding more books to the pile. Note the increase in force needed to pull the cart up the incline. Have the students locate and identify examples of inclined planes in their everyday world.

1.9 Exploring the Wedge

Make two wedges by sawing diagonally a block of wood 20 centimeters (8 in) long, 10 centimeters (4 in) wide, and 5 centimeters (2 in) thick (Figure 17.20).

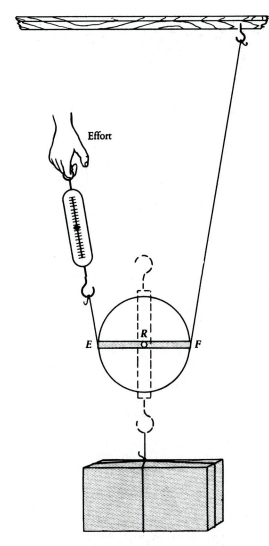

FIGURE 17.17   A movable pulley is a spinning second-class lever.

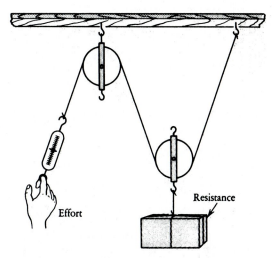

FIGURE 17.18   A block and tackle is a combination of a fixed and a movable pulley.

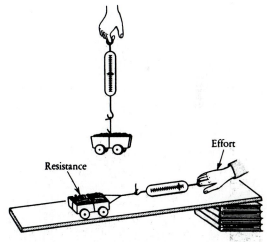

FIGURE 17.19   Less force is needed with an inclined plane.

Hold up one wedge to show that it really is an inclined plane. Place both wedges back to back and form a double inclined plane. Measure the length of the wedge and the thickness of the large end, and then calculate the ideal mechanical advantage. Insert the sharp end of the wedge a short distance under a pile of books and tap the thick end with a hammer, driving the wedge under the books and lifting them. Have the students locate examples of wedges.

1.10 Exploring the Screw

Cut out a right triangle from a sheet of white paper. Make the base of the triangle 20 centimeters (8 in) and the height 10 centimeters (4 in). Hold up the triangle

and show that the hypotenuse, or diagonal side, is an inclined plane. Make a heavy black line along the hypotenuse. Starting with the 10-centimeter (4-in) side, wrap the paper around a pencil so that the black line shows up clearly as a spiral (Figure 17.21). Hold up a large wood screw beside the pencil and show the similarity between the spiral and the screw. Point out the thread of the screw, and then find the pitch by measuring the distance between two threads. With the students, locate and identify examples of screws.

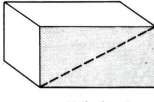

Block of wood

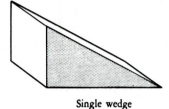

Single wedge

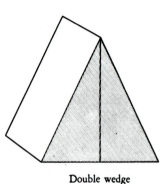

Double wedge

FIGURE 17.20 Making a single and a double wedge.

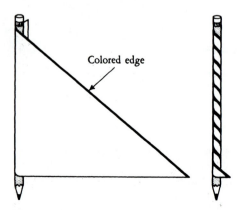

Colored edge

FIGURE 17.21 A screw is a spiral inclined plane.

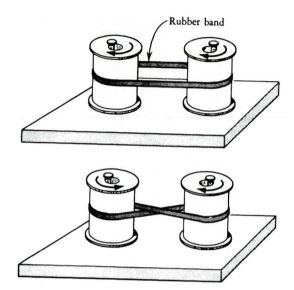

FIGURE 17.22 A belt makes it possible for one wheel to turn another wheel.

1.11 A Hunt for Compound Machines

Ask students to search at home, with a parent or guardian, to find pictures of and identify the simple machines in such everyday compound machines as scissors, playground equipment, can opener, pencil sharpener, toys, water faucet, piano, bicycle, and wrench. Have the students make collages and report to their classmates on their discoveries.

1.12 Exploring Wheels and Belts

Obtain a thick rectangular block of wood and two spools of the same size. Place the spools a short distance apart on the wood, insert loose-fitting nails into the holes of the spools, and drive the nails into the wood. Slip a wide rubber band over both spools (Figure 17.22). Have a student give one spool a complete turn and report his or her observations. (Note that the other spool also makes a complete turn, moves at the same speed, and turns in the same direction.)

Now cross the rubber band so that it makes a figure 8, and have the student give one spool a complete turn again. Ask the student to explain what happens. (This time the driven spool will turn in the opposite direction.)

Repeat both activities, using a smaller and a larger spool this time. Have students explain their observations. (When the larger spool drives the smaller spool and makes one complete turn, the smaller spool turns more than once and moves faster. When the smaller spool drives the larger spool and makes one complete turn, the larger spool turns less than once and moves more slowly. Point out that the fan belt in an automobile is an example of a belt turning a wheel.)

1.13 Finding Gears with Chains

Turn a bicycle upside down. Push the pedal with your hand and see how it turns the large gear wheel, which turns the chain, which turns the small gear wheel, which then turns the rear bicycle wheel. One turn of the large gear wheel makes the small gear wheel turn more than once and move faster. Compare the number of teeth in each gear and find the ideal mechanical advantage.

Use black crayon to place a mark on each gear. Make one complete turn of the large gear and see how many turns the smaller gear make. Count the number of teeth on the large and small gears, and find the ideal mechanical advantage of the bicycle.

1.14 Make a Pinwheel Windmill (for Older Students)

Have enough supplies so that each student can make his or her own pinwheel windmill. Use these instructions: Cut out a paper sheet 15 centimeters (6 in) square and make lines and pinholes as shown in Figure 17.23. Cut each line, and then bend in the corners to bring the pinholes in line with the center hole of the paper. Run a pin through the pinholes, and then push the pin into the eraser on a pencil or into a cork stopper. Blow on the pinwheel or hold it in front of an electric fan. Ask students to explain their observations. (The air turns the pinwheel because the air strikes the curved blades at a slant. A windmill operates in much the same way.) Ask students which type of simple machine is represented by a windmill (wheel-and-axle machine).

Have the students read about and report on windmills and their uses and how they are used today to convert energy from wind into electrical energy.

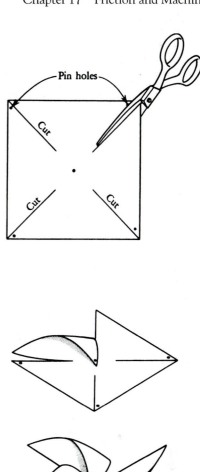

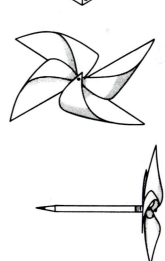

FIGURE 17.23   Making a windmill.

NOTE

1. James J. Kirkwood, "Simple Machines Simply Put," *Science and Children* 31(7) 40 (April 1994), p. 15.

STUDENT BOOKS AND OTHER RESOURCES FOR "FRICTION AND MACHINES"

Anthony, J. L. "Race Car Rally." *Science and Children* 31(5):26–29 (February 1994).

Bortz, F. *Catastrophe! Great Engineering Failure and Success.* New York: Scientific American, 1995.

Gartrell, J. E., Jr. *Methods of Motion: An Introduction to Mechanics, Book 1.* rev. ed. Washington, DC: National Science Teachers Association, 1992.

Gates, P. *Nature Got There First: Inventions Inspired by Nature.* Phoenix: King Fisher, 1995.

Kirkwood, J. J. "Simple Machines Simply Put." *Science and Children* 31(7):15–17, 40 (April 1994).

Leyden, M. B. "Gear Up for Science Fun. Teaching Science." *Teaching Pre K–8* 24(8):28–29 (May 1994).

Moody, J. C. "Let's Build a Mousetrap Car." *Hoosier Science Teacher* 19(4):111–113 (May 1994).

Shaw, E. L., et al. "Inclined to Roll." *Science Activities* 30(4):32–35 (Winter 1994).

Teachworth, M. "Build a Bed of Nails." *The Science Teacher* 61(6):54–56 (September 1994).

CHAPTER 18

Heat

THE NATURE OF HEAT

I. KINETIC THEORY OF HEAT

  A. All materials, or substances, are made of tiny particles, called molecules.

    1. Molecules are always moving, and the movement of molecules is called **heat.**

    2. The energy that molecules have is called **kinetic energy** (energy of motion).

    3. The faster the molecules of a material are made to move, the more kinetic energy they have and the hotter the material becomes; the slower the molecules of a material move, the less kinetic energy they have and the cooler the material becomes.

  B. Heat, then, is a form of energy. It is the energy of moving molecules.

II. SOURCES OF HEAT ENERGY

  A. Heat energy can be produced from at least five other kinds of energy.

  B. Heat energy can be produced from the **mechanical energy** of friction, compression, or percussion.

    1. When two surfaces rub together, friction makes the molecules move faster and the materials become hotter.

    2. When molecules of gas are crowded together, or compressed, heat is produced.

    3. When a hammer pounds a piece of iron, the molecules of iron move faster and have more kinetic energy, so the iron becomes warmer.

  C. Heat energy can be produced from **chemical energy.**

    1. When two materials react chemically, often the chemical energy that is released is changed, or transformed, into heat.

    2. The burning of a fuel, such as oil, gas, coal, or wood, is a chemical action that produces heat.

  D. Heat energy can be produced from **electrical energy.**

    1. When an electric current flows through a thin wire of a light bulb or a toaster, heat is given off.

    2. The resistance of the wire to the flow of electric current produces heat.

  E. Heat energy can be produced from the **radiant energy** of the sun or other glowing materials.

    1. The sun is our chief source of heat, obtained either directly from the sun itself or indirectly from the sun's energy stored in fuels.

    2. Radiant energy, then, is our chief source of heat energy on earth.

  F. Heat energy can be produced from **nuclear energy.**

    1. When the nucleus of an atom is split, either naturally or artificially, the nuclear energy produced can be transformed into vast amounts of heat energy.

III. EFFECT OF HEAT ON CHANGES IN THE STATE OF MATTER

  A. All materials on earth are found in any one of three forms, or states, of matter: **solid, liquid,** or **gas. Plasma,** which is gas that is electrically charged, is a fourth state of matter (see Chapter

DEMONSTRATION 18.1

Heat is the Energy of Moving Molecules

Place tumblers of cold water and hot water side by side, and add two drops of red food coloring to each tumbler. Point out that the molecules of hot water have more kinetic energy and are moving more quickly than the molecules of cold water. The faster-moving molecules of hot water disperse the food coloring more quickly than the slower-moving molecules of cold water.

DEMONSTRATION 18.2

Sources of Heat Energy

A. Friction as a source of heat

Have students rub the palms of their hands together briskly and note the heat produced by the resulting friction.

B. Compression as a source of heat

Use a pump to inflate a tire or a ball. Point out that the barrel of the pump becomes warm because the air inside has been compressed.

C. Percussion as a source of heat

Pound a block of iron with a hammer. The continued percussion makes the molecules of iron move faster, and the block becomes warmer.

D. Chemical energy as a source of heat

Strike a match and note that the friction of the match head rubbing against a rough surface produces enough heat to cause a chemical reaction to take place. The match head bursts into flame, and the chemical energy of the burning match is the source of heat.

E. Electrical energy as a source of heat

Turn on a hot plate or electric toaster. Electrical energy is being converted to heat energy.

F. Radiant energy as a source of heat

Put a match head on a pie tin. Use a magnifying glass to focus the sun's rays on the match head. The match head will burst into flame.

16). The discussion that follows, however, is limited to the three states—solid, liquid, and gas.

1. In gases, the molecules have a great amount of energy. They usually move very fast and are far apart.
2. In liquids, the molecules have less energy. They move less quickly and are closer together.
3. In solids, the molecules have even less energy. They are very close together, and each molecule seems to vibrate at one spot rather than move about.

B. Water is a material that we can find in all three forms, or states: as ice it is in the form of a solid; as water it is in the form of a liquid; and as water vapor it is in the form of a gas.

C. We can bring about a change in the state of a material by heating or cooling the material.

D. If we add enough heat energy to a solid, the solid becomes a liquid.

1. The added heat energy makes the molecules in the solid vibrate more and more quickly until they finally break away, move about freely, and are farther apart, as in a liquid.
2. When this condition occurs, we say the solid melts. The temperature at which melting takes place is called the **melting point.**
3. Every solid has its own melting point.

E. If we remove enough heat energy from a liquid, the liquid becomes a solid.

1. Removing heat energy causes the molecules to move more slowly and come closer together, until they are very close together and each molecule vibrates at one spot rather than moves about.
2. When this condition occurs, we say the liquid freezes. The temperature at which freezing takes place is called the **freezing point.**
3. Every liquid has its own freezing point.

F. If we add enough heat energy to a liquid, the liquid becomes a gas.

1. The added heat energy causes the molecules in the liquid to move more quickly and to stay farther apart until they are moving very quickly and are very far apart, as in a gas.
2. When this condition occurs, we say that the liquid **evaporates,** or turns into a gas or vapor.
3. Evaporation takes place at all temperatures, but if a liquid is heated sufficiently, at a certain temperature bubbles of gas form, which rise to the surface of the liquid.
4. When bubbles form in this way, we say that the liquid boils. The temperature at which this occurs is called the **boiling point.**
5. Each liquid has its own boiling point.

G. If we remove enough heat energy from a gas, the gas becomes a liquid.
1. Removing heat energy causes the gas molecules to move more slowly and come closer together until the gas **condenses,** or turns into a liquid.
2. For each gas there is a certain temperature at which it will condense, becoming a liquid.

IV. EXPANSION AND CONTRACTION

A. When materials are heated, the molecules move faster and spread farther apart so that the materials become larger in volume, or **expand;** when materials are cooled, the molecules move more slowly and come closer together, so that the materials become smaller in volume, or **contract.**
B. The rates of expansion and contraction are different for solids, liquids, and gases.
1. In solids, the molecules are very close together and seem to vibrate rather than move, so in relation to liquids and gases, solids expand and contract less.
2. In liquids, the molecules move about quickly and are farther apart, so liquids can expand and contract more than solids.
3. In gases, the molecules move about quickly and are quite far apart, so gases expand and contract most.

V. EXCEPTIONS TO THE RULE OF EXPANSION AND CONTRACTION

A. Most materials expand when heated and contract when cooled.
B. Water is an exception to this rule.
1. When water is cooled, it contracts until its temperature reaches 4° Celsius (39° Fahrenheit).

2. When it is cooled from 4° Celsius (39° F) to the freezing point of water, 0° Celsius (32° F), water expands slightly.
3. Because water also expands as it freezes, ice is less dense than water and can float in water.

C. This unusual form of expansion explains some of the special characteristics of water.
1. It explains why the water in a lake freezes from the top down rather than from the bottom up.
2. It explains why water pipes burst when the temperature is below freezing.
3. It also explains why huge and heavy icebergs float.

VI. EXPANSION AND CONTRACTION IN OUR DAILY LIFE

A. When the metal lid of a glass jar is stuck tight, hot water will cause the lid to expand more rapidly than the jar, allowing the lid to be unscrewed easily.
B. When two glass tumblers are stuck, one inside the other, they can be loosened by pouring hot water on the outside tumbler while filling the inside tumbler with cold water, using caution against breakage.
C. When baking powder is used in baking a cake, carbon dioxide gas forms inside the dough and expands when heated, causing the cake to rise.
D. Telephone wires that are strung in summer are allowed to sag a little so that the wires can contract without breaking in winter.
E. Engineers place one end of a bridge on rollers to allow for expansion and contraction of the bridge in summer and winter.
F. Concrete workers leave spaces between slabs of concrete road and sidewalk so that the concrete will not bulge and buckle in summer, or contract and crack in winter.
G. Metal rivets used in construction are hammered into place while red hot so that when they cool, they will contract and pull the parts together with great force.
H. Some thermometers contain liquids, which expand and rise up the thermometer tube when they are heated, then contract and fall within the tube when they are cooled.
I. Thermostats and metallic thermometers contain a bar or coil made of strips of two different metals that expand at different rates, causing the bar or coil to turn when heated or cooled.

DEMONSTRATION 18.3
Expansion and Contraction

A. Solids expand when heated and contract when cooled

Wrap one end of a wire around a nail and attach the other end to a clamp, covered with rubber or cloth, on a ringstand (Figure 18.1). Adjust the length of the wire so that the tip of the nail just clears the table and can swing freely. Now heat the wire with a Bunsen burner or alcohol lamp, moving the flame up and down the wire. The wire expands, causing the tip of the nail to touch the table, and the nail can no longer swing freely. Remove the flame and let the wire cool. The wire contracts, letting the nail swing freely again.

B. Liquids expand when heated and contract when cooled

Pour water colored dark red with food coloring into a Pyrex flask until the flask is almost full. Insert a long glass or plastic tube into a one-hole rubber stopper and fit the stopper tightly into the mouth of the flask. The amount of water in the flask will have to be adjusted so that when the stopper is inserted, the colored water will rise about one half the distance of the part of the tube above the stopper (Figure 18.2).

Place a small rubber band around the tube at the level of the liquid. Heat the flask on a hot plate just long enough to show the water expanding and rising up the tube. Transfer the flask to a pan of cold water and note that the water contracts and falls within the tube.

SAFETY NOTE: Use caution for this demonstration.

1. Use extra caution whenever using a hotplate, Bunsen burner or any heat source in the classroom, keeping curious or careless children protected from touching it.
2. Protect children from possible glass breakage (even when using Pyrex glassware) and from spattering of glass and boiling water.
3. Use care whenever pushing glass tubing through a rubber stopper. It should be done only by the teacher and after lubricating the glass rod by wetting it with water and slowly twisting the rod through.

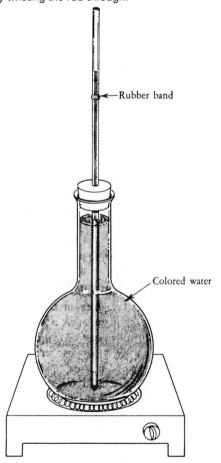

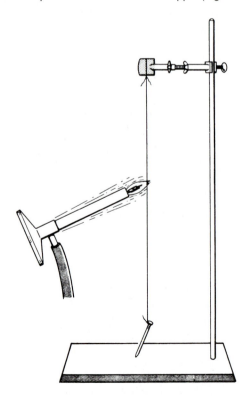

FIGURE 18.1 The wire expands when heated and contracts when cooled.

FIGURE 18.2 The water expands and rises when heated and contracts and falls when cooled.

DEMONSTRATION 18.4
Exceptions to the Contraction and Expansion Rule

A. Water is an exception to the rule of expansion and contraction

Fill a plastic bottle with water and screw the cap on tightly. Allow the bottle to stand overnight in the freezer of a refrigerator. Remove the bottle the next day and note how it bulges because the water expanded when it was cooled below 4° Celsius (39°F) and then froze.

B. Rubber is also an exception to the rule of expansion and contraction

Cut a long rubber band. Tie one end of the band around the head of a nail and attach the other end to a ringstand, as described and pictured in Figure 18.1. Now move a candle flame quickly up and down the rubber band several times, being careful not to hold the flame too close to the rubber band. The rubber band will contract when heated and will pull up the nail.

TEMPERATURE

I. TEMPERATURE

  A. Temperature describes in degrees how hot or cold a material is.
    1. Temperature depends on the speed of movement of the molecules in a material.
    2. The faster the molecules are moving, the higher the temperature of the material; the slower the molecules move, the lower its temperature.

II. MEASUREMENT OF TEMPERATURE

  A. A thermometer is used to measure temperature.
    1. The operation of a thermometer depends on the principle that materials expand when heated and contract when cooled.
  B. The thermometer commonly used to measure temperature is a sealed glass tube containing a liquid such as mercury or colored alcohol.
    1. There is a very narrow, hollow passageway running through the tube. This passageway is called the bore.
    2. At the bottom of the bore is a bulb that contains the liquid.
    3. The liquid is also part of the way up the bore.
    4. When the liquid inside the bulb is heated, it expands and rises up the bore.
    5. When the liquid is cooled, it contracts and goes down the bore.
  C. A scale on the thermometer tells us just how high the liquid is in the thermometer, and gives us the temperature of whatever is around the bulb.
    1. The scale on a thermometer is divided into many equal lines, or divisions, called degrees.
    2. The degree (°) is the unit of measurement of temperature.
    3. The two common temperature scales are the Fahrenheit scale and the Celsius scale.
  D. In the **Fahrenheit scale** the freezing point of water registers at 32° and the boiling point of water registers at 212°.
    1. There are 180 lines, or divisions, between the freezing point and boiling point of water.
    2. The Fahrenheit scale was developed by the German physicist Gabriel Fahrenheit (1685–1736).
    3. Zero on the Fahrenheit scale is the lowest temperature that Fahrenheit could get from a mixture of salt and ice in water.
  E. In the **Celsius scale**, also called the **centigrade scale,** the freezing point of water is at 0° and the boiling point of water is at 100°.
    1. There are 100 lines, or divisions, between the freezing point and boiling point of water.
    2. The Celsius scale is named after the Swedish scientist Anders Celsius (1701–1744).
    3. Scientists, and most of the world, use the Celsius scale.
  F. It is easy to convert from the Fahrenheit scale to the Celsius scale, and vice versa.
    1. Because there are 180 Fahrenheit degrees and 100 Celsius degrees between the freezing and boiling points of water, 1° F is equal to 100/180, or 5/9° C; and 1° C is equal to 180/100, or 9/5° F.
    2. Moreover, because 0° on the Celsius scale is the same as 32° on the Fahrenheit scale, we must always *subtract* 32° when changing from the Fahrenheit to the Celsius scale, and al-

ways *add* 32° when changing from the Celsius to the Fahrenheit scale.

3. So, to change from °F to °C, subtract 32° from the Fahrenheit reading and multiply the result by 5/9:

$$C = (F - 32) \times 5/9$$

4. To change from °C to °F, multiply the Celsius reading by 9/5 and add 32°.

$$F = 9/5\ C + 32$$

G. There are several kinds of thermometers.
   1. A **mercury thermometer** contains mercury, the only metal that is liquid at room temperature.
   2. Because mercury has a high boiling point (about 357° C or 675° F), the mercury thermometer can be used to measure fairly high temperatures. However, mercury freezes at −40° Celsius (−40° F), so it cannot be used to measure very low temperatures.
   3. Because mercury is a very toxic metal, mercury thermometers are no longer used in most public school classrooms.
   4. An **alcohol thermometer** looks and operates like a mercury thermometer, but in this case alcohol—colored red or blue—is used in the bulb and tube.
   5. Because alcohol has a boiling point lower than that of water (about 78° C or 172° F), an alcohol thermometer cannot be used to measure high temperatures. However, alcohol has a very low freezing point (about −130° C or −202° F), so the alcohol thermometer is used in Arctic and polar regions.
   6. Most indoor and outdoor household thermometers and those used by public schools are alcohol thermometers.
   7. The **clinical thermometer** is a mercury thermometer, but is shorter than the regular mercury thermometer and has a scale that runs only from 33° C to 43° C (92° F to 110° F).
   8. The bore of this thermometer is very narrow so that even one tenth of a degree will make a big difference in the level of the mercury and can easily be read.
   9. At one spot inside the bore there is a narrow bend or pinch. When the clinical thermometer is placed inside a person's mouth, the mercury is heated and expands, pushing its way up and beyond this pinch to give the proper temperature reading. When the ther-

mometer is removed, however, the mercury cannot fall back through the pinch, so the level of the mercury remains at the temperature of the person's body. This stationary position allows an accurate reading of the person's body temperature. To force the mercury down the tube again, past the pinch, one has to shake the thermometer quite vigorously a few times.

10. A **metal thermometer** does not use a glass tube, bulb, or liquid. It has a small coil made of two strips of metal welded together along their lengths. The inside strip of metal is usually brass, and the outside strip is steel.

11. When the coil is heated or cooled, the brass strip expands and contracts more than the steel strip, making the coil twist.

12. As the coil twists, a pointer connected to one end of the coil moves across a scale that is marked in degrees.

13. The metal thermometer is used for obtaining temperature readings in home ovens and refrigerators.

14. **Digital thermometers** are usually highly sensitive thermometers that give accurate readings on electronic meters.

15. The **strip thermometer** is a celluloid tape made with heat-sensitive liquid crystal chemicals which cause a change in the color of the tape according to the temperature.

16. Strip thermometers are useful in taking the temperature of infants because one needs only to place the strip on a baby's forehead for a few seconds to obtain a fairly precise temperature reading.

III. MEASUREMENT OF THE AMOUNT OF HEAT

   A. Two units commonly used to measure the amount of heat are the British thermal unit (Btu) and the calorie.
   B. The **British thermal unit** (Btu) is the amount of heat needed to raise the temperature of 1 pound of water 1° on the Fahrenheit scale.
   C. The calorie is the amount of heat needed to raise the temperature of 1 gram (about 3 hundredths of an ounce by weight) of water 1° on the Celsius scale.
      1. This calorie is called the small calorie and is spelled with a small *c*.
      2. The large Calorie, spelled with a capital C, is equal to 1,000 small calories.
      3. We use (large) Calories to find out how much heat energy is available from different foods.

METHODS OF HEAT TRAVEL AND THEIR EFFECTS

I. HEAT CAN TRAVEL BY CONDUCTION

   A. When a material such as a metal rod is heated, molecules next to the source of heat move faster.
     1. The molecules bump into other molecules, making them move faster.
     2. These molecules then bump into still other molecules, making them move faster too.
     3. In this way all the molecules in the material are made to move faster and have more kinetic energy, so the material becomes hotter.
     4. The heat energy has been passed, or conducted, from molecule to molecule within the material, yet the material itself does not move.
     5. This method of heat travel, whereby energy is passed along from molecule to molecule by bumping, or collision, is called **conduction.**
   B. Any material through which heat travels is called a **conductor.**
     1. Metals are good heat conductors.
     2. Good heat conductors are also good conductors of electricity.
     3. In good heat conductors the molecules are very close together and conduct the heat energy from molecule to molecule very quickly and easily.
     4. Some metals, such as silver and copper, are better heat conductors than other metals.
   C. Materials that do not conduct heat very well are called **nonconductors**, or poor conductors.
     1. Most nonmetals, liquids, and gases are poor conductors of heat.
     2. In poor heat conductors the molecules are farther apart and do not conduct the heat energy from molecule to molecule quickly or easily.
   D. A vacuum cannot conduct heat because there are no molecules to pass along the heat energy.
   E. When a nonconductor is used to stop the conduction of heat, it is called an **insulator.**
     1. Pot and pan handles are covered with insulators made of wood or plastic.
     2. Rubber and cloth are also used as insulators.
     3. Because air is a very poor heat conductor, anything with air spaces in it, such as wool or cork, is a good insulator.

II. HEAT CAN TRAVEL BY CONVECTION

   A. Convection is a method of heat travel that takes place only in gases and liquids, both of which are called fluids.

     1. When a fluid such as air is heated, the molecules move faster and spread farther apart so that the air expands.
     2. When air expands, it becomes lighter.
     3. The colder air above it is heavier, and gravity pulls down harder on the colder, heavier air than on the warmer, lighter air.
     4. Because of this greater pull of gravity, the cold air moves down and pushes the warm air upward.
     5. This cold air in turn is heated, expands, becomes lighter, and is pushed upward by colder, heavier air above it.
     6. In this way, continuous currents of rising and falling air are produced.
     7. The same currents are produced with a fluid such as water.
   B. **Convection,** then, is a method of heat travel whereby the molecules of a heated gas or liquid actually move from one place to another.
     1. The heat is carried from a place of higher temperature to a place of lower temperature by the molecules of a moving gas or liquid.
     2. The movement of the gas or liquid is called a **convection current.**
     3. There can be no convection current in a vacuum.
     4. Some ovens are convection ovens.
     5. Solar ovens heat by creating convection waves from the energy of sunlight.

III. HEAT CAN TRAVEL BY RADIATION

   A. Radiation as a method of heat travel is very different from conduction and convection, because it has nothing to do with the passing of heat by moving molecules.
   B. The sun and other glowing bodies give off, or radiate, energy in the form of invisible waves.
     1. These radiant energy waves travel out into space without the help of molecules.
     2. When radiant energy strikes a solid, opaque material, some of the energy is absorbed and makes the molecules in the material move faster, so the material becomes hotter.
   C. Radiant energy is not heat, but becomes heat when it is absorbed.
     1. The sun heats the earth, 150 million kilometers (93 million mi) away, in this way.
     2. This method of passing along heat by radiant energy waves is called **radiation.**

DEMONSTRATION 18.5
Heat Travels in Water By Convection

Fill a Pyrex container almost full of water. Shred a blotter with a food grater and place the fine particles in the water. Muddle the bits of blotting paper until they become thoroughly soaked and sink to the bottom of the beaker. Now place the container on one side of a hot plate and heat the container (Figure 18.3). The blotting paper will indicate the path of the convection current produced in the water. The bits of blotting paper will move up the side of the beaker resting on the hot coils, and travel down on the cooler side of the Pyrex container.

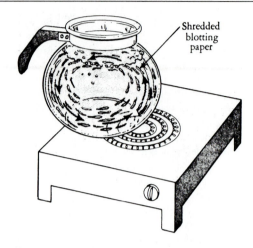

FIGURE 18.3   A convection water current.

D. The kind of material determines how much radiant energy is changed into heat.
  1. Dark, rough materials are good absorbers of radiant energy and produce much heat, as compared with light, smooth materials.
  2. Light, smooth materials reflect most of the radiant energy that strikes them, and so do not produce much heat at all.
  3. Transparent materials, such as air and glass, allow almost all of the radiant energy to pass through them, so these materials produce little or no heat.
E. Some modern cooking ovens are designed to heat either by radiant energy or by convection.
F. Radiant heat waves are part of a family of radiant energy waves called **electromagnetic waves** (see Chapter 20). This family includes radio waves, infrared rays or heat waves, light rays, ultraviolet rays, X-rays, gamma rays, and cosmic rays.
  1. Microwave ovens, for instance, heat food with electromagnetic radiation at a very special frequency that excites vibrations in water molecules.

IV. HEATING THE HOME
A. The fireplace.
  1. When a fire is started in a fireplace, the heat of the fire warms the air in the fireplace and the air in the chimney.
  2. A convection current is produced, which moves through the fireplace and up the chimney.
  3. This convection current removes cold air from the floor, but the current also carries much of the heat of the fire up the chimney.
  4. The heat that warms the room is mostly radiant heat, whereby the radiant energy from the fire is absorbed by the walls, furniture, and other materials in the room.
B. The stove.
  1. The heat from the fire in a stove passes through its metal walls by conduction, and into the air next to the walls by conduction as well.
  2. The heated air sets up a convection current that heats the whole room.
  3. The hot walls of the stove radiate some heat too.
  4. Gas, oil, kerosene, coal, and wood can be used as fuel for a stove.
  5. Today most stoves use gas or electricity, for cooking purposes only.
C. Central heating systems.
  1. Many homes and buildings are heated by central heating systems.
  2. In central heating systems the stove, or furnace, is located in the basement or utility room.

3. The heat is conducted from the furnace to the rooms by pipes or ducts.
4. The most commonly used central heating systems today are the hot-air, hot-water, steam, and radiant heating systems.

D. In a **hot-air heating system** the furnace is surrounded by a brick or iron jacket filled with air.
   1. The furnace heats the jacket by conduction, and the jacket heats the air by conduction.
   2. The hot air inside the jacket is pushed up, either by cold air entering at the bottom of the furnace or by a fan.
   3. The hot air goes up the pipes into the different rooms in the house.
   4. The hot air comes into each room through a metal grating, or register, in the floor, walls, or ceiling.
   5. The air circulates through the rooms and heats them by convection.
   6. Then the air is either carried back to the furnace through a cold-air return so that it can be reheated, or is allowed to escape and is replaced by fresh air from outdoors.

E. In a **hot-water heating system** the furnace is surrounded by a boiler filled with water.
   1. When the water is heated, it is pushed up by cold water entering the bottom of the boiler.
   2. The hot water goes up the pipes into the different rooms in the house.
   3. The hot water then goes into a metal radiator in each room.
   4. The radiator is divided into many sections of hollow pipe so that the *radiator exposes* a great deal of its surface to the air.
   5. The hot water heats the walls of the radiator by conduction.
   6. The radiator walls heat the air next to them by conduction.
   7. The hot air then heats the room by convection.
   8. At the same time, the radiator radiates some heat as well.
   9. After the hot water in the radiator gives up its heat and becomes cooler, it goes back to the boiler through return pipes and is reheated.
   10. The same water is used over and over again.

F. A **steam heating system** works very much like a hot-water heating system, but in this case steam is used instead of hot water.
   1. The boiler is only partly filled with water.
   2. When the water is heated, it is changed into water vapor or "steam."

3. The steam has great pressure and is forced up the pipes into the radiators.
4. When the steam gives up its heat to the radiators, it condenses back into water, which goes down the pipes to the boiler, where it is reheated.

G. In a **radiant heating system** hot water is circulated through copper pipes located in the floor or in the walls.
   1. The hot water heats the pipes by conduction.
   2. The pipes heat the floors and walls by conduction.
   3. The floors and walls radiate much heat energy, and this radiant energy warms the people and the furniture in the room.

H. In **solar heating systems** the sun is used to furnish some of the heat needed for the home or building.
   1. The sides of the building facing the sun are mostly large glass windows.
   2. Radiant energy from the sun passes through the windows into the rooms, where the radiant energy is absorbed and changed into heat.
   3. This type of heating, using the sun's rays to heat space, materials such as masonry, or containers that hold water, is called **passive solar heating.**
   4. Greenhouses usually use passive solar heating, as do home greenhouse window boxes.
   5. Some people use solar collector panels to heat water that is then pumped into the house to provide hot water and home heating.
   6. The use of solar collector panels to heat water or air that is then circulated to parts of the house is called **active solar heating.**
   7. Some homes, vehicles and spacecraft use photovoltaic cells on their roofs to collect the sun's energy so as to cause an electric current to flow or to be stored for later electrical use.
   8. The system of creating electricity from the sun's energy is called a **photovoltaic system.**
   9. Solar heating systems work well on clear days when it is not too cold or windy.

I. The **heat pump system** takes heat from the outside air, working like an air conditioner in reverse.
   1. A heat pump is not energy efficient at below-freezing temperatures, but in milder climates a heat pump is efficient and economical.

2. In summer a heat pump operates as a conventional air conditioner.
3. Like a refrigerator, a heat pump must be defrosted.
4. Most heat pumps defrost automatically, but when in the defrost mode a heat pump is wasting energy that could be used for heating or cooling.

V. PREVENTING HEAT LOSS

A. There are three ways in which heat may be lost in the home.
1. Heat is conducted through the windows, walls, and roof.
2. Heat is radiated through the windows.
3. Heat escapes by convection through cracks around doors and windows.
B. This heat loss can be prevented or reduced in many ways through the use of **insulation.**
1. Insulating materials can be used in the walls and under the roof.
2. These materials, such as rock wool or glass wool, contain many air spaces and are nonconductors, or insulators.
3. Insulators stop heat from being conducted out through the walls and roof.
4. Storm windows, when fitted over regular windows, create an air space between the two windows.
5. Air is a poor conductor of heat and acts as an insulator (which is why glass wool and rock wool are such good insulators).
6. This insulation prevents the windows from conducting heat out of the house.
7. Permanent double-paned windows work according to the same principle as storm windows.
8. Weather strips or special materials, when placed around windows and doors, stop heat from escaping through any cracks that may be present.
C. Insulation not only stops heat from leaving a house in winter, but helps keep heat from getting into the house in summer.

VI. COOLING IN THE HOME

A. The refrigerator.
1. A refrigerator cools by taking heat away from materials.
2. A refrigerator has a pipe running through it, and inside the pipe is a gas that is changed into a liquid when compressed.
3. In an electric refrigerator a motor runs a compressor, which compresses the gas and takes heat away from it until the gas becomes a liquid.
4. The heat that is taken away from the gas passes out into the air of the room.
5. The liquid gas then flows under pressure through the pipe in the refrigerator until it reaches a place that is to be cooled.
6. Here the pressure is taken away from the liquid gas so that the liquid evaporates into a gas again.
7. When a liquid evaporates, it needs heat, and it takes this heat from the space surrounding the liquid.
8. Taking heat away cools the materials in the space surrounding the liquid that is evaporating.
9. The gas then continues to the motor and compressor, where it is turned into a liquid again.
B. The deep freeze or freezer.
1. Special refrigeration machines freeze food quickly, until the temperature of the food in the machines is 10° to 20° below 0° Fahrenheit.
2. The freezing must be quick, or else the food will lose much of its flavor and consistency.
3. When food is frozen, the water in the food freezes and forms ice crystals.
4. When food, especially fruits and vegetables, is frozen slowly, the ice crystals are large and can break the cells of the food, killing their taste and flavor.
5. When food is frozen quickly, the ice crystals are very small and do not break the food cells.
C. Air conditioning.
1. An efficient air conditioner accomplishes three things: it cools the air in a room; it lowers the amount of water vapor (humidity) in the air; and it supplies fresh air and removes stale air.
2. The home or automobile air conditioner has a cooling unit that works like a refrigerator.
3. Warm air passes through the cooling unit, and heat is taken away from the air.
4. The heat is passed on to the air outdoors, which carries it away.
5. A dehumidifier helps the excess water vapor in the air condense as the air is cooled.
6. The air is blown by a fan through a filter, which removes dust and pollen.
7. An air conditioner usually has a fresh-air connection, which provides the conditioner with fresh outdoor air.

DEMONSTRATION 18.6
Slow Oxidation Produces Heat

Soak a wad of steel wool thoroughly in water, remove the wad, allow it to drain, and then stuff it into a Thermos bottle. Obtain a one-hole rubber stopper large enough to fit the mouth of the Thermos bottle, and insert a thermometer into the hole. After the steel wool has been in the Thermos for about 10 minutes, insert the stopper and the thermometer (Figure 18.4). The temperature will soon rise, showing that heat is being produced as oxidation takes place. The temperature will stop rising after about 20 minutes, because all the oxygen present in the air inside the Thermos will be used up. When the temperature has stopped rising, remove the stopper, allow fresh air to enter, and then replace the stopper. The temperature will begin to rise again.

Ask children to suggest safety tips for home that are related to this demonstration of slow oxidation. (Such as, slow oxidation of oily rags in a garage or of moist hay in a barn can start a fire.) Have them list things they could do at home to prevent fires that can occur from slow oxidation.

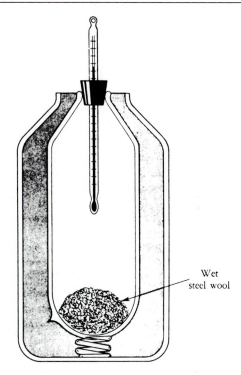

Wet steel wool

FIGURE 18.4   Wet steel wool oxidizes slowly and gives off heat.

FIRE

I. THE NATURE OF FIRE

   A. Fire, the burning of a material, is also called **combustion.**

     1. Combustion is a chemical change that takes place when certain materials combine rapidly with oxygen to give off heat and light.

     2. This chemical reaction, which takes place when a material combines with oxygen, is called **oxidation.**

   B. Materials can also combine with oxygen (oxidize) slowly and produce some heat, but no light.

     1. This combination is oxidation too, but it is a **slow oxidation** and is not called burning or combustion.

     2. The rusting of iron is an example of slow oxidation.

   C. To be called burning, the oxidation must be fast enough to produce both heat and light.

II. FACTORS NECESSARY TO PRODUCE FIRE

   A. For burning to take place, three things are needed: fuel, oxygen, and heat for ignition.

     1. A fire needs a material that will burn, which is called a fuel.

     2. The more oxygen a fuel gets, the faster the oxidation will take place, and the hotter the fire will become.

     3. Supplying the fire with more air will give the fuel more oxygen.

     4. Breaking the fuel into small pieces will expose more of the fuel's surface to the air and, in this way, give the fuel more oxygen.

     5. If a fuel is broken into pieces so small that they look like particles of dust, the fuel may combine with the oxygen so quickly that it will produce an explosion.

DEMONSTRATION 18.7
The Concept of Kindling Temperature

Attempt to light a sugar cube with a match. Then, after failing to ignite the sugar cube, rub it in some ashes that you prepared earlier (by burning a piece of paper and crushing the ash) and try again to light the sugar cube.

Ask your students why the sugar cube ignited when it was covered with ash but not before. Ask students to identify practical applications of this concept.

---

6. A fire needs a sufficient amount to heat to get the fuel hot enough to burn.
B. Some materials burn more easily than others.
   1. We say that these materials have a lower **kindling temperature,** which is the lowest temperature at which a material will ignite and burn.
   2. At this temperature, oxygen combines quickly enough with the fuel to keep the chemical reaction going steadily.
   3. Materials like phosphorus, sulfur, and paper have a low kindling temperature and burst into flame easily.
   4. When exposed to oxygen, such as in the air, pure phosphorus will ignite at room temperature, so in the laboratory this material must be kept in water in a tightly sealed container.
   5. Materials such as wood and coal have a high kindling temperature and must be quite hot before they will ignite and burn.

III. THE PRODUCTS OF FIRE

A. Fire produces a **flame,** which is a mass of burning gas.
   1. Some fuels produce a flame directly, but other fuels must be partially changed into a gas before they can burn with a flame.
   2. A gaseous fuel, such as natural gas, burns directly to produce a flame.
   3. A liquid fuel, such as gasoline or kerosene, must be heated until it turns into a gas before it will burn.
   4. Some solid fuels, like paraffin, first melt and then turn into a gas before they can burn.
   5. Other solid fuels, such as wood and coal, when heated will give off gases that burn.
B. The color of a flame depends on how much oxygen the fuel is getting.
   1. When a fuel gets all the oxygen it needs and burns completely, the flame is blue, or nearly colorless, and is very hot.

2. When a fuel does not get enough oxygen to burn completely, the flame is yellow or orange and is not as hot as a blue flame.
3. A flame is yellow because the particles of unburned fuel are glowing.
C. A **candle flame,** for example, has three parts.
   1. The center of the flame around the wick is dark, showing the presence of unburned gas.
   2. Almost all the rest of the flame is yellow, which shows that the gas is burning but not getting all the oxygen it needs.
   3. Around the edges the flame is blue or colorless, which shows that here the gas is getting all the oxygen it needs and is burning completely.
D. Fire produces water vapor and carbon dioxide or carbon monoxide gas.
   1. Most common fuels contain the chemical elements carbon and hydrogen.
   2. When a fuel burns, the hydrogen combines with the oxygen to form water vapor.
   3. Water vapor forms instead of liquid water because so much heat is given off during the burning.
   4. When a fuel has all the oxygen it needs and burns completely, the carbon combines with the oxygen to form carbon dioxide gas.
   5. When a fuel does not get enough oxygen, the carbon combines with the oxygen to form carbon monoxide gas instead.
   6. Carbon monoxide gas is made up of less oxygen than carbon dioxide gas.
E. **Smoke** is unburned fuel.
   1. Smoke is made up of particles of carbon that did not receive enough oxygen to make them burn completely.
   2. When smoke collects on walls or in chimneys, it is called **soot.**
F. Some fuels leave behind an **ash,** which is a part of the fuel that does not ordinarily burn.

DEMONSTRATION 18.8

The Effect of the Amount of Oxygen on Burning

Prepare pure oxygen by pouring some 3 percent hydrogen peroxide into a glass jar. Add a piece of liver about the size of half dollar, then cover the top of the jar with an index card or piece of cardboard. (Keep the liver cool, but do not freeze, until one hour before using.) An enzyme in the liver, called catalase, makes the hydrogen peroxide decompose, bubbling vigorously, to produce oxygen gas and water.

Untwist one end of a piece of thick picture wire or steel wool and hold this untwisted end in a flame until the wire begins to glow. Then quickly insert the glowing wire or steel wool into the jar of pure oxygen (Figure 18.5). The wire will burn like a Fourth of July sparkler in the pure oxygen.

Flames and sparks are very dangerous in the presence of high concentrations of oxygen. Ask the students to research and report their findings to the class about where high concentrations of oxygen are used, such as in industry and in medicine, and the safety measures that are in effect in those situations.

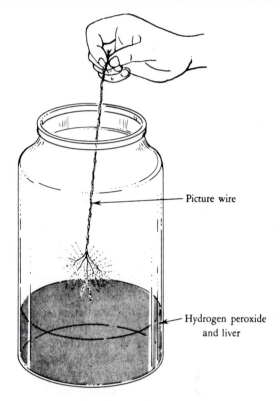

Picture wire

Hydrogen peroxide and liver

FIGURE 18.5   Picture wire burns vigorously in pure oxygen.

IV. SPONTANEOUS COMBUSTION

  A. Sometimes materials burst into flame all by themselves, a phenomenon called spontaneous combustion.

    1. **Spontaneous combustion** takes place when a slow oxidation is going on in a closed space where the air cannot circulate or escape.

    2. An oily rag in a closed closet or garage can burst into flame through spontaneous combustion, as can dust and lint caught in a hose leading from a clothes dryer.

    3. The oil, or dust and lint, combines with oxygen, or oxidizes, slowly and gives off a small amount of heat.

    4. This heat cannot escape because there is no movement of air to carry it away.

    5. The heat makes the oil (or lint and dust) combine with oxygen more quickly, which produces more heat, which cannot escape and so makes the fuel combine with oxygen even more quickly.

    6. This process continues, producing more and more heat, until the kindling point of the cloth rag (or the dust and lint) is reached, and the material bursts into flame.

  B. If green or wet hay is stored in a barn, spontaneous combustion may take place, because damp hay ferments and gives off heat.

V. FACTORS NECESSARY TO PUT OUT FIRE

  A. To put out a fire we must take away one or more of the three things needed to make a fire.

    1. We can remove the fuel.

DEMONSTRATION 18.9
Kindling Temperature

A. Demonstrating Kindling Temperature

Invert a pie tin over a tripod and put a match head on the tin (Figure 18.6). Heat the tin with a Bunsen burner. When the tin reaches the kindling temperature of the match head, the match head will burst into flame.

B. Comparing the Kindling Temperature of Different Materials

Invert a pie tin over a tripod, as described in demonstration A. Place on the tin a match head, a small amount of sulfur (if available), a piece of paper, a piece of match stick, and a piece of soft coal or charcoal. Make sure the materials are of approximately the same size, and space them equidistant from each other and from the center of the tin. Place a Bunsen burner or alcohol lamp under the center of the tin and light it. Note the order in which the materials reach their kindling temperatures. The match head will burst into flame first, followed by the sulfur. The paper will char or burn, and the wood will just char slightly. The coal will not burn, because its kindling temperature was not reached.

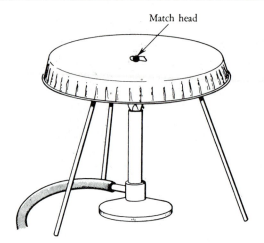

FIGURE 18.6   A match head has a low kindling temperature.

---

2. We can cut off the supply of oxygen.
3. We can cool the burning fuel, making its temperature lower than the kindling point.

B. The most common methods of putting out fires are to cut off the supply of oxygen and to lower the temperature.

C. Removing the fuel is practical only with a small fire, such as a camp fire or a fire in a wastebasket.

D. The supply of oxygen can be cut off by using sand, soil, a heavy wool blanket or coat, water, carbon dioxide gas, or any other material that will not burn.

E. The temperature can be lowered by using water or any other cool material that will not burn.

F. **Fire extinguishers** use chemicals to put out fires by cutting off the supply of oxygen and by cooling the burning fuel.

   1. The **soda-acid** fire extinguisher, when turned upside down, mixes two chemicals together to form carbon dioxide gas, which smothers a fire by cutting off the supply of oxygen.
   2. This type of extinguisher contains water and cannot be used to put out oil fires because the water, which is heavier than oil, sinks to the bottom while the burning oil floats and even spreads out farther on top of the water.
   3. Nor can this type of extinguisher be used to put out electrical fires, because the solution of chemicals in the extinguisher is a good conductor of electricity.
   4. The **carbon dioxide** extinguisher is used for putting out oil and electrical fires.
   5. This extinguisher contains compressed liquid carbon dioxide, and when the liquid carbon dioxide leaves the extinguisher, it turns into large amounts of very cold carbon dioxide gas.
   6. Because carbon dioxide is heavier than air, it will hover over the flaming material and put out the fire by cutting off the supply of oxygen and cooling the burning fuel.
   7. The **carbon tetrachloride** extinguisher is also used to put out oil and electrical fires.
   8. Liquid carbon tetrachloride is pumped out of the extinguisher.
   9. The flames heat the liquid carbon tetrachloride and turn it into a heavy blanket of gas, which pushes the air away from the fire and smothers it.

DEMONSTRATION 18.10

Flame is a Burning Gas

Light a candle and allow it to burn for a few minutes. Tilt the candle and note the liquid paraffin that drips down. Point out that when the wick first began to burn, it melted the paraffin, which rose up into the wick and was changed to a gas by the heat of the flame. The gas burned, giving off heat and light.

Snuff out the candle flame with a test tube, then immediately light a match and lower it toward the wick (Figure 18.7). You will light the candle before you touch the wick. Point out that when the candle was snuffed, the wick was still hot and continued to change the liquid paraffin to a gas for a short time. The burning match set fire to this gas, which then set fire to the wick.

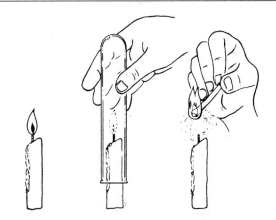

FIGURE 18.7   A flame is a mass of burning gas.

10. The **foam** extinguisher is very effective against gasoline and large oil fires.
11. It works very much like the soda-acid extinguisher, but it also contains a foam-making material, such as licorice extract.
12. When this type of extinguisher is turned upside down, the chemicals mix together and produce a tough foamy mass of carbon dioxide bubbles, which covers the burning gasoline or oil and shuts off the supply of oxygen.

VI. SAFETY PROCEDURES FOR FIRES

A. Keep matches and lighters away from heat.
B. Keep matches and lighters away from small children.
C. If you have to strike a match or a lighter, strike away from you and not toward you.
D. Be sure the flame is out when you throw a match away.
E. Surround a camp fire with nonporous stones, bricks, or bare earth; porous materials can explode when they get too hot.
F. Be especially careful when making a camp fire on a windy day.
G. Put out the camp fire thoroughly with sand or soil when you do not want it any more.
H. Never use gasoline to start a fire of any kind.

I. Put a metal screen in front of a fireplace.
J. Put hot ashes in nonflammable containers only.
K. Do not allow trash that will burn to pile up in the basement or attic.
L. Do not put oily rags in closets or other places where there is no circulation of air.
M. Keep the lint traps and hoses of clothes dryers cleaned out.
N. If a container has materials in it that will burn, keep it away from heat or an open flame.
O. Keep a carbon dioxide fire extinguisher in the home, where it can be quickly reached.
P. If your clothes catch on fire, do not run: running supplies the fire with more oxygen, allowing it to burn faster. Roll on the floor or wrap up in a rug, coat, or blanket.
Q. Learn how to telephone the fire department and turn in an alarm using a fire alarm box.
R. If a fire in a house is too big for you to put out, leave the house at once. Close the door to the room where the fire is, to cut down the supply of air in the room. Go to the nearest alarm box or telephone the fire department.
S. Keep chimneys clean.
T. In fireplaces, burn only those fuels recommended for the specific type or make of fireplace.
U. Do not use a home fireplace as a trash bin.

DEMONSTRATION 18.11
Fire Extinguishers

A. Carbon Dioxide Puts Out Fire

Place three candles of different lengths on a piece of cardboard. Prepare a cardboard trough with three holes, each hole just large enough to fit snugly over one of the candles. Fit the trough over the candles so that it is just below the top of each candle (Figure 18.8), and then light the candles.

Obtain a large glass jar or beaker. Prepare carbon dioxide by pouring some baking soda (sodium bicarbonate) into the jar, adding vinegar, and then covering the jar with a piece of cardboard or an index card until the bubbling subsides. Remove the cardboard and tilt the jar over the higher end of the trough, allowing just the invisible carbon dioxide to flow into the trough and put out the candle flames.

B. Making a Foam Fire Extinguisher

Put two tablespoons of baking soda into a tumbler of water, stir, and then pour into a quart-size glass jar. Break an egg and pour the contents into the jar. Cap the jar and shake the contents thoroughly. Obtain a large pie tin and place it on a fireproof mat. Pour some alcohol or lighter

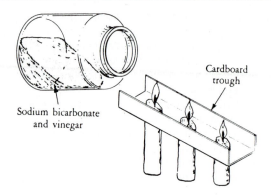

Sodium bicarbonate and vinegar

Cardboard trough

FIGURE 18.8   Carbon dioxide puts out the candle flames.

fluid into the tin and set fire to the alcohol with a lighted match (be very careful not to spread the fire). Place the jar in the center of the tin and immediately pour a cup of vinegar into the jar. A foam will form, which will overflow the jar, pour down the sides, and put out the fire. Point out that the egg made it possible for the bubbles of carbon dioxide to cling together and form a foamy mass.

FUELS

I. CHARACTERISTICS OF A GOOD FUEL

    A. A fuel is any material that is burned to produce heat for use in the home or in industry.

    B. For a material to be considered a good fuel, it should have certain characteristics.

        1. It should be inexpensive and easy to obtain.

        2. It should be easy and safe to store, ship, and use.

        3. It should burn fairly easily.

        4. It should produce a large amount of heat.

        5. It should produce very little smoke.

    C. There are three classes of fuels: solid, liquid, and gas fuels.

    D. Geothermal energy is gradually being harnessed as a clean alternative to coal, gas, and oil, but it will not be able to replace them completely.

II. SOLID FUELS

    A. Solid fuels include wood, charcoal, coal, coke, peat, and lignite.

        1. Wood has a low kindling temperature and gives a great amount of heat.

        2. However, wood gives off much smoke and leaves a lot of ash.

        3. Chimneys of wood-burning fireplaces must be cleaned out frequently; otherwise, a chimney, roof, and attic fire can result because of the buildup of soot and creosote.

        4. When metal chimneys get too hot, they can melt, creating a serious fire hazard.

    B. Charcoal is wood that is heated in the absence of air. It is an artificial fuel.

        1. The liquid and gas impurities in the wood are driven off, leaving mostly burnable carbon.

        2. Charcoal burns with a great deal of heat, gives off no smoke, and leaves very little ash.

    C. Coal consists of the remains of plants and ferns that were covered by the earth millions of years ago.

        1. Because of the action of high temperatures and tremendous pressures in the earth, the

liquid and gas impurities were driven off, leaving mostly burnable carbon.

   2. **Soft coal** contains about 70 percent carbon and burns with a great deal of heat, but it gives off much smoke and leaves quite a bit of ash.

   3. **Hard coal** contains almost 90 percent carbon, burns with a great deal of heat, gives off much less smoke, and leaves little ash.

D. Peat and lignite are coal in its early stages of formation and do not give very much heat.

E. Coke is soft coal that is heated in the absence of air. It is an artificial fuel.

   1. Gas impurities in soft coal are driven off, leaving mostly burnable carbon.

   2. Coke burns with a great deal of heat, gives off no smoke, and leaves very little ash.

III. LIQUID FUELS

A. **Petroleum**, also known as crude oil, was formed from the remains of small plants and animals that died millions of years ago.

   1. These remains were buried in mud and rock beneath shallow seas.

   2. Today most petroleum is found deep below the earth's surface in certain kinds of rock formations.

   3. In some areas petroleum is also found below the earth's surface a short distance from the seashore.

   4. Raw petroleum is not used as a fuel itself, but is broken up into different materials and refined.

   5. From petroleum we get such liquid fuels as fuel oil, diesel oil, gasoline, and kerosene.

   6. From petroleum we also get such commercially important materials as naphtha, benzene, lubricating oil, grease, and paraffin.

IV. GAS FUELS

A. Gas fuels include natural gas and the artificial gases.

B. **Natural gas** is found together with petroleum deposits and near coal fields.

   1. Because it is heavier than air, natural gas can be stored in underground caves.

C. **Artificial gases** are made from soft coal, coke, and petroleum.

D. All gas fuels have an advantage over both solid and liquid fuels in that they burn instantly.

   1. Moreover, gas fuels are clean, and easy to handle, and can be piped all over the country.

   2. Gas fuels also give much heat, produce no smoke, and leave no ash.

V. ALTERNATIVE FUELS

A. A growing environmental consciousness has spurred scientists and engineers to search for cleaner energy alternatives.

   1. The harnessing of the heat energy produced by nuclear radiation deep in the earth and the development of fuel cells may be sources of energy for the future.

B. The earth continuously produces heat, primarily by the decay of naturally radioactive chemical elements that occur in small amounts in all rocks.

   1. The annual heat loss from the earth is enormous—equivalent to 10 times the annual energy consumption of the United States—and more than that needed to power all nations of the world if it could be fully harnessed.

   2. If only 1 percent of the thermal energy contained within the uppermost 10 kilometers (62 mi) of the earth's crust could be harnessed, this amount could replace 500 times that contained in all oil and natural gas resources of the world.

   3. Scientists and engineers are working at finding ways to utilize more fully the earth's abundant thermal energy—commonly called **geothermal energy.**

C. Hot springs are formed when underground water is heated by hot rock and gases beneath the earth's surface and the hot water then flows to the surface.

   1. The passageway along which the hot water travels is wide and open, so the water reaches the surface quickly and easily.

   2. The temperature of the water may range from just warm to boiling.

   3. On its way to the surface the hot water dissolves large amounts of minerals.

   4. As the water evaporates, these minerals are deposited around the mouth of the hot spring and tend to build up colored layers or terraces.

D. A geyser is a hot spring that sprays its water high into the air at intervals.

   1. This eruption of water occurs because the geyser has to travel a narrow, twisted pathway, rather than a wide passage, to reach the earth's surface.

   2. Heated water is often trapped in the passageway, where it continues to be heated far above its boiling point of 100° Celsius (212° Fahrenheit) without being changed into steam.

   3. The reason for such superheating is that at higher than atmospheric pressure, the boil-

ing point of water increases as well. Water heated above its boiling point without turning to steam is called **superheated water.**

4. The superheated water expands and causes some of the water above it to overflow onto the earth's surface.
5. The loss of water above eases the pressure on the superheated water below, so that some of it is suddenly changed to steam, which blows all the water above it high into the air as a geyser.
6. After the geyser erupts, some of the water flows back into the passageway, where it meets more underground water coming up, and the process repeats itself.

E. In 1992, The Geysers, a hydrothermal system in northern California became the world's largest development using geothermal energy to move large turbines to produce electricity.
1. Actually, The Geysers is not a spouting geyser or system of geysers but a field of slow erupting vents, warm springs, and fumaroles.
2. Pipes set deep into ground wells carry steam to turbine generators that, in turn, generate electricity.
3. Other countries using geothermal energy to create electrical energy are El Salvador and Nicaragua, since the 1970s, and Costa Rica, since 1994.

F. In Iceland and in some areas around Paris, France, geothermal energy is used to heat water and as a source of heat for buildings.

G. The **fuel cell** may be another source of energy for the future.
1. The fuel cell was first discovered in 1839, when Sir William Grove of England discovered that electricity can be generated by supplying hydrogen and oxygen to two separate electrodes immersed in dilute sulfuric acid.
2. Today the U.S. space shuttles use alkaline potassium hydroxide fuel cells to supply electricity and drinking water.
3. A fuel cell is a form of continuously operating battery, able to transform the chemical energy of various fuels into a flow of electrons—electricity.
4. The U.S. Department of Energy (DOE) is supporting the development of buses driven by methanol fuel cells for use in urban transit systems.
5. The Southern California Gas Company has several phosphoric acid fuel cell plants on line.

Exploratory Activities For "Heat"

1. AN EXPLORATORY STUDY OF TEMPERATURE SCALES (ANY GRADE LEVEL)

Modify the activities that follow according to the interests, age, and maturity of your students.

1.1 Make Ribbon Temperature Scales

Teacher Preparatory Activity

Obtain some sturdy white cardboard about 76 centimeters (30 in) long and 25 centimeters (10 in) wide. Cut slits 2 centimeters (3/4 in) wide in the center of the cardboard near the top and the bottom (Figure 18.9). Obtain pieces of red ribbon and white ribbon, each about 13 millimeters (1/2 in) wide. Sew one end of the red ribbon neatly and firmly to one end of the white ribbon. Slip the loose ends of the red and white ribbon through the slits, as shown in the diagram. Cut off any excess ribbon and sew the other two ribbon ends together. Now, by pulling the ribbon at the back, you can make the red ribbon (which represents the mercury or alcohol in a thermometer) rise or fall. Use felt-tip marker to mark the distance between both slits in equal divisions so as to produce an accurate representation of the Fahrenheit scale.

Prepare a second ribbon thermometer illustrating the Celsius (centigrade) scale. Then prepare a third thermometer showing a Fahrenheit scale on one side of the ribbon and a Celsius scale on the other side.

Student Activity

Have the students study each scale separately. Let them take readings with actual thermometers of the temperature of the room, hot and cold liquids, and other materials for which they are interested in finding temperatures. Find the boiling point and the freezing point of water on each thermometer and scale (using a mixture of ice and water for the freezing point). Point out that the boiling point and freezing point vary, depending on how far above sea level you are located.

After the students have mastered reading each scale separately, show them the ribbon thermometer containing both scales. Compare such fixed points as the boiling and freezing points of water on both scales.

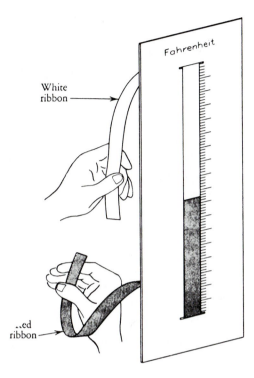

FIGURE 18.9   A red and white ribbon thermometer.

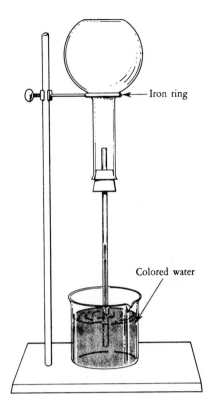

FIGURE 18.10   An air thermometer works differently from a liquid thermometer.

Show the students how to convert temperatures from one scale to another, checking the results on the ribbon thermometer.

1.2 Making an Air Thermometer

(For older students or as a teacher demonstration.) Obtain a small flask or bottle, a one-hole rubber stopper, and a narrow glass or plastic tube 45 centimeters (18 in) long. Insert the tube into the stopper and fit the stopper tightly into the neck of the flask. Support the flask with an iron ring attached to a ringstand, as shown in Figure 18.10. Place the end of the tube in a beaker or tumbler of water colored very deep red with food coloring.

Heat the flask very gently with a small Bunsen burner flame or with an alcohol lamp, moving the flame back and forth along the flask. The heat will cause the air inside the flask to expand, and bubbles of air will leave the bottom of the tube. Drive out enough air so that when the flame is removed and the air inside the flask cools and contracts, the colored water rises a sizable distance up the tube. Point out that the air pressure on the surface of the colored water forced the water up the tube, taking the place of the air that was driven out of the flask.

Now put your hands in hot water, dry them, and place them around the flask. The colored water will be driven down the tube as the air inside becomes warm and expands. Cool your hands and place them around the flask. This time the colored water will rise up the tube, as the air inside the flask cools and contracts. If you like, prepare a cardboard temperature scale behind the air thermometer and let the students take daily room temperature readings.

2. AN EXPLORATORY STUDY OF HEAT CONDUCTORS (GRADES 4–9)

2.1 Exploring Metals as Conductors

Into a cup of hot water put a sterling silver spoon, a silverplated spoon, and a stainless steel spoon. Note which spoon handle becomes the hottest. Repeat the learning activity, using rods of different materials such as brass, iron, and copper.

2.2 Exploring Other Materials as Conductors

Into a cup of hot water put rods of such materials as wood, glass, and plastic. Use rods of equal length and thickness. Note that the parts above the surface of the

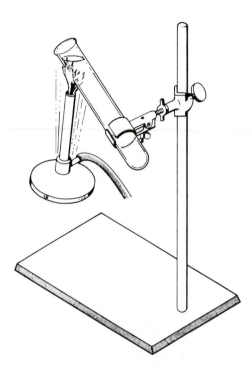

FIGURE 18.11 The water at the top of the test tube will boil while the water at the bottom is still cold.

water do not become hot, or even warm. Put a piece of rubber tubing in the hot water. The end outside the water will not become hot.

2.3 Exploring the Use of Nonconductors

Wrap some cloth around one end of a metal rod and place the other end into the flame of a Bunsen burner or alcohol lamp. Because the cloth is a poor conductor of heat, you will not burn your hand even though the metal rod becomes very hot. Repeat this learning activity, using some thicknesses of paper wrapped around the metal rod.

2.4 Exploring Water as a Conductor

Fill a Pyrex test tube almost full of cold water and clamp the test tube to a ringstand (Figure 18.11). Have the clamp nearer to the bottom of the test tube. Now heat the top of the test tube with the flame of a Bunsen burner or alcohol lamp, moving the flame back and forth, until the water boils. Carefully feel the bottom of the test tube. The water will still be cold.

2.5 Exploring Air as a Conductor of Heat

Hold one end of a short metal rod and place the other end in the flame of a Bunsen burner or alcohol lamp.

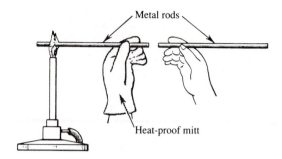

FIGURE 18.12 Because air is a poor heat conductor, the second rod remains cool.

In a very short time the end of the rod you are holding will become hot, as the heat travels along the rod by conduction.

Let the metal rod become cool and repeat the learning activity, this time holding the end of the rod with a heatproof mitt. At the same time, hold with your bare hand one end of a second short rod about 2 centimeters (1 in) away from the end of the first rod (Figure 18.12). The second rod will remain cool because air is a poor conductor of heat.

3. AN EXPERIMENTAL STUDY: CHANGING SYSTEMS (GRADES 4–9)

Overview This investigation will assist students in their understanding of what a system is and how energy affects it.

Materials Needed (One set of the following for each group of about four students): beaker, thermometer, ring stand, clamp, test tube, aluminum foil, cork straight pins, various kinds of nuts (almond, walnut, peanut), water, scales (suitable for weighing a nut).

Focusing Questions

1. What is a system?
2. Can you name some examples of systems?
3. Do systems ever change?
4. We are going to test nuts for their energy content by burning them. Which nut do you predict will cause the greatest change in the temperature of the water?

Procedure

1. Add 25 ml of water to your test tube.
2. Suspend the test tube with a clamp to the ring stand.
3. Cover a cork with aluminum foil and stick a pin in it, then place the cork beneath the test tube.

Temperature	Peanut	Walnut	Almond
Start: 0 sec.			
30 sec.			
1 min.			
90 sec.			
2 min.			
2.5 min.			
3 min.			
3.5 min.			
4 min.			

4. Select a nut and weigh it.
5. Stick one of the nuts onto the pin.
6. Record the temperature of the water in the test tube.
7. Ignite the nut with a match.
8. Record the temperature of the water every 30 seconds for 4 minutes even if the nut burns out.
9. Record the temperatures on the above chart.
10. Weigh the cooled nut after burning.
11. Graph your results.

Closing Questions

1. While the nut was burning, in what way did the water system change?
2. Is the amount of change in the water system related to the amount of change in the nut system? Is there a way you can test this?
3. As the nut and water systems changed, what other system changed?
4. Which nut produced the greatest amount of heat energy? Why do you suppose this was so?

STUDENT BOOKS AND OTHER RESOURCES FOR "HEAT"

Gardner, R. *Science Projects About Temperature and Heat.* Hillside, CA: Enslow, 1994.

Marstall, B. *Fire in the Forest: A Cycle of Growth and Renewal.* New York: Atheneum, 1995.

United States Department of Energy. *Fuel Cells for Transportation.* Washington, DC: Author, 1992.

Vogel, C., and C. Goldner. *The Great Yellowstone Fire.* Boston: Little, Brown, 1990.

CHAPTER 19

Sound

PRODUCING AND TRANSMITTING SOUND

I. SOUND AND ITS CHARACTERISTICS

  A. Sound is one of three types of radiation.
    1. There are three general categories of radiation: mechanical, electromagnetic, and particle radiation.
    2. Mechanical radiation requires a material medium to proliferate energy from one place to another.
    3. Sound is an effect of mechanical radiation.
  B. As an effect of mechanical radiation, sound is caused by an object that is moving back and forth, or vibrating.
    1. Vibrations from the source disturb the molecules in the surrounding air and establish radiating waves of sound energy.
    2. Sound vibrations can be produced by plucking, stroking, blowing, and hitting.
    3. Sound cannot travel at all in a vacuum, where there are no molecules to vibrate and transmit the sound energy.
    4. If there is a medium, such as air, vibrating waves move out in all directions from the vibrating source.
    5. Perception of sound depends on three factors: a vibrating source that sets up the sound waves, a medium such as air to carry the waves, and a receiver to detect them.

II. HOW SOUND TRAVELS

  A. When an object, such as a violin string or a tuning fork, is made to vibrate, the sound energy travels out as waves in all directions.

1. When the string vibrates, it moves back and forth very rapidly. As it moves forward, it pushes against the molecules of air in front of it and presses them closer together. The space in which the molecules are pressed closer together is called a **compression.**
2. As the string moves backward, it leaves a space with fewer molecules in it, and these molecules spread farther apart. The space in which the molecules are spread farther apart is called a **rarefaction.**
3. One compression and one rarefaction together make up one complete **sound wave,** or **vibration,** or **cycle.** As an object vibrates back and forth, it produces cycles of compression and rarefaction, one after another.
4. Sound is measured by the number of cycles produced per second. This number is referred to as the **frequency** of the sound. Frequency is measured in units called **hertz** (Hz). One hertz is one complete cycle, or vibration back and forth.
5. The presence of cycles of alternating compression and rarefaction means that the molecules of air have also been made to move back and forth, or vibrate.
6. As the molecules of air vibrate, they bump into other molecules and cause these molecules to vibrate, which then cause still other molecules to vibrate.
7. No single vibrating molecule travels very far. Each moves back and forth, pushing against other molecules, as the sound waves radiate out in all directions.

DEMONSTRATION 19.1

A Visual Simulation of Sound Vibrations

Although sound waves and water waves are quite different kinds of waves, water waves can be used to simulate sound waves. Strike a tuning fork with a soft mallet and touch the tip of the vibrating fork into the surface of a beaker of water. Ask students to describe what they see. Ask students whether effects of sound can be felt as well as heard and seen. Very low frequency sounds can sometimes be felt. (Students have probably felt the low frequency sounds that come from some car radios as they pass on the street. You can touch a radio speaker and feel the vibrations. Likewise, you can touch your throat and feel the vibrations of your vocal cords when you speak in low tones.)

B. Most sounds come to us through the atmosphere, which is composed of gases.
1. The speed of sound in air at sea level is about 336 meters (1,100 ft) per second, or about 1 kilometer in 3 seconds (1 mi in 5 secs).
2. The warmer the air, the greater the speed of sound will be. The speed of sound in air increases about 30 centimeters (1 ft) per second for every degree rise in Fahrenheit temperature, or about 60 centimeters (2 ft) per second for every degree rise in Celsius temperature.
3. High on a mountain, this air is thinner and does not contain as many molecules as the air in a valley. Therefore, in the upper atmosphere sound does not travel as fast as it does at lower elevations.
C. Sound travels faster and farther through liquids than through gases. Sound travels about 1,464 meters (4,800 ft) per second in water, or about four times as fast as in air.
D. Sound travels faster and farther through hard solids than through liquids or gases.
1. Sound travels more than 3,000 meters (10,000 ft) per second through wood, or about nine times as fast as in air.
2. Sound travels more than 5,000 meters (16,500 ft) per second through steel, or fifteen times as fast as in air.
E. Soft solids, like cork, rubber, felt, and cotton, are poor conductors of sound because they tend to absorb sound waves rather than to conduct them. Thus, soft solids that are poor conductors are used for soundproofing.

III. DIFFERENCES IN SOUND

A. Humans perceive differences in sound. These differences are pitch, intensity, and quality (or timbre).
B. **Pitch** is related to a sound's frequency.

1. When a body is vibrating, it produces a certain number of vibrations, or sound wave cycles, per second.
2. The faster a body vibrates, the more vibrations it produces a second, and the higher the sound's frequency, or pitch. The slower a body vibrates, the fewer vibrations it produces a second, and the lower the sound's frequency, or pitch.
3. The human ear cannot hear all possible frequencies, only those within a range of about 20 cycles per second to 20,000 cycles per second.
4. Frequencies lower than the human ear can hear are called **subsonic,** and frequencies higher than the human ear can hear are called **supersonic** or **ultrasonic.** Because dogs can hear sounds above the human maximum range of 20,000 cycles per second, whistles that are pitched at supersonic frequencies are used to call dogs.
5. Extremely low frequencies (below 10 Hz) and extreme high frequencies (of 100,000 to 500,000 Hz) can cause physical and chemical reactions. Ultrasonic sound waves can kill bacteria, insects, and pests; control and operate automatic garage doors; clean clothes by shaking the dirt out of them; and cause water and oil to form an emulsion.
C. A sound's **wavelength** is the distance between its compressions (or between its rarefactions), which is another way to define the pitch of a tone.
1. The wavelength of a particular sound is equal to the velocity of sound divided by the frequency of the sound. The formula is

$$\lambda = \frac{V}{f}.$$

Because in air sound travels at about 336 meters (1,100 ft) per second, to find the wavelength for a particular sound you would divide 336 by that sound's frequency.

 2. If the source of a sound is moving, such as a car's horn while the car is speeding by, the distance between the crests of the sound waves is compressed in one direction and lengthened in the opposite direction. This compression and lengthening of a sound wave will change the frequency of the sound, a phenomenon known as the **Doppler effect.**

D. **Intensity** is the loudness or softness of a sound. It has nothing to do with the pitch.

 1. The loudness or softness of a sound depends on the distance the object is vibrating, which is known as **amplitude.** The greater the amplitude, the more energy the sound wave has. The more energy put into making a sound, the louder the sound will be.

 2. The farther sound waves travel, the softer the sound becomes, because as the waves move away from the source of the sound, they lose energy and decrease in amplitude.

 3. The unit of measurement of sound intensity is the **decibel.** Decibels are measured by a machine called the sound-level or decibel meter. Whispering produces 10 to 20 decibels of sound. Talking rather loudly produces about 60 decibels. Heavy traffic noises produce about 70 to 80 decibels. Thunder produces about 110 decibels. The threshold of human pain caused by sound is 120 decibels. The loudest automobile stereos have been measured at 154 decibels.

E. The **quality** of a sound tells us the difference between various musical instruments, or between different persons who are producing a similar sound.

 1. Even though sounds have the same pitch and intensity, they can appear different.

 2. This difference occurs because, when an object vibrates, it produces a fundamental frequency and overtones, or multiples of the fundamental tone.

 3. When this multiple vibration takes place, sounds of different frequencies are heard at the same time.

 4. The lowest sound a vibrating body produces is called the **fundamental tone.**

 5. The other sounds that the vibrating body produces simultaneously, but that have different frequencies, are called **overtones.**

 6. The quality of a sound depends on the number and strength of the various overtones that are produced.

IV. HEARING

A. When sound waves reach the ear, they are changed to electrical signals that are carried by the auditory nerve to the brain, where they are then translated into what we know as sound.

B. Most animals, including humans, can hear a much broader frequency range than they can produce (see Chapter 15). This wider range of hearing likely provides a survival advantage in the wild.

C. Animals have adapted hearing mechanisms in different ways.

 1. Cicadas have hearing organs at the base of the abdomen, in their stomachs. Crickets have hearing organs in the oval slits of their forelegs. The cockroach hears with hairs on its abdomen. A caterpillar hears with the hairs all over its body.

 2. A snake picks up sound waves with its tongue.

 3. Bats and dolphins use echolocation, picking up the reflection of their own high-pitched squeaks.

 4. Some moths have developed a defensive mechanism against the bat by producing sounds that mimic the bat's, thereby jamming the bat's signal, and others by altering the frequency by which they beat their own wings, thereby confusing the predator bat.

 5. For humans, the sense of hearing is located in the ear (see Chapter 15).

V. ECHO

A. An echo is a sound wave that bounces back, or is reflected, from a hard surface such as a cliff or a wall of a building.

 1. To hear an echo we must be at least 17 meters (56 ft) away from the reflecting surface.

 2. The farther away the reflecting surface is, the longer time it will take to hear the echo. Too far away, of course, no echo will be heard.

 3. Sometimes a sound wave bounces off many surfaces and produces a series of echoes.

B. There are ways to eliminate unwanted echoes from a large room or auditorium.

 1. Soft drapes on walls and window frames, and rugs on the floor, can be used to absorb sound waves and prevent echoes.

 2. Covering the ceilings and the walls with rough materials or materials with many little holes in them can break up sound waves so that few reflect back to cause echoes.

3. Sound waves are also absorbed by people present in an auditorium, thus reducing the echo effect.

VI. THE VOICE

A. At the top of the windpipe, or trachea, in your throat is the voice box, or **larynx.**
   1. Stretched over the top of the larynx are two thin but strong bands of tissue called the **vocal cords.**
   2. When air from the lungs is blown through a narrow slit (the glottis) between these two cords, the cords are made to vibrate by the moving air and sound is produced.
B. Muscles attached to the vocal cords make the cords tight or loose and in this way control the pitch of your voice.
   1. The tighter the vocal cords, the faster they vibrate and the higher the pitch.
   2. The greater the force with which air is blown between the vocal cords, the louder the sound.
C. Men's vocal cords are usually longer and thicker than those of women and so do not vibrate as fast. This difference explains why men have lower or deeper voices than women. A young male's vocal cords become longer and thicker as he gets older. As a result, his voice changes from a relatively high pitch to a lower one.
D. The quality of a person's voice depends partly on several factors.
   1. The strength and control of the vocal cords affect the quality of a person's voice. The muscles that control our vocal cords can be strengthened and controlled through practice.
   2. Air passages in the throat, mouth, and nose, as well as the sinuses of the head, also affect the quality of the voice. Passages that are opened wide and free of mucus give a better voice quality than passages that are occluded and less open.
   3. The position of the lips, tongue, and teeth also functions in determining the kind and quality of sounds produced.

MUSIC AND MUSICAL INSTRUMENTS

I. MUSIC VERSUS NOISE

A. Pleasant sounds, produced by regular vibrations, are called **music.** Harsh or unpleasant sounds, produced by irregular vibrations, are known as **noise.**

II. MUSICAL INSTRUMENTS

A. Musical instruments are devices used to produce pleasant sounds of different pitch, intensity, and quality. Musical instruments are divided into three classes: stringed instruments, wind instruments, and percussion instruments.
B. **Stringed instruments** contain one or more strings that are made to vibrate and produce musical sounds. The strings are made to vibrate in different ways.
   1. Some strings are stroked or rubbed with a bow, as in the violin, cello, and bass viol. Some strings are plucked, either with the fingers or with a pick, as in the ukulele, guitar, banjo, and harp. In the piano, the strings are struck by small hammers.
   2. The pitch, or frequency, of all the musical sounds produced by stringed instruments can be changed in three different ways.
      a. The looser the string, the lower the pitch; the tighter the string, the higher the pitch.
      b. The longer the string, the lower the pitch; the shorter the string, the higher the pitch.
      c. The thicker the string, the lower the pitch; the thinner the string, the higher the pitch.
   3. Stringed instruments like the violin, cello, and banjo have just a few strings that are attached to pegs. The strings are of different thicknesses that produce sounds of higher or lower pitch. Pegs can be used to tighten or loosen the strings and make the pitch higher or lower. When these instruments are played, the fingers move up and down the vibrating strings, making them longer and shorter, thus producing lower and higher musical sounds.
   4. Instruments such as the harp and the piano have a great many strings. Their strings differ in length, thickness, and tightness so that they produce sounds of different pitch. The harp also has pedals that can pull the strings tighter and make them produce sounds with a higher pitch.
   5. Sounds from stringed instruments can be made louder or softer. The harder a string is bowed or plucked, the more strongly it vibrates and the louder the sound. The more gently a string is bowed or plucked, the more

weakly it vibrates and the softer the sound. Furthermore, when a string vibrates, it makes the entire instrument vibrate at the same frequency, or pitch.

6. The vibrating instrument makes the air surrounding the instrument vibrate at the same frequency as well. The large amount of vibrating air reinforces the original vibrations of the string and makes them stronger, which means the sound will be louder. In the piano, a sounding board above the strings vibrates, rather than the entire piano.

7. Some instruments, like the violin and the guitar, have openings to air spaces within them. Not only does the instrument vibrate, but because the sound waves enter the instrument, the air inside it vibrates at the same pitch, or frequency. The vibrating air joins and reinforces the original vibrations, making them stronger and producing a louder sound. Reinforcement of the original vibrations to make the sound louder is called **resonance.**

8. Sounds made by stringed instruments differ in quality.

9. When a string vibrates, the whole string vibrates. The tone produced is called the **fundamental tone.**

10. A vibrating string can vibrate not only as a whole, but also in parts at the same time. When a string vibrates in two parts, it is just as if the shorter strings were vibrating, with each part just half as long as the original string. These shorter strings vibrate twice as fast, producing a tone, called an **overtone.**

11. Vibrating as a whole, the string produces its fundamental tone, which is the lowest tone it can produce. Vibrating in parts, the string produces overtones, which are higher than the fundamental tone.

12. The quality of the sound depends on the number and strength of the overtones that are produced. The quality also depends on the size, shape, and material of the instrument, because these factors help to determine how many overtones will be produced.

C. **Wind instruments** contain a column of air that is caused to vibrate to produce musical sounds.

1. The air column can be made to vibrate by either blowing into it, as is done with the clarinet, saxophone, and trumpet, or by blowing across it, as is done with the flute and piccolo.

2. Wind instruments are divided into two main classes: woodwind and brass instruments.

3. In all **woodwind instruments,** except the flute and the piccolo, a thin piece of wood or plastic, called a reed, is used to make the air column vibrate. The reed is in the mouthpiece of the instrument.

4. Blowing into the mouthpiece makes the reed vibrate, which then makes the air column vibrate.

5. In the flute and the piccolo, we blow across a hole and start the air column vibrating.

6. Examples of woodwind instruments include the flute, piccolo, clarinet, oboe, bassoon, and English horn. The saxophone uses a reed, but is made of brass, so it belongs partly to the brass family.

7. **Brass instruments** are made of brass, and are played by vibrating the lips while they are pressed against the mouthpiece of the instrument. Examples of brass instruments include the saxophone, trumpet, cornet, bugle, trombone, French horn, and tuba.

8. The vibration of the lips starts the air column vibrating.

9. The pitch or frequency of the vibrating air column can be changed by making the air column longer or shorter. The longer the air column, the lower the pitch; the shorter the air column, the higher the pitch.

10. Woodwind instruments have a series of holes, usually covered by pads called keys. Pressing or releasing the keys opens or closes the holes, making the length of the air column inside the instrument longer or shorter.

11. Some brass instruments, like the trumpet and the tuba, have valves that are used to control the length of the air column.

12. The slide trombone has a slide that moves in and out to control the length of the air column. The valve trombone has valves; it works like a trumpet but sounds like a trombone.

13. Because it has no valves or slide to move in and out, there is no way to change the length of the air column in the bugle, so the different notes are produced by changing both the tightness of the lips and the force of the air blown into the instrument.

14. Many wind instruments, especially brass instruments with valves or a slide, also depend on the tightness of the lips and the force of the breath to produce notes of different pitch.

15. Sounds from wind instruments differ in quality. An air column not only vibrates as a whole, but also vibrates in parts at the same time, producing overtones. The quality of the

DEMONSTRATION 19.2
Sounds Produced By Musical Instruments

Obtain, or have students bring to class, a variety of instruments, making sure you have adequate representation of stringed, wind, and percussion instruments. For each instrument show how sounds are produced, made higher or lower, and made louder or softer. Have the students produce sounds of the same pitch and intensity from various instruments and note the difference in the quality of the sounds. Discuss the formation of overtones in each instrument and their relationship to the quality of the musical sounds produced.

sound depends on the number and strength of overtones produced. The quality also depends on the size, shape, and material of the instrument, because these factors help to determine how many overtones will be produced.

16. Blowing harder into a wind instrument will make the air column inside the instrument vibrate more strongly and produce a louder sound. At the same time, the air column vibrates in parts. These new vibrations join and reinforce the original vibrations produced by the air column vibrating as a whole. This combination of vibrations makes the air column vibrate more strongly and produces a louder sound. In most wind instruments, blowing harder can make the sound not only louder but higher as well.

D. **Percussion instruments** are either made of solid materials, such as wood and metal, or made of materials stretched over a hollow container.
1. The solid or stretched materials are struck by mallets, hammers, or the hands, which make the materials vibrate and produce sounds.
2. Percussion instruments made of solid materials include the xylophone, glockenspiel, triangle, cymbals, chimes, bells, castanets, and wood block.
3. Percussion instruments made of material stretched over a hollow container include the bongo drum, snare drum, bass drum, kettle drum, and tambourine.

4. In percussion instruments made of solid materials, the longer the material, the lower the pitch; the shorter the material, the higher the pitch.
5. In percussion instruments made of a material stretched over a hollow container, the pitch can be changed in different ways.
   a. The tighter the covering, the higher the pitch; the looser the covering, the lower the pitch.
   b. The thinner the covering, the higher the pitch; the thicker the covering, the lower the pitch.
   c. The smaller the diameter of the instrument, the higher the pitch; the larger the diameter, the lower the pitch.
6. Striking percussion instruments harder will make them vibrate more strongly and produce louder sounds. At the same time, the vibrating materials make the air around them vibrate at the same frequency. The large amount of vibrating air reinforces the original vibrations and makes them stronger, producing louder sounds.
7. The hollow containers of percussion instruments like the drum, the marimba, and the chimes also help produce louder sounds. The column of air inside the container vibrates at the same frequency as the original sound, reinforcing the original vibrations and making them much stronger, thus producing a louder sound.

EXPLORATORY ACTIVITIES FOR "SOUND"

1. *EXPLORING THE PRODUCTION AND TRANSMISSION OF SOUND* (ANY GRADE LEVEL)
Review the following set of 11 activities and, depending on the age and maturity of your students, decide the best approach for involving them in the activities. One approach is to establish several learning stations, each with complete instructions for doing one of the activities, and have the students take turns visiting the stations in groups of three or four. Instructions given here for each activity may have to be rewritten, depending on how it is to be used.

1.1 Sound Is Produced by Vibrating Objects

Give students the following instructions: Hold one end of a rubber band in your teeth and stretch the band. Pluck the band, noting the vibration and the sound produced. What do you notice? (The vibration is so rapid that it produces a blur. Note that when the vibration stops, the sound stops.) Now set a tuning fork vibrating by striking one prong sharply against your kneecap or the rubber heel of your shoe. (Never strike a tuning fork against a hard object.) Hold one end of a sheet of paper and touch one prong lightly to the other end of the paper. What do you conclude? (The vibrating prong will make the paper rattle, showing that the prong is, indeed, vibrating.) Feel the vibrations by touching the vibrating prongs lightly with the fingertips. Now place tissue paper against the teeth of a comb and hum a tune. What do you feel? (Students will feel the vibrations as a ticklish sensation on their lips.)

1.2 How Sound Travels

Pour some water into a tub or basin. Dip your finger quickly into the water and then pull it out. Draw a diagram of what you observe. How do you think this relates to the way sound travels? (Waves are produced and spread out in concentric spheres. Point out that sound waves themselves are not like water waves, but their methods of travel are somewhat alike.)

1.3 Sound Travels in All Directions

Place students in four corners of the room, facing the wall. Have one student in the middle of the room produce a sound. Let the students raise their hands as soon as they hear the sound. Have the students write down their tentative conclusion about the direction in which sound travels. Now place one student at the top of the stairs, a second student half-way down, and a third student at the foot of the stairs. Have the student half-way down the stairs make a sound. Have students check their original conclusion and modify it if necessary. (The sound will travel up and down, as well as in all horizontal directions.) Now fill a large beaker or tumbler full of water. Strike the prongs of a tuning fork very sharply against your kneecap or the rubber heel of your shoe, and then quickly place the ends of the prongs in the center of the water (Figure 19.1). Write down what you observed. (The vibrating prongs will make the water splash out of the beaker in all directions.) Again, what do you conclude about the direction that sound travels?

1.4 Sound Travels by Means of Compression and Rarefaction of Molecules

Obtain a "Slinky" (a walking spring coil) from a toy store. Attach one end to a hook, high off the floor, and

FIGURE 19.1   The vibrating tuning fork scatters water in all directions.

allow the rest of the Slinky to stretch to the floor (Figure 19.2). Instruct students as follows: Press together two of the stretched coils close to the floor, and then release these coils suddenly. What do you observe? (An impulse, consisting of a series of compressions and rarefactions, will travel the length of the Slinky.) Compare this movement with the way sound travels by means of compressions and rarefactions of molecules. (Point out that each coil—and molecule—moves back and forth just a little, yet the result is an extensive movement and travel of the impulse.)

1.5 Sound Travels Through Solids

Position two students at opposite ends of a table. Have one student scratch the table top so lightly with a fingernail that the other student cannot hear the sound. Now have the second student place one ear against the

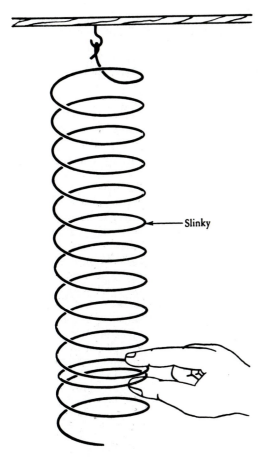

FIGURE 19.2   A "Slinky" shows how sound travels by compression and rarefaction of molecules.

Jingle bell

Water

FIGURE 19.3   The sound of the bell cannot be heard in a vacuum.

end of the table, and have the first student scratch the table top again. Ask, What do you observe? (The second student will hear the scratching sound very clearly, because sound travels faster through solids than through air.)

1.6 Sound Travels Through Liquids

Fill a large aquarium with water. Click two spoons together about 15 centimeters (6 in) from a student's ear. Have the student put his or her ear against one end of the aquarium. Click the spoons again, this time under water in the aquarium. Ask, What do you conclude about sound traveling through water? (The student will hear the sound.)

1.7 Sound Travels Through Gases

Send one student out of the room with one end of a garden hose, and have another student speak softly into

the other end. Ask, What do you observe? (The student outside will be able to hear the words very clearly. This activity also shows that sounds can be directed.) Students may want to make their own "phones," using a long piece of string with Styrofoam or paper cups or aluminum soft drink cans. The string can be connected through a hole in the bottom of each cup or can and tied off inside. Let students experiment with different kinds of containers and string to see which "phone systems" work best.

1.8 Sound Does Not Travel Through a Vacuum (Probably Best as a Teacher Demonstration)

Obtain a large Pyrex flask and a solid rubber stopper that fits the flask. Push a small hook into the underside of the stopper. From the hook, suspend a string that is attached to a small jingle bell so that the bell will hang freely inside the flask when the stopper is inserted (Figure 19.3). Place a small amount of water in the flask, set the flask on a hot plate, and boil the water until almost all the air inside the flask has been driven off and there is mostly steam inside the flask. Remove the flask, insert the stopper, and allow the flask to cool. The steam will condense, leaving a partial vacuum in the flask.

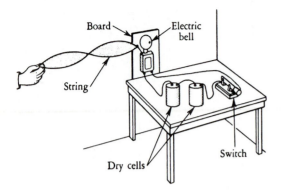

FIGURE 19.4   Forming loops to illustrate fundamental tone and overtones.

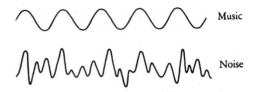

FIGURE 19.5   Diagram showing the difference between music and noise.

Set up a second (control) flask exactly like the first, but do not boil the water, so that this second flask is full of air. Now shake both flasks gently. Compare the loudness of the bell in the partial vacuum with that of the bell in air.

1.9 Investigate Pitch

Have a student draw the edge of an index card over a comb at different speeds. Ask, What do you observe? (The faster the index card moves against the teeth, the faster it vibrates and the higher the sound becomes.)

1.10 Sound Quality

Engage students in the following activity: Push a table against a wall. Attach an electric bell to a piece of wood and bend the clapper so that it will not strike the gong when it is moving back and forth. Connect the bell to two dry cells and a switch, as shown in Figure 19.4. Obtain 3 meters (10 ft) of thin, soft string and attach one end of the string to the clapper. Push down the switch to complete the electric circuit and set the clapper moving back and forth.

Stand some distance away and pull on the string as the clapper vibrates. By experimenting with the amount of pull on the string, you will be able to make the string vibrate as a whole to form just one loop, and then vibrate in parts to form two, three, or even four loops. Compare this formation of loops with the formation of the fundamental tone and overtones in vibrating objects to produce sounds of different quality.

1.11 Exploring the Voice

Have students feel their windpipes while humming or making low sounds. They will feel the vibrations of their vocal cords. Have them make loud and soft sounds, noting the greater force with which air is blown between the vocal cords to produce louder sounds. Let one student say something normally, and then repeat it while pinching his or her nostrils shut. Ask, What do you observe? (Students will note the change in quality of the sounds produced.)

Inflate a balloon and allow the air to escape while you pinch and stretch both sides of the neck of the balloon. The more you pinch and stretch the rubber, the higher the sound becomes. Ask, How does this compare with your own ability to make sounds? (This effect compares with the tightening of the vocal cords to produce higher sounds.)

2. EXPLORING MUSIC AND MUSICAL INSTRUMENTS (ANY GRADE LEVEL)

2.1 Comparing Music and Noise

Begin by having the students list unpleasant noises they have heard. Ask them why each was unpleasant. Relate noise with irregular vibrations and music with regular vibrations. Draw a diagram of both regular and irregular vibrations on the chalkboard (Figure 19.5).

2.2 Forced Vibrations Increase the Intensity of Sounds

Strike a tuning fork, hold it up, and have the students listen to the sound produced. Strike the tuning fork again, but this time touch the handle of the tuning fork to a table top or the chalkboard. The vibrating tuning fork will force the table top to vibrate with the same frequency, and the vibrating table top will now force the air around it to vibrate with the same frequency too. This large amount of vibrating air reinforces the original vibrations of the tuning fork, making them stronger so that the sound becomes louder. Show how this same effect is produced with musical instruments.

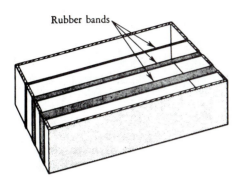

Rubber bands

FIGURE 19.6   A stringed instrument made from a cigar box.

FIGURE 19.7   Producing air columns of different sizes in soda bottles.

Now review the following four activities and, depending on the age and maturity of your students, decide the best approach for involving them in these activities. One approach is to divide the class into groups and have each group do one of the activities as a project and then show and report their finished work to the rest of the class. Instructions for each activity will have to be rewritten, depending on how it is used.

2.3   How the Pitch is Changed in Stringed Instruments

Obtain a cigar box, remove the cover, and cut three grooves on opposite edges of the box. Stretch three rubber bands of equal length, but different thicknesses, lengthwise around the box, placing them in the grooves to keep them in place (Figure 19.6). Give students the following instructions: Pluck each band and note that the thinner the band, the higher the sound will be.

Pluck one band and note the sound produced. Hold the middle of the band with your fingers and pluck either portion of the band that extends from your fingers to one edge of the box. Note that only half of the rubber band now vibrates and the sound is higher. In fact, the sound is now an octave higher than the original sound. Hold the band at different positions. The shorter the length of the vibrating band, the higher the sound will be.

Pluck one rubber band and listen to the note produced. Now pull the band at one end, making it tighter. Note that the tighter the band becomes, the higher the sound will be.

2.4   Changing the Pitch in Wind Instruments

Give the following instructions: Blow across an empty soda bottle. The sound is produced by the column of vibrating air inside the bottle. Repeat the activity, using bottles of different sizes. The smaller the bottle, the shorter the air column will be and the higher the sound will become.

Obtain eight soda bottles of the same size and line them up in a row. Pour different amounts of water in them, adding or taking away water as needed, until you can produce the eight notes of the scale when you blow across their mouths (Figure 19.7). Note the relationship between the length of the air column in each bottle and the pitch of the sound produced. Prepare a tune to play for the class.

2.5   Changing the Pitch of Percussion Instruments

Give students the following instructions: Use a toy xylophone to show that the shorter the bar, the higher the sound. Cut a piece of rubber from a large balloon or an old inner tube and place it over the mouth of a glass jar. Grasp the rubber with both hands and pull it downward while a student strikes the rubber repeatedly with the eraser end of a pencil (Figure 19.8). Note that the tighter the rubber drum head becomes as it is pulled farther downward, the higher sound will become. Repeat this activity with jars of the same size, but having mouths of different widths. The narrower the mouth of the jar, the higher the sound that is produced. Using rubber pieces of different thicknesses over the mouth of the jar will show that the thinner the rubber, the higher the sound that is produced.

2.6   Make a Musical Instrument

Give students the following instructions: Crease the ends of two straws so they are flattened. Snip off the corners at the tops of the flattened ends to form points, as shown in Figure 19.9. Cut off the bottom of one straw so that the straw is 5 cm long. Predict which straw will have the higher pitch. Blow into the straws as a clarinet player would blow through a reed mouthpiece. Explain why the two straw sounds differ in pitch.

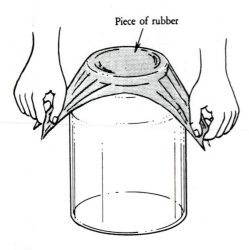

FIGURE 19.8   The tighter the drum head, the higher the sound will become.

FIGURE 19.9   Making a straw instrument.

STUDENT BOOKS AND OTHER RESOURCES FOR "SOUND"

Ardley, N. *The Science Book of Sound.* New York: Harcourt Brace Jovanovich, 1991.

Jennings, T. *Making Sounds.* New York: Franklin Watts, 1990.

Huetinck, L. "Physics to Beat the Band." *Science and Children* 32(3):27–30 (November/December 1994).

Kaner, E. *Sound Science.* Arlington, VA: National Science Teachers Association, 1991.

Skurzynski, G. *Get the Message: Telecommunications in Your High-Tech World.* New York: Bradbury, 1993.

Thompson, S. "Super Ears." *Science and Children* 32(8):19–21, 50 (May 1995).

CHAPTER 20

Light

THE NATURE OF LIGHT

I. VISIBLE LIGHT IS ONE OF THREE TYPES OF RADIATION
   A. There are three general types of radiation: mechanical radiation, electromagnetic radiation, and particle radiation.
      1. Electromagnetic radiation (ER) is also referred to as light or radiant energy.
      2. Unlike mechanical energy (sound), radiant energy can travel through a vacuum as easily as it can through air. It can also pass through some solid materials.
   B. Visible light is actually one of a group of radiant energy waves, called electromagnetic radiation.
      1. Electromagnetic radiation can be classified according to the amount of energy being moved. Starting with lowest energy (longest wavelength) and moving up to highest energy (shortest wavelength), the **electromagnetic spectrum** includes radio waves, microwaves, infrared rays, visible light, ultraviolet rays, X-rays, and gamma rays. At one end of this spectrum are those waves with long wavelengths and low frequencies, and at the other end are those waves with short wavelengths and high frequencies (see Figure 20.1).
      2. All of these electromagnetic waves are invisible to the human eye except light rays. Humans recognize the other waves by the effects they cause.

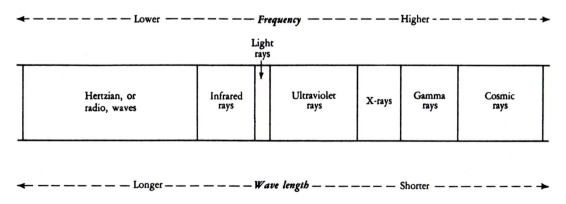

FIGURE 20.1   Diagram of the electromagnetic spectrum.

3. All electromagnetic waves, including light rays, travel in a vacuum at a speed of 299,743 kilometers (186,282 mi) per second.

II. ELECTROMAGNETIC WAVES TRAVEL AT THE SAME SPEED, BUT DIFFER IN WAVELENGTH AND IN FREQUENCY

A. **Wavelength** is the distance between corresponding parts of two waves with the same motion.

B. **Frequency** is the number of waves that pass by a point in one second.

1. Electromagnetic waves with long wavelengths, such as radio waves, have a low frequency. Electromagnetic waves with short wavelengths, such as X-rays, have a high frequency. The shorter the wavelength of the electromagnetic wave, the greater its energy and the higher its frequency.

2. A **cycle** is one complete up-and-down movement of a wave. The frequency of a wave, then, is also the number of cycles that happen in one second. In a 60-cycle wave, for example, the wave moves up and down 60 times in one second. That means that in one second, 60 complete waves pass by a given point.

3. Because electromagnetic waves have very high frequencies, their frequencies are usually given in kilocycles (thousands of cycles) or megacycles (millions of cycles). One hertz is one cycle, therefore other terms used to express frequency are hertz, kilohertz, and megahertz.

III. WAVES WITH LONG WAVELENGTHS AND LOW FREQUENCIES

A. Waves with long wavelengths and low frequencies include infrared rays and radio waves.

1. **Infrared rays** are a band of invisible waves that we perceive as heat. Much of the sun's energy comes to us as infrared rays.

2. *Infra* means "below," and infrared rays are the first band of rays below visible red light rays.

3. Infrared rays are used in taking pictures in the dark because all objects radiate heat, in obtaining special photographic effects, in detecting fingerprints or changes in documents and paintings, and in medicine.

4. **Radio waves** make up a very wide band of invisible rays that are used in various kinds of communication.

5. This band of rays is found below the infrared rays. The band is so wide that it is further divided into smaller bands or channels. Separate channels are used for AM radio, FM radio, television, police calls, military communications, radar, amateur broadcasting, aviation, and distress signals. The waves in each band or channel are often identified by their frequencies (kilocycles and megacycles) instead of their wavelengths.

IV. WAVES WITH SHORT WAVELENGTHS AND HIGH FREQUENCIES

A. Waves with short wavelengths and high frequencies include ultraviolet rays, X-rays, and gamma rays.

1. *Ultra* means "beyond," and **ultraviolet rays** are the first band of rays beyond visible blue light rays.

2. Ultraviolet rays come from the sun and cause people to tan and burn.

3. Ultraviolet rays can be produced when an electric current flows through mercury vapor. When the invisible ultraviolet rays strike certain chemicals, called phosphors, the chemicals glow and give off visible light. This effect is used in fluorescent lamps and in identifying marks made on clothing by a laundry. Ultraviolet radiation is also used for scientific research, in special lamps to kill germs, in advertising, and in safety-warning devices.

4. **X-rays** constitute a band of waves found beyond the ultraviolet rays. They have a shorter wavelength and higher frequency than ultraviolet rays.

5. X-rays can pass through nonmetals and through thin sheets of most metals. The rays are stopped by thicker sheets of metals and by certain metallic salts, such as barium sulfate.

6. X-rays are used to take pictures of the bones and organs in the body, detect cracks in metals, and inspect fruits to see whether they have been damaged by frost.

7. **Gamma rays** are tiny electromagnetic waves found beyond the band of X-rays. Radioactive materials give off gamma rays. Gamma radiation is very high energy radiation (see Chapter 16).

VISIBLE LIGHT

I. MAGNETIC CHARACTERISTIC

A. Although scientists know much about light and the other electromagnetic waves, they do not fully understand the exact nature of electromagnetic waves.
   1. Scientists know that although light travels in waves, it has certain behaviors that are better explained by assuming that light acts like a particle.
   2. When light is emitted or absorbed by atoms, it behaves as though it were composed of particles, or packets of energy called **photons.** When light travels, however, it acts like an electromagnetic wave.
   3. When light passes through a strong magnetic field, the lines that make up the light spectrum are split into two or more lines. This influence of magnetism on light is named the **Zeeman effect.**

II. LIGHT TRAVELS IN STRAIGHT LINES

A. Even when light is made to change direction, it continues to travel in straight lines.
   1. A thin line of light is called a **ray.**
   2. A **beam** of light is made up of many rays.
B. Light travels at a speed of 299,743 kilometers (186,282 mi) per second, or more than 1,060 million kilometers (660 million mi) per hour. It takes about 8 minutes for light to travel from the sun to the earth. Light traveling faster than sound waves explains why we sometimes see things before they are heard, as, for example, when a batter hits a home-run ball.
C. Because the stars and planets are so far away from the earth, astronomers use the speed of light as a unit for measuring these great distances.
   1. Until recently astronomers used only the light-year as a unit for measuring long distances. A **light-year** is the distance light will travel in one year, about 9 trillion kilometers (6 trillion mi).
   2. Proxima Centauri, the star nearest the earth (not counting the sun) is more than four light-years (42 trillion kilometers or 26 trillion miles) away.
   3. Scientists now also use the **parsec** as a unit for measuring long distances: one parsec is about three light-years, or 30 trillion kilometers (19 trillion mi).

III. TRANSPARENT, TRANSLUCENT, AND OPAQUE MATERIALS

A. Light can pass through some materials but is stopped by other materials.
   1. Materials like air, plastic wrap, water, and clear glass are called **transparent.** When light strikes transparent materials, almost all of the light passes directly through them. We can see clearly through transparent materials.
   2. Materials such as frosted glass and some plastics are called **translucent.** When light strikes translucent materials, only some of the light passes through them, while most is scattered. Because light is scattered as it passes through translucent materials, we cannot see clearly through them. Objects on the other side of a mildly translucent material are unclear. Through strongly translucent materials, we can see only light and shadow.
   3. Most materials are **opaque.** When light strikes an opaque material, none of the light passes through the material. We cannot see through opaque materials. All of the light is either reflected by the opaque material or absorbed and converted into heat.
   4. Even with transparent and translucent materials, some of the light is absorbed and converted into heat.
B. Because light travels in straight lines, shadows are formed when an opaque material is placed in the path of rays of light.

IV. SOURCES OF LIGHT

A. Materials that emit light are called **luminous** materials.
B. The sun is a natural source of light, and is our chief source of light.
   1. Light energy from the sun is produced by changes taking place in the nuclei of atoms of the materials that make up the sun.
C. Stars are also a natural source of light.
D. The moon and the planets do not produce their own light, but shine because sunlight strikes them and is reflected from their surfaces.
E. Some organisms, like the firefly, can produce their own light through a biochemical process known as **bioluminescence.**

DEMONSTRATION 20.1
Light Travels in Straight Lines

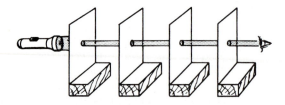

FIGURE 20.2   Light travels in a straight line through the holes in the index cards.

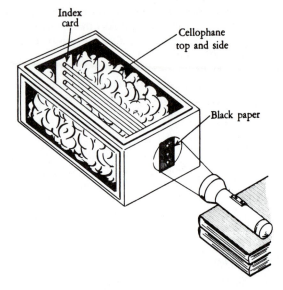

FIGURE 20.3   A light-ray box.

Obtain four index cards and find their center by drawing diagonals on each card. Make a good-sized hole at this center, and then attach each card with thumb tacks to a small block of wood (Figure 20.2). Place the index cards one in front of the other, some distance apart, making sure that the holes are in a straight line with each other. Rest a flashlight on some books set 1 meter (3 ft) from the first card, making sure that the height is just right for the flashlight to shine directly through the holes.

Turn on the flashlight and darken the room. Have a student look through the holes and see the light of the flashlight. Infer that the light can be seen only because it is passing through each hole in a straight line. (If you clap two chalkboard erasers repeatedly along the path of the light, the student can see a beam of light in a straight line.) Now move one card so that it is out of line. The student cannot see the light because it travels in a straight line but is stopped by the card.

Obtain a large rectangular cardboard carton and remove the flaps to create an open side. Put the carton down so that the open side is at the back. Remove most of the top and front side of the carton and replace these pieces with plastic wrap, pressing the plastic wrap firmly to the carton (Figure 20.3). Paint the inside cardboard of the carton with flat black paint.

Obtain two pieces of black cloth, each slightly larger than half the length of the carton, and tack them to the open back in such a way that they overlap at the middle. You can now put your hand inside the carton without permitting any light to enter. Halfway down one end of the carton, cut a window 7 centimeters (3 in) long and 5 centimeters (2 in) wide. Obtain a piece of black construction paper slightly larger than the window, punch out three holes, one beneath the other, and then tape the paper over the window. Tape a small white index card on the inside of the other end of the carton, directly opposite the black paper. The card will act as a screen.

Fill the carton with smoke by burning a rope, damp paper, or incense in an ash tray. Obtain a three-cell focusing flashlight and rest it on some books set 1 meter (3 ft) away from the carton, making sure the height is such that light from the flashlight will shine directly through the holes. Turn on the flashlight, then darken the room. Three rays of light will be visible inside the carton. The rays are parallel, showing that light travels in straight lines.

F. Common artificial sources of light include the candle, kerosene lamp, gasoline lamp, electric light, fluorescent light, neon light, sulfur lamp, and laser light.

G. The **sulfur lamp** uses microwave energy on sulfur gas to create a bright, cool, energy-efficient source of light. A bulb is filled with a small amount of sulfur in an inert gas compound. The sulfur is agitated when bombarded by microwaves. The light given off is nearly the same as sunlight, except there is little heat and very little ultraviolet emission. The bulb has no metal wire parts but does contain a small microwave generator.

H. **Laser light** does not spread out as do other forms of light energy, but travels in a narrow beam that spreads very little and is made of only one wavelength or color. Laser light is produced by a laser, which means "light amplification by stimulated emission of radiation." Laser light can be concentrated into beams powerful enough to drill holes in a diamond, can be used as a cutting tool for surgical operations, and can be used to accurately measure lines and movements.

V. MEASUREMENT OF LIGHT

A. The intensity of a light source is measured in **candles** (or candelas in the international system).
    1. Long ago a "candle" was defined as the amount of light given off by a standard candle of precise construction. We spoke of candle power.
    2. Today a candle is defined as one sixtieth of the light intensity of one square centimeter of a perfectly black object at the freezing point of platinum.
B. In determining the amount of light illuminated from a surface, given that the distance from the light source to the illuminated surface is measured in feet, the intensity of that illumination is measured in **footcandles.** At a distance of one foot the illumination provided by a light source of 100 candles is 100 footcandles.
    1. The amount of light that is illuminated from a surface depends on several factors, including the intensity of the light source, the angle at which the light hits the surface from the source, and the distance of the surface from the source.
    2. The greater the distance from the light source, the weaker the illumination from the lighted surface. The distance versus illumination follows an inverse-square law. For example, if the distance from the source is doubled, the amount of light falling on a given area is reduced to one fourth, the inverse of 2 squared. If the distance is tripled, the surface receives only one ninth of the original illumination, and so on.
C. Another unit of light power, called the **luminous flux** of a light source, is also used today. Luminous flux is measured in **lumens.** An ideal one-candle source gives off 4 lumens. One footcandle is equal to one lumen per square foot. A **photometer** (or light meter) is used to measure the amount of light given off by a source.

THE REFLECTION OF LIGHT

I. LIGHT CAN BE REFLECTED

A. To enable us to see an object that does not produce its own light, three things must happen. There must be a source of light; the light must strike the object; and the light must be reflected from the object and then travel to the eye.
B. When light is reflected, it changes direction, but it still travels in straight lines.
C. Transparent and translucent materials allow most of the light striking them to pass through, but some light is absorbed and some light is reflected.
D. Opaque materials do not allow any light to pass through, but absorb and reflect the light instead.
    1. Such materials differ greatly in how much light they absorb and reflect.
    2. Dark-colored, rough opaque materials absorb more light than they reflect.
    3. Light-colored, smooth opaque objects reflect more light than they absorb.

II. LAW OF REFLECTION

A. When a ray of light strikes a mirror perpendicular to the surface of the mirror, the ray is re-

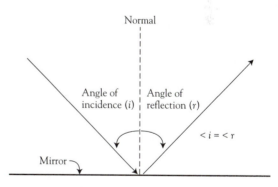

FIGURE 20.4   Angle of incidence is equal to the angle of reflection.

flected directly back. A perpendicular line has an angle of 90 degrees to the surface and is called the normal (see Figure 20.4).
B. When a ray of light strikes a mirror at a slant, or angle, the ray is reflected at a slant, or angle, in another direction.
    1. The ray that strikes the mirror is called the **incident,** or striking, ray.
    2. The ray that is reflected by the mirror is called the **reflected** ray.

DEMONSTRATION 20.2
The Law of Reflection

Place a mirror at the center of a table. Darken the room, and then turn on a focusing flashlight and aim it at an angle at the mirror. The light will be reflected and appear on the wall. Have a student clap two chalkboard erasers over the mirror and on each side of the mirror (Figure 20.5). Two rays of light, an incident ray and a reflected ray, will appear. Change the angle at which the ray strikes the mirror and note how the angle of the reflected ray changes accordingly. Point out that the angle of incidence and angle of reflection are always equal.

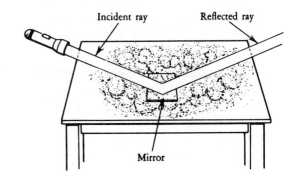

FIGURE 20.5   Illustrating the law of reflection.

3. The angle between the ray of light that strikes the surface and the normal is called the **angle of incidence.**
4. The angle between the reflected ray and the normal is called the **angle of reflection.**
5. The law, or principle, of reflection states that the angle of incidence is equal to the angle of reflection (see Figure 20.4).
C. The law of reflection holds true for all smooth, polished surfaces.
   1. When a beam of light strikes a mirror, each ray in the beam is reflected regularly.
   2. Each ray has the same angle of incidence and angle of reflection so that although the rays change direction, they all do so the same amount, and in this way continue to form a beam. This means that parallel rays of light will reflect off the mirror and remain parallel.
   3. When a beam of light strikes a rough surface, each ray is reflected irregularly but still obeys the law of reflection. The rays hit the surface irregularities, which are oriented at different angles to each other, so the rays reflect at different angles.
   4. When light strikes a sheet of very smooth paper, the light is reflected regularly to the eye, producing a glare. When light strikes a sheet of coarse paper, the uneven surface reflects the light irregularly and scatters it, so that very little glare is produced.

III. MIRRORS
   A. Some mirrors are flat or plane, and others are curved.
   B. A **plane mirror** is usually made of a flat piece of clear glass, and the back of the glass has a thin coating of silver or another shiny metal.
      1. The light striking the mirror passes through the transparent glass; then almost all the light is reflected back by the shiny, but opaque, silver.
      2. Unbreakable mirrors can be made from highly polished steel, but steel mirrors do not reflect light as well as glass mirrors.
      3. Objects that you see in a mirror seem to be behind the mirror, but they are not. What you really see is the reflection of objects in front of the mirror. This reflection is called an **image.**
      4. When you look into a mirror, you see a reversed image of yourself. The image in a mirror seems to face you so that everything is reversed.
      5. The image in a mirror is just as large as the object in front of it.
      6. The image in a mirror also appears to be just as far behind the mirror as the object is in front of it.
   C. Curved mirrors are curved either inward or outward. Mirrors that are curved give different kinds of images than plane or flat mirrors.
   D. Mirrors that curve inward are called **concave mirrors.** A concave mirror causes rays of light

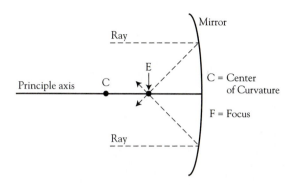

FIGURE 20.6   The point of focus of a concave mirror.

to converge at a point called the **focus** (see Figure 20.6).

1. Concave mirrors are used in some telescopes to gather the light from a distant star and concentrate the light so that the star may be examined. The important job of any telescope is to gather as much light as possible, not to magnify the image.

2. Flashlights, automobile headlights, and spotlights also use concave mirrors, made of shiny metal. However, in these instruments the mirrors work the opposite from the mirrors used in telescopes. The light source, the light bulb, is placed at the focus of the mirror. The rays of light coming from the bulb are reflected by the mirror to throw a beam, instead of being scattered in all directions.

E. Mirrors that curve outward are called **convex mirrors.**

1. A convex mirror does not bring rays of light together at one spot, but spreads them out in all directions.

2. Although images from a convex mirror are erect and smaller, the convex mirror gives an image that covers a larger area. Some rear-view side-installed auto mirrors are convex mirrors. These are often marked with a caution to the driver that the image seen in the mirror may actually be closer than it appears.

THE REFRACTION OF LIGHT

I. THE NATURE OF REFRACTION

A. When light rays strike a transparent material at an angle of 90 degrees, they travel in a straight line and gradually slow down.

B. When light rays pass at a slant, or angle, from one transparent material (such as air) into another transparent material (such as water), they are bent, or **refracted,** so that they travel in a different direction.

1. Although the rays are now traveling in a different direction, they still travel in a straight line.

2. The light rays must pass at a slant, or angle, from one transparent material into another; otherwise, they will not be bent.

3. If light rays pass from one material into another in a perpendicular line (at an angle of 90 degrees), they pass straight through without being bent and there is no refraction.

C. Light is bent because there is a change in the speed of the light as it passes from one transparent material into another.

1. Light passes at different speeds through different kinds of transparent materials.

2. The difference in speed depends on the **optical density** of the material.

3. The greater the optical density of a material, the more slowly light passes through it.

D. When light rays pass into an optically denser material at an angle, they are slowed down and bent toward the normal, but when light rays pass into a less optically dense material at an angle, they speed up and bend outward.

1. The amount of refraction depends on the optical density of the material.

2. The greater the optical density of the material, the more the light rays will be bent inward (the greater the angle of refraction).

II. LENSES

A. A lens is a piece of glass, or other transparent material, that is either curved on one side and flat on the other, or is curved on both sides.

1. Lenses are used to bend, or refract, light rays. Because the surface of the lens is curved, light rays strike the lens at a slant.

2. The curvature of the lens makes the rays of light bend as they pass through it.

DEMONSTRATION 20.3

Light Can Be Refracted

Fill a rectangular aquarium three-quarters full of water and add drops of milk until the water has a cloudy appearance. Darken the room, and then turn on a focusing flashlight and aim it at an angle at the aquarium (Figure 20.7). At the same time, have a student clap two chalkboard erasers over the aquarium to outline the path of the beam of light coming from the flashlight. The beam of light will be bent inward as it passes from the air into the water. Now hold the flashlight so that the beam of light enters the water vertically (at an angle of 90 degrees). The beam will pass from the air into the water without being refracted.

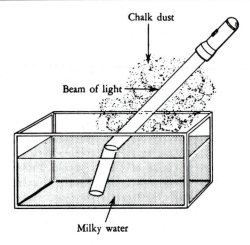

FIGURE 20.7   The light is refracted when it enters the water.

3. When light rays pass through a lens, they are always bent toward the thickest part of the lens.

B. Either on one side or both, lenses are either curved inward (concave) or outward (convex).

C. A **convex lens** is thicker in the middle than it is at its edges.
   1. When passing through a convex lens, light rays are bent toward the thicker middle of the lens. Thus, after passing through the lens, the rays come together and meet at a point.
   2. The point at which the rays meet is called the **focal point.** We say that the convex lens brings the rays into focus at this point.
   3. The thicker the middle of the lens as compared with its edges, the more the rays of light are bent and the shorter the focal length.
   4. By bending the rays of light and bringing them together, the convex lens can produce a real image.
   5. When a convex lens is placed between an object and a screen, an inverted, or upside down, image can be formed on the screen. This is called a **real image.**
   6. When a convex lens is placed between your eyes and an object, the object appears larger. It is magnified. In this case, an image that is larger than the object is formed, and

it is erect, or right side up. This is called a **virtual image.**
   7. The lens of the human eye is a convex lens (see Chapter 15).

D. A **concave lens** is thinner in the middle than at its edges.
   1. Light rays passing through a concave lens are bent toward the thicker edges. After passing through the lens, the rays are spread apart.
   2. The rays seem to be coming from an imaginary point behind the lens.
   3. The thicker the edges of the lens, the wider apart the rays are spread.
   4. A concave lens produces only one kind of image—a virtual image. It is smaller than the object and is not inverted.

E. Lenses are used in many kinds of instruments, such as cameras, microscopes, telescopes, binoculars, eye glasses, and projectors. In most instances, the instruments use complex systems of lenses, that is, more than one lens.
   1. The basic parts of a **camera** are a lightproof box, an opening in front of the camera, a shutter over the opening, a convex lens behind the opening, a film at the back of the camera, and a device to hold and turn the film.
   2. The shutter allows light to enter the camera and strike the lens, which bends the light rays

so that they come together; that is, they are brought into focus on the film.

3. The film is coated with chemicals that are affected by light. When light rays focus on the film, a chemical change occurs. The film is then treated with chemicals and becomes a "negative," where the dark parts of the object appear light and the light parts appear dark. When light is then passed through the negative to light-sensitive paper, a "positive" is produced, whereby the dark parts of the negative now become light and the light parts become dark, just as they were in the original object.

4. In inexpensive cameras the lens is fixed so that it can bring into sharp focus only light rays coming from objects that are more than 2 meters (6 ft) away from the camera. In more expensive cameras the lens can be moved back and forth so that it can bring into sharp focus light rays coming from both near and far objects.

5. A light **microscope** has two convex lenses, one at each end of a lightproof tube. The upper lens is called the eyepiece, and the lower lens the objective. Rays of light from an object pass through the lens of the objective and are bent, producing an enlarged image of the object inside the tube. The lens of the eyepiece acts like a magnifying glass and magnifies this image even more, making it much larger than the object. To focus the microscope, one part of the tube is made to slide up or down inside another part.

6. Based on the lens types and placements, their are two basic types of light telescopes. The **reflecting telescope** has a large concave mirror at one end, and at the other end there is a small convex lens that magnifies the image produced by the mirror. The **refracting telescope** works similarly to the microscope, with an objective and an eyepiece. A very large convex lens in the objective collects all the light it can from a distant object and bends the light rays to produce an image, which is magnified by the smaller convex lens in the eyepiece. One part of the tube slides in and out of another part of the tube to bring objects located at different distances into focus.

7. **Binoculars** are two refracting telescopes connected side by side, one for each eye. Prisms in the binoculars reflect the light rays so that the image is not inverted.

8. **Projectors** use one or more convex lenses to project an enlarged image onto a screen. A strong beam of light passes through the object (in the case of opaque projectors it reflects from the surface of the object), and a convex lens bends the rays of light coming from the object to produce an enlarged image on the screen.

COLOR

I. THE SPECTRUM

A. When a narrow beam of sunlight passes at a slant into a triangular transparent material, called a **prism,** the sunlight is separated into a band of colored lights, called the **spectrum,** which can be seen on a white wall or screen (see Figure 20.8).

1. There are six colored lights in the spectrum: red, orange, yellow, green, blue, and violet. A long-used mnemonic for remembering this order is ROY G BIV. However, that mnemonic was created when seven colors of the visible spectrum were identified. Today, blue and indigo are considered one color.

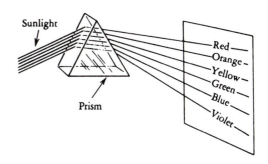

FIGURE 20.8   A prism produces a band of colored lights.

B. When a second prism (or a convex lens) is placed at just the right position in front of the rays of colored light coming from a prism, the rays of colored light combine to form white light again.

C. White light, then, is really a mixture of the six colors of the spectrum.

D. These colors are called **pure colored light,** because none of them can be divided further by another prism.

E. A prism breaks up white light into a spectrum because the colors that make up the spectrum all have different wavelengths.

1. Blue light has the shortest wavelength, red light the longest wavelength, and the wavelengths of the others are in between those of blue and red.

2. When white light enters a prism at a slant, the prism bends, or refracts, the different colors in different amounts.

3. The colors with the shortest waves are bent more than those with the longer waves.

4. Blue light has the shortest waves and is bent most, and red light has the longest wave and is bent least.

5. The other colors are bent in different amounts, so that all six colors that make up white light are separated as they pass through the prism and strike a screen at different places to form a band of colors.

II. PRIMARY AND COMPLEMENTARY COLORS

A. A colored light is only a part of white light.

1. To get a single colored light from white light, all colored lights other than the one you want must be taken away, or absorbed.

2. When white light is passed through a transparent colored material, such as red cellophane, all the colors in white light are absorbed except the red light that is allowed to pass through the cellophane.

3. The lights that have been absorbed are converted into heat.

B. Red, green, and blue are the **primary additive colors** of light. (As discussed later, these primary additive colors of light are different from the primary colors of paint pigments.) Every shade of colored light can be made by mixing or forming different combinations of these colored lights. Together, the three primary additive colors produce white light.

C. Any two colors that, when mixed together, produce white light are called **complementary colors.** The following pairs of colors are complementary colors.

Red and cyan (bluish green)
Yellow and blue
Green and magenta (purplish red)

III. COLORED MATERIALS

A. A material is of a certain color because, when white light strikes the material, some colors are absorbed and others are reflected to the eye. For example, a red dress looks red because the material absorbs all the colors of white light except red, which is reflected to the eye. Grass appears green because it absorbs all colors except green, which is reflected to the eye. The colors that have been absorbed are converted into heat.

B. A white material appears white because all the colors are reflected equally to the eye.

C. A black material appears black because all the colored lights are absorbed, so that no light is reflected to the eye.

D. The color of a material also depends on the color of light shining on it. When red light shines on a white material, the material appears red; the red light is the only color striking the white material, so red is the only color that can be reflected to the eye. When blue light shines on a red material, the material appears black because the material can reflect only red light, and there is no red in the blue light shining on the material.

E. Colors may seem different in artificial light because artificial light may have less blue and more red in it than does natural sunlight. This is the reason that when buying clothes, some people like to take an article outdoors and away from the store's artificial lighting. In some sources of artificial light blue may seem almost black because there is so little blue to be reflected. At the same time, red seems to be much brighter because some sources of artificial light have so much red, which is reflected.

F. Cyan, yellow, and magenta are called the **primary colors of paints,** or **subtractive colors** (not to be confused with the primary colors of light discussed earlier). Every other color can be produced by mixing different combinations of these pigments, such as:

Magenta and yellow paints make orange.
Magenta and cyan paints make purple.
Yellow and cyan paints make green.
Black and white paints make gray.

G. Mixing colored paints produces effects entirely different from those produced by mixing colors of light. Mixing paints is a called a subtractive process, whereas mixing colors of light is an additive process.

IV. THE COLORS OF THE SKY AND THE SUN
   A. During the day the sky appears blue and the sun yellowish white. These effects are caused by the presence of dust in the atmosphere.
      1. The sky appears blue because blue light is scattered by the dust and reflected to the eye much more than are the other colors.
      2. The yellow and red colors of sunlight are not scattered, but rather pass straight through, so that the loss of some of the blue color of sunlight makes the sun appear yellowish white.
   B. At sunrise and sunset, sunlight must travel at a greater slant, or angle, and thus it passes through more of earth's atmosphere containing particles of dust.
      1. The blue color of sunlight is now scattered much more by the dust in the atmosphere, so that there is even less blue passing straight through.
      2. The loss of more of the blue color of sunlight now causes the sun to appear reddish or orange.
      3. In addition, moisture in clouds absorbs green and blue from the sunlight, and this causes a still greater appearance of reds, oranges, and yellows at sunrise and sunset.
      4. These same principles hold for the moon when it is just rising or setting and can appear quite reddish-orange.

EXPLORATORY ACTIVITIES FOR "LIGHT"

1. *EXPLORING WITH MIRRORS* (ANY GRADE LEVEL)

Review the following four activities and, depending on the age and maturity of your students, determine the best approach for involving the students in these activities. One approach is to divide the class into groups and have each group do one of the activities as a project, then show and report their results to the rest of the class. Instructions for each activity will have to be rewritten, depending on how it is used.

1.1 Light Can Be Reflected Again and Again by Mirrors

First, have a student sit or crouch next to a wall with a window. Give the student two mirrors and have the student hold them in the position shown in Figure 20.9. By tilting the mirrors at the proper angles, the student will be able to see objects outside the window. Draw a diagram on the chalkboard to show how the light from the window strikes the top mirror, is reflected to the lower mirror, and then reflected again to the student's eye. Point out that this is how a periscope works.

1.2 Pane Glass as a Mirror

Obtain a pane of glass and tape a piece of white paper over one side. Turn on a table lamp and darken the room. Give these instructions: Stand with your back to the lamp and hold up the glass and look at it, keeping the white paper behind the glass. Record what you see. (You will see a very faint reflection because most of the light passing through the glass and striking the white paper is reflected irregularly and scattered.) Now re-

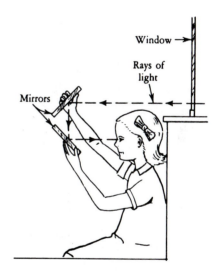

FIGURE 20.9   A periscope works by reflecting light more than once.

place the white paper with a piece of black paper. What do you see now? (You will see a very clear reflection because the black paper absorbs the light striking it, allowing a small amount of light to be reflected regularly from the surface of the glass.)

1.3 Reflection from a Concave Mirror

Have the students look into a magnifying mirror. Point out that the mirror is a concave mirror that curves inward just a little. This is the reason that the image is right side up and magnified.

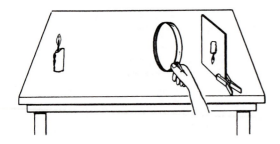

FIGURE 20.10   A convex lens held far from an object will produce an inverted, smaller image.

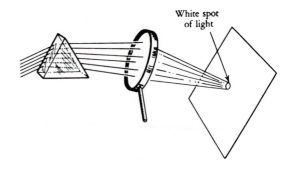

FIGURE 20.11   A convex lens recombines a spectrum to form white light again.

Obtain a large, highly polished silver tablespoon. Ask a student to look at the concave (hollow) side of the bowl, then record and explain what he or she observes. (This concave mirror curves inward a lot, and thus the image is upside down and smaller.)

1.4. Reflection from a Convex Mirror

Obtain a large, polished silver tablespoon. Give these instructions: Hold the spoon vertically and look at the convex (bulging) side of the bowl. Record and explain your observations. (You will see a long, thin image of yourself that is smaller and right side up.) Now hold the spoon horizontally and look again. What do you observe now? (The image becomes short and fat, but still is small and right side up.)

2. *EXPLORING WITH LENSES AND PRISMS* (ANY GRADE LEVEL)

Review the following five activities and, depending on the age and maturity of your students, decide the best approach for involving the students in these activities. One approach is to divide the class into groups and have each group do one of the activities as a project, then show and report their finished work to the rest of the class. Instructions for each activity will have to be rewritten, depending on how it is used.

2.1 Images Formed by a Convex Lens

Give students the following instructions: Use a spring-type clothes pin to hold a large piece of white cardboard vertically on a table. Place a lit candle about 1 meter (3 ft) away from the cardboard. Hold a magnifying glass near the cardboard and move the magnifying glass slowly toward the flame until a clear, inverted, smaller image of the candle appears on the cardboard (Figure 20.10).

Now hold the magnifying glass close to the candle and move it slowly toward the cardboard until a clear, inverted, larger image of the candle appears on the cardboard. You may have to push the cardboard far-

ther back to obtain this image. Point out that when the object is close to the lens, a large image appears. When the object is far from the lens, a small image appears. Both images are upside down.

Now use the glass as a magnifying instrument by placing the glass between your eyes and an object. Record and explain your observations. (The image produced is larger and right side up.)

2.2 Make a Spectrum

On a sunny day, when the sun's rays are coming through the window into the classroom, hold a prism (or a wedge of lucite or any other clear plastic) in the path of the sunlight. Roll the prism around until you are able to throw a rainbow on the wall (see Figure 20.8). Have a student tape a piece of white cardboard to the wall so that the spectrum will show up more clearly. Ask the students to locate and identify the different colors of the spectrum.

2.3 Colored Lights of a Spectrum Can Be Recombined

Repeat activity 2.2, but now place a magnifying glass between the prism and the cardboard (Figure 20.11). Move the magnifying glass back and forth until you make the spectrum disappear and there is only a spot of white light on the cardboard. Ask students, How can you explain this observation? (The convex lens of the magnifying glass caused the colored lights of the spectrum to converge and combine, forming white light again.)

2.4 Make a Soap Bubble Rainbow

Give students the following instructions: Punch a hole near the base of a Styrofoam cup and insert a soda straw slightly larger than the hole. Make a bubble solution by mixing thoroughly 2 cups of water, 1 to 2 tablespoons of liquid soap, and 1 cup of glycerin. Pour the solution into a soup bowl; put the mouth of the cup in the solution and shake. Lift the cup gently, upside down, and, blowing through the straw, blow a bubble. What do you see? How can this phenomenon be explained? (The thin soap film breaks up light rays to form rainbows.)

2.5 Produce Colored Lights

Turn on a focusing flashlight and darken the room. Have a student clap two chalkboard erasers together in front of the flashlight. Have students record their observations. Then ask them to note the beam of white light coming from the flashlight. Now wrap a piece of red cellophane smoothly around the glass of the flashlight. Ask, What do you observe and how can it be explained? (The beam of light is colored red because the cellophane absorbs all the colors of the spectrum except the red light, which is allowed to pass through.) Produce other beams of colored light by using pieces of cellophane of different colors.

3. *EXPLORING WITH COLORS* (ANY GRADE LEVEL)

Review the following two activities and, depending on the age and maturity of your students, decide the best approach for involving the students in these activities. One approach is to divide the class into groups and have each group do one of the activities as a project, then show and report their finished work to the rest of the class. Instructions for each activity will have to be rewritten, depending on how it is used.

3.1 Combine Primary and Complementary Colors

Give students the following instructions: Draw a circle about 10 centimeters (4 in) in diameter on a piece of white cardboard, then cut out the circle. Mark three equal sections on the cardboard and color them red, green, and blue with wax crayons. Make two small holes near the center of the circle and pass a loop of string through them (Figure 20.12). Now make the circle spin

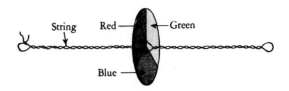

FIGURE 20.12   Combining primary colored lights produces white light.

rapidly by twisting the string, stretching it, and then allowing it to rewind. Continue stretching and rewinding to keep the card spinning constantly. What do you observe, and how can it be explained? (When the card is spinning, the primary colors will blend together to form a grayish white. If one color shows up predominantly, scrape a little of it off and replace it with more of the other two colors. Usually more blue is needed. To prevent the string from cutting through the holes, glue the cardboard circle to a large button, lining up the holes of the cardboard with those of the button.)

Repeat the activity, using another cardboard circle containing just two complementary colors, such as yellow and blue. What do you observe, and how can it be explained? (The complementary colors will blend together when the circle is spinning, forming grayish white again.)

3.2 Combine Colored Pigments

Give the following instructions: Draw some streaks of yellow and blue tempera paints separately on a piece of white cardboard. Now mix these colors and explain why the green color results. Repeat, using such combinations as red and yellow, red and blue, and black and orange. Mix the six spectrum colors together (or just red, yellow, and blue paints) and record your observations. (The resulting mixture is black because it absorbs all the colors of the white light striking it and reflects none.)

STUDENT BOOKS AND OTHER RESOURCES FOR "LIGHT"

Allen, E. W., and C. E. Matthews. "It's a Bird! It's a Plane! It's a . . . Stereogram!" *Science Scope* 18(7):22–26 (April 1995).

Ardley, N. *The Science Book of Color.* San Diego: Harcourt Brace Jovanovich, 1991.

———. *The Science Book of Light.* San Diego: Harcourt Brace Jovanovich, 1991.

Asimov, I. *How Did We Find Out About Lasers?* New York: Walker, 1990.

Austry, S. *Lenses! Take a Closer Look.* New York: Lerner, 1991.

Gardner, R. *Science Projects About Light.* Hillside, CA: Enslow, 1994.

Jennings, T. *Light and Color.* New York: Franklin Watts, 1991.

———. *Light and Dark.* New York: Gloucester, 1990.

Kipnis, N. *Rediscovering Optics.* Arlington, VA: National Science Teachers Association, 1992.

Levenson, E. *Teaching Children About Physical Science.* Arlington, VA: National Science Teachers Association, 1994.

McDuffie, T. E., Jr., and B. G. Smith. "Has Anyone Seen the I in ROY G BIV?" *Science Scope* 18(7):30–33 (April 1995).

Zubrowski, B. *Mirrors: Finding Out About the Properties of Light.* New York: Morrow, 1992.

CHAPTER 21

Magnetism and Electricity

MAGNETISM

I. MAGNETS

  A. Magnets are materials that will attract materials made of iron, steel, cobalt, and nickel. Such materials are called **magnetic materials.**

  B. There are two kinds of magnets: natural magnets and artificial magnets.

    1. **Natural magnets** are found in the earth and are called **lodestones.** They contain **magnetite,** an iron ore, and appear rocklike.

    2. **Artificial magnets** can be made from iron, steel, cobalt, and nickel (magnetic materials) and several rare earth elements called ferromagnetic elements. Sometimes aluminum is added to these materials, making lightweight but strong magnets, called **alnico magnets.** These are made of aluminum, nickel, and cobalt, from which the name "alnico" is derived.

  C. Magnets are given names according to their shapes: bar magnets, rod magnets, horseshoe magnets, and U-shaped magnets.

II. THE LAW OF MAGNETIC ATTRACTION

  A. The force (push or pull) of a magnet is strongest at its ends, which are called **poles.**

    1. All magnets have two poles: a north-seeking pole and a south-seeking pole.

    2. When a magnet is allowed to swing freely in space, its north-seeking pole points toward the earth's north magnetic pole and its south-seeking pole points toward the earth's south magnetic pole.

    3. A natural magnet (lodestone) has many poles, but there are always just as many north-seeking poles as there are south-seeking poles.

  B. When the poles of two magnets are brought near each other, they obey the **law of magnetic attraction,** which states that two unlike poles attract each other and two like poles repel each other.

III. MAGNETIC FIELD

  A. The space around a magnet also acts like a magnet. This space, within which the force of a magnet acts, is called the **magnetic field.**

  B. When iron filings are sprinkled around a magnet, the filings will arrange themselves into a pattern of parallel lines, called **lines of force.**

    1. At the ends of a magnet, where the magnetic force is strongest, the lines of force bunch closely together.

  C. Magnetic fields are present wherever electricity flows, such as near electrical appliances and power lines. When associated with electricity they are called **electromagnetic fields (EMF).**

IV. THE FORCE OF A MAGNET CAN PASS THROUGH MANY MATERIALS

  A. A magnet can attract magnetic materials (iron, steel, cobalt, nickel) without touching them. The force of a magnet can pass through nonmagnetic material, such as air, paper, wood, glass, aluminum, and brass. The nearer the

DEMONSTRATION 21.1
The Law of Magnetic Attraction

Let a magnet swing freely by cradling it in a piece of copper wire and connecting the wire with string to a ruler inserted into a pile of books (Figure 21.1). Bring the north-seeking pole of another magnet near the north-seeking pole of the suspended magnet. Bring the two south-seeking poles together. Now bring the north-seeking pole of the magnet in your hand near the south-seeking pole of the suspended magnet. Note that like poles repel each other and unlike poles attract each other.

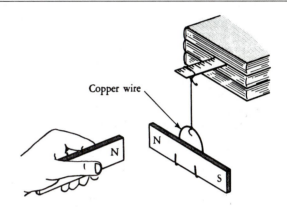

Copper wire

FIGURE 21.1 Like poles repel each other, and unlike poles attract each other.

---

magnetic material is to the magnet, the more strongly it will be attracted by the magnet.

V. THE NATURE OF MAGNETISM

A. Scientists attribute the magnetism of magnetic materials to the spinning movement of the electrons as they revolve or travel around the nucleus of an atom.
   1. In atoms of nonmagnetic materials half their electrons spin in one direction and half spin in the opposite direction, which cancels their magnetic effects.
   2. In atoms of magnetic materials more electrons spin in one direction than the other, making each atom a tiny electromagnet.

B. Magnetized atoms group together in large clusters, called domains, which line up in such a way that all the north-seeking poles face one direction and all south-facing poles face the opposite direction.
   1. This arrangement leaves free north-seeking poles at one end of a magnet and free south-seeking poles at the other end.
   2. A magnetized bar or rod, when cut in half, produces two new magnets even though the middle of the magnetized bar originally had little or no magnetic force.
   3. Each of the two new magnets now has a free north-seeking pole at one end and a free south-seeking pole at the other end.

VI. HOW MAGNETS ARE MADE

A. Only magnetic materials (such as iron, steel, cobalt, nickel, and a few rare earth elements such as dysprosium and gadolinium) can be made into magnets.
   1. These materials are termed **ferromagnetic** substances, which means that spontaneous magnetism exists in the substance even in the absence of a magnetic field. They are naturally magnetic.
   2. However, at certain high temperatures (specific for each type of material) even ferromagnetic materials will lose their magnetism.

B. It is possible to make both temporary and permanent magnets.
   1. Ferromagnetic materials are put in two categories: those with high magnetic retention and those with low magnetic retention.
   2. Ferromagnetic materials with high retention, that is, that tend to hold onto their magnetism for an indefinite period are called hard magnets, or more popularly, **permanent magnets.**
   3. Ferromagnetic materials with low retention, that is, that tend to lose their magnetism easily, are called soft, or **temporary, magnets.** Iron-silicon alloys are an example.
   4. One way of making a magnet is to place a ferromagnetic material in a magnetic field. This way of making temporary

magnets is called **induced magnetism.** The material now becomes a magnet, but perhaps only temporarily. If of a soft magnet material, the magnetism will be lost once the material is removed from the magnetic field.

5. Another way of making a magnet is to stroke a piece of ferromagnetic material (such as a nail) many times with a permanent magnet, but only in one direction. Stroking in one direction lines up the domains (or molecules) in the nail so that all the north-seeking poles are facing one direction and all the south-seeking poles are facing the opposite direction. The nail is only a temporary magnet; the domains will eventually lose their arrangement.

6. Still another way of making a temporary magnet is to wrap an insulated wire many times around a nail, or other soft ferromagnetic material, and connect the bare ends of the wire to the posts of a dry cell. This kind of temporary magnet is called an **electromagnet.** An electromagnet is magnetic only as long as the electric current flows through the wire.

7. Permanent magnets are often made from steel (an iron-carbon alloy). Needles, knives, scissors, and screwdrivers are usually made of steel.

8. Materials made of hard steel (high concentration, up to 2%, of carbon) are difficult to magnetize, but once achieved, their magnetism is more permanent; that is, they do not easily lose their magnetism. Their domains are harder to line up, but once it is done, it is just as hard to throw them out of line. A permanent magnet may be made by stroking a steel knitting needle, or a permanent magnet may be made by using a piece of steel rather than a nail (soft iron) in an electromagnet.

VII. KEEPING MAGNETS STRONG

A. There are three common ways in which one can cause magnets to lose their magnetism: by dropping or striking them; by heating them; and by placing the north-seeking poles of two magnets side by side or on top of each other. In each case the domains (or molecules) will be thrown out of line.

B. There are ways to keep magnets strong.
1. One way is to put a piece of soft iron, commonly called a keeper, across the poles of a horseshoe magnet or U-shaped magnet when the magnet is not in use. If the original keeper has been lost, any piece of soft iron will serve the purpose, or the magnet can be stored by attaching it to the side of a metal file cabinet.
2. Bar magnets should be stored in pairs with the north-seeking pole of one magnet beside or on top of the south-seeking pole of the other magnet, but separated by a nonmagnetic divider (such as a wooden stirring stick or a piece of plastic) with a keeper at each end.
3. Disk and ring magnets should be stored in pairs with opposite poles together.

C. There are ways to rejuvenate weak magnets.
1. A weak bar magnet can be rejuvenated by dragging it lengthwise across one pole of a powerful magnet, such as a large horseshoe magnet. Repeat this several times, moving the weak magnet in the same direction and across the same pole of the stronger magnet.
2. To test the poles, bring the magnet to be tested near a magnet known to be correctly marked to see that opposite poles attract and like poles repel. A bar magnet may be suspended from a string so that it swings freely. When the magnet stops swinging, its north-seeking pole should be pointed in a northerly direction. You can also test poles with a compass. The end of the compass that normally points north should point to the south-seeking pole of a bar magnet.
3. If the poles of the rejuvenated magnet are opposite to their markings, you can repeat the process of rejuvenating, this time dragging the bar magnet across the same pole of the stronger magnet, but in the opposite direction; or you can drag the bar magnet in the same direction, but across the opposite pole of the stronger magnet.
4. A weak bar magnet can also be rejuvenated by wrapping insulated wire around its full length (up to 100 or more windings) and momentarily touching the ends of the wire to the terminals of a 6-volt battery. If after doing this the magnet's poles are opposite to the markings on the

magnet, then repeat the procedure but reverse the ends of the wire that touch the battery.

VIII. THE EARTH BEHAVES AS A MAGNET

A. If a magnet is suspended so that it can swing freely, the magnet will move until it is in a north-south position, with the north-seeking pole of the magnet pointing to the north. This movement occurs because the earth behaves as if it were a huge magnet, with a north magnetic pole, a south magnetic pole, and a magnetic field.

1. The north and south *magnetic* poles are not located at the same points as the north and south *geographic* poles. The magnetic poles are about 1,700 kilometers (1,100 miles) from the geographic poles.

B. A compass tells us where the direction North is, because it contains a magnetized needle whose north-seeking pole is affected by the earth's magnetic field and points in the direction of the north magnetic pole, aligning itself with the earth's magnetic field. A compass needle always points to the north unless it is brought near magnetic materials or a magnet, which then affects its position.

IX. USES OF MAGNETS

A. Magnets are used to pick up pins and needles, to keep cabinet and refrigerator doors closed, to hold the lids of cans after a can opener has removed them, and to hold pieces of paper and other objects to bulletin boards.

B. Although it has long been known that certain organisms and animals, such as bacteria, birds, and whales, contain in their bodies or brains small amounts of ferromagnetic elements that help them to navigate, it was discovered and reported in 1992 that the human brain also contains small amounts of magnetic material, although its value in human brains is not known.

C. Magnets are used in electric motors and generators, in compasses, and in toys and games.

D. Lifted, propelled, and guided by fast-moving magnetic fields, are **magnetic levitation (Maglev) transportation systems.** Maglev vehicles are trains that are suspended on a thin cushion of air and that can easily move at a speed of more than 400 kilometers per hour (248 mph).

1. Although expensive to build, Maglev trains use less energy, make less noise, and produce less pollution than traditional rail transportation systems.

2. The first U.S. patent for a Maglev train model was obtained by Emile Bachelet in 1912, but only recently has the technology been developed, first in Japan and Germany. The German Transrapid was the first commercial passenger-carrying Maglev train in the world.

3. There are two types of suspension systems by which these vehicles can levitate above the track. They are the EMS, or electromagnetic suspension system, and the EDS, or electrodynamic suspension system.

4. **EMS, or electromagnetic suspension,** is based on the **principle of magnetic attraction.** The vehicle wraps around the steel track, leaving a gap around the sides and bottom of the track, or guideway. Electromagnets mounted in the gap between the part of the vehicle that wraps under the base of the guideway are attracted to the bottom of the guideway, levitating the vehicle. Electromagnets mounted in the gap between the vehicle and the side of the guideway are attracted to the side of the guideway, keeping the train laterally on track.

5. **EDS, or electrodynamic suspension,** is based on the **principle of magnetic repulsion.** In the EDS train, the vehicle does not wrap around the track. Instead, electromagnets mounted to the bottom of the vehicle repulse the flat steel guideway, thus levitating the train above the track. EDS prototypes are being developed in Japan.

6. For propulsion, all Maglev trains use linear electric motors built into the guideway to generate a magnetic field that attracts the vehicle, allowing the train to move.

7. In 1994, a Maglev research and development center opened at Stewart Airport in Orange County, New York.

8. The first Maglev system in the United States was built to link the Orlando, Florida, airport to Disney World in 1995.

Electromagnets

I. Magnetism Can Be Obtained from Electricity

A. Passing an electric current through a wire creates a magnetic field around the wire. When a wire carrying an electric current is placed over a compass, the compass needle turns away from its north-seeking position, seeking a position perpendicular to the wire.

B. If a wire carrying an electric current is wound into a coil, the coil acts just like a magnet, with north- and south-seeking poles. Placing a bar of soft iron in the center of the coil greatly increases the strength of this magnet. A magnet of this kind, made from electricity passing through a wire, is called an **electromagnet.**

1. Three things are needed to make a strong electromagnet: a bar of soft iron, such as a large iron nail, which is called the core; a coil of insulated wire wrapped around the core; and a source of electric current, such as a dry cell.

2. When the ends of the coil of wire are connected to the dry cell, the core and coil act like a magnet. The magnetism will continue as long as an electric current passes through the coil.

3. Soft iron is almost always used as the core of an electromagnet because it demagnetizes quickly.

4. The poles of an electromagnet can be determined simply by bringing a compass near it. If the north-seeking part of the compass needle swings toward one end of the electromagnet, this end is the south-seeking pole of the electromagnet. If the north-seeking part of the compass needle swings away from one end of the electromagnet, this end is the north-seeking pole of the electromagnet.

5. When the connections of the wire to the dry cell, or other source of electric current, are reversed, the poles of the electromagnet are also reversed.

6. Commercial electromagnets use yards of wire, one or more large cores, and a strong electric current.

7. Any electromagnet can be made stronger by
   a. Increasing the number of turns of wire around the core.
   b. Increasing the electric current. If either the number of turns of wire is doubled, or the strength of the current is doubled, the electromagnet is made twice as strong.
   c. Using a U-shaped core.

II. Uses of Electromagnets

A. An early use of the electromagnet was in the **telegraph.**

1. A simple telegraph circuit has four parts: a source of electric current, such as one or two dry cells; a key, which acts like a switch to turn the current on and off; a wire, which connects the parts of the telegraph circuit together; and a sounder, which receives the electrical energy and converts it to sound.

2. The sounder has two parts: a U-shaped electromagnet, placed so that its poles are up in the air; and a metal bar, called an armature, which is located above the poles of the electromagnet.

B. The telegraph operates as follows.

1. When the key is pressed down, a current flows through the circuit and the electromagnet becomes magnetized.

2. The electromagnet attracts the armature, which hits a metal screw below it and makes a clicking noise.

3. When the key is released, the electric current stops flowing and the electromagnet loses its magnetism.

4. The armature is no longer attracted, and a spring pulls it back into position again above the poles of the electromagnet.

5. When the armature springs back, it hits another metal screw above it and makes a second clicking noise.

6. By pressing the key down for a longer or shorter time, we can control the time between the clicks that are produced.

7. If the time between the clicks is short so that we get two clicks close together, we call the two clicks a **dot.**

8. Two clicks farther apart are called a **dash.**

9. A code of dots and dashes, called the Morse code, is used to send messages by telegraph.

C. Electromagnets today are used in other forms of communication, such as the telephone, radio, and television.

D. Electromagnets are used in industry in such devices as the motor, generator, transformer, and crane.

E. Electromagnets are found in the home in bells, buzzers, chimes, circuit breakers, VCRs, stereo speakers, and in electric toys.

DEMONSTRATION 21.2
A Simple Telegraph Set

Obtain a wood board about 30 centimeters (12 in) long, 20 centimeters (8 in) wide, and 13 millimeters (1/2 in) thick. Nail a block of wood about 7 centimeters (3 in) high to one end of the board. Use tin snips to cut a strip of iron about 10 centimeters (4 in) long and 2 centimeters (1 in) wide from a metal can. Nail the metal strip to the top of the wood block, and then bend it down to form a dip (Figure 21.2). Drive a long nail with a large head (roofing nail) into the board so that its head is just below the metal strip. This part of the set is called the sounder.

Now make a telegraph key. Nail one end of a second metal strip to the board, using two nails but driving one only partially into the board. Bend the strip back so that it angles away from the board. Drive a smaller roofing nail partially into the board so that its head is under the metal strip. Now wire the key and sounder, as shown in the diagram, using about 50 turns of wire around the nail. When you press the key, the sounder will click. (You may have to adjust the distance between the bent metal strip and the nail head of the sounder. If the click is faint, use two dry cells connected in series.)

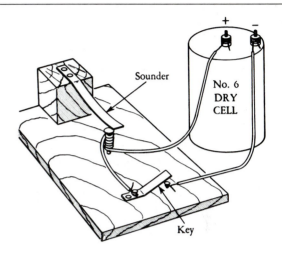

FIGURE 21.2   A simple telegraph set.

STATIC ELECTRICITY

I. STATIC ELECTRICITY AND HOW IT IS PRODUCED

  A. Static electricity is produced by friction.

    1. When two different materials, especially nonmetals, are rubbed together, they each attract light objects, such as small bits of paper and cotton thread, to themselves. We say that these materials have become **electrically charged.**

    2. The kind of electricity that is produced in these materials does not move and is called **static electricity.**

    3. When electricity does move, it is called **current electricity.**

II. THE NATURE OF STATIC ELECTRICITY

  A. All matter is made up of atoms, inside of which are three types of even smaller particles: protons, neutrons, and electrons.

    1. The protons and neutrons, which are much heavier than the electrons, are located in the center, or nucleus, of an atom.

2. The much lighter electrons are outside the nucleus and move rapidly around the nucleus.

3. The electrons move freely around the nucleus, whereas the protons are packed closely together with the neutrons in the nucleus.

4. Each proton has a positive (+) electrical charge, and each electron has a negative (−) electrical charge.

5. The neutron is neither positively nor negatively charged. It is said to be neutral.

6. Ordinarily, there are the same number of positively charged protons and negatively charged electrons in an atom. As a result, an atom is electrically neutral, neither positively nor negatively charged.

7. However, it is possible to remove electrons from the atoms in a material by rubbing the material with another material. When two materials are rubbed together, electrons pass from one material to the other.

8. The material that loses electrons now has more positively charged (+) protons than

DEMONSTRATION 21.3
Friction Produces Static Electricity

Rub a hard rubber comb briskly with wool cloth. The comb will pick up small bits of paper. Rub a blown-up balloon with the wool and put the balloon against the wall. It will stick to the wall. In each case electrons are rubbed off the wool onto the objects, charging the objects negatively and the wool positively. Hold the balloon over very fine sand. You will hear and see the sand being attracted to the balloon.

---

negatively charged (−) electrons, so this material becomes positively charged. The material that gains electrons now has more negatively charged (−) electrons than positively charged (+) protons, so it becomes negatively charged.

9. Protons cannot be removed from an atom by rubbing.

10. When a hard rubber rod is rubbed with wool or fur, some electrons are rubbed off the wool or fur and onto the rubber. The rubber has gained electrons and now has more electrons than protons, so it becomes negatively charged. The wool or fur has lost electrons and now has more protons than electrons, so it becomes positively charged.

11. However, when the rubber rod is rubbed with a plastic bag, electrons are rubbed off the rubber and onto the plastic. The rubber has lost electrons, so it is now positively charged. The plastic has gained electrons, so it is now negatively charged.

12. When a glass rod is rubbed with a piece of nylon, some of the electrons are rubbed off the glass and onto the nylon. The glass has lost electrons and becomes positively charged because it now has more protons than electrons. The nylon has gained electrons and becomes negatively charged because it now has more electrons than protons.

13. Materials will stay charged only as long as electrons have no way of entering or leaving the materials.

B. Static electricity is most easily produced in winter, when it is very cold outside and warm and dry inside (low humidity). In summer there is more water in the air, making air a better conductor. As a result, the electric charges leak away almost as soon as they are formed, so it is very hard to give the materials an electric charge that will last very long.

III. THE LAW OF ELECTROSTATIC ATTRACTION AND REPULSION

A. When two negatively charged materials are brought close to each other, they will repel, or move away from, each other.

B. The same thing happens when two positively charged materials are brought close together.

C. But when a positively charged material is brought close to a negatively charged material, they will be attracted and move closer to each other.

D. These behaviors can be stated as a law of electrostatic attraction and repulsion: like electrical charges repel each other, and unlike charges attract each other.

IV. WHY ELECTRICALLY CHARGED MATERIALS ATTRACT MATERIALS THAT ARE NOT CHARGED

A. Materials that are either positively or negatively charged will attract materials that are not charged.
   1. Materials that are not electrically charged are said to be neutral.
   2. Neutral materials have neither lost nor gained electrons.

B. When a negatively charged hard rubber rod is brought close to a small piece of paper, the paper is attracted to the rod.
   1. The negatively charged rubber rod repels electrons from the side of the paper nearest the rod.
   2. These electrons move to the other side of the paper, as far away from the rod as possible.
   3. The side of the paper nearest the rod is now positively charged, because it has more positive protons than negative electrons, so it is attracted to the negatively charged rod.
   4. When the paper touches the rod, some of the excess electrons from the rod flow into

DEMONSTRATION 21.4
The Law of Electrostatic Attraction and Repulsion

Blow up two balloons to the same size and suspend each balloon from a string so that they are 2 centimeters (1 in) apart. Rub each balloon briskly with a wool cloth. The balloons will become negatively charged and repel each other (Figure 21.3). Now rub a narrow glass jar or a test tube with nylon or a plastic bag and bring the jar near each of the balloons. The jar, having become positively charged, will attract the negatively charged balloons.

Ask students to share their experiences with electrostatic attraction and repulsion. Record their experiences on the board. After recording their ideas, with their help try to arrange the ideas into categories.

Have students brainstorm in class how knowledge of the law of electrostatic attraction and repulsion is used in technology. Record all their ideas on the board and then have students try and arrange the ideas into categories.

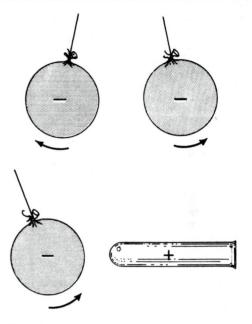

FIGURE 21.3   Like charges repel each other; unlike charges attract each other.

the paper, and the paper becomes negatively charged too.

5. The paper then drops off the rod because it now has the same electrical charge (negative) as the rod and is repelled.

C. When a positively charged glass rod is brought close to a small piece of paper, the paper is attracted to the rod.

1. The positively charged rod attracts electrons, and they accumulate on the side of the paper nearest the rod.

2. The side of the paper nearest the glass rod is now negatively charged, because it has more negative electrons than positive protons, so it is attracted to the positively charged rod.

3. When the paper touches the rod, some of the electrons from the paper flow into the rod, leaving the entire piece of paper positively charged too.

4. The paper then drops off the rod because it now has the same electrical charge (positive) as the rod and is repelled.

V.   CONDUCTORS AND NONCONDUCTORS

A. Some materials allow an electric current to flow through them easily. Such materials are called **conductors.**

1. The atoms in a good conductor of electricity do not have a very tight hold on some of their electrons, so these electrons can flow freely through a material.

2. Most metals are good conductors of electricity including gold, copper, silver, aluminum, iron, and zinc.

3. Carbon, although a nonmetal, can also conduct electricity.

4. When certain chemicals, known as acids, bases, and salts (ionic compounds) are dissolved in water, their solutions will conduct an electric current.

B. Materials that do not allow an electric current to flow through them easily, if at all, are called nonconductors or **insulators.**

1. The atoms in a nonconductor of electricity have such a tight hold on their electrons that few, if any, flow through the material.

DEMONSTRATION 21.5
Some Effects of Static Electricity

A. Charge a comb by rubbing it briskly with a wool cloth. Allow a thin stream of water to flow from a faucet, and then hold the comb near the water. The stream will be attracted by the comb and bend toward it.

B. Charge a balloon by rubbing it briskly with a wool cloth.

Pass the balloon over a student's head and cause the hair to stand on end.

C. Rub a fluorescent light tube briskly with a piece of nylon or silk in a completely darkened room or closet. The fluorescent tube will glow faintly.

---

2. Examples of insulators (nonconductors) are paper, wood, glass, porcelain, cloth, dry air, rubber, and many plastics.
C. Whenever necessary, conductors are covered with or supported by insulators.
   1. An insulator protects you against receiving an electric shock should you happen to touch the conductor.
   2. Insulators also prevent an electric current from leaving the conductor and taking an unwanted path.
D. Pure water itself is a nonconductor of electricity, but almost all water is not pure and contains ions. Even pure water has a concentration of hydrogen ions. These ions make water a good enough conductor that wet insulators can allow electricity to flow. Thus, it is never safe to touch electrical appliances or electrical wiring with wet hands or when standing on a wet floor.

VI. ELECTRIC SPARKS
   A. Ordinarily, electrons do not flow very easily through the air, because air is an insulator.
   B. Under certain conditions, however, electrons can be made to flow through the air.
      1. This flow may occur when a highly charged material is brought near an oppositely charged material, or even a neutral material.
      2. The electrostatic force of attraction between positively and negatively charged materials is very great.
      3. If the force of attraction is greater than the resistance of the air to the flow of electrons, a flow of electrons takes place between the two materials.
      4. This rapid movement of electrons through the air appears as a **spark,** and is actually a flow of current electricity.

VII. LIGHTNING AND THUNDER
   A. **Lightning** is a huge electric spark produced by static electricity.
      1. During thunderstorms rapidly rising or falling air currents may rub against the rain clouds. This rubbing can produce very large and strong electrical charges in the clouds.
      2. Sometimes one part of a cloud becomes positively charged and another part becomes negatively charged.
      3. Sometimes a cloud is ripped into two parts by the rapidly moving air, producing two new clouds, each with a different electrical charge.
      4. When a negatively charged cloud comes close to the earth's surface, the electrons in the earth's surface are repelled into the earth, leaving the surface positively charged. If a positively charged cloud comes close to the earth's surface, the electrons in the earth are attracted to the surface, leaving the surface negatively charged.
   B. Lightning is the huge spark produced when electrons leap suddenly, as follows:
      1. From one charged part of a cloud to another.
      2. From one charged cloud to another of the opposite charge.
      3. From a charged cloud to the earth.
      4. From the earth to a charged cloud.
   C. When lightning strikes the earth, it usually strikes an object located at a high point on the earth's surface, such as the top of a tall tree. Lightning strikes this object because electrons flow more easily through solid objects than through a gas such as air. Therefore, it is a good idea to stay away from trees and other tall objects during a thunderstorm.
   D. **Lightning rods** are used to protect buildings from damage by lightning.

DEMONSTRATION 21.6
The Effect of Charged Materials on Uncharged Materials

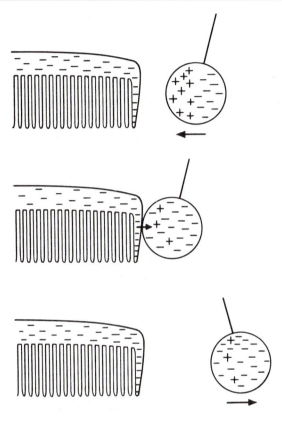

FIGURE 21.4   A charged body first attracts, then repels, an uncharged body.

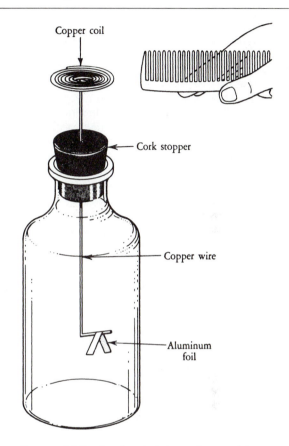

FIGURE 21.5   An electrical charge detector (electroscope).

A. Initial Demonstration

Cut out a piece approximately 6 millimeters (1/4 in) thick from a Styrofoam ball. (A ball of the same size can be obtained from a scientific supply house.) Suspend the ball from a silk or nylon thread. Charge a comb negatively by rubbing it briskly with a wool cloth, and then bring the comb near the ball (Figure 21.4). The ball will be attracted to the comb, because the negatively charged comb repels electrons from the side of the ball nearest the comb, leaving this side positively charged. Now touch the Styrofoam ball with the negatively charged comb. Electrons will flow into the Styrofoam, making it negatively charged, and the Styrofoam will be repelled by the comb.

B. Second Demonstration

Charge a glass test tube positively by rubbing it with a plastic bag or nylon. Make the Styrofoam ball neutral again

by touching it with your fingers. Bring the positively charged test tube near the neutral ball. The ball will be attracted to the test tube because the positively charged test tube attracts electrons to the side of the ball nearest the test tube, making this side negatively charged. Now touch the ball with the positively charged test tube. Electrons will flow from the ball onto the test tube, leaving the ball positively charged, and the Styrofoam ball will be repelled by the test tube.

C. Third demonstration: Make an Electroscope (electrical-charge detector)

Obtain a bottle with a narrow neck and a cork stopper to fit. Obtain some insulated copper bell wire (No. 20) from a hardware store. Use an ice pick to make a small hole through the stopper. Force a piece of the bell wire, with all its insulation removed, through the stopper. Make an

(continued)

DEMONSTRATION 21.6

Continued

---

angular bend at the lower end of the wire and wind the upper end into a close circular coil (Figure 21.5). Hang a strip of thin aluminum foil about 7 centimeters (3 in) long and 5 millimeters (1/4 in) thick over the angular bend of wire. Press the cork firmly into the neck of the bottle.

Now charge a comb negatively by rubbing it briskly with a wool cloth. Touch the comb to the wire coil on top, rubbing it back and forth a few times. Electrons will leave the comb and flow down the wire into the aluminum halves, charging them negatively and causing them to spread apart because they repel each other. Remove the comb.

The electroscope is now charged and can be used to direct and determine the unknown charges on other objects. Bring a charged object near (but not touching)

the wire coil at the top. If the charged object is negative, more electrons will be repelled from the coil down into the aluminum halves. The aluminum halves will become more negatively charged and will spread farther apart. On the other hand, if the charged object is positive, some electrons from the aluminum halves will be attracted up to the coil on top. The aluminum halves will now become less negatively charged and will come closer together.

To discharge the electroscope, touch the wire coil at the top with your fingers. Touching the coil allows electrons to leave the aluminum halves and travel through the wire, into your body, and then to the ground. The aluminum halves become neutral and collapse together.

---

1. A lightning rod is made of a metal such as copper, which is a good conductor of electricity.
2. A lightning rod's highest point is kept higher than the building so that lightning will be attracted to the rod and not the building.
3. The lowest point of the rod goes deeply into the ground so that lightning can be conducted quickly and harmlessly to the ground.

E. As lightning passes through the air, the air becomes very hot and expands suddenly. This expansion of heated air sets up giant vibrations and produces the sound we know as **thunder.**
   1. We see lightning first and then hear thunder because light travels faster than sound.
   2. Because it takes longer for sound to travel from the farther end of the lightning than from the nearer end, we hear the thunder as a long, rolling sound. Many flashes of lightning at one time also produce thunder with a long, rolling sound.
   3. Sometimes lightning is too far away for us to hear the accompanying thunder.

VIII. OTHER COMMON OCCURRENCES OF STATIC ELECTRICITY
   A. Scuffing, or even just walking across, a rug on a very cold day, when it is warm and dry indoors, can produce a shock or a spark when your finger touches a metal object. The body picks up negative electrons through the shoes and releases these electrons upon contact with the metal object. The same thing happens when you slide across the nylon seat of a car and touch the door handle.
   B. Combing your dry hair with a rubber comb will charge the hair and cause it to stand on end.
      1. The comb removes electrons from the hair, leaving the hair positively charged.
      2. Because all strands of hair have the same positive charge, they repel one another and your hair tends to stand on end.
      3. The same phenomenon is evident when you stroke a cat's fur.
   C. Nylon sweaters and undergarments can become charged as they move against a person's body, and often crackle and spark when they are removed.
   D. Trucks containing gasoline and other flammable liquids can build up a large electric charge as the liquid sloshes inside the tank.
      1. If there were no way to stop the charge from building up, a spark might be produced that would make the gasoline explode.
      2. The buildup of an electric charge is prevented by attaching a metal chain to the tank and letting the chain dangle to the ground.
      3. As soon as an electric charge is formed in the tank, the charge is allowed to escape through the chain and into the ground.

CURRENT ELECTRICITY

I. THE NATURE OF CURRENT ELECTRICITY

    A. The word *electricity* is used to describe a flow of electrons (see "The Nature of Static Electricity" in the preceding section).

        1. The electrons in a conductor "flow" very slowly through the conductor. It might be better to say that electrons "migrate."

II. THE SIMPLE ELECTRIC CIRCUIT

    A. There are three parts to a simple electric circuit: a source of electricity, such as a dry cell or electric generator; a path along which the electric current can travel, such as a copper wire; and an appliance that uses the electricity, such as a bell or a light bulb.

    B. In an electric circuit the electric current flows from the source of electricity along one path to the appliance, passes through the appliance, and then returns through a second path to the source of electricity.

    C. When all three parts of a circuit are connected so that an electric current can flow, the circuit is said to be completed or **closed.** When any of the three parts of the circuit is disconnected so that an electric current cannot flow, the circuit is said to be incomplete or **open.**

III. SWITCHES

    A. We control electricity with switches that can turn it off or on, devices that make it easy and convenient to close or open an electric circuit. When the switch is turned or pushed one way, it completes the electric circuit and the electric current will flow. When the switch is turned or pushed the opposite way, it opens or "breaks" the circuit and the electric current stops flowing.

    B. Four common types are the knife, pushbutton, snap, and mercury (silent) switches.

        1. The **knife switch** has a metallic, movable blade that moves in and out of metallic "jaws" to close or open an electric circuit.

        2. The **pushbutton switch,** used with door bells, has a flat, coil-like spring that pushes forward to close a circuit and flies back to open the circuit.

        3. The **snap switch,** used on walls, moves one way to close a circuit and the opposite way to open the circuit.

        4. **Mercury switches** use a drop of mercury to establish the electrical connection. Because mercury is a toxic heavy metal, mercury switches are not as popular as they were when first marketed.

IV. SERIES AND PARALLEL CIRCUITS

    A. If more than one battery is used in an electric circuit, the batteries are usually connected in series. When batteries are connected in series, the wires run from the outside, or negative, terminal of one battery to the center, or positive, terminal of another battery.

        1. Connecting batteries in series increases the amount of electrical force produced.

        2. An example of appliances connected in series is a single strand of Christmas tree lights. If one light goes out in a set of this type, the circuit is broken and all the lights go out. These are no longer commonly found on the market.

        3. Because all the electricity flows through each light, the more lights that are added, the more resistance the electricity meets, and the less current flows through the lamps.

        4. Because the brightness of the lights depends on the amount of current flowing through them, the lights will become dimmer.

    B. When appliances are connected in **parallel,** the electric current flows across each appliance.

        1. The appliances are connected in such a way that the electric current branches off, only part of the current going through each appliance.

        2. Each appliance can operate independently of the other, so if one appliance fails to function, the circuit is not broken and the other appliances continue to function.

        3. The electric current flowing through each appliance is completely separate from the current flowing through the others.

        4. An example of appliances connected in parallel is a set of double-strand Christmas tree lights. If one light goes out in this set of lights, there is still a complete circuit through the rest of the lights and they stay lit. Because the electricity flowing through each light is separate from the

electricity flowing through the others, the addition of more lights to the set will not affect their brightness. These are the type of Christmas tree light strands common today.

5. All house circuits are wired in parallel so that lights and other appliances can be turned on and off separately without breaking the circuit.

6. In most houses the main circuit has branches, connected in parallel, carrying electricity to different parts of the house.

V. OVERLOADING AN ELECTRIC CIRCUIT

A. Whenever there is a flow of electrons (electric current) in a wire, heat is produced. Heat is formed because the metal of the wire resists the flow of electrons through the wire. The more current there is flowing through a wire, the hotter the wire becomes.

B. In a house each branch circuit is designed to carry only so much current.

1. As appliances are connected into the circuit, each uses a certain amount of current.

2. If too many appliances are connected into a circuit at one time, the circuit becomes overloaded.

3. The combined current needed by all the appliances may be more than the circuit can carry.

4. This large amount of current may make the wires so hot that they burn away the insulation and can even start a fire.

5. A circuit can also become overloaded when a **short circuit** occurs.

6. Electricity always takes the shortest and easiest path back to its source.

7. The insulation on the wires of an electric circuit may wear off and expose the bare wires.

8. If the bare wires touch, the electric current takes a short cut, or circuit, back to its source without first flowing through an appliance that is supposed to use the electrical energy.

9. A large amount of electricity will now flow quickly through the wires, making them very hot.

C. Fuses and circuit breakers are safety devices used to prevent wires from becoming too hot when an overload takes place. They are connected in series with the circuit so that the current must pass through them on its way to the appliances. They act like emergency switches to open the circuit if too much current is flowing through it.

1. A **fuse** contains a strip of metal that melts easily when heated.

2. The metal melts more easily than the wires in a circuit.

3. When a circuit becomes overloaded, either because of too many appliances in the circuit or because of a short circuit, the wires become very hot.

4. But the metal strip in the fuse also becomes hot and melts, or "blows," before the wires do, thus breaking the circuit before any damage is done.

5. A fuse is usually enclosed in a tube or socket to prevent the melted metal from spattering and causing a fire.

6. No current will flow through the circuit until the blown fuse is replaced.

7. A **circuit breaker** has a bar, made up of two strips of metal connected together.

8. One metal strip expands more than the other strip, when heated, causing the bar to curve.

9. When a normal amount of electric current flows through the circuit and the circuit breaker, the bar remains flat and keeps the circuit closed.

10. When there is an overload, the bar becomes hot and begins to curve, thus opening the circuit.

11. A circuit breaker does not have to be replaced, but can be pushed back into place after the cause of the overloading is removed.

12. When the bar of a circuit breaker has cooled and straightened, the circuit breaker is once again ready to do its job.

13. Another and more common type of circuit breaker is **electromagnetic.** If too much current flows through a circuit, the strength of the electromagnet overcomes a spring, pulling away a metal strip in the circuit and breaking the circuit.

VI. ELECTRICAL UNITS OF MEASURE

A. A **volt** is a unit of electrical pressure. It is a measure of the push of electrons through a conductor, overcoming the resistance of the conductor.

B. An **ampere** is a unit of the rate of flow of electric current. It is a measure of the number of electrons flowing per second, or the amount of current.

C. An **ohm** is a unit of electrical resistance. It is a measure of the resistance a conductor offers to the flow of electric current.

D. There is a relationship between electrical pressure, rate of flow of current, and electrical resistance.
  1. The greater the electrical pressure (number of volts), the greater the current (number of amperes), and vice versa.
  2. The greater the electrical resistance (number of ohms), the lesser the current (number of amperes), and vice versa.
  3. This relationship, called **Ohm's law,** is expressed as follows: I = V/R, or

$$\text{Amount of Current} = \frac{\text{Electrical pressure}}{\text{Electrical resistance}}$$

  4. Ohm's law is more commonly stated in electrical units, as follows:

$$\text{Amperes 5} \frac{\text{Volts}}{\text{Ohms}}$$

E. A **watt** is a unit of electrical power.
  1. It is the measure of the rate, or how fast, electrical energy is being used.
  2. Watts can be found by multiplying the number of volts by the number of amperes. The formula is P = IV.

F. A **watt-hour** is a unit of electrical energy.
  1. It is the amount of energy used at the rate of one watt for one hour.
  2. When we pay for electrical energy, we pay by the kilowatt-hour.
  3. A kilowatt is 1,000 watts.

VII. Sources of Electricity

A. Electricity can be obtained in several different ways.

B. Electricity is a form of energy and therefore can be produced from other forms of energy. The following forms of energy can be changed, or transformed, into electrical energy.
  1. **Chemical energy,** using the wet cell, dry cell, storage battery, or fuel cell.
  2. **Mechanical energy,** using the generator or the piezoelectric cell.
  3. **Light energy,** using the photoelectric cell or the solar battery.
  4. **Heat energy,** using the thermocouple.

C. The **wet cell,** also known as the **voltaic cell,** consists of two different metals placed in a chemical solution that will conduct an electric current.

  1. The metals selected must be such that one will react faster with the solution than the other.
  2. When the metals are in the solution, they must be kept apart.
  3. A solution of an acid, a base, or a salt in water is able to conduct an electric current.
  4. A commonly used wet cell is made by inserting a strip of zinc and a strip of copper partially in a glass of water containing a little sulfuric acid.
  5. The sulfuric acid acts chemically on the atoms of zinc, leaving many electrons behind on the zinc that remains.
  6. As the negative electrons accumulate on the zinc, the strip becomes negatively charged.
  7. The zinc strip is called the negative pole of the cell.
  8. At the same time, the copper strip loses electrons to the sulfuric acid.
  9. The copper strip now becomes positively charged because it has lost negative electrons.
  10. The copper strip is called the positive pole of the cell.
  11. In this way an electrical pressure is built up between the two strips.
  12. When a wire is connected to the dry ends of the strips, there is a flow of electrons from the negatively charged zinc to the positively charged copper, and an electric current has been produced.
  13. The electric current flows in one direction only, from the zinc to the copper, and is called **direct current** (DC).

D. The **dry cell,** commonly called a battery, is a more convenient source of chemical energy.
  1. The materials of a dry cell are placed in a sealed container so that nothing can spill when the dry cell is carried or tipped.
  2. The chemicals inside must be kept moist; if the inside of the dry cell becomes dry, the cell will no longer operate.
  3. The older form of dry cell is the **carbon-zinc battery.**
  4. It includes a zinc can, which serves as the negative pole, as well as a container for the rest of the chemicals in the cell.
  5. A carbon rod in the middle of the can serves as the positive pole.
  6. The can is filled with a wet paste of ammonium chloride that has been mixed

DEMONSTRATION 21.7
Short Circuit and Fuse

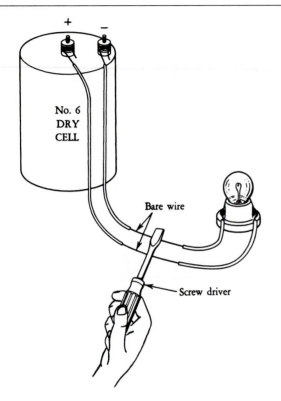

FIGURE 21.6   The blade of the screwdriver produces a short circuit.

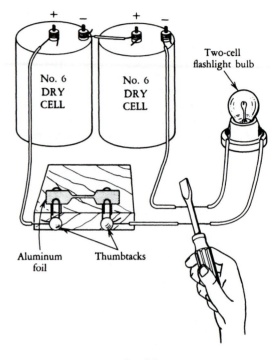

FIGURE 21.7   A simulated fuse.

A. A Short Circuit

To make a simple circuit, obtain some electrical wire and cut it into two pieces (see Figure 21.6). Remove some insulation from the middle of each wire so that the bare wires are exposed. Place the blade of a screwdriver across both bare wires, *only for a second or two,* and the bulb will go out (Figure 21.6). On paper show by lines the shorter path (or circuit) that the electric current now travels. Produce a short circuit again by pressing the bare wires together with your fingers, and feel how hot the wires become.

B. How a Fuse Works

Make a short circuit setup. Using two dry cells in series, place a two-cell flashlight bulb in the socket, and insert a homemade fuse (Figure 21.7). To make a homemade fuse, obtain two thumb tacks and two paper clips, and press them into one end of a small wood board so that the clips are upright and 2 centimeters (1 in) apart. Cut a narrow strip of aluminum foil and insert it between the paper clips. When you produce a short circuit by placing the blade of a screwdriver across the bare wires, the aluminum foil will melt and break the circuit. (If the room is darkened, you may see the aluminum glow as it becomes hot and melts.)

Have the students examine a screw-type house fuse and note the short strip of easily melted metal in the fuse. Compare the appearance of a fresh fuse with that of a burned-out fuse.

with particles of manganese dioxide and powdered carbon.

7. Metal posts, or terminals, are on top of the can: one attached to the carbon rod, the other to one end of the can.

8. The chemical action in a carbon-zinc cell is much like that in a wet cell.

9. The zinc reacts with the moist ammonium chloride and accumulates electrons, becoming negatively charged.

10. The carbon rod loses electrons and becomes positively charged.

11. An electrical pressure is built up between the zinc and the carbon.

12. When a wire is connected to the two terminals of the dry cell, an electric current flows from the zinc to the carbon terminal.

13. The **zinc-chloride battery,** commonly called a "heavy duty" battery, lasts 50 percent longer than the carbon-zinc battery and works better at lower temperatures.

14. It has a steel can filled with moist potassium hydroxide.

15. The positive pole is manganese dioxide; the negative pole is granulated zinc.

16. The **alkaline battery** outperforms both carbon-zinc and zinc-chloride batteries. The newest forms of common batteries use **lithium.**

17. Dry cells cannot give a strong, steady electric current for a long period of time.

18. Dry cells are used in flashlights, portable radios, cameras, and doorbell circuits.

E. The common **storage battery** produces electricity, just as the wet and dry cells do, from chemical energy.

1. A storage battery has lead as the negative pole, lead dioxide as the positive pole, and a solution of sulfuric acid.

2. When the two terminals are connected, an electric current flows.

3. As the battery is used, both the lead and lead dioxide poles become covered with a chemical called lead sulfate.

4. When enough lead sulfate covers the poles, the storage battery will not operate, and we say that it has lost its charge.

5. But the storage battery is different from the wet and dry cell batteries because it can be recharged and used again and again.

6. Its terminals can be connected to a source of direct electric current, which changes the lead sulfate on the poles back into lead and lead dioxide.

7. In this way electrical energy is used to give back to the storage battery its chemical energy.

8. Most storage batteries contain at least six cells, connected in series.

9. Each cell has an electrical pressure of 2.1 volts.

10. Each cell adds its voltage to the others, so if there are six cells we get a 12-volt battery.

11. The most common use of the storage battery is in an automobile, to start the motor and to run appliances if the engine is not running.

12. A storage battery is recharged while the car is running.

13. Every car has an **alternator,** which is a machine for producing electricity once the engine is running.

14. The alternator is driven by the motor of the car. When the car is running, the electricity produced by the alternator flows into the storage battery and recharges it. In this way the alternator resupplies the battery with the electrical energy that was used to start the car.

15. When the car engine is running, electricity to run lights, radio, and other appliances is provided by the alternator, not the battery.

F. The **nickel-cadmium battery** (nicad) is a small, efficient battery that performs like the storage battery.

1. A nickel-cadmium cell has a positive pole of nickel oxide, a negative pole of cadmium, and a solution of potassium hydroxide.

2. Like the storage battery, the nickel-cadmium battery can be recharged repeatedly by using a recharger that plugs into an electrical outlet and changes alternating current (AC) into direct current (DC).

3. The nickel-cadmium battery is used in cordless electrical appliances and toys.

G. The **fuel cell** may be a chemical source of energy for the future.

1. The fuel cell was first discovered in 1839, when Sir William Grove, of England, discovered that electricity can be generated by supplying hydrogen and oxygen to two separate electrodes immersed in dilute sulfuric acid.
2. Today's space shuttles use alkaline potassium hydroxide fuel cells to supply electricity and drinking water.
3. A fuel cell is a form of continuously operating battery, able to transform the chemical energy of various fuels into a flow of electrons—electricity.
4. The U. S. Department of Energy (DOE) is supporting the development of buses powered by methanol fuel cells for use by urban transit systems.
5. The Southern California Gas Company has several phosphoric acid fuel cell plants on line.

H. The **generator** produces electricity from mechanical energy.
1. When a wire is moved up and down between poles of a horseshoe or U-shaped magnet so that the wire cuts across the lines of force in the magnetic field, an electric voltage is produced.
2. The electric current can be detected by connecting the ends of the wire to the terminals of a sensitive instrument called a **galvanometer,** which is used to measure or detect weak electric currents.
3. When the wire is moved down, the needle of the galvanometer moves in one direction; when the wire is moved up, the needle moves in the opposite direction.
4. The movement of the needle shows that the electric current that is produced changes direction.
5. This kind of current is called **alternating current** (AC), because it alternates by first flowing in one direction, then in the opposite direction.
6. An alternating electric current is also produced if the wire is held stationary and the magnet is moved; if the wire or the magnet does not move, no current is produced.
7. Thus the mechanical energy of motion needed to move the wire or the magnet is changed to electrical energy by means of magnetism.

8. A generator is simply a machine used to make wires cut magnetic field lines very quickly.
9. A simple alternating current generator has four necessary parts: a coil of many turns of wire, called an armature: a U-shaped magnet, with the armature placed between the poles of the magnet; two metal rings, called slip rings, each connected to an end of the coil to collect the current produced in the armature; and brushes, made of metal or carbon, to lead the current out of the generator.
10. In small generators and many large generators, the coil moves and the magnet remains stationary; in some large generators, the magnet moves and the coil remains stationary.
11. The amount of current produced by a generator depends on how many magnetic field lines are cut and how quickly they are cut.
12. There are several ways of increasing the number of field lines to be cut: using more magnets; making the magnets stronger by using electromagnets instead of permanent magnets; using more turns of wire in the coil of wire; and inserting an iron core inside the coil.
13. Increasing the speed with which the field lines are cut can be done by moving either the coil or the magnet faster.
14. At hydroelectric power stations falling water is used to turn large wheels, called turbines, which turn the coils or magnets of the generator and produce electric current.
15. Trains and ships burn fuel to run engines or turbines, which operate generators that supply the electricity needed to drive the wheels or propellers.

I. The alternating electric current produced at power plants has a high electrical pressure or voltage.
1. This high electrical pressure is necessary to send the electricity over long distances and to overcome the resistance of miles and miles of wire.
2. Sometimes the electrical pressure in the wires amounts to several thousand volts.
3. Appliances in the home, however, use only 110 volts or 220 volts; several thousand volts in the home would be dangerous.

4. Just before the wires that branch off the main wires enter the home, the high voltage is stepped down to 110 or 220 volts by a device called a **transformer.**
5. Transformers are voltage changers. They can either step down or step up the voltage, as needed.

J. Alternating current changes its direction many times each second.
   1. Two changes in direction are called a **cycle.**
   2. In the home a 60-cycle alternating current is used.
   3. This means that in 1 second the current flows 60 times in one direction and 60 times in the opposite direction.

K. Sometimes generators are needed that will produce **direct current** instead of alternating current.
   1. Direct current over long periods of time is needed to charge storage batteries and to put metal plate on materials.
   2. To produce direct current a generator uses a commutator instead of slip rings.
   3. A **commutator** is a single ring that is split in half.
   4. The commutator automatically reverses the flow of alternating current just as the current changes direction.
   5. As a result, the current flows only in one direction and so becomes a direct current.

L. The **piezoelectric cell** is another means of producing electrical energy from mechanical energy.
   1. When certain crystals, like quartz and Rochelle salt, are squeezed mechanically, an electric current is produced.
   2. Piezoelectric cells containing such crystals are used in the cartridges of record players to "pick up" the sound as the needle moves along the groove of the record. The wiggles in the groove put pressure on the crystal, causing a voltage.
   3. They are also used in ignition systems for igniting propane gas, such as found in some recreational vehicles and outdoor gas barbecues.

M. Both the **photoelectric cell** and the **photoresistive cell** contain a light-sensitive metal and are able to change light energy into electrical energy.
   1. Certain metals, like potassium, selenium, and cadmium, are sensitive to light.

2. When light strikes such a metal, electrons flow from the metal and produce a weak electric current.
3. The stronger the light, the stronger the electric current.
4. Either of these cells is used in camera light meters to measure the amount of light that strikes the film.
5. The electricity produced by photoresistive cells is also used to open doors and operate burglar alarms.

N. The **solar battery** is used to produce and store electricity from sunlight.
   1. A solar battery contains many plates made from silicon doped with impurities such as germanium and gallium.
   2. When the plates are exposed to sunlight, an electrical current is produced.
   3. The solar battery is valuable because it needs nothing other than the silicon wafers. There are no parts to wear out.

O. The **thermocouple** makes it possible to change heat energy into electrical energy.
   1. A thermocouple can be made by twisting together an end of each of two wires of different metals and heating the twisted ends.
   2. Because the two metals expand at different rates when heated, a current flows in the direction of least resistance.
   3. When the free ends of the metal wires are connected to a galvanometer, the needle of the galvanometer moves, showing that a weak electric current has been produced.
   4. Thermocouples are used as delicate thermometers to measure very small differences in temperature.
   5. Several or many thermocouples connected together form a **thermopile,** an instrument sensitive enough to measure the temperature on distant solar bodies when connected to a telescope.

VIII. Uses of Electricity

A. Electricity can be used to produce heat.
   1. Every electrical heating appliance has a conductor that gets hot when an electric current flows through it.
   2. The conductor can be a coil of wire or a solid rod.
   3. Heat is produced by the high resistance the conductor offers to the flow of electricity through it.

4. The greater the resistance, the hotter the conductor becomes.
5. Resistance can be increased either by making the wires thinner or by using a material, such as nichrome metal, that has a high resistance to the flow of electric current.
6. Furthermore, the greater the electric current, the hotter the conductor becomes.
7. Electrical appliances that produce heat include toasters, irons, coffee percolators, hot plates, roasters, stoves, water heaters, and blankets.

B. Electricity can be used to produce light (see Chapter 20).
C. Electricity can be used to produce motion and power to run motors.
D. The parts of a **motor** are exactly the same as the parts of a direct current (DC) generator, but basically work in reverse of generators.
1. Most motors have an armature, a magnet, a commutator, and brushes.
2. A generator changes mechanical energy to electrical energy; a motor changes electrical energy to mechanical energy.
3. A generator uses magnetism to produce electricity; a motor uses electricity to produce magnetism.
4. A motor makes use of the law of attraction between unlike poles, and of repulsion between like poles of magnets, to make the armature move.
5. When an electric current passes from the brushes and commutator into the armature of a motor, the armature becomes an electromagnet.
6. The north-seeking pole of the electromagnetic armature is attracted by the south-seeking pole of the permanent magnet, and the south-seeking pole of the electromagnet is attracted by the north-seeking pole of the permanent magnet, so the electromagnetic armature moves.
7. As the armature turns, it reaches a position at which the unlike poles of the armature and the permanent magnet face each other.
8. At this point the commutator reverses the direction of the current flowing into the electromagnetic armature, which automatically reverses the poles of the electromagnetic armature.
9. Now like poles of the armature and the permanent magnet are facing each other.

10. These like poles repel each other, and the armature moves again.
11. As a result, there is continuous motion of the armature, resulting from the attraction of unlike poles and the subsequent repulsion of like poles.
12. The commutator keeps reversing the current regularly to change the poles of the electromagnetic armature.

E. The power of a motor can be increased by making the magnetic fields of the armature and the permanent magnets stronger.
1. The magnetic field of the armature can be increased by using more turns of wire around the core and by sending more current through the armature.
2. The magnetic field of the permanent magnet can be increased by using more magnets and by converting the permanent magnets to electromagnets.

F. Some motors are built to run on alternating current only, whereas others run on direct current only. Still others can run on either alternating or direct current and are called universal motors.
G. There are so many uses for motors that it would be impossible to maintain our present way of living without them.
H. Electricity can be used to plate metals.
1. Using electricity, metals can be coated, or plated, with other metals, in a process called **electroplating.**
2. Only direct current can be used for electroplating.
3. To copper plate an object, the object to be plated and a bar of copper are placed in a solution containing copper sulfate.
4. This arrangement is very much like that of the wet cell, except that in the wet cell a chemical action produces electricity, whereas in electroplating electricity produces a chemical action.
5. The object and the bar of copper are connected to a source of direct current.
6. The object to be plated acts as the negative pole and is connected to the negative terminal, or connection, of the source of direct current.
7. The copper bar acts as the positive pole and is connected to the positive terminal, or connection, of the source of direct current.
8. When a direct current flows, the copper in the solution is plated onto the object.

DEMONSTRATION 21.8
Electroplating

Obtain some copper sulfate crystals, some dilute sulfuric acid, and a copper strip. Put a heaping tablespoon of copper sulfate into a glass tumbler of warm water and stir vigorously until the copper sulfate dissolves. Then add a few drops of the sulfuric acid. Obtain two pieces of copper bell wire (No. 20), each piece 2/3 meter (26 in) long. Remove quite a bit of the insulation from the end of one piece of wire and wrap a few turns of bare wire around one end of the copper strip, making sure you have a good contact between the strip and the wire. Bend the copper strip so it will hang over a pencil placed across the rim of the tumbler (Figure 21.8).

Wrap the bare end of the second piece of wire around a house key and suspend the key in the copper sulfate solution by wrapping the wire around the pencil. Now connect the other bare ends of both wires to two dry cells connected in series, as shown in the diagram, making sure that the key is connected to a negative terminal and the copper strip is connected to a positive terminal. Allow the current to flow for 15 minutes, then disconnect the wires and remove the key. The key will be coated with copper.

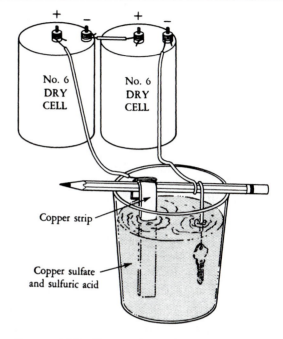

FIGURE 21.8   Coating a key with copper.

9. At the same time, copper from the bar replaces the copper in the solution.
10. The longer the current flows and the stronger the electric current used, the thicker the plate becomes.

11. Electroplating is used to plate silverware and to put chromium on automobile trimmings and zinc on the sheetmetal of cars.
I. Electricity is used in many forms of communication, such as the telephone, radio, television, computers, fax machines, and motion pictures.

ELECTRONICS AND INTEGRATED CIRCUITS

I. ELECTRONICS IS THE BRANCH OF ENGINEERING AND TECHNOLOGY THAT DEALS WITH THE DESIGN AND MANUFACTURE OF DEVICES, SUCH AS RADIOS, TELEVISION SETS, COMPUTERS, AND CD-ROM PLAYERS, THAT CONTAIN ELECTRON TUBES, TRANSISTORS, AND RELATED COMPONENTS

A. An electron tube is a device in which conduction by electrons takes place through a vacuum or an inert gas, in a gas-tight container, with operation controlled by the voltage applied at the electrodes.

B. The history of electronics began in 1883 when Thomas Edison discovered that the heated filament in his incandescent bulb gave off material that darkened the inside of the bulb.
  1. This darkening of the inside of the bulb is called the **Edison Effect,** and its principle gave rise to the **vacuum tube** that is the basis of radio, television, and computers.
C. The invention of the **transistor** in 1948 allowed for tremendous reduction in the size of electronic circuits and in their power requirements.

D. The later development of the **integrated circuit,** which is thousands of tiny circuits with thousands of transistors, resistors, and conductors imbedded in a single tiny piece of silicon, paved the way for the continued miniaturization of devices and the increase in speed with which they can operate.

II. CONVENTIONAL ELECTRONICS IS SUPPLEMENTED IN COMMUNICATIONS BY **OPTOELECTRONICS,** THE USE OF LASER LIGHT CARRIED BY OPTICAL FIBERS TO TRANSMIT INFORMATION AT HIGH SPEED

A. Laser pulses are effected by electronic signals, and the light at the other end of the fiber many kilometers away is converted back into electronic signals.

SAFETY RULES FOR ELECTRICITY AND MAGNETISM

A. Disconnect electrical appliances, especially heating appliances, when they are not being used.
B. Never touch a switch or electrical appliance when your hands are wet.
C. Never touch a switch, electrical appliance, radio, or telephone when you are in the bathtub.
D. Make sure the switch is turned off whenever you disconnect or connect an electrical appliance.
E. Do not overload your home circuit by plugging too many appliances into one wall receptacle.
F. Never touch a bare wire that is carrying an electric current.
G. Never poke around the back of a radio, television set, or computer when these appliances are plugged in.
H. Never put your finger into an open electric socket.

I. Replace electric cords when the insulation is cracked or worn thin.
J. Never touch an electric cord with wet hands.
K. Do not touch an electric cord with one hand and a water pipe, faucet, or radiator with the other hand.
L. When a fuse "blows," first find out what made it blow and correct the condition before resetting or putting in a new fuse. Always replace a blown fuse with a new one that will carry the same amount of current, never with a fuse of a higher amperage. Never put a penny in the fuse box instead of a new fuse.
M. Do not wrap or coil the cords of electric appliances that are in use.
N. Keep magnets away from computers and other electronic appliances; the magnetic field can damage the computer circuitry.

EXPLORATORY ACTIVITIES FOR "MAGNETISM AND ELECTRICITY"

1. *EXPLORING WITH MAGNETS* (ANY GRADE LEVEL)

Procedure Review the following activities and, depending on the age and maturity of your students, decide the best approach for involving students in these activities. Instructions for each activity will have to be rewritten, depending on how it is used. One approach is to divide the class into groups and have each group do one of the activities as a project, then show and report their finished work to the rest of the class. Another approach is set up the activities as learning stations around the classroom. Divide the students into groups and allow them to work at each station in turn.

1.1 Determining Which Materials a Magnet Will Attract

Have the students collect a variety of materials, such as tacks, nails, paper clips, pins, needles, coins, rubber bands, pebbles, sand, and small pieces of chalk, crayon, wood, paper, glass, cloth, leather, and aluminum foil. Let the students try to pick up or attract each object with a magnet. Put to one side all those objects that are attracted by the magnet, and ask students to explain why they are attracted. (These objects are all made of iron or steel.)

1.2 A Discrepant Event with Nickels

Give the students a handful of nickels to try to pick up with a magnet. Be sure that these coins include one Canadian nickel. Students will recognize the discrepancy: the magnet will pick up the Canadian nickel but not the American nickels. Have the students try to hypothesize an explanation. (Cobalt and nickel are also attracted by magnets. If the students comment that the American nickels are not attracted by the magnet, explain that American nickels contain mostly copper. Canadian nickels contain more nickel metal and thus are attracted by the magnet.)

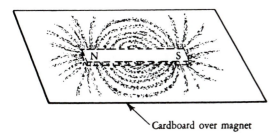

FIGURE 21.9   Lines of force in a magnetic field.

1.3 The Attraction of a Magnet—Strongest at Its Poles

Make a pile of tacks or iron filings. Obtain iron filings from a scientific supply house, or make your own filings by cutting fine steel wool into very small pieces with scissors. Now ask students to try to pick up the tacks or filings with a bar magnet, using different parts of the magnet each time. Ask, What do you observe? (The tacks or filings will be attracted most strongly to the poles of the magnet.) Repeat the activity, using a horseshoe and a U-shaped magnet. Have students record and explain their observations.

1.4 Lodestone—A Natural Magnet

Obtain a lodestone and some iron filings from a scientific supply house. You can make your own iron filings by cutting fine steel wool into very small pieces with scissors. Have students dip the lodestone into a pile of iron filings. The filings will cling in bunches at the various poles of the lodestone. Have students count the number of poles in the lodestone. Ask, What do you observe? (There should be an even number, with just as many north-seeking as south-seeking poles.)

1.5 Exploring Magnetic Fields and Lines of Force

Place a sheet of cardboard or window glass over a bar magnet. Then give students the following instructions: Sprinkle iron filings or tiny bits of cut-up steel wool all over the cardboard, and then tap the cardboard gently a few times (Figure 21.9). Diagram and explain your observations. (The filings will rearrange themselves to form a definite pattern, showing the magnetic field and the lines of force located within the field. Note how the lines of force are concentrated at the poles.)

Repeat the activity, having students use two bar magnets with the north-seeking pole of one bar magnet 5 centimeters (2 in) from the south-seeking pole of the other bar magnet (Figure 21.10). Again, ask students to diagram and explain their observations. (The lines of force seem to attract each other.) Repeat the activity, this time having student place two like poles near each other. Ask

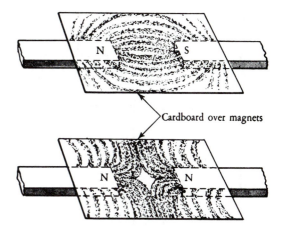

FIGURE 21.10   Lines of force between unlike and like poles.

FIGURE 21.11   The force of a magnet passes through nonmagnetic materials.

them to diagram and explain their observations. (The lines of force show the repulsion between like poles.)

1.6 Magnets Attracting Through Nonmagnetic Materials

Give students the following instructions: Place a piece of cardboard on two piles of books set a short distance apart. Put some thumb tacks on the cardboard, and then slide a magnet along the underside of the cardboard (Figure 21.11). What do you observe? (The magnet will attract the tacks and make them move.) Repeat the activity, using other materials (sheets of glass, wood, aluminum foil, and cloth), and record your observations on a data table that you devise. Now use a sheet of iron, cut from a large "tin" can with tin snips. Explain your observation. (The tacks will not move because the force of the magnet passes into the iron, making it a magnet that attracts the tacks and holds them fast.)

1.7 A Compass Needle Is a Magnet

Give students the following instructions: Examine a compass. The end of the needle that points to the north is usually colored blue, black, or red and is called the north-seeking pole. Bring the north-seeking pole of a bar magnet near the compass. Record your observations. (The north-seeking pole of the compass needle will be repelled, while the south-seeking pole of the needle will be attracted. Point out that a compass needle can be used to determine the poles of an unmarked magnet.)

1.8 The Nature of Magnetism

Give students the following instructions: Fill a test tube half full of iron fillings and stopper it. Stroke the test tube from end to end with one pole of a strong bar magnet about 20 times. Stroke slowly and gently in one direction only, being sure to lift your hand up in the air before coming down for another stroke. The test tube will now act like a magnet, because you have lined up all the filings so that they behave just as the molecules in them would behave, with their north-seeking poles pointing in one direction and their south-seeking poles pointing in the opposite direction. Bring a compass near the test tube and determine the poles of this test-tube magnet.

Now shake the test tube vigorously for some time, and then test with the compass again. What do you observe? (Mixing up the filings causes the test tube to lose its ability to behave like a magnet.)

1.9 Making a Temporary Magnet by Induction

Give students the following instructions: Plunge one pole of a bar magnet into a pile of small tacks, and then lift up the magnet. What do you observe? (There will be a cluster of tacks around the pole.) How do you explain this? Do you observe anything else? (Each tack becomes a magnet by induction and attracts other tacks. This induced magnetism is temporary because as soon as the bar magnet is taken away, the tacks do not attract each other anymore.)

Hold a large iron nail or spike quite close to one pole of a strong bar magnet. Keeping the nail and magnet in this position, dip the nail into a pile of small tacks, and then lift up the nail (Figure 21.12). What do you observe and how do you explain it? (The nail has been magnetized by induction, without even touching the magnet, and attracts the tacks. The tacks in turn are also magnetized by induction. When the bar magnet is removed, the nail loses its magnetism and the tacks fall off.)

1.10 Making a Temporary Magnet by Stroking

Give students the following instructions: Stroke a large iron nail or spike from end to end with one pole of a

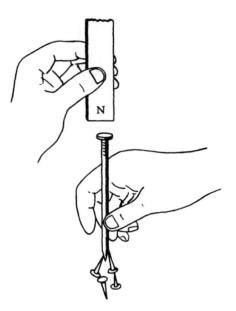

FIGURE 21.12 The nail attracts the tacks because of induced magnetism.

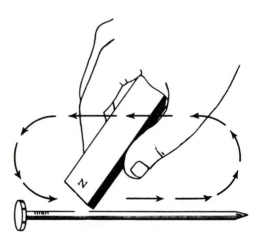

FIGURE 21.13 A nail becomes a temporary magnet when stroked with one pole of a bar magnet.

strong bar magnet about 20 times. Stroke slowly and gently in one direction only, being sure to lift your hand up in the air before coming down for another stroke (Figure 21.13). Test the nail by dipping it into a pile of iron filings or tacks. What do you observe? (The nail will become a magnet and pick up iron filings or tacks.) Set the nail aside for three to four days, and then test it again. What do you observe? (Because the nail is made of soft iron, it will have lost most of its magnetism and it will pick up very few filings or tacks.)

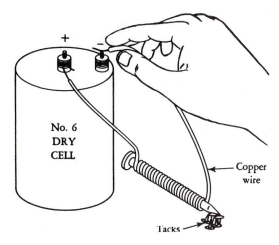

FIGURE 21.14   An electromagnet is a temporary magnet.

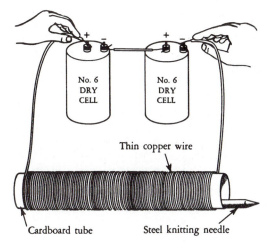

FIGURE 21.15   Making a steel knitting needle become a permanent magnet.

1.11 Making a Temporary Magnet with Electricity

Obtain some insulated copper bell wire (No. 20) from a hardware store. Give students the following instructions: Wind the wire in a coil around a large iron nail or spike about 15 to 20 times. Remove the insulation from both ends of the wire, connect one end to a terminal of a dry cell, and touch the other end to the second terminal for a few seconds (Figure 21.14). The nail will now pick up tacks and other objects made of iron or steel, and is called an electromagnet. When you remove the wire from one of the terminals, what do you observe and how do you explain it? (The electric current stops flowing and the nail loses its magnetism.) (*Note:* Keep the wires connected to the dry cell for as short a time as possible. Otherwise, the dry cell will be used up very quickly.)

1.12 Making a Permanent Magnet by Stroking

Repeat activity 1.11, having students use a steel knitting needle instead of an iron nail. Ask, What do you observe from this experiment? (The needle retains most of its magnetism after it has been set aside for three to four days.)

Have students determine the poles of this magnetized needle by bringing a compass near it. Then cut the needle in half with cutting pliers. Ask students, What do you observe and how can it be explained? (Each half will become a new magnet, with poles.)

1.13 Making a Permanent Magnet with Electricity

Obtain a cardboard tube, such as a mailing tube, about 25 centimeters (10 in) long and 2 centimeters (1 in) in diameter. Obtain some insulated thin copper wire (No.

26 or 28) from a hardware store. Give students the following instructions: Wind the wire around the tube, covering almost all of the tube, leaving about 45 centimeters (18 in) of wire free at each end. Connect two dry cells in series, as shown in Figure 21.15. Place a steel knitting needle all the way into the cardboard tube. Now touch the two end wires to the terminals of the dry cells, as shown in the diagram, for two to three seconds only. Remove the needle and test it for magnetism on tacks and other iron or steel objects.

1.1. Observing Magnets Lose Their Magnetism

Have students magnetize two large steel sewing needles by stroking them with one pole of a strong bar magnet. Let them see how many iron filings or small tacks each needle will attract. Now hold one needle with forceps or pliers in the flame of a Bunsen burner or alcohol lamp for about three minutes. At the same time, have one of the students pound the other needle repeatedly with a hammer. Now test both needles again to see how many iron filings each needle will attract. What do you observe? (Heating and striking or jarring a magnet will disarrange the molecules, causing the magnet to lose its magnetism.)

1.15 A Floating Compass

Give students the following instructions: Magnetize a steel sewing needle by stroking it with one pole of a strong bar magnet. Slice a round piece, 13 millimeters (1/2 in) thick, from a cork stopper. Cut a groove across the center of the top of the cork slice. Put the needle into the groove and place the cork slice in a

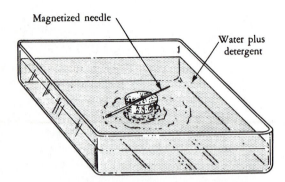

FIGURE 21.16   A floating, magnetized needle compass.

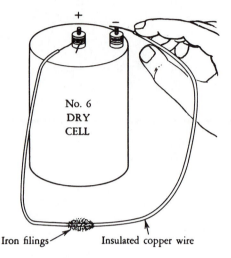

FIGURE 21.17   Wire carrying electric current acts like a magnet.

glass, china, or aluminum dish filled with water (Figure 21.16). (A teaspoon of detergent in the water will lower the surface tension of the water and prevent the cork from moving to one side of the dish and staying there. The needle will soon behave like a compass needle by assuming a north-south position because of the earth's magnetic field.)

2. *EXPLORING WITH ELECTROMAGNETS* (GRADES 4–9)

Review the following three activities and, depending on the age and maturity of your students, decide the best approach for involving the students in these activities. Instructions for each activity will have to be rewritten, depending on how it is used.

Note: Electromagnets draw a great amount of current and can use up dry cells very quickly. When working with electromagnets, keep the wires connected to the dry cells for as short a time as possible.

2.1 Testing for Magnetism in a Wire Carrying an Electric Current

Obtain some copper bell wire (No. 20) from a hardware store. Give students the following instructions: Remove the insulation from both ends of the wire and connect one end to a terminal of a dry cell. Now touch the other bare end of the wire to the second terminal of the dry cell for a few seconds and try to pick up some iron filings or finely cut-up steel wool with the middle part of the wire (Figure 21.17). (The wire will attract the filings, showing that a wire carrying an electric current has a magnetic field around it.) Place a compass beside the wire, and then touch the bare end of the wire to the terminal of the dry cell again. (The compass needle will move, showing that the magnetic field around the wire affects the magnetized needle.)

2.2 Testing for Magnetism in a Coil of Wire Carrying an Electric Current

Give students the following instructions: Wrap bell wire (No. 20) about 15 to 20 times around a pencil to form a coil, and then remove the pencil. Remove the insulation from both ends of the wire, connect one end to a terminal of a dry cell, and touch the other end to the second terminal for a few seconds (Figure 21.18). The coil will act like a magnet, picking up tacks and other objects made of iron or steel.

Determine the poles of this coil magnet by bringing a compass near it. The blue or black end of the magnetized compass needle is a north-seeking pole, so it will be attracted to the coil magnet's south-seeking pole and repelled by the north-seeking pole.

2.3 Making an Electromagnet Stronger

Give students the following instructions: Make an electromagnet as described in activity 2.2, winding the wire around the nail exactly 20 times. Count the number of tacks the electromagnet will attract. Now wind 20 more turns of wire around the same nail, and again count the number of tacks the electromagnet will pick up. (Doubling the number of turns will double the strength of the electromagnet.)

Make another electromagnet with just 20 turns of wire, and count the number of tacks it will pick up. Now connect the electromagnet to two dry cells arranged in series (Figure 21.19), and again count the number of tacks that will be attracted. (Doubling the strength of the electric current will double the strength of the electromagnet.)

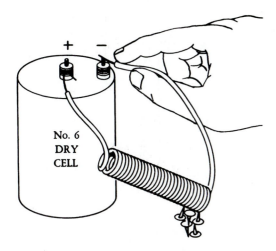

FIGURE 21.18   A wire coil carrying electric current acts like a magnet.

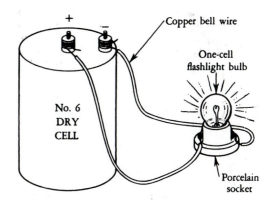

FIGURE 21.20   A simple electric circuit.

then show and report their finished work to the rest of the class. Instructions for each activity will have to be rewritten, depending on how it is used.

3.1 Making a Simple Electric Circuit

Obtain a No. 6 dry cell, some insulated copper bell wire (No. 20), a one-cell flashlight bulb, and a small porcelain socket to hold the bulb from a scientific supply house or a hardware store. Instruct students as follows: Set up a simple electric circuit, as shown in Figure 21.20, being sure to remove the insulation from the ends of the wires. Trace the flow of current through the completed circuit. Now break the circuit by disconnecting one of the wires attached to the dry cell or porcelain socket.

3.2 Comparing Conductors and Nonconductors

Give students the following instructions: Connect a dry cell, some copper bell wire (No. 20), a one-cell flashlight bulb, and a porcelain socket as shown in Figure 21.21, being sure to remove the insulation from the ends of the wires. Touch the bare ends of the two wires to a nail, the metal part of a pen or pencil, various coins, aluminum foil, and pieces of wood, rubber, cloth, and glass. Note which kinds of materials do and do not conduct electricity. Establish the relationship between electrical conductivity and how tightly or loosely the atoms hold some of their electrons.

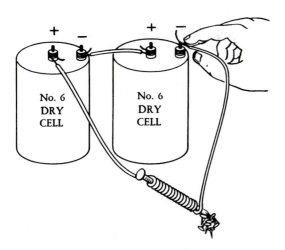

FIGURE 21.19   Increasing the strength of the electric current makes the electromagnet stronger.

Have the students predict (and test) what will happen when both the number of turns and the strength of the electric current are doubled.

3. EXPLORING CURRENT ELECTRICITY (GRADES 4–9)

Review the following eight activities and, depending on the age and maturity of your students, decide the best approach for involving the students in these activities. As a result of these experiments your students may want to design their own—to be done under your guidance.

One approach is to divide the class into groups and have each group do one of the activities as a project,

3.3 Including a Switch

Obtain a knife switch from a hardware store or scientific supply house. Give students the following instructions: Insert the switch into the simple electric circuit described in activity 3.2 (Figure 21.22). Operate the switch and show how it closes and opens the circuit. Replace the knife switch with a pushbutton switch, and then a snap switch.

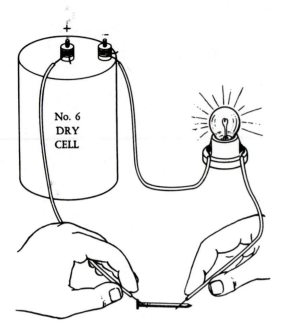

FIGURE 21.21   A nail is a good conductor of electricity.

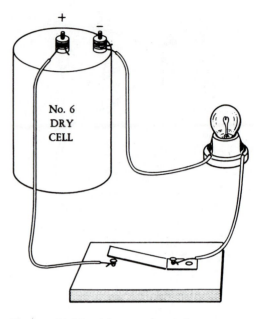

FIGURE 21.23   A homemade switch.

its head is under the metal strip. Now insert this home-made switch into your simple circuit, as shown in Figure 21.23. Operate the switch to open and close the circuit.

3.4 Series and Parallel Circuits

Give students the following instructions: Connect three porcelain sockets and three one-cell flashlight bulbs in series, as shown in Figure 21.24. Note that the electric current flows through each bulb, one after the other, and the bulbs light up dimly. Note the relative brightness of the bulbs. The bulb closest to the positive side of the bat-tery will be the brightest. Each succeeding bulb will be dimmer. Unscrewing one of the bulbs will break the complete circuit, so that the other bulbs go out.

Now connect the sockets and bulbs in parallel as shown in Figure 21.25. Point out that the current branches off, so that part of the current goes through one socket and part goes on to the next socket. Note how brightly lighted all the bulbs are. Unscrewing one of the bulbs will break only the part of the circuit that flows through that bulb, so the remaining two bulbs continue to stay lighted. If you unscrew a second bulb, the third bulb will still continue to burn. Hypothesize as to which type of circuit will run the battery down quick-est. (The parallel circuit will.)

3.5 Making a Galvanometer (Current Detector)

Obtain insulated thin copper wire (No. 26 or 28) from a scientific supply house or hardware store. Give the fol-

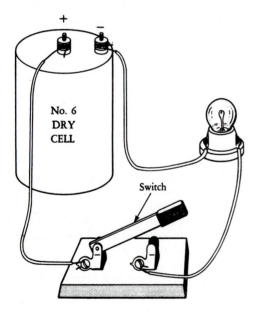

FIGURE 21.22   A knife switch can open and close an electric circuit.

Make your own switch. Using tin snips, cut a strip of metal, 10 centimeters (4 in) long and 2 centimeters (1 in) wide, from a can. Nail one end to a small board. Use two nails, but drive one only partially into the board. Bend the strip back so that it angles away from the board. Drive a small roofing nail partially into the board so that

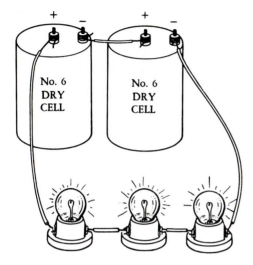

FIGURE 21.24   Flashlight bulbs connected in series.

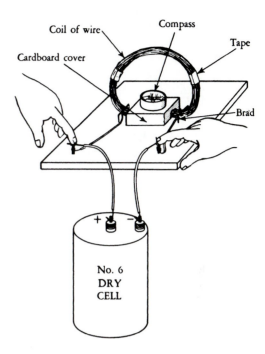

FIGURE 21.26   A current detector (galvanometer).

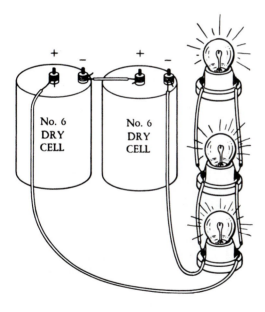

FIGURE 21.25   Flashlight bulbs connected in parallel.

lowing instructions: Wind about 100 turns of the wire around a glass jar, about 7 centimeters (3 in) in diameter, to form a narrow coil. Slip the coil off the jar and tape it at two or three points to hold the wires neatly in place. Leave some wire free at each end of the coil, and remove 2 centimeters (1 in) of insulation from each end of the wire. Use two brads to attach the coil to a small wood board and to hold the coil upright (Figure 21.26).

Place the cover of a small cardboard box inside the coil, first cutting grooves on each side of the cover so that it will rest in a stable and even position on the board. Drive two small nails almost all the way into the board and wrap the bare end of each wire around a nail.

Now rest a compass on top of the cardboard cover, and turn the board until the compass needle is parallel with the direction of the coil. Then turn the compass until the letters N and S are under the needle. Your galvanometer is now ready to operate. Connect a dry cell to the galvanometer by touching the bare ends of the wires from the dry cell to the nails of the galvanometer. The compass needle will be deflected, showing the presence of an electric current. (Point out that when an electric current flows through the galvanometer coil, a magnetic field is formed that affects the magnetized compass needle. The greater the current flowing through the coil, the stronger the magnetic field will be, and the more the compass needle will be deflected.)

3.6 Make a Simple Electric Cell

Give students the following instructions: Dissolve a tablespoon of common table salt in a glass tumbler of warm water. Obtain a metal washer, a penny, and two lengths of insulated copper bell wire (No. 20). Strip 7 centimeters (3 in) of insulation from one end of each wire and 2 centimeters (0.75 in) from the other end. Wrap the penny and the washer separately with the longer bare end of the

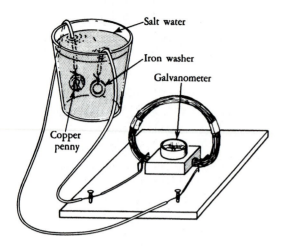

FIGURE 21.27   A simple electric wet cell.

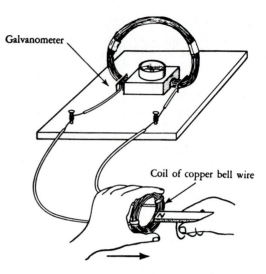

FIGURE 21.28   Generating electricity with a magnet and a coil of wire.

wire and suspend them in the saltwater by bending the wires tightly over the edge of the tumbler (Figure 21.27). Make sure that the coin and the washer are not touching each other. Now touch the other ends of the wires to the nails of the galvanometer described in activity 3.5. The compass needle will be deflected, showing the presence of an electric current. Repeat the activity, using other combinations of two different metals. (Point out that chemical energy has been changed into electrical energy.)

3.7 Generating Electricity with a Magnet and a Coil of Wire

Give students the following instructions: Wind about 50 turns of insulated copper bell wire (No. 20) around a glass jar, about 5 to 7.5 centimeters (2 to 3 in) in diameter, to form a coil. Slip the coil off the jar and tape it at a few points to hold the wires neatly in place. Leave 1 meter (3 ft) of wire free at each end of the coil. Remove the insulation from the end of the coil and remove the insulation from the end of each wire. Connect the coil to a galvanometer as shown in Figure 21.28. Hold the coil as far away from the galvanometer as possible and move the center of the coil across a bar magnet. The compass needle of the galvanometer will be deflected, showing the presence of an electric current. When you move the coil in the opposite direction, the needle is also deflected in the opposite direction. When you hold the coil stationary, there is no deflection because no lines of force in the magnetic field are being cut. When you move the coil continuously back and forth across the magnet, a continuous alternating current is produced. Repeat the learning activity, this time holding the coil

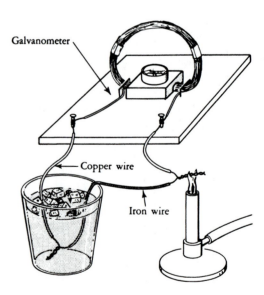

FIGURE 21.29   Generating electricity with a thermocouple.

stationary and moving the magnet. Point out that mechanical energy is being changed into electrical energy.

3.8 Using a Thermocouple

Give students the following instructions: Cut off a piece of wire from a coat hanger and scrape the paint away from both ends. Obtain two pieces of copper bell wire (No. 20) and remove the insulation from the ends of both wires. Tightly twist together one end of a copper wire to each end of the coat hanger wire and connect the other free end of each copper wire to a galvanometer. Now place one of the twisted ends into a glass tumbler containing cold water and ice cubes, and heat the other twisted end with the flame of a Bunsen burner (Figure 21.29). The compass needle of the galvanometer will be deflected, showing the presence of an electric current. Heat energy has been changed into electrical energy.

STUDENT BOOKS AND OTHERS RESOURCES FOR "MAGNETISM AND ELECTRICITY"

Cordua, W. S. "Magnetic Materials." *Science Activities* 31(1):37–38 (Spring 1994).

Dalby, D. K. "Energy Generates Excitement." *Science and Children* 31(3):27–29 (November/December 1993).

Engel, C. W., and R. R. Smith. "Gismos: Electronic Devices for Problem Solving." *Science Scope* 18(5):30–34 (February 1995).

Gardner, R. *Science Projects About Electricity and Magnetism.* Hillside, CA: Enslow, 1994.

Grosvenor, E. S. *The Alexander Graham Bell Science Kit.* Washington: National Geographic Society, 1992.

Hardy, G. R., and M. N. Tolman. "The Care and Feeding of Magnets." *Science and Children* 30(4):22–23 (January 1993).

Leyden, M. B. "Science Can Be Attractive." *Teaching Pre K–8* 24(7):26–27 (April 1994).

Moore, V. S., and W. J. Kaszas. "All Aboard! For a Lesson on Magnetic Levitated Trains." *Science and Children* 32(5): 15–18, 47 (February 1995).

Orozco, G. T., P. S. Alberú, and E. R. Haynes. "The Electromagnetic Swing." *Science and Children* 31(6):20–21 (March 1994).

Schafer, L. E. *Taking Charge: An Introduction to Electricity.* Washington, DC: National Science Teachers Association, 1992.

Skurzynski, G. *Get the Message: Telecommunications in Your High-Tech World.* New York: Bradbury, 1993.

Stwertka, A. *Superconductors: The Irresistible Future.* New York: Franklin Watts, 1991.

Van Cleave, J. *Electricity: Mind-Boggling Experiments You Can Turn into Science Fair Projects.* New York: John Wiley & Sons, 1994.

Name Index

Subject Index